MR. SUICIDE

Henry "Pathé" Lehrman
~ and ~
The Birth of Silent Comedy

BY THOMAS REEDER

Mr. Suicide: Henry "Pathé" Lehrman and The Birth of Silent Comedy
© 2017 Thomas Reeder. All Rights Reserved.

No part of this book may be reproduced in any form or by any means, electronic, mechanical, digital, photocopying or recording, except for the inclusion in a review, without permission in writing from the publisher.

All photos from the author's collection, unless otherwise noted.

Published in the USA by:
BearManor Media
PO Box 71426
Albany, Georgia 31708
www.bearmanormedia.com

ISBN 978-1-62933-161-4

Printed in the United States of America.
Book design by Brian Pearce | Red Jacket Press.

Table of Contents

Foreword by Sam Gill 7
Acknowledgements 9
Introduction by Steve Massa 13
Preface 15
Sambor: The Birth of a Notion 19
Biograph, IMP, and Kinemacolor: Baptism By Fire 23
Mack Sennett's Keystone Film Company: Creditless Where Credit is Due 37
The Sterling Motion Picture Corporation: The Grass is Always Greener 73
The L-Ko Komedy Kompany: Lehrman's Baby 101
Foxfilm and Sunshine Comedies: From Rags to Riches 179
Henry Lehrman Comedies: Overstepping His Bounds 239
Reported Missing and the Arbuckle Scandal 275
Treading Water at a Potpourri of Studios 291
The Volatile Jocelyn Leigh 303
The Brothers Warner Come Calling 307
Back Home at Fox 319
Fox, Twentieth Century, and 20th Century-Fox: This Time for Good 335
Lehrman Knocks Out Memos 349
The End 359
Lehrman's Legacy 363
The Sterling Motion Picture Corporation, Post-Lehrman: A Rudderless Ship ... 367
The L-Ko Komedy Kompany, Post-Lehrman: Soldiering On 387
Filmography 427
Endnotes 699
Bibliography 737
Index 741

For Joan, whose contributions to this book were far greater than she will ever realize.

Foreword by Sam Gill

Mack Sennett may have been the King of Comedy, but Henry "Pathé" Lehrman was the King of the Absurd; in fact, the King of the Absurd on Steroids.

Some examples in the way of explanation:

There never could be too many animals in a "Pathé" Lehrman comedy, whether lions, an elephant, ostriches, monkeys, clever dogs or two flies in the bowl of a spoon — yes, two flies. There could never be too many hazardous stunts, fast and frantic chases, high dives, hard knocks (really hard knocks), blasting or being blasted with a water hose, and treacherous falls.

Lehrman always liked water — lots of water; in fact, tons and tons of it. Lehrman also had an affinity for the extreme close-up, or in Lehrman's specific case, the most extreme close-up in the film business. A cameraman could not have been any closer to a comic's face or other player's face without being in his mouth!

Cars driving through walls or off a pier into the ocean would be good, too, as long as there were real people in the car, and no fakery. If Billie Ritchie or Ford Sterling were in a film, it would be good, in fact wonderful, at some time in the film for one grown man to aggressively jump on another grown man in order to bite his nose, his ear or his ankle, or all three.

No subtlety here.

Now on to other Lehrman "specialties."

There could never be enough fire or explosions. In fact, in a film like *Wet and Warmer*, the actors find themselves caught up in so many whirls of fire, literally fire "devils," small tornadoes of fire, that they must flee in every direction in order to avoid being burnt to a crisp — all shown in real time, in razor-sharp focus. The cameraman, along with his camera, was obviously in as much real peril as the poor actors and actresses whose terrified expressions are not faked, either. No CGI here. No camera trickery here, either.

Well, let's see, what else can be said.

There is more striking, hitting, punching, kicking and leaping in ten minutes of a "Pathé" Lehrman picture than in all thirty minutes of a "Three Stooges" comedy, or an hour-and-a-half of the most screwy screwball comedy feature of the teens, twenties, thirties and beyond. In point of fact, the creators behind the most outrageous of the Three Stooges comedies, made twenty years later, were produced, directed and created by the very same men who as boys and very young men — Jack White, his brother Jules, and their merry band of certifiable madmen — learned many of their best tricks from the master, a film magician named Henry Lehrman.

Anything else I could add? Well, yes.

Any semblance of a traditional story line was pointless because it was sure to be thrown out the window anyway, along with the flirting husband or back-stabbing friend. The action and pacing were so fast, no human eyes could possibly follow the story if there were one, and make any sense of it anyway. Also — no one was to be trusted in a Henry Lehrman comedy. In fact, there were those who worked for Henry Lehrman who said he wasn't to be trusted, either.

However, if you kept your eyes open, your mouth shut, your brain cells well-oiled and nimble, and watched this talented madman at work, you not only learned something, you could find yourself propelled (sometimes literally) into the ranks of the top directors, top gag-men, top cameramen, and top everything else in the manufacturing of the best and most inspired comedies of their day.

So, just who is this Henry "Pathé" Lehrman?

That's the point of this book, as I see it, to try and unravel the many mysteries surrounding this highly intelligent, complex and creative man and filmmaker, who to this day has been one of the most underappreciated and highly misunderstood figures in motion picture history.

In the most meticulous and careful research from a film historian who also knows the value of an informative footnote, Tom Reeder has compiled more in-depth information on this American comedy "original" than anyone I feel sure in saying, has in the past, is doing now, or will attempt in the future, who set themselves the task to find and make any more revelations of Lehrman "truths."

So there you have it. Sit down, relax, open the book and dive in. The only way I believe there is to understand Henry Lehrman, the man and legend, is to jump high and dive deep, just as if you are a participant in any one of "Pathé" Lehrman's truly unique, awesome and insane comedies.

SAM GILL
Niles, California
October 1, 2016

Acknowledgements

This book has, in a sense, been in the works for more than thirty-five years now. Its underpinnings harken back to my days as a student at NYU pursuing a Masters Degree in Cinema Studies, where I researched and wrote two Independent Study papers for the late William K. Everson. One of these, written in 1979, chronicled the films and career of silent comedy pioneer Henry Lehrman, followed in 1982 by a detailed history of the Sterling Comedies. Little was written or known about Lehrman at that time, and my fascination with this shadowy figure in film history led to a dogged pursuit of anything I could unearth about the fellow and his films. And then, degree in hand, I moved on.

Fast forward twenty-five years to 2007.

Two individuals were responsible for my renewed interest in Henry Lehrman's career. First was Wendy Warwick White, whose 2007 biography of comedian Ford Sterling prompted me to contact and congratulate her on her fine work, and share some of what I had uncovered a quarter century earlier. Wendy put me in touch with historian Joan Myers, whose considerable research into the life of Virginia Rappe had led her to Henry Lehrman, Rappe and Lehrman having been lovers. Both Wendy and Joan urged me to renew my research, and the result is now in your hands.

A book of this sort isn't written in a vacuum, and numerous individuals have contributed in ways both large and small. Three people stand out, and head up the list. Joan Myers unearthed valuable information about Lehrman during her research, and generously turned over much of this for my use. The genealogical records documenting Lehrman's early days in Sambor, as well as many of the legal records involving Lehrman's numerous law suits, real estate transactions, and probate file contents are courtesy of Joan. Words cannot express just how grateful I am for Joan's contributions, especially since she seems to love dealing with both overseas genealogists and the paperwork and bureaucracy involved with ferreting out long-buried documents; I don't.

Silent cinema historian and author Sam Gill helped to put words in the mouths of so many of the people involved in Lehrman's story. Back in the later 1960s and early 1970s, Sam interviewed dozens of individuals who were part of the silent film industry. Sam and Kalton C. Lahue co-authored the seminal *Clown Princes and Court Jesters* back in 1970, which used much of what both he and Lahue had gleaned from their interviews. Sam has graciously revisited these half-century old interviews and painstakingly transcribed many of them for my use here, and I can't thank him enough. He has also been extremely generous in allowing me to use numerous stills and other images from his incredible collection. Thanks too, of course, for his thoroughly entertaining and insightful Foreword.

Silent comedy authority Steve Massa has been of considerable help as well, guiding me through the labyrinthine holdings of the New York Public Library for the Performing Arts, and answering all sorts of questions regarding silent comedy minutia. Steve's powers of recognition of the most obscure performers in silent comedy are second to none, identifying a stunning number of the individuals in the endless stream of stills, frame enlargements, and trade publication images that I have forwarded to him. Steve has also been extremely generous with his time, reading through the first draft of the manuscript and filmography, offering helpful comments and suggestions for its betterment, and providing his gracious Introduction to this book.

Lehrman's few surviving films have become more accessible over the last decade or so, and these have facilitated further assessment of his unique approach to comedy. Ashley Swinnerton and the late Charles Silver, of the Museum of Modern Art's Film Study Center, arranged several private viewings of the museum's holdings, as has Zoran Sinobad of the Library of Congress' Moving Image Section of the Motion Picture, Broadcasting and Recorded Sound Division. The now-defunct annual *Slapsticon* conventions provided an unparalleled opportunity to view rare works of Lehrman and so many of his contemporaries, inviting comparison of both content and style. The *Mostly Lost* workshop held each year at the Library of Congress' Packard Campus in Culpeper, Virginia has shown the occasional comedy short, but more importantly has yielded the opportunity to meet and share thoughts with numerous like-minded researchers; organizers Rob Stone and Rachel Parker are to be thanked for these wonderful get-togethers. Ian Glass of T3Media, Dave Stevenson of Looser Than Loose, Paul Gierucki of CineMuseum, Jack Hardy of Grapevine Video, David Shepherd of Film Preservation Associates, the folk at A-1 Video, and private collector Bill Sprague all warrant mention as well.

Many thanks to those archivists who have provided access to one-of-a-kind documents in their respective holdings. First and foremost, Ned Comstock at USC's Cinematic Arts Library, for digging out the numerous script analyses that Lehrman undertook for Darryl Zanuck at 20th Century-Fox circa 1937-1940, as well as the story outlines by Lehrman and Nunnally Johnson for the films *Moulin Rouge* and *Bulldog Drummond Strikes Back*. Jonathon Auxier, Curator of the Warner Brothers Archives at USC School of Cinematic Arts, provided a number of in-house documents detailing the events leading up to Lehrman's dismissal as director of Warner's *Private Izzy Murphy* in 1926, and the legal issues that followed. Seth Goldman, of the Neversink Valley Museum, graciously opened the facility's doors for me on a cold Sunday and allowed me to pore through the old Caudebec Inn's guest registers with the goal of nailing down Lehrman's various stays while a member of the visiting Biograph company.

The late Robert S. Birchard, editor of the American Film Institute's AFI Catalog of Feature Films and the AFI Academic Network, had taken time out from his incredibly busy schedule to share his thoughts about the Fox Sunshine Comedies, as well as several images and documents related to Lehrman. Richard M. Roberts, whose encyclopedic knowledge of silent film history never ceases to amaze me, shared his views of Lehrman as a creative genius, and of Lehrman's last great silent comedy short, *Wet and Warmer*.

Lisa Robins should be singled out as well. As grandniece of British music hall veteran and former Lehrman star comedian Billie Ritchie, Lisa has single-handedly kept her long-departed great uncle's memory alive. She is holder of the Ritchie family records and photo albums, and has spent numerous hours researching Billie's past. Lisa conducted several interviews with Billie's daughter Wyn as well, and I am so fortunate that she initially reached out to me and was eager to share her findings.

Of course words alone cannot do full justice to a medium as visual as silent comedy, and short of viewing the films themselves the next best thing is to have images from those films. Not an easy task when so many of those films are nearly a century old or older, so a special thanks is in order to all who contributed images from their private collections. Marc Wanamaker of Bison Archives heads up the list, for responding to a hopeful request for a single studio image with a deluge of rare images. Dr. Robert James Kiss warrants mention as well, having dug into his considerable collection to provide a number of rare stills. Rob Stone and George Willeman of the Library of Congress' Packard Campus graciously provided a number of frame enlargements from their holdings. Other contributors include, and in no particular order: Elif Rongen-Kaynakci and Annette Schulz of the Netherlands EYE Filmmuseum for frame enlargements and images from several of the museum's holdings; the late Cole Johnson; Robert L. Harned and the Sally Phipps Archives; Kay Shackleton of SilentHollywood.com; Macelo Coronado and John Hillman of SilentCinema.com; and Diana R. Garcia of Heritage Auction Galleries (Ha.com). Private collectors Rob Arkus, Jim Kerkhoff, Steve Rydzewski, and Alan Herskowitz have all been similarly generous with sharing their holdings.

Additional thanks are extended to all of those who contributed in some fashion or other, be it with documents, visual identification of stills, leads, and just general encouragement. These individuals include Anthony Balducci, John Bengston, Dr. Jon Burrows of the University of Warwick, Bruce Calvert, Bob DeMoss, David Denton, Louie Despres, Jason Engle, Rob Farr, Jorge Finkleman, Frank Flood, John Hazelton of FilmPosters.com, Dave Lord Heath, Tommie Hicks, Nelson Hughes, Nina Judson, Mark Jungheim, Deborah and Christina Lane, Robin Lint, Wendy Marshall, Joe Moore, Jerry Murbach at Doctor Macro's High Quality Movie Scans, Brian Pearce and Red Jacket Press, Randy Skretvedt, Marilyn Slater, Gail Smith, Chris Snowden, Tony Susnick, Brent Walker, Richard Lewis Ward, and Steve Zalusky.

To my editor, Michael Hayde, a heartfelt thanks for the wonderful feedback that brought several factual errors to my attention, along with a number of thoughtful suggestions that went a long way to clarify some less-than-clear passages, corrections to some lingering typos, and the smoothing out some of my more fractured phrasing. Michael's knowledge of the era and attention to detail were an immeasurable asset.

Thanks to publisher Ben Ohmart as well, whose BearManor Media provides a much-needed outlet for all sorts of media-related works that might otherwise not ever make it to print. His is a valuable resource, affording authors, biographers, autobiographers, and historians the opportunity to document aspects of history that might otherwise be lost to time.

And thanks to my wife Barbara, whose patience and understanding during untold hours while I lost myself in the writing of this book was appreciated more than words can express. Her ongoing support and good nature has kept me going.

Last but not least, to the anonymous donor who has so selflessly provided me with "stuff" that will go unspecified. You know who you are, and I sincerely thank you.

Introduction by Steve Massa

The accepted mythology of American silent comedy presents Henry Lehrman as a villain — callous, egotistical, and sadistic. According to legend his misdeeds include putting extras in physical danger, bullying film newbies like Charlie Chaplin, denouncing an innocent Roscoe "Fatty" Arbuckle as the rapist and murderer of his girlfriend Virginia Rappe, and having a large hand in the death of comic Billie Ritchie. Even his nickname of "Pathé" is a source of derision — said to have come from his posing as a veteran of France's Pathé Studio to get entry into D.W. Griffith's Biograph Company.

While his infamy is played up, what's overlooked and ignored is his very real importance as one of the main architects of silent comedy. Rarely examined has been his collaboration with Mack Sennett — at Biograph and in the creation of Keystone, his work as a producer and innovator with his own companies such as Sterling, L-Ko, Fox Sunshine, and Lehrman First National, and his influence on the next generation of comedy creators like Jack White, Norman Taurog, and John G. Blystone.

That is until now.

Tom Reeder has scoured newspapers, synopses of missing films, interviews, genealogical information, pressbooks, copies of surviving films, and trade magazines (I know as I saw him busy at work at the New York Public Library for the Performing Arts at Lincoln Center) in order to present a balanced and more complete view of the demonized Mr. Lehrman and his achievements. By any stretch of the imagination a "colorful character," Lehrman was driven, could be ruthless, and was reckless with money (as well as speed limits). He was also a natural filmmaker in addition to being highly intelligent and creative, so much so that even after his glory days of the teens and early twenties his opinions and filmmaking advice were valued by no less than Darryl F. Zanuck.

Besides the new insights into Lehrman and his accomplishments, Reeder provides a detailed view of the larger world of silent film with portraits of major players such as Zanuck, Mack Sennett, D. W. Griffith, and Carl Laemmle, not to mention a "who was who" of silent comedy that includes Charlie Chaplin, Roscoe Arbuckle, Ford Sterling, Mabel Normand, Billie Ritchie, Lloyd Hamilton, Hank Mann, Alice Howell, Jimmie Adams, Dot Farley, and a slew of people you may never have heard of — Dan Russell, Gene Rogers, Sammy Cohen, and Ted McNamara — even various comedy dogs, monkeys, and lions (i.e. Ethel and Gene). All this is topped off with an amazing filmography with detailed casts and credits, synopsis, and reviews — a cornucopia of information on each individual film.

Forgotten during his own lifetime, scant attention has been paid to Lehrman in the seventy years since his death. Now we finally have an examination, thorough and unbiased, that establishes Lehrman's rightful place in film history. Silent comedy scholars and fans, in addition to anyone interested in Hollywood lore, owe a debt of gratitude to Tom for his dogged determination and accurate eye in bringing light to this dark and neglected corner of movie history.

STEVE MASSA
New York, New York
September 24, 2016

Preface

*"There's three sides to every story: yours, mine, and the truth.
Memory to each of us appears differently."*

ROBERT EVANS

How good is your memory? Not for the daily, inconsequential incidents that occur randomly, time after time, but of the more momentous occurrences. The birth of a child, the circumstances surrounding the meeting of an eventual lover, a promotion at work or the hiring for a new job, the death and the services that follow for a loved one; these are the sort of memories that stick with us, that we think about time and again. But even with these sort of deep-seated memories, do you recall the exact order of events, the specific participants or attendees, and the conversations that took place, word for word? Incidents that took place last year, ten years ago, twenty-five years ago, and, if you are old enough, forty or fifty years ago? It is doubtful, even with a diary at hand.

Henry Lehrman was a comparatively minor figure in the history of American film, and as a result few primary materials exist documenting his rise and fall in the industry. The incidents and chronology contained in the pages that follow are derived in no small part from the recollections of participants that were committed to print years after the fact. Co-workers at Biograph such as Linda Arvidson Griffith compiled her autobiography in the mid-1920s, so her memories were comparatively fresh, but others such as Mack Sennett delayed putting pen to paper for over forty years after the incidents he described took place. Biographer Gene Fowler and historian Terry Ramsaye relied on the memories and stories of others in compiling their books in the mid-1920s and mid-1930s, respectively, as did Kalton Lahue and Sam Gill more than a half century later toward the end of the 1960s.

The text that follows is liberally sprinkled with endnotes indicating the sources for the various claims and quotes made herein, so that readers can decide for themselves the veracity of each. There is little doubt that a number of inaccuracies and outright falsehoods have crept into this biography as a result, and it is hoped that corrections will be forwarded to the author as these are revealed.

As for the hundreds of films Lehrman was responsible for, only a small number have survived, and even fewer are accessible to the casual viewer. This latter group is, in many instances, one-of-a-kind copies held by various film archives throughout the world, and some of these have not yet been transferred to safety stock for viewing by historians. In discussing these films I have attempted to indicate those personally viewed, as opposed to the remainder where I have had to rely on others who had the privilege to view these rare films and/or contemporary reviews and synopses.

Two appendices are included, one detailing the fate of the short-lived Sterling Motion Picture Corporation, and the other the lengthier story of the L-Ko Motion Picture Company, both after Lehrman's departure from those studios. I felt it important to include the full history of these two studios since neither has been given this thorough treatment previously, although Wendy Warwick White's biography of Ford Sterling (*Ford Sterling: His Life and Films*, McFarland & Company, 2007) provided a good start. Both the Sterling and L-Ko companies receive complete filmographies as well.

Mack Sennett's Keystone Film Company has already been given its due in Brent Walker's meticulously researched and exhaustive *Mack Sennett's Fun Factory* (McFarland and Company, 2010), so there was no need to rehash that here. The Fox Film Company's comedy companies will receive a similarly thorough treatment in the late Robert S. Birchard's upcoming history, tentatively titled *So This Is Art: Fox Silent Comedy Shorts 1917-1928*, co-authored by Sam Gill, Robert James Kiss, and Karl Thiede; I will leave it to them to tell that story. My goal here for these two studios was to cover Lehrman's time with them, and little more.

My overall hope is to provide a reasonably accurate account of Henry Lehrman's life and career, and to engender in the reader a renewed respect for his work; heaven knows his reputation needs all the help it can get. As for any inaccuracies or outright mistakes that have found their way into the following, I take full responsibility.

A street in "Old" Sambor, circa 1900.

CHAPTER 1

Sambor: The Birth of a Notion

The city of Sambor has had a long and often tragic history. Now located in the region known as Galicia in the far western part of Ukraine (near the border with Poland), Sambor was founded in the 12th century. The town was destroyed a century later by an army of Mongol and Turk nomads known as the Tatars, partially rebuilt and burnt down once again shortly thereafter. Some of the residents relocated to a nearby village called Pohonicz, which eventually became known as Novi-Sambor, or new Sambor; the original settlement became known as Stari-Sambor, or old Sambor. Several more attacks by the ill-tempered Tatars in the late 13th and early 14th centuries resulted in yet another village-leveling conflagration. A new Sambor was built on the ruins of the old, this time optimistically — but with epic short-sightedness — surrounded by thick walls and deep trenches. As a result, the town was unable to grow beyond these barriers for the next two and a half centuries. Through the years Sambor and the surrounding region were ruled by a number of different powers, eventually becoming part of the Poland-Lithuanian Commonwealth in the mid-16th century.

Fires again decimated the city in 1585, 1637, and 1779. Nestled between the rivers Dniester and Strwionz, floods played havoc with the city as well, the worst of these in 1688 and 1700. Epidemics broke out from time to time, one in 1705 wiping out two-thirds of the population, and another in 1771 wiping out over 3,000 lives. Famine took its toll in the mid-19th century, the populace attempting to survive on wild grass and leaves.[1] All in all, it could be a hazardous place to live.

In 1772, Russia, Austria, and Prussia arrived at an agreement partitioning Poland. Austria received Eastern Galicia where Sambor was located, along with a portion of Western Galicia. The city soon became the home of Poles, Germans, Russians, and Jews. The Austrian Empire was succeeded by the Austro-Hungarian Empire in 1867, of which Sambor was a part, and remained so in the year 1881 when Henry Lehrman was born.

Lehrman arrived in this world on March 30 of that year, his birth registration giving his first name as Moses, a variation of the Hebrew name Moshe. His father, Simon Josef Lehrmann, was born twenty-five years earlier on May 13, 1855. Mother Sara, one year younger than her husband Simon Josef, was born in August of 1856. Simon Josef's parents were Moses Lehrmann and Sime Lieberman. Sara's parents were Josef Zimmermann and his wife Malka, her birth surname unknown.[2]

Lehrman had two older sisters: Ester Bina (Sabina) was born in either 1878 or 1879,[3] and Kreincze on January 28, 1880.[4] These two births predated the date given on parents Josef and Sara's marriage registry (February 15, 1880), so it is probable that this civil ceremony had been preceded by a religious ceremony. A third sister, Rachel, was born in 1882 but died a brief two months later.[5] These four are their only known children, but it is possible that there were others, unrecorded.

According to the Galicia Business Directory of 1891,[6] Simon Josef and his younger brother Osias ran a leather and farm implements manufacturing firm. Years later Lehrman referred to his father as a "successful manufacturer of steel products and agricultural implements of Austria, whose name is known throughout that country, where his implements have been in general use for years."[7] A connection to the railway network in the 1870s had proven a boon to Sambor's development, and the town rapidly became an important economic center. By the time Lehrman was eight the town's commercial enterprises included flour mills, a brewery and distillery, factories for the manufacture of oil, soap, matches, and the refining of alcohol, and so forth.[8] Simon Josef and Osias' firm was yet another beneficiary of this development.

Actress-screenwriter Salka Viertel was born in Sambor — "a provincial garrison town" as she called it — eight years after Lehrman, and affords us a glimpse of what the town was like back then in her autobiography *The Kindness of Strangers*:

> The town Sambor had a population of twenty-five thousand. There were approximately four thousand Poles, eighteen thousand Ukrainians and about three thousand five hundred Jews.[9] It also had a garrison which was very important to the younger female population, regardless of creed or nationality…. [The women] were admired by the officers loafing in the sidewalk cafés of the Promenade. The Promenade was part of the large square around the City Hall. The shops and the pharmacy were on its main sidewalk, which was called Linia A-B. At each end was the *cukiernia*, a combination of a café and *confiserie*. Old acacia trees shaded the sidewalks. In summer Sambor's "society" gathered in the kiosk in front of the *cukiernia* to sip lemonade and consume excellent ice cream and cakes. There were two kiosks, one occupied by the cavalry, the other, at the opposite end of the A-B, by the infantry. They hardly ever mixed, as members of the Austrian and Hungarian aristocracy served in the cavalry, while the infantry was mostly middle class.[10]

Available information regarding Lehrman's earliest years in Europe is sparse at best, the bulk of it coming from interviews with the fellow himself years later after he had achieved success here in the U.S. In the absence of any further collaborative or conflicting evidence, we will take Lehrman's later-life assertions about his years back in Europe at face value, reality be damned. These assertions could be conflicting at times, one blatant example the year of his birth: 1881 was instead given as 1883 in the *Los Angeles Times* biographical sketch "Henry M. Lehrman,"[11] as 1884 on his WWI Registration Card, and most frequently as 1886 in, among other places, the *1929 Motion Picture News Blue Book Booking Guide* mini-biography (p.140). This latter date was the one that made it onto his grave stone. As for his name, Lehrman adopted the first name "Henry" sometime during these early years, and his name was alternately given in later years as Henry Mauritz Lehrman and Henry Max Lehrmann, the final "n" usually, but not always, dropped from his surname. The name Lehrmann itself was likely the result of an order in the late 18th and early 19th century forcing all Jews to replace their Polish names with German names.[12]

What we do know for certain is that Lehrman's oldest sister Sabina would marry Benisch Benjamin Lauer on April 6, 1897. Lehrman's mother Sara died on February 25, 1898, and forty-eight year old father Simon Josef would remarry five years later on

Sambor's Market Place, circa 1900.

October 11, 1903 to forty-seven year old Ester Ryfka Schulsinger.[13] Simon Josef's fate is, as of this writing, unknown.

Lehrman grew up speaking German and Polish, and would eventually get by with passable French. The city's Jews were formerly taught at the progressive *Heder*, a Jewish religious school for young children, but by the 1880s they were beginning to study in the city's public schools. A commercial school for Jewish children was founded in 1891 that included a one-year business course. This taught accounting, correspondence, and the Hebrew, Polish, and German languages, so the ten year old Lehrman may have attended this school. It is likely that he was educated at the Gymnasium in Sambor, which Viertel described as "a high school equal to the American Junior College, with Latin, Greek and German as compulsory subjects." Lehrman later claimed that he was educated at the Vienna Commercial University, stating that "My parents thought they perceived in me an extraordinary talent for finance, so I was sent to the Handelsakademie, that is, College of Commerce, in Vienna."[14] A check of that institution's yearbooks during the time he would have been in attendance reportedly did not turn up any mention of Lehrman, so either he was stretching the truth to the breaking point or, less likely, attended for such a short time that he didn't make it into their pages. There was, however, a Commercial University in Sambor, so he may have attended that institution instead. The aforementioned commercial school for Jewish children also had a half-year course for adults that was held during the winter months, so he may have received some, or all, of his training there as well. Regardless, there is little doubt that Lehrman was well educated.

Lehrman's family was comparatively well off financially, and while Sambor itself was thriving at this time due to an influx of industry, there were still the less fortunate among them. "There were many beggars in the community," wrote Viertel. "Twice a week they came to the house to receive alms. The Christians on Thursday, which was also market day, the Jews on Friday. The gypsies came and went as they pleased at irregular intervals."

With the completion (or interruption) of his education, another report has him taking "a short whirl at the European music halls with several different vaudeville acts."[15] If this is true, it may have been a source of displeasure for his parents. Viertel had this to say about the traveling troupes, who had to "play before crude audiences in the dirty halls of small Galician towns:"

> Many Polish and Ukrainian companies came to Sambor. The Ukrainians had a good reputation and performed operas by Glinka, comedies, and folk musicals and dances. They had good orchestras, lovely costumes, and were enthusiastically supported by their co-nationals; but the Polish intelligentsia, always contemptuous of everything Ukrainian, never went to see them. The higher bracket of Imperial and District employees, the big landowners, also the lawyers, Jewish and non-Jewish, were Polish, but they were not interested in supporting the shabby, wandering Polish troupers, and preferred to travel two hours by train and see better performers in Lwow.[16]

A one-year term in the Austrian army was also compulsory at that time, and Lehrman claimed to have served as a lieutenant, stationed at the fortress in the city of Przemysl. "His regiment is still stationed there," wrote the *Los Angeles Times* on the first day of 1915, "and many of his former comrades are now fighting as members of Lieutenant Lehrman's garrison."[17] They wouldn't fight much longer: the fortress, while one of the largest in Europe was far from the most up-to-date, and had been surrounded by invading Russian troops since November 1914. The fortress was surrendered in March 1915, two months after Lehrman's interview.

Lehrman eventually found employment as a "correspondent," as the Austrian immigration register put it, which suggests a decently-paid white-collar profession as a private secretary or the like. One report indicates that this was in the glass business.[18] Lehrman had greater ambitions, however: "I myself perceived my ability to spend millions, but as there seemed no prospect of obtaining them in the overcrowded European field, I set out for America."[19] There's no telling what his family thought of his heading off to America, but since there is no known account of any return trips to visit them over the next forty years, it's possible that his journey to America was due in part to some friction within the Lehrmann household. Whatever the case, his real story begins with his arrival in America. Within a mere two years he would become part of the American film industry, the first step in his meteoric rise within that industry during the dozen years that followed.

CHAPTER 2

Biograph, IMP, and Kinemacolor: Baptism By Fire

As mum as Lehrman was in later years regarding the specifics of his origins back in Europe, scant little was said as well about the first half dozen years here in the U.S. What little we know about his arrival in New York City, initial employment, entry into the fledgling film industry, and subsequent positions with a trio of motion picture companies comes from official documents, a handful of interviews and press releases, and the numerous writings of others. Needless to say a lot that has been passed on is an uneasy mix of faulty recollections, colorful but potentially apocryphal stories, mere conjecture, with a dollop of accuracy thrown in just to keep things confusing.

Lehrman arrived in New York two days before Christmas, 1906, debarking from the Hamburg-American Line's steam ship *Pennsylvania* with $40 tucked in his pocket. The ship's manifest described the twenty-five year old — here named Moritz Lehrmann — as being five feet six inches tall with dark eyes, dark hair, and no visible marks of identification. His occupation was listed as "Clerk," and he had made the long journey to the U.S. in second class accommodations — not quite as comfy as those in first class but a major step up from those masses huddled in steerage. His first stop would be the home of Rudolph and Eugenie Strobach located at 524 West 151st Street.[1] Whether Strobach, who had roots in Austria and had emigrated from Bremen, Germany ten years earlier, was a relative or friend is unknown.[2] Strobach was a clerk at a clearing house, so it's possible that he had a position waiting for Lehrman in a similar capacity.[3] Lehrman later said that one of his first positions here was as a dry-goods clerk.

Lehrman couldn't speak a word of English upon his arrival, but the bright young man soon picked up the language through his interactions with others. He later claimed to have held a number of other positions during the first few years, including a stint as a bartender in an uptown German beer garden, as translator for a book agent, and as a dry goods clerk. Of this latter position he said "[Here] I began to realize the limitations of even a first-class education. I measured everything in meters and as a meter is 1/10 more than the American yard, the proprietor decided that my extraordinary generosity unfitted me for such a dry career." Yet another position supposedly held was that as a horse-drawn street car conductor on the 34th Street cross-town line.[4] Linda Arvidson,

Biograph director D.W. Griffith's wife at the time, remembered things slightly different in the mid-twenties, placing Lehrman on the Fourteenth Street cross-town line that stopped in front of the Biograph studios at number 11; Biograph was the shortened name by which the American Mutoscope and Biograph Company was more commonly known.[5] Terry Ramsey agreed with her in his *A Million and One Nights*,[6] although she may have been the source of his information.

Lehrman spent long hours in the various neighborhood nickelodeons, his fascination with the new medium taking hold while he familiarized himself with the written language. This led to an eventual job working at one of these theaters as a sweeper and cleaner, as he later told the dubiously named Mlle. Chic, writer for Universal's weekly exhibitors' paper *Universal Weekly*.[7] Lehrman's entrance into the film industry was purportedly due to a chance meeting with the young comedian Mack Sennett, who'd been working at Biograph since early 1908.

Most of what has been published about this moment in Lehrman's life comes from Mack Sennett's memory-addled autobiography *King of Comedy* (1954) and the earlier, heavily embellished, highly suspect but eminently readable biography *Father Goose: The Story of Mack Sennett* (1934) written by Gene Fowler. Both have Lehrman at the Unique Theater working as an usher when he first encountered Sennett, but Fowler is more specific giving the date as 1908 and the film screened during this chance meeting as *Coney Island*. Both accounts have Lehrman criticizing Sennett's performance in the screened film before recognizing the fellow he was speaking with and the actor on-screen as one and the same, then quickly backpedaling and turning criticism to praise. Sennett has the two of them communicating in "kindergarten-type French," and a friendship was established between the two young men, supposedly cemented over beers at Brady's Saloon on Seventh between Forty-First and Forty-Second. Given that this film was Sennett's first produced script for Biograph — featuring cops, no less — it is likely that he was soliciting opinions about the story itself as well as his performance in it.

What *hasn't* been published was Lehrman's own account of this event, relayed in an interview with Barnet Braverman in the early 1940s. His account confirms and embellishes on much of what Fowler claimed. "Lehrman was in Unique Theatre on 14th Street as usher," wrote Braverman in his summary, "looking at a slapstick comedy directed by [Griffith] which had a continuous 400 ft. scene by [Griffith]: Monday Morning in a Coney Island Court — not a cut in it! Sennett would drop in at theatre, without [Lehrman] knowing who he was, and ask what he thought of the policeman…Why do you think he's rotten?….Interest Sennett displayed made [Lehrman] alert…"[8] Fowler's account[9] pre-dated the Braverman interview, but Sennett's was written years later, so Sennett may have based his telling on either — or both — earlier source. Regardless, the three accounts are essentially consistent.

Located at 136 Fourteenth Street between Sixth and Seventh Avenues in Manhattan, the Theatre Unique was built back in 1884 as Theiss' music hall and continued as such until 1907 when it underwent $25,000 of renovation and emerged as a gaudy nickelodeon. This chance meeting of Lehrman and Sennett would have taken place sometime between September and December of 1908. The Unique showed strictly Association films — the product of Edison licensees who were members of the Film Service Association — up until July, when competition from three other area theaters for the thirteen weekly Association releases compelled the Unique to switch to independent films. The Biograph film *Monday*

Morning in a Coney Island Police Court was released on September 4, 1908, and Sennett had a small role as a policeman. Biograph lost its "independent" status in December 1908 when it teamed up with Edison and others to form the Motion Pictures Patents Company.

Sennett said that he invited Lehrman to Biograph to see the filming of the D.W. Griffith-directed *Nursing a Viper*, but the timeline gets a bit murky here. It may have been some other film that Sennett invited him to see, or it was some months after their initial meeting that the invitation was extended. Regardless of the details behind Lehrman's introduction to Biograph, the fact remains that he found work with the company, and that *Nursing a Viper*, filmed on September 24 and 29, 1909, and released on November 4, 1909, is the earliest Biograph with Lehrman in a blink-and-you'll-miss-it bit part as one in a large mob of French revolutionaries.

The Biograph had been in business since its initial appearance late in 1896, their projector an evolution of the company's Mutoscope peep show device of a year earlier. A competitor of Edison's projecting Kinetoscope and long-standing thorn in the side of that litigation-prone inventor, the Biograph had successfully weathered the numerous camera patent lawsuits filed by the Edison Manufacturing Company due to the unique design of the Biograph camera. Other film companies were not so fortunate; their camera designs were essentially the same as Edison's, thereby leaving them vulnerable to patent infringement suits. These suits decimated American film production, effectively leaving Edison and Biograph as the two survivors, while former competitors folded or were reduced to importing foreign-made films. In 1907, Edison's competitors broke down and negotiated a licensing agreement with their tormentor that allowed them to resume production. Brooklyn's American Vitagraph Company, Chicago's Selig Polyscope Company and Essanay Film Manufacturing Company, New York's Kalem Company, Philadelphia's Lubin Manufacturing Company, and France's Pathé Frères and George Méliès' Star Films (both of whose films were imported and distributed in the U.S.) were now back in business, and the doors were closed to any future applicants for licenses. Biograph remained the sole outsider, Edison hoping to force his long-standing competitor out of the market. It was around this time that Lehrman sought employment with Biograph.

The Biograph's films up to this time were typical of the era and competition: topical news and actualities, comedies, and melodramas, of either a half- or full-reel in length, of approximately five to ten minutes' duration. Most of these films had been directed by Wallace "Old Man" McCutcheon in earlier years, but illness and other duties prompted him to cede the directorial chores to others. His son Wallace Jr. was his first choice, but Wallace's interests were elsewhere and his performance in this capacity workmanlike at best. A number of others were assigned the job, but one by one their efforts proved unsatisfactory. As the company's output deteriorated and financial difficulties mounted, McCutcheon grew desperate to find someone up to the task. He found that person in David Wark Griffith.

Griffith, a thirty-three year old stage actor and aspiring playwright, had reluctantly entered the film industry as an actor in early 1908 for purely mercenary reasons. Working under his stage name of Lawrence Griffith, he landed a starring role in the Edison drama *Rescued from an Eagle's Nest*, where he rescues a child and gets to struggle with a ridiculous looking stuffed eagle. When another role proved elusive, Griffith applied at Biograph where he was quickly put to work as part of their stock company. While the five dollar a day paycheck proved useful, Griffith soon found that he could sell story synopses to Lee Dougherty in the story department for some extra cash ranging anywhere from $5 to $30. His writing abilities proved to be much better than his acting.

Impressed by Griffith's energy and creativity, and at Dougherty's urging, McCutcheon offered Griffith a job directing, with the promise that he could go back to acting for the studio if the challenge proved to be a fiasco. After testing the waters by directing a few of the company's Mutoscopes, Griffith was assigned his first film, the drama *The Adventures of*

LEFT: *David Wark Griffith.* COURTESY OF JERRY MURBACH AT DOCTOR MACRO'S HIGH QUALITY MOVIE SCANS, WWW.DOCTORMACRO.COM. RIGHT: *Michael Sinnott, better known as Mack Sennett.*

Dollie (released July 14, 1908). Griffith exuded confidence overseeing the film, his instinctive sense of drama and story construction resulting in a smooth shoot. Some practical advice from his new friend, Biograph cameraman G.W. "Billy" Bitzer (*not* Griffith's cameraman on this first film), certainly didn't hurt. Released in July 1908, the picture proved to be a success, if only with the public. According to Bitzer, exhibitors did not care for the film, but the public liked it. Word of mouth led to increased business, so the exhibitors changed their collective mind and requested more films like it. Biograph signed Griffith to his first director contract in August 1908, and he was off and running.[10] In a 1935 interview, a former Biograph property man had this to say about Griffith's direction of *Dollie*, although he may have been confusing it with a later film:

> Griffith wasn't the least bit nervous…. [T]he minute he walked on the scene we knew we were working for a real master. He gave orders clear and direct and had the whole thing done in a couple of days.[11]

Griffith directed more than sixty films during the remainder of that first year, a combination of dramas and comedies of a reel or less in length. It was baptism by fire, but Griffith was a quick learner. Not satisfied with the way things had been done previously and the static, stage-bound nature of the films that preceded him, Griffith introduced new innovations or built on others' while rewriting the art of visual storytelling, and eventually introduced a more natural, less flamboyant style of acting among his stock company of regulars. He would be Biograph's sole director through most of the following year, and the director of more than four hundred fifty films by the time he left Biograph in 1913.

While Griffith preferred filming dramas over comedies, he directed a fair number of the latter, and effectively so, the first the aforementioned *Monday Morning in a Coney Island Police Court*, his fifteenth film. One of the members of his stock company and a participant in that film was the young Canadian transplant Michael Sinnott, now using the more stage-friendly name Mack Sennett. Sennett had joined Biograph early in 1908 after several years in burlesque and on the legitimate stage both as actor and singer, and by the end of that year had appeared in more than forty films for the studio, primarily in small, supporting parts. While the majority of these were dramas, his real love was the occasional comedy he'd eventually get to play in. As he put it in an interview two decades later:

> They didn't make comedies then, just sentimental romances and very meller melodramas and tragedies — what tragedies! These were awfully funny to me; I couldn't take them seriously. I often thought how easy it would be, with the least bit more exaggeration — and they were exaggerated plenty as it was — to turn those old dramas into pure farce.[12]

Sennett's fascination with the new medium and his determination to star in and, ideally, make comedies spurred him on to learn as much about filmmaking as possible. And who better to learn from than the director he was working for, and whose fame was growing with each new release. Griffith would become his unwitting teacher and mentor:

> D.W. Griffith was teaching me how to direct, although he did not know it. He was my day school, my adult education program, my university. This was possible for two reasons: I was not regularly employed in the occasional bit parts that they gave me or as an extra, and this gave me plenty of time to watch Griffith and his remarkable cameraman, the late Billy Bitzer. And I had discovered that Griffith liked to walk.
> When Griffith walked, I walked. I fell in, matched strides, and asked questions.
> Griffith told me what he was doing and what he hoped to do with the screen, and some of what he said stuck. I thought things over. I began to learn how to make a motion picture. I even offered a few suggestions to D.W. Griffith, but I discovered he was not so fascinated by comedy as I was, and he went into silence when I brought up my favorite people, policemen. I never succeeded in convincing Mr. Griffith that cops were funny.[13]

Sennett's perseverance paid off as he landed roles in most of the comedies that Griffith directed. Sennett's big break came in February 1909 when he landed the lead in *The Curtain Pole*, a wild comedy based on another Sennett script wherein a curtain pole-wielding Frenchman rides through the streets of Fort Lee, New Jersey, leaving in his wake a jumble of human bodies and overturned carts. The film was a comedic success, an early blueprint of sorts for the chase films in Sennett's future; it still delights today. Sennett appeared in more than one hundred fifty films in the two years that followed, and his talent and creativity were duly noted. In March 1911, Sennett was rewarded and put in charge of his own comedy unit.

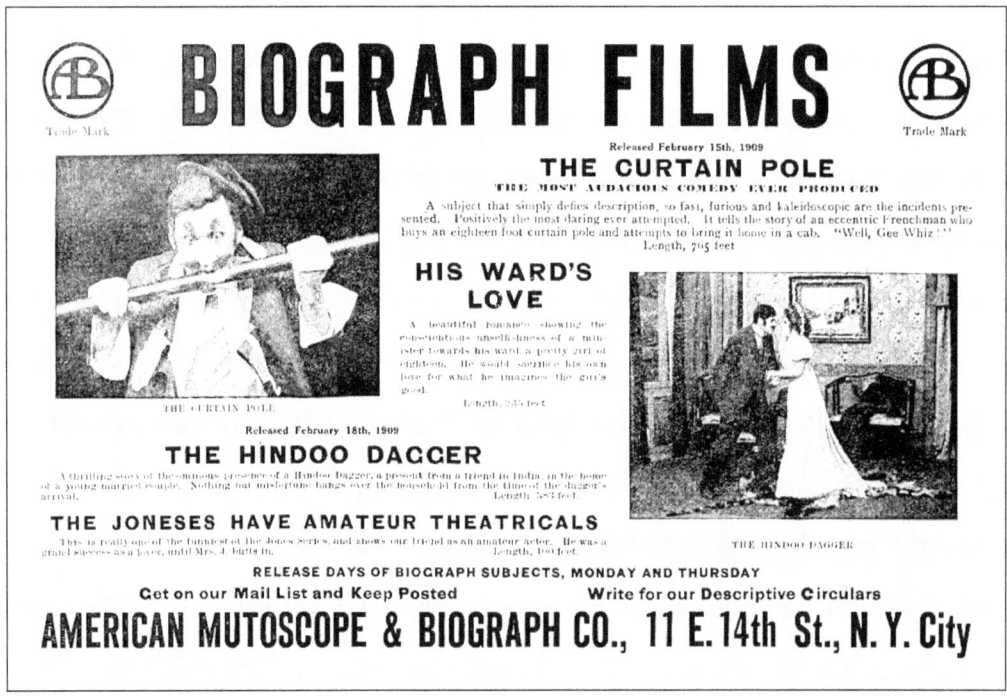

Biograph's ad for The Curtain Pole, *as it appeared in February 20, 1909 issue of* The Film Index.

In the meantime, Biograph had retaliated against the Edison closed-door policy of licensing, purchasing the patent for what was known as the Latham film loop. A vital component in virtually all film cameras of that era, it was an essential component in the smooth advancement of film stock through both camera and projector without fear of film tearing and breakage. Stymied by this action, it was now Edison's turn to negotiate, approaching Biograph to reach an amicable settlement. This led in late 1908 to a pooling of sixteen patents that related to the production and projection of motion pictures. The result was the creation of the Motion Picture Patents Company, also known as The Trust. With motion picture cameras, projectors, and film stock all falling under these patents, production companies were now licensed by The Trust to use the affected equipment and film. Distributors were licensed to handle films made solely by The Trust's licensee companies, to use projectors manufactured by Edison, and to pay ongoing fees for the privilege. Any company that balked at doing so was threatened with patent infringement and the inevitable lawsuits that would follow. The Trust's goal was simple: eliminate the remaining independent film producers and the roughly 1,000 independent film exchanges and exhibitors operating at the time. And now that Biograph had dropped the manufacture of the Mutoscopes and was focusing solely on motion pictures, the company shortened its name to The Biograph Company.

Lehrman had arrived at the studio sometime most likely in mid- to later-1909. He was dressed in an "old suit of clothes," said actor Al Ray years after the fact; his "dialect was so thick everybody looked at him."[14] As legend has it, Lehrman boasted that he had learned about the art of film at Pathé Frères in Paris. Terry Ramsey told it this way:

> [T]he adventuring young man presented himself at the Biograph studios and intimated that he would confer the favor of an interview upon the management. His bearing was dignified and distinguished, and his accent foreign, "M. Henry Lehrman of Paris."
>
> The management learned to its entire excitement and delight that the caller was a celebrated motion picture expert, recently connected with the Pathé establishments in France and that he would consider an American connection. M. Henry Lehrman was welcomed to Biograph's staff. He seemed to have a leaning toward comedy and was cast for it.
>
> Presently a faint tinge of suspicion arose that perhaps M. Lehrman was not, after all, a French motion picture expert. The story was whispered about and soon a nickname was born on it. He was "Pathé" Lehrman thence forward.[15]

The nickname stuck, and Lehrman must have embraced it; he used it extensively throughout his career, and in many instances in promotional pieces where he would have had the ability to suppress it. Asked a few years later about the origin of the nickname, Lehrman expressed ignorance:

> Where I got the name "Pathé"? I don't know myself, though I am certain that it did not come from Pathé Frerès, with whom I am not, and never have been, connected. I have an idea that D.W. Griffith was responsible for it in the beginning, and I suppose I objected strenuously, and that is the reason the name stuck to me. Perhaps he thought I was French, as I speak the language, but I was born in Austria, where I grew up speaking German and Polish.[16]

Griffith was the logical source; he was known for assigning nicknames to many of the members of his stock company, given the size of the group and the multiplicity of common first names.

Lehrman was a warm and willing body, but one without any perceptible previous experience. "The last thing that I ever thought of becoming was an actor, a moving picture actor at that!" he later said about his arrival here in the states. Griffith put him to work, nonetheless, albeit in the smallest of bit parts and as an extra in group shots. Griffith grew to respect and utilize the well-schooled European's knowledge of history, and the inaccuracies that would inevitably surface in the filmic recreation of those eras. Lehrman is identifiable in thirteen films made during the four month period from late September 1909 into the beginning of January 1910, and in an additional thirty-four films made during late April 1910 through early May 1911. There's little doubt that he appeared in more films than these, either wholly unidentifiable in crowd scenes, in films no longer available for viewing, or in footage that ended up on the cutting room floor.

The first of these, *Nursing a Viper*, is readily available for viewing, and Lehrman is there in the mob scenes, buried under a thick beard and heavy wig; sharper eyes than mine have isolated him in the surging crowds. There is the apocryphal story told by Fowler and mirrored by Sennett of Lehrman's "audition" for this film, wherein he performed an unexpected leap from a window (or rooftop, depending on the teller), plunging twenty

Lehrman leads the pack in The Redman's View.

feet before landing — and not once, but twice. For this his daily salary was doubled to the princely sum of ten dollars.

Lehrman's second recorded appearance — appearances, actually, as he's present in three different group scenes — is in the death-of-the-neglected-child weepie *Through the Breakers* (December 6, 1909). He is prominently on display in *The Redman's View* (December 9, 1909) as one of a dozen callous westerners who drive the Indians from their land, as well as one of the horde of brokers excitedly milling about the floor of the exchange in *A Corner in Wheat* (December 13, 1909). In the Sicilian-out-for-revenge drama *In Little Italy* (December 23, 1909) he is buried among a group of guests at a ball. Sennett had small roles in all five films as well, which may or may not have played a part in Lehrman's landing his bit parts.

Other appearances followed — all minor as well — with Lehrman among guests at a party, as a member of an audience, one of a group of stockbrokers, as a soldier or bar patron, and others of that sort.

Lehrman grew more comfortable with his acting ability, and would hang around the studio hoping for another role. Unfortunately for the ambitious young man, the available openings at Biograph were sporadic at best and frequently parceled out to members of the company of longer standing. As Linda Arvidson put it:

> Henry Lehrman, alias Pathé, hung about. How he loved being a near-actor! How he adored getting fixed up for a picture! He was satisfied by now that his make-ups were works of art. From the dressing-room he would emerge patting his swollen chest, with the laconic remark, "Some make-up!"[17]

Lehrman's friendship with Sennett grew over the next few years, and the two would share lodging at different times. The Bartholdi Inn at the corner of Broadway and 45th Street was one of their stops, although it is unclear if they were tenants at the same or different times. Victor Heerman described the Inn and its tenants to Kalton Lahue and Sam Gill:

> At that time just about everybody was living at the Bartholdi Inn. It was a boarding house run by a wonderful woman named Polly Bartholdi. It catered to the theatrical people and those in the movies. If you got a bit behind in rent, it was okay, pretty much the only place in New York where it was okay. Well, some of the top players lived there, like King Baggot and Bob Daly from the IMP, Dell Henderson and his wife from the Biograph, lots of picture people there…. In fact, Mack Sennett, Ford Sterling, Henry Lehrman, oh everybody, used to come to the Bartholdi Inn.[18]

According to Sennett's autobiography, however, Sennett, Lehrman, and Henderson shared a small apartment somewhere (and assumedly before Henderson's marriage) living as he put it "in a kind of competitive socialism, sharing everything and fighting each other for clothes, money, and girls."[19] Fowler goes into more (questionable) detail, stating that the apartment was Sennett's and cost thirty dollars per month, with the second-best room sublet to Henderson for sixteen dollars per month, and the smallest to Lehrman for ten dollars per month.

> These three men devoted most of their spare time to talk of pictures. All three had native ability in the field. Henderson knew how they should be acted. Sennett had a fine critical sense and could foretell what the public would like and what it would not like. He was a dependable barometer, because he himself had the average man's amusement tastes. Lehrman soon demonstrated that he had a natural creative bent and a flair for story construction.[20]

Lehrman had small parts in at least thirteen films shot between late September 1909 and early January 1910, and then there is a break that doesn't resume until late April. This period coincides with Griffith's first trip out to California where the weather was far more conducive to year-round film production. Both Sennett and Fowler have Lehrman as part of the group that headed out for the three month stay, but that is doubtful given the gap of his appearances. Lehrman did accompany the group the following January, however, so they've most likely confused the two trips. With the company's return in April, Lehrman resumed his small roles; how he occupied himself during those three previous months is unknown.

Towards the end of June 1909, Griffith had taken his troupe on the five hour trip out to the small town of Cuddebackville, New York, the company's base of operations the Caudebec Inn. This hilly area in Orange County bisected by the Neversink River offered settings and historic structures ideal for films of a variety of genres, and a climate far more pleasant than in the hot city. Griffith, Dougherty, and three others arrived in advance of the group on June 20, to make plans and scope out the area; the rest of the group following a week later on the 27th. Lehrman, who had by now been accepted by the group as one of their members, arrived for the tail end of the stay, signing the inn's guest register on October 17, 1909. A note of curiosity here: Lehrman was signed into room 18, the same room that has a June 27 register entry for a "Miss Behrman" of the Biograph group. The name "Behrman" is crossed out on the June 30 entries, and there are no further entries until October 17. Just who "Miss Behrman" was remains a mystery, and there is the distinct possibility that Lehrman and "Behrman" are one and the same, the gender and misspelling the work of a harried clerk furiously entering the large group's names.

A year later, Griffith made a return trip to Cuddebackville and the Caudebec Inn, arriving on July 20. Lehrman was part of this initial group as well, and stayed for the duration as evidenced by additional guest register entries for July 24 and August 28, 1910. Eddie Dillon, a Sennett favorite who later starred in a number of his Biograph comedies, was Lehrman's constant roommate throughout the trip, and presumably one of his better friends within the company. Lehrman appeared in at least two of this second visit's productions, the charming *Wilful Peggy* (August 25, 1910) starring Mary Pickford as the feisty peasant bride of the lord of an Irish manor, and *In Life's Cycle* (September 15, 1910), another one of those there-but-for-the-grace-of-God melodramas with the abused unwed mother crawling back to daddy.

Sennett, not yet directing at this time, had his sights set on overworked director Frank Powell's job. Powell was in charge of Biograph's second film company, primarily handling the comedies that Griffith no longer wanted to be associated with. Powell's health and/or mental stability was shaky at best, and Sennett waited for the fellow to snap.

> The Powell "crack-up" was not to come for many months, but the three men waited patiently. To be prepared for the Powell decline and fall, Sennett kept Lehrman working incessantly. At night he would bludgeon him for ideas, nor would he let Pathé go to sleep until some worth-while suggestion had been made. Sometimes they concocted a saleable scenario, and Mack would peddle it next day. Lehrman profited from these nocturnal sessions, for Sennett always handed over the entire proceeds of the sales to his guest.[21]

Sales of these scenarios would typically result in a windfall in the area of fifteen dollars to twenty-five dollars for the author. Mary Pickford, in her autobiography, wrote that Sennett was jealous of her ability to sell scenarios to Griffith, and approached her with the arrangement that she would put her name on his stories, and in return receive a commission for each one sold. This arrangement was short-lived due to the raucous nature of his stories, totally out of character with the ones she wrote and sold, and not ones with which she wanted her name associated.[22]

Lehrman, seemingly indispensible to Sennett by this time if only for his fertile creativity, was also part of Griffith's troupe that returned to California for the 1910-11 winter season, arriving on January 3, 1911 and remaining through the better part of May. Lehrman shared a room with Sennett at the Alexandria Hotel, and received two dollars a day (as did everyone else) for expenses. He is identifiable in over a dozen films made during that stay, including the amusing *Comrades* (March 13, 1911), wherein he plays a butler. This film heralded Sennett's directorial debut, his patience having finally paid off, but not as a replacement for Powell, who continued directing comedies and an increasing number of dramas for the next two years before exiting Biograph.

Sennett would continue with direction for Biograph for the next year and a half, and while his films were quite popular with audiences and exhibitors alike, his preference — and Lehrman's for that matter — for none-too-subtle slapstick and borderline vulgarity was kept in check by the more conservative tastes of the front office and Griffith, whose approval was required on all scripts and cast choices. Sennett yearned for the freedom to make the sort of outlandish comedies that he preferred, ones deeply rooted in the tradition of the burlesque houses that he used to frequent in the Bowery: "The round, fat girls in nothing much doing their bumps and grinds, the German-dialect comedians, and especially the cops and tramps with their bed slats and bladders appealed to me as being funny people."[23]

There is a noticeable break in the production dates for the California-based films in which Lehrman appeared, which lasted from late March until early May. This may have been while Lehrman was (according to Fowler) hospitalized for jaundice. The *Blind Princess and the Poet* (August 17, 1911), filmed in early May, is the last of the California films in which Lehrman is known to have had a role.

After the group's return to New York, Griffith and company made a third trip out to Cuddebackville, arriving on July 30, 1911. Lehrman was along for this trip as well, rooming with buddies Sennett and comedian Fred Mace, but has not been identified in any of the films made at that time. This would be Griffith's final trip to Cuddebackville, but other competitor studios took notice of what this rural area had to offer from the Biograph releases, and followed on Griffith's heels: the Pathé Frères company arrived at the Caudebec in June 1912, another group from Gem arrived in July 1912, a third group from Thanhouser in October 1912, and another from Victor in June 1913.

Lehrman, probably feeling that he was being underutilized, began to look elsewhere for a more productive position with another of the area's film companies. In the meantime, The Trust's stranglehold on the industry was beginning to show cracks. Its onerous rules, regulations, and fees didn't sit well with everyone, resulting in a proliferation of independent companies. One of these was Carl Laemmle's Independent Motion Picture Company — aka IMP — formed in June 1909 and initially working out of a makeshift studio just a few blocks east of Biograph's on Fourteenth Street. The impishly-named IMP was soon cranking out a slew of low budget one- and two-reelers, and was looking for talent; early successes in that regard included the luring away from Biograph of Florence Lawrence ("The Biograph Girl") in 1909, and Mary Pickford a year later. Lehrman, always looking to better himself, took a job with the young studio in their scenario department, by now relocated to West Fifty-Sixth Street. Julius Stern, Laemmle's brother-in-law and part of the company "family" as the IMP's general manager, reminisced in 1915 about his part in furthering Lehrman's career:

> I am always watching for fresh talent, and if I think I see promise in a person, absence of past reputation doesn't count an iota.... Under this system I have given many of the "big lights" of the business help in their early picture days that I know has been fruitful of results. Pathe Lehrman, for instance, was in the scenario department when I encouraged him to do a picture. It was a slap-stick comedy and I must admit that it wasn't well thought of at the time of its premiere about four years ago. That was because Lehrman was ahead of his time: slap-stick of that order is today the demanded film of the business.[24]

In a *Los Angeles Times* biography that appeared a mere three years later, and assumedly based upon an interview with Lehrman, former Biograph and current Keystone star Mabel Normand is given credit for prompting Lehrman to think big:

> Mr. Lehrman left the Biograph Company to accept a position as director for the Imp Company in New York, making a specialty of comedy work. Here his ideas in the game of comedies, he being only a youngster himself, were advanced and strengthened by the encouraging advice of Mabel Normand a most popular star, who being keen of perception, realized young Lehrman had undeveloped talent. She talked the work over with him on more than one occasion, and, with her assistance…he produced a number of brilliant and popular plays.[25]

It is not clear from the article's vague timeline just when this encouragement took place. Early on at Biograph? Normand did not work at Imp, but perhaps their friendship continued during Lehrman's employment there. Fowler, it is worth noting, wrote that some "members of the troupe thought [Normand] liked Pathe better [than Sennett], but Sennett did not appear to take notice."[26]

The one film that we know of that Lehrman directed under the nom de plume "Henry Pathé" was the split-reel comedy *Beat At His Own Game* (March 2, 1912), along with the top-of-the-bill *The Right Clue*. Star John R. Cumpson (whom Lehrman had probably met back at Biograph) appears as a jealous lover who decides to test his equally jealous fiancé, played by Grace Lewis. The test involves having a friend dress as a woman, but the fiancé catches on and turns the tables on him. The sole review that I've found gives the rather obtuse assessment "A prettily set farce pure, but one that leaves something in its situation still obscure.... It is amusing." The photography, however, was deemed "a bit foggy."[27]

Jack Cohn, who worked in the IMP's darkroom while Lehrman was engaged by the studio (and was later one of the founders of what would become Columbia Pictures), commented on the short films made for IMP at the time and Lehrman's contributions:

> A good many of our pictures were so short we had to go out to find a little scenic to put into it to make it a full reel. It is not so long ago that Henry Lehrman made a couple of half-reel comedies. He was years ahead of the crowd on slapstick comedies, but there was no one in the organization who appreciated these pictures, and he was laid off before he ever screened his work.[28]

Evidently Lehrman and IMP were not a good fit. Lehrman was replaced in his position as scenario editor by Herbert Brenon, who had been running a small theater up until that time and would move into direction soon after his hiring.

Lehrman returned to Biograph for a few more films made during the trip to California at the beginning of 1912, and assumedly to help out Sennett wherever his assistance was needed. There has been the occasional past attribution that Lehrman co-directed some of Sennett's comedies for Biograph, but historian Brent Walker found no evidence of this while researching his wholly dependable account of the life and films of Sennett. Still, while there may be no documentary evidence, there is no real reason why Lehrman may not have lent a directorial hand while Sennett was performing in front of the camera, or sent off to film additional, "second unit" shots while Sennett concentrated on the main action.

Lehrman's on-the-job education at Biograph was summarized several years later in the fawning *Los Angeles Times* piece:

> For a year and a half he struggled hard to win recognition. He had many obstacles thrown in his way, but he won out.
>
> During these days of hard work and slow progress he met Mr. David W. Griffith, the noted director, then rehearsing the actors and players in motion-picture work, who seemed to appreciate young Lehrman's ability and hard work. Mr. Griffith encouraged him, gave him a chance to stick to the game and live. His work was of the right kind, and he began climbing the ladder of achievement. He was given a part here and there, later a lead, and his work was so satisfactory that his prestige was established, and he became a real actor familiar with the details of motion-picture work.[29]

A rosy picture painted here, but one with a basis in truth. Lehrman learned a lot about acting and the craft of filmmaking while with the company, and from the unrivaled likes of Griffith and Bitzer. As for comedy construction, his close association with Sennett during this time proved to be career-altering. The two fed off each other, and both participants benefitted; their respective careers would be intertwined for the rest of the decade, as co-workers in close collaboration, and later as fierce competitors. As for Biograph, the final film that Lehrman is known to have appeared in was the Sennett-directed comedy *His Own Fault*, filmed in May 1912 and released on July 25. And then on to seemingly greener pastures, if only for a very short while.

It would appear that Lehrman was engaged by The Kinemacolor Company of America around this time. Kinemacolor was the dominant color film process up until the First World War, originating in Great Britain and a huge success in Europe. Utilizing its own proprietary cameras and projectors that ran at twice the speed of conventional equipment — thirty-two frames per second versus sixteen — the system utilized alternating red and green filters that, when projected, resulted in the approximation of natural color (forget about blues, though). First exhibited here in the states in late 1909 in an effort to interest investors, patent rights were secured and The Kinemacolor Company of America was established in early 1910. In addition to existing films brought over from Great Britain — typically actualities involving British royalty — early home-grown fare was shot in and around New York; studios were set up out in Hollywood late in 1912. The

Kinemacolor system never really caught on since most theaters balked at the notion of having to acquire the special projectors required to show the films. The fact that more experienced technicians were needed to oversee the cameras, that more light was required to expose the faster-moving film, and that the films themselves were more expensive to produce didn't help matters. And then there was the issue of eyestrain, and the matter-of-fact, less-than-engaging nature of the films themselves. Victor Heerman, who was employed by Kinemacolor to manage its road show presentations, gave his opinion of the company's films years later to historian Anthony Slide, saying that "Looking at these Kinemacolor pictures every day! And nothing quite in focus. They were beautiful pictures and all that, but there was no expression."[30] The Hollywood studio was sold to D.W. Griffith in 1913 and renamed the Fine Arts studio; production such as it were returned to New York, and ceased by 1915.

Given that few mentions were made in later years regarding Lehrman's employment with this firm, one can only assume that it was brief. A piece in *Motography* a mere four years later stated that Lehrman "soon rose to a directorship with Kinemacolor,"[31] but as with a number of other later claims resulting from interviews with the man himself or in the fertile imaginations of publicity scribes, this was probably an exaggeration at best. Regardless, Lehrman's tenure with the New York City based film industry would soon come to a close, and recent past associations would be renewed.

CHAPTER 3

Mack Sennett's Keystone Film Company: Creditless Where Credit is Due

So much has been written about the Keystone Film Company and its origins, most recently and reliably by Brent Walker in his authoritative *Mack Sennett's Fun Factory*, that there is no need to hash over the details here. Let it suffice to say that Sennett's talents as director of nearly one hundred comedies for Biograph had caught the eyes of Adam Kessel and Charles O. Baumann, heads of the New York Motion Picture Company, aka NYMPC. Kessel and Baumann had recently broken ties with Carl Laemmle's Universal distribution exchange, switching over to The Mutual Film Corporation, a rival exchange set up by Harry Aitken and John R. Freuler of the Western Exchange Service, along with Charles Hite and Samuel Hutchinson of the H. & H. and Majestic Film Services. The NYMPC had a steady output of dramas and westerns through their Domino, Kay-Bee, and Broncho brands, but needed a comedy company to balance out their offerings. Sennett provided a young, energetic, time-tested solution to their needs. A deal was struck, and the Keystone Film Company was formed in August 1912 to provide a single reel of comedy per week, with Sennett as director general and part owner.

Sennett needed a cast to populate his films. Comedienne Mabel Normand, the star of so many of his previous films as director and with whom he worked so well, was an obvious choice. Ford Sterling hooked up with the new company as well, and while Sterling is now viewed as a huge talent in early film comedy, he was at this time a relative newcomer, with few more than a dozen films at Biograph to his credit, all of them for Sennett. The fledgling company went to work immediately, filming in and around the streets of Manhattan while the NYMPC's former Bison studio out in the Los Angeles suburb of Edendale, California, was retrofitted. These earliest films were rough and tumble affairs, filmed in a slapdash, spontaneous, seat-of-the-pants fashion, and on the most meager of budgets. One of Sennett's less fanciful comments about these early days gives an idea of the initial, bare-bones approach: "We didn't have any studio. We just carried the cameras and props on our shoulders and started off somewhere on a street car. Usually we hung around near Fort George."¹ Victor Heerman remembered it this way: "It was [at the Barthodi Inn] where Sennett pretty much cast his first two pictures — all from the people staying there at the Inn. Anyone who wasn't working was hired for these two pictures, made down at Coney Island. They got five dollars and a chance to work in these two pictures. Well, believe it or not, these two films were a big hit."²

After a few short films were completed, including the Normand and Sterling half-reeler *At Coney Island*, the small company headed west.

Adam Kessel, Charles O. Baumann, and Mack Sennett, circa 1918.

Sennett, Normand, and Sterling arrived in California sometime in early September. They were accompanied by Henry Lehrman, whom Sennett had hired for the valuable assistance he could provide both in front of the camera as part of the growing stock company, and behind as idea man and general, all-around help. Heerman spoke of Lehrman's value to Sennett, stating that "Sennett hung onto him because Lehrman *did* know — he *knew* — there wasn't anybody or anything he didn't know; or if he didn't know, he'd find out."³ Ambitious, no doubt, and possessed of an inquisitive mind.

Kessel and Baumann joined the group towards month's end to inspect the extensive changes and additions taking place at the former Bison plant on Allesandro Street. Also on hand was Kessel and Baumann's one-third partner in the NYMPC, Fred J. Balshofer. Comedian Fred Mace, who had remained behind in California after the Biograph company's last visit, was brought on board as well.⁴

The Los Angeles area was experiencing growing pains at this time. The population back in 1880 had been a mere 11,093, which had grown in ten years to 50,395, with that number doubling over the next ten years to 102,479 in 1900. By 1914 the population increased five-fold to roughly 550,000, with the surrounding county adding more than 750,000 to that count.⁵ The locals had the burgeoning film industry to thank — or curse — for that latter leap in growth.

Among the earliest releases filmed out west was the reteaming of Sennett and Mace as a pair of bumbling sleuths. The film, *At It Again* (November 4, 1912), was the first in this series and, according to Walker, the first documented assemblage of ineffectual cops that served as a rough prototype for the famed Keystone Cops yet to come. The meerschaum

LEFT: *Mabel Normand*. RIGHT: *Henry Lehrman, sans his familiar mustache.*

pipe-smoking characters, decked out in Holmesian garb complete with deerstalker hats, had been made popular back at Biograph in films such as *Caught With the Goods* (December 25, 1911).⁶

Lehrman's first on-screen appearance was in *A Temperamental Husband* (November 11, 1912), probably filmed in October and with Lehrman in the role of a cop. *The Cure That Failed* (January 13, 1913) and *The Stolen Purse* (February 10, 1913) were his next two appearances, always in a support of Sterling and his costars, and directed by Sennett. Lehrman's "leading man" break came when he was made one of the two leads in the Sennett-directed *Her Birthday Present* (February 13, 1913; extant), costarring with Mace as a pair of larcenous tramps who end up in a gun battle over a stolen necklace. Lehrman gets into the spirit of things here, holding his own against Mace and running, leaping about, and gesticulating wildly in true Keystone fashion when the situations call for it, although his athletic abilities appear somewhat wanting when he executes a rather labored-looking somersault.

The films were an immediate success, with the ubiquitous Ford Sterling, Mabel Normand, and Fred Mace embraced as three of the film-going public's most popular comedians. Scenarios were solicited for "split reel light and farce comedies," promising budding authors that they "may get more than $50 if your script is worth it."[7] Then again, maybe less. Encouraged by the response from exhibitors for the new company's output, Kessel and Baumann informed Sennett that they wanted to supplement the current Monday releases with a second weekly release on Thursdays, effective February 3, 1913. Realizing that an additional weekly reel of film would be an impossible burden to add to his existing workload, Sennett assigned Lehrman to direct a second comedy unit. Actress

The Stolen Purse *co-starred Sennett (holding purse), a bearded Lehrman, and Fred Mace (holding pistol).*

Betty Schade, formerly with Selig, Essanay, and American, was announced to be the new unit's leading lady,[8] although it's somewhat doubtful that it worked out that way given that she doesn't appear in any of the existing credits for Lehrman's films, and most likely ended up working for others at the studio.

Lehrman directed his maiden effort, *Murphy's I.O.U.*, at the very end of December 1912, with Fred Mace as cop "Murphy" in debt to Lehrman's moneylender "Cohen;" Sennett and comedienne Dot Farley co-starred. This was Farley's first for Keystone, and she would appear in a number of films for both Lehrman and others over a brief three month period before leaving the company to join the St. Louis Motion Picture Company as their female lead.[9]

Lehrman assisted Sennett on January 1 and 2 with the direction of *The Sleuths at the Floral Parade*. With that film's completion, Lehrman concentrated on creating a backlog of films while Sennett's efforts continued to fill the schedule for the first month of these twice-weekly releases. By March 3, however, Lehrman's initial efforts were ready to be added to the weekly schedule. *A Deaf Burglar* was the first to be released, costarring Mace and Charles Avery as a pair of inept burglars oblivious to the noise their safecracking is making. *The Two Widows*, costarring Ford Sterling as "Schnitzel" and Dot Farley as one of the widows he is thinking of marrying, followed on March 13th. The Keystone stock company members were all utilized by both Sennett and Lehrman depending on availability and need, and soon included Arthur Tavares, Nick Cogley, Charles Avery, Bert Hunn, Evelyn Quick, Chester Franklin, Laura Oakley, Josef Swickard, Rube Miller,

Tramps Lehrman and Fred Mace have robbery in mind in Her Birthday Present.

Edgar Kennedy, Jack Leonard, Raymond Hatton, Fred Happ, and Bill Hauber. The two directors managed to keep the product flowing.

Beatrice Van, who worked for the studio at this time as an extra, said that "During the early years, Sennett had the reputation of using more extras than anyone else in town. That was due to the fact that since he was turning out so many comedies, many of them one reel in length, and many of them split reels, the word got out that Keystone had a constant, great need for extras."[10] While lead players received ten dollars for each day worked and contract players received twenty-five dollars a week, "As an extra, I got paid three dollars a day and was given a box lunch with a bottle of milk — on the days that I worked. The box lunch and milk kept me alive so that I could save the three dollars for the streetcar fare and for my baby.... In those early years, you had to work steadily to make any money at all, even enough to live modestly."[11]

Lehrman worked non-stop to keep up with the demanding schedule, turning out a steady stream of half-reelers with eye-catching titles such as *Foiling Fickle Father* (March

13), *Love and Pain* (March 17), *Cupid in a Dental Parlor* (April 21; "Lots of action but a slight plot," said *Moving Picture World*[12]), *Algy on the Force* (May 5), and *That Dark Town Belle* (May 8), starring Mace "as a negro barber [who] has many rows with the dusky wooers who come to see his flirtatious intended."[13]

His most famous film from this early period is *Bangville Police* (April 24) with Normand as the farm girl terrified that burglars are loose in her barn. Fred Mace is the sheriff of Bangville who rides to the rescue in his ancient jalopy, accompanied by five deputies who

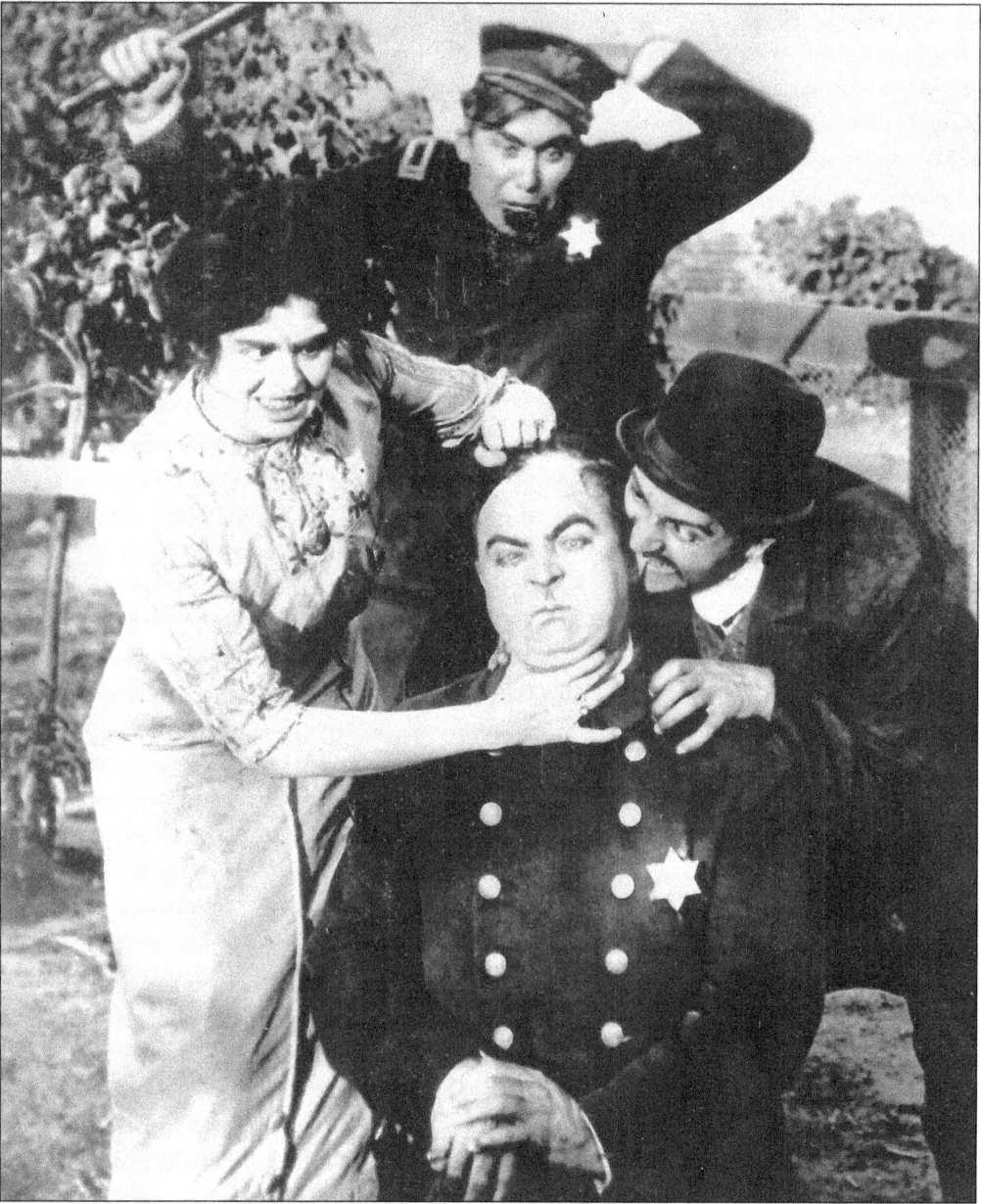

Fred Mace getting the worst of it as Dot Farley strangles him, Lehrman latches on to his ear, and Sennett wields his billy-club in the Lehrman-directed Murphy's I.O.U. COURTESY OF SAM GILL

can't seem to get out of each other's way. Only Lehrman's eleventh as director for Keystone, the surviving film shows what an assured craftsman he was at this early stage. The visuals are striking, especially when compared to some of Sennett's efforts from this period. Instead of the usual right-to-left or left-to-right movements of characters carried over from the stage, Lehrman rarely settles for such routine staging when he can instead have characters move to or from the foreground, and at a more visually interesting diagonal trajectory. He utilizes rapid cross-cutting between the farm and the sheriff and his depu-

Fred Mace and Mack Sennett in character on the set of The Sleuths at the Floral Parade, *while assistant director Lehrman sweet-talks Mabel Normand.*

ties, and provides some nice tight close-ups of Normand while she's hiding in the closet. And Normand's performance here demonstrates what a good actress she had become in just a few short years. Her terrified state while hiding in the closet has moments that, while not quite in the same league, remind one of Lillian Gish's performance while holed up in the closet in the later Griffith-directed *Broken Blossoms*, this latter performance one that *Photoplay* deemed "the screen's highest example of emotional hysteria."[14] Elsewhere, Normand incorporates little bits of "business" to render her character more natural, such as her playful interaction with her dad (Nick Cogley) in the opening scenes. Lehrman had learned much about comedy from Sennett, but significantly more about the art of filmmaking from the acknowledged master, Griffith. It should be noted here that this film is the earliest surviving example of the Keystone Cops, albeit in a more simplified rural form. "As a whole, this reel is very pleasing and full of laughs," reported *Moving Picture World*.[15]

Toplitsky and Company (May 26; extant) is another good example of Lehrman's work during this period, this his first full-reel film. Set in the Jewish section of town, second-hand clothing store owner Toplitsky (Nick Cogley) suspects his partner (Sterling) of messing around with his wife, and with good reason. When he finds the two together,

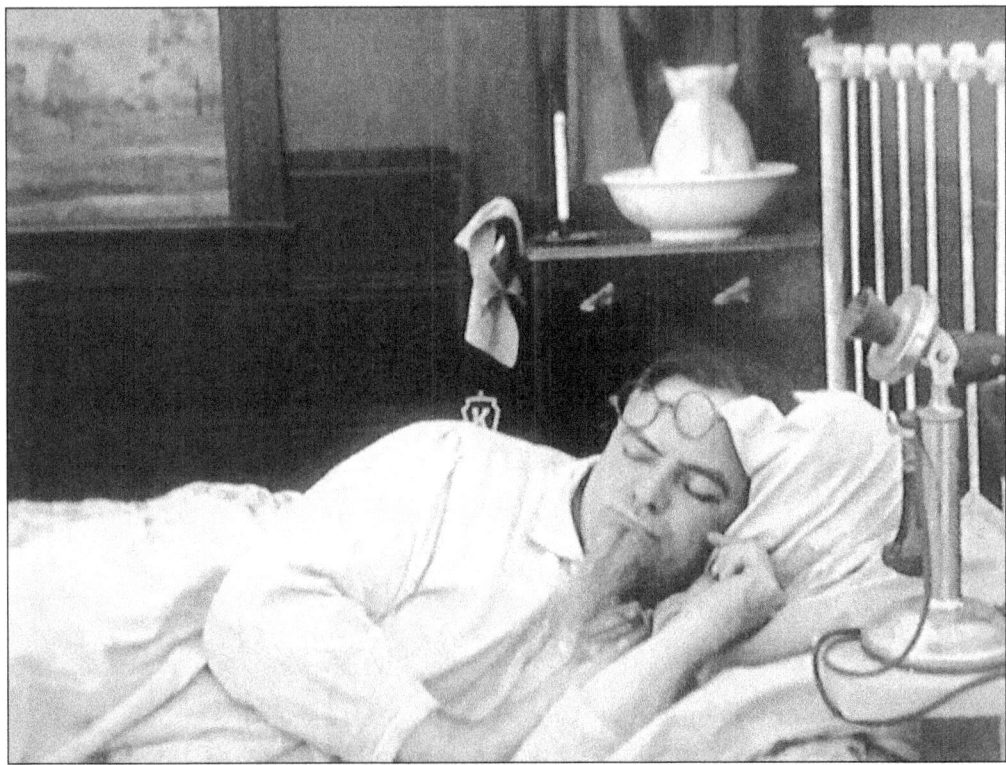

Sheriff Fred Mace rests soundly in Bangville Police, *the Keystone logo posted prominently beyond him.*

Sterling flees and takes refuge in a bath house. A gypsy's bear breaks loose of its chains and gives chase, with Sterling taking refuge in the wife's bedroom and under the sleeping woman's bed. Toplitsky, about to forgive his wife, spots Sterling's legs sticking out. All hell breaks loose in a fight upon the bed, with everyone trapped when the bed collapses under the massive headboard.

Lehrman's direction here is vigorous, with some great mugging-filled close-ups of Sterling while hiding under the bed, and three-way cross-cutting early on between the store interior, the store exterior, and the Toplitsky home, with more excitement-building cuts throughout the extended chase that follows. Interesting camera angles abound as well, as usual for Lehrman. The use of a bear on the loose, it should be noted, is a harbinger of things to come, a hint of Lehrman's coming interest in using animals in his films, and the lions-on-the-loose of his later Sunshine Comedies.[16] While the film is populated by Jews and set in the Jewish quarter of town, there's very little, if any, stereotyping; the film could just as well taken place in a general store run by Baptists. The characters are the usual Keystone types, and their buffoonery transcends religion and ethnicity. Sterling, true to form, does some extensive nose biting.

At the end of March into early April, Lehrman was assigned to direct a newcomer to Keystone, the actor named Roscoe Arbuckle. Soon to become more commonly known to filmgoers by the affectionate but unflattering nickname of "Fatty," the three-hundred pounder had years of stage experience behind him, but aside from a short stint with Selig

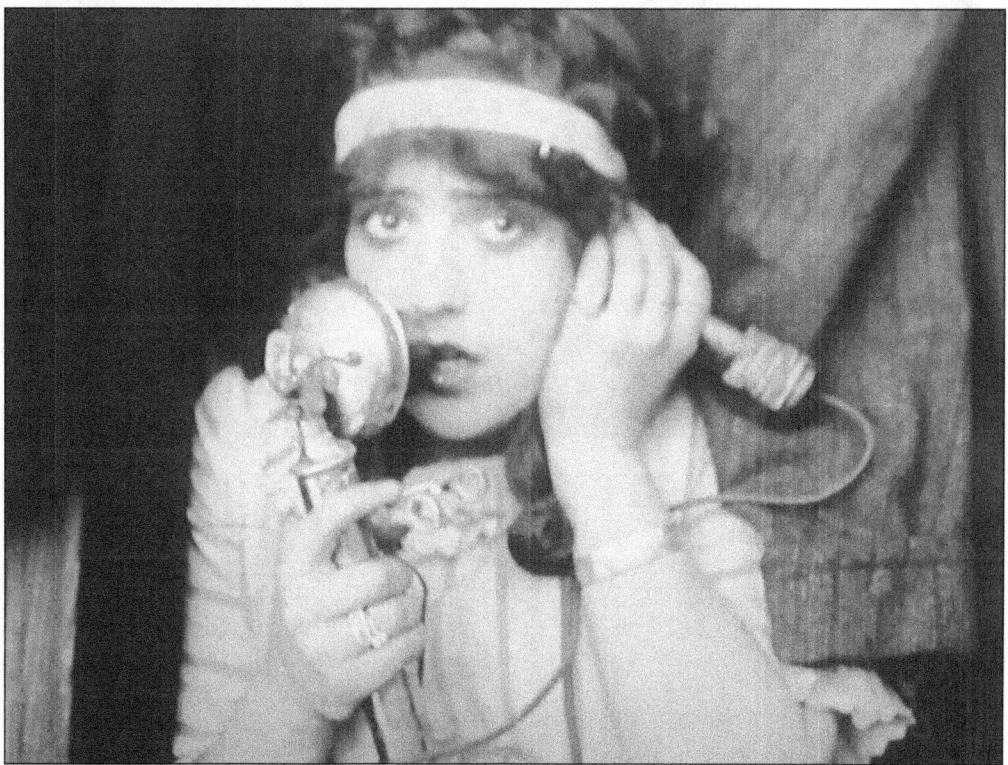

Mabel Normand pleads for help in Bangville Police.

several years earlier and at least one film for Nestor, was otherwise new to this medium. The resulting one-reel film was *The Gangsters* (May 29; extant), with cop Arbuckle arousing the ire of tough guy Spike (Mace, all puffed-chest swaggering bravado here) and his gang of toughs when he's caught flirting with Spike's girl (Evelyn Quick). After Arbuckle is stripped of his uniform, he hatches a plan to get even by using a dummy dressed in a cop's uniform to lure the gang out onto a barge. This being a Keystone, it is the cops instead who end up in the drink.

Arbuckle is thoroughly at ease in his first film for the studio. His shy smile and bashful demeanor when meeting the flirtatious Quick, here bubbling with youthful sexiness, fades when confronted by the scowling Spike. It isn't long before Arbuckle is delivering belly-whomps to Spike, repeatedly bouncing him to the ground and dominating this first encounter. Arbuckle worked well with Lehrman, who would go on to direct the comedian in a long string of films that included *Passions — He Had Three, Help! Help! Hydrophobia!* (both June 5), *For the Love of Mabel* (June 30), *Love and Courage* (July 21), and a slew of

ABOVE: *Irate husband Nick Cogley threatens Ford Sterling as Alice Davenport looks on, in* Toplitsky and Company. BELOW: *Roscoe Arbuckle, Emma Clifton, and Frank Opperman (left to right) in a scene likely from the George Nichols–directed* A Robust Romeo *(02/12/1914).* COURTESY OF SAM GILL

others over the year that followed. The last of their productive relationship was *A Rural Demon* (March 19, 1914) before Sennett promoted Arbuckle to direct his own starring roles, *Barnyard Flirtation* (March 28, 1914) the first of these.

Arbuckle would go on to direct more than fifty additional films for Sennett over the next two years. Arbuckle was hugely popular with audiences, but after three years toiling under the legendarily tight-fisted producer, left Sennett when offered an unprecedented, highly lucrative contract with Paramount. This gave him complete artistic control of the Comique Film Corporation, a new company set up specifically for him where he would function at the creative end as well as headlining. Arbuckle and Lehrman remained close friends during these years, and in 1920 the rotund comedian would acknowledge his debt to his friend: "All my mechanical knowledge of pictures I learned under the direction of Lehrman, who directed all but about two of my pictures."[17] Their close friendship would, by the end of the following year, take an unexpected turn.

Actress Quick, by the way, provided some unintentional problems for the young film company. Actress Beatrice Van recalled the event in detail in an interview with historian Sam Gill, saying that Fred Balshofer had appeared on the studio lot for an impromptu meeting with Sennett. Sennett found her soon after in the dressing room:

> Sennett appeared at the door and said to me, "Don't make up this morning, Miss Van. We're going down to San Diego to shoot a picture." He then told me to go home and pack a suitcase and be at the railway station that afternoon…. Later I found out that I was only going along because Mabel Normand had insisted on it…we were the only two women in this group.[18]

San Diego turned out to be an interim stop, with Tijuana the final destination.

> It was not until we reached Tijuana, and after Mabel and I were settled into our room, that Mabel explained the real reason we were in Mexico rather than San Diego. Mabel said that an underage girl who had been working at Keystone — a girl by the name of Evelyn Quick — had had sexual relations with several of the males among the Keystone comedians, that she had been arrested by the police, and was "naming names" as Mabel explained it.[19]

The *Los Angeles Times* reported Quick's implication in a blackmail and "white slavery" ring, and while the article spared the more lurid details, Quick's testimony did not; it resulted in two prominent businessmen being hit with statutory offenses against Quick, believed to be only a fifteen year old. Any concerns about Quick mentioning additional names in her testimony that could result in further charges against studio employees turned out to be unfounded. The trip south proved to be beneficial to Van, however, if only in terms of roles:

> Mabel was furious and in a rotten mood, because she had been looking forward to making the trip north to San Francisco [to take part in a parade] rather than being taken down to Tijuana where she felt she was being held prisoner, which was the way she looked at it…. Mabel refused to work at all,

which meant that by default I was going to be playing the female lead in this picture. It was a way for Mabel to get back at Sennett, but for me it was a wonderful opportunity.[20]

Sennett managed to shoot two half-reelers and Lehrman one additional short, *Out and In* (June 19, 1913) during their stay. Van stated that four films were shot with her in the lead, but went on to state that "whether or not any of these pictures were actually released, I don't know…," so the fate (or reality) of that fourth film is unknown.

With the threat of any legal ramifications resulting from the Quick affair now lifted, the group returned to California. Quick, who had made a handful of films for Keystone, including *The Two Widows* (March 13) and *Cupid in a Dental Parlor* (April 21) for Lehrman, moved over to Al Christie's Nestor studios for a couple of more shorts before disappearing for a few years and resurfacing as Jewel Carmen. As for Van, "now that Evelyn Quick, whose loose tongue had driven the company to Mexico, was out of the picture," she said, "I inherited Evelyn's 'domain' [as] female lead in the split-reel comedies" and the five dollars per day that went along with it.[21]

Beatrice Van, unidentified pup, and Roscoe Arbuckle in Help! Help! Hydrophobia!. *The pup may — or may not — be a very young Luke.*
COURTESY OF SAM GILL.

Another important figure was to enter Lehrman's world in early 1913, the pint-sized toddler Paul Jacobs, not even three years old at the time. Born in Laclede, Idaho on July 31, 1910, Jacobs' family relocated to California in 1911 and landed in a house "immediately in front of the back end of the Keystone studio."[22] As the story goes, Lehrman needed a child to act in one of his films and spotted Jacobs playing in his yard; the purchase of an ice cream cone supposedly sealed the deal, and Jacobs had a job.[23] Accurate or not, Jacobs' first appearance in a Keystone film was the Sennett-directed half-reel *Hide and Seek* (April 3, 1913), where he appears in two brief shots with three other children, one "riding" a Bull Terrier, and the other perched atop a sand pile. Jacobs' acting was limited, to be sure, with outrageous mugging (crying with balled fists rubbing his eyes, anger shown by a clenched fist and lower jaw stuck out, etc.), stiff and mechanical movements, and repeated glances for guidance to the director out of camera range. He was so damn cute about it, however, his awkwardness really didn't seem to matter much, or at least not to the viewing public. His next few films were for Lehrman, the first *Love and Rubbish* (July 14; extant), filmed in part by Echo Park Lake, followed by *Just Kids*

(July 28). From that time on Jacobs bounced back and forth between the company's units, appearing wherever a pudgy, young, mop-haired ragamuffin was needed.

Lehrman's *Love and Rubbish*, with Sterling and Charles Avery as a pair of park sweepers competing for the attention of the park lovelies, has a climactic scene where the adults desperately attempt to stop a runaway barrel they erroneously believe contains a young girl. The girl and three of her young friends — Jacobs is one of them — stand on the sidelines, amused by the adults' ridiculous antics. One only needs to compare the direction of this

LEFT: *Paul Jacobs, off the job.* RIGHT: *Paul Jacobs at the feet of studio cops, likely taken at Keystone. Left-to-right: George Ramage (?), Hank Mann or Bill Hauber, unknown, and Bobby Dunn.* COURTESY OF SAM GILL.

film to Sennett's *Hide and Seek* to see how wildly divergent the two directors' techniques were, and how much more visually interesting Lehrman's was. Already Lehrman was well into his use of cutting to quicken a film's pace, the jumps here between individual shots during the climax increasing in frequency and leaving the viewer breathless; the film itself has one hundred twenty-four separate shots in its nine hundred eighty-two feet. (The downside to the rapid cutting is that some of what goes on in the frame is missed as the viewer struggles to keep up.) There are some interesting camera angles and compositions here as well, one standout with Sterling in the foreground, trees in the background silhouetted by the lake and its boaters in the far background. There are numerous — and atypical for Keystone — close-ups employed: the fat man's foot as it is stabbed; his grimacing face; the young daughter in foreground, an infant playing on the ground beyond; and several close shots of the quartet of kids watching the adults, laughing, and ultimately thumbing their noses at them! *Moving Picture World's* reviewer took issue with this last shot, calling it "a bad piece of business in an otherwise fairly good reel.

Many exhibitors will prefer to cut this off."[24] It's a terrific little film for its time, complete with ear-, nose-, and ankle-biting!

The unrelenting demand from the NYMPC for a steady stream of product began to take its toll on the two harried directors, particularly on Sennett who had far more to worry about running a studio than solely the direction of films. Their ranks needed to be supplemented, and to that end director Wilfred Lucas, formerly with Biograph, Rex, and Bison, was brought in to head a third comedy unit in mid-1913. Later that same

Matty Roubert (left) and Gordon Griffith aboard the Venice Miniature Railway in a scene from How Villains Are Made. COURTESY OF ROBERT JAMES KISS.

year director George Nichols, formerly with Biograph, Thanhouser, Gem, and Lubin, was engaged; he would on occasion take acting roles as well. Both were former acquaintances and coworkers of Sennett's back at Biograph, and no doubt hired as much for their familiarity of Sennett's approach to comedy as their directorial talents. Robert Thornby, a former actor, writer, and director at Vitagraph with no previous ties to Sennett, joined the studio toward the end of the year to direct.

While Paul Jacobs didn't have a lot to do in these early films besides mug and look cute, audiences liked what they saw in such Lehrman-directed films as *The New Baby* (September 4), *Our Children* (November 17), and *How Villains Are Made* (March 14, 1914). *The Motion Picture News* elaborated on the theme of this latter film and the preproduction work required:

> Henry Lehrmann, Keystone director, has just completed a two-reel "Kid" melodrama featuring the abduction of a juvenile heroine by the juvenile villain. The Venice Miniature Railway, near Los Angeles, with engines, coaches, roundhouses,

depots and several miles of track, was leased especially for this feature. Besides the railway, all of the remaining sets and furnishings, down to the last detail, were in small scale.[25]

Motography commented on the young actor's abilities in this film:

> Billy Jacobs, just two [sic] years old, plays his part so naturally that one wonders if he knows it is being done in front of a camera. He is a chubby, curly-headed little fellow and already is on the regular list.[26]

Given Jacobs' proximity to the studio and the willingness of his mother to let him work, either Sennett or Lehrman — or together as a creative team — came up with the idea for a series of kid comedies starring the disciplined and malleable young man. The three year old was turned over to director Robert Thornby and christened "Little Billy." The success of the first series entry, *Our Children* (November 17, 1913), led to a string of "Little Billy" films such as *Little Billy's Triumph* (January 29, 1914), *Little Billy's Strategy* (February 5), and *Little Billy's City Cousin* (February 26). Thornby's unit included Thelma Salter, Charlotte Fitzpatrick, Buddy Harris, and Gordon Griffith.[27] Lehrman snatched up the young actor for one last film — the aforementioned *How Villains Are Made* — between the first and second of these "Little Billy" films, after which Jacobs remained under Thornby's care. Both director Thornby and his diminutive actor would in short order play a new role in Lehrman's career.

As busy as he was cranking out reel after reel of comedy, and with random appearances in his own efforts, Lehrman was occasionally called upon to act in crowd scenes in other directors' films as well. These included *The Speed Kings* (October 30, 1913; directed by Wilfred Lucas) and *A Film Johnnie* (March 2, 1914; directed by George Nichols). Sennett's *Cohen Saves the Flag,* a Civil War "epic," has co-stars Sterling (as Cohen) and Lehrman (as Goldberg) vying for lovely Normand's attention. When Cohen enlists in the Union army and is made sergeant, he is soon chagrined to find that Goldberg is his bossy (and ruthless) lieutenant. The film is "epic" in that it looks like it had a much bigger budget than was the case, the extensive battles taking place in the background actually scenes being filmed for the Thomas Ince drama *The Battle of Gettysburg.* While not released until late in the year on November 27, 1913, it was filmed back in late January shortly after Lehrman had begun his directorial duties.

There has been some confusion in the past as to whether or not Lehrman co-starred in the Sennett-directed film *The Fire Bug* (August 21, 1913; notable as Keystone's first two-reeler). One contemporary review in *The New York Clipper* was confident in its assertion that Lehrman was one of the leads:

> On Aug. 21, 1913, the Keystone Film Company will release a distinct novelty in their comedy entitled "The Firebug." It is in two reels a fact alone which claims attention in a comedy, and the story is a realistically clever intermingling of humor and pathos. The scenes laid in New York's Ghetto, that great Melting Pot of the Hebrew and Italian races, are full of life, animation and color. The daily life of the New York Jew, his work, his play, his little foibles, his failings and his attributes,

ABOVE: *Ford Sterling and Lehrman in* The Speed Kings. BELOW: *Ford Sterling's "Cohen" wraps himself in the American flag in* Cohen Saves the Flag. COURTESY OF SAM GILL

all are shown in crystal-like clearness and telling accuracy to detail, and it might well be said that the mirror is indeed held up to nature. Screamingly funny and natural situations pervade the film. Ford Sterling and Henry (Pathe) Lehrman's delineation of the Jewish character are true to the life, showing the touch of long study and real artistry.[28]

To further add to the confusion, Lehrman later claimed to have directed this film as well. Walker has determined that the official records indicate otherwise, and a still from the film in Moving Picture World clearly shows Sennett and Nick Cogley as the rival arsonists.[29]

While Lehrman's schedule was a full one, there was some free time to unwind and — for lack of a better word — get into trouble. Now that the money was rolling in, Sennett indulged in a rare luxury, a $6,000 imported red Fiat. Lehrman borrowed the car one night and didn't return, and when Sennett grew worried the next day, the car was found parked with its engine still running — outside a brothel. Or at least according to Sennett,[30] who in recording his reminiscences a good forty years later relayed stories about Lehrman no doubt tinged with some level of bitterness over what he considered his trusted co-worker's eventual betrayal and desertion. By September 1913, Lehrman had acquired and registered a car of his own, so there was no further need to borrow Sennett's Fiat.[31]

Another such story has to do with Lehrman's propensity for studio gossip, much of it delivered to Sennett himself and frequently involving Sennett's girlfriend Normand. According to Sennett, it was "all disturbing and all inaccurate." The supposed reason? "Pathé was in love with Mabel [Normand] himself." Lehrman had her linked with a young Rudolph Valentino and Jack Mulhall, and told Sennett that she "was pretty much upset and grieved by [his] oafishness." And, as icing on the cake, Lehrman started a rumor that Sennett had broken Normand's arm during a confrontation in Mulhall's apartment. Later on, Lehrman would inform Normand that Sennett was out on the town squiring other actresses about. Lehrman informed Sennett that "In your best washed and polished job, [Normand] says you look like a Hoboken store detective." Again, all according to Sennett, and all quotes his.[32]

According to Beatrice Van, "Sennett's mother was always trying to get [Mabel and Sennett] to marry, but Mabel said that she was not interested, and didn't want to marry Sennett." And what about Lehrman?

> I know that "Pathé" Lehrman…was in love with Mabel, too. In fact, he was nuts about her, and just like Sennett, he would try to buy her favors with jewelry. Lehrman had come down to Tijuana on our trip to Mexico, and was directing pictures there as was Sennett…. I remember one afternoon when Mabel told me she was going to visit "Pathé" Lehrman in his hotel room. She was gone for a while, and I didn't think anything of it, but she came back with a gorgeous sapphire bracelet, which she immediately hid in the chamois bag full of jewels they made me wear around my neck all the time we were in Tijuana.[33]

Competition between Sennett and Lehrman must have made for some awkward moments at the studio, and fed a growing rift between the two. As for that chamois bag full of Normand's jewelry, Van was required to wear it "for the very real fact that I was considered expendable and Mabel wasn't!"[34]

By now heady with his new found popularity and success, Fred Mace defected from Keystone and moved over to Majestic in late April 1913. Keystone needed to replace this key player and, if Sennett's later recollections served him correctly, have a backup if Sterling, who was now top dog at the studio, decided to follow.

Vaudevillians were prime source material, their fifty-week tours of the various circuits originating in New York and concluding in California. As a result, filmmakers could head over to the area theaters and check out the talent to see if there were any reasonable prospects. Charles Chaplin was discovered in such a way, but where and by whom is up for debate. Sennett claimed that he and Normand had first spotted the young comedian late in 1912 during a performance of Fred Karno's *A Night in an English Music Hall* at New York's American Theatre on Forty-Second and Eighth.[35] Ramsaye has Adam Kessel (or his brother Charles, according to other sources) discovering Chaplin at New York's Hammerstein Theatre.[36] Historian Kevin Brownlow received information that strongly suggests that it was Harry Aitken, a NYMPC executive, who first saw him at the Pantages Theatre in Los Angeles.[37] Less than two years after the fact Chaplin himself in an interview had Sennett approaching him in Los Angeles at the Empress Theatre on Spring Street,[38] but that may have been after one of the Kessel and Baumann team had first seen him. Lehrman, in a typical display of self-promotion, even claimed in 1916 that he had "discovered" Chaplin.[39] But nearly a half century later, Chaplin in his autobiography recounts much the same story that Sennett had a decade earlier.[40] Regardless of where the truth lies, Chaplin was contacted, terms were discussed, and a one-year contract was signed for $150 per week for the first three months, after which it would be increased to $175 per week.[41] Chaplin finished the year's tour of the Sullivan and Considine circuit at the end of November 1913, and headed for the Keystone studios to commence work on December 16. Sennett assigned the new recruit to Lehrman's care, to show him how things worked at the studio, to introduce him to the mechanics of making a film, and to guide him through his initial effort at Keystone.

This was not an ideal time for anyone at the studio to treat a newcomer with kid gloves. Sennett's bosses back at the NYMPC were all over him to keep on schedule with his delivery of finished product. Films were being completed and shipped only weeks before their scheduled release dates, which caused numerous production problems (and angst) for the NYMPC. An excerpt from a heated telegram sent to Sennett in mid-January 1914 illustrates:

> WE CANNOT RUN SO CLOSE IT TAKES ONE WEEK AT LEAST TO GET POSTERS AND WE MUST SHIP TO EXCHANGE AT LEAST ONE WEEK IN ADVANCE OF RELEASE DATE BESIDES OUR CONTRACT CALLS FOR US TO NOTIFY THE MUTUAL OF RELEASE DATES AT LEAST ONE MONTH IN ADVANCE CANNOT UNDERSTAND WHY KEYSTONE IS SO FAR BEHIND WHILE INCES COMPANY ARE SO FAR IN ADVANCE[42]

The pace must have been grueling, and even with the addition of several more directors — the company now had seven units working — it was barely able to keep its head above water. Some of the films were by now comparatively more sophisticated than the output of a mere year earlier, and therefore took slightly more time to produce. Sennett's introduction of two-reelers was throwing production further out of balance, and Mutual was unhappy that these were now being submitted as part of Keystone's weekly contractual obligation of three single-reelers. The two-reelers were originally intended to be once-a-month "specials" that Mutual could sell independent of the regular weekly release schedule, and therefore considered lost revenue. The NYMPC was taking the heat from Mutual, and passing it on to Sennett. One of the films referenced in this telegram as not yet having been delivered was Chaplin's maiden effort for the studio, *Making a Living*, which began production the day after Chaplin arrived at the studio.

Chaplin acting belligerent while Lehrman observes, amazed at the fellow's gall, in Making a Living. *Chaplin's impromptu outfit and characterization would be mothballed after this one film.*

Lehrman didn't have any time to waste on niceties or hand-holding. His primary focus was getting the current production filmed and out of his hair as quickly and efficiently as possible so that he could move on to the next one on his list. Chaplin, in his first "autobiography" published in 1916, recounted his first meeting with Lehrman:

> The director was standing in his shirt-sleeves beside a clicking camera, holding a mass of manuscript in his hand and clenching an unlighted cigar between his teeth. He was barking short commands to the company which was playing…. The scene over, he welcomed me cordially enough, but hurriedly.
> "Glad to see you. How soon can you go to work? This afternoon? Good! Two o'clock, if you can make it. Look around the studio a bit, if you like. Sorry I haven't

a minute to spare; I'm six hundred feet short this week, and they're waiting for the film. G'by. Two o'clock, sharp!" Then he turned away and cried, "All ready for the next scene. Basement interior," and was hard at work again.[43]

This was an autobiography in name only. In fact it was authored by Rose Wilder Lane, a feature writer for the *San Francisco Bulletin* who'd written a series of pieces on Chaplin after a number of face-to-face interviews with him. These were expanded into his "autobiography" without his knowledge, but have a basis in truth, and give a sense of that first encounter and the pressure that Lehrman was under.

Lehrman himself commented on this first film with Chaplin some years later. Director Robert Florey, a friend since the early twenties, interviewed Lehrman some years later when they were neighbors:

> I had never heard of Chaplin. I knew that he was a Limey, some said he was an acrobatic dancer, others that he had been a clown in a circus. To me it made no difference at all. I asked Sennett what clothes he should wear and Sennett said that as he was a Limey he had better dress himself as a lord.[44]

Which Chaplin did, decked out in a long waistcoat, top hat, cravat, and monocle, and sporting a long, droopy mustache not unlike Kaiser Wilhelm's in reverse. The result was about as far removed from his famous "tramp" costume as imaginable, and reportedly a throwback to some of his old costumes with the Fred Karno company productions.

Chaplin wasn't used to working in such a hectic, seemingly slap-dash fashion, and the filmmaking approach to shooting individual scenes out of sequence proved totally baffling to the young comedian. Chaplin had been indoctrinated in the ways of the music hall stage, where individual gags and skits evolved over time, and productions were performed in a linear fashion, from beginning to end. Differences in the working style of the director and actor created immediate conflicts, conflicts that no doubt would have arisen had Chaplin's first effort been for any other director at the studio. Chaplin, a success on stage for a number of years now, felt like a fish out of water.

Lehrman costars in *Making a Living* as a newspaper reporter whose job Chaplin's character, a dandified swindler, is out to get. When a horrific auto accident takes place, Lehrman rushes to the scene, but while he is otherwise occupied rescuing the driver, Chaplin makes off with Lehrman's notebook and camera, and the first of the film's two chases begins. Lehrman ends up in bed with another man's woman, and Chaplin inadvertently stabs a cop in the stomach(!), after which he presents the notebook and camera to the paper's editor as his own work. Finding out that he has been scooped by his own material, Lehrman gives chase, and both end up scooped by a street car's cowcatcher.

Given Chaplin's years of training and experience on stage, coupled with Lehrman's antic sense of humor and technical experience, the film itself is much better than one would think reading the various participants' comments about it, and the interplay between the two stars often quite amusing. Lehrman, who plays it relatively straight here, grows increasingly frustrated with his ongoing interactions with the obnoxious Chaplin, who plays it anything but straight. And while his character's looks are far removed from the "popular" Chaplin's, a number of very familiar mannerisms are on display. The film itself looks good, with several scenes shot on site at the *Los Angeles Times'* linotype and press rooms.[45] Lehrman, it was reported at the time, took an almost new $1,500 Studebaker and sent it over a cliff for the accident sequence. And in spite of the usual Keystone mayhem, it is a shock to see Chaplin jab that knife into the cop's midriff, although the latter jumps back up, seemingly unaffected — as would countless comedians to come who get shot in the posterior with no apparent ill effect.

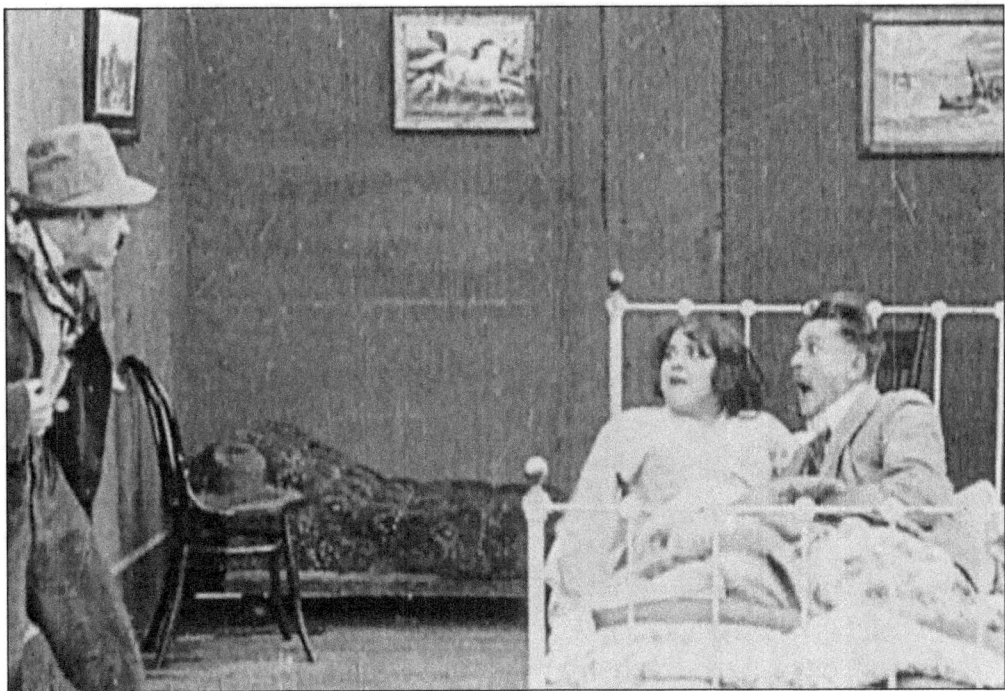

Lehrman, busted! From Making a Living.

Chaplin wasn't at all happy with the experience, and if his reminiscences of a half century later are to be believed, he wasn't happy with Lehrman either: "Lehrman was a vain man and very conscious of the fact that he had made some successful comedies of a mechanical nature; he used to say that he didn't need personalities, that he got all his laughs from mechanical effects and film cutting." Chaplin, it would seem, was still mildly bitter about the director not using some of Chaplin's suggestions and bits:

> When we started I could see that Lehrman was groping for ideas. And of course, being a newcomer at Keystone, I was anxious to make suggestions. This was where I created antagonism with Lehrman. In a scene in which I had an interview with an editor of a newspaper I crammed in every conceivable gag I could think of, even to suggesting business for others in the cast.... But when I saw the finished film it broke my heart, for the cutter had butchered it beyond recognition, cutting into the middle of all my funny business. I was bewildered, and wondered why they had done this. Henry Lehrman confessed years later that he had deliberately done it, because, as he put it, he thought I knew too much.[46]

What a whiner. In the film that survives Chaplin monopolizes the screen, and the scene with the editor is still jam-packed with Chaplin business. What he fails to acknowledge is that the film was a one-reeler, that there's only so much that can be crammed into a film of that length, and only so much time to devote to the making of a film of that length. Chaplin should have been content to spread "every conceivable gag" over the following year's films rather than expect them to be committed to a single film. His naivety, or perhaps ego, blinded him to reality.

Lehrman on location at the Los Angeles Times *facilities, in* Making a Living.

Sennett, evidently, was not happy with the results, a reaction he said was shared by Kessel and Baumann as well but not, it would seem, with contemporary reviewers: "The clever player who takes the role of nervy and very nifty sharper in this picture," wrote *Moving Picture World*, "is a comedian of the first water, who acts like one of Nature's own naturals."[47] Sennett claimed the film was a flop, and felt the costume was all wrong for American audiences — and he hated the mustache. Chaplin was told to find a new costume for his next film, scheduled to be shot around a coaster car race taking place in Venice, California on January 10, 1914. Lehrman was to direct and costar in this as well, released as *Kid Auto Races at Venice*. He spoke some years later of Chaplin's thoughts for the new costume:

> [Chaplin] told me that in his next film he was considering dressing himself up as a tramp. A few days later we were getting ready to go out to Venice...and I saw Chaplin arrive wearing the costume that was to make him famous.... And that's how we got to see Charlie Chaplin for the first time in his "Trampy" disguise, in the

film *Kid Auto Races*, which wasn't supposed to be anything more than a lighthearted documentary about kids, but which became his second film. I finished it the same day; Chaplin acted without rhyme or reason in some of the scenes in the film.[48]

Chaplin had cobbled together a costume of threadbare gentility. Reports vary slightly on the origin of some of the items, but it's generally accepted that the oversize shoes were borrowed from Sterling and the huge trousers from Arbuckle (Chester Conklin's trousers,

Chaplin in his now-familiar costume as the pesky onlooker in Kid Auto Races at Venice. *Lehrman can be seen over Chaplin's shoulder, standing by the cameraman.*

according to some sources). A tight cutaway coat reportedly belonged to Charles Avery (or Conklin), and a scrap of crepe hair was trimmed from one of Mack Swain's backup mustaches. Add in Arbuckle's father-in-law's derby hat, a checkered vest, along with Chaplin's own rattan cane, and you had the genesis of the costume that Chaplin would inhabit for most of the next quarter century.

The story, what there is of it, is simplistic. Lehrman and his cameraman are at the races to film the day's events when a slightly inebriated, chain-smoking Chaplin arrives on the scene. Curiosity gets the best of him, and his fascination with the filmmakers' activities results in the ruination of practically every shot as he repeatedly maneuvers himself in front of the camera. As his frustration with the pest mounts, Lehrman progresses from issuing polite requests to move, to commands to do so, to gentle pushes and, finally, to violent shoves that have Chaplin tumbling over backwards. As with the previous film, Lehrman

ABOVE: *Lehrman's at wit's end over Chaplin's annoying antics, from* Kid Auto Races at Venice.
BELOW: *Cameraman Frank D. Williams, Chaplin, and Lehrman.* COURTESY OF SAM GILL.

and Chaplin appear to work well together, although Sennett's later claim that Lehrman "gave himself the best camera angles" is demonstrably untrue and rings of sour grapes.

With the completion of *Kid Auto Races at Venice*, Lehrman was ready for his next assignment. This too would involve Chaplin, as Lehrman recalled years later:

> Two days later, after he had seen the rushes, Mack Sennett told me that he thought the Limey was very funny and that, together with me, he was thinking

Chaplin seated in the hotel lobby, while Lehrman — hands in pockets — chats in the background. From Mabel's Strange Predicament.

> of making Chaplin's third film; Mabel Normand should also have a part. Our co-operation was rapid and simple: Mack directed some scenes with Mabel while I photographed the scenes with Chaplin. We worked with two cameramen and this one-reel film, which we completed in the course of the day, was given the title *Mabel's Strange Predicament*.[49]

Walker asserts that neither Sennett nor Lehrman had anything to do with this film, attributing the direction to Mabel Normand. But working under the premise that Lehrman's recollections were accurate, and that *Mabel's Strange Predicament* was filmed over the period January 6, a Tuesday, to January 12, a Monday — four days of filming that would have preceded the Venice shoot — how would one account for Chaplin's presence in such a good portion of the film? Perhaps some footage shot over those first few days was sidelined for replacement with some new footage with Chaplin, or that footage shot with Chaplin before *Kid Auto Races* was beefed up now that Sennett saw what Chaplin was capable of. Either way, the film was completed on schedule, and it would appear that Sennett and Lehrman doubled up and worked in concert. Lehrman could have filmed Chaplin's (additional) scenes over the course of the final day, while Sennett assisted Normand with the remaining scenes required to tie it all together — and allowed Normand to receive sole credit for the direction of this film. It wouldn't have been the first time that Lehrman assisted with direction in a secondary capacity, and without credit.

Chaplin is in his element here as a falling-down drunk with an eye for the women. He eventually zeroes in on pajama-clad Normand who has inadvertently locked herself out of her hotel room, and manages to end up under the bed of another married man, here played by Chester Conklin. This is early Chaplin here, rough, crude, vulgar, and aggressive, and not the "nice" Chaplin he would evolve into within the next few years and, arguably, the funnier Chaplin. Lehrman manages a very brief appearance in this film as well in one of the crowd scenes as a guest in the hotel lobby.

All reports would indicate that there was much contention between director and his new comedian, the age-old conflict between commerce and art. The Keystone films had to be ground out as quickly and efficiently as possible without sacrificing the comedy within, but Chaplin proved to be an ongoing impediment, constantly arguing for new gags, bits of business, and retakes. Lehrman's patience wore thin. Still, Lehrman agreed to helm a third film, the one-joke *Between Showers* that was shot over several days immediately following a days-long downpour. The plot is simple: Sterling, as Mr. Snookie, steals an umbrella not realizing that it belongs to cop Conklin, and it ends up in Chaplin's hands. After some arguments over a female bystander (Emma Clifton), Sterling grabs cop Conklin to complain that his umbrella has been stolen. When Conklin recognizes the umbrella as his own, he arrests Sterling instead of Chaplin.

Sterling and Chaplin work well together here, with the former's typically outrageous mugging and grand gestures offset by Chaplin's comparatively subdued approach. Lead actress Clifton, who slightly resembles a much chunkier Mabel Normand, is not above the physical aspects of the comedy, going one-on-one with both Sterling and Chaplin, having her hair pulled and even the recipient of one of Sterling's famous nose bites!

Fowler alludes to Lehrman's seat-of-the-pants approach to filmmaking during the making of *Between Showers*, which contrasts the comedic styles of its two stars:

> It had been raining. The skies made the Californians wince as they apologized for the deluge to tourists. Lehrman wanted to get away from the studio — the world's most depressing place on a wet day. He took Sterling, Chaplin, a girl and a policeman, put them in a car and started down Main street. When Lehrman saw a wide puddle, he stopped and began the picture.
>
> The background consisted of citizens hopping across the street and wading through the puddle.
>
> Lehrman called: "Places." He gave final instructions to the principals and the action began. Charlie Chaplin was never more deliberate. Sterling plunged into the routine. The two styles clashed violently. Sterling's over-emphasis, all the muscular resources of his repertoire were called upon to engulf Chaplin. Goliath made his first rushing bid for victory. David, calm, detached and a little sad, stood

ABOVE: *Mabel Normand arrives at the Hollywood Hotel to film* Mabel's Strange Predicament. *Keystone writer/director Frank Cooley can be seen over her shoulder.* BELOW: *Alice Davenport and Chester Conklin follow Normand into the Hollywood Hotel to film* Mabel's Strange Predicament. COURTESY OF SAM GILL.

his ground. A twirl of the cane, a lift of an eyebrow, a mournful wiggle of his mustache, a chivalrous raising of his derby and a tentative little kick against his own posterior — these deadly pellets brought the giant to earth.[50]

Written twenty years after the filming of *Between Showers*, Fowler's focus was on the film's two stars, with nary a reference to the friction between Lehrman and Chaplin. After the completion of *Between Showers*, however, Lehrman could no longer tolerate Chaplin's constant belligerence and balking at taking orders. As writer Harry C. Carr told it a year later based on his conversations with Chaplin:

> They quarreled all the time during the first of Chaplin's work. Mabel Normand and Chaplin fought like a black dog and a monkey. Lehrmann [sic] finally appealed to Mack Sennett: he said he couldn't do anything with Chaplin. Sennett called Chaplin to time. The Keystone people say that the hardest "call down" anybody ever got at the Keystone was that handed to Charlie Chaplin by Sennett because he refused to obey the director. Chaplin took the boss's breezy remarks as toasts to the President are drunk — standing and in silence. But he went right on acting in his own way. Finally Lehrmann passed him on to another director, who had an equally bad time with him.[51]

The other director was George Nichols, too old for Chaplin's nonsense and equally frustrated by the young man's behavior.

Much has been written regarding Chaplin's and Lehrman's intense dislike for each other, and while that may have been true I suspect that their relationship was not nearly as contentious as one would be led to believe. Both had egos that knew no bounds, and there is little doubt that the two would frequently butt heads while actual production was taking place, but there's some evidence that their relationship outside of business hours was less contentious. Mary Pickford, formerly with Biograph, and with Famous Players while Lehrman and Chaplin were working together, recalled the two together at the beach:

> And then one time later, there was a big ball given at Long Beach, and [Chaplin] and a man called Pathé Lehrman, who was a big actor…and Charlie Chaplin took off his shoes, and was imitating J. Warren Kerrigan — did you ever hear of him? You didn't? Well, he was the Clark Gable of the day, or the Brando, or any attractive…. He was one of the great stars. And I thought it was very undignified. Now I'd think it funny, but I didn't think so then. And Pathé Lehrman introduced Chaplin to me, and he gave me a — my mother used to call it a "cold fish hand" — you know, sort of limp and kind of cold. But I was completely disgusted with his behavior. It wasn't naughty, it was very funny — they were imitating this very handsome — Charlie was playing my part, you see, and Lehrman was Kerrigan, and that was my first meeting with Chaplin.[52]

Perhaps theirs was an uneasy alliance: adversaries while at work, but friendly acquaintances on the outside.

ABOVE: *Chaplin and Sterling face off, while Chester Conklin and Emma Clifton observe from a safe distance, in* Between Showers. COURTESY COLLECTION EYE FILMMUSEUM. BELOW: *Wilfred Lucas is about to be caught in Lehrman's* Baffles, the Gentleman Burglar *(02/16/1914).*

Chaplin wasn't the only one on staff who Lehrman managed to rub the wrong way. William S. Campbell, who would later direct for Lehrman's Sunshine Comedies at Fox, claimed in a much later interview that he was with Sennett and Keystone from nearly the very beginning in 1912. Campbell recalled Lehrman's fatherly advice to him regarding the fine art of writing for comedies:

> We never wrote anything down in those days. I remember I thought, Now I'm a big-shot, and I went and got a big stack of paper and a big sharp pencil and sat down at a desk to write. Well, Henry "Pathé" Lehrman came up and stood behind me breathing heavily. He was the meanest, most sarcastic so-and-so you ever knew and he said to me slowly, like talking to a baby: "Waddya doin' here wid your pencil and your paper?" So I say, just as sarcastically, "I am writing a story." And he says, "Dis is de way you should write a story," and he picked up all my paper and pencil and scattered them to the winds. "IN YOUR HEAD," he shouts.[53]

Walker places Campbell's assignment to Keystone's scenario department much later in 1915, and long after Lehrman had left the studio. There's solid evidence that Campbell was at Keystone much earlier than that, based on a piece that appeared in the November 14, 1914 issue of *Motion Pictures News* that stated that "W.S. Campbell, formerly with Keystone, Mace comedies and R.B. producing companies, in capacity of scenario editor, is now sole occupant of the script room at Sterling studio."[54] Depending on when exactly Campbell had been hired by Sennett, this opens the possibility that Campbell's and Lehrman's days at Keystone may have overlapped.

While Lehrman's primary function at Keystone was as director, he would on occasion be told to step in and help flesh out crowd scenes or bit parts whenever he was otherwise unoccupied and available. Lehrman appears, albeit very briefly, as part of a congratulatory crowd after the climactic race in *The Speed Kings* (October 30, 1913), casually removing his hat, patting down his hair, and replacing his hat with moves that may or may not have been consciously executed to "upstage" and draw attention away from others in the crowd. In the recently rediscovered *A Thief Catcher* (February 19, 1914), Lehrman has a slightly meatier role as the police station's desk sergeant, his face partially obscured by the cap he keeps pulled down low over his eyes. Given the loss of the bulk of the Keystone output from these early years, it is anyone's guess as to how many other bit parts Lehrman assumed.

The origins of various well known gags, comic routines, assembled groups of cops, bathing beauties, and the like have been made repeatedly over the years and attributed to various individuals, but Lehrman figures into the recollections of some as being the source or receptive recipient of another's suggestion. According to Fred Balshofer in his memoir *One Reel a Week*,[55] Mabel Normand's form-fitting bathing suit worn in one of the early East Coast films, *The Water Nymph*, inspired Lehrman to suggest to Sennett the forming of a group of bathing beauties to appear in some of the films. This concept would eventually evolve into the Mack Sennett Bathing Girls. While Lehrman wasn't the first to use an assemblage of ineffectual cops, his *Bangville Police* was one of the earliest uses of a group of bumbling lawmen. Then there were the Keystone Kids with Paul Jacobs as their lead, nurtured from the beginning by Lehrman before entrusting them with director Thornby. And as for the age old gag of throwing pies, director Craig Hutchinson claimed

ABOVE: *Lehrman pats his hair as Mabel Normand congratulates the race's winner, from* The Speed Kings. BELOW: *Lehrman is all bluster as the desk sergeant in* A Thief Catcher.

a half century after the fact that he suggested a lobbed pie to Lehrman over lunch: "At first reluctant, Lehrman raved 'funniest thing you ever saw,' after viewing film rushes of comic Rube Miller being hit by pies."⁵⁶

It should be noted here as well that in a trade ad that ran in April 1914, Lehrman laid claim to having directed, co-directed, or been the original inspiration of a number of films for Keystone that aren't found in the filmography compiled by Walker, one that supersedes all its predecessors for accuracy and completeness. Based on the Keystone ledger entries,

Eight of the Sennett bathing beauties, striking a pose. COURTESY OF JERRY MURBACH AT DOCTOR MACRO'S HIGH QUALITY MOVIE SCANS, WWW.DOCTORMACRO.COM.

Walker credits Sennett with the direction of *The New Neighbor* (September 30, 1912), *The Battle of Who Run* (February 6, 1913), *The Fire Bug* (August 21, 1913), and *Mabel's New Hero* (August 28, 1913). The claim in the trade ad was that "Up to the time that he severed his connection with the Keystone, Mr. Lehrman directed every Keystone picture in which Mack Sinot (Sennet) [sic] appeared." Perhaps "co-directed" would have been the more accurate assertion. While the ledger entries credit Sennett, it is not at all improbable and wholly believable that Lehrman assisted whenever Sennett appeared before the camera, as he did in the first three of these films, all of which were filmed before any additional directors were added to the studio rosters. As for *Mabel's New Hero*, Lehrman and Sennett had taken turns directing Arbuckle from his very beginning at Keystone, so he may have lent Sennett a hand on this film as well. The ad also claimed that Lehrman had originated the ideas for the Sterling vehicle *Heinze's Resurrection* (February 17, 1913), *The Riot* (August

11, 1913) with Roscoe Arbuckle, and Mabel Normand's *Love and Gasoline* (February 21, 1914), a claim that Walker neither disputes nor addresses. That said, Lehrman was clearly full of himself, and not above making the occasional outrageous claim, as he did at the beginning of 1916 when he stated that "My best ideas were in the line of comedy. Mack Sennett worked under me. I discovered Ford Sterling and Charlie Chaplin made his screen debut under my auspices."[57] Sennett must have hit the ceiling when he read that!

While the area's film industry was growing daily, it was still comparatively small at this

Humble beginnings: the original Keystone and Broncho studio, 1912. COURTESY OF SAM GILL.

time. Lehrman did his best to socialize and make himself known to others, attending local parades, auto races, boxing matches, and industry banquets, and frequenting the area's various night clubs such as Baron Long's Vernon Country Club and Café Nat Goodwin in Santa Monica. One such industry affair was the 1913 Christmas dinner dance given by the Balboa Feature Film Company and held at the Hotel Virginia in Long Beach. Lehrman's fellow guests included the aforementioned Mary Pickford and J. Warren Kerrigan, as well as a fellow named Isadore Bernstein, a general manager over at Universal.[58] Whether Lehrman met Bernstein at this time or knew him previously is unknown, but within a year Bernstein would play an important part in the furthering of Lehrman's career.

Lehrman's dissatisfaction with his role at Keystone was mounting steadily by this time, and for good reason. With the company since its inception and one of the two directors responsible for the creation of the Keystone style, Lehrman was only a paid employee and one whose name was unknown to the public at large. It is arguable that the look and feel of Lehrman's early films for Keystone are more in line with what audiences came to regard as the company's norm, and casual viewing of both Sennett and Lehrman's output from these early years demonstrates some obvious stylistic differences in their respective techniques. Lehrman's films tended to be more energetic and, in many instances, more violent, eschewing depth of plot and characterization for action of the slapstick variety. Visually they were far more interesting, with some thought given to camera placement and the movement of the actors, as well as attention to cutting and the assemblage of shots that further accelerated the pace of the on-screen action. Lehrman's films such as *Bangville*

The new and thriving Keystone studio, circa 1915. COURTESY OF SAM GILL.

Police and *Love and Rubbish* would average a cut every eight seconds, while Sennett's *The Gusher* (December 15, 1913) and *A Bandit* (June 23, 1913; extant) would average a cut every ten seconds. These averages would be reversed on occasion, with Sennett's *Mabel's New Hero* (August 28, 1913; extant) averaging a cut every seven seconds, but the rapid cutting in Lehrman's films frequently has a better pace and flow to it. It would seem that when it came to visuals — and film is, after all, a visual medium — that Lehrman had absorbed more in this regard during his years at Biograph than Sennett had. He was a prolific idea man as well, coming up with the framework for the plots of both his films and those of others at the studio, skimpy though they may have been.

But in spite of his considerable contributions it was Sennett who was reaping all the acclaim for the company's meteoric rise in popularity and demand for its output, while Lehrman was just another company functionary. According to Fowler, Lehrman was earning $125 a week while his good friend Sterling was pulling in $200.[59] What probably stuck in his craw, however, was the money being thrown at Chaplin, brought in at $150 back in December, raised to $175 in January and, according to Sennett, raised again $250 a week with the completion of *Between Showers*.⁶⁰ Lehrman most likely would have felt deserving of some credit for Chaplin's growing success, having guided him through his first films at the studio and overseeing the comedian's character's metamorphosis from the slick dandy of *Making a Living* to the shabbily clothed working stiff of *Kid Auto Races*, the character he'd go on to inhabit and embellish for years to come.

Terry Ramsey made a point of acknowledging Lehrman's worth:

> In the opinion of not a few of his contemporaries, Lehrman added importantly to the development of screen comedy technique and, as an assistant to Mack Sennett, helped to evolve the style of screen extravaganza which, in after years, made Keystone and Sennett famous.... His humorous quips and quirks were an early part of the evolution of the now well-recognized craft of the picture specialist known as "gag-man."⁶¹

With Chaplin out of his hair, Lehrman went to work at the beginning of February on what would become his last film directing Arbuckle, *A Rural Demon* (March 19, 1914), and took some spare moments along with most of the other personnel at Keystone to play themselves in bits in the Chaplin vehicle *A Film Johnnie* (March 2, 1914). Little did Sennett realize at the time that these would be Lehrman's last for the studio as well, although he probably should have.

CHAPTER 4

The Sterling Motion Picture Corporation: The Grass is Always Greener

The enterprise that ultimately evolved into The Sterling Film Company was the brainchild of thirty-six year old, New York-born filmmaker Fred J. Balshofer. As told in his autobiography, Balshofer got his start in the mid-1890s as a photographer for the New York-based Stromeyer and Wyman stereoptican company. His position was retained when the company sold out to Underwood and Underwood, and after eight years of this he spent another two years with the Shields Lantern Slide Company. His initial exposure to the fledgling industry came with his employment by Philadelphia's Sigmund Lubin in 1905, where he served for a couple of years as photographer and lab man. This position included the additional duties of frequent illegal duping of competitors' motion picture prints for resale. Balshofer returned to New York City in October 1907 where he served a half-year stint as photographer for the Mosher and Harrington film exchange, after which he and partner Herman Kolle formed The Crescent Film Company in Spring of 1908.

Balshofer's autobiography, it should be pointed out, was published in 1967 as he was approaching his ninetieth year, well over a half century after most of the events described took place. Like so many other published reminiscences, it is his version and perspective of these events; there is little doubt that these various memoirs place the teller in the best of lights, at the occasional expense of the other participants involved.

Based in South Brooklyn, The Crescent Film Company released its product through Adam Kessel and Charles Baumann's Empire Film Exchange on Fourteenth Street near Third Avenue. After several months of comparative success, Kolle decided he wanted out and sold his interest in the company to Kessel and Baumann for $500, who were both pleased with Crescent's output. Putting up an additional $1,500 against Balshofer's filmmaking experience, Kessel and Baumann went in on a three-way split with Balshofer in early 1909 on a venture to be named The New York Motion Picture Company. Working out of the loft of a three story building in Brooklyn, Kessel served as President, Baumann as Vice President, and Balshofer as Secretary-Treasurer. The 101 Bison Company was formed to make motion pictures for release, with Balshofer handling the direction, photography, and cutting of the initial releases until competent individuals could be hired to assume those tasks. Stars Charles Inslee and Charles French eventually assisted with the direction of their own films, with French contributing stories as well. As the company grew more successful, it quickly became the primary target of the Motion Picture Patents Company detectives, which resulted in a hasty move out to California in November 1909. Intended only as a stay for the winter months, it eventually became permanent with studios first on Alessandro Street in Edendale, and later at a fenced-in property at Santa Ynez Canyon in the Santa Monica Mountains.

LEFT: *Fred Balshofer.* RIGHT: *Carl Laemmle.*

Production proceeded comparatively smoothly for the next couple of years, with the Bison brand steadily growing in popularity. Audiences nationwide were thrilled by the realism provided by the scenic California locales and the rugged western types that Balshofer assembled to appear in these dramas. The widespread success of these films along with those of a growing number of other independents did not sit well with the Patents Company's members, whose membership in the company was exclusive. Its goal, as mentioned earlier, was to drive non-participant film companies and exchanges out of business by prohibiting the use of patented cameras and projectors, which in theory would dry up product.

The independent exchange owners weren't about to fold without a fight, however, and had formed their own companies in order to ensure a steady flow of film. As a result, the Patents Company had embarked on a policy of continuous harassment that was growing nastier as time went on. The threat of infringement suits hung over the independents' heads, and each producer was well aware of what a costly legal battle would mean to the financial stability of his company. In order to protect themselves, eight of the independents banded together on June 8, 1912, as The Universal Film Manufacturing Company, to present a united front against their common enemy. Comprising The New York Motion Picture

Company, Carl Laemmle's IMP, Pat Powers' Powers Picture Plays, David Horsley's Nestor, Charles Jourjon's American Éclair Company, William Swanson and Joe Engel's Rex, Mark Dintenfass' Champion Film Company, and William Steiner's Yankee film companies, each was issued stock in the new concern in direct ratio to his assets.

According to Balshofer, the members all managed to coexist peacefully for the first several weeks, with temporary positions of President for Baumann, Vice President for Powers, Treasurer for Laemmle, and General Manager for Balshofer. With the first meeting came a greedy scramble for the top position, which Baumann thought belonged to either Kessel or himself due to their ownership of the largest block of stock. The others disagreed, with the result that an incensed NYMPC pulled out of the combine on June 27. The other members insisted that the NYMPC's assets were committed, and took physical and legal steps to gain possession of them. As the new President and Vice President, Laemmle and Powers made behind-the-scenes overtures to Balshofer of a healthy bonus and block of stock if he would defect, but he steadfastly refused. Legal maneuvers broke down when it was discovered that Balshofer had never signed the contract turning over the NYMPC's assets for stock. The decision was handed down that Universal could retain only the Bison name and $17,000 in cash.[1] Balshofer's company was rechristened Kay-Bee, and resumed production at Santa Ynez with the newer Broncho and Domino western units. The power struggle within Universal continued for a short while until Laemmle managed to buy out each of his competitors, with Swanson receiving $750,000 and Powers $1,000,000.

The Patents Company's draconian policies lost some of their clout over the following years as patents expired and member patent holders adopted a less aggressive stance. The death knell was finally sounded on October 1, 1915 when a federal court decision ruled against The Trust for its illegal restraint of trade in *United States v. Motion Picture Patents Co.* After a failed appeal The Trust was officially terminated in 1918.

A month after their defection from Universal, Kessel, Baumann, and Balshofer joined up with another independent distribution exchange, The Mutual Film Corporation. This is the time when their association with Mack Sennett began and the Keystone Film Company was formed. As the NYMPC's West Coast Operations Chief, Balshofer was to oversee the operations of the new filmmaking concern.

By mid-1913, Balshofer had become a comparatively wealthy figure in the industry, pulling in weekly dividends on top of his considerable salary. Time was taking its toll on Balshofer's relationship with Kessel and Baumann, however, and he eventually sold his one-third interest in the NYMPC to them for $100,000[2] and moved forward with plans to go it on his own. In his autobiography, Balshofer claimed that the split was due to his partners' decision to take part in the formation of the new Triangle Film Corporation, a decision he disagreed with. Since Triangle didn't become a functioning entity until mid-1915, however, it would seem that his memory was playing tricks on him.

Balshofer set out for New York City with the goal of drumming up a deal with Carl Laemmle for a production company under his sole control. In spite of the friction between his former partners and Laemmle, Balshofer remained on good terms with Laemmle and his associates, and the two were able to do business. Laemmle had been peeved by Kessel and Baumann's defection from his distribution exchange two years earlier, and with the ascendency of Keystone had created his own competitor comedy production company, Joker, in 1913. While Joker filled a niche in the Universal's weekly release schedule, it was only moderately successful and its output paled in comparison with Keystone's. Laemmle felt that another, higher profile comedy unit was needed to balance the weekly schedule, and was receptive to Balshofer's proposal. There was a proviso, however: Balshofer would need to come up with a comedy lead whose popularity had already been established. Hiring known and proven entities rather than nurturing new talent was an approach of Laemmle's that had met with past success, with the acquisition of talents such as Biograph's Florence Lawrence and Mary Pickford; there was no reason to believe that it wouldn't have the same success in the field of comedy. Balshofer seemed to think that he would be able to lure either Mabel Normand or Ford Sterling away from Sennett,[3] and Laemmle agreed that either one of the popular comedians would be more than acceptable, but expressed doubts that the two candidates weren't tied up with contracts. Balshofer knew otherwise, for contracts were the exception rather than the rule at Keystone. As Sennett put it, "With Kessel and Bauman riding me about expenses all the time, I gave out as few contracts as possible. This meant that when there was an overcast, or rain, or when my rambunctious geniuses in the story departments failed to come up with what they called a script, I could lay off the actors and cut down the overhead."[4] With Laemmle's blessing, Balshofer headed back to California hoping to sign Normand. His luck failed him, for word of his intentions had somehow leaked to Sennett, who promptly committed her to a contract of his own. Balshofer turned to Sterling with considerably more success.

In the earliest days of 1914, Ford Sterling was among the three most popular comedians in film, vying for top honors with Vitagraph's John Bunny and the European Max Linder, both whose styles differed radically from Sterling's grotesquely funny caricatures. Born George Ford Stich in La Crosse, Wisconsin, on November 3, 1883, Sterling recounted late in 1914 the years before entering the film industry:

> [We] moved early to Texas, where dad was engaged in the cattle business. After his death I found it necessary to get out and hustle. I did — hustled right onto the stage, at the advice of James O'Neill, a graduate of my alma mater, Notre Dame College, at South Bend, Indiana. I went first with George Whittier, by dint of much persuasion and sundry promises that were almost threats, to make good. This was a repertory show. I then made up my mind for musical comedy, but my start in this profession was by no means prepossessing. I acted, did a song and dance, was property man and even helped load the cars, but it didn't hurt me, and it taught me a lot. I was with a circus for a time, billed as "Keno, the Boy Clown," and then when I left the circus I acted and played professional baseball. I played ball seven summers, with Gulfport, Mississippi; Mobile; McKeesport, Pennsylvania; Saginaw; Toledo, and two seasons with Duluth. And then I drew pictures (remember the "Sterling Kids"? I'm the originator and artist of those) for the Chicago *American*.... [T]hen I played stock, and also in vaudeville, and, in fact, it was while doing a vaudeville act with Tom McEvoy, called "Breaking into Society," that I got into the picture game. "Pathé" Lehrman saw me, told me he was convinced I'd make good in pictures, and then followed an engagement with Mack Sennett, of Biograph then, who had been looking around for some time for a comedian. Then, as you know, I went to Keystone, in the same bunch with Mabel Normand, "Pathé" Lehrman, Fred Mace and Mack Sennett.[5]

Lehrman, it would seem, was the one who "discovered" Sterling and encouraged him to become a part of the film industry.

The Keystone comedies were cranked out at a furious pace, and Sterling starred in virtually all but a handful of the first half year's releases. His roles varied from film to film, but several character types eventually predominated, with Sterling's Dutch-German impressions (Schultz, Hoffmeyer, Heinze, Schnitzel, Schmidt, Meyer, etc.) and the character of Cohen taking the lead. Audiences fell in love with Sterling and his rather

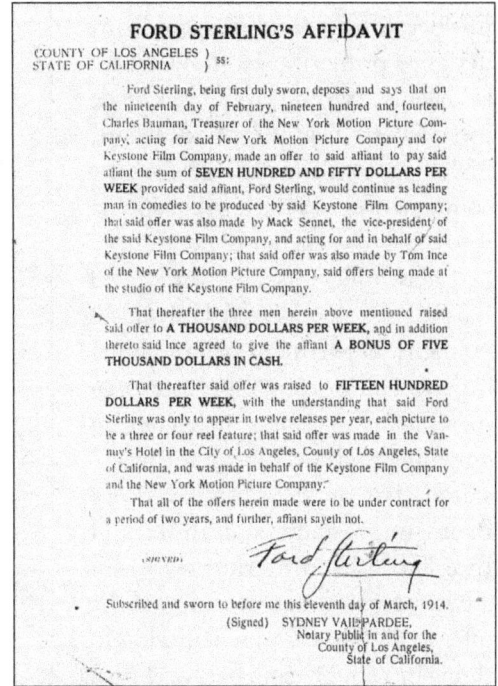

LEFT: *Ford Sterling*. RIGHT: *Sterling's affidavit detailing the history of offers made to induce him to stay at Keystone, as reproduced in the March 21, 1914 issue of* Universal Weekly, *Universal Studio's weekly publication for exhibitors.*

bizarre comedic style, one in which every thought and action to come is telegraphed to the viewer through his wild gesticulations. They became his not-so-silent partners, and reveled in his blustering lechery and cantankerousness. Sterling haunted the screen from the company's inception, and was elemental to its initial overwhelming success.

"No milder or more subtle form of comedy is difficult," reminisced Sterling a dozen years later, "if you have once played slapstick comedy. It is like hitting one of those machines they have at Coney Island. If you hit it as hard as you can, you ring the bell. More gentle blows send the weight up to various heights, but they don't sound the gong. In slapstick every effort must ring the bell, and all the other degrees of humor are touched on and passed."[6]

At Keystone, Sterling tried to dislodge the bell.

In April 1913, Fred Mace, Keystone's other male lead and Sterling's rival for audience popularity, departed from the company for what he hoped would be greener pastures. This left Sterling as the company's unrivaled top star. In order to meet the public's demands, Sennett would have as many as three production units working simultaneously, with Sterling shuffling from set to set for actual filming. Sterling's talents eventually involved the writing and direction of his films as well, and his salary increased accordingly to a hefty $250 a week. Said Sennett: "Kessel and Bauman pleaded with me that this was an impossible sum for a Keystone cop, even the chief cop, because those quick two-reel features were not sold on a percentage basis…and there had to be a limit to their cost."[7] Requests for an additional salary increase were put off, and Sterling, never one to underestimate his worth, began to think in terms of a possible move; Lehrman too was making similar noises of discontent.

With Balshofer's overtures and the prospect of a production company designed primarily as a showcase for his talents, Sterling's mind was made up; Sennett was informed accordingly. Sennett claimed to have made a counter-offer of $400 a week, upping it to $750 a week, but to no avail.[8]

Laemmle was informed of Balshofer's success, and Universal's publicity department began churning out all sorts of promotional materials trumpeting their coup in obtaining Sterling. One of the pieces stated that on February 19, 1914, Baumann, Sennett, and Thomas H. Ince had offered Sterling $750 for a two-year contract, then upped the offer to $1,000 with Ince offering to throw in a $5,000 cash bonus. A final offer had taken place at Vannuy's Hotel in Los Angeles: a two-year contract at $1,500 a week, for twelve three- to four-reel releases per year.[9] All of these offers were nixed by Sterling; the decision had been made to go with Balshofer, and he was going to honor it.

This portrait of Henry Lehrman first appeared in ads for the new Sterling Comedies. This same portrait would be used time and again up until the early 1930s. COURTESY OF MUSEUM OF MODERN ART/ FILM STILLS ARCHIVE.

And Sterling wasn't the only loss the Keystone was about to suffer. Balshofer and Sterling also lured Lehrman into the new company with the promise of partial ownership and the opportunity to write and direct his own comedies, with full credit for his efforts. This, needless to say, was just what Lehrman wanted to hear. Director Robert Thornby was enticed away to head up a kids' unit in the new company. Actresses Emma Clifton and Peggy Pearce, along with diminutive star Paul Jacobs, were to jump ship as well, moving over to the fledgling new company.

Adam Kessel was shocked by this turn of events and the various articles and ads appearing in the trades. One of these, appearing in the *New York Dramatic Mirror* under the bold heading "Another Smashing Universal Scoop!", listed the four key figures and went on to say that "The Directors and Actors that made Keystone Comedies famous — Artists who have made the world laugh — have joined the constellation of Stars under the banner of Universal Moving Pictures. You Asked Us to Give You More Comedy — You Never Dreamed We'd Give You Such a Sterling Answer!"[10] In that same issue appeared a small article that went on to say that "Ford Sterling has for years been the chief loadstone of the Mutual funmakers, while Lehrman, besides being an able director, has provided many of the ideas introduced in the whirlwind comedies."[11] After initially denying the rumors of the wholesale defection, Kessel adhered to the old adage that the best defense is a good offense, and responded with a disingenuous piece that followed in the trades:

> The statement that H. Pathe Lehrman and Fred Balshofer have been permanently identified with the Keystone Company is not correct. Fred Balshofer has never been connected with the Keystone Company. He was a camera man and factory man for the New York Motion Picture Corporation. It is said that Lehrman has introduced many of the ideas in Keystone comedies. This is also incorrect, as Mr. Mack Sennett is the originator of all Keystone comedies and has made Fred [sic] Sterling the comedian he is to-day. Pathé Lehrman never to our knowledge acted or directed in a comedy on his own prerogative.[12]

There was another defector from the Keystone ranks as well, a fellow named Beverly Griffith. The Georgia-born Griffith had held a few menial jobs before and after moving out to Los Angeles, eventually landing a position in 1913 as assistant property man with Keystone. He made a few appearances in some of the early Keystone shorts (including Lehrman's *Making a Living*), and it wasn't long before Griffith was promoted to assistant to Sennett himself, a position he held until early 1914 when he accompanied Sterling and Lehrman over to the new firm. Here he became Balshofer's assistant and was eventually placed in charge of the business end of the four Sterling units to come.[13]

Another to make the move was seventeen year old Jack White. White had entered the film industry two years earlier as office boy to Sennett and company messenger, receiving the princely sum of eight dollars a week. According to White almost seventy years later in a lengthy interview with David N. Bruskin, he was a victim of circumstances:

> A manager by the name of Barry Griffith, who knew me well, couldn't seem to get any messages to Ford Sterling…so he called me on the switchboard and sent a coded message through me to Ford Sterling. Sterling then left Sennett to form his own company. Mack heard I had delivered the message that lost him Ford Sterling and thought that I had done it knowingly, which I hadn't. I thought I was doing a friend a favor. Mr. Sennett called me in and said, "As of Saturday, your employment here is terminated." I had to look it up in the dictionary — what the hell is terminated? So I was fired. I went to Ford Sterling for a job, and he gave me one right away at ten dollars a week. My salary was improving.[14]

The "Barry Griffith" he referred to was in all likelihood a misremembered Beverly Griffith. White was put to work at Sterling developing and printing still pictures, moving on to work in the motion picture lab. White was soon joined by his friend Charles Hochberg, another defector from Keystone, who was put to work cutting negatives. In his interview with Bruskin, White also claimed authorship of a story involving a mailman and bulldog that he had written back at Keystone but was never filmed. It resurfaced months later at the new studio where Lehrman and Sterling supposedly filmed it, forgetting its origin, but paid the young author when reminded.[15] White would continue his association with Lehrman through the rest of the decade, eventually forming his own comedy brands releasing through the Educational Exchange throughout the twenties.

The Universal publicity machine went into hyper-drive touting Laemmle's coup, planting numerous two-page blurbs in the *Universal Weekly*, the company's exhibitors' publication, and in the trades alike. "We did not stop at getting Ford Sterling," stated one of them, which went on to bellow "WE GOT THE MAN WHO HAS WRITTEN AND DIRECTED MOST OF HIS SCREAMING SUCCESSES, MR. LEHRMAN. THEN WE GOT THE MAN WHO HAS WRITTEN AND DIRECTED OTHER OF HIS SUCCESSES, Mr. Thornby."[16] Another ad touted Lehrman as "the man who has written and directed most of the Keystone comedy successes. His work is famous. But now he is working with the Universal instead of against it."[17] Laemmle made it known to the Universal exchanges "that this contract is one of the most expensive we have undertaken and that the film would cost more than the regular price," but they were (reportedly) not overly concerned, well aware of the drawing power of the Sterling name.[18]

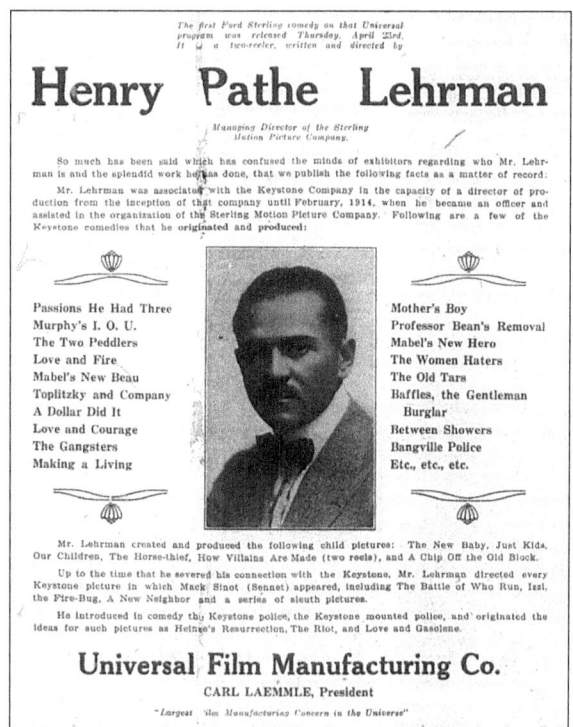

The Universal publicity machine touted Lehrman's many successes and achievements while at Keystone, in the April 25, 1914 issue of Universal Weekly. *Some of these are questionable, or overstatements of fact.*

Sennett claimed the last word to the two key defectors as they packed to leave his studio, "shouting back and forth through the dressing rooms about the marvels they were going to put on film." "All right, you guys, tell you something," shouted Sennett. "I can *act* in the pictures, I can *direct* the pictures, I can *produce* the pictures, I can *advertise* the pictures — and damn it, I can *finance* the pictures. I'll be a success when you fellows have fallen on your cans and been forgotten!"[19]

Years later, Sennett lamented about his good friend Lehrman's departure and, it would seem, his feelings of betrayal. A mixture of sadness and bitterness crept into his words: "As the years went on I found increasing use for Pathé, and it is certainly a fact that he used me."[20]

Laemmle had left New York for California on February 12, and word of the new company was released to the press on February 18,[21] the morning after his arrival by train in Los Angeles. The March 11 installment No. 5 of Universal's *Animated Weekly* newsreel featured a jubilant Laemmle engaged in vigorous handshakes with Balshofer, Sterling (in his Dutch getup), Lehrman, and Thornby, reportedly taken at the signing of contracts.[22]

Response to the announcement was both positive and reactionary. Universal's exchangemen and exhibitors nationwide were jubilant at the news, flooding Universal's New York City–based home office with telegrams and letters of congratulations. Biograph responded with a more defensive move, calling its Los Angeles–based comedy unit back to the east coast after a mere seven week stay, no doubt concerned that some of its more

The signing, as pictured in the March 21, 1914 issue of Universal Weekly. *Left to right: Fred Balshofer, Ford Sterling, Carl Laemmle, Robert Thornby, and Henry Lehrman.*

prominent members might be caught up in the new studio's aggressive acquisition of talent and the resultant ripple effects. And with good reason: While actor Gus Pixley heeded the call to return, star performer and assistant producer Charlie Murray jumped ship and headed over to Keystone, reportedly to fill Sterling's now vacant shoes. A number of the group's other performers decided to remain behind in sunny California as well, including Louise Orth, Bud Ross, and several others whose names have collectively faded from popular memory.[23]

The three principals incorporated the new film company as the Sterling Motion Picture Company in late February 1914, with capital stock of $10,000 and subscribed stock of $300. The incorporators' names, as they appeared on the official documents, were Fred J. Balshofer, Henry M. Lehrman, and George F. S. Stich,[24] Sterling's real name. Balshofer was appointed president and Sterling vice president, while Lehrman wore the dual hats of both secretary and treasurer. Balshofer's self-serving autobiography would lead one to believe that he was the sole owner of the company, and that Sterling and Lehrman were

Charlie Murray in the Keystone His Second Childhood *(12/26/1914). Left-to-right: Frank Opperman, Dixie Chene, Grover Ligon (bald man in back), unknown, Murray in drag, and Phyllis Allen.* COURTESY OF SAM GILL.

his employees, when in reality the three of them were all stockholders in the new firm. Balshofer said that Sterling's salary was $250 and Lehrman's $200, with both to receive a cut of the profits. In light of Sennett's and the NYMPC's reported counter-offers, if factual, these figures sound low.[25]

Robert Grau, in his concise *The Theatre of Science: A Volume of Progress and Achievement in the Motion Picture Industry* published later that same year, summarized the birth of the new studio as such:

> Probably the greatest coup that was accomplished up to now was the acquisition in the latter part of February, 1914, of the quartet of comedy producers, Ford Sterling, for a long time the chief lodestone of the Mutual fun-makers; H. Pathé Lehrman, who was not only an able director of Keystone comedies, but the provider of most of the ideas introduced in the whirlwind burlesques; Fred Balshofer, skilled as an executive in such matters, an official of the New York

Motion Picture Company, and Robert Thornby, who gained fame in Vitagraph dramas and comedies and who had been with the Keystone for several months prior to the change. The comedies in which Mr. Sterling had become famous were the only competition which had annoyed the Universal. That being the case, the Universal went out, paid the price and secured not only Mr. Sterling, but his companions.[26]

Universal ran a nationwide contest soliciting a name for the new comedy brand, offering a twenty-five dollar payout to the winner; suggestions were to be forwarded to Balshofer care of Universal.[27] He was inundated with over three thousand submissions that ran the gamut from creative to absurd, including potential brand names of "Sterling Silver," "New Era," "Humorous," "Tip-Top," "Crackerjack," "Excelsior," "Target," "Mirth," "Skylark," "Stetson," "Bohemian," "Star," "Lodestone," "Standard," "Funny Film," "Orpheus," "Uni-Ford," and "Universal Ford."[28] The winning name, "chosen solely on the basis of Sterling's popularity," was the obvious, but rather unimaginative, name of "Sterling." Mrs. Frieda Decker of Brooklyn was the winner, even though several hundred other similarly unimaginative contestants submitted this same name, her submission chosen solely because it was the first of these received.[29] *Universal Weekly* touted the new brand's registered trademark as the letter "S" in a circle, but unlike the other Universal brand logos it never appeared in print on those pages (it did make it onto theaters' posters, however). According to Fowler, Lehrman had grave reservations regarding this new name, and the character Sterling had made famous as well:

> "We can't do that," Lehrman said, "because you're a German. And if we put your name up too prominently, it may offend anti-German customers. And another thing, Ford, you've got to stop playing German roles."
> Sterling bridled. "For two years I've worked all the time to establish myself. I became the greatest Dutch comedian in the world, and I'll not give up the character."
> "You'd better be just a plain American comedian," said Lehrman. "We can't take chances."
> "I refuse to do that," said Sterling. "I'll play the Dutchman or nothing. And we'll name it the Sterling Company."[30]

Accurate or not, these arguments don't make a lot of sense, given that the name Sterling has Scottish origins, and that Sterling's Dutch character had been embraced by the public with few signs of resistance. The Sterling name would be the company's name.

Balshofer had conducted a search in late 1913 to lease a studio to house whatever film company he would be able to establish. He found just what he needed in David Horsley's former Nestor studio, situated at the northwest corner of what would become Gower Street and Sunset Boulevard. Originally built back in 1889 to house The Cahuenga House, a roadhouse that came to be more commonly known as the Blondeau Tavern, that business had gone belly-up soon after the institution in 1904 of a local ordinance prohibiting the sale of liquor. Horsley had leased the property in 1911 and converted it to Hollywood's first studio, but had moved on by the time Balshofer ended up purchasing the place on

January 1, 1914.³¹ Balshofer put down $500 towards the property's $11,000 cost, with monthly installments of $125 towards the balance. Complete with offices, a lab, dressing rooms, and a backyard open air stage surrounded by a six foot high fence to keep the nosey locals at bay, the property occupied an approximately one hundred eighty foot frontage on Sunset by two hundred eighty feet on Gower.³² The small studio was ready for immediate occupancy once the deal with Laemmle was finalized.

Universal's schedule in early 1914 was a full one, with nearly a third of the thirty (on

Gale Henry held prisoner by (left to right) Bobby Vernon, Heinie Conklin, and William Franey, as Lillian Peacock looks on; from an unidentified Joker comedy. COURTESY OF ROBERT ARKUS.

average) reels released weekly devoted to comedy. Although only a couple of the brands releasing through Universal were geared solely towards comedy, most of the remaining dozen or so had the occasional release in that vein. Joker was the most prominent of the comedy outfits, having gained nationwide acceptance in the year since its inception. Developed primarily to cash in on Keystone's popularity, directors Allen Curtis and Hampton Del Ruth were cranking out two comedies a week with the stars Max Asher, Harry McCoy (paired in the "Mike and Jake" series as well as in numerous roles both co-starring and solo), Louise Fazenda, Bobby Vernon (initially as Sylvion De Jardins), and William Franey; Joker's initial offering, *The Cheese Special*, was released on October 25, 1913. Crystal's mainstays were the popular Pearl White and Chester Barnett co-starrers which had been on the market since October 1912, and in their expanded, two-reel format since May 1913. Crystal's schedule was increased in late summer 1913 with the addition of Vivian Prescott and Charles DeForrest who were to co-star in a series of single-reelers commencing with *Midnight Soaring* (January 20, 1914). Al Christie churned out an endless stream of shorts for Nestor starring Eddie Lyons, Lee Moran (not to be officially teamed for another year), seventeen year old Victoria Forde, Ramona Langley, and John Steppling. IMP released occasional comedies with King Baggot and Ethel Grandin among many others, as did Rex every week or so with its Robert Leonard vehicles, and Powers with its Donald MacDonald and Laura Oakley starrers. Éclair's comedies included the "Nutty" series starring René Gréhan. Frontier's lone comedy series featured J. Arthur Nelson as Slim of Bungville, but would drop comedies altogether by mid-year. Victor offered only

The Nestor Comedy Company's Al Christie, Eddie Lyons, Lee Moran, and Victoria Forde.

an occasional excursion into the field and of varying tastes, with drawing-room comedies such as *The Imp Abroad* (January 12) co-existing with more vulgar fare such as *Irene the Onion Eater's Daughter* (February 6). One of Universal's most popular brands of the day was its Universal Ike series featuring Augustus Carney in a role originated at Essanay as Alkali Ike. Carney's temperament got the best of him, and he was promptly replaced a mere two months after the formation of his own company by a character named Universal Ike, Jr. (Bobby Fuehrer), who also proved short-lived. The addition of Ford Sterling to the Universal rosters seemed a sure-fire move, offering a star with considerable name recognition and proven popularity who could serve as the linchpin of a comedy schedule that heretofore had lacked any real cohesion or direction.

With all of the hype promoting Lehrman's seemingly endless talents and the major contributions he had made to help build the Keystone brand into the success it had become, Lehrman knew that his first film had to be a big one, loaded with outrageous laughs and plenty of violent action in a fast moving two-reeler to help set it apart from the single-reel norm. It needed to showcase the star's undeniable talents along with enough action and comedy to please a diehard Keystone fan. It needed to be spectacular, at least within the modest limits of the genre. Knowing that they had a two month buffer before exhibitors were to receive the first of the brand's releases, Lehrman and Sterling went to work immediately after the contracts were signed to build up a backlog of comedies for eventual release. They couldn't get bogged down with too many time consuming two-reelers, however, so they decided that after a first two-reel spectacular they would follow with several less ambitious single reelers, followed again by another two-reel special.

Continuing with the cost-effective Keystone approach to building a film around a pre-existing event, the upcoming Vanderbilt Cup auto race at Santa Monica was chosen not only for the on-screen thrills it would provide, but for its close proximity as well. The Vanderbilt Cup race was by now an institution with ten years under its belt, its origins back in Long Island, New York in 1904, where posters warned neighbors to "Chain your dogs and lock up your fowls."

Lehrman, Sterling, and actress Emma Clifton headed out to the track where filming would take place over two days, first on February 26 when the Vanderbilt Cup race itself was held, and again on the 28th when the grand finale International Grand Prix event took place. The footage that Lehrman's cameraman was to take would be supplemented — and in a very big way — by additional footage taken by a dozen of Universal's other cameramen covering the race from all angles for a rush five hundred foot newsreel. Stationed at various points around the 8.4 mile track (where a

Ford Sterling in costume for the Sterling Comedies.

total of forty-eight laps would cover more than four hundred three miles), the results were as good as anyone could have hoped for. There were numerous skids and near crashes, but the topper was a breathtaking five rollovers of the Sunbeam driven by the current first position holder, John B. Marquis, as he failed to navigate the so-called "Death Turn."

Frank B. Goode, a former professional race car driver new to the acting profession, was hired by Lehrman for a part in the film and to take part in the race as well. Goode's choice was a logistically savvy one, as it would further facilitate shooting and the integration of race footage with Sterling's antics. "[Goode] is picked as a likely place man by many of his admirers. His car is particularly fast and Goode knows full well that he is to travel in fast company. As a result of his knowledge, he will prepare carefully for the big event," said the *Los Angeles Times*.[33] Driving a yellow Apperson Jack Rabbit that the *Times* said "looked like a gunboat in wartime paint," Goode attracted attention during the speed trials when he temporarily lost control and nearly crashed.[34] As for the final race on the 28th, Goode had to drop out midway with a broken valve. Goode's previous role had been in director Robert Thornby's *The Race* (September 25, 1913) for Vitagraph, but he cut his acting career short and moved over to cinematography where he remained up until his death in the late 1930s.[35]

For added public relations value, Universal president Laemmle, Fred Balshofer, and their guest Herman Fichtenberg[36] tagged along as well to observe the races and the filming.

As a tip of his hat to his new associates, Lehrman shot some additional footage of the group for inclusion in the finished film. Look closely at the shots where Clifton cheers on Goode from the bleachers and you'll spot "spectator" Balshofer seated to her left, and Laemmle in the row behind.

Lew Carter, another professional driver with ten years experience, was pressed into service playing one of the film's cops. Carter fell victim to one of Lehrman's potentially dangerous gags, one that was unannounced and off-the-cuff, a precursor to many more gags of this sort in years to come. Carter was hanging by one foot from a tree branch over a canal, intending to drop, when Lerhman decided to lend him a hand by backing his car into the tree. He did so, and at quite a clip, knocking Carter nearly senseless. It made for good footage, though, reportedly ending up in the finished film,[37] although not in the print I was able to view.

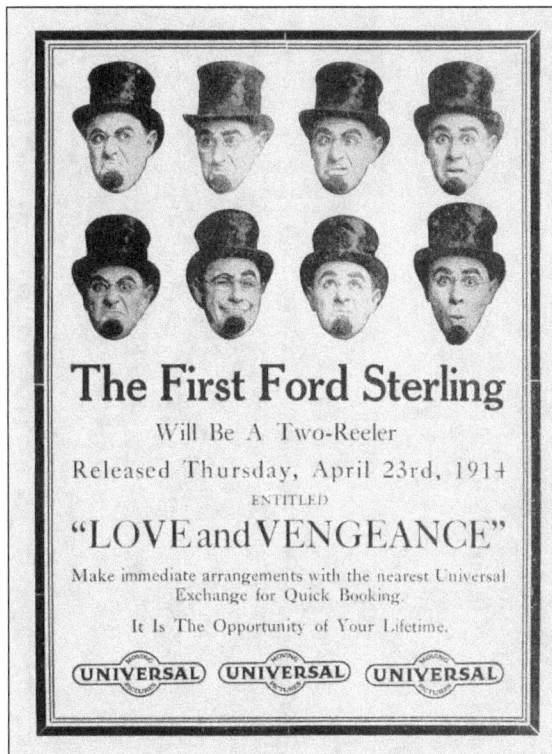

Ad promoting the soon-to-be-released Love and Vengeance, *from the April 18, 1914 issue of* Universal Weekly.

With the footage taken at the race track under their belts, additional connective and introductory material was shot and the whole assembled under Lehrman's guidance and titled *Love and Vengeance*. The completed two-reeler was screened for the press a week before its scheduled April 23rd release:

> When this picture was shown in the Universal projection-room for the press and National Board of Censorship, there was difficulty in getting into the room. Naturally the widespread publicity given the fact that Ford Sterling was with the Universal has caused a national interest in this his first production, "Love and Vengeance," in two reels. It is perfectly safe to predict that this film will have a larger circulation than almost anything the Universal has yet placed on the market, and that is a large statement. Mr. Sterling's undoubted popularity and H. Pathé

Lehrman's cleverness as a director make a combination which should be difficult to circumvent. The Universal's statement that these two men are in a class by themselves, that they fear no competition, seems very true.[38]

The completed film was slapstick of the roughest sort, and demonstrated that Keystone now had a very worthy competitor. The first reel has little to do with the race itself, set in a park and introducing Sterling as Snookee, who flirts with a heavyset woman played

Sterling latches onto Lehrman's nose in Love and Vengeance.

by actress Lucille Ward. When Ward's beau arrives, here played by Lehrman himself and dressed in garb vaguely reminiscent of Chaplin's outfit (though admittedly less shabby), the fun begins and the confrontation over Ward quickly escalates. Lehrman and Sterling go at it, employing shoes, bricks, and the inevitable bites to the nose and thigh, and two cops are soon brought into the melee. When the dust settles, Sterling returns to Ward, but soon drops her when the younger, more attractive Clifton flirts with him from afar. Sterling professes his undying love for her with the usual jumble of broad, sweeping gestures. She is amused, but her heart is with race car driver Goode, who arrives on the scene and spirits her away. Rebuffed by Ward, who is now fed up with his fickleness, Sterling feigns suicide with a single pistol shot to the ground. His subterfuge is revealed when Lehrman, suspecting such a trick, places the pistol to the "dead" Sterling's temple for a second shot. Sterling is out of there.

In reel two, Sterling accompanies Clifton to the Vanderbilt Cup race, but she soon abandons him to support her lover in auto number 2. As she cheers for Goode from the bleachers,[39] a frustrated Sterling decides to get even. Sneaking off, he heads for a bend in the track and proceeds to soak the corner with water from a neighbor's hose. This has little impact on the race, however, as one auto after another skids around the corner, most of them barely missing Sterling. Goode wins the race, and Clifton's heart.

Universal, with its typically shameless lack of subtlety, billed the film as "Two reels of laughing, screaming, side-splitting fun; two reels of real comedy — real action — real wit; two reels of the kind that will keep the crowds in your house roaring with laughter from the first picture to the last fade-away."[40] Frontier's output was reduced to open up a Thursday slot in the release schedule for the eagerly awaited Sterling comedies.

Sterling's fans were not at all disappointed with the results, which were full of his usual amusing throw-away bits: He hefts a rock and accidentally hits himself; he drops the rocks which accidentally land on his toes; he purchases a sandwich at the race and takes a huge bite before handing the mangled remains to Clifton; he sits on the bleachers only to land on the one spot with a huge, loose splinter, and beside the fellow with the crossed legs, whose shaking foot continuously makes contact with Sterling's thigh; and other bits of business too numerous to mention.

Lehrman's penchant for close-ups and rapid-fire cutting are on display as well. During the two antagonists' initial encounter, Sterling and Lehrman face off mad as hell, and stomp into the foreground where their two faces fill the screen in extreme close-up, culminating in an aggressive bite to Lehrman's snout. Lots of tight cross-cutting is employed during the fight that ensues, but really shifts into high gear once the auto race begins. The action is covered from an array of well-chosen angles, with in-the-action footage shot from one auto of the others fast approaching from behind, and some good close-ups of Goode and his mechanic maneuvering down the track.

The *New York Dramatic Mirror*'s reviewer was pleased with the results:

> [T]his two-reel comedy, of heterogeneous complexion, without any very noticeable plot, although there is a slight sign of one, manages to bring out more real laughter, more solid mirth to the foot, than anything we have seen in some time. No, it is not a gentle form of humor. You would hardly call it ladylike action when one man jumped upon another and bit him on the nose, and when that person retaliated in kind and bit a piece out of the leg of the other. This is the type of fun, rough, boisterous, slapstick comedy that, in spite of the educated predelictions [sic] of the spectator, gets beneath the veneer of his higher pretensions and brings him to the common ground of laughter. To tell why one laughs at Ford Sterling is to give an analysis of humor itself. Suffice it that he at all times — and he is on the screen for the major part of the play — brings laughter.[41]

Reviewer George Blaisdell of the *Moving Picture World* concurred:

> We are not going to attempt to outline the many good things in this unusual production. Suffice it to say, an exhibitor may go the limit on it, confident that from his grouchiest patron he will pull a laugh and also a real thrill. Furthermore, it is as clean as a whistle.[42]

And Great Britain's *Bioscope*, which would quickly become the new studio's cheerleader, was beside itself with glee:

> [A] screamingly funny farce. Mr. Sterling's particular form of humour is inimitable and undescribable. His tempestuous method is equally provocative of mirth, whether making love or besieging his enemies with brickbats, and his unflagging acrobatic efforts keep the fun going fast and furious from start to finish…a most ingenious comic film.[43]

Actress Emma Clifton, Sterling's co-star in this romp, had appeared in a number of films for Lubin in 1912-13, after which she moved over to Keystone for a short while before moving to Sterling to become this company's leading lady. Philadelphia born and the daughter of Selig screenwriter Wallace C. Clifton,[44] Emma made a few more films for that studio after the Sterling studios ceased operations, switching over to screenwriting for the remainder of her short career. Blaisdell singled her out for comment and her similarity in appearance to Mabel Normand:

> There will be many who see "Love and Vengeance" who will believe that the young woman playing opposite Mr. Sterling is none other than the one with whom he has appeared in so many pictures. There is a strong resemblance. Emma Clifton will make an effective foil for the comedian; it is quite safe to say we will hear much of her in time to come.[45]

Lucille Ward, the film's only other visible actress, had a long career on both the stage and in film, starting out in vaudeville and graduating to replacement for Marie Dressler in *Tillie's Nightmare*. She moved over to the film industry in 1913 where she made a handful of films primarily for Keystone before joining Sterling. She has been associated with at least four Sterling releases.

Sterling and Clifton portrayed a bride and groom whose wedding is interrupted by a gun-toting crook in the single reel *A Fatal Wedding*, the next of the series to be filmed. Scheduled for an April 30 release, that almost didn't happen when a temporary injunction was secured on April 24 restraining Universal from releasing the film. Theatrical producers Marcus Klaw and A.L. Erlanger, who had co-produced (with Biograph) *The Fatal Wedding* due for May release, claimed that the Sterling film "might cause considerable misunderstanding through the similarity of titles with [their] film version…."[46] It's doubtful that Sterling's raucous antics would ever be misconstrued for the hankie-wringing melodramatics of German playwright Theodore Kremer, but since the trade press kept misprinting the short comedy's title with *The* instead of *A*, confusion no doubt could have resulted. Universal and Sterling quickly regrouped and replaced the title with *His Wedding Day*, and the film was released to most theaters as such — most, but not all; reports emanated from Philadelphia's new Stanley Theater that "Ford Sterling scored a hit in 'The Fatal Wedding' and brought laughter from all sides."[47] Curiously, Universal came up with a lame excuse for the last-minute title change, jumping on the coattails of a suit brought by the Jesse L. Lasky Feature Play Company against the Eastman Kodak Company. Lasky had sued due to a batch of raw film stock whose perforations were inconsistently punched, requiring a number of scenes for their upcoming *The Squaw Man* to be refilmed, and at great cost. Universal claimed this as the reason for the retitling of the Sterling film![48]

Moving Picture World was slightly less enthusiastic about this second offering. While judging the film to be "rapid fire," its final assessment was that "the first part of this offering is very laughable, but toward the last the pie-throwing and other sloppy scenes interfere with the humor, as invariably happens when these things are overdone."[49] H(arry). B. Harris, Sterling's chief cinematographer, was commended for his work here.

LEFT: His Wedding Day *was the final release title of* A Fatal Wedding. *Left to right: Emma Clifton, Ford Sterling, and Harold "Josh" Binney.*

The third film to be released finally put Paul Jacobs to work, and in a lead (of sorts) role. Sterling is police *Sergeant Hofmeyer*, hoping to acquire a coaster for his young son. Spotting an abandoned coaster, Hofmeyer appropriates it and takes it home. Little Billy (Jacobs), who is also coaster-less, follows Hofmeyer and takes the coaster for his own. When Hofmeyer finds the coaster missing and tracks it down to Little Billy, he hauls Billy off to the station and reports the kid for stealing "his" coaster. Unfortunately for Hofmeyer, the coaster's true owner is the police captain's son, and the captain pegs Hofmeyer for the liar and thief that he is. All hell breaks loose in the station with a flurry of fists and swinging billy clubs, rendering all participants unconscious. Outside, Billy roars with laughter.

Sterling's anticipated over-the-top performance doesn't disappoint here, with alternating displays of bravura and cowardice. He is delightfully antisocial in this one, his actions ranging from benign (bumming a smoke from a hobo), to corrupt (lying to his superior on multiple occasions), to outrageously nasty (bullying and threatening little kids with his billy club and, in the film's coup de grâce, wrestling with one of them and blackening his eye!). As usual, Sterling gets his comeuppance, and in an apocalyptic fashion during the station free-for-all that leaves seven cops battered and unconscious. The final battle is an amusing melee, Hofmeyer's last stand a visual treat as he wobbles, spins in place, and finally crashes to a bench unconscious.

The culminating police station sequence is typical Lehrman overkill, and his black sense of humor permeates the film. Lehrman uses his close-ups to good effect with lots

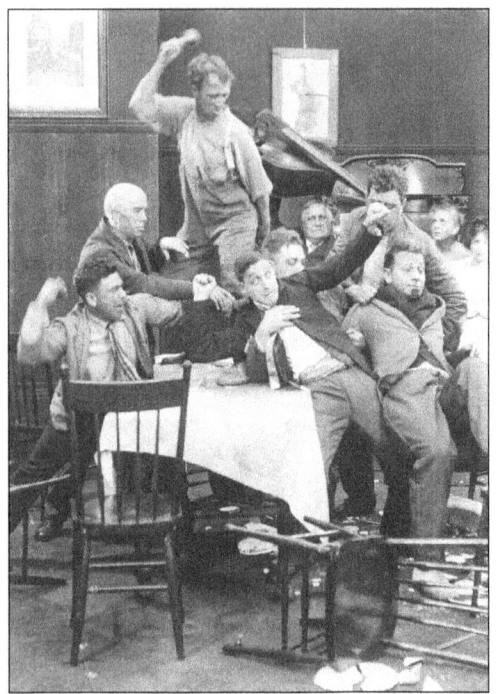 

LEFT: *Other studios were seemingly less concerned about the reuse of titles. Essanay's* In and Out *(08/03/1914; pictured here) starred Wallace Beery (with the tiny goatee, dazed look, and leaning back on table) and was released a mere seven weeks before the Sterling Comedy of the same title,* In and Out *(09/21/1914), starring Max Asher, William Franey, and Bobby Dunn.* COURTESY OF MUSEUM OF MODERN ART/FILM STILLS ARCHIVE. RIGHT: *Paul Jacobs sticks his tongue out as Sterling tells him to beat it, from* Sergeant Hofmeyer. COURTESY OF SAM GILL.

of cute ones of Jacobs, mugging shamelessly for the camera. While not much of an actor at this moment in his youthful career, he gets a pass for enthusiasm and likability. The final extreme close-up is the film's highlight, with Jacobs' mirth-filled face filling the screen, and for an extended shot without cuts. Lehrman's friendship with the young boy and working knowledge of his weaknesses went a long way in eliciting Jacobs' winning performance. "Lehrman even used to stand on his head to get a desired laugh out of the sober little man," revealed *Moving Picture World* in a piece on the pint-sized thespian. "Faces and funny gestures fell shy with Billy's laugh nerves, but when Pathe stood on his head Billy laughed — but Pathe laughed last — in the projection room where he would chuckle at the kid's little screen smile."[50]

Lehrman's method of producing these one- and two-reel comedies was analyzed in a piece in the *Universal Weekly*, purportedly based on a lengthy interview with the director:

> Funny situations are never a matter of chance in the production of film comedies. They are a matter of deep thought and constructive thinking. H. Pathé Lehrman knows just exactly why he places every piece of business in Sterling comedies. First, he chooses a situation and he works with this situation exactly in the same manner that a composer of music works with a given theme or melody. He develops to the principal situation and away from it. In his mind the story is in small pieces, card-catalogued and arranged systematically. He wishes to get over a certain idea, and if it takes twenty scenes he "gets over" the idea so that there will never be any question in anybody's mind as to the significance of what is taking place. He has a rare faculty for comprehending the value of anticipation. The "punches" in his comedies are never lost to the audience. He allows the audience to suspect what might happen. He never startles them with something they cannot immediately grasp. He understands these things should be accomplished and Ford Sterling understands how to accomplish them.... When a person talks about picture with Mr. Lehrman he does most of the talking — not because he likes to talk, because he is a very good listener, but because the person soon realizes that he understands the business from its depths. He has penetrated into the soul of it.[51]

The article's author goes on to describe Lehrman's dependence — or lack thereof — on a script, and his work in the cutting room:

> Mr. Lehrman works without a script; that is, a scenario is never written for the comedies which he produces. He has the scenario in his mind. At first he has only the principal idea, but he never transfers any of his ideas to paper. When the comedy of two or three hundred scenes is completed, he places the scene together from memory. He has a remarkable memory. He never places the scene in its wrong place in relation to the continuity of the story. He is interested in his work and never forgets any point in connection with his story.[52]

Production was halted, if only momentarily, on April 1, and the studio's personnel assembled on the stage. Announcing that it was Lehrman's birthday — it wasn't; they were two days late — Sterling and Balshofer presented Lehrman with a gold watch.[53] Then they sent everyone back to work; there was, after all, only so much time for frivolity.

Papa's Boy was the next Sterling and Jacobs co-starrer, initially scheduled for release before *Sergeant Hofmeyer*, but bumped to the following week when it wasn't completed in time for public consumption. The story is a trifle: Sterling and wife Emma Clifton deal with all sorts of kitchen-based mishaps while attempting to prepare dinner, so Little Billy makes off with a jar of blackberry jam. Billy uses the jam to woo the little girl next door, but when a rival shows up the two boys struggle, unaware when the little girl takes off with the jam to share with yet another boy. Billy and the rival, now both in the same boat having been dumped by the fickle little girl, settle their differences.

Released on May 14, a *Motion Picture News* reviewer had mixed feelings about the results, sniping that there was "not enough Sterling in the comedy. It will appeal to children, for the little ones play the prominent parts."[54] Children, evidently, but perhaps not adults. *Motion Picture Magazine*'s reviewer was far more charitable, focusing primarily on Jacobs and his pint-sized compatriots:

> He is one of the most wonderful child actors, and from the moment he flings his irresistible smile across the screen until he winks his left eye in mimic imitation of his father, Ford Sterling, he is just the best little scream ever. Ford Sterling is as funny as a Sunday supplement, but this little youngster that takes the part of papa's boy is as funny as a child of four in mischief every minute can be.[55]

Jacobs' initial roles for the studio paired him with Sterling under Lehrman's guidance, while they waited for Thornby's arrival. The twenty-four year old filmmaker was currently at work elsewhere at Universal writing and directing the two-reel Edwin August drama *Old California* (April 25, 1914) for 101 Bison, after which he would devote his full energies to the Sterling Kid Comedies[56] building a similar stockpile of one-reelers for later release. Born in New York City in 1889, Thornby had previous experience in stock with the Keith and Proctor circuits before moving to Vitagraph where he played heavies in their Western dramas. He made the switch to comedy, appearing in a series of tramp comedies that he directed as well as starred in. Thornby was hired by Sennett in later 1913 along with Rube Miller and Charles Avery, upping Keystone's production to seven active units. There he was assigned by Lehrman to helm the initial Little Billy single reel, and his facility for (or tolerance of?) directing young children soon became apparent. Paul and Thornby worked well together, and the public's acceptance of their efforts was proven, so it made sound business sense to bring them over as a team of sorts, ending Thornby's brief several month stint at Keystone. Thornby's kid comedies would eventually alternate on the release schedule with the Ford Sterling vehicles. While Jacobs was repeatedly referred to as Little Billy in the press (and never by the name Paul), none of the eventual Sterling releases bore any more than the shortened name "Billy."

Neighbors followed on the release schedule, this one with Sterling starring as Schlitz. Schlitz and Mulligan (comedian Max Asher) are deep into a card game in Schlitz's home, while their wives hang out at Mulligan's home and gossip. Schlitz's blatant cheating finally causes Mulligan to snap, and the two card players go at it, mano a mano. The wives return and join in the free-for-all, which leads to a wild chase through hotels and alleyways. The police arrive and Schlitz receives his comeuppance as the target of a skillfully aimed fire hose.

Reviews were few for this release, with the *Motion Picture News* briefly commenting on the results in a less than satisfactory fashion: "Neighbors will quarrel, and this comedy proves it. Pie, brick-throwing and shooting cause many laughs, and the picture ends with a hose-fight."[57]

Lehrman's name was never tied to this film in the trades, or at least not that I've been able to track down. The concluding scene's use of a fire hose, however, would suggest that Lehrman was indeed the director, as he would revisit that comic device in several films yet to come at L-Ko such as *Silk Hose and High Pressure* (1915) and *Cold Hearts and Hot Flames* (1916). Revisit, and expand exponentially!

While maintaining a hectic pace to build up a backlog of films for release, Sterling made it a point to take time off for some relaxation and to indulge his love of baseball. A Pacific Coast movie league was formed — the Photo-Players League — with competing teams from the Universal, Vitagraph, American, Broncho, Biograph, Reliance, and the Universal Ranch. Sterling and Robert Leonard of Rex, both having played ball prior to their becoming a part of the film industry, headed up the Universal team. Lee Moran, Eddie Lyons, and Herbert Rawlinson were on board as well, with a pre-season dance given to raise funds

LEFT: *Sterling has his hands full in this ad for* Papa's Boy. COURTESY OF JIM KERKHOFF.
RIGHT: *Paul Jacobs is up to his usual mischief in this still from* Papa's Boy. COURTESY OF SAM GILL.

to fit up the team. Sterling assumed the role of short stop, and within the first month of play the two Universal teams were tied for first place.[58] The B.H. Dyas Sporting Goods Company contributed a silver loving cup to be awarded the eventual winners.

Lehrman took some time out as well to become a member of the Photoplay Authors' League, newly formed in Los Angeles in March 1914. The league's stated purpose was "to do for photoplaywrights what the Authors' League of America is doing for other branches of the literary profession. Only photoplaywrights having ten or more produced scripts to their credit are eligible." Lehrman was among the thirty-six founding members.[59]

Lehrman saved up his energy for the company's second two-reeler (and what would prove to be his last for the studio), the action-packed *Hearts and Swords*. Co-starring Emma Clifton and recent arrival Peggy Pearce, it was lensed by former Keystone cameraman Frank D. Williams,[60] the plot such as there is involves rivals fighting over not one, but two young ladies. Sterling bests his opponent in love for the hand of a woman they both encounter in a park, and takes her to an outdoor dance. The rival, meanwhile, makes the acquaintance of a "Salome dancer," and brings her to the dance as well. True to form, Sterling dumps the first young lady and throws himself upon the rival's girl, which leads to the usual confrontation. I'll let the *Universal Weekly* describe this culminating event:

> The rivals turn out to do battle, neither of them having a taste for such an affair. They prove to be terrible cowards, and the fight results in a fiasco. In the mix-up that follows the Salome dancer escapes into a public park with the Park police

LEFT: *Lovely Peggy Pearce, in a promotional portrait from her days with Keystone.* RIGHT: *Sterling glowers as Peggy Pearce flirts with an unidentified actor in* Hearts and Swords.

> in hot pursuit trying to cover her up. They chase her to a bridge where the rivals, in mortal combat, pitch head-long into the water, sixty feet below. The efforts to save the rascals from drowning results in the most comical incidents imaginable.[61]

It isn't clear from contemporary writings as to which of the two female roles was played by Clifton and Pearce, but given various descriptions of the "Salome dancer" as "a scantily clad maiden" having a "shapely form and grace," my money would be on Pearce as the dancer. Sterling's rival in love remains unidentified. Pearce, who had her start at Biograph in 1913 before moving over to Keystone that same year, had the dubious distinction of being Chaplin's first love back during his early days at Keystone.

The film's May 28 release was greeted with enthusiastic reviews rivaling those for *Love and Vengeance*. The *New York Dramatic Mirror*'s reviewer was particularly enthused by this one, but seemed to have some difficulty explaining *why* he liked it so much. His words, however, bear testimony to the audience acceptance and embracing of Lehrman's anarchic style, combined with the outrageous antics of Sterling's lovable rogue:

Ford Sterling assumes the lead under the direction of Henry Lehrman in this two-reel rollicking revel of joy. We laughed for thirty minutes, and positively cannot say what we laughed about. To those who have seen these pictures this statement will be understandable. To others let us say that the film consists of a series of make-ups, grimaces, and expedients all centered about nothing in particular, but funny every foot of it. It is the height of the ridiculous and the burlesque on whatever action happens. A chase, sword play, diving off a high bridge, and comic slaughter in the water, and a lot of other diversions, including the Divorce Dance, are what enable the cast to keep the humor alive.[62]

Bioscope's reviewer verged on ecstasy, praising both Sterling and the release for possessing "in liberal measure all the qualities which have rendered these films so widely popular, [with Sterling showing] no trace of falling off in his own peculiar humour. In fact, it will probably be thought by many that this film…is one of the best samples of the brand. It is as impossible to describe a Sterling comedy as it is to resist its humour."[63] *Moving Picture World* concurred, calling it a "two-part rip-roaring comedy that gains hearty and continuous laughter…. Ford Sterling at his best. This strenuous comedy will make any audience laugh like the dickens." The reviewer had one minor criticism of the film, however, stating that the "photography is not of the best in some places."[64]

It is clear that the Sterling-Lehrman teaming was living up to audience and exhibitor expectations. The two-reelers were rapturously received, and the interim single-reelers deemed acceptable and better than the norm; ongoing success seemed assured. But it was not to be: Less than three months after the formation of the Sterling studio and the release of Lehrman's first four comedies, came the stunning mid-May announcement: Henry Lehrman had sold his interests in the company to Balshofer and Sterling![65]

The reasons for Lehrman's abrupt departure remain unclear, and Balshofer's autobiography does little to clarify matters given that there are so many obvious inconsistencies cited. The distribution of shares among the founders is unknown, so Balshofer may or may not have had a controlling interest. Regardless, Balshofer leads the reader to believe that he was the sole owner with comments such as "In February, 1914, I incorporated the Sterling Film Company," and that the others were all employees when he says "No one, however, had any idea that I was also after Ford Sterling, and before anyone found out, I had him signed to a contract," and "I signed 'Pathé' Lehrman as my director." And his comment that "I declared a dividend at the end of four months from the day we started shooting pictures" is just dead wrong since Lehrman didn't even make it to the three month point. The tricks of memory? Perhaps, but Balshofer is so specific as to the date that it hints of pure fabrication.

Are we to believe any of the reasons he laid out for Lehrman's departure? In Balshofer's words:

> Production of Sterling comedies continued to be a big success for a while, making it appear that my troubles were over, but toward the end of the year, the continued success had so affected both Sterling and Lehrman that it became impossible to get a day's work out of either. They would argue for hours at a time over how to play a scene as the crew stood around and waited. They came to

hate each other so much that when Lehrman ordered Sterling to be on the set at nine in the morning ready to work, Sterling, who resented Lehrman's ordering him around, would show up at noon. Lehrman, to show his importance, would be gone when Sterling arrived. The following morning Sterling would be ready to go to work at nine but Lehrman wouldn't show up until noon. This nonsense went on until it got so that it took two weeks to make a five hundred-foot film, whereas Bob Thornby was knocking out one of our child comedies every week. The feud between Sterling and Lehrman reached a point where I just had to fire Lehrman rather than Sterling since Sterling was the basis of my contract with the Universal company.[66]

Toward the end of the year? Curious, since Lehrman was out of there by mid-May and hard at work with his own studio by year's end. And he and Sterling did manage to turn out eight reels of comedy in no more than twelve weeks — not speedy, but not too shabby either. Fowler is more specific to the moment when things fell apart at the studio:

Lehrman was making a picture called *Hearts and Swords*. He was faced by financial hazards. If the picture required an extra day in the shooting, the profit would be jeopardized. Lehrman decided to make a seven o'clock call, so that a good start could be made. Sterling didn't show up until after noon, and he seemed exhausted. Lehrman was furious. "If I'm able to get up at seven, so are you. I'm quitting."[67]

Given that this was indeed Lehrman's last film for the studio, Fowler's anecdote rings true. Unfortunately, aside from his earlier comments regarding the disagreement over the studio name and Sterling's Dutch character, Fowler doesn't mention any other incidents that would reflect on the rift growing between director and star. That said, there most likely is some truth to Balshofer's itemization of the infighting between the two, in spirit if not in fact, but we will never know for sure.

A possible explanation for Sterling's evident distraction from the all-consuming filming schedule could be of a romantic nature. A brief mention in the May 23 issue of *Moving Picture World* touches on his growing relationship with pretty young actress Teddy Sampson:

It was rumored, only rumored, that Ford Sterling, who has taken pretty Miss Teddy Sampson away from the Mutual, and made her his leading lady, had married her early in the week. When seen personally, the funny man only smiled and said n – o. But there was a queer hesitation in his voice. It would seem rather funny at that. He has dodged the belles of Pasadena society for some time — to become the hubby of a leading lady.[68]

While Sampson was never Sterling's leading lady in film, the two did end up marrying, although the exact date is unclear.

A not unlikely alternative to the various reasons given for Lehrman's departure could be that Laemmle, observing Lehrman's potential based on his initial filmic efforts, may have approached the creative young man with an offer to back yet another studio with Lehrman at the helm, figuring that Sterling and Balshofer would have sustained success due to the comedian's popularity. Or perhaps the other way around, with the ambitious Lehrman approaching Laemmle with the concept of a new studio. Again, we probably will never know for certain, but the bottom line was that Lehrman was gone, leaving Balshofer and Sterling to their own devices. (The rest of the Sterling Comedies story can be found in Appendix A.)

The Universal baseball team. Left to right: unknown kid, Eddie Lyons, Lee Moran, George Marshall, unknown, Ford Sterling, Harry Tenbrook, unknown, unknown, Herbert Rawlinson, unknown, Victoria Forde. COURTESY OF ROBERT S. BIRCHARD.

With its incorporation, Lehrman now needed a cast and cr[...]
Lehrman attempted to lure Mabel Normand away from Keysto[...]
per week to star in his new company, a hefty increase over the $1[...]
was currently paying her. Sennett matched Lehrman's offer, so Le[...]
$400, which Sennett again matched, and Normand stayed put.[13]
and fellow actress Beatrice Van remembered it in a more simpl[...]
somewhat from Fowler's account, but warrants repeating here:

> Mack Sennett was terribly stingy when it came to salaries [...]
> anywhere near what they were worth. However, on that iss[...]
> revenge in an unexpected way. When "Pathé" Lehrman left [...]
> own pictures for Universal, he offered Mabel $400 a week to [...]
> Keystone, it was some time before Sennett paid Mabel mo[...]
> dollars a week, and only then in order to keep Mabel from lea[...]
> Lehrman offered Mabel the $400 a week, and Sennett was [...]
> was seriously considering it. Sennett then had no choice but [...]
> offer so that Mabel would stay, and so that's how Mabel got [...]
> in salary.[14]

The details aside, Normand was out of the running. Lehrma[...]
York to acquire some fresh talent as leads. By the end of August [...]
heading back to Los Angeles with three performers in tow. Engl[...]
Ritchie would be the L-Ko's lead comedian, supported by vaudev[...]
Selby and 300 pound heavyweight Henry Bergman to serve as R[...]

Eighteen year old Selby was the eldest of three children born [...]
William and Olga Selby.[16] Born and raised in Philadelphia, the [...]
Bronx in 1910 when the cute young brown-haired, black-eyed fif[...]
on a three-year career on the stage. This included two season[...]
opportunity to dance with Gertrude Hoffman, a stint with G[...]
company, as well as her own singles act.[17] Lehrman's arrival in [...]
of female lead in the new company brought Selby's career on [...]
Upon her arrival in Los Angeles it was noted that "Miss Selby i[...]
soon to be Mrs. Lehrman," and that she and Lehrman would be [...]
while honeymooning" in the studio owner's new Fiat,[18] which w[...]
a then-considerable $7,000.[19] Where this supposed rumor origi[...]
but apparently there was nothing to it.

According to a 1931 interview cited in David Robinson's C[...]
Bergman said he received his "histrionic" training in Wagnerian r[...]
Augustin Daly's theatrical company in New York for nine years. Th[...]
after several weeks' rehearsal and only a few performances left the [...]
Fortuitously, a friend put him on to the opportunities the film indu[...]
led Bergman to Pathé and a job in Pearl White's *The Perils of Pau*[...]
followed — at least one of them for Universal's Crystal — before f[...]
introduced him to Lehrman, who offered the imposing forty-six [...]
with L-Ko.[20]

CHAPTER 5

The L-Ko Komedy Kompany: Lehrman's Baby

Lehrman's departure from Sterling in May 2014 was accompanied by the announcement that he planned a return trip to "his native land," Austria, of several weeks duration.[1] His availability was quickly noted, however, and offers from five other film manufacturers followed. The offer from Carl Laemmle and the Universal won out,[2] and may already have been agreed upon before the competing offers were made. The June 27 issue of *Universal Weekly* heralded the agreement, announcing that Lehrman, "the king of comedy directors," would "soon begin the production of his own comedies on the Universal program."[3] Lehrman's new production company, unnamed in the Universal piece, had an official name by the time the news hit the streets: the L-Ko Motion Picture Company. Lehrman's European trip never came to be, nor would he ever again return to the land of his birth.

The L-Ko — which stood for "Lehrman Knock-Out" — was incorporated in Los Angeles, California, on July 22, 1914 by Lehrman, along with Isadore Bernstein, Abe Stern, Sam Behrendt, and Alfred P. Hamberg. The new company's capital stock was $10,000, divided into one hundred shares with a par value of $100 per. The five subscribers each shelled out a modest $100 for an equal number of shares — one — to start out with. The agreement was notarized by Helen Morrison, who would soon become Lehrman's personal secretary and remain as such for the rest of her life.

Lehrman's associates in the new company came from a variety of backgrounds, both within and outside the industry. Philadelphia-born Alfred P. Hamberg had been employed in the advertising departments of several of that city's newspapers back at the turn of the century before relocating in 1902 to New York for a similar position with the *American and Journal*.[4] By 1912 Hamberg had made a career switch to management of theatrical productions, Broadway's Globe Theatre presentation of *The Rose Maid* among them. By 1913 he was managing one of the city's new film venues, the Park Theatre, acquiring some small level of notoriety when he was served a summons for the public display of the then-sensational *The Inside of the White Slave Traffic*, on the grounds that the film "was likely to impair the morals of young girls."[5] A year later Hamberg was slated to join Dallas, Texas' Southern Feature Film Association as a director, but ended up with Lehrman's group and L-Ko instead. Hamberg's role with the new company was according to at least one source, assistant director.⁷

Twenty-three year old Abe Stern was a former manager Illinois Exhibiting Companies.⁸ Stern, with "considerable expe of the motion picture business," was to serve as the company likely that Lehrman had to make some concessions in his agree it would appear that Stern was one of them; Stern was Unive

LEFT: *Abe Stern.* RIGHT: *Isadore Bernstein.*

brother-in-law as a result of Laemmle's 1898 marriage to Rec

Thirty-seven year old, New York-born Isadore Bernstein ha position with the Monopole Film Company to become gener Pacific Coast studios on June 28, 1913. Prior to that he had been *Christian Herald* for fourteen years as a reporter, and was superinten at the Five Points Mission.¹⁰ Bernstein too was credited as the c

Sam Behrendt had only indirect ties to the industry. A well- with deep pockets, Behrendt had a piece of a number of Los A These included the theatrical publicity firm Angelus Publicity Building Company — Lung Yep having a momentary claim to f Chinese police officer — and the Behrendt-Levy Company. It wa founded in 1900, that he made a fortune by taking a gamble wit While other local financiers were reluctant to invest in the new the first studio insurance policies for William Selig and William F the policies for many other filmmaking concerns.¹² What Behre was, if nothing else, a willingness to invest in the startup.

The hiring of Billie Ritchie, of course, was Lehrman's coup, providing him with a veteran performer with decades of experience and time-tested routines under his belt. Born on September 5, 1874 in Glasgow, Scotland, Billie's father Thomas Hill was a merchant seaman who may never have met his newborn son. Billie's mother Mary, a dressmaker and sometime entertainer known as the Scottish Soprano, remarried a fellow named Munro a year later. Munro would father the rest of Billie's seven siblings over the following years and give Billie his surname. Entertainment seems to have been in the family's blood, and

LEFT: *Gertrude Selby.* RIGHT: *Henry Bergman.*

Billie joined his mother's company in 1888, then known as Mary Hill's Concert Company, wherein he took small parts.²¹ By 1891 he was performing a singing and acrobatic dancing act as Willie Munro, followed by several years' dramatic work with the Gower family company, in repertoire under Rollo Balmain's management, and with various Christmas Pantomime companies. Ritchie's career as a comedian was set in motion when he joined Fred Karno's company in 1898, touring all of the big England theatrical circuits over the next seven years performing in sketches such as *Love in a Tub, Hilarity, Early Birds, The New Woman's Club, Her Majesty's Guests*, and *Jail Birds*.²²

According to biographer J.P. Gallagher, Karno was a penny-pinching, sadistic, and sexually perverse autocrat, but when it came to entertainment a creative genius both in storytelling and in set design and construction. Born Frederick John Westcott in 1866, Karno ran away from home while a teen and took on a succession of jobs for survival. These included tours with circuses as a budding gymnast, and a stint with Harry Manley's Circus in Burton-On-Trent where he learned pantomime. Karno hooked up with two other gymnasts to create an act, the group assuming the name The Three Karnos when they were pressing into service to replace another act that failed to show, The Three

Carnoes. Karno later acquired an Edison phonograph and introduced it into the act as the "Karnophone," and was soon working without his two former partners. Karno's initial slapstick mime acts were *Love in a Tub* and *Hilarity*, both introduced in 1895. From there on Karno's fame grew to international proportions as the genius behind "The House That Karno Built," the training ground for a number of comedians who would find even greater fortune in the years to come in the nascent film industry.[23] Ritchie was one of those who benefitted from the experience.

LEFT: *Billie Ritchie*. RIGHT: *Young Billie Ritchie*. COURTESY OF LISA ROBINS.

Ritchie assumed the lead of the drunk in Karno's *A Night in an English Music Hall* in 1903, and it was this show and role that brought him to the United States. Ritchie, his wife Winifred whom he had married in 1901,[24] and eight other members of Karno's music hall troupe, came over on the S.S. *Philadelphia*, arriving in New York City on October 14, 1905. Impresario Oscar Hammerstein had closed a deal for the troupe — billed as the London Comedy Company — to appear in *A Night in a Music Hall* starting on October 16 at the city's Victoria Theater. By November the troupe had moved on to the Orpheum Theater, and a reviewer for the *Brooklyn Daily Eagle* commented on an unnamed performer who no doubt was Ritchie: "There is an intoxicated youth in the lower right hand box whose continual interference with the performance is one of the most amusing things seen at the Orpheum in a long while. The man who plays the part ought to have his name on the programme. As a rough and tumble comedian he is a star and he has a gift of facial expression that might be copied by many a better actor."[25]

Within a year Ritchie had broken off from Karno and set up his own troupe, Ritchie's London Pantomime Company, under vaudeville entrepreneur Gus Hill's management.[26] Accompanied by a fellow Karno comedian named Rich McAllister, the two headlined a new musical comedy titled *Around the Clock*. Ritchie had the lead of "Bill Smith, the drunk, the man from nowhere," while McAllister assumed the role of "Johnny Mack, the bell boy, full of mischief."[27] Reviewers in Syracuse took note: "For those whose eyes are quicker than their ears it is a howling success. Billy [sic] Ritchie has a skate when the curtain rose up and also when it comes down and he skates continually. Back of him is the athletic Rich McAllister...." (*Syracuse Journal*, October 16, 1906). "Mr. Ritchie is always funny and his pantomimes and unique antics caused much laughter." (*Post-Standard*, Syracuse, October 16, 1906). Ritchie's wife was an ongoing part of the cast as

LEFT: *An early photo of Billie Ritchie taken in Belfast, Northern Ireland.* RIGHT: *Billie Ritchie in costume for an early, unidentified production.* PHOTOGRAPHS COURTESY OF LISA ROBINS.

well, billed as Winifred Frances ("Francis" in numerous sources) and acknowledged to have a pleasing singing voice.[28]

A year later *Around the Clock* was back in New York, the troupe now billed in ads as "Billie Ritchie's London Comedy Company." The show continued touring through 1908. "Ritchie cannot be imitated in this role, and he scored a complete success last evening. In parts of his work he doubled with Rich McAllister, a diminutive specimen of humanity, who made good with the audience from the start.... Especially funny was the wrestling bout. The house roared with laughter when Billie Ritchie took the terrible Turk on and put his shoulders to the mat." (*Trenton Evening Times*, August 28, 1908). *The London Fire Brigade* was another show that debuted during this time, a "pantomimical satire" co-written and co-starring Ritchie and Tom Hearn (a British vaudevillian billed as "The Laziest Juggler in the World") and copyrighted in August of that year; the Ritchie-Hearn London Pantomime Company production premiered at Proctor's in Newark the last week of July.

By 1909 Ritchie and McAllister were headlining the musical satire on nightlife in New York, *Vanity Fair*, now billed as the Ritchie Comedy Company. Both *Around the Clock* and *Vanity Fair* incorporated *A Night in a Music Hall* as part of the show, bolstered by other acts and routines. *Vanity Fair* toured well into 1911. *Around the Clock* resurfaced in late 1911 and continued into 1913, followed once again by *Vanity Fair* in late 1913. *Vanity Fair* continued touring through the end of May 1914, wife Winifred by his side on stage through the very last performance. With Ritchie's departure for Hollywood, Winifred remained behind to appear in at least one more show, the Drury Lane Company's *Hop O' My Thumb* in November 1914.

Billie Ritchie in costume for another early, unidentified production. COURTESY OF LISA ROBINS.

Once Lehrman had his core stock company assembled there were two items requiring immediate concern: the acquisition of a studio, and the generation of a backlog of product to be readied for the eventual, unrelenting release schedule. Back in October 1911, Universal had taken over David Horsley's first Nestor studio through a merger, which it sold to Balshofer at the beginning of 1914 for his Sterling Comedies. Universal had acquired the plot of land across the street soon after that initial purchase, and built some additional, modest studio facilities. The facilities, then in the process of being vacated as part of Laemmle's consolidation of operations in the newly-built Universal City scheduled for completion in early 1915, became the new home of the L-Ko company. In the meantime, temporary facilities were arranged and utilized, and Bernstein had a stage "100 feet square" erected so that the new company could go to work within days of their arrival in Los Angeles and hours of the stage's completion.[29]

As with Sterling, Lehrman went to work directing his new stock company with the goal of completing several comedies while finding some other comedy directors to hire to share the burden. His first film needed to establish the brand in the minds of audiences, and to that end it would be a no-holds-barred two-reel special loaded with gags and violent action. The result was *Love and Surgery*, one of a handful of L-Ko's known to have survived. Much of the film was shot at exterior locations, with only a couple of interiors required for scenes set in a police station and another set in a hospital operating room. Lehrman co-stars, with new hire Eva Nelson backing up Ritchie, Selby, and Bergman.

The story, such as it is, opens in a park. Lehrman has callously shunned his girl Nelson, but returns in a fit of jealousy when he sees Ritchie flirting with her. The inevitable battle between the two ensues, Lehrman first delivering multiple brick blows to Ritchie's head, only to be driven off in a hail of gunfire directed at his posterior. Ritchie then moves on to another young lady, this time Selby, whom he first entices with a milk shake. He is soon driven off due to his boorish behavior. She scurries off and informs her fiancé Ignatz (Bergman) of Ritchie's uninvited advances. Confrontation number two is set in motion,

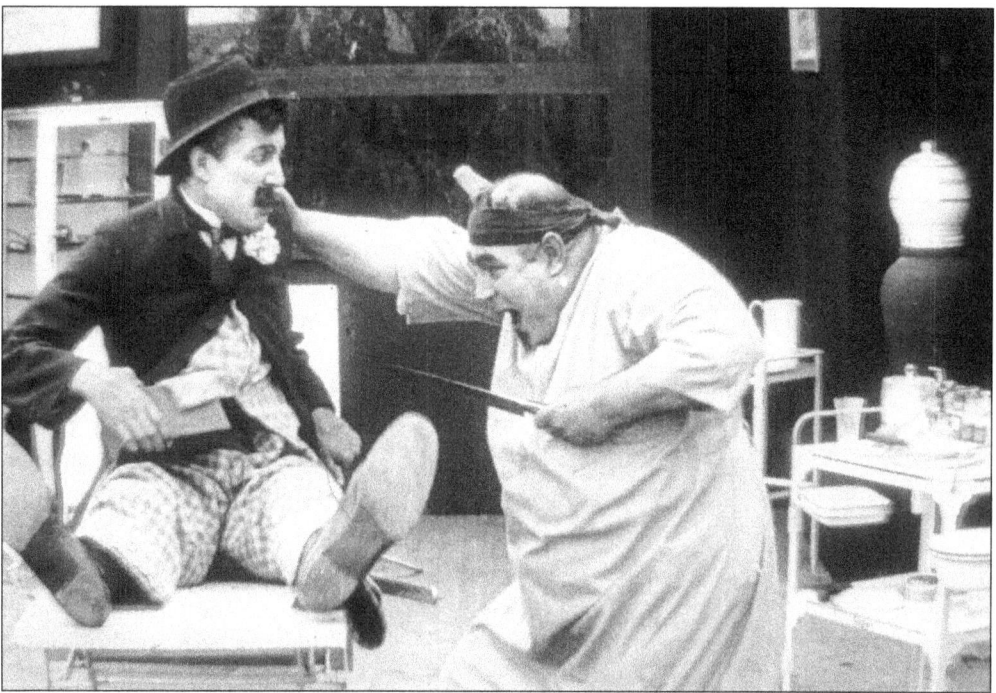

Surgeon Ignatz (Henry Bergman) has his nemesis, Billie Ritchie, at his mercy, in Love and Surgery. COURTESY OF LIBRARY OF CONGRESS.

Ritchie initially getting the worst of it until he manages to clobber Bergman twice with a huge mallet — modest-sized mallets will never do in the L-Kos when huge ones are available — resulting in two large, horn-like protuberances atop the dazed fellow's head. The fight continues, with Ritchie eventually propelled through the brick wall of the police station. Inside, he is set upon by a bevy of cops who proceed to pummel him into a helpless heap. He is carted off to the hospital, only to find that the surgeon about to operate on him is none other than Ignatz, who takes his time selecting the sharpest, most painful looking instrument to inflict upon his captive. Seeing this, Ritchie flees, racing across rooftops one step ahead of his pursuer, only to crash through a roof and through several floors below, landing back in the police station. The cops once again descend upon him, and beat him senseless for a second time.

With *Love and Surgery*, Lehrman delivered the goods. Subtle it was not, rather a fast-paced, action- and gag-filled romp that rivaled the best of what Keystone had to offer. Was it an out-and-out imitation of Keystone's product as some claimed at the time? That's arguable, since Lehrman was one of the two architects of the so-called Keystone style, and it was only natural that he would continue with a style that he felt was in no small part his own. And there was no doubt that this was a Lehrman film: Once it gets moving, the film unspools at a breakneck speed, with Lehrman's blink-and-you-miss-it, rapid-fire cutting propelling it forward inexorably to its apocalyptic conclusion, an orgy of visual mayhem as Ritchie receives his comeuppance at the hands of a phalanx of brick-wielding cops. Lehrman introduces one delightfully extended close-up as well: Lehrman, while doing battle with Ritchie, comes upon a stray brick. He picks it up, looks at it, then over at Ritchie, and back and forth several times more as it slowly dawns on him that this could be a very effective weapon, whereupon he launches into his attack wielding his new find. Lehrman's acting here, I might add, is spot-on.

With his decades of experience on the music hall and vaudeville stages, Ritchie's on-screen persona arrived nearly fully-formed. His character was a 140 pound, five foot seven-and-a-half inch tightly-wound package of compressed energy that would soon evolve into a liquor-loving, playfully lecherous dynamo with a perpetually sour expression evinced by a downturned mouth. Cockily belligerent, he was a dirty, unfair fighter, with moments of cowardice when it best suited his interests. Oversized mallets seemed to be a preferred weapon during these encounters, but swords, pistols, shotguns, and dynamite would always do in a pinch. Ritchie's character would waddle about on his heels, feet splayed, acquiring a hopping gallop whenever the pace needed to be picked up, chest puffed out and straining his waistcoat, his prodigious protruding posterior reminiscent of Syd Chaplin's.[30] The one accommodation that Ritchie would need to make in his transition from stage to screen would be for Lehrman's judicious use of close-ups. Since Ritchie's facial gyrations were already fully-formed, this only required an acknowledgement of, and slight adjustment for, the camera that was only a few feet from his face rather than a spectator far away in his seat. The other change that would soon take place and obvious from a viewing of Ritchie's first and second starring film was with his mustache. In *Love and Surgery* it is a long, scraggly affair that covers his mouth, rather than the neatly-trimmed brush that resides upon his upper lip in his follow-up film *Partners in Crime*.

As for the slapstick itself, there are a number of alternately absurd and charming little bits courtesy of the star and his director. One cute bit has flirtatious Nelson hiding behind a very tiny tree, more a five-foot stick with a few paltry leaves at its top. Ritchie appears and does not at first spot her in this "hiding" place, an obvious impossibility. Later, when Selby storms off in disgust over Ritchie's clumsy advances, he pursues her, the two milkshake straws protruding from his mouth like a walrus' tusks, dripping milkshake as he follows.

One should mention Lehrman's acting in this and previous and subsequent films. His performances could be effective when he played it straight, as in the earlier Biograph dramas and in the comedy *Comrades* as a butler, as well as in his Keystone *Making a Living* where he was the jealous reporter. But when he went for broad comedy such as in the Sterling *Sergeant Hofmeyer*, however, it was more of a hit-or-miss affair. He tried too hard and overacted as a result, with an accentuation of gestures and moves that appear forced rather than smooth. In *Love and Surgery*, this accentuation occurs when Ritchie has him by the seat of the pants and collar and marches him to the lake, Lehrman's high-step more clumsy-looking than humorous. And while physically in great shape, Lehrman was no acrobat, and attempts at tumbles and rolls lacked the "grace" of so many

ABOVE: *Billie Ritchie's scraggly mustache, from* Love and Surgery. BELOW: *Henry Lehrman considers the possibility of using a brick as a weapon, in* Love and Surgery. PHOTOGRAPHS COURTESY OF LIBRARY OF CONGRESS.

of comedy's stage- and circus-trained comedians who possessed a well-honed athletic ability. The results can look awkward. That said, audiences and reviewers of that era were less demanding and accepted his screen characters in all their clumsy glory. Peter Milne, reviewer of *Motion Picture News*, had this to say about one of Lehrman's performances: "Mr. Lehrmann has a strong line of business, peculiar to himself. He has a humorous series of facial expressions and many eccentric little bits of action that bring laughable response from an audience."[31]

Love and Surgery hit the theaters on October 25, 1914. Universal had announced a change to its weekly release schedule earlier that month effective October 19, with Wednesday's Nestor transferred to Tuesdays to replace the discontinued Universal Ike series, and Sunday's Frontier offering switched to Saturdays to make way for Lehrman's upcoming comedies.[32] The film's opening credit — only the title card survives in the print at the Library of Congress — is surprisingly crude and primitive in design when compared to other films of that era, with the appearance that it had been quickly executed by an amateur. Clearly, money wasn't spent on an artist or title service, but it is unclear whether this was due to budgetary constraints or lack of time. The title cards for subsequent releases were an improvement, if only by comparison.

The film was enthusiastically received, and Peter Milne's *Motion Picture News* review was typical:

> We have seen all varieties and brands of slapstick comedy that the market of today offers, but "Love and Surgery" contains more slapstickism, so to speak, than all the rest.
>
> The L. Ko. is a new brand added to the many now under the Universal banner, and if more follow and come up to the standard set by this, they will establish a name for themselves, a name to be smiled at whenever it be heard.
>
> Slapstick comedies have for some time been great favorites with some people, but, like all great favorites, they have those who do not look upon them in such a favorable light. The farcical burlesque elements of this picture will be enjoyed to the fullest extent by most of the male audiences. And by those who do not mind the extreme rough work, perhaps a little suggestive in its roughest moments, a warm welcome will be awaiting the picture.
>
> Henry Pathé Lehreman [sic] is the director and second leading man of this picture and Billy [sic] Ritchie is the star to whom the final honor of creating laughs must be allotted. But it is the ingenious mind of the director that conceived the plan and to him must go a great amount of praise.
>
> As is usual with this variety of picture, there is no plot; if there is, it will be completely obliterated in the mass of uproarious events. Brick throwing, punching, running, daring falls, diving through walls and roofs, flirting, shooting and countless other varieties of furnishing hilarity are linked together in this picture with such startling rapidity that he will be a morose individual indeed who is not aching and crying from laughter at the end of the farce.[33]

Lehrman's first L-Ko comedy was a howling success, and Ritchie, in what was purported to be his first film, went over big with audiences and exhibitors alike.

But things are not always as they seem, for Ritchie had actually made another, little-seen film just months before. Less than a year earlier, Ritchie's vaudeville manager Gus Hill had decided to venture into film, and to that end formed the Nonpareil Feature Film Co. in late 1913 with partner William Counihan. Several popular comic strips were announced ("Mutt and Jeff" and "Bringing Up Father" among them) as potential offerings in one-reel shorts, Hill having earlier presented sketches on stage featuring these same characters. States rights were offered as early as May 1914 before a single foot of

LEFT: *Gertrude Selby, Henry Lehrman, and Billie Ritchie in a scene from* Love and Surgery, *featured on the cover of the October 17, 1914 issue of* Universal Weekly. RIGHT: *Billie Ritchie's first film role as* Happy Hooligan, *appearing on the bottom half of the bill with headliner* The Line Up at Police Headquarters *in this Nonpareil Feature Film ad. From the February 24, 1915 issue of* New York Dramatic Mirror.

film had been taken, but Hill already had one drama available for release, *The Line-Up at Police Headquarters* "starring" Police Commissioner George S. Dougherty, to lend his new firm some legitimacy.[34] Cartoonist Frederick Burr Opper's "Happy Hooligan" was to be Nonpareil's first comedy, and Paul Arlington, author of many comedies for both Kalem and Mutual, was assigned to adapt the cartoons for the screen.[35] Jack Mahony, formerly with Reliance, was assigned to direct, and Billie Ritchie was to star in the lead of "Happy."[36] The announcement was greeted with enthusiasm: "Unless our predictions fail, Billy [sic] Ritchie will make an unparalleled success as a motion picture comedian, inasmuch as he combines wonderful pantomime ability with a keen sense of the ridiculous." (*New York Clipper*, June 20, 1914). Just when and where Lehrman was introduced to Ritchie and his considerable comedic abilities is unknown, but his decision to make him his company's lead some months hence was already being prophesized as a wise choice.

The Lox Club, a New York-based chartered social organization open to all burlesque performers, was formed that same year, and Ritchie became a member. The organization's first outing was held at Boehm's Picnic Grounds at New Dorp, Staten Island on June 16, 1914, and Ritchie was there in his "Happy" costume along with a cameraman and director. Scenes were filmed during an interruption in the outing's ball game for an upcoming film tentatively named *Hooligan at the Lox Outing*. Later on after dinner, the participants all retired to the beach where "a picture of Hooligan being rescued from the water was staged on the pier."[37] *Billboard* additionally reported that footage was shot "of Hooligan's antics evading two cops."[38] Two weeks later the film, heralded as firm's first comedy and now bearing the simple title *Happy Hooligan*, was announced as completed,[39] but doesn't appear to have actually made it into theaters until early 1915. Nonpareil's days were numbered, however; aside from a filmed version of *Alice in Wonderland* that actually made it into theaters, and the John and Emma Ray comedy *A Hot Old Time* that was announced but never filmed, no other films were produced by the doomed company.[40] A suit was brought against them in November by the Star Company, successor to the *New York Journal* and *Evening Journal* claiming copyright infringement on their acquired rights to the strip, demanding that Nonpareil forfeit all reels and negatives.[41] This suit most likely delivered Nonpareil its death blow, for it ceased to exist by early 1916.

Lehrman[42] followed his first slam-bang release a week later with the single-reel *Partners in Crime*, a far less ambitious effort more in keeping with the standard weekly releases of competitor comedy companies, but still a frenetic, action-filled (if somewhat incomprehensible), thoroughly enjoyable romp. Ritchie and Bergman co-star, with Selby interjected as a curvy, flirtatious young lady seemingly present solely to elicit lustful responses from the various dice-rolling vagrants around her. The two leads have a love-hate relationship in this one, working together at one point in an attempt to rob a house in order to "buy a saloon" with the hoped-for proceeds, but more often at odds primarily over Selby's affections and the necklace that Ritchie manages to pilfer from the chief of police's home. There is no end to the fisticuffs, pistol shooting, water dumping, and so forth, with Ritchie even tearing the mustache off the saloon keeper who has attempted to eject him from his establishment. The film concludes with not one but two spectacular leaps from a window several stories above, first Ritchie followed by Bergman, their descents slowed as they both crash through a store-front awning before hitting the sidewalk below.

Ritchie interjects all sorts of throw-away business that enlivens the proceedings. Whenever a thirst for liquor overcomes him — and that's often — his tongue darts in and out of his mouth like a lizard's. Finding a carafe of booze in the home he has entered to rob, he hesitates, then finally succumbs and pours himself a shot, thinks better of it, and switches over to the carafe itself which he proceeds to empty. Later on, when he is unsuccessful at snapping his fingers, he licks his fingers several times, his tongue once again darting in and out, until he is successful in accomplishing this superfluous task. His look of bewilderment as Selby attempts to entice him, attempting to locate the target of her affections while totally oblivious that he himself is the target, is priceless.

Lehrman's direction is assured as always, with one standout sequence during a heated encounter between the two leads shot in stunning close-up. Bergman and Ritchie face off for a fight, the former approaching to extreme close-up from left middle ground to right foreground and out of frame, followed by a reverse of Ritchie approaching to a screen-filling close-up, delivering a series of anger-fueled epithets that leaves the viewer wishing he could read lips. Lehrman, sporting a trim little beard, assumes a role in this film as well, as the chief of police whose intended gift of a necklace for his wife is stolen by Ritchie, a sequence and eventual conclusion very reminiscent of Keystone's *Her Birthday Present* in which he co-starred a year and a half earlier. Once again, Lehrman's physical attempts at comedy appear somewhat labored in several instances of action, his energetic hopping about just a bit too, shall we say, *enthusiastic*; they come off more absurd than humorous.

Two more single-reelers — *The Fatal Marriage* (November 8, 1914) and *Lizzie's Escape* (November 15, 1914) — followed, both featuring Lehrman's trio of comedians and the former with the director assuming another role. *The Fatal Marriage* has Lehrman and Ritchie both trying to foist off an unattractive girl on another poor fellow while competing for the affections of Selby, while *Lizzie's Escape* has the pair as city slickers both attempting to bilk country girl Selby of her money. Exchange operators and exhibitors were quick to write in to Universal with reports of the acceptance of the new L-Ko's: "Let me congratulate you on having the funniest picture I ever saw…. Billy [sic] Ritchie and the gentleman that played 'Lonesome Ignatz' are the funniest things I ever saw, barring none. Hoping you will book me many more L-Ko comedies of the same calibre." (L.L. Epstein, Plaza theatre, Brooklyn) "I certainly am pleased with the new L-Ko comedies. They surely will have to go some to make a better comedy than this first release, 'Love and Surgery'. My patrons all tell me that it was the best comedy they have ever seen." (C.A. Ledgewood, Marple theatre, Wichita, Kansas) The occasional theater patron took the time to write in as well: "I recently observed, in the *Motion Picture Magazine*, a notice that Pathé Lehrman had a new comedian whom he hoped would take. You just tell Mr. Lehrman for me that you took. You took the theatre by storm, and won at once a place among famous comedians. 'Love and Surgery' — 'The Fatal Marriage' were both screamingly funny. Nearly every one will agree with me when I say good comedians are scarce. But if you keep up the good work and the director hustles, why the number should increase." (Vance Caroll, location unspecified) [43]

Production of *The Fatal Marriage* was marred by an incident that would be added to the eventual growing list of mishaps and accidents that would plague Lehrman's career and, ultimately, his reputation. These would garner him the nicknames "Mr. Suicide" and "Suicide Lehrman" for his supposed insensitivity and lack of concern when ordering stuntmen and actors alike to perform hazardous stunts for the future amusement of filmgoers. Former professional driver and fledgling actor Lew Carter was once again involved, although in this instance he was not entirely without fault. Carter was instructed to attempt near-right angle turns in his big racing car at speeds between forty and fifty miles an hour, and lost control — not once, but twice! The first time his auto merely left the road and screeched to a halt within feet of someone's home. The second time was a more serious accident, the auto rolling over twice and pinning Carter under the vehicle. Miraculously (or at least according to the press releases), he was pulled out without any major physical harm, and Lehrman's cameraman caught both instances on film. Resourceful to the end, Lehrman altered the film's storyline to accommodate both pieces of action.[44]

The pace, of course, would be impossible to keep up for a single individual and his cast. An attempt was made to streamline production by limiting output to single reels, the initial two-reel *Love and Surgery* followed by seventeen single-reel comedies before another multi-reel comedy would be released. Lehrman went about signing new cast and crew members to help shoulder the burden and attain his immediate goal of three active units.[45] Victor Heerman was one of the first,[46] a British-born New Yorker who since 1901 had been involved not only with the legitimate theater but with the film industry as well, acting in some early Biographs and later behind the scenes at Thanhouser, Kinemacolor, and Mutual, and rooming at the Bartholdi Inn where he had met co-roomers Lehrman and Sterling. Heerman recalled their (and others) return to the city after two years in California reaping some of the fortunes the film industry had to offer:

> [A]ll these people who had gone to L.A. with Sennett were coming back, and staying at the Astor Hotel, and throwing money around like you couldn't believe. And these were the same guys a year before I was lending fifty cents or a dollar to. So anyway, they began drifting back to New York, and instead of living at the Bartholdi Inn where most of us lived, they lived at the Astor or other places down there. They would come back east and rent five dollar-an-hour cars to go riding in the park, and I said "There must be gold in them thar hills."[47]

One of these return trips led to a job offer:

> I was down at the old Weber and Fields Music Hall when Pathé Lehrman, whom I had known around here for years, who was sort of an advisor for Mack Sennett, stopped by.... [He] came back and said "I'm starting my own company." Holy Mackerel! So I said, "How about a job?" He said, "You want to come to the Coast?" I said, "Yeah." He said, "Well, I'll be here at the Astor Hotel," and then he said, "I wish you had talked to me before." I said, "Why?" "Oh, I made some arrangements to pick up tripods in Chicago, and they're not ready yet. We have to go straight through Chicago to get back in time. If you can leave here, pick up the tripods, and bring them to the Coast, the rest of us can go straight through Chicago and not stop."[48]

Heerman jumped at the offer, and arrived in Los Angeles with the tripods. His first position with L-Ko was supposed to be as assistant to Albert P. Hamberg, but that didn't last very long.

> After about three days that I was here, and I hated to see it, but Lehrman sent back the fellow who was brought out as his assistant, and he made me his assistant. Lehrman then took me in and showed me the assembling and the cutting. That's where all pictures are made. You show me a director who has no experience in cutting, and I'll show you a director who doesn't know what it's all about.... The one little projection room was a tiny little room to look at your pictures; but a lot of them never saw their pictures because they just cut the negative, and never made up prints. We never had a script in our lives. I never knew what a script looked like other than those I got from Thanhouser.[49]

Heerman's duties would soon include title and gag writing.

Twenty year old Texas-born actress Eva Nelson was among the first hires, described at the time as five feet four, brown hair, and "the eyes of a sorceress set in a dark, oval face."[50] Some work with Keystone followed a several-year stint on the stage in musical comedy where she was one of the "Bloomer Girls" in an ill-fated California-based show of the same title back in 1913.[51] Eva was with the L-Ko from the very beginning with her smaller role in *Love and Surgery*, and would remain there for the duration of Lehrman's tenure with the company.

Lehrman brought several others on board in the months that followed as well. Louise Orth was among the first,[52] a graduate of the Hinshaw Conservatory of Music. Born in Denver, Colorado in 1891, Orth had appeared in Blanche Ring's *Yankee Girl* in 1910 (along with Henry Bergman in the cast), spent two seasons — 1911 into 1913 — with Julian Eltinge in *The Fascinating Widow*, ending up in a San Francisco-based presentation of *The Isle of Bang Bong* in mid-1914.[53] Back east, Louise landed with the Biograph in 1913 where she co-starred in nearly two dozen films into 1914 before breaking loose to make a few more films for random studios before Lehrman hired her. Described at the time as "a 'real-for-sure blonde' with blonde hair and a complexion as pure as cream with the faint blush of the peach to it,"[54] Orth brought an air of elegance to her roles at L-Ko, in contrast to the rough-hewn characters portrayed by Nelson and the girl-next-door parts assigned to Selby. Orth's first for L-Ko was most likely *The Manicure Girl* (December 27, 1914) starring Ritchie, although some other, less reliable sources have attached her name to several earlier films.

Lehrman was quick to address the open director positions as well. The first of these was filled in September by thirty-six year old Canadian Harry Edwards, who had his start as a property boy at the Universal two years earlier. Edwards had worked his way up to direction of the Universal Ike series within a year or so, and the Universal Ike Jr. series that followed when disgruntled star Augustus Carney quit the studio. Edwards made the lateral switch over to L-Ko, and would marry the Ike series' co-star Louise Glaum the following year.[55]

Heerman described working conditions at the comparatively primitive studio at this time:

> They had built a little stage on the corner of El Centro and Sunset Boulevard. You used to get off the streetcar at Gower Street, walk down to Sunset, and there was the Universal studios. At that time it was one great, long stage, and all the diffusers, strings and dressing rooms were in the back. The offices were over there; the rest was an open lot, and the mud was up to your knees when the rain came. Uh![56]

By November the three intended units had increased to four due to the L-Ko's growing popularity, with the announcement that Lehrman and Edwards had been joined by directors George Nichols, a Sterling defectee after only a couple of months with that studio, and Rube Miller.[57] The fifty year old Nichols came into the fold with a load of experience behind him, entering the industry in 1906 after twenty years in theater as stage manager and director. Nichols acted for Griffith at Biograph from 1908 through 1912, with that important association opening doors to positions as director for Thanhouser, Gem, and Lubin. Joining Keystone in 1913, Nichols directed scores of comedies from *Fatty at San Diego* (November 3, 1913) through *A Fatal Flirtation* (May 25, 1914) during his nine month stay. After his short stint with Sterling, Nichols moved over to L-Ko. It is unclear what Nichols' contributions were, if any, to L-Ko's output, so it is possible that his stay with the studio was just as brief, if not briefer.

Rube Miller, an Ohio-born twenty-seven year old former clown, had worked at Keystone since 1912, initially as an actor and stuntman before advancing to direction in early 1914. His stay with L-Ko proved to be brief, with only four known credits during this period. Miller co-starred with Ritchie and Peggy Pearce, who had joined the studio late in 1914, in *Through a Knot Hole* (January 10, 1915), and headlined *The Butcher's*

LEFT: *Eva Nelson.* RIGHT: *Louise Orth from one of her early stage roles, possibly* The Isle of Bang Bong. COURTESY OF STEVE MASSA.

Bride (February 3, 1915) with Henry Bergman as co-star, and *Every Inch a Hero* (January 20, 1915) and *Peggy's Sweethearts* (February 14, 1915), both with Peggy Pearce, before departing for Kriterion in March 1915.[58] Miller directed this latter film, and while he most likely directed the other three films as well, this has not been confirmed. The direction of *Every Inch a Hero*, a copy of which is held by the Library of Congress, is rudimentary and workmanlike at best.

The studio facilities were being enhanced during this period of anticipated growth. In addition to the erection of a new 114-by-60-foot stage, a second story with ten new rooms was added to the dressing room building, and a new prop room and cutting room were added as well.[59] One of the other enhancements to the studio was in the area of lighting, which Lehrman recalled nearly a quarter century later, and in a surprising amount of detail:

> …Cooper-Hewitt lights were used extensively in New York as early as 1908. The trouble with them, although thoroughly satisfactory for photographic purposes, was the fact that they were terribly heavy and clumsy. As a consequence, the over-head Cooper-Hewitts had to be stationary and permanently attached. The

mobile Cooper-Hewitts took up a tremendous lot of space and were very difficult to handle. The portable arc lights, however, were the ones that were developed here on the West Coast, and these were the lights we began using here extensively around 1914. We also employed Cooper-Hewitts with four tubes instead of eight, and of much smaller dimensions.[60]

Jack White had followed Lehrman from Sterling to L-Ko, where he would work in the cutting room and project the dailies for Lehrman's approval. Working under the cutting department's head (whom he named as Bob Roberts), White said that he would work hand-in-hand with Lehrman cutting some of the films, and would ship the original cut negatives to New York where anywhere from fifty to a hundred prints would be struck for release. "I would contact him before cutting anything and have a confab with him about just what he thought he got on film," said White. Their approach to editing differed somewhat, however, as White's technique evolved into one all his own that would serve him well in the coming years. "I only agreed with him on a limited number of things. If some cuts didn't satisfy me, I would cut it the way I saw fit instead of the way he thought it should be." Charles Hochberg followed from Sterling and would join the cutting staff as well, and would remain with Lehrman for a number of years to follow.[61] Ira H. "Joe" Morgan was head cameraman by mid-1915, the beginning of a long career that would span into the late 1950s, with an assist by cameraman William J. Piltz. Piltz was vice president of the two year old Static Club, a society of active motion picture cameramen.[62] French born A.H. Vallet, another Static Club member and former Nestor employee, joined Piltz in the L-Ko camera department, and was noted by one reporter for his clever nighttime photography in a Billie Ritchie comedy.[63] Frank Crompton, formerly with Powers, moved over to L-Ko as head carpenter.[64] Henry Roberts Symonds, who was brought on as a writer, would follow Lehrman to his next two studios before breaking off to write for features in the 1920s, and former IMP writer George Edwardes-Hall was added to the staff as well.[65]

The remainder of the year's six releases were, for the most part, all directed by Lehrman and starred one or more members of his original troika of comedians, with the director himself taking the occasional role. *The Groom's Doom* (November 22, 1914) had Ritchie involved in the ubiquitous park flirtation that led to a marathon boxing match complete with mudhole finale.

A Blighted Spaniard (November 29, 1914; extant) co-starred Henry Bergman as "Bombardio" and newcomer Peggy Pearce as "Sunshine" in a south-of-the-border tale involving the former's attempts to win her affections away from her lover "Tomalio." This latter role was played by Canadian-born actor Wallace MacDonald, fairly new to the industry with a dozen or so films for Keystone under his belt. Victor Heerman commented on the seat-of-the-pants nature of filmmaking at this time, and the resourcefulness that was needed to complete this particular film:

> While on location, every now and then, something would come up, and Lehrman would say, "What do you think, Vic? Wonder if we can get a banjo somewhere?" Well, we're out in the middle of San Fernando Valley, about eight miles from the nearest anything. One stand-by car has gone back to get some cold water somewhere because there's no water. There were no gas stations. It was just desert. "What are we going to do?" he says. There's a little front, with a door, and a

senorita up on this thing, and the fellow wants to serenade her.... Lehrman says, "Where can we get a banjo? Where can we get an instrument?" I said, "What about a comb and a paper?" Holy Golly, Lehrman throws his arms around me. "Oh, say, that's good!" Every time something would come up, I'd have a suggestion.⁶⁶

The Baron's Bear Escape (December 20, 1914) once again co-starred Bergman and MacDonald as rival suitors, with Bergman portraying the wealthy "Baron Wilhelm

Henry Bergman and four-legged friend from The Baron's Bear Escape. COURTESY OF ELIF RONGEN-KAYNAKCI, EYE FILMMUSEUM.

von Hasenpfeffer" favored by the girl's father, and the youthful, twenty-three year old MacDonald favored by the girl herself. A print of the film is held by the EYE Filmmuseum.

Fido's Dramatic Career (December 6, 1914) was a novelty of sorts for the studio, a first not only in that it was director Harry Edwards' maiden effort for L-Ko, but also with its large animal cast. Fido, a stray from the streets, dreams that he is the pampered pet of a beautiful woman, which allows him to exact revenge on all those who had treated him roughly in the past. Later, seated in a private box, he is treated to a match between Mike's Billy Goat and Fritz's Grizzly Bear. His dream comes to an abrupt end when the sprinkler is turned on. As one reviewer noted, "A collection of well-trained dogs, with a monkey, a goat and a few other animals perform in this picture and will furnish great amusement."⁶⁷ Another noted that "Fido drives an auto to the fight and smokes a pipe during the rounds. Other dogs and a chimpanzee and goat add to the fun, which ends up with a big chase. A good animal yarn, well-pictured throughout."⁶⁸ Yet another praised the film, saying that "The situations are unique in view of the fact that all of the participants are animals, and throughout the picture the comedy interests are capably sustained."⁶⁹ Edwards had demonstrated a facility for working with animals.

Lehrman's *The Rural Demons* (December 13, 1914; extant) co-starred the director with Ritchie as two country bumpkins both vying for the hand of pretty lass Selby, resorting to battle with eggs, bricks, and whatever else is at hand whenever their paths cross. Ritchie elopes with Selby, making off in Lehrman's jalopy, but when he gets a flat it is, improb-

Eloping Billie Ritchie and Gertrude Selby in a panic over their flat tire, in The Rural Demons. COURTESY OF LIBRARY OF CONGRESS.

ably, in front of a tire manufacturing business. Ritchie heads inside for a replacement, and urges through each phase of the manufacture of the new tire. "The comedy is interrupted when at its height," the *Motion Picture News* reviewer commented, "to introduce scenes showing the manufacture of automobile tires, which is most interesting but seems rather out of place."⁷⁰ *Moving Picture World* agreed, adding that "This would have been an excellent half reel feature by itself, and is very interesting." The reviewer added one additional observation, one that crops up far too often in these early offerings: "The photography was not very clear in places."⁷¹ For the record, the film ends with Lehrman winning the girl, and a frustrated Ritchie attempting to get a refund on his new tire.

Lehrman managed to make the papers around this time, and not in the most flattering of fashions. The possessor of a heavy foot and a so-called "monster" Fiat that would respond to his urgings, Lehrman was stopped on October 2 while speeding from the studio. He was ticketed, and then sped off, much to the amazement of the two officers who once again gave chase. Stopped a second time, he was directed to the Central Police Station, which he set off for once again at a high speed. He was stopped a third time, ordered out of the car, and hauled off to court. When it was revealed that he had been arrested twice before in the past six weeks, Lehrman, "attired in a brown suit of the latest cut [and] shorn of his diamonds by the desk sergeant,"[72] was thrown in jail for the night, the judge refusing to accept the $10,000 bail money friends had brought to the courtroom.[73] "I'll sell my car and never drive again if you give me a chance," pleaded the director. "I am sorry. I was tired and wanted to go home in a hurry." "You mean you are sorry that you were caught," responded the Judge, not buying a moment of it.[74] The following day, Police Judge Chambers sentenced Lehrman to serve thirty days in the city jail, thoroughly annoyed that the director had not only a history of speeding, but was insulting and dismissive of the arresting officers as well. Lehrman gave notice of appeal to the Superior Court, and was released on $500 bond.[75] The sentence was later set aside "on the grounds that Lehrman was not informed of his right to have an attorney represent him," and a trial scheduled for the following February.[76] The results of the trial (assuming it took place) were of sufficient disinterest to not warrant any further press. The incident itself — albeit a comparatively minor one — proved to be the first blemish on the director's budding reputation, but most surely not the last. As for his Fiat, it was crippled soon after when L-Ko cameraman Walter Stradling rear-ended Lehrman's prize possession, wrecking the vehicle's gas tank[77] and forcing the filmmaker to find alternate transportation between the studio and his residence at the Hotel Alexandria.

Lehrman wasn't the only one at L-Ko who had a tangle with the law, the second instance occurring only days after his own encounters. J.H. McDaniel was arrested on a petit larceny charge on a warrant issued at the insistence of Roy Kohler, a Coast League baseball player. McDaniel was thrown in jail along with his dog, known as "Montana Kid." The dog, unfortunately, was currently co-starring with Louise Orth in L-Ko's *Gems and Germs* (January 3, 1915), bringing production to a halt. Lehrman made a quick trip back to the station to bail out both the dog and his owner, reportedly complaining "That makes $525 I have got up here now."[78]

The Manicure Girl (December 27, 1914) was the last of the year's offerings, this one co-starring director Lehrman with Ritchie, Louise Orth, and newcomer Hank Mann. Ritchie and Mann play rivals for the hand of manicurist Orth, only to find a third rival in her workplace's head barber (Charles Dudley). Ritchie wins out this time around after a chase through sewer pipes, with Mann and Dudley disposed of in a dump cart and hauled off to the city dump. *Motion Picture News* commented on a bit player in a fashion typical of those times: "Many of the scenes transpire in a barber shop in which the colored bootblack is the shining light (not literally)."[79] Universal issued a challenge to exhibitors with the release of this film, wherein they would choose any other comedy short released in the past six months by another studio, show it on the same bill as *The Manicure Girl*, and have their patrons vote on which film was the best. Universal expressed its conviction that the L-Ko would be the winner, "believing that there is no program on earth that contains comedies which surpass its new L-Ko comedy releases." No prize was offered.[80]

Mann, formerly with Keystone in small roles from 1913, had been an acrobat and steeplechase during the years before that, or at least according to Walker. In an interview from early 1915, Mann described his start in the industry following work as a sign painter, painting ads for a Durham, North Carolina tobacco company on the sides of barns and other structures. "From my scaffold one day I saw a comedy company playing. It looked like play to me then. I found out that they were the Keystone company, and when I was out of a job I joined them as an extra. Being a good runner I usually led the cops in the chases."[81] An accurate quote, or a press agent's pipedream? Who knows?

Mann's second for L-Ko was directed by Lehrman as well, the thoroughly enjoyable single reel *Cupid in a Hospital* (January 6, 1915), co-starring Ritchie and Orth. Ritchie, hospitalized after losing out in a park-based altercation over pretty nurse Orth, befriends a crippled Hungarian patient played by Mann. The friendship turns sour when Mann

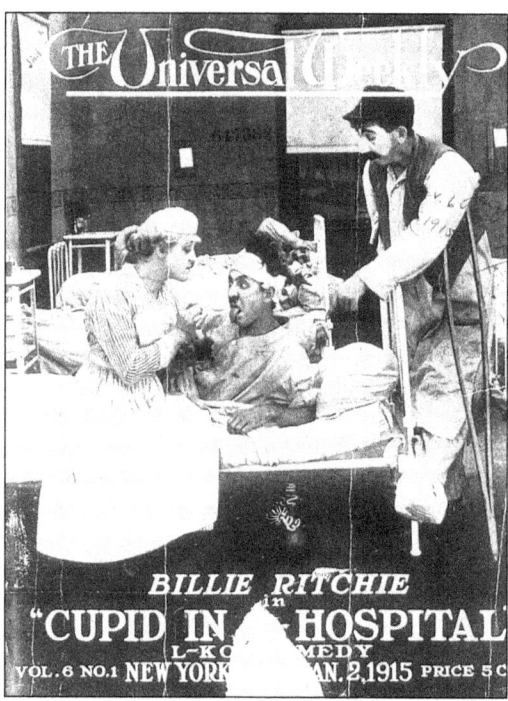

LEFT: *Hank Mann in costume for an L-Ko Comedy, in this promotional postcard issued by Trans-Atlantic Film Co., Ltd., Universal's distributor in Great Britain.* RIGHT: *Nurse Louise Orth tends to bedridden Billie Ritchie in* Cupid in a Hospital, *featured on the January 2, 1915 cover of* Universal Weekly. *Hank Mann on crutches.*

observes Orth showering affection on Ritchie, whom she previously thought dead. Mann turns out to be an anarchist, and with a bomb provided by two of his cohorts plans to blow up Ritchie. His plans go awry, however, and both he and Ritchie are blown into the heavens — a clumsy double exposure — and end up in a lake, their final resting place marked solely by the anarchist's floating crutch. Mann has a second, earlier role in the film as a clean-shaven cop, in stark contrast to his Hungarian's bushy mustache and corked-on "five o'clock shadow."

Ritchie once again inserts all sorts of throw-away business into the resulting film, which survives in a print held by the Library of Congress. A pair of cops attempts to revive the unconscious Ritchie, first with a gentle shove, then a billy-club to the gut, followed by a brick to the head, all without success. Only when they offer a whiff of gin do they receive any sort of response: first a shudder, then a sniff, followed by the lizard-like darting-in-and-out of his tongue as he finally comes to. Later, when he can't find a match to light his pipe, he instead eats the tobacco. When he first accepts the Hungarian's offer of a drink, Ritchie pulls his hospital gown up over his head to do so surreptitiously. When he offers a drink of the Hungarian's booze to another patient, the fellow points to the bandages covering his mouth, so the resourceful Ritchie instead dabs the liquor onto those same bandages. And after his initial victory over the rival suitor, Ritchie delivers one of his familiar dismissive finger snaps.

Mann's next two for L-Ko were *Father Was a Loafer* (February 10) and *Almost a Scandal*

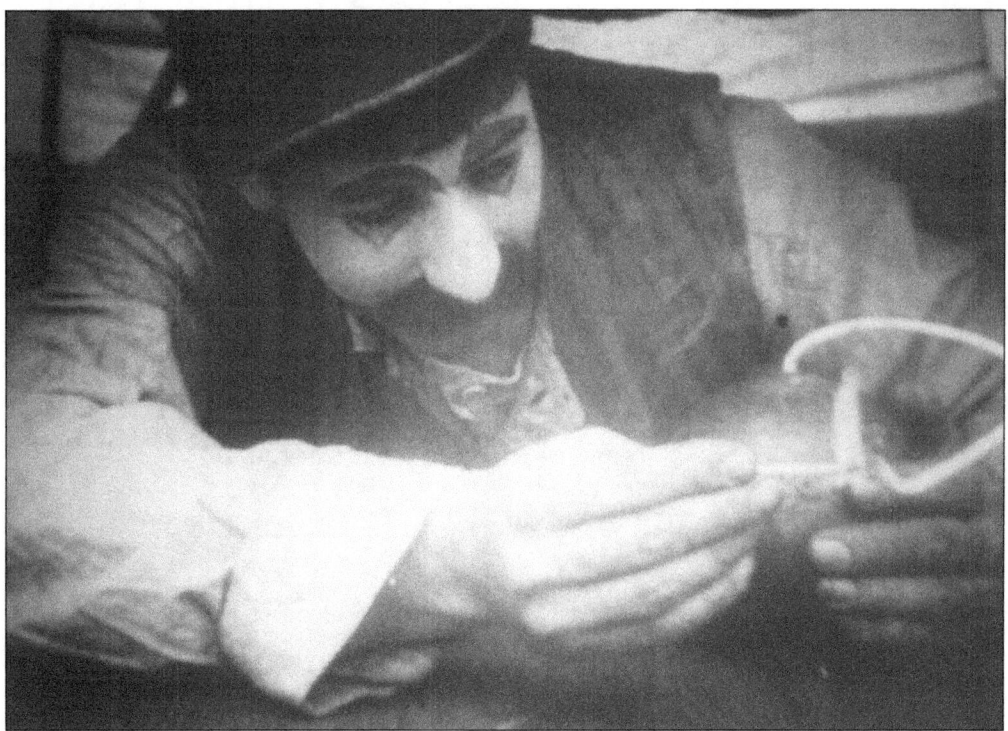

Hank Mann as anarchist, lighting a bomb while hiding under a bed in Cupid in a Hospital.
COURTESY OF LIBRARY OF CONGRESS.

(February 17), the former directed by Lehrman and the latter most likely directed by him as well, but this has not been confirmed. *Father Was a Loafer* stars Ritchie and Selby, along with newcomer Alice Howell, another recent acquisition from the Keystone studios. A former vaudevillian, the five foot, two inch, 130 pound Howell was forced to seek work when her second husband and fellow performer Dick Smith contracted tuberculosis, bringing their act to an end. Bit parts at Keystone followed in 1914, and her comedic talents and go-for-broke attitude were quickly noted. With the appearance of a disheveled, overworked cherub, Howell soon came to be known as "the scrub woman" due to the plethora of characters of that ilk that she was assigned to portray. And her hair:

> It is the sort of hair that you can do anything you like with. She makes a big asset out of it, doubling it with a huge cock-a-too knot over her forehead as a kitchen mechanic; piling it into an enormous pompadour as a lovesick waitress; fluffing it into a huge grotesque mass of curls as a caricature of a society woman.[82]

While Selby, Orth, and Nelson were all attractive additions to the L-Ko roster, none of them were rough-and-tumble comedians, and Lehrman found such a woman in Howell. After a year with Keystone, the twenty-eight year old actress moved over to L-Ko and more prominent roles both in a supporting and starring capacity. *Father Was a Loafer* was the first of these.

We are fortunate that a print of *Father Was a Loafer* survives, one of the few L-Ko's available for viewing. Howell plays Ritchie's wife and mother to their four children.

LEFT: *Alice Howell*. RIGHT: *"Father's Private Car." Poster art for* Father Was a Loafer.
COURTESY COLLECTION EYE FILMMUSEUM.

Summoned home from the tavern he frequents, Ritchie is horrified to find that she has just given birth to triplets, with doctor (Mann) and two nurses (Orth and Nelson) in attendance. This pushes Ritchie over the edge, and he flees their home. Spotting heiress Selby at the mercy of her runaway horses, Ritchie rescues her and in recognition of the heroic act he has just performed is offered her hand in marriage. Meanwhile, a family friend takes advantage of Howell's distraught condition and proposes to her, but when she reads of her husband's impending nuptials, she races off to the wedding pushing a wheeled basket with the triplets aboard. The ceremony comes to a raucous end, Ritchie as usual getting the worst of it when he is forced out of his hiding place with a fork jabbed into his rear, then beaten senseless by his outraged spouse. Ritchie is hauled back home in a daze, deposited in the basket the triplets had arrived in and pulled behind Howell's car.

Howell, her hair pulled tightly back and sporting a huge mole by the corner of her mouth, has a prominent role here and ample opportunity to display her talents. Mann sports bushy mutton chop whiskers as the attending physician, and Selby, as Ritchie's intended, is all dolled up here and far more attractive in appearance than in the earlier surviving films in which she appears in less glamorous roles. Ritchie, of course, is the focus of the film, and doesn't stint on the amusing bits and moments of absurdity. In the tavern and obviously tipsy, he attempts to light the sausage in his mouth thinking it's a cigar, later stuffing it into the open neck of the bottle from which he's just poured a drink. Then his hat is sucked up to an overhead fan. Arriving home, his mounting shock as one after another of the triplets is brought out and placed in his arms. After leaving his wife, he hesitates momentarily upon seeing his children's toys on the porch steps, but resumes

A dazed Billie Ritchie is dragged home in the newborns' basket, in Father Was a Loafer.
COURTESY OF LIBRARY OF CONGRESS.

his flight after counting to seven on his fingers. Posting his goodbye letter to his wife, his finger gets stuck in the mailbox. And later at the Rocks' residence, pouring an open bottle of booze into a can in his coat pocket, then planting the empty bottle in the butler's back pocket so that the poor fellow takes the blame. There is one seemingly risky shot here: Ritchie, holding three live babies, falls over backwards in shock, but is caught at the last moment before he falls too far. All in all, *Father Was a Loafer* is hysterical viewing, and one of the better Ritchie films known to survive.

Almost a Scandal survives as well, with Ritchie flirting with Louise Orth while her jealous husband (Bergman) flirts with another woman (Eva Nelson). When Bergman stumbles across Ritchie and his wife, a battle ensues between the two men, culminating with a four foot long sword driven through Bergman's middle, all with no discernible ill effect! Mann has a smaller role as a drunk in the tavern, and in that capacity has a lot of humorous interaction with Ritchie. He is an enjoyable, if disappointingly underused, asset to the film.

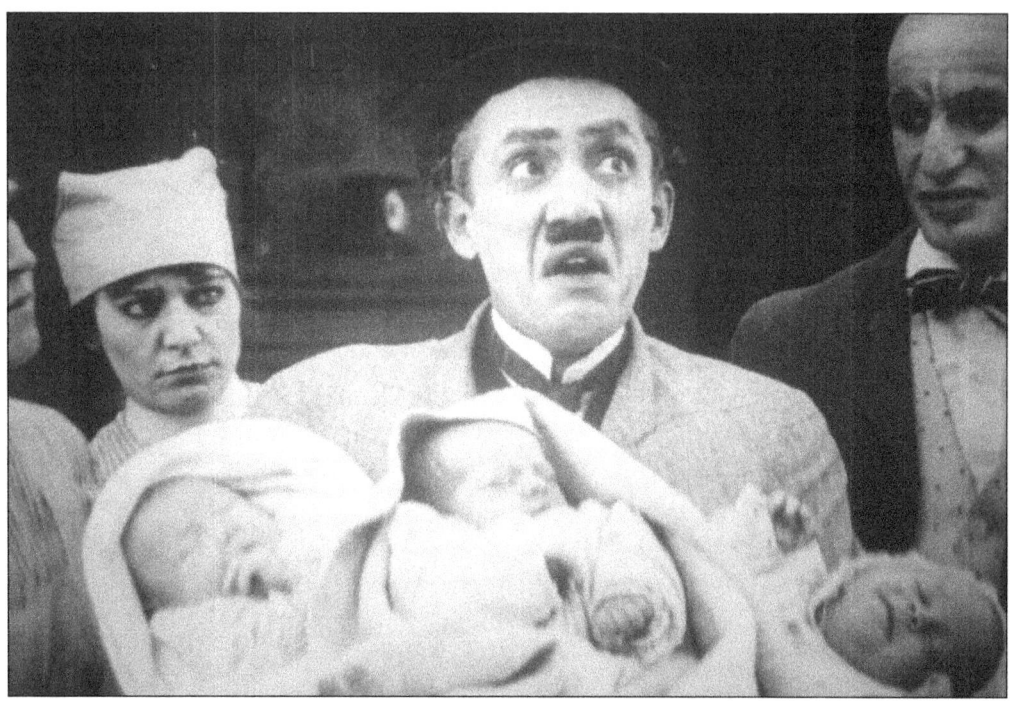

ABOVE: *Billie Ritchie discovers that wife Alice Howell has given birth to triplets; he isn't happy. From* Father Was a Loafer, *nurse Eva Nelson to his left, expressing concern.* COURTESY OF LIBRARY OF CONGRESS. BELOW: *Love-struck Billie Ritchie presses his face against the bank window for a better look at Louise Orth, in* Almost a Scandal. COURTESY COLLECTION EYE FILMMUSEUM.

This is a surprisingly savage, though admittedly very funny, comedy. Aside from the usual knockabout stuff, at one point in the cafe Billie kicks a chair out from under a drunken sleeping patron, who falls to the ground flat on his face. The sword duel that climaxes the film is a jaw-dropper, Billie shoving the huge four foot sword through Bergman's midsection (mercifully, off-screen), a good foot-and-a-half protruding from the irate fellow's back. The fact that it doesn't seem to faze Bergman neutralizes what otherwise would have been horrific.

Sporting a pointy, upturned mustache and goatee, Bergman does a lot of broad mugging here, at one point making a ponderous attempt to look nimble as he hops in the air and clicks his heels together. His character is at turns pompous, lecherous, and bloodthirsty — and utterly foolish. As his wife, Orth struts her stuff and flirts throughout with any male that crosses her path. While elegant, her physical appeal is elusive, but perhaps she was considered a "looker" to 1915 eyes.

Ritchie, of course, steals the show, and during his climactic encounter with Bergman, clad only in baggy pants, suspenders, and striped T-shirt, reveals a physique toned and hardened from years of strenuous workouts both on and off stage. He again injects all sorts of amusing bits into the proceedings. While consuming the last drops of drink in the cafe with the glass held over his open mouth, his tongue catches every last drop, lizard-like. A request from Bergman for money can't be heard, so the resourceful Billie grabs a funnel, sticks it in the Bergman's ear, and repeats his comments full volume. Later, when confronted by the angry Bergman over being with Bergman's wife, Ritchie ends up nervously eating his cigar. And finally, in a move worthy of Ford Sterling and perhaps added at Lehrman's insistence, Billie leaps onto Bergman and chomps down on his ear!

1915 had opened with a big promotional push for the new studio's releases. Perhaps the most conspicuous display appeared in Manhattan, where the executive offices of the Universal Film Manufacturing Company resided in the Mecca Building located at 48th Street and Broadway. There, overlooking "The Great White Way" from high up on the building's north wall, appeared a huge promotional sign with the six story tall image of a smiling Billie Ritchie, cane in hand and tipping his hat, billed as "The Man Who made Laughter Famous" and promoting L-Ko's "fifty other celebrated stars," perhaps a slight exaggeration. At over 9,000 square feet, the sign was touted as the largest painted sign in the U.S. A photo published at the time shows several painters on scaffolding, no taller than the nearby image's head.[83]

The other promotional piece was a detailed two-column biography that appeared in the *Los Angeles Times*. It detailed Lehrman's life and career to date as well as his working methods, and while the accuracy of some of its assertions is questionable, most of it rings true. One curious paragraph explains Lehrman's thoughts on comedy, and touches on some eyebrow-raising goals for the studio:

> Mr. Lehrman's view of comedy is anything that resembles life — that is true to nature. He now plans a series of comedy pictures based on exposition life and specialties, the principal object being a combination of educational features that will blend and harmonize with comedy. This will make scenes more attractive and individual, as well as educational and instructive.[84]

ABOVE: *Billie Ritchie, "The Man Who Made Laughter Famous," as he appeared bigger-than-life on the side of Broadway's Mecca Building. From the January 30, 1915 issue of* Universal Weekly. BELOW: *Another, closer look at the side of the Mecca Building. (Note the size of the men on the scaffold in the bottom right.) Universal was going all-out promoting its new comedian, with the hope that he would be the next Chaplin.*

Was Lehrman actually serious about this, or was it sheer puffery? The L-Ko's that followed certainly didn't deviate much from the established norm, but perhaps Lehrman's goals were undercut by the suits at Universal, who may have "requested" more of the same. A small piece appeared a year later that suggested as much, stating that "Upon advice from the New York office of the Universal Film Company, a new policy was inaugurated last week by the Christie Film Company, which provides that all future subjects shall contain more characters of eccentric or comedy make-up."[85] *Pancakes and Lunatics* was to be the first Christie release filmed under these strictures (apparently not with that title), and the front office's demands may have played a part in Christie severing his ties a few months later. The same pressure may have been placed on Lehrman.

A series of one-reelers greeted the new year, the release schedule now upped to two per week on Sundays and Wednesdays. *Thou Shalt Not Flirt* (January 13, 1915) starred Ritchie as a husband with a wandering eye, his dalliances revealed to his wife as a theater's newsreel unspools; Lehrman directed and co-starred as well. *The Death of Simon Legree* (January 24) has Ritchie as a property man ruining a traveling troupe's performance of *Uncle Tom's Cabin*. *Variety* was favorably impressed by this film, commenting that the L-Ko output "appears to have considerably improved of late, as attested by some recent pictures. In 'The Death of Simon [Legree],' there was some stage horseplay that elicited prolonged laughter with a genuine ring. The L-KO appears to be working along better lines."[86]

Henry Bergman was terrorized by Bolivar the Baby Bear in *Caught with the Goods* (January 17), while Peggy Pearce had *Every Inch a Hero* (January 20) all to herself as poor farm girl Nell, lusted after by the rent-demanding villain. No cast or credits have been connected to the film *Merry Mary's Marriage* (January 27), but given that the main character's name is "Rube" it may very well have been another of Rube Miller's films for the studio.

After Her Millions (January 31) finished off the month with a splash, the company's first three-reeler following a string of seventeen single-reels. As such it was heavily promoted by Universal ("MOST UPROARIOUS, SIDE SPLITTING LAUGH SPLITTING LAUGH PRODUCER EVER THROWN ON THE SCREEN") in a garish two-page ad featured in *Universal Weekly*. Lehrman directed, and co-starred with Ritchie and Selby. Millionaire heiress Selby is the object of both their affections, but she wants nothing to do with the two hard-drinking fellows. Their pursuit of her leads to a hotel where all hell breaks loose. *Universal Weekly's* synopsis mentions one long-running gag that is indicative of the level of humor:

> A guest, all through the hall scenes, causes roars of laughter by his desperate but vain efforts to "make" the bathroom. Driven to despair, the harassed guest makes a wild dash into the hotel corridor, maims and brains Billie and Henry, frightens the millionaire heiress into hysterics with his sledge-hammer war club, and finally slams the bathroom door after him.[87]

"It is unfortunate that a higher notch of the art had not been aimed at," sniffed the *Moving Picture World* reviewer. "The humor of the picture is based on an abnormal degree of drunkenness, and is at times unpleasantly vulgar and suggestive."[88] Not high art, for sure, but the film-going public loved it. The first of L-Ko's three-reel specials, Lehrman would soon come to restrict his efforts behind the camera to these occasional offerings, with his dwindling acting appearances restricted to these as well.

After Hank Mann's initial four efforts for director Lehrman, he was assigned to another unit, that of twenty-two year old John G. Blystone, known around the studio as "Jack." Blystone was the company's newest addition, directing for the studio by the end of 1914.[89] Blystone likely filled the position originally intended for Nichols, who by early 1915 was directing for Majestic.[90] Blystone had only one previous known credit to his name at the time (but reportedly had directed others), the single reel comedy for Joker, *On Again, Off Again Finnegan* (October 14, 1914) co-starring Eddie Boland and Ernest Shield. Mann

LEFT: *Billie Ritchie in costume for* After Her Millions. COURTESY OF JIM KERKHOFF.
RIGHT: *John G. "Jack" Blystone.*

became the star of this unit, and his name finally found its way onto the posters for his films. *Their Last Haul* (February 21, 1915) was the first of these, wherein Mann stars as a burglar reformed by his girl Alice Howell. Reformed only up to a point, though, deciding to make one last haul with his cohort played by Wallace MacDonald. The heist goes awry when another group of robbers arrive, observed by the cops who are on to their plans. Mann ends up locked in a safe along with a bomb set to blow in five minutes, dangling from the top of a twenty-story building. True to silent comedy form, the bomb blows, Mann ends up in a lake, and vows to go straight. As tantalizing as the synopsis and ads for this film sound which suggested a thrill ending ("If you want to see the desperate chances moving picture comedians take to make you laugh, see this wonderful picture. IF EITHER SIDE LETS GO — GOOD NIGHT!"), the fragments held at the Library of Congress disappoint, consisting solely of four brief snippets of film, one of them from the credits.

Production would, out of necessity, shut down during rainy spells. L-Ko and the other studios were all affected come February, when the previous five full days of rain were predicted to extend to three weeks in total.[91] *Los Angeles Times* reporter Grace Kingsley has left us with a fascinating glimpse of how the time was spent at Universal during one late 1914 downpour:

> What do the motion-picture actors at the Universal studios do when it rains? Sit around and shiver and hate themselves? Not they. They have organized a vaudeville company, and everybody that can do a stunt that either looks or listens well does something. The prop-room is the theater.... The programme was impromptu on Thursday afternoon, but was plumb full of pep. To the accompaniment of piano and ukelele, Lee Moran and Lon Chaney put on a nifty soft shoe dance; Carmen Phillips sang Spanish songs and did a fancy dance; William Worthington played and sang a solo from "Madame Butterfly;" William Clifford gave a reading from "The Bells;" and Gertrude Selby and Lon Chaney danced some society and interpretive dances.[92]

The rain would return with a vengeance in May, when three weeks of precipitation resulted in little or no work at a number of the studios.[93]

Victor Heerman commented on the toll the rainy season would have on some of the studio's employees, and the steps required to keep them on the lot:

> During this time, the rainy season had come, and if you weren't on the payroll, you were out. We had a pretty good bunch around there. They got five dollars a day, would pick up twenty-five, thirty dollars a week, or thirty-five dollars a week because we worked every Sunday. But when the rainy season came, they were leaving the lot and going off. I had a hell of a time trying to get them to hang around. The only ally I had was Abe [Stern].
>
> I said, "Now Abe, if we don't keep these people, we can't make the pictures. Now let me make a deal with some of them. I'll get them for what I can — three days a week guaranteed." So, like Hank Mann, three-day guarantee; Ray Griffith, three-day guarantee; Alice Howell, three-day guarantee, but nothing for her husband, he got paid when he worked. That was a tough job. And you had people like Bert Roach, for three dollars a day, guarantee him nine dollars a week, nothing for his sister. When you had one, you knew you always had another one in case you needed a bit.[94]

Lehrman took time out at the beginning of February to join up with a number of other motion picture company heads to discuss plans for a Motion Picture Producers' Association, a mutual benefit organization. Fellow directors included Mack Sennett, Jesse Lasky, D.W. Griffith, Thomas Ince, David Horsley, and nineteen others.[95] One of the primary goals of the association was to counter the call for a censorship board as promoted by the Public Welfare Committee. To that end screen editorials were being prepared to help sway public opinion, with Griffith, Sennett, and Ince leading the charge. One of the earliest Fine Arts film's editorials ran as follows:

> We have no wish to offend with indecencies or obscenities, but we demand as a right the liberty to show the dark side of the wrong, that we may illustrate the

bright side of virtue, the same liberty that is conceded to the art of the written word, the art to which we owe the Bible and the works of Shakespeare.[96]

With comparisons like that, how could the public refuse?

Lehrman also took part organizing Motion Picture Day at September's San Diego Exposition, working hand-in-hand with fellow committee members Chaplin, Fred Mace, Mack Sennett, and Al Christie (along with several others), any standing grievances among them assumedly set aside during this period.[97] Tiring of living out of a room in the Hotel Alexandria, Lehrman also went ahead and purchased a house located on a corner property at 6717 Franklin Avenue and Highland Avenue in Los Angeles, which he would occupy by year's end and reside in for the remainder of the decade.

Much has been made over the years belittling Ritchie's accomplishments as merely a Chaplin imitator, but the reality is that Ritchie himself may have started the controversy. As far back as April 1914, when Chaplin had only a dozen films to his credit and was still a newcomer to the screen, Ritchie was claiming to be the originator of the act. This was a full three months before Lehrman hired him and a good half year before the release of his first L-Ko. A review of the Gus Hill production *Vanity Fair* stated as much: "Ritchie is a grotesque acrobat, his specialty being given as the 'drunk,' an act that he is said to have originated."[98] Less than a year later when Ritchie himself had a dozen films in release, he elaborated:

> I first used my present make-up in my vaudeville act with my three sisters in 1887. I also played and used the same make-up with Fred H. Graham in the English pantomime, "Cinderella," playing "Baron Near Broke." Two years later I again used the same make-up in the character of a street musician in "Early Birds" while with the Karno Company. I claim I am the originator of this make-up and of the comedy which is associated with the make-up.

1887: That would be two years before Chaplin was born. The article goes on to state that he was "the original 'Drunk'" in *A Night in an English Music Hall*, playing from coast to coast here in the U.S., and originated the part of Bill Smith, the Man from Nowhere, in Gus Hill's musical revue *Around the Clock*. Ritchie estimated that he had played the role of the drunk then being popularized in the L-Ko comedies more than five thousand times in America, England, and France.[99] *Universal Weekly* came out with both guns blazing a month later with the two-page article "Billie Ritchie's Make-up Is All His Own," which included an itemized listing of his accomplishments up until his hiring by Lehrman, accompanied by an article embellishing the provenance of the character. One's interest is piqued when the article went on to say that

> The Universal will shortly publish photographed excerpts from London theatrical journals, as well as from other English dailies, proving, by photographs of Billie Ritchie in costume and press notices, that the Universal comedian is now wearing the same style of costume which he introduced into the English halls during the early 90's.[100]

Alas, it never happened.

```
                      OFFICE.
                                         January 21st, 1915.

Mr. R. H. Cochrane.
Dear Sir:-

Attached find copy of data just received by Mr. Brandt
from Mr. Ritchie.

Mr. Ritchie before coming to this country, was one of the
best known comedians on the English stage, especially in
the "halls" (vaudeville.)  As such he was the type of ac-
tor that an aspiring comedian would be sure to copy.  For
instance right now in this country, Frank Tinney might be
the kind, whom a boy who thinks he is going to make a black-
face comedian, would imitate, because of Tinney's popularity;
and Joe Weber and Lew Fields might be the type of German
comedian that a youth who aspires to be a German comedian,
would naturally pay attention to.

Ritchie in his statement says that he first used the present
make-up (of which he affirms, "I am the originator; also of
this kind of comedy) in the year 1887.

In an interview in "Motography," published January 16th,
Chaplin gave his age as 25, which would make the year of his
birth 1890, three years after Ritchie had started to popular-
ize his style of comedy in England, which is Chaplin's heath,
and which he did not, in fact, leave until just a few years
ago.  It is therefore, entirely conceivable that young Chaplin
(you see that he IS young) having stage aspirations of the slap-
stick order, paid attention to the famous Billie Ritchie, who
during Chaplin's boyhood and for many years before was the lead-
ing exponent of stage slapstick in England.

In fact a few years after Chaplin's stage debut, we have him
actually following Ritchie into a comedy role.

The following will prove THAT:--

RITCHIE'S STATEMENT:  I am America's original "Drunk" in a
"Night in an English Music Hall" playing the Orpheum time from
Coast to Coast.

CHAPLIN'S STATEMENT:  My first visit to this side of the
water was made while I was playing the lead in a pantomime pro-
duction "A Night in an English Music Hall."  It was my work
in this production that attracted the attention of Mack Sennet
and when an opening occurred in the Keystone forces he wired
east for me.

I think that about clinches our case.

BA:SS                            B. ADLER.
```

"Ritchie in his statement says that he first used the present make-up (of which he affirms, 'I am the originator; also of this kind of comedy) in the year 1887." Letter to Universal's Robert H. Cochrane asserting Billie Ritchie's claim as the prototype, and not imitator, of Chaplin's character. This was in part the basis for the article "Billie Ritchie's Make-up Is All His Own" in the March 20, 1915 issue of Universal Weekly. COURTESY OF LISA ROBINS.

"Not so fast!" chimed in British comedian Billie Reeves. "There has been a lot of discussion as to who was the original drunk, but after all the talk has simmered down you will find that I myself played the part. I first played the famous drunk part in an act produced by Fred Karno."[101] He went on to say that this was in 1904, which may be accurate as far as the Fred Karno appearances were concerned, but Ritchie was laying claim primarily to the make-up and character. Regardless, it is somewhat difficult to believe that someone else didn't portray a drunk on the stages of the British music halls or here in the U.S. before any of these three. Vaudevillian Charles Barnold even had his "Barnold's Drunken Dog" act in that same year of 1904.[102] When you come right down to it, however, aside from similar garb in some of Ritchie's films and a mustache cut down to a Chaplinesque square after his first release (likely at Lehrman's insistence), there really isn't much similarity between the two comedians' characterizations. *Motion Picture Magazine*'s "Answer Man" responded to a writer's expressed abhorrence of Ritchie and his supposed purloining of all things Chaplin, stating that "have you forgotten that Billie, who also comes from the London music halls, charges that Charlie has stolen his 'thunder' and, consequently, that Billie is not an imitator of Chaplin methods? To tell you the honest truth, however, I cannot see the slightest resemblance in the work of the two comedians."[103] Another reviewer said as much, but with a proviso: "Billie Ritchie has developed into a very good screen comic, with a method more or less his own. It seems too bad, though, aside from who is the originator of the derby hat, small mustache and cane, attributes of both Chaplin and Ritchie, that Ritchie continues to use these comedy accessories. Inasmuch as Chaplin used them first, at least on the screen, and additionally because Ritchie, who is naturally a clever comedy pantomimist, doesn't need to use anybody's make-up there seems no reason why the latter should continue them."[104] And, eventually, Ritchie would heed this advice.

Carl Laemmle's dream of a huge central location to consolidate all production was realized on March 15, 1915, with the gala opening of Universal City. More than ten thousand people were in attendance for the event, with many members of the Universal rosters on hand, some of whom put on performances for the assemblage of star-crazed filmgoers. L-Ko was represented by Ritchie, Selby, Orth, and Pearce,[105] but tellingly Lehrman remained behind at the old studio at 6100 Sunset Boulevard. The studio was otherwise vacant now, with L-Ko the sole holdout.[106]

L-Ko released a total of seventy-seven films during 1915, their twice-a-week release schedule more of a hit-or-miss goal with some months having as many as nine films in the marketplace while other months as few as four. Ritchie, who was turned over to Harry Edwards' unit and care, averaged two releases per month with twenty-three films (give or take) unspooled over the course of the year. These were greeted enthusiastically by audiences and exhibitors alike, as one Chicago-based theatre owner was quick to note: "I wish to say that since I started to advertise Billie Ritchie as a drawing card for Monday nights, I have found my receipts have been double what they are on other nights."[107] The Ritchie releases currently believed to be lost include the two-reel *The Avenging Dentist* (February 28), with Ritchie going to work on Henry Bergman's teeth, first with his fists and later as his patient. *Bill's New Pal* (March 3) had café waiter Ritchie and chef Bergman doing battle over cashier Selby; Ritchie ends up in the oven. *In and Out of Society* (March 7) may or may not have had an appearance by Ritchie; *Universal Weekly* listed him in the cast, but the film was headlined by Peggy Pearce and Dick Smith, who are the only two mentioned in that publication's synopsis.

Hearts and Flames (March 31) stars Ritchie as a plumber who shares a mutual infatuation with Louise Orth. He manages to mess up some connections in the basement, resulting in a fire and gas explosion. He rescues Orth from the flooded cellar by rowing her out in a bathtub. Bergman is the jealous rival, as he was in *Father Was Neutral* (May 5), vying with Ritchie for Peggy Pearce's love, much to the annoyance of her father. Ritchie

LEFT: *"The Nerve of the Man!" The cover of the January 1916 issue of* Film Fun *magazine exploited the so-called Chaplin-Ritchie "controversy."* RIGHT: *Billie Ritchie's getting ready to slap Gene Rogers, who is preoccupied with Peggy Pearce. From the ad for* Father Was Neutral *that appeared in the May 22, 1915 issue of* Motion Picture News.

is married artist Bill de Boozer who convinces Bergman's wife Pearce to disrobe and pose for him in *Bill's Blighted Career* (June 9). His wife is posing as well for a sculptor in an adjacent room, and during the requisite confrontation loses her drape, fleeing "garbed in nature's pristine beauty." Reviewers commented favorably on the concluding chase sequence, but were less than complimentary about the film's general tone. "The rest of the picture we regret to say, shows a reversion of form on the producing company's part," complained *Motion Picture News*' reviewer. "A good many of the scenes are disgusting in their suggestiveness and spoil any humor that might be in the actions of the players."[108]

Bootblack Ritchie saves wealthy heiress Orth from a group of thugs in *The Curse of Work* (July 4), and assumes the identity of a baron to crash an heiresses' reception in *A Doomed Hero* (July 18). Edwards took Ritchie to the Los Angeles Benevolent Order of Elks convention to film *Hello Bill* (August 11), which co-stars Orth and Reggie Morris, the latter hired by the studio earlier that year after several years' work primarily for Biograph.

Ritchie's initiation into the Elks is a rather humiliating affair, culminating with a forced ride on a goat. Ritchie, Lehrman, Nelson, and Selby appear in a film within the film *Life and Moving Pictures* (July 28), most likely helmed by Lehrman while Ritchie's usual director Edwards was laid up with influenza.[109] Another film likely helmed by Lehrman was *Room and Board–$1.50* (October 20), with Ritchie attempting suicide when shrewish wife Howell threatens to elope with their star boarder (Bergman), and Ritchie is a street car conductor in *Stolen Hearts and Nickels* (November 24).

Promotional ad for A Doomed Hero.

The Fatal Note (April 7) is thought lost as well, which is unfortunate since there was an incident of note attached to the screening of this film over in England. While the film's plotline with Ritchie and Pearce as newlyweds doesn't suggest anything noteworthy (aside from a climax that involves a fire hose — the first of many at L-Ko), the film evidently was funny enough to be the cause of a miraculous "cure." Manchester Corporal Robert Beck, A.S.C, was wounded while on duty as a motorcycle dispatch rider in France, leaving him both deaf and dumb. Recuperating from his wounds in Maghull Military Hospital in Liverpool, he and some fellow patients were treated to a film showing at the Palace Theatre in the village of Aintree. As the Billie Ritchie comedy *The Fatal Note* was screened, Beck was reduced to convulsive laughter that somehow, miraculously, restored both his speech and hearing.[110] Billie Ritchie: Miracle Worker!

Evidently Beck wasn't the only one tickled by the film, as one California exhibitor was quick to note in a letter to Universal: "The Marysville Theatre played 'Tillie's Punctured Romance' here on Monday and Tuesday last. Many people utilized the opportunity to compare Chaplin and Ritchie (we played Billy [sic] in 'The Fatal Note' on Tuesday). The verdict of nearly all is that Ritchie is the better comedian of the two and that his work is much cleaner."[111]

Ritchie's films and the Universal comedies in general were gaining wide acceptance and popularity at this time in war-stricken England due to the efforts of George Stevenson, former head of Universal publicity and now head of Universal's British arm, the Trans-Atlantic Film

Company, Ltd. Known across the pond as "House of Comedies," "Billy [sic] Ritchie and his L-Ko comedians; Eddie Lyons, Lee Moran and the Nestor Comedy artists have become household words in the United Kingdom," according to *Moving Picture World*.[112] It didn't hurt that the quality of the general output of Universal competitor Essanay had plummeted to such an extent that British exhibitors were refusing to sign block contracts with the firm solely to get the new Chaplin releases, his home after leaving Keystone. As a result, exhibitors were advertising Chaplin on the bill but not giving the names of his films since these were older Keystones. One annoyed reporter griped that "At a leading West End theatre I visited last night the Chaplin shown was a Keystone the age of which may be gauged from the fact that Pathé Lehrman who appeared in it left Keystone rather more than a year ago."[113]

Billie Ritchie in costume from another unidentified L-Ko Comedy. COURTESY OF JIM KERKHOFF.

A handful of Ritchie's films from 1915 are known to survive, some almost in their entirety and others as brief fragments. The Lehrman-directed *Vendetta in a Hospital* (September 8) is one of the latter, with only its climactic bomb-throwing sequence available in the brief sequence held by the Library of Congress. *Poor Policy* (April 25) survives nearly intact, wherein the beautiful bracelet Ritchie has purchased for his girl (Pearce) is swallowed by an ostrich. What to do? Ritchie sets his house ablaze in order to collect on a $500 fire insurance policy, the proceeds of which are intended to purchase a replacement bracelet. His rival — Bergman, of course — thwarts his plans, leading to Ritchie's arrest. Of primary interest in this film is the star's interaction with the ostriches at the ostrich farm. Ritchie wrestles one of them to the ground to retrieve an apple, and later engages in an extended fight with another hoping to retrieve the bracelet, grabbing it by the neck with much strenuous tugging and pulling. Several wild rides on the back of the ostrich do little to endear the comedian to the swift-running bird.

> In this picture several of the scenes are laid on an ostrich farm, which gives Billie an opportunity to spring one of his greatest and funniest surprises. Imagine if you can Billie Ritchie chasing an ostrich down a road, the bird galloping at top speed. As fast as his peculiar trot will permit him, Billie sometimes nearly comes up with great bird; sometimes falls over with a terrific bang that would send any

ABOVE: *Frame enlargement featuring Billie Ritchie from* Vendetta in a Hospital. *Gene Rogers behind and to the left.* BELOW: *Rivals Billie Ritchie and Henry Bergman, from* Poor Policy. PHOTOGRAPHS COURTESY OF LIBRARY OF CONGRESS.

ordinary individual to sleep for ever; and eventually vaults on to the ostrich's back and triumphantly rides his queer steed almost up to the camera's lens. Of course you cannot really imagine the scene. You must actually see it to believe it.[114]

Viewing this footage is somewhat unsettling armed with the knowledge that in just a few years Ritchie would suffer severe internal injuries from an ostrich attack; it's not overly surprising they would respond in such an aggressive fashion if on the receiving end of similar treatment. The ostriches aside, it would appear that a real house was burnt to the ground for the fire sequence. As passersby attempt to call in a fire alarm, Ritchie knocks one after another unconscious with one of those really huge mallets that always seem to be conveniently at hand.

Ritchie co-starred in *Love and Sour Notes* (May 19) with Frank Voss, a heavyweight comedian with former stage experience, hired by L-Ko to be the studio's resident fat man. Born Franklin H. Voss and raised in Chicago in 1890 (some sources say 1888), Voss was dubbed "Fatty" for his screen appearances. Fat and stocky but with the appearance of muscle under the girth, Voss was a rather coarse looking fellow, lacking Roscoe Arbuckle's impish attractiveness. In this film Voss is a musician much admired by Peggy Pearce, and Ritchie the jealous rival determined to bring him down. After an opening altercation initiated by Ritchie, Voss ends up pinned to the ground, his trombone's slide piercing the ground on either side of his neck. Later on, the "prodigy makes his debut" at the local church. Voss, dressed to the nines, mounts the stage along with a pianist and small choir. As he performs, Pearce, seated in the front row, makes goo-goo eyes at him. Enter Ritchie, bound and determined to wreck the poor fellow's performance. In the riotous sequence that follows,

ABOVE: *Promotional ad for* Poor Policy, *featuring Billie Ritchie riding one of those damned ostriches. From the May 11, 1915 issue of* Universal Weekly.

Ritchie first produces a lemon from his coat and, coming up with a brilliantly devious idea, goes to work on the lemon, at first fondling and rolling it between his hands, then chomping it in two, sucking, squeezing, and so forth with increasingly sadistic glee. On stage, Voss falters as juice is squirted first in one eye then the other, all the while interrupting his performance while drooling profusely all over his coat! Ritchie goes nuts on the lemon. Pearce is in tears over the ruined performance. Ritchie roars with laughter. And then Ritchie produces a pie from somewhere, and tosses it directly into Voss' face. Voss

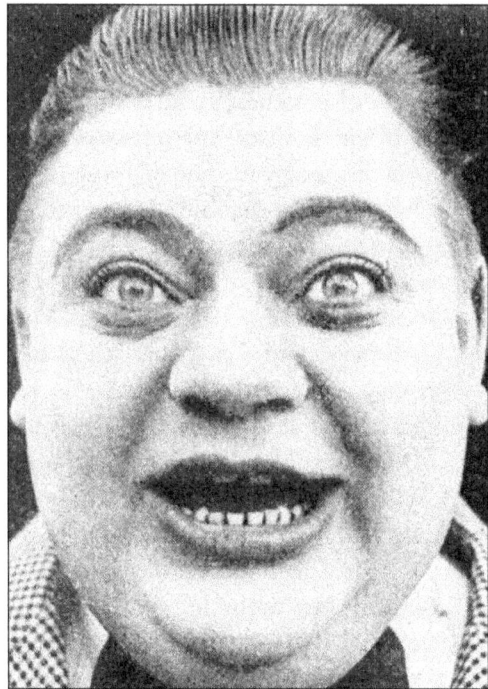

LEFT: *Franklin H. "Fatty" Voss.* RIGHT: *Gene "Pop" Rogers, as he appeared in* Silk Hose and High Pressure. COURTESY OF LIBRARY OF CONGRESS.

fires back, instead hitting some audience members. Voss goes after Ritchie, who clambers up into the church's bell tower and clings to the bell for dear life as Voss pulls its rope from below. Voss then climbs up and pursues Ritchie out onto the church's roof, which collapses under his considerable weight. Unfortunately, the print held by the Museum of Modern Art terminates just before this last scene of spectacular destruction, which a *Motion Picture News* reviewer described in tantalizing fashion: "In the finale the two rivals are reposing on the roof of a church, which caves in, in such a realistic manner that one would imagine the two actors received injuries."[115] This is a very funny film, with Ritchie's most antisocial tendencies on full display.

Ritchie wants to marry Louise Orth in *Married On Credit* (September 29), but can't come up with the two dollar fee demanded by the Reverend B. Goode (Gene Rogers). When he heads off to dig up the cash, another fellow arrives and decides to marry Orth, but he too has insufficient funds. Billie eventually gets his hands on a purse full of cash, but upon his return to the church is confronted by Orth's father (Bergman), who has an intense dislike for Ritchie. A wild chase follows, with the frustrated groom-to-be pursued by a trio of cops, his fiancé's father, and the rival. Billie falls into an open manhole, followed one-by-one by his pursuers. This finale is typical L-Ko, furiously paced with lightning-fast cuts, culminating with a string of cops dragged off by the car they attempted to stop with a trip-line. There are, of course, the numerous gunshots that fly back-and-forth across the screen in smoky streams, another staple of the L-Ko's and Keystones.

Born in 1869 or 1866, depending on whether you believe him or his death certificate, Gene "Pop" Rogers had joined L-Ko earlier in the year after twenty-five years spent on

Henry Lehrman and the Gaiety Girls Company arrive at the Hotel Harmony, from Silk Hose and High Pressure. COURTESY OF LIBRARY OF CONGRESS.

the legitimate stage. This earlier work included light opera as a comedian with both the Wilbur Opera and Boston Lyric Opera Companies, and touring the Orpheum circuit in vaudeville for six years. Having made the leap from stage to film with L-Ko, Rogers commented on his preference for the latter, saying that "I am frank enough to say that I infinitely prefer pictures. The constant variety is a relief after long runs, and helps to keep the mind young."[116] At five feet six inches tall and two hundred ten pounds, Rogers was a jovial fire-plug of a man and an effective foil for the L-Ko comedians.

Some Ritchie highlights in *Married On Credit:* when he grabs the purse full of money and is followed by the owner's dog, a humorous tug-of-war ensues between Billie and the determined mutt. Later, while Billie sits at one end of a park bench, a heavy-set woman sits down beside him. When the woman moves to the far end, Billie is catapulted through the air and lands in her lap, a flawlessly-executed gag that is a crowd pleaser. All in all, an enjoyable effort, a surviving print held by the George Eastman House.

ABOVE: *Gaiety Girl performer Louise Orth flirts with Billie Ritchie, who is preoccupied by the kid on his lap in* Silk Hose and High Pressure. COURTESY OF ROBERT ARKUS. BELOW: *Billie Ritchie shows two of the Gaiety Girls his sausages, in* Silk Hose and High Pressure. COURTESY OF LIBRARY OF CONGRESS.

Silk Hose and High Pressure (October 30, 1915) was a three-reel, Lehrman-directed epic of sorts, its middle reel a reworking of Fred Karno's old *Mumming Birds* sketch, coincidentally arriving in theaters three weeks before Chaplin's take on the sketch, *A Night in the Show*. Reel one finds former actor Ritchie and his roommate Gene Rogers — souses both — living in a flat in the Hotel Harmony. Other tenants include former actress Alice Howell and her jealous police captain husband Henry Bergman. The Gaiety Girls Company arrives at the hotel for a stay, accompanied by Henry Lehrman who, according to *Universal Weekly*, is their manager, but you'd be hard put to determine that from viewing the film. Ritchie and Rogers are introduced to one of the troupe's actresses, played by Louise Orth. The hotel's strict, steely-eyed female janitor oversees the hotel's patrons to ensure that the two sexes remain separated.

In reel two, Ritchie and Rogers go to the local theater to see the Gaiety Girls at work, and here is where we get a reworking of the *Mumming Birds* sketch. Billie flees his front row seat after continued annoyance by a nearby little girl, taking refuge in a vacant box seat. He flirts with the onstage girls, but when he finds himself competing with Rogers, who now occupies the opposing box seat, some brick throwing follows. Billie's unwelcome involvement with another performance (as Julius Caesar?) results in the reanimation of an onstage "corpse," who joins Billie back at the box seat for some swigs of booze.

Reel three takes place after the show back at the hotel. Rogers has purchased provisions for a party and leaves them in his room, heading off to find the Gaiety Girls. Ritchie returns and finds the provisions, so he ties off the legs of his pants and proceeds to stuff the bounty into his pant legs. He waddles off to find the party, his pants bulging with the contents within. Finally locating the girls, they inquire about the provisions. In one of the film's borderline-salacious moments, Billie pulls out his pants' waist and has them look down the front. The girls squeal with delight as he yanks out a long string of sausages! Howell has joined the party and ends up dancing with Billie, while elsewhere in the hotel her husband has planned a party of his own, with all of his fellow police officers in attendance. When he stumbles across Howell in Billie's arms, jealousy flares, and soon a free-for-all follows. Guns are pulled and a hailstorm of shots fired, with the melee finally spilling out onto the street. Billie mans a fire hose and blasts one after another of his pursuers into the air, each of his victims flailing helplessly at the end of the heavy streams of water. The film ends with a bang when the gasoline leaking from a police car's tank explodes, engulfing all in a conflagration of fire, smoke, water, auto parts, and gasoline.

Lehrman's filmmaking style is much in evidence here, with his typically lightning-fast, breathless editing, and several extreme close-ups of the various participants, most notably of Orth and Ritchie. The climatic gun battle between Ritchie, Bergman, and the cops is over-the-top, with the smoke trails of the dozens of bullets flying every which way filling the screen and nearly obliterating the attendant action. Subtle this film is not, but it is extremely funny in its crude, knockabout way. The final sequence, of course, is the film's pièce-de-resistance, a cleverly-executed filmed "ballet" of sorts, its dancers performing at the end of the fire hose's stream. This had been done before, of course, in a lesser fashion in *The Fatal Note,* and would be revisited the following year in *Cold Hearts and Hot Flames,* but was at its best and most outrageous here in Lehrman's film. It was audacious comedy filmmaking at its best, tagged by *Motion Picture News'* reviewer as "one of the best low comedies that the L-Ko organization has turned out."[117] A print of the film is held by the Library of Congress.

Ritchie's numerous contributions to the storyline and isolated bits of business are on full display. When Rogers attempts to wake Ritchie with the lure of alcohol, the latter crawls from his bed, following the trail of drizzled booze on all fours, sniffing and licking as he goes. Later, he attempts to navigate the hotel's staircase with his pants stuffed with foodstuffs, culminating in the lewd payoff of having the girls look down his pants at the goodies within. After Ritchie and Howell perform a very close dance at the party, Ritchie and Bergman's follow-up "dance" is punctuated by a slap to the other's face with each successive step.

Less ambitious, but to my way of thinking the funniest of the Ritchies that survive, is *Sin On the Sabbath* (December 8, 1915), wherein frustrated suitor Billie attempts to win over the father (Rogers) of his girl (Orth) by treating him to numerous rounds of drink in the back room of his pharmacy. As the two descend into blissful inebriation, a slick young rival suitor (Reggie Morris) hatches a plot to bring the drinking to an end. He slaps a "Poison" label on the bottle from which they are drinking, and then brings it to their attention with a display of horrified surprise. Ritchie's reactions to the news are delightful as he confronts his assumed upcoming demise with a string of amusing reactions. Rogers, meanwhile, heads home, followed by Reggie who reveals his prank. Rogers is at first incensed, but quickly calms down when he realizes that he still has the half-full bottle of booze in his possession. He returns to the pharmacy and sets Ritchie's mind at ease, after which they both take big, celebratory drinks. Ritchie smiles broadly as the film ends.

This is Ritchie's show, and the gyrations he goes through after learning he has been "poisoned" are priceless. Upon this revelation, Ritchie flops around on the floor in wide-eyed horror, while father flees back home, belching all the way. Ritchie gallops all over the pharmacy, pours milk from a pail into a big pan on the floor, then lies on his belly lapping it up like a dog. Reggie produces a coffin-sized box from the back room and proceeds to explain to Ritchie — now finished with the milk and the empty pan on his head — what it's for. Ritchie, seemingly in shock, is propped up on a counter stool by Reggie, who crosses Ritchie's arms across his chest, tilts his head to one side, and closes his eyes; Ritchie is now ready for death! Reggie stops a conveniently-passing mortician, sending him in to the pharmacy to give a non-responsive Ritchie his card. The mortician, joined by his associates, places a belching Ritchie into a coffin; it's a tight fit, and Ritchie's head is propped up at the far end, wide-eyed in horror. And so on, one side-splitting reaction followed by another, a tour de force performance in which the comedian digs deep into his bag of tricks.

Harry Edwards was most likely responsible for this film's direction, and he has either adopted much of Lehrman's style or had the studio's head looking over his shoulder for much of the filming. There are a generous amount of tight close-ups, first in the introductory scene with the three family members, Orth, Rogers, and his wife as portrayed by Alice Howell. Later on, Ritchie's face fills the screen as he takes his initial swigs, followed by close shots as he and Rogers smoke from a hookah (really!) with one so tight here you can clearly see Ritchie's capped front tooth! There is a generous amount of cross-cutting as well during the climax, between the events at the pharmacy and back at the family home.

Ritchie's appearance here differs somewhat from the stock photos many have come to accept as his usual garb. Decked out in the opening scene wearing a sporty, belted sports jacket with generously padded shoulders, necktie, bowler, and bamboo cane, he looks almost dapper. It doesn't hurt that for once he smiles a lot, particularly when the liquor is introduced, and it is a very nice, engaging smile. Orth, as usual, has a quirky attractiveness to her that is reminiscent of today's Chloe Sevigny, but stockier and with a much thicker neck. Howell is very amusing in her fussy minor role, trimmer in appearance than in later films and, aside from the ridiculous mess of hair tangled atop her head, rather pleasing in appearance. Rogers amuses as the blustery father, perfect for the role in that he has the appearance of a heavy drinker. As the scheming rival, Morris is adequate with his bland good looks.

Apart from the studio, Lehrman seemed to have a knack for making it into the papers, and not always in the most flattering of ways. In mid-1915 he was once again arrested for violating traffic laws when he sped past a standing street car. Patrolman Culp pursued Lehrman back to the Hotel Alexandria and cornered him inside, where Lehrman insisted he was sick and demanded that a taxi be called to drive him back to the police station. Culp instead called a patrol wagon, and Lehrman was unceremoniously driven to the station where he was charged and released on bail.[118] Alas, Lehrman had a heavy foot and was arrested yet again in December for speeding on Sunset Boulevard.[119] So he hired a chauffeur to drive him, but within a week Lehrman and his driver were pursued down a country road by a car loaded with men, one of whom was on the running board and attempted to board Lehrman's car. Fortunately the chauffeur was a better driver than Lehrman, and managed to escape the assumed robbers.[120]

Hank Mann, now L-Ko's second biggest star, appeared or starred in more than twenty films over the course of the year. In the Blystone-directed *Rough But Romantic* (March 17), Mann struggles to protect his girl Selby from the amorous advances of his father (John Rand), and this on dad's wedding day! *A Change in Lovers* (March 28) involves a watch stolen from Selby by (assumedly) Mann that eventually lands him in jail; "not a dull moment appears through the entire picture" said *Motography*'s reviewer.[121] *Moving Picture World* summarized the plot of *Under the Table* (April 14): "The prudish young wife is shocked by her husband's pictures and statues. Later she gets up a flirtation. Her parents also become entangled in affairs and several couples wind up in the same restaurant, where a rough house ensues — a very rough house."[122] Reggie Morris, Dick Smith, and Selby rounded out the couples.

Señor La Bullio (Mann) loses sweetheart Señorita Hitchy Koo (Eva Nelson) to another, only to find the boasting rival in Bullio's barber chair asking for a shave in *Shaved in Mexico* (April 28). Neither would appear to win the Señorita's hand, however, since they and two other suitors, spurned by the fickle woman, decide on a quadruple suicide at film's end! Mann rats out his two crook friends (Dick Smith and Vin Moore) in order to keep them away from his girl Howell in *A Stool Pigeon's Revenge* (May 12), a print of which survives at the UCLA Film and Television Archive. *Broken Hearts and Pledges* (May 26) is another park-based comedy with Mann fighting with both his girl Selby's dad and a pesky rival, while new-to-L-Ko Harry Gribbon plays a penniless and hungry fellow with a very faithful dog. Gribbon, who had extensive stage experience behind him, had entered film with Keystone at the beginning of 1915, only to jump ship a few months later to hook up with L-Ko.

The Child Needs a Mother (July 7), a print of which survives at the Library of Congress, co-starred newcomer Jay Howe (aka Kitty Howe) as father to three-hundred pound, sixteen year old Gwendolyn, in search of a mother to help shoulder the growing burden of child rearing. This takes him to a park and encounters with Mann, Peggy Pearce, and Gene Rogers. While not a particularly amusing film, heavyweight Frank "Fatty" Voss' antics as the overweight teen are the funniest thing here. Aside from the ridiculous visual of a grown man in a "little" girl's clothing, at one point early in the film "she" throws a hissy-fit, slowly

Hank Mann flirts with Peggy Pearce in The Child Needs a Mother. COURTESY OF LIBRARY OF CONGRESS.

demolishing a sturdy chair with bare hands. *Motion Picture News* thought more highly of the results, declaring it "One of the best of the recent L-kos."[123]

Mann and Howe play a penniless and hungry duo who set their sights on May Emory in *Love On an Empty Stomach* (August 15). Emory was Harry Gribbon's wife, and had abandoned years on stage for Keystone along with her husband; she followed him to L-Ko as well. In *A Tale of Twenty Stories* (August 22), striped pajama-clad Mann finds himself high up on the ledges of the Hotel de Bunion while fleeing a growing number of jealous husbands, Voss and Vin Moore among them. One of the earliest examples of the so-called "high and dizzy" comedies, the fragments that survive at the Museum of Modern Art reveal some edge-of-the-seat rooftop antics. *Motion Picture News* was impressed by these, stating that "The latter scenes of the picture are thrillingly uproarious, due to the manner in which the various characters fearlessly cavort on the edge of the building." The reviewer had reservations about the film as a whole, however: "When this subject was seen for review it contained many scenes that were disgusting. The censors have doubtless had these eliminated."[124]

Gertie's Joy Ride (September 5; extant) was simply an excuse for a one-reel thrill ride, with crazed Mann and passengers Selby and Morris tearing through town, culminating with a thirty mile per hour crash off the end of a pier at Ocean Park into the drink below.[125] The exciting climax and its apparent risk to the on-screen vehicle's occupants caught the attention of the *Moving Picture World*'s reviewer:

> [I]n spite of the fact that the object is to raise a laugh, it is often quickly hushed by a gasp…a closer inspection of the moving picture…proves conclusively that the occupants [of the car sailing off the pier] were real people and not dummies such as are sometimes employed by mollycoddle directors when they have similar scenes to be photographed.[126]

The film was one of L-Ko's more popular releases, and was one of the best sellers over in England with more than seventy prints sold.[127]

Mann and his boss (Dick Smith) flirt with each other's wife (Peggy Pearce and Sylvia Ashton), the four of them eventually ending up in jail for disobeying the park's rules of *No Flirting Allowed* (September 19). This leads to a battle between the two husbands that escalates to include a fellow prisoner and some on-duty cops as well, moving from cell to cell as holes are punched in one wall after another, huge blocks of stone used as bludgeons all the while. Smith produces a bomb — heaven only knows where it came from — and reduces the police station to rubble. The film, a print of which resides at the Library of Congress, is of sufficient entertainment value.

Scandal in the Family (September 22) is yet another park-based comedy of errors, this one affording Reggie Morris the opportunity to masquerade as a young lady, fooling flirtatious Mann and Dick Smith in the process. In *A Mortgage On His Daughter* (October 3), Mann uses the mortgage he holds as leverage to force Kitty Howe's permission to allow marriage to his daughter Peggy Pearce. His plans crumble when he is trumped by the holder of an even larger mortgage. *A Bath House Tragedy* (October 10) features Mann as a life guard tangling in the bath house with Dick Smith, who has made advances towards Mann's girl Peggy Pearce while his fat wife is in the steam tank trying to drop some pounds. In *Poor But Dishonest* (October 24), brick yard worker Mann is promoted to yard foreman when he rescues the daughter of the company's owner, placing him a position to fire his rival; Pearce and Smith again costar. Lovers Mann and Pearce are forced to act as butler and maid in *Disguised, But Discovered* (November 17) when their respective parents marry under the pretense of both being childless. Issues arise when innocent kisses are observed among some of the participants, and misconstrued as more lecherous and inappropriate behavior.

Mann and Pearce's relationship is threatened in *Father's First Murder* (October 31) when her father (Dan Russell) asserts his preference for a rival. This was the introduction to film for the five foot nine, two hundred seventy pound comedian Dan Russell. Born Herbert Charles Dunn in Birmingham, England in 1875, Russell's family had relocated to California soon after. Russell gravitated to the stage, appearing in vaudeville from the earliest part of the century. At first teamed with wife Blanche O'Neil in acts such as *A Matrimonial Tangle* (1906) and *The Package Party* (1907), leading up to *The Matinee Girl* later that same year which had seventeen year old Maggie Ray in a small part. The couple separated by the end of the year and Russell would take on a new partner and wife, the bit player now billed as Marguerite Ray. Ray would be rechristened as Marjorie Ray by 1912 when they co-starred in *Ma Gosse*, and would continue on the stage until she joined her husband at L-Ko later in 1917.

Sometime during the spring Lehrman was forced to slow down, "handicapped in the carrying out of his ideas during the spring by attacks of illness," as *Moving Picture World* put it.[128] By mid-1915 most of L-Ko's trustees had severed their involvement with the company. Alfred Hamberg had headed to Dallas, Texas soon after L-Ko's incorporation where he was to direct films for the Southern Feature Film Association,[129] and by the beginning of 1915 had filed a suit against Universal to recover the three weeks salary owed to him.[130] He would go on to work for D.W. Griffith in various capacities up until his death in 1922. Isadore Bernstein had severed all ties with Universal by April 1915 as well,[131] and aside from his short-lived Bernstein Film Productions — notable for introducing Stan Laurel to film with *Nuts in May* (1917) — would continue in the industry primarily as a writer through the late 1930s. Sam Behrendt, aside from the money he invested and hobnobbing with the various studios' elite, had nothing further to do with L-Ko. Which left Abe Stern, the company's business manager, to keep an eye on Lehrman. While the fate of the three former trustees' stock is unknown, it is likely that Stern and his brother Julius acquired some, if not all, of it, thereby making them the majority stockholders.

Lehrman had taken ill with inflammatory rheumatism, and was confined to bed. "There he was, flat on his back," said Victor Heerman. "At last, they put his leg in a cast, with a great wire thing over his leg. Even a sheet couldn't touch it. That was the agony that he went through"[132] During Lehrman's absence from the studio, Heerman was put to work directing and running the company. Lehrman remained in tight control, however, reviewing every foot of film that was shot and keeping tabs on the studio's day-to-day workings.

> Lehrman wanted to see every picture. We had to rent a little one-reel projector. I would go down there and try to show him multiple reels of pictures, which could take about three hours. There weren't any motors then, you cranked them by hand.... At last, the doctor said "No more of that," because Lehrman would get all excited. "What's that? Why didn't you tell him this?" And so on and so on.
>
> We had meetings down there. I was trying to keep harmony. You would go down there for an eight o'clock meeting. He would want to see so-and-so for a story talk or something, and they would stay in the Alexandria Bar, and have a few extra drinks. They would get a little tipsy. He had a weight and pulley on this thing to keep the leg from shrinking. It went down to the foot and over the pulley, and there was a sandbag at the end, situated just right.
>
> This fellow, three sheets to the wind, said, "Now, I'll tell you, Henry, what you should do, in..." and Henry said, "No, wait a minute, this..." and then leaned over the bed while he was talking. "Look," the fellow said. Then the fellow went to put his foot down, and caught it in the sandbag. Up and around and across the fellow went. You couldn't help but laugh. That was just like one of our own gags! At long last we got him out. That was the end of the conferences at the hospital.[133]

Meanwhile, the Universal's program underwent yet another shuffling of its release schedule, but the L-Ko releases emerged untouched, retaining their Wednesday slot along with a Victor and Animated Weekly offering, and Sunday slot accompanied by a Rex and Laemmle release.[134]

During Lehrman's absence, Heerman was plagued with the day-to-day operations at L-Ko. Production was nip-and-tuck, and they were experiencing great difficulties getting the films cut and sent to New York:

> Abe is saying to me, "What are we going to do? What are we going to do? We need to get these pictures off." He was upset because if your picture didn't leave for New York Tuesday night, there was no payroll in Los Angeles Saturday morning. Those on the East Coast would look at the thing, wire the money to the bank, and the checks on the West Coast would be okayed. "We can get them out," I said. Just keep him quiet.
>
> The telephone would ring, and Abe would want me to come down to the train station with the films. I told Abe, "I can't go down there and get the pictures out." I worked, I would say, from seven o'clock in the morning to nine or ten o'clock in the evening, sometimes to midnight. I had to work those hours in order to get all the company out first thing in the morning. I had to, in order to make one picture a week and to cut three more. Cutting them, I had to do at night. I think I worked two or three years before I had Sunday off. Anyway, I enjoyed it. It was tough, but a lot of fun.[135]

L-Ko's staff of directors was increased with the hiring of David Kirkland.[136] Born in San Francisco in 1878, and with several seasons of stage experience with Maude Adams and Robert Edeson,[137] Kirkland had entered the industry as an extra with the Méliès Company in 1911, followed by comedy work in Essanay's Snakeville series in late 1912 to early 1914. Moving over to Universal in late March 1914, Kirkland did some acting and directing for Nestor[138] and Joker before joining Sterling in June; Kirkland signed with L-Ko in April. After his one film for Blystone, Harry Gribbon was assigned to Kirkland's unit where he starred in a string of comedies including *Blue Blood and Yellow Backs* (June 20), *A Dismantled Beauty* (June 23), and *Avenged By a Fish* (September 26). Perhaps Gribbon's biggest contribution to L-Ko was his creation of the character Mr. Rawsberry, the randy, skirt-chasing flirt reduced to cowardice whenever he is confronted by the boyfriends or husbands of the objects of his lust. The series opened with *Park Johnnies* (June 6) wherein Rawsberry pursues Louise Orth back to her apartment building only to be confronted by irate husband Vin Moore. Rawsberry's attempts to escape by fleeing to adjacent apartments only gets him in deeper, culminating in a mass confrontation and chase that ends up back at a police station. In *The Curse of a Name* (July 21), Rawsberry is a janitor who dresses above his means, steals some money from his boss' safe and heads to a fancy hotel with intentions of picking up a girl. To that end he hires a page to bellow his name throughout the lobby and corridors; Peggy Pearce co-stars as one of the women who catches his roaming eyes. Pearce co-stars *In the Claw of the Law* (August 4) as well, where all that is required to send Rawsberry off on his amorous ways is to spot his wife in an innocent conversation with a grocery boy. After knocking out the tooth of a father who had objected to Rawsberry's advances towards his daughter, Rawsberry spots his wife again, this time with a cop, and makes a scene. Annoyed, his spouse pretends she doesn't know Rawsberry, and Rawsberry is hauled off to the station and taken before the judge, who just happens to be the same fellow whose tooth he had knocked out earlier. When things look darkest for Rawsberry, his wife appears and, the judge recognizing her as a former "acquaintance," hastily dismisses Rawsberry! *Does Flirting Pay?* (October 17) has Rawsberry hiding behind a screen door and pouncing on women who stop to browse

Harry Gribbon, in drag, isn't fooling the girls at the beach in Avenged By a Fish. COURTESY OF SAM GILL.

at a lingerie store's window, later moving in on May Emory at a restaurant only to find himself stuck with her departed companion's tab. In *The Idle Rich* (November 3), Rawsberry acquires a black eye from annoyed May Emory after confronting her in a park. Heading back to the lawn party thrown by his wife Eva Nelson, he regales the participants with a fanciful story about how he acquired the shiner. Which they all believe, that is, until Emory herself turns out to be the party's guest of honor. Rawsberry is a department store floorwalker in *Mr. Flirt in Wrong* (August 25), who heads to the beach and poses as a bathing suit-clad millionaire in his ongoing struggle to attract members of the opposite sex. Emory is one of the objects of his affections and, once again, delivers a staggering blow, this time to Rawsberry's chin. *Mr. Flirt in Wrong* is notable in that it was the film debut of Charles Winninger in the role of Rawsberry's boss, who pursues the hapless fellow, guns blazing, after advances were made to his wife. This time Rawsberry ends up in a bathhouse trapped with two bears recently escaped from the zoo, along with their unconscious keeper!

Lehrman must have thought he found the next great star when he signed the Wisconsin-born, thirty-year-old Charles Winninger. A member since childhood in his parents' touring vaudeville act, the Winninger Family Variety Company, along with his five brothers and one sister, Winninger spent later years in stock and repertory companies as a single where the short, chubby actor took on roles ranging from slapstick to the dramatic. His lucky break came in 1910 when lead Lee Kohlmar broke his leg and Winninger became the last minute replacement in Lew Fields' musical comedy *The Yankee Girl*. Here he met

LEFT: *Director David Kirkland.* ABOVE: *Harry Gribbon as "Mr. Rawsberry" getting the worst of it in* Does Flirting Pay? *From the March 1916 issue of* Film Fun.

and later married co-star Blanche Ring, and leads followed over the next few years in the companies headed by his wife,[139] including *The Wall Street Girl* (1912) and *When Claudia Smiles* (1914). At Louise Orth's insistence, Lehrman first met Winninger in Los Angeles where he was appearing with his wife in the sketch *Oh, Papa!* Lehrman was so taken with the fellow and his credentials that he hired him at $250 a week, or at least according to Linda Arvidson.[140] Now with L-Ko, it was announced that Lehrman would personally direct all of the two- and three-reel comedies in which the well known vaudeville star would appear.[141] Lehrman took Winninger, Gertrude Selby, and a dozen others to the mountains at Arrowhead for a two month stay, planning to complete at least five films there while more construction went on at the growing studio.[142]

Aside from *Mr. Flirt in Wrong*, Winninger appeared in two additional films during 1915. *Lizzie's Shattered Dreams* (December 12) had country girl Alice Howell sheltered from her cruel stepfather by two city strangers who have less than honorable intentions; assumedly one of them was portrayed by Winninger. He had the lead as *The Doomed Groom* (December 19), getting cold feet on the day he is to be married — to Fatty Voss! Winninger would have one more starring role in early 1916 that will be touched on in a few pages.

Another addition to the roster of comedians was twenty year old Ray Griffith, on stage for a good portion of his young life until his vocal chords were damaged, followed by stints with a circus, on the vaudeville stage as a dancer, as a pantomimist with a French troupe, and in the U.S. Navy. While it has been rumored that he may have had some initial bit parts at both Vitagraph and Kalem earlier in the year, Griffith's first known credits are at L-Ko, first in (unconfirmed) bits in Hank Mann's *Gertie's Joy Ride* and *Scandal in the Family*, followed by his first credited role in *Under New Management* (October 13; extant).

LEFT: *Raymond Griffith.* RIGHT: *Director Craig Hutchinson.*

Here he co-stars with Fatty Voss as a pair of office clerks both smitten by stenographer Selby, who in turn has her sights on boss Gene Rogers only to run afoul of his wife Alice Howell. Griffith's comedic talents were evident, and he was quickly cast in five additional films released through the end of the year. *Tears and Sunshine* (October 27) starred Gene Rogers and Griffith as father and son whose collective grief over the loss of a loved one is back-burnered when they find that neighboring mother and daughter Alice Howell and Getrude Selby are in the same position, grieving the loss of Howell's late hubby. In *Ready for Reno* (November 21; extant), Griffith portrays Peggy Pearce's short-tempered husband, at odds with Dan Russell who has made advances towards Pearce after stomping out on his endlessly-complaining wife. Griffith and Russell are rivals at odds once again in *A Saphead's Revenge* (December 5) when the latter takes Peggy Pearce to a dance; Griffith schemes to keep them from winning a dancing competition. *Blackmail in a Hospital* (December 15) co-stars Griffith as a crutches-bound patient and Pearce as the hospital's pretty young nurse whom all the patients are in love with. *A Scandal at Sea* (December 29; extant) rounded out the year, this time with Griffith flirting with Louise Orth, the wife of gruff ship captain Russell. These last four films, it should be noted, were all directed by newcomer Craig Hutchinson. A former story editor at Keystone for the previous two years, the twenty-three year old was new to direction with L-Ko; Hutchinson's sole earlier credit for the studio was Hank Mann's *Father's First Murder*.

A few of the remaining release slots were filled with leads other than Ritchie, Mann, Gribbon, and Griffith. Fatty Voss was the headliner of *Itching for Revenge* (August 8) and *A Game of Love* (September 1), but while the title of *Fatty's Infatuation* (February 24) would suggest another Voss vehicle, it instead featured Willard Gardner as young Fatty, infatuated with thirteen year old actress Gertrude Short in her sole film for L-Ko. Short, it might as well be noted, went on to marry silent comedy director Scott "Perc" Pembroke, thirteen years her senior, and continued with acting well into the 1940s. *Easy Money* (March 10) and *Too Many Bachelors* (March 21) co-starred Peggy Pearce and Dick Smith, while *Cupid and the Scrub Lady* (November 7) and *From Beanery to Billions* (December 22) provided leads for Alice Howell. Gertrude Selby was the star of *Zip and His Gang* (February 7, with a plot that sounds very similar to that of *The Gangsters*)[143] and co-starred with Reggie Morris and Fatty Voss in *Greed and Gasoline* (December 26). This latter film also co-starred Dave Morris — no relation to Reggie — a comedian with a vast amount of stage and film work already under his belt. Having taken an initial stab in the industry with Pathé in 1911, he hooked up with Biograph two years later followed by work for Klaw and Erlanger, Keystone, and Kalem. *Greed and Gasoline* is his first confirmed film for L-Ko, and would be followed by a dozen more films over the better part of a year before moving over to work at Al Christie's studio. Most of these L-Ko's would co-star Gertrude Selby and Reggie Morris as well.

Lizzie's Watery Grave (December 1) is notable in that it was one of only two films that both Paul Jacobs and Olive Johnson starred in for L-Ko. Former Powers director Harry Matthews was originally slated in July to direct these children's subjects,[144] but by September it was announced that Victor Heerman would direct.[145] The other was *Little Billy's School Days* (April 23, 1916) with Fatty Voss playing one of Jacobs' classmates, and the completion of these would mark the point where Jacobs would transition from shorts to features, entering a more profitable stay with Lasky where he appeared in more than a half dozen films including *The Heart of Nora Flynn*, *The Valiants of Virginia* (both 1916), *Unconquered*, and *The Tides of Barnegat* (both 1917). With a few other films for Essanay and Selig thrown into the mix, Jacobs retired from the industry in July 1918 at the ripe old age of eight after appearing in Colleen Moore's *Little Orphant Annie* (1918). His only connection with the industry in the years that followed was as a writer for various Hollywood publications. Years later and far removed from the numerous roles of his childhood, Jacobs explained the risk of youthful stardom to interviewer Sam Gill:

> It wasn't until I was well into it that I began to be endlessly apprised of what was presumed to be an exalted position for a child star. I had no idea what any of that meant. All small children, when they are given consistent and intense attention, presume that they must be special. I took it for granted that I was special because everybody said so.[146]

A film reviewed and promoted as *Beach Birds* is the one anomaly of 1915 in that it is unclear what its actual release title was or, for that matter, if it even saw release. Originally scheduled for September 19 release, much of the confusion arises from Universal alternately listing cast members in ads and synopses as either Hank Mann, Peggy Pearce, and Fatty Voss or as Louise Orth, Henry Bergman, and Dick Smith. Given these two groups of cast members it is reasonably safe to assume that it was eventually released as either *A Bath House Tragedy* (October 10) which was promoted as having Mann and Pearce in the cast, but *Avenged By a Fish* (September 26) is a possibility, but only Bergman stars in this latter film along with Harry Gribbon and May Emory. There is overlap in the synopses of the three titles, but each is sufficiently vague that it is impossible to make a final determination.

LEFT: *Promotional ad for the short-lived Pyramid Comedies, featuring Chaplin "look-alike" Ray Hughes. From the January 12, 1918 issue of* Moving Picture World. RIGHT: *Billie Ritchie and Henry Lehrman return from a trip to New York, January 1916.* COURTESY OF LISA ROBINS.

And that's assuming that *Beach Birds* was possibly released under a new title. To add to the confusion was another comedy actually released two years later with this same title. Starring a little known and very Chaplinesque vaudevillian named Ray Hughes, short-lived Pyramid Comedies managed to film four comedy shorts released in 1918. *Beach Birds* was accompanied by *In and Out*, *Love and Lunch*, and *Beauties and Bombs* before the company folded and Hughes faded into obscurity.

With the arrival of 1916, Los Angeles was hit with its first snowfall in twenty-five years, and the comedy companies were quick to take advantage of it.[147] Operations at L-Ko were now functioning like a well-oiled machine, and a second, much larger stage had been erected to accommodate the four production units, over three hundred feet in length and seventy feet deep.[148] L-Ko leased the balance of the old Universal studio at Gower and Sunset, and moved their offices into the building formerly occupied by the Universal.[149] While a number of the weekly releases were still a single reel in length, the number of two-reelers produced had been growing steadily. Lehrman had made a trip to New York in October 1915 to secure the services of Stanley C. Kingsbury as his special representative in that city. A former showman, Kingsbury had years of experience as a rep at different times for Warners and Famous Players, both in New York and Toronto.[150] The goal, of course, was to drum up new licensees of the L-Ko output.

Charles Winninger's highest profile film for the studio was released in early 1916, but may have been delayed from the previous year due to censorship issues. Several years

LEFT: *Detail from Paul Émile Chabas'* September Morn. RIGHT: *Comedian Gale Henry spoofed* September Morn *in the March 10, 1917 issue of* Moving Picture Weekly.

earlier in 1912, French painter Paul Émile Chabas had executed what was perhaps his most famous piece titled *September Morn*. The subject was a nude young girl modestly posed standing ankle-deep in a body of water, and the picture eventually made it to our shores where it was consigned to the likes of calendar art. That is until May 1913, when future publicist Harry Reichenbach managed to convince Anthony Comstock, head of the New York Society for the Suppression of Vice, that the picture was obscene and immoral. It immediately became a *succès de scandale*, and sold briskly for years to come. Not one to miss out jumping on the coattails of a newsworthy event, Lehrman threw together a story that would, with a play of words, reference the "notorious" painting and, perhaps, entice audiences with the hope that the on-screen antics would be of a similar titillating nature. *A September Mourning* (February 6, 1916) was the result, co-starring Winninger and Ray Griffith as novice artists who decide to try their hand at painting "September Morn," but encounter difficulty in finding models willing to pose for them. Arriving at a park, the two novice artists stumble upon a group of lovely young ladies — Gertrude Selby among them — performing Greek dances in diaphanous costumes. Having found their "models," the artists set to work, only to be interrupted by a picture-snapping fellow who crowds their space. A dispute and tussle follows, cut short when the cops arrive and declare the dancers' costumes to be indecent. The girls rebel at this, and the cops end up in the lake. Lehrman has a role as a disgruntled art dealer, who shows up at the park wielding a pistol. All hell breaks loose but the girls, seemingly unfazed, continue to dance.

Heerman was pressed into service once again, and commented on the making of this film:

> When Lehrman got well, the doctor said what he should do is go up to Arrowhead Springs and take the mud baths. They took him up in an ambulance…. So immediately, Lehrman said "Alright, I'll take Winninger, Ray Griffith and Gertie Selby," this and so-and-so and so-and-so and…." He left nothing for the four other companies.
>
> Well, here we are running around trying to make pictures with extras. I don't think anybody got five dollars a day in those pictures. They were all three dollar people. Couple of days later, Lehrman's up there and calls, "Send me dancing girls." I said "What do you mean, dancing girls?" He says, "You know. I'm going to do a picture of an artist, and I want wood nymphs jumping and playing." So I said "Alright, well, when do you want them?" He said, "Right away, right away." I said "Well, I don't know any wood nymph dancing girls." I said "I'll call you back. I'll call you tonight."
>
> I talked it over with everyone and someone said, "Well, that Denishawn school, why don't you go down and talk to them?" I went to Denishawn. The school was down on Sixth Street overlooking the city, just where it went down the hill, between Sixth and Seventh. I went down there and talked to him [Ted Shawn]. Of course, coming at this time, it was winter. I suppose I had on a cop's uniform. If it was raining and you didn't have a raincoat, you'd go into wardrobe and take a cop's uniform or anything that would keep you dry.
>
> So I had quite a time talking to them, but there were two or three mothers or grandmothers down there, and this one woman said "Why yes." She then asked another, "Do you want to do it?" "Why yes, I think it would be fun for the girls." So everything was all set. I said "I'll pick you up and put you on a train tomorrow." So I called Lehrman and said, "I'm bringing up the girls on the train tomorrow. Get some cars to meet us." He said "Alright."
>
> The next day we left. We had Phoebe Brown, who worked with Ivan Bankoff, who was a great little Russian dancer. He took her under his wing and the next thing you know, she was ballerina at the Metropolitan in New York. We had a girl named Pearce who seemed the best of the lot. I don't know what ever happened to her. And there was Carol Dempster who afterward became a Griffith star. And a couple of others, who were all in this group.
>
> By golly, a couple of days later, Lehrman is up there taking these mud baths, and he's dancing, of course with a limp, but nevertheless, he's dancing.[151]

"The censors objected to the costumes and to the lack of costumes," said an article in *Film Fun*. "After a week or two of wrangling over the matter, they compromised. The censors cut out a couple of scenes that did not appeal to them, and the show went on."[152] Judging from the stills that survive, it is difficult to see just what all the fuss was about, but those were different times. "This, of course, is not in the best of tone, but it escapes any pronounced vulgarity" commented *Moving Picture World*.[153] It would prove to be Winninger's last film before returning to the stage — for a while, at least — reportedly because his blue eyes didn't register on the orthochromatic film used at the time.[154] Winninger would make a few sporadic appearances during the twenties once the more forgiving panchromatic film was introduced, but would become a regular on screen as a character actor in sound films with a career that would last up until 1960.

Aspiring artist Charles Winninger can't get a lot accomplished with those Greek dancers swarming around him, in A September Mourning.

Billie Ritchie continued to be L-Ko's big draw, appearing in another fifteen films throughout the year. He took ill in March, however, and was out of the studio for a month while he recuperated. "He has just returned to work," it was reported in early April, "but looks thin,"[155] his month-long absence resulting in a dearth of Ritchie releases from May into July. Ritchie was feeling good enough a few weeks later to commit to joining a bunch of other Universal personalities to take turns occupying a booth at the First National Motion Picture Exposition, held mid-May at New York's Madison Square Garden.[156]

Some of Ritchie's releases for the year were single-reel quickies, such as *Twenty Minutes at the Fair* (February 20; extant) and *A Friend, But a Star Boarder* (March 26), both co-starring Peggy Pearce; *A Meeting for a Cheating* (April 19) and *Billie's Waterloo* (June 7; extant), both co-starring Eva Nelson; *A Bold Bad Breeze* (July 19), and *She Wanted a Ford*

(October 22) appearing opposite Gertrude Selby. Reviews for *Twenty Minutes at the Fair*, which was filmed at the San Diego Fair, questioned its tastefulness: "[T]he action is altogether much too risque for a mixed audience. A model leg is brought into play, and it introduces much that is a little offensive"[157] and "Particular audiences will not like this because of the vulgarity of many of the bits of small business."[158] Gene Rogers is *A Friend, But a Star Boarder*, so taken with Ritchie's wife Pearce that he sets out to feed her lies and half-truths about her hubby. In *A Meeting for a Cheating*, Ritchie asks friend Dan Russell

The L-Ko Motion Picture Company posed for a group photo on April 22, 1916. Left to right, front row seated: Editor Charles Hochberg second from left, Jack White, Billy Bevan (straw boater), Lucille Hutton, director Jack Blystone, and Billie Ritchie (tie and flat cap) after the two women to the right of Blystone. Dan Russell seated on ground in front of Ritchie, and Bert Roach seated on ground at far right. Fatty Voss in back row with dark hat and bow tie, dwarfing the others. Is that Lehrman in the far back with the flat cap and bow tie? COURTESY OF MARC WANAMAKER AND BISON ARCHIVES.

to pose as a burglar to teach wife Nelson a lesson about leaving her jewelry lying about. Ritchie attempts to blackmail philanderer Gene Rogers into letting him marry daughter Nelson in *Billie's Waterloo*,[159] and attempts to impress Gertrude Selby in *She Wanted a Ford* by taking her for a ride in his engineless jalopy, locomotion provided by Dan Russell and friends hiding under the hood!

In *A Bold Bad Breeze*, Ritchie falls in love with the married woman next door, much to the annoyance of her jealous husband. The woman was portrayed by actress Lucille Hutton, and her husband by the Australian comic Billy Bevan, both of whom had been hired earlier in the year. The single-reel was helmed by first-time director Noel Smith.

One of the film's stunts was a bit riskier than in previous films, and Ritchie was reportedly offered a stunt double, a first for him at L-Ko. "I certainly can do anything that anybody that looks like me can, so here goes" he was supposed to have replied.[160] If accurate, it may have been a stance he would later come to regret.

Ritchie's two-reelers for 1916 included *Billie's Reformation* (January 9), *Knocks and Opportunities* (January 26), *False Friends and Fire Alarms* (March 8), *Scars and Stripes Forever* (March 22), *Bill's Narrow Escape* (April 26), *His Temper-Mental Mother-In-Law*

LEFT: *Director Noel Smith.* RIGHT: *Another stunt from* A Bold Bad Breeze *had four cops dangling precariously from the side of a high structure.* COURTESY OF ROBERT JAMES KISS.

(August 16), *Crooked from the Start* (September 6), *Cold Hearts and Hot Flames* (September 20), and *Where is My Wife?* (November 22). Ritchie's wife harps endlessly about their money woes in *Billie's Reformation*, but matters only get worse when he inherits a half million dollars and falls for a blonde (Louise Orth); this would be Henry Bergman's last film for the studio before joining Charlie Chaplin over at Mutual for what would prove to be a long and fruitful relationship.

Ritchie puts ingratitude on display in *Knocks and Opportunities* when he is rescued from near-death by a young man (Reggie Morris), only to begin a campaign of lies about the fellow in hopes of winning over his fiancé, played by Louise Orth. *False Friends and Fire Alarms* is an anomaly, with Ritchie for once playing an honest character, a jockey who wins the big, fixed race, the heart of his girl (Peggy Pearce), and the gratitude of her oil magnate dad (Gene Rogers). And in *Bill's Narrow Escape*, Ritchie is saddled with a wife (Eva Nelson) who dreams of becoming a movie star, the opportunity arising when a film director (Gene Rogers) asks for permission to shoot on their front lawn. L-Ko constructed "an attractive California bungalow" across the street from the studio that would shortly be burnt to the ground for one of the film's climatic scenes.[161] Ritchie is at his mean-spirited best in *His Temper-Mental Mother-In-Law*, having his pesky mother-in-law tied to her bed by some hired thugs, then dragging the house down to the railroad tracks and delighting as a locomotive roars by and demolishes the place. Not surprisingly, he receives his comeuppance when he climbs to the top of the engine for a better look at his handiwork but inadvertently sits on the steam pipe and is blown sky high. Motorcycle cop Ritchie has a nice little income generator in *Crooked from the Start*, accepting bribes

Eva Nelson's about to give it to hubby Billie Ritchie in Bill's Narrow Escape.

from speeders. Romantic friction erupts when he falls for speeder Gertrude Selby, who is also the object of affection of Ritchie's chief, played by Dan Russell. Hotel proprietor Ritchie has a wandering eye in *Where is My Wife?* and finds himself in deep trouble when he attempts to assist a married tenant with preparations for her bath. In true L-Ko fashion, he finds himself afloat in a runaway tub.

Ritchie starred in a three-reeler in 1916 as well, the amusing *Live Wires and Love Sparks* (March 19) which not only survives but has received more exposure than any of his other L-Ko's due to its presence on David Shepard's *Slapstick Encyclopedia* set of silent comedy releases. Here he is Billie Steele, married to Eva Nelson and plagued with a family of four rambunctious children and a very sleepy teenage daughter. The pretty young roomer across the hall (Peggy Pearce, whom he calls "Goldilocks" throughout) catches his eye, so as one would expect Billie schemes to invite her to his company's masked ball. His wife gets wind of this and shows up in Pearce's place hidden behind a mask and wig of long blond curls, fooling her unsuspecting hubby. It isn't long before Billie learns the awful truth, while his enraged wife enlists the aid of the other male attendees in a bloodthirsty pursuit. The grand finale takes place with Billie attempting an escape via the telephone wires high above the street, pursuers behind him on the wires as well as on the ground below. This sequence is flawlessly executed, without a hint of artifice. Unfortunately, the surviving print is missing the final few feet of action, but the synopsis in *Moving Picture Weekly* offers an enticing glimpse at what we are missing: "Telephone repair wagons roll

Lucille Hutton attempts to break up a fight between hubby Billie Ritchie and her mother, played by Margaret Joslin. From His Temper-Mental Mother-In Law.

up and attempt to rescue the stranded wire dancers, all of whom take fearsome tumbles to the ground. There is no switching of scenes here. The actors actually tumble from the telephone wires to the ground as the camera does a vertical top to bottom panorama and catches them as they smash holes in the turf."[162] *Moving Picture World*'s reviewer offered an objective assessment of the spectacular climax, stating that the "scramble across roof tops and telegraph wires in the last reel contains some really sensational acrobatic stunts."[163]

While *Live Wires and Love Sparks* might have fared better as a taut two-reeler, the result is still very enjoyable fun. Ritchie's philandering knows no bounds, and as he digs himself a deeper hole through his unrestrained antics at the masked ball, we watch with mounting amusement and confidence that he will, as always, receive his comeuppance, and in spectacular Lehrman style. (Lehrman has been credited in a few unofficial sources as the director of this film, but that has not been confirmed by any contemporary sources.) One brief but amusing bit occurs as Ritchie's annoyed wife hauls him back into their flat, carrying him in the air by the back of his vest, one-handed (via wirework), his arms and legs flailing ineffectually. Much of the film's humor derives from the mayhem created by his four young children, and his unsympathetic treatment of his kids is almost understandable. Adorned with jet black eyebrows and oversized slap shoes, some of them don small bowler hats and little canes when they head outside. As for the unknown actress who played his Olive Oyl-ish teen-aged daughter, she provides some of the film's funnier moments, shuffling about half asleep throughout, her face disappearing behind her frequent, cavernous yawns. And when she inadvertently intrudes upon her father's amorous advances towards the neighbor, one of Ritchie's backward kicks promptly propels her from the room. Gene Rogers provides additional laughs as a new acquaintance of Ritchie's who attends the ball dressed in a Scottish kilt, only to lose it to another attendee (Joe Murphy) who is scrambling to cloak himself. Ritchie, true to form, has stolen the fellow's outfit to further disguise himself from the growing number of others who are annoyed with him.

Billie Ritchie dances with his unmasked wife Eva Nelson in the three-reel Live Wires and Love Sparks. COURTESY OF ROBERT ARKUS.

"Billie Ritchie is seen to very good advantage in this subject," stated the *Motion Picture News* reviewer, "in fact to better advantage than he has been in many of past L-Ko subjects."[164]

Cold Hearts and Hot Flames is one of the other L-Ko's that survives in a two-reel print held by the Museum of Modern Art, and it is a corker! Ritchie is in love with Gladys Tennyson, daughter of hotel proprietor Vin Moore. Moore can't stand Ritchie, but has a change of heart when the mortgage holder shows up threatening to close down the place, and is appeased when Ritchie writes him a check for the full amount. Gratitude reverts to hatred when the check bounces, but Ritchie squirms out of this by fooling Moore into thinking that Ritchie will soon come into a huge inheritance. Moore sets aside his plans to burn the place down to collect on a $50,000 insurance policy, and hastily sets up a wedding between his daughter and his soon-to-be-benefactor. Unfortunately, Moore's set-aside plans are put back in motion by a playful cat, and the service is interrupted when the place catches fire. The finale is another L-Ko whirlwind, with fire hoses once again put into creative play, tearing the skirt from a female observer, aiding as well as hindering the firemen attempting to stanch the blaze, and lending a final assist to Ritchie with his rescue of Tennyson. The minister is quickly put back to work to complete the marriage, but the service is cut short when the furnace blows up (a very clumsy miniature). The trio is last seen atop a table blown sky high, three faint haloes appearing above their heads! Ritchie is atypically attired here, more formally dressed in top coat, top hat, and gloves

Billie Ritchie, barely tolerant of his four young children and perpetually yawning, Olive Oyl-ish teenage daughter, from Live Wires and Love Sparks. COURTESY OF ROBERT ARKUS.

with striped backs. He is dapper in appearance, well groomed with perhaps a more modest-sized mustache and hair grayed at the temples.

Aside from the extensive use of the "Lehrman" fire hoses, *Cold Hearts and Hot Flames* is full of numerous other "throw-away" gags that help maintain its brisk pace. Ritchie does battle with an oversized fly in a lengthy sequence, and comes to the rescue of a woman and her young daughter, both floating above the room, their skirts filled with the hot air from an enormous heating grate below. Another heating grate provides one of the film's more risque (by 1916 standards) shots, with Tennyson's skirt billowing seductively about her like a hot air balloon while considerable rivulets of sweat streak her pretty face. During the film's climax, Moore's rear end is singed in the fire, and relief is provided by the water running in the gutter in which Moore scoots about, dog-like, attempting to douse his butt. The film's most callous bit — though admittedly very funny — involves a parasol-wielding woman who keeps getting in the way of the arriving fire trucks. When she won't move, they simply run her over! Jack Blystone was credited with the direction of this one, and it is evident that he has learned well at the school of Lehrman. Too well, perhaps; Blystone would soon claim credit for a lot of other recent L-Ko's, and in the most public of forums.

All was not well in the industry, however, given its increasingly fractious relations with the city of Los Angeles. *Moving Picture World* summed it up thusly:

> For some time the film men have realized, and have had to realize, for their own benefit, that the city of Los Angeles does not appreciate its motion picture industry. This is an astonishing statement to make — astonishing when you consider that the industry brings to the city approximately $20,000,000 a year and work for 20,000 people. It looks however from past experiences and especially from recent activities that such a complaint would be justified. Producers complain of everlasting interference from the city with petty regulations; permits for this and that; interfering with the taking of pictures and the building of sets.
>
> And this is not all! The censorship matter is still on the boards, and there is no real immediate action being taken — the meddlers still try to cut the essence from the films.
>
> The last kick — the straw that fractured the back of the camel, is the heralded and talked of vicious and unjust attacks on the moral conditions in the studios by a publicity-hungry clergyman in the "chemically pure" city.[165]

Lehrman and his fellow business men resurrected the Motion Picture Producers' Association and finally got around to incorporating it in an attempt to come to terms with the city. They maintained an air of diplomacy in the meetings that followed while letting it be known that both the cities of San Francisco and San Diego were attempting to entice a number of the studios to relocate, and in some instances with attractive inducements. The city panicked at the prospect of the potential loss of revenues and jobs — it was estimated later in the year that the industry spent $35,000,000 annually[166] in the city — and an agreement was quickly hammered out. The result was the Motion Picture Conservation Association, with the city agreeing to commit to a climate of fair play — the cessation of hassling by do-gooders, moralists, newspapers, permits and fees — in return for the producers slapping the title "Made in Los Angeles" on most of their upcoming releases. That, and for staying put, of course.[167]

Lehrman and his fellow filmmakers had another objective as well. The industry had created a National Board of Censorship back in 1909 that was intended to ward off any sort of legal film censorship through self-regulation. The growing consensus was that this board was too liberal and self-serving, resulting in the House of Representatives Sixty-Fourth Congress hearings in mid-January 1916 before the Committee on Education. The hearings were to discuss a bill to create a new division of the Bureau of Education, to be known as The Federal Motion Picture Commission. Its mission was to control the content of film, a prospect that terrified Hollywood. Lehrman and a number of other prominent directors signed their names to a group statement protesting such a commission:

> As a moving-picture director we know them to be made with greater regard for public morality. In consequence cleaner than average newspaper and least need of outside censorship. Proposed bill imposes tax which must ultimately fall on public. We protest passage of bill.

Billie Ritchie, Gertrude Selby, Alice Howell, and a number of other actors and actresses joined in to affix their signatures to a similar statement that "earnestly protest passage of censorship bill."[168] This led to the film industry establishing the National Association of the Motion Picture Industry later that year setting up its own guidelines and standards with the renewed hope of avoiding any sort of external censorship. The association lasted until 1922 when it was replaced by the Motion Picture Producers and Distributors Association (MPPDA) in the wake of several unfortunate high profile industry scandals.[169]

There was a shuffling of directors in early 1916 when L-Ko lost two of its workhorses to other studios. Harry Edwards headed over to Kalem in March to direct Lloyd Hamilton and Bud Duncan in their popular Ham and Bud series,[170] while Craig Hutchinson headed elsewhere at Universal to direct for several other companies;[171] he would return to L-Ko later in the year. Guy Hedlund, an actor since 1906 primarily with Biograph, was reported to have directed a few comedies for L-Ko before his termination in April, but this has not been confirmed.[172] A similar, unconfirmed report had former Keystone director Edwin P. Nolan credited with some direction at L-Ko before departing for Continental Players in late March-early April.[173]

Meanwhile, Victor Heerman, who had only been connected with the direction of the Paul Jacobs films, was less than thrilled by Lehrman's return. He complained about the experience decades later:

> Lehrman came back, and I had just finished this picture, and he looked at it, and said, "It's fine." When I saw the film, the title came on, "Directed by Henry Lehrman," I said, "What the hell is this? You weren't even in the studio when I made this, and you put your name on it." He said, "You should be proud that I'm willing to put my name on your picture." That was the end![174]

Heerman's response to Lehrman's claim of direction seems somewhat petty, and suggests that there was something more left unsaid. This was, after all, standard operating procedure at L-Ko during Lehrman's stewardship, and should have come as no surprise to Heerman; Lehrman was the studio's director general, and as such he oversaw and approved everything that left the place with the L-Ko name on it. Heerman should instead have been grateful for the opportunity to direct, which opened numerous doors for him in the years to come.

Heerman's dissatisfaction lingered into 1916, however, and when the staff was ordered to work Sundays, Heerman refused and was fired sometime in June.[175]

> Abe [Stern] would give me twenty-five dollars a reel for every picture I made. He says, "Don't ever tell Henry. Don't ever tell Henry." So Lehrman came back and felt I should work every Sunday. I said I was not going to work any more Sundays for a time. He said, "You can't disrupt the studio." I said, "Well, I disrupt the studio all night long cutting these pictures, making these stories and writing

these titles. Doesn't that count for anything?" He said, "You work tomorrow." I said, "I won't work tomorrow." I said that was it. Everybody was at the studio and I didn't show up. The next day he said, "You're fired for insubordination." I said "That's fine." I left, and that was that.[176]

Sennett snapped him up to direct for Keystone.[177]

Lehrman's departure from Keystone two years earlier and the subsequent competition he provided, first with Sterling and now with L-Ko, still stuck in Sennett's craw. If the arguable quality of the output and the performers therein were not enough to distinguish the output of the two, Sennett had in August of the previous year switched to an all two-reel and feature policy, one that L-Ko wouldn't adapt until May of 1917 with the release of *Tom's Tramping Troupe* (May 9, 1917). As a dig at L-Ko and other competitors whom he all felt were shamelessly stealing the Keystone style, Sennett adopted a verse from Rudyard Kipling's *Mary Glouster* as his company's new motto:

> *They copied all they could follow,*
> *But they could not copy our mind,*
> *And we left them sweating and swearing,*
> *A year and a half behind.*[178]

Sennett's new motto failed to gain traction, and little more would be heard or seen of it.

Alice Howell, Ray Griffith, and Dan Russell were all well served during the year, both as headliners and in supporting roles. Howell was most prominent, with fifteen films to her credit, among them *Flirtation A La Carte* (January 16), *Saving Susie from the Sea* (January 19), *Her Naughty Eyes* (February 9; a rehashing of the old plot about an involuntarily winking eye and the problems it causes with the opposite sex), and *Dad's Dollars and Dirty Doings* (February 27). Jack Blystone assumed the direction of the comedienne with *The Double's Trouble* (April 16), and would remain in that position for all of her subsequent films including *Pirates of the Air* (June 28), with its midair plane-to-plane transfer:

> The stellar feature of this rapidly moving L-Ko number is an aeroplane chase. Two machines take part and the passengers think nothing of sprawling all over the wings and dropping from one to another. Now anyone, with half a brain can tell that such action could never transpire on real aeroplanes, and the fact that the machines are palpably products of the L-Ko property department does not detract from the credit that should go to the director for attempting such a difficult bit of comedy. He has succeeded in making these scenes funny although the element of realty is not pronounced.[179]

Blystone would also direct Howell in *Unhand Me, Villain* (August 9; promoted pre-release as *The Villain Still Pursued Her*), with a character memorably named Lena Genstyou, and *Tattle-Tale Alice* (December 1). Howell's demonstrated ability to carry a film resulted in a handful of three-reelers as well, *Lizzie's Lingering Love* (July 25), *Tillie's Terrible Tumble* (September 12), and *Alice in Society* (November 7) among them.

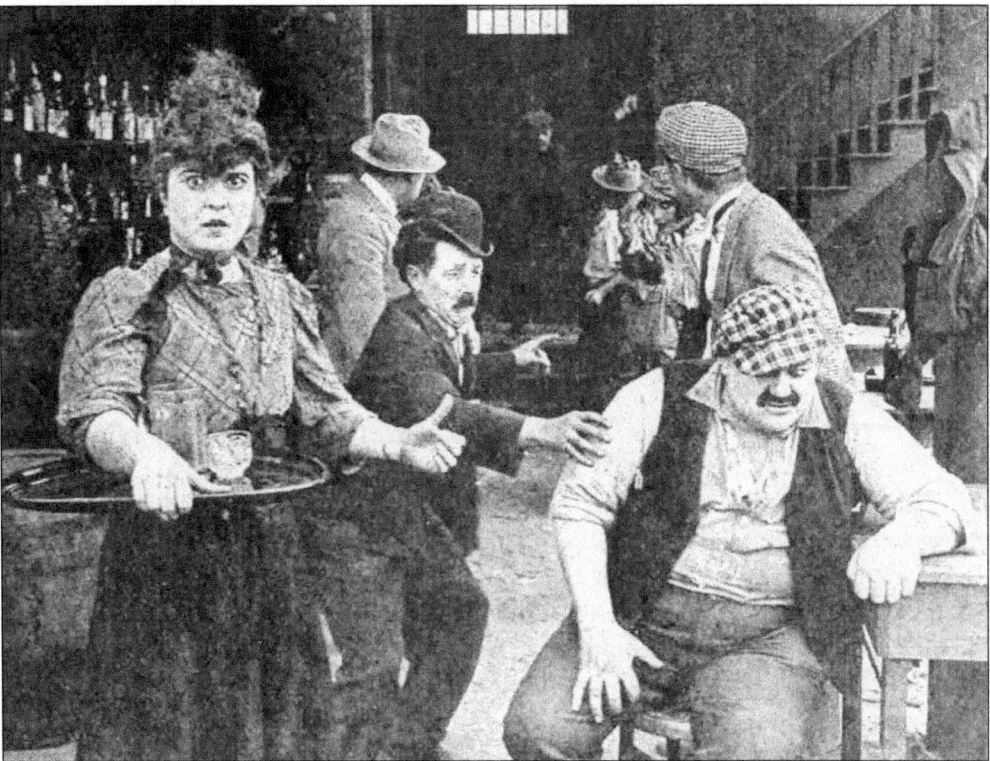

ABOVE: *The L-Ko cops creating the usual mayhem in* Unhand Me, Villain. COURTESY OF ROBERT JAMES KISS. BELOW: *Alice Howell and Phil Dunham trying to avoid trouble with gang boss Fatty Voss, in* Lizzie's Lingering Love.

Raymond Griffith was Howell's co-star in *The Bankruptcy of Boggs and Schultz* (May 3), the three-reel *The Great Smash* (May 10), *A Busted Honeymoon* (May 24), and *How Stars Are Made* (June 14), this latter film extant and a copy held by the Library of Congress. Griffith's others for L-Ko before his unofficial teaming with Howell included *Mr. McIdiot's Assassination* (January 23), *Cupid at the Polo Game* (January 30), *Elevating Father* (February 16), and *Blue Blood and Black Skin* (March 1) before departing for Keystone and greener pastures mid-year. This last film co-starred Dan Russell as a murderous barber and Louise Orth as his girl Pinky, with Griffith a stranger from up north who comes between them. A notable curiosity in that all of the participants performed in blackface.

The spectacular climax of *The Great Smash* was heavily promoted in the film's ads — "Ye gods — what a thrill!" headlined one of *Moving Picture Weekly*'s ads — and elicited enthusiastic responses from reviewers. Peter Milne gave a particularly effusive report:

> Without stretching the point this three-reeler is candidly the best L-Ko we have seen, and we have seen them all. And that statement is made considering and in the face of the wonderful improvement visible in the recent output of this company.... [The film's] most startling point is its chase. Chases have become things to shy at owing to the manner in which they have been overworked, but this one is unusual. A steam engine, an automobile, and the land and harbor police partake therein, and every scene of it offers a laugh and a thrill. Houses are knocked over or torn open, an entire village is put to confusion, vehicles and pedestrians are menaced by the chasers, until at last the engine runs upon the draw of a bridge and there blows itself to atoms. This last is done in miniature, but it is so cleverly welded in with the real scenes that the thrill is carried out to the very end. The mechanical side of this miniature is practically perfect.[180]

Dan Russell was seemingly everywhere in the L-Ko releases for 1916, making appearances in more than a quarter of them whenever a burly, imposing character was needed. These characters spanned the spectrum of classes from crooks, assassins, prize fighters, and tramps, to middle-class laborers with even the occasional high society millionaire thrown into the mix. One recurring character was Dinty in films such as *Where is My Husband?* (August 2), *A Surgeon's Revenge* (September 27), and *Heartsick at Sea* (January 17, 1917; as Dinty Doozleberry).

Without question, Russell's highest profile picture for the year was the Lehrman three-reel special *For the Love of Mike and Rosie* (April 5). The film marked the return of Lehrman to the screen in a starring role as another of his Jewish characters, and the film was heavily promoted at the time for its epic — by L-Ko standards, that is — qualities. The plot centers around the Goldfinger family and their inheritance of a large fortune. As a result, daughter Rosie (Louise Orth in an uncharacteristic dark wig) is surrounded by suitors, and the Goldfingers favor Dr. O'Briensky. O'Briensky doesn't last for long, however, when the famed fighter A. Cross Leech (played by Lehrman; the character's name a playful sendup of famed boxer Leach Cross) — aka "The Jewish Lion" — arrives on the scene and ejects him. The Goldfingers aren't very happy about this turn of events, but matters turn from bad to worse with the arrival of Mike McGinnis (Russell) — aka

"The Irish Terror" — who ejects Leech and decides to stay. Leech makes a triumphant return and through a turn of events ends up in a boxing ring for a no-holds-barred climatic boxing match, Lehrman outfitted in a ludicrous striped and sleeveless T-shirt. "Boxing matches, when burlesqued, are to our previous recollections quite dull, but Mr. Lehrman's affair is arranged and carried out excellently" reported Peter Milne at the time.[181] Surrounded on three sides by bleachers filled with wildly cheering locals, the match came to a typical Lehrmanesque end: "The battle was a hard one and after

The climactic train crash in The Great Smash, *done with miniatures.* COURTESY OF ROBERT JAMES KISS.

repeated knock-downs the fight was stopped by a gent without a cent, who scrambled into the ring and brought the whole house down to assist. The ring collapsed, precipitating Irish and Jews together, and a grand free-for-all international fight followed."[182] The "gent" referred to in the previous quote was slyly inserted into the film by Lehrman, and from several accounts another reference to the character he helped create with Chaplin back at Keystone:

> Interspersed between glimpses of the ring wherein the fight is in progress are scenes displaying the efforts of a gentleman in high hat, loose clothing, little moustache and slight cane, to view the fight without a pasteboard. This actor is surprisingly funny, considering the origin and adaptation of his make-up, and his appearance aids in no small measure in putting the laughs in the fight.[183]

Universal filled the trades with full-page ads touting that "thousands of dollars we're [sic] spent to take the side-splitting boxing exhibition, as well as other scenes making this without doubt one of the greatest L-KO subjects ever released."[184] The stills accompanying these ads along with the various contemporary synopses and reviews suggest that this film was one of the more ambitious and important L-Ko's, and its assumed loss one to be regretted. The subject matter was close to Lehrman's heart: he was in real life a frequenter of the area boxing matches, as were a number of his fellow filmmakers. Jack Doyle's fight club in Vernon was the usual destination, where Lehrman would hang out with Fatty Voss and run into his old friend Chaplin.

Mike McGinnis, "The Irish Terror" (Dan Russell) and Lehrman at odds over dark-haired Louise Orth in For the Love of Mike and Rosie.

Fatty Voss plugged away during the year with roles in more than a dozen comedies, initially in support of Gertrude Selby, Dave Morris, and Reggie Morris in four shorts before donning a child's clothing to co-star with Paul Jacobs in *Little Billy's School Days*. After that most of his appearances were with Alice Howell, although he did land a leading role in *A Gambler's Gambol* (July 5) where he feigns suicide in response to his wife's complaints about his obsessive gambling.

Another newcomer to the L-Ko ranks was London-born, thirty year old Phil Dunham who was hired late in 1915. After years of stage experience in England and Ireland followed by some work in vaudeville here in the U.S., Dunham had entered the film industry back in 1913 with roles in productions for Nestor, Joker, and Powers and, more recently, Kalem. At five feet six and one hundred forty pounds, the compact comedian quickly found himself playing a variety of roles in more than a dozen films during the course of the year, and would remain with the studio until its eventual demise. He would move into direction as well later the following year.

Other new hires included the aforementioned Lucille Hutton and Billy Bevan. Seventeen year old Hutton hailed from Indiana and was schooled in Los Angeles, with a stage career that began at the tender young age of ten in amateur theatricals. This led to a stint with the Morosco stock company in Los Angeles and some ingénue roles in musical comedy. Before joining the L-Ko, Hutton had several uncredited bits in films,

LEFT: *A dapper, mustachieod Phil Dunham.* RIGHT: *Lucille Hutton graced the cover of the November 11, 1916 issue of* Moving Picture Weekly, *promoting* The Million Dollar Smash *(11/15/1916).*

D.W. Griffith's *A Timely Interception* (1913) and director Tod Browning's *The Woman from Warrens* (1915) among them. Her pretty young countenance was thrust upon the Los Angeles public when she was chosen as that year's official herald for Fall Dress-Up Week, during which the city's "niftiest dresser" would be chosen.[185]

Born in Australia in 1887, Billy Bevan came to North America with one of the Pollard Opera Company's touring theatrical troupes. After performances throughout Alaska and Canada, Bevan ended his eight year association with Pollard and joined Vancouver's Fletcher stock company. This led to a stint with Anderson's Gaiety Company in San Francisco as well as some time spent in vaudeville and musical comedy before hooking up with L-Ko in late 1915. His early roles in films such as *Lizzie's Shattered Dreams* and *Gaby's Gasoline Glide* (May 17, 1916) were sans the familiar "walrus" mustache that has come to be associated with him from his later, higher profile films for Mack Sennett.

Twenty five year old Billy Armstrong joined the L-Ko as well, another Brit with Karno experience who spent a year at Essanay most prominently with roles in some of Chaplin's early films for that studio. A few starring roles in Cub Comedies preceded his hiring by L-Ko, where he would remain for the better part of the next few years, with a break in late 1917 into 1918 for a stint with Sennett. One of Armstrong's more memorable roles at L-Ko — memorable in that the film actually survives and is available for viewing — is *Gaby's Gasoline Glide*,[186] with Armstrong vying with Phil Dunham for the heart of Gertrude Selby's Gaby, cute as a button and exuding roly-poly, girlish charm. It doesn't help matters that Gaby is fickle, bouncing back and forth between the two suitors. When

Minister Billy Bevan performs the nuptials for Gertrude Selby and a nervous looking Phil Dunham in Gaby's Gasoline Glide.

she eventually decides to marry Dunham, however, Armstrong vows revenge, luring the two newlyweds into his large touring car and embarking on a hair-raising ride that ends with a spectacular crash off the end of a pier, taking all to a watery grave below. Based on some stills from contemporary publications of the previous year's *Gertie's Joy Ride*, it would appear that the climatic footage was reused from that earlier film.

Carmel Myers, the seventeen year old daughter of Australian rabbi Isadore Myers, landed her first credited roles[187] at L-Ko in a trio of films before being hired by D.W. Griffith later in the year to become a member of the Triangle-Fine Arts Company. Myers eventually graduated to even greater roles in greater films such as the MGM epic *Ben Hur: A Tale of the Christ* (1925). When asked years later if she had a role in D.W. Griffith's *Intolerance*, she was quick to distance herself from her admittedly humble beginnings: "No. I was working at another studio, my first job, at a comedy studio called L-KO — Lehrman's Nut House….It was a dreadful studio, a grade or two lower than Mack Sennett, if you can imagine."[188]

Other additions to the L-Ko stock company during 1916 included Katherine Griffith, a forty-year-old comedienne with fifteen years of vaudeville, stock, and musical comedy experience, and child actor Gordon Griffith's mother; Belle Bennett, who entered the industry three years earlier and only stuck around at L-Ko for a single film before moving elsewhere; and baby-faced Joe Moore, arguably the least successful of his actor siblings Owen, Tom, and Matt.[189] Moore married his lot mate Grace Cunard early in 1917,[190] but left the L-Ko lots soon after to make a few more random films before being drafted into the army.

Lehrman had managed to balance work and play during this period, even though much of the latter would have an industry connection. Always an avid dancer, Lehrman had the previous summer competed against his former co-worker Ford Sterling, actor Wallace Reid, and others in a dancing championship held at the Vernon Country Club. It is unknown who took home the $200 cup, but the fact that only previous cup winners were eligible to participate was a measure of Lehrman's talents.[191] Earlier in 1916, L-Ko was represented by Lehrman and Abe Stern at a "surprise" forty-ninth birthday party for Universal owner Carl Laemmle held at the Los Angeles Athletic Club. "This has been a jolly dinner" was the birthday boy's response.[192] These birthday parties were an annual event that both Lehrman and Stern had attended the year before as well.[193]

The outside activity that garnered the most ongoing press, however, was the drive to solicit monies for the Actors' Fund. Headed by committee president Jesse L. Lasky, a dinner held in March generated more than $5,000 in contributions from attendees. While the $250 ponied up by L-Ko paled in comparison to Fine Arts' $10,095 donation, it was only a notch or two behind Universal's $480 and Lasky's $325, and far more than the paltry $85 put forth by the actors at Keystone.[194] It was a start, but it was quickly decided that contributions from the various studios' actors alone would need a boost from another source. To that end, Lehrman and others put their heads together and came up with a plan that would ultimately result in an automobile race to be held at Ascot Speedway on Memorial Day, May 30. A committee was formed that reunited Lehrman with a number of former and current co-workers, among them Mack Sennett, Ford Sterling, Fred Mace, Harry Gribbon, and Eddie Dillon, as well as a number of other industry notables.[195] The event came to be known as the Automobile Fashion Show, with each car and driver entered backed and supported by the various studios. This support included the broad clowning by the stars of the Keystone and L-Ko comedies, Alice Howell strutting her stuff as an ineffectual emergency nurse.

> There was a comedy race in which the clowns of the Keystone and L.K.O. companies competed. This was one of the funniest events ever staged. The comedy producers had their cars rigged up with smoke pots, bombs and other smoke and noise-making equipment, and in the race the drivers stopped to present each other with bouquets and to engage in slapstick battles.[196]

The Fashion Show, in which the cars and their drivers would be judged on their appearance, was preceded by a five-mile motorcycle race; an L-Ko employee named Wake Walters won this event. The Fashion Show participants included actress Priscilla Dean, who won first place, along with Mabel Normand, Universal comedienne Lillian Peacock, and many others. L-Ko was represented by an aspiring actress named Virginia Rappe, heretofore known — if known at all — for her fashion modeling; she drove a Fiat.[197] Was it Lehrman's so-called "monster" Fiat? Or perhaps Sennett's? Neither; local auto dealers lent the vehicles on display for the event, and the Fiat was one of them. While little known in mid-1916, Rappe's name would be on everyone's lips a mere five years later after another, more notorious holiday weekend event.

The L-Ko comedies were going strong during this period. They had their detractors, for sure, those who considered them "lower rent" rip-offs of the more popular Keystones, or who disdained anything even hinting of slapstick. Billie Ritchie had his own thoughts on the matter, and gave *Film Fun*'s reviewer Elizabeth Sears an earful in a spirited defense of his and Lehrman's type of humor during an interview earlier that year:

> I haven't any ambitions to play anything but comedy. To make two laughs grow where only one grew before is a good work, it seems to me. I don't claim to be the man who put the laugh in laughter, but I've done my share in keeping it there. Audiences are made up of all sorts of people, you know. There are thousands of people, especially the younger ones, who cannot appreciate the more subtle forms of humor. They want to know right out what they are laughing at. They have lively imaginations, and they want to see something happening right along.
>
> Go to any theater and watch the better class of slapstick stuff. You'll hear the crowds roaring at it, won't you? Sure you will. You may not like it yourself, but there are plenty who do. And they pay to see the show just as often as you do. We must please them as well as the other crowd. Half the audiences at the picture houses are young people, and it is safe to say that they prefer comedy of the action type. I study out my parts patiently before I go before the camera, to get every bit of comedy action out of them.
>
> I have the highest admiration for the highbrows. I'd be tickled to death if I could go 'round looking as if I had swallowed the dictionary. But remember that of all the population of this world, the highbrows occupy a comparatively small portion. And somebody must amuse the rest of the crowd. Think of that sometimes, won't you, when you are knocking slapstick?[198]

Lehrman was ready to take his studio to the next level with the announcement of a five-reel war comedy, then in the planning stages. Lehrman authorized the expenditure of $500 — $100 per word — solely for the five word title to a story written by H.H. Van Loan, *The Mirth of a Nation*. No doubt an intended pun on the title of D.W. Griffith's *The Birth of a Nation* from the previous year, this may have also been Lehrman's response to Sennett's feature length *Tillie's Punctured Romance* from late 1914. *The Mirth of a Nation* was to star Billie Ritchie, and would be an ambitious first for the studio.[199]

And then, four days after Independence Day, Lehrman declared his independence from L-Ko by selling his interests in the company.[200]

What happened? The much-touted explanation that has gained traction over the years may have originated in Kalton Lahue and Sam Gill's indispensible *Clown Princes and Court Jesters*. "Lehrman had become more obnoxious to Carl Laemmle daily," Lahue stated matter-of-factly,[201] and while there may be some truth to this assertion there are some other possibilities worth considering that do not involve Lehrman's personality. One of these would be monetary: Laemmle may have been tightening the purse strings, making it increasingly difficult for Lehrman to produce the kind of comedies he wanted, leading to a growing dissatisfaction that resulted in his decision to leave L-Ko behind and start fresh elsewhere. Lehrman's recent expenditure of the then unheard of sum of $500 for a mere five-word title may have been the tipping point, further annoying Laemmle and the deciding factor that led to Lehrman's departure.

Another possibility is that there were other studios with deeper pockets that were attempting, behind the scenes, to lure the creative and successful Lehrman away from the more parsimonious Universal family, that may have played into Lehrman's confidence to make the break and place himself on the open market.

A more likely explanation has to do with Laemmle's unparalleled reputation for nepotism; Abe Stern was, after all, Laemmle's wife's brother. And while the "L" in L-Ko stood for Lehrman and the company itself was initially promoted as Lehrman's, there had been a dearth of promotional materials issued of late citing Lehrman's considerable contributions, while the press for Abe Stern and his brother Julius had been on the increase. And there is the distinct possibility that by this time Abe, or the two Stern brothers jointly, had acquired a controlling share of the L-Ko stock.

Julius Stern had nothing to do initially with L-Ko, given his position on the opposite side of country as manager of the eastern studios. Word went out in mid-May that he and his brother had teamed up with a mid-western theater manager named Louis Jacobs to form a new $50,000 producing company, and contracts had been secured with popular film stars Francis Ford and Grace Cunard.[202] Ford and Cunard had recently left Universal after filming five episodes of the serial *Peg O' the Ring*, with Ruth Stonehouse assuming the lead role. Stonehouse was now out of the film, and the initial stars were to reassume their roles and finish the film under the Sterns' leadership. Initial reports stated that the production would not take place at Universal City, but at some other undisclosed studio on one of the two coasts.[203] The situation became clearer a month later, however, when it was announced that Julius Stern was "no longer connected with the Universal Company. It is reported on good authority that he will become an important factor in the L-Ko organization, which makes pictures independently for release by Universal."[204] No longer connected as an employee, that is, but he was still a major Universal stockholder[205] and had those all-important familial ties. "I regret that I am leaving the Universal," stated Stern. "But there comes a time in every young man's life when he wants to spread out and go into business for himself. I have that desire now, and it is this ambition which is causing me to leave this great organization."[206] Stern had relocated to the L-Ko studios by the end of June.

What probably galled Lehrman was the announcement that partner Abe Stern was to be married to a woman from Milwaukee named Jessie Jacobs, who it turned out was the daughter of the Stern brothers' new production company partner. Abe's marriage took place earlier in May, and on the newlyweds' return trip to Los Angeles Abe wired Lehrman from St. Louis "requesting" that that a few moving picture cameras be set up at the station for their grand arrival — cameras, and a few other things. The newlyweds arrived decked out in "full wedding regalia."[207]

> Five automobile loads of employees of the company accompanied by two automobiles filled with flowers and a moving picture camera met Mr. and Mrs. Stearn [sic].... After a parade through the business district the party returned to the studios of the company at Hollywood, where a reception was held.[208]

Julius' arrival in California was no less grand:

> All members of the four Universal L-Ko comedy companies…assembled in front of the studio recently to greet the new general manager, Julius Stern, upon his arrival…. At the head of the receiving line was Abe Stern, brother of Julius, who presented him with a gigantic key to the film world's production center. Stanley C. Kingsbury, who was formerly the New York representative of the L-Ko Company, and is now at the studio as business manager, was at Mr. Stern's elbow, and beside him were the directors, players, cameramen and others.[209]

Clearly this wasn't Lehrman's company any more. But perhaps, in a sense, it hadn't been for awhile. Lehrman's dissatisfaction with the whole situation and its attendant disinterest may have been festering for the better part of 1916, and the eventual breakup a mutually agreeable, quietly orchestrated affair. One possible clue is a report that appeared at the end of 1915 stating that Lehrman was returning to Hollywood from a trip to New York where he was "arranging details in his contract with the Universal Film Mfg. Company."[210] Perhaps the two parties could not come to terms on a renegotiated contract, and agreed to part ways come the following July. That could explain the departure of so many personnel and the hiring of fresh new replacements.

The exact reasons for Lehrman's departure from L-Ko most likely will never be known for certain, and perhaps Lahue's comment was spot on. Lehrman's behavior over subsequent years would reveal a reckless streak, the occasional lack of sound judgment, and an inability or unwillingness to manage money. A tendency to speak before taking a moment to objectively consider what he was about to say, and the potential ramifications of those words didn't help, but that could be due in part to the fact that English wasn't his native language; I'm being charitable here. He could, at times, be his own worst enemy. (The rest of the L-Ko story can be found in Appendix B.)

Production still from Cupid in a Hospital, *featuring cast, crew, and visiting executives. Left to right, seated: Gertrude Selby, Abe Stern, Carl Laemmle, Louise Orth, unknown. Standing: Hank Mann on crutches, Billie Ritchie with bandaged head, Alice Howell behind Stern, Eva Nelson behind Laemmle, Henry Lehrman with bowtie, and Rube Miller at right with goatee.*
COURTESY OF MARC WANAMAKER AND BISON ARCHIVES.

CHAPTER 6

Foxfilm and Sunshine Comedies: From Rags to Riches

During the three years that followed where the Sterns were busy reinventing and ultimately dismantling L-Ko, Henry Lehrman had moved on to what appeared to be an even greater opportunity. A little more than a month after disposing of his interests in that company on July 8, 1916, it was reported that Lehrman would "assume the management of an organization of his own devoted entirely to the production of comedy feature pictures."[1]

Concurrent with Lehrman's departure from L-Ko came the announcement that William Fox, owner of the Fox Film Corporation, was leasing the National Drama Corporation Studio with the intent of installing companies to produce "two-reel comedies patterned on the general lines of the famous Keystone pictures.... Photoplays of the slapstick type will be attempted, but will not dominate, as it is also planned to produce comedies of the polite variety."[2] Charles Parrott was already at work directing Hank Mann, with an additional four companies in the planning stages.

Lehrman's name resurfaced in the press in October when it was reported that he had begun production of his first comedy at the studios of the Christie Film Company. Within a few days it was revealed that Lehrman had been engaged by Fox[3] to make comedies.

> Henry R. [sic] Lehrmann, former president and supervising director of the L-Ko Comedies, has already gone to Los Angeles to negotiate with actors, directors and a large corps of technical workers for this purpose. He left for the West Coast immediately after a protracted conference with Mr. Fox and General Manager W.R. Sheehan.
>
> Mr. Fox intends that this important addition to his organization shall become as strong immediately upon its inception, as the firmly based dramatic release each week. To this end, Mr. Lehrmann has been instructed to engage scores of the silent drama's best known and most capable photoplayers in the laugh-making films.
>
> "I can assure exhibitors and motion picturegoers everywhere," Mr. Fox said, "that the comedies will set a new mark in the field. Each of the manuscripts which I have already selected for screening is literally a mine of laughs, and I will not release a single comedy which does not show clearly that it is an uproarious success."[4]

The film currently under production by Lehrman would be his first for Fox, under way on a new, large stage built by Christie to accommodate Lehrman and his Fox comedies.[5]

By year's end Fox's upcoming Foxfilm Comedies were announced, two-reelers to be released weekly effective January 1, 1917. These were to be released independent of the regular Fox program, and would be made available to all exhibitors. Six production companies were reportedly at work making product for the upcoming schedule, a claim that would

LEFT: *William Fox.* RIGHT: *Hank Mann's Foxfilm Comedy unit.*

later ring hollow in an interview with Lehrman a month later. Director ranks included Charles Parrott, Harry Edwards, and Walter C. Reed, and the roster of comedians including Hank Mann, Charles Arling, Frank Alexander, Lee Morris, William Hauber, Anna Luther, Carmen Phillips, Amy Jerome, and Annette De Foe.[6] Cowboy star Tom Mix and his leading lady Victoria Forde were lured away from Selig soon after, to star in Foxfilm comedies of the western sort.[7]

Lehrman's first contribution to the schedule, initially announced with the tentative title *The Society Buzzard*,[8] would ultimately bear the title *The House of Terrible Scandals* (March 19, 1917).[9] It would star Billie Ritchie,[10] Gertrude Selby, Dot Farley — all newly brought on board — and Lehrman himself, as well as a return of the comedy dog "Montana Kid." Selby's interim career had failed to catch fire in a handful of dramas and short comedies in Universal's Rex, Imp, Bluebird, and Red Feather productions, as well as a couple of Selburn Comedies, so she returned to her comfort zone. David Kirkland was lured away from Universal to direct, the finished film coming in at a reported cost of $7,500.[11] J.H. Walraven wrote about the film's climactic scene:

Lehrman was anxious to get a scene showing a man at the end of a balanced ladder extended high over one of the business streets of Los Angeles. No one would undertake the risk, which looked like certain death. One morning Mr. Lehrman called the company together and told them to be ready to go down to make the scene. There was much speculation as to who he had secured to perform the hazardous feat. When they arrived at the top of the tall building in the centre of the business district there was Henry Lehrman made up and ready to do the part himself. The director protested, members of the company pleaded, but his mind had been made up, and with Billie Ritchie straddling one end of the ladder, he worked his way out to the other end suspended in mid-air, and high above the street below he performed what is probably the most daring feat ever enacted before a motion picture camera.[12]

The scene, according to J.C. Jessen, was supposed to take place atop a "twenty-two story building. Los Angeles does not have any skyscrapers this high, so it was necessary for the Lehrmann Company to build several additional stories to one of the highest Los Angeles buildings."[13] One can assume that the newly-built structure was set up in such a fashion so that any unanticipated mishaps would merely deposit the unfortunate victim to the actual building's rooftop rather than the street many stories below, and that Walraven exaggerated a bit on the risks involved. Given Lehrman's risk-prone approach to filmmaking and anything for a laugh mentality, however, one can only assume.

Fox's goal of a January 1 release wasn't met, however. *Social Pirates*, the very first Foxfilm Comedy to make it to the screen, went into release two weeks later than promised, on January 15. Starring Charles Arling and directed by Walter C. Reed, the film edged out Hank Mann's first effort for Fox, *His Ticklish Job*, by two weeks.

Fox's publicity department went into overdrive promoting the new comedies, touting William Fox's past success as a reliable barometer of the quality of the new releases:

> YOU know the FOX reputation and you know that Mr. Fox would never endanger that reputation by releasing comedies unless he knew they were bigger, better, funnier than any other comedies in the market; unless he knew that his comedy producing organization is so good, so reliable and so experienced that he can depend on it for a two-reel laugh producer every week in the year.[14]

Praise was heaped on Lehrman as well:

> Motion picture comedy in its highest development today is the product of the brain of one man. That man is Henry Lehrman, hardly thirty years old, who has gained fame for himself as director, actor and producer.
> Within a few weeks Mr. Lehrman's first comedy for William Fox's Foxfilm brand will be released. He is making it now and all the genius which has been manifested in his previous comedies will be used to evoke laughs from the most serious-minded observer.[15]

Lehrman elaborated on his vision for the upcoming Fox comedies, an approach that would distance the output from that of his former studio:

> It's the most difficult thing in the world to produce comedy today if you adhere to the old line methods. Real comedy must bring laughs. All the laughs have been squeezed out of pie-throwing and the like, so something entirely new must be substituted. My aim in comedy-making is to produce laughs by unusual methods, and unusual situations. I am strongly opposed to the use of character make-up by principals in particular, and all the leading players in my comedies will appear in their regular faces.
>
> It is my intention to have six comedy companies at work in a few weeks. Every picture they make, I will supervise in person. I will act in some of them, but I do not care for it particularly. My principal work will be direction.[16]

Nine Foxfilm Comedies — five of them starring Hank Mann — were released before Lehrman's *The House of Terrible Scandals* made it to the screen. The first part of Lehrman's film consists of an extended, alcohol-fueled dream sequence wherein among other curiosities a cat chases a mouse into Lehrman's open mouth, and culminates with a hair-raising sequence in which Lehrman and Ritchie — sans his usual costume and playing it comparatively straight — are perched on opposite ends of that ladder balanced on the building's railing. The second, gag-filled part takes place at a reception given in honor of Ritchie's bride-to-be, played by Gertrude Selby. Ritchie's alcohol-tinged breath catches fire when Lehrman places a lit match in front of him, and Lehrman has an extended sequence to himself as he attempts to deal with the soup-slurping woman seated beside him. When the building catches fire, Lehrman aims a nearby hose at the structure with the intention of dousing the flame, only to find that the hose is attached to a gasoline truck. Both the fire and police departments arrive and ineffectually attempt to deal with the disaster and, according to a contemporary synopsis, "a runaway locomotive crashed through a string of box cars"[17] in typical Lehrman excess.

Lehrman's usual approach to launching a new brand was to create the best film possible for its initial offering, and *The House of Terrible Scandals* appears to have been another example. William Fox kept his promise to exhibitors, who were extremely pleased with the results. "This comedy was so good that I consider it the week's best picture," enthused one exhibitor. "It is a combination of Keystone and Chaplin comedy that keeps the audience in one continual roar. Much time and money was spent on this comedy."[18] "One of the most wonderful comedies ever produced," gushed another. "My patrons never laughed so much at any other offering. It was liked by everyone."[19] The first reel survives and is held by the EYE Filmmuseum.

Cinematographer Jerome Ash, who worked as a cameraman on some Francis Ford films during the later teens, told a story — perhaps apocryphal — about the release of this film. The Stern brothers were worried about the competition that Lehrman might provide once he was settled in at Fox, so they sent a scout to a showing of *The House of Terrible Scandals*. "The scout reported there was nothing to worry about — that Stern's comedies were every bit as good. 'Don't tell me,' erupted Abe Stern, 'that they're as bad as all that!'"[20] If the story is true, the scout was lying to his boss.

With the completion of *Terrible Scandals*, Lehrman headed back east for a month's stay, and in all likelihood to meet with William Fox to discuss the future of Foxfilm Comedies. Fox, it was reported, was "[n]ot satisfied with his new Fox Film comedy program," but he evidently was very impressed with Lehrman's first film. Together they agreed to form the

ABOVE: *Billie Ritchie (left), sans his familiar mustache, teeters at the opposite end of the ladder from a panic-stricken Lehrman in* The House of Terrible Scandals. COURTESY OF COLE JOHNSON. BELOW: *Lehrman awakens from his alcohol-fueled dream in* The House of Terrible Scandals. COURTESY OF ELIF RONGEN-KAYNAKCI, EYE FILMMUSEUM.

Sunshine Comedy Company as an eventual replacement for the Foxfilm Comedies. Fox would serve as president of the new concern, and Lehrman as vice-president and general manager.[21] The plans were to have four production companies at work supplying a two-reel comedy every other week. While the Foxfilm units continued production, two units went to immediate work on the Sunshine Comedies, David Kirkland at the helm of one and Lehrman himself heading the second. Ads were placed in the trades extolling the virtues of the yet-to-come comedies while soliciting scenario writers, actors, and "ingenues with

Lehrman is frustrated in his attempts to gain access the bathroom, Sid Smith seated in the background, from The House of Terrible Scandals. COURTESY OF ELIF RONGEN-KAYNAKCI, EYE FILMMUSEUM.

good looks — youth — personality" to staff four additional companies. "It is our purpose that Sunshine Comedies shall represent the greatest possible advance in motion picture production.... To achieve new lines of thought, to abandon conventional ideas, and to discard time-worn methods is our aim."[22] Former auto race driver and Christie Company leading man Harry Ham was brought on board primarily to handle the films' various automotive stunts. "From the way they look," reported *Motion Picture Magazine*, "they ought to be some thrillers on the screen."[23]

One of the problems facing the various studios in Fox's neck of the woods was the discussion of a proposed ordinance that would create a moving picture zone. This was a result of complaints by individual property owners in the residential district, resulting in a tour by the Los Angeles City Council and the decision to have the City Attorney draw up the ordinance. If it were to go into effect, Fox along with Lasky, Christie, L-Ko, Kalem, Fine Arts, Vogue, Chaplin, Mabel Normand, and Yorke-Metro would all be forced to relocate their studios.²⁴ This was put on hold when the president of the Merchants and Manufacturing of Los Angeles made an impassioned plea, pointing out that the loss of Fox alone would result in the monthly loss of $125,000 paid for supplies and salaries.²⁵ One of the residents' biggest gripes was the presence of a planing mill on the Fox grounds, and William Fox sought to have his property rezoned as an industrial tract. His application was denied, forcing the removal of the mill. Two of the more vociferous of the locals kept up their condemnation of the Fox lot, citing "the scandalous conduct of the actors, [and] the conduction of a crap game which tended to injure the moral standard of the youngest boys of the neighborhood."²⁶ Complaints continued into the latter part of the year, but action was delayed by the City Council, one prominent member stating that "We want to please the property owners, but we must also be careful in taking action affecting one of the biggest industries in the South."²⁷ As it turned out, the best action was no action, or at least none that negatively affected the studios. By the beginning of 1918 Fox was enlarging his studio and "building enough glass stages to accommodate ten companies."²⁸ The Fox studios were located on thirteen acres straddling Western Avenue, the dramas filmed on the west lot, and the Sunshines on the east lot.²⁹

Ad for the upcoming Fox Comedies, from the July 14, 1917 issue of Moving Picture World.

Gloria Swanson, one of the silent era's most popular stars, had started her acting career at Essanay while in her mid-teens, followed by a year-and-a-half stint for Sennett lasting well into 1917. She wasn't happy with the type of film that was Sennett's bread and butter, and quit, complaining in her autobiography that

> I knew the world of slapstick was not for me...and I hated the vulgarity that was just under the surface of it.... It was a world of falling planks and banana peels and wet paint and sticky wads of gum, of funny-looking fat men with painted moustaches blowing the foam off beer at each other, of stern battle-axes wielding rolling pins and wearing curlers in their hair, and of cute giggly hoydens getting teased, tickled and chased."³⁰

She went on to report that after a three month period of unemployment she took control of her life, contacted Triangle, and went to work for that company making features.

What Swanson conveniently failed to mention was a short period of employment between these two jobs: The trades reported in October 1917 that she had been hired by Lehrman to star in his Sunshine Comedies.[31] Swanson's good friend Sylvia Godwin elaborated:

> At the time I met Gloria, her contract with Mack Sennett had just expired, and a new one had been signed with Pathé Lehrmann, a producer of comedies. For some reason — fortunately for her — he did not start production, so she was enjoying day after day of vacation, and depositing one hundred and twenty-five dollars in the bank each week.... After securing her release from Pathé Lehrmann, Gloria was given a leading role in a five-reel feature at the Triangle Studio and from then on she climbed consistently ahead.[32]

This brief period of employment by Sunshine had concluded by the following March when it was reported that she was "formerly a Keystone player and more recently with the Henry Lehrman Sunshine Comedies Company,"[33] so it would appear that Swanson's determination to distance herself from the types of films that Sennett was making was not immediate.

Another of Lehrman's new hires was his former associate from Keystone, writer and director William S. Campbell. Campbell, it was reported a few years later, hailed from Ashley, Pennsylvania, running away and joining the circus due to his love of animals; there he assisted the assistant to the animals' trainer. He ended up in Los Angeles where he opened a movie theater, eventually drifting into scenario writing for Selig. A short stint with Universal was followed by an extended stay with Keystone before defecting for Sunshine.[34] Jack White, who had followed Lehrman from L-Ko and initially put to work as a cutter and given odd jobs to do as needed ("a jack-of-all-trades" as he put it), was assigned to Campbell as his assistant. "When there was any extraneous shooting to be done, Jack would do it," said White years later in an interview with David N. Bruskin. "They gave me a scene to co-direct with Bill Campbell, who was like a father to me. He let me direct while he sat back and observed. Years later, he remarked to my brother Jules that he made a director out of me, which he did."[35] White and Campbell's initial collaboration would result in *Roaring Lions and Wedding Bells* (November 11, 1917), the first official Sunshine release. More than two dozen more Foxfilm Comedies had gone into release before the program was turned over to Sunshine with this film, the bulk of those comedies directed by Hank Mann, Charles Parrott, and Tom Mix. The Foxfilm Comedy name was shelved.

One of the stars of *Roaring Lions* was comedian Lloyd Hamilton who, after a year with Universal's Frontier, had risen to fame in the recently-folded Kalem's Ham and Bud comedies (1914-17) opposite diminutive Bud Duncan. Norman Taurog, who caught the acting bug at age four and got his start in the industry as one of the IMP Kids, was working at Sunshine at the time. Taurog had joined L-Ko as a property man and actor, and eventually migrated to Sunshine at age seventeen where he assisted Jack White, who had been promoted to director. In an interview with Leonard Maltin conducted nearly sixty years later, Taurog got his timelines and some of his facts a bit confused, but he spoke of his contributions to the reinvention of the "Ham" character:

One of the first things that I did was take that big mustache off of him and they thought I had gone crazy. Here the man had created a great character and I said "Yes, but there is no expression in his face with that size mustache." Lehrman was a good scout and he said, "Let's take a chance." Once they saw a picture of Lloyd with just a straight face and that little cap and the little cutaway coat, they liked him very much.... The character was created by Henry Lehrman, Lloyd, and a little bit of Jack White and a little bit of me, little by little. I'm the fella that insisted on that

LEFT: *Writer-director William S. Campbell.* RIGHT: *Lloyd Hamilton, out of costume.*
COURTESY OF SAM GILL.

walk, as if he always had tight underwear. Lehrman insisted on the cap because it gave him a boyish look, which was right. Jack White cut off the cutaway coat one day on the set with a tailor and made the short cutaway coat and the baggy pants.[36]

Hamilton was still wearing his bushy mustache in *Roaring Lions and Wedding Bells* and wouldn't lose it for several more films, indicating that the character's evolution took place over a number of films for the company. It's also a possibility that Taurog was confusing Sunshine with Henry Lehrman Comedies or spoke of an evolution that transcended the two; Taurog followed White to that studio as his assistant,[37] and both worked on the studio's first film which starred Hamilton.

The plot of *Roaring Lions* was the usual absurdist nonsense, with Hamilton and Jimmie Adams as rivals for the hand of Mildred Lee, competing in a contest set up by her father to see who would be the lucky winner. The goal: retrieve a watch placed in a lion's cage. The lion's trainer (Mario Bianchi) gets into the act hoping to beat out the others, but when he loses he proves to be a very sore loser, unleashing his lions at the wedding party.

"When we went out to make *Roaring Lions and Wedding Bells* for Fox, I hadn't the slightest idea of how I was going to wind up the picture. I had to shoot off the cuff," explained White in a way that makes it sound more like Campbell was his assistant rather than the other way around, "but the rushes were so goddamned good that the front office encouraged me to keep on shooting. I never thought of asking how much it was going to cost. They were supposed to tell me, 'Slow down, you're spending too much.' When I saw the advantage I had, I took it."[38]

Variety was enthusiastic about the film and the promise it held for future Sunshine releases, although the reviewer made the common assumption that Lehrman was the director.

> The Sunshine lives up to its trademark. It not only casts a laughing ray from start to finish, but it also has some uproariously funny scenes in which wild animals have as much prominence as the men and women in the film. If the succeeding subjects furnish as much honest laughter as the first film, then their success is assured. Henry Lehrman directed it. Lehrman has staged thousands of funny scenes and directed innumerable camera "bits," but he seems to have outdone himself with his first Sunshine. After looking at "Roaring Lions and Wedding Bells" the task of making film comedies seems to be getting tougher, harder and more difficult and calls for almost superhuman and impossible feats of man and beast to keep up their piston-rod comedy effect. This first Sunshine is funny and capable of handing the most tired business man the surcease from his physical and mental toil he has been looking for. The principals are working all the time. So are some trained lions and ostriches. A trained elephant also shows amazing camera training. All sorts of mixups, confusions, chases, monkeyshines, clashes, jams, roughhouse, slapstick, photographic tricks, illusions, legitimate screen artifice, natural didoes and the Lord knows what-not are utilized in making the Sunshine subject rank among the best in modern day film comedy. It can't miss, either ahead or following a dramatic.[39]

Moving Picture World, on the other hand, correctly attributed the direction to Campbell.
"The picture was a big smash," said White. It grossed more money than some of their features. It played first-run houses."[40] While the actors all emerged unscathed at the end of production, the lions fared less well: "One of them lost a tooth during the action, another received a severe cut on the flank, and a third had his leg skinned and scarred."[41]

One gag impressed *Photoplay* writer Randolph Bartlett, who claimed to have seen the film three times. "If some one will explain to me how [Lehrman] made the scene in which a lion sits on the foot of the bed, and tickles the feet of two sleeping colored gentlemen with the brush on the end of his tail, I will be much obliged. One of the funniest things ever projected is the result on the gentlemen of color. The face of one turns white as he wakes, while the other turns over in bed, and a pale streak — probably yellow — slowly runs up his spine."[42]

William Fox, who was located on the East Coast in New York and loathed traveling out to the West Coast studios by train, had in 1916 left those studios under the care of his general representative Abraham Carlos. Carlos was not the man for the job, evidently, and Fox's growing dissatisfaction with Carlos' performance led him to send out twenty-seven

ABOVE: *Lloyd Hamilton, Mildred Lee, and a friendly ostrich in* Roaring Lions and Wedding Bells. COURTESY OF ROBERT JAMES KISS. BELOW: *Lloyd Hamilton encounters a lion in* Roaring Lions and Wedding Bells. COURTESY OF COLE JOHNSON.

year old Sol Wurtzel as a replacement. "This is to advise you that Mr. Sol Wurtzel, my former secretary, who is now in Los Angeles, and who, you no doubt met by this time, is entrusted with the same powers held by Mr. Carlos up to this time," wrote Fox to Lehrman. "May I ask you to be good enough to give Sol every possible assistance and advice that you can so that he can make good at his new post?"[43]

David Kirkland's *A Milk-Fed Vamp* (November 25, 1917) was the second Sunshine to be released, starring Dot Farley as a farmer's daughter who charms a city boy and, in spite

Dot Farley, looking particularly attractive in A Milk-Fed Vamp, *Ernest Shield on left.*

of the fact that he already has a wife and three children, elopes with him. She eventually encounters the wife, who has an organ and monkey, the latter the source of much of the film's entertainment. "[T]his monkey is one of the most amusing things in the picture," said *Moving Picture World*. "Its antics and the things the director has thought up for it to do are both fresh and compellingly laughable."[44] As for the film itself, it "is a laughmaker and can be safely depended on to make good in the average theater. It has touches of vulgarity that will make it the more acceptable with most of the people; but are just enough to keep it from being a sure choice for a children's party or Sunday school entertainment." The *Los Angeles Herald* elaborated about the monkey, "this latest recruit to Lehrman's large group of players," saying that "His name is at present unknown, though he is generally addressed as either 'Jocko' or 'Tony.'…[He] wears a red coat and a red cap and has a long tail. He's just like every other monkey in existence, except that he's funnier."[45]

Lehrman sang the praises of one of these early comedies in an interview. "The distinctive feature of this new comedy is that it presents a comedy that is interesting and clever from the standpoint of the story. It has hundreds of funny incidents that are new and will inevitably cause the wildest sort of laughter, but without them a decidedly good and absorbing story has been told."[46]

Lehrman's reputation for recklessness and risking the lives of his actors, extras, and stuntmen has by now become legend. Stuntman Harvey Parry is credited with tagging him with the less-than-flattering nickname "Suicide Lehrman," a variation of the "Mr. Suicide" moniker attributed to Lehrman by Kalton Lahue. "By the time L-KO was under way, Lehrman had been nicknamed 'Mr. Suicide' by actors and especially by extras. Lehrman had little respect for human life," claimed Lahue, "especially that of actors…. He would go to any length to obtain the desired effect or scene, regardless of the hazards to life or limb. Thus, his nickname and a reputation which actually caused extras to refuse work calls from L-KO."[47] Lahue makes this claim for when Lehrman was associated with L-Ko, but was that really the case or might the reputation have come later during his time with Fox, and the studios confused over the haze of elapsed time? The article "Fox Films Have Daring Stunts" appeared at the end of December, 1916, and details some of the hair-raising stunts being performed for the new Foxfilm Comedies:

> In William Fox's new series of comedy pictures, the Foxfilm comedies, brand new methods of laugh production have been resorted to. Camera trickery, mechanical effects and disregard for life and limb on an unusual scale characterize every one of the forthcoming fifty-two releases. Here are a few examples of screen comedy of the modern school selected at random from some of Mr. Fox's new offerings:
>
> Thousands of gallons of water are released from a broken gravity tank on the roof of a hotel and out into the street. There is no question as to the volume of water or power of the current. Every piece of furniture and every human being in the six sets that are wrecked is swept along in the rush of water. The carrying away of a huge banquet table, at which are seated fifty guests in evening clothes, comes as the startling climax. Property destroyed in obtaining this one effect represents thousands of dollars.
>
> In another picture an entire village is submerged by a cloud burst. A hundred or more dwelling houses and business places are inundated, the water in the streets extending to the roofs of the structures. It is no miniature set. The main village street with all its activities are shown close up. Then the cloudburst begins. Water accumulates in the gutters, backs up over the sidewalks and gradually rises to the roofs as the villagers climb higher and higher for safety. The cost of this effect in dollars and cents is equal to an amount large enough to produce an ordinary two-reel comedy.
>
> Another early release features a unique race effect. The leading comedian, in the guise of a Marathon runner, is shown passing a bird in full flight and an automobile traveling at a high rate of speed.
>
> One of the biggest "chases" ever shown in pictures is the feature of a Fox film comedy soon to be released. A gang of crooks on a handcar is pursued by officers on a locomotive, motorcycle, automobile and police launch. All are shown in action at once. The climax comes when the crooks, deserting the handcar, board an electric engine, which tears its way through a courthouse wall and into a courtroom. Several retakes were necessary for this scene. Once the engine got

beyond control of the motorman and wrecked three other sets in which players were at work.

These are just a few of the remarkable effects shown in Foxfilm comedies and Mr. Fox intends that all future comedy releases will contain features equally distinctive.[48]

This article appeared while Lehrman was wrapping up production of his initial effort for Fox. It is unclear when exactly Lehrman and Fox came to terms for the former's participation, and when Lehrman was able to impose his vision for the upcoming productions. That said, the films referred to and the "disregard for life and limb on an unusual scale" may have been a result of Lehrman's vision as conveyed to Fox, or already been in effect independent of Lehrman's arrival. With the evolution of Foxfilm Comedies into Sunshine Comedies and Lehrman's association with the latter, it is possible that this seemingly reckless approach was imposed on Lehrman, and that he gained his reputation more by association rather than cause.

Historian Sam Gill took exception to this notion when forwarded to him for his comments:

> I strongly believe that it was Lehrman's brand of comedy, and approach to comedy, that Fox wanted, and why Fox acquired his services. I definitely do not believe that it was the other way around. I think I am correct when I say that if you look at the films Lehrman had made and continued to make, one is struck with a style of outlandish and often surreal comedy. Mack Sennett may have had a tendency to such humor, but not nearly as marked and well-defined as Lehrman's. At least, that is my opinion.
>
> When you look at the earliest L-KO films…and Lehrman's use of Billie Ritchie in these films, I would say that Lehrman was going the direction of a consistently broader and more anarchic type of comedy than Mack Sennett was directing and producing at the same time.[49]

I wholly agree with Gill's assessment of Lehrman's approach to comedy, and how it differed from Sennett's. Fox wanted his new comedies to stand in stark comparison with those of his competitors, and Lehrman was the logical choice to shepherd this new brand of comedy to the screen. And while it is very likely that Lehrman's reckless approach to physical stunts was fully formed as he emerged from L-Ko, the possibility remains that it may instead have been imposed on him by Fox, wanting to make his comedies bigger, better, and without peer when it came to on-screen mayhem.

That, or the big budgets now available to Lehrman simply allowed his most outlandish impulses freer reign.

Regardless, one of the Sunshines that Lehrman wrote and directed and the next to be released garnered a lot of press for a stunt gone wrong. *His Smashing Career* (December 9, 1917) starred Billie Ritchie, Gertrude Selby, Billy Bevan, and Vic Potel in a story vaguely reminiscent of the very first Sterling Comedy, *Love and Vengeance*. The plot revolved around race car driver Hundred Horsepower Harry (Ritchie, also referred to as the cheekily named Little Peter), his efforts to win the girl (Selby), her father (Bevan) who wants better for

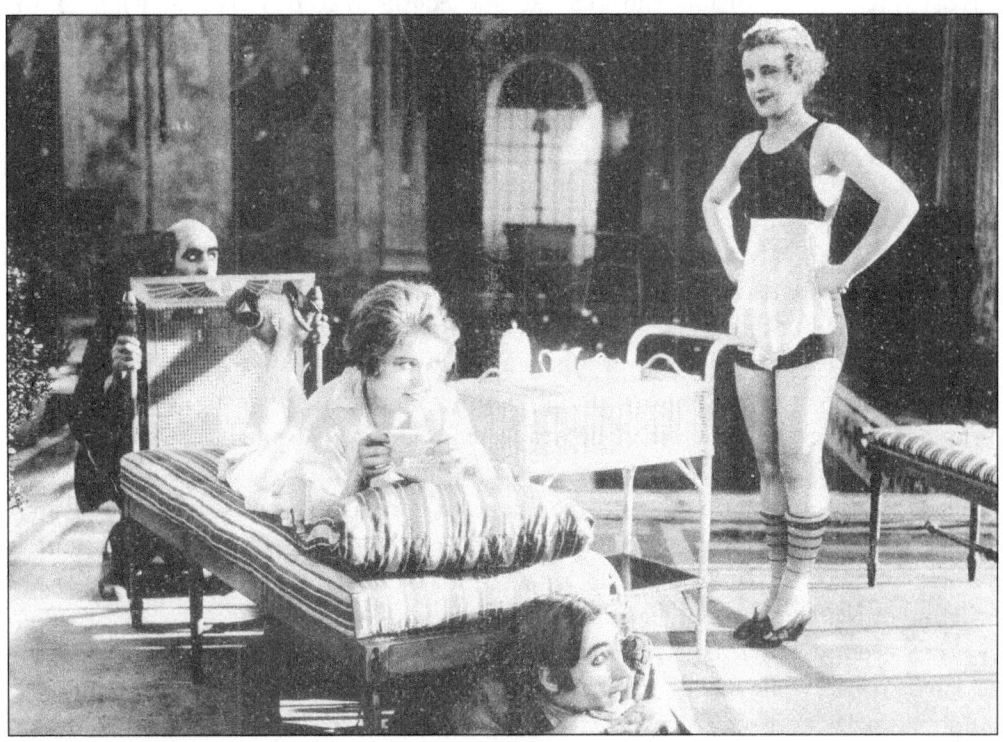

ABOVE: *Gertrude Selby lounges, unaware of the intruders behind and under her couch in* His Smashing Career. COURTESY OF ROBERT JAMES KISS. BELOW: *The Sunshine cops are about to be in deep water in this shot from* His Smashing Career. COURTESY OF HERITAGE AUCTION GALLERIES, HA.COM.

his daughter, and the villains who go to extreme lengths to keep Harry from winning. The judge (Potel) of the big race views the proceedings from atop a tall tower, built adjacent to the grandstand.

Stuntman Leo Houck doubled for Potel in one of the film's big scenes which took place on April 24. "The scene in which I was hurt was supposed to be funny," said Houck. "To make the people laugh a grandstand collapsed and a 40-foot tower fell over on it. The construction was of the 'break-away' type; that is, it was built to fall properly, without injuring anyone. Only, as often happens, something went wrong. I was hit by the 40-foot tower." Hit hard enough that he was laid up for five weeks.[50] Stuntman Joe Miller was injured as well, but didn't take it in stride, claiming that no one alerted him in advance as to what to expect (a number of others hired to fill the stands testified that they too had not been given any advance warning). During an exciting moment in the race, poles supporting the grandstands where he was seated were dislodged and the whole structure collapsed, dropping the unsuspecting Miller to the ground "twenty or forty feet" below. Miller sued the Sunshine Comedy corporation and Lehrman for a total of $6,100 dollars.[51] Miller seemed to be a magnet for bad luck, for less than two years later he was severely burned from an acetylene tank explosion while making a film for Selig.[52] It is not known whether or not he filed another suit.

Half a century after the fact, Norman Taurog gave his recollection of the event to historian Sam Gill, while shedding some light on Lehrman's apparent go-for-broke approach to obtaining his on-screen gags: "Henry Lehrman had a great talent for comedy, but sometimes he achieved his end in a bad way. On one particular occasion, he pulled the supports out from under a small stadium bench, resulting in three or four broken legs. He said 'Gee, I didn't know anyone would get hurt,' and he really didn't. He just didn't realize what he was doing. He was out after gags; and when he was, he was often oblivious to people around him."[53]

Cameraman William McGann offered a similar account of the event to Gill, again a half century later: "I was a cameraman for Henry Lehrman when he was at Fox, and I can tell you that the story is true that he had a bleacher full of extras during the filming of one scene, and for a thrill sequence he had the supports pulled out from under the stands, and all the people seated there came crashing down. There were injuries, and the word did get out that you took your life in your hands if you were working for Henry Lehrman."[54]

His Smashing Career and its attendant injuries were the single most publicized mishap in Lehrman's career to date, and if not the origin of his reputation for disregarding the safety of those working for him, it surely cemented it. But there were others. Sylvia Day, Betty Carpenter, and Mae Eccleston were all badly bruised while filming a Sunshine when a locomotive struck the wagon in which they were riding, and the three of them were ejected.[55] And actor John Rand, best remembered for his association with Chaplin during the Essanay and Lone Star years, brought suit against Sunshine complaining that someone struck him with a "property" rock, stating that these property rocks were much harder than genuine rocks. Lehrman claimed otherwise, stating (as paraphrased in the *New York Telegraph*) that "a regular rock would kill a man, while a 'property' rock would only nearly kill him."[56]

Harvey Parry tells another story about one of Lehrman's Sunshine Comedies that featured lions. "We had a bank set, with dress extras in all their finery. They put the dog on more than the stars. Most of them had money and big cars and the best of clothes, and they appeared in movies for fun. Out of no place comes this lion. Ohhhh! Well, fellows walked up the walls, you know, knocked each other down to get out of the way. Lehrman got a hell of a scene out of it, but it scared them to death. The lion was, in a sense, harmless, but these were Lehrman's — what do you call them? — idiosyncrasies."[57]

These accidents — both unplanned and planned — were nothing new in the industry, where stuntmen like Eugene Adams was run over by a chariot while filming a scene for the Crest Film Company, and Billy Williams fell from atop a windmill and suffered

A stunt man takes a leap from Hollenbeck Park bridge in an unidentified Keystone comedy.
COURTESY OF SAM GILL.

broken ribs when a restraining strap broke.[58] The comedy industry had the highest rate of injuries due to the fact that the comedians themselves were in many instances expected to perform the stunts rather than have a double fill in for them. "Our stuff cannot be faked," said Roscoe Arbuckle. "When people see it they know they are seeing real stunts. Of course, now and then we do a trick film, but everyone knows it is a trick when they see it — there is no bunk about it." Given that many of the comedians had backgrounds in vaudeville or the circus, a lot of them had considerable acrobatic skills that served them well in avoiding injury. Preplanning helped as well, but things would inevitably go wrong with unfortunate, sometimes disastrous, and on rare occasion lethal results. "[W]e figure [the stunt] out on paper, and if it looks as if it will work we do it. That's all there is to it. Now and then it doesn't work, and we either have to plan it a different way, or do it over again until we get it."[59]

"Directors in those days didn't give a damn about a person's life," said Parry in an interview with the *National Enquirer*. "They'd outline a stunt they wanted you to do and when filming was under way you'd discover they'd fooled you by adding something which made the stunt far more dangerous. For example, they'd tell you your job called for you to be on a wall to make a jump — but just when you'd be ready to jump the wall would begin collapsing under you."⁶⁰ While Lehrman wasn't singled out by name, Parry's example sounds suspiciously like the collapsing grandstand in *Her Smashing Career*. Parry was far more specific — if somewhat inaccurate — in an interview with the *Chicago Tribune*: "Another time this guy — his name was Henry Lehrman — put 300 people on some bleachers that he'd rigged to collapse. Only nobody knew it was going to collapse, except Lehrman. The bleachers went down, and one guy was killed and another was badly injured."⁶¹

Another stunt that resulted in injuries most likely took place during the filming of *His Smashing Career* as well, and this one was related by Lehrman himself. Recent hire (and soon to be cameraman) George Meehan was instructed to pilot a "Police Ambulance" off the Venice Pier. When Lehrman spotted the vehicle filled with what he considered "unconvincing" dummies, he quickly took charge. "What are you going to do with those dummies?" he demanded to know. "Use real people." The switch was made, and a number of people were injured as a result.⁶²

Arbuckle was more fortunate than most, or at least in terms of on-set accidents. Steve Rydzewski's biography of Ben Turpin *For Art's Sake* details a staggering number of injuries sustained by the comedian during his earlier years of filmmaking. Art Gibson of the Sterling Film Company was shot in the hand, the wad of the blank cartridge penetrating the flesh and lodging between the bones of the palm.⁶³ Leo White was injured while working with Billy West in a Bulls Eye Comedy when a trick car collapsed at the wrong moment,⁶⁴ and S.A. Moorhouse suffered a fractured skull and internal injuries while portraying a drunk on an amusement ride for that same studio.⁶⁵ Bud Duncan nearly drowned when he was required to enter a body of water wearing a full suit of armor while filming a Ham and Bud Comedy for Kalem, and was dragged back to land in an unconscious state.⁶⁶ Wanda Wiley was hospitalized for two weeks with sprains and fractures when she was thrown from her horse while filming a comedy for Universal, the horse spooked by the noise from a nearby wind machine.⁶⁷ And at Fox, Bill Hauber and Clarence Reedscale were both injured while filming an escape from an airship to an automobile when they came in contact with the motor's revolving blades; both were hospitalized.⁶⁸

L-Ko and Century had their share of accidents. Billie Ritchie's suspenders became entangled in an airplane propeller used off-stage for wind effects; his trousers were shredded before stage hands could come to the rescue.⁶⁹ Alice Howell was trapped in a runaway balloon while filming *Balloonatics*, a journey that lasted for half a dozen miles before setting down in a farmyard.⁷⁰ The former "Baby Peggy" Montgomery, Diana Serra Cary, recounts the story of her co-star, the "giant" Jack Earle, who fell fourteen feet from a scaffold attached to one of the Century cars, then struck by a falling two-by-four. He eventually went blind from the accident.⁷¹

Physical injury, of course, was not the worst fate that could befall an actor or stuntman. Actress Lillian Peacock suffered serious internal injuries in 1916 leaping from one moving automobile to another while filming a comedy for Joker. She returned to work after a partial recovery, but was soon incapacitated and eventually died from those injuries after a six-month illness in 1918.⁷² Stunt pilot Earl Burgess was filming an airborne stunt for a Chester Conklin film where he needed to climb out on a wing, fake a fight with a (dummy) villain, and knock his adversary off the plane's wing. During a retake, the exhausted stuntman lost his grip and fell 500 feet to some telephone wires below.[73] Needless to say, this was Burgess' last stunt. While the film company was not named in any of the accounts that appeared at the time, the accident took place in early February 1920, placing it at Fox.

Photoplay Magazine once said that the "Keystone company has a record for freedom from accident and sickness that is the envy of the craft."[74] While that may have been accurate, numerous reports in the press would suggest that Keystone had its fair share, although no doubt a function of the company's size and level of output. Director Frank C.

"*The leading lady refuses to do stunts.*" From the April 28, 1917 issue of Moving Picture World.

Griffin's *The Feathered Nest* (1916), for example, was the poster child for on-set accidents. Louise Fazenda, stranded on a rock out in the ocean with the tide rising around her, had to be rescued — sort of — by co-star Harry Booker and director Griffin. A rip tide impeded their return to shore, sending them repeatedly into the rocks before a life saving crew came to the battered and bruised group's rescue. The following day Fazenda was rapped on the head by the bow of a boat in yet another water scene, and on the third day was once again struck on the head in a similar scene, reportedly rendered unconscious for the next three days. Booker was hospitalized for two days after being struck in the nose by a croquet ball, while actor Wayland Trask took a header off a bicycle when the handlebars came loose, resulting in three days off with a lacerated shoulder. Charlie Murray was sidelined for a week when a hansom cab ran over his foot, and two stage carpenters were knocked unconscious while filming a boat scene, necessitating another rescue. While none of these accidents were the result of outlandishly planned stunts, they are illustrative of the risks the actors took on a day-to-day basis. All told, production was delayed three weeks by the laying off of the injured performers.[75] In another incident, Chester Conklin was badly burned from a gasoline explosion while filming a scene aboard an airplane with Mabel Normand; she emerged unscathed.[76] As for the bombs and explosives used in so many of the Keystone productions, it was reported that the position of inspector of explosives was created to safeguard against accidents, this decision a result of a massive explosion when the wrong, far more powerful bomb was detonated.[77]

Nor was death a stranger to the Keystone company. Cameraman L.B. Jenkins was killed by an out-of-control race car. As Gene Fowler put it, Jenkins had "set up his tripod between two fairly large trees.... [O]ne of the machines blew a tire. The car headed straight for Jenkins, cut the two trees off as evenly as though they had been carefully hewn down, smashed Jenkins against a stump, and killed him."[78] Three others were killed in the accident as well.[79] The film, according to Brent Walker, was most likely *Skidding Hearts* (1917). Stuntman Bernard Harris spoke of his tenure with Keystone in a 1973 interview with

---

Two Film Men Killed in Grand Prize Race.

This year was a disastrous one at the Santa Monica races, when Lewis Jackson, chauffeur for Grace Cunard and Francis Ford, lost control of his car while doing a hundred-miles-an-hour on a dangerous curve, and crashed into four trees. Jackson was instantly killed. His mechanic, John Ghianda, escaped by "stepping out of" the machine before it was torn to pieces. After the flying piece of steel and wood hit the first tree, it crashed into L. B. Jenkins, cameraman of the Keystone Film Company, killing him, and demolishing his camera, which he had been grinding until the impact. A woman running a soda stand was killed. A spectator standing beyond the cameraman was also killed. Grace Cunard and Francis Ford and company were in a box at the grandstand when the wreck occurred and did not learn of the death of their champion until some time later. Miss Cunard was nearly prostrated over the accident. The whole company, which was making a picture around the races, stopped work and went home after the terrible news reached them.

The account of L.B. Jenkins' death, as it appeared in the December 9, 1916 issue of Moving Picture World.

writer Joann Roberts, wherein he said that he witnessed several serious accidents during stunts gone wrong. The worst was the result of a smoke bomb that accidentally exploded, setting off the rest of the smoke bombs. Four actors escaped with only smoke damage but a fifth, who dived over the back of a moving car in an attempt to escape, eventually died of his injuries.[80]

Accidents aside, the critics liked what they saw when *His Smashing Career* was reviewed. "It has the expected Lehrman quality in its wealth of dashes, splashes, jumps and almost unthinkable combinations," wrote *Moving Picture World*. "It is so filled with the unexpected and the astonishing that it baffles any description at all."[81] Lehrman inserted some suggestive footage into the proceedings as well, and this was duly noted. "The director pulled something unusual in the handling of a disrobing act when a gracefully formed young woman prepares to dive into a swimming pool. A few of these go close to the border line of what is permissible, but the director always stopped just in time to prevent an argument with the censors. Men, in particular, will find the picture entertaining."[82]

Damaged — No Goods (December 23, 1917) rounded out the year, co-directed by Jack White and Jay Howe. Father dislikes his daughter's choice of a beau, so the fellow dresses as a woman to gain entrance to the house. As such he wins the father's admiration, but his charade is uncovered just as he and the girl are set to elope. "The greatest fault to be found with [the film], is the lack of clearness in plot in the opening reel," wrote Margaret I. MacDonald in *Moving Picture World*. "The rapid action of the play continues from the very start, but fails to make itself thoroughly understood; and the comedy saves its reputation principally by the funny business toward the end of the second reel, where it works up to a hilarious climax."[83]

In spite of William Fox's commitment to a Sunshine release every other week, a mere sixteen comedies were offered to the public in 1918. These were *Shadows of Her Pest* (January 6, 1918), *Son of a Gun* (February 3), *Hungry Lions in a Hospital* (February 3), *Are Married Policemen Safe?* (February 17), *My Husband's Wife* (March 3), *A Self-Made Lady* (March 24), *A Waiter's Wasted Life* (April 7, 1918), *A Neighbor's Keyhole* (May 5), *Wild Women and Tame Lions* (June 2), *Who's Your Father?* (June 30), *A Tight Squeeze* (July 28), *A High Diver's Last Kiss* (August 25), *Roaring Lions on the Midnight Express* (September 22; extant), *Mongrels* (November 17), *The Fatal Marriage* (December 15), and *The Son of a Hun* (December 29). William Fox gave his reaction to the initial film Lehrman presented to him for his approval, and the films that followed:

> [Lehrman] showed me a comedy on a new idea that took me off my feet. So I put that away and told him to go ahead on some more. This one was too good to be true. When I got back to New York another one followed, and then another, until we have ten of them on hand that have never been seen, except by our branch managers at the Convention. At the same time, some remarkable accounts followed the films from the coast, one of them for $32,000, another for $28,000 and so on. I wired Lehrman to keep on going and not to stop at anything. I wanted fifty more of them. He took it seriously and answered that it would be beyond human possibility to make more than sixteen more this year.[84]

Lehrman lived and breathed film during this time while he was furiously producing the initial ten comedies. "Mr. Lehrman is one of the hardest workers in motion pictures," stated *Moving Picture World*. "While he is making a comedy he generally forgets to eat. As one of his colleagues says, 'He lives on laughs.'"[85] Lack of sleep and food may have impaired Lehrman's judgment, however, leading to a bad outcome for the fellow. He hired a car from S.A. Elmore for use in one of the Sunshines, with the understanding that it was "only to be slightly damaged." Instead, the car was "demolished beyond all hope of recovery." When Lehrman refused to pay for the damage, an enraged Elmore proceeded to do damage to Lehrman's face. Lehrman was hospitalized, and Elmore found guilty of battery and fined $100. "Judge White stated that the attack made by Elmore on Lehrman was, in his opinion, the most vicious in his four years' experience as a police court judge."[86]

It wasn't all work for Lehrman, however, as he managed to fit in a number of extracurricular activities that were for the most part industry related. Lehrman and Ritchie went off on several hunting trips and were joined by actor Tom Mix on one of them. Lehrman reportedly used these trips away from the studio to come up with new ideas for his films, returning "with a considerable amount of written material."[87] Lehrman took part in a late night event at the Bristol café, held by the theater owners and managers of Los Angeles. Lehrman served as one of the principal speakers, along with Hughie Mack and current L-Ko owner Julius Stern.[88] If crossing paths with Stern wasn't enough, Lehrman later attended the grand opening of Sid Grauman's palatial "Egyptian" Theater, sharing the space with former associates Sennett and Chaplin.[89] Several months later in July, 1918, Lehrman was reunited with both Chaplin and Sennett when the three of them joined up with a number of other Hollywood notables in a committee to organize a patriotic event called the "Great War Parade." Put on by the Motion Picture War Service Association, the pageant heralded the two-week long War Exposition.[90]

Dancing was a passion of Lehrman's as well, and when he wasn't competing he would occasionally sponsor a competition. One of these took place at Baron Long's Watts Tavern, where Kenneth Harlan and Lottie Pickford were the winners; they were awarded the Henry Lehrman dancing trophy.[91] And now that he had money burning a hole in his pocket, Lehrman decided to spend some of it on things both worthwhile and frivolous: the former, a $110 contribution to the Jewish Relief Fund;[92] the latter, an auto he helped design to be built on a Packard twin-six chassis by the Earl Auto Works. Its cost? The modest sum of $10,000. The *Los Angeles Times* provided a lovingly detailed description of the finished auto's design and appointments, concluding with "In all its appointments the car shows most exquisite taste and expert artisanship and reflects credit both on Lehrman as its designer, and Earl[e C. Anthony], who built the body under his personal supervision."[93]

"Laugh with Lehrman, The Wizard of Wit." From the August 11, 1917 issue of Moving Picture World.

Billie Ritchie, quickly adapting to American ways, took part in a benefit baseball game organized by the Red Cross, wherein the "Comics" team played against the "Tragics" team. Ritchie's teammates on the Comics team included Hank Mann, Harold Lloyd, Charlie Murray, Eric Campbell, Chester Conklin, Slim Summerville, Bobby Dunn, Ed Kennedy, Ben Turpin, Rube Miller — and Charles Chaplin![94] Not to be outdone, Lehrman staged a baseball benefit at Vernon Park the following May, proceeds going to the Red Cross. Lehrman's team, the Sunshines, played against the All Stars, teamed by actors from a variety of studios. The makeup of Lehrman's team is worth noting as it gives us a listing of those working for Sunshine at the time. Aside from Lehrman, who served as manager, the team comprised Sunshine personnel Lloyd Hamilton, Hugh Fay, Slim Summerville, Bobby Dunn, Billie Ritchie, Tom Kennedy, Al Breslau, Kite Robinson, Bill McDermott, Clarence Dickenson, Al Burns, Ross Lederman, Larry McGrath, Charles Hochberg, Jack White, William Campbell, Al Herman, Jimmie Adams, Chester Thomas, and Roy Del Ruth.[95] "Everyone should aspire," said Lehrman, "to use each spare moment in furthering the interests of some 'win-the-war' branch or society of the U.S. service."[96]

Some exhibitors may have been confused at the beginning of 1918 when a new comedy manufacturer was announced. Located in New York, Sunshine Film, Inc. optimistically promised fifty-two one- and two-reel comedies per year, with former Biograph comedian Gus Pixley to star. Perhaps as a response to a threatened legal action which Fox's lawyers may or may not have made, the comedies were quickly christened Moon Comedies. *No Money — No Fun* and *The Bogus Uncle* were the two single-reels that resulted, which *Moving Picture World*'s reviewer Hanford C. Judson dismissed with the terse "They are disappointing."[97] The series failed to garner any interest and Pixley departed. Sunshine feebly announced several more intended Moon Comedies in the year that followed to star Lola Venus and Gus "Shorty" Alexander: *Their Unexpected Job*, *His Finish*, *Their Downfall*, and *Trouble Inn*, the latter to star someone referred to as "Funny Face" Ascott.[98] It does not appear that any of these were ever released, and Sunshine Film, Inc. became one more footnote in studio history.

Son of a Gun starred Billie Ritchie and was directed by Richard Jones, recently hired away from Sennett and later to add his first initial "F." to his name. A spirited letter from a woman named Phyliss Carr to the editor of *Motion Picture Magazine* is worth quoting in full, given that it provides a synopsis of the film buried within the writer's diatribe about the awfulness of the film.

> If some companies must produce comedies, WHY dont they at least produce DECENT ones? I have had to sit and endure many perfectly abominable slapstick comedies to see the feature picture of the evening, but one I saw the other evening, called "The Son of a Gun," produced by the Sunshine Comedy co., was the worst ever and my patience is exhausted. From start to finish the picture was thoroly [sic] disgusting; in fact, I should call it a satire on the U.S.
>
> Will you please tell me why the censors allow things like this to pass?
>
> "The Son of a Gun" was a two-reel slapstick Sunshine comedy. Most of the scenes were supposed to be laid in Mexico and the star of the picture was supposed to be "General Chronico Appendecito," who, by the way, was a typical little slapstick "runt" with the usual mustache about a yard long, cross-eyed, and with his clothes half falling off of him. I wont [sic] tell you all the horrors that were in this picture, but only the ones that made me the most provoked.
>
> "General Appendecito" wanted some excitement and ordered his soldiers to execute two men for him. One of the men was a drunkard and the other was dressed to represent Uncle Sam. While I didn't mind the drunkard getting executed (as I think they all should be) it surely made me peeved to see them shoot Uncle Sam, even if it was only in the movies. Then again the leading-lady, who was supposed to

be a second Lillian Gish, goes to the American Consul to save her fiancé, and the Consul is a *very, very* poor representation of Colonel Roosevelt, and my opinion is that it shouldn't be allowed, altho [sic] I suppose a great many people would find no fault with this as they dont [sic] all admire him as I do. In another scene, the leading-man is all covered up with dynamite, nitro-glycerine, bombs, etc., with the exception of the soles of his feet, and is about to be blown to atoms, when in rushes a typical Keystone policeman, who looks at the leading-man's feet and

Uncle Sam and Teddy Roosevelt hold off some banditos in Son of a Gun. *Left to right: unknown, Guy Woodward, Edgar Kennedy, and Sid Smith.* COURTESY OF ROBERT JAMES KISS.

exclaims: "He is an American; I must save him." Now I wish some one would be kind enough to tell me how long since it is possible to distinguish Americans by their feet? An automobile chase then follows of more imitation Keystone "cops" and another auto full of Red Cross nurses, speeding to the Mexican border. The auto containing the policemen breaks down and they all jump out and hold up the auto containing the Red Cross nurses and have a regular fist-to-fist fight with them to gain possession of their auto, leave them strewn along the road, take the auto and start along again. In all probability the Red Cross nurses were men dressed up as women, but that scene added nothing to the value of the picture nor was it in the least funny.

Here is the last and, in my opinion, the worst offense. There is a locomotive rushing to the supposed battle laden with still more policemen and it is completely covered with the American Flag. Now if that is the best use the Sunshine Company can think of to put "Old Glory" to, that of being trampled all over by a lot of crazy-acting, crazy-looking men, I think they had better go out of business until they find something better.[99]

Hungry Lions in a Hospital is one of the few Sunshine comedies from the Lehrman period that has survived, less several minutes of footage, and reunites Lloyd Hamilton with his oversized feline friends. Directed by Jack White, with actor Albert Ray serving as his assistant, Hamilton (as Ham Bohn) still sports his "Ham and Bud" mustache in this tale that lives up to its title's promise. The medical facility's doctors all wield huge, nasty-looking knives and are buddies with the local morticians, M. Balmer and Cough Finn. A couple of lunatics — anarchists, perhaps — are loose in the hospital as well. Once the lions (played by Ethel and Gene) are introduced there are some truly hair-raising scenes, and one can appreciate just how terrified those extras must have been that Harvey Parry spoke of. The lions, needless to say, are the primary reason for this film's existence, and figure in the most memorable scenes. There's the obligatory scene of a black man asleep in bed dreaming of his girlfriend, caressing the lion sleeping next to him, the discovery of which causes his hair and eyebrows to go white with fright in a nicely executed dissolve. Ham triumphantly traps one of the lions in a large barrel, but when he enlists the aid of his friends to haul it away discovers that the barrel has no bottom. The patients in the hospital erect a huge barrier of bed-springs turned on their sides and stacked in a futile attempt to keep the lions at bay. As one would suspect, the police are called and rush to the scene in their open-top police car. When one of the lions joins them, all of the vehicle's passengers leap out while driving over a high bridge, plummeting down to the river far below. The unmanned vehicle ends up crashing through the first floors of several buildings. Besides the lions and cops are the ubiquitous bathing beauties, here bathing in an indoor pool. Ham observes them from beneath the surface via a periscope while breathing through a jerry-rigged device, air provided by a pump operated by one of those "lunatics."

Is it funny? Absolutely! Coherent? Well, that's the problem. With all of the introductory scenes and setup missing, coupled with Lehrman's — okay, Jack White's — lightning-paced editing and frenetic action, it is difficult to follow. One just goes with the flow, a "problem," if you will, shared with several of the L-Ko films; *Love and Surgery* comes to mind. Visually the film is much more expensive looking than a number of competitors' comedies, with a lavish indoor pool and elaborate hospital sets. So elaborate that a victim of an auto accident on Santa Monica Boulevard was allegedly rushed to Lehrman's "hospital." Understandably unable to provide the required assistance, Lehrman instead lent his Fiat to transport the poor fellow to the nearest medical facility.[100]

Are Married Policemen Safe? was set both here in the United States and across the border in Mexico, wherein the chief of police of a large Mexican city is able to exact revenge on the U.S. cops who had earlier tormented him in the states. The film, which starred Billie Ritchie, Charles "Heinie" Conklin, and Hugh Fay, is believed to be lost. Based on contemporary reviews, however, it sounds as though it was a typical Lehrman whirlwind of action. "There are as many stunts pulled in this one as in the ordinary serial installment," said *Wid's*. "For instance, two automobiles were shot off into the surf, their occupants spilling all over the screen."[101] *Motography* also mentioned a "railroad train running straight

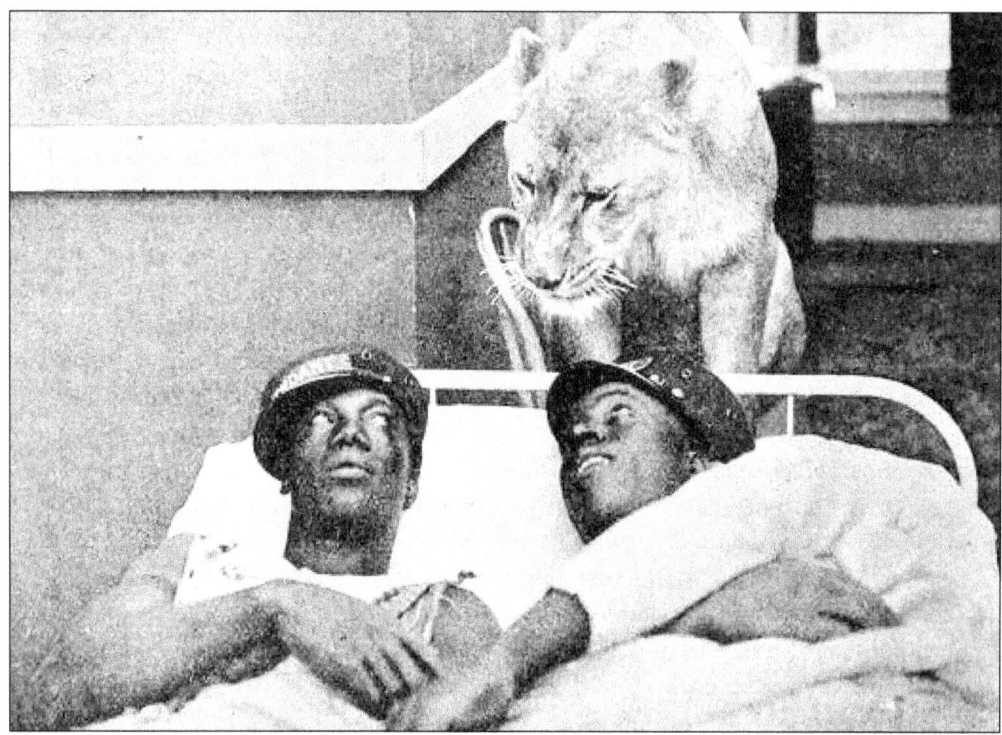

ABOVE: *A rude awakening in* Hungry Lions in a Hospital. BELOW: *Another confrontation in* Hungry Lions in a Hospital.

through a station,"[102] while *Moving Picture World* elaborated on the basic plot somewhat: "The story of the comedy seemed to hinge around the love affairs of a couple of married policemen who tried to marry other wives and were foiled in the attempt."[103] Pretty girls were present in this release as well, their abbreviated clothing landing them in court before a judge ("Hugh Fay as a nance Judge in the picture got laugh after laugh," reported *Variety*[104]). One of them bares her legs to demonstrate what all the fuss was about, forcing the flustered judge to tell her to cover them up. "Now that your charms are covered," read the intertitle, "I can give a just decision." The Kansas Board of Review ordered both the footage and intertitle removed.[105]

Are Married Policemen Safe? was the second Sunshine directed by Richard Jones, and turned out to be his last, Jones bitterly departing from the studio soon after and suing the company $10,000 for breach of contract. "Jones maintains he was under contract to produce pictures for a stated time at a salary of $300 per week, with a bonus of $500 for each successful picture. The company, according to the director, refused to recognize the contract after it had been in force for three months."[106] Jones returned to Sennett and far greater success, later hooking up in the mid-1920s with Hal Roach where he served in multiple capacities as director, supervising director, and producer. Jones left Roach in 1927 to direct features up until his untimely death in 1930 at the comparatively young age of thirty-seven.

Little is known about *My Husband's Wife* aside from the fact that it was both written and directed by Lehrman, and starred Hugh Fay. *A Self-Made Lady* starred Dot Farley as "a 'she crook' who was sentenced to seven days in prison, but through a slight error was behind the bars for seven years. When the 'she crook' gets out she wants to go straight but circumstances won't let her."[107] Reviewer Peter Milne described one of the film's running gags:

> The head crook keeps a package of money lying on a table toward which he leads all disagreeable personages such as policemen. When greedy fingers seize on the package they innocently spring a trap door beneath and the intruder is projected into a tank of water. The first time this is pulled it is uproarious, for the unfortunate cop discovers a dozen of his companions waiting below to welcome him.[108]

Bobby Vernon and Edgar Kennedy co-starred, with David Kirkland directing a story written by Lehrman. Kirkland was drafted shortly midway through filming and had to leave in a hurry for San Francisco. He took actor-writer Al Ray with him, discussed the finish of the film, and Ray then returned to Los Angeles and completed the film.[109] Kirkland's drafting brought his association with Sunshine to an end, but he would return to the industry a year later once his tour of duty was completed. Comedy shorts would for him be a thing of the past, however, his focus now on feature work, hired by Constance Talmadge to helm a trio of her vehicles.

Lloyd Hamilton, meanwhile, was sidelined for four weeks due to an injury incurred while filming *Hungry Lions in a Hospital*. A swinging door was the culprit, striking Hamilton's shoeless left foot and breaking the big toe's bone in two.[110] His first film after he returned to the studio was *A Waiter's Wasted Life*, which *Moving Picture World* called "[a] roaring comic picture with witty subtitles and fresh ideas that positively compel hearty

ABOVE: *"Nance judge" Hugh Fay checks out Marvel Rae, as Sid Smith (far right) looks on, in* Are Married Policemen Safe? COURTESY OF ROBERT JAMES KISS. BELOW: *Dot Farley tempts Victor Potel with some cash in* A Self-Made Lady. COURTESY OF MUSEUM OF MODERN ART/FILM STILLS ARCHIVE.

laughter."¹¹¹ Set in both a lunch room and the jail next door, Hamilton starred as the luckless waiter who ends up on the gallows in lieu of the murderer, who has escaped. This was the first film in which Hamilton appeared without his famous mustache.¹¹²

Winifred Westover was Billie Ritchie's co-star in *A Neighbor's Keyhole*, with Hugh Fay and Charles Dorety lending support. Reviewer Peter Milne commented on the comparative lavishness of the tale unspooling on the screen: "This appears to be one of the most elaborate and extravagant comedies that Henry Lehrman has ever produced for the Fox program. Its special effects include a hurricane and a violent rainstorm which continues throughout the two reels. The wild chasing...goes on through wind and rain.... The two reels must have cost a sum equal to that expended on the average five-reel feature, perhaps more."¹¹³ One of the film's sequences involved the flooding of a swank hotel, and production involved a lot of water for this and other scenes. The *Dramatic Mirror* reported on the impact this had on the neighborhood, stating that "pedestrians on the East side of Western Avenue where the Sunshine Comedy studios are situated have, during the past week, skirted the studios and taken to the road. Henry Lehrman has been making a comedy, employing much water, some sets being completely submerged and the overflow has kept Western Avenue a correct imitation of a small river."¹¹⁴

Full-page Sunshine Comedies ad, from the March 9, 1918 issue of Moving Picture World. *That's Lehrman astride the bomb in the lower left-hand corner!*

Wild Women and Tame Lions is a curiosity in that it appears to have undergone some considerable changes after its initial release on June 2, 1918 and its re-release a year later. Reports surfaced towards the end of 1917 that comedian Ford Sterling had been engaged by Lehrman to star in Sunshine comedies.¹¹⁵ Several weeks later another account stated that Sterling was acting in a comedy being made by Lehrman. "Ford Sterling plays the leading part. Among other things it is remarkable for its presentation of the famous humorist in an entirely new make-up."¹¹⁶ Charles Parrott was pegged as Sterling's director in the February issue of *Motion Picture Magazine*,¹¹⁷ the publication then changing its tune a month later when it reported that former Keystone director Harry Williams had been engaged to direct Sterling.¹¹⁸ And then nothing further was printed in 1918 associating Sterling with Sunshine Comedies, and Sterling was back with Sennett by May. It wasn't until mid-1919 after Lehrman's departure from Sunshine when Fox quickly re-released thirteen of Lehrman's best comedies that Sterling's name resurfaced as the star of *Wild Women and Tame Lions*:

> Ford Sterling plays the hero in "Wild Women and Tame Lions," and is given ample opportunity to show his talents as a tailor and a lover — making a much greater success as the latter despite irate husbands. The lions are used in bedroom and parlor scenes. A fighting kangaroo is one of the features of the comedy.[119]

Everyone is checking out Winifred Westover (right), including janitor Charles Dorety, in A Neighbor's Keyhole. COURTESY OF ROBERT JAMES KISS.

The problem with this report is that for the initial release of this film there was absolutely no mention of Ford Sterling's presence, instead Tom Kennedy and Ethel Teare were cited as the stars. Further complicating matters is the original copyright synopsis for the film deposited with the Library of Congress, which details a typical lions-on-the-loose bit of slapstick with nary a mention of a tailor and his philandering. The late researcher Robert Birchard, former editor of the American Film Institute's AFI Catalog of Feature Films and the AFI Academic Network, had been researching the Fox comedies for what promises to be the definitive history of that studio's output. He obtained not only this synopsis but a number of stills credited to this film as well, and a number of these stills clearly show a clean-shaven and bespectacled Sterling along with co-stars Hugh Fay and Virginia Rappe, while others look like they've come from another film altogether. In a correspondence with this author, Birchard speculated that "perhaps what happened is they shot with Sterling, but didn't complete the film. Then shot the synopsized version, and only later for the reissue resurrected Sterling's footage, which allowed them to claim that this was 'better and funnier' than the original."[120] While merely supposition on his part, it sounds reasonable. An amusing sidenote: In the synopsis, the three lions are named Abie, Julius, and Jacob, a subtle dig at L-Ko owners Abe and Julius Stern and their partner Louis Jacobs.

Cowboy actor Tom Mix, who was Selig's big star for nearly eight years and well over one hundred fifty shorts, had been signed by Fox at the beginning of 1917 to star in the new Foxfilm Comedies opposite Victoria Forde.[121] A series of two-reel comedies followed that included *Hearts and Saddles*, *A Roman Cowboy*, *Six-Cylinder Love*, *A Soft Tenderfoot*, and

Jimmie Adams (left) and Tom Kennedy react to a snarl in the original Wild Women and Tame Lions.

Tom and Jerry Mix before Mix made the switch over to dramatic western features based on the success of his five-reel *Durand of the Badlands* (August 12, 1917). While Mix was filming *Fame and Fortune*, Lehrman was busy looking for an actor for his next film which would eventually be released as *Who's Your Father?* The film was to be a western comedy, and Lehrman needed someone who would look at home in the role both on horseback and on foot. Not having much luck with the actors on hand, Lehrman mentioned his predicament to his friend Mix, perhaps with the hope that Mix would offer his services. Not only did Mix agree to star and direct the comedy, "he jumped at the chance of getting into a rapid-fire comedy," or at least according to *Motion Picture News*.[122] The plot had to do with a cowboy's rescue of a baby adrift in a tiny crib, and the spinster (a jaw-dropping Frank Hayes!) who claimed the infant was hers in hope of forcing the cowboy to marry her. Concurrent with this is the kidnapping of Mix's girl Colette (Gertrude Selby) by the town's sheriff (Heinie Conklin) and his dimwitted deputy (Vic Potel). There is some mistaken identity confusion at one point between a white baby and a black baby, and the Chicago Board of Censors went scissor-happy over this subplot. Excise "all scenes of colored woman talking to white man outside her cabin door," was one of their dictates, along with "colored man looking at self in mirror and at white child on couch," and "colored man apologizing to white man and scene of his talking to him." And while they were at it,

ABOVE: *Hugh Fay, Virginia Rappe, and Ford Sterling in the reworked* Wild Women and Tame Lions. COURTESY OF ROBERT S. BIRCHARD. BELOW: *Is this Abie, Julius, or Jacob having his hair done by Frank Hayes in* Wild Women and Tame Lions?

they cut out the shot of the "man pulling fish out of his trouser front" as well.[123] The film fared less well in Ohio, where it was rejected outright due to its title.[124] This would prove to be Mix's very last comedy short, with the western star reportedly issuing the departing comment "Never again! This comedy stuff is too fast for me!"[125] The film survives in a print held by the Library of Congress.

Lloyd Hamilton's next release was *A Tight Squeeze*, co-starring Ethel Teare, Jimmie Adams, and Tom Kennedy. This reunited Hamilton and Teare after their years working together in Kalem's Ham and Bud comedies. Hamilton had asked for Teare when he was hired to work in the Sunshine comedies, but had to wait for a contract she was then working under to expire.[126] Exhibitors seemed to like the results, one of them reporting that it was "A good comedy; one that you hear loud and continued laughing from. Animals worked very cleverly,"[127] while another reported that "This is the best two-reel comedy I have looked at in a long time. Who ever [sic] directs the animals around the Fox shop deserves a medal for this."[128] That director was Jack White, assisted by William H. Watson, their second joint effort; *A Waiter's Wasted Life* was their first.

Glass slide for A Tight Squeeze. COURTESY OF JIM KERKHOFF.

Director William Beaudine affords us a glimpse into the making of one of the Sunshine Comedies. Beaudine had entered the industry back in 1909 with Biograph, initially doing whatever he was told to do but eventually working up to assistant director, primarily for Mack Sennett where he received his first taste of filmmaking of the comedic sort. With Sennett's departure in 1912, Beaudine spent the next year and a half in Dell Henderson's unit as his assistant before moving over to Kalem in 1914. There he directed Bud Duncan and Ethel Teare, and with Duncan and Lloyd Hamilton's teaming some of the Ham and Bud Comedies. A move to Universal followed in 1916 where he directed dozens of comedies for Joker, followed by a brief stint with Triangle at the end of 1917 into 1918 when one after another of the eight comedy units was let go, Beaudine's being the last.[129] With his dismissal, Beaudine made the rounds of the studios and was offered a job by Lehrman at $100 a week, a $50 decrease from his previous salary. Beaudine was to assist director Noel Smith on the film *A High Diver's Last Kiss*, starring Slim Summerville, Bobby Dunn, and Betty Carpenter. Production issues had plagued the film, and at the end of a month only one reel was in the can, so Beaudine was brought on board to help get the film completed in a more timely fashion. Lehrman promised Beaudine that with the completion of this film he would have full responsibility for the direction of the next one. It wasn't to be. After five weeks on the job, "I came home from location on Saturday," said Beaudine, "and Al Herman, Lehrman's hatchet man, was waiting for me at the studio. 'Mr. Lehrman says you don't

ABOVE: *Frank Hayes at his loveliest, from* Who's Your Father? BELOW: *Heinie Conklin (left) and Vic Potel are the law in* Who's Your Father? PHOTOS COURTESY OF LIBRARY OF CONGRESS.

have to show up on Monday,' he told me. Lehrman got sore because I dozed off during the gag meetings, and that was that."[130]

The plot had something to do with a high diver's insistence upon marrying his boss' daughter before he'll make a dangerous dive. When he is kidnapped, his girl decides to take his place. "A bomb which has been placed at the top of the ladder is discovered by the girl and thrown into the assembled throng," said a synopsis in *Exhibitors World*, "her one-piece bathing suit is snatched from her back by her sweetheart, who seeks to rescue her in an airplane, and she rushes from the tank to his arms, an aerial elopement providing the ending."[131] The eloping couple was portrayed by Summerville and Carpenter.[132]

The dive, according to a contemporary account, was staged in Venice by champion high diver Mae Eccleston, from a reported height of one hundred feet into four feet of water.[133] Beaudine, remembering her solely as "this dame," claimed years later that it was only a sixty foot dive.

According to Beaudine, Dunn had quit two weeks into production after an on-set argument, and an intertitle was written providing an explanation for his absence. Filming took place in June and into early July, 1918, but Dunn and Summerville "of the Sunshine Comedies" were performing together at a Red Cross benefit in August,[134] which would seem to indicate that Dunn was still affiliated (or re-affiliated) with Sunshine. Regardless, Dunn had moved back to L-Ko by November.[135]

Norman Taurog told interviewer Sam Gill about how, after acting as Lehrman's assistant, he was "eased" into directing chase sequences:

> How I got established as a director was from chases. Lehrman was a very lazy man and he hated to do chases. He would get up to a certain point in the picture — of course he was a great comedy director — and he'd always try to slough off the chase because that was the toughest thing to do. In those days we didn't have process. You had to go out to Hillcrest in Hollywood and on those wide streets going up and down there by Vitagraph, and make all your chases — of course, you had permits. So he used to slough them off and say, "Norman, you go out and do them. You start it, then I'll be out." Well, he never showed. Loving the business the way I did, wanting to direct as badly as I did, naturally I worked it out as much as I could.
>
> So there it was: all of a sudden one day, go out and do the chase. Of course, having assisted Lehrman, knowing how meticulous he was, what a good comedy director he was, I picked up an awful lot from him.[136]

This experience eventually led to Taurog's first onscreen credit:

> When I started with Lehrman, the credit on the pictures was "Henry Lehrman — Sunshine Comedies." It took a long time before I got screen credit. Then one day, he couldn't help himself because I made a very outstanding chase that really rocked him. It was with speed boats and was such a great chase and got so many laughs in the theater, he said "I'm going to give you credit as my co-director." So it said "Directed by Henry Lehrman and Norman Taurog." You couldn't get a bigger boost for a start in your career because he was just like Mack

ABOVE: *Gertrude Selby and her daddy, Jimmie Adams, in* Who's Your Father? COURTESY OF LIBRARY OF CONGRESS. BELOW: *Lloyd Hamilton and Ethel Teare have a visitor in* A Tight Squeeze. COURTESY OF ROBERT JAMES KISS.

Sennett. The minute people saw that, they said "Oh, this guy's got something or Lehrman wouldn't share credit with him." Little by little, Lehrman started to turn over pictures to me. I started to make pictures, then he became the supervising director of all the units.[137]

The fourth of the Roaring/Hungry Lion entries, *Roaring Lions On the Midnight Express*, co-starred Billie Ritchie, Jimmie Adams, and Hugh Fay, and Lloyd Hamilton may have had a bit part in blackface, but that has not been confirmed; Lehrman directed. The film's paper-thin plot involves just that as several lions break loose from their cages in the baggage car and proceed to terrorize the rest of the train's passengers. Filming took place on tracks near the Salt Lake Station in Long Beach. A complete Pullman train was secured along with a crew to operate it on a section of track long enough for it to get up to speed when filming. In keeping with the films of this era, on-screen blacks were the butt of many gags. The lions went through their various paces obediently, but would on occasion get carried away. Actor Hugh Fay and several fellow actors were at the receiving end of one of these incidents that took place on top of the train, and no doubt were terrified as a result:

> The same lion was used on top of the train in another scene and was behaving beautifully, when all of a sudden he seemed to take a striking fancy to [Hugh] Fay, who was playing in the scene, and started to run after him. The trainer, followed by his assistant, with gun in hand, tried to quiet the beast which insisted on following the actors along the top of the moving train. When he leaped lightly into the engine, the engineers scrambled for their lives. The old fellow seemed to pay but little attention to them, however, but after sniffing about the cab awhile discovered that his prize was cornered on the top of the great iron monster. As he stepped through the window in pursuit, the cameramen were photographing him from a speeding automobile running alongside the train. Again a wonderful comedy situation had been photographed for the screen, and the terror of the actors' faces, together with the angry snarls of the great beast, promised a thrill of delight to the thousands of people who would roar at the seemingly comical situation, which promised in the making to be turned into a tragedy at any moment.[138]

One of the film's noteworthy gags involves "a mysterious passenger whose odd appearance is explained by a startling discovery." Evidently the economy-minded fellow hoped to get the most bang for his buck as it is revealed that he has brought along a small horse in his oversized suitcase, and his son in a carpet bag. The conductor explores further, finding the wife and the rest of the family both huddled under and sitting upon the shoulders of others, all hidden beneath a very roomy shawl![139]

Not surprisingly, the success of the Sunshine lion comedies was noted by opportunistic Julius Stern over at L-Ko, who quickly put a series together co-starring comedian Charley Dorety with the Century Lions. Initial entries starting at the beginning of 1919 sported such titles as *Lions and Tin Horn Sports*, *Looney Lions and Monkey Business*, *Frisky Lions and Wicked Husbands*, and *Howling Lions and Circus Queens*, and were directed by Vin Moore. There would be more than a dozen additional outings with lions before interest waned and the series had run its course.

ABOVE: *Billie Ritchie takes an impressive tumble in* Roaring Lions on the Midnight Express.
BELOW: *More passengers in harm's way in* Roaring Lions on the Midnight Express. PHOTOS COURTESY OF ROBERT JAMES KISS.

Lehrman's love and use of animals in his comedies was a topic of considerable comment in the press, and this extended well beyond the lions that made it into the titles and were foremost in the movie-going public's conscience. There were ostriches, of course (fifty-seven of them in one film), elephants, ducks, rabbits, and even a trained bumblebee if one of the more far-fetched claims was to be believed. This latter flying insect had a role in one of the films where it stung a mouse on its tail, which swelled and carried the rodent aloft as if a helium-filled balloon.[140] Grace Kingsley wrote of a "party" that actress Gertrude Griffith gave for the Sunshine menagerie, stating that most of them had names such as "Joe, the monkey; Theodore, the cat; Billy, the goat; Bum, the bulldog; Rats, the terrier; Ludwig, the dachshund;" along with three nameless white mice and four nameless canaries.[141]

Full-page ad for Roaring Lions on the Midnight Express, *from the August 10, 1918 issue of* Moving Picture World.

Dogs were, perhaps, Lehrman's favorite, appearing and reappearing in his films at regular intervals. "Dogs are the smartest of all animals," said trainer Rennie Renfro. "You pick 'em and train 'em for six months, and you have something. I got Buster from Henry Lehrman, the producer. He was the runt in a mongrel litter of nine. Lehrman made me give him $25 for him. Six months later he worked him in a picture, tried to buy him back for $5,000. I wouldn't sell him. I love that dog."[142] Another canine "star" at Sunshine was Lehrman's brown and yellow brindle bull Jess, who went missing at the Exposition park one day in August during some location filming. A despondent Lehrman offered a reward for the dog's return, but Jess' fate was never reported.[143]

Montana Kid, the dog, had roles in several of Lehrman's comedies over the years, but it was with director Jack White's *Mongrels* that a quartet of the four-legged canines took center stage. Teddy the dog starred, with Lloyd Hamilton, Gertrude Selby, and Jimmie Adams lending support. The human part of this amusing bit of propaganda involves "a gang of Hun spies," led by top Hun Adams, out to destroy a munitions factory, while Hamilton and Selby provide the love interest. Adams eventually gets the worst of it, hung from a flag pole and sagging out of sight as the American flag flaps in the foreground. As for the dogs:

> …Lehrman had printed a big sign reading, "Enemy aliens must not cross this line." On one side of the line is shown a French poodle gnawing a bone.

ABOVE: *Sylvia Day and a top-hatted, mustached Billie Ritchie expose the "mysterious passenger's secret, while Hugh Fay and Slim Summerville observe. From* Roaring Lions on the Midnight Express. COURTESY OF MARC WANAMAKER AND BISON ARCHIVES. BELOW: *Production shot likely from Century's* Lonesome Hearts and Loose Lions *(08/27/1919). Foreground left to right: Phil Dunham, Marjorie Ray, and Dan Russell. The fellow in the background is probably lion trainer Charles Gay of Gay's Lion Farm in nearby El Monte, California.* COURTESY OF SAM GILL.

A dachshund, wearing a Hun helmet, comes along, crosses the line and attacks the poodle. The poodle puts up a valiant defense of his rights, but as he is fighting, a vapor bursts, from the dachshund's mouth, representing the Germans' poison gas.

The English bulldog comes to the aid of the poodle, and the two pursue the dachshund into a kennel, which rocks and rolls violently during the conflict.

Then, seeing that the dachshund is still full of fight, the poodle runs away and brings back an American terrier. The American terrier, the French poodle and the English bulldog pitch into the German dachshund and clean him up with neatness and dispatch.[144]

The English bulldog, American terrier, and French poodle await their enemy, in Mongrels.

"Dandy comedy," said one theater owner. "Everyone liked it."[145] "A regular riot," said another. "Sunshine comedies are in a class by themselves."[146] But while Lehrman's dogs were kicking German butt onscreen, an increasing number of U.S. soldiers were needed to do the real thing in a war that we'd been a part of for over a year. The threat of an increase of the draft age — the originally twenty-one to thirty-one years to the much broader eighteen to forty-five years — had the studios scrambling, with big stars like Douglas Fairbanks and William S. Hart soon to be in the crosshairs. A so-called "War Squad" followed through on its "work or fight" promise to go after anyone of draft age engaged in film extra work, arresting, detaining, and ultimately inducting a number of unlucky individuals.[147] The studios responded by quickly putting in motion a plan to "comply" by creating a central pool of full-time extras, paid a flat twenty dollars to thirty dollars a week, to be used by anyone requiring their services. The downside was that of the 1,200 people currently on the "extras" list, only 400 of them were to be hired; the rest of them were out of luck.[148]

Lehrman, who had registered for the draft on September 10, joined the Hollywood Officers' Training School. The school had been organized on January 18, 1918 to prepare studio employees for eventual induction into the armed services, and ten of his Sunshine employees soon followed suit.[149] The ten are worth naming as they indicate who was working for Lehrman at this time: Hugh Fay, Lloyd Hamilton, Jimmie Adams, William Watson, Glen Cavender, Frank Coleman, Tom Kennedy, Harry Lorraine, William Campbell, and Al Herman.[150] Sunshine cinematographer George Meehan was on his way to France in the U.S. Army's camera division,[151] former Foxfilm comedian Hank Mann was already there with the Fortieth Division,[152] and directors David Kirkland and Noel Smith had both been called up. Scenario and title writer Ralph Spence, formerly with Keystone, had been called a year earlier but was spared enlistment, so Lehrman promoted him to managing editor of the Sunshine Comedies.[153]

Lehrman had come to love the U.S., a country that had afforded him considerable wealth and prestige, and had made his name known throughout the film industry. When the Studio Liberty Loan Campaign was announced, Lehrman made certain that his studio purchased Liberty Bonds. (Whether this and subsequent contributions were made solely out of unbridled patriotism, untinged by a lingering concern that being foreign by birth might cast a jaundiced eye towards his presence here, is unknown.) For the third campaign held in mid-1918 which collected a total of $1,274,900, Sunshine's purchase amounted to a modest $8,000, less than most of the other comedy companies' contributions: the Chaplin studio purchased $52,000 worth of bonds, Sennett $48,000, Christie $18,500, and even the Sterns' L-Ko $11,000, but a few thousand more than King Bee's $3,600. These purchases were all comparatively small potatoes when compared to the big boys: the Lasky studio's $302,700, Fox's $141,700, Hart's $122,000, and Universal's $102,400.[154] As they said, though, every penny counted. When the fourth drive rolled around in October, Lehrman was one of two (Lasky was the other) to contribute two days in advance of the official beginning of the drive, personally contributing $5,000.[155] The Fourth Liberty Loan Tank meeting was held at Los Angeles' Central Park, and Lehrman, as chairman of the affair, appeared "with his entire company" that included Ritchie, Hamilton, Hugh Fay, Mack Swain, Fred Fishback, Hampton Del Ruth, Roy Del Ruth, Gertrude Selby, Betty Carpenter, Vera Steadman, Jimmie Adams, Mae Eccleston, Hazel Deane, Harry Lorraine, Frank Coleman, Ethel Teare, Jack White, Billy Watson, William Campbell, Charles Dorety, and Leach Cross.[156] Within a month Lehrman had upped his personal contribution to $10,000, with his studio adding another $27,600 to the Liberty Loan pot. All told, the fourth drive collected a whopping $4,860,450.[157]

Adding to the studios' woes were the extra costs incurred due to the war. Both negative and positive costs had increased by a half-cent per foot, which Fox estimated would add an additional annual cost of $40,000. On top of that was another quarter cent-per-foot tax levied on positive stock, adding considerably to the release cost of each film.[158]

If the increased costs, the prospect of a staff slowly decimated by the draft, and the threat hanging over their own heads wasn't enough to cause headaches for the studio owners, the growing demands of organized labor were. In late August, 1,100 members of the International Association of Theatrical Stage Employees and Motion Picture Operators walked out over demands for a flat wage of six dollars per eight hour day, and nine dollars for overtime. A number of studios, including Fox, gave in rather than face a shutdown, but others refused including Sunshine (which was semi-autonomous from Fox), Christie, Lasky, Triangle, Morosco, and Vitagraph.[159] Chaplin, L-Ko, and Sennett were among those who caved.[160]

And that wasn't all. Elsewhere, all hell had broken loose, both here in the U.S. as well as internationally. People everywhere were panic-stricken over the spread of what had by now come to be called the Spanish Influenza pandemic. While its exact origin is unknown, the consensus seems to be that it was here in the heartland, in Kansas.

This occurred just as we were gearing up to enter the European war, so as raw recruits were shipped from one army outpost to another, squeezed into overcrowded barracks, and eventually sent overseas, it didn't take long for this virulent strain of the flu to spread from one carrier to the next. The first wave in March and April of 1918 was deadly, but comparatively less so than the second, more virulent wave that surfaced in August and hit its peak in October. It spread from port cities on both coasts and along rail lines and rivers as carriers moved about and unknowingly passed it to most anyone they came in contact with.

The symptoms could be terrifying. As an individual's condition worsened, blood could flow from his or her nose, from violent coughing, and even from the eye sockets. Bodies would turn a dark blue, almost black as cyanosis set in, a coloration one witness described as "a dusky, leaden hue." Philadelphia was hit hardest, with a peak of 4,597 deaths in a single day. New York City witnessed more than 33,000 deaths in all, and eventually 30% to 40% of the country would be affected. By the time it had run its course it has been estimated that there were more than 675,000 deaths here in the U.S. alone. Worldwide estimates were staggering, with anywhere from 21 million to more than 100 million deaths attributed to the Spanish Flu.[161]

By the time the flu reached the West coast, however, the experience of others had given local officials a good idea of how to react, and in a proactive fashion. In October, the Los Angeles Public Health Director ordered that all schools be closed, and that all public gatherings be forbidden — and this only two days after announcing that there was "No cause for alarm." The studios were quick to respond, stating that most of their work was outside, and with smaller groups of people. Some agreed to a voluntary plan of curtailed production that involved a four week "vacation" — without pay — as each unit completed current filming.[162] Metro, Universal, and Fox all adopted this plan, but Lehrman chose to ignore it, reportedly requesting permission to do so since he was behind schedule. Sunshine continued with full production, its four companies trying to keep up with the demanding schedule.[163] Lehrman wasn't alone in this decision, with the Chaplin and Griffith studios among several others following suit.[164] Lehrman himself was stricken with a mild attack of the flu in January, and confined to bed for ten days with a hired nurse at his side.[165]

Theater owners, needless to say, were not happy with the enforced closings, but kept their patriotic lips sealed — for awhile, at least. A rumor spread that Julius Stern had brought the flu to Los Angeles after a stay in New York. "That's a Spanish disease," Stern was reported as saying, "not Jewish."[166]

Sunshine was growing as a result of the popularity of its comedies. A new administration building was constructed on the Western Avenue side of the studios that housed Lehrman's executive suite as well as the general offices, the purchasing, scenario, accounting, and publicity departments, and the cutting and assembling room.[167] Additional staff was brought in as well. In October, Lehrman hired Hampton Del Ruth, former production manager and scenario writer at Keystone, to serve in a similar capacity at Sunshine.[168] The trades indicated that Del Ruth had voluntarily left Keystone, but former Sennett editor William Hornbeck said otherwise in an interview with Kevin Brownlow: "A title on Sennett comedies said 'supervised by Mack Sennett in collaboration with Hampton Del Ruth.' The story goes that when Sennett found out what collaboration meant, he fired Hampton Del Ruth."[169]

Twenty-four year old director Fred Fishback was hired a month earlier, another Sennett defectee.[170] Romanian-born Fishback had come to the U.S. around the turn

LEFT: *Hampton Del Ruth*. RIGHT: *Jack Cooper*.

of the century and, after a short stay at Thomas Ince's Broncho, was hired by Keystone in 1914 as a bit player, prop man, and when needed, as a stunt man. He moved up to assistant director later that same year, becoming a full-fledged director in 1916. He was prolific and proficient in this capacity, helming comedies starring Mack Swain, Chester Conklin, Ford Sterling, Ben Turpin, and Polly Moran. Lehrman put him to work directing both Swain and Ethel Teare, both of whom he had worked with back at Keystone.

Another new hire was "society girl" Virginia Rappe. "So clever has she proven herself in the art of creating laughter," stated a studio press release, "that Mr. Lehrman will probably offer her a long-term contract.... Her rare beauty, combined with an exceptional understanding of just what is required to secure a laugh, promises a most brilliant future for this young girl, who but a short time ago knew absolutely nothing about the motion picture art...."[171] It probably didn't hurt that the two had known each other for several years now, and that she was Lehrman's girlfriend ("quite the season's best-looking New Yorker," wrote the *Los Angeles Times*' "Bishop of Broadway"). Rappe would play a big part in Lehrman's career in a few years, and not necessarily a good part.

To show that there were no hard feelings over any earlier publicity-related swipes, Lehrman hired his old protégé Jack Blystone away from L-Ko at the end of the year. Blystone's contributions and importance to the L-Ko had been built up at Lehrman's expense after Lehrman's departure from L-Ko, and some of those press releases must have proved irksome. But that was past history now, and Blystone resigned his position as general supervisor of production for the Sterns to return to direction at Sunshine.[172] Salaries and, it would appear, working conditions were more appealing at the Sunshine studios than at either L-Ko or Keystone. Norman Taurog put it this way: "[W]hen we worked with Fox, who had the world by the tail, then we spent money because they had great faith in Lehrman."[173] If Fox's press releases were to be believed, Sunshine's annual expenditure for twenty-six comedies was $1,500,000; "This cost is greater than that of all other comedies combined!" crowed one full-page ad.[174] Blystone was to head up a new fourth unit, desperately needed to meet exhibitor expectations and achieve Fox's stated goal of twenty-six releases for the upcoming year.[175] On the alternate weeks starting January 12, 1919, Tom Mix comedies would be released, with five of his past best being re-titled and re-edited as initial offerings while Mix went to work creating new product.[176]

Lloyd Hamilton, Hugh Fay, and Mack Swain took time out in November to put on a show for the soldiers at nearby Camp Kearney. Hamilton and Swain's comedy double "pretty nearly caused the army men to laugh themselves to death," reported the *Oakland Tribune*. "Lloyd and Swain work wonderfully well together — I'd like to see them do a regular vaudeville turn — or even in the pictures together."[177]

The last two releases of 1918 were *The Fatal Marriage* and *The Son of a Hun*. Little is known about either film, aside from the fact that the former starred Billie Ritchie — almost unrecognizable in a top hat, monocle, and an even bushier mustache than the one made familiar back at L-Ko — along with Hugh Fay, Sylvia Day, and Joe, the orangutan; William Campbell directed. "Joe is called upon to express his opinion of a German in this production," reported *Motion Picture News*. "According to those producing the film Joe expresses this opinion to the satisfaction of all patriotic Americans."[178] One can only imagine. Jack White helmed *The Son of a Hun*, which starred Lloyd Hamilton, Gertrude Selby, Dave Morris, and Jimmie Adams in a tale of a wedding that devolves into a battle, culminating with a tank demolishing a house. Reviews were sparse for both of the films, neither of which — along with the bulk of the Sunshine Comedies — appear to have survived the ravages of time.

We are more fortunate with the first two releases of 1919 — *Oh! What a Knight!* (January 26) and *His Musical Sneeze* (February 23) — in that they are among the few Sunshine Comedies from the Lehrman era known to have survived. *Oh! What a Knight!*, new-hire Fred Fishback's first effort for Sunshine, starred Mack Swain and Ethel Teare, with Jack Cooper and Glen Cavender rounding out the cast. The film is a terrifically amusing spoof of western melodramas and their time-worn conventions, with just about every cliché in the book thrown in for good measure. Jam-packed with a feature's share of broad action and stunts, the film boasts some truly spectacular horse work that would have the SPCA up in arms these days. The intertitles are hilarious, and a major contributor to the film's overall entertainment value.

Swain plays mama's boy Sunny Jim Arsenic, the boastful but ineffectual and cowardly sheriff of Dead Horse. Teare is his girl, Black-Eyed Susan, but she falls for dastardly Jack

ABOVE: *Hugh Fay kisses Sylvia Day's hand while Billie Ritchie lifts Fay's pocket watch, in* The Fatal Marriage. BELOW: *The wedding in* The Fatal Marriage. *Left to right: William Irving, Hugh Fay, Phyllis Allen, Frank Hayes (minister), Sylvia Day, and Frank J. Coleman (with cup).* COURTESY OF ROBERT S. BIRCHARD.

Rancid (Cooper), who later holds up the Pink Garter saloon and makes off with a bag of cash. Jim actually manages to corner Rancid, but Susan convinces Jim to let the robber go. Jim heads back to town to return the retrieved cash, but a turn of events cause him to relinquish his badge: "Boys, I may be western but I'm squar'," he tells the posse that intercepted him on the road, "and when a woman's honor is at stake Sunny Jim's lips is sealed!" Returning home in shame, his mother restores his courage: "We ain't never had a coward in the house of Arsenic!" Jim heads out and confronts Rancid, first in his hideout

Lloyd Hamilton is caught by Jimmie Adams in The Son of a Hun. COURTESY OF ROBERT JAMES KISS.

where a knock-down, drag-out fight ensues, and finally in a climatic free-for-all in the saloon where, after an exciting chase on horseback, Jim lassos and overcomes Rancid. Now a hero, Jim's badge is returned and he is reunited with Susan. As the two kiss, Jim's ma arrives and smacks him on the rear with a rolling pin. "Mother, you've broken my heart," he responds. She drags Jim off by the hair, leaving Susan behind.

The film is a faster, funnier, more frenetic redo of Fishback's 1916 Sennett Keystone-Triangle *His Bitter Pill*, with Swain reprising his earlier role of Big Hearted Jim, Teare assuming Louella Maxam's earlier role of Sun Kissed Nell, and Cooper in Edgar Kennedy's earlier role of Diamond Dan. The little kid who plays Susan's younger brother carries his part well enough, and proves to be a trooper as Cooper throws him across a room, and later on as he's picked up by his two arms as a pair of horseback rider gallop past on either side of him, a painful looking "rescue" at best. Fishback's direction keeps things moving at a breakneck pace, with tongue firmly tucked in cheek. As historian William K. Everson once put it, "nobody here merely mounts a horse when a spectacular leap will do instead."[179] *Oh! What a Knight* would be re-released over the years with the alternate titles of *The Sheriff's Mustache* and *Cowboy Ambrose*, the latter no doubt chosen to associate the film with Swain's popular character of the same name.

His Musical Sneeze is another delight, with Lloyd Hamilton in the lead as Casper, whose father (Jimmie Adams) takes the disinterested fellow to the exclusive Rocky Bed Lodge; retired Woodrow Butts and his daughter Lucy (Virginia Rappe) are already there. Casper is saddled with a very bad cold, his sneezes so violent and musical that they launch

"Nobody here merely mounts a horse when a spectacular leap will do instead." From Oh! What a Knight! COURTESY OF ROBERT S. BIRCHARD.

an Oriental rug into the air, clear a dining room table of its contents, and are eventually mistaken by a group of assembled hunters as the call to embark on a fox hunt. Baron Charles Peabody (Charles Dorety) arrives on the scene, and professes undying love to Lucy in hopes of getting his hands on her wealth. Casper intervenes, so Lucy tells them that "Whoever gets the fox — gets me." This doesn't go as planned, so Peabody proposes a duel, which is interrupted by the arrival of a lion! Casper incapacitates the lion with the odor from a skunk he caught earlier in the belief that it was a fox, and is hailed a hero. Butts awards his daughter to Casper.

Jack White directed what turns out to be one of the more outlandish comedies of the period, essentially a vehicle for the film's two set pieces, the rabbit hunt and the later fox hunt. In the former, a totally disorganized group of hunters run about and fire their shotguns willy-nilly at the fast-moving rabbit in a mind boggling melee, each shot causing the ground to erupt in huge explosions, with nearby hunters tossed in the air like rag dolls. Casper goes after the rabbit on foot, following it into its hole and burrowing through the earth in dogged pursuit. The rabbit has the upper hand, taunting Casper by flicking sand in his face, nipping at his fingers and reducing Casper to tears, and eventually biting at his rear and tearing off a long piece of under drawers. The latter fox hunt culminates with Casper's capture of the skunk, Casper's horse collapsing to the ground unconscious as a result of the odor while Casper is oblivious due to his cold.

Lloyd Hamilton averts his gaze from lovely Vera Steadman in His Musical Sneeze.
COURTESY OF ROBERT JAMES KISS.

Aside from these two lengthy sequences, gags abound throughout the film. Rappe's reflection is seen in a vanity mirror, and she is assumed to be the woman sitting before it with her back to the camera. When the woman turns, however, she is revealed instead to be Rappe's black maid (Madame Sul-Te-Wan). As Adams and Hamilton drive to the lodge, a rabbit hopping down the road outpaces their vehicle. Hamilton and Dorety engage in a gravity-defying fight, Hamilton first easily tossed dozens of feet through the air, exacting revenge by violently shaking Dorety in an action akin to a dog killing a squirrel, ending with Dorety flung through the air and landing in a distant rubbish can. Dorety's reaction to the arrival of the lion is arguably the film's funniest moment, his knocking knees a fast-moving blur, followed by a labored attempt to flee by manually lifting one paralyzed leg after the other.

Lehrman once again spent a lot of money on a set, this one the impressive interior of the lodge shown to full advantage in the wide opening shot; A.H. Giebler, having visited the set during filming, called it "one of the largest I have ever seen used in a comedy."[180] Whether or not White was instructed by Lehrman to do so, the bulk of the film's close-ups are reserved for Virginia Rappe. These include close shots of her in her swimsuit before each of her two dives from a cliff to the pool of water below, her later arrival in the lodge hall decked out in her fox-hunting togs, and her final arrival at the film's end on horseback. When the camera wasn't lingering on Rappe it was otherwise trained on Casper's horse's face as it reacted in several shots to the overpowering odor of the skunk.

LEFT: *Fox general manager Winfield "Winnie" Sheehan.* RIGHT: *Billie Ritchie in costume for* The Fatal Marriage.

There is a nice, wide tracking shot as the mounted fox-hunters approach on horseback, the camera drawing back and "joining" in the chase. All in all, a delightfully surreal comedy, one that *Moving Picture World* called "one long laugh, with a refreshing amount of new material in its two reels."[181]

Unfortunately for Lehrman, he wasn't around at Sunshine to see either of these two initial 1919 releases. Nor, for that matter, was the bulk of his staff.

Lehrman and Fox's relationship came to an unceremonious end, at least according to a story that circulated at the time. Arriving at the studio for work one morning, Lehrman was stunned to find that wherever his name had resided side-by-side with William Fox's on the exterior studio walls, now only Fox's name now remained. Winfield "Winnie" Sheehan, Fox's general manager, had one of the studio's painters remove Lehrman's name the night before.[182]

The excessive costs of the Sunshine Comedies had become a sore point between Fox and Lehrman, in spite of Fox's earlier assertions that cost was inconsequential, and quality foremost. Sheehan had been instructed to keep an eye on the activities at Sunshine, and had confronted Lehrman mid-January demanding to know some details of the operation. This was several days after Helen Morrison, Lehrman's personal secretary for the past five years and the studio's current business manager, had died on January 13, 1919, a victim of influenza. Lehrman had assumed personal charge of the services and burial, which took place in one of the plots he owned, Lehrman and his staff serving as pallbearers.[183] Sheehan grilled him for information, but Lehrman, put on the spot so soon after her passing, responded that Morrison "was in close touch with the financial affairs," and that "her demise left him slightly in a quandary."[184] It didn't help matters that Lehrman was sick with the flu, and probably not at his sharpest.[185] Was Sheehan's confrontation coincidental, or did he take advantage of the situation? We'll never know, but one thing is for certain: He used Lehrman's inability to answer specific questions to his advantage, sealing the fate of the Fox-Lehrman relationship.

On Saturday, January 18, the Fox Film Corporation terminated its contract with Lehrman and, it was reported, fired Lehrman's entire staff. The supposed victims of this mass firing included directors Jack White, Jack Blystone, and Fred Fishback, business manager Al Herman, and the actors Billie Ritchie, Gertrude Selby, Hugh Fay, Lloyd Hamilton, Ethel Teare, and more than fifty other actors and technicians. The unofficial reason was that the Fox Film Corporation and Lehrman could not come to terms on the financial details of their contract. Lehrman claimed that the move was an outgrowth of the trend to eliminate the middleman in the production and distribution of films.[186] Sheehan stated that the reason was the unreasonable production expenditures that Lehrman had insisted on making: "Sunshine Comedies, Inc., has terminated its contract with Henry Lehrman for the best interests of the business," stated Sheehan. "The Fox Film Corporation intends to continue producing and distributing comedies on a greater scale than ever. Definite plans of enlarged project will be announced later."[187] Fox wanted his comedies held to a cost of $20,000 to $22,000,[188] and Lehrman's were exceeding this guideline.

An article that appeared in the *Los Angeles Herald* earlier in January regarding Lehrman's plans for "the greatest of all his splendid achievements as a comedy maker" that would be "built on scientific lines…every situation being figured out before Mr. Lehrman will begin to direct it" suggest why Sheehan's patience may have run out:

> For this purpose the carpenter staff have been given instructions to build in miniature every known character, including animals of all kinds, that is extant. Also working models of a submarine, battleship, balloon, aeroplane, trolley car, steam engine, interior of a laundry, a hotel roof garden, and numerous other models. The biggest cast ever assembled for any one comedy is to be seen in this production.[189]

Gone were the days of "seat-of-the-pants" script-less direction. Lehrman, it was reported, was going to institute a suit against Fox for the amount of $200,000, "a just rating of damages sustained by [Lehrman]."[190]

Of course now that the Sunshine ranks had been decimated, Sheehan and Fox needed to regroup and make plans for the "new" Sunshine. To that end directors Fred Fishback and Jack Blystone weren't fired as initially reported, but retained to continue making comedies for Sunshine.[191] Or at least that was the plan; Fishback, perhaps after directing one last comedy *The Merry Jailbirds*, packed his bags and headed over to Century. There were a handful of lesser comedies in the can that could be released to plug some holes in the schedule, but only two remained that were made under the Lehrman regime. *Money Talks* (March 23, 1919) was the first, directed by Fishback with Jack Cooper, Mack Swain, and Gertrude Selby starring. *Moving Picture World* liked the film, stating that "The subtitles are witty, the action is astonishing, and the whole, though indescribable, is certainly amusing."[192] *Wid's Daily* thought well of the pairing of Swain and Cooper, calling them "a contrasting pair who work well together."[193] *Variety*'s reviewer, on the other hand, sat through a showing at the Rivoli, and later wrote that "A Fox Sunshine comedy, 'Money Talks,' closed the film entertainment without getting a laugh."[194] None of the reviews mentioned what sounds like it would have been the film's high point:

> One of the greatest thrillers staged in Los Angeles for a film was shot this week when Bobbie [sic] Dunn jumped from the eleventh-floor fire-escape of the Bryson Apartments while five cameras played upon him. This scene is for the Lehrman Sunshine comedy released by Fox, titled "Money Talks," and in which Dunn plays the part of a man 80 years of age, when unable to get an apartment with bath, has his tank of cold water placed outside his window, but eleven floors below. Fred Fishback is directing this subject, and had use of several hundred wealthy tourists, who witnessed the thriller and played the part of atmosphere in the scene.[195]

Buster Keaton recalled this filming some forty years later for his autobiography, in a more detailed, albeit slightly different, fashion:

> Lehrman offered him five dollars to jump off the Hotel Bryson roof into a mortar box full of water. The Bryson, in downtown Los Angeles, was eight stories, and from its roof eighty feet above the street the mortar box, which was nine feet long, five feet wide, and five feet deep, looked about the size of a domino. When Bobby accepted the offer Lehrman asked him if he could make the jump on that Friday afternoon. "I'm making a picture for Sennett all this week," he said thoughtfully. "They'll be shooting on Friday, but I doubt that they'll be using the Cops that afternoon. I'll be able to sneak out all right." Bobby made the dive headfirst. Diving eighty feet into water five feet deep meant he must hit just right with his chest, then immediately cut upward in an arc. He came up without a scratch, collected his five dollars, dressed, and hurried back to the Sennett lot before he could be missed.[196]

Reports had surfaced a month earlier which stated that Lehrman had "found an old man of 76 years, who in his youth, was an expert swimmer, and [had] agreed to make a 100-foot dive into four feet of water."[197] The article's wording indicated that the dive was yet to take place, and one would assume that this was merely a figment of some publicist's over-active imagination. If true — and that would be difficult to swallow — it would suggest that perhaps the elderly fellow got cold feet and backed out at the last moment. Either that, or died in the interim.

The other film, originally scheduled for release before *Money Talks*, has a rather bizarre history behind it. The negative for *A Lady Bell-Hop's Secret* disappeared one day before Lehrman's termination, and it was hinted at the time that this was another reason for the split. Fox Film Corporation posted semi-accurate accounts of the mysterious disappearance a month later in the trades:

NEGATIVE STOLEN

On Friday afternoon, January 17, 1919, a Sunshine Comedy negative, measuring 1,800 feet, was stolen either from the Fox Studio, 1401 North Western Avenue, Los Angeles, California, or while in transit, care American Railways Express Company.

Shipment of negative was made from Fox Studio in a sealed wooden case. When the case was opened the cans were found to contain gravel and dirt.

The negative was entitled *"A Lady Bell-Hop's Secret,"* valued at $50,000.

Notice is given to all branches of the trade that if this negative, or positive prints thereof, be offered for sale, hire or lease, immediate telegraph notice should be given to the undersigned.

The robbery is now under investigation by Criminal Authorities. The title of this Sunshine Comedy may be changed by those responsible for the theft. Briefly, the story is that of a girl who works as a bell-hop in a hotel. Her sweetheart has knowledge of the location of six million dollars in gold hidden in a sand pit. The gold is recovered by the villain, who escapes in an aeroplane and drops from the parachute into an open cage of lions, etc., etc.

Information with reference to the theft or location of negative may be given to either the nearest Police Authorities, the Sheriff or direct to

FOX FILM CORPORATION
130 West 46th Street New York City[198]

While it was hinted in previous press releases that Sol Wurtzel, general superintendent of the Fox studio, had strong suspicions of who was involved in the theft, it wasn't until the beginning of February before names were named. Film cutter Charles Hochberg was accused of embezzlement in a complaint issued by Deputy District Attorney McCartney. Wurtzel stated that the film had cost $32,000 to produce (rather than the $50,000 stated in the later full-page ad), and that Hochberg had been instructed to package the negative, insure it for $25,000 with Wells Fargo and Co., and ship it to the Fox Film Company in New York. "Wurtzel said he became suspicious and informed the express company, which opened the metal box at San Bernadino." Only sand and rock were found inside.[199] Lehrman's attorney Milton Cohen took on Hochberg as a client, and Hochberg was arrested but released on cash bail of $2,500. The grand jury's investigation of the theft began on February 19.[200] Six days later, both Lehrman and Hochberg were charged with acting in collusion in the theft, and were indicted on two counts, one alleging grand larceny and the other for embezzlement. A parade of witnesses was brought before the grand jury, which along with Wurtzel included Julius Stern of L-Ko. Lehrman was released on

$2,500 cash bail as well.[201] On April 1 both Lehrman and Hochberg pleaded not guilty, and Cohen filed two demurrers which were overruled. The trials were set for May 22.[202] "I financed the Sunshine Comedies for a year and a half and devoted my entire energies to making a success of the work," said Lehrman. "It would be suicide to my career for me to have stolen a film that would be valueless to me."[203] The case against Lehrman was dismissed on April 10 due to insufficient evidence, but Hochberg was still on the hook.[204] His trial began on May 6,[205] but on May 14 he was freed of the charge.[206]

LEFT: *"Lost Negative Found!" But where? Full-page ad for* A Lady Bellhop's Secret, *from the May 3, 1919 issue of* Moving Picture World. RIGHT: *Betty Carpenter cuddles up to Hugh Fay in this poster for* A Lady Bellhop's Secret.

The *New York Dramatic Mirror* made a telling statement about the charges made against the two of them: "When Henry Lehrman was indicted for larceny recently he claimed 'frame up.' When he was exonerated at his trial before Judge Willis in a Los Angeles court later, many skeptics granted that, perhaps, he was right."[207] Perhaps those skeptics were right, but we will never know for sure.

But then, just as mysteriously as the negative disappeared, it reappeared. *The Lady Bell-Hop's Secret*, originally scheduled for a February 2 release, finally went into release on May 4, two days before Hochberg's trial began. A full page ad announcing the film's upcoming release appeared in the April 27 issue of *Film Daily*, declaring "LOST NEGATIVE FOUND! $50,000 PICTURE A LADY BELLHOP'S SECRET NOW READY FOR RELEASE." [208] The details behind the film's return — or *was* it found? — were never reported.

A Lady Bell-Hop's Secret starred Hugh Fay and Betty Carpenter, with direction attributed to William Campbell, who had left the studio the previous September.[209] *Moving Picture*

World liked the belated results, if in a somewhat less-than-informative way, calling it "[t]wo reels that will surely make a houseful of laughter. A farce of comical characters as well as comical doings, it is replete with good old doings worked up anew. A flood in an upper room of a hotel, caged lions and buried gold are some of its fun-making things."[210] A.H. Giebler had visited the Sunshine set while the aforementioned scene was being shot, and said that "I got out on the stage at the same moment that Hugh Fay made his entrance into a scene that represented the hallway in a hotel. Hugh was accompanied by 37,000 gallons of water — and they let all that good water run around all over the place, and nobody tried to mop it up."[211]

Betty Carpenter and Hugh Fay in A Lady Bellhop's Secret. COURTESY OF COLE JOHNSON.

With the release of *A Lady Bell-Hop's Secret*, the last of the new Lehrman productions had its premiere. Lehrman may have been gone from the studio, but the films he was responsible for during his less than two year stay remained, and whatever feelings Fox had toward Lehrman at this time, he knew the films themselves were gold. Given the impending gap in product for release, *The House of Terrible Scandals* was re-released as a Sunshine Comedy on April 20, 1919. "[O]ne of the best slapstick comedies that has been released in a long while, reported *Variety* on its return, "and it had the blasé Broadwayites practically falling out of their seats."[212]

In late May, Fox Film Corporation assistant general manager Herman Robbins announced the upcoming "second edition" of thirteen of the best of Lehrman's output. Packaged as "The Lucky Thirteen," new prints were struck from "revised and re-edited negatives," offering a potential clue as to how Ford Sterling came to be in *Wild Women and Tame Lions*. Scheduled for release weekly during the months of June, July, and August, the other films in the package included *Roaring Lions and Wedding Bells, A Milk-Fed Vamp, His Smashing Career, Damaged — No Goods, Shadows of Her Pest, The Son of a Gun, Hungry Lions in a Hospital, Are Married Policemen Safe?, A Self-Made Lady, A Neighbor's Keyhole, A Tight Squeeze*, and *Roaring Lions on the Midnight Express*.[213] "The Lucky Thirteen" were thrown together "By Command of the Exhibitors of America" who no doubt fretted over the news of Lehrman's termination and the looming hole in the upcoming release schedule.

Hampton Del Ruth, who had been promoted to head supervisor of the studio after Lehrman's termination, signed Chester Conklin and Billy Armstrong as a first step in dealing with the depleted ranks, along with directors Vin Moore, Eddie Cline, Mal St.

Clair, Roy Del Ruth, and Frank Griffin. Del Ruth also assembled a so-called "Beauty Brigade," which was described in *Variety*: "[Del Ruth] claims that it takes the prize for variety, versatility and pulchritudinous charm. It is said to possess members who not only can act, but can dance, sing, dive, swim, run, wrestle, box, drive motor cars and speeding motor cycles, climb — girls, in fact, who will take all sorts of dare-devil chances on sea and land, or in the air."[214] Some girls! The thirty bathing beauties included Marvel Rea, Dorothy Lee, and Vera Steadman among their ranks.

Two-page ad promoting "The Lucky 13." Lucky for Fox, who needed to fill a gap in Sunshine's production schedule. From the June 28, 1919 issue of Moving Picture World.

It wasn't long before Del Ruth fell out of favor with the penny-pinching Fox and his right-hand man Wurtzel. "It was DelRuth's [sic] ambition to make comedies irrespective of cost so that Del Ruth's name could be glorified," wrote Wurtzel to Fox. "[I]nstead of making comedies for quality with a view of cost, he made them for quality only,"[215] an approach akin to Lehrman's. A contract was drawn up for Blystone with an eye to the future, and within a few years Blystone would, once again, assume his superior's position when Del Ruth was let go.

One of Fox's complaints about both Lehrman's and Del Ruth's reigns as the Sunshine comedies' supervisors was that "neither one of the two succeeded in developing a single comedian that became an asset to the company."[216] Keeping an eye out for just such a comedian, Fox felt that Australian-born acrobat and pantomimist Clyde Cook would be the studio's great white hope. "Fox Film Corp. feels reasonably sure Cook will ultimately take Chaplin's place," telegraphed an overly-optimistic Fox to Wurtzel.[217] It didn't turn out that way, and by 1925 Cook had moved over to the Roach studios.

Without Lehrman's creative energy, imagination, and seeming willingness to throw money at any given production, the Fox Sunshines that followed devolved into slick but predictable slapstick, still better than a lot of smaller comedy companies' output, but lacking that unique inspired quality that the Lehrman touch imparted to them. Winnie Sheehan quickly tired of them, and felt that the public had as well. In early 1921, he wrote a strong, impassioned memo to Fox detailing their shortcomings and the new direction he felt they needed to take.

The Sunshine Beauties. Left to right: Anita Burrell, Hazel Deane, Mildred Lee, Betty Carpenter, and Mae Eccleston. COURTESY OF ROBERT JAMES KISS.

I feel that the Sunshine staff and their idea appears to be concentrated on violent and rough comedies. By this I mean that the story, gags and sequences carry with them acts of violence of a character that is bitterly opposed by censor boards and people interested in combating censorship influence and expansion.

The use of bombs, bottles labeled poison, gun play, pick-pocketing, robbery, theft, appear too frequently in Sunshine Comedies. Also the dress of our comedies is too grotesque and inhuman.

ABOVE: *Slim Summerville, preoccupied with his ice cream cone, in the Sunshine* Comedy Pretty Lady *(11/22/1920).* BELOW: *Jimmie Adams appears fascinated by the wrangling of a goat in this production still from an unnamed Fox comedy.* COURTESY OF MARC WANAMAKER AND BISON ARCHIVES.

In almost every Sunshine Comedy of late there has not been a central idea or plot in connection with the picture. It is simply a series of hokum, rough gags, even depicting criminal acts, which do not get a laugh and are only interesting because of the rapid action involved....

Sunshine Comedies has depended upon rapid action more than situation, story or plot for their appeal. I believe the public is tired of this type of comedy. For instance in Harold Lloyd, Buster Keaton and even in the Charlie Chaplin

The Fox Imperial comedy Wine, Women and Sauerkraut, *directed by Jess Robbins (05/22/1927).*

picture The Kid, there is a central idea behind each comedy and the action is much slower than Sunshine but the laughs are more frequent, wholesome and sure.

I therefore recommend that we have more plot, story and slower action, with the additional rearrangement of more modern clothes and elimination of grotesque facial make-up on the part of our actors in future Sunshine Comedies. I do not mean to kill the finish of the story by slow action, because I realize the importance of a fast finish to any comedy.

I realize that this is a vital and drastic change in the class of Sunshine Comedies, but I believe the time has arrived when the public demand the exhibitors are loud in their requests for a rearrangement in the type and style of Sunshine Comedies.[218]

A number of Sheehan's points are well taken, but delivered from the point of view of a New York city sophisticate most likely lacking a real sense of what a large segment of undemanding, escapism-seeking middle America was quite happy with. It didn't help that the stuffy, moralistic Sheehan seemed to lack a sense of humor, and probably would have been happier had Fox never gotten into the comedy business in the first place. Few of the Fox comedies of the 1920s have survived, but some that do, such as *Wine, Women and Sauerkraut*, *Twenty Legs Under the Sea* (both 1927), and *The Lady Lion* (1928), would suggest only a partial evolution. The grotesque caricatures, outfits and makeup that Sheehan abhorred appear to have been minimized in place of clean-cut youthful types, but the scantily clad beauties are still quite in evidence, and the broad slapstick remains. And, for that matter, there was at least one toothless lion still hanging around the studio.

The Sunshine comedies were to be comingled with other brands such as Imperial, Fox, and the Van Bibber offerings. They would continue for several more years, finally disbanding at the end of the 1928 season with the coming of sound. Lehrman, of course, was long gone by the end of the previous decade, but as fate would have it he would reconnect with Fox in the future, and not just once.

CHAPTER 7

Henry Lehrman Comedies: Overstepping His Bounds

The termination of Lehrman's contract with Fox may very well have played into some simmering, vaguely formulated plans on Lehrman's part. The Fox publicity machine had been unstinting in its promotion of Lehrman as the second-to-none genius of comedy, with a seemingly endless stream of articles appearing weekly in the trades touting his unparalleled creativity and imagination. As often as not the ads in local papers included Lehrman's name along with the title of that week's Sunshine offering, and not always accompanied by Fox's. Lehrman's reputation was by now well established among those in the industry, and had taken hold in the minds of the public as well. As for Lehrman himself, there was little doubt that his films were every bit as good as those of his former cohort Sennett, and in some aspects even better given their inflated budgets and, of course, the Lehrman "genius" behind their frenetic storylines.

Soured by his eventual unhappy relationships first with Laemmle and the Sterns, and then with Fox and his bean-counting sycophants, Lehrman had little appetite for entering into another business relationship of that sort. The solution must have seemed obvious to him: he would explore creating his own studio of which he would be his own boss, answerable only to whatever distributor he could come to terms with to deliver a steady and dependable flow of comedy shorts for an agreed-upon cost. To that end, and within less than a month of his exit from the Fox family, Lehrman announced in the trades the formation of his own studio. Initially heralded in a full-page ad that appeared in the February 15, 1919 issue of *Moving Picture World*, the studio-to-be would be called Lehrman Comedies, and would produce twelve two-reel comedies per year.[1] Promising to "unearth new and elaborate angles in production" for release on the open market[2] "of the usual intense character," eventual output was soon upped to include five-reel comedy dramas.[3] Curiously, it was rumored that Charlie Chaplin was to be one of the principal backers of Lehrman's new studio, but that report proved to be just that — a rumor.[4]

The studio was officially incorporated on March 21, 1919, under the name of Henry Lehrman Productions, Inc. There were three trustees of the new studio: Lehrman, his lead comedian Billie Ritchie, and Lehrman's cameraman George B. Meehan, Jr. Capital stock was set at $100,000, with one thousand shares of a par value of $100 each. Subscribed stock opened at $20,200, with Lehrman owning two hundred shares and both Ritchie and Meehan owning a single share each.[5]

Born on July 19, 1891 in Brooklyn, twenty-eight year old George Meehan had relocated to California in 1910. Eventually entering the industry as a mechanic and tester, Meehan was reportedly involved with some stunt work as well. Lehrman took notice of the young man and hired him to work for Sunshine as an assistant cameraman. A six month stint followed in the U.S. Army's Signal Corps, where Meehan served as official photographer

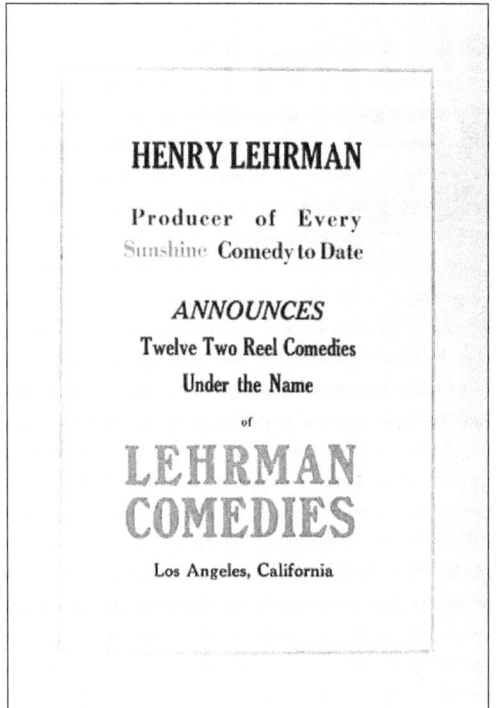 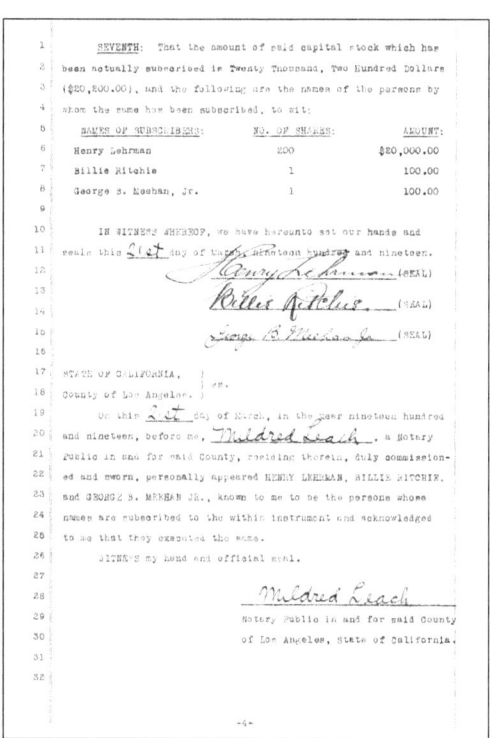

LEFT: *Lehrman's full-page announcement in the February 15, 1919 issue of* Moving Picture World. RIGHT: *Page four of the* Articles of Incorporation of the Henry Lehrman Productions, Inc., *dated March 21, 1919.*

attached to the General Staff. After being mustered out, he reconnected with Lehrman and, with the purchase of this single share of stock, became part of what would more commonly be known as Henry Lehrman Comedies.[6]

Harry A. Sherman, a former Minneapolis exchange man and president of Sherman Productions, Inc., was hired and sent to New York in late March to negotiate for the distribution of the upcoming comedies. Several weeks passed before Sherman struck a deal with First National Exhibitors' Circuit, the details as reported by *Variety* to distribute twelve two-reel comedies a year, with a $40,000 advance on each negative. As Lehrman's official representative, Sherman signed the one-year agreement on April 25 with an option for an additional twelve month period.[7] *Moving Picture World* reported that the "deal involved a sum said to exceed $1,000,000," and went on to say that this "sum of money is said to be the largest ever paid for two-reel comedies, with the exception of one or two comedy star contracts, and is undoubtedly the highest financial return ever recorded for comedies of the shorter length, minus a star. This transaction is made all the more extraordinary by the record breaking time in which it was concluded, not more than an hour having been required to consummate." The deal as reported here was for a two-reel comedy every six weeks rather than monthly.[8] Monthly or every six weeks, it really didn't matter since there was no time limit set in the contract.[9]

First National Exhibitors' Circuit had been organized two years earlier by Thomas L. Talley and J.D. Williams. Its membership was made up of independent exhibitors nation-

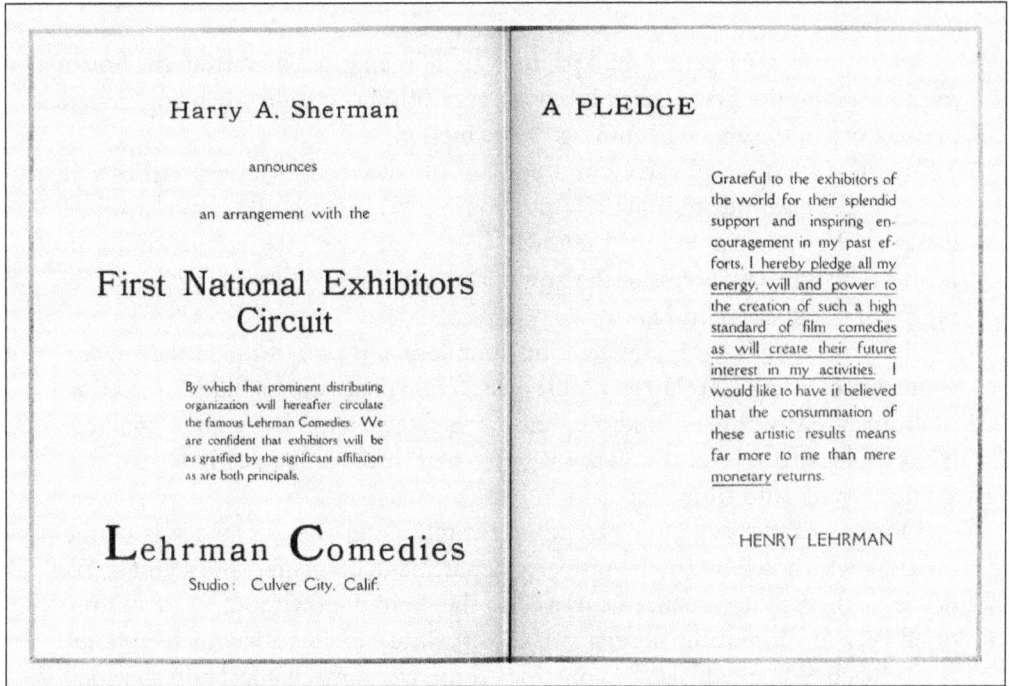

Lehrman's pledge, as it appeared in the May 10, 1919 issue of Moving Picture World.

wide who banded together to use their collective resources to acquire films directly from established stars and directors, thereby avoiding the high rental costs, block booking, and other ills previously forced upon them by producers — Adolph Zukor and his Famous Players-Lasky Corporation output the biggest offender.[10] One of the circuit's most notable arrangements took place in June 1917 when they signed Charles Chaplin to a "million dollar contract" calling for eight two-reel comedies per year with a $125,000 advance on each negative. Chaplin, needless to say, was one of the "comedy star contract" exceptions.

Lehrman was quick to tout the new arrangement in an awkwardly worded testimonial that was part of a two-page ad appearing in *Moving Picture World*: "Grateful to the exhibitors of the world for their splendid support and inspiring encouragement in my past efforts. I hereby pledge all my energy, will and power to the creation of such a high standard of film comedies as will create their future interest in my activities. I would like to have it believed that the consummation of these artistic results means far more to me than mere monetary returns."[11]

Meanwhile, Lehrman acquired a ten acre piece of property on Washington Boulevard in Culver City just north of the recently built Ince studio. Located on a sub-division of the south portion of Rancho Rincon de Los Bueyes, the deal was closed on April 7, 1919.[12] Plans were drawn up for the new studio by the Hollywood-based architectural firm of Meyer and Holler (aka Milwaukee Building Company).[13] The planned studio would be the fifth in the area joining Ince, the Goldwyn company which was leasing the Triangle studios, producer Wayne Mack who was leasing the Essanay studios, and the Culver City Film Company; ground was broken on May 27.[14] As the new studio neared completion in early July, the *Los Angeles Times* detailed the plant's setup and features:

> Large forces of carpenters and painters are now engaged in putting the finishing touches on the first of the big stages, and diffusers are already being placed, preparatory to the actual beginning of production.
>
> The new studios will carry out a number of advanced ideas, evolved by Mr. Lehrman. The administration building, fronting Washington Boulevard, will be distinctly Venetian in design. There will be a great lake, 600 feet in length, in front of the property, access to the grounds and business offices being gained by means of ornamental bridges.
>
> The first of the stages, now nearing completion, is one of the largest in the country, measuring 100x250 feet, and construction plans also include the erection of an inclosed [sic] glass studio of the same dimensions. Three large concrete tanks are located at intervals on the stage, so that three companies, if desired, can produce water stuff simultaneously.
>
> Opening off the stage, and extending entirely along one of its sides, is a large building which will house the property department, carpenter shops and scene decks, so that any article may be moved to the desired set without waste of time or effort, and without the necessity of moving it off the floor on which it stands.
>
> In this building will also be constructed the weird mechanical effects which enter into the making of the modern comedy, and enable the cavorting comedians to defy everything from the law of gravity to the police force. Flanking the stage on the opposite side are two large two-story buildings, one of which will be given over to dressing-rooms and temporary business offices, while the other will be devoted to various technical departments.
>
> The Lehrman studios, when completed, will represent an investment of approximately $200,000…[15]

The estimated $200,000 price tag was a considerable increase from the originally reported cost of $75,000 a mere two months earlier,[16] upped once before in the interim to $100,000. When one considers that the Thomas Ince Studios next door came in at $200,000 as well just a year before,[17] and for a much larger setup, this final cost is considerable and, in retrospect, probably far too extravagant. The doubling in cost, it was reported, was the result of an arrangement to lease space at the opposite end of the lot to his old friend Roscoe Arbuckle to make films for release through Paramount-Artcraft. Arbuckle was said to have an equal partnership arrangement with Lehrman,[18] but the latter was quick to put the rumor to rest: "The new studios are entirely my own property," said Lehrman. "I have no partners nor associates whatever in their ownership. Mr.

ABOVE: *Exterior view of the Henry Lehrman Studios, 1919.* BELOW: *Aerial view of the Henry Lehrman Studios, 1919.* PHOTOS COURTESY OF MARC WANAMAKER AND BISON ARCHIVES.

Arbuckle's…position at the studios will be solely that of a tenant. I am moved to make this point clear in justice to both Mr. Arbuckle and myself."[19]

The diffuser system that Lehrman was having installed warranted note in the press due to its unprecedented practicality. "Henry Lehrman is equipping his new studio at Culver City with an ingenious diffuser system that gives perfect protection to the diffusers without the necessity of a covered stage," wrote *Moving Picture World*.

> Above the center of the stage is a small A-shaped glass roof, under which all the diffusers are pulled in case of rain, or when work is finished at the end of the day. The system is made up of two sets of diffusers meeting in the center, all made so that they may be pulled in either direction, so that light may be admitted to any desired spot on the stage and nowhere else. To keep out undesired streaks of light, each diffuser is hung at a slight angle and overlaps its neighbor for about a foot on each side. The result is a stage covering that is absolutely light-tight. The system prolongs the life of a great expanse of diffuser canvas, and other studio heads on the west coast are considering plans for using the system on their open stages.[20]

Lehrman began assembling a staff of players, directors, and technicians, many of whom had worked for him formerly, and three — Billie Ritchie, Lloyd Hamilton, and Jack White — who had been on Lehrman's payroll continuously since their collective departure from Sunshine.[21] White was assigned to direct, with Norman Taurog brought on as his assistant. Hamilton and Ritchie, of course, were to be the brand's lead comedians. Henry Roberts Symonds, who was with Lehrman at both L-Ko and Sunshine, was signed to the producing staff. Al Herman was appointed general superintendent, Earle Olin was hired as technical director, E.M. Popper as purchasing agent, and A.L. Barnes as auditor. George Meehan was the studio cameraman, and Charles Hochberg, now absolved of those lingering charges of theft, was appointed film editor of the upcoming comedies; Arthur Roberts was hired to assist Hochberg. Edward C. Thomas, formerly West Coast manager of the *Exhibitors Trade Review*, was hired as publicity director.[22] By mid-August, Olin was erecting sets for Arbuckle, who was now on the lot. By October Edward Thomas had resigned, teetering on the brink of a nervous breakdown; he made a hasty retreat to the countryside on the advice of his physician.[23] Lehrman put pencil to paper conjuring up new ideas for storylines, refusing all inquiries from outsiders hoping to get in on the act; "the producer himself originates all the stories for Henry Lehrman Comedies."[24]

Olin came up with an idea that was quickly adapted for use in the new studio:

> One of the great items of waste in studio technical departments is involved in the damage which is done to "flats" and scenery by the constant nailing of stage braces, which are attached to the flats only to be torn off again within a few days. This necessitates constant replacing of wooden strips, and proves a considerable item of expense. Mr. Olin's device entirely eliminates nailing, and consists of two jaws which are actuated by a tapered steel pin, and tightly bind two sections of scenery together. A slot in the clamp receives the end of the brace, the other end of which is nailed to the stage floor. A single tap of a hammer effectively locks the clamp, while another tap on the other end is all that is necessary to release it.

The device, which was estimated would result in the saving of thousands of dollars annually by the producers of motion pictures, was patented by Olin. Arbuckle became a financial backer, and Lou Anger, Arbuckle's business manager, was put in charge of marketing the new device.[25]

One interesting report surfaced at the end of July that flies in the face of the notion that Lehrman and Chaplin were somewhat less than friendly. "Charlie Chaplin visited the Henry Lehrman studios in Culver City last week," wrote the *Los Angeles Herald*, "and spent

Interior view of the Henry Lehrman Studios, 1919, with the overhead diffuser system in place.
COURTESY OF MARC WANAMAKER AND BISON ARCHIVES.

the afternoon in going over the new plant with Mr. Lehrman and swapping reminiscences of the early days."[26] Another report followed in mid-September which only adds to the notion that the two were very friendly; it took place at the Ship Café in Venice:

> The music that rang through the night air was refreshing, machines whirled up to the door, when along came Charles Chaplin accompanied by Henry Lehrman. They quickly stepped in and were seated at a table, when Roscoe Arbuckle loomed in sight, and he entered the same door, followed by Larry Semon and Lucile Carlisle, James W. Horne, his charming wife, kiddies and others, Antonio Moreno, George Beban, Frank Berzage [sic] and his friend wife (Rena Rogers), Lew Cody, Louis Gasinier [sic], Will Rogers, Tom Mix and Victoria Forde, Mitchell Lewis, Russell Simpson, Fred Fishback and wife (Ethel Lynne), Buster Keaton, Al St. John and wife, Albert Ray and wife, Earle Williams and wife, Kennth Harlan, Lottie Pickford, James Morley, Tim McGrath, Viola Dana and party, Teddy Sampson, Eddie Ring, Louie and Oscar Jacobs, and hundreds of others of filmland.[27]

Other of Lehrman's outside activities involved both work and play. Back in April he had met with a number of film men to set up an exclusive club whose membership would be restricted to a one hundred maximum. "It is designed to be quite exclusive," reported *Variety*. Initial members included Lehrman, Chaplin, Douglas Fairbanks, Sid Grauman and others, with meetings scheduled for the mezzanine floor of the Hotel Alexandria.[28] Lehrman also found time to take up piloting an airplane, being coached by early aviation pioneer and Venice's first official aerial policeman Orvar Meyerhoffer.[29] More affectionately known as "Swede," Orvar's life came to an end a year later when he had the misfortune of backing into his plane's spinning propeller.[30]

While waiting for his studio to be built, Lehrman went to work in May shooting some preliminary footage for his first production at the newly-built Astra Studios in Glendale. Production moved into the Culver City studio once it was ready in mid-August with Jack White — touted as the youngest director working in the U.S. — calling the shots.[31] Lloyd Hamilton and Ritchie co-starred, although the latter, while named in prerelease promotional materials, was curiously absent in the finished film's credits. Also in the cast were Lehrman's girlfriend Virginia Rappe, recently signed after a reported — and difficult to swallow — seven months of negotiations,[32] along with seasoned second-string comedians Harry Todd, Harry McCoy, Rube Miller, and Charles Dorety; Ernie Shield and Charles Dudley were brought on as well.[33]

Henry Lehrman Comedies' new hire, Lloyd Hamilton. PHOTO COUTESY OF JIM KERKHOFF.

Lehrman's evolving thoughts on the business of comedy were detailed in an "interview" that appeared in numerous publications at this time, and warrants repeating here:

> To the superficial observer, the creation of film comedy appears to constitute the easiest branch of production endeavor. The novice in scenario writing almost invariably begins by dashing off a succession of comedies, leaving the more serious themes for treatment after he shall have acquired a certain facility of expression in the language of the screen, and a more accurate knowledge of the so-called mechanics of the art. The comedy director is often looked upon as having failed to reach the pinnacle of artistic accomplishment occupied by his brethren of the drama, and the idea persists that anyone can make comedies.

Nothing could be further from the actual facts. The production of comedies is the most serious in the film world — (even as it is the most interesting) — and involves the exercise of the utmost in resourcefulness and ingenuity. It is probably true that more thought, more labor and more painstaking care are lavished on a successful two-reel comedy than on the average dramatic feature of more than twice its length. Indeed, in the case of Lehrman Comedies, this comparison applies as well to the time consumed in production, since my pictures of two-reel length require an average of ten weeks each for filming.

To these facts can be attributed much of the progress made in film comedy during the past two years — an advance which has far exceeded that made in the dramatic field within the same period, and has wrought a complete change in the standards of humorous productions. While producers of film drama have given scant evidence of progressive thought, pictured comedy has shown a constantly changing improvement of method and execution. The forcible contact of the common chicken egg with human visage is now in distinctly bad odor, whatever the age of the egg. The custard pie as a weapon of defense is more than apt to prove offensive. No longer can the kick in comedies be registered entirely with the feet. New lines of "business" or action must be constantly devised, new "gags" introduced, new situations contrived; always it must be something new and always it must be either funny or breathlessly thrilling. In these days of the sophisticated audience it is not sufficient to do the unexpected. The blasé film fan is constantly expecting the unexpected, and it becomes necessary to cap the "unexpected" action with some further bit of humorous by-play to induce a laugh.

And a film comedy is not simply a motion picture with some laughs in it. A successful comedy must be an unbroken succession of laughs, resulting either from purely humorous action or speech on the part of the performers; from the prompting of humorous thought on the part of the audience; or from the depiction of thrilling situation or action which culminates so disastrously or so miraculously that the spectator must laugh from the very force of pent-up emotion. There must be a continuously ascending degree of the ludicrous, and never a lag in the tempo of the action, once the pace is established. It is difficult enough to wring a laugh from an audience, but to pile laugh on laugh, and to keep it up for forty minutes, requires not only a thorough understanding of the possibilities of pictured action and the ingenious application of such knowledge, but unlimited patience and hard work. I once spent more than three weeks in securing a few short close-ups of a pair of flies in the bowl of a spoon, and considered myself fortunate in finally obtaining just the action I desired.

All wild animals, be they flies or lions, are more temperamental than the most intractable star, and this fact only adds to the woes of the man whose business it is to be funny. The constant demand for thrills has made the production of comedies the most dangerous branch of film work, and has necessitated the tedious repetition of hazardous "stunts" in an effort to secure a few seconds of satisfactory action on the screen.

Since the province of the motion picture is to amuse and entertain, the comedy must be accorded a high position in the film world. Many a theatre owner has seen a good comedy bolster up a weak feature and literally "save the show." And I am starting production on the new Lehrman Comedies with the conviction that the possibilities of future development are unlimited, and that the coming years will see every motion picture judged not upon its length, but on the quality of the entertainment which it offers.[34]

Whether Lehrman himself actually wrote these words or left it up to his publicist Edward Thomas is questionable, but if the latter it would have been with Lehrman's input and guidance. Either way, the piece indicated a departure from the rougher slapstick of the earliest Sterling and L-Ko comedies, a trend evidenced in the more recent Sunshines. Appearing as it did while the first Henry Lehrman Comedy was still in production, it remained to be seen where Lehrman's sensibilities — and public reaction — would guide him now that he was his own boss.

Lehrman's willingness to lavish money on the look of his films became evident early on via a press release touting the "construction of a magnificent set…which represents a corridor in a million-dollar apartment house" by technical director Olin. "[It] is of the most elaborate construction," the release went on to say, "and is expected to set a high standard for future Lehrman productions. It is stated that Mr. Lehrman is to give particular attention to the matter of settings and will make them as fine as those used by any company in existence, irrespective of the length or magnitude of pictures produced."[35]

The few reports that emerged from the sets of Lehrman's maiden production mostly involved Lloyd Hamilton. Production was momentarily delayed when a deputy game warden from the California fish and game commission came to arrest Hamilton for hunting (and bagging) ducks out of season, this based on a recent newspaper article wherein the writer had inadvertently written "ducks" while the reality was "doves," then currently in season. His arrest was averted, so it was said, when Lehrman himself intervened and identified the dead avians — one of which he had dined on the night before — as such.[36]

Another report, if it was to be believed, had Hamilton actively trying to find a new home for his bulldog, intending to replace it with a young pup. Billie Ritchie had questioned the reason for the desired exchange. "I tell you," Hamilton was said to have responded, "my dog, he fights all the time. Some day he's gonna lick Mr. Lehrman's dog, and then I get fired."[37]

The production's biggest mishap occurred during the filming of a scene wherein a cop was to ascend a marble staircase and fall into a large square bathtub in the floor. The scene was shot over and over again, each time the action deemed not quite right. Lehrman wanted the actor to emerge from the tub and violently shake off the water in the fashion of a dog doing the same. The actor didn't quite get what Lehrman was alluding to until the producer demonstrated. "Oh," the actor responded. "You mean shimmie," after which he nailed it.[38] Unfortunately on the day's final take the tub sprang a leak, and a massive deluge followed. "Chairs, megaphones and carpenters went floating off the stage and dropped into the bean field next door." Production was shut down for the day while the mess was cleaned up and repairs made.[39] Or so it was reported.

The four-reel *A Twilight Baby* was finally completed by November 1 after ten weeks of production. The negative was shipped to First National headquarters in New York where prints were struck for nationwide distribution.[40] The film had its Los Angeles premiere at Tally's Kinema in on December 21, and went wide in early 1920. Lehrman went all out

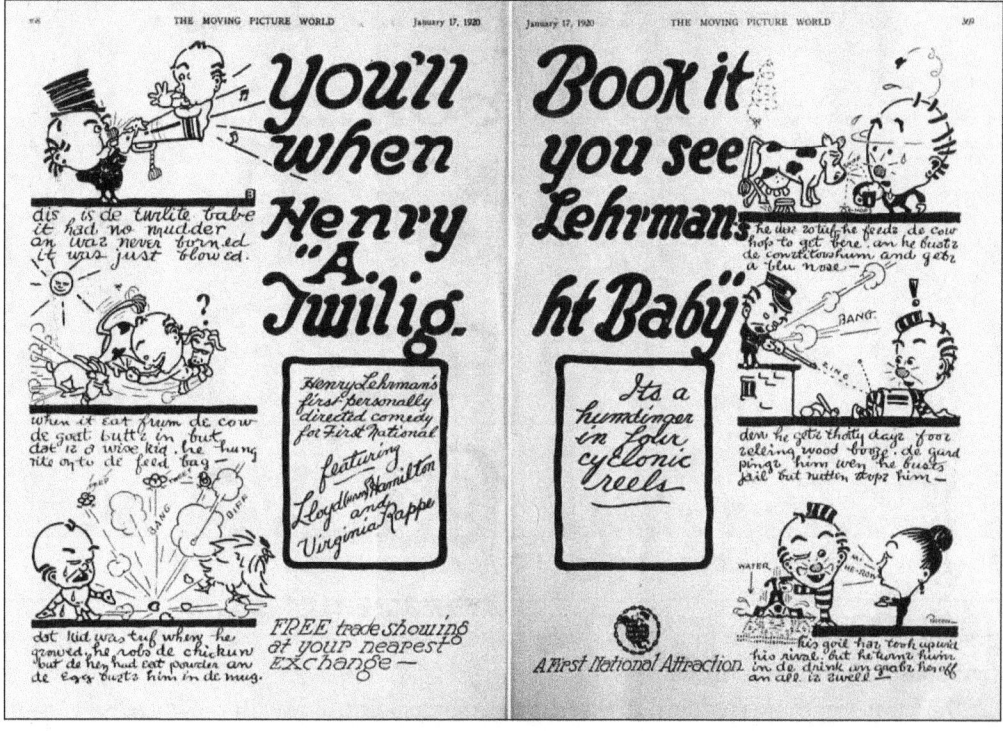

ABOVE: *One of the two two-page ads for* A Twilight Baby *that appeared in the January 3, 1920 issue of* Moving Picture World. BELOW: *The two-page ad for* A Twilight Baby *from the January 17, 1920 issue of* Moving Picture World.

with promotional materials that employed both humorous illustrations and text. A pair of cartoonists were hired, one to illustrate a huge four-page ad that appeared in *Moving Picture World* on January 3, and the other for a two-page ad on January 17; both displayed numerous whimsical moments from some of the film's highlights and were intended to whet the exhibitors' appetite. Additional, comic strip-like images accompanied a number of the theatrical ads that appeared in the larger city papers, with witty text alone or in conjunction with the film's iconic "leaping baby" image for the smaller ads. Large photo-

Ham (Lloyd Hamilton) flirts with his girl Virginia (Rappe) in A Twilight Baby.

graphic images from the film itself were reproduced on the front page of *Wid's Daily* on four subsequent days in December.

The film's length was reduced to three reels at some point, although the four-reel version continued to be advertised into 1921, so it would appear that two alternate versions of the film were made available to exhibitors. The extant print held by the Museum of Modern Art clocks in at twenty minutes, and represents the last half of the film. Neither the earlier mentioned tub sequence nor the apartment house corridor appear in this print, casualties of either the editor's shears, the latter reduction of the film's initial length, or part of the two reels of footage lost to deterioration over the intervening years.

What survives is a delightful epic of absurdity. The extant footage opens with Ham (Hamilton) in prison, working on a rockpile. His adopted father (Harry Todd) thinks he is overseas fighting the Germans, but his girl Virginia (Rappe) knows better, that he went to prison for bootlegging. After an unsuccessful attempt to escape, Ham is eventually released and returns home to his dad, his girl, and his faithful dog Happy. Also vying for Virginia's hand is Jake (Charles Dorety, in vaguely Keaton-ish attire), son of Nasty Harold (Billie Ritchie, unbilled and barely recognizable behind his huge paintbrush mustache). There's a lot of bad blood between Ham and Nasty Harold and his son, but after a lot of roughhouse business Ham ultimately proves to be a coward. This is a turnoff for Virginia, her "dream world coming to an end." Ham's dog Happy overhears Nasty Harold tell Jake that he is going to kill Ham with his shotgun, but when Happy rushes to Ham's side in a failed attempt to alert him, it is Happy who appears to be mortally wounded while Ham suffers a slight injury to his wrist. Thinking his dog has been killed, Ham acquires the courage to go after Harold, and after a wild melee in Harold's cabin, Harold is finally dispatched, his head put through a door and the door set adrift. Only Harold's squirming body is visible, his head beneath the door and under water. "Beware! I'm a caveman!" bellows Ham as he grabs Virginia under one arm and a minister under the other, hauling them both off with marriage the goal. The film concludes with Ham and Virginia arriving at the cottage he had purchased for the two of them, an idyllic scene with a garden full of flowers gently swaying in the breeze, a shimmering lake beyond. Fade to an abrupt end.

Newlyweds Ham and Virginia at the door to their cottage, in A Twilight Baby. COURTESY OF JOAN MYERS.

What hasn't survived involves Ham's arrival in the world. *Moving Picture World* gives us a taste of what is missing:

> Most remarkable is the act of a mothering dog, who leaves her litter of pups to care for the abandoned baby. She drags the tiny helpless human creature to where it can suckle directly from a cow and there stands guard until the infant

is fed. There is a really talented rooster, who not only officiates as an alarm clock, but pecks at heavy sleepers to rouse them and raises the shade of their window. There are puppies who follow the baby's example in getting sustenance direct from the cow.... When the baby, supposedly of noble birth, is grown, the result is a clownish and cowardly fat boy.[41]

Lehrman needed a baby for the filming of these early sequences, and found one in the unlikeliest of places. The entire troupe of the Singer Midgets, then currently appearing at the Pantages theater, visited the Culver City studios as Lehrman's guests. As the name would suggest, this was a talented group of little people who performed (and sang) under the leadership of European-born Leo Singer. Julius,[42] the smallest member of the group, was pressed into service in the role of the baby, makeup applied and dressed in a "little nightie." Lehrman, it was reported, "required the services of a tiny child, but was unable to find one with the strength necessary to perform the acrobatic stunt required, so the little midget filled the bill completely."[43] A report that makes one miss the loss of the film's earliest scenes all the more.

Another missing sequence involves Ham feeding hops to a cow, the result being the cow's production of beer rather than milk. This illegal production of alcohol lands Ham in prison. Nasty Harold is a rival bootlegger, hence the bad blood between him and this upstart "rival."

Hamilton is again clean-shaven in this film, although it was reported that he reverted briefly to his old "Ham" make-up for a scene where he disguises himself.[44] Rappe's character is introduced, swinging on a swing, her posterior repeatedly making contact with a spiky cactus. While facially attractive, she is a big, hefty girl who doesn't always film well; one is left with the impression that she probably came across more physically attractive when posed for fashion stills. "Miss Rappe," wrote Ray Frohman, "[is] of the dashing, black-haired, magazine cover type of beauty, rather big for a comedy 'lead,' as the studio 'panners' would mutter."[45] As for her acting chops, the evidence here where she was given a larger part than previously is that they were somewhat limited. In the scene where she and Ham grieve over the supposed death of his dog, her emoting looks forced and not at all convincing. One could argue that director White wanted her to play it broadly for comic effect, but I am doubtful.

As for Ritchie, he looks lean and haggard and almost unrecognizable in his guise as Nasty Harold. Ritchie was on the mend from ostrich-induced injuries most likely sustained while still back with Sunshine. A press release back in September 1918 reported that the actor had moved into a new home in Laurel Canyon. "So enthusiastic has Mr. Ritchie become over his new residence that the white lights of Los Angeles haven't seen him for a long time, and Mr. Ritchie says it will be a pretty distant day before they will again."[46] This break from filmmaking may very well have been for quiet, unreported recuperation.

The film (or the portion that has survived) is full of wildly inventive and visually satisfying gags and stunts, including Hamilton's unsuccessful escape attempt from the prison, the no-holds-barred melee in Todd's general store, Hamilton and Dorety's less-than-friendly encounter, and in what is arguably the film's funniest sequence, the culminating face-off between Hamilton and Ritchie. Here the two are on either side of a locked door and the former ponders just how to get at the latter, in spite of the fact that there are no walls left

ABOVE: *As Nasty Harold, a barely-recognizable Billie Ritchie confronts Ham, cowering behind brave Virginia, in* A Twilight Baby. COURTESY OF JIM KERKHOFF. BELOW: *Another scene missing from the surviving print of* A Twilight Baby.

standing to either side of the door. Other throwaway bits are of varying success: in one of the funnier moments a gunpowder-eating hen lays her eggs, and the resultant explosion blows the tail feathers off a stunned rooster. Hamilton's attempts to converse with Rappe while a mackerel flops around inside his pants, however, while amusing is a rather worn gag. Lehrman was interviewed about the rooster gag soon after the film's release, a conversation that sheds light not only on the scene in question, but on his method of working with animals and his approach to comedy in general:

> "Where did you get the inspiration to blow off the rooster's tail?" I asked.
> Henry Lehrman looked at me seriously, almost with a frown, puffed at his cigarette and after a moment's thought answered;
> "It's one of those things you can work out with mathematics and psychology."
> "You are the Henry Lehrman that makes comedies?" I asked. I thought for a moment I might have wandered into the wrong room at the Claridge. He smilingly assured me that he was.
> "Then maybe I did not make myself clear. What I asked was: Where did you get the idea that it would be funny to blow off the rooster's tail and that the crowds would laugh at it?"
> For three weeks I had been waiting to ask that question. Lehrman was out in California the day I sat in the Rialto Theater and in company with thousands of others laughed myself almost sick when in "A Twilight Baby," a Lehrman comedy, a bomb had blown the tail off the proud cock of the walk. The actual amputation was funny, but the look on the rooster's face as he turned around and saw that his glory was gone had sent the audience into hysterics.
> "That," said the director, looking at me owl-eyed and speaking as if he weighed every word, "was a natural thing to do. The rooster was king of his domain; he was vain and his great vanity lay in the beautiful tail feathers. I hit him — or, in this case, fate or the bomb hit him — in his vainest spot, and the crowd laughed. It always has been so. The fall of a vain person always amuses the public."
> The very serious creator of mirth thought for a moment.
> "Did you notice," he went on, "how the laugh at this point was kept up? It wasn't a mere flash, was it?"
> When assured that it wasn't he revealed one of the secrets of the business. "I was afraid the laughter would die down — and that was one place where I wanted it to be continuous. So I threw the amputated feathers into the air and had them fall as the rooster gazed sadly at the missing part. I felt certain that the public would howl at the slowly departing glory."
> "I like to use animals in my pictures," said Mr. Lehrman, "and birds and fowl. Somehow the public is happiest when it can get a laugh out of a cat or a dog or a bird. There is never any danger that the humor will be unsavory. I understand that is one of the reasons why Hugo Riesenfeld bought 'A Twilight Baby,' to run at the Rialto. He felt that children could see it with pleasure — and it was still funny enough for the grown-ups.
> "No, I never use trained animals in my comedies. The only dog I use is the one you saw come out of the pound. I study my dogs and cats and birds just as

ABOVE: *Virginia Rappe, in* A Twilight Baby. BELOW: *Ham tries to figure how to get through a locked door to Nasty Harold, who is backed up by Charles Dorety. This production still from* A Twilight Baby *was used by King Features Syndicate to illustrate news articles during the Roscoe Arbuckle trials for the death of Virginia Rappe, which explains why the arrow has been added pointing at her.* COURTESY OF HERITAGE AUCTION GALLERIES, HA.COM.

I study my human actors and fit the work to their characteristics. I can always find some way to make animals do what has to be done for the pictures. And I find there is more spontaneity, more pep in the mut [sic] than you can ever find in the trained dog."

"How do you ever get your human beings, dogs, cats, cows, goats, birds and fowl to work together in your rather complicated plots?"

"I don't," he answered, smiling. "I have never written out a scenario. I begin something and leave it to my wits, chance and the actors and animals to finish it. I am sometimes in the position of the housewife who starts out to make an omelet and finds she has a perfectly good custard."

"When did you start making the world laugh? Were you a comedian or cartoonist?"

Again the young man — he can't be over thirty-two — looked at me with that owl-like look.

"I don't believe I ever cracked an original joke in my life, and I know I never told a funny story," he said. "The farce comedy of the movies, to be successful, must be humor, not wit. Good titles can't save bad comedy. There is always something funny in every situation in life, and that's what I seek."

"Didn't the loss of his tail spoil the rooster?" I asked.

Mr. Lehrman spoke slowly and with emphasis. "The loss of the rooster's tail feather did not in the least affect his value as chicken stew."[47]

Hamilton and Todd's reunion provides another of the film's funniest sequences. The two rush to each other with open arms but miss, Ham's head going through the barn's siding. A ram proceeds to ram Ham's butt, Ham registering pain on the other side of the wall. Others attempt to pull him free, but he instead crashes through the wall and into the barn. A cranky mule kicks him back through the wall, Ham landing on a bull's back and off they go. One laugh follows another, and just as they are about to subside, Ham engages in his epic tangle with Dorety. Some of the highlights of this encounter include a split telephone pole driving a bystander into the ground, and Ham rolling a somersaulting Dorety into another group, arrayed and tumbled as if bowling pins.

While the bulk of the film involves non-stop laughs, an admittedly touching moment of pathos takes place after Ham's dog Happy has been shot. Near death, the wounded dog struggles forth by the side of a creek, lit by a patch of sunlight. As his struggles subside, an overhead cloud turns the patch of sunlight dark, visual imagery suggesting the dog's death. It is a beautifully shot sequence, and surprisingly moving. That the dog makes a reappearance later on, evidently healthy aside from a bandaged leg, provides a happy end and does little to diminish the power of the earlier scene.

Critics for the most part were enthusiastic about the results. "All in all, it is a comedy which rates with the topnotchers," reported J.S. Dickerson of *Motion Picture News*, "and worth a million of the majority of releases of its type placed upon the market in the past couple of years."[48] (Dickerson must not have been overly familiar with the stars of these comedies, repeatedly misidentifying Hamilton as Hank Mann!) *Moving Picture World* concurred: "We laugh at the ludicrous; we laugh at the ridiculous; we laugh anyhow until we are tired. 'A Twilight Baby' made a great hit at the Rialto, and it is one of the best farces ever shown on the screen."[49] *Wid's Daily* advised exhibitors that "Numerous farm scenes in which domestic animals are seen, and bits that carry considerable appeal will put this slapstick comedy, a three-reeler, over.... The production has been screened nicely and will fit well on your program."[50] *Exhibitors Herald* observed that "Care has been lavished upon its preparation, and it shows the results in genuinely laughable incident."[51]

Exhibitor response ran the gamut from unbridled enthusiasm to out-and-out disgust, with length frequently an issue. "Good four reel comedy. Very well liked. Good business" reported a Buffalo, New York theater owner.[52] Goose Creek, Texas agreed: "This picture

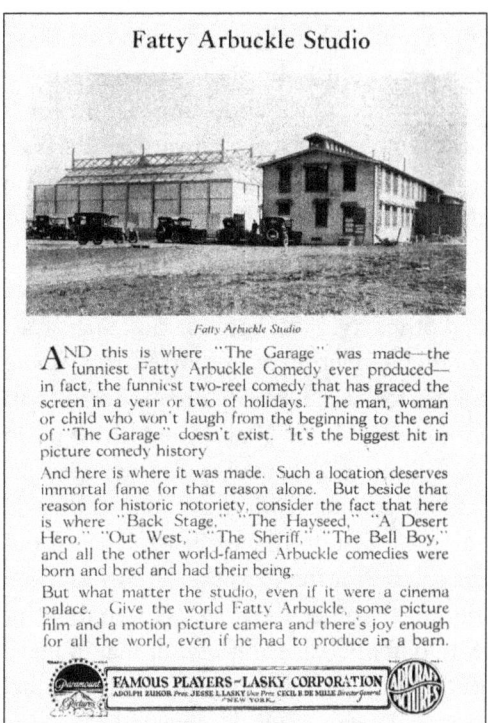

LEFT: *"Biff! Right on the Funny Bone!" Full-page ad for* A Twilight Baby, *from the December 13, 1919 issue of* Exhibitors Herald. RIGHT: *Lehrman's studios were advertised as the Fatty Arbuckle Studios in this piece promoting Arbuckle's two-reel comedies. The list of films actually made at this location is somewhat exaggerated.* COURTESY OF MARC WANAMAKER AND BISON ARCHIVES.

pulled big."[53] Less enthusiastic responses focused primarily on the film's length and the fact that it deviated from the standard two-reels. "Good comedy. Probably too long. Two reels long enough for laughs" was a report from Lafayette, Colorado;[54] "Too long. The first half is great, then it begins to drag. Two reels is long enough for a comedy" was Detroit, Michigan's reaction.[55] "Something different in this one. First two reels continual laughter, when it begins to drag. Four reels too long," was the feeling in Kalamazoo, Michigan, but agreed that it was an "exceptional comedy."[56] Perhaps the most virulent feedback came from a small town theater owner in Idaho, who didn't mince with words: "This comedy became a tragedy. We wonder from what asylum Lehrman escaped. Lost in a night what it has taken all winter to build up, namely, the high quality of First National. No producers are so blind as those who won't see."[57] As they say, you can't please everyone.

A series of mishaps plagued Lehrman during this period. Perhaps the biggest blow came from the joint defection of his lead comedian Hamilton and boy wonder protégé Jack White, who headed off to make their own Mermaid comedies for release through Educational. The second issue was Roscoe Arbuckle's departure from the lot after filming only two comedies — *The Hayseed* (October 26, 1919) and *The Garage* (January 11, 1920) — thereby depriving Lehrman of much-needed lease income. (Or perhaps not. When questioned a year later about his presence at the Lehrman Studios and this lease arrangement, Arbuckle responded "Yes, it was the only way I could get back money he owed me."[58] Which would seem to indicate that no money changed hands, rather a debt being paid off.) The shortfall was short lived, however; Lehrman would soon lease the extra space to Jack and Harry Cohn for filming of their new Hall Room Boys comedy series to co-star Neely Edwards and Hugh Fay.[59]

A curious side note regarding Hugh Fay: Aside from the alleged selling of drugs back during the Keystone days, Fay had one of the stranger collections in all of Hollywood. He collected the footwear of famous people: "In his residence in the foothills of Hollywood he has a room filled with big glass wall cases which in turn are filled with boots, shoes and other styles of footwear that once graced the pedal extremities of some of the world's foremost celebrities," reported the *Sunday Oregonian*. Among the more recognizable names listed as former owners of said footwear were Abraham Lincoln, Ulysses S. Grant, Geronimo, Carrie Nation, and Grover Cleveland.[60] To each his own.

Adding to Lehrman's woes was a suit brought by Harry A. Sherman against Lehrman and his company. Sherman alleged that the two had entered into a contract for a weekly salary of $250 from March 13, 1919 through May 10, 1920, and that he had not received his salary "for many weeks." Lehrman, he claimed, had within a month of the contract's signing modified the price per film that Sherman was sanctioned to accept in negotiations with potential distributors, but that in no way should have impacted any of the other terms of the contract.[61] The resulting writ of attachment included both the studio and Lehrman's personal residence in Hollywood.[62]

What Lehrman wasn't aware of was what was going on behind his back. Fox had gotten wind that Lehrman was boasting of misreporting his 1918 earnings of $36,533.33 to Internal Revenue, and decided to take a bit of vindictive action towards their former employee. To that end, Joseph R. Darling was instructed to surreptitiously contact the Bureau of Investigation in Washington to inform them of same. "Please do not use my name nor that of the Fox Film Corporation in the investigation," implored Darling in one of his follow-up telegrams. Darling's telegram was acknowledged with the terse response "Impossible to secure confidential information of this character." Darling's comments were then forwarded to Internal Revenue in the Treasury Department to be looked into.[63]

Concurrent with this was the organization of Associated First Pictures, Inc. to fight the four big motion picture corporations, who were alleged to be backed by Wall Street interests with plans to create a monopoly of the motion picture business. A "war chest" was set up to fund the acquisition or construction of movie houses in every state. Affiliated with First National Exhibitors' Circuit, the new organization would have control of the productions of Lehrman as well as those of Charles Chaplin, his wife Mildred Harris, Norma Talmadge, Constance Talmadge, Anita Stewart, Marshall Neilan, Charles Ray, Catherine McDonald, and King Vidor.[64]

Lehrman's monetary woes soon became apparent, a combined result of the money poured into building his state-of-the-art studio and the land it sat upon, his lack of discipline lavishing money on expensive sets while making *A Twilight Baby*, the salaries that needed to be paid during the break from Sunshine and actual production of his own comedies, and an extravagant personal lifestyle that continued unabated. Lehrman was desperate for an infusion of cash to keep things going.

LEFT: *Aerial view of Lehrman's studios in 1921, a year after it was reincorporated under the name Henry Lehrman Comedies.* COURTESY OF MARC WANAMAKER AND BISON ARCHIVES. RIGHT: *C.L. Chester.*

On April 17, 1920, a new company was incorporated under the name Henry Lehrman Comedies, Inc., and Lehrman himself was *not* one of the directors. The new directors were Joseph LaRose, A.L. Barnes, and Laura Lindsay.[65] LaRose, formerly production manager for New York's Rialto and Rivoli theatres, had a month earlier accepted a position of assistant to C.L. Chester Productions, Inc. and relocated to the West Coast.[66] Barnes was Lehrman's auditor at Henry Lehrman Productions, and Laura Lindsay was a legal secretary.

This was the result of an agreement between C.L. Chester, Allen Dudley, and A.B.W. Hodges. Lehrman had borrowed $25,000 from them, to be paid back with seven percent interest within the following two years. This loan was secured by a Deed of Trust for the Culver City property, and in return Lehrman agreed to the establishment of the new company to oversee operations and, it is assumed, keep him on a tighter leash.[67] Additionally, Chester had loaned Lehrman an additional $5,000 on May 7, 1919, shortly after Henry Lehrman Productions had been incorporated.[68] C. L. Chester was a comparatively well known filmmaker at the time for his production company's "Chester-Outing Scenics," and had in February announced an upcoming series of two-reel comedies. The first of these, *Four Times Foiled*, was released at the end of February and starred Snooky the "Humanzee" under William Campbell's direction. Chester had taken over the contract to supply the twelve Lehrman two-reel comedies to First National for the upcoming year, and was now handling the business management of the new series of two-reel comedies. Lehrman would continue to produce these at his Lehrman studios in Culver City, while Snooky was kept at a safe distance at Chester's own studios back on Hollywood's Western and Ferndale Avenues. A.B.W. Hodges, formerly of the short lived Brentwood Film Corporation of 1919-20, was made vice-president of the new Henry Lehrman Comedies, Inc., and Allen Dudley was made treasurer.[69] Hodges was now in active charge of the business end of the studio, and would keep a close eye on both costs and schedules. On June 4, 1920, Lehrman turned over the deed to the Culver City property to Henry Lehrman Productions, Inc.[70]

Lehrman moved forward in an attempt to better market his upcoming comedies. In late summer he announced plans for a direct exploitation service with exhibitors, to augment the publicity and advertising service of the First National Exhibitors Circuit distributors. It was intended to "present one of the most thorough producer-exhibitor co-operative arrangements ever attempted." The staff he assembled, it was said, included "men who are familiar not only with the needs of the newspapers, magazines and other periodicals but who have had years of experience in the co-operative exploitation of amusement stunts with exhibitors direct."[71] Little more was ever reported about this service, so it is unknown just how long it was in existence or, for that matter, whether it actually even came to be.

Albert Ray, Fox Picture Star. PHOTO COURTESY OF JIM KERKHOFF.

With the departure of Hamilton and White, Lehrman had been left scrambling for a new lead comedian and someone he could oversee to direct his next film. Comedian Charles "Heinie" Conklin was hired to star, by now a veteran of film comedy after serving a two-year stint with Joker before joining Sennett in 1915, then relocating to Sunshine where he had taken part in a trio of Lehrman's productions. Conklin, aka Charles Lynn, was perhaps most recognizable for his rather bizarre mustache, an outlandish affectation that drooped down to his chin, ending in two tight curls. As his co-star, Lehrman hired Albert Ray, a good looking, youthful leading man-type in his mid-twenties. "Albert Ray is regarded as typifying on the screen all that is likeable and best," wrote one columnist. "Youthful and the possessor of an illimitable fund of pep and vigor, he is regarded as ideally suited for the speedy, good humored type of American screen entertainment."[72] Ray had entered the industry years earlier as a director for the East Coast Ramo Film Company, later heading down to Jacksonville, Florida where he directed some comedies for Vim.[73] More comedy direction followed back up north after Vim folded before Ray relocated to the West Coast and starring roles in features, as well as some comedy work for Lehrman at Sunshine.[74] Given Ray's experience with direction, Lehrman assigned him to direct as well as act in the studio's second feature, tentatively titled *Springtime* but eventually released as *The Kick in High Life*; Al Herman would act as his assistant. Ray's boy-next-door looks would be in stark contrast to Conklin's caricature, with seventeen year old ingénue Charlotte Dawn hired for the female lead as the girl they both lust for.

Lehrman decided to take a different approach with this film. "Abandoning his effort to draw on the elusive laugh as a result of satire on romance and the present day film," wrote *Exhibitors Herald*, "Mr. Lehrman has brought forth, it is said, a picture that is built only for laughing purposes and stops at no clean ends to get the applause of the audience."[75]

The film wrapped in late July and the negative was shipped to the Rothacker lab in Chicago where prints were struck.[76] Released on September 13, 1920, the film involves the characters of Bud Weiser and Lotta Sherry attending the birthday party of a "precocious youngster." Contemporary reviews of the film, which is believed lost, were short on details, but a number of them referred to a hair-raising scene where a baby girl wanders out on a plank protruding from the window of a skyscraper, rescued at the last minute as the plank appears to be about to topple down into the street far below. A slightly more detailed promotional piece gives a hint of what the film was about, and the ends to which Lehrman would go to achieve the desired results.

> Three supposedly jealous suitors, engaging in a free-for-all fight as the result of attention paid to the young woman of their combined hearts, recently wrecked the perfectly good house in which the battle was staged.
> The interior of this home was badly battered, plaster and paintings being knocked down and much of the furniture demolished....
> Henry Lehrman, the producer of the picture, insisted that the realistic results obtained could be had only by using (or abusing) the genuine article, so he moved his actors and actresses into the bungalow and let them do the rest.
> Al Ray, Hugh Fay and Charles Conklin were the actors who did most of the damage, wielding clubs, smashing furniture, throwing plates and dynamite.
> The resulting picture is an attraction said to contain more novel fun features than any yet produced by Lehrman, who says that the damage done was well worth the cost.[77]

One humorous bit that Lehrman inserted into the film was based on a real life incident that he saw at a society affair, and thought was one of the funniest things he had ever witnessed. One couple's dancing was brought to an abrupt, mortified halt when the fellow's false teeth fell out and clattered to the floor. One suspects that the incident didn't seem quite as amusing to the couple whose dance routine was prematurely interrupted.[78]

Laurence Reid, in his review for *Motion Picture News*, had a lukewarm response to the film. "This Henry Lehrman comedy for First National presents an assortment of tried and true tricks, with no original effort being visible anywhere. The slapstick brush is applied quite strenuously…. The weakness of this comedy is the absence of spontaneity. They are conceived and executed for the mere sake of slapstick. It's a knockabout piece with a good deal of tumbling and falling and spanking on the part of the tumblers and spankers." Al Ray's comedy chops were singled out for comment as well, saying that "it strikes us that he is not exceptionally talented in a comedy direction. He should be used as a straight foil to Charles Conklin or some other player who is gifted with a sense of the burlesque."[79]

Reid may not have been impressed, but it was a return to the old Lehrman style, and the exhibitors loved it. "Had large business and kept the house in an uproar continually," reported one.[80] "One of the best slapstick comedies we have ever shown," said another.[81] "One of the best slapstick comedies I have ever run," chimed in an exhibitor from Minnesota. "They laughed so hard that one patron broke a seat back."[82]

C.L. Chester, as it turned out, had a very abbreviated stay as business manager for the Lehrman comedies, severing connections in mid-July to devote his entire time and energy to his own comedies and Chester-Outings.[83] Lehrman went to work personally directing the company's third film from his own script, with final scenes completed in mid-September.[84] *Wet and Warmer* again co-starred Charles Conklin, Al Ray, and Charlotte Dawn, with Billie Ritchie brought back for another appearance that, sadly, would also be his last. Released on November 1, 1920, the film survives in a print held by UCLA and is one of the few surviving Lehrman films I've not yet had the pleasure of viewing.

According to contemporary reviews, the story involves a number of guests at a hotel where illegal spirits — it was filmed during the earliest days of Prohibition — are hidden in the establishment's fire extinguishers. When a fire breaks out, the residents rush for the extinguishers only to find that their contents serve to accelerate the fire rather than extinguish it. Conklin takes part in one of the film's more thrilling bits, clad in a nightshirt and out on the building's ledge attempting to escape the fire. "He leans over to catch the telephone receiver and nearly loses his balance and a stream of water sends him scurrying along the ledge," wrote reviewer Laurence Reid.[85] Billie Ritchie sleeps through the fire, the edges of his bed ablaze all around him.

Film historian Richard M. Roberts gave his thoughts about the film in an online post. "WET AND WARMER (First National 1921) was the hit of the 2005 Slapsticon, a wild and nightmarish comedy that shows Lehrman's notorious excesses in full flower. When he wants to show a burning building, he doesn't set a few smoke-pots about the windows, he gasolines the flats and sets the whole set aflame, sending comics running for their lives. This short moves a mile a minute, but the gags are all beautifully punctuated, moving in a speedy-but-dreamlike flow that tops anything Sennett ever did for weirdness."[86]

I contacted Roberts and forwarded my cobbled-together summary of the film, hoping that he would elaborate on the film's plot. In his usual generous fashion, he gave a lengthy response that exceeded my expectations. His recollections follow, relayed years after last having seen the film, one he has viewed numerous times:

> This is another of those shorts that could be cut into two one-reelers with no-one realizing they were ever parts of the same film.
> The whole first part had Heinie Conklin and Albert Ray running around a park doing bizarre, off-the cuff gags with Charlotte Dawn (including a very risqué gag

ABOVE: *Heinie Conklin (aka Charles Lynn) caught in the act by chef Tom Kennedy (?), from* The Kick in High Life. BELOW: *Al Ray (left) and Heinie Conklin appear to have the upper hand over dazed Phil Dunham, from* The Kick in High Life. PHOTOGRAPHS COURTESY OF ROBERT JAMES KISS.

involving a canvas-painted sign for a cootchie-dancer (or was it a fortune teller) that starts to undulate when either Conklin or Ray (can't recall which at the moment) backs into it as we get shocked reactions from folk standing in front of it….

All of this first part is tied to the hospital stuff in the second half by one intertitle: "and then she woke up….."

As I recall, it's not a Hotel, but a rest home for looneys, which the film indicates that Dawn, Ritchie, and Conklin are. Upon awaking, Charlotte Dawn

Heinie Conklin has lost his pants in this lobby card for Wet and Warmer; *Al Ray and Charlotte Dawn do their best to avoid looking.* COURTESY OF JIM KERKHOFF.

actually has a nice comic scene where she sets out to casually eat something like a dozen or more donuts rolls, or some such, idly stuffing them into her mouth endlessly and casually without an obvious cut, it's a wonderfully timed and executed bit. Ritchie, considering how ill he was at the time, is remarkably agile, even if he is nearly unrecognizable and heavily made up (he also only appears in the Hospital scenes as I recall, not in the first part). The bit of his sleeping through the fire is more elaborate than you describe, it is again a razor-sharp-timed and, in typical Lehrman fashion, dangerous, bit where a sleeping Ritchie keeps shifting position on his burning bed while flames shoot up through holes in the bed that he had lain parts of his body on just a second before. Ritchie then ends up out on the window ledge with Conklin, doing some decent acrobatics for a dying man.

ABOVE: *Bellboy Heinie Conklin taking a small monetary bribe from Al Ray, unbeknownst to Charlotte Dawn, in* Wet and Warmer. COURTESY OF ROBERT JAMES KISS. BELOW: *Charlotte Dawn, in drag, is confronted by the law. Heinie Conklin sporting pajamas and a Coolie hat, in background. From* Wet and Warmer.

The Hotel Conflagration is truly a textbook example of Lehrman's "suicide" moniker, it's obvious he cares not one whit for any actor's safety, he's just set fire to the set and let them fend for themselves. You can actually see gasoline being thrown on the flames from offstage by the stagehands, and at one point, the heat is so great that the camera catches a fire-funnel shooting straight up in the middle of the set! There are moments when the actors are definitely running off the burning set for their lives.

WET AND WARMER really is one of the most insane short comedies ever made, one of the first that made me begin to admire Lehrman for his darker and weirder-than-Sennett comic style, even if he endangered his comics way more often.[87]

Roberts also added that he thought that "Virginia Rappe makes a very quick appearance as someone in the park who walks into a scene and reacts to Conklin being soaked by water." Historian and Rappe authority Joan Myers commented on this Rappe sighting in her usual humorous fashion: "I indeed spotted a woman who could have been Virginia Rappe, or perhaps she was just wearing Virginia Rappe's clothing. So I've now seen it in 35mm on the big screen and I can confidently and categorically state: that woman may be Virginia Rappe or perhaps it's a woman wearing Virginia Rappe's clothing. I can't ID the woman any more firmly than that so you're all going to have to live with 'maybe'."[88]

The film, screened at Cinecon 49 in 2013, elicited several other comments. One viewer elaborated on the cootchie-dancer/fortune teller bit that Roberts alluded to, calling it "a funny gag in which a small dog caught under a paper billboard causes a Theda Bara poster to undulate indecently...." Another viewer stated that some of the film's scenes were filmed "in and around Hollenbeck Park, and above the Hill Street Tunnel and Hotel La Crosse," and offered "glimpses of the Hall of Records from a building's roof." I'll take their collective words for it.[89]

Contemporary reviewers were pleased with the results. *Moving Picture World* called it "A lively little farce,"[90] and *Motion Picture News* agreed, remarking that "Henry Lehrman has done a first rate job of it in his latest comedy.... It is a sure laugh provoker and carries some incidents which are uproariously funny."[91] Exhibitor reactions were mixed. "An absolute knockout.... It is too bad that Lehrman does not make at least one a month. If you want to make your audience laugh, get this one,"[92] was one of the more positive reactions, while "Some one [sic] should take out Lehrman's brains and cleanse them. People called me down for showing this"[93] fell at the other end of the spectrum. This latter exhibitor, it should be noted, was the same one who turned in a scathing reaction to Lehrman's *A Twilight Baby*; it would seem that Lehrman's sensibilities were at odds with the good citizens of Salmon, Idaho! And, for that matter, the state of Kansas' censor who, among other things insisted on the removal of the play-on-words intertitle "My but it is hot."[94]

Director Noel Smith was hired to direct Lehrman's fourth for First National, or at least the film was copyrighted as such; other sources credit the direction to Lehrman and Roy Del Ruth. *The Punch of the Irish* went into production in September and was completed by the end of October,[95] with exteriors filmed at the opulent residence later known as the McKinley Mansion, located at the corner of 3rd Street and S. Lafayette Park Place. Built in the mid-teens, the French-Renaissance style home served as a background for numerous other silent comedies starring the likes of Harry Langdon, Harold Lloyd, and Poodles Hanneford.[96] Lehrman had two elaborate sets built for the film, one the salon of a large ocean liner and the other the partial exterior of the mansion. "Henry Lehrman has

ABOVE: *Al Ray is greeted at the gate by Suzanne Avery, in* The Punch of the Irish. COURTESY OF ROBERT JAMES KISS. BELOW: *Billy Engle looks on with some concern as his wife (Frank J. Coleman) partakes of the spiked punch.* COURTESY OF LIBRARY OF CONGRESS.

discarded the pet idea of comedy producers that it is unnecessary to give any elaborate touches to a fast-moving comedy production," it was reported in yet another hint of the producer's extravagance. "Lehrman says that in his belief it is just as necessary to provide comedy kings and queens with gorgeous backgrounds, as is the case in dramatic pictures. The reason, adds Lehrman, is that by this method the comedy character is accentuated and is even more ridiculously funny to the beholder."[97] Perhaps, but it would suggest that Lehrman was digging an even deeper hole for himself as well.

A surviving print held by the Library of Congress would appear to be the bulk of the film, and clocks in at roughly fifteen minutes. Most of it takes place around the McKinley Mansion and the sets built to mimic it, but the German intertitles — in the absence of translation — render some of the storyline somewhat less than clear. Al Ray and Phil Dunham arrive at the mansion, rivals for the hand of Virginia Rappe. Ray presents her with a bouquet of flowers, but Dunham has snuck in a note that leaves her furious. Ray catches up to Dunham inside the grounds, where a bunch of partygoers cavort around the pool. A brawl follows between the two rivals that lands them, along with most everyone else and Rappe, in the pool. Soon after the two water-logged combatants emerge from the pool, a smaller group sits down for an outside meal at a table overseen by Rappe's father (Billy Engle) and mother (Frank J. Coleman, in drag). Mother tries the punch and, finding it to be spiked, likes it very much. It goes to her head, though, and when one of the pontificating diners (George Rowe) annoys her, she grabs him and tosses him all over the place. That done, she goes after her husband with a vengeance. Momentarily dazed by a falling plant, she revives and tears a small tree from the ground and swings it wildly at her husband. The two square off but it is an uneven match, each one of her punches sending him eight feet into the air. Bystanders attempt to restrain her to no avail, so Rowe sneaks a horse shoe into pa's glove and now it is ma who flies eight feet into the air with each of pa's punches, crashing into and destroying a sizable pergola. Ma is ready to give up, but when she discovers the horse shoe she goes ballistic, pummeling her poor husband senseless and punching the others into the pool. Pa flees into the mansion with his enraged wife in full pursuit, several near misses propelling ma out a second story window crashing to the earth below. The chase and fight conclude with all present falling into the pool, its contents ejected in a massive gush that pours through the mansion. The closing shot is of the now-waterless pool's drenched occupants.

It is a terrifically funny film. Once the dinner and resultant fight ensues, the remainder of the film is non-stop, over-the-top action, and Rappe, Ray, and Dunham effectively disappear from the story. The culminating donnybrook between ma and pa is an amazing bit of filmic mayhem, and beautifully orchestrated for maximum impact. Unlike the rougher L-Ko's, the wirework is slickly done, with no wires visible when the two are propelled into the air, one after the other, with each of the other's punches. The direction is handled well by whomever was actually in charge of this one, and there are a series of nice tight close-ups of the various diners seated around the table. As for the spiked punch, it is notable in that illegal alcohol had a place in every one of the Henry Lehrman Comedies to date.

There are some wonderful gags in the first part as well, several of them based around a pair of butlers — obviously white actors in exaggerated blackface — who get stuck in a tar puddle. One of them gets globs of tar on his hands, and when he and the other get into an argument and trade blows, his tar-covered fist gets stuck to the other's face. His initial punch keeps the other fellow's head snapping back due to the tar, rendering him

ABOVE: *George Rowe sneaks a horseshoe into Billy Engle's glove, giving him an edge.* COURTESY OF LIBRARY OF CONGRESS. BELOW: *Glass slide for* The Punch of the Irish, *"A Comedy Wallop."* COURTESY OF JORGE FINKLEMAN.

senseless after repeated contact with his opponent's fist. Later, as Ray and Dunham duke it out, the two of them end up on either side of the pool, on tippy-toes stretched over the water, their extended hands both on an overweight floater's tummy for support. The tar gags culminate when a butler's tar-covered feet come in contact with Dunham's rear end, the two of them exiting the scene in a bizarre, crab-like walk.

As for Rappe, she has little to do here other than look good in various states of undress, appearing to have slimmed down somewhat since her previous appearance on screen. Hers is the lead "eye candy" role.

Several reports had surfaced in October 1920 indicating that Lehrman had contracted with B.P. Schulberg to be his exclusive representative in the east.[98] Lehrman, it was said, "declared that his realization of the importance of producer and exhibitor being in close touch had lead him to contract with the man who was at one time general manager of Famous Players-Lasky and who was one of the organizers of United Artists." Schulberg worked on Lehrman's behalf behind the scenes, but would later come to regret taking on a client with such rocky financial underpinnings.

The fifth and final of the Henry Lehrman Comedies, *A Game Lady*, is somewhat of a mystery due to a dearth of contemporary reviews and its assumed loss. The director of the film is as vague as that for *The Punch of the Irish*, with Noel Smith once again credited in the copyright records, but

A slimmed down Virginia Rappe in one of several costume changes, flanked by Al Ray (left) and Phil Dunham. COURTESY OF JOAN MYERS.

both David Kirkland and Roy Del Ruth named elsewhere. Kirkland was credited by *Wid's Daily* in an article that appeared in early September: "The most unique vacation of the summer is that of David Kirkland, director for Constance Talmadge during the last season, who has returned to Los Angeles to make a slap stick comedy with Henry Lehrman. Kirkland, who first achieved fame as a director of these pictures, plans to enjoy his month's rest in making a real, old fashioned comedy, replete with wild animals, tame cops and custard pies."[99] Another article about the completion of *The Punch of the Irish* appeared nearly two months later at the end of October issuing a similar statement. It reported that "David Kirkland is supervising the direction of the next Lehrman production which is already under way."[100] A month later, however, *Wid's Daily* cited Roy Del Ruth as the director.[101]

The film itself didn't see release for a good six months after *Punch*, however, quietly making it onto the schedule on June 27, 1921. Given the increasingly shaky state of

Lehrman's business affairs and the fact that Lloyd Hamilton, who had left Lehrman's employ along with Jack White long before, was in the cast offers the possible explanation that the resultant film comprised footage both old and new. The Hamilton footage may have been outtakes from *A Twilight Baby* or footage shot for another aborted project, pieced together with newer footage of co-stars Al Ray, Phil Dunham, Frank Coleman, and Virginia Rappe. Rappe, it had been reported the previous November, had returned from a vacation in Canada and was back at work on another film.[102] This later footage may

Virginia Rappe and her hunter friend (unknown) in A Game Lady. COURTESY OF JOAN MYERS.

also have been filmed on an on-again, off-again basis as money became available and with different directors. *Motion Picture News*' Laurence Reid commented on the film's disjointed structure: "There is no logic and [Lehrman] did not intend there should be any. He has assembled a cast of fairly clever comedians, a lot of trick incident, some hokum atmosphere, plenty of comedy properties and pieced them together in a crazy quilt pattern — without any attention being placed to law or order.... 'A Game Lady' may be topsy-turvy but it succeeds in sending the 'peepul' forth laughing as they say goodby."[103] Curiously, most of the ads that I have found for the film indicate combinations of Rappe, Coleman, and Ray as the film's stars, with no mention of either Hamilton or Dunham. The latter two, however, are the sole cast members mentioned in Reid's review.

Money was so tight for Lehrman at this time that, aside from a single payment of $110, he defaulted on the interest payments for the loan of $25,000 from Chester, Hodges, and Dudley. Notice was given on December 15, 1920 that due to the breach of obligation the whole amount plus interest was immediately due and payable. Lehrman had three months to pay up, failure to do so would result in the sale of his property.[104] Lehrman could not make the payment. To compound his problems, Lehrman lost his Franklin Avenue house of five years to Chester as well.[105]

Lehrman put on a game face during this period, with the occasional promotional article appearing in the general press extolling his comic creativity, with nary a hint of any of his personal problems. One such piece is typical:

> Henry Lehrman is one of the leaders in the field of creating screen comedies of the cleaner sort and many thousands of people owe many happy moments to his capacity for visualizing and exaggerating humorous sides of every-day life as he and everyone else sees it. Here is a man who actually sits up nights planning new ways in which to make people laugh with the aid of the motion picture camera. It is not at all unusual for him to work all night on an idea or an inspiration which seems to promise fun for the masses and classes of photoplay fans. It is said that Mr. Lehrman comes so enthusiastic over his work that he frequently forgets to eat his meals regularly and those who will take the time to study the present up-to-minute, rapid-fire comedy of the silversheet will readily understand that the thousand and one details which go to make up a few minutes of such diversion inevitably require many hours of the art of inoffensively turning life's foibles to good account in sending sunshine into the darkened lives everywhere.[106]

This piece describes a man who is totally preoccupied with his art and, if accurate, is suggestive of a person removed from most all other daily considerations. Considerations, for instance, such as running and ensuring the viability and survival of a business. The two, of course, do not go hand in hand.

Lehrman's legal problems began to pile up during this period. The Behrendt-Levy Company was one of the first, issuing a complaint against Henry Lehrman Productions, Henry Lehrman Comedies, and Lehrman himself for monies owed in the amount of $1,676.85 for policies on Lehrman's studio and place of business, plus interest and the costs incurred in the suit; Hodges and Dudley and several others were named in the suit as well.[107] Hodges, Dudley, and Chester filed an answer to the complaint several months later denying that they had anything to do with the policies.[108]

Show business attorney Nathan Burkan filed a suit in New York in February for services rendered in 1919 that involved the drawing up and modification of Lehrman's contract with First National, along with general counseling. The amount was for $750 plus 7% per annum.[109] Lehrman, represented by attorney Milton M. Cohen, responded a week later denying that he had promised or agreed to pay for any services,[110] and issued an amended response a week later specifically naming Burkan.[111] To no avail; Lehrman failed to respond to a summons issued by the court on April 2, so a judgment was eventually made against Lehrman in the amount of $1,099.97.[112] These complaints and judgments were just the tip of the iceberg, however, and would continue to resurface over the coming years.

As for *A Game Lady*, the reason behind the delay of its release involved negotiations between First National and Educational Pictures in the early months of 1921. A meeting took place in Chicago in late December or early January where First National presented upcoming productions from their so-called "Big Five" producers. The franchise holders who were present expressed their desire that the First National circuit should, in the future, handle features only. Rumors followed in late January that First National and Educational had negotiated a deal wherein the former would turn over its Lehrman Comedies and Toonerville Trolley Comedies to Educational, who would have use of First National's exchanges for distribution of its films. First National would, in return, no longer handle short features. Neither company would comment on the rumors, however.[113] In

Aerial view of the Henry Lehrman Comedies studio in 1921, the new Hal Roach Studios now looming in front of it. COURTESY OF MARC WANAMAKER AND BISON ARCHIVES.

mid-March *Variety* reported that the Lehrman Comedies were to become part of the Educational program, and that this arrangement was "the reason for the discontinuance of the Lehrman contract with First National."[114] Lehrman himself announced on March 29 that he had signed with Educational to make thirteen two-reel "super-comedies" during the coming year, and that the contract called for "one of the largest remunerations paid to a comedy producer." Tellingly, Educational refused to confirm or deny Lehrman's claims. The article went on to say that the final three comedies produced for First National had been turned over to Educational. The titles of the three named comedies? *The Punch of the Irish*, *The* [sic] *Game Lady*, and another film never mentioned before or after in the press, something titled *Mile-a-Minute*.[115] Neither deal appears to have gone anywhere, as First National announced in June that *A Game Lady* was one of its upcoming releases.[116] As for

Mile-a-Minute, the film remains a mystery. Lehrman would later claim to have produced six special comedies for First National,[117] so it would appear that the film was completed, but was never released as such. Which raises the question: Was the finished film acquired by another company and released under a different title? We may never know. One possible clue appeared in the January 15 and 22, 1921 issues of *Camera!* where it was stated that Al Ray was directing a one-reel comedy for Lehrman starring Jimmy Savo,[118] so this may have been what was later referred to as *Mile-A-Minute*.

Lehrman was left searching for work, his Henry Lehrman Productions having died a slow death with the expiration of his contract with First National. Whether it occurred to Lehrman at the time or not, the death of Henry Lehrman Productions signaled the death of his dreams and aspirations as well. "I have a scheme at present which promises so fairly that I am afraid to queer it by telling you what it is," said Lehrman in an interview five years earlier. "Next time you come to see me you may find me either in a palace or in the poor house."[119] If Henry Lehrman Productions was the eventual goal of Lehrman's "scheme," the latter part of his prophecy had finally come true.

CHAPTER 8

Reported Missing and the Arbuckle Scandal

Lehrman was left saddled with debt and scrambling for work. He even considered a return to Fox in late April, entering negotiations to discuss the possibility of the resumption of his former position as head of Sunshine.[1] This didn't happen, although there would be positions with Fox in his future.

Another blow came on July 6, 1921, with the passing of his "discovery" and good friend Billie Ritchie in his current home at 2050 Ivar Avenue. Papers nationwide all gave the cause of death as the result of "injuries suffered two years ago when he was attacked by ostriches at a motion picture studio," as the Associated Press put it.[2] This only added to Lehrman's reputation for risky stunts since everyone in the industry knew that Ritchie had worked solely for Lehrman and no one else. And while there is little doubt some element of truth regarding the injuries sustained, none were reported in the press at the time they would have occurred, and the real cause of death as documented on Ritchie's death certificate was "carcinoma of stomach," or stomach cancer. Regardless, it was the loss of a good friend and close working companion of the past six years. Ritchie's funeral was held at the Highland Avenue parlors of Gates, Crane & Earl, Reverend Neal Dodd officiating. He was interred at Forest Lawn cemetery.[3]

There is an interesting story regarding Ritchie's death, as told by his daughter Wyn decades later to his grandniece Lisa Robins. As Lisa put it, "When I visited Wyn she showed me the family albums.... She spoke of Billie playing the cello and she would often listen to him play. Then on the day of the funeral she heard a very loud noise coming from the music room. When she went to see what had happened she stated that the cello was laying on the floor with a split from top to bottom."[4] Coincidence, but a rather unsettling one.

While Lehrman's confidence in his abilities to successfully manage a business may have been shaken by the failure of his studio, and his star comedian was now just a sad memory, there was still no doubt in his mind that he had a unique facility for creating crowd-pleasing comedies, and that his talents as a director were undiminished. Lehrman decided that a move into feature film production would be a logical — and profitable — next step. It is unknown how many (if any) offers came his way during this period, nor how many doors he may have knocked on seeking a position, but we do know that he was ultimately successful in securing a contract with Myron Selznick in July 1921.

Twenty-two year old Myron Selznick, son of famed film producer Lewis J. Selznick, was president in charge of the East Coast productions of the Selznick Pictures Corporation. After several years of learning the trade in his father's organization out in California, the senior Selznick disposed of some of his interests and offered a management position of one of his studios to his son. By the age of twenty Myron was reportedly the industry's youngest producer, and by 1920 the entire organization was relocated from the West Coast to the East Coast where space was leased at the old Universal studio in Fort Lee.

LEFT: *Myron Selznick, circa 1917.* RIGHT: *Owen Moore.*

Additional studio space was acquired to handle Selznick's four companies, including the old Biograph studios in the Bronx, and the former Fort Lee studios of Alice Guy Blaché and Peerless. The productions at these studios featured the stars Olive Thomas, Elaine Hammerstein, Louise Huff, William Faversham, Eugene O'Brien, and Owen Moore.[5] According to *Moving Picture World*, Lehrman approached Selznick and "expressed a desire to work with Mr. Moore, convinced that from such a combination of star, director and producer there must logically develop screen comedies of unusual merit."[6] Lehrman and Moore had first met back at Biograph in 1909, and Lehrman may have been urged by the actor to approach Selznick in a gesture to help get him back on his feet. A deal was struck and it was announced that Lehrman would both write and direct the film which would co-star Moore with his new bride, Kathryn Perry, followed by three more Moore starrers tentatively titled *The Forgetters*, *Rest for the Weary*, and *Oh Professor*.[7]

Lehrman moved into an apartment in Manhattan at 25 W. Fifty-First Street, his various creditors left behind back in California. When the couple returned from their honeymoon up in New England, Lehrman would spend most of his time at Douglaston Manor, Moore's home on Long Island, where the two of them talked over various ideas for the film. The film's working title was announced as *Love is an Awful Thing*.[8] Unfortunately, Lehrman would not get to make this film — or at least a film with this title.

Lehrman had emigrated to the U.S. in December 1906 when he was a youthful twenty-five years of age, and had not seen any of his family in the fifteen years since. A stranger in a strange land, the ambitious fellow was determined to make a success of himself. He made a number of friends along the way, but many of these were mere passing acquaintances as he moved from one studio to the next. Billie Ritchie was significant in that he

LEFT: *Virginia Rappe with her friend Helen Patterson in January 1914. The two were models in the Wonder Models of Fashion troupe, and this photo was taken sometime during or after their trip to Europe.* COURTESY OF HERITAGE AUCTION GALLERIES, HA.COM. RIGHT: *Virginia Rappe, posing in Los Angeles circa 1916.* COURTESY OF JOAN MYERS.

was a steady companion during the greater part of Lehrman's ascension in the industry, but now he was gone. And that left one other close friend: Virginia Rappe.

Rappe, whose thirtieth birthday fell one day after Ritchie's death, had been in a romantic relationship with Lehrman for at least two years by this time. There's little doubt that the two were acquaintances back in June 1916 when she took part in the Automobile Fashion Show at Ascot Speedway, representing the L-Ko studio. It is possible — not probable, but possible — that the two had met as far back as 1912-13 during Lehrman's brief tenure with Kinemacolor. An article reporting on Rappe's fashion modeling at an Indianapolis department store stated that she "poses for the Kinemacolor fashion section and drives a regular racing car."[9] Assuming that their paths did not cross at this time, this early indicator of her love for fast cars may have been a passion that made Lehrman take notice at a later date.

It has yet to be verified whether Rappe appeared in any films prior to 1917. Her first confirmed credit was in Fred Balshofer's *Paradise Garden*, a Yorke-Metro feature released in October 1917, starring matinee idol Harold Lockwood. "Watch Virginia Rappe," said *Moving Picture World*'s Marion Howard in one of the more favorable assessments of Rappe's thespic abilities, "for she has a great future as vampire or heroine."[10] We'll need to take her word for it, since the film is thought to be lost. A co-starring role followed with then unknown Rudolph Valentino, supporting famed cross-dresser Julian Eltinge in Balshofer's *Over the Rhine*, but the film was shelved when the war's end rendered its subject matter of little public interest. The film would be recut and re-released in 1920 as *An Adventuress* with little success, and again in 1922 with lots of new humorless comedic footage added as the incoherent comedy *The Isle of Love*, primarily to cash in on Valentino's newfound popularity and the name recognition that Rappe would by then have acquired.

Lehrman took note. Her talents as an actress aside, Rappe's independent spirit, healthy good looks, and considerable accomplishments appealed to Lehrman. She had travelled to London and Paris, and had achieved success as a model, a line of work she had entered back in 1908. More recently she had taken on fashion design, and in 1916 set her sights on the burgeoning film industry. "She was not at all like picture people," wrote actress Miriam Cooper, who met Rappe at that time. "She didn't wear makeup, and wore her hair parted in the middle and drawn back into a knot at the nape of her neck. With her pale skin and dark eyes she was plain but beautiful. She dressed expensively but simply."[11] It didn't take long for Lehrman and Rappe to become romantically involved, and Rappe moved into his house on Franklin Avenue. The two became fixtures at the area's restaurants, nightclubs, and charity events.

Lehrman hired her for a lead role in the Sunshine comedy *His Musical Sneeze*, and had previously given her roles in at least one other Sunshine, the aforementioned *Wild Women and Tame Lions*. "Let me make you a star to rival Bebe Daniels, Mary Pickford and all the rest," he was reported as telling her in a quote of dubious reliability.[12] With the formation of his own studio, Lehrman had starred her in its maiden production *A Twilight Baby*, with roles in *The Punch of the Irish* and *A Game Lady* following. While an attractive presence in these films, her comedic abilities were marginal and she was used to best advantage in the former capacity. With the failure of his company and the loss of the Franklin Avenue home, their relationship underwent some strain and the two quarreled. Rappe moved into a rental on Ivar Avenue close to Billie Ritchie's current home and, when her financial situation grew more perilous, into the home of her "aunt" and "uncle" Kate and Joe Hardebeck on N. Wilton Place. Lehrman relocated to New York to make the Owen Moore film, but would later claim that despite the strain in their relationship, he and Rappe were engaged to be married. "I think the only man she cared anything in the world about was Henry Lehrman," confided her good friend and aspiring actress Helen Hansen. "She was awfully fond of him and kept wishing that he would hurry back from New York. He was never out of the girl's thoughts. You know how girls will talk, but during all our conversations she has never mentioned liking another man — even casually"[13] Lehrman's feelings towards Rappe at this time are unknown, but after her death he professed to have loved her, and the fact that he still had photos of her in his wallet and framed in his apartment lends more than a little credence to his assertion.

So when he received a telegram from his and Rappe's good friend Sidi Spreckels that the actress was in a local San Francisco hospital and in serious condition,[14] he was understandably concerned. Lehrman reportedly sent a telegram to Rappe urging "his sweetheart to have hope and to recover,"[15] but it is doubtful that she was ever in any sort of condition to read or comprehend its contents in the days leading up to her death on Friday, September 9, 1921. "I first heard of it about one o'clock on Friday afternoon," said Lehrman. "The telegram just told me that she was dead and I had no inkling as to what had happened until I saw it in the newspapers."[16] And what he saw in the newspapers wasn't pretty. On the day after her death, the police announced that they had placed Roscoe Arbuckle under arrest on a charge of murder. "This woman without a doubt died as a result of an attack by Arbuckle," stated San Francisco Detective Captain Duncan Matheson.

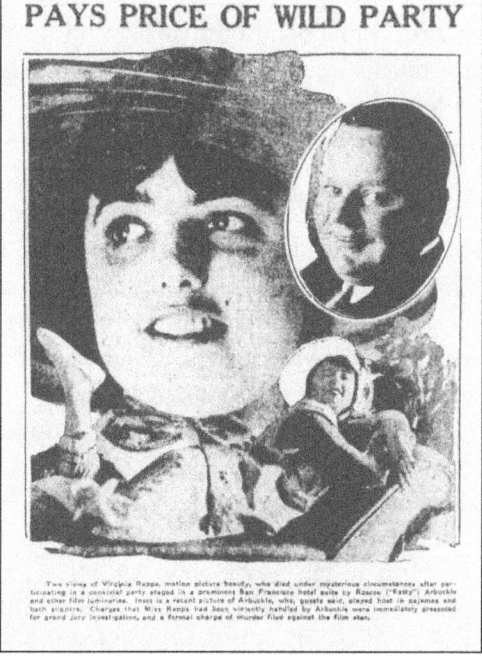

LEFT: *Virginia Rappe in a happier moment, posing with her dog Jeff circa 1918.* COURTESY OF JOAN MYERS. RIGHT: *Sensational photo spreads and equally sensational captions were the norm.*

"That makes it first degree murder without a doubt. We don't feel that a man like 'Fatty' Arbuckle can pull stuff like this in San Francisco and get away with it."[17]

What had actually happened? On Labor Day weekend, Roscoe Arbuckle and two of his friends — actor Lowell Sherman and director Fred Fishback — traveled north to San Francisco, their final destination that city's elegant St. Francis Hotel. Liquor was acquired, an impromptu party thrown, and attendees both invited and uninvited came and went. One of the guests was Virginia Rappe. The events that followed have been chronicled in detail elsewhere, most recently in Greg Merritt's excellent *Room 1219* (Chicago Review Press Incorporated, 2013), the most thoroughly researched and objective accounting of the affair to date; skip its predecessors. Suffice it to say that Rappe incurred a ruptured bladder some time during the party — the exact cause of which has never been conclusively determined — and died four days later. The nation's newspapers went into a feeding frenzy over the scandal, brimming over with articles filled with speculation, innuendo, and outright falsehoods, fueled by the contradictory accounts provided by the various participants and assorted "specialists" brought in by both the prosecuting and defense attorneys.

What did Lehrman actually know during the early days that immediately follow Rappe's death? Only what he read in the papers and the scant information he received from the West Coast, primary of which were the vituperative, self-serving telegrams and phone calls from one Maude Delmont. Delmont and Rappe were both friends of Al Semnacher, a small-time film publicist, and the trio were among the party's attendees. Delmont told Lehrman that she was Rappe's friend, but had in actuality only just met her that weekend. Her initial telegram insisted that "I'll tell the truth, if I have to die.... Virginia did not die from congestion of the lungs, as first reported. An autopsy disclosed that she was crushed and injured, proving violence."[18] It was the subsequent information provided by Delmont that really grabbed Lehrman's attention. "Miss Delmont, who accompanied Miss Rappe to Arbuckle's suite in the Hotel St. Francis, has had several long-distance telephone calls with me," reported Lehrman. "She said: 'Mr. Arbuckle telephoned Miss Rappe to come see him on business. She distrusted him and had me come along. We had a few drinks, when he leaped up and seized her, carried her into another room and locked the door. I pounded on the door and I could hear her struggle and scream. After a quarter of an hour, she gave a terrible scream. I threatened to telephone the office of the hotel, and Arbuckle appeared at the door. Every bit of Miss Rappe's clothes had been torn to shreds. She was unconscious.'"[19] Lehrman continued to take Delmont's assertions as gospel, and even wired her some money to foot her hotel bill so that she could remain in San Francisco to aid the police in their investigation.[20]

Reporter Louis Fehr headed to Lehrman's apartment, intending to get a statement from the one person who was closest to Rappe. Understandably outraged by what he believed to be the actions of his former good friend, Lehrman unleashed an impassioned, subjective tirade about the man who he felt had betrayed his trust, and the woman he professed to love. It is worth repeating at length, given the impact it most likely had on Lehrman's career in the years that followed. The wording varied slightly from one newspaper to the next, but here's how the copyrighted interview appeared in the *San Francisco Examiner*:

> My prayer is that justice be done. I don't want to go to the coast now. I could not face Arbuckle. I would kill him.
>
> *(reading from the affidavit of nurse Mrs. Jean Jameson)* She said she blamed Arbuckle for her injuries and want him punished for it. That is just like Virginia. She had the most remarkable determination. She would rise from the dead to defend her person from indignity.
>
> I had a talk over the long-distance telephone with Mrs. Sydia Spreckels, former wife of John D. Spreckels Jr. She said that before she knew she was going to die Virginia kept saying: "Don't tell Henry. Don't tell Henry." That means one thing. She had lost the battle to defend herself. She didn't want me to know. She knew what I would do.
>
> Arbuckle is a beast. I directed him for a year and a half. I finally had to tell him if he didn't keep out of the women's dressing room I would see that he was through. He boasted to me that he had torn the clothing from an unwilling girl and outraged her.
>
> That's what comes of taking vulgarians from the gutter and giving them enormous salaries and making idols of them. Arbuckle came into the pictures nine

years ago. He was a bar boy in a San Francisco saloon. Not a bartender, a bar boy; one of those who wash glasses and cleans cuspidors.

Such people don't know how to get a kick out of life, except in a beastly way. They are a disgrace to the film business. They are the ones who resort to cocaine and the opium needle and who participate in orgies that surpass the orgies of degenerate Rome. They should be swept out of the picture business.

I'm no saint, but I have never attended one of those parties. Virginia wouldn't associate with anyone she knew was vile like that. Her friends were people like Charlie Chaplin and other decent people.

Despite his weight, Arbuckle was a powerful man. I remember a few years ago, when we were making a picture at Tijuana, Mexico, he weighed 210 pounds.

He entered a hundred-yard dash against Mexican athletes. Some of them were bull fighters. They laughed at his entry. But he beat them all.

It is a silly lie to say that Virginia died of pneumonia. I have here a telegram from Dr. Rumwell of the Wakefield Sanitarium, San Francisco, that her bladder was ruptured and that this led to peritonitis, causing her death.

Since I got that telegram I have talked to some of the best doctors in New York. They tell me that only the most crushing exterior force could cause an internal rupture.

Virginia always had a violent physical aversion for Arbuckle. When we three worked together I wanted everything to be like a happy family. One time when he attended a party her aversion sort of dampened things. I took her aside and said: "Cheer up. Treat him pleasantly. He's a good fellow." She replied: "He's coarse and vulgar. He nauseates me. He is cheap and thinks he's funny."

I can see now in my mind's eye how she must have fought him like a tiger, even if she had had a couple of drinks.

I remember once there was a terrible assault case in the newspapers. She said to me, quietly: "Henry, if anyone tried to do a thing like that to me, he'd have to kill me." Well, she's dead.

She had been in the pictures four years. She was born in New York and brought up in Chicago. She had never been sick a day in her life. She always held herself aloof from the vulgar crowd in pictures. She was clean, decent, high-spirited, and to think she had to die like that!

I have telegraphed to the coast to give her a wonderful funeral.

Look, see this telegram. When I got the first wire from Mrs. Spreckels that she (Miss Rappe) was in the hospital, I started to wire Arbuckle to look after her. He knew what she and I were to each other. I never suspected that, beast that he was, he would lay a finger on her.

I feel as though I had died and that my being here in these rooms isn't quite real. I haven't been out of these rooms since I got the wire that she was dead. But I want to live now to see that justice is not cheated.

Nobody can pull me off. Arbuckle has powerful friends, and much influence and money will be used to save him. But he will have me to reckon with, even if he succeeds in buying his freedom.

God, give justice.[21]

Needless to say, Lehrman didn't mince with words — words he may have come to regret in the years to come.

"I cannot understand how Henry Lehrman could have said such a thing, because he must have known better," stated Minta Durfee Arbuckle, the arrested comedian's estranged wife. "Roscoe and Henry Lehrman were inseparable pals, and I am sure my husband still considers Lehrman one of his very best friends."[22] Best friend? Still? Rather doubtful.

Bits and pieces of Lehrman's comments from that day resurfaced in subsequent articles, but aside from some follow-up entreaties to the prosecutors to do their best to see that justice was served and Arbuckle made to pay, Lehrman was actually rather mum regarding his "friend" from that time on. He did, however, issue some rather blistering statements involving the industry as a whole and those in power. "[T]here is a certain element in the motion picture world that is trembling just now in the efforts to prevent the making an example of Arbuckle. They fear that if he is punished they cannot avoid the exposure and ruin which will follow."[23] Given the financial impact that the scandal was having on Paramount Pictures — they had four completed Arbuckle features sitting on the shelf waiting for a now doubtful release — and the nationwide attention now focused on Hollywood's excesses — stories of drunken orgies, widespread drug use, and just about any other sort of sensationalism that could be conjured up — Lehrman's words were not ones to please those who would be in a position to provide future employment.

Given what he knew at the time, combined with a feeling of betrayal from his friend Arbuckle and helplessness being a continent away from what was taking place, Lehrman's impassioned, off-the-cuff response is somewhat understandable. "I'll have to get out of here," he said. "[The telephone] rings all the time and everyone wants to talk to me about Virginia. Each time someone calls and asks questions it brings the whole terrible thing back to me. The loss of Miss Rappe has nearly driven me crazy."[24]

Unfortunately, Lehrman was required by Selznick to remain in New York and continue working on the Moore film, or at least that's what he claimed. Regardless, a trip to the West Coast, feasible in those days only by train, would require at least a two week interruption of production, an interruption that Selznick was not about to entertain. About the best Lehrman could do — and he did it willingly — was to assume responsibility for all of Virginia Rappe's funeral arrangements, believing that she had no living relatives. Former employee Norman Taurog, now directing for comedian Larry Semon, contacted Lehrman and offered to handle the local arrangements. "I don't know of anybody more faithful and sincere than you am glad to avail myself of your offer to assist," responded Lehrman by telegram.[25] Lehrman contacted Halsted and Company, the San Francisco funeral home holding her remains, and instructed them to ship the body back to the Strother and Dayton Funeral Home on Hollywood Boulevard in Los Angeles. Her remains were shipped by train on the night of September 16, arriving in Los Angeles the following morning. Lehrman secured a burial plot in Hollywood Cemetery next to the one he had acquired for his secretary Helen Morrison a mere two years earlier.[26]

On Sunday, September 18, a viewing was held in the chapel at Strother and Dayton, open to the public for six hours. Friends and employees of the film industry shuffled past the open casket, but they were far outnumbered by total strangers, estimates ranging anywhere from 6,000 to 8,000 depending on the observer.[27] The funeral was held the following day with an Episcopalian clergyman officiating, this time the chapel open only to friends while an estimated 1,500 curiosity seekers milled about outside; Norman Taurog and former Lehrman employee Al Herman guarded the door against any potential "crashers." "There were a number of beautiful floral offerings," reported the *Kingston Daily Freeman*, "the most pretentious being a blanket of 1,000 Tiger lilies sent by Miss Rappe's fiance, Henry Lehrman."[28] Across the blanket lay a white satin ribbon, the words "To my brave sweetheart, from Henry" emblazoned in gold letters.[29] Other floral arrangements included those from Winifred Ritchie, Lloyd Hamilton, George Meehan, and numerous others.[30]

Actor Tom Wilson, in blackface.

The pallbearers comprised former Lehrman associates Taurog, Herman, David Kirkland, Frank Coleman, and Frank Olin (as reported, but assumedly misnamed Earle Olin), accompanied by Larry Semon and Oliver Hardy.[31] Taurog, Semon, and Hardy had interrupted the filming of the comedy *The Sawmill* to attend to matters.

It was reported in October that Kathryn Perry had been replaced by Pauline Garon as the female lead for Lehrman's film. Garon, who was starring in *Lilies of the Field* at Broadway's Klaw Theatre, would need to shuttle between the city and the Fort Lee studios to make the film.[32] Also selected for the cast were Tom Wilson, who specialized in blackface roles for the screen, and Japanese actor Togo Yamamota; both were brought in from Los Angeles for the film. Nita Naldi was chosen as well, having previously co-starred with Moore in *A Divorce of Convenience* (1921) for Selznick.[33] Production was under way by November, the film still being referred to as *Love is an Awful Thing*.

The story that Lehrman came up with, and that Lewis Allen Browne adapted for the screen, was designed to be a spoof of sorts on the melodramatic serials of the day, loaded with non-stop action and plenty of laughs. It was designed as entertainment and nothing else, and the final release would open with a foreword stating just that. For scenes involving a shipwreck, Lehrman hired the schooner *Nancy Hanks* and instructed the captain to sail well out into the Atlantic. According to a press release, "Lehrman insisted that sea pictures should be taken at sea," a stance that undoubtedly added to the realism and resulted in some pictorially pleasing footage, and "two dozen sea-sick people."[34] A piece that appeared during the film's production gives a sense of one of the more exciting sequences in the film, now believed to be lost:

Among the last shots to be made are a number of marine scenes to be taken off the Atlantic Coast near Keyport, N.J. A new type of sea-sled, capable of making a speed of seventy-eight miles per hour, has been secured to engage in a race with a six-passenger hydroplane from the Aero Marine Works at Keyport. The United States Government is providing two torpedo boat destroyers for these scenes.

It is of interest to know that when asked for depth bombs to be used in conjunction with some of these marine scenes, Government officials said there were practically no depth bombs to be had in this country at the present time. The desired effect of an explosion under water is to be accomplished through the use of a charge of 300 pounds of dynamite.

The film had become the biggest production ever made to date by the Selznick Organization, and it was announced to exhibitors that for the 1921-22 season the Owen Moore vehicles would be handled as "specials" and sold individually. During the previous season the Moore films were sold as a star series, as were the films of a number of Selznick's other contract stars. This new approach to selling the Moore comedies had been decided on earlier, and Lehrman chosen to handle the first of the new releases to kick-start the new and improved series. Still, exhibitors were skeptical. "When it is recalled that there have been a number of Owen Moore pictures made by the Selznick company — and all of them of the program variety insofar as cost of production is concerned," questioned *Exhibitors Trade Review*, "there is considerable curiosity as to just what this new production is to be…. It is a natural query as to just how a forthcoming release starring Owen Moore, whose forte is farce comedy, is to surpass all previous Selznick studio efforts."[35]

By February 1922 the film had acquired the title *Sink or Swim*, and various articles commented on how long the production had been taking place.[36] That title had a short shelf life, with the final title of *Reported Missing* announced a mere month later.[37]

With shooting completed, editing and titling of the film took place at the Selznick studios in East Forty-eighth Street in Manhattan. Myron Selznick appeared to be distancing himself from Lehrman by now, either that or he wanted a larger share of the credit for the completed film. "Henry Lehrman, who wrote and directed the new Moore comedy, is contributing his ideas to the completion of the presentation," commented one piece, "but Myron Selznick is giving his personal attention to every detail."[38] Five popular columnists were engaged to write the intertitles, three of whom were humorists for various New York dailies. This trio included H.I. Phillips of the *New York Globe*, John Medbury of the *New York Journal*, and Will B. Johnstone of the *New York Evening World*. Lehrman wouldn't be able to contribute many more ideas at this time, since he had departed for the West Coast a month earlier, arriving in Los Angeles in mid-March; he headed north to San Francisco, arriving on Monday, April 10. There was much speculation as to whether Lehrman would testify for the prosecution in the Arbuckle trial, and he had expressed a willingness to do so.[39] That never happened, however, no doubt a disappointment to the members of the press who had been eagerly anticipating a courtroom confrontation between Arbuckle and his "friend."

Lehrman's reputation was in somewhat of a freefall by now, both within the industry and the public at large. Initially a sympathetic presence in the earliest days of the scandal, people were beginning to question his sincerity and motives. Perhaps the single biggest blow came courtesy of William Randolph Hearst's International Feature Service, Inc., which published a scathing full-page article that appeared in papers nationwide. Titled "$1,000 for Lilies But Not One Cent for a Lovely Wrap," the article was accompanied by a photo of Lehrman and an even larger photo of the aggrieved woman at the center of the piece, one Jocelyn Leigh. Dripping with sarcasm toward Lehrman, the story went on to claim that within a month of Rappe's death, Lehrman had promised a mink coat and a job in the movies to Miss Leigh. She acquired the coat but was shocked — *shocked* — when Lehrman's seventy-five dollar check for down payment bounced and her dreams

"$1,000 for Lilies But Not One Cent for a Lovely Fur Wrap." Lehrman as cad.

for a mink coat shattered. Photos of the front and back of the bad check were included, lest anyone doubt the veracity of the story being told.[40] The article made Lehrman out to be a two-faced cad of the worst sort, never questioning the motives of the woman at the center of the story. The rest of the story came out two months later in a far smaller piece, wherein Miss Leigh admitted that the previous story was "not exactly correct." In this telling she claimed that Lehrman had given her the seventy-five dollar check as a first payment of a $700 debt he owed her for work already done, and that she had used it as down payment for the coat. When the store owner refused to alter the coat and refused to accept a return, she said, Leigh complained to Lehrman, who immediately stopped payment on the check.[41]

As if those stories weren't sufficient in presenting the director in a less than favorable light, another piece appeared once again dredging up those 1,000 Tiger lilies. Albert O. Stein, the San Francisco-based florist who had filled the order for that floral arrangement, insisted that numerous attempts to collect the $150 owed him by Lehrman had all met with failure. And so he filed suit.[42] But perhaps the most damaging failure to honor his debts were the ones that never made it into the press, the ones that were known primarily among various industry insiders. Lehrman, it appears, failed to pay the funeral home and cemetery bills as well, leaving Norman Taurog on the hook. Taurog had sent a bitter telegram to Lehrman back on January 26 while the director was still in New York:

Reported Missing *was well received, as this ad from the April 23, 1922 issue of* Film Daily *promoted.*

> News papers have asked me for story about unpaid bills unless you forward money immediately, I will be forced to tell the truth, and show people you are not such a martyr The worry you have caused me, and the shifting of your responsibilities is at an end. Your friends the one or two you had are done. Send money immediately to Strother and Dayton and Hollywood Cemetery, if you do not, you will have to take the consequences. Answer by return wire.[43]

It is assumed that Lehrman paid these bills since there were no suits filed by either Strother and Dayton or Hollywood Cemetery, but it is clear from Taurog's telegram that Lehrman had managed to burn a lot of bridges and leave a number of unhappy former friends and acquaintances in his wake. It did not bode well for his future in the industry.

ABOVE: *Owen Moore holds court in* Reported Missing. COURTESY OF ROBERT JAMES KISS.
BELOW: *Pauline Garon and Owen Moore, shanghaied in* Reported Missing. COURTESY OF HERITAGE AUCTION GALLERIES, HA.COM.

Meanwhile back in New York, so confident was Myron Selznick that he had a smash hit on his hands, that he arranged a special showing of the film on April 7 to 1,500 people at the Ritz Carlton Hotel's grand ballroom. Attendees, it was reported, were "thoroughly representative of the industry, and many other prominent in the New York social and literary world." The film was deemed "a genuine box-office attraction." The occasion was also designated as a farewell party for Myron and his stars and production staff, all of whom would soon relocate to the West Coast.[44] Lehrman, of course, was not in attendance; he was back on the West Coast. One attendee's reaction to the film was fairly typical, stating that the film "is not only one of the best pictures ever made by the Selznick company but one of the most thoroughly satisfactory ever made by any company."[45]

More promotional materials for Reported Missing. COURTESY OF JIM KERKHOFF.

Released on April 5, *Reported Missing* follows the exploits of a wealthy young Richard Boyd (Moore) who inherits a steamship line. His girl Pauline (Garon) wants him to utilize the ships, but one of his advisors is in cahoots with a Japanese businessman named Young (Togo Yamamoto) and unsuccessfully tries to convince Boyd to sell out. Young has Boyd shanghaied and Pauline is forced to accompany him. Boyd's faithful black servant Sam (Tom Wilson) follows and joins them on the boat on which they are captives. A storm strands the boat on a reef, and as the situation on board grows more dire with each passing day, rescue appears at hand when Boyd is able to attract the attention of a passing warship. Young grabs the girl and makes off for land in a motor boat. The warship provides a plane and drops some bombs in the path of the boat, but Young and his captive make it to land. Joined by the warship's sailors, Boyd and the others pursue Young in an exciting auto chase, Boyd crashing over an embankment to avoid hitting a child. Arriving at Young's hideout, a climactic chase and fight ensues in the building's labyrinthine tunnels. Boyd emerges victorious after killing Young.

The film proved to be a big hit with reviewers, most of whom were taken with Lehrman's mix of comedy and action. Laurence Reid's review in *Motion Picture News* was typical:

> Henry Lehrman, who wrote and directed this melodramatic comedy, has been given free rein to add to the gayety of a nation. And he has contributed a feature which will be talked about for its adventurous action, its novel gags, its subtle and broad humor, its quaint characterization, its development toward a climax

which carries explosive qualities and its overwhelming suspense. This compelling element causes the spectator to grip the arms of his seat despite the fact that the incidents and gags are charged with humor. Even though you wonder if Owen Moore, "shanghaied" by his enemy, will ever see land again, you laugh over his embarrassing moments.[46]

By the end of May *Exhibitors Trade Review* reported that "To date bookings on the feature registered at the Selznick offices in New York surpass in number and importance the bookings on any other photoplay which the firm has ever released."[47] The film proved to be a hit with audiences, and exhibitors were thoroughly pleased with its performance. "First showing in Northwest," wrote one. "Raised prices from thirty cents to forty and stood 'em out for three days. Wonderful audience picture. Not even one dissatisfied patron."[48] "If they don't like it they're dead and don't know it," raved another. "Comedy and excitement rarely blended. Tom Wilson is a new Bert Williams. Play it up big."[49]

Of course there always has to be one dissenting voice, this one provided by the New York *Evening World*'s reviewer Don Allen. It is worth repeating here in part, primarily because it is so at odds with practically every other review written about the film.

> Never in the wildest days of Mack Sennett did he ever descend to the hokum that Henry Lehrman…does in "Reported Missing." The good points…are several really excellent photographic shots, many of which are ruined by inaccuracies and absurd carelessness of direction. Moore…works like a Trojan to get across and keeps everlastingly at it, but the hardest worked man in the whole production is the one who throws teaspoonfuls of water through the portholes in an effort to simulate a terrific storm at sea. The storm is, indeed, terrible, but not in the sense Lehrman wishes it to be. In fact, the adjective could be used to advantage in describing almost every inch-fraction of the whole too long footage."[50]

Evidently a reviewer taken with his own words.

Tellingly, in spite of all the praise heaped upon *Reported Missing* and its director, Lehrman was one-and-done with Selznick. As for the title *Love is an Awful Thing*, it was reassigned to Owen Moore's follow-up film, to be directed by Victor Heerman, one of Lehrman's former directors back at L-Ko. Heerman had previously directed two other Moore vehicles for Selznick — *The Poor Simp* (1920) and *The Chicken in the Case* (1921) — and had acted as Lehrman's assistant on *Reported Missing*,[51] so he was a natural choice to helm Moore's next film, given that Lehrman was out of the running. With the completion of *Reported Missing*, Myron Selznick and his company packed up and vacated the East Coast studios to relocate to the West Coast. *Love is an Awful Thing* and all future Selznick productions would be made there, putting an end to Myron's earlier contention that "All this stuff about California being the only place to make moving pictures is bunk."[52]

Absent from the film's credits and promotional materials was a claim commented on several times shortly after the film's release: David Kirkland, Lehrman's former director and more recently Constance Talmadge's director-of-choice, sent a telegram ostensibly to the *New York Times* stating that he was both co-author and co-director of *Reported*

Missing.[53] It was a claim that found no support anywhere else, but one he would stick with and make more than once.[54]

Arbuckle, his charges lowered from murder to manslaughter, was finally acquitted in a third trial, the previous two resulting in hung juries. "Acquittal is not enough for Roscoe Arbuckle," began the one hundred thirty-five word statement signed by the twelve jurors. "We feel that a great injustice has been done him." Given the length of the statement and the thought that went into its composition, one marvels at how the twelve jurors had time to sign it, let alone write it, in the mere five minutes that elapsed from when they left the courtroom until a verdict was reached.

Arbuckle's acquittal aside, the final result of the scandal was that the reputation of one of the world's most popular comedians was severely tarnished, and his on-screen career ruined. As for Rappe, the reputation of an innocent young woman was trashed, no thanks to the prosecuting attorneys who did their best to shift blame from the defendant to the deceased, aided and abetted by the press who feasted on every sordid tidbit that was presented across the three trials. Sadly, that undeservedly sordid reputation lingers on to this day, regurgitated and embellished from one lazy writer to the next. "Millions of pretty girls turn their faces toward the gilded west and sigh for celluloid stardom," wrote *Variety*. "Thousands venture to go after the pot of brass at the end of the Cooper-Hewitt rainbow. Virginia Rappe was one of those. She yearned for stardom. She made it — at last!"[55]

The press eventually soured on Lehrman, casting him in a less than favorable light in the years to come; *Variety* referred to him as the "film director who obtruded himself into notoriety through a verbal assault in the press upon Fatty Arbuckle."[56] And if Lehrman's employment situation and future weren't looking bleak enough at this time, some prankster placed the following ad in the *Los Angeles Times'* "personal" column, an obvious dig at the director's failings: "Personal — Wanted, the address of Henry Lehrman. Have $1,000,000 to start motion picture business. Cash waiting." It was followed by a P.O. address for reply.[57]

CHAPTER 9

Treading Water at a Potpourri of Studios

If Lehrman had expected the success and surrounding publicity for *Reported Missing* to open some doors for him at major studios, those expectations were soon dashed and he was left saddled with debt and scrambling for work. It was the Stern brothers at Century who initially expressed interest back in February, stating that Lehrman had been engaged to produce twelve "super-comedies" over the following year,[1] and by April it was reported that Lehrman was actually directing a film for them.[2] *Camera!* elaborated somewhat, stating that Lehrman was directing Lee Moran in a comedy for Century, with Jack Dawn assisting, working from a scenario by Lehrman.[3] Little more was heard about this arrangement, leading one to believe that this may have been Lehrman's sole Century before a falling out between the two parties. If Lehrman actually did direct more than one film for Century, those titles have not been identified.

Columnist and screenwriter Jimmy Starr had an interesting anecdote to relate years later regarding an uneasy encounter he had with Lehrman around this time. He was on his way to a menial job sorting mail for Harry Brand, who was at the time head of Buster Keaton's publicity department. He was intercepted by A.M. Brettinger who asked if Starr would recognize Lehrman, and breathlessly went on to say (as paraphrased by Starr) that "Lehrman's coming into the studio. Just coming through the gate about now. You've got to stop a murder! Lehrman's carrying a gun. He's going to try to kill Arbuckle — and Arbuckle is in with Mr. Schenck! Just stall him until I get Arbuckle out through the back gate. Now Hurry!" Starr went on to relate his somewhat twisted knowledge of the Arbuckle-Rappe scandal, and his growing apprehension as Lehrman approached.

> I put on my best smile as I approached Lehrman, who seemed to be casually inspecting the studio street. His thin lips formed a half-smile as I greeted him.
>
> "Mr. Lehrman, I am glad I ran into you. I admire your style of comedy and I was hoping you might give me a chance to be your gagman on some two-reelers."
>
> My eyes searched his clothing for a possible concealed pistol, but I found no suspicious bulges. Lehrman was obviously pleased with the compliment.
>
> "Jimmy, I am very honored that you would like to work with me. I could teach you the continental style of comedy that this country should know more about.

I hope to return to filming very shortly — probably at Fox — and perhaps I can find a place for you."

"I certainly appreciate your thinking of me," I said, wondering how I could inquire of his current mission. "Are you looking for anyone in particular? I could direct you to the office. I know this studio like the back of my hand."

Lehrman's small, beady eyes darted up and down the studio street.

"No," he drawled. "I dropped in to see Sam Rork. He has a comedy property he wanted to talk to me about it. I doubt if anything will come of it. He hasn't much of a sense of humor."

My relief must have been obvious. Lehrman asked: "Why are you so intent on my visit?"

"I guess it was the chance of seeing you," I stammered. "I had been hoping for so long…and, well, here you were, and I just had to put in a bid to — for a crack at working with you."

Lehrman patted me on the shoulder. He moved on, saying: "Keep in touch."[4]

And Lehrman kept his word, eventually hiring Starr in 1928 to write gags for the feature he was then working on.

Lehrman surprised everyone with his April 26, 1922 marriage in Santa Ana to Jocelyn Leigh, now described as "Chicago's leading representative in Ziegfeld's Follies." Leigh, whose real name was Mary Alice Simpson, described Lehrman as a "friend of her father." According to the *Los Angeles Times*, news of their marriage "caused a sensation among Lehrman's friends and acquaintances…especially those who knew him when he was devoted to Virginia Rappe."[5] Given the earlier publicity surrounding Lehrman, Leigh, and the mink coat, one can just imagine what form that "sensation" took.

Lehrman continued to be hounded by creditors during this time, hoping to collect debts accrued by Henry Lehrman Productions and the studio associated with them. Frustrated by Lehrman's lack of acknowledgement of their repeated demands for payment, they turned to the courts. A $722.65 judgment was awarded to S.G. Levy and associates back in October of 1921,[6] and another was awarded the Pacific Coast Electrical Company on April 1922 in the amount of $760.12 "for fixtures sold and delivered."[7] Yet another suit was filed in November by the Hammond Lumber Company in the amount of $4,000, claiming that Lehrman had refused payment on three promissory notes.[8] The Pacific Coast Electrical Company debt proved to be a thorough embarrassment to the director when it was trumpeted in the papers: Lehrman's failure to appear in court on September 15 led to an arrest on a contempt charge later that night.[9] Lehrman claimed that he had misunderstood the original summons, but the fellow who served said summons claimed that Lehrman "tore up the subpoena and threw it in his face."[10] The press had a field day with that one.

The Collection Service Corporation was engaged on behalf of two creditors, the Western Union Telegraph Company, pursuing a $159.13 debt, and the Southern California Edison Company, pursuing a $320.03 debt. The defendants named included "Henry Lehrman Studio," "Henry Lehrman," "C. Fred Grundy," "Grundy Comedies," and a whole lot of "John Doe"s. Grundy is somewhat of a mystery, appearing sporadically in the press in the years leading up to this in a less than flattering light for alleged stock fraud,[11] but never in connection with the film industry. Grundy issued a series of denials through his attorney, denying "that he was associated with Henry Lehrman Studio, or that he was an owner thereof, or had an interest therein," and further denying that "Grundy Comedies Company is now or was ever a corporation," and that he was in any way responsible for the named debts.[12] The collection company went after every film company they thought may have employed Lehrman in an attempt to garnish his wages. Century Films came first in May, but they responded by stating that "Mr. Lehrman is not in our employment and has no interest in our pictures,"[13] nor had they any "property in [their] possession, or under [their] control, belonging to said defendant."[14] Century's terse responses suggest that Lehrman's employment by them was brief, and possibly for only that sole Lee Moran comedy.

The H.G. Bittleston Law and Collection Agency filed a complaint in June on behalf of four other companies as well, seeking payment for services rendered in the lines of wearing apparel, printing, gas and oils, and advertising; their claims totaled $551.68 with interest.[15] They attempted to garnish any outstanding wages owed to Lehrman by Robertson-Cole Studios only to be informed that there was nothing owed, and that in fact Lehrman was "in debt to the company and overdrawn."[16] Further evidence of this referenced employment of Lehrman by Robertson-Cole has yet to be discovered.

Newlyweds Jocelyn Leigh and Henry Lehrman. The calm before the storm.

An association with Robertson-Cole was announced several months later, however, when it was reported that Lehrman was to direct the remaining six Carter De Haven two-reelers. He was to take over for director Mal St. Clair, who was reassigned to the upcoming *Fighting Blood* series of two-reel fight films. Filming would take place at the R-C studios, for release through F.B.O (Film Booking Office).[17] Two shorts are definitely known to have resulted from this arrangement, the first with the working title *False Alarm*[18] and released in January 1923 as *A Ringer for Dad*. Starring De Haven and his wife from a story by Monty Brice and Ethel Foreman, the *Chicago Daily Tribune* deemed it "a little domestic comedy that is not as good as the ones the Sidney Drews put out, but which passes the time away pleasantly."[19] Lehrman was cited as working on a second comedy at the end of December tentatively titled *Baby Ben*, with a script by De Haven and Monty Banks.[20] None of the remaining five comedies was released with that title, so one is left to guess whether it was the following film, *Say It With Diamonds*, or one of the others. With the completion of this series, De Haven left the business to sell real estate in West Hollywood.[21]

The Collection Service Corporation, dogged in its pursuit to garnish wages for its two clients, may have jumped the gun on this one. Based on the reports in the press, they went after the Los Angeles offices of Film Booking Offices of America in late October, only to receive the curt reply that "Mr. Lehrman is not connected with this office."[22]

LEFT: *Promo for* A Ringer for Dad. Exhibitors Herald, *January 20, 1923.*
RIGHT: *Carter De Haven, looking cool.*

Lehrman followed his brief stint with Robertson-Cole for a comparatively more lucrative job with Universal to both write and direct a feature starring the popular western star Hoot Gibson. Announced in early 1923 with the tentative title *The Poor Worm*,[23] the result was released in May as *Double Dealing*. The story, such as it was, involved a small-town "boob" named Ben Slowbell (Gibson) who loses his drug store when his mortgage is foreclosed. Enter a fast-talking city slicker (Eddie Gribbon) who colludes with the town skinflint to unload a seemingly worthless parcel of land, convincing Slowbell to borrow the cash from his grandmother. What appears at first to be a disastrous move eventually pays off handsomely when some strangers arrive in town and purchase the land at a tidy profit. "Looking at this picture in the most sympathetic light possible," wrote reviewer Laurence Reid, "we cannot offer many praises for it."[24] *Film Daily* agreed, taking Lehrman to task for the disappointing results. "Henry Lehrman, erstwhile short reel comedy director, is doubly responsible for this very weak Hoot Gibson feature inasmuch as he is both author and director and has done a fairly poor job in each instance…. Lehrman has only succeeded in dragging his story out to feature length through a lot of unnecessary footage and slap stick stuff that gets laughs not because it is funny but because it is so ridiculous."[25] *Motion Picture Magazine* jumped in, calling it "a wild, wild story fit only for infantile minds."[26] *Exhibitors Trade Review* and *Exhibitors Herald* were seemingly the two dissenting voices, the former calling it "a pleasing bit of entertainment [that] should make a good box office attraction,"[27] and the latter judging it a film "that will no doubt please [Gibson's] admirers. Quite funny in spots and plenty of action in others."[28] The exhibitors themselves gave mixed results, ranging from "Patrons very well pleased"[29] to "They don't make them any worse than this one."[30] One exhibitor offered a more balanced report, stating that "Personally I liked it. It demonstrates that Hoot can act other parts than woolly Westerns. Had much good clean comedy. A top-notch fight scene and was clean with a good story."[31] The reviews and reactions aside, *Double Dealing* was nothing more than a minor offering, a far cry from the heavily promoted success of *Reported Missing*. As a director of features, Lehrman's second proved to be a step in the wrong direction. And to add insult to injury, Universal would later attribute this film in print to director Edward Sedgwick, who helmed many of the other Gibson features for that company.[32]

Cowboy star Hoot Gibson, as pictured on Universal Weekly's *cover, November 15, 1924.*

The Bittleston Collection Agency, in its ongoing pursuit to collect on behalf of its clients, contacted Universal in January 1923 and had better luck this time, collecting fifty percent of his weekly paychecks.[33] Two other aggrieved parties attempted to garnish Lehrman's wages from Universal as well: Charles Levy and Son had been awarded a judgment of $722.65 for a debt that dated back to 1921, and they were successful. B.P. Schulberg, Lehrman's former East Coast representative, wasn't as lucky. Awarded a judgment of $1,714.60 on June 20, 1922 for services rendered to Lehrman, his attorneys learned of Lehrman's employment by Universal and attempted to garnish his wages. Too early, as it turned out; Lehrman hadn't started yet.[34]

Lehrman was jobless once again, but only for several months. His fortunes shifted in May when F.B.O. contacted him to assume direction of the second series of twelve two-reelers in the popular *Fighting Blood* films. The first series of twelve, released between February and July 1923, were all the work of prolific comedy director Mal St. Clair who was reported as taking "a much needed rest." Based on H.C. Witwer's "Fighting Blood" stories that had first appeared in *Collier's Weekly* and were adapted for the screen by Beatrice Van, by now a respected screenwriter, the first series had proved to be extremely popular with bookings in over 7,000 theaters nationwide.[35] Initially relying on title recognition to lure patrons into the theaters, it didn't hurt that Universal had adapted Witwer's popular *Leather Pushers* book of 1920 as a series of twenty-four two-reelers starring Reginald Denny for release in 1922, and to overwhelming success. According to Mal St. Clair biographer Ruth Anne Dwyer, F.B.O. intentionally created confusion about the two series: They brazenly advertised their films as a "Leather Pusher" series, relying on the fact that the term was a generic one for boxers, and apparently got away with it.[36] Witwer, who was only thirty-nine when he died in 1929, was known primarily for his humorous boxing and baseball stories, written largely in slang. In addition to over 400 stories and magazine articles, he also scripted nearly 125 films and authored a pair of comic strips.[37]

Filming at the Powers Hollywood Studios, the new offerings would again co-star George O'Hara and Clare Horton, with supporting players Albert Cooke, Kit Guard, Mary Beth Milford, Joe Rivers, and "Petey," the "droll canine performer with the ring around his eye;" Louise Lorraine replaced Horton midway through the series.[38] Each film included a boxing match with star O'Hara as Gale Galen, aka "Six-Second Smith" and contender for the world lightweight crown, with the occasional appearance by real-life celebrity boxers. Sports writer and former professional boxer Larry McGrath had a role in at least three of the new series' entries,[39] while Leach Cross, Kid McCoy, and Al Wolgast had roles in the former series.[40] Lehrman's first in the new series was titled *So This is Hollywood* (August 5, 1923), and he would go on to direct at least four more entries that have been confirmed, *She Supes to Conquer* (#2), *Long Live the Ring* (#3), *The Three Orphans* (#4), and *A Comedy of Terrors* (#7). (Al Santell directed at least two of the entries, *Babes in the Hollywood* (#10) and *The Switching Hour* (#12), respectively.)[41] The first of the new series was released on August 5, arriving in theaters immediately on the heels of the last of the first series. Each episode had a budget in the neighborhood of $2,000.[42]

Variety was impressed with the results, reporting that the second entry was billed above the five-reel feature, "and it should be. It has snap and action and, above all, a wealth of low comedy. That would recommend any picture, and this one looks like a clean-up. Any picture that can make a film audience laugh right out loud so you can hear 'em on the sidewalk is in a way to returns."[43] *Film Daily* concurred, reporting that the "brand new series…looks like ready money and lots of it in the box office…. There is a lot of comedy introduced and if the remainder of the series live up to what developed in the first three stories they are going to prove a mighty good bet."[44] Sounds like Lehrman was the right man for the job. Exhibitors were seemingly unanimous with their praise. "The second series is even better than the first series," reported one. "Just finished 'Fighting Blood,' second series, and broke all house records," wrote another.[45] "We have played twelve and not a bad one in the lot. Everyone likes them, all classes alike" and "To say that these are good would be putting it mildly" were additional accolades.[46]

Lehrman was up to his old tricks while filming *She Supes to Conquer*. During a sequence that involved the shooting of a film set in ancient Rome, comic Al Cooke was to be chased by lions. His mad dash to escape them resulted in a severe cut to his elbow and a sprained knee, neither severe enough to get in the way of resumed shooting once he was patched up.[47] "The hero is instructed in the next scene to step into the arena as a lion crouches to

ABOVE: *Production shot taken during the first* Fighting Blood *series. Left to right: unknown, director Mal St. Clair, Frankie Adams, and star George O'Hara.* BELOW: Fighting Blood *series screenwriter Beatrice Van, hard at work.* COURTESY OF SAM GILL.

spring upon the pale, blonde heroine, and choke the lion to death." wrote *Variety* of the sequence. "It is urged by a nancified lion tamer that it is perfectly safe. They release the lions and for 400 feet or so it becomes a lion chase equal to the classics in some of the earlier Sunshine subjects put out by Fox."[48]

Shooting of *A Comedy of Terrors*, the series' seventh entry, took place during September. Lehrman was under considerable financial strain by this time, hounded by creditors and drowning in debt. He finally gave up and filed a voluntary bankruptcy petition in Los Angeles through his attorney, Nathan Goldberg. Lehrman's listed liabilities were in excess of $43,000, while his assets only amounted to $5,300. Fifty-four creditors were listed, including the actor Francis X. Bushman, who was owed $760.[49] For someone as vain as Lehrman, it must have been the ultimate humiliation.

Lehrman's run with the *Fighting Blood* series may have come to an end with the offer in November from Abe Carlos to direct another feature. Carlos and Lehrman had met back in late 1917 when their positions with Fox overlapped for a brief time before Carlos was relieved of his position as General Superintendant of the West Coast studios, to be replaced by William Fox's private secretary Sol Wurtzel. Carlos had returned to the East Coast and remained in Fox's employ until 1923 when he resigned to go into independent production with his Carlos Productions. After the single Henry B. Walthall starrer *The Unknown Purple* (1923), Carlos engaged former Thanhouser and Douglas Fairbanks stunt man Richard Talmadge to be featured in a string of films for release through Truart Film Corp. Lehrman was hired to direct the series' second entry, tentatively adopting the title of the novel from which it was being adapted, *To Live or Die*.[50] Re-titled *On Time* shortly thereafter, casting was completed in December with German-born Talmadge to be supported by Billie Dove, George Siegmann, Stuart Holmes, and Charles Clary. *Reported Missing*'s standout performer Tom Wilson was brought on as well to supply the comedy relief as Talmadge's valet, appearing once again in blackface as a character named Casanova Clay.[51] Filming was completed by early January, but release was delayed until March 1 while Truart hammered at a deal with F.B.O. to distribute the bulk of their product.[52]

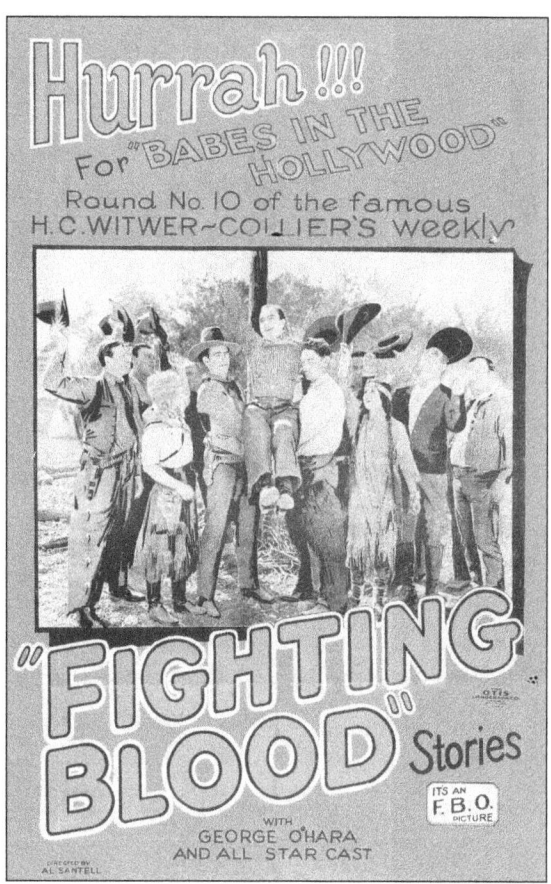

Poster for episode #10 of Fighting Blood *series 2:* Babes in the Hollywood. COURTESY OF HERITAGE AUCTION GALLERIES, HA.COM.

ABOVE: On Time *lobby card. Left to right: Richard Talmadge, Tom Wilson, and Douglas Gerrard.* BELOW: *Billie Dove looks away as Talmadge looks confused, from* On Time. *The fellow in the doorway is actor Fred Kirby (unconfirmed).* PHOTOS COURTESY OF MACELO CORONADO AND JOHN HILLMAN, SILENTCINEMA.COM.

Talmadge stars as Harry Willis, who promises fiancé Dove that he will amass a fortune within six months. To that end he accepts a challenge from a mysterious Chinese stranger: if he follows a series of rather bizarre challenges for the course of a day, he will be awarded $10,000. "He agrees and action follows," wrote *Exhibitors Trade Review*. "He attempts to rescue a woman in distress and falls into the hands of an insane doctor who tries to operate on him. Later he is mixed up in a series of exciting incidents in a Chinese temple. He has many fights, but escapes."[53] The challenges, of course, were

LEFT: *William Fox short subject lineup for 1924*, Moving Picture World, *October 11, 1924.*
RIGHT: *Jimmy Parrott and friend in the Fox Imperial Comedy,* Sweet Papa. Exhibitors Trade Review, *August 16, 1924.*

there primarily to show off Talmadge's considerable athletic abilities, but that's pretty much what his fan base wanted to see. The film concludes with the revelation that the challenges were merely a means to an end, to see whether Willis has the stuff to become a movie star. He does, and is awarded the bucks along with a movie contract and Billie Dove's admiration.

The movie received mostly lukewarm reviews. "Richard Talmadge doing athletic stunts around a very poor story,"[54] reported *Photoplay*, unimpressed with the adaptation by relative newcomers Garrett Fort and Al Cohn and, one would assume, the intertitles by Ralph Spence. *Harrison's* stated that "This comedy-melodrama does not measure up to the standard set by previous Richard Talmadge productions,"[55] while *Moving Picture World* decreed it "a film that starts out with promise but soon develops into such a bewildering maze of nonsense that there is one hope left in the mind of the observer — that the end may soon arrive."[56] *Exhibitors Trade Review* put a more positive spin on their review: "For those who like thrills and stunts at the sacrifice of plot, 'On Time' will offer great appeal. From start to finish it is a series of stunts and knock-down-drag-out fights in which Richard Talmadge occupies the center of the limelight."[57]

It was paying work, but not the sort likely to reignite Lehrman's career. Fortunately, his abilities and reputation as a creative talent in the realm of short comedy were undiminished. The powers at Fox had come to realize what a loss his dismissal had created for the company. With his fall from fortune and willingness to resume working, it would be a good time to bring him back under terms more favorable to the studio — and very quietly. With no fanfare whatsoever in the trades, Lehrman was hired in early 1924 to supervise twenty-six comedy productions[58] of the fifty-two planned for the new season — one per week. Twenty Sunshine Comedies and seventeen of the new Imperial Comedies were scheduled — Lehrman would contribute to these two brands — along with seven Monkey Comedies and a series of eight films based on Richard Harding Davis' Van Bibber stories. Ralph Spence was now editor-in-chief of the Fox comedy units, which included the directors Benjamin Stoloff, Lewis Seiler, Norman Taurog, George "Slim" Summerville, Roy Del Ruth, and Albert Ray, with George Marshall handling the Van Bibber series.[59] George Meehan was back as Lehrman's cameraman for most of his films.[60]

While the titles of most of Lehrman's films for Fox during this period are unknown, we do know that he directed *Children Wanted* (Sunshine; June 22, 1924), *Sweet Papa* (Imperial; August 17, 1924) starring Sid Smith and James "Paul" Parrott, *The Diving Fool*[61] (Sunshine; September 21, 1924), and *Heavy Swells* (Imperial; December 13, 1925). Neely Edwards and Charlotte Merriam starred in one of his comedies as well, but whether it was one of the other three just named or another film altogether is unknown.[62]

George Gray, a jack-of-all-trades in the industry who got his start at Keystone and at various times served as stuntman, actor, writer, director, co-director, and makeup man, claimed to have served as co-director on some of Lehrman's Fox films. He didn't think much of his director:

> Oh, Henry Lehrman was a stinker! I worked as an assistant director to him. One time he was chewing out everybody, but as he started on me I stood up and said, "Look, Mr. Lehrman, you can get by with that with everyone else, but I am *not* going to take it...." Lehrman quieted down, and said to me, "Now, George, don't say that...." And honest to God, he *almost* apologized.[63]

Lehrman's former director Jack White, now supervising director of E.W. Hammons' Educational-Mermaid Comedies, noted the shift taking place in short comedies at this time due to changes in the public's tastes and other outside influences. "The bathing girls who decked every comedy a few years ago have put on their clothes. They have been found out," he said. "There is nothing funny about a bathing girl. She may be pretty to look at, but she isn't funny. The marital infidelity and bedroom comedies have been discouraged by the censor boards and by public taste to the point where making them is a financial risk. That means they will never come back." What did that leave? "[T]he fast-action comedy, with its limitless possibilities for ingenuity on the part of the actor and director, is here to stay."[64] While Lehrman now toiled in comparative obscurity, his former pupil was doing quite well. The Mermaid comedies were supplement by the Tuxedo and Cameo brands, with star comedian Lloyd Hamilton soon moving from the Mermaids to his own unit.

White had learned and fully absorbed the art of comedy from Lehrman, but had a far better business sense, avoiding the various pitfalls that had felled his mentor; he kept a low profile and spent the company's money wisely. A lot of the Educational output was modestly budgeted and had an assembly line look to it, but White maintained a steady output, adhered to schedules, and kept the exhibitors satisfied.

Money, alas, always seemed to burn a hole in Lehrman's pocket, so with his new found employment and guarantee of same for at least the upcoming year, he once again splurged. Making a beeline for the Stanley W. Smith auto dealership, he purchased a Peerless six sedan.[65] It wasn't too long before the heavy-footed director was in Dutch with the law, pulled over for doing thirty-five miles per hour, evidently well above the posted limit. Upon receiving the ticket, Lehrman drove off, but with the officer's gloves sitting on his running board. The officer followed in an attempt to retrieve his gloves, but when he noted that Lehrman was now doing forty, pulled him over a second time and presented him with a second ticket. Lehrman failed to report on the second charge and was later hauled in on a bench warrant, receiving a two-day jail sentence for his forgetfulness.[66] Some habits were hard to avoid.

And with an influx of cash came the greed of others. Lehrman became the supposed target of two rather inept robbers, reported as E.O. Parks and B.M. Putnam. The two loitered outside of Lehrman's home and confronted an approaching stranger they assumed to be him. It wasn't, rather a mere passerby named Larry Richardson. Upon realizing their mistake, one of them was reported as saying "Beg pardon, I thought you were Lehrman." The duo fled, but not before Richardson noted their license plate number. Based on that information, the two were arrested two days later on a charge of suspicion of robbery.[67] The two claimed that they were so drunk that night that they had no recollection of the event. The moral: Crime does not pay.

CHAPTER 10

The Volatile Jocelyn Leigh

If Lehrman had anticipated a life of marital bliss as a result of his union with Jocelyn Leigh, the reality was anything but. Lehrman, who gave his middle name as Mauritz and a Jack Benny-like age of thirty-seven on his April 26, 1922 marriage certificate, didn't know what he was getting into when he said "I do," but perhaps he should have had an inkling sometime over the previous four months that he had known her. News of their marriage sparked a new wave of sarcastic reportage, with a posed photo of the two lovebirds appearing in newspapers nationwide, relaxing in an easy chair, Jocelyn gazing at Lehrman with rapt adoration. Lest anyone forget his back-story, this photo was usually accompanied by text such as "Bought Tiger Lily Blanket for Miss Rapp [sic]; Loses Heart Again" and "Virginia Rappe's Fiance is Married."[1] Elsewhere, solo photos of the attractive bride appeared — both head shots and one long shot of the shapely red-head decked out in a one-piece, body-hugging affair and spiked heels — with similar scandal re-invoking blurbs, always reminding the public of Lehrman's former fiancé.[2] When asked, Jocelyn would say that she had no intention of getting into the picture business, in spite of conflicting reports as to why she relocated to Los Angeles from her hometown of Chicago in the first place.

The couple moved into an apartment on Irolo Street (reported as *Irol* Street), but it wasn't long before her fiery temperament erupted. "Lehrman stated that the first quarrel they had," reported *Variety*, "was when he came home and told his wife about a girl he had met on the street who had smiled at him."[3] The first public airing of any sort of discord in the Lehrman household appeared in late December 1922 when it was reported that the police had been called in to intervene in a "dispute" that had risen over the purchase of a new automobile, although the actual purchaser was not named.[4] This wasn't the first big blowup, however; they didn't last long at the Irolo Street address, another disturbance caused by Jocelyn forcing them to vacate in August 1922 and relocate to an apartment house on Western Avenue between Sunset and Hollywood Boulevards. Numerous violent disturbances brought an end to their stay here after a mere three months, their landlord forcing them out in October. Lehrman's lack of any meaningful employment during this time and the constant hounding by creditors didn't help matters, and Jocelyn was probably miffed that her marriage to a "successful" Hollywood director wasn't panning out as she had hoped.

From then on it was a nomadic existence, each new dwelling giving way to the next when one landlord after another gave them their walking papers. A home on North Bronson Avenue followed and actually lasted for six months until March 1923 when they moved once again, this time to Detroit Street. Six weeks later, with Lehrman suffering "great mental anguish, humiliation and embarrassment" — or at least according to his *Complaint on Divorce* — they were forced to seek yet another residence. Several more dwellings followed between March and November 1923 before they "settled" into a

Jocelyn Leigh, circa 1926. She had changed the spelling of her last name to "Lee" by this time.

residence at 1800 North Normandie Street. While Lehrman had managed to score a few paying jobs with the *Double Dealing* feature and the *Fighting Blood* series, it wasn't enough, and it is anyone's guess how the necessity to declare bankruptcy in September affected Jocelyn. The tipping point came in November when, in the presence of Lehrman's friends, Jocelyn called Lehrman "vile and vulgar names, and created such disturbances of such a violent nature" that he told her to pack up and get out. The couple entered into a separation agreement and Jocelyn moved in with her mother. But Jocelyn had a rather warped view of just what a separation involved, returning to his home during his absence and, upon his return, greeting him with a barrage of thrown items that included knives and drinking glasses, and threatened to kill him — again according to his *Complaint*.[5] Lehrman relocated to 6600 Sunset Boulevard, but Jocelyn followed late one night in July, smashing a pane of glass to gain entrance, requiring Lehrman to drive her to the hospital to have her injuries dealt with. *Variety* euphemistically reported that she had "caused a stir," while Lehrman was a bit more succinct, stating that she had "her hysterical moments." But, he added, they were "good friends."[6]

Luther Reed, participant in round two.

It got worse. Jocelyn ratcheted it up a notch by threatening to "create a scandal of such character as would force the plaintiff out of the moving picture business and thereby to permanently incapacitate him in the industry...."[7] To that end she repeatedly broke into his house while he was in the midst of business conferences, and made such a scene that his associates in one instance and a director in another fled the place while the police were called in. In another incident Jocelyn threatened to kill Lehrman, and in the presence of his landlady. All this while Lehrman was attempting to resurrect his standing in the industry with his return to the Fox comedy unit. It must have weighed heavily on him.

A temporary restraining order was issued in late October 1924 prohibiting Jocelyn from entering into any and all verbal communication and physical interaction with Lehrman. She filed a demurrer a few weeks later, but it was overruled on November 17, 1924.[8] Lehrman filed for divorce in mid-December, and was granted same the day after Christmas 1924; the continuance of the restraining order was part of the judgment. Jocelyn didn't walk away empty handed, however, Lehrman earlier having agreed to pay her $8,500 in monthly installments of $200 — a bribe of sorts to get her to agree to move out — and threw in a Chrysler valued at $2,000 as part of the deal.[9] It was a clean break, at least on paper. When asked about the divorce, a weary Lehrman responded "We have been ordered out of so many places, that I'm tired. I didn't want to fight forever."[10]

One might be somewhat skeptical of Lehrman's allegations, believing them to be exaggerations embellished to make for a stronger complaint, but aside from the initial demurrer filed by Jocelyn she never issued any sort of vigorous rebuttal. A further bolstering of the validity of Lehrman's allegations surfaced six years later. Jocelyn, by now foregoing the stage surname Leigh for Lee, had remarried, this time to RKO director Luther Reed. That union didn't last as long as Lehrman's had, the harried director filing for divorce only a few months after tying the knot. "Director Reed couldn't believe the stories Lehrman and his lawyers had related in court," reported the *San Antonio Light*, "and with no more qualms concerning his own domestic happiness he led the pretty little redhead to the alter…. His plea is almost identical with the one that won another director, Henry Lehrman, his freedom from Jocelyn in 1926 [sic] — he just can't be healthy and happy…in the midst of the wild tantrums that, he asserts, Jocelyn stages when something annoys her."[11] One could argue that Reed and his lawyers were embracing a previously used strategy that had met with success, but only after a few months of marriage? Doubtful.

Lehrman's divorce from Jocelyn wasn't the last of his unfortunate interactions with the woman, the final reported incident occurring a year later in January 1926 and saddling the hapless director with charges of intoxication, possession of liquor, and transportation of same. The account of the incident is worth repeating here due to its rather bizarre nature:

> Lehrman was arrested by Police Officer Donlan at Hollywood Boulevard and Cahuenga Avenue early Tuesday morning. Donlan said he saw a man chasing a screaming woman down the street, and arrested him just as he caught her. He searched the man's car, he said, and found six bottles of beer. Lehrman was a motion picture director. He gave his occupation on the police blotter as "retired." His divorced wife, who is said to have been in the Follies under the name of Jocelyn Lee, had been chasing him down the street in her car, he is said to have told Donlan.
>
> "I was told by Lehrman that he had been driving on the boulevard with his former wife following him," Donlan said. "He told me this had irritated him, and he had swerved his car into the curb to head her off. Her car then scraped his machine.
>
> The woman, the officer said, accompanied Lehrman to the police station, where she gave the name of Helen Bryant, but later admitted she was Mrs. Alice Lehrman.

It is probably safe to assume that Lehrman's patience had grown thin with his erratic former wife's antics. He was released on $400 bail, but when sought for his side of the story at his Fernwood Avenue address, he had already moved out.[12] Lehrman would never remarry.

Jocelyn Lee, for what it is worth, became a moderately successful actress in a two-dozen film career that began shortly after her divorce from Lehrman until it sputtered out in the early 1930s. These were supporting roles with the sole exception her lead in the Leo McCarey-directed Hal Roach comedy short *Madame Q* (1929) opposite Edgar Kennedy. She married for a final time in 1935, this time to screenwriter James Seymour. By all accounts this was a happy, peaceful marriage, which would suggest that she had either matured out of her temper-tantrum phase, or her choice of a third partner was a far more compatible one.

Or, perhaps, that both Lehrman and Reed were somewhat less than blameless.

CHAPTER 11

The Brothers Warner Come Calling

Lehrman's contract with Fox came to an end in mid-1925, but the reason for this is unknown. He may have fulfilled their needs in building up a new brand and was no longer of use to them, he may have wanted too much money for a second year, or the distraction of a tumultuous marriage and Jocelyn's shenanigans may have had an impact on his performance. Or, just as likely, a better offer may have come his way. Regardless of the reason, a better offer did come his way, this time from Warner Brothers. It would be for a feature-length drama — a decided change of pace for Lehrman — to star Kenneth Harlan and Patsy Ruth Miller. It was a one-shot deal, but with the promise of a longer-term contract if Lehrman delivered.

Warner Brothers had announced the signing of Harlan along with Bess Meredith and Huntley Gordon as new members of the permanent Warner stock company earlier in 1925.[1] Harlan's first for Warners was *Bobbed Hair* (1925), a comedy co-starring Marie Prevost and Louise Fazenda. It was quickly decided to pair Harlan with actress Patsy Ruth Miller in a series of films to be part of the forty productions scheduled for the 1925-26 season, a plan that was hoped would repeat the past success of the other studio pairings of Marie Prevost with Monte Blue, and Irene Rich with Huntly Gordon. *The Fighting Edge* was to be the first of these, and it was announced that Lehrman would direct. The film went into pre-production in August.[2] Charles "Heinie" Conklin was added to the cast to add some comedic moments to the drama, adapted for the screen by Edward T. Lowe, Jr. and Jack Wagner from the 1922 novel by William McLeod Raine. Camerawork was handled by Allan Thompson and Robert Laprell. Actual filming began in September, but was delayed for three weeks when Miller was confined to her home due to a bout with influenza.[3] Filming resumed in October and wrapped in early November, with editing spilling into December.[4] A January 16, 1926 release date was announced, but ultimately moved up a week to January 8.

Harlan and Lehrman had a past with each other, and not always a pleasant one. Aside from assumedly more pleasant encounters at dancing competitions in the teens, Harlan had for reasons unknown acquired a dislike for the director. This dislike came to a head sometime in 1921 when Harlan spotted Lehrman speaking with his wife of the time, former Ziegfeld Follies star and aspiring film actress Florence "Flo" Hart. "I saw my wife in the company of Henry Lehrman and another man," stated Harlan in an answer affidavit to his wife's complaint for divorce, "both of whom were engaged in the moving picture business, and neither of whom were of the character or bore reputations of the kind of men with whom I desired my wife to associate. Upon that occasion at Long Beach I got into an altercation with Henry Lehrman and it was because of that incident that my wife secured a summons against me...."[5] The altercation resulted in the two of them being hauled off by the police, and Harlan fined $10 for his aggressive actions. Flo claimed that he beat her as well, but Harlan insisted that the fine was solely for "thrashing Henry

LEFT: *Patsy Ruth Miller, circa 1922.* RIGHT: *Lehrman's nemesis, Kenneth Harlan, with his gloves off.*

Lehrman."[6] Harlan, it should be noted, was married a total of nine times, Hart only the second in the long line of spouses. One would assume that the actor-director relationship was all business on this particular production, but perhaps the two had patched up previous disagreements and/or misunderstandings by this time.

Spanish-Irish U.S. Government agent Juan O'Rourke (Harlan), living in Mexico, is assigned to rescue another agent being held prisoner by a gang of smugglers. The other agent's daughter Phoebe (Miller) gains access to the smugglers' house by feigning unconsciousness after a staged auto accident. O'Rourke connects with Phoebe and the two work together to locate and free her father, but are pursued by the vengeful smugglers after doing so. U.S. troops arrive in the nick of time to save the day, and O'Rourke marries Phoebe.

Reviewers seemed pleased with the results. "Henry Lehrman has been eminently successful in packing action into this story of romance and smuggling along the Mexican border," wrote Frank Elliott in *Motion Picture News*.[7] "Smuggling aliens across the Mexican border is an exciting subject to begin with," added the *National Board of Review Magazine*, "and when the story starts off with races, auto spills and disguises and continues such thrills to the end, with plenty of good comedy added, interest never lags."[8] Pat Hartigan, Lew Harvey, and W.A. Carroll rounded out the cast, with Heinie Conklin suppling the film's moments of broad humor as the smugglers' cook. Hungarian-born ex-boxer Jack Herrick had a small role as one of the gang's lecherous toughs, moving in on the imprisoned but physically resistent Miller with the memorable lines "Ah-ha, my little gal, you're a regular li'l wildcat, heh? Come on, sweetie, lambast your lovin' papa! Papa likes 'em rough!"[9] Clearly one of the bad guys.

Patsy Ruth Miller feigns unconsciousness after her staged auto accident, from The Fighting Edge. COURTESY OF ROBERT JAMES KISS.

With the completion of *The Fighting Edge* and his one film contract with Warners, there was some brief talk about Lehrman joining Famous Players as a director in a unit headed by B.P. Schulberg,[10] but that never amounted to anything. Lehrman was sidelined for a while when he suffered a serious injury to his knee — or a fractured leg, depending on the report — while reportedly working on some unnamed production in an unstated capacity in late February or early March 1926.[11] Warner Brothers, evidently pleased with the work he had done on the Harlan production, waited for Lehrman to recuperate before offering him another contract, one that had the potential to carry him through the rest of the decade. The contract stipulated $7,500 for a single picture paid in weekly installments of $500, with Lehrman to not only direct a yet-to-be-specified film, but to assist with writing the story and scenario, and cutting, titling, and editing should the producer request assistance. It was the stated options that held the most promise: Warners could extend Lehrman's employment for another year and an additional three films, with compensation for the first of these $8,000, payable at $500 per week; the second for $9,000, at $500 per week; and the third for $10,000, at $500 per week. Additionally there were the options of a second one-year extension at $1,000 per week, a third one-year extension at $1,250 per week, and a fourth one-year extension at $1,500 per week. All Lehrman had to do was deliver the goods, and in a manner satisfactory to all involved. Lehrman signed the contract on May 12, 1926.[12] It appeared that his foundering career had been resurrected.

Lehrman's first assignment under the new contract was for popular comedian Syd Chaplin's next film, to follow his recently released *Oh What a Nurse*. Chaplin, Lehrman, and Rex Taylor began collaborations on a story for the upcoming film.[13] Within a month, however, Lehrman was reassigned, this time to the upcoming feature *Private Izzy Murphy*, to be headlined by Broadway star George Jessel. The film had been announced as part of Warners' lineup for the 1926-27 season back in April, initially with Herman Raymaker slated to direct.[14] Chuck Reisner was announced to replace Raymaker as director in mid-May,[15] the Warners finally settling on Lehrman by June.[16]

Jessel, who was a big hit in the starring role of *The Jazz Singer* on Broadway at the time, had been friends with Sam Warner since the teens, the two of them having met back in 1919 when Jessel played a small supporting role in director Carl Harbaugh's *The Other Man's Wife*, filmed at a Long Island studio. Sam visited Jessel in his dressing room and tried to interest him in *Private Izzy Murphy*. Jessel countered with making *The Jazz Singer* into a film instead. "If this Vitaphone thing goes through by next year," Jessel later paraphrased Warner as having responded, "we could make *The Jazz Singer* with sound and then you could sing the songs."[17] Vanity prevailed and Jessel was sold on the idea; filming was scheduled for a break in his Broadway performances. Filming commenced on July 1 on a script written by Edward Clark, Raymond L. Schrock, and Philip Lonergan especially for Jessel. Patsy Ruth Miller was reunited with Lehrman in a costarring role. Regarding Jessel's claims, it turns out that Warner Brothers had secured the rights to film *The Jazz Singer* for Jessel sometime in July.[18]

The *Private Izzy Murphy* filming didn't go well.

On Sunday afternoon, July 11, after only a week and a half of shooting, Lehrman was called into Ray Schrock's office for a three-way discussion that included Jack Warner. Evidently Schrock and Warner had "a great many discussions for the good of the picture" over the first few days of filming, and felt that things were not progressing to their satisfaction. Warner wrote at the time that "in the presence of Mr. Schrock and myself Mr. Lehrman made the direct statement that if we were not satisfied with his method of directing the picture, 'PRIVATE IZZY MURPHY', that he would release us and call the contract off." Warner went on to say:

> I told him (Mr. Lehrman) we would let him continue until the next day (July 12th) when I would see the film he had photographed on the Saturday night previous (July 10th) which were scenes in the New York subway, and if we were not satisfied we would then relieve him of the contract.
>
> Upon seeing the film, and not being satisfied with Mr. Lehrman's method of directing the picture, Mr. Schrock and myself had a meeting and we both came to the conclusion that we would take up Mr. Lehrman's proposition and relieve him of his duties of the fulfillment of the contract with us.

Thereupon, Mr. Schrock personally met Mr. Lehrman Tuesday morning, July 13th, at approximately eight thirty A.M. and informed him that we would relieve him of his obligations under the contract, as per our conversation Sunday previous.[19]

Had Lehrman called their bluff, hoping that they would back down? We don't have any clue as to the cause for the dissatisfaction with Lehrman's output, so it may have been the result of a clash of personalities rather than the actual work that Lehrman was doing. Or was Lehrman's performance actually substandard for the first time? We will never know the specific cause, but whatever the reason Lehrman had managed to flub the first real opportunity to resurrect his career since the Arbuckle scandal.

This was, of course, all behind closed doors. The press reported that recent hire Lloyd Bacon, previously scheduled to direct *What Happened to Father?*, was to assume direction of *Private Izzy Murphy*. "Ordered by his physician to take a long rest, Henry 'Pathe' Lehrman has yielded the megaphone to Lloyd Bacon," wrote *Variety*. "Lehrman started shooting recently, but his condition was such that he was forced to discontinue."[20] Was this simply a ruse to mask the real reason for Lehrman's dismissal, or perhaps a genuine illness had impacted his work on the film and truly was the cause for the split. Then again, perhaps Lehrman suffered some sort of breakdown as a result of the dismissal, providing a convenient excuse. Jessel had this to say about this initial experience working with Lehrman:

> Private Izzy Murphy was in the hands of a former Keystone comedy director. "Pathe," they called him. He had never seen me on the stage, had no idea what I did and for four or five weeks kept me sitting on the sidelines while he played mechanical-device scenes with several comedians. We were making one scene at five o'clock in the morning, which he made me do over and over again, insisting that I was not sparkling enough. Whereupon I told him that I did not know that I had been engaged to be a bottle of Canada Dry. Pathe and I were friends off the set, but had nothing in common in our work. He became ill and an assistant director, Lloyd Bacon…was given his job…. He immediately took out all the slapstick stuff and played the picture for its melodramatic value…. To undo what had been done in the picture necessitated working forty-eight hours at a stretch.[21]

Based on his comments, it would appear that Jessel had no idea what Lehrman did, either.

Lehrman, once again out of work and strapped for cash, hired a lawyer to press Warner Brothers for the balance of the money he felt he was due. Lehrman had been paid $4,500 up to the date of his termination, and now wanted the balance of the $7,500 stipulated by the contract. In a letter to attorney William A. Bowen at the Warner Brothers' law firm of Flint and MacKay, "Mr. Warner stated that neither he nor Mr. Schrock notified Lehrman in writing that they relieved him of the contract," wrote Warners' comptroller P.A. Chase, "nor did Mr. Lehrman state anything in writing concerning his willingness to terminate the contract."[22] Given that the contract was still, technically, in effect, Lehrman's position was not unreasonable. Lehrman filed suit against Warner Brothers in October, alleging that the terms of his contract had been broken and that he was still owed another $3,000 in pay.[23]

While Jack Warner stalled and Lehrman's attorney Leo V. Silverstein persisted, a letter was received by Warner Brothers from the Treasury Department Internal Revenue Service attaching and seizing a total of $1,029.96 wages due to Lehrman to enforce payment of income tax owed for the year 1924.[24] A month later at the end of November, Lehrman quietly settled with Warner Brothers for $1,500.[25]

Lehrman may have had a drinking problem, or at least a tendency to do stupid things on those occasions when he consumed too much of the then-illegal but easily obtainable beverage. As a result, he landed in the headlines once again in early September, and in an even less flattering fashion than usual. A complaint was lodged by one Alla Sebastian, niece of the former mayor of Los Angeles Charles E. Sebastian, claiming that she had been "annoyed" by Lehrman and an associate of his. According to her complaint, Lehrman had approached her while she was waiting for a bus, offered her a drink from his pocket flask, and tried to induce her to join him in his car. She refused and boarded the next bus, but claimed that they had followed her in his car, and again accosted her when she arrived at her destination. Lehrman pleaded not guilty and was released on $500 bail. Three months later and for reasons unknown, Sebastian sent a letter stating that she no longer wanted to prosecute the charge, and dropped her complaint.[26]

Lehrman needed paying work, and was now willing to do just about anything industry-related in return for a paycheck. He hooked up once again with Rex Taylor, and the two of them knocked out a script that was tentatively titled *The Speed Boy*. The script landed with Richard Talmadge Productions which had just entered into a six-film contract with Universal. According to promotional materials in *Universal Weekly* intended to interest exhibitors in the upcoming series, the features were to be "of a super-quality, far in advance of his former output," and would be "a great advance in box-office value over his prior successes…production costs on the new pictures are almost double what they were on former vehicles for this star."[27] George Melford was assigned to direct, with a release date of March 13 scheduled.

It didn't happen. Abe Carlos intervened with a pair of suits filed by Carlos Productions against Talmadge and his production company, taken to court two days before the film's intended release. One asked for a judgment of $39,280 allegedly advanced by Carlos Productions, and the other involved the soon-to-be-released initial offering now titled *The Poor Millionaire*. Carlos Productions claimed ownership of the finished film, and asked for either its return or, in lieu of that, $45,000 as its value along with an additional $20,000.[28] The film remained on *Motion Picture News'* "Coming Attractions" listings for Universal up through December 9, 1927, and then disappeared from sight. Universal terminated its contract with Talmadge, and he returned to his more modestly-budgeted independent output the following year.

As for *The Poor Millionaire*, it eventually was released on April 7, 1930, distributed by Biltmore Pictures; it had the reported distinction of being the last silent film released during the sound era. "Crude production rates among the lowest seen this season, with amateurish directing and acting," railed *Film Daily*. "Here is one which looks as if it had been made over the week-end. It is pretty terrible any way you figure it…. Even for an independent this picture has little excuse, and looks as if it had been shot on a very limited bankroll. The production is handled in the style of the old serial thrillers of 15 years ago and is amateurish throughout. Only good as filler for small stands with uncritical patronage."[29] Ouch.

Lehrman received another offer to direct, this time at Columbia Pictures, but it is impossible to say just what his contributions, if any, were to the finished film. This was *For Ladies Only* (July 20, 1927; extant), a romantic comedy co-starring Jacqueline Logan and John Bowers, based on George F. Worts' story "Down with Women." The film was announced in March as one of the studio's "Big Twenty-Four" releases scheduled for the 1926-27 season, but by early April it was announced that Lehrman had "surrendered the megaphone" to Percy Pembroke for the supposed completion of the film.[30] Confusion arises in that actual film-

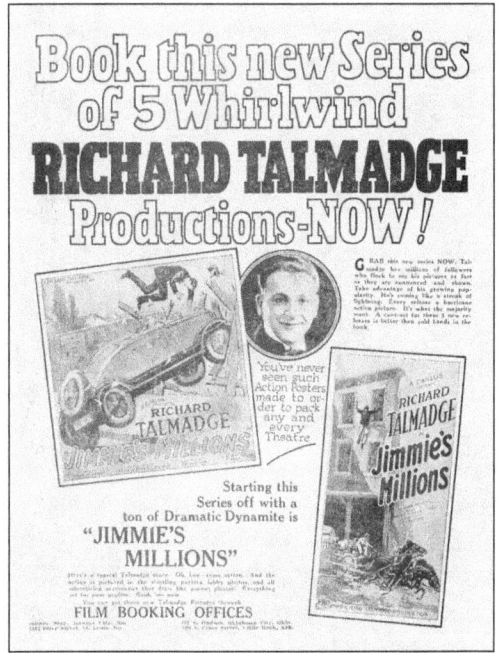 

LEFT: *Full-page ad for Richard Talmadge Productions, releasing through Film Booking Offices, circa 1925.* RIGHT: *Richard Talmadge and unidentified starlet, from* The Poor Millionaire.

ing didn't begin until sometime mid-June, a couple of months after Lehrman's departure,[31] so unless he shot some earlier footage that was scrapped — unlikely given that the studio was penny-pinching Columbia — perhaps the most he did was some pre-production work.

Regardless, the reason for his apparent hasty departure was due to an offer by Hal Roach, one that provided an opportunity to return to the industry niche in which he felt most comfortable. As head of the Roach story department, Lehrman would handle the written material for the various directors working on the lot, getting it into final shape for shooting. This placement was widely reported in numerous trade publications during the months of April and May, but as with so many other seemingly "solid" offers, nothing ever came of it.[32] Whether Lehrman actually spent some time working at the Roach studios is unknown, so either the deal fell through at the last minute or another, better offer came his way. And that offer may have been the surprise one that came from — of all studios — Warner Brothers!

Warners wanted him back, this time to direct the sequel-of-sorts to *Private Izzy Murphy* — the film he had been thrown off a year earlier — to be titled *Sailor Izzy Murphy*.

George Jessel, who had completed his second season on Broadway in *The Jazz Singer* back in May, had returned to the West Coast and Warners with the intention of starring in the upcoming production of the show. "My first look at the motion picture scenario, *The Jazz Singer*, threw me into a fit," recounted Jessel years later. "Instead of the boy's leaving the theatre and following the traditions of his father by singing in the synagogue, as in the play, the scenario had him return to the Winter Garden as a blackface comedian, with his mother wildly applauding in the box. I raised hell. Money or no money, I would not do

LEFT: *John Bowers, looking stern.* RIGHT: *Jacqueline Logan, looking relaxed.*

this."[33] Al Jolson had no such compunctions, and took the role. Good choice on Jolson's part, bad one on Jessel's.

Jessel was contracted to make a couple of films, so they immediately reassigned him to the second film they had planned for him, the bizarre comedy *Sailor Izzy Murphy*. Lehrman was hired in late June or very early July to direct, an offer that once again held promise of resurrecting his moribund career and reunited him with Jessel.[34] Shooting commenced in August and lasted into December, with Audrey Ferris co-starring as Jessel's love interest, Warner Oland as her father, and John Miljan as one of the film's several lunatics.

The story — a sequel to its predecessor in name only — has Izzy (Jessel) unsuccessfully attempting to interest his girlfriend (Ferris) Marie's perfume manufacturer father M. Jules (Oland) in the scent he has concocted. M. Jules and his daughter are to sail on a yacht, but persistent Izzy follows and manages to climb on board just as it sets sail. The three of them are horrified to find that the yacht's crew is made up solely of lunatics whose sole intent is to do away with M. Jules due to some past slight to their leader and the yacht's captain (Miljan). The film eventually builds to a dramatic climax in which Izzy is forced

ABOVE: *Warner Oland and George Jessel face off, while John Miljan looks on. From* Sailor Izzy Murphy. BELOW: *Helene Costello and John Miljan, their passion somewhat cooled, from* Husbands for Rent. COURTESY OF KAY SHACKLETON.

to stoke the boiler to a point where it is expected to explode. Needless to say it doesn't, and Izzy emerges victorious over his crazed oppressors.

The reviews were mixed for this one, which the press book called "a battle of wits and half-wits." "Deep melodrama is served in the guise of comedy in this latest vehicle for George Jessel," wrote reviewer Chester J. Smith. "Perhaps originally it was intended to be a comedy, as the press sheets so advise, but it goes completely melodramatic as the story progresses."[35] *Photoplay* felt otherwise: "It is to laugh. There is no other purpose behind

John Miljan and Helene Costello almost lock lips in Husbands for Rent. COURTESY OF ROBERT JAMES KISS.

this picture and you will laugh. There are moments when Georgie Jessel suggests that in time he will be another Chaplin in the mixing of comedy and pathos…. Audrey Ferris is the girl and very likable."[36] *Film Daily*, on the other hand, found the film essentially humorless: "Jessel fails to build comedy atmosphere in story that runs wild with melodramatic trimmings and foolish plot…. Jessel looks like the goat in an impossible story that handicaps him and kills off all his comedy. Warner Oland a sterling player swamped in an unconvincing role. Audrey Ferris does some mechanical posing."[37] One exhibitor went so far as to say "What a piece of cheese this turned out to be — no sense to it. Patrons wanted their money back. Leave it alone."[38] Even Lehrman didn't fair too well in their assessments: "Henry Lehrman: handicapped" sniped *Film Daily*,[39] while *Photoplay* was more charitable, stating that "Henry Lehrman directed fairly well."[40] The one aspect of the film that everyone seemed to agree on was that John Miljan gave a great performance as the head lunatic.

And how did Jessel feel about being reunited with Lehrman after their first, somewhat less-than-successful collaboration? "In this picture the director (Pathe again) had me act the part of a lunatic who believed he was an admiral," wrote Jessel. "I was thrown into the water off San Pedro, in full admiral's uniform, sword and all, to be picked up, of course, in a boat near by. After doing this scene six times and nearly drowning, the day's work was ended by my throwing several bottles at the director, and meaning it."[41]

Lehrman's working relationship with the powers at Warners must have gone a lot more smoothly this time around, for with the completion of *Sailor Izzy Murphy* they offered him a second film. It was initially announced in October that Lehrman would direct the upcoming Irene Rich vehicle *Powder My Back* (erroneously reported as *Powder My Neck*) as soon as she completed *Beware of Married Men*.[42] The film was instead turned over to Roy Del Ruth to direct, and Lehrman was reassigned to the film version of the Edwin Justus Mayer play *In Name Only*. Owen Moore was loaned out by Metro-Goldwyn-Mayer to star, with Helene Costello, John Miljan, and Moore's wife Kathryn Perry co-starring. Shooting was completed by mid-November, and the film re-titled *Husbands for Rent* for its December 31, 1927 release.[43]

Moore plays a rather naïve and timid Englishman initially engaged to Kathryn Perry's character, but their upcoming nuptials look increasingly doubtful when she meets and falls for Miljan. Moore meanwhile finds himself attracted to Costello, so plans are shifted and Miljan is now set to marry Perry, and Moore now plans to marry Costello. Those plans fall apart when Miljan and Costello elope, so Moore and Perry go through with their original plans. And, once they get over their misgivings about each other, settle into a happy marriage.

The film, a slight one that *Motion Picture News* deemed "slim enough to be told in a single reel and seems interminable when stretched out to five or six,"[44] received consistently lackluster reviews, several of which took issue with the more risqué elements of the storyline. "The story offers a negligible pick-up of situations that fail to arrive at anything very close to entertainment, at least for those who prefer good clean comedy," wrote *Film Daily*. "The business of the honeymoon and the attempts of the valet to suggest the marital duties to his embarrassed employer immediately taboo the picture for juvenile trade or church going communities." Adding insult to injury, the anonymous reviewer went on to judge Lehrman's direction as "poor."[45] *Variety* damned the film (along with so many of its ilk), complaining that "Stories of this type, which are being put into production consistently, never carry. Use of material of this kind often raises conjecture regarding the mental balance of the supervisor, director or producer responsible for the choice. Without merit of any kind, timeworn, and lacking a single incident or combination of sequences productive of a laugh or even getting attention, this story could have been taken from any one of 50,000 magazine stories which have appeared in print in the past 20 years. There is no particular idea to the story and very little comedy."[46] The film survives and is held by the UCLA Film and Television Archive.

It would be the last film that Lehrman would make for Warner Brothers.

Sally Phipps strikes a sexy pose while Sammy Cohen, sporting a halo, looks on in this poster for Why Sailors Go Wrong. COURTESY OF JIM KERKHOFF.

CHAPTER 12

Back Home at Fox

Lehrman was approached by Fox yet again with the offer of a one year contract, to take over the direction of a yet-to-be-titled comedy co-starring Sammy Cohen and Ted McNamara.[1] The film had originally been shot by a fellow named Frank O'Conner at a cost of $110,000, but the results were so poor that the film was deemed unreleasable, and scrapped.[2] The film's story was of a broad, slapstick nature with lots of low humor, so Lehrman seemed like a logical choice to salvage the project. O'Conner, now canned by Fox, had started out in film as an actor back in 1915, but switched over to direction in 1921 where he helmed a number of modest films for independents such as Realart, B.P. Schulberg's Preferred Pictures, and Gotham Productions. His hiring by Fox was a step up to a more prestigious company and, arguably, fare, but his talents, such as they were, were not up to the task. With his termination from Fox, O'Conner would direct several more low-budget films for Chadwick, Chesterfield, and C.C. Burr before returning to his comfort zone of acting in 1930. He would continue on for the next thirty years in mostly uncredited bit parts, ending up in roles on various television productions until his death in 1959.

Sammy Cohen and Ted McNamara were being groomed by Fox as an up-and-coming comedy team based on their on-screen chemistry in Raoul Walsh's *What Price Glory?* (1926). The pair headlined director Ben Stoloff's *The Gay Retreat* ten months later with acceptable results; *Variety*'s reviewer opined that the film "is no world-beater and is not going to do more than favorably introduce McNamara and Cohen," and went on to characterize the production as "a frugally produced feature, utilizing sets and props of a caliber and number not much beyond the character of the average Fox-Sunshine comedy."[3] This last comment is suggestive of why Lehrman was chosen to helm their resurrected follow-up film, the first in a planned series of five-reel comedy pairings.[4]

Lehrman took over the production, scrapping the bulk of what O'Conner had shot with the exception of a mere reported 309 feet of the original footage. When Lehrman's version was completed, an additional $46,000 had been added to the budget.[5] The finished film, which was released on March 25, 1928 as *Why Sailors Go Wrong*, co-starred Nick Stuart and former Wampas Baby Star Sally Phipps as the requisite love interest.

The paper-thin story involves rival cabbies Cohen and McNamara who are engaged by Stuart to help rescue his fiancé Phipps. She has been spirited away by wealthy yacht owner Carl Miller and his skipper, Jack Pennick, who have attempted to convince her that Stuart no longer loves her. The trio manages to board the yacht, but is quickly imprisoned.

After some imposed manual labor that opens the door for some gags and visual humor, a raging storm leaves the yacht stranded. Cohen, McNamara, Phipps, and her father (E.H. Calvert) are set adrift in a lifeboat, but eventually land on the island of Pogo Pogo. A passing battleship spots the stranded yacht and rescues its passengers, a quick explanation from Stuart resulting in the arrest of Miller and Pennick. Meanwhile on Pogo Pogo, Cohen and McNamara are separated from Phipps and her father, leading to all sorts of encounters with the island's wildlife before being captured by natives. They are given a

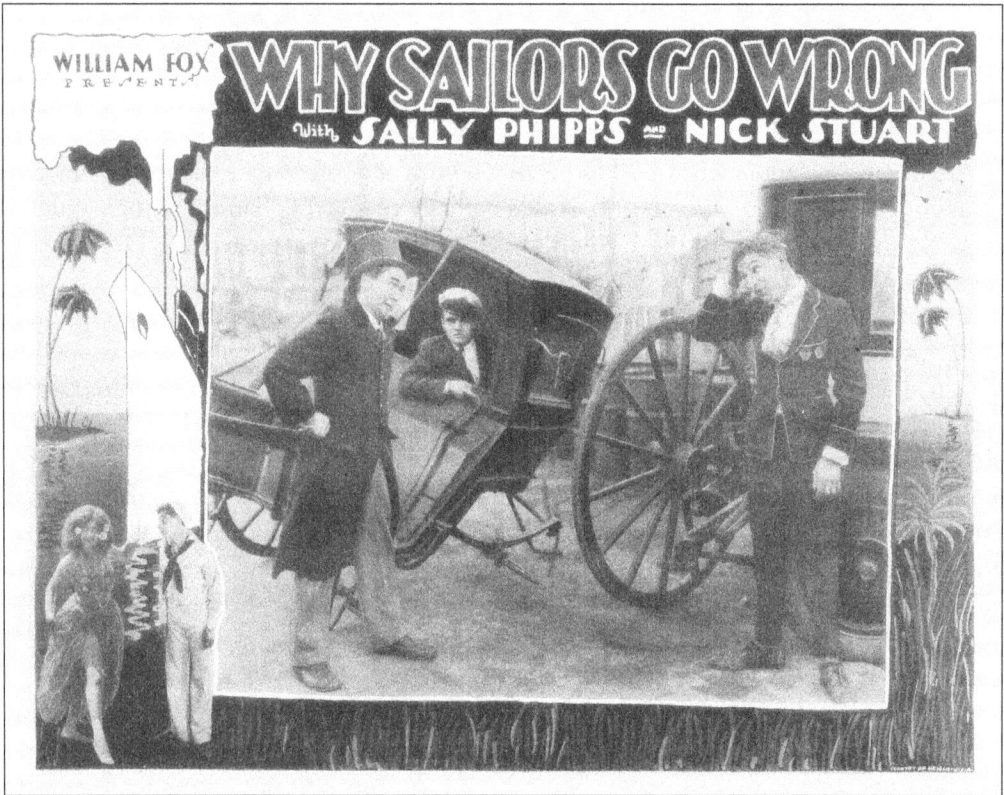

Cabbies Ted McNamara and Sammy Cohen survey the wreckage while annoyed passenger Nick Stuart looks on in this lobby card for Why Sailors Go Wrong. COURTESY OF HERITAGE AUCTION GALLERIES, HA.COM.

choice: marry the chief's two husband-hungry but unattractive daughters, or beheading; they chose the latter. They are saved at the last moment by Stuart and a bunch of sailors from the battleship.

The film, which survives, is somewhat of a disappointment and not particularly funny, but in all fairness most likely plays better with a receptive audience rather than a solo viewing. The film is technically well done, with handsome cinematography by Sidney Wagner and solid, if unimaginative, direction by Lehrman. Much of the film was shot on location, the ocean-based footage shot twenty-five miles off the coast of San Diego and the island-based sequences at Laguna Beach and in Balboa Park. There is some nice staging and camerawork, including several tracking shots as the skipper stalks Cohen and McNamara along the yacht's deck, and later, McNamara's vertigo when forced to

ABOVE: *The cabbies and their passengers assemble at the docks in* Why Sailors Go Wrong. *Left to right: Ted McNamara, Nick Stuart, Carl Miller, Sally Phipps, and Sammy Cohen.* COURTESY OF ROBERT HARNED. BELOW: Why Sailors Go Wrong: *Sammy Cohen in place for a beheading as Ted McNamara looks on in horror.* COURTESY OF ROBERT JAMES KISS.

climb the mast, conveyed through a series of dissolves. The storm-at-sea sequence is visually exciting as well. As for the film's fistfights, they are utterly convincing, with punches actually appearing to connect.

Unfortunately, the film's five-reel length is somewhat of a stretch, accomplished in part by a lot of padding with gags that run on far too long for their own good. One of these involves both Cohen and McNamara taking turns falling into the drink and being pulled to safety by the other. This goes on for an interminable length, with each subsequent dunking resulting in a loss of additional clothes until both are safely back on board but absent some key articles of clothing, Cohen's privates covered only by a seaweed "skirt." Cohen paints a shirt on McNamara, which works up to a point, but a prolonged struggle between the two for what little clothing remains ends up with them sharing a single shirt pulled down to their knees. This extended sequence eats up over eight minutes of screen time, but admittedly has some amusing moments.

Another lengthy sequence involves the pair of them attempting to escape from lions by climbing two very tall and spindly trees. These bend and sway under their weight, threatening to deposit them in the crocodile-infested pond below. This too goes on for far too long, although it is competently executed and has its amusing moments as well.

Other gags fare better, although it's questionable as to how they went over back in 1928. The film's closer with the castor oil gag — they feed it to a crocodile in hopes of recovering an ingested roll of money — is laugh-out-loud funny, but admittedly of questionable taste. Another one has Cohen, beset by seasickness, vomiting over the side of the boat while gulls collect for the "chum." He manages to stifle a second wave of nausea, and thumbs his nose at the eagerly awaiting birds. The skipper's mirth at Cohen's plight is cut short when one of the gulls poops on his face. You get the idea.

Reviewers were lukewarm to the results, commenting on the film's low humor but acknowledging that it would likely be a crowd pleaser. "All the newspaper lads and lassies on the metropolitan daily ritzed this one," wrote the *Film Daily*, "but the fact still remains that an intelligent and select Roxy clientele laughed in their well-bred way throughout. And if you can get that kind of an audience to chortle, it's a cinch that it will knock 'em off their seats in the popular houses. Just goofy nonsense, but the Hebe and Scotty taxi drivers shanghaied on a private yacht and forced to act as gobs keep the fun going at a fast clip. There's a wild storm and they land on a cannibal island. Here they pull a series of gags with the wild animals and natives that make you laugh in spite of yourself. The story's a flop, but the laughs are undeniably there."[6] *Motion Picture News* concurred, but commented on the overlong gag sequences and directed blame at Lehrman: "Sammy and Ted are a combination bound to provoke mirth and their all too ridiculous exploits here will doubtless be appreciated despite poor direction which prolongs many of the sequences to an impossible point in an effort to promote laughs."[7] Historian William K. Everson called the film "one of the most monumentally foolish comedies ever made."[8] The film was a success, however, with worldwide rentals of $347,000 and a profit of $63,000.[9]

As for the hoped-for comedy team of Cohen and McNamara, those plans evaporated with McNamara's untimely death before the film's release. The official word on his death was relayed by *Brooklyn Daily Eagle* reviewer Martin Dickstein along with a swipe at the finished product: "It was in the course of filming the yachting scenes, it will be regretfully recalled, that young Mr. McNamara contracted the illness which resulted in his recent death. It is something approaching the irony of such things that this talented comedian should have died for a cause so utterly undeserving."[10] Jimmy Starr, who was writing titles for Warners at the time and would soon work with Lehrman on his next film, recalled the event in a more cynical fashion: "Ted was pretty much of a drunk. Success had merely provided him with more money for booze. On a binge one rainy night, Ted fell in a gutter that was rushing with icy water and he just lay there. He caught pneumonia and died."[11]

LEFT: *Same lion, different tree. McNamara and Cohen in an uncomfortable spot in* Why Sailors Go Wrong. COURTESY OF ROBERT JAMES KISS. RIGHT: *"A Sugar Papa Tries to Save the Starving Broilers of Broadway."* Chicken a la King. COURTESY OF HERITAGE AUCTION GALLERIES, HA.COM.

Either way, McNamara's untimely death would prompt Fox to reteam Cohen with Pennick for a couple of films in an attempt to make up for their loss.

Lehrman's follow-up assignment at Fox reteamed him with his old buddy Ford Sterling in the film adaptation of the play *Mister Romeo* by Harry Wagstaff Gribble, Wallace M. Mannheimer, and Isaac Paul. Sterling, now finished with his contract with Paramount, was in the midst of a divorce initiated by wife Teddy Sampson, charging desertion and claiming that Sterling had an income of $5,000 a week and community property of $50,000.[12] Former stage actress Nancy Carroll was borrowed from Paramount to play the feminine lead, and comedian Arthur Stone was loaned by First National.[13] George Meeker was hired for the hard boiled hoofer role when director Lehrman spotted him on the set of the actor's previous film, *A Thief in the Dark*, entertaining his fellow cast members with some soft shoe dancing and impersonations of a burlesque performer. Frances Lee and Carol Holloway rounded out the cast.

The story involves married tightwad Horace Trundle (Sterling) who sets out to "save" his brother-in-law Oscar (Stone) from flashy chorus girl Maisie DeVoe (Carroll), but ends up falling head over heels for the girl and her good-looking pal Babe Lorraine (Lee). Throwing caution to the wind, he ends up blowing a lot of money on them and making a fool of himself. Oscar gets wind of this and informs Horace's wife Effie (Carol Holloway), who gets in touch with Maisie and Babe and cooks up a scheme with the two girls to "cure" hubby of his philandering. Needless to say, with success. George Meeker provided more youthful love interest for Carroll.

Filming started in March. A call was issued for two dozen beautiful girls who could dance and assume the roles of the other chorus girls, and one of Los Angeles' largest theaters was utilized for six days of interior footage. Lehrman reportedly placed a one-sheet out in front of the theater inviting passers-by to come in and watch a film being shot, obtaining extras to fill the theater's seats for free.[14] Filming wrapped in April, and after dabbling with the tentative title *Husbands Are Liars*,[15] *Chicken a la King* was finally settled on. Jimmy Starr, who had provided titles and comedy construction for twenty Warners and First National productions during 1927-28, was hired by Fox in a similar capacity for the film. The results were good enough that Fox trotted the film out along with a handful of others at its silver anniversary sales convention in New York in May, screening it for the home office executives, district and branch managers, and foreign representatives who were in attendance.[16]

Released on June 17, 1928, reviewers were pleased with the results and the film's leads. "Altogether it is a tidy little picture," wrote Laurence Reid, "one which is sophisticated without going too snappy. It is excellently mounted, superbly directed and acted with genuine color." He went on to single out female lead Nancy Carroll as "a treat to the eye."[17] *Film Daily* agreed, calling it "Corking light comedy stuff, done with class," and judging Carroll "a knockout for looks, and she can troupe."[18] Mordaunt Hall concurred, stating that "Nancy Carroll is so pretty that one almost sympathizes with [Arthur Stone] in his helplessness."[19] As for the male leads, "Mr. Sterling and Arthur Stone a real comedy team," wrote *Film Daily*.[20] "Mr. Sterling gives an able characterization here, except for an occasional desire to make extravagant gestures," wrote Hall.[21] "Mr. Sterling, himself, it may be added, gives an excellent performance and otherwise does much to relieve the plot of its more banal moments."[22] The film proved to be successful reteaming of Lehrman and Sterling, and helped in a small way to reestablish Lehrman as a competent director, if only of programmers of this ilk.

Meanwhile, the slow forward march from silent film to sound was taking place. While there had been sporadic attempts to marry audio to visual earlier in the century, it wasn't until the mid-1920s when real progress began to be made. One of the first was Lee DeForest and Theodore Case's Phonofilm system, which placed sound directly on the film itself so that absolute synchronization would be maintained. The Phonofilm system would evolve into the Movietone system, the development of Case and his assistant Earl Sponable after the former's split with DeForest. Sensing that sound films were the future, William Fox bought the patent rights to the Case-Sponable system in July 1926 and gave it its new name.[23] Fox was beaten to the punch by Warner Brothers, however, when they

ABOVE: *The cast of* Chicken a la King *surrounds director Lehrman. Left to right, background: Arthur Stone, Ford Sterling, Carol Holloway, George Meeker. Foreground: Nancy Carroll, Lehrman, Frances Lee. The rather amusing inscription: "To Jimmy Starr, from his son, Henry Lehrman."* BELOW: *Nancy Carroll and Frances Lee at their eye-catching best in* Chicken a la King, *while Ford Sterling looks on with disapproval.* COURTESY OF ROBERT JAMES KISS.

premiered their sound-on-disc Vitaphone system a few weeks later, and their part-talking *The Jazz Singer* became a nationwide sensation when it premiered on October 6, 1927. But it was Fox's superior sound-on-film approach that would win out in the end.

Construction began in June 1928 on the new $500,000 state-of-the-art Fox Film Laboratory where, among other things, research and ongoing development of the new sound system would take place. This would occupy a thirteen and a half-acre site, formerly a citrus grove and alfalfa-dominated field that had once been the home of *The Clansman*

Ford Sterling is hiding under a bed once again, this time with Frances Lee; Carol Holloway and Arthur Stone have a heart-to-heart.

author Thomas Dixon before its acquisition by Fox Films in 1916. The first two films made at this site were reported to be Lehrman's two reel comedy *The House of Terrible Scandals* twelve years earlier, and Raoul Walsh's feature *The Honor System*. A cornerstone laying ceremony took place on Friday, June 29, and both Lehrman and Walsh were invited as honorary guests to speak at the event. Icing on the cake for Lehrman was the fact that some footage of *The House of Terrible Scandals* was placed in the cornerstone for posterity, along with a segment of Walsh's feature.[24]

At the beginning of June, Fox announced ambitious plans for the upcoming 1928-29 season. Vice president Winfield Sheehan tossed out a budget with the nicely rounded number of $100,000,000 to be allocated to fifty-two features, twenty-six comedies, twenty-six variety subjects, and an unspecified number of Movietone entertainments.[25] Also scheduled were the studio's short subjects, which included one hundred four issues of

Fox News and twenty-six two-reel comedies, this latter group consisting of ten Imperial Comedies, eight Sunshine Comedies, and eight Fox Animal Comedies.[26]

Lehrman's name was bandied about in the press with several films that may or may not have come to fruition. One of these was *A Night in a Pullman*, mentioned in passing in June as one of his upcoming assignments.[27] Another title mentioned at this time was *The Fatal Wedding*, with John Stone working on the adaptation and continuity.[28] Yet another title announced in late May which received more press was something called *Vampire a la Mode*. An original by Renee Marie, it was slated to star Marjorie Beebe as soon as she finished shooting *The Farmers Daughter*. John Stone was named as the scriptwriter for this one, so it may be the same film as the aforementioned *The Fatal Wedding*.[29] Whether any of these titles actually made it to the screen under another title (and, potentially, another director) is unknown, but the fact that Stone was the screenwriter for Lehrman's next film, *Homesick*, suggests that perhaps one or more of these titles evolved into this film.

Homesick was originally scheduled to co-star the new team of Sammy Cohen and Jack Pennick, who had just finished filming Benjamin Stoloff's *Plastered in Paris* with Marjorie Beebe. Stoloff was set to direct this new film as well, with Nick Stuart and Sally Phipps once again providing the love interest.[30] There was the usual last minute shuffling of cast and crew members, when Stoloff was yanked to instead direct the Movietone short *The Bath Between* starring the popular team of Bobby Clark and Paul McCullough, with Lehrman now reassigned to direct. The fledgling Cohen-Pennick team was broken up when director F.W. Murnau requested Pennick's services for his more prestigious cinematic reworking of the play *The Mud Turtle*, tentatively titled *Our Daily Bread* but with the final title of *City Girl* when it was released in 1930. Pennick was replaced by Harry Sweet,[31] a comedian who had his start working for the Sterns in their Rainbow and Century comedies and had moved over to Fox in 1924; Henry

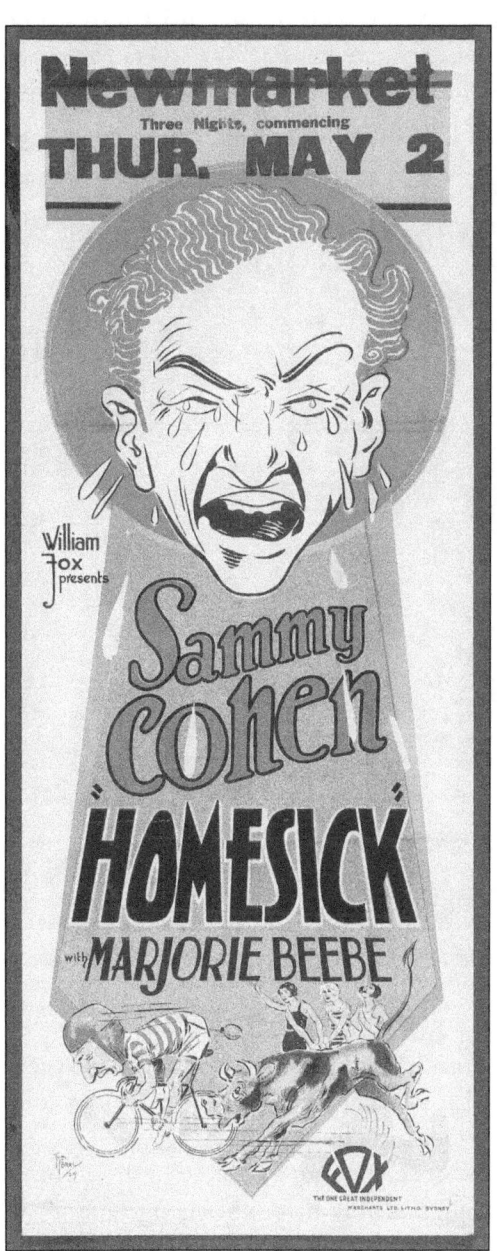

Sammy Cohen sobs up a storm in this poster for Homesick. COURTESY OF HERITAGE AUCTION GALLERIES, HA.COM.

Armetta and Pat Harmon rounded out the cast. Filming was under way in August, with some of it shot on location in the deserts of Arizona where the temperatures soared, only cooling to a stifling 104 degrees at night. While there, Cohen was introduced to a dance then known as the Huachuca Crawl and was so taken with it that he insisted that it be incorporated into the film. The dance, it was said, originated in Arizona where Negro soldiers improvised on the dances of the local Navajo and Hopi Indians, and would perform the amusing variation at the annual ball held at Fort Huachuca.[32]

Sammy Cohen flashes a winning smile while a disinterested Frank Alexander stares into the distance, in Homesick.

The finished footage was in editor Ralph Dixon's hands by September.[33] Shot as a silent, the completed film was released at year's end with a synchronized score and promoted as "A Roaring Farce of Thrills, Romance and Hilarious Situations."

Sammy Schnable (Cohen), flat broke in New York, spots an ad placed by a California girl named Babe (Beebe). She wants a husband, but only if he has enough money to bankroll a chicken ranch. The only way Sammy can get the money is if he can win a transcontinental New York-to-Los Angeles bicycle race and its prize of $25,000. The problem is the entrance fee, so Sammy borrows a dollar and joins a poker game that lasts two days before he wins enough for the entrance fee and a bicycle. Ambrose (Sweet), the poker game's loser, is convinced that Sammy won through less than honest means. He vows to get even and joins the race as well, with the same goal of winning Babe's love. Along with the other contestants (Armetta and Harmon among them), the race is on, and during its course all sorts of obstacles are encountered. Sammy takes repeated aim at Ambrose's

ABOVE: *Sammy Cohen gets the best of Harry Sweet in* Homesick. BELOW: *Harry Sweet seems to have the upper hand — and Marjorie Beebe's arm — while jealous Sammy Cohen glares, from* Homesick. COURTESY OF ROBERT JAMES KISS.

painful corn in an effort to slow him down, and Ambrose responds by engineering a number of impediments to Sammy's progress, including "a cattle stampede, desert hardships, and a forest fire." Sammy ends up winning the race, but neither he nor Ambrose win Babe's hand in marriage; she has married her butler. *Film Daily* gave an enthusiastic review: "This is a rollicking comedy with the fun coming steadily throughout the reels. It is mostly broad slapstick, but the kind that makes you laugh in spite of yourself.... From the time the race starts it is a series of good hearty laughs." Lehrman's direction was given a simple thumbs-up with the concise rating of "boxoffice."[34] *Movie Age* agreed, calling it a "Broad, slap-stick comedy of the kind that sends the folks away laughing."[35] Clearly, Lehrman was in his element with this one: published reports suggest that it was a return to the milieu he was most at home in, with exhibitors reporting 80% to 90% attendance to their showings.

A cautious Fox had sound tests run with his contracted actors and actresses to determine the risk the studio was taking with a switchover to talking films. He also had his staff directors assigned to shorts to see how each would fare with the new medium. Lehrman's next assignment was the three-reel (or two-reel, depending on the source) all-talking Movietone short based on the story *The Cornet Rehearsal*, written by Sidney Lanfield and William Halligan. Paul Girard Smith adapted it for the screen as *The Blew Danube*, but the title was quickly changed to *Sound Your "A"* to avoid a potential conflict with Pathé's upcoming Leatrice Joy feature *The Blue Danube*.

The film, a Fox Movietone Entertainment, was to star sixty-five year old George Bickel, newly signed by Fox after a ten year absence from the screen. Most recently the star of Broadway's *The Circus Princess*, Bickel had a long and varied career that included work as a clown for the Ringling Brothers Circus, in vaudeville as part of the team of Bickel and Watson, and in short comedies during the mid-teens for George Kleine appearing with Harry Watson in his "Musty Suffer" series and later in his own George Bickel Fun Subjects.[36] The years after that were spent performing in George White's Scandals 1919-21 and in various musical comedies on Broadway. Co-starring with Bickel in *Sound Your "A"* were Arthur Stone, Marjorie Beebe, Henry Armetta, Jerry Madden, Arnold Lucy, Stuart Erwin, Virginia Sale, and Donald MacKenzie. Filming began the first week in November and wrapped mid-month.

Bickel stars as German-born Conrad P. Schultz, whose ongoing practice with his cornet gets him thrown out of his apartment. As he wanders down the street tooting on his cornet, he is overheard by Charlie, the landlord of a bunch of flats. Charlie's tenants all make so much noise that he hits upon an idea: He gives Schultz a room and free rent, encouraging him to practice as much as he wants, hoping that the racket will drive the other tenants away. Schultz's music has the desired effect, but annoys the area's dogs as well, one of which runs off with and destroys Schultz's prize Stradivarius fiddle. When the tenants all depart, Charlie now demands that Schultz turn over his cornet, never to play it again, which he does. Later, however, more musical racket draws Charlie back to Schultz's room where he finds the musician playing a replacement cornet. "Here, here, here — what do you mean — didn't you promise not to play that anymore?" asks the infuriated landlord. Schultz responds: "I ain't playing dot — I'm playing dis."[37]

There was no official release date for this film, and reviews, if any, were sparse. "A little pruning would have helped," wrote *Variety*. "Drags somewhat at the three-quarter mark,

ABOVE: *George Bickel, second from right, rehearses with friends in* Sound Your "A". COURTESY OF COLE JOHNSON. BELOW: *Mary Astor looks somewhat hesitant to take gambler Earle Foxe's loan, in* New Year's Eve.

but ends logically and funny. Recording is clear. So is photography. Funny enough to go in anywhere."[38] Not a glowing review, to be sure, but it would appear that Lehrman had handled his first talking picture in a workmanlike fashion and with no apparent problems.

One major obstacle faced Lehrman and the other silent comedy directors attempting the awkward transition to sound. While he had fully mastered visual storytelling and sight gags, the new sound comedies relied primarily on verbal jokes, the cameras locked down by the primitive microphones of the day. It must have been a frustrating challenge for many, and an exciting one for others.

Lehrman was immediately assigned to his follow-up production, this one released silent to theaters not yet wired for sound, as well as in an alternate version with music score and sound effects. Based on the short story "One Hundred Dollars" by Richard Connell, the author perhaps most famous for "The Most Dangerous Game," it was retitled *New Year's Eve* in Dwight Cummins' adaptation for the screen.[39] 1926 Wampas Baby Star actress Mary Astor was signed to star opposite lead Charles Morton, with Earle Foxe, Florence Lake, and Arthur Stone in supporting roles. Originally announced in September as an intended Christmas offering, the film was delayed and shooting didn't begin until December 13. The finished film was ready for release on February 24, 1929, well in advance of the following Christmas holiday season, a decision most likely prompted to avoid non-talkie obsolescence.

Astor plays an unemployed woman who wants to raise enough money to buy Christmas toys for her sick little brother. She finds a dropped wallet with ten $100 dollar bills in it, and returns it to owner Morton who rewards her with one of the bills. She rushes out to buy toys and has them sent to her home, but is horrified to find that a pickpocket has stolen the bill. Her landlady, having paid for the toys upon delivery and now unable to recoup her losses, evicts Astor. Desperate for a loan, Astor goes to see a gambler who had made unwelcome advances to her earlier. An altercation with the pickpocket results in the gambler's death, and that is how Astor finds him. In a story not short on coincidence, Morton heads to the gambler's joint as well and finds Astor and the body. The butler spots them and, thinking them to be the murderers, calls the police. Some of the gambler's cohorts are ready to take Morton out and bump him off. In an attempt to escape the premises, the pickpocket falls to his death, and Astor is able to set things straight and save the day.

"Fox rushes holiday season with Santa Claus film," wrote *Film Daily*, "but it is excellent program picture with nice action and love story." The reviewer went on to declare Lehrman's direction "adequate."[40] *Motion Picture News* warned readers to harbor "no illusions about this being one of the current 'whoopee' pictures because of the title. It is a dank, cold drama, with tears aplenty, lots of worry over the poor heroine, with everything hotsy-totsy at the final fadeout."[41]

Much was made in the press about one of the film's sequences wherein a gangster shoots at Morton, narrowly missing him and shattering a plate glass window inches from his head. Lehrman insisted on real bullets, much to Morton's chagrin. Lehrman reassured him, explaining that he had hired a fellow named Charley Hall to do the shooting, a former U.S. sniper during the war and an expert marksman. Hall gave an exhibition of his marksmanship to convince the reluctant actor, who finally agreed to go through with it. "At that I did no acting, when I registered fear" commented Morton after the fact.[42]

While the Hollywood studios had by now reluctantly grown to accept the sound film as an inevitability, the jury was still out on whether or not it was here to stay or just a passing fad — or at least in the minds of the thousands of theater owners who remained unwired, and their patrons. A survey was conducted by Associated Publications among those unwired exhibitors to get their feelings about the looming trend to sound. Some of the results reflected a stubborn belief — perhaps wishful thinking — that silent films were here to stay. When asked "Can you meet the competition of sound pictures satisfactorily

Charles Morton, second from right, is in hot water when the mobsters discover Earle Foxe's dead body, from New Year's Eve. COURTESY OF ALAN HERSKOWITZ.

with really good silent pictures — productions that are as good as any silent pictures made before the coming of sound?" a resounding ninety-six percent responded "Yes." Only forty percent were dead set against ever wiring their theaters, however, while another thirty percent intended to and the remaining thirty percent said they might. Their patrons told a slightly different story, seemingly content with the status quo. Only six percent of them really wanted their local theater to convert to sound, and forty-four percent of them were strongly opposed to "canned music, unnatural voices, squeaks and phonograph noise." Thirty-six percent were on the fence and didn't care one way or the other, but with the proviso that there was at least one wired theater within riding distance where they could view and hear the occasional, exceptional sound release. Interestingly, a full eighty percent were against — and some vehemently so — silent versions of talking or sound films. The survey results were summarized: "It is generally agreed that talking pictures at first created a tremendous impetus in box-office receipts in those theatres, wired to take care of such pictures, but that it was true that the novelty is worn off or is rapidly becoming so, and that today each can go in his own chosen way without additional loss or profit than suffered before sound."[43] That didn't last.

Regardless of what the great unwired masses thought, Fox was committed to sound and had erected twenty-five buildings in the Fox Hills on forty acres of "cactus-strewn scrubland." Dubbed Movietone City, the new facilities were designed and erected specifically as a plant for the production of sound films.[44] While competitor studios were cautiously moving forward into sound film production, MGM, United Artists, Warners, RKO, Universal, Pathé, Columbia, and several other studios stated a commitment to releasing silent versions of all or most of their new sound productions. Fox was the lone wolf, announcing that it would drop all silent films from its upcoming 1929-30 season.[45]

Unfortunately for Lehrman, and in spite of the fact that he had successfully shepherded a sound film into the theaters, his luck and the offers from the studios had run out. *New Year's Eve* turned out to be his swan song, or at least as far as feature film direction was concerned. In March, *Motion Picture News* reported that Lehrman was "through at Fox."[46]

CHAPTER 13

Fox, Twentieth Century, and 20th Century-Fox: This Time for Good

If Lehrman was "through" at Fox, however, it's not entirely clear what that actually meant. A photo has surfaced that appears to show Lehrman sitting among the cast and crew of the musical *Married in Hollywood*, another Fox production underway in June 1929. Since that film's story takes place in Vienna not too far removed from where Lehrman was born and raised, he may have been rehired as a technical consultant or in some other short term capacity. Verifiable photos of Lehrman from this period have not been discovered, so with no other images for comparison it is possible that the individual pictured is someone other than Lehrman. Another hint that he was still or re-affiliated with Fox came in the form of a press release in October listing him as one of the attendees at a "Cock-Eyed World" frolic held in the Blossom Room of the Roosevelt, where Sol Wurtzel and his wife were the official honorees.[1]

By mid-1929, it was reported that there were 382 foreign-born individuals working in the American film industry, but only 122 of them currently under contract. Lehrman, it would seem, was among the 260 left scrambling for work.[2]

Perhaps in an attempt to remain relevant in an industry where he was becoming increasingly irrelevant, Lehrman took to the press to elucidate on the art of filmmaking. One of his new innovations was something he called "triple tempo," wherein a different tempo was applied to the different recurring themes of comedy, drama, and romance. While the overall theme of a film should remain fairly constant, each individual scene should have its own "speed" to achieve the appropriate effect. *New Year's Eve*, he said, had employed three tempos, in rotation, "to enhance the entertainment qualities of the picture."[3]

It was the subject of camera angles and their relationship to the written word, however, on which Lehrman expounded, and at length:

> A great deal of foolishness has been written about "camera angles" by people who have tried to make it a mysterious subject. In reality there is nothing secret about it. The only thing to keep in mind is to let the camera take the place of the spectator's eye. The spectator, in this sense, is a mythical character, just as an author

in writing a story in the third person tells it from the viewpoint of a mythical being who can be in a number of places at once, read the minds of the characters in the tale, and otherwise take certain permissible liberties that are not possible in real life.

In a similar manner it is permissible to mount the motion picture camera in a spot where an actual eye-witness would not ordinarily be, if by so doing the director can present a scene more clearly.

The same principle applies to the so-called "truck" or "trolley" shots, in which

The cast and crew of Married in Hollywood *(10/27/1929). Is that Lehrman all the way to the left, second row?*

the camera operates on a perambulator or a moving platform, and approaches an object or person to give a close-up without breaking the continuity of the scene. This type of shot is almost an exact parallel to the device of a fiction writer describing a general scene and then narrowing down to a detailed description of a certain person in it.

After all, the object of an author and of a director is virtually the same — to tell his story as graphically as possible. If the former is allowed the privilege of being omnipresent in order to make his story more convincing, the latter should likewise be given the right to take liberties with his camera for the same purpose.[4]

Towards the end of 1930, *Los Angeles Times* columnist Philip K. Scheuer reported on the fallout of the transition from silent to sound films, stating that "A survey today of the first class — the directors — reveals virtually no casualties. A few faded away when sound hit them, but it is more than likely that their days were numbered anyway." After citing numerous examples of former silent directors who seemed to be flourishing in the new medium, he turned to those less fortunate. "Directors you don't hear about any more — as directors — are Henry Lehrman, Irvin Willat, Gregory La Cava, Frank O'Connor, Joseph Henabery, Charles Klein, Albert Parker, Russell Birdwell, William Christy Cabanne, Raymond Cannon, Paul Fejos, Lambert Hillyer, James Hogan, E. Mason Hopper, James Horne, Emory Johnson, David Kirkland, Willard Mack, Roy Pomeroy, R. William Neill, James Tinling, Robert Vignola, and Maurice Tourneur."[5] While Scheuer may have been a tad premature in issuing a death sentence to some of the aforementioned directors, his first-named casualty proved to be prescient.

And yet the comedy short, the field in which Lehrman was most at home, was doing well with the coming of sound. Educational president E. W. Hammons was bullish — or at least early on — about the boost sound had given to his short comedies, calling it "one of the most remarkable changes in program building methods the industry ever has witnessed. This change in policy," he went on to say, "has been so drastic that even the most optimistic short feature booster has been somewhat surprised at the sudden swing that short dialog subjects have taken. Practically overnight they are becoming the backbone of many exhibitor's [sic] programs.... [It] is possible to point to many instances where the live exhibitor is devoting the major portion of his newspaper 'ad' copy to short features."[6]

Lehrman made another six-week trip to New York at the end of the 1929. On his return to Los Angeles aboard the Chief, Lehrman said he had "seen every play — at least every one worthwhile" during his visit, and claimed he was now connected with Warners in some fashion or other.[7] That "connection" was not elaborated upon, and no further evidence has surfaced to indicate any sort of renewed business relationship with Warners. Aside from the April 7, 1930 release of *The Poor Millionaire*, the Richard Talmadge feature Lehrman had co-written filmed three years earlier, Lehrman was conspicuously absent from the press for the better part of that year.

Lehrman did have one last sound film in him, a short for Universal announced late in 1930 and released in early 1931. "A new series of two-reelers, described as a 'distinct departure' in shorts production is planned by U[niversal]," reported *Variety*. "Henry P. Lehrman, oldtime director," worked out the idea, presented it to Universal and would "work on the first immediately as an experiment."[8] The result, *The Big Butter and Yegg Man*,[9] co-starred George Sidney and Charlie Murray and involves a banker (Sidney) whose testimony results in a crook's imprisonment. The crook breaks jail and gains entrance to the banker's home by posing as the new butler. The banker gets wind of this and disguises himself as his wife in an attempt to avoid detection. "A few good laughs, and fairly wide appeal," reported *Motion Picture Herald*,[10] whose reviewer seemed to like it more than *Film Daily*'s, who dismissed it as "Pretty mechanical stuff that lacks any real gags to score the laughs."[11] No more was heard of this "distinct departure," so it would appear that the proposed series never came to be. And with this final inconsequential film, Lehrman's career as a director, one which showed such great promise during the teens and into the twenties, sputtered to an end.

But not his career in the industry itself; Lehrman's mercurial relationship with Fox brought him back into the studio fold yet again, with occasional, teasing mention of directorial assignments that never materialized. He was for the most part exiled to a position behind the scenes.

Lehrman was re-signed by Fox to direct early in 1931, joining the other seventeen directors then on staff.[12] Only one project was announced with Lehrman's name attached to it, the El Brendel vehicle *Sink or Swim* slated to co-star Marjorie White, Cecelia Parker,

Thirteen of the eighteen directors at Fox in 1931, from an ad in the May 14, 1931 issue of Film Daily.

Rosalie Roy, Joyce Compton, Dixie Lee, and Peggy Ross.[13] It never came to fruition, and Lehrman lost his position with Fox after a mere seven months.[14] For reasons unknown, Lehrman quietly disappeared from any further mention in the press for close to two years, most likely unemployed for some, if not all, of that time.

This could have marked the end of Lehrman's career in Hollywood, and may have but for the intervention of a friend — or at the very least an acquaintance — that he had made sometime in the past. This individual was Darryl F. Zanuck.

Zanuck had entered the industry at a very young age, having already sold some stories to both Fox and Universal by the time he was twenty. He spent some time with Sennett as a gag writer, followed by brief stints in a similar capacity with Charles Chaplin and Harold Lloyd. This led to a job writing a series of scripts for F.B.O. for that studio's twelve-part

The Telephone Girl series of two reelers and, Zanuck later claimed, the first *Fighting Blood* twelve-part series that predated it.¹⁵ Both of these were directed by Mal St. Clair, whom Zanuck had befriended a year or so earlier at Sennett's. The two of them had moved over to Universal for that studio's *The Leather Pushers* series, but with its completion once again found themselves without jobs. A move to the Warner Brothers studio in 1923 proved fortuitous, and the writer-director team single handedly saved that concern from looming bankruptcy with their series of films starring the canine wonder Rin-Tin-Tin. Zanuck quickly became the studio's fair-haired wonder, and within two years was promoted to head of production. So prolific was he with the churning out of scripts that he was forced to adopt three pseudonyms so that his name in the credits would not be so ubiquitous. Zanuck remained at Warners through the transition to sound, and ushered in their series of wildly popular gangster and crime films of the early 1930s. Zanuck's relationship with the brothers Warner came to an abrupt end in April 1933 over a disagreement about the draconian studio-wide salary cuts that had been imposed on all but the Warners themselves.

Poster art for the unrealized film Sink or Swim, *from an ad in the May 14, 1931 issue of* Film Daily.

He wasn't without a job for very long. Within two days of Zanuck's resignation from Warners and with financial backing from Louis B. Mayer, Zanuck joined up with Joseph Schenck to form a new independent production company, Twentieth Century Films. Zanuck and Schenck were both one-third owners of the new company, along with Mayer's son-in-law William Goetz whose involvement with the new firm likely the motivating force behind Mayer's largesse. Twentieth Century was committed to delivering eighteen films over as many months to their distributor United Artists, where Schenck still served as president. They set up shop on the Sam Goldwyn lot, working out of rented space and renting whatever else they needed until they were up and running.

After a few months getting organized, Twentieth Century was finally able to announce in July its schedule for the first season's twelve releases. Under contract to Twentieth was the actor George Arliss and the actresses Loretta Young, Constance Bennett, and Constance Cummings, as well as the directors Gregory La Cava, Lowell Sherman, Walter Lang, and Sidney Lanfield. A scenario staff of nineteen was assembled, and among this group was Nunnally Johnson, a former journalist and short story writer who had relocated to Hollywood in the late 1920s. Johnson was known primarily for the humorous stories and scripts he had written since then. Another of the nineteen was Henry Lehrman,[16] but this hiring proved to be too little, too late; his recent period of inactivity resulted in the filing of a voluntary petition in bankruptcy with the Los Angeles Federal court.[17]

It isn't clear as to when Lehrman and Zanuck first met. It may have been back at Robertson-Cole, when Zanuck's claimed involvement with the first *Fighting Blood* series or the later *The Telephone Girl* series may have resulted in some overlap at the studio with Lehrman, then working on the second *Fighting Blood* series. More likely it was at Warner Brothers, where Lehrman's on-again, off-again employment back in 1926-27 would have taken place midway through Zanuck's ascendancy there. But it may just as well been outside of the studio at one of the many social events they may have jointly attended. And there is always the possibility that Zanuck had nothing to do with Lehrman's hiring, that it was instead undertaken by Schenck, who would have known Lehrman from that brief period back in 1920 when Roscoe Arbuckle had set up shop at the Henry Lehrman studios. Or, perhaps, the doing of Raymond Griffith who worked for Lehrman back at L-Ko nearly twenty years earlier and was now an associate producer at Twentieth, and the associate producer on Lehrman's first scripted film there.

Constance Bennett *graces the poster for* Moulin Rouge. COURTESY OF HERITAGE AUCTION GALLERIES, HA.COM.

Zanuck assigned Johnson to his first project, a script for the romantic musical comedy *Moulin Rouge*, and handed him his writing partner. "[Zanuck] put a fellow with me named [Henry] Lehrman," recalled Johnson years later, "a wonderful fellow who came out of Keystone and claimed to have devised Charlie Chaplin's little tramp outfit. I know he worked close to Chaplin for many, many years, and he kind of lives on in history."[18] Either Johnson's memory was cloudy regarding Lehrman's "many, many years" with Chaplin, or Lehrman himself may have exaggerated the duration of their working relationship. The script was reported to be based on a French play by Lajon de Bri, and bore the title *Girl from Moulin Rouge*. The film went before the cameras from early September through the month of October. William Goetz teamed with Raymond Griffith as the film's associate producers.

The film as directed by Sidney Lanfield was released at the end of January 1934. Lanfield had entered the industry in the mid-1920s as a gag writer for Fox, moving into direction for that studio in 1930 and remaining there until his hiring by Twentieth Century for this film. The story is a slight one of the back stage variety, with Constance Bennett starring as Franchot Tone's wife Helen. Tone, as Doug, is the author of a stage show that his wife longs to star in, but he belittles her abilities and refuses to let her star. The couple separates over this disagreement. A foreign entertainer named Raquel is hired to star (also played by

Franchot Tone has the hots for "Raquel," not realizing that she is his wife (Constance Bennett) in disguise, from Moulin Rouge. COURTESY OF COLE JOHNSON.

Bennett), but it turns out that Helen and Raquel were fellow performers in a "sister" act several years earlier, and convenient spitting images of each other. When Raquel learns of Helen's predicament, she insists that she will step aside and allow Helen to take her place, and Helen, donning a blond wig, assumes the identity of Raquel and the lead role. Naturally, she's a smash in it, and soon finds her husband falling for her alter ego. She conspires to test his loyalty or lack thereof, with all sorts of awkward and uncomfortable situations following. This being a romantic comedy, however, the film comes to a happy conclusion.

Reviewers were for the most part happy with the results, which the *Film Daily* called a "Smart and Lively Musical with Better than Usual Story."[19] Bennett was singled out for the most praise, with the *New York Times* declaring that "Miss Bennett shines as a comedienne"[20] and *Motion Picture Herald* promoting that her "singing should prove a new attraction for her regular fans, and should make it possible for exhibitors to stir up new interest in this personality."[21] Johnson and Lehrman's script was deemed "so smart and sophisticated that the wiseacres will have to be alert or they will miss the best points so easily brought to them on a silver platter by the adapters, Nunnally Johnson and Henry Lehrman."[22] While it is impossible to determine which contributions to the script were Lehrman's, or the extent of them, one could guess that the pompous Russian baritone and the cartwheeling acrobats auditioning behind the stars were his doing, reminiscent as they are of some of the ridiculous acts on stage in the early *Silk Hose and High Pressure*. Let's hope that he wasn't responsible for the broadly-acted drunk (Hobart Cavanaugh) who shows up four or five times during the action.

Contemporary reviews aside, the film is an enjoyably amusing bit of fluff. Bennett is the film's highlight, of course, in a dual role that requires her to act as a French woman for the bulk of the film and sing for a first time on screen, and in a wholly acceptable and pleasing fashion. Her discomfiture over the awkward romantic situation she finds herself in is palpable, having first wooed Doug but now the target of his dogged advances, and this leads to their first passionate tangle, off-screen and in a highly suggestive sequence. The rest of the cast shines, Tone — on loan from MGM as a last minute replacement for originally scheduled Robert Taylor[23] — annoyingly smug as her conflicted husband, Tullio Carminati as the show's producer Le Maire infatuated with "Raquel," and Helen Westley as Bennett's friend Mrs. Morris, delivering her lines in a no-nonsense, wise-cracking fashion

Poster art for Ronald Colman's first stint as Bulldog Drummond *(08/03/1929).* COURTESY OF HERITAGE AUCTION GALLERIES, HA.COM.

and bristling when Helen as Raquel refers to her as her maid Fifi ("Sounds like a lap dog!"). Sidney Lanfield's direction is competent, and Russell Markert's choreography adequate (and shamelessly evocative of Busby Berkley) in the film's culminating "Moulin Rouge Revue" stage extravaganza. Charles Rosher's cinematography is fine but workmanlike, and there are a handful of technically well-executed travelling matte shots where Bennett appears with herself in the two roles, one character passing in front of the other with little evidence of optical fringing.

Lehrman's next assignment was for a lavish musical tentatively titled *The Love School*, to be co-written with Sam Mintz from a story by Jerome Kingston; Blossom Seeley was to star.[24] This film never got beyond the planning stages. Twentieth Century, dependent upon the rental payments from United Artists, found that not only was their distributor slow to pay the money owed them but also that UA was retaining the lion's share of the receipts due to its creative interpretation of the terms of their contract. As a result, Zanuck was forced to switch production plans to some smaller budgeted films.

Lehrman was teamed once again with Nunnally Johnson, fresh off the latter's writing assignment for *The House of Rothschild*. Their project: the comedy mystery *Bulldog Drummond Strikes Back*, with Johnson receiving credit for the screenplay and dialog, and Lehrman for the adaptation. Based on the character created by H.C. McNeile under the

Ronald Colman and Loretta Young, about to get "up close and personal" in Bulldog Drummond Strikes Back. COURTESY OF HERITAGE AUCTION GALLERIES, HA.COM.

pen name "Sapper," the film was to co-star Ronald Colman and Loretta Young, with Charles Butterworth providing comedy relief as Drummond's assistant Algy. Colman had portrayed the character once before in the stylish, F. Richard Jones-directed *Bulldog Drummond* for United Artists in 1929, but with Claud Allister in the role of Algy. Actual production took place from mid-February 1934 into early April, with Roy Del Ruth directing, and Goetz and Griffith again serving as associate producers.

The plot involves a half-million pound illegal shipment of furs hidden in the hold of the cargo ship *Bombay Girl*, newly arrived in London. The problem for Prince Achmed (Warner Oland), owner of the furs, is that a cholera epidemic aboard ship has contaminated the furs, a fact that could become common knowledge if the contents of a radiogram are revealed. Achmed intends to ensure that the radiogram remains unseen, leading to a string of disappearances and murder. Drummond (Colman), newly retired, is pulled into the investigation by lovely Lola Field (Loretta Young), who is concerned about the disappearance of her uncle. Drummond enlists the aid of his newly-married friend Algy to help with the investigation and to decipher the contents of the radiogram. After a series of far-too-coincidental occurrences, Drummond finally solves the mystery and sets fire to the furs, destroying them. A defeated Achmed conveniently shoots himself, bringing the film to an end.

The film is an enjoyable romp, with Colman perfect in the lead as the devil-may-care, quick-witted amateur sleuth. Young is at her loveliest, and Butterworth a hoot as the timid newlywed repeatedly denied bedding down his bride Gwen (Una Merkel) by Drummond's persistent demands of him. Oland plays yet-another "insidious Oriental," with C. Aubrey Smith continuously at wit's end due to Drummond's presence in the affair, a running gag that garners its share of laughs. Del Ruth's direction is fine,[25] and Peverell Marley's cinematography is wonderfully atmospheric, especially during the opening, fog-bound scenes. Alfred Newman's ominous score is a bonus. Once again it is anyone's guess just what Lehrman's actual contributions were to a storyline that, while enjoyable, is cluttered with far too many disappearances, last minute rescues, and coincidental situations that stretch credulity.

Critics were almost unanimous with their praise for the film. "A thriller all the way through," wrote *Motion Picture Herald*, "it appears not only to be a super-baffler for the mystery fans, but a romantic love story with special appeal for the women and a situation — action comedy that opens the door wide to intriguing, spectacular showmanship."[26] "Comedy mystery melodrama is the entertainment and showmanship center of this picture," enthused *Motion Picture Herald*. *Film Daily* called it "a fitting vehicle for Ronald Colman's return to the screen. It is an ideal mixture of comedy and melodrama...[that] should please every type of audience."[27]

There was, of course, the occasional dissenting opinion, such as that expressed by Norbert Lusk in *Picture Play Magazine*: "Ronald Colman's return to the screen is made in an attempted sequel to his admirable 'Bulldog Drummond,' but the follow-up is inferior and, strangely, with no virtues of its own that I can see. Characters and incidents recall an old-time serial more than the suavely polite dramatics expected. Even Mr. Colman's jauntiness is jaded. It suggests nervous fatigue rather than nonchalant humor, probably because of bad photography."[28] He must have seen a poor print.

Nunnally Johnson shed some light on one of Zanuck's more famous quips: "[O]ne of Zanuck's sharp remarks to [Lehrman] is famous. After we ran a picture one night... Henry Lehrman said, 'Darryl,' and Darryl said 'Goddamnit, don't say yes until I finish.' This was Henry Lehrman, and he worked with me." Johnson immediately followed that comment with another, dismissive of Lehrman's contributions to their final collaboration. "[Zanuck] saw I wasn't doing anything with him, since he was an aging fellow and he was just on the payroll."[29]

Another assignment for Lehrman followed, this time reportedly to direct retakes for the montage sequences in the Roy Del Ruth-directed film *Folies Bergère de Paris*. This is a charming musical comedy wherein a stage performer (Maurice Chevalier) is hired to impersonate a wealthy Baron (also Chevalier) at a social function while the Baron heads off to line up a loan when he goes broke on a worthless mine. The Baroness (Merle Oberson) is in on this, but all sorts of marital and lover mix-ups ensue before Chevalier, impersonating the Baron, inadvertently manages to agree to a $25 million buyout of the mine, so all ends well for the Baron.

ABOVE: *Maurice Chevalier as popular stage entertainer Eugène Charlier of the* Folies Bergère. COURTESY OF COLE JOHNSON. BELOW: *Maurice Chevalier transforms himself into the likeness of Baron Cassini, urged on by the Baron's protective friends in* Folies Bergère.

The only montage sequence that exists in the print I viewed runs a brief five or six seconds, and is a series of close-ups shot from below of various theatre folk repeating the Baron and Baroness' names upon their arrival at the theatre. There are two musical dance numbers, one early on and the other at the film's conclusion, and both are very evocative of Busby Berkeley. The former, to the song "Rhythm of the Rain," involves umbrellas, clouds, and faux lightning bolts. The latter, to the song "Singing a Happy Song," involves straw hats (aka "boaters") in all sorts of sizes. Both are handled adequately, and assumedly staged by Dave Gould and filmed by Peverell Marley; it's doubtful that Lehrman had any part of this, but we'll probably never know for certain. This film too had Goetz and Griffith as associate producers.

Twentieth Century's impatience and growing resentment of its distribution arrangement with United Artists resulted in a merger with Fox Films. This would prove to be a good solution for the two studios. "Fox still has the best distribution system in the movie business," said Joe Schenck at the time, "and it makes the worst films. The reverse is true of us."[30] Zanuck promised at least thirty-five films a year, and gained control of the new studio, christened 20th Century-Fox when the merger was completed at the end of June 1935. Schenck resigned his position as president of UA and became chairman of the board of the new company, while Zanuck and Winfield Sheehan were made vice presidents.[31] A purge of former Fox employees followed, but some of that company's more popular stars (such as Shirley Temple, Will Rogers, Warner Oland, and Warner Baxter) were retained. Nunnally Johnson and fellow screenwriter Bess Meredyth were brought over from Twentieth, as were associate producers Griffith and Goetz.[32]

Lehrman wasn't as lucky, and once again found himself without a job. He took a writing job at Metro-Goldwyn-Mayer, and along with Arthur Kober wrote the script for the film *Calm Yourself* based on Edward Hope's book. George Seitz directed with Robert Young and Madge Evans starring, the film released to theaters at the end of June. And with that, Lehrman's uncredited assignment with Metro came to an end and he was once more unemployed.[33]

But not for long. By August he had been rehired by the new 20th Century-Fox and was at work on the screenplay for a film tentatively titled *Snatched!*, a project that had its roots back at Twentieth Century. This was among the first eight films announced for production by the new company, based on a hard-hitting story by Kubec Glasmon, of *The Public Enemy* fame[34] and loosely based on the recent, sensational Weyerhaeuser kidnapping. Glasmon went on to write the screenplay while Lehrman again handled the adaptation.

The project ran into some criticism from the Hays office due to growing criticism of the large number of crime films being produced. The production code had been recently amended by Joseph I. Breen to read "Crime stories are not to be approved when they portray the activities of American gangsters armed, in violent conflict with the law enforcement officers." *Snatched!*, which followed the violent exploits of a group of kidnappers, flew directly in the face of this amendment. Because it was already in production, however, the *New York Times* reported that "exceptions were made,"[35] although some changes were made to the script to mollify the Hays office. Irving Cummings, who was originally announced to direct,[36] was replaced by George Marshall, and the film was made without any apparent further interference aside from the Hays office's insistence on a title change. After some back-and-forth, it was released as *Show Them No Mercy*.[37]

ABOVE: *The kidnappers with the ransom money in* Show Them No Mercy. *Left to right: Edward Brophy, Cesar Romero, Warren Hymer, and Bruce Cabot.* BELOW: *Some dissention among the ranks, from* Show Them No Mercy.

Released on December 6, 1935, the result is a surprisingly brutal film. Four kidnappers exchange the young boy they have taken for $200,000 ransom. Returning to their hideout they find a young couple — Joe and Loretta Martin — who have taken shelter from a violent storm, sick infant included. The Martins are held prisoner while the kidnappers take steps to see if the money is safe to spend. It isn't, having been eyeballed by the FBI and the serial numbers made public. Tensions rise among the four kidnappers, leader Tobey (Cesar Romero) trying to keep Gimp and Buzz (Warren Hymer and Edward Brophy, respectively) mollified while heavy-drinking, loose cannon Pitch (Bruce Cabot) lobbies for killing the couple (Rochelle Hudson and Edward Norris) and their child. As usual during this era, crime doesn't pay. Buzz is killed at a roadblock, Gimp is shot down trying to board a train, and Pitch turns on Tobey and shoots him to death when his back is turned. Joe Martin attracts Pitch's attention and gets shot for his efforts, but gives Loretta enough time to grab the kidnappers' machine gun and blast Pitch into the next world, "the blood bubbling from the perforations" as *New York Times* reviewer Andre Sennwald put it.[38]

This is a terrific little film, and one that deserves wider circulation. One touch that harkens back to Lehrman's *A Twilight Baby* and suggests that it was his contribution, is the shooting of the Martin's dog Sport, left (the viewer assumes) to die but later revealed to have dragged itself to town and, once patched up, leads the FBI to the hideout. Cabot's on-screen death is especially effective and atypical of the usual off-screen shootings, here machine-gunned in close-up, the bloody bullet holes appearing one-by-one across his torso before he drops from sight, dead as a doornail. Hymer and Brophy, more often found in lighter roles, are allowed some room to provide random moments of humor, a decided break from the bleak story being told. Sennwald called it "a modern morality tale, made out of cold brutality and macabre humor," and singled out Cabot for giving "a terrifying performance as a surly killer who is transformed by liquor and nerve into an irresponsible madman."[39] While Lehrman's contributions to the script may never be known with any certainty, it is probable that the film's random moments of humor — as dark and mean-spirited as they sometimes are — were provided by him.

Show Them No Mercy would be the last film in which Lehrman's name would appear in the credits, his remaining years spent behind the scenes.

CHAPTER 14

Lehrman Knocks Out Memos

Lehrman's name disappeared from the trades during 1936. In March 1937 it was announced that he was to be pulled from the writing staff to direct a film tentatively titled *Everybody Sing*, to star Tony Martin, Leah Ray, Dixie Dunbar, Joan Davis, and Helen Westley. The film soon acquired its release title of *Sing and Be Happy*,[1] but would end up directed by James Tinling. Production took place in April, and since Lehrman was named as director well into that month it isn't clear whether he started the film and was replaced, or was replaced earlier on. There was a report in mid-May that Lehrman was recuperating in Wilshire Hospital following an operation,[2] so health reasons may have had a part in his replacement. If that was the case, however, he was not rewarded with another opportunity to direct once he recuperated.

Another conflicting report had surfaced in mid-March as well, indicating that Lehrman's comeback as a director was for an unnamed film built around the character of P.G. Wodehouse's fictional butler "Jeeves."[3] Whether a reworked *Sing and Be Happy* was the result or this was another, briefly considered follow-up to the Arthur Treacher vehicles *Thank You, Jeeves!* and *Step Lively, Jeeves!* is unknown. Nothing more was heard of this project.

Lehrman returned to the story department and was assigned to reading and evaluating treatments, scripts, and rewrites. Lehrman had by now become part of Zanuck's inner circle, having earned a place there as a result of his thoughtful evaluations and comments regarding the various stories submitted at all stages of their development, and the filmed footage that resulted from same. It didn't hurt that Zanuck found him to be an amusing fellow. Lehrman seemed assured of a job for the long run. Mel Gussow said this about their relationship in his biography of the producer:

> Zanuck had his private projection room with his private projectionist, Irving Holden…. He would watch the rushes of every movie shot by Fox, and he would screen rough, and then final, cuts of all of his pictures, and when there was time would show film from rival studios. His closest associates would attend these screenings; producers, directors, and writers involved in the film…, top personnel not involved in that picture (other producers and directors, Lew Schreiber, Henry Lehrman), his favorite film editor, Barbara McLean, Molly Mandaville, Edward Leggewie, and his trio of house critics: Sam Silver, Nick Janios, and Harry Wardell, a jury of peers that he trusted probably above all others.[4]

Screenwriter Philip Dunne was less charitable in his assessment of this "jury of peers," commenting on their attendance at story conferences, and likely holding a grudge over one or more of their assessments of one of his scripts:

> [Zanuck] used to have a bunch of stooges that came to story conferences: Fidel LaBarba, the flyweight champion, and Henry Lehrman, the old comedy director, and Jacques Surmagne, his French teacher, and even Sam, the studio's barber. Sometimes he would pick on a stooge in our discussions to incite me, and out of that we got a solution to problems in the script we were analyzing. Zanuck could be very cruel to his stooges....[5]

Whether Lehrman had to occasionally swallow his pride to put up with Zanuck's abrasiveness, insults, and chronic practical joking is questionable, but one account of this era would suggest that he did. Milton Sperling, Zanuck's personal secretary back at Warners and a screenwriter at 20th Century–Fox, remembered Lehrman from one of these early studio affiliations, and Lehrman's somewhat awkward relationship with Zanuck:

> I've mentioned that [Zanuck] used to go around the studio swinging a polo stick — or, rather, a cut-off version of one to strengthen his wrist. But not always. Shortly after I got there, I found he has swapped the polo stick for what was known as a goosing-stick. It was like a cattle prod. He used to walk around the studio with one in his hand, and he would unexpectedly goose people whenever they turned their backs on him. Only certain people, though, his stooges. There was one man who worked for him for years and years, a man known as Pathé [Lehrman], a pratfall artist in silent pictures (named after the company that first hired him). When he goosed him, Pathé would leap high in the air like a ballet dancer. And Zanuck would scream with laughter.[6]

Sperling remembered this as being at Warner Brothers, the studio where he had his first job in 1932. If that is the case, then perhaps Lehrman was employed by Warners during that "lost" two-year period, but no other evidence has been turned up so far to confirm that. Sperling was hired by 20th Century–Fox in mid-1935,[7] so it is entirely possible that he was confusing his studios and this marginally humiliating treatment took place during this later period.

Lehrman's primary function at the studio from mid-1937 to mid-1940 was to evaluate and critique the various treatments and scripts that crossed his desk. His notes — and they were voluminous — were forwarded to Darryl Zanuck for his review, and there was a healthy back-and-forth between the two. It is clear from the reading of some of these that Lehrman took this assignment seriously and gave some long, hard thought to each and every one of them — or at least for those that he felt had any worth. Zanuck's responses, terse as they were, indicated a respect for Lehrman's comments even in those many instances when he didn't agree with them.

Some of the films made from the writings reviewed by Lehrman in 1937 included *Sally, Irene and Mary*, *My Lucky Star*, and *Wife, Husband and Friend* (working title *Career in "C" Major*); in 1938 *The Story of Alexander Graham Bell* (working titles *Alexander Graham Bell* and *American Miracle*), *Tail Spin*, *The Three Musketeers* (working title *One for All*), *Belle Starr*, *Hotel for Women*, *Hollywood Cavalcade*, and *Everything Happens at Night*; in 1939 *Hudson's Bay* (working title *Hudson's Bay Company*), *Little Old New York*, *Johnny Apollo*, *Maryland*, *The Blue Bird*, *Lillian Russell*, and *Song of the Islands*; and in 1940 *Four Sons*, *The Return of Frank James*, and *How Green Was My Valley*.

Lehrman's reaction to Sam Hellman's treatment that would eventually become *My Lucky Star*, at this stage referred to simply as *Sonja Henie No. 4*, is of primary interest in

Producer Mark Hellinger "consults" with Darryl F. Zanuck. The inscription: "Looks as 'tho I'm saying 'No!'"

that it displays a trace of the moralism that got him so much grief sixteen years earlier during the Arbuckle scandal. Based on a play by Sheridan Gibney and Victor Wittgenstein, Lehrman responded that "Under no circumstances would I want to see Sonja Henie in a story of this nature. She is an idol of children and clean-minded people, and to associate her with a story of such suggestiveness is liable to do her terrific harm. On the other hand, this story could be whipped into shape for entertainment with different casting."[8] Zanuck's reaction to the acceptability of the treatment differed from Lehrman's, but he agreed (using his typical economy of words) on its unsuitability as a vehicle for Henie: "not for Henie — why make this type of story while clean but not for her audiences." It would appear that the script actually used when the film went into production the following April was not based on this treatment, or if it was it was heavily rewritten and scrubbed clean of any potential suggestiveness, if any actually existed.

Reading through Lehrman's comments during the development of a screenplay for the film *Johnny Apollo*, it is clear that a number of his suggestions were considered and implemented. Made over a five month period spanning April to August the previous year, Lehrman reviewed first the treatment by Curtis Kenyon, followed by both the first draft continuity and the revised "final" screenplay by Rowland Brown. Philip Dunne, it would appear, was brought in at the end to clean up loose ends since a large number of Lehrman's observations regarding this "final" screenplay have either been made, or entire sequences removed or rewritten.

Some of what Lehrman had to say is rather amusing in retrospect: "On page 14, sc. 29, there is an insert of a sign reading: 'Pi Phi Fraternity.' I believe there is no such thing; they only have a Pi Phi Sorority. I checked with the Research Department on that." Later on, when Apollo (Tyrone Power) asks gangster Mickey Dwyer (Lloyd Nolan) about the six slugs still imbedded in his body, "Mickey says: 'When it rains and then other times my eyes go back on me. Some day I'm going up to State Prison and have them taken out.' Although I know the reference is to the bullets, it very nearly reads as if he means to have his eyes taken out." And when Apollo arrives in prison: "[Apollo], speaking to the newly arrived prisoners, says something about the prison haircut he received, how his head was shaved to look like an ostrich egg, etc. etc. As I do not expect that our lead is going to have a shaved head, I would like to see the reference to the haircut eliminated." In all three instances Lehrman's advice was heeded.

One of Lehrman's more substantive suggestions involved the character of Robert Cain Sr., Apollo's father played in the film by Edward Arnold:

> As the story turns out to be a racketeer story, we ought to sound a note at the beginning of it by having the boy's father, who has been a Wall Street operator but is now in bad shape financially, implicated in a deal to finance illegal liquor shipments for the purpose of recuperating. Having him involved in liquor traffic, of course, is only an illustration, but the result would be that he is caught and finds himself in a jam. By sounding this kind of a note, the development of the story as it stands will have a correct foundation and will not be jarring, as it is at present; there won't be the abrupt transition from the college and financial background to the underworld.[9]

The final film opens with Cain Sr., owner of Cain and Company, thrown off the stock exchange when he is indicted for embezzlement, and eventually thrown in prison. His son, at first angry with his father's actions, soon realizes that he overreacted. The film's plot revolves around Apollo's film-long quest to have his father paroled.

The Return of Frank James' pivot point comes when James (Henry Fonda) learns that his trusted farmhand Pinky has been jailed and is to be hung for a crime he didn't commit. James needs to decide whether to continue his vengeance-filled pursuit of Bob Ford, the man who murdered Frank's brother Jesse, or return and attest to Pinky's innocence. As the film stands, James at first tells Eleanor (Gene Tierney), the young reporter who believes in Frank's innocence, that he intends to continue his pursuit. Lehrman gave a lot of thought about the treatment's handling of this and scenes to follow:

> The scene between Frank and Eleanor, upon his being informed that Pinky is going to be hanged, should be pitched a little bit higher, because as it stands now Frank is rather callous and indifferent to the fate of his devoted darky. Frank

should display a fanaticism and a deadly determination to get Ford, and it should be played so strongly that he actually does not realize at the time that he is sacrificing the life of his innocent friend.

The film reflects these comments, with Frank merely offering the tepid response "What can I do?" and dismissing the issue by saying that he will turn himself in, but only after he has dealt with Ford. Lehrman continued:

> Later, when Frank changes his mind and decides to go back to save Pinky, I wonder whether it constitutes real melodrama. The action is played against a mere statement of fact that someone is going to be hanged. The real melodrama would be if we played the action of the chase across country to rescue Pinky against the business centering around the darky as the time for his execution draws nearer.
> Further, when the girl speaks to the Major, denouncing Frank, etc., I don't believe we get the full drama out of it if we are aware of the fact that Frank is on his way back; if the audience does not realize that Frank has changed his mind, his reappearance as the girl finishes denouncing him would carry more kick and relief. Of course if we don't know that Frank is going back to save Pinky, all the incidents — swapping horses, fording the river, stopping the train, etc. — would lose some of their value if we employ them. I am mentioning this point for you to decide where the higher melodramatic value lies.

Zanuck must have felt that the "higher melodramatic value" was in Frank's mad dash back to the town of Pinky's imprisonment, since this is the way the film plays out.

> I still feel, as I did in my previous comment, that we should have a scene showing Pinky behind bars, perhaps being taken to another cell for a last meal, or something of the sort. As it stands now, we never get a glimpse of him, and I believe a short and effective scene could be written in which he pleads his innocence and insists that they are hanging a man who is not guilty, etc.[10]

Zanuck chose to ignore Lehrman's last comments, as Pinky is never again seen in the film after Frank learns of his plight. It is worth noting in these "politically correct" times that Lehrman's use of the word "darky" merely repeats the treatment's use of the same term when referencing Pinky, and its use in the final script and completed film.

Upon reading the first draft continuity for Richard Llewellyn's *How Green Was My Valley*, Lehrman delivered his heartfelt thoughts to Zanuck. The story touched on labor unrest in a Welsh mining village, and the callous disregard with which the miners were treated by management:

> I am hardly in a position to give an unbiased opinion on the merits of this story. There are some good situations, good characters, etc., but, underneath, the story deals with the fight of labor against a system — and the average man, in his heart, cannot be sympathetic to the cause of that system.

> With the Nazi socialist army on the march and fundamentally condemning and decrying the system of democratic countries, I feel the time is very inopportune for dealing with a subject of this kind. All stories that are more or less a condemnation of the capitalistic system — in this case, the English system — seem to me to be in extremely bad taste and almost constituting a condemnation of England. With the whole existence of England at stake at the present time, I don't believe it's any time for us to be throwing stones at them. And I imagine the majority of Americans might feel the same about it as I do.
>
> The subject has tremendous possibilities, but I would like to see the making of it postponed until the military and political situation of the whole world becomes more defined and clearer.[11]

Lehrman's bias is understandable. Not only was Great Britain at war, he no doubt had a personal hatred of the Germans in that he was Jewish and still had family back in Sambor; his sister Sabina would perish two years later, a prisoner at Auschwitz. His comments, it would seem, fell on deaf ears; Zanuck assigned John Ford to direct Phillip Dunne's screenplay a year later.

Some of Lehrman's suggestions for the Alice Faye starrer *Tail Spin* are of interest in that they were embraced and utilized almost in their entirety. In this instance, however, they were directed to Harry Joe Brown, the film's associate producer, rather than Zanuck. The film follows the exploits of a group of female flyers who are set to compete in the Powderpuff High Speed Race. When fellow pilot Lois' husband is killed during a test flight, it leads her to contemplate suicide:

> For a dramatic highlight I have a suggestion which I think is a pip, if properly worked, will give it an emotional wallop which will unquestionably be the highlight of the picture. The suggestion is this: When Lois takes her plane out to commit suicide, Trixie [Faye] appears a minute or so later. Finding that Lois has left, she senses the situation, hops in her plane and climbs for altitude to catch up with Lois. They level off at 10,000 feet, flying side by side, with Trixie trying to make her plea heard above the roar of the plane motors. Lois then noses over with an idling motor, followed by Trixie. With no other sound except the swish of the air, Trixie makes an impassioned and hysterical plea to Lois, asking her not to do the terrible thing she contemplates. In scene and dialog, the writing should be in keeping with the terrific situation the thing offers. Lois, to shut herself off from the heart-rending appeal Trixie is making, turns the motor on, power-dives and crashes with a hysterical shriek accompanying her to her death.
>
> If shot properly, that scene — to my way of thinking — is as terrifically dramatic scene as I have ever seen on the screen.[12]

Brown liked the suggested climax, and screenwriter Frank Weed rewrote the ending. As filmed by director Roy Del Ruth, the sequence mirrors Lehrman's words with little change. Curiously, Lehrman's comedic suggestions for this film — ones that he concluded would be "a thrill and a belly laugh" — were completely ignored.

While Lehrman looked for the potential in most every treatment that crossed his desk, pointing out weakness and offering creative improvements, there was the occasional reject. One example was the first draft continuity for *Sally, Irene and Mary* written by Leonard Praskins and Morris Musselman that Lehrman read on July 14, 1937; he didn't mince with words:

> The incidents in this script individually are stupid. Collectively they are horrible and don't even deserve the name of a yarn. I cannot find any excuse for high-priced writers turning out such an awful mess. They should be ashamed of it. It is impossible to make any constructive suggestions.[13]

The piece was turned over to Karl Tunberg and Dot Ettinger for a rewrite, which Lehrman reviewed on August 2, eliciting a far more favorable reaction: "Quite an improved version over the previous treatments of this. It is shaping up into something promising."[14]

Lehrman's comments about Curtis Kenyon's revised treatment for the film that would become *Hudson's Bay* are equally dismissive, and provide a look at an awareness of his reputation among his co-workers:

> After reading the script, I began to question my own sanity and it was some time before I recovered enough to realize that it was the script that was at fault. It all seems a hodge-podge of impossible conceptions, and when the aurora borealis hit me in the puss and I found myself in King Arthur's Court, I gave up the struggle. In other words, the whole thing is pretty terrible. As I don't wish to add the writers to the host of enemies I already have, my comment is herewith concluded.[15]

Lehrman's penchant for speeding and questionable judgement while behind the wheel landed him back in the press once again at the end of 1937 into 1938, and not in a flattering way. On Christmas night he was driving — perhaps speeding — down Ventura Boulevard, pretty twenty-four year old aspiring actress named Eva Winter at his side. Deciding to pass the slower vehicle in front of him, Lehrman pulled out to pass unaware of the other vehicle headed towards him. Lehrman slammed on the breaks, reportedly skidding a full thirty-eight feet before crashing head-on with the other vehicle. Winter's right eye was torn out and she suffered severe facial injuries. Virginia Hamp, the sixteen-year-old driver of the other car and daughter of radio entertainer and passenger Charles Hamp, received severe bruising and leg lacerations. All four were taken to Van Nuys hospital for treatment. Lehrman, complaining at first of an injured wrist and shock, and later of chest pains, was booked on a charge of reckless driving and suspicion of drunk driving, and released on a $1,000 dollar bond pending trial.[16] After several postponements while Lehrman recuperated from his chest injuries, Lehrman pleaded not guilty to the drunk-driving charges on February 28, and was ordered to stand trial on April 11.[17] At the trial that followed, Hamp testified that she saw and heard Lehrman "staggering about and using profane language" when she revived at the hospital. Four other witnesses said that Lehrman appeared to be sober earlier that evening, and a fellow named George E. Vogt explained away the presence of liquor on Lehrman's breath by testifying that he had given

Lehrman a drink while they waited for the ambulance to arrive. Eva Winter testified that he was sober as well, so the jury acquitted him of the drunk-driving charges.[18] A skeptic might conjecture that some money changed hands to ensure testimonies favorable to the defendant, but I'll take the reports at face value.

Reputation-compromising articles featuring Lehrman took a break until September 1938, when it was reported that an income tax lien was filed in Los Angeles against Lehrman in the amount of $823, an amount that paled in comparison to B.P. Schulberg's $9,741 and Stepin Fetchit's $3,615.[19] Four months later another lien in the amount of $387 for 1933 was filed against Lehrman by the federal collector of internal revenue.[20]

Lehrman received more positive, if only fleeting, mention in the press mid-year when he was ostensibly reunited with his old friend Sennett. Columnist Philip K. Scheuer summarized the background, albeit in a slightly inaccurate fashion:

> Many years ago, as the Hollywood clock turns, Henry Lehrman was a gag man at the Mack Sennett studio. Ensued a falling-out with Boss Sennett, and Lehrman betook his gagging elsewhere....
>
> Today an office door at 20th Century-Fox reads, "Henry Lehrman" — and beneath, "Mack Sennett." The pair, their differences forgotten, are engaged in re-creating the slapstick milieu for "Hollywood Cavalcade," a new technicolor feature presenting Alice Faye as a bathing beauty who rises to dramatic stardom, Don Ameche as her director-discoverer, and Alan Curtis as a Gable of the period.[21]

This $2,000,000 production, a thinly veiled and highly fictionalized romantic comedy loosely based on the exploits of Sennett, his lead actress and girlfriend Mabel Normand, and the Keystone studios, spanned the industry from its infancy in 1913 up until the coming of sound. Irving Cummings directed the bulk of the film, but Mal St. Clair was brought in to handle all of the recreated slapstick comedy sequences. Numerous performers from silent comedies — several of whom had absolutely nothing to do with either Sennett or Keystone — were hired to take part in these latter recreations, including Buster Keaton, Chester Conklin, Ben Turpin, Hank Mann, Heinie Conklin, Jack Cooper, James Finlayson, Victor Potel, and Snub Pollard. Jed Prouty stood in for the ailing Ford Sterling, and Marshall Ruth impersonated the permanently unavailable Roscoe Arbuckle. Sennett, who played himself in the film, also served as an associate producer and technical advisor, and was trotted out for numerous interviews about the good old days and his unparalleled achievements in silent comedy.[22] The *New York Times*' reviewer gave the completed film a qualified endorsement, but finished his review by pointing out that "the real talent, of course, and 'Hollywood Cavalcade's first line of defense against cynical criticism belongs to the boys of the slapstick brigade — to Keaton, Jed Prouty, Eddie Collins, Jimmy Finlayson, Hank Mann, Chester Conklin and Ben Turpin. We have no case against them."[23]

As for Sennett, the film's positive reception signaled a return to the screen for the Keystone Cops, or at least in print. It was announced that 20th Century-Fox had signed Sennett to collaborate with associate producer Harry Joe Brown on a proposed series to feature the bumbling force. The first film was tentatively titled *Left at the Alter, or*

Love in a Pullman Car, and was planned to have sequences in both black and white and Technicolor.[24] It never came to pass.

Conspicuously missing from all of Sennett's interviews and any further articles about the production was mention of Lehrman, which leads one to believe that the door with his name on it belonged to his office at the studios, and that Sennett's name was hastily added below it for the duration of the production. Instead, Lehrman remained behind and continued his script analyses, objectively commenting on the film's December 1938

Mack Sennett standing with Buster Keaton seated to his left in this scene from Hollywood Cavalcade. COURTESY OF HERITAGE AUCTION GALLERIES, HA.COM.

treatment by Hilary Lynn: "The general outline of this story looks very promising and I have no doubt that, with further development, we will succeed in making an excellent vehicle." He did have some issues with the treatment's ending, but offered some useful suggestions for an alternate approach:

> As for the actors chipping in to finish the picture, I don't believe this is a good incident. I would suggest that the leading lady, who has been making quite a bit of money, might try to offer him the necessary capital, which he refuses. She realizes he might not be able to get the money otherwise, and she hires, unbeknown to him, a man who supposedly in appreciation of his former accomplishments, is willing to advance him two hundred thousand dollars or so at a nominal banking interest rate of six or seven percent. This way, he could make a deal with a producing company for a high interest in the profits, and presumably through that he will eventually become financially independent. I would prefer that to the actors chipping in.

Zanuck reviewed the ending as well and responded with a short but withering comment directed at the treatment, "Finish hoke of the worst sort — if we are to make a film of our own industry let us at least be honest and legitimate."[25]

Lehrman's interest in younger women didn't end with the Eva Winter affair. There were several reports in the press in early 1940 listing those he was escorting around Hollywood. Olive Hatch, a bit player of little note who started with Sennett in 1928 and had a handful of mostly uncredited roles in her resume, was one of these. Twenty-seven years Lehrman's junior, the two were spotted at Kerwin's Lodge in March, but by April she had been replaced by another named Kay Sabichi.[26] Sabichi, a society girl who hung around with the movie crowd and appeared in several bit parts as Katherine Sabichi, was even younger at thirty-one years Lehrman's junior.

Unfortunately for Lehrman, and in spite of his usefulness to Zanuck, his luck was about to run out. War had broken out in Europe back in September 1939, sending economic jitters throughout the industry. This resulted in the studios' pruning of expenses, and wholesale personnel layoffs at MGM and 20th Century-Fox. These layoffs affected more than four hundred employees, the bulk of them from the white-collar and technical ranks. Lehrman was among the unlucky chosen, losing his job in mid-1940.[27]

CHAPTER 15

The End

Lehrman had hit rock bottom. Already an essentially irrelevant figure when he was canned from 20th Century-Fox, he would be out of a job for more than two years, an eternity in the film business. With no steady source of income, Lehrman moved from his Beverly Hills residence at 704 N. Elm Drive to 1759 Orchid Avenue, and shortly after that to 1560 N. Hobart Place, filing for bankruptcy at the end of 1941. His listed liabilities amounted to $17,031, with assets only $750. Liabilities included $1,800 in Federal and $600 in State taxes, along with $1,000 owed to Mack Sennett.[1]

Sennett must have regretted "sharing" that office with his old buddy a year earlier.

Lehrman had one last break, however, one that would carry him through his remaining days. In February 1943, Lehrman was hired by 20th Century-Fox once again after his extended period of inactivity. "Henry Lehrman, former production biggie, has returned to the studio to work on the script of Jitterbugs" reported *Boxoffice*.[2] His assignment was to collaborate on the script for the new Laurel and Hardy film, the third under their new contract for the studio.[3] The comedy team's contract with Hal Roach had expired back in April 1940, and hopes for landing a distributor for their newly-incorporated Laurel and Hardy Feature Productions had proved fruitless, thereby leading them a year later to accept a non-exclusive agreement offer from 20th Century-Fox for a first film, with an option to make nine more over the next five years. *Great Guns* and *A-Haunting We Will Go* (both 1941) were the comedy team's two previous films for the studio, along with *Air Raid Wardens* (1942) made on loan out to MGM, which preceded Lehrman's arrival.

One would assume that Lehrman's rehiring was Zanuck's doing since he was the one with the most clout at the studio and had a fondness for Lehrman. The film's producer was Sol Wurtzel, however, so it is possible that he now took pity on the fellow who was once a thorn in his side back at Fox Sunshine twenty-five years earlier, and was the force behind the hiring. Wurtzel was in charge of the studio's B unit, which primarily churned out series films that included Charlie Chan, Mr. Moto, and The Cisco Kid, as well as star vehicles featuring Jane Withers and The Ritz Brothers. The studio wanted to beef up its lower-budget comedy offerings as a response to the wild success of Universal's initial Abbott and Costello offering, *Buck Privates*. Former silent comedian Monty Banks had directed the first film and Alfred L. Werker the second, and the screenplays for both were by Lou Breslow, but with uninspired results. Wurtzel decided to put together a new, more suitable team to make the upcoming comedies, so he turned to in-house director Mal St. Clair to direct. St. Clair was a good choice with a solid background in comedy, a former cartoonist who joined Keystone as an actor in the mid-teens, graduating to writer and gagman soon after, and switching to direction in 1919 for Sennett, Keaton, and several other comedy outfits. Feature work followed in the mid-twenties, signing with 20th Century-Fox in the mid-thirties. Mal St. Clair was scheduled to direct *Jitterbugs*, and most likely knew Lehrman from back at F.B.O. where their directorial assignments had overlapped.

Scripting was turned over to new hire W. Scott Darling, whose career in the industry dated back to the late teens with work for Al Christie, followed by a lengthy stint in the

LEFT: *Director Mal St. Clair's self portrait, 1930.* RIGHT: *Laurel and Hardy demonstrating how it's done in this poster for* Jitterbugs. COURTESY OF HERITAGE AUCTION GALLERIES, HA.COM.

twenties at Universal where he both wrote and directed comedies. The intervening years had been consumed primarily with pounding out unimaginative, workman-like scripts for programmers. With his hiring by 20th Century-Fox and assignment to Wurtzel's Laurel and Hardy unit, Darling would return to his roots. Wurtzel may have felt that Darling could use some help with comedic ideas and gags, so it is entirely possible that Wurtzel was behind Lehrman's return. Lehrman would work with Darling on the script for *Jitterbugs*, but only Darling would receive on-screen credit when the film was released in June.

Jitterbugs was followed by three more films for which Lehrman reportedly contributed "uncredited gags:"[4] *The Dancing Masters* (1943), *The Big Noise* (1944), and *The Bullfighters* (1945). All four films were made by the same creative team, but *The Dancing Masters* was the sole film produced by Lee Marcus. Darling would in many instances substitute research for creativity, reusing a number of gags and routines from the earlier films of the comedy team. Whether or not Lehrman bore any responsibility here is unknown, but historians have placed the blame squarely on Darling's shoulders. As Stan Laurel put it, the Fox films "weren't the caliber that we made at Roach,"[5] a vast understatement in the opinion of many, but at best an oversimplification. The films were popular with the masses and always turned a profit, so 20th Century-Fox was pleased with the results.

With these four final efforts, Lehrman's known contributions to film came to an unremarkable, unheralded end. We can assume that he rode out his remaining days in quiet anonymity, making the daily trip to and from the studio in his 1941 black Packard 6 Club coupe, a considerable step down from the "monster" Fiats of his earlier career, but still a respectable vehicle. His contributions during his final year with the studio are unknown, and most likely minor.

Lehrman's health was none too good by this time. He had been under the care of his personal physician, Dr. Maurice W. Rosenberg, for the past five years for arteriosclerosis and arterial hypertension. His last two appointments with the doctor were on November 4 and 5, 1946, when Lehrman was unwell and Rosenberg made house calls. During each of these visits Rosenberg administered 300,000 units of penicillin in oil.[6] Two days later on Thursday the 7th, Rosenberg made another house call to check on his patient, and found Lehrman dead. It was determined that he had suffered a massive cerebral hemorrhage at approximately 7:30 that evening, and the sixty-five year old died shortly thereafter. Among the numerous, superficial, inaccuracy-filled obituaries that appeared in papers across the country, the *Los Angeles Times*' assertion that Lehrman had been married twice stands out as a curiosity, and one that given the available evidence was in error.[7]

Lehrman's body was removed to Pierce Bros. mortuary on Santa Monica Boulevard, where Joseph E. Wiley handled the embalming.[8] Services were scheduled for 2:00 P.M. on Sunday the 10th in the Pierce Bros.' Hollywood Chapel, and burial followed at Hollywood Cemetery on Santa Monica Boulevard. Lehrman had handwritten a simple will a year earlier and left it with his attorney Ewell D. Moore. Dated July 29, 1945, it read:

> In case of my death I hereby leave my belongings in my apartment to Del Henderson a friend of many years standing. Mr. Henderson will take care of my funeral. I wish to be interred near Miss Virginia Rappe in the Hollywood Cemetery.

His wishes were honored. Lehrman was buried on the eastern side of the cemetery's lily pond in Section 8, Lot 257, beside the graves of Virginia Rappe and his late secretary, Helen Morrison.

His will was interpreted to mean that he wanted Henderson to act as executor, but for whatever reason Henderson refused. As for those personal belongings intended for Henderson, it was later reported that "Petitioner was unable to carry out the bequest to Del Henderson as no personal belongings came into the possession of petitioner."[9]

When all was said and done, Lehrman's assets amounted to $2,582.55. This included $698.41 stashed away in a savings account and $1,275 received at auction for the sale of his Packard. Outstanding debts amounted to $2,446.91, which included $1,257.19 owed to Internal Revenue for delinquent federal income taxes dating back to 1939. Which left a balance of only $135.64.

According to his probate file, Lehrman had two surviving relatives. His older sister Kreincze — by then "Karoline" Liebermann — resided in Manhattan at 300 West 72nd Street. Lehrman had a nephew as well named Julian Lynn, who resided with Karoline in December 1946. By the time of her deposition dated October 27, 1947, Karoline had moved to 401 West End Avenue. In her deposition Karoline stated that Lehrman's and her older sister Sabina had perished at Auschwitz in 1942. Karoline went on to state that Sabina's son by husband Benisch/Benjamin Lauer, Heinrich Lauer, age forty-six, resided at 12 Telhai Street, P.O.B. Haifa, Palestine. By 1949, when Lehrman's probate was completed, Heinrich Lauer had relocated to 6 Keith Roach Avenue, Har Hacarmel, Haifa, Israel. After Lehrman's debts were settled, the two surviving relatives — sister Karoline and nephew Heinrich Lauer — received a modest $67.82 each.

So who was Julian Lynn? Were Heinrich Lauer and Julian Lynn one and the same, or was Lynn unrelated and simply a case of mistaken identity? It remains a mystery for now.

There's a rather sad side note to this. Karoline, who became a naturalized citizen of the United States in 1951,[10] stated that she had not seen her brother since 1905 back in Vienna, Austria, nor had she received any letters from him in over twenty years.

His final years must have been lonely ones.

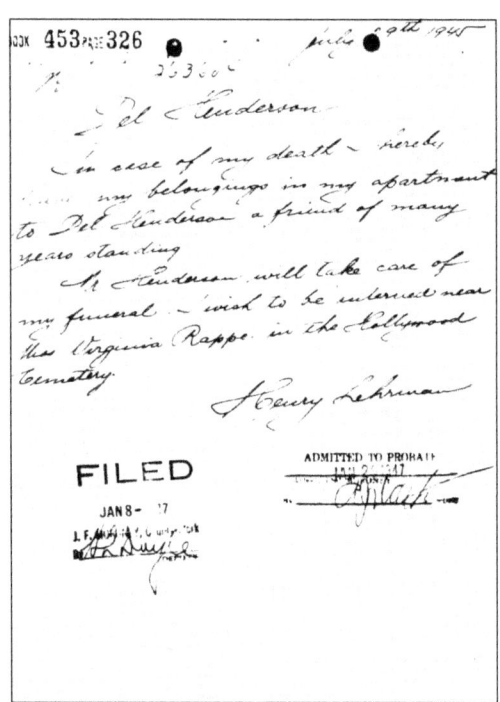

LEFT: *Dr. Maurice W. Rosenberg's claim against the estate of Henry Lehrman for services rendered.* RIGHT: *Henry Lehrman's handwritten will, dated July 29, 1945.*

CHAPTER 16

Lehrman's Legacy

Lehrman may have been marginalized in the industry for the latter part of his career, but his influence carried on for years to come. Most notable are the films of his protégé Jack White, who went on to form several successful comedy companies in the 1920s, and the films of Jack's brother Jules White, whose comedy unit at Columbia produced many hundreds of knockabout comedies from the 1930s up until the mid-1950s. Director Norman Taurog was another success story, his roots with Lehrman during the latter's peak and moving on to a rich and varied career in features that lasted well into the 1960s. Taurog never failed to credit Lehrman as the source of much of his knowledge regarding film construction. During his 1966 interview with historian Sam Gill, Taurog elaborated on Lehrman's considerable and lasting influence:

> He was a wonderful man to me. He was one of the most wonderful men I ever worked for. I could do no wrong with him. I speak of people as I find them, and he was one of the finest men as far as I was concerned. He was one of the few who educated us, helped us get our bearings, taught us how to dress, taught us everything we knew — Jack White and myself.
>
> Henry Lehrman was our teacher. Lehrman's influence over young people was tremendous. He knew the business. He was a perfectionist, and all you had to do was watch him and learn. Ask him a question, 'Why do you do it that way, Mr. Lehrman?' If he was in a good mood he would tell you. If he was in a bad mood, he would say, 'None of your goddam business!' Later on, he would come back to you and say, 'You asked me a question this morning. I was in a bad mood. I'll tell you why I did it.' If you paid attention, and you kept your mind and your eyes open on your work, you learned from him.

Taurog would move on to direct for Larry Semon, and from there to Educational where he would direct the comedies of Lloyd Hamilton, Lige Conley, Spencer Bell, and Sid Smith.

> And all that led me to a career directing feature films, right up to today. For any success I have had, Henry Lehrman must receive a great deal of the credit, for giving me, Jack White, and others, the opportunities he did, teaching us what he did, and having faith in us. For that, I will be always grateful.

Taurog also commented on Lehrman's apparent generosity, stating that "he had a heart of gold, and it mattered little if a person hard up requested five dollars or five hundred dollars."[1] One example of this was Lehrman's support of Lloyd Hamilton. By the late 1920s Hamilton had descended into alcoholism, his career in a nosedive due to a blacklisting by the Hays office. Hamilton biographer Anthony Balducci wrote that "whenever [Hamilton] was especially desperate for money, he was able to depend on Henry Lehrman," his debt to Lehrman having grown to $350 by early 1930.[2] Lehrman, it was reported, helped his old friend out by forcing him to take a cure for his addiction, from which the comedian emerged alcohol-free.[3] The MPAA lifted its ban on the comedian, and his career resumed.

Historian Joan Myers tells a story about an interview with former child actor Coy Watson, Jr., who was said to have worked for Lehrman when a child. "When I spoke to Coy Watson, Jr.….it was interesting because I asked him…'What did you think about Henry Lehrman?' and he didn't hesitate a second; it was like that, he said 'he was a very sensitive man, and my father thought he was one of the best directors working in Hollywood.' He didn't have time to think about it, it just popped out; he didn't have time to rehearse it or anything"[4]

So what was Lehrman like in private life? It is evident from his writings that he was well educated, and the examples we have of his penmanship display a beautiful and fluid use of cursive handwriting. An interviewer from the *Los Angeles Times* reported in 1915 that "like many educated and highly-sensitive Europeans, he has an extensive imagination."[5] Another reporter stated that "Like all real comedians, he is very serious in private life."[6] He was a proficient and self-assured dancer, evidenced in the numerous dancing competitions in which he took part. As for sports, boxing appeared to be his one interest, if not passion, although there was a passing interest in flying as well. Expensive automobiles were another passion of his, or at least in the earlier years when he could readily afford them. As for dress, he was always immaculately attired in the few images that survive. From the few written accounts that remain (primarily from his years at Fox), it would seem that he was somewhat of a dandy. While at the studio he would adorn himself in his version of the "official" director's attire, reported as wearing horn rimmed glasses and officers' puttees.[7] Another writer snidely remarked on Lehrman's appearance at one affair, commenting on his "little waxed moustache just so, and his hair bandolined so tight and his feet in such snug pumps and himself in steinblochian attire."[8] Screenwriter Lenore J. Coffee, whose career spanned well over forty years and who was employed by practically every studio functioning between 1919 and 1959, rented a chauffeur-driven car at some unspecified time. "[The] chauffeur was permitted to rent the car at his discretion," she wrote. "It suited me beautifully, but from the very first I noticed that there was always a scent of violets in it. I said to the chauffeur, 'The woman who owns this car must be very fond of violet perfume.' 'It's not a woman. The car belongs to Mr. Lehrman.' I said, 'Henry Pathé Lehrman?'"[9]

Ray W. Frohman, a former newspaper reporter turned freelance writer on motion pictures, had conflicting thoughts about Lehrman in an article he wrote regarding a visit to the Henry Lehrman Studios. The visit had taken place during post-production of *The Punch of the Irish*, and the article appeared shortly after Virginia Rappe's death:

In the studio projection room watching the "rushes" of "The Punch of the Irish" for titling and cutting purposes, Miss Rappe, who was seeing the film for the first time, giggled and giggled at the comedy "gags" in its entire two reels — giggled at "her own stuff," too.

Any other comedy producer would have been tickled a delicate pink at this supreme tribute to his successful laughmaking. But the wily and sardonic Lehrman — not so he. With a good-humored sneer, he chuckled to all of us: "Virginia laughs as if she were paid for it."

A New York interviewer was impressed to find Lehrman surrounded by Japanese prints and "such books as Wells' 'Outline of History'." Culture and breeding are not the impressions he conveys at the studio, glowering when something goes wrong or roaring threats to "fire you right at your projection machine" at the projectionist who failed to heed his "not so fast!" at the unreeling. "His nose meets his chin," one of his discontented players sneered about him, out of distance of his terrifying frown.

He has a sense of humor, however, chuckling like a boy over his "happy thoughts" in conference of titlists — for the main title of "The Punch of the Irish" and most of the subtitles are suggestions by Lehrman himself, "sprung" upon his co-executive, David Kirkland, now a Universal director.[10]

Lehrman certainly seemed to have a knack for rubbing some people the wrong way, but that really doesn't come as a surprise. The unrelenting release schedules, the persistent headaches associated with running a company, and the threat and ultimate realization of financial ruin can bring out the worst in a person's personality. But there was another side to Lehrman, one that never makes it into the various film books that bother to mention his name, and the occasional online post. Dixie Chene, an actress who had known Lehrman at Keystone, told a story about Lehrman during an interview with Sam Gill. Dixie's husband, former fighter Charles Armistead, had been hired by Lehrman for some stunt work at Keystone, and later worked for Lehrman at both L-Ko and Sunshine. Armistead died overseas during the war, one day before he was to return home to the states.

At the time of Charley's death, I was working at a popular roadhouse near L.A. One night I noticed Henry Lehrman in the audience with a group of actor friends. He waved at me several times while I was singing. As soon as I finished my song, I went backstage to change, and he was there. I said, "Excuse me, Mr. Lehrman, but I have to change." He told me he had learned of Charley's death, reached out his hand and placed a bill in my hand. It was a one hundred dollar bill. He said Charley would be making this if he were alive, and that I should have it. As long as I sang there, Henry Lehrman showed up over and over again, and every time he came backstage, he gave me a one hundred dollar bill.[11]

As with any artist, it is the artist's work that counts, and that which should be evaluated independent of its creator's personal traits and private exploits. Whatever sort of fellow Lehrman was — and heaven knows there have been conflicting reports through the years — the films are what he should be remembered for, and not his private life which was, in a word, *colorful*.

And at his peak these films were second to none. During the teens Lehrman would put his heart and soul into each new studio's first offering: both the initial Sterling release *Love and Vengeance* and the L-Ko opener *Love and Surgery* are manic displays of creativity and unfettered, good-natured violence every bit as good as — if not better than — anything Keystone was churning out at the time. *The House of Terrible Scandals*, Lehrman's first for Fox, is of a similar piece, featuring Lehrman himself in a lead role doing battle with Billie Ritchie in what *Variety* called "one of the best slapstick comedies that has been released in a long while…." The Sunshines displayed a growth and maturity from his earlier, rougher films, and benefitted greatly from enhanced budgets that resulted in a more polished product. And it was with his own Henry Lehrman Comedies where his creativity reached its peak, as evidenced by the three surviving films, *A Twilight Baby*, *Punch of the Irish*, and *Wet and Warmer*.

Sadly only a very few of his hundreds of films survive, and of those only a handful have at different times been commercially available for viewing. This lack of availability, coupled with the disparaging remarks regarding Lehrman that have made it into print over the years, have led to a dismissal of L-Ko's output as substandard and routine. The fact that the Stern brothers' post-Lehrman L-Ko's and later Century comedies are often lumped together with Lehrman's output hasn't helped matters in terms of differentiating the earlier product from the latter. Additionally, the comparative abundance of surviving Keystone and later Sennett comedies along with the Hal Roach output has unfairly elevated their films in the minds of the more casual writers about film.

Film historians are reevaluating their opinions, however, slowly but surely gaining a renewed respect and admiration for Lehrman's work as more surviving films of his are unearthed throughout the world.

APPENDIX A

The Sterling Motion Picture Corporation, Post-Lehrman: A Rudderless Ship

With Lehrman's departure and the essentially humorless Fred Balshofer now in charge, the Sterling Motion Picture Company would become a rudderless ship. And with Lehrman's creativity and directorial abilities now a thing of the past, an even greater burden fell upon Sterling's shoulders. He now had to direct as well as star in his comedies, while maintaining a constant stream of product for the unforgiving Universal release schedule; it must have felt like the bad old days back at Keystone. Balshofer, desperate for a quick infusion of creativity, advertised in the trades that he was offering "top-notch prices" for one- and two-reel scripts "compelling in action and virile of plot."[1]

New York Dramatic Mirror writer William Lord Wright wrote of the Sterling company's handling of submitted photoplays, based on an interview with Balshofer:

> Sterling and Balshofer never work from a script, they do not follow a written story in photoplay form, according to Mr. Balshofer. At times the two spend several hours together discussing a plot or a unique idea and then they build it up until the farce commences, and the action must be rapid until the finish. Scenes at the Sterling studios are never timed and very rarely is a farce rehearsed. If the scenes taken are not satisfactory they are taken over until proper results are obtained. It is nothing unusual, according to Mr. Balshofer, for four or five thousand feet of negative to be taken for a single-reel story and this is later cut and trimmed down to one thousand feet to eliminate poor acting and to gain smooth running qualities.

The twice-used phrase "according to Mr. Balshofer" might suggest that Wright wasn't fully embracing Balshofer's puffery regarding the modus operandi at the studio. As for those contemplating a submission to the studio, he tacked on a warning of sorts to temper expectations, stating that "your photoplay, if accepted by the Sterling Company is not apt to 'be produced as written.' It will likely be taken carefully apart, the idea only retained, and then the director and the cast will work out their own situations."[2]

Fortunately, production of the Sterling Kid Comedies was ongoing and consistent. The company's Thursday release was to be supplemented by a Monday Kid Comedy, effective June 1. Monday's slot had been held by a Powers release, with Powers now to join Frontier (and Crystal) in the one-release-per-week club; *Universal Weekly* somewhat half-heartedly suggested that the reduction to one release each per week would result in a "material improvement in the artistic quality of [these] pictures,"[3] but less-of-the-same seemed more accurate. The Universal program would now be a weekly twenty-eight reels of film. With this announcement, Universal adopted the rather disconcerting habit of reporting Billy's age — and it was always Billy rather than Paul in their articles — in a haphazard and totally inaccurate fashion. While in reality Paul Jacobs was forty-five months old, they reported him as twenty-nine months old and elsewhere as "not more than five" and "not more than seven." Four and a half months later, he was reported as thirty months old, and so on. At any rate, Jacobs' cohorts in these earliest Kid films were pretty, golden-haired, brown-eyed, five-year-old Carmen DeRue, a child actress on stage and in film for most of her handful of years, and Chandler House, who was several years older. Thornby's theory was that well-rested and well-fed children perform best, so he insisted upon twelve hours sleep for each of them, and stuffed them four times a day with bread, milk, and ice cream.

While the Sterling Kids and Sennett's Keystone Kids-Little Billy comedies were among the first children's series in this country, there were a few others. Predecessors here in the U.S. date back to Edison's Buster Brown series of 1904, which Edison resurrected in the summer of 1914 with Norris Millington in the lead. Essanay released *Peck's Bad Boy* in 1908, and Vitagraph had their Sonny Jim series starring Bobby Connelly in 1914-15. In France there was the Bébé series with René Dary in 1910-13, and the Bout-de-Zan series with René Poyen in 1912-16. Universal's Éclair brand introduced a series of single reel juvenile comedies at the beginning of 1914 co-starring Clara Horton and Willie Gibbons, which the *New York Clipper* deemed "the prettiest novelty that has been offered the exhibitors in many months....These photoplays have the sweetest appeal imaginable."[4] With summer came the introduction of a new brand, "Universal Boy," starring Little Matty Roubert, formerly of Powers. June also saw the inauguration of a short-lived series by Child Players Co. of America whose first offering was the one-reel *Kids of the Movies*.

Complicating matters for the Sterling brand was the disastrous fire at New York City's Colonial Hall Building at 101st Street and Columbus Avenue which destroyed well over $300,000 of Universal's negatives and positives. Most of the Universal affiliates were affected to some degree, requiring varying amounts of reshooting on yet-to-be-released productions. *Kids*, the initial Sterling Kid Comedy, was among the casualties, forced to relinquish its scheduled June 1 slot to a last minute replacement, Powers' split-reel *All the Dog's Fault* and *The Arsenal of Lloyd at Triest*.

Kids finally made it to the screen on June 15; Universal ads declared it to be an "original, classy, clean comedy...every mother in town should bring her child to see it,"[5] perhaps in an attempt to allay the fears of every mother in town that it would be as crass and tasteless as some of its "adult" counterparts. No need to worry, for the plot was squeaky-clean and typical of the series that followed, most of which dealt with puppy-love and jealousy, pie stealing, infants wandering off and saved by the household pooch, missing or stolen dolls, and similarly innocuous storylines. Little Billy reappeared three days later in *Billy's Riot* (June 18), and four days after that in *The Flirt* (June 22) with co-star Carmen DeRue.

Sterling made it back to the screen on June 25 in *A Jealous Husband*, which had initially been scheduled for a week earlier, followed by yet another Little Billy comedy *It's a Boy* (June 29; extant), co-starring Charles Inslee as his father. In this latter film, a dog pulling a cart containing an infant is spooked by an explosion, and runs wild over hills and through streams. It eventually overturns and spills its youthful contents at the conclusion of what is admittedly a rather hair-raising viewing experience. The Kid Comedies were thoroughly competent and enjoyable, and reviewers took note: "In their way, the clever Sterling Juveniles are even

Paul Jacobs looks on as father Charles Inslee cuddles the new baby brother, in It's a Boy.
COURTESY OF LIBRARY OF CONGRESS.

more amusing than the members of the elder company....Little Billy will speedily rival Ford Sterling himself."[6] Which, it would appear to some, wouldn't be too large a challenge. Sterling's next two starring vehicles had him as an ineffectual cop in *Snitz Joins the Force* (June 4), and bogus cop in *Smaltz Loves* (June 11; aka *When Smaltz Loves*), and were met with somewhat less enthusiastic reviews; criticism was leveled squarely at their sameness and predictability, and at the less than adequate performances of his supporting cast.

By late June, Balshofer's director shortage problem had been resolved. In addition to Thornby, who was consistently dependable in his rigid adherence to schedules and budgets, and could be relied upon to produce acceptable fare, Sterling had now assumed direction of a number of his starring vehicles. The remaining films were turned over to newly hired directors David Kirkland and George O. Nichols.[7] Balshofer lured Nichols away from Sennett, placing him in charge of a third unit and putting him to work on *The Crash*, "one of the biggest, if not the most spectacular comedy production ever attempted."[8] A generous and outgoing individual, Nichols was never without his ever-present hip flask of bourbon, and he frequently partook of it, urging those about him to join in. With the hiring of Nichols and the less-experienced Kirkland soon after, the ranks now appeared to be more than adequate to handle the twice-weekly releases.

July opened with a bang with the release of the Nichols-directed *The Crash* (July 2), a lightning-paced chase revolving around the well-worn premise of rivals at love. During the course of its single-reel, the foes destroy their car and motorcycle as well as a pair of gasoline trucks, a house, and a barn.[9] Wild and woolly fare, to be sure, followed by the more peaceful

LEFT: *Ford Sterling administers one of his trademark nose bites in* Snitz Joins the Force. *Is that Charles Inslee on the receiving end?* RIGHT: *Ad for* The Crash, *promoted as a "Ford Sterling Spectacular Comedy." Patrons were no doubt annoyed to find that Sterling himself was not in the film. From the June 27, 1914 issue of* Moving Picture World.

Billy's Vacation (July 6). Sterling reappeared in *Snookee's Flirtation* (July 9; originally scheduled for June 25) as a chronically lazy husband henpecked into getting a job in a shoe store. When his jealous wife is informed of his flirtations with numerous female customers — Peggy Pearce and Emma Clifton among them — she confronts him, and the film concludes with an avalanche of shoes. *Moving Picture World* found it "a rough and knockabout farce in the usual Sterling style…not so funny as the best of this brand; for the scheme calls for business a bit too rough for more discriminating patrons."[10] *Bioscope* was, as usual, more charitable, stating that "Ford Sterling is again at his best in a screamingly funny farce."[11] A print of the film is held by the Museum of Modern Art, and it is typical Sterling.

With the increase of production capacity and the growing paucity of its stock players, the company's ranks were increased with the acquisition of additional actors and actresses. These included Mae Wells, Margarete Whisler, Al Garcia, Arthur Tavares, and Keystone's kid comedian Gordon Griffith. Wells' film career began in 1904 with Edison's *Memories of a Trunk*, followed by roles for Powers, Éclair, Keystone, and Frontier. Former Selig lead Garcia had dozens of films to his credit from his start in 1911, with an occasional effort for Kalem and Powers before hooking up with Sterling. Tavares, a handsome former cabaret performer and light opera singer, got his start with Kalem and had worked for Keystone soon after Sennett's arrival in California. Seven year old Griffith, son of actors Harry and Katherine Griffith, co-starred in several dozen Keystone comedies over the past year, primarily the Kid Comedies opposite Paul Jacobs; his first at Keystone was Lehrman's *Just Kids*.

Also joining the studio was Charles Inslee, a former legitimate actor who had worked briefly for Griffith (a fistfight with the Master brought that relationship to an end) and later for Balshofer's 101 Bison Company. Inslee was at this time going through a period of some embarrassment as a result of his wife's suit for divorce. Her grounds, as was widely circulated in the press, were that he was a peculiar man, and cruel "in not letting her hug, caress and kiss him."[12] He had the last laugh, though, for she was refused alimony on the basis that as an actress she was making much more than he was in his present state of affairs. Inslee's first at Sterling was *It's a Boy*, with the other newcomers relegated to such films as *Almost Married* (July 13) and *The Circus* (July 20; extant). Little Billy never missed a beat, featured in *A Beach Romance* (July 16), *A Wild Ride* (July 27), and *A Race for Life* (August 3; extant), which Thornby had filmed at the amusement area at Venice-By-The-Sea. This latter film featured a dream sequence that was staged as if an old-fashioned melodrama, with Gordon Griffith the mustache-twirling villain. Nestor, meanwhile, had released the Allan Dwan-directed *The Great Universal Mystery* on July 10. This one-reel promotional short was chock full of Universal's East and West Coast personnel, including Sterling, Balshofer, and Thornby.

Ford Sterling's next release for his company was the well-received two-reel *Love and Lunch* (July 23). Browbeaten by his fiancé Peggy (Pearce; unconfirmed) into getting a job at a lunch counter and forfeiting his usual pastime of flirting, our hapless hero is outraged when he finds her marrying the fellow whose job he has taken. The inevitable fight ensues, with the lunch wagon rolling away and having its gas tanks explode. *Bioscope* approved, of course: "Sterling…bubbles over with fun, and manages to get a laugh out of the most absurd situation. Moreover, there is an apparent lack of effort in all that he does, and the amount of work he puts into his 'business' is something to marvel at. There is nothing so amusing as a Sterling comic, so fresh is its humour and so remarkable its acting."[13] *A Dramatic Mistake* followed on August 6, with Sterling as Snitz, seeking a job in the theater in his periodic effort to pay the rent. Landing the role of "Virginius" when the show's lead arrives drunk, Snitz's family thinks he's being murdered when they overhear his exuberant rehearsing. *At Three O'Clock* (August 13), scripted, cut, and directed by Kirkland, had Sterling suffering a fit of despondency upon learning that his girl (Peggy Pearce) has spurned him for a gangster. Joining a suicide club, Professor A.A. Sassan is scheduled to put the comedian out of his misery at the title's time. *His Wife's Flirtation* (August 20) was next with Sterling as the homicidally jealous farmer Reuben,[14] followed a week later by the extant *Snookee's Disguise*, with Sterling a flirtatious cornet player who finds his wife to be equally unfaithful. *Moving Picture World* dismissed it as a "characteristic Ford Sterling number,"[15] while *Bioscope* found it "even more remarkable than the many hilarious productions of this wonderful comedian."[16] August proved by far to be the comedian's most prolific month in terms of released films, rounded out by a guest appearance in Paul Jacobs' *Lost in the Studio* (August 17), wherein Little Billy wanders about the Sterling studios getting into all sorts of trouble. The idea for this film was a natural, as it mirrored the real-life exploits of the curious child. In an effort to keep him out of trouble, studio carpenters had made Paul a toy movie camera several months earlier, which enabled him to traipse about the facilities continuously "directing" scenes.

Meanwhile, Balshofer returned from an early August trip to New York City and the

Ford Sterling as Virginius, emoting over a pile of downed cops, in A Dramatic Mistake.

home offices of Universal, which was planned as a "short respite from his arduous duties." He continued to paint a rosy picture of his studio for the press, telling them that while the comedies were doing quite well commercially, they were "continuously on the improve."[17] Problems persisted, however, with the most nagging one being the continuous shortage of workable scripts now that Lehrman's fertile and creative mind was elsewhere, many of which Balshofer was forced to write himself as well as providing plot ideas. Further complicating matters was the abrupt departure after only two months' stay of George Nichols,[18] forcing Balshofer to once again return to direction while attempting to fill the vacancy.[19] A replacement was found almost immediately with the acquisition of twenty-five year old Frank C. Griffin from Lubin's Jacksonville, Florida studio. Associated with

ABOVE: *Sterling at the hands of his would-be assassins Bobby Dunn (left) and Lee Morris (right), in* At Three O'Clock. COURTESY OF COLE JOHNSON. BELOW: *Sterling as the flirtatious cornet player in* Snookee's Disguise, *soon to fall head over heels for neighbor Peggy Pearce.* COURTESY OF LIBRARY OF CONGRESS.

that company since 1906 as an actor, Griffin had made the switch over to comedy direction a year or so earlier, a vocation that had almost proved fatal when the young director was accidentally dragged under the sea by an ocean liner's anchor while participating in a comedy sequence.[20]

One of the company's biggest coups was the hiring of popular comedian Max Asher. Born in Oakland, California, on May 5, 1880, Asher appeared in his young teens in Oakland's People's Theatre before moving on to vaudeville. After a start as "Mysterio, the

Butcher Schultz (Max Asher) wields a huge hunk of something as a battering ram, with the assist of Bobby Dunn (sideburns), from In and Out.

King of Cards," a long association followed with Kolb and Dill's famous Dutch dialect musical comedy productions, with additional musical comedy performances throughout Western Canada where he perfected his Dutch characterization.[21] After a three month stint with Keystone, Asher moved over to Universal and Powers in April 1913 where he remained until Joker was formed to showcase his talents. Joker's first Asher release was *The Cheese Special* in October 1913, with an endless stream of comedies following on its heels. Usually teamed with Harry McCoy (the "Mike and Jake" series, etc.) and Louise Fazenda, and directed by Allen Curtis, Asher's position as top dog was somewhat diluted in the months that followed, with Joker expanding its roster of top comics to five. Friction resulted, and Asher moved across the street to Sterling when he felt that a complaint he had made had been insensitively brushed off.[22] His first for the new studio was the aforementioned *Neighbors*, followed by his appearance as Schultz in the single reel *In and*

Out (September 21), a well-received bit of slapstick with grocer battling butcher in a hail of food.²³ Asher promptly acquired the services of Velma Steck, formerly a soubrette with the Kolb and Dill act, as his co-star.²⁴

Further additions to the Sterling company included former race car driver and aspiring actor Frank Goode as Thornby's assistant on the Kid Comedies,²⁵ and former vaudevillian Gus Erdman. Actress Bobbie Gould, late of L. Frank Baum's ill-fated Oz Film Company,²⁶ was brought over to co-star with Erdman in *Snookee's Day Off* (October 26). Emma Clifton

LEFT: *Paul Jacobs and Olive Johnson in an unidentified Sterling Comedy.* COURTESY OF SAM GILL. RIGHT: *Sterling's "Snitz" is about to clobber Dave Anderson's "Hans" (center), his rival for the hand of Emma Clifton (right) in* A Shooting Match. *From the cover of the September 19, 1914 issue of* Universal Weekly.

returned to the ranks after an extended stay in the east with her parents²⁷ to star with Charles Inslee in *A Strong Affair* (August 10) and *The Tale of a Hat* (August 31), followed by *Trapped in a Closet* (September 14). Scenario editor Charles Hagenios, late of Kalem and Frontier, was pressed into service to helm *The Tale of a Hat*, taking his cast to San Pedro harbor to film exteriors. This film is his only known credit with the studio.

Paul Jacobs continued with his regular appearances, though less frequently so, in three more comedies before being yanked from the company by his parents. *A Rural Affair* (August 24) featured the usual prepubescent love affair, this time with Billy fixated on newcomer Olive Johnson who, with dark hair in bangs, blue eyes, and Jacobs' approximate age, size, and shape, was cute as a button. "I even had my own leading lady," commented Jacobs about Olive much later in life in an interview with historian Sam Gill. "We assumed when we grew up, we'd get married. When she became older, she and her mother went on the road in vaudeville as a song and dance act, and I don't know what happened to her afterwards."[28] The other two Jacobs releases were *The Broken Doll* (September 7), and *The Battle* (September 28). At two reels, *The Battle* was not only Jacobs' longest film to date, but also his most ambitious and, in the estimation of some reviewers, his best. Little Billy's despondency over not having a girlfriend(!) is interrupted when an old soldier, stricken by Billy's resemblance to his dead son, takes him home with him. The two play and Billy listens in fascination as the old fellow recounts his military exploits of days gone by. Eventually they both fall asleep, with Billy dreaming of himself taking part in the exploits for the better part of the second reel. Billy's mother conducts a frantic search for the missing child, but when she finally finds Billy asleep with his arms around the old man's neck, she understands and lets them be. *The Battle* was a welcome change of pace from the usually predictable Kid Comedies, though somewhat overlong for the material presented, occasionally hindered by substandard photography, and marred by a blatantly obvious substitution for Billy in the dream's horseback ride. Nevertheless, Paul Jacobs' assumed swansong was a distinctive one.

Problems with the Sterling releases were not limited to *The Battle* by a long shot, and were surfacing with an increasing regularity. The quality of the photography was degenerating on a number of the more recent releases, and reviewers were quick to point it out ("…uneven and quite below the standard in some places" snapped *Moving Picture World* in its review of *The Battle*).[29] Furthermore, exhibitors had been screaming from the first that the titles in Sterling Comedies refused to stay in frame, and it wasn't until the end of September that the problem was resolved.[30] The company's biggest problem, however, was its growing inability to meet its announced schedules. Substitutions had been made on a sporadic basis and for varying reasons from as early as June, but cancellations became standard operating procedure as of September when two of its eight bi-weekly releases were postponed. It wasn't long after that *Universal Weekly* gave up completely with its usual policy of announcing the following week's release titles for the increasingly undependable studio.

Ford Sterling plodded on amidst the confusion, however, producing a pair of comedies for release in both September and October. *A Bogus Baron* (September 3), featured Peggy Pearce and Sterling's "right-hand man" Beverly Griffith, with Sterling as Snitz posing as an aristocrat to help discredit a young suitor's rival. Snitz was again the hero of the two-reel *A Shooting Match* (September 24), engaged in the match of the title with romantic rival Hans for the hand of the lovely Emma (Clifton). Sterling took over the directorial duties when director David Kirkland left early for a vacation in San Francisco.[31] *Hypnotic Power* (October 8) followed with Sterling as Snookee, who hypnotizes his rival in order to get him out of the way;[32] David Kirkland co-starred as the hypnotist, with Clifton the object of their desires. Sterling's last in October and, as it turned out, his last for the studio, was *Secret Service Snitz* (October 22) co-starring Pearce, a last minute replacement for Clifton. Following the improbable exploits of a Secret Service agent cracking down on moonshiners, the action became so frenetic during shooting that a badly bruised and scratched Clifton was put under a doctor's care and withdrawn from production for several days.[33] Pre-release materials listed Clifton in the cast, but the battered actress was replaced by Peggy Pearce who appeared in the finished film. *Variety* dismissed the released film as "uninteresting," and *Motion Picture News*, while deeming the film to be "very laughable," went on to say that the print viewed "seems lightstruck in parts."[34]

ABOVE: *Max Asher's character of Myers being prepped for the grave,* in Myer's Mistake. *Arthur Tavares on left wielding the mallet.* BELOW: *Heinie Plitzer (Max Asher) and his girl Lena (Vilma Steck) at the picnic,* in Heinie's Outing. COURTESY OF LIBRARY OF CONGRESS.

Also released in October were Max Asher's next efforts for the studio, a pair of Kid Comedies sans Jacobs, and Gus Erdman's first two vehicles. *Myer's Mistake* (October 5), director Frank Griffin's first for the studio, is notable for two reasons: not only did Asher almost suffocate while filming a scene in which he was buried alive both in script and reality, but the film received the usually generous *Bioscope*'s first negative review of a Sterling release ("There is really very little that is amusing in this…hardly in good taste")[35] while *Moving Picture World* praised it. The two publications took almost identical opposing stances on Asher's *Heinie's Outing* (October 15; extant), with hero Heinie Plitzer at odds with gangster "Knock-out" Jim at a Dutch picnic. The Kid Comedies comprised *The Close Call* (October 12; extant) and *Carmen's Wash Day* (October 19), starring Olive Johnson and Carmen DeRue, respectively; the former of these, according to *Motion Picture News*, had a new, unidentified lead: "A kid named Felix assumes Billy's role in this juvenile comedy, but he isn't as good as his more noted predecessor."[36] The "unidentified" lead was three year old Felix Walsh, a terrible substitute for Jacobs and as wooden as a cigar store Indian. Erdman's first two efforts were the *Snookee's Day Off* (October 26), which *Motion Picture News* deemed "funny in parts, risque in others, with a few vulgar moments,"[37] and *A Race for a Bride* (October 29), which *Variety* called "the cheapest kind of picture. Poor."[38]

Variety was the first trade publication to leak word of rumored internal problems in Balshofer's company, stating that the increasingly shaky enterprise might soon be dissolved "by mutual consent of parties interested."[39] Reporters descended upon Sterling soon after his arrival in New York City on October 5 and "a close conference with the heads of the Universal," but the characteristically secretive actor would only reveal that he was there "on a double mission and that none of his plans could be made public." It was never made clear just what those "plans" involved, but little work was gotten out of Sterling following his return to California on November 5, and no more films were ever completed with him for the rest of his stay. Balshofer had taken a vacation during this time as well, heading off to Bakersfield with former boxing champ Jim Jeffries for some hunting.[40] How those two hooked up is anyone's guess.

Problems with Sterling aside, Balshofer plugged along with his little company with an eye to possible future expansion. His late November duck and quail hunts with Thornby were more jubilant affairs due to the recent reacquisition of the services of Paul Jacobs. Furthermore, thirty-year-old comedian William Wolbert had been brought into the fold from Joker, where his Willie Walrus series — *Willie Walrus, Detective* (June 3), *Willie Walrus and the Baby* (May 27), *Willie Walrus and the Awful Confession* (July 15), etc. — had achieved a fair amount of success and exposure. After having spent thirteen years in legitimate theater, another two years with Balboa, and the past year bouncing around Universal making films for Victor, Powers, Nestor, and Joker, Wolbert now found himself with yet another studio. While Wolbert continued to be promoted as the Willie Walrus character, his Sterling character was tagged Noodles and his first release was the Kirkland-directed *Noodles' Return* (November 19). The Kids Comedies added *The Wall Between* (November 2), *A Bear Escape* (November 16), and the amusing *Black Hands* (November 23), wherein a nervous father mistakes his young son's jam-soaked handprints as a death sign from the Mafia after arguing with an Italian organ grinder. *Billy's Charge* (December 7) marked Jacobs' return to the screen, reuniting him with fellow kids DeRue and House, followed by *Carmen's Romance* (December 21) towards year's end.

Other of Sterling's bi-weekly releases included Asher in drag as *Dot's Chaperone* (November 5), with Bobbie Gould introducing the character of Dot (and Gould herself to be rechristened as "Dot" Gould in all subsequent *Universal Weekly* references). The comic duo reappeared in *An Ill Wind* (November 9) with Asher the tight-laced police chief of Pumpkin Center, but with Gould in a pre-Dot characterization. *Dot's Elopement* (November 26) teamed them for a third time with backing from Gus Erdman, whose *The Dog Raffles* (November 12) had appeared two weeks earlier co-starring him with Peggie, the studio's dog, in a tale of a thief and his trick dog. Dot became Dolly in Asher and Gould's *Love, Luck, and Candy* (December 3) which involved the intended poisoning of an unfaithful sweetheart, but the two went their separate ways for his *Lizzie's Fortune* (December 14) and her *Love and Water* (December 31; extant). *Lizzie's Fortune* suffered not for her absence, with nineteen-year-old Sterling newcomer Louise Fazenda taking her place. Fazenda had started in the industry a year earlier with Joker, appearing with Asher in that company's maiden film *The Cheese Special* in October. After a year of co-starring roles with Lee Morris, Harry McCoy, Bobby Vernon, William Franey (her co-star after Asher's departure), Gale Henry, and others, Fazenda made the gradual switch over to Sterling, but fame would await another year or so until her eventual employment at Keystone.[41] The December 10 slot originally announced for *Lizzie's Fortune* was instead filled by Wolbert and Erdman's *His New Job*, with Wolbert reappearing a week later in *The Fatal Hansom* (December 17), a wildly humorous destructive piece with Noodles and rival cabby Bobby Dunn[42] at each other's throat over potential fares. *The Chef's Revenge* (December 28) almost didn't make it, with Universal announcing its intended release, later cancelling that date, and then dumping it on its exchanges on the date originally announced. Emma Clifton co-starred with former stage director, Griffith alumnus, and recent Essanay and Rex comedy director Lloyd Ingraham. Director David Kirkland seemed unable to keep his new lead under control, with results that *Motion Picture News* leaped upon: "There is slightly too much gesticulating by the principal players of this comedy to be enjoyed. A little less of it and the picture would be more pleasing." The reviewer threw the struggling studio a bone, however, stating that the "comedy is better than the Sterlings have been of late, but could be improved upon if the movements before spoken of were omitted."[43]

Sterling made a late November trip to San Francisco where he attended the first annual ball of the Screen Club along with Chaplin, Roscoe Arbuckle, and a number of other film notables.[44] Sterling's comparative inactivity became complete in mid-December, the result of a reported "severe attack of Typhoid Fever and Pneumonia" which left him "seriously ill." Supposedly caused by a severe cold caught on his return trip from New York, it "later went to Pneumonia when he became overheated one day last week while working at the studio," reported *Universal Weekly*. "[His] condition is so precarious that immediate recovery is doubtful."[45] Other accounts had him dropping twenty-two pounds[46] and dragging his weakened shell to the doctor's office.[47] Balshofer insists that the entire incident was a sham, and that after three weeks of a messenger arriving to collect Sterling's paychecks, someone clued Balshofer as to "what his 'sickness' really was; Sterling had been spending his nights at Baron Long's night club whooping it up."[48] Balshofer says that he put in an unannounced appearance at the club soon after, catching Sterling "there in all his glory, putting it on high, wide, and handsome." This was the straw that "broke" Balshofer's back, and he resolved to remove the popular though decreasingly seen and uncooperative comedian from the company's employment.

Sterling's shenanigans aside, an attempt had been made to maintain business as usual at the studio. Harry W. Wulze, who had a year or two's experience writing for Flying A, was added to the scenario staff,[49] as was William F. Adler, who worked in the lab when not stationed behind the camera.[50] Balshofer himself was pressed into service to direct, helming at least two films that we know of, *Those German Bowlers* (January 14, 1915) and *Raindrops and Girls* (March 18). Comedian Ernest Shield was brought over from Joker, by now fully recuperated after an extended hospital stay; he had suffered a brain concussion in April from a twenty-five foot fall to rocks while on loan-out to the *Lucille Love, the Girl of Mystery* serial. But there were losses as well: William Wolbert had left the company to succeed Marshall Neilan as a comedy producer at Kalem,[51] and Peggy Pearce had by now left for L-Ko.

With an eye to that elusive but sorely needed increase in production, Balshofer was having the studio overhauled and refurbished, nearly doubling the working space and bringing it "out from under the trees" with the addition of five thousand square feet of new stage.[52] Complementing the increased working space was the addition of Winfield Kerner electric lights, which would enable filming to continue "no matter how many clouds hide California's Old Sol."[53] Canvas covers were added to facilitate production during inclement weather, which had been blamed as the cause of the company's frequent cancellations.[54] These latter additions came too late for the beleaguered studio, however; the cancellations resulted in a return to a single release per week, effective January 1915. A poke in the eye here, as Lehrman's new company L-Ko would be upped from one release per week to two with this move; the ailing Frontier and Crystal brands were to be dropped completely.

More important was the December hiring of forty-nine year old John E. Brennan, late of Kalem.[55] Brennan, an overweight comedian of Irish parentage with a sharp pointed nose and perpetual grin, was at various times in his career a clog dancer (world champion, supposedly), a blackface comedian with Primrose and West's Minstrels, a stock comedian at Keith's in Boston, and performer of the role of Hi Holler in close to three thousand performances of *Way Down East* (among many other plays) before joining with Kalem in support of Ruth Roland.[56] Going independent in July 1914, Brennan's small Santa Monica studio turned out several single-reelers with Betty Teare[57] for Kalem (*Daub Has a Dream*, *Waiting at the Church*, etc.) before heading over to Sterling. Brennan's first with the new studio was *Innocent Dad* (December 23), a beachside farce co-starring Gould and Erdman which did little to help the flagging brand. Balshofer's *Those German Bowlers* followed with Brennan as bowling nut Grousmeyer who takes an argument with neighbor Schmaltz to the alleys for final settlement.

Sterling's departure from the company was not announced as such, but his subsequent availability became public knowledge with the new year. Rumors abounded in the trade papers in late December and throughout January as to what his next move would be. On December 25, *Variety* announced his probable return to Keystone to coincide with Chaplin's departure for Essanay.[58] On January 14, *Variety* squelched a rumor that Sterling would be taking up an Orpheum tour by reporting that Orpheum's New York office had totally denied such an arrangement (although it was mentioned in passing that the offices in San Francisco might be setting up some sort of deal for a tour).[59] January 20th's *New*

York Dramatic Mirror confirmed a forty week Orpheum contract[60] (which never came to pass), while the 23rd's *Moving Picture World* indicated that Sterling was looking to start another company of his own. By February all rumors were put to rest with the announcement that Sterling had been signed by the New York Motion Picture Corp. to a two year contract and would be returning to Keystone and Sennett forthwith. Two months later, *Variety* made the rather telling observation that Sterling had signed "for considerably less" than they had offered him not to leave a year earlier.

LEFT: *John E, Brennan.* RIGHT: *Violet Radcliffe (right) joins Paul Jacobs (center) in an unidentified Sterling Comedy.* COURTESY OF SAM GILL.

Balshofer announced an upcoming business trip to New York, unconvincingly asserting to reporters that Sterling's departure "makes no difference whatever, as the demand for comedies continues and the company will resume work on his return." He went on to say that while in New York he "will be on the search for good talent as he intends to enlarge the company and put on a different line of comedy, doing away with the slapstick variety as much as possible."[61] With Sterling's departure from the company bearing his name, however, there seemed to be little reason for its continued existence. Exhibitors and audiences alike were becoming increasingly frustrated with the dwindling number of Sterling comedies to actually star the comedian. As theater owner Frank C. McGray put it in a letter to *Universal Weekly*: "They go away hollering their heads off because they expect to see Sterling whenever his name is mentioned." McGray went on to say that the Kid Comedies, which had become very routine and predictable by this time, "don't go strong."[62] Universal had been generous with the promotion of the company at its inception, but Laemmle was not loose with a buck and the purse strings had been pulled in as soon as it was confirmed that the Sterling releases were short of the blockbuster hits he had hoped for. Allotted space in *Universal Weekly* diminished, slowly but surely, in favor of other more promising and prestigious brands and releases, and by August 1914 Lehrman's L-Ko Komedies were getting the sole push for films of that ilk. As for space in the trade publications, it became non-existent. The writing was on the wall, and Balshofer tossed in his cards and called a cease to active production in mid-January, giving his employees their two-weeks' notice and leasing the studio at Gower and Sunset to another company.[63]

Balshofer had a fair backlog of films, however, and intended to get every last penny out of them that he could. The weekly releases continued for several months in a somewhat slipshod fashion, with some occasionally interesting results. Paul Jacobs appeared in one film per month through March: *Olive's Love Affair* (January 7) with Violet Radcliffe again playing the tough male bully with curls securely hidden under cap as in her previous *Carmen's Wash Day* (October 19, 1914); *Billy Was a Right Smart Boy* (February 11); and *Olive's Pet* (March 25). Two final Kid Comedies followed with Olive Johnson soloing: *Olive's Hero* (April 1); and *Playmates* (April 15). Wolbert's final release was the Kirkland-directed *Treasure Seekers* (January 28), a "cannibal comedy" filmed on location at a place supposedly named Dead Man's Island,[64] while Emma Clifton's was *The Fox Trot Craze* (February 18). Other releases included the Brennan and Gould co-starrers *Love and Dough* (February 4) and *When Snitz Was "Married"* (March 4), Gould's *The Runaway Closet* (February 25), Brennan's *The Knockout Wallop* (March 11), and Louise Fazenda and Gus Erdman's *Raindrops and Girls*[65] and *The Butler's Busted Romance* (April 8). The previous year's November 12 release *The Dog Raffles* resurfaced as *Dude Raffles* (January 21), while December 28's *The Chef's Revenge* was rereleased on April 29 untouched.

Balshofer claims in his autobiography to have fashioned thousands of feet of unused footage of Sterling into a number of additional releases, with connecting scenes filmed of twenty-four year old George Jeske in Sterling's garb and running through his supposedly convincing Sterling imitation. Jeske is cited by the *Universal Weekly* for only two Sterling releases (*When Snitz Was "Married"* and *The Knockout Wallop*) and by *Motion Picture News* for a third (*Black Hands*), under his birth name of Jaeschke. Neither *Universal Weekly*'s synopses suggest, nor do reviewers assume him to be Sterling, and the *Black Hand*'s reviewer commented that the story's police force was "led by a comedian who gives promise of a bright future."[66] Sterling's name had not been associated with any of the releases in a starring capacity since October's *Secret Service Snitz*, so Balshofer's memory concerning his assertion that "in this way we made Sterling comedies long after I had let him go"[67] seems faulty at best. Only April 22's *His Smashing Career* in which both *Moving Picture World* and *Bioscope* assumed the lead character of Snooks to be portrayed by Sterling seems a likely candidate, with its favorable reviews lending some credence to Balshofer's contention that "one of the comedies we made in this fashion was perhaps the best in the entire series."

The Sterling Company's final three releases in May offered a few surprises that might earlier have amounted to something. *Counting Out the Count* (May 6) co-starred Billie Reeves and Johnny Doyle as a pair of down-on-their-luck vaudevillians posing as a count and his valet in hopes of attracting a millionairess. The fifty year old Reeves, formerly a lead with Fred Karno's touring troupe and a prominent participant in Flo Ziegfeld's Follies of 1906, 1909, 1910, and 1911, made his first appearance in film in this Sterling release before signing a six month contract with Sigmund Lubin in March 1915, to be directed by Arthur D. Hotaling. *Counting Out the Count* met with mixed reviews, and when the following twenty-six one-reel comedies for Lubin failed to go over in a big way, a frustrated Reeves returned to the stage.

Pokes and Jabbs (May 13) followed, with former Lubin, Komic, and Royal comedians Bobbie Burns and Walter Stull introducing to film the characters they would continue to inhabit, first for World Film's Wizard Comedies and later for General Film's Vim Comedies, from November 1915 into 1918. *Motion Picture News* shed some light on the film's origins, and perhaps on a level of craftsmanship a notch or two above the recent Sterling fare, when it reported that "This was made by an outside company, but the Sterling brand has seldom been honored with a more acceptable slapstick."[68]

Billie Reeves, Lubin star — for a short while at least.

The Sterling Film Company's final release on May 20 was *The Battle of Running Bull*, "two reels of Sterling slaughter" with John Brennan, Bobbie Gould, Ernest Shield, and Arthur Tavares co-starring in a tale of the battlefields which did little to prove that war is Hell. This trio of comedies suggests that Balshofer had been attempting to put some new life into the Sterling brand with the introduction of some virgin (to the screen) talent, perhaps hoping in the case of Reeves that what had worked with Chaplin might reoccur with someone of such similar background and experience, and that with Burns and Stull the presentation of a clearly defined set of comedic characters might gain acceptance from an audience thirsting to see their further exploits. *The Battle of Running Bull* was clearly a more ambitious project for Brennan than his previous single-reelers, and might have been a sign of bigger and better things to come from this jovial individual. Alas, the release of these three films sounded the studio's death knell, and whether their presence in the company's closing lineup was by design or mere coincidence remains a moot point. Balshofer's rudderless ship had finally run aground.

With the official dissolution of the Sterling Film Company in January came a mass exodus of the talent involved to the far corners of the industry. Max Asher resumed his work with director Allen Curtis at Joker, followed by a return to the stage and occasional appearances in comedy shorts and in supporting character roles in film throughout the remainder of the silent era. Curtis continued directing with a similar sound-era induced retirement. William Wolbert had already moved over to Kalem, and Peggy Pearce to Lehrman's L-Ko Komedies towards the end of 1914. Pearce's departure may have been precipitated by an accident she had while at Sterling, when a needle that penetrated her foot led to a serious illness and extended hospital stay while she convalesced.[69] Pearce returned to the Sennett fold at Triangle in 1916, followed by work in several features for other studios in the late teens before retiring near the end of the decade. Lucille Ward spent the next thirty-plus years primarily in character parts for numerous studios. Arthur Tavares headed for Fiction Pictures and assorted comedy parts including some Vogue comedies for director Rube Miller,[70] and Ernest Shield joined Eddie Boland and Bertha Burnham in a new unit at Joker under director Archer McMackin. George Jeske returned to Sennett and acting for several years before switching over to direction, with jobs at Reelcraft directing William Franey and at Roach directing Snub Pollard and Stan Laurel. Jeske turned to screenwriting in 1926, and with only a few exceptions remained in that capacity for the next twenty years. John Brennan left to produce a series of comedies titled *The Adventures of Hi Holler*,[71] but these plans seem to have fallen apart, and after a few more sporadic film appearances his acting career appears to have ended in 1920.

Paul Jacobs relocated briefly to Majestic for *Her Filmland Hero* and L-Ko for *Lizzie's Watery Grave* and *Little Billy's School Days*, followed by appearances in more than a half dozen features and the occasional short. Jacobs retired from acting in 1918. As for the rest of the Sterling Kids, none of the before-the-camera careers of Olive Johnson, Violet Radcliffe, Carmen DeRue, and Chandler House lasted more than a few years at various studios, Johnson and Radcliffe immediately moving over to Balboa's Kids Komedy Kompany under Frank D. Williams' guidance.[72] Only Gordon Griffith had any sort of staying power as an actor, with sporadic appearances well into the 1930s before switching over to assistant direction and production. Chandler House continued in the industry, and for decades to follow, but in a behind-the-scenes capacity briefly in the 1920s as a cinematographer, followed by more than thirty years as editor in both film and television.

Louise Fazenda found her niche with Sennett at Keystone where her popularity blossomed and flourished throughout the teens, eventually settling into character roles in a staggering number of features in the twenties (more than seventy from 1921 to 1930) and thirties. Mae Wells continued with acting, co-starring in *The Grey Nun of Belgium* (1915) before settling in with Sennett for the rest of the teens, followed by a handful of films during the twenties for Universal, MGM, and several minor studios.[73] Bobbie Gould headed over to Reliance where she made the single-reel *An Independent Woman* with former "Alkali Ike" star Augustus Carney, after which she withdrew from the industry.

Sterling himself led a checkered existence in the industry following his unsuccessful bid for independence. His welcomed return to Sennett and Keystone resulted in *Hogan's Romance Upset* (February 13, 1915) with Charlie Murray, filmed in late January, and *That Little Band of Gold* (March 15) with Roscoe Arbuckle and Mabel Normand. This was followed by a series of two-reel comedies lasting until the expiration of Sterling's two-year contract, which he did not renew. The comedian would reunite with Lehrman briefly at Fox's Sunshine Comedies at the end of 1917, and again in 1928 with a lead role in the director's feature for Fox, *Chicken a la King*. At the end of the twenties Sterling made an effortless switch into sound with another dozen features and several less-successful two-reel comedies. Sterling retired in the early thirties with nearly a million dollars in the bank, but a succession of bad investments rapidly depleted these reserves. In April 1937, the penniless actor announced his return to show business with the optimistic claim

"I'm at the beginning of my second million." Little came of it, however, and in June 1938 the actor was admitted into a Los Angeles hospital for some tests. Two months later, Sterling's left leg was amputated above the knee, and his condition grew progressively worse from that time on. A sixteen-month hospital stay terminated with his death on October 13, 1939 of thrombosis of the veins at age fifty-five; wife Teddy Sampson was at his bedside.

The former Sterling studio undergoing a face lift during its retrofitting for Quality Pictures.

David Kirkland directed several comedies for Keystone before moving to L-Ko in April, where he remained until mid-1917 and a move to Fox Film's Sunshine Comedies. Feature direction followed in the twenties, and a demotion to B westerns with the coming of sound. Robert Thornby headed for Knickerbocker Star Features in Flushing, followed by stays with World Pictures, Famous Players, Fox, and several other companies where he directed features into the twenties, and Frank Griffin headed to Keystone, L-KO, and Fox for similar chores. With the notable exception of Louise Fazenda, none of the other Sterling alumni had any more than a moderately successful career, and few lasted beyond the silent era.

Balshofer fared well with the aborted studio, claiming to have "made something like $75,000" during its year or so of existence. His trip to New York on January 20, it was revealed, was instead to complete arrangements for a new company.[74] An attempt to sign Chaplin a short while before for $500 a week plus 25% of the profits had fallen through when Chaplin accepted a more lucrative offer from Essanay. The studio was completely rebuilt in later 1915, the old frame buildings and stage removed, replaced by a new 100 by 150 foot open air stage and 30 by 50 foot enclosed studio fitted with all new lighting devices.[75] Balshofer now had his eye towards feature production, and Quality Pictures Corporation was the immediate result, organized in New York with Joe Engel and Richard Roland for release through Metro. Quality was followed in 1916 by his Yorke Film Corporation which lasted through the teens, and the Gower and Sunset studio was sold in January 1916 for $22,000 to Al and Charles Christie. Balshofer was experiencing problems with his hearing in the early twenties, and decided to take a short respite from his duties until treatment improved his impairment. Aside from a few sporadic features, his comparative inactivity in the film industry lasted through the silent era. After a single Spanish language talkie, Balshofer eased into a retirement that lasted until his death in 1968.

The Sterling Film Company could have been a successful venture. The quality of its earliest releases and the favorable critical reaction to them would indicate that more of the same would have been heartily welcomed by exhibitors, critics, and the public alike. Unfortunately, Sterling and Lehrman functioned best under the strict control and guidance of a man like Sennett. Balshofer had given them virtual free reign, closed his eyes, and hoped that all the pieces would fall into place. They didn't, and it may have led to Lehrman's departure. Without a gifted director and creative mind at the helm, and with little if any guidance from the essentially humorless Balshofer, Sterling foundered and the comedies that followed lost that special magic with which Lehrman was able to infuse them. Of the non-Sterling starrers, the Kid Comedies fared best, but audiences soon tired of their routine nature and lack of inventiveness. Furthermore, while these films were still a novelty in their earliest days, and audiences found the inexperienced and awkward little tykes "cute" as they hopped and mugged their collective way through their small roles, overexposure and a lack of anything new soon took its toll. The series quickly grew wearisome to the audiences subjected to them each and every Monday. As for the remaining Sterling fare, most of it devolved into filler indistinguishable from the Joker brand and offered the filmgoing public little that was new or different. The fact remains that the Ford Sterling vehicles were the brand's backbone and its raison d'être, and without them life ceased. The brand deserved to die as quickly as it did, and in the final analysis it becomes apparent that Balshofer should never have attempted to break into comedy production.

APPENDIX B

The L-Ko Komedy Kompany, Post-Lehrman: Soldiering On

Upon Lehrman's departure in July 1916, and the ascendancy of the Sterns to full ownership, the L-Ko underwent immediate changes. The Sterns' partner Louis Jacobs was made the firm's business manager, and Abe began calling the Gower Street studio "Universal City Junior."[1] Billie Ritchie, who was under contract to Lehrman rather than L-Ko, departed with Lehrman. Gertrude Selby departed as well, heading elsewhere at "Universal in a more gentle kind of comedy," but after a single short for IMP ended up in a few dramas instead, a stated goal of hers.[2] Only a handful of the more prominent players from Lehrman's heyday remained with the Sterns, Vin Moore, Dan Russell, and Marjorie Ray among them. Phil Dunham stayed on as well, but he was a comparatively recent newcomer, as was Billy Armstrong. Alice Howell, who had by now become the company's darling, was signed to a new two-year contract and would work exclusively under Jack Blystone's direction.[3] As for the directors, Dave Kirkland hung around for a short while, but Craig Hutchinson, Harry Edwards, and Victor Heerman had all departed by this time, although Hutchinson, having directed a few comedies elsewhere under the Universal banner, would return in short order. Noel Smith stayed on, and L-Ko actor Jay Howe would soon be given some opportunities behind the camera, as would Vin Moore, Dick Smith, and Frank Voss, who was given a shot a directing — himself — in at least one comedy. It was reported in August that Lehrman was still contracted to film his five-reel war burlesque for L-Ko, a job that would take three or four weeks to finish, before settling in elsewhere. That never came to pass.[4]

Lehrman's protégé Jack Blystone, on the other hand, not only stayed on, but was assigned the position of Director General as well, and from this time on the more familiar "Jack" would be replaced with "J.G" or "John" in the company's promotional materials — and there was a noticeable increase in those materials with the ascension of the Sterns to full ownership. Numerous ads and articles credited a large number of the latter half of the year's transitional L-Ko releases to him:

> Mr. J.G. Blystone, Director-General of L-KO Komedies, is the man that has been described as "The Man with a million comedy ideas." Mr. Blystone's versatility in the producing of film comedies is amazing. The best answer to his

brilliance in the Komedy field is the endless number of L-KO productions that have brought instantaneous popularity, prestige and packed houses to thousands of Exhibitors the world over.[5]

and

All these L-Ko's made exclusively under the direct supervision of J.G. Blystone, since the advent of Mr. Stern as President of L-Ko: "Crooked from the Start," "Cold Hearts and Hot Flames," "A Surgeon's Revenge," "Tillie's Terrible Tumble," "A Rural Romance," "Terrors in a Turkish Bath," "Alice in Society," "Murdered By Mistake," "A Mid-Air Mixup," "Unhand Me, Villain," "Lizzie's Lingering Love," "Where is My Husband?," "Temper-mental Mother-in-Law," "The Right Car But the Wrong Berth," "Where is My Wife?," "Pirates of the Air."[6]

One senses that the above list played a bit fast and loose with the facts, since *Pirates of the Air* had its special effects discussed in a *Moving Picture Weekly* article a full month before Stern had left the east coast for California.[7] As for *A Mid-Air Mixup*, no L-Ko was ever released under this title, and none of the synopses for other films suggest a possible re-titling. Except, of course, for *Pirates of the Air*, but that film was in release well before these promotional pieces, and was listed as a separate credit in them.[8] And while Blystone was credited for the actual direction of a number of the above titles, David Kirkland is known to have directed at least one of them and Craig Hutchinson at least three others. Blystone was following in his mentor's footsteps here, with the lines between actual direction and supervision of other directors frequently blurred.

Regardless, it would appear that Blystone worked feverishly during this mid- to latter-part of 1916, saddled as he now was not only with direction but with the supervision of the other directors as well. Alice Howell received his particular attention, appearing in five more comedies during the second half of 1916, three of which were the atypical three-reelers. While there was an ongoing controversy among exhibitors over the pros and cons of the three-reeler, one convert to the pro camp made his feelings known in a letter to Universal:

Gentlemen: All that you have heard about comedies not being well done in three reels is a mistake. I write you of my own experience, not of my own opinion. My audience the other night saw your three-reel comedy entitled "ALICE IN SOCIETY" and laughed from the time the picture went on until it was finished. I have been an exhibitor for many years and have played all sorts of pictures, and I can say to you that I never heard an audience laugh so much as they did at your feature. I am converted to the three-reel comedy because it has proven to me that people who come to my theatre want that kind of subject.[9]

For the record, *Alice in Society* would be the last three-reel comedy released by L-Ko during the rest of its existence.

It was close to year's end before the backlog of Lehrman's L-Ko product was used up and the Stern brothers' output took over. The usual Wednesday-Sunday, two-per-week release schedule had fallen apart during this period while the studio was regrouping. Most releases now fell on Wednesdays, but given the unreliable availability of product there were the occasional gaps and switching-off with other companies' release slots.

In a promotional piece placed by Universal that appeared in early November, Julius Stern made it clear that all things "Lehrman" were now history, and that he had a new vision for his studio.

Alice Howell (center) from an unidentified L-Ko or Century comedy. COURTESY OF ROBERT JAMES KISS.

The old adage, "A new broom sweeps clean," seems to have unusual realization in the recent reorganization of the L-Ko Komedy Co.'s forces at Hollywood, California. Since the advent of Julius Stern at the L-KO studios things have been happening thick and fast. Now that Mr. Stern has been elected to the office of President and General Manager he has swept aside all the old time methods of comedy productions, surrounded himself with the most capable comedy people in the business and is headed on the straight road to a huge success. Associated with Mr. Stern at the L-KO studios in Hollywood are his brother, Abe Stern, as Secretary and Treasurer, and J.G. Blystone as Director General, plus a combination of other clever minds not found in the comedy field in this or any other country. The old regime has been entirely discarded. Entirely new and cleverer methods have been instituted throughout the entire plant. The vulgar slap stick has been "canned." The old time thread bare "love in the park — brick throwing["] picture has also been sent to the scrap heap. L-KO'S from Mr. Stern's advent have taken on a new dress. Newer in idea — newer in props, newer in every detail of production and no expense being spared now to make L-KO the topnotchers in the entire comedy producing field. Mr. Stern can feel complimented by the associates who have surrounded him and thru whose loyalty and brains, plus Mr. Stern's own initiative, augur a huge success for L-KO films and for all Exhibitors who are now showing them or who will show them.[10]

With approximately 21,000 theaters operating nationwide and a daily attendance in the range of 25,000,000 tickets sold, the Sterns felt the prospects for their revitalized studio were promising.[11] Stern had outlined his plans for the "new" L-Ko, but a mere two years earlier had given his unwavering approach to dealing with a company's talent, an approach that no doubt would extend to the employees of L-Ko as well:

> [M]y plan of giving aspiring persons a hearing and an opportunity has netted me as fine results as it has those persons. It has brought new, forceful ideas into the production end, and new, popular faces into the acting end. I do believe, however, in strict discipline at a studio — to which the biggest star and director should adhere. A film producing studio, in my eyes, is just like a big business office, and while there are certain conditions that make office rules useless in a studio, I do believe in a firm and rigorous general system.[12]

It would be a new L-Ko. One thing became immediately apparent: Lehrman's stock company had for the most part remained unchanged during his leadership, a "family" of sorts. Patrons attending an L-Ko showing took comfort in the knowledge that some combination of the regulars would be starring, be it Ritchie, Selby, Bergman, Rogers, Orth, or Nelson; it was tightly knit group while Lehrman was in control, his employees displaying a devotion to their boss, and he reciprocated. With the Sterns' takeover, however, the company's method of doing business became an assembly line affair, one with a revolving door at either end.

By the time 1917 arrived, the Sterns' studio was operating close to normal. Phil Dunham now appeared to be the company's lead performer, starring in an impressive fourteen comedies released by the beginning of August. All of these co-starred Lucille Hutton, who was hired as the departing Gertrude Selby's replacement,[13] and at least half of them were directed by Vin Moore, who would on occasion appear before the camera as well; Jay Howe eventually took over from Vin Moore for the direction of four of these. This unit was filled out with the addition of newcomer Merta Sterling who appeared in the third release — *Faking Fakirs* (January 31, 1917) and all of the subsequent films. Actor Charles Inslee joined the unit with the fourth film — *After the Balled-Up Ball* (February 21) — and stayed on for the rest of them as well.

Wisconsin born Merta Sterling had been a stenographer in the office of Klaw and Erlanger and reportedly had managed to convince producers to let her take part in a revival of *The Prince of Pilsen*.[14] Success in this role led to some work in vaudeville, after which she joined up with Kalem in 1915 and appeared in films primarily for that company (as Myrtle Sterling) before moving over to L-Ko and the Dunham unit.[15] Charles Inslee had followed his earlier work at Sterling Comedies with a stint at Kalem, where he supported Bud Duncan and Lloyd Hamilton in some of their Ham and Bud comedies, and at Essanay where he appeared in a few of Chaplin's comedies before joining L-Ko.

On the Trail of the Lonesome Pill (January 3) is a curiosity in that the film revolves around Dunham's visit to an opium den, the bulk of the film his drug-induced dream. In *A Limburger Cyclone* (January 10), Dunham and his cabaret dancer girl find themselves in prison and at the mercy of a cyclone that deposits the prison, its occupants, and the two leads in a heap at the bottom of a cliff. "The wind storm at the close is one of the best things of the kind ever staged," stated *Moving Picture World*, "in fact it may be a pioneer achievement of the sort."[16] We will have to take his word for it. *Summer Boarders* (March 14) fared less well, with Dunham as a paperhanger in a plot that reviewers collectively panned. Dunham and Inslee were a pair of rube gumshoes in *Defective Detectives* (March 21), a film that culminated with yet-another rooftop chase. Dunham's Fire Chief and Inslee's Chief of Police are at odds over the mayor's daughter Hutton in *Love and Blazes* (April 18), and Dunham and Merta Sterling are the proprietors of a boarding house in *Tom's Tramping Troupe* (May 9), the resting place of a theatrical group in town for a performance of *Uncle Tom's Cabin*.

Phil Dunham appears to be fighting a hangover in this poster from After the Balled-Up Ball.
COURTESY OF HERITAGE AUCTION GALLERIES, HA.COM.

The other films of the Dunham-Hutton-Sterling-Inslee unit included *Nabbing a Noble* (April 4), *Good Little Bad Boy* (May 16), *Dry Goods and Damp Deeds* (June 6), *Chicken Chased and Henpecked* (June 13), *Blackboard and Blackmail* (August 1), and *The Little Fat Rascal* (August 8). With the completion of *The Little Fat Rascal*, star Phil Dunham moved behind the camera as the studio's newest director, joining Noel Smith, Dick Smith, and Vin Moore in that capacity;[17] Dunham's only previous experience behind the camera had been assisting Vin Moore on *Love and Blazes*. For his first solo effort, Dunham guided Billy Bevan and Lucille Hutton in *Backward Sons and Forward Daughters* (September 5). Dunham would continue to direct the team of Bevan and Hutton for the remainder of 1917 in *Counting Out the Count* (October 3), *Even As Him and Her* (October 31), and *The Joy Riders* (November 21).

With Dunham now removed from the unit, Merta Sterling went on to star in a reconfigured unit that initially added newcomer Al Forbes into the mix, with Babe Emerson joining for the second and subsequent films as Lucille Hutton's replacement. These included *Her Daring, Caring Ways* (June 27), *A Prairie Chicken* (September 19), *Fat and Furious* (October 24), and *Deep Seas and Desperate Deeds* (December 12). Both Emerson and Forbes were new to film, and while Emerson's career didn't exist beyond the four films she made for L-Ko, Forbes managed to land a few more jobs after L-Ko at Hal Roach's studio in 1924. "Such mere men as Al Forbes help in the comedy to be sure, but the bulk of the work falls upon the rotund Miss Sterling to be gotten away with after the slap-stick and speedy fashion L-KOs are famous for" commented *Moving Picture World* about *The*

Merta Sterling has her arm around Lee Morris in this production still from Cannibals and Carnivals *(01/02/1918, filmed after Dunham had left the unit to direct). Queenie Emery can be seen sitting at the right side of table, front.* COURTESY OF DEBORAH AND CHRISTINA LANE.

Donkey Did It (February 6, 1918), the trio's final effort.[18]

L-Ko's other workhorse during this same period was Dan Russell, with eleven films to show for his efforts by mid-August. Vin Moore co-starred in the first three of these, while Russell's wife Marjorie Ray took some time off from her stage work to appear in the second through fourth film. Actress Gladys Roach took over as the female lead after that, appearing in at least six of these and undergoing a name change midway to Gladys Varden for her appearance in *Beach Nuts* (May 23); Gladys' older brother, comedian Bert Roach, joined his sister for one of these.[19] Vin Moore's wife Eunice Moore — occasionally billed as Eunice Murdock — took part in a couple of the releases as well. Direction of the initial releases was handled by whomever was available, divided among Charles Hutchinson, Blystone, Jay Howe, and Noel Smith, with Smith eventually taking the reins and handling the final four. Titles included *Heartsick at Sea* (January 17), *Spike's Bizzy Bike* (Febuary 28), *Dippy Dan's Doings* (March 28), *Where Is My Che-ild?* (June 20), *Surf*

ABOVE: *Phil Dunham is reprimanded by teacher Lucille Hutton and taunted by student Merta Sterling (far left) in* Blackboard and Blackmail. *Queenie Emery, an uncredited bit player at L-Ko, is in the far back immediately to the right of Hutton.* COURTESY OF DEBORAH AND CHRISTINA LANE. BELOW: *Phil Dunham and Merta Sterling would be reteamed at Century for* Brownie, the Peacemaker *(08/23/1920).* COURTESY OF SAM GILL.

Scandal (July 18), and *Rough Stuff* (August 15). Russell portrayed a shepherd boy in *Little Bo-Peep* (April 25; extant), a heroic lifesaver in *Beach Nuts*, found himself quarantined in a house full of people in *The Cabaret Scratch* (May 2), and in *Ring Rivals* (April 11) reprised his role of "the Irish Terror" from *For the Love of Mike and Rosie*. The creativity of *The Battle of "Let's Go"* (January 24), a military spoof with Russell as General Debility doing battle with Vin Moore's General Concarne, was particularly well received by Robert C. McElravy of the *Moving Picture World*:

> There have been any number of military burlesques since the inauguration of the comic film, but Dan Russell and his assistants, including Vin Moore and Marjorie Ray, prove that good things bear repetition. To follow in the wake of so many previous attempts along this line and still make a favorable impression is no small feat, but it is accomplished in good style in this offering.[20]

For the most part, Russell's films were favorably reviewed, and a reviewer for *Motion Picture News* offered a hint of Russell's versatility and popularity when he stated that "Dan Russell seems to have risen to the point where his presence in any comedy is a sufficient guarantee of its success. With his smiling countenance and generally gratifying presence he fills the bills every time, almost regardless of the story or production."[21]

As for Alice Howell, she was busy working under Blystone's guidance on a trio of comedies, the first of which was in production at the end of 1916. Tentatively titled *The Balloon Bandits*,[22] it would eventually be retitled as *Balloonatics*, followed by *Automaniacs* and *Neptune's Naughty Daughter* (working title *The Worshippers of the Cuckoo Clock*). The three comedies were initially promoted as upcoming L-Ko releases, but the Sterns and Blystone decided to distance the comedienne from the L-Ko output, providing her with a production company all her own. Julius Stern announced the upcoming brand in May as Howl Comedies, but Howell herself objected to that name and finally agreed to the more dignified Century Comedies.[23] The Howell brand was to be released in the U.S. by the Longacre Distributing Company (conveniently located in New York's Mecca Building) on a state rights basis.[24] The first of these finally went into release in September, and while her comedies would continue to be filmed on the L-Ko lot, Howell was no longer a member of the L-Ko family.

Which was most likely a savvy and prescient move by the Sterns and Blystone. Universal had been undergoing some reorganization for the past year, the first worrisome signs of which had taken place at the end of 1915 when it was announced that H. O. Davis, director general of the San Diego Exposition, was hired as the chief executive of Universal's Pacific coast studios. The announcement "exploded like a bombshell this week in Los Angeles filmdom," stated *Moving Picture World*. "It certainly was a great surprise to the trade in general and kept so secret that only a very few on the inside might have had an inkling of what was going to happen…. There have been rumors of late that there has been trouble at Universal City because of divided authority."[25] Henry McRae, up until then the director general at Universal City, got the news in a letter from Laemmle informing him that Davis would now have complete control over the studio and the productions therein. McRae put on a happy face about the change as he packed to take a production unit to the Orient to do some far-removed filming there. Reorganization plans were to stretch into April 1916

ABOVE: *Dan Russell as chauffeur "Speedometer Bill," in* Dippy Dan's Doings. COURTESY OF STEVE MASSA. BELOW: *Dan Russell and some of the participants in his hotel's fashion show, in* Rough Stuff. COURTESY OF SAM GILL.

amidst other rumors that Universal and Mutual were planning to combine their interests so, as *Variety* put it, "the entire picture business [would] be under their control."[26] It was later reported that Spreckels' Sugar had acquired a large amount of Universal stock, and that Davis was there to represent their holdings. "Efficiency engineer" Davis received a tidy $100,000 a year for his services, and set out to earn every penny of it. One of his earliest reforms was "the issuance of an order calling for the entire roster of camera men, players and directors on the salary roll to report for duty at the hitherto unheard of hour of eight A.M," reported the *New York Clipper*. "Naturally, the drastic ruling caused the actor folk much uneasiness and not a little inconvenience."[27] Another of Davis' reforms dictated that the Universal's editorial department was to up its weekly output to fifty reels a week, a twenty-five percent increase over the former forty reels a week.[28] Needless to say, some of Davis' efficiencies were causing some friction at the studio.

As a result of the Universal's reorganization, some contracts were not being renewed, and both Dunham and Russell were casualties. As for Frank Voss, however, there was no need to let him go. Voss had appeared in three comedies during the first four months of 1917 — *Brave Little Waldo* (February 16), *Fatty's Feature Fillum* (March 7), and *Crooks and Crocodiles* (April 8) — and had turned to direction as well for the second of these. And then his career was unexpectedly cut short when the twenty-eight year old comedian died in his apartment of heart failure on April 22. Voss had been a huge sports enthusiast, and a frequenter of the prize fights at Jack Doyle's Vernon Athletic Club. Doyle kept Voss' seat open the night after his death, and the audience was provided an unexpected tribute by Guy Woodward, a good friend of Voss and a supporting actor over at Keystone. Woodward stepped into the ring with a huge bouquet of flowers:

> I came to pay tribute to Frank Voss, friends. A good sportsman, a good fellow and a real man — that was Fatty Voss. I am going to place these flowers before his vacant chair, and I would ask that every man and woman in this arena arise for ten seconds in respect to the memory of Fatty Voss.[29]

Voss' wife of a mere four months escorted his body back to their hometown of Chicago, and there would be no further L-Ko's released with Voss in the cast.

Another casualty of the Sterns' housecleaning was Billy Armstrong, who had hooked up with L-Ko in 1916 with a first appearance in *For the Love of Mike and Rosie*. Some of his other films from that year included the aforementioned *Gaby's Gasoline Glide*, *The Jailbird's Last Flight* (June 21), *Pirates of the Air*, *Ignatz's Icy Injury* (July 12), *Spring Fever* (July 23), and *A Double Double Cross*[30] (August 23). Armstrong's antics fit in well with the L-Ko crowd, and they were usually appreciated by reviewers as in this comment about *The Jailbird's Last Flight*: "Billy Armstrong and Gene Rogers do excellently as the flirts in this while Carmel Myers makes a very pretty foil."[31] There was the occasional quibble, however, as in the same publication's review of *Ignatz's Icy Injury*. In this film Armstrong had the opportunity to display his considerable roller skating abilities, likely a talent picked up during his Karno training. The reviewer complained "that there is just a little too much of Armstrong."[32] The athletic Armstrong was as game as the other comedians on the lot to take risks for a given film's stunts, and usually without undue harm. One trick went frighteningly wrong however, while performing a stunt for a film to follow *Spring Fever*:

Since the finishing of this picture, Armstrong has been working in another in which he attempted to do a wire walking act, and fell from the top of a telegraph pole. At first it was thought he was fatally injured, but he is now on the road to recovery, and will be able to resume his work shortly.[33]

Armstrong appeared in two more films in 1917, *Up the Flue* (January 21) and *Crooks and Crocodiles*, the former most likely the scene of his accident and the latter released well after he had returned to Sennett.

Dan Russell in an unidentified L-Ko, being strangled by Vin Moore. Katherine Griffith to the left of Moore, William Irving on his knees, and Marjorie Ray (Mrs. Dan Russell) with her hand on Irving's shoulder. COURTESY OF STEVE MASSA.

Promotional releases in May shortly before Dunham and Russell's release listed the other current L-Ko stock company members, some few of them holdovers but the bulk of them recent newcomers being groomed as replacements. The males: Charles Inslee, Harry Lorraine, Bert Roach, Chester Ryckman, Robert McKenzie, Russell Powell, "Shorty" Richards, Jerry Asch, Porter Strong, Dick Smith, Charles Post, and Walter Stephens; the females: Merta Sterling, Lucille Hutton, Eva Novak, Gladys Varden, Kathleen Emerson, and Lou Bolton.[34]

Aside from Inslee, Sterling, and Hutton, the most prolific of the above performers at L-Ko was Dick Smith, with Eva Novak a close second. Smith had come to L-Ko along with his wife Alice Howell in late 1914 or early 1915, and stayed with the studio well into 1919 with dozens of appearances in both supporting and lead roles, many of them with wife Howell. Smith moved into direction in 1917 with *Hearts and Flour* (July 11, 1917) and continued in that capacity with another five efforts before abandoning that position and returning to acting in *Barberous Plots* (January 30, 1918). Smith would resume direction after leaving L-Ko and joining Howell in her Reelcraft Comedies in 1920.

Nineteen year old Eva Novak received her first film credit at L-Ko in Craig Hutchinson's *Roped Into Scandal* (May 30, 1917) and would remain with the studio until its demise, her last film the extant *All Jazzed Up* (June 4, 1919) co-starring with Dan Russell, Phil Dunham, and Hughie Mack. Novak, along with co-stars Russell, Dunham, and Mack,

Production shot from Century's Neptune's Naughty Daughter. *Left to right, foreground: Robert McKenzie, unknown, Eva Heazlett (Mrs. McKenzie), Abe Stern, Alice Howell, Sam H. Comly (of* Moving Picture World), *and Charles W. Painter. Background: A.L. May (head of scenario and publicity departments), John G. Blystone, unknown, Louis Jacobs (business manager), and Fatty Voss. From the February 10, 1917 issue of* Moving Picture World.

had all been appearing separately in films for Century as well during this period, as had Billy Armstrong and Merta Sterling. Novak would move into features where she would find far greater fame as Tom Mix's leading lady. Her popularity waned with the coming of sound, but she would appear in mostly uncredited bit parts well into the 1960s.

Twenty-one year old Gladys Varden only lasted at L-Ko for another year and a total of eighteen films, her career in the industry coming to an end of sorts after her departure. She reportedly made a brief return in 1924 with appearances in a few shorts directed for Universal by her husband Erle C. Kenton, and again in a few uncredited bits much later in life. Her brother Bert Roach, after a three year career on the stage, had an uncredited role in *Fatty's Magic Pants* for Keystone in 1914 before moving over to L-Ko at the end of the year. A few more uncredited roles followed at L-Ko before his presence was finally acknowledged in *For the Love of Mike and Rosie* in early 1916. Roach has been connected to more than a dozen roles for the studio before rejoining Sennett in 1918, but the odds are there were many others that have gone unrecognized due to a scarcity of published credits and the paltry survival of the L-Ko's.

Norman Taurog was hired by the Sterns during this post-Lehrman period, initially serving as a property man and actor. He was given his initial, inauspicious opportunities to direct here — very likely due to need — with questionable success: "I made one pic-

LEFT: *This promotional piece for Frank "Fatty" Voss'* Brave Little Waldo *appeared on the cover of the February 10, 1917 issue of* Moving Picture Weekly. RIGHT: *Full-page ad for* Barberous Plots, *from the January 12, 1918 issue of* Moving Picture Weekly.

ture with Hughie Fay, one with Alice Howell, a picture with Vin Moore…and I made one picture with Bob McKenzie. They saw that one, the McKenzie one, they didn't like it, so they took me off it, which happens. That's when I left there and went over to Henry Lehrman."[35] There are no known L-Ko or Century credits for Fay, so it is likely that Taurog was misremembering Fay from one of the later Sunshine Comedies.

There were several anomalies during this period, perhaps most notably the May 6, 1917 release of the Billie Ritchie comedy *Scrambled Hearts*. Ritchie was long gone from L-Ko by this time, and given that the film was a single-reel — L-Ko's last before committing solely to two-reelers — and that it co-starred Anna Darling, who had appeared a year earlier in a trio of May-released L-Ko's, would seem to indicate that it was a year-old film held from release for one reason or another. Darling, it should be noted, was hired by Universal as Anna Schraeder, had the name change forced on her, starred in these four films, and then appears to have faded into obscurity — unless, of course, you consider her role as stage mother of The Darling Twins, a vaudeville act that toured through the twenties into the thirties.

Another anomaly was Sammy Burns, a former acrobatic dancer and comedian who toured vaudeville from 1909 through 1914 with partner and spouse Alice Fulton before moving into film with a handful of comedies for Vogue in 1916. "Sammy Burns shows that he is not only an acrobat of parts, but also thoroughly up to snuff in the tricks of the slapstick art," wrote one reviewer of his part in one of the Vogues. "Many of his mannerisms are borrowed from other screen fun-makers, while others are quite new and excellently conceived."[36] L-Ko took note, and he was hired away from Vogue after a mere four films

LEFT: *Eva Novak in* All Jazzed Up *(06/04/1919)*. COURTESY OF LIBRARY OF CONGRESS.
RIGHT: *Gladys Varden, formerly Gladys Roach, actor Bert Roach's younger sister.*

that same year. His fortunes don't seem to have been any greater at his new home. After co-starring with Dan Russell and Carmel Myers in *Tough Luck on a Rough Sea* (May 31, 1916), Burns would not have another role at L-Ko until early 1917 when he was ostensibly assigned to a unit under Dick Smith[37] that produced a sole comedy, *That Dawgone Dog* (February 7). There was one last film, *Bombs and Bandits* (July 4; not directed by Smith), before Burns moved on. A single film for Nestor, *A Poor Prune*, surfaced in 1919, followed by a number of aborted projects for Long Island's K.B. Clarendon Comedies, Staten Island's King Cole Comedies, and his own Sammy Burns Comedies which never had a release and filed for bankruptcy in 1922. 1920's *Oh! Buoy!*, a short for Reelcraft's Royal Comedies, was squeezed in during this, but Burns finally gave up and returned to vaudeville where he ended up as a dance director.

There were two early 1917 releases starring Hank Mann as well, who was at that time working at Fox. Given that *End of a Perfect Day* (February 14) co-starred Gertrude Selby, this was most likely a holdover from when they both worked at the studio. His other film was *Love on Crutches* (March 16) which, given its synopsis, appears to be *Cupid in a Hospital* with a new title.

ABOVE: *Sammy Burns and Dolly Dimples in* Bombs and Bandits. BELOW: *Chinese laundry owner Wun Lung Woo's back-room torture chamber, filled with such pain-inflicting devices as a "mechanical beating apparatus, feather ticklers for the soles of the feet, and a wash-wringer adapted to taking the starch out of victims." From* Ash-Can Alley *(01/23/1918). Left to right: Eva Novak, Eddie Barry, Eva Heazlett, Bob McKenzie, and two unidentified Chinese.* COURTESY OF SAM GILL.

And then there was Frank Klein, a circus strongman hired by L-Ko in early 1917 to "do all of the heavy work in these comedies." Klein's numerous claims to fame were not theatrical, rather (if the press release was to be believed) "lifting a horse with his teeth, breaking rocks with his bare fists and juggling half-ton weights." For his debut performance in *Defective Detectives,* Klein allowed "a fully loaded automobile to run over him."[38] Since this was the first and last to ever be heard of Klein, one wonders if his filmic stunt soured him to the industry.

The other newcomers to the studio were for the most part unknowns, although Harry Lorraine had been in the industry since 1912. With more than fifty films to his credit, the British born actor had starred for several years in homegrown product before relocating to the U.S. in 1914 where he made films primarily for Lubin. Hired by L-Ko in 1917, Lorraine would make a handful of films over the next year with lead roles in *Roped Into Scandal* (May 30) with Eva Novak and Bert Roach co-starring, and *Soapsuds and Sirens* (September 26) where he starred as dance teacher Prof. Thinem. Newcomer Walter Stephens co-starred in this latter film as a janitor named Nibbs, having recently joined Bert Roach and Gladys Varden in Noel Smith's unit.[39] Based on Stephens' performance in this film which survives in a print held by the Library of Congress, Stephens was one of the less inspired comedians to grace the screen. One particularly unfunny dud of a gag involves Stephens chasing after an elusive bar of soap scooting about the hallway floor, finally capturing it and holding it from then on in his teeth. Stephens appeared in at least seven other L-Ko's including *Props, Drops, and Flops* (August 29) and *From Cactus to Kale* (September 12) before leaving the studio and soon fading into well-deserved obscurity. Future Hal Roach star Jimmy Finlayson pops up as well in a small supporting role as Roach's assistant. There is one amusing sequence that stands out where a trio of old men sit on a curb leering up at Gladys Varden's window, her exposed leg repeatedly popping into view as she executes a dance routine. Moments later, a lineman loses hold of a live wire which falls through her window and lands on her leg; sparks follow! A climactic runaway barrel sequence, while nothing new, is reasonably well done and rather amusing.

Ireland born Robert McKenzie joined L-Ko after appearing in roughly forty films for Essanay over the two preceding years. His stint with the studio resulted in more than a dozen films before he departed later in 1918 and went on to a lengthy career that lasted another thirty years with more than three hundred films to his credit, westerns primarily. Some of McKenzie's L-Ko's include *Sign of the Cucumber* (July 25; extant), *Street Cars and Carbuncles* (August 22), *The Nurse of an Aching Heart* (October 10), *Vamping Reuben's Millions* (October 17), and *Double Dukes* (November 7). The aforementioned films also co-starred Eva Novak, Eddie Barry, and another fledgling actor, twenty year old Chester Ryckman. Barry was brought on in mid-1917, with a year's experience starring in Christie Comedies and, it was reported, some work at Keystone and for Universal's Nestor and Joker Comedies as well, and would continue cranking out films for L-Ko throughout the following year.[40] Chester Ryckman would make only eight films in his brief career — all of them for L-Ko — before being drafted in 1918 and heading off to Camp Rosecrans where he contracted influenza and died shortly thereafter.[41]

L-Ko's one other female addition was Katherine Young, who must have been thoroughly annoyed by the ongoing misspellings in the press of her first name as "Katheryne" and "Catherine." Drafted from a musical comedy show playing locally, Young was touted

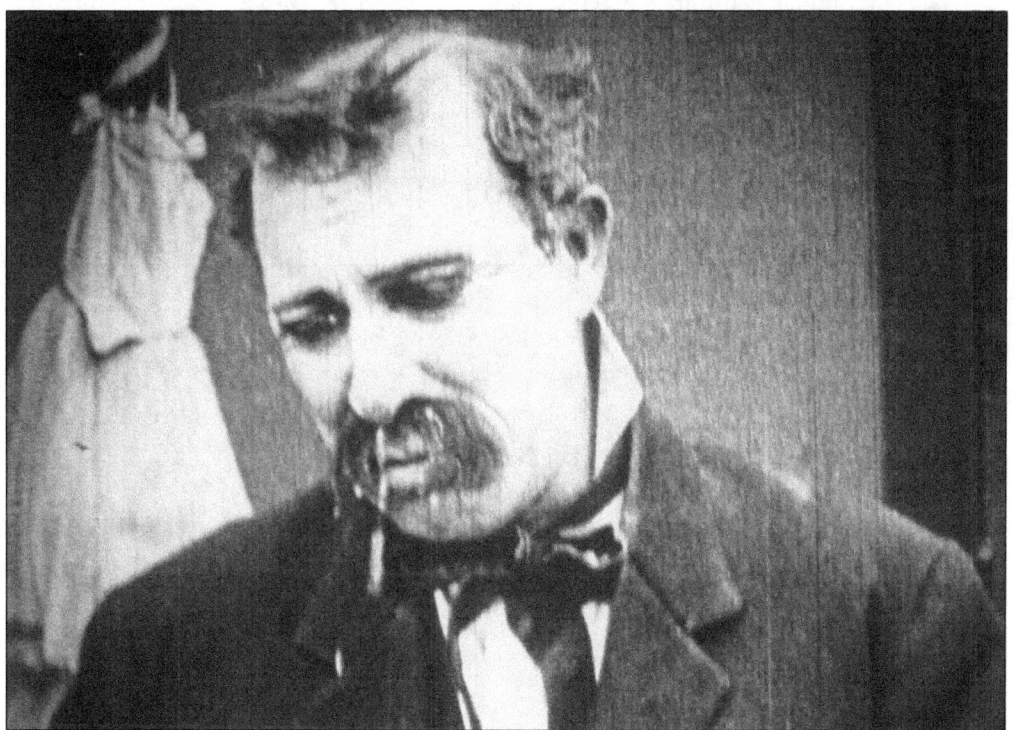

ABOVE: *Harry Lorraine as Prof. Thinem in* Soapsuds and Sirens. BELOW: *Gladys Varden wants to learn how to dance in* Soapsuds and Sirens. PHOTOS COURTESY OF LIBRARY OF CONGRESS.

as L-Ko's unofficial "vampire," playing wanton women in *Torpedo Pirates* (January 9, 1918), *A Rural Riot* (April 24) and, most notably, man-eater Miss Gettem in *Vamping Reuben's Millions*.[42]

Aside from so much of the comparatively low wattage talent that was now featured in the L-Ko output, the Sterns did manage to attract a few "name" performers to its ranks, if only for a few films each. Bobby Dunn was the first of these, who got his start at Sterling in 1914 but quickly moved over to Sennett where he made dozens of films

Production shot from an unidentified L-Ko comedy. Standing at the far side of the pool are Dave Morris (left) and Robert McKenzie; Mario "Frenchy" Bianchi — soon to change his name to Monty Banks — stands at the far right. COURTESY OF MARC WANAMAKER AND BISON ARCHIVES.

over the next three years. Dunn appeared in a trio of films at L-Ko before moving on: *A Hero for a Minute* (December 5), which featured actor Edgar Kennedy in a smaller role, *Barberous Plots* (January 30, 1918), and *A Flyer in Folly* (March 6, 1918). Dunn co-starred in these latter two films with another of the Sterns' laudible acquisitions, the super-sized, Brooklyn-born comedian Hughie Mack. Mack had been hired in a supporting capacity by Vitagraph back in 1913, but over his four year stint and more than one hundred forty films with that studio had worked his way up to headliner status. Many of Mack's later films were directed by Larry Semon before Semon attained immense popularity as an on-screen comedian. Mack signed his contract with the Universal to appear in L-Ko's on August 2, 1917,[43] and worked under director Noel Smith (with James Davis assisting) on his first for the studio, *Hula Hula Hughie* (November 14), co-starring Eva Novak and Rae Godfrey. Archie Mayo, the latest addition to the L-Ko's directorial staff, was announced as

Mack's future director,[44] but that never came to pass. Noel Smith helmed Mack's second release as well, *Torpedo Pirates*, with James Davis and Robert Kerr takings turns directing for the remainder of Mack's releases in 1918. Kerr had been hired away from Sennett, bringing comedian Bobbie Dunn along with him, and Davis had been brought over from Vogue when L-Ko learned that they were going to lose Noel Smith to the draft.[45] Mayo, an untested entity who had been hired as well due to the draft news,[46] ended up with only four films to his credit before he too was called up to serve. Some of Mack's other

Production still from Hula Hula Hughie, *which* Moving Picture World *panned by saying "There is a note of vulgarity running through many scenes which keep this from becoming really humorous; it is too much like a return to the crude efforts of the early comics." Hughie Mack is the huge fellow in the center, Eva Novak to the left of his arm, Harry Lorraine at the desk, and the bald guy left foreground is James Finlayson.* COURTESY OF SAM GILL.

films for L-Ko during 1918 included *Barberous Plots*, and *Pearls and Girls* (February 13).

L-Ko's two biggest and most significant acquisitions came late in 1917 with the hiring of popular comedians Gale Henry and Mack Swain. Henry and Swain, along with Merta Sterling, Hughie Mack, and Bobbie Dunn, were all hired as a result of Julius Stern's decision to adopt the star system, with a separate production unit for each star and his or her dedicated director — or at least that was the plan. Stern's intention was to couple the names of comedy stars along with their respective films in advertising for upcoming releases. "The players we begin with have all established an individual reputation for fun-making with theatregoers," said Stern, "that cannot fail in adding to the attractiveness of L-Kos in their representation of clean, wholesome and inoffensive comedies of the strenuous type."[47] Henry was well established in the industry by this time, with close to two hundred comedies to her credit primarily at Universal's Joker brand before her transfer to L-Ko. Henry was to co-star along with Hughie Mack and, for a short while, Bobby Dunn,[48] assuming roles with such outlandish names as Henrietta Hamaneggs, Pygmalion Prune, Theodosia Thimble, and Prunella Pip. Henry's L-Ko's included *A Flyer in Folly* (March 6, 1918), *Cooks and Crooks* (March 20), *Gowns and Girls* (April 3), *Saved from a Vamp* (April 10), *A Rural Riot*, and *Her Movie Madness* (May 8), the earlier releases well reviewed. Henry's stint with L-Ko was a short one, however, resulting in only six films released over a three month period in early 1918 before she departed to set up her own comedy company for eventual release through Bull's Eye Film Corporation.[49]

Mack Swain was hired away from Sennett, with whom he had had a fruitful four year relationship that resulted in nearly seventy-five films and the establishment of his popular character of Ambrose. Swain brought the character over to L-Ko, along with William S. Fredericks, a non-entity who had only a few stories for Sennett to his credit. Fredericks was to direct, a position at which he had no prior experience, and why he was given this opportunity is unknown. It would appear that he did a good enough job at it, though, as the reviews for *Ambrose's Icy Love* (December 26, 1917), *Home Run Ambrose* (January 16, 1918), *Ambrose the Lion-Hearted* (February 27), *Ambrose and His Widow* (March 13), *Sherlock Ambrose* (March 27), and *Adventurous Ambrose* (April 17) were for the most part good: "An unusually funny L-Ko"[50] and "It is one of the best L-KO's recently shown"[51] were two of the comments, praise of this level not typically doled out during this period for the L-Ko's. Swain's co-star in these films was young Jack Perrin, a one-year veteran of the Keystone/Triangle Sennett comedies who would later go on to appear in hundreds of films in a career that spanned nearly fifty years, most visibly in westerns. Swain's feminine co-star was pretty Rae Godfrey, who previously starred throughout 1916 in Vim's Plump and Runt comedies with Oliver Hardy and Billy Ruge. As the series wound down and Vim headed towards extinction, Godfrey packed for Hollywood and landed a job at Triangle making single reel comedies[52] before Universal hired her in later 1917.

Adventurous Ambrose, a copy of which survives at the Library of Congress, is an amusing tale wherein farmer Ambrose (Swain) inherits the Wavecrest Inn at Seaside from his late uncle Ebenezer Noodlesoup. Arriving there with his wife, played by Molly Malone — Godfrey was absent from this film — Ambrose gets caught up in an honest mistake. Two separate couples were previously booked for upcoming arrival, and as only could happen in a comedy short, both husbands happened to have the same name, U.R. Dunn. Garbage can manufacturer Dunn (Bob Higgins) arrives first and is assigned a room (unlucky room 13!), his wife to arrive later. After Dunn heads out to the beach to frolic with a bevy of bathing beauties, broker Dunn's wife arrives (Lily Loney) and is directed to the other Dunn's room, where she unpacks and then heads out. The first Dunn's wife (Mabel Healy) now arrives and is directed to the same room by Ambrose's wife, unaware that Ambrose had earlier directed the other Mrs. Dunn to that room. When she finds another woman's garments in her husband's room, she naturally assumes the worst. And then the broker (Perrin) arrives, and just as all hell is about to break loose the film comes to an abrupt end; the surviving print only includes reel one.

There are several memorable moments in this film, one involving Ambrose and his wife's arrival at the Inn, riding in an open wagon powered by a goat underneath. When the goat balks and starts backing up, Ambrose redirects it by tossing a stick of dynamite behind the vehicle. Later on, Malone lifts a window shade to watch the goings on at the

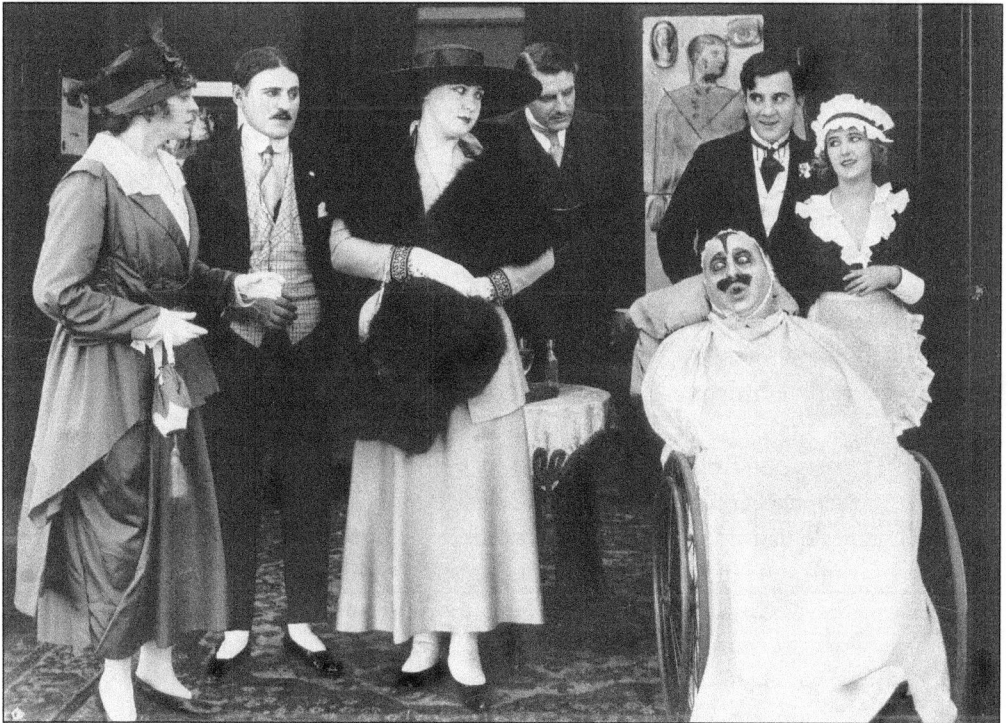

ABOVE: *Rae Godfrey and Mack Swain in* Ambrose's Icy Love. COURTESY OF SAM GILL.
BELOW: *Jack Perrin and Rae Godfrey at far right, hovering over an "ill" Mack Swain, in* Ambrose and His Widow. *Dick Smith is second from left and May Emory to the right of him.* COURTESY OF STEVE RYDZEWSKI.

beach. When she pulls it back down her skirt gets caught in it, and when it unexpectedly reopens it lifts her skirt along with it, much to the pleasure of a bystander. Six year old Coy Watson, Jr. has a bit part in the film's opening playing mailman George Washington Wilkins, delivering Ambrose's letter of inheritance in a dog-powered wagon. While only the first reel survives, it is a crisp 35mm print, which makes the loss of the second reel all the more saddening.

Swain lasted at L-Ko about as long as Gale Henry did, resulting in six films released into early 1918; it would appear that they had both been signed to six-film contracts, as likely as not to give the flagging brand a boost in the minds of exhibitors and viewers alike. "President Julius Stern, of L-Ko Comedies, remains on the Pacific Coast for another month to observe the outcome of several changes he has made," commented *Moving Picture World*. "There has been a general shift of players and directors brought about by the addition of new stars for the L-Ko list, and the new schedule of operations is depended upon to work a general benefit to the product."[53]

Europe had been at war since July of 1914, but it was another three years before the United States was goaded by the Germans to join in April 1917. The Selective Service Act was passed a month later with the goal of building the country's small military force into a large fighting machine. Within a year, 10,000 new troops were being sent over to France on a daily basis, so a lot of warm bodies were needed, and quickly. Hollywood provided its fair share of recruits and, noting that film production in Europe had plummeted with the outbreak of war, provided its fair share of increased product to fill the void. "Exhibitors and manufacturers had found that the condition of public mind created by the war has provoked a demand for comedies that is daily increasing," wrote *Motion Picture News*. "President Julius Stern and General Director J.G. Blystone have decided to increase their forces and turn out more merrymakers to keep 'the folks at home' in better spirits as the tension increases."[54] Comedian Dave Morris was rehired at the end of the year as part of this buildup, starting, as the management put it, a "star series" of his own. *Bullets and Boneheads* (December 19, 1917) was the first of these, "confidently depended upon to give L-Ko's 'star series' a good send-off."[55]

In preparation for this increased production, an 80 by 120 foot addition was built off the main stage, along with a new wardrobe department[56] and an 8,000 square foot extension to the property department.[57] During this expansion, the L-Ko lots were opened up as a drilling area for the 2,000 man strong local Los Angeles unit of camoufleurs, a division of the U.S. Army consisting primarily of former employees from the area's studios.[58] The camoufleurs were to head over to France to design and execute military camouflage.

Carl Laemmle had imposed a temporary suspension of operations at some of the production companies late in 1917, citing several reasons for his actions. "[W]e intend to take advantage of the fact that we have accumulated the largest reserve stock of negatives in our career," explained Laemmle. "The fact that the cloudy and rainy season are about at hand helped us to arrive at this decision.... By suspending operations until we have used up a certain amount of our big reserve supply of negatives, we avoid the heavy loss of having several companies idle on cloudy or rainy days." These points sound reasonable enough taken by themselves, but the overriding reason was the upcoming war tax on theater tickets that left some unanswered questions in the minds of producers, and the suspension would be in effect "[u]ntil we know exactly how seriously the war tax is going to affect us, and until we

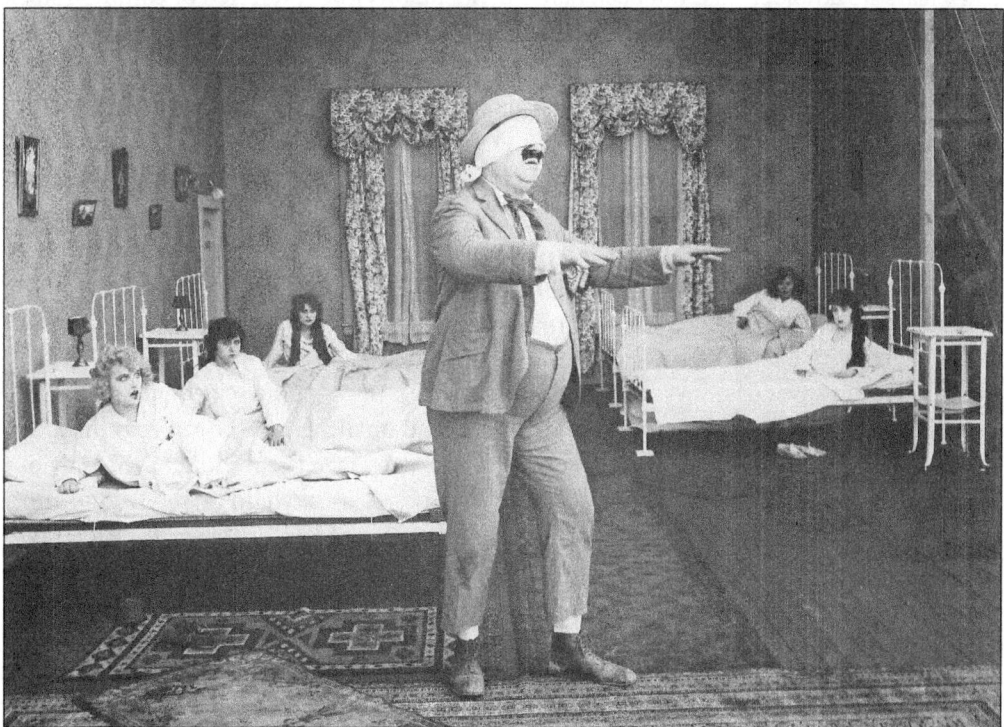

ABOVE: *Blacksmith Mack Swain gives Rae Godfrey a helping hand, in* Ambrose the Lion-Hearted. BELOW: *Blind-folded Mack Swain loose in the girls' dorm at Cornyell College, from* Home-Run Ambrose. PHOTOS COURTESY OF SAM GILL.

are positively convinced that the exhibitors will co-operate in collecting the money from the public...."[59] Universal threatened to do away with comedy productions altogether. R.H. Cochrane explained that the company had "on hand about 350 one and two reel films, which have never been shown. These we expect to release, as usual; and at the usual rate of time this will stretch over at least a year's time. There will, however, be no further production of pictures of this length as a result of the war tax, which will render them temporarily unprofitable." The Nestor and Joker Comedy brands were affected, as were a number of other companies, but the L-Ko seems to have been spared. Nestor comedians Eddie Lyons and Lee Moran had a contract with another year to run, so they were luckier than most, receiving a salary while sitting around with nothing to do.[60] The less fortunate who were not under contract sought employment elsewhere during this lull in production.

By May of the following year, however, Laemmle did a one-eighty in a drive to re-establish the popularity of the short subject, announcing that the week of May 13 would be free of five-reel features, instead consisting solely of serial episodes, comedies, and the usual split-reel releases of *Universal Animated Weekly* and *Current Events and Screen Magazine*. It was an experiment, he said, to gauge the public's preference for shorts or features, or a combination of both.[61] A short-lived experiment, but it probably helped to clear some space on the shelves of those previously unreleased shorts.

By the beginning of 1918 Laemmle was bemoaning the state of the short film industry and his company in general, insisting that exhibitors start paying more for rentals or "we can all get ready for the damndest crash that ever resounded in any industry in the land." Universal's stockholders had not been paid a dividend on either preferred or common stock for over a year, and the short film was much to blame: "An audit of our books shows that in a recent 6-months period we lost $3.08 on every positive reel of short stuff shipped from our plant — not on every negative reel but on every positive. And in that period we shipped 24,810 such reels." 371,000 feet of good negatives of one, two and three reels sat on the Universal's shelves that could not be marketed except at a loss.[62] Only L-Ko and Nestor Comedies continued to be released into the first half of 1918, so it would appear that either there was a healthy backlog of unreleased Nestor's sitting on the shelves or, just as likely, Laemmle decided that if he was paying those two he would get something tangible from them — like releasable product. It's little wonder why the Universal was undergoing reorganization.

At L-Ko, however, 1918 was more of the same, with the Swain, Henry, and Mack offerings filling the bulk of the first four months' releases. Actually less of the same, as the L-Ko releases were now down to one per week, and had been since the middle of the previous year. By May, however, it was announced that L-Ko's releases would be reduced to three per month, with an Alice Howell Century Comedy as a replacement every fourth week.[63] Aside from Dave Morris, Eva Novak, and Eddie Barry, there seemed to be little continuity among the cast lists for the later part of the year. Rube Miller would make a return for a nine comedies, as would Harry Gribbon, who starred in four comedies during the later part of the year that included *Business Before Honesty* (August 21, 1918), *A Pullman Blunder* (September 18), the extant *King of the Kitchen* (December 4), and *Work or Fight* (December 25). Gribbon's a chef, and not a very good one, in *King of the Kitchen*. Most of the laughs in this one — and they are few — revolve around his cooking, with bits involving a live fish jumping from a bowl of soup and latching on to a diner's beard, and a demanding patron

ABOVE: *Dave Morris (left) in* Bullets and Boneheads. BELOW: *Left to right: Rube Miller, Caroline Wright (?), Eva Novak, and Eddie Barry, from an unidentified L-Ko.* COURTESY OF SAM GILL.

(Oliver Hardy) who is served soup laced with kerosene resulting in the expectoration of a flash of flame. Rosa Gore and May Emory supply the so-called "love interest," with Eva Novak stirring up jealousy. *Work or Fight* was a parody of the National War Labor Board's recently enacted "work or fight" rule which threatened any unemployed male with being immediately drafted. Production on this latter film was suspended for two weeks while director Craig Hutchinson was hospitalized with blood poisoning, the result of wounds from an exploding bottle of peroxide.[64]

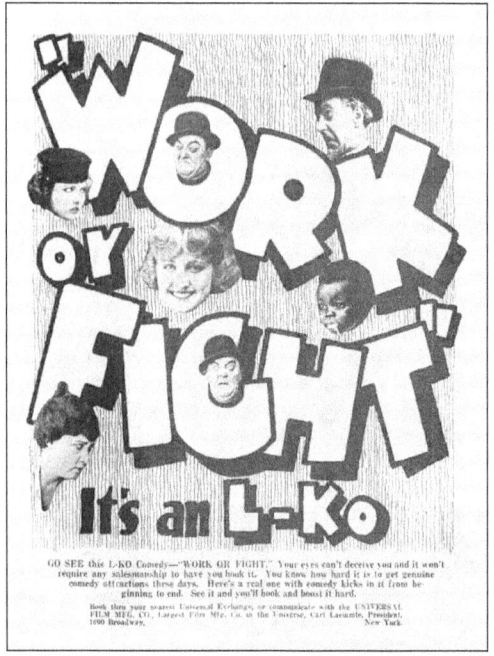

LEFT: *Full-page ad for* Work or Fight *from the January 18, 1919 issue of* Moving Picture Weekly. RIGHT: *Full-page ad for* The Freckled Fish, *from the January 25, 1919 issue of* Moving Picture Weekly, *featuring Oliver Hardy (left) and Chai Hong (center), aka "Charlie of the Orient.*

Two more additions to the staff in 1918 were the comedians Oliver Hardy and Stan Laurel during their pre-teaming years. During a break between his stints in Billy West's King Bee Comedies and Vitagraph, Hardy, a veteran of roughly one hundred seventy-five previous films, had a co-starring role in two of the Harry Gribbon films, and in another six films that reached into 1919. These included *Hello Trouble* (September 25, 1918), *Painless Love* (November 27), *The Freckled Fish* (January 22, 1919; extant), *Hop the Bell Hop* (February 5), *Lions and Ladies* (February 26), and *Hearts in Hock* (March 19). Hardy's director for five of these films was Charles Parrott, a former actor-director at Keystone, Fox, and Rolin who would eventually go on to far greater fame as the comedian known as Charley Chase.

Stan Laurel, on the other hand, was relatively new to film, with only the ill-fated Stanley Comedy *Nuts in May* for former L-Ko trustee Isadore Bernstein, and Nestor's *Hickory Hiram* (April 8, 1918) to his credit. Laurel would have only two supporting roles at L-Ko, one in support of Rube Miller in *Who's Zoo?* (May 22; previously announced as a upcoming

ABOVE: *Stan Laurel at the mercy of the cops, from the Nestor* Hickory Hiram. *Herbert Prior in the back with the mustache.* BELOW: *Stan Laurel strangled in* Phoney Photos. *Rena Rogers at far left, and Neal Burns far right.* PHOTOS COURTESY OF MARK JUNGHEIM.

Nestor back in February) and the other with Neal Burns in *Phoney Photos* (July 3) before joining with Larry Semon over at Vitagraph. In an interview with John McCabe, Laurel commented on his experience with Universal: "I made only three or four of them, and there was some jealousy on the lot from other comedians because I was a newcomer who might possibly be cutting in on their livelihood. In any case, the films were pretty bad...."[65]

Several other former players made a return as well. Phil Dunham was resigned and appeared in at least four films, while Billy Armstrong returned for another eight films. The one fresh-faced comedian to join the L-Ko ranks was the Chinese comedian[66] Chai Hong, frequently billed as Charlie of the Orient. According to Julius Stern (as filtered through the pages of *Moving Picture World*), "Hong has a style peculiarly his own. More important is the fact that he admits never having been filled with the ambition to imitate Charlie Chaplin."[67] Little is known of Hong's origins, but the comment about Chaplin suggests the possibility that he may originally have been the find of a Russian named Benjamin Brodsky, who modestly billed himself as the "D.W. Griffith of China." Brodsky claimed to have introduced film to China, and said that the "Chinese like American slap-stick comedy, but they won't stand for the Chinaman making a fool of himself.... We have a Chinese Charlie Chaplin. His name is Chan and he is a wonderful acrobat. He's the only Chinese slapstick comedian we have ever got them to stand for. He gets $12 a month, but it's so much money the other actors refuse to believe him."[68] It is anyone's guess whether Hong and "Chan" was the same person given the lack of information regarding Hong's pre-L-Ko days. What we do know is that Hong, who could speak three different languages, was lured from his position as a bellhop at the Hotel Alexandria by someone from L-Ko.[69] Hong's first films in 1918 for the studio[70] were *Romance and Dynamite*, *A Clean Sweep* (July 24), and *Nuts and Noodles* (October 2), with more following in 1919 that included *Klever Kiddies* (January 1), *Charlie the Little Daredevil* (January 15), *The Freckled Fish*, *A Movie Riot* (April 9; with Hong dressed in Chaplin garb), *Good-Night, Turk!* (May 7), *A Pair of Deuces* (July 9), and *Charlie the Hero* (August 20). "The small Chinaman and young alligator contribute a few laughs in the first reel"[71] wrote one reviewer, in one of the few reviews of Hong's films; the

Chai Hong may not have been "filled with the ambition to imitate Charlie Chaplin," but you wouldn't know it from this still that appeared in the February 1919 issue of Photoplay.

L-Ko's, while initially reviewed with each new release, were now reviewed less frequently. Based on "the comments he has received from exhibitors on Chai Hong's fun making ability," Stern signed Hong to a long term contract,[72] but his appearances were not solely confined to L-Ko's. One notable appearance during Hong's tenure with L-Ko was in one of Universal's many Germany-bashing propaganda films. Released as a more important sounding "Master Comedy," *A Kaiser There Was* (December 16, 1918) co-starred fellow-L-Ko comedians Eva Novak, Billy Armstrong, and Charles Inslee. Hong would soldier

Chai Hong and Rube Miller are leery of the club-wielding cop while admiring a group of L-Ko Beauties, possibly from A Movie Riot. COURTESY OF ROBERT JAMES KISS.

on in shorts after L-Ko ceased to exist in films for Century and Rainbow, and researcher Steve Massa has placed Hong in small roles during 1919 for Rolin (Harold Lloyd's *Count Your Change*) and Vitagraph (Larry Semon's *His Home Sweet Home*) as well. Hong's career eventually fizzled, and by mid-1925 he was found working as actor Lew Cody's valet and houseman, reportedly with a "contract for life." "Even if I never become a star myself," said Cody, "it isn't every actor who has the satisfaction of having a former star for his valet."[73]

The lines between Century and L-Ko tended to blur around this time, with more frequent releases from the studio mentioning both brands in the same breath. Cast lists of films from the two studios show a large degree of overlap, and by mid-1918 Blystone had relinquished his position as Century's sole director to the other directors working at L-Ko. It would appear that the Sterns were slowly but surely setting in motion the eventual discontinuation of the L-Ko brand to be replaced by their own Century brand, the final nail in the coffin of anything to do with Henry Lehrman. Quality of the L-Ko's was reasonably consistent with those of Lehrman's later tenure, and a perusal of the reviews for the films of 1918 into 1919, while frequently including variations of the words "vulgar," "coarse," "rough," and "knockabout," almost always gave the films average to above average ratings. One notable exception was the review for Hughie Mack's *Hula Hula Hughie* that damned the film for being "too much like a return to the crude efforts of the early comics."[74] Even the films released during the transitional year of 1916 tended to receive favorable reviews, with only the occasional mention of substandard photography (*False Friends and Fire Alarms*) or a difficulty to recommend a particular film (*Billie's Reformation* and *Twenty Minutes at the Fair*), films all starring Billie Ritchie and notably all without a director accreditation. Perhaps the worst reviewed film of 1916 was the Noel Smith-directed Billy Armstrong comedy *Spring Fever*, where in one fell swoop *Motion Picture News* suggested what an aberration this particular offering was from the usual L-Ko releases: "When a company such as the L-Ko, can and do turn out excellent comedies, one is forced to wonder why they should make such a poor picture as 'Spring Fever.' There is no story whatsoever and the business is rather poor…."[75] Even the earlier films from 1915 tended to receive average to above average reviews, which leads one to pose the question as to just why did the L-Ko's have such a reputation for sub-par quality? Abe Stern's now-classic (and possibly apocryphal) rejoinder, in later years erroneously attributed to Sam Goldwyn,[76] was reported in *Photoplay* at this time in a piece worth repeating in full, in that it indicates the general opinion of the L-Ko's. Out of "respect" for their subject, however, Abe remained unnamed.[77]

> Not long ago the middle-aged Hebraic head of a great film manufacturing concern came from New York to visit his Los Angeles plant. Among other things assuredly needing managerial attention was the quality of the firm's comedies, which had become more funereal than funny.
>
> On an automobile trip with two of his executives the comedy subject came up, and the department heads were loud in their derision of the trash that passed as humor. The producer endured their guffaws for awhile, and then turned on them in sharp reproof:
>
> "Boys, our comedies are no laughing matter!"
>
> Still less did he comprehend their shouts at this sally, and when miles had been rolled in on the speedometer, and they were still chuckling, he explained, with exasperated finality:
>
> "Say — now quit it, will you! I tell you again, our comedies are not to be laughed at!"[78]

Evidence that Stern could be funny, but only when he didn't intend to be.

So, why did the L-Ko's have such a shabby reputation? It would appear that it was not so much the quality of the films themselves, rather the borderline suggestive nature of a number of the gags, situations, and plotlines coupled with the aggressive nature of the rough slapstick unfolding on the screen that went over big with the common folk but flew in the face of the highbrows. And, admittedly, Billie Ritchie's music hall routines and the

ABOVE: *Phil Dunham is barely recognizable without his mustache and bushy eyebrows in this bit part from* Gymbelles and Boneheads *(03/26/1919)*. COURTESY OF ROBERT JAMES KISS.
BELOW: *New hire Bartine Burkett (far right) co-starred in* It's a Bird *(01/29/1919) along with Harry Mann (left) and Eddie Barry (right)*. COURTESY OF MARK JUNGHEIM.

unfettered licentiousness of his filmic incarnation frequently brought on the complaints. One telling review of *A Stool Pigeon's Revenge* from 1915 indicates the writer's perceived "improvement" over a number of the films that preceded it: "The L-Ko assemblage has omitted the dirt from all their releases of recent weeks, which has raised their standard considerably."[79] In all fairness to the Sterns, the lowly reputation of the L-Ko films, while unwarranted, appeared to be deep-seated and unshakeable, or at least in the minds of many.

A few of the other new faces that surfaced during this period included Bartine Burkett, Kathleen O'Connor, Coy Watson Jr., Mario Bianchi, Caroline Wright (occasionally spelled as Carolyn), and Helen Lynch. They would appear and, just as quickly, disappear from one film's credits to the next. Bianchi, who had his first job in this country as an exhibition dancer in a New York café, had attracted Lehrman's attention. Recognizing the young Italian's possibilities, Lehrman offered him a job at L-Ko where he acted in bit parts for a couple of years before moving on.[80] Bianchi would eventually undergo a name change and achieve a fair degree of success in comedy shorts and several features as Monty Banks, eventually branching out into direction as well.

The Sterns kept raiding the current and recent Sennett ranks for behind-the-scenes talent as well. Anthony W. Coldewey was hired to head up L-Ko's scenario department[81] and Frank Griffin[82] was hired to direct. By year's end L-Ko's roster of directors included Charles Parrott, Griffin, Noel Smith, Craig Hutchinson, James Davis, Vin Moore, and Joseph LeBrandt,[83] formerly a writer at IMP. Former Selig actor William Hutchinson was brought in to co-star in Charles Parrott's *Hearts in Hock*, but succumbed to an attack of appendicitis which required a hasty rewrite of the film's plotline.[84]

Julius Stern began a big promotional push in early 1918 for a fluid group of nameless L-Ko ingénues who would come to be known as the L-Ko Beauties. A not-so-subtle riding on the coattails of Sennett's Bathing Girls, the idea may have taken hold back in summer of 1917 when the Seal Beach Bathing Suit Contest took place. Sixty entrants from the various studios paraded in front of 30,000 spectators, and four of the L-Ko's eight entrants took home prizes: Eva Novak won first prize, Babe Henderson second, with Gladys Varden and Nell Christie tying for third. Reported as such in Universal's weekly publication *Moving Picture Weekly*, the article's title — "Edith Roberts and the L-Ko Beauties Take Bathing Suit Prizes" — may have given Stern the moniker he was looking for his loose assemblage of women,[85] heretofore unofficially known as the L-Ko Komedy Girls; June Rush and Caroline Wright rounded out the group. The first official word of the group came early in 1918 when Stern announced the results of a questionnaire recently sent out to a representative sampling of exhibitors nationwide that indicated a "growing demand for screen comedies in which feminine pulchritude figures importantly…. The new L-Ko releases will feature girls — lots of them — rather than just one or two players."[86] Stern seized upon this notion that a bunch of pretty girls would boost his brand's popularity and rushed them into a bunch of films to be released one after another. L-Ko followed Keystone director Eddie Cline's lead in clothing them in men's bathing suits "so they could actually swim." Said Cline of his pragmatic decision to switch suits, "And so they'd maybe look funny. I had no thought of sex appeal…. I wasn't interested in girls. My job was making a movie about fish."[87] Sennett, needless to say, viewed Cline's results with a view towards the box office.

Initially billed as the L-Ko Beauty Girls, the Beauties were now prominently added to the cast lists of films usually starring Rube Miller such as *Her Movie Madness* (their

L-Ko Comedy Girls in Bath-Suit Contest
Eva Novak Won First Prize and Gladys Varden and Nell Christie Seconds, at Seal Beach, California

ABOVE: *L-Ko's participants and winners of the Seal Beach Bathing Suit Contest, from the August 18, 1917 issue of* Motion Picture News. *The caption is slightly at odds with the Moving Picture Weekly's article; Varden and Christie tied for third.* BELOW: *The L-Ko Beauties.*

first, and pre-teaming with Miller), *Pretty Babies* (May 15), *Merry Mermaids* (June 5), *A Blind Pig* (June 12), *Romance and Dynamite* (June 19), and *The Belles of Liberty* (July 10; extant) before their popularity waned.[88] Stern even went so far as to have special projection instructions printed and shipped with the reels of these comedies:

> On these the attention of the operators is called to the fact that L-Ko comedies should be run at a speed much slower than the usual feature. This is necessary, it is explained, to give the feminine portion of the audience an opportunity to grasp the detail of the costumes worn by the beauties and the male portion to thoroughly assimilate every detail of the work of nature.[89]

The Beauties were often the targets of censors, with those in Chicago — a puritanical, scissor-happy group — going after *Her Movie Madness*'s "eight near views of a woman in underwear," "near view of woman in bedroom undressing," and "man pulling woman from under bed and following scene showing her in underwear."[90] These were excised from the prints shown locally, and we can assume that the woman in question was *not* Gale Henry.

The Spanish Influenza pandemic arrived on the West Coast in October. As a result, those in power had learned some lessons from those exposed earlier, and hit harder, on the East Coast. A mass closing of public buildings was ordered in an effort to control the spread. Most studios shut down for a four week period that resulted in a forty percent decrease in production[91] and a seven week break in L-Ko's release schedule that lasted through October and well into November; both Universal and L-Ko reopened for business on November 18.[92] George H. Binns, one of L-Ko's recent acquisitions from the Sennett ranks, was one of Hollywood's less fortunate, succumbing to the dreaded illness.[93] Due to the interruption of production, however, the occasional need for filler spilled into 1919. One such instance was the release of *Fools and Duels* (January 8, 1919), a "new" film co-starring Ford Sterling and Peggy Pearce with direction by Henry Lehrman that was a re-titled re-release of the 1914 Sterling Comedy *Hearts and Swords*.

By year's end, several articles appeared listing cast members of L-Ko productions taking place during that period of time. These included names both known and obscure, and some brought in solely for a single production. Among the listed were Phil Dunham, Rube Miller, Billy Armstrong, Harry Gribbon, Mae Emory, Babe Hardy, Merta Sterling, Dick Smith, Eddie Barry, Peggy Prevost, Chai Hong, Marvin Loback, Russ Powell, Harry Griffith, Harry Mann, Eddie Boland, Harold Lockwood, Charles De Lea, "Musty Suffer" alumnus Dan Crimmons, Jack Henderson, Eddie De Comas, Owen Evans, Charles A. Millsfield, Bartine Burkett, Helen Lynch, Loretta Wilson, Jim Donnelly, and Grace Orma. Directors included Charles Parrott, Frank Griffin, Noel Smith, Craig Hutchinson, James Davis, Vin Moore, Joe LeBrandt, and Ferris Hartman.[94] There was increased spillover taking place from the ranks of L-Ko to Century productions, so while all of the above were indicated as L-Ko hires, in some instances these individuals — Loback for example — worked almost exclusively on films for Century. *Wid's Daily* reported in mid-January that L-Ko manager Louis Jacobs had three companies at work,[95] which if accurate would suggest that a lot of L-Ko's directing power was taking place on films for Century.

There were numerous uncredited participants at work as well, both in front and behind the cameras. One such bit player was a young lady named Queenie Emery. Born in

England circa 1899, Emery came to the U.S. in 1907 and landed in Boise, Idaho. A movie magazine contest win in 1915 resulted in a trip to Hollywood where she landed in L-Ko comedies and, it would appear, was assigned to Merta Sterling's unit. These lasted until 1919 when she became pregnant, quit the business, and relocated to Denver, Colorado.

Perhaps our best glimpse of what life was like in the later days of L-Ko comes from Diana Serra Cary. As Baby Peggy, she was the pint-sized queen of Century Studios in the early 1920s, the studio that L-Ko was soon to morph into. While her words describe

Another scene from It's a Bird, *with Bartine Burkett (in doorway), Harry Mann (center), and Eddie Barry (striped pajamas).* COURTESY OF MARK JUNGHEIM.

the studio's physical condition and the working atmosphere during the early 1920s, it provides a very strong suggestion of what the place looked like just a few years earlier, and the mindset of its owners.

> Century Studio occupied a full city block on the southwest corner of Gower Street and Sunset; it had been built in no style at all except what might be described as Early Hollywood. The buildings were mostly made-over barns dating from when it had been a humble farm. Remodeled frame California bungalows served as offices, relics of a slightly later period when L-KO (Lehrman's Knock-Out Comedies) had operated on this site…. Although the lot was not yet ten years old, including the brief reign of L-KO, it was in an advanced state of decay. Once-gaily-striped awnings hung in sun-bleached shreds over windows fogged with grime. The owners-producers toiled in cubicles euphemistically

referred to as offices, but their raw lumber walls, door jambs, and windowsills had yet to be framed, painted, or sealed. A dressing room at Century was nearly as bare as a jail cell. My own — despite the star on the door — was windowless, uncarpeted, and all of ten feet square. It was equipped with a rough-hewn make-up bench and mirror framed in wire-caged light bulbs, an unyielding army cot…, two straight chairs, a curtained pole to serve as a closet, and an antique kerosene stove for chilly dawns and nights when we worked overtime. These

Newcomer Peggy Aarup co-starred along with Dick Smith, Billy Bevan, and a mutt in Let Fido Do It. COURTESY OF HERITAGE AUCTION GALLERIES, HA.COM.

spartan quarters bespoke the studio's philosophy of total commitment to the product. Everything and everyone had been stripped for action, every needless creature comfort jettisoned to ensure expediency, speed, and profit. At Century time was money, and one always had the uneasy feeling that both were running out.[96]

As for Julius Stern, one of the more complimentary things Cary was able to say about him was that "Julius Stern allowed himself no more creature comforts or perquisites as president than his lowliest employee…. His penuriousness was thoroughgoing and even-handed, and while it scorned preferential treatment, it also made grousing about one's own stark accommodations an exercise in futility."[97]

The Sterns' intention to deep-six L-Ko and replace it with Century became increasingly apparent at the beginning of 1919 when *Wid's Daily* reported that "In all this talk of billion dollar mergers, the name of the L-Ko Company is being mentioned by

ABOVE: *The happy newlyweds of* The Belles of Liberty *(07/10/1918; Director: James Davis). Left to right: Eva Novak, Dave Morris, Caroline Wright (?), and Rube Miller.* COURTESY OF SAM GILL. BELOW: *Waiter Phil Dunham is in a panic over beating the odds at the gambling table in* All Jazzed Up. COURTESY OF LIBRARY OF CONGRESS.

the wise ones as the dark horse in the back ground whose decision as to amalgamating will clarify the present chaotic condition in the industry. In the meantime," concluded *Wid's*, "they are now closed, taking stock."[98] After a pow-wow at L-Ko and Century's "greatly enlarged [corporate] quarters" resulting from a move from the fourth to eighth floor of Manhattan's Mecca Building at 1600 Broadway,[99] Julius Stern headed back to California leaving brother Abe behind to manage the office and sales department.[100] Over the next few months Julius and studio manager Louis Jacobs would take turns overseeing operations at the studio while the other headed back east to attend to business affairs.

L-Ko's releases during 1919 were a mixed bag of offerings featuring familiar names along with newcomers such as former Sennett Bathing Beauty Peggy Aarup, Lois Neilson, Harry Keston, and Cub Comedies alumnus Clair Alexander. Director Fred Fishback, formerly with Keystone and most recently with the Fox Sunshines, was announced as L-Ko's newest catch, along with Universal actress Edith Roberts.[101] They were both put to work, but on Century Comedies. The same applied to comedian Bud Jamison, who left Hal Roach's employ ostensibly to star in L-Ko comedies.[102] He too found himself working instead for Century, now in support of the Century Lions rather than Harold Lloyd. For that matter, many of the L-Ko comedians now relegated to the casts of Century Comedies found themselves in support not only of Stern's beloved lions, but Brownie the Dog and the orangutan Joe Martin as

Full-page ad for Rainbow's initial release of A Roof Garden Rough House *(09/10/1919), from the August 30, 1919 issue of* Moving Picture Weekly. *This film was originally announced as an upcoming L-Ko production, and is occasionally credited as such.*

well. Veteran comedienne Dot Farley was yet another L-Ko hire,[103] and was featured in two of that studio's comedies before being consigned to the Century menagerie.

Few of the L-Ko's survive from this final year, but those that do show occasional moments of inspired lunacy buried within familiar, unimaginative plots. Newcomer director William Watson's *All Jazzed Up* (June 11, 1919) takes place at the "Drop Inn," a roadside café with all manner of sausage-related items on its menu. The shady proprietor (Dan Russell) obtains customers by flattening passing vehicles' tires, and entertains them with food cooked by chef Toddles (Hughie Mack) and served by waiter Wilbur (Phil Dunham), dancing girl Dainty Dotty (Eva Novak), and gambling rigged so that the house can't lose. In the event that the gambling is going the customer's way, he is quickly dispatched down a chute that leads to the basement where a huge, muscle-strapped black man awaits with a sledge hammer! The customer is conked, the won money retrieved, and the unconscious fellow dumped outside. The film is rather funny, moving at a good clip and peppered with a number of decent, if time-worn, gags, some of them laugh-out-loud funny. One of the better bits involves a patron's string of sausages, arriving after having been dragged all about the place by a hungry dog. When they finally land on his plate they take on a life of their own, squirming about in a roughly pixilated fashion. A first bite reveals a metal dog license inside, followed by a cut to Toddles outside chasing down a pack of stray dogs. At another point, Russell peeks out the window to view long strings of autos lined up on either side of the road, frustrated drivers furiously pumping up flattened tires intercut with a title card that suggests heavy cursing. Moments of creativity are counter balanced with such ho-hum bits as Toddle's extended struggle with flypaper, stuck first to his hands and then to his feet, and his later sweeping of dust back and forth between kitchen and dining area that ultimately leads to a predictable broom fight with Wilbur. All in all, however, *All Jazzed Up* is a pleasant surprise and painless viewing, and we are fortunate that one of the last L-Ko's survives; a print is held by the Library of Congress.

Abe Stern headed west at the end of May to meet with his brother to discuss the future of L-Ko, although that in all likelihood had already been determined. The future, or lack thereof, was announced in mid-June: the L-Ko comedies had been discontinued, the last of which was to be released in July. The L-Ko comedies were to be replaced by a new brand, Rainbow Comedies, which would be released every other week alternately with the Century Comedies. Universal's weekly publication *Moving Picture Weekly* drastically reduced its full-page ads for the L-Ko comedies, replacing them with ads heralding the upcoming Rainbow and Okeh Comedy brands. The brothers Stern would both remain at the studio throughout the summer to oversee production.[104]

> At the studio owned by Messrs. Stern, quite a bit of commotion is to be seen. They are producing high class two-reel slapstick comedies, animal comedies with lions, bears, monkeys and snakes, and last but not least a serial is being produced. The high class two-reel slapstick comedies will be released under the brand name of Rainbow, and the animal comedies will come under the Century banner.[105]

"High class" says it all. And twice.

The L-Ko studios were promptly renamed Century Studio.[106] Within a year Abe took a leave of absence from L-Ko, having left that company to succeed P.A. Powers as treasurer of Universal;[107] Oscar Jacobs would be Stern's temporary replacement. In August 1920, the board of directors, as represented by president Julius Stern and vice president Louis Jacobs, voted to increase the capital stock of L-Ko from its original one hundred shares with the par value of one hundred dollars per share to seven hundred fifty shares.[108] The company would soldier on for another eight years before being voluntarily dissolved in mid-1928,[109] with well over five hundred comedy shorts to its credit. But it wasn't L-Ko that was dissolved, it was Century Film Corporation, for back in September of 1920 an application had been filed with the clerk of the Superior Court of the State of California to officially change the company's name from L-Ko Motion Picture Kompany to Century Film Corporation. The application was approved by Superior Court judge Grant Jackson on October 26, 1920.[110]

And with that approval, the last remaining vestiges of Henry Lehrman's L-Ko studios were put to rest. Or so thought Stern. Old habits die hard, the press stubbornly continuing to refer to his studio using the "L-Ko" moniker right up until it burned to the ground in 1926.

Filmography

Biograph Company

For the following Biograph releases, Lehrman appearances noted as "identified" in most instances means that his presence in a given film was noted through either the author's viewing of that film, or through the collective identification of the authors of *D.W. Griffith and the Biograph Company*: Cooper C. Graham, Steve Higgins, Elaine Mancini, João Kuiz Viera, and their associates (Metuchen, N.J.: The Scarecrow Press, Inc., 1985). All other sources of identification are specifically noted.

Actor: 1909

Nursing a Viper: *Released 11/04/1909.* 1 reel. DIRECTOR: D.W. Griffith. CAST: Arthur V. Johnson, Marion Leonard, Frank Powell, George Nichols, James Kirkwood, Mack Sennett, Frank Evans, Anthony O'Sullivan, Owen Moore, J. Waltham, Henry Lehrman *(identified as one of the members of the bloodthirsty mob)*

Through the Breakers: *Released 12/06/1909.* 1 reel. DIRECTOR: D.W. Griffith. CAST: James Kirkwood, Marion Leonard, Adele De Garde, Kate Bruce, George Nichols, Charles Craig, Arthur Johnson, William Quirk, Mack Sennett, Ruth Hart, Jeannie MacPherson, Grace Henderson, Donald Crisp, Owen Moore, Robert Harron, Gertrude Robinson, Frank Evans, J. Waltham, Henry Lehrman *(identified in several group scenes set at a ball, in a club, and at a soiree)*

The Redman's View: *Released 12/09/1909.* 1 reel. DIRECTOR: D.W. Griffith. CAST: Owen Moore, James Kirkwood, Charles West, Mack Sennett, George Nichols, William Quirk, Arthur Johnson, Anthony O'Sullivan, Frank Evans, Charles Craig, W. Chrystie Miller, Dorothy West, Kate Bruce, Ruth Hart, Edith Haldeman, Henry Lehrman *(identified as one of the conquering settlers)*

A Corner in Wheat: *Released 12/13/1909.* 1 reel. DIRECTOR: D.W. Griffith. CAST: Frank Powell, Grace Henderson, James Kirkwood, Linda Arvidson, W. Chrystie Miller, Gladys Egan, Henry B. Walthall, Mack Sennett, George Nichols, Frank Evans, Arthur Johnson, Charles Craig, William Quirk, Robert Harron, Owen Moore, Anthony O'Sullivan, William J. Butler, Henry Lehrman *(tentatively identified as one of the brokers on the exchange floor)*

In Little Italy: *Released 12/23/1909.* 1 reel. DIRECTOR: D.W. Griffith. CAST: Marion Leonard, George Nichols, Henry B. Walthall, Gladys Egan, Charles Craig, Owen Moore, William Quirk, Gertrude Robinson, Dorothy West, Kate Bruce, Jeannie MacPherson, Mack Sennett, Ruth Hart, Blanche Sweet, Henry Lehrman *(identified as one of the guests at the ball)*

To Save Her Soul: *Released 12/27/1909.* 1 reel. DIRECTOR: D.W. Griffith. CAST: Arthur V. Johnson, Mary Pickford, W. Chrystie Miller, George Nichols, Kate Bruce, Jeannie MacPherson, Gertrude Robinson, Paul Scardon, Linda Arvidson, Henry Lehrman *(identified as an audience member)*

The Day After: *Released 12/30/1909.* ½ reel. DIRECTOR: D.W. Griffith. CAST: Arthur V. Johnson, Marion Leonard, George Nichols, James Kirkwood, Mack Sennett, Henry B. Walthall, Jeannie MacPherson, Gertrude Robinson, Anthony O'Sullivan, Frank Evans, Dorothy West, Henry Lehrman *(identified as one of the guests at the party)*

Actor: 1910

The Rocky Road: *Released 01/03/1910.* 1 reel. DIRECTOR: D.W. Griffith. CAST: Frank Powell, Stephanie Longfellow, George Nichols, Edith Haldeman, Blanche Sweet, Charles Craig, Kate Bruce, W. Chrystie Miller, Henry Lehrman *(identified standing at an outside bar)*

The Last Deal: *Released 01/27/1910.* 1 reel. DIRECTOR: D.W. Griffith. CAST: Owen Moore, Ruth Hart, Edith Haldeman, George Nichols, James Kirkwood, Frank Powell, Dell Henderson, Guy Hedlund, Anthony O'Sullivan, Charles Perley, Charles Craig, Frank Evans, Adolph Lestina, W. Chrystie Miller, Henry Lehrman *(tentatively identified as one of the card players)*

The Cloister's Touch: *Released 01/31/1910.* 1 reel. DIRECTOR: D.W. Griffith. CAST: Henry B. Walthall, Marion Leonard, Edith Haldeman, Arthur Johnson, Mack Sennett, Ruth Hart, Charles Craig, Francis J. Grandon, Alfred Paget, Frank Evans, Dorothy West, Henry Lehrman *(identified as one of the men at the palace)*

The Woman from Mellon's: *Released 02/03/1910.* 1 reel. DIRECTOR: D.W. Griffith. CAST: William Quirk, George Nichols, Mary Pickford, Mack Sennett, Dell Henderson, Alfred Paget, Francis J. Grandon, Henry Lehrman *(identified as a stockbroker in a second office)*

The Course of True Love: *Released 02/07/1910.* 1 reel. DIRECTOR: Frank Powell. CAST: Florence Barker, Owen Moore, Elinor Kershaw, Henry Lehrman *(identified in the role of a servant)*

The Love of Lady Irma: *Released 03/17/1910.* 1 reel. DIRECTOR: Frank Powell. CAST: Florence Barker, Dell Henderson, Mack Sennett, Henry Lehrman *(identified as one of the thugs)*

A Child of the Ghetto: *Released 06/06/1910.* 1 reel. DIRECTOR: D.W. Griffith. CAST: Dorothy West, Kate Bruce, Dell Henderson, Charles West, W. Chrystie Miller, George Nichols, Henry B. Walthall, Clara T. Bracey, Anthony O'Sullivan, Charles Craig, Guy Hedlund, J. Waltham, Henry Lehrman *(identified as one of the individuals in the sweatshop)*

A Victim of Jealousy: *Released 06/09/1910.* 1 reel. DIRECTOR: D.W. Griffith. CAST: James Kirkwood, Florence Barker, Mary Pickford, Charles West, Charles Craig, Alfred Paget, Joseph Graybill, Edward Dillon, Grace Henderson, Henry Lehrman *(identified as one of the attendees at the reception)*

In the Border States: *Released 06/13/1910.* 1 reel. DIRECTOR: D.W. Griffith. CAST: Charles West, Gladys Egan, John T. Dillon, Alfred Paget, Mack Sennett, Henry Lehrman *(identified as one of the Union soldiers)*

The Face At the Window: *Released 06/16/1910.* 1 reel. DIRECTOR: D.W. Griffith. CAST: Verner Clarges, Henry B. Walthall, Joseph Graybill, Vivian Prescott, Francis J. Grandon, Dell Henderson, George Nichols, Grace Henderson, Charles West, Alfred Paget, William Quirk, Guy Hedlund, Henry Lehrman *(identified among those at the second club)*

A Child's Impulse: *Released 06/27/1910.* 1 reel. DIRECTOR: D.W. Griffith. CAST: Vivian Prescott, Charles West, Mary Pickford, Joseph Graybill, William J. Butler, Guy Hedlund, Frank Evans, Alfred Paget, Dorothy West, Edward Dillon, Dell Henderson, John T. Dillon, Anthony O'Sullivan, Henry Lehrman *(identified as one of the guests at the second party)*

A Child's Faith: *Released 07/14/1910.* 1 reel. DIRECTOR: D.W. Griffith. CAST: George Nichols, Florence Barker, Alfred Paget, Mack Sennett, Gladys Egan, W. Chrystie Miller, Gertrude Robinson, Charles Craig, Guy Hedlund, Dorothy West, Edward Dillon, Clara T. Bracey, Jeannie MacPherson, Henry Lehrman *(identified as one of the well-wishers)*

A Flash of Light: *Released 07/18/1910.* 1 reel. DIRECTOR: D.W. Griffith. CAST: Charles West, Vivian Prescott, Stephanie Longfellow, Verner Clarges, Joseph Graybill, Guy Hedlund, Ruth Hart, John T. Dillon, Henry Lehrman *(tentatively identified as a guest at the second party)*

As the Bells Rang Out!: *Released 07/21/1910.* ½ reel. DIRECTOR: D.W. Griffith. CAST: George Nichols, Stephanie Longfellow, Charles West, Grace Henderson, George Siegmann, Gladys Egan, Joseph Graybill, Gertrude Robinson, Henry Lehrman *(tentatively identified as one of the wedding guests)*

An Arcadian Maid: *Released 08/01/1910.* 1 reel. DIRECTOR: D.W. Griffith. CAST: Mary Pickford, Mack Sennett, George Nichols, Kate Bruce, Edward Dillon, John T. Dillon, Joseph Graybill, Charles Craig, Vivian Prescott, Henry Lehrman *(tentatively identified as one of the men on the train)*

Wilful Peggy: *Released 08/25/1910.* 1 reel. DIRECTOR: D.W. Griffith. CAST: Mary Pickford, Clara T. Bracey, Henry B. Walthall, Claire McDowell, Henry Lehrman *(tentatively identified as one of the bumpkins)*

Little Angels of Luck: *Released 09/08/1910.* 1 reel. DIRECTOR: D.W. Griffith. CAST: George Nichols, Grace Henderson, Verner Clarges, Gladys Egan, Edith Haldeman, Jeannie MacPherson, Dell Henderson, Edward Dillon, Henry Lehrman *(identified as a co-worker)*

A Mohawk's Way: *Released 09/12/1910.* 1 reel. DIRECTOR: D.W. Griffith. CAST: George Nichols, Claire McDowell, Edith Haldeman, Henry Lehrman *(identified as a patient)*

In Life's Cycle: *Released 09/15/1910.* 1 reel. DIRECTOR: D.W. Griffith. CAST: George Nichols, Stephanie Longfellow, Henry B. Walthall, Charles West, Edith Haldeman, Francis J. Grandon, Frank Evans, Edward Dillon, Joseph Graybill, Charles Craig, Henry Lehrman *(identified among a bar's patrons)*

Rose O'Salem Town: *Released 09/26/1910.* 1 reel. DIRECTOR: D.W. Griffith. CAST: Dorothy West, Clara T. Bracey, Henry B. Walthall, George Nichols, Francis J. Grandon, W.C. Robinson, Henry Lehrman *(identified as one of the girl's captors)*

The Iconoclast: *Released 10/03/1910.* 1 reel. DIRECTOR: D.W. Griffith. CAST: Henry B. Walthall, Claire McDowell, Edith Haldeman, George Nichols, Gladys Egan *(Lehrman has been identified as a fellow printer by Billy Bitzer from the* Biograph Bulletin *image.)*

The Message of the Violin: *Released 10/24/1910.* 1 reel. DIRECTOR: D.W. Griffith. CAST: Charles West, Clara T. Bracey, George Nichols, Stephanie Longfellow, Grace Henderson, Verner Clarges, Dell Henderson, Lily Cahill, Henry Lehrman *(identified as a music student)*

Sunshine Sue: *Released 11/14/1910.* 1 reel. DIRECTOR: D.W. Griffith. CAST: Marion Sunshine, W. Chrystie Miller, Clara T. Bracey, Edward Dillon, Charles West, George Nichols, Donald Crisp, Henry Lehrman *(tentatively identified as the boarder's friend)*

A Child's Stratagem: *Released 12/05/1910.* 1 reel. DIRECTOR: D.W. Griffith. CAST: Edwin August, Stephanie Longfellow, Gladys Egan, Claire McDowell, Linda Arvidson, Lily Cahill, Guy Hedlund, Henry Lehrman *(identified as the lawyer's aide)*

Happy Jack, a Hero: *Released 12/08/1910.* ½ reel. DIRECTOR: D.W. Griffith. CAST: Dell Henderson, Grace Henderson, Florence Barker, Mack Sennett (Happy Jack), Lottie Pickford, Henry Lehrman *(identified as one of the party guests)*

His Sister-in-Law: *Released 12/15/1910.* 1 reel. DIRECTOR: D.W. Griffith. CAST: Lottie Pickford, Gladys Egan, Edward Dillon, Claire McDowell, Jeannie MacPherson, Harry Hyde, J. Jiquel Lanoe, Dorothy West, Guy Hedlund, Henry Lehrman *(identified as one of the wedding guests)*

White Roses: *Released 12/22/1910.* ½ reel. DIRECTOR: Frank Powell. CAST: Mary Pickford, Edward Dillon, W. Chrystie Miller, Jack Pickford, Francis J. Grandon, Henry Lehrman *(identified as one of the people at the station)*

Actor: 1911

The Two Paths: *Released 01/02/1911.* 1 reel. DIRECTOR: D.W. Griffith. CAST: Dorothy Bernard, Wilfred Lucas, Adolph Lestina, Clara T. Bracey, Grace Henderson, Harry Hyde, Jeannie MacPherson, John T. Dillon, Vivian Prescott, Lottie Pickford, Henry Lehrman *(tentatively identified as one of the party guests)*

The Italian Barber: *Released 01/09/1911.* 1 reel. DIRECTOR: D.W. Griffith. CAST: Joseph Graybill, Mary Pickford, Marion Sunshine, Mack Sennett, Kate Bruce, Robert Harron, Adolph Lestina, Henry Lehrman *(identified as one of the men buying newspapers)*

The Midnight Marauder: *Released 01/12/1911.* ½ reel. DIRECTOR: Frank Powell. CAST: Edward Dillon, Lottie Pickford, Kate Bruce, Harry Hyde, Henry Lehrman *(identified as one of the party guests)*

Conscience: *Released 03/09/1911.* 1 reel. DIRECTOR: D.W. Griffith. CAST: Edwin August, Stephanie Longfellow, Joseph Graybill, Gladys Egan, Dell Henderson, Alfred Paget, Henry Lehrman *(identified as the stenographer)*

Comrades: *Released 03/13/1911.* 1 reel. DIRECTOR: Mack Sennett. CAST: Mack Sennett, John T. Dillon, William J. Butler, Grace Henderson, Vivian Prescott, Jeannie MacPherson, Kate Toncray, Francis J. Grandon, Henry Lehrman *(appears as the family's butler)*

Priscilla and the Umbrella: *Released 04/03/1911.* 1 reel. DIRECTOR: Frank Powell. CAST: Florence Barker, Joseph Graybill, Edward Dillon, Grace Henderson, William J. Butler, Blanche Sweet, Kate Bruce, Alfred Paget, Guy Hedlund, Henry Lehrman *(identified as one of the club members)*

The Broken Cross: *Released 04/06/1911.* 1 reel. DIRECTOR: D.W. Griffith. CAST: Charles West, Florence La Badie, Grace Henderson, Dorothy West, Vivian Prescott, John T. Dillon, Jeannie MacPherson, Henry Lehrman *(identified as a boarder)*

Madame Rex: *Released 04/17/1911.* 1 reel. DIRECTOR: D.W. Griffith. CAST: Edwin August, Stephanie Longfellow, John T. Dillon, Francis J. Grandon, Joseph Graybill, Edward Dillon, W.C. Robinson, Vivian Prescott, Alfred Paget, Jeannie MacPherson, Verner Clarges, Henry Lehrman *(identifiable in one of the group scenes)*

A Knight of the Road: *Released 04/20/1911.* 1 reel. DIRECTOR: D.W. Griffith. CAST: Dell Henderson, George Nichols, Dorothy West, John T. Dillon, Edward Dillon, Alfred Paget, Francis J. Grandon, Guy Hedlund, Henry Lehrman *(identified as one of the dishonest tramps)*

The New Dress: *Released 05/15/1911.* 1 reel. DIRECTOR: D.W. Griffith. CAST: Wilfred Lucas, Dorothy West, W. Chrystie Miller, Vivian Prescott, Henry Lehrman *(identified as a drinking companion)*

Enoch Arden: Part II: *Released 06/15/1911.* 1 reel. DIRECTOR: D.W. Griffith. CAST: Wilfred Lucas, Linda Arvidson, Francis J. Grandon, Robert Harron, Florence La Badie, Joseph Graybill, Guy Hedlund, Henry Lehrman *(identified as one of the seamen on the rescue ship)*

Her Sacrifice: *Released 06/26/1911.* 1 reel. DIRECTOR: D.W. Griffith. CAST: Vivian Prescott, Grace Henderson, Charles H. West, Florence La Badie *(Lehrman tentatively identified by Billy Bitzer from the* Biograph Bulletin *image.)*

The Blind Princess and the Poet: *Released 08/17/1911.* 1 reel. DIRECTOR: D.W. Griffith. CAST: Blanche Sweet, Charles West, Francis Grandon, Dell Henderson, Jack Dillon, Joseph Graybill, Flo La Badie, Marguerite Marsh, Kate Toncray, Grace Henderson, Wilfred Lucas, Hazel Buckham, Gladys Egan, Jeanie MacPherson, Frank Opperman, Alfred Paget, Henry Lehrman *(The* Photo-Play Journal, *June 1916, p.28 gives full list of cast and characters, including Lehrman who is named in the role of a courtier. Some of the cast members named are at odds with other sources.)*

Actor: 1912

Iola's Promise: *Released 03/14/1912.* 1 reel. DIRECTOR: D.W. Griffith. CAST: Mary Pickford, Alfred Paget, Frank Evans, Dorothy Bernard, Frank Opperman, Kate Toncray, William Carroll, Charles Hill Mailes, Henry Lehrman *(tentatively identified as one of the cutthroats)*

A Beast at Bay: *Released 05/27/1912.* 1 reel. DIRECTOR: D.W. Griffith. CAST: Mary Pickford, Edwin August, Alfred Paget, Mae Marsh, Charles Hill Mailes, William Carroll, W.C. Robinson, Henry Lehrman *(identified as one of the prison guards)*

His Own Fault: *Released 07/15/1912.* DIRECTOR: Mack Sennett. CAST: Fred Mace, Kate Bruce, William J. Butler, Harry Hyde, Frank Evans, Antonio Moreno, Henry Lehrman *(identified as one of the gamblers in the gambling hall)*

IMP — Independent Moving Pictures Company

Beat At His Own Game: *Released 03/02/1912.* ½ reel. DIRECTOR: Henry Pathe (Henry Lehrman). CAST: W.R. Cumpson [John R. Cumpson], Grace Lewis, E.L. Leigh. On split reel with **The Right Clue**.
SYNOPSIS: "Harry Spencer [Cumson] is jealous of his fiancé, Pearl Brown [Lewis], and Pearl is jealous of Harry, and each resolve to cure the other. Harry persuades a friend [Leigh] to dress up as a woman and sent him (her) to commiserate with Pearl. He did it so thoroughly that Harry becomes alarmed at the display of affection on the part of the disguised man towards the unsuspicious girl. After a series of cross purposes, however, the disguise of the

spurious woman is accidentally revealed and he is ejected from the house. Harry confesses his fault and then learns that the original suspicions were unfounded and that Pearl's alleged admirer was only her cousin." *Moving Picture World*, February 23, 1912, p.718.

REVIEW: "A prettily set farce for sure, but one that leaves something in its situation still obscure. There is a clever female impersonation in it. Mr. Gumson [sic] plays in it a man in love and somewhat jealous. The girl is played by Miss Grace Lewis. The man gets his friend and room mate to impersonate a girl and takes him to call. His sweetheart, however, soon sees through the trick and manages to get one back on the jealous lover. It is amusing. The photographs are a bit foggy." *Moving Picture World*, March 16, 1912, p.963

Keystone Film Company

1912:

A Temperamental Husband: *Released 11/11/1912.* ½ reel. DIRECTOR: Mack Sennett. CAST: Ford Sterling, Mabel Normand, Mack Sennett, Henry Lehrman, Laura Oakley

1913:

The Cure That Failed: *Released 01/13/1913.* ½ reel. DIRECTOR: Mack Sennett. CAST: Ford Sterling, Fred Mace, Henry Lehrman, Arthur Tavares

The Stolen Purse: *Released 02/10/1913.* ½ reel. DIRECTOR: Mack Sennett. CAST: Mack Sennett, Fred Mace, Ford Sterling, Henry Lehrman, Nick Cogley, Arthur Tavares

Her Birthday Present: *Released 02/13/1913.* ½ reel. DIRECTOR: Mack Sennett. CAST: Fred Mace, Henry Lehrman, Ford Sterling

A Deaf Burglar: *Released 03/03/1913.* ½ reel. DIRECTOR: Henry Lehrman. CAST: Fred Mace, Charles Avery, Dot Farley, Rube Miller, Ford Sterling, Bert Hunn, Chester Franklin, Carmen Phillips
REVIEW: "This…has quite an amusing idea in it. The deaf burglar awakens the whole neighborhood by his noisy work as a yeggman. A good burlesque." *Moving Picture World*, March 8, 1913, p.998

The Sleuths at the Floral Parade: *Released 03/06/1913.* ½ reel. DIRECTOR: Mack Sennett (ASSISTANT DIRECTOR: Henry Lehrman). CAST: Mack Sennett, Fred Mace, Mabel Normand, Ford Sterling, Beverly Griffith (Henry "Pathé" Lehrman)

The Two Widows: *Released 03/13/1913.* ½ reel. DIRECTOR: Henry Lehrman. CAST: Ford Sterling, Dot Farley, Evelyn Quick, Bert Hunn, Chester Franklin, Hale Studebaker, Arthur Tavares
REVIEW: "A hurly-burly plot, in which Schnitzel has trouble in wedding the right widow." *Moving Picture World*, March 22, 1913, p.1222

Foiling Fickle Father: *Released 03/13/1913.* ½ reel. DIRECTOR: Henry Lehrman. CAST: Mabel Normand
REVIEW: "Father and son love the same girl, but the son palms off another on dad, getting Mabel for himself. Rather amusing." *Moving Picture World*, March 22, 1913, p.1222

Love and Pain: *Released 03/17/1913.* ½ reel. DIRECTOR: Henry Lehrman. CAST: Ford Sterling, Dot Farley, Nick Cogley, Arthur Tavares
REVIEW: "Another case of extreme farce, which has funny moments…. As a whole, the reel is successful, of its type." *Moving Picture World*, March 22, 1913, p.1222
"['Love and Pain' does] not appeal to the writer. The comedy is much too forced, and the farcical nature in which the Keystone comedies are carried out savor too strongly of an imitation of the poorer class of European farce-comedies." *Moving Picture News*, March 15, 1913, p.17

Her New Beau: *Released 03/31/1913.* ½ reel. DIRECTOR: Henry Lehrman. CAST: Mabel Normand, Fred Mace, Mack Sennett
REVIEW: "Mack Sennett and Fred Mace in a series of park scenes, in which there is more action than plot." *Moving Picture World*, April 5, 1913, p.50

The Land Salesman: *Released 04/03/1913.* ½ reel. DIRECTOR: Henry Lehrman. CAST: Ford Sterling
REVIEW: "This…gives a slight story in connection with stump blasting scenes. The blasting is very interesting." *Moving Picture World*, April 5, 1913, p.50

Father's Choice: *Released 04/10/1913.* ½ reel. DIRECTOR: Henry Lehrman. CAST: Mabel Normand, Fred Mace, Ford Sterling
REVIEW: "This…shows us how Fred Mace and Mabel Normand black up to deceive the irate parent who opposes their marriage. Fairly interesting." *Moving Picture World*, April 19, 1913, p.282

Murphy's I.O.U.: *Released 04/17/1913.* ½ reel. DIRECTOR: Henry "Pathé" Lehrman. CAST: Fred Mace, Mack Sennett, Dot Farley, Henry "Pathé" Lehrman, Nick Cogley
REVIEW: "A fair, half-reel comedy, in which Murphy, a policeman, gives his wife's jewels to a creditor, and learns to regret it. His wife pursues him and finally procures her jewels again." *Moving Picture World*, April 19, 1913, p.282

A Dollar Did It: *Released 04/17/1913.* ½ reel. DIRECTOR: Henry Lehrman. CAST: Fred Mace, Nick Cogley, Dot Farley, Laura Oakley
REVIEW: "This…is better than ['Murphy's I.O.U.']. It has many uproarious moments of the slapstick variety." *Moving Picture World*, April 19, 1913, p.282

Cupid in a Dental Parlor: *Released 04/21/1913.* ½ reel. DIRECTOR: Henry Lehrman. CAST: Fred Mace, Evelyn Quick, Charles Avery, Joseph Swickard
REVIEW: "A short reel, in which the love episodes occur in a dental parlor. The girl is the dentist's daughter. Lots of action but a slight plot." *Moving Picture World*, April 26, 1913, p.381

Bangville Police: *Released 04/24/1913.* ½ reel. DIRECTOR: Henry Lehrman. CAST: Fred Mace, Mabel Normand, Nick Cogley, Dot Farley, Charles Avery, Rube Miller, Edgar Kennedy, Jack Leonard, Fred Happ, Raymond Hatton
REVIEW: "More laughable absurdities, in which Fred Mace appears as a police captain in a home-made automobile. As a whole, this reel is very pleasing and full of laughs." *Moving Picture World*, April 26, 1913, p.381

Algy On the Force: *Released 05/05/1913.* ½ reel. DIRECTOR: Henry Lehrman. CAST: Fred Mace, Nick Cogley, Dot Farley, Ed Kennedy, Charles Avery
REVIEW: "Fred Mace as Algy, on the police force, gets tangled up and arrests the new mayor. There is some amusement in this." *Moving Picture World*, May 10, 1913, p.597

That Dark Town Belle: *Released 05/08/1913.* ½ reel. DIRECTOR: Henry Lehrman. CAST: Fred Mace, Charles Avery
REVIEW: "A half reel, showing Fred Mace as a negro barber. He has many rows with the dusky wooers who come to see his flirtatious intended. Not especially interesting." *Moving Picture World*, May 3, 1913, p.489

'Twixt Love and Fire: *Released 05/19/1913.* ½ reel. DIRECTOR: Henry Lehrman. CAST: Charles Avery, Edgar Kennedy (not to be confused with the George Nichols-directed 1-reel film starring Roscoe Arbuckle)
REVIEW: "In this half-reel…there is a lot of hilarity. You can feel the humor coming up as situations progress and the general havoc wrought by the jealous husband toward the close is very funny. It is exceptionally good of its type." *Moving Picture World*, May 17, 1913, p.706

Toplitsky and Company: *Released 05/26/1913.* 1 reel. DIRECTOR: Henry Lehrman. CAST: Ford Sterling, Nick Cogley, Alice Davenport, Raymond Hatton, Edgar Kennedy, Charles Avery, Bill Hauber, Rube Miller, Bert Hunn, Jack Leonard, Beverly Griffith
REVIEW: "This is a knockabout comedy, in which one Jew clothing merchant falls in love with his partner's wife. A live bear appears in the latter part of the film and some scenes are taken in a bath house. The humor, however, does not come up very strongly." *Moving Picture World*, May 31, 1913, p.921

The Gangsters: *Released 05/29/1913.* 1 reel. DIRECTOR: Henry Lehrman. CAST: Fred Mace, Nick Cogley, Roscoe Arbuckle, Hank Mann, Charles Avery, Bill Hauber, Edgar Kennedy, Evelyn Quick
REVIEW: "Fred Mace appears as the leader of a gang of toughs, who make things lively for the police force. A favorite pastime of the gang is stripping trousers from the members of the force. This renders the film a little rough for presentation in some houses. There are humorous moments, but the film does not show the company at its best." *Moving Picture World*, May 31, 1913, p.922

Passions — He Had Three: *Released 06/05/1913.* ½ reel. DIRECTOR: Henry Lehrman. CAST: Roscoe Arbuckle, Beatrice Van, Charles Avery, Nick Cogley, Alice Davenport, Rube Miller
REVIEW: "The fat boy again appears in this. The milking scene will not appeal to refined audiences. There is not much motive to the story…." *Moving Picture World*, June 7, 1913, p.1033

Help! Help! Hydrophobia!: *Released 06/05/1913.* ½ reel. DIRECTOR: Henry Lehrman. CAST: Roscoe Arbuckle, Beatrice Van, Nick Cogley
REVIEW: "Some mad dogs and a scared fat boy combine to bring about a series of wild happenings in this half reel. Trained Boston bulldogs are employed to good advantage in this." *Moving Picture World*, June 7, 1913, p.1033

Feeding Time: *Released 06/09/1913.* ½ reel. DIRECTOR: Henry Lehrman. Educational short subject showing a visit to an alligator farm
REVIEW: "This…gives an interesting view of the way alligators are fed." *Moving Picture World*, June 14, 1913, p.1138

The Tale of a Black Eye: *Released 06/19/1913.* ½ reel. DIRECTOR: Henry Lehrman. CAST: Fred Mace, Alice Davenport
REVIEW: "A half-reel comedy in which Fred Mace appears as a flirtatious married man. He is thrown out of a department store and gets a black eye. Later, he is humiliated by seeing himself in moving pictures in company with his wife. Quite entertaining." *Moving Picture World*, June 21, 1913, p.1254

Out and In: *Released 06/19/1913.* ⅓ reel. DIRECTOR: Henry Lehrman. CAST: Ford Sterling, Edgar Kennedy, Rube Miller, Charles Avery, Dave "Andy" Anderson
REVIEW: "This…shows Ford Sterling as an escaped convict. He eludes the officers and enjoys a straw ride, but is recaptured. Very slight." *Moving Picture World*, June 21, 1913, p.1253

For Love of Mabel: *Released 06/30/1913.* 1 reel. DIRECTOR: Henry Lehrman. CAST: Mabel Normand, Roscoe Arbuckle

Love and Rubbish: *Released 07/14/1913.* 1 reel. DIRECTOR: Henry Lehrman. CAST: Ford Sterling, Charles Avery, Virginia Kirtley, Dave "Andy" Anderson, Alice Davenport, Roscoe Arbuckle, Edgar Kennedy, Bill Hauber, Paul Jacobs
REVIEW: "Ford Sterling appears in this as Mr. Fickle. He flirts with women in the park and starts considerable trouble. His rival rides down hill in a barrel into the lake. The children thumbing their noses at the close was a bad piece of business in an otherwise fairly good reel. Many exhibitors will prefer to cut this off." *Moving Picture World*, July 19, 1913, p.321

The Peddler: *Released 07/21/1913.* ½ reel. DIRECTOR: Henry Lehrman. CAST: Ford Sterling, Henry "Pathé" Lehrman
REVIEW: "This…shows Ford Sterling as a peddler. The action is vulgar in this and it is scarcely the thing for a mixed audience." *Moving Picture World*, July 26, 1913, p.429

Love and Courage: *Released 07/21/1913.* ½ reel. DIRECTOR: Henry Lehrman. CAST: Roscoe Arbuckle, Mabel Normand
REVIEW: "Mabel's lovers become involved in a running fight. There are touches of vulgarity in this which might well have been avoided." *Moving Picture World*, July 26, 1913, p.429

Just Kids: *Released 07/28/1913.* 1 reel. DIRECTOR: Henry Lehrman. CAST: Gordon Griffith, Thelma Salter, Paul Jacobs, Charles Avery, Edgar Kennedy, Ford Sterling, Alice Davenport
REVIEW: "Quite an amusing story, worked out by child actors until toward the close. The boys are rivals for the little girl and fight over her. Later her doll gets into the pond and the sailor proves himself a hero by rescuing it. A pleasing comedy." *Moving Picture World*, August 2, 1913, p.537

Professor Bean's Removal: *Released 07/31/1913.* 1 reel. DIRECTOR: Henry Lehrman. CAST: Mabel Normand, Ford Sterling, Roscoe Arbuckle
REVIEW: "Quite an amusing number, in the rough style of this company's well-known nonsense. Mabel and Ford practice so violently on their trombones that the neighbors move the house one evening. An actual moving house is shown, and it is some time before the audience learns what is going on. Something new and different, without any particular offensiveness." *Moving Picture World*, August 9, 1913, p.637

A Chip Off the Old Block: *Released 08/14/1913.* 1 reel. DIRECTOR: Henry Lehrman. CAST: Nick Cogley, Gordon Griffith, Hank Mann, Bert Hunn, George Jeske
REVIEW: "This reel begins with rather neat flirtation between a widow and a widower, and a separate flirtation between their two children. The four meet at the beach later and the children begin trying out the various 'concessions.' The Dippy Dan finally claims their attention and quite a novel comedy situation results. For light nonsense of an inoffensive sort this is quite enjoyable." *Moving Picture World*, September 23, 1913, p.845

The New Baby: *Released 09/04/1913.* 1 reel. DIRECTOR: Henry Lehrman. CAST: Nick Cogley, Gordon Griffith, Paul Jacobs
REVIEW: "There is quite a little laughter brought out by this, but the humor is of a very coarse grained variety. It concerns the arrival of a new baby in the home of a Jewish family, the other children being greatly put out over the occurrence." *Moving Picture World*, September 20, 1913, p.1285

Mother's Boy: *Released 09/25/1913.* 1 reel. DIRECTOR: Henry Lehrman. CAST: Roscoe Arbuckle, Alice Davenport, Nick Cogley, Bill Hauber, Billy Gilbert, Edgar Kennedy, Al St. John, George Jeske
REVIEW: "The Fat Boy smokes a cigarette in bed and sets the house on fire. Later several love affairs develop; a neighborhood row ensues; two bear chase the combatants up a telephone pole. The Fat Boy hangs out on the wires with a remarkable indifference to life and limb. Later the police force appears and the officers climb the pole. A good rough and tumble number, free from offense." *Moving Picture World*, September 27, 1913, pp.1393-1394

The Abalone Industry: *Released 10/06/1913.* ½ reel. DIRECTOR: Henry Lehrman. Educational short subject showing abalone divers at work
REVIEW: "Interesting and instructive views of the abalone fields, where the valuable shell fish are pried loose from their rocks and manufactured into ornaments…. A good number." *Moving Picture World*, October 18, 1913, p.265

Two Old Tars: *Released 10/20/1913.* 1 reel. DIRECTOR: Henry Lehrman. CAST: Roscoe Arbuckle, Nick Cogley
REVIEW: "One of the Keystone laugh producers which would make a confirmed dyspeptic forget his troubles. The rescue of the drowning man with a derrick was most ludicrous, and the antics of the police force in the ocean also brought laughter. A good release." *Moving Picture World*, October 25, 1913, p.381

Our Children: *Released 11/17/1913.* 1 reel. DIRECTOR: Henry Lehrman. CAST: Paul Jacobs, Gordon Griffith, Thelma Salter, Matty Roubert, Charlotte Fitzpatrick
REVIEW: "A story played entirely by children, containing some coarse spots and nothing of a particularly commendable nature." *Moving Picture World*, November 29, 1913, p.1009

Cohen Saves the Flag: *Released 11/27/1913.* 1 reel. DIRECTOR: Mack Sennett. CAST: Ford Sterling, Mabel Normand, Henry Lehrman, Nick Cogley, Dot Farley, Laura Oakley, Evelyn Quick, Charles Avery, Bill Hauber, Bert Hunn, Beverly Griffith, Chester Franklin
REVIEW: "A burlesque on war, in which Ford Sterling appears as a Yiddish private. The photography is not very good in places, and while there are humorous moments, the story is not very strong. A few of the scenes will get laughs." *Moving Picture World*, November 29, 1913, p.1009

The Woman Haters: *Released 12/01/1913.* 1 reel. DIRECTOR: Henry Lehrman. CAST: Roscoe Arbuckle, Nick Cogley
REVIEW: "Two old salts, baching it together, become acquainted with their lady neighbors. Gossip ensues and a row follows, in which women pull hair and there is a general mixup. This is fairly amusing." *Moving Picture World*, December 6, 1913, p.1153

San Francisco Celebration: *Released 12/04/1913.* ⅓ reel. DIRECTOR: Henry Lehrman. Educational short subject showing San Francisco's Portola Festival
REVIEW: "Views of the manner in which the Golden Gate city celebrated the anniversary of Balboa's discovery. Views of a characteristic West Coast parade are shown. A pleasing half reel." *Moving Picture World*, December 6, 1913, p.1152

The Horse Thief: *Released 12/11/1913.* 1 reel. DIRECTOR: Henry Lehrman. CAST: Gordon Griffith, Thelma Salter, Matty Roubert, Charlotte Fitzpatrick
REVIEW: "In which some children get a hobby horse and two of them make away with it. Ten cents is offered for the capture of the thief. The trial scene was amusing. Quite an entertaining little offering of the kind." *Moving Picture World*, December 13, 1913, p.1280

Protecting San Francisco from Fire: *Released 12/18/1913.* ½ reel. DIRECTOR: Henry Lehrman. Educational short subject showing San Francisco's fire department at work
REVIEW: "Views of the fire-fighting apparatus employed in the Golden Gate city. The view of the fire boat in action was particularly good." *Moving Picture World*, December 20, 1913, p.1413

The Speed Kings: *Released 10/30/1913.* 1 reel. DIRECTOR: Wilfred Lucas. CAST: Mabel Normand, Ford Sterling, Earl Cooper, Teddy Tetzlaff, Roscoe Arbuckle, Barney Oldfield, Paul Jacobs, Edgar Kennedy, Billy Gilbert, Bert Hunn, Henry Lehrman *(congratulatory man in crowd)*

The Champion: *Released 12/27/1913.* 1 reel. DIRECTOR: Henry Lehrman. CAST: Mabel Normand, Henry "Pathé" Lehrman
REVIEW: "A first-rate horse racing number, in which Mabel Normand plays the part of the driver after her lover has been bound and hidden away by the villain and his tools. The police force is called out and the film runs along in the usual burlesque style for which this company is noted. In this instance both the story and the settings are exceptionally interesting." *Moving Picture World*, December 27, 1913, p.1545

1914:

Too Many Brides: *Released 01/19/1914.* 1 reel. DIRECTOR: Mack Sennett and Henry Lehrman. CAST: Ford Sterling, Mack Swain, Peggy Pearce, Hank Mann, Charles Avery, Grover Ligon
REVIEW: "Sterling courts a number of sweethearts at the same time and succeeds in stirring up a lot of trouble for himself. The chase scene is full of funny antics and moves on to a laughable close." *Moving Picture World*, January 24, 1914, p.414

Making a Living: *Released 02/02/1914.* 1 reel. DIRECTOR: Henry Lehrman. CAST: Charlie Chaplin, Virginia Kirtley, Henry "Pathé" Lehrman, Alice Davenport, Chester Conklin, Emma Clifton, Billy Gilbert, Charles Inslee, Eddie Nolan, Beverly Griffith, Grover Ligon, Edgar Kennedy
REVIEW: "The clever player who takes the role of nervy and very nifty sharper in this picture is a comedian of the first water, who acts like one of Nature's own naturals. It is so full of action that it is indescribable, but so much of it is fresh and unexpected that a laugh will be going all the time almost. It is foolish-funny stuff that will make even the sober minded laugh, but people out for an evening's good time will howl." *Moving Picture World*, February 7, 1914, p.678

Kid Auto Races at Venice, Cal.: *Released 02/07/1914.* ½ reel. DIRECTOR: Henry Lehrman. CAST: Charlie Chaplin, Henry "Pathé" Lehrman

Mabel's Strange Predicament: *Released 02/09/1914.* 2 reels. DIRECTOR: Mabel Normand. CO-DIRECTORS: Mack Sennett and Henry Lehrman. CAST: Mabel Normand, Charlie Chaplin, Chester Conklin, Alice Davenport, Harry McCoy, Al St. John, Billy Gilbert, Bill Hauber, Frank Cooley, Henry Lehrman *(Brent Walker asserts that only Normand was involved in the direction of this film)*

Baffles, the Gentleman Burglar: *Released 02/16/1914.* 2 reels. DIRECTOR: Henry Lehrman. CAST: Wilfred Lucas, Ford Sterling, May Wells, Peggy Pearce
REVIEW: "In which Ford Sterling appears as chief of police. The gentleman burglar robs police officers at will and the whole plot hinges on the efforts to capture him. This makes a very good burlesque of a presentable sort. It is entirely nonsensical and contains many laughable situations. A good offering of its kind." *Moving Picture World*, February 28, 1914, p.1089

A Thief Catcher: *Released 02/19/1914.* 1 reel. DIRECTOR: Ford Sterling. CAST: Ford Sterling, Edgar Kennedy, Mack Swain, Charles Chaplin, Henry Lehrman

Between Showers: *Released 02/28/1914.* 1 reel. DIRECTOR: Henry Lehrman. CAST: Charlie Chaplin, Ford Sterling, Chester Conklin, Emma Clifton, Eddie Nolan
REVIEW: "Ford Sterling and the new English comedian of the Keystone Company, play the leads in this comedy. A crook (Ford Sterling) changes umbrellas with a policeman, and then loans it to a girl who insists later that it is hers. The crook recovers 'his' property, but the girl sends a friend to get it back. The friend is successful, but the cop arrives, and on seeing him the crook refuses the contrivance. They are all arrested." *Motion Picture News*, March 7, 1914, p.40

A Film Johnnie: *Released 03/02/1914.* 1 reel. DIRECTOR: George Nichols. SCREENPLAY: Craig Hutchinson. CAST: Charles Chaplin, Peggy Pearce, Edgar Kennedy, Hampton Del Ruth, Roscoe Arbuckle, Ford Sterling, Henry Lehrman, Minta Durfee, Hank Mann, George Jeske, Billy Gilbert, Harry McCoy, Frank Opperman, Bill Hauber, George Nichols, Bert Hunn, Dan Albert, Walter Wright

How Villains Are Made: *Released 03/14/1914.* 2 reels. DIRECTOR: Henry Lehrman. CAST: Thelma Salter, Gordon Griffith, Charlotte Fitzpatrick, Paul Jacobs, Matty Roubert
REVIEW: "Charlotte Fitzpatrick, nine years old, is the girl in the story. Thelma Slater [sic], five years old and curly-headed, is in the story also, but Thelma is supposed to be a boy and wins the hand of the fair Charlotte in the face of a rival, Gordon [Griffith]. So Thelma and Charlotte marry and keep house and Gordon hires Matty [Roubert] and another villain to help him tie Charlotte to the railroad track, and then they steal an engine and dash madly away to run down the helpless heroine.

"Thelma, at work in over-alls and nifty cap, pursues the villains in a buggy and a wild race ensues. Charlotte loosens her skirt but when she finds that to save herself she will have to walk off skirtless, she refuses to save herself, remains on the track but of course is rescued, skirt and all, by the brave Thelma, as the train is almost upon her." "Another Keystone Kid Production: Child Actors Featured," *Motography*, March 21, 1914, p. 200.

A Rural Demon: *Released 03/19/1914.* 1 reel. DIRECTOR: Henry Lehrman and Mack Sennett. CAST: Roscoe Arbuckle, Eva Nelson
REVIEW: "Here is one of Mack Sennett's comedy pictures. It is a hummer in every way. It has a regular rural twang and never hesitates from start to the finish. It embraces all kinds of characters, including a fractious goose. There is a bomb effect, a chase and a wind-up where everybody gets soaked but the cameraman, in the river. If you want a good laugh see it." *Moving Picture World*, March 21, 1914, p.1526

San Francisco and Her Environs: *Released 03/21/1914.* ⅓ reel. DIRECTOR: Henry Lehrman. Educational short subject showing a tour of San Francisco

Some Questionable Credits

Universal Weekly of April 25, 1914, p.17, ran a biography of "Henry Pathe Lehrman" that credited him with some Keystone films not otherwise credited to Lehrman:

Mabel's New Hero: *Released 08/28/1913.* 1 reel. DIRECTOR: Henry "Pathé" Lehrman *(according to the article)*, or Mack Sennett *(Walker, according to the NYMPC ledger)*. CAST: Roscoe Arbuckle, Charles Inslee, Virginia Kirtley, Charles Avery, Edgar Kennedy, Hank Mann
REVIEW: "[A] comedy of errors in which a young husband is obsessed with much groundless jealousy of his wife and comes to amusing grief for his folly. The fun is extremely lively." *Moving Picture World*, October 12, 1912, p.144

Universal Weekly: "Up to the time that he severed his connection with the Keystone, Mr. Lehrman directed every Keystone picture in which Mack Sinot (Sennet) [sic] appeared, including..." Walker asserts that these listed films were all directed by Sennett, but acknowledges that Lehrman may have assisted whenever Sennett was in front of the camera.

The Battle of Who Run: *Released 02/06/1913.* 1 reel. DIRECTOR: Henry "Pathé" Lehrman *(article)*, or Mack Sennett *(Walker)*. CAST: Mack Sennett, Fred Mace, Ford Sterling, Mabel Normand, Nick Cogley
REVIEW: "This film contains a masterly burlesque on real warfare. There are a number of cowering officers and privates, mixed messages, bursting bombs, and side-splitting situations. Mabel Normand appears in an officer's uniform, and has some trouble picking out the real hero of the occasion. A surprisingly good army burlesque." *Moving Picture World*, January 25, 1913, p.365

The Firebugs: *Released 08/21/1913.* 2 reels. DIRECTOR: Henry "Pathé" Lehrman *(article)*, or Mack Sennett *(Walker)*. CAST: Ford Sterling, Nick Cogley, Mack Sennett, Edgar Kennedy, Charles Avery, Alice Davenport, Arthur Tavares. Henry Lehrman was also credited as one of the co-stars in a *NY Clipper* review, 09/06/1913, p.13, but this is incorrect.

The New Neighbor: *Released 09/30/1912.* ½ reel. DIRECTOR: Henry "Pathé" Lehrman *(article)*, or Mack Sennett *(Walker)*. CAST: Fred Mace, Ford Sterling, Mabel Normand, Mack Sennett
REVIEW: "A full reel comedy containing much that is genuinely funny, but also many broad, suggestive situations which will not commend it to the best houses; in fact, much of it is unfit for presentation anywhere." *Moving Picture World*, September 6, 1913, p.1069

Universal Weekly: "[Lehrman] introduced in comedy the Keystone police, the Keystone mounted police, and originated the ideas for such pictures as…" Walker does not comment on any of these claims.

Heinze's Resurrection: *Released 02/17/1913.* 1 reel. DIRECTOR: Mack Sennett. Ideas: Henry "Pathé" Lehrman *(article).* CAST: Ford Sterling, Fred Mace, Laura Oakley, Arthur Tavares

The Riot: *Released 08/11/1913.* 1 reel. DIRECTOR: Mack Sennett. Ideas: Henry "Pathé" Lehrman *(article).* CAST: Roscoe Arbuckle, Mabel Normand, Charles Inslee, Alice Davenport, Charles Avery, Paul Jacobs, Gordon Griffith, Nick Cogley, Virginia Kirtley, Bill Hauber, Al St. John, Hank Mann, Edgar Kennedy

Love and Gasoline: *Released 02/21/1914.* 1 reel. DIRECTOR: Mabel Normand. Ideas: Henry "Pathé" Lehrman *(article).* CAST: Mabel Normand

Other sources have credited Lehrman as a member of the cast of the following films, but these remain unconfirmed:

Stolen Glory: *Released 10/14/1912.* 1 reel. DIRECTOR: Mack Sennett. CAST: Ford Sterling, Fred Mace, Alice Davenport, Charles Avery, Victoria Forde, Frank Opperman; Henry Lehrman *(Walker: no mention)*

Saving Mabel's Dad: *Released 01/06/1913.* ½ reel. DIRECTOR: Mack Sennett. CAST: Mabel Normand, Fred Mace; Henry Lehrman *(Walker: unverified)*

A Landlord's Troubles: *Released 02/20/1913.* ½ reel. DIRECTOR: (Mack Sennett). CAST: Ford Sterling, Mack Sennett; Henry Lehrman, Fred Mace, Edgar Kennedy, Al St. John *(Walker: all highly unlikely)*

A Tangled Affair: *Released 02/24/1913.* ½ reel. DIRECTOR: Mack Sennett. CAST: Mabel Normand; Henry Lehrman, Harry McCoy *(Walker: both highly unlikely)*

The Sterling Motion Picture Corporation
(released through Universal Film Manufacturing Co.)

These are the films released by the Sterling Motion Picture Corporation, 1914-1915, copyrighted (in a few later instances) by Universal Film Manufacturing Company, Inc.

Universal Weekly (retitled *Moving Picture Weekly* effective July 3, 1915) was a weekly publication provided to industry trade publications and exhibitors to promote current and upcoming studio releases. Synopses were included for most of the Universal films, and printed either verbatim or with minor editing in trade publications such as *Moving Picture World* and *Motography.* The synopses that follow for both the Sterling and L-Ko releases are in some instances taken directly from the pages of one of these publications, and in other instances are an abridgment of the originals. The abridgments were employed whenever the original text was deemed overly verbose.

It should be noted that in a few identifiable instances the synopsis provided was inaccurate. Since most of these films are now considered "lost," these instances would remain undetected. When a film survives, however, these inaccuracies become evident. An example of this is for the Sterling release *The Close Call* (October 12, 1914), the synopsis of which appeared under the byline "Dog Averts Tragic Death of Baby" and goes on to tell a tale in which the two young leads fail to keep an eye on a baby who wanders off after a bulldog and ends up at a cliff's edge. Viewing the film itself reveals that there is neither a baby nor bulldog; instead it is one of the young leads who gets into trouble, tumbling down the cliff-side itself. Did the writer work from a rough treatment of the storyline that later underwent director-imposed changes? Was the writer's memory affected by the sheer number of films viewed for review on a given day? Or was it merely an example of laziness? We'll never know.

There was also at least one synopsis provided for a film that was for a different film altogether. This was caught and corrected here, but it is possible this mix-up occurred elsewhere and went undetected. Similarly, *Universal Weekly*— all of the trade publications for that matter — would on occasion list actors or actresses as cast members for films in which they did not appear. I apologize in advance if any of these errors have made it into the following filmographies.

Cast listings and credits for these films have been derived solely from contemporary sources, from viewing the few films that survive, or from other films' stills. Film listings and credits from other, newer sources have proven to be wholly unreliable in far too many instances; these have been avoided altogether while compiling the following, which is the most accurate filmography to date. That said, any documentable additions or corrections to the following would be welcomed by the author.

The *Universal Weekly* entries for Henry Lehrman were alternately given as *H. Pathe Lehrman*, *Pathe Lehrman*, and *Henry Lehrman*.

Love and Vengeance: *Released 04/23/1914 Thursday.* No copyright entry — 2 reels/1975 feet. DIRECTOR, SCRP: Henry Lehrman. CAST: Ford Sterling, Henry Lehrman, Emma Clifton, Lucille Ward, Frank Goode, Carl Laemmle, Herman Fichtenberg, Lew Carter, Fred Balshofer
SYNOPSIS: "'Love and Vengeance' is a characteristic Sterling production. It is not enough to say that there are no dull moments in it, for there are many that will cause hearty laughter. In the beginning, Snookee, portrayed by Mr. Sterling, has an altercation with a man [Lehrman] who fights with his right shoe, which he hurls with most unerring aim. Snookee retaliates with various loose bricks. The cause of the disturbance is a rather stout woman [Ward]. Snookee gets the best of the argument and also the woman, but it is not long before his eye rests on the figure of a younger woman [Clifton], who with a circular pocket mirror has been reflecting in the eyes of the two the rays of the sun. Snookee remonstrates with the mischievous young person, but under the charm of her eyes his wrath fades. His affections experience most rapid transference; there is a fly in the ointment in the form of a racing driver [Goode], however. It is for him that the new charmer has eyes only.

"Snookee gets desperate when it looks like No. 2 coming in a winner. With a hose he sprinkles the course. Then things happen in chunks. Machines skid all over the road. Always, Snookee seems right in line for a bump. He gets it going and coming. Automobiles go backward and forward and sometimes sideways. Policemen essay to straighten matters out and instead are themselves straightened out. It's all a new kind of machine-made comedy — and that is no disrespectful pun, either. What those skidding machines do in the way of stunts is almost past belief." George Blaisdell, *Moving Picture World*, April 18, 1914, p.341

REVIEWS: "We are not going to attempt to outline the many good things in this unusual production. Suffice it to say, an exhibitor may go the limit on it, confident that from his grouchiest patron he will pull a laugh and also a real thrill. Furthermore, it is as clean as a whistle. There will be many who see 'Love and Vengeance' who will believe that the young woman playing opposite Mr. Sterling is none other than the one with whom he has appeared in so many pictures. There is a strong resemblance. Emma Clifton will make an effective foil for the comedian; it is quite safe to say we will hear much of her in time to come. Mr. Lehrman has got together a most efficient company. Every member of it displays the agility and the absolute disregard for the retention of anatomical unity which seem so essential these days in the making of this popular style of comedy." Reviewed by George Blaisdell, *Moving Picture World*, April 18, 1914, p.341

"'Love and Vengeance,' the first Universal comedy, like other productions in which Mr. Sterling has been featured, contains little of a story or plot. Were there one, the film would not be half as funny as it is, for it is not the plot that attracts people to a Sterling comedy." *Motion Picture News*, April 18, 1914, p.46

"While no problem is solved, nor light shed on an existing evil or any of the other difficulties attempted that seem to tempt the dramas of to-day, this two-reel comedy, of heterogeneous complexion, without any very noticeable plot, although there is a slight sign of one, manages to bring out more real laughter, more solid mirth to the foot, than anything we have seen in some time. No, it is not a gentle form of humor. You would hardly call it lady-like action when one man jumped upon another and bit him on the nose, and when that person retaliated in kind and bit a piece out of the leg of the other. This is the type of fun, rough, boisterous, slapstick comedy that, in spite of the educated predelictions [sic] of the spectator, gets beneath the veneer of his higher pretensions and brings him to the common ground of laughter. To tell why one laughs at Ford Sterling is to give an analysis of humor itself. Suffice it that he at all times — and he is on the screen for the major part of the play — brings laughter. Wound up with the plot is the Vanderbilt cup race. One of the scenes in the play shows the upset of a speeding automobile. The scenes, as the speeding machines round the turn and sweep along the straightaway, are full of breathless interest. It is supposed that the sweetheart of the girl that Ford Sterling wants is piloting car No. 2 in the race, and that Sterling attempts to wreck the car by watering the turn in the road. What the automobiles do when they strike the slippery turn constitutes but one of the series of funny features with which the film is filled. The offering brings out with great success the expression of which Ford Sterling is the master. The play is well staged, and possesses, as usual, some unusual examples of trick photography." Reviewed by F., *New York Dramatic Mirror*, April 29, 1914, p.39

His Wedding Day: *Released 04/30/1914 Thursday.* No copyright entry — 1 reel/1000 feet. DIRECTOR: Henry Lehrman. CAST: Ford Sterling, Emma Clifton
(Pre-release promotional materials title: **The Fatal Wedding** and **A Fatal Wedding.** Last minute title change due to conflict with K. and E.'s film of play of same title, *The Fatal Wedding*.)
SYNOPSIS: Wedding between groom Sterling and bride Clifton interrupted by gun-toting crook; can of milk poured over Sterling; Sterling tries to kill himself, but self-preservation gets the best of him and he tries to save himself. Synopsis adapted from the plot summary in *Universal Weekly*
REVIEWS: "…a can of concentrated lacteal poured over a muchly prized suit…" *Bioscope*, July 9, 1914, p.XXXI

"This introduces Ford Sterling in a rapid-fire one reel offering. All of the first part of this offering is very laughable, but toward the last the pie-throwing and other sloppy scenes interfere with the humor, as invariably happens when these things are overdone. The photography is good." *Moving Picture World*, May 2, 1914, p.674

"Ford Sterling scored a hit in 'The Fatal Wedding' and brought laughter from all sides." *Motion Picture News*, May 9, 1914, p.20

Sergeant Hofmeyer: *Released 05/07/1914 Thursday.* No copyright entry — 1 reel/1000 feet. DIRECTOR: Henry Lehrman. CAST: Ford Sterling, Paul Jacobs
SYNOPSIS: "Sergeant Hofmeyer's son wants a new coaster. Hofmeyer schemes to get one. Meantime, the neighborhood kids decide to have a coaster race and little Billy, who wants to be in on it, hasn't his coaster. While Hofmeyer does his best, he observes a coaster in the street out of commission. Hofmeyer walks off with it and presents it to his son. Billy steals off with the coaster when Hofmeyer is in the house. Before he goes far the machine breaks down. Hofmeyer comes up and takes the youngster to the police station. Billy then declares that the coaster does not belong to Hofmeyer — that he stole it. At this moment the captain's boy enters and accuses Hofmeyer of taking his machine. The captain smashes Hofmeyer and a general fight commences. Billy looks on, proud that he can at least cause such trouble." *Moving Picture World*, May 9, 1914, p.358
REVIEWS: "Ford Sterling appears in this amusing trifle as a police sergeant. The number has strong juvenile interest, Little Billy being one of the leading participants. The action is not so pronounced as usual, but brings numerous smiles." *Moving Picture World*, May 9, 1914, p.821

Papa's Boy: *Released 05/14/1914 Thursday.* No copyright entry — 1 reel/1000 feet. DIRECTOR: Henry Lehrman. CAST: Ford Sterling, Emma Clifton, Paul Jacobs
SYNOPSIS: Father (Sterling) and son Billy (Jacobs) await dinner being prepared by mother (Clifton). Father rushes out to the kitchen when his wife burns the meal, and Billy snatches up and rushes out with the blackberry jam that his dad had been so generous in helping himself to, and so stingy when it came to sharing with his son. Taking the jam as a gift to his sweetheart, Billy runs into his rival George and the two get into a fight over the stuff. A cop arriving on the scene manages to get a face full of the jam, and Billy and George flee. They find that their girl has made off with the bulk of it and is sharing it with another boy. In their sorrow, Billy and George shake hands. Synopsis adapted from the plot summary in *Universal Weekly*, May 9, 1914, p.24

REVIEWS: "It's human stuff, human and fun-loving that one gets in this picture." *Universal Weekly*, May 9, 1914, p.24

"Not enough Sterling in the comedy. It will appeal to children, for the little ones play the prominent parts." *Motion Picture News*, May 16, 1914, p.56

Neighbors: *Released 05/21/1914 Thursday.* No copyright entry — 1 reel/1012 feet. DIRECTOR: Henry Lehrman? CAST: Ford Sterling, Max Asher, Lucille Ward
(Lehrman included here as director solely based on cast and chronological order.)
SYNOPSIS: Schlitz (Sterling) plays cards by himself while his wife attempts to make dinner. They work up to a quarrel, but then make up, hugging and kissing in front of the open window. The Mulligans watch for a while. Later, Mulligan (Asher) heads over to Schlitz's to play cards, while Mrs. Schlitz goes over to Mrs. Mulligan's for some gossip. Schlitz wins time and again because of his blatant cheating, and soon the two card players are at each other's throat in battle. The wives return and join in the free for all, and soon the battle leads to a knock-down, drag-out chase through hotels and alleys. The police arrive and ineffectually attempt to put a halt to it, but are given a welcoming blast from a fire hose for their efforts. Synopsis adapted from the plot summary in *Universal Weekly*, May 16, 1914, p.21
REVIEWS: "I laughed til my throat was sore and the tears poured down my cheeks. It put me in good humor for the day's work." (an "unbiased" Carl Laemmle in) *Universal Weekly*, May 23, 1914, p.32

"Neighbors will quarrel, and this comedy proves it. Pie, brick-throwing and shooting cause many laughs, and the picture ends with a hose-fight." *Motion Picture News*, May 16, 1914, p.56

Hearts and Swords: *Released 05/28/1914 Thursday.* No copyright entry — 2 reels/1869 feet. DIRECTOR: Henry Lehrman. CINEMATOGRAPHY: Frank D. Williams. CAST: Ford Sterling, Emma Clifton, Peggy Pearce
(This film, which was not copyrighted, was most likely re-released as **Fools and Duels** on Wednesday 01/08/1919, and copyrighted © 01/02/1919 as an L-Ko release)
SYNOPSIS: While boating, Sterling spots a pretty girl alone in her craft and decides to follow her, unaware that another fellow with similar intentions is doing the same. Sterling becomes aware of his rival and through dubious means puts him temporarily out of the running. Having made the pretty girl's acquaintance, the two attend a lawn party and Sterling is the envy of all the other males. That is, until his rival arrives with a sexy, scantily clad "Salome dancer." Naturally, Sterling is smitten by her, and makes advances towards her. The rival is understandably furious, and a sword duel soon follows. Both turn out to be cowards, however, and the duel ends in a fiasco with Sterling and the rival plunging from a bridge to the water sixty feet below. Humorous efforts to save the floundering men follow, and the dancer flees through the public park with the park police in hot pursuit attempting to cover her up. Synopsis adapted from the plot summary in *Universal Weekly*, May 23, 1914, p.12
REVIEWS: "Ford Sterling assumes the lead under the direction of Henry Lehrman in this two-reel rollicking revel of joy. We laughed for thirty minutes, and positively cannot say what we laughed about. To those who have seen these pictures this statement will be understandable. To others let us say that the film consists of a series of make-ups, grimaces, and expedients all centered about nothing in particular, but funny every foot of it.

It is the height of the ridiculous and the burlesque on whatever action happens. A chase, sword play, diving off a high bridge, and comic slaughter in the water, and a lot of other diversions, including the Divorce Dance, are what enable the cast to keep the humor alive." *New York Dramatic Mirror*, May 20, 1914, p.3

"This is a two-part rip-roaring comedy that gains hearty and continuous laughter. It is crammed with funny situations and characters and what they don't do in the action of the picture never happened. There is a scantily clad maiden who is some dancer. Ford Sterling is at his best. This strenuous comedy will make any audience laugh like the dickens. The photography is not of the best in some places." *Moving Picture World*, May 30, 1914, p.1262

"A comedian of Sterling's quality is not to be hampered by the conventions of a connected story…a ferocious duel (is) fought according to rules which occur to Sterling during the progress of the fight…the beauty of the setting and the perfect quality of the photography add enormously to [the film's] attractiveness. Ford Sterling's eccentric comedy and wonderfully ingenious bits of 'business' gain greatly by the contrast." *Bioscope*, June 25, 1914, p.1361

"Ford Sterling at his best. As usual there is no real plot or story, just a conglomeration of slap stick comedy that will always amuse. Rivals in love as usual. They fight a duel with sabers, but these get mixed up with their feet. Finally they all land in the water and there we leave them." *Motion Picture News*, May 30, 1914, p.66

Films from here on most likely produced after Lehrman's departure for L-Ko:

Snitz Joins the Force: *Released 06/04/1914 Thursday.* No copyright entry — 1 reel/965 feet. CAST: Ford Sterling
SYNOPSIS: Snitz (Sterling) awakens after a lavish dream of extreme wealth. Meeting a police sergeant's girl, he is completely taken with her and makes her acquaintance during the sergeant's absence. He declares his love for her, but she informs him that she prefers brass buttons and blue uniforms. Snitz decides to join up, and finds himself appointed to the sergeant's precinct. When the sergeant finds Snitz wooing his girl, he sends him out alone to round up a ring of gangsters in hopes of getting him out of the way. The gangsters pursue a terrified Snitz, and after a chase that leads through streets and alleys, a rooftop struggle sends all crashing down a chimney into the awaiting arms of the police. The captain awards Snitz the sergeant's badge. Synopsis adapted from the plot summary in *Universal Weekly*, May 30, 1914, pp.20-21
REVIEWS: "A Ford Sterling number, in which he appears as a police officer. He falls in love with the captain's sweetheart and a chase ensues, over house tops, etc. This is a characteristic offering, but not quite as amusing as some." *Moving Picture World*, June 6, 1914, p.1410

Smaltz Loves (aka When Smaltz Loves): *Released 06/11/1914 Thursday.* No copyright entry — 1 reel/948 feet. CAST: Ford Sterling
SYNOPSIS: Smaltz's (Sterling) girl Gretchen loves cops. Smaltz "finds" a uniform. Smaltz spoils a bathing excursion. Smaltz wins Gretchen for good.
REVIEWS: "Ford Sterling is the same as ever and his queer Dutchman, Smaltz, will excite laughter. Yet there are moments when his supporting company fails to hold up its end and lets some of the picture fall flat. The plot (it is merely a scheme on which Sterling plasters

the fun) is typical of this kind of offering — there is apt to be a good deal of sameness in them all. It will probably be acceptable to Sterling's following." *Moving Picture World*, June 13, 1914, p.1542

Kids: *Released 06/15/1914 Monday.* No copyright entry — 1 reel/1000 feet. DIRECTOR: Robert Thornby. CAST: Paul Jacobs, Chandler House, Charlotte Ford
SYNOPSIS: Jimmie stands beneath Charlotte's window serenading the girl he assumes to be home. She isn't, and her ma chases him away. Finding her in the park with Chandler, Jimmie challenges his rival to a fight, with Little Billy serving as Jimmie's second. Chandler gives him a sound thrashing, and Jimmie scurries under Charlotte's skirt for shelter! Later, while Chandler and Charlotte are playing hide and seek, Jimmie approaches her with ice cream, and she accepts. Chandler returns and throws mud at Jimmie, but it hits Charlotte instead. She leaves with Jimmie, and the two head off for a boat ride. A jealous Chandler sets them adrift without oars, and Little Billy rushes (successfully) to Charlotte's ma for help. Synopsis adapted from the plot summary in *Universal Weekly*, June 13, 1914, p.21
REVIEWS: "A story featuring principally a group of children, with love and jealousy to keep the plot in action. Some of the scenes are quite laughable and the motor boat chase toward the close was very good. This is entertaining." *Moving Picture World*, June 20, 1914, p.1960
"Sterling must really look to his laurels, for his juvenile rivals enter into the sport of the play with much zest and plenty of humor." *Bioscope*, September 17, 1914, p.VIII

Billy's Riot: *Released 06/18/1914 Thursday.* No copyright entry — 1 reel/990 feet. CAST: Paul Jacobs
(**A Jealous Husband** previously announced for release on this date)
SYNOPSIS: A little girl's flirting causes problems, but Little Billy gets even with his pea-shooter.
REVIEWS: "Little Billy's efforts as an actor grow funnier the more you see of him. He is always clever and amusing, but he needs a little more definite plot some times. This number contains a lot of good fun and is sure to please." *Moving Picture World*, July 11, 1914, p.256

The Flirt: *Released 06/22/1914 Monday.* No copyright entry — 1 reel/981 feet. CAST: Carmen DeRue, Paul Jacobs
SYNOPSIS: A quartet of rivals: the two boys get into plenty of trouble; the two girls fall in the river and the police fish them out.
REVIEWS: "This is a number enacted principally by children. Two couples come to grief in their love affairs. Not enough plot to hold the interest very strongly. The chief action occurs at the last when they all get into the water, followed by the police force. Only fairly entertaining." *Moving Picture World*, June 27, 1914, p.1830

A Jealous Husband: *Released 06/25/1914 Thursday.* No copyright entry — 1 reel/925 feet. CAST: Ford Sterling.
(**Snookee's Flirtation** previously announced for release on this date)
SYNOPSIS: Snookee (Sterling) rescues his neighbor who misconstrues the facts, resulting in a riotous chase.
REVIEWS: "This farce has the peculiar qualities found in Ford Sterling's pictures. He himself in this offering is very comical and will provoke much laughter. The plot or scheme is of the

slightest; but the business is not allowed to drag and there is a constant changing of the same situation that often takes on very amusing phases. It is a good offering of rough and tumble stuff and will be welcomed by audiences." *Moving Picture World*, June 27, 1914, p.1830

It's a Boy: *Released 06/29/1914 Monday.* No copyright entry — 1 reel/956 feet. CAST: Paul Jacobs, Charles Inslee, Violet Radcliffe
SYNOPSIS: Little Billy is jealous of the new baby in the house, and conspires with a friend (Radcliffe) to get rid of him. Billy carries the swaddled baby out of the window and puts the infant in a dog cart, then off they go. A nearby explosion spooks the dog, who takes off in a panic dragging the cart along. Billy pursues the cart on foot, fearful that harm may come to his little brother. Finally, the cart overturns and the dog comes to a stop, resting beside the cart and infant. Billy arrives and finds the baby unharmed, and realizes the foolish, dangerous thing he's done. He carries the baby back home where he presents it to his mom and dad (Inslee), with a tearful explanation of jealousy and guilt. Synopsis adapted from the plot summary in *Universal Weekly*
REVIEWS: "Little Billy is the chief figure in this film story. When the new baby comes he conspires with a friend to make away with it. They place it in the dog cart and there is an exciting pursuit. This is not strong, but proves quite entertaining." *Moving Picture World*, July 4, 1914, p.65

The Crash: *Released 07/02/1914 Thursday.* No copyright entry — 1 reel/950 feet. DIRECTOR: George Nichols
SYNOPSIS: An extended chase: rivals in love, one making off with the girl in his car while the other follows in hot pursuit on his motorcycle. The cops follow on "fractious bronchos," but can't catch them. During the course of the film, a gasoline wagon explodes taking a house and barn with it. The chase terminates with the auto driving off a cliff, the cycle following and landing in the midst of the wreckage. As the rivals emerge from the debris, they spot the girl leaving with yet another man. Synopsis adapted from the plot summary in *Universal Weekly*, June 27, 1914, p.21
REVIEWS: "The last third of this comic picture is so unusually speedy that it hardly fails to take strongly with the gallery and the downstairs too. It uses an old situation, but goes its predecessors one better in startling incident at the close and is truly laughable." *Moving Picture World*, July 11, 1914, p.255

Billy's Vacation: *Released 07/06/1914 Monday.* No copyright entry — 1 reel/987 feet. CAST: Paul Jacobs
REVIEWS: "A very clever picture, abounding in good-humoured fun." *Bioscope*, October 15, 1914, p.XXI

Snookee's Flirtation: *Released 07/09/1914 Thursday.* No copyright entry — 1 reel/982 feet. CAST: Ford Sterling, Peggy Pearce, Charles Inslee, Emma Clifton, Lucille Ward, Merta Sterling, Arthur Tavares
SYNOPSIS: Chronically lazy Snookee (Sterling) is sent out by his wife (Ward) to look for work. After much procrastination, Snookee finds a shoe store well attended by females and decides that it's as good a place as any. His suspicious wife wises up to his continuous

flirting, and the film concludes with a climactic chase and fight that culminates with all being buried under an avalanche of shoes. Synopsis adapted from the plot summary in *Universal Weekly*

REVIEWS: "A rough and knockabout farce in the usual Sterling style. It is not so funny as the best of this brand; for the scheme calls for business a bit too rough for more discriminating patrons. It is a sort of 'Merry Wives of Windsor' picture without the humanity and wit, but will make laughter." *Moving Picture World*, July 18, 1914, p.433

Almost Married: *Released 07/13/1914 Monday.* No copyright entry — 1 reel/880 feet.
CAST: Mae Wells
SYNOPSIS: Farmer John Smith has two daughters: May, who is pretty, and Lizzie, who is fat and ugly. He wants to marry off Lizzie, but prospective husband Reuben falls for May instead. Lizzie complains about this turn of affairs to her dad, and he tosses Reuben out of the house. Reuben hires a pair of thugs to kidnap May, but the inept duo mistakenly makes off with Lizzie while May elopes with her lover. Smith, thinking that they have May, chases them to the J.P.'s where Reuben awaits. The neighbors join in on the chase, but when Smith realizes that it's Lizzie and not May, he holds the neighbors back in order that the wedding may proceed. Reuben discovers the error and pushes Liz out the window. Smith shoves her back in. A mad scramble follows and Reuben beats a hasty retreat down the empty country road. Synopsis adapted from the plot summary in *Universal Weekly*, July 18, 1914, p.25
REVIEWS: "Rough farce that is a bit more vulgar than usual with this make. There is nothing offensive in it, but the business is rougher and broader. The gallery may like it very well." *Moving Picture World*, July 25, 1914, p.572

"...more remarkable for its swift action and the weird antics of its comedian than for its humour." *Bioscope*, January 28, 1915, p.X

A Beach Romance: *Released 07/16/1914 Thursday.* No copyright entry — 1 reel/979 feet.
DIRECTOR: Robert Thornby. CAST: Paul Jacobs, Olive Johnson
(**Love and Lunch** previously announced for release on this date)
REVIEWS: "Robert Thornby produced this picture featuring 'Billy' and three other youngsters who have become well known in pictures. The story is, of course, nothing; but the acting of the kids will delight spectators who like a little quiet amusement with their more vigorous offerings. It is a cute picture." *Moving Picture World*, July 25, 1914, p.572
"A delightful absurdity." *Bioscope*, October 15, 1914, p.273

The Circus: *Released 07/20/1914 Monday.* No copyright entry — 1 reel. DIRECTOR: George Nichols
SYNOPSIS: The local villagers and the village boob go to the circus that has just arrived in town. The boob is soaked by the elephant that he's been annoying, so he storms off and complains to the circus manager. The manager already has a chip on his shoulder concerning Bill, the elephant's trainer, as they are rivals for the same circus performer, so he tracks him down and the two get into a fight. The manager is knocked into the elephant's trough, and is soaked once again when Bill ties the elephant's rope to a lemonade stand which is pulled down, dispensing its contents on him. Meanwhile, the show is on but is

judged to be terrible by the hard-to-please villagers who shower the performers with tossed vegetables. The fire eater accidentally knocks over his burner of coals, and in an attempt to douse the resulting fire mistakes bottled gas for bottled water. Spitting it onto the flame, things worsen and the local fire department is called in. They prove to be inept with their hose, and all are soaked, including Bill and the manager, whose fight has progressed to the stage. Synopsis adapted from the plot summary in *Universal Weekly*, July 25, 1914, p.20

REVIEWS: "This is a knockabout comedy, with a circus side-show setting. The fire-eater sets the tents ablaze and a wild scramble ensues. Good stuff of its kind, but the photography is only average." *Moving Picture World,* August 1, 1914, p.705

"The adventures of a country rube at the circus, ending with a free-for-all fight, create a roar of laughter throughout the reel. Ford Sterling himself does not appear. The photography is slightly below standard." *Motion Picture News*, August 1, 1914, p.62

Love and Lunch: *Released 07/23/1914 Thursday.* No copyright entry — 2 reels/1745 feet.
CAST: Ford Sterling, Peggy Pearce *(unconfirmed),* Charles Inslee, Arthur Tavares
SYNOPSIS: Sterling is forced to go job hunting when his fiancée Peggy's parents insist on his being employed before they can be married. Jones, a single waiter at Smith's lunch wagon, flirts with all the girls. Smith's wife has Jones fired and replaces him with Sterling, who assures them that he is married. Peggy arrives at the wagon and Sterling, not wishing to jeopardize his job, treats her very roughly and throws her out. Jones comforts her, proposes to her, and marries her, and the newlyweds return to the wagon for a meal. Sterling is upset by this all and is fired by Smith when he begins to neglect his work; Jones is rehired now that he is married. The mandatory fight follows, with the lunch wagon set free, rolling down a hill, and reduced to rubble when its gas tanks explode. Sterling lands in the river "struggling and furiously angry." Synopsis adapted from the plot summary in *Universal Weekly*, July 18, 1914, p.16

REVIEWS: "A two-reel farce picture in which the many will find laughter even in the first reel which is, to the reviewer, rather dry from repetition. In the second reel, when the lunch cart is running away and the cops are in full chase, all will laugh and heartily, for it is very funny." *Moving Picture World*, July 25, 1914, p.573

A Wild Ride: *Released 07/27/1914 Monday.* No copyright entry — 1 reel/984 feet. CAST: Paul Jacobs, Carmen DeRue
SYNOPSIS: Little Billy (Jacobs) and Olive (DeRue) are in "love," and Desmond is furiously jealous. His repeated advances are rebuffed, and he is finally slapped. Swearing revenge, he follows them about the seaside amusement area, from the gondola to the roller coaster. Setting their coaster running free, Desmond flees. An attendant calls the cops, and upon their arrival they board another coaster car to aid their pursuit. Billy and Olive's car comes to a halt, but the cops' car continues on its mad runaway ride. Billy and Olive head for the beach and the rocks, and the film closes with Olive's head resting on his shoulder. Synopsis adapted from the plot summary in *Universal Weekly*, July 25, 1914, p.20

REVIEWS: "This film story is enacted by children. The boy rivals strive over their lady love at a beach resort, the wild ride being taken on a scenic railway. In this they were pursued by a burlesque police force. Not much plot to this; it proves fairly amusing." *Moving Picture World*, August 8, 1914, p.837

"The feature of the picture is a wild ride taken by two of the children in a scenic railway car with the burlesque police following in the next. The picture is good throughout, but this last event is a crackerjack." *Motion Picture News*, August 8, 1914, p.61

"…in seriousness and intelligence, [the Sterling Juveniles] rival an actor of many years experience. Moreover, they play with an utter lack of self consciousness; they are just happy children, with that delightful quality of youth — unspoiled, free, and natural — for which we elders sigh in vain…the inimitable Sterling police — among whom, by the way, the 'casualty list' must be very severe…" *Bioscope*, October 1, 1914, p.82

Troublesome Pets: *Released 07/30/1914 Thursday.* No copyright entry — 1 reel. CAST: Charles Inslee, Margarete Whisler, Al Garcia
SYNOPSIS: Farmer Reuben (Inslee) hates animals, but his wife (Whisler) likes them. When the farm hand (Garcia) gives her a chattering monkey, Reuben locks it in the pantry. The farm hand points out a traveling peddler who has a parrot for sale, and she buys it. She puts it in the house when she heads to town with a neighbor, and its repeated screams of "I WANT A CRACKER" continue to waken the sleeping Reuben who returns to the kitchen time and again trying to figure out just what the racket is. Finally finding the parrot, he tosses it into the well and then heads for the basement to drink hard cider. His wife returns and, hearing the parrot's screeches from the well, thinks that it's Reuben calling for help. She coerces the farm hand into climbing down to rescue Reuben. The parrot flies out. Reuben emerges from the basement, and his relieved wife hugs him. Synopsis adapted from the plot summary in *Universal Weekly*, July 25, 1914, p.24
REVIEWS: "The master of the house, tired of the monkey and parrot, kept by his wife, puts one in the pantry and the other down the well. The parrot's cries for help rouse the neighborhood. There are no extremely laughable places in this, but it is lightly amusing throughout." *Moving Picture World*, August 8, 1914, p.837

"A good comedy, but not as good as the majority of this brand. His wife owns a parrot which her husband doesn't fancy, and he throws it down a well. The whole village is aroused by cries of 'help' emitting from the well. A monkey is also introduced which adds to the fun." *Motion Picture News*, August 8, 1914, p.61

A Race for Life: *Released 08/03/1914 Monday.* No copyright entry — 1 reel/980 feet. DIRECTOR: Robert Thornby. CAST: Paul Jacobs, Gordon Griffiths, Chandler House, Carmen DeRue
SYNOPSIS: Billy (Jacobs) snatches one of his mother's pies from the window sill and shares it with Chandler. Chandler offers a piece to Carmen who is with Gordon, and he picks a fight with Chandler. Billy's ma arrives and he's put to bed. He dreams: Gordon is forcing himself on Carmen, and swears revenge on the intervening Chandler. He abducts Carmen and makes off with her on a handcar. He ties her to the tracks when she refuses marriage. Billy enlists a friend's aid, and the two speed off in a car. They engage in a race with a train, and Billy leaps and pulls her from the tracks in the nick of time. He returns her to Chandler. Billy awakens. Synopsis adapted from the plot summary in *Universal Weekly*, August 1, 1914, p.20
REVIEWS: "A 'kid' story, with Little Billy and his pals in the cast. The girl is abducted by the boy villain and the miniature engine bears down upon her as she lies tied to the railroad tracks. This gets up quite a little suspense, even though of a burlesque nature. The whole

experience turns out to be Billy's dream. A good number enacted entirely by children." *Moving Picture World*, August 15, 1914, p.960

A Dramatic Mistake: *Released 08/06/1914 Thursday.* No copyright entry — 1 reel/993 feet. DIRECTOR: David Kirkland. CAST: Ford Sterling, June Clark, Harry Griffith, Alberta McCoy, Jack Dillon, Arthur Tavares
SYNOPSIS: Snitz (Sterling) is such an admirer of the stage that he never finds time to work. The landlady (McCoy) demands the overdue rent from Snitz's wife (Clark), and has her burly husband (Griffith) back up the request with Snitz. Facing reality, Snitz turns to the stage for employment, but his audition is grotesque and he is rudely sent away. When the company's lead actor (Tavares) arrives too drunk to play the part of "Virginius," the stage manager (Dillon) heads for Snitz's apartment with the costume and tells him to prepare for the matinee. Snitz rehearses with great enthusiasm, but his family overhears and mistakes his bellowing for the cries of a murder victim. They call the cops, who pursue him to the theater thinking him to be the murderer. The audience is impatiently waiting when Snitz arrives with the cops in hot pursuit, and matters are further complicated when the show's lead arrives unannounced. There is much to-do. Synopsis adapted from the plot summary in *Universal Weekly*, August 11, 1914, p.21
REVIEWS: "This is a typical Ford Sterling number, with the comedian in the part of Virginius. His performance is interrupted by the police and there is a grand scramble on all hands. A lot of fun in this of the rough-house sort and it will bring many laughs." *Moving Picture World*, August 15, 1914, p.961

A Strong Affair: *Released 08/10/1914 Monday.* No copyright entry — 1 reel/972 feet. CAST: Charles Inslee, Al Garcia, Emma Clifton, Mae Wells, Harry Griffith
SYNOPSIS: Cobbler Mier (Inslee) falls hopelessly in love with the girl (Clifton) when she brings in her slippers for repair. Soon after, Schultz the baker (Garcia) arrives with his shoes and tells of his wedding later that day, producing a picture of the girl Mier has fallen in love with. Mier seeks revenge and places limburger cheese in Schultz's shoes. At the wedding, the minister drops his bible at Schultz's feet and catches the "aroma" as he picks it up. He eyes him up and down. The girl drops her handkerchief, reaches for it, and stops the wedding when she catches the smell. Her father (Griffith) throws Schultz out of the church. Schultz discovers the problem, but returns to the church to find the girl marrying Mier. He throws the cheese, and a fight ensues. The minister calls the cops. When they arrive, all find the smell growing to an intolerable level, and they all seek refuge in a nearby wagon. Unfortunately, it turns out to be a limburger cheese wagon. Synopsis adapted from the plot summary in *Universal Weekly*, August 8, 1914, p.20
REVIEWS: "A low comedy number which will not suit particular audiences. Limburger cheese placed in the groom's shoes by his rival breaks up the wedding. Cheese is thrown freely by the guests at the wedding. This sort of humor has its admirers, but it is very offensive to some. The construction and photography are good." *Moving Picture World*, August 23, 1914, p.1100

"An amusing farce of a knockabout character. One sadly misses the ridiculous antics of Ford Sterling, who is a host of humour in himself. Nevertheless, the film is quite acceptable." *Bioscope*, October 29, 1914, p.XXI

At Three O'Clock: *Released 08/13/1914 Thursday.* No copyright entry — 1 reel/973 feet. Director, SCREENPLAY: David Kirkland. CAST: Ford Sterling, Peggy Pearce, Arthur Tavares, David Anderson

SYNOPSIS: Sterling is spurned by his girl (Pearce) for a gangster (Tavares). Despondent, he joins a suicide club for $5, and Prof. A.A. Sassan (Anderson) and his undertaker M. Balmer are scheduled to take care of him at 3:00. The girl tires of the domineering gangster and returns to the elated Sterling, and he forgets about the 3:00 appointment. Not for long, however. Sassan, having drunk his "killer liquid," is in hot pursuit, with the gangsters close behind. Sterling and his girl flee to a building full of explosives, and exit just as the others all enter and are blown up. Synopsis adapted from the plot summary in *Universal Weekly*, August 8, 1914, p.21

REVIEWS: "In this number Ford Sterling appears at his best. He determines to die because of a girl and arranges with Profs. A. Sassin and M. Balmer for his death a three o'clock. Later he changes his mind and there is the usual wild chase. This contains a lot of funny situations." *Moving Picture World*, August 15, 1914, p.961

"[Sterling] is, undoubtedly, one of the greatest screen comedians." *Bioscope*, October 15, 1914, p.273

Lost in the Studio: *Released 08/17/1914 Monday.* No copyright entry — 1 reel. DIRECTOR: Robert Thornby. CAST: Paul Jacobs, Robert Thornby, Ford Sterling

SYNOPSIS: Billy (Jacobs) arrives at the studio and greets his director, Robert Thornby. Sterling arrives, and Billy follows him to his dressing room, pestering him with questions until the actor gently throws him out. Billy plays with some friends until he spots a cameraman putting some candy into his film case. As he watches, he accidentally backs into a scene that Sterling is directing. He is forgiven. Later, Billy sneaks into the case and takes the candy. The cameraman soon realizes that his film has somehow been exposed, and heads to the vault to replace it. Billy pursues some kittens into the vault, and is locked in when the watchman closes the door. When Thornby is ready to direct a scene, it is discovered that Billy is missing. A massive search follows, with the vault the last place to be checked. Billy comes out crying. Synopsis adapted from the plot summary in *Universal Weekly*, August 15, 1914, p.20

REVIEWS: "Little Billy visits the moving picture studio in this number and gets lost while playing with some kittens. Pictures of Ford Sterling and his director, Robert Thornby, are shown. The plot is not very strong in this and it depends largely on Billy's popularity for interest." *Moving Picture World*, August 29, 1914, p.1242

His Wife's Flirtation: *Released 08/20/1914 Thursday.* No copyright entry — 1 reel/980 feet. CAST: Ford Sterling

(*Moving Picture World* attributes the role of Reuben to Sterling, but this is not substantiated in other sources, and is unlikely)

SYNOPSIS: Reuben stomps off to work, furious about his wife's flirting with the farm hand. He finds his clerk flirting with the customers, calls him down, and settles in waiting on the customers himself. His wife arrives at the store and, when Reuben's too busy to talk to her, begins flirting with a traveling salesman. Reuben sees this and kicks the salesman out. The wife feels sorry for the salesman, and he apologizes for getting her into trouble. A cop witnesses this from afar, and tells Reuben of her further flirting. Reuben shoots the place up, the salesman flees, and a burglar, dressed similarly to the salesman, jumps out the window. A chase involving the cop, the salesman, and the burglar follows, ending with the salesman losing the bulk of his clothes (they are lifted while he's taking a swim) and hiding under the wife's bed. Reuben returns and sits on the bed with his wife for a talk. He feels hands on his feet, pulls the salesman out from under the bed, and resumes his shooting. The salesman flees with Reuben close behind. Synopsis adapted from the plot summary in *Universal Weekly*, August 15, 1914, p.21

REVIEWS: "This tells the story of a flirtatious young wife. The traveling man loses his clothes and goes through most of the scenes in a bathing suit. Some of the situations are too suggestive and the humor is not strong." *Moving Picture World*, August 29, 1914, p.1242

A Rural Affair: *Released 08/24/1914 Monday.* No copyright entry — 1 reel/994 feet. CAST: Paul Jacobs, Carmen DeRue, Gordon Griffith, Olive Johnson

SYNOPSIS: Billy loves Carmen, who is older and larger than he is, but she loves Gordon who is more her age and size and has little difficulty shoving Billy aside. Billy secures a rabbit as a gift for her in hopes of winning her affections, but it escapes into a hole. He follows it and gets stuck. Olive, who loves Billy, runs and gets Carmen and Gordon to help rescue him. They do, and all four are now happy. Synopsis adapted from the plot summary in *Moving Picture World*, October 3, 1914, p.98

REVIEWS: "This features Little Billy with a cute little girl. He brings her a rabbit and this escapes down a bluff. Billy goes after it fearlessly and both he and the rabbit have to be rescued. An interesting number enacted entirely by children." *Moving Picture World*, September 5, 1914, p.1373 (At different times, *Moving Picture World* referred to this film under the alternate titles of **A Rural Love Affair** and **A Rural Romance**)

"It is a film which we certainly recommend." *Bioscope*, November 5, 1914, p.XXXVI

Snookee's Disguise: *Released 08/27/1914 Thursday.* No copyright entry — 1 reel/1002 feet. CAST: Ford Sterling, Peggy Pearce, Dave Anderson, Katherine Griffith, Bobby Dunn, Hank Mann

SYNOPSIS: Snookee (Sterling) is a cornet player with a wife — Mrs. Snookee — who loves to shop. She leaves him alone to practice, and heads for the Palace Café where the owner flirts with her –"An Innocent Flirtation." Meanwhile, Snookee is practicing beside an open window when the pretty young girl (Pearce) across the way begins to flirt with him, first getting his attention by using a mirror to reflect light in his eyes –"Not-So Innocent." Her husband catches her in the act and threatens Snookee from afar. Snookee responds with some violent blasts from his coronet. Meanwhile, offended by the café owner's advances, Mrs. Snookee returns home. Informed of the owner's actions, Snookee decides to catch him in the act. He dresses as a heavily-veiled woman and heads for the café.

The girl's husband, as it turns out, is a waiter at that same café, and the girl is there as well. The owner discovers Snookee's disguise and calls a cop. Snookee beans the girl's husband, mistaking him for the owner, and panics. The girl discovers Snookee's disguise as well. Her husband pulls a gun and begins shooting, and a wild chase ensues throughout the café. Some more cops arrive and join in. Snookee and the husband face off in battle, as does the girl and Mrs. Snookee, who has just arrived, in a battle of hair-pulling. At the climax, Snookee takes a wild swing and knocks himself out. Synopsis based on the print held by Library of Congress.

REVIEWS: "Characteristic Ford Sterling number. He appears as a cornet player who flirts with a girl across the way. His wife also flirts with a clerk and the principals meet in a restaurant where rampant trouble ensues. There is shooting, broken crockery, and some of the usual slapstick work." *Moving Picture World*, September 5, 1914, p.1373

"…even more remarkable than the many hilarious productions of this wonderful comedian. It is a weird and wonderful film, and its humour is contagious." *Bioscope*, October 29, 1914, p.XXI

The Tale of a Hat: *Released 08/31/1914 Monday.* No copyright entry — 1 reel/970 feet. DIRECTOR: Charles Hagenios. CAST: Emma Clifton, Charles Inslee, Harry Orr
SYNOPSIS: Three tramps arrive in town in a boxcar. The two tell the littlest third to go out begging, and beat him up when he refuses to do so, leaving him behind. A bill collector (Orr) browbeats the young wife (Clifton) to pay up the balance owed on a furniture loan. Her husband (Inslee) overhears, and when the collector leaves tells his wife that he'll withdrawal the last of their savings, $1000. The two tramps overhear and follow him. He makes the withdrawal and puts the $1000 bill in the band of his straw hat, and when he emerges from the bank he's attacked by the tramps. He flees and drops the hat, and they unknowingly toss it aside; the third little tramp picks it up and puts it on. When the duo catches the exhausted husband, they force him to tell of the money's whereabouts. He does, and they set out in pursuit of the little tramp on handcars. The husband enlists the aid of the marchers in a police parade, and they give chase in a police wagon. The pursuing tramps fall through an open drawbridge, the hat flies through the air and lands at the wife's feet. As the sheriff and his men begin to move the furniture out, she produces the $1000 and pays off the bill. The cops arrive shortly after the tramps, who are now madly shredding the hat in search of the money. The furniture is returned. Synopsis adapted from the plot summary in *Universal Weekly*, September 12, 1914, p.24
REVIEWS: "An eccentric comedy number in which the husband puts the rent money in a straw hat. The hat blows off his head and falls into the clutches of some tramps. Later it again gets away and blows into the wife's hands just in time to pay the rent. There are amusing spots in this and one thrill where the handcar falls through the open bridge draw." *Moving Picture World*, September 5, 1914, p.1373

"A breathless 'chase' comic." *Bioscope*, November 12, 1914, p.XXI

A Bogus Baron: *Released 09/03/1914 Thursday.* No copyright entry — 1 reel/994 feet.
CAST: Ford Sterling, Dave Anderson, Peggy Pearce, Arthur Tavares, Beverly Griffith
SYNOPSIS: Andy (Anderson) loves the landlady's daughter (Pearce), but the landlady objects. When a Count arrives, the landlady "chooses" him as a potential suitor. In an attempt to discredit his "rival," Andy coerces park worker Snitz (Sterling) to dress up in the Count's uniform and pose as Baron von Glutz with the understanding that when the Count is out of the picture, Snitz will step aside for Andy. Naturally, Snitz enjoys himself so much that he refuses to defer to Andy, so Andy tells the Count of the theft of his uniform. The Count goes after Snitz with the usual results. Synopsis adapted from the plot summary in *Universal Weekly*, September 12, 1914, p.24
REVIEWS: "Ford Sterling appears as a gardener in this number and is bribed by the girl's lover to aid him in forestalling the Baron's attentions. Ford pretends to be a band leader

and the usual mix-up ensues. There are no big features in this comic number and it is only fairly entertaining." *Moving Picture World*, September 12, 1914, p.1513

"...quite one of Mr. Sterling's best efforts." *Bioscope*, October 29, 1914, p.XXI

The Broken Doll: *Released 09/07/1914 Monday.* No copyright entry — 1 reel/747 feet. DIRECTOR: Robert Thornby. CAST: Paul Jacobs, Olive Johnson, Gordon Griffith, Carmen DeRue
SYNOPSIS: Billy and Gordon are brothers, with Olive and Carmen their respective sweethearts. Gordon excuses himself from Carmen's presence to go milk the cow. Billy makes fun of him and is squirted in the eye with cow's milk. Billy helps Olive reach the pump for water, then walks her home. They part at the crossroads. Gordon hears a yell and sees dust in the distance, and rushes over thinking that a car has hit Olive. It ran over her doll, however, and he sits down, kisses her on the cheek to comfort her, and attempts to mend the doll. Billy witnesses this and misunderstands, and in a fit of jealousy tells Carmen of her sweetheart's assumed perfidy. All is eventually explained and settled. Synopsis adapted from the plot summary in *Moving Picture World*, October 3, 1914, p.98
REVIEWS: "A child story, with Little Billy and three other children in it. One of the girls has her doll run over by an auto. The children are cute and attractive, but the plot in this offering is very thin." *Moving Picture World*, September 19, 1914, p.1645

"Billy almost precipitates a quarrel between two lovers, and nearly breaks off his own engagement. But things are settled in a happy way. An amusing offering." *Motion Picture News*, September 19, 1914, p.61

"Quite the best juvenile series we have seen, and deserves widespread popularity." *Bioscope*, November 19, 1914, p.XIII

09/10/1914 Thursday: release cancelled; **Trapped in a Closet** *previously announced for release on this date*

Trapped in a Closet: *Released 09/14/1914 Monday.* No copyright entry– 1 reel/910 feet. CAST: Emma Clifton
(retitled **Trapped in a Wardrobe** for British release)
SYNOPSIS: Bill and his wife (Clifton) battle constantly. To make amends, he has an old fashioned armoire delivered to his house which arrives while his wife is at the market. Burglars break into the house and gather up numerous belongings, but when the wife returns, they pack the belongings and themselves in the armoire until the coast is clear. Noticing that her silverware is missing, she calls the cops. She also calls the furniture men and tells them to take the bulky armoire out of her house. The cops realize that the goods must be in the armoire that the furniture men are carrying off, and set out in pursuit on mule-back. After using all of the ammo in their wild firing, an ancient artillery piece is called into service. The furniture men and the burglars alike flee the wagon, which spills. The cannon explodes and all are blown up with it. Synopsis adapted from the plot summary in *Universal Weekly*, September 12, 1914, p.20
REVIEWS: "This comic film reverts somewhat to the old-style eccentric. Two men are hauled away in a wagon, locked inside a wardrobe. The police follow and there is a lot

of wild revolver firing. This has amusing spots in it, but not much plot." *Moving Picture World*, September 19, 1914, p.1646

"Two burglars are the ones to get trapped, and then the closet is carried off on a moving van. They are chased by the comical Sterling police, who are mounted on quadrapeds [sic] of various species and sizes. A great amount of shooting occurs." *Motion Picture News*, September 19, 1914, p.61

09/17/1914 Thursday: no release

In and Out: *Released 09/21/1914 Monday.* No copyright entry — 1 reel/995 feet. DIRECTOR: David Kirkland. CAST: Max Asher, Bobby Dunn, Lucille Ward, Miss Clark, William Franey
SYNOPSIS: Schultz (Asher) the grocer and Murphy (Dunn) the butcher play cards in the back of the grocer's store while Mrs. Schultz and Mrs. Murphy gossip. Their gossip develops into a heated quarrel, while Schultz and Murphy break into a fight over Murphy's cheating. All four move into battle with much of the grocery's food tossed back and forth and a side of beef used as a battering ram. Mounted cops are summoned by a neighbor and arrive amidst a shower of eggs and ham. They beat a hasty retreat from the crossfire. Synopsis adapted from the plot summary in *Universal Weekly*, September 19, 1914, p.20
REVIEWS: "A number in which Max Asher appears as a grocer at war with his neighbor, the butcher. Real stores are used in the settings. They get into a quarrel and their wives follow suit. Egg throwing is the chief diversion. This is fairly humorous." *Moving Picture World*, September 26, 1914, p.1777

"Quite good fun, although one sadly misses the peculiar antics of Ford Sterling himself." *Bioscope*, November 26, 1914, p.XI

A Shooting Match: *Released 09/24/1914 Thursday.* No copyright entry — 2 reels/1905 feet. Directors: David Kirkland and Ford Sterling. CAST: Ford Sterling, Emma Clifton, Dave Anderson
(pre-release title: **At the Shoot**)
SYNOPSIS: At an aristocratic trap shooting club, rivals Snitz (Sterling) and Hans are in a deadlock over their love for the lovely Emma (Clifton). Being of an indecisive nature, Emma suggests that they engage in a shooting match to decide who shall have her for his own. They agree, and go off to practice with their shotguns for the big day. Snitz realizes that Hans is the better shot, so he pays Louie to remove the shot from Hans' shells. Snitz wins by one point, but finds that Emma has fallen for Louie during the match. Snitz refuses to pay Louie, who divulges Snitz's subterfuge to Hans. A free-for-all breaks out among the contestants, and Snitz seeks refuge in a tree. Hans and the others cut it down. Synopsis adapted from the plot summary in *Universal Weekly*, September 19, 1914, p.17
REVIEWS: "Two thousand feet of a Ford Sterling burlesque seems excessive, unless the plot has enough variety to warrant such a liberal allowance. 'A Shooting Match' is padded. Antics that may appear funny at first sight, lose their power to amuse when repeated with little variation, and in this picture Sterling is forced to repeat himself. As a comedian,

he gives himself a difficult task, for the story does not suggest more than one reel…. Photography is not of the best." Reviewed by D., *New York Dramatic Mirror*, September 23, 1914, p.31

"A Ford Sterling number. Hans and Snitz prepare for the shooting match. Snitz arranges with the score-keeper to extract shot from Hans' cartridges. This leads to a general scramble and Snitz takes refuge in a tree, which Hans and his friends cut down. This is very amusing in spots. The plot itself could have been compressed into one reel to advantage. Men of a sporting turn will appreciate the shooting contest." *Moving Picture World*, October 3, 1914, p.65

The Battle: *Released 09/28/1914 Monday.* No copyright entry — 2 reels/1776 feet.
DIRECTOR: Robert Thornby. CAST: Paul Jacobs, Olive Johnson
SYNOPSIS: Billy is despondent over being the only kid without a girlfriend. An old soldier spots the child while passing by, and his heart is softened by the child's resemblance to his dead son. He lures him home with candy. At the old soldiers' home, they play with a toy rifle and a drum, and then the old soldier lines up some toy soldiers on the floor and recounts exploits of days gone by. Years earlier he had been stationed at a fort on the plains, and had been in love with the Colonel's daughter. When the fort seems doomed during an Indian attack, the soldier had shown his heroism by sneaking out and going for help. Impressed by the soldier's bravery, the Colonel had consented to the match between his daughter and the soldier. The story being done, Billy and the old soldier both fall asleep, and Billy dreams the exploits with himself and Olive in the soldier's and daughter's positions. Meanwhile, Billy's ma is frantic over the disappearance of her child with the man with sweets, and enlists the aid of neighbors in her search. She finally finds them asleep, Billy with his arms around the old man's neck. She comes to understand what has happened, and leaves them undisturbed. Synopsis adapted from the plot summary in *Universal Weekly*, September 26, 1914, p.11
REVIEWS: "A two-reel juvenile offering, with Olive and Little Billy in the leading parts. The story is not strong, the first reel being slow and uncertain in development. Billy's dream, in the second reel, where he takes part in some genuine Indian warfare and saves the fort from destruction, was interesting. But it was necessary to make a substitution in the horseback ride. The photography is uneven and quite below the standard in some places. This is only moderately entertaining, though Billy and the little girl are very captivating." *Moving Picture World*, October 3, 1914, p.65

"In the two reels of this picture produced by Robert Thornby, the footage is divided about equally between the Universal Company's juvenile players and frontier battle scenes, in which Indians attack and soldiers defend a fort. To all intents and purposes, there are two totally dissimilar subjects included under one head: for the first reel offers a rather slow moving child story, whereas the second shows the adult battle, and little else. Billy strays away from his playmates, and wanders into the home of a kind-hearted old gentleman, who tells him a story of his experiences in the West. Both fall asleep, and Billy dreams of the thrilling events., in which he plays the part of the volunteer that rides through the Indian lines and summons reinforcements. Plenty of men are engaged, and a great quantity of powder is burned in the assault on the fort. These scenes are very well arranged, although it is something of a surprise to find that an early frontier fort is protected by modern machine guns." *New York Dramatic Mirror*, September 23, 1914, p.34

"Quite the best of the series, and should prove a big attraction." *Bioscope*, December 3, 1914, p.IX

10/01/1914 Thursday: no release

Myer's Mistake: *Released 10/05/1914 Monday.* No copyright entry — 1 reel/979 feet. DIRECTOR: Frank C. Griffin. CAST: Max Asher, Arthur Tavares, Miss Elliott, Mr. Quinn
SYNOPSIS: Emil Myer (Asher) comes to realize that his sweetheart Fannie (Elliot) is fickle, so he decides to shoot himself. His roommate Arthur Schultz (Tavares) intercedes at the last moment, fighting for the revolver which goes off harmlessly. Count Gasco (Quinn) is annoyed by the gunshot, but softens at Myer's story and suggests a plan. Myers fakes the suicide to elicit a response from Fannie. Informed, she calls to view the dearly departed. Schultz immediately falls for her, so he nails the lid on the coffin and carries it in a wild dash to the graveyard where he buries it. Returning to the house, he finds Gasco wooing Fannie in the kitchen. Realizing his mistake, he returns to the graveyard to save Myers, but finds that he has already escaped. Meanwhile, Myers stumbles across Gasco and Fannie, and returns to the graveyard for a renewed attempt at suicide. Finding Schultz, the two break into a fight and both fall into the open grave. Synopsis adapted from the plot summary in *Moving Picture World*, October 3, 1914, p.98
REVIEWS: "Max gets into rivalry with a younger man over a girl and pretends to be killed. He is placed in a coffin and buried, but digs out again. This contains considerable humor of the slapstick sort and is amusing in its way. The photography is good." *Moving Picture World*, October 17, 1914, p.337

Hypnotic Power: *Released 10/08/1914 Thursday.* No copyright entry — 1 reel/1011 feet. CAST: Ford Sterling, Dave Anderson, David Kirkland, Emma Clifton
SYNOPSIS: In an attempt to get his rival (Anderson) out of the way, Snookee (Sterling) takes a crash course in hypnosis. Using his new-found talents on his rival, he has him jump in a lake. Snookee gathers up his girl (Clifton) and heads for the preacher's home to make hasty wedding preparations. The master hypnotist (Kirkland) runs into the rival wandering about aimlessly, and brings him to. The rival breaks into the preacher's home before the knot has been tied, with the usual climactic results. Synopsis adapted from the plot summary in *Moving Picture World*, October 3, 1914, p.98
REVIEWS: "Ford Sterling appears in his usual eccentric characterization. Jealousy of a rival leads him to study hypnotism. He makes the rival jump in the lake. All goes well until the professor of hypnotism shows up. This contains a lot of amusing nonsense and is quite pleasing." *Moving Picture World*, October 10, 1914, p.189

"Usual type. Rough house stuff good for laughs. Sterling at his best." *Variety*, October 17, 1914, p.24

The Close Call: *Released 10/12/1914 Monday.* No copyright entry — 1 reel/945 feet. CAST: Olive Johnson, Felix Walsh
(erroneously credited as **A Close Call** in several sources)
SYNOPSIS: A young boy Felix (Walsh) and girl Olive (Johnson) wander down a country path, holding hands. After announcing their affection for each other, Olive heads for home

promising to return shortly. With a bowl of jam provided by her mother in hand, she heads back to share it with Felix. Stumbling on a cliffside path, the jam topples over the side. Her attempt to retrieve it results in Olive sliding half way down the cliff, landing in some brush.

An older boy and girl hear Olive's cry for help, so they rush back to her home and alert her mother. Accompanied by two neighbor women and three farmers, they rush to the scene to affect a rescue. Meanwhile, Felix has discovered Olive's predicament, and heads to the base of the cliff where he manages to rescue her. The group of adults arrives at the scene and one of the farmers is lowered by rope, only to find that Olive is no longer there. He's pulled back up, explains what he didn't find, and is again lowered for a second look. When Felix and Olive arrive unharmed, the jubilant adults rush to them, leaving a single farmer struggling with the rope. Seeing his predicament, the other farmers return and the two haul their friend to safety. The overjoyed parents, holding the two youths in their arms, smother them with hugs. Synopsis based on personal viewing of film

After school, Olive and her boyfriend are given bread and jam on the porch and told to keep an eye on the baby. They don't, and the baby crawls off after the bulldog. The baby plays at a cliff's edge, but is "rescued" by the bulldog who eats the baby's jam and lures him away from danger. Meanwhile, ma and the neighbors are frantic. Finding one of the baby's shoes by the cliff, they all climb down in search. After numerous mishaps, the baby is found safe and sound. Synopsis adapted from the plot summary in *Universal Weekly*, October 10, 1914, p.24

REVIEWS: "Little Olive drops her piece of bread and jam over the cliff and slides down after it. Felix comes to her rescue and great excitement is caused among the older folks. A child story with some clever little actors in it. The plot, of course, is very light." *Moving Picture World*, October 17, 1914, p.337

"A child named Felix assumes Billy's role in this juvenile comedy, but he isn't as good as his more noted predecessor. But he rescues Olive from the side of a cliff where she has fallen, and his act and the whole picture is very amusing." *Motion Picture News*, October 17, 1914, p.54

Heinie's Outing: *Released 10/15/1914 Thursday.* No copyright entry — 1 reel/930 feet.
CAST: Max Asher, Velma Steck, Arthur Tavares
SYNOPSIS: Gangster "Knock-Out" Jim*(Tavares) and Heinie Plitzer (Asher) are both in love with Lena (Steck). Jim asks her to attend the Dutch picnic with him. The neighborhood gang is at odds with Jim over the theft of their crap money, so they inform Plitzer. Plitzer asks Lena to attend, and she accepts when Jim knocks him down. Arriving at the picnic, Plitzer excuses himself and goes to wash his hands in the river. He falls in. Meanwhile, a man in a checkered suit accidentally bounces a croquet ball off Jim's head and makes a hasty exit. He removes the checkered suit to go bathing, and Plitzer, emerging from the river soaked, spots the dry suit and makes off with it. When Jim sees Plitzer in the checkered suit, he assumes him to be his attacker. He empties his revolver at him without scoring a hit. An ambulance is summoned by witnesses to the action. Plitzer discovers two revolvers in the suit's pockets, opens fire, and chases a panicky Jim out of the picnic. Plitzer is the hero of the day.

*"Spike" in the title cards of the Library of Congress print. Synopsis adapted from the plot summary in *Universal Weekly*, October 10, 1914, p.20

REVIEWS: "Max takes his girl on a picnic. He borrows a bather's checked suit and finds himself in a peck of trouble as a result. There is an ambulance runaway and a general scramble toward the last. This is well photographed and quite amusing." *Moving Picture World*, October 17, 1914, p.337

"Few laughs." *Variety*, October 17, 1914, p.24

"An indifferent knock-about comic." *Bioscope*, December 24, 1914, p.XI

Carmen's Wash Day: *Released 10/19/1914 Monday.* No copyright entry — 1 reel/973 feet.
CAST: Carmen DeRue, Max Asher, Chandler House, Violet Radcliffe
SYNOPSIS: While Carmen is washing her doll's clothes, Radcliffe approaches. He teases her and tries to kiss her, and she strikes him with the wet wash. He plans revenge and throws mud on the clothes. When she returns and sees the mess, she begins to cry. Chandler consoles her and offers to rewash them. Radcliffe makes fun of him and they get into a fight. Radcliffe shoots at Chandler and misses, but hits a servant girl inside a window. She looks out and sees an innocent man with a gun and hits him with a rolling pin. The gun discharges, hitting a painter and knocking him from a ladder. He throws his paint in anger, accidentally hitting the servant girl. While the fight among the neighbors grows larger, the children make up. Synopsis adapted from the plot summary in *Universal Weekly*, October 17, 1914, p.20
REVIEWS: "This starts out with a number of children, but later older people appear in the cast. The bad boy, who put dirt on Carmen's clean clothes, succeeds in starting a neighborhood rumpus. There are amusing moments in this, but the plot itself is very slight." *Moving Picture World*, October 24, 1914, p.493

"The Sterling kids start a regular riot in this picture between the older people by careless manipulations of a sling shot and bow and arrow. Max Asher appears in a comical role. A chase ends the picture." *Motion Picture News*, October 31, 1914, p.52

"Capable kid comics. More laughs than usual." *Variety*, October 1914

Secret Service Snitz: *Released 10/22/1914 Thursday.* No copyright entry — 1 reel/965 feet. CAST: Ford Sterling, Peggy Pearce, Emma Clifton
SYNOPSIS: Secret Service agent Snitz (Sterling) is cracking down on moonshiners. Spotting a moonshiners' daughter (Pearce) in a perilous situation, Snitz rescues her. She shows her gratitude, but this is seen by her lover who decides to kill Snitz. He enters the cabin and attempts to knock the stuffing out of Snitz, who escapes and is hidden by the girl in a whiskey barrel. Her man realizes this, nails the lid on, and rolls it down the hill. It crashes into the moonshiner's house and explodes. Snitz runs off with the gang of moonshiners in pursuit. Snitz's aides, hidden in the mountains and waiting for a signal, descend upon the moonshiners. After a wild fight, the moonshiners are all arrested. Synopsis adapted from the plot summary in *Universal Weekly*, October 17, 1914, p.24
REVIEWS: "Ford Sterling here appears as sheriff in a moonshiners' district. He gets on trail of the gang and takes a ride in a barrel over some cliffs. This runs along in about the same style as former productions, none of the action being particularly new." *Moving Picture World*, October 31, 1914, p.642

"Amusing burlesque on the moonshiner-secret service agent story. Ford Sterling is Snitz. Very laughable. The film seems lightstruck in parts." *Motion Picture News*, October 31, 1914, p.52

"Uninteresting." *Variety*, October 24, 1914, p.22

Snookee's Day Off: *Released 10/26/1914 Monday.* No copyright entry — 1 reel/995 feet.
CAST: Gus Erdman, Bobbie Gould
SYNOPSIS: Louie Myer (Erdman) is forced by his wife to accompany her to the beach. He misses the trolley, but is scooped up by the fender of the next one and has a free trip to his destination. His wife tells him to wait while she changes in the bath house. He moves closer when he spots a shapely leg under a parasol, but his wife cuts him short. He again tries to flirt, but is rebuffed by the young lady. The girl and his wife use neighboring bath houses (mounted on wagons), and Louie decides to kidnap the young lovely. Dragging the wagon to a secluded spot, he realizes his goof when he finds his wife inside. He locks the door. Meanwhile, the wagon that he assumed contained his wife and that he had set adrift now bobs about with the young lady on its roof calling for help. Her lover saves her and she points an accusing finger at Louie. Her lover pummels Louie. The horse runs off with his wife's wagon and it crashes. Louie's wife emerges from the crumbled bath house and rescues Louie from his beating. They return home on the trolley. Synopsis adapted from the plot summary in *Universal Weekly*, October 24, 1914, p.24, under the title **Snoopee's Day Off**)
REVIEWS: "Shapely misses on the beach cause husband trouble. Only fair." *Variety*, October 31, 1914, p.26

"This number deals with a married man who does some snooping around bath houses on a beach. The scenes are vulgar and suggestive and the number has little to commend in it except the good photography." *Moving Picture World*, October 31, 1914, p.642

"Snopee [sic] is henpecked and when he sees an attractive young woman disporting herself on the beach in an abbreviated bathing suit, we can excuse him in his attempt to roll his wife's bathhouse into the water, but he gets the wrong house and the girl goes instead. Funny in parts, risqué in others, with a few vulgar moments." *Motion Picture News*, October 31, 1914, p.63

"An indifferent, slapdash comic, whose humour degenerates to something approaching coarseness." *Bioscope*, January 7, 1915, p.X

A Race for a Bride: *Released 10/29/1914 Thursday.* No copyright entry — 1 reel/1011 feet.
CAST: Gus Erdman, Emma Clifton, Arthur Tavares, Dot Gould
SYNOPSIS: The girl's (Clifton) father promises her hand to the first suitor (Erdman and Tavares) to bring back a Justice of the Peace. One of them gets thrown in jail for his less than subtle attempts to coerce a J.P. to go with him; the other is pursued by a gun-wielding J.P. Synopsis adapted from the plot summary in *Universal Weekly*, date unknown
REVIEWS: "An eccentric comedy number, in which the girl's father promises her hand to the one who first brings in a justice of the peace. One of the lovers is thrown in jail, escapes, and is followed by the justice with a gun. He wins. This is fairly well presented and moderately amusing." *Moving Picture World*, November 7, 1914, p.788

"Good comedy of the two suitors for the girl. The one who brings the justice of the peace to the house first is to win her. The race is the most comical feature." *Motion Picture News*, November 7, 1914, p.51

"Cheapest kind of picture. Poor." *Variety*, October 31, 1914, p.26

The Wall Between: *Released 11/02/1914 Monday.* No copyright entry — 1 reel/964 feet.
CAST: Chandler House, Carmen DeRue, Carl Formes, Miss O'Connor
SYNOPSIS: The estates of Mr. Smith (Formes), a widower, and the widow Mrs. Jones (O'Connor) are separated by an English brick wall. He repeatedly has words with her about her chickens crossing into his yard, and neither seems to have much patience with the other. Smith's nephew (House) is home visiting from boarding school, and begins to conduct an over-the-wall flirtation with Mrs. Jones' niece (DeRue). They are caught by their guardians as they attempt to cross the wall, and warned not to do it again. Their persistence warms the guardians' hearts, and the two former enemies become friends. Synopsis adapted from the plot summary in *Universal Weekly*, October 31, 1914, p.24
REVIEWS: "A comedy number based on the familiar situation of a widow and widower living on opposite sides of a dividing stone wall. They quarrel and the children bring them together. The idea has, of course, been used frequently; the settings and photography are attractive." *Moving Picture World*, November 7, 1914, p.788

"Quite a pleasant comedy that will please." *Motion Picture News*, November 7, 1914, p.51

"Camera splendid." *Variety*, November 7, 1914, p.22

Dot's Chaperone: *Released 11/05/1914 Thursday.* No copyright entry — 1 reel/980 feet.
CAST: Dot Gould, Max Asher
SYNOPSIS: When his sweetheart (Gould) decides to date another, Max dresses as a woman and acts as her chaperone. Synopsis adapted from the plot summary in *Universal Weekly*, date unknown
REVIEWS: "A Max Asher number, in which Max disguises himself as a woman and hires out as chaperone for his sweetheart. The action does not lead up to any very humorous situations. It makes altogether a fair offering." *Moving Picture World*, November 14, 1914, p.933

"Only two or three laughs. Lacks class." *Variety*, November 7, 1914, p.22

"An indifferent comedy of a familiar, and none too amusing, type." *Bioscope*, January 14, 1915, p.XI

An Ill Wind: *Released 11/09/1914 Monday.* No copyright entry — 1 reel/957 feet. CAST: Max Asher, Carl Formes, Miss Bobbie Gould
SYNOPSIS: The police chief of Pumpkin Center rules his men with an iron hand. After a hard day of drilling them, he heads for home to sign some valuable documents. One of the important papers blows away, and the chief sets off in hot pursuit. It blows into a pretty young girl's bedroom, and the chief crawls in after it. Her boyfriend, a police lieutenant, stumbles across him and not realizing who he is, ropes him up in the couch and has him and the couch hauled down to the station where he's released…to everyone's horror. The furious chief takes revenge Synopsis adapted from the plot summary in *Universal Weekly*, November 7, 1914, p.20
REVIEWS: "An eccentric number with some quite amusing situations in it. The chief of

police becomes locked in a clothes box in the girl's room and is given a wild ride inside it. The photography is good and this succeeds very well for an old type of film story." *Moving Picture World*, November 21, 1914, p.1076

"The methods of the Sterling police are so certain in their appeal to the general public, that no very great originality is required of them, but in this instance their exuberance supplies all deficiencies, and the film is certain to create merriment." *Bioscope*, January 21, 1915, p.IX

The Dog Raffles: *Released 11/12/1914 Thursday.* No copyright entry — 1 reel/700 feet.
DIRECTOR: David Kirkland. CAST: Arthur Tavares, Gus Erdman, Peggie the dog
SYNOPSIS: A gentleman crook (Tavares) has his trick dog (Peggie) trained to enter guests' rooms and remove their valuables via the fire escape. During a caper, the thief doesn't realize that a second crook, Yeggman (Erdman), is also in the process of burgling the room. The dog emerges with a lit stick of dynamite, and both crooks flee. They race across rooftops with the dog close behind, and jump down a chimney (coincidentally the police station's) in an attempt to escape. The cops chase them out into the street, and the duo end up diving into the river with the cops, now aware of the danger, following. The dog drops the dynamite into the river where it explodes harmlessly, and the crooks are arrested. Synopsis adapted from the plot summary in *Universal Weekly*, November 11, 1914, p.20
REVIEWS: "The dog's master, being out of food and money, teaches the animal to invade other people's rooms and steal. All goes well till the dog picks up a lighted bomb and then a wild chase results. This is well pictured and makes a fairly amusing number." *Moving Picture World*, November 21, 1914, p.1077

"…a roaring farce…plenty of go in this strenuous little piece." *Bioscope*, January 21, 1915, p.IX

A Bear Escape: *Released 11/16/1914 Monday.* No copyright entry — 1 reel/758 feet.
DIRECTOR: Robert Thornby. CAST: Carmen DeRue, Buddie Harris, Chandler House, Buster Emmons
SYNOPSIS: Two country boys (House and Emmons) decide to scare the city boy (Harris) who has won their sweetheart (DeRue). One of them dresses as a bear while the other joins a group of children. The phony bear meets up with a real bear and flees in terror, hiding in a tree. Later, thinking it's safe, he comes back down only to have the chase resumed. The chase leads into the group of kids, and all flee for their lives. Slowly but surely the boys get back together and realize that the girl is nowhere to be found. They conduct a search and eventually find her feeding sugar to the apparently harmless bear. She refuses to have anything more to do with such cowards. Synopsis adapted from the plot summary in *Universal Weekly*, December 26, 1914, p.28
REVIEWS: "A boy and girl story, in which one of the lads makes up as a bear. A real bear chases him up a tree. This situation affords quite a little amusement. It turns out that the real bear is tame and eats sugar from the girl's hand. This should interest children." *Moving Picture World*, November 1914

"Comedy to big laughter…great for kids." *Variety*, November 21, 1914, p.26; among its six "Best Reels of the Week")

Noodle's Return: *Released 11/19/1914 Thursday.* No copyright entry — 1 reel/1000 feet.
DIRECTOR: David Kirkland. CAST: William Wolbert
SYNOPSIS: Meek Noodles (Wolbert) is incessantly hounded by his wife. He writes her a goodbye note and heads for the saloon. He realizes how much he loves her and eventually returns. He climbs into bed, not realizing that his fellow occupants are the newlywed couple that his wife has rented the house to. His wife realizes the errors of her ways and returns to Noodles. Synopsis adapted from the plot summary in *Universal Weekly*, date unknown
REVIEWS: "Old-time stuff for laughs. Medium." *Variety*, November 21, 1914, p.26
"Played very brightly…calculated to afford plenty of amusement." *Bioscope*, May 13, 1915, p.X

Black Hands: *Released 11/23/1914 Monday.* No copyright entry — 1 reel/985 feet.
DIRECTOR: Robert Thornby. CAST: Carl Formes, Seymour Hastings, Felix Walsh, George Jaeschke
SYNOPSIS: Mr. Craig (Formes) argues with an Italian organ grinder and later worries when he receives a threatening note. During his absence, his boy (Walsh) gets into the jam and leaves jam-soaked handprints all over the walls, and then retreats to the attic for a nap. When his dad returns and sees the mark of the black hand on the front door, he calls in detective Skylark Fumes (Hastings). Fumes decides that there must be at least a thousand black handers on the loose, so with the aid of trained police pigeons calls in the force. After many deductions and some "clever" police work, the boy is found. Synopsis adapted from the plot summary in *Universal Weekly*, November 21, 1914, p.20
REVIEWS: "A small boy with a pot of jam leaves numerous imprints around his father's premises. Skylark Fumes, the celebrated detective, is called and an amusing investigation follows. This idea has been used before, but is here handled fairly well and makes quite a pleasing offering." *Moving Picture World*, November 28, 1914, p.1233
"The police are the funniest part of the picture; they are led by a comedian who gives promise of a bright future." *Motion Picture News*, November 28, 1914, p.49
"Idea good, but overdrawn." *Variety*, November 28, 1914, p.23
"…hardly equal in merit to the majority of the…juvenile series, this is quite an acceptable little trifle." *Bioscope*, February 4, 1915, p.XIX

Dot's Elopement: *Released 11/26/1914 Thursday.* No copyright entry — 1 reel. DIRECTOR: Frank Griffin. CAST: Bobbie Gould, Max Asher, Gus Erdman, Frank Griffin, Miss Lewis, John Brennan
SYNOPSIS: Dot (Gould) and Gus (Erdman) are in love, but her father (Asher) forbids it because Gus isn't good enough for her. Father prefers Max (Griffin), who holds his mortgage. Gus returns home in a funk, but finds a letter informing him that he's heir to $50,000. He rushes off and tells Dot, and they mount a sprinkling cart and head off for the minister's home. Max spots them and tells her pa and ma (Lewis), and they hop into their car and drive off in pursuit. Max follows, and all repeatedly skid on the water put down by the cart. During the wild ride, Gus loses the letter and pa finds and reads it. Having a miraculous change of heart, pa beats up Max and tears up the mortgage. He heads to the church and confronts Gus, who is ready to fight. To his surprise, pa greets

him like a long lost brother. Synopsis adapted from the plot summary in *Universal Weekly*, December 26, 1914, p.21

REVIEWS: "Conventional knock-about comedy, in which the girl is about to marry the real estate agent at her father's request, when her lover falls heir to a fortune. They elope and a chase ensues. This proves moderately amusing." *Moving Picture World*, November 28, 1914, p.1233

"The most laughable feature of this comedy is the chase, in which a watering cart and two automobiles partake. Dot, who is the daughter of a poor man, is given as the wife-to-be of the mortgage holder. Then her real beau discovers he has inherited a fortune, which leads to the elopement and a hasty marriage. Max Asher has a small part as the father." *Motion Picture News*, November 28, 1914, p.49

*11/30/1914 Monday: release cancelled (**His New Job** previously announced for release on this date)*

Love, Luck, and Candy: *Released 12/03/1914 Thursday.* No copyright entry — 1 reel/999 feet. CAST: Max Asher, Bobbie Gould, Arthur Tavares
SYNOPSIS: Max (Asher) calls on his sweetheart Dolly (Gould) and finds her with his rival (Tavares). He heads to the pharmacy for some poison but the chemist, suspecting the worse, gives him sugar instead. Max "poisons" some candy and sends it to her. Dolly, finding the rival to be a flirt, drops him and sends a love note to Max. Receiving the note, he rushes to her house. Meanwhile, she's fainted at the sight of a rat, and when he finds her and the partially consumed candy, he assumes the worst. He calls an ambulance and then eats some of the candy to commit suicide. He imagines he's dying, and when she gets up he thinks her to be a haunting spirit. She convinces him otherwise. The ambulance is accidentally blown up by a construction gang. Synopsis adapted from the plot summary in *Universal Weekly*, November 28, 1914, p.20
REVIEWS: "Park, girl, male flirt, policeman, trouble. This eccentric comedy is well-photographed, but the humor is not very pronounced. The latter scenes leading up to the explosion were best." *Moving Picture World*, December 12, 1914, p.1524

"Fair comedy of average merit." *Bioscope*, February 18, 1914, p.1524

Billy's Charge: *Released 12/07/1914 Monday.* No copyright entry — 1 reel/977 feet. CAST: Paul Jacobs, Carmen DeRue, Chandler House
SYNOPSIS: Billy is given bread, jam, and his baby sister to watch. He doesn't, instead strolling off with Carmen and Chandler. The child wanders off towards the lake, Billy and Chandler steal a bird's nest, but Carmen is furious, tells them that "God will not like it if they steal it," and insists that they replace it. They do, and Chandler fakes a fall from the tree in hopes of some sympathy. Billy remembers the child and heads back. Finding a shoe by the lake, he assumes the worst. He soon realizes that a strange dog has lured the child away from the lake and is protecting it. Billy grabs the child and returns him to his home moments before his ma returns. He resolves to be a little more careful the next time. Synopsis adapted from the plot summary in *Universal Weekly*, December 5, 1914, p.21
REVIEWS: "Little Billy neglects his baby sister. The big dog proves her friend and saves her from drowning. The latter feature was the most interesting, but would have gotten over

more strongly if the baby had not cried so continuously. The picture closes with everyone safe at home." *Moving Picture World*, December 12, 1914, p.1524

His New Job: *Released 12/10/1914 Thursday.* No copyright entry — 1 reel/982 feet. CAST: Agnes Copelin, Arthur Tavares, Gus Erdman, William Wolbert
(**Lizzie's Fortune** previously announced for release on this date)
SYNOPSIS: Mabel (Copelin) arrives at a hotel for a stay, but is put off by flirts Arthur (Tavares) and Mr. Stue (Erdman), so she packs to leave. Stue follows her, so she hides in the room across the hall under the bed. Arthur arrives — it's his room — while Noodles the porter (Wolbert) goes to Mabel's room for her trunk. He stumbles across Stue in her room, a fight ensues, and Stue is thrown across the hall, crashing into Arthur's room. He rolls under the bed and finds Mabel, but is quickly dragged out again by Arthur. A free-for-all follows and Mabel escapes while Stue falls into her trunk, is imprisoned, and is dragged bumpily down the hotel steps by Noodles. Noodles loses his footing and he, the trunk, and Stue end up in the hotel fountain covered with various pieces of Mabel's lingerie. Stue falls peacefully asleep. Synopsis adapted from the plot summary in *Universal Weekly*, December 5, 1914, p.24
REVIEWS: "Willie Walrus appears in this burlesque number as porter in a hotel. There is a mix-up among the various guests and some rather rough knock-about work. This is amusing in spots." *Moving Picture World*, December 12, 1914, p.1524

"…indifferent…of no very great humour or originality." *Bioscope*, February 18, 1915, p.X

Lizzie's Fortune: *Released 12/14/1914 Monday.* No copyright entry — 1 reel/977 feet. CAST: Max Asher, Arthur Tavares, Louise Fazenda, Gus Erdman
SYNOPSIS: A trio of lazy boarders (Asher, Tavares, and Erdman) is short on money and incentive, but long on appetite. Their landlady, the homely widow Lizzie Prune (Fazenda), is in love with the handsome boarder Arthur, but all three despise her, tolerating her only for the free ride they're receiving. After extended grumbling about the latest meal, they head for the garden to relax. Arthur finds a young boy playing with a scrap of paper, and upon reading it comes to the conclusion that she's to be a heiress of $50,000. He smothers her with affection while she does the dishes, and the other two find the note. All three get into a fight and take turns proposing, and she relaxes while each tries to outdo the others in cleaning, cooking, chopping wood, and so on. She chooses Arthur and they are married. While strolling, he finds the remainder of the note: the uncle leaving the money had remarried and his widow got it all! Arthur attempts to escape but is chased by Lizzie. They end up in the river, and she plants an affectionate kiss upon his brow. Synopsis adapted from the plot summary in *Universal Weekly*, December 12, 1914, p.21
REVIEWS: "Not a laugh." *Variety*, December 19, 1914, p.26

"The girl in the boarding house finds her stock rising when a letter arrives saying she has inherited $5,000. Three boarders try for her hand, but it develops later she is to get nothing. A familiar plot, full of action and carrying the interest quite well. The photography is uneven but generally good." *Moving Picture World*, December 19, 1914, p.1681

"The reel is rather dull." *Motion Picture News*, December 19, 1914, p.84

"Bright comedy, with the usual rushabout finale." *Bioscope*, March 11, 1915, p.X

The Fatal Hansom: *Released 12/17/1914 Thursday.* No copyright entry — 1 reel/993 feet. CAST: Bobby Dunn, William Wolbert
SYNOPSIS: Irish cabby Casey (Dunn) kisses his wife goodbye and heads for work. Riding to the stand, he gets into his usual fight with rival cabby Noodles (Wolbert) over a fare, and both lose it. Noodles heads to a saloon. Noodles' girl arrives but Casey begins to flirt with her and invites her for a ride. She accepts. He puts her in the hansom cab and hires Noodles to drive the cab, unaware that the girl is Noodles' girl. As the trip progresses, Noodles grows curious about Casey's girl's looks and takes a peak. Now furious with the two of them, he's off on a wild ride. Casey's wife spots his predicament and follows the runaway hansom on horseback. The horses break loose from the cab on a hillside, and the cab rolls down and off a pier with all three still aboard. Some dockworkers go to the rescue, and Casey's wife accidentally falls in. After several unsuccessful attempts at rescue, the dockworkers give up in disgust, leaving the four to their own devices. Synopsis adapted from the plot summary in *Universal Weekly*, December 12, 1914, p.24
REVIEWS: "William Wolbert appears in this as Noodles, a cab driver. He and another are rivals for a girl. The most amusing situations are toward the latter part of the reel where Noodles backs the hansom off the pier. Eccentric comedy somewhat better than the average." *Moving Picture World*, December 19, 1914, p.1681

"Two cabmen are rivals in love as well as business, and their antagonism leads them into many a quarrel. When one of them is seated in the cab with the object of his and the other's affections, and the other is perched aloft driving the vehicle at great speed, the chances are that the spectacle will strike many on the humorous side. All the principals end up struggling in the water in the finale." *Motion Picture News*, December 19, 1914, p.84

"The film is of a riotously humourous order, and has scenes which would never gain approval of the Royal Humane Society…brisk, well-played…" *Bioscope*, February 11, 1915, pp. 562-563

"…of no very great merit and very little real humour." *Bioscope*, February 25, 1915, p.X

Carmen's Romance: *Released 12/21/1914 Monday.* No copyright entry — 1 reel/998 feet. DIRECTOR: Robert Thornby. CAST: Carmen DeRue, Paul Jacobs, Buster Emmons, Chandler House
SYNOPSIS: Country boy Buster is jealous when city chap Chandler makes eyes at Carmen. Buster picks a fight, but is thrashed soundly by Chandler. Carmen takes a walk with Chandler who goes to a well for water. Buster hits him with a stick, accidentally knocking him in. Buster attempts to rescue him but also falls in. Both call for help, but Carmen is not strong enough to hoist them both up. She finds Billy and together they succeed. Billy scolds Buster while Chandler and Carmen leave together. Synopsis adapted from the plot summary in *Universal Weekly*, December 19, 1914, p.20
REVIEWS: "A juvenile offering of about the average interest. The main situation is where the two rival boys fall into the well. Little Billy and the girl rescue them with great difficulty. The photography is good." *Moving Picture World*, December 26, 1914, p.1841

"It is funny, most of the humor resulting from the antics of two of the members of the cast, the villain and the hero, while in the well. Billy plays the part of the peacemaker and smoothes things over in the finale. This will please more than the ordinary kid comedy, although it might be appreciated more if childish actions were resorted to by the children instead of their emulation of grown-ups." *Motion Picture News*, December 26, 1914, p.50

Innocent Dad: *Released 12/24/1914 Wednesday.* No copyright entry — 1 reel/645 feet. DIRECTOR: Frank Griffin. CAST: John Brennan, Bobbie Gould, Gus Erdman, Mr. Rooney SYNOPSIS: Father (Brennan) and son Arthur (Erdman) are separated at the beach, so dad heads to the café. He gets into an argument with a burly waiter and ends up hiding under a table. The son and a new girl (Gould) that he met on the boardwalk arrive and sit at the table, barring dad's escape from beneath it. The girl's jealous gangster lover (Rooney) arrives and flies into a raging fit when he finds her with Arthur. Arthur flees when a gun is drawn, and dad tries to follow, taking the table with him. The gangster mistakes dad for Arthur and opens fire. Dad swims out to the mast of a sunken ship, and the gangster opens fire with an old cannon. The third shot destroys the cannon, sending the gangster flying through the clouds. He lands on dad, and the fight continues in the water. Synopsis adapted from the plot summary in *Universal Weekly*, December 19, 1914, p.21
REVIEWS: "A burlesque offering with John E. Brennan and Dot Gould in the cast. This is a reiteration of numerous stunts that have been done frequently; it is well photographed but has not much novelty in the main situations." *Moving Picture World*, December 26, 1914, p.1841

"[I]t is poor Dad who gets into a whole lot of trouble when he is the most innocent one of the crowd. There is a grand mix-up in a dining room which is fairly humorous. The picture is a comedy of the average order, nothing startlingly funny, but everything passably humorous." *Motion Picture News*, December 26, 1914, p.50

"There is nothing particularly humourous in the film, and its 'comedy business' is extravagant in the extreme." *Bioscope*, March 4, 1915, p.X

The Chef's Revenge: *Released 12/28/1914 Monday.* No copyright entry — split reel/617 feet. DIRECTOR: David Kirkland. CAST: Lloyd Ingraham, Emma Clifton, Arthur Tavares SYNOPSIS: A crowded restaurant's patrons impatiently await the arrival of the establishment's chef while the proprietor (Tavares) wrings his hands with worry. Chef DeBean (Ingraham) eventually arrives, going through his protracted ritual of greeting the pretty young cashier (Clifton) good morning, slowly removing his kid gloves, surveying the hungry crowd, and then entering the kitchen after an enthusiastic reception from the proprietor. He puts his army of assistants to work. Mr. Millions, an important but grouchy man about town, arrives at the restaurant. The proprietor, to show his great esteem for the wealthy and influential Millions, summons DeBean so that the man may place his order directly with the chef. DeBean and his men proceed with the preparation of the fellow's steak, which includes the group jumping upon it before cooking to tenderize the steak. Finally, DeBean personally presents the meal in grand style with everything just so. Unfortunately, Millions is in a worse mood than usual and finds fault with everything. He gets into a fight with the proprietor and, using the steak as a weapon, knocks other patrons senseless with it. After much damage has been caused, Millions is ejected from the premises and DeBean is scolded. In a rage, DeBean and his crew quit. Later, DeBean spots the proprietor fooling around with the cashier and flies into a jealous rage. Sneaking into the restaurant's kitchen, he plants a bomb in the boiler. In his haste to escape, however, he manages to lock himself in. The resulting explosion leaves DeBean buried in an avalanche of pots and pans. Synopsis adapted from the plot summary in *Universal Weekly*, December 28, 1914 p.29

REVIEWS: "Restaurant scenes predominate in this burlesque number. The chef becomes angered and he and the waiters jump on a steak before cooking it. This is only moderately amusing, the final scenes being the best." *Moving Picture World*, January 2, 1915, p.76

"There is slightly too much gesticulating by the principal players of this comedy to be enjoyed. A little less of it and the picture would be more pleasing....This comedy is better than the Sterlings have been of late, but could be improved upon if the movements before spoken of were omitted." *Motion Picture News*, January 2, 1915, p.50

"...little originality, but plenty of rough humour." *Bioscope*, July 1, 1915, p.IX

Love and Water: *Released 12/31/1914.* No copyright entry — 1 reel/989 feet. DIRECTOR: Dave Kirkland. CAST: Dot Gould, Lloyd Ingraham, Arthur Tavares
SYNOPSIS: Pedro the park sweeper (Ingraham) sits down to the lunch his wife has brought him. Dot (Gould), "a young lady of leisure," is rowing about on the park lake. A flirt (Tavares) spots her and, hiring a boat, sets out after her. He ends up accidentally capsizing both of their boats, and Pedro rescues Dot while his wife rescues the flirt. The flirt kisses her in gratitude, but when Pedro sees this the hot-blooded Italian flies into a rage, pulls his stiletto, and heads after the flirt. A grateful Dot follows him and all end up thrashing about in the lake. Synopsis adapted from the plot summary in *Universal Weekly*, December 26, 1914, p.20
REVIEWS: "A typical eccentric comedy number with no very distinguishing features about it. The scenes take place in a park; the plot is very slight. Photography good." *Moving Picture World*, January 2, 1915, p.76

"Jealousy is the cause of a great deal of trouble between two couples who appear in this reel. There is a lot of action that takes place on and in the water, which is fairly funny." *Motion Picture News*, January 2, 1915, p.50

"...of no very great humour." *Bioscope*, March 25, 1915, p.XI

1915:

Olive's Love Affair: *Released 01/07/1915 Thursday.* No copyright entry — 1 reel/992 feet. DIRECTOR: Robert Thornby. CAST: Paul Jacobs, Olive Johnson, Violet Radcliffe
SYNOPSIS: Billy (Jacobs) and Bob (Radcliffe) both love Alice (Johnson), but she prefers Billy. Bob steals her doll, throws it into a cave's waters, and sends Alice a note informing her of such. Billy intercepts the messenger carrying the note and sets out to rescue the doll with his dog Fido. Billy slips into the cave and gets stuck on a ledge above the water. He sends Fido with his handkerchief to Alice and she returns with the dog but is unable to reach him. She sends Fido for some rope, and when he returns Billy is rescued, doll in hand. Bob is nearby laughing over the affair, so Billy sends Fido after him. Synopsis adapted from the plot summary in *Universal Weekly*, January 2, 1915, p.20
REVIEWS: "A juvenile number, with Olive and Little Billy in it; also a big dog. The children really do some exciting work in their rescue over the side of the cliff. The best of these juvenile numbers shown for some time." *Moving Picture World*, January 9, 1915, p.222

Those German Bowlers: *Released 01/14/1915 Thursday.* No copyright entry — 1 reel. DIRECTOR: Fred Balshofer. CAST: Louise Fazenda, John Brennan
SYNOPSIS: Lazy bowler Grousmeyer (Brennan) loafs around the house spending all of his time reading the bowling news. His neighbor Schmaltz stops by for a visit, but soon the two are doing battle in an argument over technique, and the house gets wrecked. They head for the alleys intending to prove their respective points, but when Schmaltz's method appears to be the better of the two, Grousmeyer smears the alley with soft soap in an attempt to make him look bad. The deception is discovered and everyone in the alley breaks into a big fight. Mrs. Grousmeyer returns home and blames the wreckage on Mrs. Schmaltz's husband, and soon the two of them are in their own fight which carries them down to the alleys and into the major battle in progress. Synopsis adapted from the plot summary in *Universal Weekly*, January 9, 1915, p.21
REVIEWS: "A good burlesque on the popular sport of bowling. Two married men sally forth to the alleys to try their skill. The result is highly amusing and the game will please professional bowlers particularly. Good photography." *Moving Picture World*, January 16, 1915, p.370
"Rough knockabout comedy." *Variety*, January 23, 1915, p.25

Dude Raffles: *Released 01/21/1915 Thursday.* No copyright entry — 1 reel/700 feet. CAST: Arthur Tavares, Gus Erdman, Peggie (dog)
(This is a re-titled re-release of 11/12/1914's **The Dog Raffles**)

The Treasure Seekers: *Released 01/28/1915 Thursday.* No copyright entry — 1 reel. DIRECTOR: David Kirkland. CAST: Dot Gould, William Wolbert, John Brennan
SYNOPSIS: Delicatessen owner Meyer visits neighbor Heinzie (Wolbert) at the latter's grocery. They sit about drinking hard cider, discussing the possibilities of a treasure map one of them has stumbled across. They fall asleep and dream: both are aboard a ship bound for the cannibal island holding the buried treasure. After the usual mishaps they land and are captured by the cannibals. Plump Meyer is selected as their next meal and is "prepared" accordingly, but is saved at the last moment when the Queen (Gould) falls in love with him. She orders Heinzie thrown into the pot. While Meyer implores her to spare Heinzie's life, the cannibals gather driftwood for the fire. One of them accidentally gathers some dried out dynamite and the fire explodes. Meyer and Heinzie awaken as they both fall to the store's floor, and a small fire caused by Heinzie's cigar adds realism to their dreams. They mutually swear off hard cider. Synopsis adapted from the plot summary in *Universal Weekly*, January 23, 1915, p.29
REVIEWS: "In this eccentric comedy number Wm. Wolbert appears as a cobbler. He finds a treasure map in an old shoe and he and his companion dream of exciting experiences among cannibals. This is well-pictured, but only fairly successful from a humorous standpoint." *Moving Picture World*, January 30, 1915, p.673

Love and Dough: *Released 02/04/1915 Thursday.* No copyright entry — 1 reel/937 feet. CAST: Dot Gould, John E. Brennan
SYNOPSIS: Bakery foreman Heinze (Brennan) is put in charge of the establishment when his boss is called away on business. In addition to assuming clerk duties, Heinze takes up flirting with every girl that enters, and unwittingly makes the same four o'clock appointment to meet

three different girls at the corner. Four o'clock rolls around and the trio of girls are outraged at his callousness. The chase follows, with Heinze seeking refuge in the bakery. Sneaking from box to barrel, Heinze finally finds a secure hiding place in the baking oven. Meanwhile, the other bakers become involved and get the worst of it, being knocked into the flour bin before beating a hasty retreat to the upstairs. As the girls try to follow, the bakers pour out the contents of a barrel of flour, swamping the women below. The film ends on Heinze, still in the oven amidst a jumble of squashed pies and tarts, sadly awaiting the girls' departure. Synopsis adapted from the plot summary in *Universal Weekly*, January 30, 1915, p.21

REVIEWS: "A knockabout number, with John E. Brennan and Dot Gould in the cast. The scenes in the restaurant kitchen would have been funnier if they had not been so dirty and unattractive. The action in this is good, but it suffers from the slovenly character of the settings and costumes." *Moving Picture World*, February 6, 1915, p.828

Billy Was a Right Smart Boy: *Released 02/11/1915 Thursday.* No copyright entry — 1 reel/ 985 feet. CAST: Paul Jacobs, Olive Johnson, Carmen DeRue
(pre-release title: **Billie's Strategy**)

SYNOPSIS: Billy breaks off his flirting with Olive to pursue Carmen. She wants a doll, so Billy brazenly steals Olive's. Olive is furious, so Billy replaces her doll with one that he steals from some black children. The black kids go after Billy and in his flight he runs across their doll which Olive has tossed aside. He returns it to them. Billy returns to Carmen, spirits her away from her new sweetheart, and buys her some ice cream. Having no money, he borrows some from Olive to pay for it. Carmen's sweetheart witnesses this incredible display and goes over and tangles with Billy who gets the worst of it. He is shunned by Carmen and Olive alike. Synopsis adapted from the plot summary in *Universal Weekly*, February 6, 1915, p.20

REVIEWS: "A juvenile number in which Billy and a rival aspire to Olive's hand. Billy borrows money from the rival with which to entertain the girl. The plot is slight but it makes an entertaining offering of its kind." *Moving Picture World*, February 13, 1915, p.985

"Good story, excellent acting." *Variety*, February ?, 1915, p.?

"The Sterling juveniles are less mechanical and more childlike than ever...." *Bioscope*, September 9, 1915, p.VII

The Fox Trot Craze: *Released 02/18/1915 Thursday.* No copyright entry — 1 reel. CAST: Ernest Shield, Arthur Tavares, Emma Clifton

SYNOPSIS: Hall room boys Harold (Tavares) and Percy (Shield) decide to attend the hotel's dance. They possess a single suit each; Harold sends his out for pressing, while Percy presses his own. Percy manages to burn a hole in the seat of the suit's pants, so he steals Harold's suit as it is being returned by the bellboy. Harold grows impatient waiting for his suit and sneaks into the hall in his underwear for a look. He learns of the theft and, covering himself with a portiere, heads for the ballroom. Meanwhile, Percy has managed to set himself smoldering on a discarded cigarette butt, and seeks seclusion in an out of the way corner to remove the suit and douse the fire. Harold arrives and the two grapple over the suit, both losing their coverings during the fight. Retreating in their underwear, they both swear off dancing and ballrooms. Synopsis adapted from the plot summary in *Universal Weekly*, February 13, 1915, p.21

REVIEWS: "Picturing the adventures of two Willie boys at a hotel. They quarrel over a suit of clothes and run about in summer underwear. This is mildly amusing, but needs more plot." *Moving Picture World*, February 20, 1915, p.1140

"No plot." *Variety*, February 1915

The Runaway Closet: *Released 02/25/1915 Thursday.* No copyright entry — 1 reel/714 feet. CAST: Dot Gould, Ernest Shield, Arthur Tavares, Charles Hygenios
(retitled **The Runaway Wardrobe** for release in Britain. Released on a split reel with the 210 foot educational **Swan Life**)
SYNOPSIS: Mrs. Jones' maid dot (Gould) loves Charley (Hygenios), but has a brass button fetish. Resultantly, she flirts with all of the neighborhood cops. Charley steals a police sergeant's uniform and returns. Dot is entertaining her newest cop friend (Shield) who takes Charley for the real sergeant and flees. Charley woos Dot, but when the real sergeant arrives looking for his uniform, Charley is forced to take refuge in a stand-alone closet. Mrs. Jones returns and mistakes Charley for a burglar, but Charley doesn't want to face the cop and remains locked inside. Instead, he takes off with it, feet protruding from its splintered bottom. A zig-zag escape blindly leads him to the edge of a cliff and over, smashing on the ground below. Charley swears off buttons and uniforms. Synopsis adapted from the plot summary in *Universal Weekly*, February 20, 1915, p.21
REVIEWS: "A frivolous [sic] maid, a flirtatious cop and a masquerading hobo appear in this. The latter hides in a wardrobe and runs away with it, finally falling over a cliff. This is fairly amusing." *Moving Picture World*, February 27, 1915, p.1289

"…conventional in plot but amusing in its treatment." *Bioscope*, May 27, 1915, p.XI

When Snitz Was "Marriaged": *Released 03/04/1915 Thursday.* No copyright entry — 1 reel. CAST: John Brennan, Dot Gould, George Jaeschke, George Smith
SYNOPSIS: Dot (Gould) and her family await at their home for the groom Snitz (Brennan). They call on the phone and awaken him, and he hurries over, bumping into others and creating "a vengeful mob." He finally arrives but realizes that he's forgotten the minister. He rushes out and finds one and puts him in a hack which bolts away with him, the minister, and its cabby (Smith). It crashes off a cliff, and Snitz gathers up the minister from the wreckage and moves on. When they get to Dot's he finds that she has eloped with the milkman (Jaeschke). Snitz and the others set off in pursuit, arriving at the train station in time to see the train pull out with Dot and the milkman waving from its rear platform. Synopsis adapted from the plot summary in *Universal Weekly*, February 27, 1915, p.21
REVIEWS: "A low comedy number with John E. Brennan and Dot Gould in the cast. The bridegroom's appearance was unattractive throughout the film and many of the scenes were in like character. The fall over the cliff was a scene worthy of a better story." *Moving Picture World*, March 6, 1915, p.1449

The Knockout Wallop: *Released 03/11/1915 Thursday.* No copyright entry — 1 reel. CAST: John Brennan, Gus Erdman, George Jaeschke, William Hunn
SYNOPSIS: Candy puller Louie (Brennan) gets into an argument with his assistant (Erdman) and they decide to settle it in the ring. A fight fan gives Louie an intensive training, while a dope addict flunky (Jaeschke) puts the helper through a similar "nerve-wracking,

death-defying test of his bravery." They ultimately meet at the Knockout Club, and as the fight progresses Louie gains the upper hand. Between rounds the flunky gives the helper an injection of pure Tabasco sauce with one of his needles, and the helper goes wild. He Ko's Louie with a single punch, and then proceeds to take out the seconds in both corners. Still keyed up, he wrecks the place and then heads outside. He pushes in one of the walls, heaping wreckage on those inside, and then knocks over a pillar which brings down the roof on himself. The entire building collapses burying everyone. Synopsis adapted from the plot summary in *Universal Weekly*, March 6, 1915, p.20

REVIEWS: "The general uncleanliness of the settings interfere with the humor of the first part of this eccentric comedy. The fighting scenes are better, but as a whole it is not very successful." *Moving Picture World*, March 13, 1915, p.1608

Raindrops and Girls: *Released 03/18/1915 Thursday.* © 03/08/1915 — 1 reel/855 feet. DIRECTOR: Fred Balshofer. CAST: Gus Erdman, Louise Fazenda, Nana King, Arthur Tavares
SYNOPSIS: Snoopy (Erdman) and his wife (Fazenda) go to the shoe store. She's interested in a pair of shoes, but the clerk (Tavares) sells them to a young lovely (King). Snoopy's wife wrecks the store. As they head home they find it's raining, and she waits while Snoopy goes for an umbrella. He snitches one in a nearby saloon, but on the trip back runs across the lovely young girl. He gallantly carries her across a puddle, but his wife sees this and demands similar treatment. He drops her, however, and both get soaked and she loses her hat. To make amends, he takes her to a hat store where they once again run across the young lady. Snoopy resumes his flirting and his enraged wife engages in battle, with the store getting wrecked and Snoopy knocked cold. Synopsis adapted from the plot summary in *Universal Weekly*, March 13, 1915, p.21

Olive's Pet: *Released 03/25/1915 Thursday.* © 03/12/1915 — 1 reel/408 feet. CAST: Olive Johnson, Paul Jacobs
SYNOPSIS: Olive drops and breaks her doll. She announces that the boy who replaces it will be her sweetheart. The boys run about grabbing dolls. Billy takes his dog Ted out and finds "Snow White, a pickanniny, busily engaged playing with a nigger doll." Ted diverts her attention while Billy grabs the doll. The child is broken-hearted over the loss of her doll, but it is soon returned. Later, Ted is set adrift on a raft. The cops mistake Ted for a child and are constantly falling in the water while attempting to perform acts of heroism in the rescue of him. Synopsis adapted from the plot summary in *Universal Weekly*
REVIEWS: "A juvenile number, featuring Olive, Little Billy and other children. The boy swipes some dolls for his sweetheart and later there is an adventure in which a dog takes part. This has no particular plot, but is well photographed and quite pleasing." *Moving Picture World*, March 27, 1915, p.1933

Olive's Hero: *Released 04/01/1915 Thursday.* © 03/25/1915 — split reel/746 feet. CAST: Olive Johnson
(**Olive's Hero** also appeared on a split reel with the 210 foot educational **Swan Life**)
SYNOPSIS: Olive displays her new kewpie doll to her sweetheart Jimmy who props it against a tree. Skinny swipes it, intending to present it to Rose, his idol. Olive asks Jimmy to "rescue" the kewpie, so he sets out after Skinny and corners him on a bridge. Skinny tosses the

doll into the water, but Jimmy finds a rope and rescues the doll. Skinny grabs it back and again tosses it into the lake, and this time Jimmy dives in after it. Unfortunately, Jimmy can't swim, and Skinny is forced to rescue both Jimmy and the doll. Synopsis adapted from the plot summary in *Universal Weekly*, April 10, 1915, p.20

REVIEWS: "This juvenile number has a lot of fun in it. Skinny steals Olive's kewpie doll and throws it into the lake. The hero comes and tries to save it, but Skinnie [sic] has to save both doll and hero at the end. A good 'kid' number." *Moving Picture World*, April 3, 1915, p.66

"…these exceptionally clever and attractive children play a miniature burlesque melodrama with great charm and effect." *Bioscope*, June 24, 1915, p.X

The Butler's Busted Romance: *Released 04/08/1915 Thursday.* © 03/25/1915 — 1 reel/945 feet. DIRECTOR: David Kirkland. CAST: Ernest Shield, Gus Erdman, Louise Fazenda, Raymond Russell, Agnes Copelin, Bert Hunn

SYNOPSIS: Jiggs (Russell) is informed by letter that he'll inherit a large fortune if he marries the girl specified (Copelin). While he's away on business, his butler (Shield) finds the letter. Learning that the girl is on her way over, the butler decides to impersonate Jiggs in hopes of winning the girl for himself. When she arrives, he makes his moves. The ugly cook (Fazenda) loves the butler, however, and does all she can to thwart his advances towards the girl. He dumps the cook in the coal bin. The chauffeur finds the letter and decides to make his own moves. When the cook escapes from the bin, she vents her wrath on the unfortunate trio and all hell breaks loose. Jiggs returns home in time to save the girl and toss out the trio of troublemakers who land in the estate's fountain. Synopsis adapted from the plot summary in *Universal Weekly*, April 3, 1915, p.21

REVIEWS: "This is a comedy number in which Ernest Shield appears as a butler. He poses as his master and attempts to marry the heiress, but the chauffeur and the maid foil his scheme. The humor is of the knockabout type and is quite in evidence. The settings are unusually attractive for this sort of production." *Moving Picture World*, April 10, 1915, p.237

"Ernest Shield and Louise Fazenda were directed by David Kirkland in this comedy, and succeeded in making a very excellent one. Its situations are well developed by the two principals and the supporting cast, and the dirty comedy has been left out, showing a wise move on the director's part. Learning that the master's wife-to-be is to arrive at the house, he takes off his master and the results are of course humorous." *Motion Picture News*, April 10, 1915, p.70

Playmates: *Released 04/15/1915 Thursday.* © 04/07/1915 — split reel/606 feet. CAST: Olive Johnson, Paul Jacobs

(**Playmates** was on a split reel with the 240 foot educational **Where Our Morning Paper Comes From** which, according to *Bioscope* [June 17, 1915, p. IX], showed "the various processes in the manufacture of the materials for the newspapers.")

SYNOPSIS: Playmates Olive and Margie are allowed to go out by her ma to play marbles, but are warned to stay clean. They join a game with "Tough-guy" Jack, Harry, and Little Billy. As marbles are won they are put in a cigar box, and Billy in turn puts them through a knothole in the fence. Soon the game is over for lack of marbles. Olive and Margie head for a dirty pond to make boats and are soon covered with mud from head to toe. They sneak home and into the bathroom, and soon the room and tub are as dirty as they were. In the bedroom they engage in a pillow fight and one breaks open, spilling feathers into the room. Ma comes to the "rescue." Synopsis adapted from the plot summary in *Universal Weekly*, April 24, 1915, p.22

REVIEWS: "This very amusing juvenile offering will take the average observer back to his childhood days with a vengeance. The manner in which the kids fall into a muddy pond and try to clean up in the bathtub afterward is very funny. A fine juvenile subject." *Moving Picture World*, April 17, 1915, p.394

"A group of children tiring of playing marbles adjourn to a mud hole, and before they are through every one is coated thick with dirt. The best part of the reel comes when the three boys of the party are washing themselves. This is by all means one of the best juvenile comedies that the Sterling company has produced as of late. The situations are humorous, and the child players enter well into the spirit of the thing." *Motion Picture News*, April 17, 1915, p.89

His Smashing Career: *Released 04/22/1915 Thursday.* © 04/14/1915 — 1 reel/780 feet.
CAST: Ford Sterling (unconfirmed)
SYNOPSIS: Musical conductor Snooks (Sterling?) tires of practicing and goes for a walk. Spotting a pretty young lady accompanied by a boob in the park, Snooks tries to steal her away and is forced to toss the boob into the lake. He is chased by two of the boob's friends through town and country on foot and in auto. He crashes his car through a prison and the cops set out after the fleeing cons and Snooks. The cons are caught, and Snooks makes off with the girl. Synopsis adapted from the plot summary in *Universal Weekly*, May 1, 1915, p.22

REVIEWS: "Ford Sterling appears in this low comedy number as a man with musical ambitions. He gets into a love affair and leads a wild chase in an automobile. His performances in the latter are decidedly interesting. A lively number of the kind." *Moving Picture World*, April 24, 1915, p.558

"A burlesque on the lines of which Mr. Ford Sterling has rendered so widely popular, in which a motor-car, which goes through some remarkable evolutions, plays a prominent part. This is a good sample of a type of farce which never fails to please." *Bioscope*, July 15, 1915, p.IX

The Chef's Revenge: *Released 04/29/1915 Thursday.* © 04/22/1915 — split reel/617 feet.
CAST: Lloyd Ingraham, Emma Clifton, Arthur Tavares
(this was a re-release of the December 28, 1914 release [see synopsis and reviews], this time on a split reel with the 350 foot educational **After Big Game of the Sea** [© 04/22/1915 — split reel] which follows a Byron Chandler expedition showing the methods for capturing a crocodile, a porpoise, and a shark)
SYNOPSIS OF **After Big Game of the Sea**: "Expedition leaves Key West, Fla., for Bermuda. Encounter huge crocodile, which is captured, after big fight. Then is shown another big fight with porpoise, which is also captured and hoisted on to ship. Bait is thrown out later to catch shark. Shark bites and is captured." *Moving Picture World*, May 5, 1915, p.960.
REVIEWS: "The photography is magnificent, and some wonderful views are the result." *Bioscope*, July 1, 1915, p.IX

Counting Out the Count: *Released 05/06/1915 Thursday.* © 04/27/1915 — 1 reel/1018 feet. CAST: Billie Reeves, Johnny Doyle

SYNOPSIS: Variety actors Billy [sic] and Johnny's act fails and they are ejected from the theatre. Learning that millionaire's daughter Rita Canarsie has decided to marry a nobleman, Billy hatches a scheme in which he will disguise himself as a Count with Johnny posing as his valet. All of the girls love the Count, but the village boys bribe a gigantic Belgian cook to play a practical joke on him. His true character is exposed and he is thrown from the premises. Rita marries the nobleman. Synopsis adapted from the plot summary in *Universal Weekly*, May 1, 1915, p.22

REVIEWS: "Billy Reeves and his pal appear in this as two vaudeville actors. He poses as a count and gets a jag on at a society function. The humor of this is not very strong. The closing scenes are of the knockabout type." *Moving Picture World*, May 8, 1915, p.901

"The plot of a penniless vaudevillian who assumes the person of a count is taken as a vehicle to introduce Billy Reeves to patrons of the picture theatre. Some of his antics are funny, but the picture is poorly put on, and even the details of this simple and well known story are sometimes terribly jumbled." *Motion Picture News*, May 8, 1915, p.78

"A typical Sterling farce, which will cause much amusement." *Bioscope*, July 8, 1915, p.X

Pokes and Jabbs: *Released 05/13/1915 Thursday.* © 05/06/1915 — 1 reel/970 feet. CAST: Bobbie Burns, Walter Stull

SYNOPSIS: The Pokes and Jabbs families live in apartments across the hall from each other. Mr. Pokes admires Mrs. Jabbs' new fur coat when he sees her in the hall, but their spouses, each peeking through their respective keyholes, assume that they are flirting. Arguments follow, and the two wives stomp out, Mrs. Jabbs heading for her mother's and Mrs. Poke heading to a Suffragette meeting. Later, Mr. Pokes and Mr. Jabbs learn of a masked ball and decide to go, with Jabbs in drag as a woman. They arrive to find the ball postponed, and after a series of wild mishaps manage to make it back home. They go into Pokes' apartment and both fall asleep on the bed, Jabbs still in woman's clothing. Mrs. Pokes returns and is horrified to find whom she thinks to be her husband in bed with a woman. Jabbs flees via the fire escape and returns to his apartment where he again falls asleep. Mrs. Jabbs returns and fails to recognize her husband and assumes that he has a woman in his room. He again flees through the window but is eventually caught by Mrs. Pokes who tears his dress off. Explanations follow and all is cleared up. Synopsis adapted from the plot summary in *Universal Weekly*, May 8, 1915, p.22

REVIEWS: "The plot of this low comedy number is very much jumbled, though it is not very important. The incidents, of the knockabout sort, are rough but quite laughable." *Moving Picture World*, May 15, 1915, p.1073

"A strenuous slapstick in which two henpecked husbands go out for a 'time,' one of them dressing as a woman. The situations resulting on their home-coming and during their tour of the saloons are humorously conceived and very well carried out by the cast.

"The majority of the male comedians who appear seem confirmed acrobats, and their actions have obviously been well guided by a director who knows his business. This was made by an outside company, but the Sterling brand has seldom been honored with a more acceptable slapstick." *Motion Picture News*, May 15, 1915, p.73

"A very involved comedy in which the humour is not entirely free from suggestiveness." *Bioscope*, September 9, 1915, p.VII

The Battle of Running Bull: *Released 05/20/1915 Thursday.* © 05/13/1915 — 2 reels.
CAST: Ernest Shield, John E. Brennan, Arthur Tavares, Dot Gould
(The *Universal Weekly* synopsis for this film ["Hero Routs Army with Asafetida Bomb," May 15, 1915, p. 27] is the most confusing one to appear in that publication for a Sterling release. The author evidently was quite taken with his own cleverness and sense of humor, but it's such a disjointed jumble of vague but flowery prose as to be virtually unreadable. The synopsis below is a very rough approximate of its contents, but it's difficult to even place the story in time. *Moving Picture World* further complicates matters by referring to characters General Delivery, Capt. Smear, and so on, none of whom are mentioned in *Universal Weekly*)
SYNOPSIS: Tin Ear Charlie (Tavares) joins up with the Pea-Green Army, a regiment of cripples, drunks, ex-cons, and so forth. He falls in love with Dot (Gould), the daughter of Colonel Bunk (Shield), but finds that he'll allow no one save a hero to marry his pretty offspring. Lt. Wampus (Brennan) is also infatuated with Dot, and he decides to make life in the service as rough as possible for Charlie. Dot takes pity on Charlie, however, and pity soon turns to love. The enemy attacks and a massive poisonous asafetida shell is fired at the regiment. Charlie picks up the shell in an effort to protect his own hide and tosses it back at the invaders, who are wiped out by it. Charlie is hospitalized when struck by a fragment, and Wampus attempts to convince everyone that Charlie is a coward. Dot and Bunk think otherwise, however, and Charlie and Dot are married. Synopsis adapted from the plot summary in *Universal Weekly*, May 15, 1915, p.27
REVIEWS: "A two-reel war burlesque, with Dot Gould, John E. Brennan and others in the leads. The officers are known as General Delivery, Captain Smear, etc. The first reel is given up entirely to flirtations and wrangles over the girl; the battle scenes come in the second. This would have been much more amusing with a stronger plot to hold it together. There are a number of funny situations as it stands, but they are not of the cumulative sort and get only scattering laughter. The battle scenes are the strongest in the production." *Moving Picture World*, May 22, 1915, p.1262

"A burlesque war offering, in which the cook of the regiment turns out to be the hero of the day.

"The definition of the picture running under the main title is given as comedy-drama, but why the drama? There's not a bit of it in the story, which is evidently intended to be totally humorous. And as for that, the picture is very funny in a great many scenes of the second reel, and some few of the first.

"It would make an excellent one reel subject, but as it stands some of the action tires because there is little plot to sustain the interest. The battle scenes, by the way, are very good. Perhaps this is where the drama comes in." *Motion Picture News*, May 22, 1915, p.75

L-Ko Motion Picture Kompany, Inc.
(released through Universal Film Manufacturing Co.)

These are the releases of Henry Lehrman's L-Ko Motion Picture Kompany, Inc., aka Lehrman-KnockOut, 1914-1919, copyrighted (in most instances) by Universal Film Manufacturing Company, Inc.

Unless otherwise noted, synopses have been taken from the plot summaries in the *Universal Weekly* publication (retitled *Moving Picture Weekly* effective July 3, 1915). These synopses are frequently paraphrased and shortened, as the originals tend to be overlong and verbose, with fanciful character names that may not have appeared in a released film's intertitles. Other sources for synopses include *Moving Picture World*, which tend to be slightly reworked versions of the *Universal Weekly-Moving Picture Weekly* synopses, and personal viewing of the films when possible. In some instances the synopses are quoted verbatim, and in most instances the source, date, and page number have been included.

Cast and crew attributions have been taken from a variety of sources, primarily contemporary reviews and synopses, as well as visual identification of cast members from surviving films or stills. A film's director is listed when known. Given that both Lehrman and John Blystone after him were supervisors — akin to today's producers — films were frequently touted as having been made under "the personal direction of" that individual. This results in some understandable confusion as to whether they simply supervised or actually handled the direction, or both.

Universal Weekly-Moving Picture Weekly entries for Henry Lehrman were alternately given as H. Pathe Lehrman, Pathe Lehrman, and Henry Lehrman.

1914 Releases (Sundays):

Love and Surgery: *Released 10/25/1914 Sunday.* No copyright entry — 2 reels. DIRECTOR, SCREENPLAY: H. Pathe Lehrman. CAST: Billie Ritchie, Gertrude Selby, H. Pathe Lehrman, Henry Bergman, Eva Nelson, Dave Anderson
SYNOPSIS: After a callous Lehrman belittles his girl (Nelson) and leaves her alone in a park, Ritchie ("a cross between a hobo and a superannuated flirt," as *Universal Weekly* put it) arrives on the scene and flirting ensues between him and the girl. Lehrman returns and in a fit of jealousy the two males do battle over the young lady. Lehrman delivers multiple brick-blows to Ritchie's head, but Ritchie recovers and goes after Lehrman with a pistol, shooting his rival in the rear.

Having struck out with this young lady, Ritchie moves on to another young lady (Selby) he spots sitting at a nearby table. He purchases a milk shake along with two straws and offers it to her along with some overly flirtatious comments. When she gives him the brush-off, Ritchie grabs the milk shake and stomps off, the two straws in his mouth spewing and dribbling their contents as he does so. When her jealous fiancée Ignatz (Bergman) arrives, Selby informs her fiancé of Ritchie's shabby behavior. Enraged, a fight ensues between the two men, the smaller Ritchie getting the brunt of it. Ritchie grabs a huge mallet and delivers two massive blows to Ignatz's head, resulting in two tall bumps that look more like horns. They continue to tangle, and Ritchie is knocked through the brick wall of a police station. He is arrested on the spot and brutally beaten into a helpless heap. He's taken to the hospital, and the surgeon arrives to operate. Much to Ritchie's horror, the surgeon turns out to be none other than Ignatz, the fiancé whom he'd fought with earlier. The surgeon takes his time deciding just what pain to inflict upon his patient. Ritchie flees, running for his life across rooftops, ultimately crashing through a roof and several floors below, ending up back in the police station. Ritchie is once-again beaten into insensibility by the cops. Synopsis based on the print held by the Library of Congress

REVIEWS: "A two-reel number introducing a new company for the first time in slapstick humor of an uproarious sort. Billy [sic] Ritchie and Henry Lehrmann make an immediate hit as a pair of flirtatious 'ginks.' The first scenes are taken in a park and the latter ones in a hospital. There are some screamingly funny things in this, but the fun is of the roughest sort such as squirting water from the mouth, kicking a woman in the stomach, tearing off a woman's dress and the like. There is no connected plot, but merely a series of rough-house scenes from start to finish. None of the scenes are impossible and this will no doubt prove successful before audiences that are not overly particular." *Moving Picture World*, October 24, 1914, p.493

"Tiresome first reel and corking second. Many good comedy bits, but picture too long." *Variety*, October 29, 1914, p.26

"We have seen all varieties and brands of slapstick comedy that the market of today offers, but 'Love and Surgery' contains more slapstickism, so to speak, than all the rest.

"The L. Ko. is a new brand added to the many now under the Universal banner, and if more follow and come up to the standard set by this, they will establish a name for themselves, a name to be smiled at whenever it be heard.

"Slapstick comedies have for some time been great favorites with some people, but, like all great favorites, they have those who do not look upon them in such a favorable light. The farcical burlesque elements of this picture will be enjoyed to their fullest extent by most of the male audiences. And those who do not mind the extreme rough work, perhaps a little suggestive in its roughest moments, a warm welcome will be awaiting the picture.

"Henry Pathé Lehreman [sic] is the director and second leading man of this picture and Billy Richie [sic] is the star to whom the final honor of creating laughs must be allotted. But it is the ingenious mind of the director that conceived the plan and to him must go a great amount of praise.

"As is usual with this variety of picture, there is no plot; if there is, it will be completely obliterated in the mass of uproarious events. Brick throwing, punching, running, daring falls, diving through walls and roofs, flirting, shooting and countless other varieties of furnishing hilarity are linked together in this picture with such startling rapidity that he will be a morose individual indeed who is not aching and crying from laughter at the end of the farce." Reviewed by Peter Milne, *Motion Picture News*, October 31, 1914, p.48

Partners in Crime: *Released 11/01/1914 Sunday.* No copyright entry — 1 reel. DIRECTOR: Henry Lehrman. CAST: Billie Ritchie, Pathe Lehrman, Gertrude Selby, Henry Bergman, Hank Mann
SYNOPSIS: A street tough (Mann) loses his girl (Selby) to an overweight bruiser (Bergman). Meanwhile, penniless Billie (Ritchie) is thrown from a saloon and returns to do battle with the bartender. Enter the bruiser who enters the fight, unaware when Billie lifts his pocket watch. Billie wanders off and encounters the girl. Attracted to her, he goes to present her with the pocket watch, but when the bruiser wanders over Billie sheepishly returns the watch to him. Realizing that Billie is a crook like him, the bruiser shoos the girl away and enlists Billie's aid in robbing a house, the spoils to go towards buying a saloon of their own. Billie enters the house but is forced to flee when he is discovered by the lady of the house. He encounters the girl once again, but the bruiser's arrival leads to another confrontation that ultimately involves a cop.

Elsewhere, the Chief of Police (Lehrman) admires a necklace that's intended as a surprise for his wife. He places it on a chair and covers it, then goes to retrieve his wife. Billie, passing by, sticks his head in the open window and, finding the necklace, steals it. The chief goes to present it to his wife and is furious when he discovers it missing. The bruiser spots the necklace in Billie's possession and snatches it, but Billie responds in kind, the necklace passing back and forth several times. After a wild chase, the bruiser ultimately gains possession of the necklace. Billie wants it back, so he searches out the nearest cop who turns out to be the chief. Billie drags the chief to the bruiser hoping to regain the necklace, but when the chief sees the necklace he's ecstatic, grabbing it and heading back to present it to his wife. Synopsis based on a print of the film held by the author

REVIEWS: "An eccentric offering with Billy [sic] Ritchie playing the light-fingered tramp. There is considerable jumping, running and shooting in this, but the humor does not come up very strongly except in occasional places." *Moving Picture World*, October 31, 1914, p.642

"Not as good as it could be, as it is practically incoherent. A good many laughs are produced by the actions of Billy [sic] Ritchie, but if the scenes fitted in together there would be more laughs still. Rough slapstick work throughout." *Motion Picture News*, October 31, 1914, p.52

"Good comedy with lots of laughs." *Variety*, November 7, 1914, p.22

The Fatal Marriage: *Released 11/08/1914 Sunday.* No copyright entry — 1 reel. DIRECTOR: Henry Lehrman. CAST: Billie Ritchie, Pathe Lehrman, Gertrude Selby, Lew Carter, Henry Bergman

REVIEWS: "The marriage was, indeed, fatal. Autos were overturned, lives were risked, property was destroyed in this mad, wild round of fun and laughter. The best slam-bang bunch of fun in a long time." *Universal Weekly*, October 31, 1914, p.30

"Two comical gentlemen have rather an ugly woman whom they want to marry to some misguided person, but they are unsuccessful as a younger and prettier girl puts in her appearance and wins the attention of the applicants. A comical chase is the feature of the picture in which some acrobatic work takes place. Rough slapstick action marks the entire reel." *Motion Picture News*, October 31, 1914, p.52

"Trick photography, chases, water-soaked principals, etc. Funny in spots." *Variety*, November 12, 1914, p.24

"A Universal picture of LKO brand entitled 'A Fatal Marriage' headed the entertainment program. It was a comedy of successive laugh-creating incidents. One incident in particular which elicited a round of acclamation was where the automobile of the would-be police department in its pursuit of abductors turned several complete sommersaults." "Bronx Exhibitors Hold Ball," *Moving Picture World*, November 14, 1914, p.907

Lizzie's Escape: *Released 11/15/1914 Sunday.* No copyright entry — 1 reel. DIRECTOR: Henry Lehrman. CAST: Henry Lehrman, Billie Ritchie, Gertrude Selby

REVIEWS: "Two mashers both try their hands at striking up an acquaintance with a country girl. They meet with varying success, and then try to take her money, but are frustrated. A fair slapstick." *Motion Picture News*, November 7, 1914, p.50

"A side-breaking L-Ko comedy with the well known trio of fun-makers, Billie Ritchie, Henry Schermann [sic], and Gertrude Selby." *The Cedar Rapids Daily Republican*, November 21, 1914, p.11

"A short reel comic, showing the adventures of a country girl with a couple of city ginks, the latter played enjoyably by Henry Lehrmann and Billy Ritchie. The girl has her money taken from her in the back end of a saloon and it has various adventures before she recovers it. Low comedy that will cause some laughter." *Moving Picture World*, November 21, 1914, p.1077

"Laughs by usual bomb explosion and pistol firing." *Variety*, November 21, 1914, p.26

The Groom's Doom: *Released 11/22/1914 Sunday.* No copyright entry — 1 reel. CAST: Billie Ritchie

REVIEWS: "Usual mess and roughhouse stuff. Intermittent laughter."*Variety*, November 28, 1914, p.23

"A park flirtation followed by a boxing match is the chief amusement in this. The principals all wind up in a mud puddle. Not very strong, the situations having been overworked considerably." *Moving Picture World*, November 28, 1914, p.1233

"Rather low comedy, which is humorous until the finale, when all the actors end up wallowing in a mudhole. The muscular suitor finally meets his superior when he forces that gentleman into a boxing match. The photography is poor in places." *Motion Picture News*, November 28, 1915, p.49

A Blighted Spaniard: *Released 11/29/1914 Sunday.* No copyright entry — 1 reel. DIRECTOR: Henry Lehrman. CAST: Henry Bergman, Peggy Pearce, Wallace MacDonald

SYNOPSIS: Tomalio (MacDonald) and Sunshine (Pearce) are lovers, and he plays love tunes for her from below her window — much to the annoyance of her neighbors. Bombardio (Bergman) is also taken with Sunshine, but she thinks little of him, and his attempts to woo her by following Tomalio's lead and playing tunes for her fall flat. Frustrated, Bombardio stomps home, accidentally stumbling across the cave of a band of Federal spies, filled with a huge amount of dynamite. He makes a deal with the spies to kidnap Tomalio, but "tables are turned upon Bombardio and all his base designs are perpetuated upon himself." Synopsis adapted from the plot summary in *Universal Weekly*, November 21, 1914, p.20

REVIEWS: "The opening scenes in this low comedy of Mexican life are pretty and attractive. The fun is also appealing, but drops off in quality when Bombardio loses his trousers and begins running around in his underwear. A barrel of dynamite is introduced to keep things moving." *Moving Picture World*, December 5, 1914, p.1385

Fido's Dramatic Career: *Released 12/06/1914 Sunday.* No copyright entry — 1 reel. DIRECTOR: Harry Edwards

SYNOPSIS: Fido, an abused stray dog of the streets, crawls onto the lawn of a beautiful residence and falls asleep. He dreams he's a pampered pet of a beautiful lady he'd spotted earlier, and that he gives all of those who treated him roughly their comeuppance. Later he's the guest of honor, seated in a private box, of a contest between Mike's Billy Goat and Fritz's Grizzly Bear. Fido's blissful dream comes to an abrupt end when a nearby sprinkler is turned on." Synopsis adapted from the plot summary in *Universal Weekly*, November 28, 1914, p.24

REVIEWS: "…a comedy played exclusively by animals — See dogs drive automobiles, etc." *Coshocton Morning Tribune*, January 2, 1915, p.8

"The situations are unique in view of the fact that all the participants are animals, and throughout the picture the comedy interests are capably sustained." *Motography*, December 5, 1914, p.793

"This is full of interest. Fido drives an auto to the fight and smokes a pipe during the rounds. Other dogs and a chimpanzee and goat add to the fun, which winds up with a big chase. A good animal yarn, well-pictured throughout." *Moving Picture World*, December 12, 1914, p.1524

"A collection of well trained dogs, with a monkey, a goat, and a few other animals perform in this picture and will furnish great amusement." *Motion Picture News*, December 12, 1914, p.49

The Rural Demons: *Released 12/13/1914 Sunday.* No copyright entry — 1 reel. DIRECTOR: Henry Lehrman. CAST: Henry Lehrman, Billie Ritchie, Gertrude Selby
SYNOPSIS: Billie (Ritchie) and Henry (Lehrman) are jealous rivals for the hand of a lovely farmer's daughter (Selby), going into battle whenever they encounter each other in her vicinity. Billie has a short-lived triumph when he elopes with the girl in Henry's auto, but escape comes to a grinding halt when he gets a flat. Fortunately, it's in front of a tire factory, so Billie tries to buy a replacement. Unfortunately, they don't have the correct size, but the superintendent agrees to manufacture one on the spot while an impatient Billie waits. Meanwhile, Henry informs the girl's father of the elopement, and with sheriff and constables assembled all give chase. When they arrive and find the auto, Henry's further outraged by the flattened tire. Inside, Billie reluctantly agrees to pay for the finished tire, but when he heads out and sees that he's lost both the girl and the auto, attempts to get his money back from the superintendent. A fight between the two breaks out, and escalates when Billie's pursuers enter the fracas. Henry is the victor. Synopsis adapted from the plot summary in *Universal Weekly*, December 5, 1914, p.20
REVIEWS: "Billy [sic] Ritchie and H. Pathe Lehrmann appear in this as eccentric rube characters on a farm. Gertrude Selby is the girl. The action is the usual knockabout sort. The egg throwing was not an attractive feature. Sandwiched into this are a number of scenes showing how automobile tires are made. This would have been an excellent half reel by itself, and is very interesting as it stands. The photography was not very clear in places." *Moving Picture World*, December 19, 1914, p.1681

"A slapstick comedy in which the profuse use of bad eggs occurs. The comedy is interrupted when at its height, to introduce scenes showing the manufacture of automobile tires, which is most interesting but seems rather out of place. Billie Ritchie and Henry Lehreman [sic] are the lovers seeking the hand of Gertrude Selby, supposedly a dainty rural maid. Lehreman has a small cyclecar in which and out of which he furnishes a lot of laughter." *Motion Picture News*, December 19, 1914, p.84

The Baron's Bear Escape: *Released 12/20/1914 Sunday.* No copyright entry — 1 reel. DIRECTOR: Henry Lehrman. CAST: Henry Bergman, Peggy Pearce, Wallace MacDonald
SYNOPSIS: Baron Wilhelm von Hasenpfeffer (Bergman) and youthful Wallace (MacDonald) are rival suitors, and while the girl favors Wallace, her father favors the Baron due to his

wealth and prominence. Her father drives poor Wallace away with a flurry of blows from his cane. Seeking revenge, Wallace seeks out and dons a bearskin and hides on the wagon carrying the Baron and his hunting party. Making a threatening appearance, Wallace terrifies the Baron, who flees and manages to tumble off a cliff, hanging for dear life to a limb halfway down. In a panic, Wallace rushes for help, first to the mounted police, then to the girl's family, and finally to the local storekeepers, all of whom set out for the rescue. The police are first to arrive, but one of them takes a tumble, falling and dislodging the Baron. Both land in a heap in a huge mud puddle below. One-by-one the would-be rescuers arrive, and one-by-one each slips off the cliff's edge, joining the Baron whose bulk serves as a "pillow" in the mud below. Synopsis adapted from the plot summary in *Universal Weekly*, December 12, 1914, p.27

REVIEWS: "A hunting yarn chiefly interesting for its good photography and fine scenic effects. Henry Bergman is enjoyable as the baron, but the plot of having the lover disguise as a bear has been used so often that it lacks freshness. A familiar subject well presented." *Moving Picture World*, December 19, 1914, p.1681

"Henry Bergman is featured as Baron Hazenfeffer [sic] in this comic offering. He has amorous intentions toward a young girl, and is furthered in his suit by father, but daughter has a young American in mind. The baron goes hunting and the other man dresses as a bear and scares the wits out of the professed hunter. The thread of the story is lost in the mud hole appearing in the last scene in which all the characters are splashing in when the picture closes." *Motion Picture News*, December 26, 1914, p.50

The Manicure Girl: *Released 12/27/1914 Sunday.* No copyright entry — 1 reel. DIRECTOR: Henry Lehrman. CAST: Billie Ritchie, Hank Mann, Louise Orth, Charles Dudley
SYNOPSIS: Fickle manicure girl Louise (Orth) has numerous affairs and lovers, but manages to keep them secret from each other. When an encouraged Billie (Ritchie) follows her into the barber shop, however, the head barber (Dudley) becomes insanely jealous. He follows the girl out of the shop but now finds her with yet-another fellow, and in the confrontation that follows the barber gets the worst of it and flees back to his shop. The victor soon finds Louise with another lover, and in the struggle that follows he thinks he's drowned the newcomer. He heads for the barber shop to have his moustache removed, hoping that no one will recognize him in his clean-shaven state. The head barber recognizes him, though, and he and his assistants go after the rival with revenge in mind. Outside, however, they find Louise back with Billie. Totally frustrated, the barber and the rival throw themselves into a nearby dump cart, soon to be carted off to the city dump. Synopsis adapted from the plot summary in *Universal Weekly*, December 19, 1914, p.20
REVIEWS: "This reel shows the scrimmages that take place between a number of rivals for the hand of a manicurist. Billie Ritchie is the leading rival. Quite a number of scenes depict the characters drinking water and then spirting it out of their mouths at each other. Louise Orth plays the name part. Many of the scenes transpire in a barber shop in which the colored bootblack is the shining light (not literally)." *Motion Picture News*, January 2, 1915, p.50

"A characteristic comedy-burlesque, with Billy [sic] Ritchie in his familiar part. He and the barber become rivals for the girl. Toward the close there is a chase through some large sewer pipes. This contains laughable moments." *Moving Picture World*, January 2, 1915, p.76

1915 Releases (Sundays and Wednesdays from this date on):

Gems and Germs: *Released 01/03/1915 Sunday.* No copyright entry — 1 reel. DIRECTOR: Henry Lehrman. CAST: Louise Orth, Harry Russell, Montana Kid the dog, Frank Lanning
SYNOPSIS: A chemist (Lanning) concocts what he feels to be a wonderful new poison, and invites two leading scientists to test the mixture. The chemist's willful daughter Gem (Orth), whom he's locked in her room in a futile attempt to keep her away from her determined suitor (Russell), manages to escape. To get even, Gem and her lover replace the new mixture with a harmless one, accidentally leaving her energetic dog (Montana Kid) behind when they leave. The chemist and his two guests arrive to find the dog drinking the now-harmless mixture and, fearing the dog is mad, flee when they think the dog will bite. Assuming it's all a game, the dog pursues them. Meanwhile, Gem and her lover have coerced a minister into performing a marriage ceremony by the lake's edge. The dog chases the chemist and scientists onto a bridge where they plunge into the lake below to escape the "mad" canine. Spotting his owner Gem, the dog goes after her, panicking the minister, whose panic scares Gem and her lover into following him into the lake. The terrified yells of those in the lake attract the police, who arrive on the scene as well. Synopsis adapted from the plot summary in *Universal Weekly*, December 26, 1914, p.20
REVIEWS: "Eccentric comedy of a fairly amusing sort. The dog drinks the professor's liquid containing germs and starts a wild chase. The girl and her bald-headed lover start another and every one winds up in the lake, also the dog. This has amusing moments." *Moving Picture World*, January 9, 1915, p.222

Cupid in a Hospital: *Released 01/06/1915 Wednesday.* No copyright entry — 1 reel. DIRECTOR: Henry Lehrman. CAST: Billie Ritchie, Louise Orth, Hank Mann, Eva Nelson, Charles Dudley
SYNOPSIS: "A pretty nurse [Orth] makes an impression on Billie [Ritchie]. Her flirtation arouses the jealousy of the crippled anarchist [Mann], who gets even by bouncing a basin on Billie's head. The young interne, also in love with the pretty nurse, makes a date to meet her, but Billie, waiting for another sight of his lady fair, forestalls him. The interne's jealousy aroused, he proceeds to punish Billie. Believing him dead, the frightened nurse and interne make off for the hospital. Found unconscious by a couple of policemen, Billie is restored by a whiff of his beloved gin. He is carried into the hospital, where his head is bandaged, and he is prepared for bed. When turned into the ward he is treated by the anarchist. The ungrateful Billie manages to steal the bottle, but is not able to get away with the contents before the arrival of the nurse. The nurse recognizes him and showers attentions upon him, much to the jealousy of the anarchist, who plants a bomb under the bed of the sleeping Billie. The anarchist, awaiting the explosion, is horrified to discover the nurse sitting on the bed with Billie. He endeavors to drag her away as the bomb is discovered. Thoroughly alarmed, the entire hospital force endeavors to throw the bomb out of the window. In the confusion the anarchist is thrown on the bed, and together with Billie, both are blown through space into infinity." *Universal Weekly*, January 9, 1915, p.20
REVIEWS: "A burlesque number with some decidedly laughable spots running through it. Billy [sic] Ritchie invades a hospital, where he makes love to one of the nurses and creates

a riot among the patients. A bottle and a bomb add to the excitement. A successful comic offering." *Moving Picture World*, January 9, 1915, p.222

Through a Knot Hole: *Released 01/10/1915 Sunday.* No copyright entry — 1 reel.
DIRECTOR: Rube Miller. CAST: Billie Ritchie, Rube Miller, Peggy Pearce
SYNOPSIS: A married man glimpses the pretty bride next door through a knot hole in the fence. His admiration becomes evident to her, and she amuses herself by playing up to him. Her jealous husband gets wind of this, however, reprimands the neighbor, and sets out to forgive his wife. Spotting the neighbor's eye back at the knot hole, the jealous husband flies into a rage and jabs his finger through the hole. When he puts his eye to the hole to see what damage he's inflicted, he finds himself on the receiving end of a reciprocal poke. Further enraged, he rushes into the house and returns with a gun, prompting the peeping Tom to grab a gun of his own. A chase ensues but is brought to an end when the intruder's wife applies "her washtub-developed muscle." Synopsis adapted from the plot summary in *Moving Picture World*, January 2, 1915, p.130
REVIEWS: "In this number, which is well photographed, two sets of married people become involved in a jealous quarrel. The fun is mere horseplay and has not much real humor in it." *Moving Picture World*, January 16, 1915, p.369

Thou Shalt Not Flirt: *Released 01/13/1915 Wednesday.* No copyright entry — 1 reel.
DIRECTOR: Henry Lehrman. CAST: Billie Ritchie, Henry Lehrman, Louise Orth, Henry Bergman
SYNOPSIS: When his wife catches him flirting with the housemaid, she forces him to promise to call and check in every five minutes from the office. He agrees, but once in the office delegates the task of calling her to his assistant. He heads out for a day on the town, but flirtations with a young lady lead to a pummeling from her jealous husband. Returning home, he explains the shabby condition of his clothes with a tall story about rescuing a child about to be run over by a street car. His wife insists that he take her to the movies, and as coincidence would have it the jealous husband and his wife are there as well. And there, projected on the screen, are images of the flirtatious husband taken earlier in the day. He flees from the wrath of his wife only to come face-to-face with the jealous husband. The pummeling this time around tops the former. Synopsis adapted from the plot summary in *Universal Weekly*, January 16, 1915, p.21
REVIEWS: "An eccentric number in which the flirtations of a married man create trouble. There is some amusement in the latter scenes, though it is of a rough character." *Moving Picture World*, January 16, 1915, p.369

Caught with the Goods: *Released 01/17/1915 Sunday.* No copyright entry — 1 reel. CAST: Henry Bergman, Bolivar the Baby Bear
SYNOPSIS: The undersheriff, taken with his superior's wife, flatters her with attention, to which she happily responds. The sheriff has a hot temper, and finding the two together threatens to kill his subordinate. The second time he catches them together he means business, and the undersheriff flees. Hiding out in a bath house, he decides to kill some time by donning a swim suit and going for a swim. Meanwhile, a bear escapes from a local menagerie and ends up in the same bath house. The undersheriff is forced to flee along

with the other bathers, clad only in his swim suit. Terrified, he takes refuge in the sheriff's house, hiding in the wife's bedroom. Where, of course, he's found by the wife, who proceeds to beat him into submission with her fists. Seeing this, the sheriff is delighted, and finally forgives the undersheriff. Synopsis adapted from the plot summary in *Universal Weekly*, January 9, 1915, p.21

REVIEWS: "An eccentric number in which the undersheriff makes love to the sheriff's wife. The latter scenes, in which a bear invades a bath house and later chases the bathers up a telephone pole, are quite amusing." *Moving Picture World*, January 23, 1915, p.516

Every Inch a Hero: *Released 01/20/1915 Wednesday.* No copyright entry — 1 reel. CAST: Peggy Pearce, Rube Miller

SYNOPSIS: A poor young farm boy (Miller) is loved by Nell (Pearce). When the villain spots Nell, he's determined to have her, but the farm boy intercedes until the constable arrives. Later, the villain confronts Nell's mother, telling her to pay the rent or out she goes. Spotting Nell, he makes the connection and then makes an offer: he'll take Nell in lieu of the rent, but the mother must decide in five minutes. When the farm boy hears this, he's off to dig up his buried savings. He returns and pays off the debt, and the villain is once again foiled. But not for long; He kidnaps Nell, ties her to a rope, then dangles her off a cliff. When the farm boy tries to rescue her, he's knocked unconscious. Awakening, he's told to hang on to a tree, the rope tied to his legs and Nell still dangling. When his hold gives out, he and Nell will plummet to their deaths. His hold does indeed give out, but he manages to grab the villain's legs, and the two struggle. Rescuers arrive and the heroic boy is reunited with Nell. Synopsis adapted from the plot summary in *Universal Weekly*, January 23, 1915, p.21

REVIEWS: "A well-photographed eccentric number, with a sort of Desperate Desmond villain. This works up quite a lot of amusement and is better than the average offering of the kind." *Moving Picture World*, January 23, 1915, p.517

The Death of Simon Legree: *Released 01/24/1915 Sunday.* No copyright entry — 1 reel. DIRECTOR: Henry Lehrman. CAST: Billie Ritchie, Eva Nelson, Louise Orth

SYNOPSIS: When an acting troupe arrives in town to put on "Uncle Tom's Cabin," a young lovely falls for Simon Legree, one of the troupe, who gives her a free pass to the show. Her lover Fatty is dismayed by this and threatens suicide, but then decides to take in the show. At the night of the performance, Legree takes a bow and tosses the love-struck girl a rose. Fatty tosses a pie into Legree's face. As a result of this, Fatty decides that the only way to win his girl back is to become and actor himself, so he goes to work practicing the play. Meanwhile, the play goes on, and when it comes time for Little Eva's tragic death and ascent to heaven, the property man (Ritchie) messes things up and ruins the performance. Enraged, Legree pulls a revolver, which panics the audience into fleeing the theater. Sheriffs arrive and confront the troupe. When the girl and her friends arrive home, they overhear Fatty practicing and take him to be one of the troupe, and rush forward to throw him out of the house. Frightened, Fatty attempts to escape but lands in a barrel, which rolls and threatens the safety of the girl and her friends. They run for their lives but find themselves at the edge of a bank along with the sheriff and the troupe. All of them topple off the edge and land in a heap at the bottom, the barrel with Fatty crashing nearby shortly after. The property man arrives and, assuming all to be dead, pulls a stave from

the barrel to use as a shovel to bury them. Slowly but surely, the mass of bodies awaken one-by-one, and untangle themselves from the others. Synopsis adapted from the plot summary in *Universal Weekly*, January 16, 1915, p.21
REVIEWS: "A very good burlesque on 'Uncle Tom's Cabin.' The characterizations are good and the scenes of the famous old story are brought out in a laughable manner. This is a good offering of the type." *Moving Picture World*, January 30, 1915, p.672

Merry Mary's Marriage: *Released 01/27/1915 Wednesday.* No copyright entry — 1 reel.
SYNOPSIS: Merry Mary marries Rube, in spite of the sheriff's warnings that Rube is a heavy drinker. After the wedding, Mary's focus is on baking a pie, Rube's favorite dish. His real favorite, though, is the bottle, and when he finally comes across one he drinks himself into a stupor. Mary's shocked to find that the accusations were true, and is in a panic when the local serenaders come to sing to the newlyweds. Wanting to avoid the comments she knows will be made, she dumps Rube into an empty barrel. She is spotted doing this, however, and Rube's limp body is taken for that of a corpse. Mary is arrested and in spite of denying any wrongdoing, she's given the third degree. Rube awakens and crawls from the barrel just in time to prove Mary's innocence. Synopsis adapted from the plot summary in *Universal Weekly*, January 23, 1915, p.20
REVIEWS: "Several rube characters supply the action in this number. The girl puts her drunken husband in a barrel and the police, thinking he is dead, give chase. This proves fairly amusing." *Moving Picture World*, January 30, 1915, p.673

After Her Millions: *Released 01/31/1915 Sunday.* No copyright entry — 3 reels. DIRECTOR: Henry Lehrman. CAST: Billie Ritchie, Henry Lehrman, Gertrude Selby
SYNOPSIS: Henry (Lehrman) and Billie (Ritchie) both spot millionairess Gertrude (Selby) in her limousine, and are immediately smitten. Billie takes off after her in his car, and Henry, left behind and heartbroken, must console himself with a photo of the young lady. Later, Henry again runs into Gertrude, and attempts to woo her. She rebuffs him with a garden hose, which the annoyed Henry turns back on her. Her screams alert her father, who bodily removes Henry from the premises. Billie, still searching for Gertrude, comes across Henry, and the two fight over the photo. Billie finally convinces Henry to sell it, and the two head into a bar to drink. The cherished photo reverts back to Henry when he takes it from Billie, now thoroughly drunk. When Billie recovers enough to comprehend his loss, he follows Henry back to the hotel where, coincidentally, Gertrude has a room as well. Billie retires to his room with a bottle. When Henry's photo blows out the window and into Gertrude's window, Henry follows. Gertrude flees and ends up hiding under Billie's bed, until driven out by the arrival of a mouse. Billie professes his love, Gertrude flees into the hall, and a riot breaks out. One poor guest, whose attempts to get to the bathroom are repeatedly thwarted, finally knocks both Henry and Billie into insensibility, terrorizes Gertrude into hysterics, then triumphantly claims the bathroom for himself. Unable to choose between these two characters, heiress Gertrude announces that she intends to marry Englishman Lord Bolingbroke. Synopsis adapted from the plot summary in *Universal Weekly*, January 23, 1915, p.7
REVIEWS: "This picture…is laid out on farce comedy lines. It is unfortunate that a higher notch of the art had not been aimed at. The humor of the picture is based on an abnormal

degree of drunkenness, and is at times unpleasantly vulgar and suggestive." *Moving Picture World*, February 6, 1915, p.829.

The Butcher's Bride: *Released 02/03/1915 Wednesday.* No copyright entry — 1 reel. CAST: Rube Miller, Henry Bergman
SYNOPSIS: A butcher finds that the butcher boy is flirting with his new bride. Enraged, the butcher pulls a gun and the boy is quickly driven away. He thinks his troubles are over, but returns home to find Mr. Peabody flirting with his bride. He again produces his gun, Peabody flees, and the butcher's offended bride leaves. Later, Peabody and his wife go to the beach, but when he spots the butcher's bride there, he loses his wife and again hooks up with the bride. The butcher boy spots the two of them together, and rushes off to inform the butcher. The butcher grabs his guns, locates Peabody and his wife, and confronts Peabody. "A denouement, entirely unexpected by the unhappy families, follows." Synopsis adapted from the plot summary in *Moving Picture World*, January 30, 1915, p.724
REVIEWS: "An eccentric comedy number with the opening scenes in a butcher shop. None of the characterizations are particularly appealing; the best scenes are toward the close at the beach resort." *Moving Picture World*, February 6, 1915, p.828

Zip and His Gang: *Released 02/07/1915 Sunday.* No copyright entry — 1 reel. CAST: Gertrude Selby, Henry Lehrman, Henry Bergman, Ted Mulford
SYNOPSIS: Zip and his gang, "protected" by the local ward boss, are merciless in their torment of each new cop on the beat, taking his clothing, humiliating him, and sending him packing battered and bruised. The Star Policeman decides to put an end to all this, managing to arrest Zip and stealing Zip's girl for good measure. This is a short-lived triumph, as the ward boss has Zip released and goes on to make life miserable for the police. Humiliated, the police plan to capture the gang, luring them out on to a pier. They are almost successful, but the tide is turned when the gang manages to dump their captors into the ocean. Spotting this, the Star Policeman comes forward and pushes the gang into the ocean. Their frantic efforts to keep from drowning delight the assembled police. Synopsis adapted from the plot summary in *Universal Weekly*, January 30, 1915, p.20
REVIEWS: "An eccentric comedy number of the familiar type, featuring a gang of toughs and the police force. Some of the latter situations become quite amusing." *Moving Picture World*, February 13, 1915, p.985.

Father Was a Loafer: *Released 02/10/1915 Wednesday.* No copyright entry — 1 reel. DIRECTOR: Henry Lehrman. CAST: Billie Ritchie, Hank Mann, Gertrude Selby, Alice Howell, Louise Orth, Eva Nelson, Bert Roach, John Rand, Violet Radcliffe
SYNOPSIS: "Bummel [Ritchie] is blessed with a family of four when his wife [Howell] presents him with triplets. This addition to the family causes him to leave home. He meets Miss Rocks [Selby], the multi-millionairess. She is out driving when her horses run away. Bummel rescues her at great risk to himself. Out of gratitude her father bestows her hand and fortune on the needy Bummel and the marriage day is set.

"In the meantime the deserted wife outgrows her sorrow in the company of Baldwin. The latter gentleman does not mind the seven children Bummel has left behind. He has just about landed her when she reads of the approaching marriage of her spouse and the multi-millionairess. Her arrival at the Rocks mansion at the moment her husband is about to marry the heiress is scarcely as dramatic as the subsequent attempts of Bummel to escape." *Universal Weekly,* February 6, 1915, p.21

REVIEWS: "An exceptionally funny Billy [sic] Ritchie number. He plays the part of a married man whose wife presents him with triplets. He leaves home and contemplates marrying an heiress whose life he has saved, when the wife appears. This is well-photographed and full of eccentric humor." *Moving Picture World*, February 13, 1915, p.985.

"When an L-Ko comedy is announced the Orpheum patron usually looks forward to a half hour of unadulterated fun, and this latest release…will supply thirty minutes of the keenest kind of humor. Billie Ritchie is fun-master in chief and Gertrude Selby gives able assistance as the youthful mother of seven children." *Fort Wayne Journal-Gazette*, February 13, 1915, p.9

Peggy's Sweethearts: *Released 02/14/1915 Sunday.* No copyright entry — 1 reel. DIRECTOR: Rube Miller. CAST: Peggy Pearce, Rube Miller, Bobby Mack, and Jack Clifford

SYNOPSIS: When Peggy (Pearce) goes in wading and loses her slipper, passing Oscar (Miller) recovers it. He asks to meet her father, who turns out to be the Constable Oscar had an argument with earlier. Not only does the Constable not care for Oscar, he's had the Head Constable in mind for his daughter, and takes this opportunity to force the issue. Oscar's not about to give up the fight: "His misery calls forth the cunning of a demon which results in the Head Constable being locked in the closet with the hired girl. Various other unpleasant things happen." Synopsis adapted from the plot summary in *Universal Weekly,* February 13, 1915, p.20

REVIEWS: "A country youth meets a girl wading in a stream and an attachment is formed. Later her father objects and brings in a rival. The fun is fairly good, being of the knockabout type. Photography fair." *Moving Picture World*, February 20, 1915, p.1140

"[This] is one of the amusing L-Ko comedies telling of a certain maiden — fair of face and figure, who is constantly beset by the attentions of a horde of love-lorn swains. Needless to say, Peggy's final selection creates a tremendous amount of havoc among her unsuccessful suitors, and their actions keep the spectator in an uproar of laughter." *Fort Wayne Journal-Gazette*, February 17, 1915, p.9

Almost a Scandal: *Released 02/17/1915 Wednesday.* No copyright entry — 1 reel. DIRECTOR: Henry Lehrman (unconfirmed). CAST: Billie Ritchie, Louise Orth, Henry Bergman, Hank Mann, Eva Nelson

SYNOPSIS: Billie (Ritchie) meets a blonde (Orth) and flirts with her, with her approval. She returns home with a love-struck look on her face, arousing the suspicion of her jealous husband (Bergman). He reminds her that he carries loaded pistols. Later on at a saloon, Billie calls her at her home and arranges a meeting. The husband enters the saloon and greets Billie, not realizing who Billie is talking to on the other end of the line. The husband grabs the phone and is entranced by the woman at the other end, who is sending kisses. Billie leaves the saloon to hook up with the blonde, much to the envy of the husband and the establishment's patrons.

Billie and the blonde meet up at a café and are seated. The blonde's husband arrives shortly thereafter with a date (Nelson), neither couple aware of the other's presence. The husband makes an advance towards his date and is slapped for his efforts, so he leaves

the table. He encounters Billie who, after describing the beauty he's with, borrows some money from the husband to pay his check. After the husband strikes out a second time with his date, he abandons her and looks for Billie, wanting to see the "beauty" he is with. Shocked to discover that the woman with Billie is his wife, the enraged husband gives chase. The two end up fighting, and onlookers intervene and present them with swords for a duel. Billie manages to disarm the husband, and drives his long sword through the husband's belly. Looking like a human shish kabob, the husband resumes his pursuit of Billie, both pistols blazing, the astonished onlookers trailing behind. After briefly boarding a passing trolley, the two resume the chase on foot. Billie knocks the husband to the ground, pulls the sword from his belly, then kicks and stabs the pursuing onlookers to the ground. Synopsis *based on the print held by the EYE Filmmuseum, Amsterdam*
REVIEWS: "An eccentric comedy number.... The opening scenes in a park are the usual knockabout sort and not of much interest. The sword duel scenes at the last are quite amusing." *Moving Picture World*, February 20, 1915, p.1140

Their Last Haul: *Released 02/21/1915 Sunday.* No copyright entry — 1 reel. DIRECTOR: John G. Blystone. CAST: Hank Mann, Wallace MacDonald, Alice Howell
SYNOPSIS: Reformed by a girl (Howell), crooks Rudolph (Mann) and Gustave (McDonald) decide to pull one last heist before going clean. They go to rob a safe, but Rudolph doesn't realize that Gustave has planted a time bomb in the opened safe, and Gustave doesn't realize that Rudolph would want to revisit the safe after he planted the bomb. And neither realizes that another gang of crooks are planning to haul away the safe, and that a bunch of cops are watching from afar. Rudolph ends up locked in the safe suspended from a 20-story skyscraper, with 5 minutes to go before the explosion. The other gang of crooks struggle with the safe, but the explosion puts an end to that. Rudolph is blown clear, landing in a nearby lake. He decides to go straight. Howell has a role in the film as "The Girl." Synopsis adapted from the plot summary in *Universal Weekly*, February 13, 1915, p.20
REVIEWS: "This eccentric comedy number works up very gradually into a hilarious affair. The would-be safe robbers not only perform some extremely laughable feats, but take all sorts of chances in their fight on the roof and use of the rope up and down the sides of the high building. This is an extremely good offering of the nonsencial [sic], combining laughter with thrills." *Moving Picture World*, February 27, 1915, p.1289

Fatty's Infatuation: *Released 02/24/1915 Wednesday.* No copyright entry — 1 reel. CAST: Willard Gardner, Gertrude Short, George Short
SYNOPSIS: Young Fatty (Gardner) has a sweetheart (Gertrude Short), but she shares her affections with Fatty's rival, Johnny Boston Beans (George Short). Fatty's parents give him a dollar to go pay the gas bill, but on the way he encounters his sweetheart looking longingly at the confections in a store window. When Johnny arrives and butts in, Fatty succumbs and buys his sweetheart ice cream and candy and, to rub it in, buys the same for Johnny. Out a dollar, though, Fatty wanders home without having paid the bill. Arriving home, he finds that the gas has been turned off, and he confesses to what he did, all for love. Expecting the worst, Fatty finds that they are touched by his explanation, and Fatty is forgiven. Synopsis adapted from the plot summary in *Universal Weekly*, February 20, 1915, p.20

REVIEWS: "A juvenile number with a slight but rather amusing plot. Willard Gardner is the fat boy who uses the gas money to buy candy and ice cream for his young sweetheart. He afterward confesses that he did it for love. Not strong but pleasing in its way." *Moving Picture World*, February 27, 1915, p.1289.

The Avenging Dentist: *Released 02/28/1915 Sunday.* No copyright entry — 2 reels. DIRECTOR: Harry Edwards. CAST: Billie Ritchie, Louise Orth, Henry Bergman (pre-release title: **Wounded Feelings**)
SYNOPSIS: A dentist (Ritchie) is out with his girl when he spots a stout older man (Bergman) out with his girl. The dentist is taken with the stout fellow's girl, so he ditches his partner and confronts the other fellow, accusing him of flirting with his girl. This leads to a fight, and Ritchie flees after knocking out several of the stout fellow's teeth. Later, the stout fellow is at his home, his battered jaw still bothering him considerably. His daughter (Orth) brings home her sweetheart, and she insists that the two meet. Her sweetheart, however, turns out to be the dentist, and the fight quickly resumes. The stout fellow gets the worst of it, his few remaining teeth knocked out. In pain, his daughter convinces him to go see a dentist, neither realizing that the cause of her dad's pain is a dentist. The stout fellow settles into the dental chair, but is shocked when his mortal enemy enters the room. Another struggle ensues, and the stout fellow is knocked out cold. Thinking himself to be a murderer, the dentist flees but in his haste falls into an open manhole, and is carried through the sewer out to the sea. Synopsis adapted from the plot summary in *Universal Weekly*, February 20, 1915, p.13
REVIEWS: "A two-reel eccentric comedy number.... The action in the first reel is very conventional and the plot as a whole is slight. This might have been condensed into one reel. The main situations occur in a dentist's office and are of a familiar type. This makes a fairly humorous offering." *Moving Picture World*, March 6, 1915, p.1449

Bill's New Pal: *Released 03/03/1915 Wednesday.* No copyright entry — 1 reel. DIRECTOR: Harry Edwards. CAST: Billie Ritchie, Gertrude Selby, Henry Bergman, Louise Orth
SYNOPSIS: A café's 300 pound chef (Bergman) and waiter (Ritchie) are roommates who have issues with each other, one of them being the chef's propensity for stealing all of the bed's blankets, leaving the waiter shivering. Both are in love with the café's cashier (Selby), and their demonstrations as such work to the annoyance of the patrons and the displeasure of the proprietor. The competition for her affections grows to the breaking point, and the chef unleashes a volley of knives and other cooking instruments. When it appears that the chef has killed a man, he quickly stuffs the "body" into a barrel. Everyone else goes after the chef, and all of them except the waiter end up falling into the cellar. The waiter seeks refuge in the oven, and is almost incinerated before he is rescued. Synopsis adapted from the plot summary in *Universal Weekly*, February 27, 1915, p.20
REVIEWS: "The scenes are of the usual knockabout sort, followed by a chase after the man in the garbage can. This is a fair number of its kind." *Moving Picture World*, March 6, 1915, p.1449

In and Out of Society: *Released 03/07/1915 Sunday.* No copyright entry — 1 reel. DIRECTOR: Harry Edwards. CAST: Peggy Pearce, Dick Smith
SYNOPSIS: Reuben (Smith) attempts to cut into society by charming a young lady (Pearce) in the lobby of a fashionable hotel. She offers him the loan of a pair of trousers to wear to

that evening's ball, which he accepts, unaware that the young lady is married and that the trousers belong to her husband. When the husband realizes that Reuben has his trousers, they are quickly removed and Reuben is left at the ball trouser-less. He manages to extricate himself from this humiliating situation, but accidentally ends up in the husband's room, hidden away in the Murphy bed. He's discovered by the husband, and in his attempts to escape ends up in another lady's bath room. This lady's husband discovers Reuben, and chases after him armed with two revolvers. Reuben escapes only after the two revolvers have been emptied. Synopsis adapted from the plot summary in *Universal Weekly*, March 6, 1915, p.20
REVIEWS: "An eccentric number featuring a rube character who rips his pants at a dance and runs about in his B.V.D.'s while they are being mended. Some of the situations are quite funny but it is a rather coarse type of humor." *Moving Picture World*, March 13, 1915, p.1608

Easy Money: *Released 03/10/1915 Wednesday.* No copyright entry — 1 reel. CAST: Peggy Pearce, Dick Smith
SYNOPSIS: When Reuben (Smith) wanders into town and is lured into a card game, the local gamblers think he's going to be easy pickings. He turns out to be a much better card player than they'd anticipated, so they turn sexy Gertie (Pearce) loose on him to divert his attention. When this ploy is successful, however, the gamblers and Gertie argue over the spoils. Peeved, Gertie informs the police of the gamblers' cheating, and they go and bring a halt to the game. Reuben grabs the pot and high-tails it out through the skylight. When the commotion subsides, the gamblers reluctantly admit that Reuben got the best of them. Synopsis adapted from the plot summary in *Universal Weekly*, March 6, 1915, p.20
REVIEWS: "The rube arrives in the city, is picked up by the adventuress and lured to a hotel. He is fleeced in a poker game and considerable excitement follows. This type of plot is very familiar and is handled here in average fashion." *Moving Picture World*, March 27, 1915, p.1933

No release 03/14/1915 Sunday

Rough But Romantic: *Released 03/17/1915 Wednesday.* © 03/08/1915 — 1 reel. DIRECTOR: John G. Blystone. CAST: Hank Mann, Alice Howell, Johnny Rand, Gertrude Selby
SYNOPSIS: Father (Rand) is about to be married to his homely sweetheart (Howell) when he spots his son's (Mann) pretty girl (Selby) in the audience. He's immediately infatuated with the pretty girl, but his son notes this unwelcome interest and quickly informs the bride-to-be's hulking brother of same. The brother refocuses father's attention. Father orders the pretty young girl out of the house, but takes note of where she lives. His bride-to-be heads to the girl's house to plead with her to leave her fiancé alone. Father heads there as well with some henchman with the intention of kidnapping the young girl, but his henchmen accidentally stuff his bride-to-be in the sack instead. The police are called and father realizes his mistake, but not soon enough. Pursued by the police, father ends up driving off a cliff. His son and the young girl are reunited. Synopsis adapted from the plot summary in *Universal Weekly*, March 13, 1915, p.20
REVIEWS: "This eccentric comedy number deals with the matrimonial adventures of Mr. Nappy and his son. The chase scenes with an auto and bike are funny and the acrobatics with ropes over the side of the cliff combine laughter and thrills. A good low comedy offering." *Moving Picture World*, March 20, 1915, p.1765

Too Many Bachelors: *Released 03/21/1915 Sunday.* © 03/11/1915 — 1 reel. CAST: Peggy Pearce, Dick Smith
SYNOPSIS: Bachelors Moses (Smith) and Abe are madly in love with Peggy (Pearce), but she can't stand either of them. In hopes of solving this problem, she decides to elope with another fellow. Seeing the elopement taking place, Moses intercedes and gets a suitcase in the eye, then yanks the ladder from beneath Peggy, leaving her hanging. Meanwhile, Abe enlists the help of a pair of tramps and another old bachelor, with the kidnapping of Peggy the goal. The tramps throw a bag over Moses and haul him away in a wagon while Abe and the older bachelor kidnap Peggy. The tramps eat too much ice cream and fall off the wagon. Peggy manages to escape from Abe and the older bachelor. Moses and Abe fight over possession of the wagon, which rolls off a cliff. The pair end up in the mud far below, joined soon after by the older bachelor. The three of them engage in a free-for-all. Synopsis adapted from the plot summary in *Universal Weekly,* March 27, 1915, p.20
REVIEWS: "This is a low comedy number featuring Peggy Pearce as a country girl beset with many admirers. There is an elopement, a chase and a bad spill over a cliff. The number has amusing spots and is on the whole one of average merit." *Moving Picture World*, March 27, 1915, p.1933

No release 03/24/1915 Wednesday

A Change in Lovers: *Released 03/28/1915 Sunday.* © 03/18/1915 — 1 reel. DIRECTOR: John G. Blystone. CAST: Hank Mann, Gertrude Selby, Reggie Morris
SYNOPSIS: Father gives his watch to his daughter to take to be fixed, but she entrusts it to her sweetheart who manages to lose it. His rival finds it and, when father spots this stranger with his watch and attempts to retrieve it, he gets a black eye for his efforts. Later, the daughter and the rival are arrested and taken to court and, lo and behold, father is the sitting judge. The rival is thrown into prison. Undeterred, he uses a sledgehammer to break through the jail's stone wall, while the guards slumber nearby. Synopsis adapted from the plot summary in *Universal Weekly,* March 20, 1915, p.21
REVIEWS: "One of the inimitable comedies in which Hank Mann and Gertrude Selby are featured and which is filled with laughs from start to finish. The incidents are so arranged that not a dull moment appears through the entire picture." *Motography*, March 27, 1915, p.508

Hearts and Flames: *Released 03/31/1915 Wednesday.* © 03/19/1915 — 2 reels. DIRECTOR, AUTHOR: Harry Edwards. CAST: Billie Ritchie, Louise Orth, Henry Bergman, Bob Mack, Eva Nelson
SYNOPSIS: Plumber Billie (Ritchie) falls for lovely Louise (Orth), and she falls for him. Jealous rival Henry (Bergman) follows as she takes Billie home. Henry confronts Billie and a fight follows, ending up inside. Her parents can't stand Billie either, and the two descend upon him with fists and broom. The next day, Billie goes to the father's office and flirts with his stenographer Eva (Nelson). Henry arrives and Billie gets the worst of it in yet another fight. Henry takes Eva home, Billie follows, and the fight resumes. Louise arrives at Eva's home and finds Billie, whom she's now madly in love with. She takes him home with her. Her father's there, though, so Billie cannot enter. Louise heads up to her room and hatches a plot. Clogging the sink's drain with some of her mother's false hair, the sink soon

floods. Mother and father, in a panic, call the plumber — Billie. Billie arrives and heads to the cellar to work, followed closely by Henry. Billie turns off both the water and gas and attempts to make repairs, inadvertently making the wrong connections. Louise goes to make tea but finds the water shut off. Water spurts out of the gas jets upstairs, soaking the guests assembled there. Billie lights a match to see if he's reconnected the pipes correctly, but ends up blown across the cellar. The building catches fire, and Billie and Henry run for help. Louise is trapped by the fire in her upstairs bedroom, screaming for help. A series of rescue attempts follow using ladders, a net, and finally a chute, but all fail due to incompetence or the resumption of fighting between Henry and Billie. A final attempt is cut short by several explosions, Henry blown down the chute and Billie blown out the window. Billie returns and manages to shove Louise down the chute, but she ends up in the flooded cellar. Billie dives in, rescuing Louise by rowing her out in a bathtub. Synopsis adapted from the plot summary in *Universal Weekly*, March 27, 1915, p.24

REVIEWS: "A two-reel nonsense number.... This gets a conventional start but later works up to some amusing low comedy situations. The incidents in the plumber's shop and those later when the house is ravaged by fire and flood have much laughter in them. This will please lovers of slapstick comedy very much and is a good offering of the kind." *Moving Picture World*, April 3, 1915, p.66

No release 04/04/1915 Sunday

The Fatal Note: *Released 04/07/1915 Wednesday.* © 04/01/1915 — 1 reel. DIRECTOR, AUTHOR: Harry Edwards. CAST: Billie Ritchie, Peggy Pearce

SYNOPSIS: The wedding dinner is under way, and the groom (Ritchie) and his bride (Pearce) are having a grand time. A jealous rival is present, however, and he writes a note full of disparaging remarks about the groom and sends it along to the bride. The groom intercepts it, however, and sends it back with a note to meet "her" in a room across the hall. The rival hurries over, expecting to meet the bride there. The groom heads there as well, intending to mete out punishment, but he quickly realizes that he's no match for the rival, and flees for his life. He doesn't get far, however, hindered by some of the guests who get in his way, including a man with gout and a woman with an overly-jealous husband. The bride's family is "drawn into the unpleasantness," a fire hose finally adding to everyone's misery. Synopsis adapted from the plot summary in *Universal Weekly*, April 10, 1915, p.20

REVIEWS: "A two-reel low comedy number of fair strength.... Billie flirts with a girl on a bench and brings her to an apartment house. Here a rival lover turns up and their jealousy leads to prolonged knockabout scenes of a mildly amusing character. The tone of this plot is not the best, and some of the photography was too light. A fair number of its kind." *Moving Picture World*, April 10, 1915, p.238

"The gallant swain is engaged to be married. At the breakfast before the wedding the defeated rival slips him a note under the table, thinking that it has fallen into the hands of the girl he still loves. Of course a grand rough house ensues ending in a house fight, in which some of the funniest scenes in the picture occur. Billie Ritchie and Peggy Pearce are the leads. This comedy ought to amuse, although nothing original is introduced until near its termination. Several rather risqué scenes appear." *Motion Picture News*, April 10, 1915, p.70

No release 04/11/1915 Sunday

Under the Table: *Released 04/14/1915 Wednesday.* © 03/31/1915 — 2 reels. DIRECTOR: John G. Blystone. CAST: Reggie Morris, Dick Smith, Hank Mann, Gertrude Selby SYNOPSIS: When newlywed Gertrude (Selby) finds a photo of a pretty young lady in her husband Reggie's (Morris) pocket, he flees and heads to the park. There he meets and flirts with a woman sporting a black eye, not realizing that she is his mother-in-law. Hank (Mann) shows up and flirts with her as well, and a fight ensues; Reggie triumphs. Meanwhile, an angry Gertrude heads for the park. Hank spots his wife flirting with another man, who turns out to be Gertrude's father. Another fight ensues, with Hank once again the loser. Reggie and Gertrude's mother head to a café together. Soon after Gertrude's father and Hank's wife arrive and sit at a nearby table. Gertrude's ma hides under the table to avoid her husband's wrath. Reggie and father get in an argument over seating. Next, Gertrude and Hank arrive, having teamed up earlier in a row with a cop. Mother watches her husband flirt with Hank's wife from beneath the table. Father spots Gertrude coming and ducks under the table, his wife escaping to under another table in the nick of time. Reggie spots his wife, so he too ducks under the table, followed by Hank's wife who spots her husband. The cop enters and Hank ducks under the table, and he and his wife are soon in a fight. The table is tipped, exposing everyone. A huge free for all follows. Synopsis adapted from the plot summary in *Universal Weekly,* April 10, 1915, p.30
REVIEWS: "The prudish young wife is shocked by her husband's pictures and statues. Later she gets up a flirtation. Her parents also become entangled in affairs and several couples wind up in the same restaurant, where a rough house ensues — a very rough house. There is no absolute vulgarity in this; the photography is good and there is considerable amusement of the knockabout in it. A very fair example of the slapstick comedy." *Moving Picture World*, April 17, 1915, p.394

"This farce depicts the [illegible] that result when three married couples quarrel. All six air their heated minds by a stroll, and the final scenes, which are laid in a restaurant, find each husband with another wife.

"Consternation reigns after the couples are enlightened to the actions of their better halves. Unlike most multiple reel comedies, this one fully deserves the space furnished by the two thousand feet. Hank Mann, who is by all odds the star, and a clever one at that, registers some original tricks that are bound to produce laughter, while the rest of the cast, which includes Gertrude Selby and Reggie Morris, is good to furnish many a laugh.

"The farce is by no means vulgar, and besides it is literally clean. It will offend no one, and should surely please the lovers of slapstick comedies." *Motion Picture News*, April 17, 1915, p.89

No release 04/18/1915 Sunday

No release 04/21/1915 Wednesday

Poor Policy: *Released 04/25/1915 Sunday.* © 04/16/1915 — 1 reel. DIRECTOR, AUTHOR: Harry Edwards. CAST: Billie Ritchie, Peggy Pearce, Henry Bergman, Gene Rogers SYNOPSIS: "Billie [Ritchie] took out a policy which worked two ways. It was good for a loan of $3.75 or $500 in case of fire. He tried to collect on both clauses but had not counted on rivals and sweethearts. His rival [Bergman] extinguished Billie's insurance blaze and to cop Billie's troubles an ostrich swallowed the bracelet he had bought for his girl [Pearce]. In addition, an unkind note he had written in his rival's name fell into hostile hands and was read by unfriendly eyes. When the fire department and hoses had their turn, Billie found himself completely cured of any inclination to realize on fire insurance policies." *Universal Weekly*, April 17, 1915, p.20

REVIEWS: "A pretty girl and an empty pocket cause an outclassed rival to burn his house to collect the insurance, but he is arrested as a fire-bug, and rather than suffer the ignominy of a jail sentence he heroically takes his own life. In this Billie Ritchie appears at his best supported by Peggy Pearce and Henry Bergman. Those scenes, which were taken on an ostrich farm, are uproarious, and the remainder of the picture will hardly leave the spectator time for breath, so thick and fast are the laughs. A mallet is used by Ritchie and several other characters with an effect that is as laughable as it is disastrous to the rest of the players." *Motion Picture News*, April 24, 1915, p.78

"This is a pleasing low comedy, except for one vulgar touch at the end, which may be eliminated. The ostrich farm incidents were amusing and novel. The insurance policy scheme to raise money also worked out pleasingly. A good comedy of the type...." *Moving Picture World*, May 1, 1915, p.729

Shaved in Mexico: *Released 04/28/1915 Wednesday.* © 04/22/1915 — 1 reel. DIRECTOR: John G. Blystone. CAST: Hank Mann, Eva Nelson

SYNOPSIS: Senor La Bullio (Mann) is the village barber and the lover of Senorita Hitchy Koo (Nelson). She proves to be fickle, though, when newcomer Si Perkins woos and wins her affections. Perkins goes to the barber for a shave, and foolishly boasts of his conquest. He realizes his mistake when he sees Bullio reach for the sharpest straight razor, with fire in his eyes. Perkins attempts escape, but is outrun by Bullio. The Senorita has two other suitors as well, but when she sees the squabbles erupting between the bunch of them, decides to dump them all. The four spurned suitors decide on a quadruple suicide. Synopsis adapted from the plot summary in *Universal Weekly*, April 24, 1915, p.30

REVIEWS: "Hank Mann exhibits promising characteristics in this slapstick number. He gets many laughs throughout the film, which pictures a Mexican story in costume. This is much better than the average offering of this company." *Moving Picture World*, May 1, 1915, p.729

No release 05/02/1915 Sunday

Father Was Neutral: *Released 05/05/1915 Wednesday.* © 04/26/1915 — 1 reel. DIRECTOR, AUTHOR: Harry Edwards. CAST: Billie Ritchie, Peggy Pearce, Henry Bergman, Fatty Voss

SYNOPSIS: Father is a flirt, and so is Billie (Ritchie). When both set eyes on the same girl in the park, push comes to shove and father gets the worst of it. Back home, father's daughter (Pearce) brings home her sweetheart, who turns out to be Billie. Spotting father, Billie takes off in a hurry. Later, Henry (Bergman) moves in on the girl, and father dislikes him even more than Billie. Henry wants to marry the girl, but when father balks Henry slaps him repeatedly until father agrees to the marriage. The girl balks, however, so Henry turns to father with a second round of slaps. Father gives in once again, and tells Henry that he should kidnap the girl to achieve his goal of marriage. Henry hires a third party to kidnap the girl, but it turns out that the kidnapper is Billie. Billie and the girl are reunited, and both father and Henry lose out. Synopsis adapted from the plot summary in *Universal Weekly*, May 1, 1915, p.22

REVIEWS: "A low comedy number.... [Ritchie] flirts with the girl and goes home with her; the father objects and he carries the girl off in a trunk, over the roof. The humor does not come up very strong in this; an average number." *Moving Picture World*, May 8, 1915, p.901

"Father cares little as to which of his daughter's three suitors she accepts, as he has a deep dislike for all of them. It comes down to the survival of the fittest, and Billie Ritchie is the winner. This is an ordinary slapstick, which will produce laughs, without exhibiting anything extraordinarily clever. Henry Bergman and Peggy Pearce are also in the cast." *Motion Picture News*, May 8, 1915, p.78

No release 05/09/1915 Sunday

A Stool Pigeon's Revenge: *Released 05/12/1915 Wednesday.* © 05/05/1915 — 1 reel. DIRECTOR: John G. Blystone. CAST: Hank Mann, Vic Moore, Dick Smith, Alice Howell, Peggy Pearce

SYNOPSIS: Hank (Mann) attempts to discourage his crook pals (Smith and Moore) from pursuing his girl (Howell), but when he's unsuccessful at this he takes another approach. Informing the cops of a planned robbery, the two are arrested and out of Hank's hair. Not content to have the girl, however, he heads for the site of the robbery hoping to collect the spoils left behind by his former friends. Meanwhile, the two have broken out of jail and are heading back to the site with the same intentions. When he hears them coming, Hank hides in a trunk, but it's the trunk they want and they carry him off. The cops arrive and unleash a hail of bullets at the crooks, hitting the trunk instead. The crooks finally manage to escape with the trunk, but when they open it and find Hank inside all hell breaks loose. The stolen money is lost in the melee. Synopsis adapted from the plot summary in *Universal Weekly*, May 8, 1915, p.31

REVIEWS: "There is a lot of good action in this number, but unfortunately it has not enough plot to hold it together properly. Many of the incidents, such as the runaway trunk, are funny, but the plot should have been stronger to get the best results." *Moving Picture World*, May 15, 1915, p.1073

"Hank Mann again supported by Peggy Pearce and a number of other funny people in another acrobatically strenuous farce.

"The plot revolves about the act implied in the title and is developed well by the daredevil cast. This will surely get over. The L-Ko assemblage has omitted the dirt from all their releases of recent weeks, which has raised their standard considerably." *Motion Picture News*, May 15, 1915, p.73

No release 05/16/1915 Sunday

Love and Sour Notes: *Released 05/19/1915 Wednesday.* © 05/11/1915 — 1 reel. DIRECTOR: Harry Edwards. CAST: Billie Ritchie, Peggy Pearce, L-Ko Fat Boy (Fatty Voss), Henry Bergman, Frank J. Coleman

SYNOPSIS: "Billie [Ritchie] was playing a cornet and thought he was the only fellow making a noise. Oscar [Voss], his rival, however, was blowing a trombone in the near vicinity and the girl [Pearce] evidently preferred sonorous notes to light airy ones, as she picked Oscar and left Billie blowing flat notes.

"This made him sore and he attempted to throw Oscar into the creek. They both fell into a sand pile. Her ill feeling was not helped when Oscar got a job playing solos in the village meeting house which Billie had been trying to land for a month.

"Billie took a lemon to the concert, however, and when Oscar commenced his solo, Billie sat in the front row and squeezed the sour fruit. This so puckered Oscar's tonsils that he couldn't blow a note.

"The concert was upset and Oscar chased Billie onto the roof. Billie thought he was going to escape in the bell but he didn't know Oscar was going to ring it from below. Neither did Oscar realize the roof was going to collapse when he chased Billie out on it. Also the girl did not realize the roof was going to fall on her, nor did the congregation want to get hit with plaster. But they all did." *Universal Weekly,* May 15, 1915, p.22

REVIEWS: "Billy [sic] Ritchie, Peggy Pearce and a corpulent youth appear in this. The rival horn blowers indulge in numerous antics while striving for the girl's hand. The last scene, in which the church falls down, was quite novel. The number as a whole is only fairly good." *Moving Picture World*, May 22, 1915, p.1261

"Zu Zu, an accomplished musician and Nightingale, one of the bogus variety, are rivals for the hand of Peggy, and their rivalry leads to innumerable hot encounters. Billie Ritchie and Peggy Pearce are the leads in this slapstick which is of the terrific rough and tumble variety. In the finale the two rivals are reposing on the roof of a church, which caves in, in such a realistic manner that one would imagine the two actors received injuries. This is not while Zu Zu is playing a wind instrument, causing his thoraxial organs to contract." *Motion Picture News*, May 22, 1915, p.75

No release 05/23/1915 Sunday

Broken Hearts and Pledges: *Released 05/26/1915 Wednesday.* © 05/18/1915 — 1 reel. DIRECTOR: John G. Blystone. CAST: Hank Mann, Gertrude Selby, Harry Gribbon, Neal Burns, Peggy Pearce

SYNOPSIS: Penniless Harry (Gribbon) is hungry, but the store owner is unsympathetic and sends him packing. Harry sends his dog back in to steal some food, but when a cop intervenes the dog bites him on the calf and then Harry and the dog take off. Meanwhile, Hank (Mann) argues with both his girl's (Selby) father and his rival, and takes a few kicks to the face. Father throws him out the window, but Hank perseveres and meets his girl in the park. Another fellow flirts with the girl, but Hank quickly disposes of him. Harry and his dog arrive in the park, followed by the cop with the sore calf. A struggle follows between Harry and the cop, and Hank and a bystander are pulled into the fight. The dog once again bites the cop, and then the four of them end up in the lake. The girl, still ashore, goes off with another fellow. Synopsis adapted from the plot summary in *Universal Weekly*, May 22, 1915, p.22

REVIEWS: "Rivals in love are the causes for a great bit of confusion in this strenuous slapstick. Hank Mann has the principal part and is uproariously funny in those scenes in which he appears, which scenes are not numerous enough. Aside from the fact that there is a little too much tumbling this reel is most acceptable." *Motion Picture News*, May 29, 1915, p.80

"A knockabout comedy number.... There is no particular plot; an average offering of the kind." *Moving Picture World*, May 29, 1915, p.1433

No release 05/30/1915 Sunday

No release 06/02/1915 Wednesday

Park Johnnies: *Released 06/06/1915 Sunday.* © 05/28/1915 — 1 reel. CAST: Louise Orth, Harry Gribbon, Fatty Voss, Vin Moore
SYNOPSIS: In pursuit of a woman who had rebuffed him in the park, flirtatious Mr. Rawsberry (Gribbon) follows her into a police station, interrupting and annoying a sitting judge. Rawsberry promptly removes himself, but spotting another attractive lady (Orth), decides to follow her. He does, and into her into the apartment house where she lives, encountering her ill-tempered husband (Moore) who is not amused. Rawsberry attempts to flee via another apartment, but finds himself confronted by a gun-toting sharpshooter. Rawsberry flees into yet-another apartment where a young lady is bathing. Another flirt whom Rawsberry had encountered earlier in the park arrives on the scene, and in the mass confrontation and chase that follows everyone ends up back at the police station, further infuriating the judge. A cop (Voss) gets knocked through a wall, and Rawsberry hits the judge in the stomach with a mallet. The sharpshooter opens fire. When the film concludes, Mr. Rawsberry is cured of flirtation. Synopsis adapted from the plot summary in *Universal Weekly*, May 29, 1915, p.22
REVIEWS: "A rather conventional low comedy number, the scenes being taken in a park, an apartment house and a police court. The situations are amusing in spots, but the number is only fairly strong." *Moving Picture World*, June 12, 1915, p.1778

Bill's Blighted Career: *Released 06/09/1915 Wednesday.* © 06/01/1915 — 2 reels. DIRECTOR: Harry Edwards. CAST: Billie Ritchie, Peggy Pearce, Henry Bergman
SYNOPSIS: Bill de Boozer (Ritchie) is a married artist. Monty Lizzio (Bergman) is a portly brewer and patron of the arts, and he too has a lovely wife Peggy (Pearce). Lizzio visits a sculptor friend, and as he leaves passes Bill's wife who is arriving. The sculptor befriends her and finally convinces her that she should pose, and she agrees, disrobing in a dressing room and emerging wrapped solely in a drape. Meanwhile, Bill meets Peggy — he already knows she's Lizzio's wife — and convinces her that she'd make a wonderful model. He takes her to the sculptor's studio and shows her the wonderful paintings on the wall. She's inspired and agrees to pose, and retires to another dressing room to prepare for her posing. Bill proceeds to paint a portrait of Peggy until he hears Lizzio and the sculptor approaching, at which time he hides, coincidentally in the room in which his wife is posing. Lizzio discovers his wife Peggy, and decides that the sculptor is responsible. Bill, meanwhile, thinks that Lizzio's responsible for his wife being there. All hell breaks loose. The sculptor is thrown from one end of the studio to the other, and Lizzio produces a pistol. Bill hides in a suit of armor and poses as a statue. The studio porter arrives and is pulled into the melee, and the cops arrive soon after, pistols blazing. Bill's wife loses her drape, and flees "garbed in nature's pristine beauty." A wild chase ensues, culminating in a cemetery. Bill tumbles into a very large open grave, joined soon after by Lizzio, the studio porter, the cops,

Peggy, and Bill's wife — it is one crowded grave! Bill digs furiously, and eventually digs his way out to the surface, followed closely by a polecat. Bill shoves the polecat into the open grave with its remaining residents, then shovels dirt in on top of them. When they've all been carefully interred, Bill stamps the dirt down solidly, then plants geranium seeds in a decorative design upon the surface. He departs, leaving the filled grave and its inhabitants behind. Synopsis adapted from the plot summary in *Universal Weekly,* June 5, 1915, p.13
REVIEWS: "Ritchie in the role of an artist and minus a good bit of his usual getup, uses another man's wife as his model. Another artist in the same apartment is doing the same thing with Billie's wife, and these two precarious situations mixed in with any number of scantily draped models causes great commotion.

"Strange to say the funniest part of the picture is the chase which brings it to a close. It is these scenes that Ritchie puts across his most humorous incidental capers, which are sure to create laughter. The rest of the picture we regret to say, shows a reversion of form on the producing company's part. A good many of the scenes are disgusting in their suggestiveness and spoil any humor that might be in the actions of the players. Some of them will doubtless be eliminated." *Motion Picture News*, June 12, 1915, p.79

"A two-reel knockabout number.... The scenes are in an artist's studio and some of them are not free from vulgarity. The principal humor comes in the latter scenes, when a rough house occurs after Billy [sic] discovers that his wife is acting as a model. This is well photographed, but not up to this company's standard in certain other respects." *Moving Picture World,* June 12, 1915, p.1779

No release 06/13/1915 Sunday

No release 06/16/1915 Wednesday

Blue Blood and Yellow Backs: *Released 06/20/1915 Sunday.* © 06/12/1915 — 2 reels.
DIRECTOR: David Kirkland. CAST: Harry Gribbon, Gertrude Selby, Reggie Morris, Sylvia Ashton, Alice Howell
SYNOPSIS: Baron Peastring (Gribbon) has written a love letter to wealthy heiress Miss de Millyun (Selby) professing his love, but in actuality the penniless baron is interested solely in her money. The baron meets a maid (Howell) in the park and, unfamiliar with the ways of Americans, mistakes her for a wealthy woman. She invites him back to the place she works — coincidentally the home of Miss de Millyun and her mother — and the baron accepts, thinking it's the woman's home. He can't go penniless, though, so he convinces passerby Reggie (Morris) to loan him a few dollars. The baron arrives at the de Millyun house and realizes his mistake in time to make it appear as a planned visit. The heiress and her mother are immediately infatuated with the baron. Meanwhile, Reggie, the wealthy scion of a "blue blood" old money family, arrives at the house as well. He's truly in love with the heiress and had intended to propose to her, but when she ignores him for the baron it's too much for the poor fellow. He retires to an adjacent room and pulls a pistol, intending to kill himself. The butler sees what he's about to do, however, and in the struggle that follows the pistol fires several times through the curtain separating the two rooms, hitting both the baron and the mother in their respective posteriors. In the excitement that follows, the baron sees an opportunity to rob the family's safe. As he's scooping up the money he's

spotted by the maid who wants in, and she grabs half of it. Meanwhile, Reggie has reloaded his pistol and decides that if he's going to go, everyone's going to join him. He opens fire in a haphazard fashion, and a passing cop hears the shots and calls for reinforcements. A patrol wagon arrives and is greeted by some of Reggie's wild shots, so they pull their own guns, open fire, then wade into the melee with billy clubs flailing. Miss de Millyun realizes that she actually loves Reggie, and the two are reunited. The baron beats a hasty retreat. Synopsis adapted from the plot summary in *Universal Weekly*, June 12, 1915, p.26
REVIEWS: "A number of the types are appealing, notably the Baron, the maid, the grouch and the pretty girl. The incidents contain considerable amusement of the nonsensical sort, but the plot hardly justifies two reels. The final scenes take place in the ball room, with a general rough house in action." *Moving Picture World*, June 19, 1915, p.1941

A Dismantled Beauty: *Released 06/23/1915 Wednesday.* © 06/17/1915 — 1 reel. CAST: Harry Gribbon, Gene Rogers
SYNOPSIS: Harry (Gribbon) finds a wallet in the park, stuffed with bills. Spotting a "fat beauty" approaching, Harry drops the wallet to attract her and pretends it is hers. She pockets the money. Later, Miss Jane, the "fat beauty," carries on similar flirtations with other admirers and scores a valuable necklace from one of them. Harry sees this transaction and, hoping to get hold of the necklace, follows her to her room. Watching her disrobe, she removes her wig and is exposed as a male. Harry disguises himself as a burglar hoping to recover the necklace. Miss Jane discovers him in the act, however, and he runs away. A real burglar arrives on the scene and attempts to steal the necklace, the police arrive, and in the chase that follows gunshots blow off Miss Jane's wig, revealing her ruse. Synopsis adapted from the plot summary in *Moving Picture World*, July 3, 1915, p.126
REVIEWS: "A park flirtation and a diamond necklace lead to a lot of trouble later. This has plenty of action, but is only fair in plot." *Moving Picture World*, June 26, 1915, p.2097

"Three men are rivals for a woman who turns out to be a crook. This isn't much good except in the final scenes when a few real comedy touches appear. Harry Gribbon is in the cast and doesn't do much that is original." *Motion Picture News*, June 26, 1915, p.83

No release 06/27/1915 Sunday

No release 06/30/1915 Wednesday

The Curse of Work: *Released 07/04/1915 Sunday.* © 06/26/1915 — 2 reels. DIRECTOR: Harry Edwards. CAST: Billie Ritchie, Louise Orth, Henry Bergman
(plus the split reel **Educated Roosters**; see below)
SYNOPSIS: Bootblack Billie (Ritchie) spots several thugs following the wealthy heiress (Orth) to whom he'd given a shine earlier that day. Sensing that they are up to no good, he follows them. His instincts are right: the thugs attempt to rob her, and Billie comes to the rescue, beating the fellows until they scurry off in defeat. The heiress doesn't recognize Billie as the bootblack from earlier that day, and insists on taking her rescuer home to meet her father, the owner of a steel company. The three go out to dinner at a fancy restaurant, and the father takes a liking to Billie as well. He's about to offer Billie a job when Billie realizes he's late for work. The bill for the meal arrives, and Billie makes a bluff of paying

for it. Unfortunately, the father lets him take the check. When Billie's unable to pay, the waiters drag him out and dump him in the garbage receptacle outside the kitchen. Billie heads back to work but he's late, and his boss (Bergman) is angry. To add to his woes, the heiress and her father, deciding they both need a shine, show up at his establishment. Billie attempts a quick disguise of fake whiskers, but his boss has had enough of this nonsense. Billie is punched in the stomach and knocked through a brick wall. The boss pulls a big knife, but manages only to stab himself in the rear. Synopsis adapted from the plot summary in *Universal Weekly*, June 26, 1915, p.27

REVIEWS: "An average low comedy number with Billie Ritchie, Louise Orth and Henry Bergman leading the cast. Ritchie is a bootblack and poses as a baron while out of the shop. He is shown up finally. There is much of the same thing toward the end, but there are quite a number of laughable scenes throughout the two reels." *Motion Picture News*, July 3, 1915, p.81

"Billy [sic] is a bootblack with a fondness for women customers. He follows one of these to the park and has numerous adventures. The humor is rather broad and not quite so complicated as in some numbers, but it will serve to amuse observers who enjoy this class of film." *Moving Picture World*, July 10, 1915, p.309

Educated Roosters: Photo Vaudeville Act — split reel
SYNOPSIS: "First is shown the 'Barnyard Foxtrot,' under Professor Kurtis' direction. Then 'Bobby' is shown climbing the golden stairs. 'Banty' then walks the slack wire with much grace. 'Billikens' next shows his skill on the revolving hoop, while the wonderful mathematical roosters next come forward and answer all sorts of intricate mental arithmetic problems. Then is depicted the Ferris Wheel with the rooster engineer, followed by the grand finale, in which the entire rooster company takes part." *Moving Picture Weekly*, July 10, 1915, p.45

The Child Needs a Mother: *Released 07/07/1915 Wednesday.* © 06/29/1915 — 1 reel. DIRECTOR: John G. Blystone. CAST: Hank Mann, Peggy Pearce, Gene Rogers, Kitty Howe, Fatty Voss, Vin Moore
SYNOPSIS: "Little Gwendolyn [Voss] was just sixteen years old, but she resembled a young pachyderm more than a human being. Her disposition also resembled a young calf's and she loved to romp with father [Howe], who unfortunately was inclined towards anemia and only weighed ninety pounds. Father couldn't stand these gambolings and went out in the park to look for a mother for his child. Not being particularly attractive, he attempted to win by wits what he couldn't by beauty, and wrote a note to a lady [Pearce] sitting on a bench. This note contained belittling remarks about Hank [Mann], her escort. Hank unluckily got the note, but threw it away. It lit on the next bench where a prize fighter was talking with his lady friend. The prize fighter naturally thought the disparaging remarks were intended for him and went over to remonstrate with Hank. Meantime, little Gwendolyn's huge heart got to fluttering like a trip hammer and she went out in the park to look for a mate. Hank was the first specimen she encountered and she then and there decided he was her ideal. Hank tried to shake her but she wouldn't shake. Also her new found love made her frisky and she wanted to gambol about with Hank. Meantime, her papa had nearly landed a wife, when daughter breezed in with her 300 pounds, and

ruined the match. Hank now decided this mastodon must be painlessly although surely murdered. In making the attempt everything went wrong. The cops were involved, papa was also revolved, and Hank got dissolved. After the unpleasantness had subsided, papa found that he had no wife, Gwendolyn had no mamma or no Hank, and Hank had no girl. In fact, no one accomplished anything they had started out to do." *Moving Picture Weekly*, July 3, 1915, p.26

REVIEWS: "One of the best of the recent L-Kos with Fatty playing the role of the capricious Gwendolyn. Gwendolyn's father desires to procure a mother for his bouncing child but instead he procures a million hard knocks and messes several other people's love affairs in general. Hank Mann is in the cast. This is exceedingly laughable and should go very well." *Motion Picture News*, July 10, 1915, p.79

"Featuring Hank Mann, Peggy Pearce and a fat young man dressed up as a baby girl. The scenes are mostly of a knockabout type, rough in spots, but quite laughable." *Moving Picture World*, July 10, 1915, p.309

No release 07/11/1915 Sunday

No release 07/14/1915 Wednesday

A Doomed Hero: *Released 07/18/1915 Sunday.* © 07/08/1915 — 2 reels. DIRECTOR: Harry Edwards. CAST: Billie Ritchie, Peggy Pearce, Henry Bergman, Dick Smith
SYNOPSIS: Billie (Ritchie) has high social aspirations, and when a baron fails to show at an heiresses' reception, Billie assumes his identity. Billie attempts to make love to the heiress, but the maid he has promised to marry recognizes him and tells her hot-tempered brother, forcing Billie to back off. But not for long, and he resumes his charade. A bunch of terrorists think Billie's the real baron, and disrupt the dinner party with their bomb-throwing. Billie hides in a shed, but a bomb explodes in his rear, blowing him sky-high, with a descent more painful than his ascent. Another man ends up with the maid. Synopsis adapted from the plot summary in *Moving Picture World*, July 10, 1915, p.382
REVIEWS: "The plot concerns a baron and his groom, pursued by anarchists. Ritchie rides a bucking horse and saves a girl's life by sliding down a wire. The bombs come into play later and there is a lot of good nonsense as the picture progresses. The feature of the deaf man, impervious to the noise about him, was a good one. This is better than the average offering of this company and altogether quite amusing." *Moving Picture World*, July 17, 1915, p.487

"This subject much resembles the general run of L-Ko's. It contains scenes that are very funny and others that are boresome. The Baron's groom, played by Ritchie, poses as the baron and the consequences can best be imagined." *Motion Picture News*, July 17, 1915, p.124

The Curse of a Name: *Released 07/21/1915 Wednesday.* © 07/13/1915 — 1 reel. DIRECTOR: David Kirkland. CAST: Harry Gribbon, Peggy Pearce, Alice Howell, Dick Smith
SYNOPSIS: Mr. Rawsberry (Gribbon), a janitor who dresses above his means, steals some money from his boss' safe and heads to a fancy hotel with intentions of picking up a girl. To that end he hires a page to bellow his name throughout the lobby and corridors. Meanwhile, his boss arrives at the hotel as well, hoping to calm his nerves after discovering

the theft. To compound matters, another fellow whom Rawsberry had had a previous park encounter with also arrives at the hotel. Rawsberry spots the two men's arrival and quickly attempts to silence the page, but without luck, and too late. Rawsberry tries to escape, but encounters a fire hose wielded by the page. The fellow from the park draws a pistol, and a melee follows. Synopsis adapted from the plot summary in *Moving Picture World*, July 17, 1915, pp.547, 553

REVIEWS: "Harry Gribbon, Peggy Pearce and others disport themselves in this laughable low comedy. Both the park and the office scenes are amusing and the film winds up with a rough house finish. This is acceptable throughout." *Moving Picture World*, July 24, 1915, p.651

"Much better than the average run of L-Kos. The story is strong enough to hold the many laughable scenes together while the entire cast evidences more than ordinary care in effecting incidental actions. Henry Lehreman [sic], Harry Gribbon and Peggy Pearce are in the cast. Alice Howell as the stenographer is an excellent comedienne in this case." *Motion Picture News*, July 24, 1915, p.73

No release 07/25/1915 Sunday

Life and Moving Pictures: *Released 07/28/1915 Wednesday.* © 07/20/1915 — 2 reels.
CAST: Billie Ritchie, Harry Gribbon, Gertrude Selby, Henry Lehrman, May Emory, Dick Smith, Eva Nelson, Alice Howell
(based on the song "He's a Cousin of Mine, Just a Cousin of Mine")
SYNOPSIS: Newlywed Dick O'Dunimwell (Smith) is madly in love with his new bride (Emory). When her former lover Mr. Peastring (Gribbon) arrives, however, she hastily introduces him as her "cousin." O'Dunimwell's suspicions quickly turn to jealousy as he observes the more-than-plutonic interaction between the two. That night the three of them go to the movies, but enjoyment quickly turns to rage on O'Dunimwell's part, and extreme discomfort on the part of his wife and her "cousin" as the on-screen actors (Nelson, Lehrman, Ritchie, and Selby) enact a story that closely mimics the situation they've found themselves in. When the on-screen "cousin" is about to break up the filmic marriage, Peastring decides to flee. O'Dunimwell pulls his pistols and the place is soon in an uproar. Some cans of film explode and the theater catches fire. The angry crowd turns on O'Dunimwell, so he and his wife make a quick exit. Spotting Peastring up ahead, O'Dunimwell opens fire. Peastring jumps into a lake to cool his wounded hide. O'Dunimwell takes his wife to a restaurant, but she's despondent over the fate of her "cousin." O'Dunimwell commandeers the restaurant's musicians in an effort to cheer her up, but all he manages to do is to antagonize the establishment's owner, who throws the couple out. Meanwhile, the fire department is having difficulty extinguishing the theater's fire. A drunk is convinced there are people inside the empty building, and persists in going back in repeatedly in an effort to rescue them. He finally crashes through the theater's screen, taking the on-screen actors with him. Synopsis adapted from the plot summary in *Moving Picture Weekly*, July 24, 1915, page number illegible
REVIEWS: "A two reel low comedy number…. This is characteristic and has many laughs in it for admirers of this type comedy. There is nothing of an objectionable nature in the number." *Moving Picture World*, July 31, 1915, p.818

"This contains more laughs than the average output of this concern. Alice Howell as the boarding house slavey, is good for a laugh every time she appears, while others in the cast are Billie Ritchie, Henry Lehreman [sic], Gertrude Selby, May Emory and Harry Gribbon, quite an aggregation of good comedians." *Motion Picture News*, July 31, 1915, pp.81-82

No release 08/01/1915 Sunday

In the Claw of the Law: *Released 08/04/1915 Wednesday.* © 07/27/1915 — 1 reel. CAST: Harry Gribbon, Peggy Pearce, Fatty Voss, Alice Howell
SYNOPSIS: Chronically jealous Mr. Rawsberry (Gribbon), having spotted his wife talking with the grocery boy, decides to head out and flirt with some girls. He approaches a pretty blonde in a cafe, but her father will have none of this and drives off Rawsberry with a seltzer bottle. Rawsberry waits outside for the father, and knocks out one of his teeth with a thrown brick when he emerges. Rawsberry flees but soon runs into his wife flirting with a cop. Rawsberry is incensed, but his wife pretends she doesn't know who he is, so the cop hauls him off to see the judge — who turns out to be the fellow whose tooth Rawsberry knocked out. Rawsberry braces himself for the worst, but when his wife appears the judge recognizes her as a former "acquaintance," and hastily decides to let Rawsberry off the hook. Rawsberry and his misses make a quick retreat from the courtroom. Synopsis adapted from the plot summary in *Moving Picture World,* July 31, 1915, p.888
REVIEWS: "Everybody sees red in this number and takes to flirting as a cure for the ailment. It is quite a poor comedy, exhibiting nothing new or even laughably old." *Motion Picture News*, August 7, 1915, p.83
"The plot is not strong and the humor is only fair. The settings and photography are better than usual." *Moving Picture World*, August 7, 1915, p.998

Itching for Revenge: *Released 08/08/1915 Sunday.* © 07/30/1915 — 1 reel. CAST: Fatty Voss, Louise Orth, Bud Ross
(pre-release title: **Shot in a Bar Room**)
SYNOPSIS: The village loafer (Voss) is drinking in the town's bar when a stranger arrives. Spotting the loafer, the stranger shoots him, and the loafer is assumed dead. The posse captures the stranger and as they are about to hang him he asks them to wait until he's had his say. His story: The two were friends as boys until a girl (Orth) appeared. The stranger won her, and soon the two were to be married. The loafer had others plans, however, and on the day of the wedding the loafer filled the groom's wedding clothes with fleas. During the ceremony, the groom began to act very strangely, and in his agony stripped down to his underwear. The girl, shocked at his actions, sent him packing. She married the loafer. The stranger, having caught on to his false friend's actions, swore he'd search until he found and killed him. Which he supposedly has done. The posse, moved by the tale, decides to let him go. The loafer, long thought dead, revives. The girl now knows the truth. Synopsis adapted from the plot summary in *Moving Picture Weekly,* August 14, 1915, page number illegible
REVIEWS: "A rampant wild man tells the manner in which his contemplated victim ruined his romance by 'flicking aunts [sic]' on him during the marriage ceremony, breaking it up and afterwards marrying the girl himself. A fair farce with Fatty Voss and Louise Orth appearing." *Motion Picture News*, August 7, 1915, p.84

"Fatty has run away with another man's bride and great consternation follows when the other shows up. There is some amusement in this, though it is not quite so laughable as other numbers have been." *Moving Picture World*, August 14, 1915, p.1162

"Bud Ross appears as an eccentric character in love with an eccentric servant girl. For purposes of revenge the girl puts cowitch on the clothing of her mistress's beau. The result contains some amusing moments." *Moving Picture World*, September 4, 1915, p.1645

Hello Bill: *Released 08/11/1915 Wednesday.* © 08/04/1915 — 1 reel. DIRECTOR: Harry Edwards. CAST: Billie Ritchie, Louise Orth, Reggie Morris, Alice Howell
SYNOPSIS: Bill (Ritchie) and Reg (Morris) are both attendees at the Elks' club house during the National B.P.O.E. Convention in Los Angeles. Both have eyes for the girl (Orth), but she falls for Reg. Bill writes a note full of disparaging comments about Reg, but when he attempts to pass it to the girl Reg intercepts it. Bill is thrown out of the club. He sneaks back in, however, and locks Reg in a closet, stealing his uniform. He makes another attempt to attract the girl. Reg escapes and catches up with Bill, and Reg and his buddies decide that if Bill wants to be an Elk so badly, they'd see to it that he is initiated. Which he is, in a rather humiliating fashion, with the goat-riding the final straw. Bill is sorry he ever wanted to be an Elk. Synopsis adapted from the plot summary in *Moving Picture Weekly*, August 7, 1915, p.44
REVIEWS: "This film was made courtesy of the Benevolent Order of Elks at Los Angeles. Billie Ritchie is featured in the picture, which is developed into an amusing comedy." *Moving Picture World*, August 14, 1915, p.1162

Love On an Empty Stomach: *Released 08/15/1915 Sunday.* © 08/06/1915 — 1 reel. DIRECTOR: John G. Blystone. CAST: Hank Mann, May Emory, Vin Moore, Kitty Howe
SYNOPSIS: Hank (Mann) and his pal Kitty (Howe) are penniless and hungry. Both of them set their sights on a young lady (Emory) in spite of the fact that her escort (Moore) has just proposed to her, and has headed off to get a ring. Hank has a mallet hidden in a bouquet of flowers, and uses it on the fiancé when he returns. Unfortunately for Hank, the fiancé recovers more quickly than anticipated, and takes off after the fleeing Hank. Kitty, who was temporarily waylaid by Hank in the same fashion, recovers and joins in the chase. The fiancé finally catches Hank, and Hank's the worse for it. Synopsis adapted from the plot summary in *Moving Picture Weekly*, August 7, 1915, page number illegible
REVIEWS: "Two tramps acclaim themselves motion picture actors, and, on the strength of this, attempt to win the hand of a young maiden. There is much fighting, kicking and the like in this subject. Hank Mann is featured, and is good for a number of hearty laughs." *Motion Picture News*, August 14, 1915, p.91

"Hank Mann and his hobo partner visit the park. They meet another man's girl and some knockabout scenes occur. No particular plot, but fairly amusing as to action." *Moving Picture World*, August 21, 1915, p.1318

No release 08/18/1915 Wednesday

A Tale of Twenty Stories: *Released 08/22/1915 Sunday.* © 08/13/1915 — 2 reels. DIRECTOR: Henry Lehrman. CAST: Hank Mann, Vin Moore, May Emory, Fatty Voss, Gene Rogers
SYNOPSIS: Hank (Mann), weekending at Los Angeles' Hotel de Bunion, has a run-in with

a portly man (Voss) in the hotel's lobby, made worse when the fellow's wife loses her dress. Hank takes refuge in his room. Later, clad only in his pajamas, Hank steps out into the hall to see if his missing hat dropped there. As luck would have it, a gust of wind blows his door shut, locking him out of his room. Hank figures he can take the fire escape to his open window if only he can gain access to it through an unoccupied room. The first room he tries is occupied by a young couple (Emory and Moore), and the irate husband goes after Hank. One after another, unlucky Hank finds himself in the rooms of more married couples, and it isn't long before a large group of angry husbands are out for blood. The hotel clerk calls the police. Hank flees to the rooftop only to find himself cornered by the husbands and police, teetering on the building's ledge twenty stories above the street. He loses his balance, but grabs the coping and hangs on for dear life. His pursuers begin to fight among themselves for the "privilege" of stepping on his fingers, and soon an invalid and the police find themselves teetering on the edge as well. The invalid falls, but has a soft landing on some pedestrians hundreds of feet below. Meanwhile, the young lady who was the cause of this all sits in her room reading quietly, unaware of the mayhem above. Synopsis based on the print held by the Museum of Modern Art, and the synopsis in *Moving Picture Weekly*, August 14, 1915, p.41
REVIEWS: "When this subject was seen for review it contained many scenes that were disgusting. The censors have doubtless had these eliminated.

"If not the picture is still to be avoided. The latter scenes of the picture are thrillingly uproarious, due to the manner in which the various characters fearlessly cavort on the edge of a twenty-story building." *Motion Picture News*, August 21, 1915, p.91

Mr. Flirt in Wrong: *Released 08/25/1915 Wednesday.* © 08/18/1915 — 2 reels. CAST: Charles Winninger, Harry Gribbon, Vin Moore, May Emory, Gertrude Selby
SYNOPSIS: Rawsberry (Gribbon) is a chronic flirt. A mere floorwalker in a department store by day, he heads to the beach in his off-hours and poses as a bathing suit-clad millionaire. One day, his interactions with a lovely young customer (Emory) are not appreciated by her hot-headed husband (Moore), who proceeds to knock Rawsberry silly with a punch to the chin. When he recovers, the department manager thinks it best that Rawsberry take a short vacation. Strolling through a park, Rawsberry sets his sights on another young lady, who as luck would have it turns out to be the wife of his boss (Winninger). Rawsberry flees the scene, pursuing another young lady while his boss pursues him. A newspaper accidentally dropped from an apartment window gives Rawsberry the brilliant idea of evading his pursuer by grabbing the paper and returning it to its rightful owner inside the building. The owner turns out to be the boss' wife, and before Rawsberry can collect his thoughts, his boss arrives. Rawsberry flees in a hail of bullets. Arriving at the beach, Rawsberry takes refuge in a bathhouse, only to find himself trapped inside with two bears recently escaped from the zoo, and their drunken, unconscious keeper. Rawsberry flees for his life, ending up back in his boss' apartment, where all hell breaks loose. Synopsis adapted from the plot summary in *Moving Picture Weekly*, August 21, 1915, p.33
REVIEWS: "The department store owner discovers that his floorwalker is the man who has been flirting with his wife and a mix-up of huge dimensions follows as a result of his detection. Harry Gribbon again appears as the floorwalker, while the supporting cast includes a number of young ladies in one-piece bathing suits." *Motion Picture News*, August 28, 1915, p.81

No release 08/29/1915 Sunday

A Game of Love: *Released 09/01/1915 Wednesday.* © 08/25/1915 — 1 reel. CAST: Fatty Voss, Reggie Morris, Peggy Coudray
SYNOPSIS: Reggie (Morris) likes Peggy (Coudray), but so does Fat (Voss), who schemes to win her. Her father isn't very fond of her male suitors in general, but he has a genuine dislike for Fat. An unpleasant encounter between the two works solely in Reggie and Peggy's favor, and a second encounter has father in a killing mood. Reggie and Peggy head straight to the minister's home. Synopsis adapted from the plot summary in *Moving Picture Weekly,* September 4, 1915, p.37
REVIEWS: "The plot is farcical and has to do with the rivalry of two men for the girl's hand. The story is not strong but has amusing moments." *Moving Picture World*, September 11, 1915, p.1834

"The rivals in love again; this time they are Reggie Morris and Fatty Voss. It's only a fair picture with few real laughs, save for the titters provoked by the ridiculous physique of Fatty." *Motion Picture News*, September 11, 1915, p.88

Gertie's Joy Ride: *Released 09/05/1915 Sunday.* © 08/27/1915 — 1 reel. DIRECTOR: Henry Lehrman and John G. Blystone. CAST: Gertrude Selby, Hank Mann, Reggie Morris, Raymond Griffith
SYNOPSIS: An innocent smile from Gertie (Selby) has Hank (Mann) head over heels for her. When he later spots her with her boyfriend Reggie (Morris), however, he decides that they all should die. He takes their chauffeur's place, and then sets off on a wild ride down wet pavements, plowing through traffic, unlucky pedestrians, irate cops, and anything else that gets in his way. This includes a house that gives up its side, spilling its sleeping occupants into the yard in their pajamas. Finally, with the police in hot pursuit, Hank heads for the pier, through its railing, sailing 18 feet into the drink below. Gertie and Reggie float to the surface on a tire, but Hank never surfaces. Synopsis adapted from the plot summary in *Moving Picture Weekly,* August 28, 1915, p.30
REVIEWS: "…a comedy thriller…in spite of the fact that the object is to raise a laugh, it is often quickly hushed by a gasp…a closer inspection of the moving picture…proves conclusively that the occupants [of the car sailing off the pier] were real people and not dummies such as are sometimes employed by mollycoddle directors when they have similar scenes to be photographed." *Moving Picture World*, September 18, 1915, p.2012

"A very snappy knockabout number…. The photography is clear and attractive and many laughable stunts are shown, all of acceptable sort. The joy ride at the close is overrunning with action and almost breaks all precedents for this sort of thing." *Moving Picture World*, September 4, 1915, p.1645

Vendetta in a Hospital: *Released 09/08/1915 Wednesday.* © 08/31/1915 — 2 reels. DIRECTOR: Henry Lehrman. CAST: Billie Ritchie, Henry Bergman, Louise Orth, Hank Mann, Gene Rogers
(**Silk Hose and High Pressure** previously announced for release on this date)
SYNOPSIS: Senorita Paprika (Orth) flirts with the fellows in view from her window: Fat La Jolla (Bergman), a bomb-carrying thug; Mr. Jowlfish (Mann), enjoying a bottle of liquor;

and another fellow. Billie (Ritchie) is nearby, sleeping off a drunk. The Senorita tosses a rose, and there's a mad scramble for it. Enraged at the competition, La Jolla throws his bomb at the Senorita's house, but ends up being its sole casualty. Billie works himself up over all of this and eventually comes to the conclusion that the Senorita is at the root of the problems, so he too throws a bomb at her house. This time La Jolla and the two other flirts are the victims, and an ambulance is called. When it arrives it accidentally runs over poor Billie, and when the drivers see the number of bodies that need hauling to the hospital, they quickly dump the truck's current occupants! Later at the hospital, a male nurse (Rogers) needs to examine Billie, and instructs him to remove his clothes. This is all new to Billie, who is shocked at the request and refuses. The nurse perseveres, and Billie loses his trousers. There's a hopeless drunk who is continuously chased by unseen creatures, the result of his DTs. Later on, this fellow mixes all sorts of noxious concoctions to drink in hopes of a high. When he acquires a genuine bottle of liquor, however, Billie picks up the scent and rushes over to join him. After receiving a swig, Billie's forced into bed by the nurse. Soon after, La Jolla attempts to join Billie in the bed, and a fight breaks out that quickly involves the nurse, the drunk, and a number of other patients as well. La Jolla is given some more bombs by his thug friends and explodes them. Billie is blown through the roof and into the clouds, then slowly drifts back to earth, a harp in his hands. Synopsis adapted from the plot summary in *Moving Picture Weekly,* September 4, 1915, page number illegible

REVIEWS: "A wild riot mélange of bomb throwing and mirth-making mixups. The greatest laugh-provoking picture you ever saw." *The Otsego Farmer* (Cooperstown, NY), January 7, 1916, p.3

No release 09/12/1915 Sunday

No release 09/15/1915 Wednesday

No Flirting Allowed: *Released 09/19/1915 Sunday.* © 09/10/1915 — 1 reel. CAST: Peggy Pearce, Hank Mann, Sylvia Ashton, Dick Smith
SYNOPSIS: Hank (Mann) sits on a park bench with his wife (Pearce), attempting to eat a very tough sandwich. He gives up and hands it to her to use as a sole for her shoe. Hank heads to work and arrives as his boss Ignatz (Smith) flirts with his young secretary in another room. Ignatz's wife (Ashton) arrives and catches hubby in the act. Annoyed, she convinces Hank to retrieve some money from her husband's strong box, which he does by placing a wad of her gum on the tip of his cane. She kisses him as thanks, which her husband sees. Ignatz stomps out of the office and heads to the park. Spotting a pretty young lady — Hank's wife — the boss gives in to some shameless flirting. Flirting, unfortunately, is not allowed in the park, and a cop arrests the two of them and hauls them off to the station where they are thrown in a cell. Ignatz calls Hank and asks him to come to the station and bail him out, so Hank obediently obeys, stuffing wads of cash from the strong box into the front of his pants. When he arrives at the station, however, Hank is shocked to find that the lovely young lady is his wife, so he bails her out but leaves his boss in jail, and tells her he wants nothing more to do with her. Hank heads to the park to brood over this disturbing situation. Coincidentally, the boss' wife shows up in the park as well, and

decides she wants Hank. Hank wants nothing to do with her, but the park cop misreads the situation and arrests the two of them for flirting. Hauled down to the station, the two of them are thrown in the cell next to the boss' cell, but neither they nor the boss are aware of the identities of the occupants of the adjacent cell. The boss attempts a break for it, but only manages to break into the cell holding his wife and Hank. The two males go after each other tooth and nail, the fight escalating to include the on-duty cops and a fellow prisoner as well, moving from cell to cell as holes are punched in one wall after another. Ignatz produces a bomb — heaven knows where it came from — and blows up the police station. Synopsis based on the print held by the Library of Congress.
REVIEWS: "One of the funny low comedies with Hank Mann leading. Both Hank and his boss flirt with each other's wife, and finally the entire quartette lands in jail. Peggy Pearce, Dick Smith and Sylvia Ashton lend support to Hank." *Motion Picture News*, September 18, 1915, p.96

Beach Birds: Originally scheduled for release 09/19/1915 Sunday, but replaced by **No Flirting Allowed**. It was never released under this title, and may not ever have been released under another title. No copyright entry — 1 reel. CAST: Hank Mann, Peggy Pearce, and Fatty Voss, according to *Moving Picture World*, 09/25/1915, p.2177; Louise Orth, Henry Bergman, and Dick Smith, according to *Moving Picture Weekly*, 09/04/1915, p.55
SYNOPSIS: "Papa, mamma and their daughter, all went down to swim, but in this case daughter did not go near the water without even hanging her clothes on a hickory limb, and in addition went in with a gink by the name of Hank. Worse yet, Hank had a wife, but she didn't get lonesome, as daughter's parent got acquainted with her and sat under an umbrella on the beach. But daughter had a sweetheart, and mamma had leisure, and so they became acquainted.

"Everything was going nicely, but when six people all go swimming on the same beach, some one is going to see some one else. Unluckily, however, no one realized the meeting was going to be so soon and was going to be so unpleasant.

"As is well known, the facilities for hiding on beaches are very few and far between, and every one stood out bold and unhidden in the bright sunlight. Everyone lost out except the bathhouse man, who collected in full for his bathing suits and umbrellas." *Moving Picture World*, September 4, 1915, p.1730
REVIEWS: "A low comedy number, with Hank Mann, Peggy Pearce and Fatty Voss in the cast. Three married couples mix up in a general flirtation, all attired in bathing costumes. The tone is not good and the fun, such as it is, is entirely of the knockabout sort." *Moving Picture World*, September 25, 1915, p.2177

Scandal in the Family: *Released 09/22/1915 Wednesday.* © 09/14/1915 — 2 reels. CAST: Gertrude Selby, Hank Mann, Dick Smith, Reggie Morris, May Emory, Ray Griffith
SYNOPSIS: Father (Smith), an inebriated old fellow, hangs out at the park enjoying his drunken state. When he spots a lovely young lady, the liquor gets the best of him and he begins to flirt with her. Two younger fellows arrive on the scene, however, and the young lady's interest is quickly swayed towards the new arrivals. Father's miffed at first, but when the lady's escort Hank (Mann) arrives and proceeds to pummel the two flirts, father congratulates himself for dodging a confrontation. He's not as lucky as he thought he

was, Hank turning on him once he's finished with the two flirts. Father is knocked for a loop, crashing into a passerby named Percy (Morris). Percy, annoyed by this transgression, slaps father. Fearing for his life, father flees for home. His daughter (Selby) is home, and she wants father to meet "Sweetie," who should be arriving shortly. "Sweetie" turns out to be Percy, so father throws him out of the house. Persistent Percy disguises himself as a girl and returns to the house. The disguise fools both father and Hank, who has spotted Percy on his return trek. Father and Hank both try to elope with "Sweetie," and are soon doing battle with each other. Father ends up hanging from a live cable car wire, and when some cops attempt to get him down they too are shocked. Hank discovers Percy's subterfuge, and dumps him for father's daughter, whom he hauls down to the minister's to marry. Synopsis adapted from the plot summary in *Moving Picture Weekly*, September 18, 1915, p.33
REVIEWS: "This begins with a conventional park flirtation with some rather laughable incidents. Later the plot is complicated by Reggie disguised as a flirtatious young lady and a general mixup follows. There is not much novelty in this, but it will bring some laughter." *Moving Picture World*, September 25, 1915, p.2177

Avenged By a Fish: *Released 09/26/1915 Sunday.* © 09/18/1915 — 1 reel. CAST: Henry Bergman, Harry Gribbon, May Emory, Gertrude Selby
SYNOPSIS: Father (Bergman) and daughter go to the beach, but father wanders off by himself. Daughter is terrorized by a large fish, but is saved by a flirt whom she quickly takes a liking to. When he heads off to get an umbrella, a life saver shows up and flirts with her, much to her annoyance. When the flirt returns, daughter tells him about the life saver. The flirt decides to dress as a girl, attract the life saver, then beat the daylights out of him. Meanwhile, father's flirtatious encounter with another woman has led to the loss of his bathing suit. Scrambling for a replacement, he finds one with "Life Saver" printed on it. When the flirt spots father in this suit, he thinks it's the live saver who annoyed his girl. In the confrontation that follows, matters escalate to such a level that some officers fall into the ocean where a shark greets them, an innocent old lady falls in as well, followed by some gentlemen who can't swim. The real life saver becomes a hero when he rescues daughter from the surf. Synopsis adapted from the plot summary in *Moving Picture Weekly*, September 18, 1915, p.?
REVIEWS: "A seaside comedy with Harry Gribbon, May Emory and Henry Bergman leading. It's a fairly good reel, although nothing uproariously funny is introduced." *Motion Picture News*, September 25, 1915, p.128
"A typical knockabout beach comedy. A number of amusing incidents are pictured. The closing scenes show a man-eating shark doing comedy stunts." *Moving Picture World*, October 2, 1915, p.80

Married On Credit: *Released 09/29/1915 Wednesday.* © 09/22/1915 — 2 reels. DIRECTOR: Harry Edwards. CAST: Billie Ritchie, Louise Orth, Henry Bergman, Gene Rogers, Fatty Voss
SYNOPSIS: When the Reverend B. Goode (Rogers) demands cash up front before he'll perform the $2 wedding ceremony, groom-to-be Billie (Ritchie) has a problem — he's broke. He leaves his intended Helen (Orth) behind at the altar while he heads out to raise some

cash. Another fellow arrives and tries to marry Billie's fiancé, but the minister's insistence on cash up front places him in a similar situation. He too heads out to find some money, passing the young lady's father (Bergman) as he arrives. Meanwhile, Billie has managed to get his hands on a purse full of money. Returning to the church, Billie encounters the other fellow who relieves Billie of the purse, but Billie manages to regain possession of it. Entering the church, Billie is confronted by his fiancé's father, who has an intense dislike for Billie. After a struggle, Billie flees, pursued by father. The other fellow is still there, now joined by a bunch of cops. Pursued by the cops, his rival, and his fiancé's father, Billie falls into an open manhole, followed by the father and the others, one-by-one. Synopsis based on the print held by George Eastman House

REVIEWS: "This really has some funny situations in it, and will register a success with the lovers of slapstick comedy. Neither of the rivals have money, and both get half way through the wedding ceremony before they go in search of it." *Motion Picture News*, August 14, 1915, p.91

"All this comedy results from a minister demanding C.O.D. in the midst of the marriage ceremony. Billie has no cash and is obliged to step out and look for some. In the meantime another suitor arrives, but he encounters the same difficulty, and in the end neither one gets the girl. This is very funny slapstick with Billie Ritchie and Louise Orth." *Motion Picture News*, October 2, 1915, p.86

"A low comedy…. This is the conventional knockabout comedy with a mixup in the park. The action toward the close is rapid and some of the humor fairly good." *Moving Picture World*, October 16, 1915, p.441

A Mortgage On His Daughter: *Released 10/03/1915 Sunday.* © 09/24/1915 — 1 reel.
DIRECTOR: Henry Lehrman. CAST: Peggy Pearce, Hank Mann, Kitty Howe
SYNOPSIS: Hank (Mann) holds a mortgage against a father (Howe), but is willing to cancel it if father okay's his daughter's (Pearce) hand in marriage. Father agrees, but soon after makes the same deal with another fellow who holds an even larger mortgage. When Hank arrives to claim his bride, he finds the other fellow on the verge of marrying her. Hank raises such a stink that the wedding is called off, but now the daughter is peeved with Hank. Despondent, Hank decides to end it all with poison and drinks some, but father unknowingly drinks some of the liquid as well. Hank has a change of heart, and father realizes what he's consumed, so both of them are now in a panic over their impending deaths. They waylay a milk wagon and consume gallons of the stuff. Doctors and nurses arrive in an ambulance, and the cops show up for good measure. The ambulance filled with a lot of sick people ends up driving off a cliff. Hank and father find out that what they consumed was not poison after all, and perfectly harmless. When all is said and done, neither fellow married the daughter, and both lost the mortgages they'd held. Synopsis adapted from the plot summary in *Moving Picture Weekly*, September 25, 1915

REVIEWS: "This features Peggy Pearce and Hank Mann and contains some lively and quite amusing scenes of a nonsensical character. The reverse of the runaway picture gives a laughable effect." *Moving Picture World*, October 9, 1915, p.254

"The funny L-Ko performer, Hank Mann, appears here as a deep-dyed villain. He holds a mortgage on a pretty girl (Peggy Pearce) and determines to marry her. But he is unsuccessful, as the girl refuses him, so he decides to take poison. Her father also sips a little and thereafter the fun is fast and furious, a chase is introduced and some originality goes along with it. All in all, this is a very funny feature and as a slapstick it ranks as high as low comedies can." *Motion Picture News*, October 2, 1915, p.86

No release 10/06/1915 Wednesday

A Bath House Tragedy: *Released 10/10/1915 Sunday.* © 10/02/1915 — 2 reels. DIRECTOR: Jack Blystone. CAST: Hank Mann, Dick Smith, Peggy Pearce, Kitty Howe
SYNOPSIS: A husband (Smith) tells his chunky wife that she's grown too fat and needs to do something about it. Taking the not-so-subtle hint, his wife heads for the bath house and the steam tank, hoping to quickly drop some pounds. Meanwhile, her husband spots a lovely young lady (Pearce) while taking a walk, and immediately sets out after her, following her into the same bath house. Her sweetheart happens to be Hank (Mann), the bath house's life saver, and Hank doesn't take kindly to the husband's attentions. He pulls a gun and chases the husband into a pool, and soon ends up in there himself. Hank's pet gold Oscar is in there as well, and bites Hank on the nose. The husband emerges to find his wife flirting with Dick, another of the bath house's overweight clients. In the excitement that follows, a rubbing table breaks loose with Hank and some cops on it, and rolls out onto the building's roof where it skids around on the eaves. Synopsis adapted from the plot summary in *Moving Picture Weekly*, October 2, 1915, p.33
REVIEWS: "The opening scenes are disgusting because of dirty settings; cleanliness and humor are the best affinities. Plain soap and water and fresh, clean costumes would help the work of the company greatly. Some of the bath house scenes are quite amusing, though somewhat vulgar. Love and jealousy are the chief plot ingredients. This is only fair." *Moving Picture World*, October 16, 1915, p.442

Under New Management: *Released 10/13/1915 Wednesday.* © 10/06/1915 — 2 reels. DIRECTOR: Henry Lehrman. CAST: Gertrude Selby, Gene Rogers, Alice Howell, Ray Griffith, Fatty Voss
SYNOPSIS: Ray (Griffith) and Fat (Voss), fellow office clerks, are taken with the boss's pretty stenographer Gertie (Selby), but she has her sights set on the boss himself (Rogers). When the boss takes her into his office for "dictation," Ray and Fat watch through the keyhole. Unbeknownst to them, however, the boss's wife Alice (Howell) arrives and sees them spying on her hubby. When she too sees what they are looking at, the enraged wife storms into the office, wallops her husband, and demands that Gertie be fired. Hubby reluctantly obeys. Gertie doesn't give up easily, and when she reads an ad for a male stenographer at her former place of employment, she disguises herself as a man and applies. Alice is doing the interviewing this time, and she's so taken with the young "man" that she hires Gertie on the spot. Later, Alice takes Gertie to lunch while Ray, Fat, and her husband look on. Ray and his boss follow, but end up thrown out of the restaurant. Alice attempts to ply Gertie with highballs. The two return to the office after lunch, and when Alice attempts to make love to her new hire, Gertie's long hair falls to her shoulders. Ray and his boss enter just as the discovery is made. Synopsis adapted from the plot summary in *Moving Picture Weekly*, October 9, 1915, page number illegible
REVIEWS: "The situations are farcical and bring out considerable laughter. The plot is one in which the boss flirts with the stenographer, who already has the rest of the office force

at her feet. The wife comes and finds her husband flirting. She proceeds to take charge of the office and discharges the stenographer. The latter seeks reemployment in boy's clothes. This plot has been used before, but is here handled without offense and is quite amusing." *Moving Picture World*, October 16, 1915, p.442

Does Flirting Pay?: *Released 10/17/1915 Sunday.* © 10/08/1915 — 1 reel. DIRECTOR: David Kirkland. CAST: Harry Gribbon, May Emory
SYNOPSIS: Mr. Rawsberry (Gribbon) is a chronic flirt. Hiding behind a screen door, he pounces on the women who come to look in a lingerie store's window. One such lady (Emory) catches his eye, but her hulking escort quickly scares Rawsberry away. Rawsberry relocates to a café where he hopes his luck will improve. He spots the lady he'd approached earlier sitting with her escort, and they make eye contact. When the escort departs, Rawsberry rushes over to join her, only to be handed the escort's dinner tab. Rawsberry balks at paying this, demanding to see the proprietor. As bad luck would have it, the proprietor turns out to be someone who Rawsberry had wronged decades earlier, and who has been looking for Rawsberry and revenge ever since. A fight ensues which leaves the café in a shambles, with edibles everywhere. Synopsis adapted from the plot summary in *Moving Picture Weekly*, October 9, 1915, page number illegible
REVIEWS: "The restaurant scenes contain some amusement of a distinctly low comedy sort. The reel closes with a rough house in the eating place." *Moving Picture World*, October 23, 1915, p. 621

Room and Board — A Dollar and a Half: *Released 10/20/1915 Wednesday.* © 10/14/1915 — 2 reels. DIRECTOR: Henry Lehrman. CAST: Billie Ritchie, Louise Orth, Henry Bergman, Alice Howell
SYNOPSIS: Billie's (Ritchie) shrewish wife Alice (Howell) has threatened to elope with her star boarder (Bergman). Deciding to end it all, Billie leaves a suicide note for his wife and wanders down to the river where he intends to drown himself. He's saved from this by Madame La Rue (Orth), a hypnotist, who through some strange power lures Billie to her place and puts him to work helping her to scam new customers. Billie's wife shows up accompanied by the star boarder, wishing to see into the future. Alice asks Madame La Rue for a message from her presumed departed husband, and Billie, behind the scenes, accommodates, telling her he's happier where he now is than she'll ever be with her new boyfriend. Alice breaks into tears, while Billie proceeds to "hypnotize" his rival with a blow from his huge mallet. Billie quickly proves his value to La Rue as he administers "hypnotic" blows from his mallet to each and every new customer. His rival receives so many blows to the head that when he finally comes to he flees, leaving Alice behind. When Alice finds that Billie is still alive she's repentant, and willingly returns home with him. Synopsis adapted from the plot summary in *Moving Picture Weekly*, October 16, 1915, p.33
REVIEWS: "[T]wo reels of eccentric comedy. The photography is very good throughout, the settings clean and attractive, and the incidents quite amusing for this type of low comedy. Billie appears as a henpecked husband. He is saved from this by a lady hypnotist and later becomes her assistant. He soon has a chance to revenge himself upon his unfaithful wife and her friend. This contains some laughable moments." *Moving Picture World*, October 23, 1915, p.621

Poor But Dishonest: *Released 10/24/1915 Sunday.* © 10/15/1915 — 1 reel. DIRECTOR: John G. Blystone. CAST: Dick Smith, Peggy Pearce, Hank Mann
SYNOPSIS: Hank (Mann) is a lowly worker at a brick yard, and hopelessly in love with the owner's daughter (Pearce). The foreman is also infatuated with her, so Hank doesn't stand much of a chance. Things change quickly, however, when Hank accidentally saves the daughter in her runaway car, and her father (Smith) promotes him as foreman to show his gratitude. Hank wants to fire his rival, but circumstances get in the way when he's given a lot of grief from a brick maker for not being in good standing with the bricklayers' union. Hank, the rival, and the brick maker all end up in the dynamite building just as it's about to explode. Which it does, sending the trio skyward. Synopsis adapted from the plot summary in *Moving Picture Weekly,* October 16, 1915, p.37
REVIEWS: "The chief scenes are of a rough house character and occur in a brick yard. The incidents are clearly pictured and contain a fair amount of amusement." *Moving Picture World,* October 30, 1915, p.793

Tears and Sunshine: *Released 10/27/1915 Wednesday.* © 10/20/1915 — 1 reel. CAST: Alice Howell, Gertrude Selby, Gene Rogers, Ray Griffith
SYNOPSIS: Father (Rogers) and his son (Griffith) grieve over the loss of a loved one, but put aside their grief when they find that their neighbors, Mrs. Whosis (Howell) and her pretty daughter (Selby) are in a similar position, Mr. Whosis having just passed on. Father and the Mrs. are soon getting along famously, even though their children frequently interfere. Father decides to surprise his new lady friend with the purchase of a necklace, but another admirer of hers gains possession of the necklace and intends to present it to her. Father manages to get it back and presents it to her, and it makes a big hit. Synopsis adapted from the plot summary in *Moving Picture Weekly,* October 23, 1915, p.37
REVIEWS: "A burlesque comedy.... A widow and widower become involved in a flirtation. The plot is not very strong, but there is nothing objectionable in the story and it has amusing moments." *Moving Picture World,* October 30, 1915, p.793

Father's First Murder: *Released 10/31/1915 Sunday.* © 10/22/1915 — 1 reel. DIRECTOR: Craig Hutchinson. CAST: Peggy Pearce, Hank Mann, Dan Russell
SYNOPSIS: Father (Russell) dislikes his daughter's sweetheart Hector Peastring (Mann), and demonstrates as much by tearing a photo of Hector into tiny pieces. Undaunted, daughter (Pearce) attempts to elope with Hector, but father catches them in the act at chases Hector away. Father thinks that perhaps his friend Mr. Sweetgrass would be a better match, so he attempts to interest his daughter in the fellow. When daughter refuses, though, Sweetgrass takes to slapping father. Taking pity on her dad, daughter agrees to marry the brute. Meanwhile, Hector writes her and tells her to hang a rope out the window which he'll later pull as a signal that he's there and ready to elope. Both Sweetgrass and father get wind of the plan, with the unintended result that father's pulled from the window by his big toe, and Sweetgrass tumbles out as well. The finale is a whirlwind of confusion, with Hector mistaken for an assassin, father attempting to escape in a minister's clothing, and kidnappers getting father mixed up with the minister. Hector, father, and Sweetgrass end up in a big fight. Synopsis adapted from the plot summary in *Moving Picture Weekly,* October 23, 1915, p.42

The Idle Rich: *Released 11/03/1915 Wednesday.* © 10/27/1915 — 2 reels. DIRECTOR: David Kirkland. CAST: Harry Gribbon, May Emory, Eva Nelson
SYNOPSIS: Mr. Rawsberry (Gribbon) is awakened from his slumber by his wife (Nelson) who informs him that she's planning to give a lawn party that very afternoon. He heads for the park where he spots a lovely young lady (Emory). Attempts to flirt with her are greeted with a fist, a black eye the result. Rawsberry returns home to find the party has begun, and is quickly confronted with questions regarding his shiner. He conjures up a fanciful story about saving a child from an oncoming streetcar, and being punched by the conductor and motorman for delaying their trip. His audience falls for it, but when Rawsberry spots a guest who had witnessed the real affair go down, he quickly shoves him into a coal cellar. A highlight of the party's entertainment is provided by a woman dressed in prehistoric garb doing a prehistoric dance. Rawsberry flirts with her as well, or at least until her angry husband appears and kicks him out. Rawsberry's wife ushers her husband over to meet the guest of honor, having explained what a hero he is, and the guest turns out to be the woman from the park who gave him the black eye. A wild free-for-all follows. Synopsis adapted from the plot summary in *Moving Picture Weekly,* October 30, 1915, p.33
REVIEWS: "A two reel subject, featuring Harry and Mrs. Gribbon. Mr. Rasberry [sic] is at his best in this number, and does some very amusing stunts of a low comedy type. He shoots the bird in the cuckoo clock because it wakes him up in the morning. Then he gets a black eye while flirting and tells his wife he got it while saving a child from death. The scenes at the lawn fete are also amusing. This is free from vulgarity and better than the average offering of the sort." *Moving Picture World*, October 30, 1915, p.969

Cupid and the Scrub Lady: *Released 11/07/1915 Sunday.* © 10/29/1915 — 1 reel. CAST: Alice Howell, Fatty Voss, Luciebelle Ivey
(pre-release title: **Her Ups and Downs**)
SYNOPSIS: Gwendoline (Howell), a scrub lady, is in love with a businessman whose office is on the top floor of a skyscraper. Forbidden to use the elevator, Gwendoline climbs the stairs many times a day in hopes of getting a glimpse of the object of her affections. He, in turn, ignores her. Her sentimental daydreaming angers the janitor, who happens to have a similar crush on a stenographer. A clerk is equally infatuated with the stenographer, but she's in love with the boss. Cupid run wild. A Black Hand thug has been refused money by the boss, so the thug wrecks the boss's office. Gwendoline saves the day. The boss rewards her handsomely, and she sinks into his arms in a blissful state. Synopsis adapted from the plot summary in *Moving Picture Weekly,* October 30, 1915, p.42
REVIEWS: "A very funny low comedy number, featuring Alice Howell as a scrub lady. She is very much in love with the boss and desires to become a real lady. Her chance comes when she saves his safe from being robbed. A good offering of the burlesque type." *Moving Picture World*, November 6, 1915, p.1140

Silk Hose and High Pressure: *Released 11/10/1915 Wednesday.* © 10/30/1915 — 3 reels. DIRECTOR: Henry Lehrman. CAST: Billie Ritchie, Gene Rogers, Henry Bergman, Alice Howell, Louise Orth, Henry Lehrman, Eva Nelson
SYNOPSIS: Alice (Howell), a former actress, lives in the Hotel Harmony with her jealous police Captain husband (Bergman). In a nearby flat lives Billie (Ritchie), a former actor,

and Gene (Rogers), a pair of confirmed souses. Gene has difficulty awakening Billie from his sound sleep on a trundle bed hidden behind a curtain in the wall, so he creates a trail of booze from the bed to the kitchen table. Billie wakens to the smell, crawling out to the kitchen on all fours, sniffing and licking each drop that he encounters. The jealous cop husband Bergman soon suspects Billie of flirting with his wife, and a fight ensues with Gene joining in. The hotel's strict Janitress observes all with a steely demeanor.

The Gaiety Girls Company arrives at the hotel, followed by a cane-wielding hanger-on (Lehrman; their manager, according to *Moving Picture Weekly's* synopses, but it sure doesn't look that way). Billie and Gene are introduced to beautiful blonde actress Louise (Orth). The Janitress takes it upon herself to ensure that the two sexes remain separated. When the cop exits the hotel he spots Lehrman and confronts him. Lehrman reveals a badge pinned behind his lapel, but when Bergman reveals his as well, Lehrman beats a hasty, limping retreat.

That night, Billie and Gene go to the local theater — the Gaity (as the sign reads) Vaudeville Theatre — to see the girls at work. Taking front row seats in the crowded theater, Billie is repeatedly annoyed by a little girl seated nearby, so he sneaks up into a vacant box seat. Billie's excited when the girls flirt with him, but when he turns his attentions to Louise, she turns her attentions to Gene who has appropriated a box seat at the opposite side of the stage. Annoyed, Billie throws a brick at Gene, who returns the "favor." Billie's unwelcome involvement with a following performance (Julius Caesar?) causes the on-stage "corpse" to become very lively, the actor joining Billie in the box seat for some quick drinks of booze.

Meanwhile, Alice is there at the theatre as well, and she catches her husband flirting with an actress. After the show, Billie and Gene return to the hotel separately, Gene stopping on the way to purchase provisions for a big party. Leaving them in his room, he heads for the showgirls' room to invite them up. He invites Alice to attend as well, she having left her flirtatious husband behind at the theatre. Billie returns during Gene's absence and, spotting the food and alcohol, quickly ties off the legs of his pants and proceeds to stuff everything into his pant legs. He heads for the girls' room, missing them as they follow Gene up to his room by a different staircase. Finding his bounty missing, Gene and the girls go looking for Billie. They find him, his pants bulging with the contents therein. When they inquire about the missing provisions, Billie pulls out his pants' waist and has them look down the front. They squeal with delight.

Bergman, meanwhile, has planned a party as well, and gathers all of his cop friends to attend. Returning to his flat, he finds the other party in full swing, and Alice in Billie's arms. Louise shows concern for Alice's husband, provoking Alice's jealousy and a tussle between the two. Seeing Louise in trouble, the other girls join in. The husband and his fellow cops pull guns, and Billie's revolver is no match. Billie flees and takes refuge in a manhole. As a cop approaches, Billie takes hold of a high-pressure hose and blasts the fellow across the road. When a cripple has the misfortune of wandering onto the scene, Billie shoots him high into the air with the hose — and keeps him there. When Billie accidentally drops the hose, he too is shot into the air. With all of the participants "dancing" at the end of a stream of water, the gas from a police car's leaking tank explodes, engulfing all in a conflagration of water, smoke, auto parts, and gasoline. Synopsis based on the print held by the Library of Congress

REVIEWS: "Three reels of low comedy. The action follows no definite plot and does not hold the interest very strongly until the last reel. There are amusing spots in this number, but the tone is not of the best. The events in the final reel, when the hose is brought into the action, will bring considerable laughter." *Moving Picture World*, September 11, 1915, p.1834

"This is one of the best low comedies that the L-Ko organization has turned out. Billie Ritchie, Louise Orth and Henry Bergman are featured. Ritchie's foolish adventures with a burlesque queen make the plot. An amusing incident is the scene in which Ritchie, pointing a hose straight in the air, balances a man on the summit of the stream. There is much trick work in these three reels." *Motion Picture News*, September 11, 1915, p.90

"The Universal has released a three-reel L-Ko comedy entitled 'Silk Hose and High Pressure,' with Billie Ritchie as the star. Assisting him are Louise Orth and Henry Bergman. The comedy is one that takes some time to get started and is made up of 'bits,' some of which were used in 'A Night in an English Music Hall.' There is also one little moment that carries rather too much suggestion and the picture would have been better had it been left out. This is where Richie holds out the front of his trousers to permit a girl to look into them. The three principal scenes in the picture are the interior of a hotel patronized by actors; the street in front of the hotel and the interior of a burlesque theater. It is in the latter that all of the old English bits are done, including the pillow in the prima donna's face, the brick hurled across the auditorium, and the falls from the box. The greatest comedy scenes are from the 'high pressure' end of the picture, which is about the last half of the closing reel. The high pressure hose is used to keep the police from getting to Ritchie, who keeps them at a distance with it and finally shoots a victim up to about the third story of a building on the stream. The theatre bit with a number of chorus girls working was very well done, for the chorus actually knew what steps they were doing and managed to work as though they actually knew what a stage was. The picture will get lots of laughs in any house, for it has all of the slapstick 'hokum' that is enjoyed by movie audiences." Reviewed by Fred., *Variety*, November 5, 1915, p.23

No release 11/14/1915 Sunday

Disguised, But Discovered: Released 11/17/1915 Wednesday. © 11/10/1915 — 1 reel.
CAST: Dick Smith, Peggy Pearce, Hank Mann
SYNOPSIS: Papa (Smith) tells his prospective bride that he's childless, and she claims to be childless as well. In reality, he has a grown daughter Peggy (Pearce), and she has a grown son Hank (Mann). The two get married, but papa has Peggy pose as a maid so that he won't have to fess up. Arriving home, papa's surprised to find he has a butler as well. The butler is actually Hank, who is in disguise so that he can be near his girl — Peggy! Matters grow progressively more confusing when Hank finds his mother kissing some strange old man, not realizing that she's married to the fellow. And when she spots papa kissing the "maid," her anger is aroused. The situation goes from bad to worse before everything is straightened out. Synopsis adapted from the plot summary in *Moving Picture Weekly*, November 13, 1915, p.27
REVIEWS: "Hank Mann and Peggy Pearce appear in this low comedy number. Her father marries unexpectedly, and when he brings his bride home the daughter is acting as maid and Hank as butler. The fun is of the knockabout type and will create some laughter." *Moving Picture World*, November 13, 1915, pp.1313-1314

Ready for Reno: *Released 11/21/1915 Sunday.* © 11/12/1915 — 1 reel. DIRECTOR: Craig Hutchinson. CAST: Peggy Pearce, Ray Griffith, Dan Russell, Fatty Voss, George Gebhardt SYNOPSIS: When his wife complains about the noise he's making drinking his soup, the annoyed husband (Russell) stomps off and heads elsewhere in the park. Encountering an unfamiliar lady (Pearce) sitting on a bench, he strikes up a conversation. This lady's short-tempered husband (Griffith) spots them and rushes over to give the intruder a flurry of slaps. The battered husband's wife shows up. The one husband and the other fellow's wife find "themselves under the glare of publicity through an unfortunate accident on the telephone wires. In fact, the whole affair was one unfortunate thing after another, and about the only individual who was not ready for Reno was a policeman. This individual was burned by hot telephone wires while attempting to rescue husband and wife." Synopsis adapted from the plot summary in *Moving Picture Weekly,* November 1, 1915, p.28
REVIEWS: "A lively burlesque number beginning with the usual park flirtations and winding up with a bed falling out of a house onto some telephone wires. The closing scenes are laughable and novel." *Moving Picture World,* November 20, 1915, p.1501

Stolen Hearts and Nickels: *Released 11/24/1915 Wednesday.* © 11/17/1915 — 2 reels. DIRECTOR: Harry Edwards. CAST: Billie Ritchie, Reggie Morris, Louise Orth, Eva Nelson SYNOPSIS: Reggie (Morris) contacts sisters Sarah (Orth) and Ethel (Nelson) and asks them to meet him in the park. He heads there as well, and finding Sarah there takes her to a bench where he flirts with her. Billie (Ritchie), a street car conductor with an unusual business sense, arrives at the park and, spotting Sarah, is smitten. He's shameless in his efforts to win her over, finally drenching Reggie and driving him from the park. When Ethel comes along, however, Billie's even more smitten by her, and ends up leaving the park with her, arm in arm. Reggie sees this and returns to Sarah. After attending a concert in the park which Billie conspires to conduct, Billie and Ethel walk by a jewelry store and she falls for a bracelet in its window. Billie vows to get it for her. Later, Sarah spots the same bracelet, and Reggie vows to get it for her. Billie goes to work with a plan to bilk his passengers out of extra money, while Reggie ends up stealing the bracelet. Sarah and Ethel board the street car, followed by Reggie who is pursued by the police. Billie spots the bracelet in Reggie's possession and, cutting the electricity to the car, makes off with the bracelet while the passengers are engulfed in darkness. Reggie puts the police on to Billie, who they pursue. Billie climbs into a hot air balloon and ascends into the sky, but a hail of gunfire causes the balloon to explode. Billie plummets back to earth in a tangle of ropes, flame and smoke. The police are hampered by the crowd that has gathered, and Billie escapes with the two girls. Synopsis adapted from the plot summary in *Moving Picture Weekly,* October 20, 1915, p.23
REVIEWS: "A two-reel low comedy number.... Billy [sic] appears as a streetcar conductor, who gains prosperity at the expense of his passengers. There are numerous flirtations, much of the action centering about a bracelet he purchases for his girl. The humor in this number seems forced in many instances and is never very strong. It is, however, free from any objectionable features." *Moving Picture World,* November 20, 1915, p.1501

No release 11/28/1915 Sunday

Lizzie's Watery Grave: *Released 12/01/1915 Wednesday.* © 11/24/1915 — 1 reel. DIRECTOR: Victor Heerman. CAST: Billy Jacobs, Olive Johnson
SYNOPSIS: Billy (Jacobs) and Jimmy both love Olive (Johnson), but in spite of Billy's triumph in a bout of fisticuffs, Olive prefers Jimmy. In order to win Olive over, Billy "borrows" his little sister's doll Lizzie and presents it to Olive, who is easily swayed. In a fit of anger, Jimmy takes the doll and attempts to "drown" it in a nearby lake. Billy hears Olive's cries of anguish and runs to help, diving into the lake and rescuing Lizzie. Synopsis adapted from the plot summary in *Moving Picture Weekly*, November 27, 1915, p.27
REVIEWS: "An amusing juvenile subject, introducing Little Billy and Olive again after a considerable absence from the films. Billy's rival throws the girl's doll in the lake, in a fit of jealous rage. Billy plays hero and rescues it. A slight plot, but well pictured and pleasing." *Moving Picture World*, November 27, 1915, p.1665

A Saphead's Revenge: *Released 12/05/1915 Sunday.* © 11/26/1915 — 1 reel. DIRECTOR: Craig Hutchinson. CAST: Ray Griffith, Peggy Pearce, Dan Russell
(**Blackmail in a Hospital** previously announced for release on this date
SYNOPSIS: Mr. Slidewell (Griffith) calls on Miss Gaby (Pearce) intending to take her to the dance. While she prepares for the evening, Slidewell's rival arrives with similar intentions, and the size and bulk to back them up. Gaby drives off with the rival while Slidewell searches for pocket change to pay a chauffeur. Slidewell arrives at the dance in time to see his rival and Gaby readying themselves for the prize cup contest. Spotting a can of soft soap, Slidewell sneaks onto the dance floor and spreads the stuff around where his rival is soon to dance. It works, and the rival takes a terrible tumble. Slidewell moves in and takes over as Gaby's dancing partner, only to fall victim to his own trap. A fight follows and Slidewell is bested. Gaby leaves with the rival. Synopsis adapted from the plot summary in *Moving Picture Weekly*, November 27, 1915, p.26
REVIEWS: "An eccentric comedy number.... The girl goes to a dance with one admirer and the other puts soft soap on the floor. The fun is of a rough, knockabout sort and the number proves fairly amusing." *Moving Picture World*, December 4, 1915, p.1854

Sin On the Sabbath: *Released 12/08/1915 Wednesday.* © 12/01/1915 — 2 reels. DIRECTOR: Harry Edwards. CAST: Billie Ritchie, Louise Orth, Alice Howell, Reggie Morris, Gene Rogers, Gertrude Selby
SYNOPSIS: Daughter Louise (Orth) is in the garden fussing with her blonde hair, assisted by mother (Howell), with father (Rogers) nearby. Suitor Billie (Ritchie) arrives and sits with mother while waiting for Louise, but father thinks Ritchie is flirting with his wife and knocks him about. A slick young rival suitor (Morris) arrives, and Ritchie gives him a vigorous face-push. Father throws Ritchie out, and off Reggie and father go, arm in arm.

Ritchie heads back to his pharmacy-soda fountain. Alone, he grabs a bottle of booze from behind the counter, first taking a small sip from a tiny ladle, then a huge swig from the bottle itself. Invigorated, he chugs across the room with his characteristic splayed-foot waddle. Father and Reggie arrive, and father quickly makes amends with Ritchie — clearly, father is a drinker, and he knows Ritchie has the goods. Together, Ritchie and father head into the back room. Father takes a small drink, then he too chugs directly from the bottle. Reggie, annoyed with their drinking, comes and hauls resistant father out into the pharmacy. Ritchie follows, impishly balancing the bottle atop his head, finally luring thirsty father back to the back room. Ritchie pulls out a hookah, and he and father start smoking.

Reggie hatches a plot to put an end to their drinking: he returns to the back room as if to apologize, surreptitiously slaps a "Poison" label on the bottle, pours them each another drink, then displays the label in "horror" right after they down the drinks. Both are in shock at the revelation, Ritchie flopping around on the floor in wide-eyed horror, while father flees back home, belching all the way. Ritchie gallops all over the pharmacy, pours milk from a pail into a big pan on the floor, then lies on his belly lapping it up like a dog. Reggie produces a coffin-sized box from the back room and proceeds to explain to Ritchie — now finished with the milk and the empty pan on his head — what it's for. Now seemingly in shock, Reggie props Ritchie up on a counter stool, crosses his arms across his chest, tilts his head to one side, and closes his eyes — Ritchie is now ready for death!

Meanwhile, father has returned home and, having alerted his wife and daughter to his plight, continues his belching while Louise calls the pharmacy in a panic and mother shrieks in horror, arms flapping about. Reggie has stopped a passing mortician, sending him in to the pharmacy to give a non-responsive Ritchie his card. Louise and mother work father's arms up and down like pump handles. Reggie returns to their home now with the bottle and explains to mother and Louise the prank he has played; they are both relieved and amused. He then goes and tells father the same, but father's not amused, rather mad as hell; he punches Reggie. Father quickly calms down, though, when he realizes that not only is his life not in danger, but he now has the half-full bottle in his possession! The mortician, joined by his associates, places a belching Ritchie into the "coffin." It's a tight fit, and Ritchie's head is propped up at the far end, wide-eyed in horror. Father arrives, bottle in hand, and quickly sets Ritchie's mind at ease with news of the hoax. Both take a big celebratory drink, and Ritchie smiles broadly. Synopsis based on the print held by the Museum of Modern Art
REVIEWS: "A two-reel low comedy number.... Billy appears first as an unfortunate flirt and later as a clerk in a drug store. His job is to dispense booze to men customers in the back room. The situation around which the story is built is familiar to the average small town resident and has a humorous side. There is some funny business in this, particularly in the closing scenes, where the back room is suddenly converted into a place of worship. When the women appear the men are reading Scripture lessons and singing hymns." *Moving Picture World*, December 4, 1915, p.1854

Lizzie's Shattered Dreams: *Released 12/12/1915 Sunday.* © 12/03/1915 — 1 reel. CAST: Alice Howell, Charles Winninger, Fatty Voss, Billy Bevan
SYNOPSIS: Country girl Lizzie (Howell) is at the mercy of her cruel stepfather, who works her hard. When two strangers show up from the big city, she's won over, stealing her stepfather's savings and eloping with one of the strangers. Enraged, the stepfather gathers his farmhands and sets out after the gang. Lizzie and her friends take refuge in an abandoned house, and a battle ensues. It ends up a draw, the two sides equally banged up. Synopsis adapted from the plot summary in *Moving Picture World*, December 4, 1915, p.1895
REVIEWS: "Alice Howell and Fatty Voss are featured in this comedy of country life. The eccentric types are funny, including the cruel stepfather, romantic girl, fat boy who sucks eggs, and the city villains. The elopement and chase are well pictures and the number is a good one of its kind. This is laughable." *Moving Picture World*, December 11, 1915, p.2033

Blackmail in a Hospital: *Released 12/15/1915 Wednesday.* © 12/08/1915 — 1 reel.
DIRECTOR: Craig Hutchinson. CAST: Peggy Pearce, Ray Griffith, Dan Russell
SYNOPSIS: The hospital patients all love the beautiful young nurse (Pearce), but there's one tough admirer who pummels anyone who shows any interest. Crutches-bound Cookie (Griffith) steps in and thrashes the fellow within an inch of death, and a trusty who witnesses this demands $10 from Cookie or he'll expose him to the authorities. Cookie's penniless, but when he hears that his victim will die unless he gets a blood transfusion, and that the hospital authorities are offering $10 for blood, Cookie reluctantly steps forward. As the blood flows from Cookie into his rival, Cookie grows weaker and the rival stronger, so Cookie pinches the tube and regains his strength. The rival, now revitalized, asks to see the generous fellow who donated blood. When they meet, the rival goes after Cookie, who pulls a pistol and fires. Patients scatter as Cookie and the rival go into battle, but exhaustion finally takes over and they both sink to the floor. Some spilled chloroform finishes them off. Synopsis adapted from the plot summary in *Moving Picture Weekly*, December 11, 1915, page number illegible
REVIEWS: "Once more has this company staged a knockabout reel in a hospital where the opportunities for the slapstick art are many. Peggy Pearce is in the cast, which proves itself capable of any task allotted to it. Of its kind it is a good picture with nothing vulgar and doubtless will be well received." *Motion Picture News*, December 18, 1915, p.98

The Doomed Groom: *Released 12/19/1915 Sunday.* © 12/10/1915 — 1 reel. CAST: Charles Winninger, Fatty Voss
SYNOPSIS: Already late for his wedding, the groom (Winninger) runs across a very attractive woman and proceeds to tell her his tales of woe. Her husband arrives on the scene and is not at all happy with the groom's familiarity with his wife, so he tells him in no uncertain terms that he'd better be out of town by a specified time, or else. Fearing for his life, the groom heads for the home of his bride-to-be (Voss!) to inform everyone that he must leave town, and immediately. His bride-to-be's irate father makes it plain that the groom better stay in town, and to make sure takes all of the groom's money. The groom fears the irate husband more than the irate father, so he decides to steal his money back and skip town — without much success, running afoul of both father and husband. He gives up, crosses his fingers, and has the ceremony rushed to a quick conclusion. Synopsis adapted from the plot summary in *Moving Picture Weekly*, December 11, 1915, p.27
REVIEWS: "An eccentric comedy number, picturing the adventures of an unwilling bridegroom. Fatty Voss, attired in woman's clothes, plays the blushing bride. A pleasing idea handled in a fairly amusing way." *Moving Picture World*, December 18, 1915, p.2204

From Beanery to Billions: *Released 12/22/1915 Wednesday.* © 12/1915/1915 — 2 reels. CAST: Alice Howell, Dick Smith, Louise Orth
SYNOPSIS: Upon her father's death, Alice (Howell) is willed to a cafe owner to whom her father had been indebted. Forced to work in the cafe, she soon meets a young man and the two eventually marry. Her husband's father disapproves of the union, however, and disinherits the son leaving the couple to live in poverty. The three are reunited sometime later when the couple's young son is injured in an auto accident involving the disapproving father. The couple moves in with the father, only to find that the cafe owner, now penniless, has gone to work in the home as a butler. The butler forces Alice to open the safe, steals the contents

therein, and attempts to escape with the family members close on his heels. The butler's auto blows up, and when he comes down the money and jewels are recovered. Synopsis adapted from the plot summary in *Moving Picture World*, December 18, 1915, p.2240
REVIEWS: "A two-reel burlesque number, featuring Alice Howell and others. She is first seen as a waitress who marries the son of a rich man. Later she breaks into high society. Some of the scenes are funny in this, but the production has drawbacks and is coarse in several situations. The chase at the close is the best feature." *Moving Picture World*, December 18, 1915, p.2204

Greed and Gasoline: *Released 12/26/1915 Sunday.* © 12/17/1915 — 1 reel. DIRECTOR: Reggie Morris. CAST: Gertrude Selby, Dave Morris, Reggie Morris, Fatty Voss, Alice Howell
SYNOPSIS: Newlywed Reggie (Morris) and Gertie (Selby) mortgage their home to buy an auto. A pair of tramps (Dave Morris and Voss) come up with a scheme to make some money, one of them pretending to be hit and injured by the couple's auto. Fearing a lawsuit and filled with sympathy, the couple takes the "injured" fellow to their home to nurse him back to health, but he quickly takes advantage of the situation and their guilt. He appropriates their bed leaving them to sleep in uncomfortable chairs, and his demands grow increasingly bold and unreasonable. Later while the husband is at work, the "injured" tramp's overweight partner arrives and the two set out to rob the house. Gertie calls her husband who in turn calls the police, and the bunch of them arrives in time to arrest the tramps. Synopsis adapted from the plot summary in *Moving Picture World*, December 18, 1915, p.2240
REVIEWS: "Gertrude Selby and Reggie Morris are featured as a young married couple who are victimized by two tramps. The opening scenes are quite amusing. The offering as a whole is fairly strong." *Moving Picture World*, December 25, 1915, p.2390

A Scandal At Sea: *Released 12/29/1915 Wednesday.* © 12/22/1915 — 1 reel. DIRECTOR: Craig Hutchinson. CAST: Dan Russell, Louise Orth, Ray Griffith
SYNOPSIS: A flirt (Griffith) makes a pass at a lovely young blonde (Orth), not realizing that she is married. Her husband (Russell) turns out to be the gruff captain of a ship, and he isn't happy about the flirt's antics. He gives the flirt an hour to get out of town. The flirt decides to stow away on a ship that's ready to sail, and while his intentions are good his choice of ships is bad, and he soon comes to realize that this ship's captain is the blonde's humorless husband. His presence is discovered by the captain, and there's hell to pay. Synopsis adapted from the plot summary in *Moving Picture Weekly*, December 11, 1915, p.5
REVIEWS: "A flirtatious admirer follows the wife of a sea captain aboard his passenger ship. The male flirt has many troubles of a quite amusing sort and saves himself at the end by stopping a leak in the vessel. This is acceptable throughout and contains a fair amount of humor. *Moving Picture World*, December 25, 1915, p.2390

1916 Releases:

Pants and Petticoats: *Released 01/02/1916 Sunday.* © 12/24/1915 — 1 reel. CAST: Reggie Morris, Gertrude Selby, Fatty Voss, Dave Morris, Gladys Roach
SYNOPSIS: Gertie (Selby) loves Reggie (Morris), but cannot stand Reggie's rival Fat (Voss), who is infatuated with her. When her judge father finds that it was Reggie who almost ran him over with his auto, her father sends Reggie packing and insists that she marry

Fat. When Gertie spots Reggie innocently kissing his sister, she's unaware of the girl's identity, breaks her engagement to Reggie, and reluctantly agrees to marry Fat. In an attempt to discredit Fat, Reggie dresses as a woman and waits for him. Unfortunately, the judge arrives, falls for this "woman," and takes "her" to dinner. He later writes her a note on his business card, inviting the "woman" to his chambers. Later, a disguised Reggie meets up with Fat and embraces him. This somehow leads to Fat's arrest, causing Gertie to call off their engagement. Reggie's exultation soon turns to dismay when he's arrested for impersonating a woman. He and Fat are both hauled into court — Gertie's father presiding! The judge gives Reggie twenty-five years in prison, but when Reggie produces the incriminating business card the sentence is quickly dismissed. Reggie and Gertie are reunited. Synopsis adapted from the plot summary in *Moving Picture Weekly*, date and page unavailable

REVIEWS: "A comedy number of the farcical type…. [Reggie Morris] attires himself as a girl, and breaks up his rival's love affair. The situations are amusing and the general tone of this production better than average." *Moving Picture World*, January 1, 1916, p.98

"A very good comedy void of the slapstick, and containing an interesting plot and capable and humorous interpretation. Reggie Morris dons feminine garb once more and is ably supported by Gertrude Selby and Fatty Voss, who is in this picture an excellent comedian." *Motion Picture News*, January 1, 1916, p.96

No release 01/05/1916 Wednesday

Billie's Reformation: *Released 01/09/1916 Sunday.* © 12/31/1915 — 2 reels. CAST: Billie Ritchie, Louise Orth, Reggie Morris, Gene Rogers, Ray Griffith, Fatty Voss, Henry Bergman, Gertrude Selby, Luciebelle Ivey

SYNOPSIS: Billie (Ritchie) has a job where he's well-liked by all, but the weekly pay is barely enough to make ends meet. Throw a short-tempered wife into the mix who won't let him forget about their money woes and rails on about his friends, and it's no wonder that Billie prefers the pool hall and his card-playing friends to life at home. When a solicitor shows up and informs Billie that a long-forgotten aunt has died and left him her entire estate valued at half million dollars, Billie quits his job and goes on a spending spree. Now his wife sees even less of him as he spends his time out on the town, and matters grow even more complicated when he falls for a blonde (Orth). Synopsis adapted from the plot summary in *Moving Picture Weekly*, December 18, 1915, p.30

REVIEWS: "Billy's flirtations lead to trouble on a sleeping car, from which the occupants flee in night attire. There is so much vulgarity in this that it hurts the humor very much. Some of the scenes toward the close, on the roofs of high buildings, are better, but the offering as a whole is difficult to commend." *Moving Picture World*, January 8, 1916, p.263

"In a story of good quality and humorously tangled situations, Billie Ritchie here disports himself supported by almost all of the L-Ko company. Louise Orth, Gene Rogers, Ray Griffith, Fatty Voss, Henry Bergman and Reggie Morris are chief of the assistant funmakers. The last reel closes with several hair raising stunts staged on a high roof. Billie Ritchie's admirers will like this as he is always prominent." *Motion Picture News*, January 8, 1916, p.106

Gertie's Busy Day: *Released 01/12/1916 Wednesday.* © 01/05/1916 — 1 reel. CAST: Gertrude Selby, Reggie Morris, Fatty Voss, Dave Morris
SYNOPSIS: All Gertie (Selby) wants to do is spend a peaceful day at the park. Reggie (Morris) arrives at the scene and begins to flirt with her and, after some initial resistance finally wins her over. A fat friend (Voss) shows up and starts to flirt with Gertie as well, and soon Reggie and the friend are at each other's throat. While they are at it, a park attendant (Dave Morris) arrives and he too makes moves towards Gertie. She rebuffs him and flees, only to be descended upon by even more flirts. She calls for a cop who attempts to drive the amorous group away, which results in a free-for-all. Reggie arrives and rescues Gertie, much to the dismay of the others. Synopsis adapted from the plot summary in *Moving Picture Weekly,* January 8, 1916, p.20
REVIEWS: "An exceptionally pleasing number. Gertrude Selby has indeed a busy time in the park, meeting Reggie, the tree sprayer, the ladylike cop, a hobo, an old gentleman and Fatty. The mixups that occur are genuinely funny and the photography is clear and pleasing. A good number." *Moving Picture World,* January 8, 1916, p.263

"By all odds one of the best of the recent output of this company introducing a lot of flirtatious horseplay that accomplishes its comedy mission in most excellent style. Gertrude Selby, Fatty Voss and Reggie Morris are the leads." *Motion Picture News,* January 15, 1916, p.264

Flirtation A La Carte: *Released 01/16/1916 Sunday.* © 01/07/1916 — 1 reel. CAST: Alice Howell, Dick Smith, Phil Dunham, Fatty Voss
SYNOPSIS: Phil (Dunham) and his wife Alice (Howell) have an argument, and Phil stomps out. Elsewhere, Dick (Smith) and his wife have quarrel as well, and Dick leaves home. Alice decides to get even with her husband, and heads out for some flirting. She runs across Dick and flirts with him, but Phil shows up and she runs home. Phil and Dick argue and vow vengeance on each other. That night, Phil and Dick meet up again in a gambling room. Phil tries to cheat Dick but is caught and a fight ensues. The cops arrive and everyone flees. In a panic, Dick takes refuge in Phil's house, hiding under a bed. Phil finds him there and they resume fighting. Alice's screams alert the police, who enter the house and find some of the other gamblers there as well. A free-for-all follows and everyone is knocked senseless. Synopsis adapted from the plot summary in *Moving Picture Weekly,* January 8, 1916, p.28
REVIEWS: "A low comedy number.... Two quarreling married couples get into some flirtations. The poker game is the best feature. A fair number." *Moving Picture World,* January 8, 1916, p.263

"It pictures the flirtations of two old salts. The photography is uneven and the opening scenes are slow. There are some laughable moments at the close." *Moving Picture World,* January 15, 1916, p.443

"This knockabout affair is based on an old plot while its situations present nothing original in the way of laughable entertainment. Alice Howell and Fatty Voss are in the cast and manage to produce a few laughs." *Motion Picture News,* January 15, 1916, p. 264

Saving Susie from the Sea: *Released 01/19/1916 Wednesday.* © 01/12/1916 — 1 reel.
DIRECTOR: Noel Smith. CAST: Alice Howell, Dick Smith, Joe Moore
SYNOPSIS: Penniless Dave (Smith) and well-to-do Joe (Moore) are both in love with Susie (Howell), but she strongly prefers Dave. Her father disagrees, however, and insists that she

marry Joe. Dave takes a job as a street cleaner, and when he sees Susie, her father, and Joe in an auto, he hitches his street sweeper's little barrow to the auto axle and is towed down the road to the beach. Once there Dave takes a job as a lifeguard. Susie hires a boat but loses her oars, so Dave rushes to her rescue in a boat, pushing aside her father and Joe. Rowing her back to shore, Joe attempts to wrest her from Dave, but Dave responds by knocking down both Joe and the father, and driving off with Susie. Joe and the father summon the police and follow in hot pursuit, the chase continuing "through fences, around sharp corners, up and down hills, along the edge of precipices and finally ends in the swimming tank." Synopsis adapted from the plot summary in *Moving Picture World*, January 15, 1916, pp.477, 480
REVIEWS: "Rivalry in love is the chief plot ingredient in this knockabout comedy. Some of the action takes place at the beach. The automobile and motorcycle chase is well pictured. A characteristic number." *Moving Picture World*, January 15, 1916, p.443

Mr. McIdiot's Assassination: *Released 01/23/1916 Sunday.* © 01/14/1916–2 reels.
DIRECTOR: Craig Hutchinson. CAST: Ray Griffith, Dan Russell, Louise Orth
SYNOPSIS: Mr. McIdiot (Griffith), depressed over the loss of his love (Orth), decides to end it all. Looking into various methods of self-extermination, he soon comes to realize that he's not up to the task, so he decides to enlist outside help to do the dirty work. He goes to the Murderers' Association, a business that specializes in painless killing for a price. He makes arrangements with the Chief Assassin (Russell), who then demands payment in advance. McIdiot is penniless, so he wants the job done on credit. Needless to say, the two cannot come to terms. A frustrated McIdiot is soon cheered when he finds that his girl still loves him after all. Synopsis adapted from the plot summary in *Moving Picture Weekly*, January 15, 1916, p.23
REVIEWS: "Ray Griffith first appears in this nonsense number. He is a young man addicted to flirting in the park. He disports himself for some time picking flowers illegally, and finally comes upon a fair charmer impersonated by Louise Orth. He makes advances and is making satisfactory progress in the love affair when a portly rival comes to the scene. The latter part is played by Dan Russell who, as well as Mr. Griffith, is making a good impression in this line of comedy.

"Thinking he has lost his lady love, the young man becomes desperate and decides to kill himself. He lacks the nerve to do this and finally visits a murder bureau. The chief assassin turns out to be his rival, and he agrees to kill the young man within twelve hours. This is agreeable to Ray and he wanders out to the park again, wondering just when death will come.

"The main situation appears to be very creepy as described, but it carries very well on the screen and there are numerous laughable scenes to offset the sanguinary nature of the plot. Moreover, a happy ending is brought about, by the sudden decision of the chief assassin to give up murder as a business. The girl also relents and looks up the despondent lover, telling him she loves him alone. The final scenes are good, picturing the three leading characters climbing a high ladder upon the park bridge, from which one dives into the water below." Reviewed by Robert C. McElravy, *Moving Picture World*, January 1, 1916, p.93

"This is a purely nonsensical production and brings out numerous laughs. The main situation has a grim aspect in the telling, but seems merely amusing as pictured. It concerns a despondent young man who desires to die, but hasn't the nerve to commit suicide. He employs a professional assassin to kill him. Then the girl forgives him and he desires to live.

There are many laughable scenes in this and it is free from offense of any sort." *Moving Picture World*, January 22, 1916, p.626

"Henry Lehrmann offers in this number, to be released January 23, two reels of unsullied comedy, quite void of the slapstick and containing much 'business,' effected by a pair of most capable comedians.

"Ray Griffith and Dan Russell, comparatively new arrivals at the L-Ko studio, seem to have a brilliant sense of comedy values along such lines. They are capable men and will undoubtedly add much to the popularity of these pictures.

"'Mr. McIdiot's Assassination' offers them a picture quite unlike the usual run of Mr. Lehrmann's comedies. There is no strenuous slapstick work, and no wild chase through town and country.

"The picture has a plot, and it is interesting, though of a familiar sort, but the work of Griffith and Russell is responsible for the greater number of the picture's merits. They furnish laughs that come unaccompanied by blushes.

"McIdiot, having lost in love, goes to the Murderers' Association, and pays a large sum to have his life ended. Then, horror of horrors, he discovers that his girl still loves him, and consequently he is in fear that his life will be forfeited from him at any minute; but the proprietor of the Murderers' Association decides to mend his way and consequently the lovers are left unmolested.

"Louise Orth as the girl presents an attractive appearance, while the few remaining roles are carried by players who have been well tutored. Save for the fact that the photography in the print shown was poor in a few places, the picture is by all odds the best of the two-reel L-Kos." Reviewed by Peter Milne, *Motion Picture News*, January 8, 1916, p.98

Knocks and Opportunities: *Released 01/26/1916 Wednesday.* © 01/19/1916 — 2 reels.
CAST: Billie Ritchie, Louise Orth, Reggie Morris
SYNOPSIS: Down on his luck Billie (Ritchie) appropriates a jitney with the hope of making some money. The jitney's owner isn't happy about this, and tosses Billie into the street, where a wealthy young lady (Orth) accidentally hits him with her car. Billie feigns injury, and she takes him home to tend to him. When her father discovers this freeloader, however, he throws him out of the house. Billie decides to end it all, and throws himself in front of a truck. He's rescued at the last moment by a young man (Morris) who takes pity on him. Taking Billie under his wing, he buys him a whole new wardrobe. Billie decides to revisit the wealthy young lady, hoping that her father won't recognize him now that he's all dressed up. His hopes are rewarded, and Billie actively pursues her. When he finds out that she's engaged to the young man who had helped him out, Billie does his best to turn her against the fellow by telling all sorts of lies about him. The fellow, unaware that Billie even knows his fiancé let alone has eyes for her, eventually finds them together and catches on. He throws Billie back into the street, where Billie resumes his quest for another opportunity. Synopsis adapted from the plot summary in *Moving Picture Weekly*, January 22, 1916, p.23
REVIEWS: "The opening scenes are given up to picturing a rivalry over the girl and witness Billy's regeneration from a bum to a gentleman. The humor is not very strong until the incident at the wedding reception, when Billy puts all the guests to sleep by pouring ether on the bride's bouquet. The latter part of the production is very funny." *Moving Picture World*, January 22, 1916, p.626

"This release has a good plot that holds of itself and a lot of humorously effective trick work, while Billie Ritchie's horseplay strikes an unusually funny chord. Louise Orth and Reggie Morris take other leads. The settings are particularly expansive for comedy while the wedding scenes add a humorous touch of spicy unconventionality." *Motion Picture News*, January 29, 1916, p.570

Cupid At the Polo Game: *Released 01/30/1916 Sunday.* © 01/21/1916 — 1 reel. CAST: Ray Griffith, Louise Orth, Dan Russell
SYNOPSIS: Polo champion Ray (Griffith) is engaged to Louise (Orth), and is looked upon favorably by her flirtatious father (Russell). A shifty count decides that he wants Louise for himself, but when his attentions are rebuffed he concocts an insidious plan. He replaces the polo ball with a lit bomb, but Ray's skillfully-wielded mallet sends the bomb sailing into an innocent bystander. He in turn tosses the bomb into the club house where it lands on a billiard table. Louise's father is about to hit it with his billiard cue when Ray comes to the rescue. The villain is defeated. Synopsis adapted from the plot summary in *Moving Picture Weekly*, January 22, 1916, p.28
REVIEWS: "A particularly good knockabout comedy number…. The settings are fine and the photography good. The scenes are taken during a real polo game and the humor is the best of its kind." *Moving Picture World*, January 22, 1916, p.626
"This is by far the best of the L-Kos that we can remember. It has good comedians, original funny business, while the scene of action, the polo field, affords many opportunities for refreshing work. Ray Griffith, Louise Orth and Dan Russell, all real comedians, furnish the fun." *Motion Picture News*, January 29, 1916, p.571

Sea Dogs and Land Rats: *Released 02/02/1916 Wednesday.* © 01/26/1916 — 1 reel. CAST: Dave Morris, Reggie Morris, Gertrude Selby, Fatty Voss
SYNOPSIS: Gertie (Selby) is in love with barber Reggie (Morris), but her father, whose credit has been cut off at the barber shop, forbids her from seeing him. Gertie arranges to meet Reggie in the park, but while waiting for his arrival is annoyed by a stranger (Dave Morris) and two sailors. Unable to discourage them, Gertie heads back home, with the three of them following close behind. Her father blows up when he finds these persistent pests bothering her, and a free-for-all ensues. Reggie arrives and tries to save Gertie, but the floor gives way and all are deposited on the bridal couple on the floor below. That floor gives way as well, and all end up in the basement. Synopsis adapted from the plot summary in *Moving Picture Weekly*, January 29, 1916, p.20
REVIEWS: "A knockabout number featuring Gertrude Selby, Fatty Voss and Reggie Morris. Two sailors join in the park flirtations and some rapid fire competition takes place. The humor is of a rough sort. There is a laugh at the close." *Moving Picture World*, February 5, 1916, p.802

A September Mourning: *Released 02/06/1916 Sunday.* © 01/28/1916 — 2 reels. DIRECTOR: Henry Lehrman. CAST: Charles Winninger, Gertrude Selby, Henry Lehrman, Gene Rogers, Ray Griffith, Eleanor Pierce
SYNOPSIS: Two artists (Winninger and Griffith) try their hands at painting "September Morn," but have difficulties hiring models. One of them attempts to paint a model against her will, while the other sells a phony painting to an art dealer (Lehrman). Later, still

attempting to find models willing to pose for them, they come to a park where a group of lovely young ladies (Selby and Pierce among them) are performing Greek dances in costume. The artists watch the dancers but are annoyed when a picture-snapping fellow arrives and moves into their space. This results in a dispute and tussle. Some cops arrive and think the young ladies' garments to be indecent, but when they attempt to place overcoats on them the ladies rebel and the cops end up in the lake. Then the art dealer arrives with gun in hand and murder in his eyes. All hell breaks loose but the girls, unfazed, continue to dance. Synopsis adapted from the plot summary in *Moving Picture Weekly*, January 29, 1916, p.23

REVIEWS: "This eccentric comedy number pictures the experiences of two talented but hungry artists. It begins with the usual park flirtations, in which they are joined by a number of hangers-on, the object of rivalry on the part of all concerned being a pretty girl, portrayed without the slightest effort by Gertrude Selby.

"The opening reel is devoted to some diverting and nonsensical small business. Some of these whimsical antics prove vey laughable, though they would have been more so with a little more definite plot to hold them together. The funmakers comprise H. Pathe Lehrman, Charles Winninger, Gene Rogers and others.

"The second reel pictures the artists in the act of invading a girls' school. Numerous young ladies, clad in scant, but artistic, attire, are the object of their interest. There are moments when an apprehensive observer thinks matters may go too far, but there is really no actual vulgarity, and while the general tone of the comedy is not of the best, it is after all a harmless sort of fun.

"The photography is very good throughout and some of the settings are quite picturesque." Reviewed by Robert C. McElravy, *Moving Picture World*, November 13, 1915, p.1319

"The action of the first reel contains some laughable moments, centering about the usual park flirtations. In the second reel the two artists invade the grounds of a girls' school, where they watch the girls dancing and try to choose a subject to pose for September Morn. This, of course, is not in the best of tone, but it escapes any pronounced vulgarity and has enough amusing features to keep the observer interested. Some of the settings in the second reel are quite picturesque." *Moving Picture World*, February 12, 1916, p.979

Her Naughty Eyes: *Released 02/09/1916 Wednesday.* © 02/02/1916 — 1 reel. CAST: Alice Howell, Harry Coleman, Dick Smith

SYNOPSIS: Harry (Coleman) and Alice (Howell) are engaged, but Harry's jealous rival Dick (Smith) vows to make her his own. When Harry is called out of town, Dick engages a hypnotist to make her fall in love with him, but the hypnotist is a substandard one and manages only to give Alice an uncontrollable and naughty little wink. Her winking starts to drive all of the men about her wild with desire, and when Harry returns he's shocked to find swarms of men doing battle over Alice's charms, his uncle included! Matters escalate until the hypnotist fights with Dick for his fee, and Dick's trickery is revealed. Alice is "cured" of her affliction, and Dick is punished. Synopsis adapted from the plot summary in *Moving Picture Weekly*, February 5, 1916, p.26

REVIEWS: "Another version of the familiar plot in which the leading lady has a winking eye. In this case Alice Howell is the victim of a hypnotist, who causes her to flirt with every man she meets, including the minister when he is marrying her to another. This is not new but quite amusing." *Moving Picture World*, February 12, 1916, pp.978-979

"Alice Howell gets the wink habit and the 'come over here' look in her eyes in this production which is fairly amusing, despite the fact that it is an old idea." *Motion Picture News*, February 12, 1916, p.876

Firing the Butler; or, The Butler's Fire: *Released 02/13/1916 Sunday.* © *02/04/1916* — 2 reels. CAST: Reggie Morris, Dave Morris, Gus Leonard, Gertrude Selby, Fatty Voss, Luciebelle Ivey

(originally reviewed as **Firing the Butler or The Butler Fired** in *Moving Picture Weekly*, 02/05/1916, p.23)

SYNOPSIS: Hubby (Reggie Morris) fires his amorous butler, and then goes to the employment agency where he hires a new, awkward Dutch butler named Hans (Dave Morris). Hans heads for the house while hubby goes off to work, having informed his wife (Selby) that both the new butler and her father-in-law — whom she's never met — are both on their way. Hans arrives first and the wife mistakes him for her father-in-law, treating him lavishly and affectionately. When her father-in-law (Leonard) arrives, she thinks he's the new butler and banishes him to the kitchen. He's beside himself as a result of his daughter-in-law's cold treatment, and when he sees her kiss Hans that's the last straw. Hans goes to the kitchen and accidentally sets the place on fire. Hubby arrives soon after and manages to save his wife and father. She's heartbroken over the loss of her new home, but is consoled when hubby produces an insurance policy on the house. Hans retires to the smoking ruins to finish his lunch. Synopsis adapted from the plot summary in *Moving Picture Weekly*, February 5, 1916, p.23

REVIEWS: "Slapstick as defined a year or so ago, and applied to comedies in which real slapstick, bricks, pies, fruit and other fodder supplied appropriate ammunition for the comedian's catapult arm has been misused of late. The real slapstick affairs have almost wholly given way to the comedy in which horse play and 'business' is perpetrated.

"Consequently the picture in hand is popularly known as a slapstick comedy to distinguish it from its halfbrother that moves about as a 'parlor' comedy, but 'Firing the Butler; or, the Butler's Fire' is void of bricks, hen fruit and miscellaneous products of the country fields. It is 'business' comedy from start to just before the close when a fire scene is introduced, adding the spectacular touch.

"In the great majority of scenes the 'business' falls to one Dave Morris, whom many will remember as a Biograph and Keystone player. He is ridiculously laughable in these two reels.

"A ludicrous makeup, eccentric clothes, and original tricks aid him to a praiseworthy extent. As a butler he is mistaken for a father-in-law by pretty Gertrude Selby and so the elaborate plot can be easily imagined, but the laughs can not.

"Morris carries a huge carpet about with him and when hungry extracts from the middle of it a yard loaf of bread, sliced lengthwise and containing varieties of ham from the Virginia kind to just plain delicatessen stuff. Salt is in his vest pocket, and the appetite lies in his stomach; and there you are, and there's a lot more that we vouch for but tremble at describing.

"The finicky would prefer it cut to a flash, but that's the only fault. Reggie Morris is the husband while Fatty Voss as usual has his humorous little bit as the effeminate job-hunter. He finally finds one as a trim parlor maid and he gets a laugh.

"Mr. Lehrmann has produced a real winner in this." Reviewed by Peter Milne, *Motion Picture News*, January 29, 1916, p.562

"This is well constructed and enjoyable throughout. The home settings are particularly attractive and the low comedy free from offense, though the kissing scene seemed inappropriate considering the difference in make-up of the two characters. The plot itself is clever and a step ahead of this company." *Moving Picture World*, February 19, 1916, p.1152

Elevating Father: *Released 02/16/1916 Wednesday.* © 02/09/1916 — 2 reels. CAST: Louise Orth, Dan Russell, Ray Griffith
SYNOPSIS: Ray (Griffith) owes a lot of money. He's also in love with Louise (Orth), but has never had the pleasure of meeting her father (Russell). When Ray is informed that a bill collector is planning to gain access to him disguised as a woman, Ray arms himself with a huge mallet. Louise's father is a confirmed flirt, and disguises himself as a woman in order to follow a girl. He ends up in the same hotel as Ray and, having lost the girl, knocks on Ray's door. Mistaking father for the bill collector, Ray knocks the man senseless, then proceeds to thrash him mercilessly. Father's taken away in an ambulance. The next day, Louise takes Ray to meet her father. Entering the poor fellow's bedroom, both father and Ray immediately recognize each other. Ray flees for his life, pursued by the pistol-wielding father to the far corners of the hotel. Ray heads for an elevator, and father attempts to lasso him. When the elevator races up the shaft, poor father, tangled in the rope, is dragged up behind it. The elevator reaches the top, crashes through the roof, and heads into the clouds with father helplessly dragged behind. The elevator, Ray, and father come crashing back to the rooftop, where father has his vengeance on his daughter's suitor. Synopsis adapted from the plot summary in *Moving Picture Weekly*, February 12, 1916, p.30
REVIEWS: "The first reel does not develop much plot. The second is better and contains some amusing moments. On the whole this is only fairly strong. The elevator scenes make the best feature." *Moving Picture World*, February 19, 1916, p.1152

"The work of Ray Griffith, Dan Russell and Louise Orth is as usual very good, but 'Elevating Father' makes entirely too much of the same incidents to really amuse. It has some novel stuff in it, at that, but virtually the story is a one-reeler." *Motion Picture News*, February 19, 1916, p.1033

Twenty Minutes At the Fair: *Released 02/20/1916 Sunday.* © 02/11/1916 — 1 reel. CAST: Billie Ritchie, Peggy Pearce, Gene Rogers
SYNOPSIS: Billy (Ritchie) stumbles across the San Diego Fair during his wanderings. Thinking that he might benefit somehow by getting inside, he sneaks in under another visitor's coat tails. After some aimless wandering, Billy settles down on a bench for a rest. A girl (Pearce) is followed by an unwanted admirer (Rogers). She heads to the store of a friend, an excitable Italian, who stops the admirer in his tracks and gives him a thrashing. Later, Billy and the admirer, both old friends, meet. Billy picks up two girls and invites them to dinner. When it comes time to pay, however, Billy is broke and suggestions to toss dice to see who pays are ignored. Billy and the admirer come to blows over the bill, and the Italian arrives and joins in the fight. Billy overcomes the two. The girls call in the police, who chase Billy to one of the fair's concessions, the Painted Desert. Billy scales

the highest peak. The Italian throws bomb after bomb at him, but Billy tosses them back. He misses one, though, and disappears in the explosion that follows. At which time Billy awakens on the park bench to find himself covered with pigeons. Once they are driven away Billy discovers that two eggs have been laid in his hat. Annoyance quickly turns to satisfaction when he realizes that he's actually gotten something out of his trip to the fair. Synopsis adapted from the plot summary in *Moving Picture Weekly*, February 12, 1916, p.32
REVIEWS: "This reel was made at the Fair, and shows some interesting views of it, but the action is altogether much too risqué for a mixed audience. A model leg is brought into play, and it introduces much that is a little offensive. Billie Ritchie, Gene Rogers and Peggy Pearce are the leads." *Motion Picture News*, February 19, 1916, p.1033

"A low comedy number, featuring Billy [sic] Ritchie and others. Particular audiences will not like this because of the vulgarity of many of the bits of small business. None of the humor is very good and the production as a whole has not much to commend in it." *Moving Picture World*, February 26, 1916, p.1319

No release 02/23/1916 Wednesday

Dad's Dollars and Dirty Doings: *Released 02/27/1916 Sunday.* © 02/18/1916 — 2 reels.
CAST: Alice Howell, Dick Smith, Phil Dunham, Fatty Voss, Dan Russell, Louise Orth, Billy Bevan
SYNOPSIS: Farm girl Alice (Howell) wants to go to the big city and become an actress, but neither her musician boyfriend Dick (Smith) nor her father wants her to go. Determined to go, Alice locks Dick in the rat-infested cellar and makes off with one of her father's bags of coins. Father rescues Dick, who heads to the city after Alice. Arriving in the city, naive Alice is soon taken of all her money by a crook (Dunham) and his female accomplice. Later, a cop misconstrues her situation and arrests her for vagrancy. In the meantime, her father has died and left Alice a fortune, word of which quickly makes the papers. The crook spots this notice and heads to the jail to pay her fine. He attempts to abduct her, but Dick arrives in the nick of time, and a fight follows between Dick, some cops, and the crook and his accomplice. Alice now realizes that her dreams of becoming an actress are just that, She returns home with Dick. Synopsis adapted from the plot summary in *Moving Picture Weekly*, February 19, 1916, p.23
REVIEWS: "Several novel touches, such as a scene in which an automobile whisks off a lady's skirt, make this picture quite distinctive, although appealing more to unconventional folk.

"The story is a burlesque on the melodrama in which a girl is lured from the farm by the bright lights. Alice Howell is the girl, and cuts many funny figures in the city.

"It was unfortunate that the producer chose to picture a death scene. It is totally out of place in a burlesque that is otherwise very good." *Motion Picture News*, February 26, 1916, p.1182

"A two-reel low comedy number, featuring Alice Howell as a country girl who goes to the city. She gets a jag on in a cabaret, drinking milk punch, and falls into the toils of the villain, from whom her country lover eventually saves her. This is laughable in places, but the humor is of a vulgar type in almost every instance. The number has some few good points, but is unfortunate in its general tone." *Moving Picture World*, March 4, 1916, p.1495

Blue Blood and Black Skin: *Released 03/01/1916 Wednesday.* © 02/23/1916 — 2 reels. CAST: Dan Russell, Ray Griffith, Louise Orth
(**Blue Blood and Black Skin** was the *Moving Picture Weekly* review title. The film was alternately reviewed as **Blue Blood But Black Skin** in *Moving Picture World* (and copyrighted under that title as well), and **Blue Blood But Black Skins** in *Motion Picture News*)
SYNOPSIS: George (Russell), a black barber, is the terror of Darktown, a bully feared by everyone. He loves Pinky (Orth), but is enraged by her tendency to flirt with others, thrashing anyone who makes the mistake of responding to her teasing. A stranger (Griffith) from the north arrives one day and, after flirting with Pinky, is awarded a photo of her. He makes the mistake of going to the barber shop and launching into an exaggerated retelling of his "conquest" of Pinky. George responds predictably, chasing the stranger with razor in hand. Soon the town is in an uproar, and when George finally catches up with the stranger and is about to reduce him to ribbons, Pinky strolls by with a new lover, one whom she's just wed. George faints and the stranger from the north flees. Synopsis adapted from the plot summary in *Moving Picture Weekly*, February 26, 1916, p.30
REVIEWS: "A two-reel low comedy number, done entirely in black face. The action consists largely of rivalry over a dusky belle, to whose hand the village barber lays first claim. He deals in turn with numerous rivals, not hesitating to employ his razor when necessary. In the end the girl marries a man whom he had not suspected of intimacy with her. This makes quite a pleasing burlesque number. While the scenes are of a rough, acrobatic sort, they are free from any great vulgarity. The closing scenes are of a riotous sort." *Moving Picture World*, March 4, 1916, p.1495

"Dan Russell, Louise Orth, Ray Griffith and a large supporting company appear here, all in black face.

"The reels have a good bit of funny acrobatic action while the plot is quite straight enough to hold the laughs together. There are minutes when the business grows a little tiresome but on the whole it is a good number." *Motion Picture News*, March 4, 1916, p.1328

Gertie's Awful Fix: *Released 03/05/1916 Sunday.* © 02/28/1916 — 1 reel. CAST: Gertrude Selby, Reggie Morris, Dave Morris, Eva Nelson
SYNOPSIS: Newlyweds Gertie (Selby) and Reggie (Reggie Morris) invite neighbors Mr. (Dave Morris) and Mrs. Chilfoot (Nelson) over. Mrs. Chilfoot grows envious of her hosts' fine statuary, so she smashes a few pieces. Reggie, annoyed, tells her what he thinks of her, which upsets Gertie. Hoping to please Gertie, Reggie buys her a necklace. Later, Gertie shows the necklace to an admiring Mr. Chilfoot, but Mrs. Chilfoot shows up turning it into an uncomfortable situation. Demanding to know what's going on between the suspicious looking twosome, Mr. Chilfoot reluctantly shows her Gertie's necklace. Mrs. Chilfoot, thinking it's her husband's necklace, takes it for her own, leaving Gertie in an awkward position. She wants the necklace back, of course, so she sneaks into the Chilfoot's apartment late that night hoping to retrieve it. Mrs. Chilfoot awakens and calls the police, which leads to a fight and chase. Reggie awakens Gertie, who now realizes that this has all been a bad dream. Synopsis adapted from the plot summary in *Moving Picture Weekly*, March 11, 1916, p.32
REVIEWS: "An average L-Ko concerning the mixup which the flirting of two married couples causes. It is laid in a hotel and the situations are familiar, once or twice quite risqué but withal very funny.

"It develops that the whole thing has been a dream in the end. Gertrude Selby, Reggie and Dave Morris are the principals." *Motion Picture News*, March 4, 1916, p.1328

"The scenes occur in an apartment house, where two families indulge in a number of laughable incidents, though the plot is slight." *Moving Picture World*, March 11, 1916, p.1667

False Friends and Fire Alarms: *Released 03/08/1916 Wednesday.* © 03/01/1916 — 2 reels.
CAST: Billie Ritchie, Gene Rogers, Peggy Pearce
SYNOPSIS: Billie (Ritchie) the jockey is an honest fellow. He's in love with the daughter (Pearce) of a wealthy oil magnate (Rogers) who has an unscrupulous, dishonest partner, but naively trusts him completely. The partner schemes to bilk the magnate out of his wealth by bribing a foreman to convince his boss the magnate that his oil wells are soon to run dry, and that he'll soon be ruined financially. The magnate, despondent over this bad news, is now convinced by his partner to bet a fortune on Billie's mount at the big race at Ascot Park. The partner attempts to bribe Billie to throw the race, but Billie refuses. Billie borrows a speedy fire horse, thinking this is what it will take to assure a win. Finding another jockey that's involved in the plot, Billie slugs him and then enters the race. Billie's mount quickly moves to the front of the race, and the partner is now in a panic. Just then a fire breaks out at the magnate's house, and when the fire horse hears the fire bell, it responds instinctively, jumping the fence and racing after the fire engines, Billie now powerless to alter the horse's course. The magnate and his family fear that they'll lose everything when they see the horse exit the race. Learning of the fire, they quickly return home, assuming that all of their cash and valuables will have been destroyed. Billie saves the day, however, rushing into the house and returning with the valuables. The villainous partner's schemes are exposed. Synopsis adapted from the plot summary in *Moving Picture Weekly*, March 4, 1916, p.21
REVIEWS: "Billy appears in this as a flirtatious jockey. The photography is not up to standard at times and the humor not very strong. The most interesting scenes are toward the close, when a spirited horse race and the burning of a bungalow take place simultaneously. The number as a whole is only fairly strong." *Moving Picture World*, March 11, 1916, p.1667

"Devotees of Billie Ritchie will enjoy this two reel farce for he is very much in evidence from first to last.

"A horse race is one of the prominent features of the picture in which Bill's horse hears the old familiar sound of the fire gong and leaves the race flat.

"Gene Rogers and Peggy Pierce [sic] are also in the cast. The photography is not what is to be expected from L-Ko pictures." *Motion Picture News*, March 11, 1916, p.1475

No release 03/12/1916 Sunday

No release 03/15/1916 Wednesday

Live Wires and Love Sparks: *Released 03/19/1916 Sunday.* © 03/10/1916 — 3 reels. CAST: Billie Ritchie, Peggy Pearce, Eva Nelson, Gene Rogers, Joe Murphy, Charles Inslee, Bert Roach, Gladys Roach
SYNOPSIS: Telephone worker Billie Steel (Ritchie) and his wife (Nelson) live in their furnished flat with their five children. When his pretty neighbor (Pearce) from across the hall asks to use their phone, Billie is smitten. He later places a call to her to ask her to meet him

at his company's masquerade ball, but her husband — a telephone company employee — intercepts the call and reroutes it to Billie's own wife. She recognizes his voice and accepts the invitation, pretending to be the neighbor, who Billie refers to as "Goldilocks."

Meanwhile, Billie has been avoiding bill collectors, and one envelope wielding fellow (Rogers) in particular. The fellow finally confronts Billie, who is stunned and overjoyed to find that instead of an unpaid bill the envelope actually contains $854.86 in cash along with a note explaining this windfall. The two are now the best of friends.

That night, Billie arrives at the ball and while searching for "Goldilocks" manages to annoy a number of the other attendees. Billie's wife and her five children arrive, his wife's identity hidden by her costume and long curly blonde wig. She enters the ball while her sleepy teenage daughter sits with the kids. Billie sees his wife and, thinking her to be the neighbor, asks her to dance. She goes along with it. The teen falls asleep, so the four youngsters wander off and all hide in a cupboard. Billie accidentally opens the cupboard and when he sees them he pretends they aren't his. This makes his wife even madder.

Back on the dance floor, his wife reveals her identity and hauls off and slugs Billie. Now in a panic, Billie flees. His wife enlists the aid of the other male attendees, who all join in bloodthirsty pursuit. Billie exits from a top floor window onto the telephone wires outside, grabs a long pole, and executes a tightrope walk from one telephone pole to the next. A trio of pursuers follows, two of them firing rifles, and Billie ascends to an even higher set of wires. More pursuers on the ground appropriate a lineman's wagon, his ladder falling and the poor fellow left hanging from the wires above. The three pursuers lose their balance and all fall into a wagon below. A cop on horseback arrives and is hauled up by the balancing pole Billie was using to a higher set of wires. The cop attaches a phone to the wires and calls the station, and a cop car is dispatched leaving the place in a shambles while exiting. The three pursuers place a ladder against the wires and climb up to rescue the cop, at which point the only known surviving print ends abruptly, the final few feet of action missing. According to the synopses in *Moving Picture Weekly*, everyone drops from the wires, one-by-one, smashing large holes in the ground below. Synopsis based on the print on the *Slapstick Encyclopedia* DVD.

REVIEWS: "Billie Ritchie is seen to very good advantage in this subject, in fact to better advantage than he has been in many of past L-Ko subjects. The comedy has a holding plot and a considerable amount of original business, but hardly enough to adequately and untiringly fill three reels. The fun is not crude and there is nothing to offend. Gene Rogers and Peggy Pearce also appear." *Motion Picture News*, March 18, 1916, p.1626

"Mr. Bringumyoung and his wife are first discovered in bed with their five children and the pretty neighbor across the hall starts complications. The action is almost entirely of a rough house character. Some of it is very amusing, but the split-trousers feature in the second reel will not appeal to particular exhibitors. The scramble across roof tops and telegraph wires in the last reel contains some really sensational acrobatic stunts. The action is pleasing, but the general tone not of the best." *Moving Picture World*, March 25, 1916, p.2032

Scars and Stripes Forever: *Released 03/22/1916 Wednesday.* © 03/13/1916 — 2 reels.
CAST: Billie Ritchie, Jerome Ash, Peggy Pearce, Gene Rogers, Joe Murphy, Gladys Roach
SYNOPSIS: Billie (Ritchie), chief of the Black Handers, delights in the group's anarchistic ways. When he suspects that the cops have gotten wise to him, however, he double-crosses his pals by turning State's evidence on them. He thought this would leave him in the clear, so

he's shocked when he's thrown into prison as well. He writes threatening letters to the warden (Ash), but when they are traced back to him he's thrown into the dungeon. The rest of his gang is locked up in the prison as well, leading to more threats by Billie. All he receives for these newest efforts is a pummeling by the guards. Some of the gang members escape and kidnap the warden's pretty daughter (Pearce). Billie manages to rescue her, and turns the gang over to the police in the process. They want Billie's head for this, but while they are unable to lay their hands on him they instead squeal on him and his past exploits, landing him back in prison. Synopsis adapted from the plot summary in *Moving Picture Weekly*, March 18, 1916, p.19
REVIEWS: "Billy and his band of Italian anarchists are thrown into prison after abducting the warden's daughter. There are a number of laughable moments in the prison scenes. The prisoners get a bottle of booze from the visiting minister and much trouble follows. This is free from offense and contains considerable humor of the burlesque sort." *Moving Picture World*, March 25, 1916, p.2032 (reviewed as **Scars and Bars Forever**)

"A Billie Ritchie comedy in which he shines to advantage. There is a great lot of business laid in a prison which is very funny — in fact, the entire release, save in the matter of photography, is one of the best of L-Kos. Gene Rogers and Peggy Pearce support Ritchie." *Motion Picture News*, March 25, 1916, p.1779

A Friend, But a Star Boarder: *Released 03/26/1916 Sunday.* © 03/17/1916 — 1 reel. CAST: Billie Ritchie, Gene Rogers, Peggy Pearce
SYNOPSIS: Billie (Ritchie) and his wife (Pearce) have been happily married, but that all changes when they take on the star boarder (Rogers). He's immediately taken with the wife, so he sets out to feed her lies and half-truths about Billie with the goal of poisoning her mind against him. And he's successful, resulting in a divorce between Billie and his wife. The star boarder quickly proposes, and she accepts. It rains heavily during the wedding ceremony, so the star boarder calls a cab. It arrives and in they climb. The cab's driver turns out to be Billie, and when he discovers who his fares are proceeds to give them the ride of their lives, with cops and pedestrians soon in hot pursuit. The wild ride continues until the cab blows up with all occupants still inside. Synopsis adapted from the plot summary in *Moving Picture Weekly*, March 18, 1916, p.28
REVIEWS: "Skidding automobiles on wet streets make the chief attraction in this reel, and these scenes, which form the climax and the greater part of the last half of the reel, are hilariously funny.

"The leads, Billie Ritchie, Peggy Pearce and Gene Rogers, do acceptable work." *Motion Picture News*, March 25, 1916, p.1779

"A very funny low comedy number.... The star boarder stirs up trouble between Billy and his wife. Not much in plot, but full of amusing antics and ends up with a wild ride in the rain. A good number of the type." *Moving Picture World*, April 1, 1916, p.106

No release 03/29/1916 Wednesday

Caught On a Skyscraper: *Released 04/02/1916 Sunday.* © 02/24/1916 — 2 reels. CAST: May Emory, Gertrude Selby, Harry Gribbon, Reggie Morris, Vin Moore
SYNOPSIS: Mr. Rawsberry (Gribbon) spots a woman in the park and, infatuated with her, dashes off a love note. He hands it to a passerby to give to her, not realizing that the fellow

is her sweetheart. The fellow instead hands the note to another woman (Emory) who is there with her husband (Moore). Incensed at Rawsberry's brazenness, the husband threatens Rawsberry with bodily harm if he ever comes near his wife again. Rawsberry rushes home to his hotel room, taking refuge in his bed. It turns out that the husband and wife reside in the room directly across from Rawsberry's, and to make matters worse the wife is a sleepwalker. In a deep sleep, she enters Rawsberry's room, at which time her husband spots her and assumes the worst. Things look bad for Rawsberry, but all is soon forgotten when the wife walks to the rooftop and proceeds to pace along the roof's edge. Rawsberry's so alarmed that he accidentally falls through a skylight. The wife eventually awakens and is now safe in her husband's arms. Synopsis adapted from the plot summary in *Moving Picture Weekly,* March 25, 1916, p.21

REVIEWS: "A sleep walking wife furnishes the risqué element of this film, but the scenes are handled in a clever and humorous manner, hardly liable to give any but the severely straight laced offense.

"The final scenes show the sleep walker parading about on the edge of a high roof. These scenes are the sort that make the spectator either marvel or shut his eyes in terror.

"Gertrude Selby, Reggie Morris, Harry Gribbon and May Emory are the leads." *Motion Picture News,* April 1, 1916, p.1924

"This two-reel number begins with park flirtations and some breezy mixups in an apartment house. The woman sleepwalker invades a man's room at night and goes to an empty bed. Her husband later discovers her there. This is accomplished without any great offense. The sleep walker, impersonated by May Emory, does some really sensational stunts later, traversing the edge of a high roof and crossing between two tall buildings. This is a very diversified number and makes a good offering of the low comedy type." *Moving Picture World,* April 8, 1916, p.285

For the Love of Mike and Rosie: *Released 04/05/1916 Wednesday.* © 03/28/1916 — 3 reels. DIRECTOR: Henry Lehrman. CAST: Louise Orth, Henry Lehrman, Dan Russell, Billy Armstrong, Bert Roach

SYNOPSIS: The Goldfingers have just inherited a small fortune and have moved into a grand apartment. There are many suitors for the hand of lovely young Rosie Goldfinger (Orth), but Dr. O'Briensky is looked upon most favorably by the family. This courtship is interrupted with the arrival of A. Cross Leech (Lehrman), a local fighter known as The Jewish Lion, who ousts the doctor. Grandpa Goldfinger isn't happy about this, and comes up with the idea of bringing in feared fighter Mike McGinnis (Russell), the Irish Terror, to drive Leech away. The plan works, but with the unintended consequence that McGinnis now falls for Rosie and refuses to leave the house. Mr. Goldfinger pleads with McGinnis to leave, but to no avail, and calling in the cops fails to succeed as well. Deciding that McGinnis is even worse than Leech, the latter's return the next morning is greeted with open arms. He's induced to drive the Irishman away, and manages to do so through some trickery. McGinnis returns and challenges Leech to a fight, which commences later that day in a well-attended boxing match. After much fighting a small fellow enters the ring and incites the large audience to join in, which they do, causing the ring to collapse. A massive free-for-all ensues between the rival factions. Synopsis adapted from the plot summary in *Moving Picture Weekly,* February 19, 1916, page number illegible

REVIEWS: "Controversies between the Irish and the Jews have long possessed humorous possibilities and present indications point to the future success of such conflicts.

"However, 'For the Love of Mike and Rosie,' though centering about this clash of races, is void of the conventionality of the past and has little to do with the future save for its individual prospects which seem unusually promising.

"It is a funny picture and needs not the assistance of decorative adjectives to strengthen its significance.

"Henry Lehrmann, the man who put the L in the L-Ko organization, who awaits a good opportunity before thrusting his comical figure before the camera lens, features himself in this picture.

"Mr. Lehrmann has a strong line of business, peculiar to himself. He has a humorous series of facial expressions and many eccentric little bits of action that bring laughable response from an audience.

"Mr. Lehrmann is the Jew in the case and the Irishman is played in equally capable manner by Dan Russell, whose exaggerated swagger and weird make-up gets over in fine style. Louise Orth is the girl over whom the two gentlemen come to blows, but neither one wins her, as the picture ends in a riot.

"The immediate cause of the riot is a boxing match between the Irishman and the Jew. Boxing matches, when burlesqued, are to our previous recollections quite dull, but Mr. Lehrmann's affair is arranged and carried out excellently.

"Interspersed between glimpses of the ring wherein the fight is in progress are scenes displaying the efforts of a gentleman in high hat, loose clothing, little moustache and slight cane, to view the fight without a pasteboard.

"This actor is surprisingly funny, considering the origin and adaptation of his make-up, and his appearance aids in no small measure in putting the laughs in the fight.

"The film, however, is not all fight. The business done at the outset is funny to the extreme and the plot is holding. All in all, we can unhesitatingly say that 'For the Love of Mike and Rosie' is a highly laughable and acceptable comedy." Reviewed by Peter Milne, *Motion Picture News*, April 8, 1916, p.2070

"A three-reel prize fight offering, done in burlesque comedy fashion. H. Pathe Lehrmann, Louise Orth and Dan Russell shoulder the chief responsibilities and succeed in getting much laughter. The trouble comes up when a Jewish family invites in an Irishman to help eject an unwelcome guest. The Irishman clears the premises, but then refuses to leave himself, having fallen in love with the daughter of the house. His chief rival returns and they finally meet in the prize ring. This will please fight fans mightily. A good offering of the low comedy type." *Moving Picture World*, April 8, 1916, p.286

No release 04/09/1916 Sunday

No release 04/12/1916 Wednesday

The Double's Trouble: *Released 04/16/1916 Sunday.* © 04/07/1916 — 2 reels. CAST: Alice Howell, Harry Coleman, Billy Bevan
(copyrighted as **A Double's Troubles**)
SYNOPSIS: Countess Troubleskoy (Howell) checks in at a fashionable hotel. The hotel

chambermaid (also Howell) bears a striking resemblance to the countess, and yearns to try on her clothes if only for a night. The chambermaid is in love with Mr. Oscar Yeppenger, but he'll have nothing to do with such a lowly woman. As it turns out, the countess is actually the head of a gang of pickpockets who pass on their ill-gotten gains to her for safe keeping. She plans to bilk the hotel's residents out of even more money by holding a ball that night that all will attend. In the meantime, however, she's spotted by the baron, a jealous old flame who follows her to her room and strangles her. The chambermaid, finding the countess in a faint, makes off with her clothes and attends the ball posing as her. In so doing, she is able to attract Yeppenger. The crooks, thinking her to be their boss, deposit their newest load of loot with her. The chambermaid, hoping to further entice Yeppenger, passes the loot on to him. This action is spotted by the crooks, who go after Yeppenger. The baron makes matters worse by throwing a few bombs among the assembled guests. The hotel ends up a destroyed wreck, and the chambermaid rues the day she donned the countess' clothes. Synopsis adapted from the plot summary in *Moving Picture Weekly*, April 16, 1916, p.13

REVIEWS: "Alice Howell in her usual eccentric role and also as a conspiring countess together with Harry Coleman are the leads in this comedy which is fair, while not presenting anything uproariously laughable.

"The slavey in the hotel usurps the place of the countess and then innocently betrays a gang of crooks. The finale introduces a laughably sensational climax." *Motion Picture News*, March 15, 1916, p.2221

A Meeting for a Cheating: *Released 04/19/1916 Wednesday.* © 04/12/1916 — 1 reel. CAST: Billie Ritchie, Dan Russell, Eva Nelson, Lucille Hutton
SYNOPSIS: Billie (Ritchie) is worried about the jewelry his wife (Nelson) leaves lying around the house, but his expressions of concern go unheeded. Hoping to teach her a lesson, he writes a note to a friend asking him to pose as a burglar. His wife sees the note before it's sent, alerting her to the plan. That night the friend is late showing up so Billie, thinking that his friend is not coming, assumes the role of burglar. Coincidentally, a genuine burglar breaks into the house, followed shortly by the friend in disguise. The three of them stumble about, dodging each other. The police arrive and a wild chase follows, with all three eventually apprehended. Billie and his friend finally convince the police of their identity, and the real burglar is carted away. Synopsis adapted from the plot summary in *Moving Picture Weekly*, April 15, 1916, p.27
REVIEWS: Film not shown for review.

Little Billy's School Days: *Released 04/23/1916 Sunday.* © 04/14/1916 — 1 reel. DIRECTOR: Victor Heerman. CAST: Billy Jacobs, Olive Johnson, Fatty Voss
REVIEWS: "A comedy with little Billy and Olive, that contains a welcome touch of drama here and there. It concerns itself largely with the capers cut by school children of which Billy and Fatty Voss are the leaders. The spectacle of Fatty and Billy side by side is one of the funniest sights in the reel." *Motion Picture News*, April 22, 1916, p.2388

"A country school number, featuring Little Billy, Olive and Fatty Voss. A juvenile love affair and amusing mischief in school are the chief ingredients. It brings forth considerable laughter and is appealing." *Moving Picture World*, April 29, 1916, p.824

Bill's Narrow Escape: *Released 04/26/1916 Wednesday.* © 04/19/1916 — 2 reels. CAST: Billie Ritchie, Eva Nelson, Gene Rogers, Louise Orth

SYNOPSIS: Billie (Ritchie) works in the kitchen of his wife Eva's (Nelson) boarding house. She dreams of becoming a movie actress, and slowly but surely Billie gets the acting bug as well. A movie company approaches for permission to film in Eva's front yard, and she happily agrees. When the wadding from a prop pistol strikes Billie, he drives the cast and crew away, unaware of who they are and thinking them to be hooligans. Eva sets him straight, and explains the situation to the film's director (Rogers). Later, Billie flirts with an actress boarder (Orth) who convinces him he should be in movies. When the director hires Eva for a part in the film, Billie poses as a dummy to gain access to the studio as well. Once inside, Billie manages to inadvertently ruin a number of scenes, and soon the studio is in turmoil. An accidental explosion blows them from the studio, both landing outside the complex's walls. They decide that life in the film industry is a bit too exciting for them, and they return to the comparative tranquility of the boarding house. Synopsis adapted from the plot summary in *Moving Picture Weekly*, April 22, 1916, p.26

REVIEWS: "A two-reel low comedy number.… This consists largely of knockabout situations. Billy's wife rents the house to some moving picture people and jealousy results. This gets up a fair degree of humor in spots, but has numerous vulgar touches which keep it from being the best sort of comic. The last reel closes with the studio on fire and some explosions." *Moving Picture World*, April 29, 1916, p.825

"Although this picture gets away with a poor start, the closing reel brings to light some excellent studio burlesque in which Billie Ritchie manages to stop all production at the L-Ko plant. There is less story than usual in these subjects and the supporting players, especially in the first reel, are not properly handled. Eva Nelson, Gene Rogers and Louise Orth are others." *Motion Picture News*, April 29, 1916, p.2561

No release 04/30/1916 Sunday

The Bankruptcy of Boggs and Schultz: *Released 05/03/1916 Wednesday.* © 04/26/1916 — 1 reel. CAST: Alice Howell, Ray Griffith, Dick Smith, Anna Darling, Phil Dunham

SYNOPSIS: Business partners Boggs (Griffith) and Schultz (Smith), two deeply suspicious souls, don't trust anyone — not even each other. They quarrel constantly, and their distrustful nature extends to the combination of their safe, with each having only one half of the combination. When they let their old stenographer (Darling) go, their dishonest janitor (Dunham) comes up with a scheme to rob them, arranging it so that a cohort (Howell) is hired as a replacement. Both partners fall for the new hire, and each plans to rob the safe and elope with her. Come midnight both the janitor and the new stenographer are in the office to rob the safe, but when Schultz arrives the two hide inside it. Boggs arrives shortly thereafter, and unbeknownst to each other Boggs drills holes in one side of the safe while Schultz prepares to dynamite it from the other side. Synopsis adapted from the plot summary in *Moving Picture Weekly*, April 29, 1916, p.27

REVIEWS: "A knockabout number.… The partners try to rob their own safe, in which the janitor and stenographer are hiding. The situation is a funny one, but the knockabout scenes seem a little overdone. The number is fairly strong." *Moving Picture World*, May 20, 1916, p.1357

"This concerns the squabble of jealous partners over the contents of the safe and the favor of the stenographer. It is fairly humorous, Ray Griffith creating most of the laughs. Dick Smith and Alice Howell are others." *Motion Picture News*, May 20, 1916, p.3112

Mr. Buddy Briggs, Burglar: *Released 05/07/1916 Sunday.* © 04/28/1916 — 1 reel. CAST: Dave Morris, Gertrude Selby, Reggie Morris, Eva Nelson
(pre-release title: **Spring Fever**)
SYNOPSIS: When his wife departs to visit her supposedly ailing father, Mr. Briggs (Dave Morris) wastes no time in contacting some friends at his club to come over for a party. Mrs. Briggs cuts her trip short when she receives a telegram at the station stating that an error had been made regarding her father, who's actually okay; she heads back home. When she arrives, one of Mr. Briggs' buddies (Reggie Morris), knowing what a temper she has, hides under the bed while Mr. Briggs ushers the rest of his guests out. Mrs. Briggs discovers the buddy under the bed and lets out a scream. Mr. Briggs comes running and immediately figures a way out of his uncomfortable situation. Climbing under the bed, he convinces his buddy to pretend to be a burglar so that he — Mr. Briggs — can haul him off to the "police station," in reality a local café. The ruse works, and soon Mr. Briggs and his buddy are rejoined at the café by their friends. An informer soon alerts Mrs. Briggs to her husband's trickery, and she storms down to the café, huge cleaver in hand. Mr. Briggs comes to realize the downside to his plan. Synopsis adapted from the plot summary in *Moving Picture Weekly*, April 29, 1916, p.38
REVIEWS: "Showing the various efforts that a henpeck makes to amuse himself with friends not to his wife's liking, while that lady has been purporting to go on a trip. Dave Morris is in this and neither he nor the comedy is as good as he can be and his pictures can be. Others are Gertrude Selby and Reggie Morris." *Motion Picture News*, May 6, 1916, p.2730

"A comedy number of a slightly burlesque sort.... The flirtatious husband is entertaining friends when his wife returns and he pretends one of them is a burglar. The number has no great novelty, but is fairly strong." *Moving Picture World*, May 13, 1916, p.1183.

The Great Smash: *Released 05/10/1916 Wednesday.* © 05/03/1916 — 3 reels. CAST: Alice Howell, Dick Smith, Ray Griffith, Billy Bevan
(pre-release title: **A Millionaire's Son**)
SYNOPSIS: Millionaire John D. Rock (Smith) deplores his son (Griffith) John Jr.'s fast living and lack of ambition, so he arranges to send Jr. out to work on a railroad section gang. His section boss, John Blake, is a humorless brute. Jr. meets up with little Nell (Howell) at the railroad camp, and falls head over heels for her. The problem is that Nell is Blake's "girl," and when she reciprocates his attention, Blake gives Jr. some rough treatment. Jr.'s stubborn streak kicks in, and he refuses to give up in his pursuit of Nell. Blake has enough of Nell's unfaithfulness, and with the aid of some assistants kidnaps the girl and ties her to the railroad track. He appropriates a train with the intention of running over the poor girl. Jr. gets wind of this and hops in a racing car to try to rescue Nell before Blake's train kills her. Jr. manages to avoid the drawbridge opening as he arrives at it, but Blake, close behind, fails to notice it. Blake's train plummets off the open span and into the river below. Jr. uses a motor boat to rescue Nell, while Blake and his cohorts crawl out of the ruined locomotive's smoke stack. Synopsis adapted from the plot summary in *Moving Picture Weekly*, April 29, 1916, p.33

REVIEWS: "This three-reel offering is very successful for a purely comic production. It is a big step in advance for this type of eccentric comedies, in which the characters are really 'caricatures' with human impulses of an exaggerated sort. The fun starts at the very beginning and is maintained at high speed throughout. There is no vulgarity, except perhaps in the kicking scenes, but these are harmless. The offering is one that will appeal to all observers and shows what can be done by sticking to straight humorous action. The events of the last reel are both thrilling and extremely funny. An excellent comic number." *Moving Picture World*, May 13, 1916, p.1183

"Spontaneity as applied to comedy, of whatever species, is almost a guarantee in itself of that comedy's success. The various tricks, business and thrills, if there are any, must be voluntary in order to put to rout the thought that they are acted. Such is the excellent accomplishment of those who produced and appeared in 'The Great Smash.' Without stretching the point this three-reeler is candidly the best L-Ko we have seen, and we have seen them all. And that statement is made considering and in the face of the wonderful improvement visible in the recent output of this company.

"Its most startling point is its chase. Chases have become things to shy at owing to the manner in which they have been overworked, but this one is unusual. A steam engine, an automobile, and the land and harbor police partake therein, and every scene of it offers a laugh and a thrill. Houses are knocked over or torn open, an entire village is put to confusion, vehicles and pedestrians are menaced by the chasers, until at last the engine runs upon the draw of a bridge and there blows itself to atoms. This last is done in miniature, but it is so cleverly welded in with the real scenes that the thrill is carried out to the very end. The mechanical side of this miniature is practically perfect.

"Ray Griffith, Alice Howell and Dick Smith are the principals. Griffith, with only a moustache as makeup, creates a laugh with every move. He is a real comedian, finished and with a keen sense for that which is humorous. Miss Howell plays another of her eccentric parts, Romantic Rosie, the light house keeper's daughter, while Dick Smith is the villain.

"The first part of the picture transpires in a train yard, where Ray has been sent by his irate parent to learn the business from the bottom up. His meeting with Rosie, who is loved ardently by the villain, results in the chase.

"The business in the train yard is done chiefly through the medium of mallets, but, strangely enough, the fun is fast and furious even with such conventional means of producing it.

"The photography of the picture is as good as that seen in the best photographed dramatic subjects." Reviewed by Peter Milne, *Motion Picture News*, May 20, 1916, p.3103

No release 05/14/1916 Sunday

Gaby's Gasoline Glide: *Released 05/17/1916 Wednesday.* © 05/10/1916 — 2 reels. DIRECTOR: John G. Blystone. CAST: Gertrude Selby, Billy Armstrong, Phil Dunham, Billy Bevan, Dave Morris
(pre-release and copyrighted title: **Gertie's Gasoline Glide**; title change announced in *Moving Picture Weekly*'s 05/06/1916 issue)
SYNOPSIS: Both Bill (Armstrong) and Phil (Dunham) are in love with Gaby (Selby), but Phil has the advantage in that he has a car while Bill only has a motorcycle. Bill arrives to take Gaby out for a ride, but Phil shows up and steals her away with his more comfortable

ride. Bill follows and shoots out Phil's tires, then convinces the stranded Gaby to leave with him. When he hits a bump with his fast-moving motorcycle, however, Gaby is ejected from the back. Bill doesn't even notice this for awhile, but when he does he turns back to retrieve her, but to no avail; she's back with Phil. Not giving up, Bill goes out and purchases a large touring car, then learns how to drive it. Once he's mastered the handling of the vehicle, he goes looking for Gaby, only to find that she's just married Phil. He invites the newlyweds for a ride in his car, but once they're on board he announces that this is the last ride they'll ever take. A wild ride follows, with more and more cops joining in pursuit as the ride progresses. Bill heads for a pier and drives the vehicle off its end, taking all "to a watery grave." Synopsis adapted from the plot summary in *Moving Picture Weekly*, May 13, 1916, p.23

REVIEWS: "Billy and Gertie go for a motorcycle ride. She is tickled to death until the other chap comes along with a cycle car built for two. But when that bucks and throws her down a manhole Gertie gets peeved. By this time Billy has acquired a flivver. She is on the upward scale all right, and goes for another ride. But she has the manhole habit by this time, and finally marries the guy with a cycle car. Billy then takes bride and groom for a honeymoon ride and for one solid roaring, screaming reel he makes the Ford do stunts and flip-flops, being merrily chased by a police auto patrol and a cycle cop in the meantime. For sheer fun and for clever, original and daring auto stunts this comedy is positively in a class by itself. It has more punch than any slapstick laughmaker you ever saw. Don't overlook this one if you want to give the comedy-loving fans a genuine treat." *Motion Picture News*, April 29, 1916, p.2542

No release 05/21/1916 Sunday

A Busted Honeymoon: *Released 05/24/1916 Wednesday.* © 05/17/1916 — 1 reel. DIRECTOR: John G. Blystone. CAST: Alice Howell, Ray Griffith, Fatty Voss, Anna Darling SYNOPSIS: On the day he's to be married, the groom (Griffith) heads to his favorite bar and has too much to drink. Wandering into the park, he proceeds to flirt with a married lady. Her husband (Voss) isn't amused, and gives the groom a thrashing. The groom scurries back home and the wedding ceremony takes place. Once it's over, however, the groom takes his poor wife's (Howell) hard-earned savings and heads back to the bar. She's had enough of her new husband, and returns home to mom and dad, leaving the deserted apartment behind. The landlady quickly rents the apartment to another couple, who turn out to be the couple from the park. After a night of drinking, the groom stumbles back to his old apartment and, thinking his wife is in the bed, climbs in. It turns out to be the husband who gave him a thrashing in the park, and the groom is saved from certain death by the man's wife and brother. Synopsis adapted from the plot summary in *Moving Picture Weekly*, May 20, 1916, p.23

REVIEWS: "Ray Griffith does the drunk very well in this and gets himself into a number of ticklish situations. The laughs are plentiful. Alice Howell, Fatty Voss and Anne [sic] Darling are the chief support." *Motion Picture News*, May 27, 1916, p.3372

"This is done in a low comedy style and the treatment is rough, though not extremely so. It makes a fair number of the eccentric type." *Moving Picture World*, July 8, 1916, pp.268-269

Gamboling On the Green: *Released 05/28/1916 Sunday.* © 05/19/1916 — 1 reel. CAST: Gene Rogers, Elsie Cort, Reggie Morris, Anna Darling, Dan Russell, Dave Morris, Gladys Roach, Fatty Voss

SYNOPSIS: Pa (Rogers) ditches his wife (Cort) and runs off with Reggie's (Morris) sweetheart (Darling). Reggie's not happy about this, and when a bum approaches with pa's stolen watch, Reggie buys it from him. Reggie takes a job as janitor in pa's office, and when he sees pa with his former sweetheart he makes a vow with pa's wife to get even. The bum reappears and makes off with a watch and the wife's purse. Everyone gives chase, but arrives a moment too late — the bum has sold the purse to a pawnbroker for $1. The pawnbroker opens the purse and finds a fortune in it, and the bum — witnessing this — dies on the spot of heart failure. Crime doesn't pay. Synopsis adapted from the plot summary in *Moving Picture Weekly,* May 20, 1916, p.33

REVIEWS: "A flirtatious husband and several janitors are used around which to hang the slim idea of this comedy. It will produce some laughs, no doubt, but taking it from the standard of the recent L-Kos it is lacking in many respects. Reggie Morris and Gene Rogers are the principals, while Dave Morris has a small part." *Motion Picture News*, May 27, 1916, p.3372

"[An] eccentric comedy. Paw and Maw visit the park and Paw flirts with Reggie's girl. There is some amusing small business, though scarcely enough plot and action to make an unusual subject. This is fairly strong." *Moving Picture World,* July 8, 1916, p.269

Tough Luck On a Rough Sea: *Released 05/31/1916 Wednesday.* © 05/24/1916 — 2 reels. DIRECTOR: Craig Hutchinson. CAST: Dan Russell, Sammy Burns, Carmel Myers

SYNOPSIS: Commodore Alimonio (Russell) falls for his son's girl (Myers), and his son (Burns) isn't happy about. He shoves his father out to sea, and then takes passage on the S.S. *Sinkatania* to escape punishment for a crime he's committed; his girl accompanies him. When the voyage is under way, the ship stops to rescue a fellow who turns out to be Alimonio. Both he and his son are unaware of the other's presence aboard the ship, but a violent storm throws the two of them together. It's an unhappy reunion, but when the storm causes the ship to start to sink, father and son put differences aside in an effort to survive. Hearing that women and children may board the lifeboats first, the two quickly dress as women, but their disguises fail to fool the ship's captain. The ship finally sinks and father and son go down with it. The son's sweetheart survives, however, falling in love with another occupant of her life boat. They marry. Synopsis adapted from the plot summary in *Moving Picture Weekly,* May 22, 1916, p.21

REVIEWS: "This two-reeler has some most humorous action transpiring on a ship at sea while it also introduces a clever contortionist and acrobat who plays the leading role with comical results. The rolling ship movement done by rockers is not always consistent with weather conditions outside, but on the whole is a most satisfactory release. Dan Russell is among the cast." *Motion Picture News,* June 3, 1916, p.3434

"Dan Russell stars in this burlesque sea story as a retired commodore. He and his son fall in love with the same fair charmer. His son sets his father adrift in a small boat, but he manages to board the son's vessel and starts to get his revenge. The scenes on the 'Sinkatania' are cleverly staged, a special set built for this purpose. There are laughs running all through this, the humor being of the slapstick, knockabout type." *Moving Picture World,* July 1, 1916, p.108

No release 06/04/1916 Sunday

Billie's Waterloo: *Released 06/07/1916 Wednesday.* © 05/31/1916 — 1 reel. CAST: Billie Ritchie, Gene Rogers, Eva Nelson, Lucille Hutton
(copyrighted as **Billy's Waterloo**)
SYNOPSIS: Billie (Ritchie) wants to marry his young sweetheart, but her father (Rogers) will have none of it, and lets Billie know that he's no longer welcome in the house. Later, Billie stumbles across the father having an affair with another woman, and grabs the father's hat as evidence. Confronting father, Billie threatens to expose the affair to his wife (Nelson) unless father agrees to Billie's marriage. Reluctantly, he agrees. At the wedding ceremony, the minister demands that Billie remove his silk top hat. Billie is very proud of the hat and refuses, but the minister is adamant. Billie challenges the minister to a fight, thinking he'll be a pushover. The minister proves otherwise, thrashing Billie all over the apartment house, out into the street, and back into the house where the fighting becomes so strenuous that the floor gives way depositing them into the water-filled basement below. Synopsis adapted from the plot summary in *Moving Picture Weekly,* June 3, 1916, p.28
REVIEWS: "Billy [sic] Ritchie as a strong man and Gene Rogers as his rival furnish fair comedy in 'Billy's Waterloo.' Quite naturally the reel closes in a wild fight, that is about average." *Motion Picture News,* June 10, 1916, p.3605

"A low comedy number, featuring Billy [sic] Ritchie and Gene Rogers. The acrobatic lover is not a favorite with the girl's father, who throws him out. A series of rough-house, knock-about scenes occur. The action is fast and furious and has a climax that will be appreciated by those who like this type of humor." *Moving Picture World,* July 1, 1916, p.108

Phony Teeth and False Friends: *Released 06/11/1916 Sunday.* © 06/02/1916 — 1 reel. CAST: Gene Rogers, Reggie Morris, Billy Bevan, Eva Nelson
SYNOPSIS: Dentist Reg (Morris) sends his apprentice Bill (Bevan) on an errand to deliver a box of candy to his sweetheart. Bill gets sidetracked in the park, leaving the box of candy on a bench. When he returns he finds that Gene (Rogers) has found the candy and eaten it. Annoyed that he doesn't have the funds to replace the box, Bill knocks out several of Gene's teeth. Gene stumbles home and is consoled by his daughter, and she sends him off to her dentist sweetheart — Reg — for repairs. Meanwhile, Reg has learned that Bill never arrived with the candy, so he goes out looking for him. Bill returns to the office during Reg's absence, and is there when Gene arrives. Bill goes to work on Gene, leaving him in worse shape than when he arrived. Returning home, his daughter announces that Reg is on his way over, and Gene, thinking that it was Reg who caused him so much trouble, waits with murder in his eyes. Reg arrives and Gene promptly works him over before discovering that Reg was not the culprit. Together Reg and Gene return to the dental office and find Bill working on another unfortunate patient. They pounce on him and send him to his doom in a nearby lake. Synopsis adapted from the plot summary in *Moving Picture Weekly,* June 3, 1916, p.20
REVIEWS: "The greater part of the action taking place in a dentist's parlor, this comedy in respect to locale and plot is rather worn. The action while provoking laughter to a certain extent is only fair measured by the recently attained high standard of the company. Reggie Morris and Gene Rogers are included in the cast." *Motion Picture News,* June 10, 1916, p.3605

"A knockabout number, featuring Reggie Morris as a young dentist. His assistant creates trouble by maltreating the girl's father in the dental chair. Some characteristic chase and slapstick scenes follow, the assistant finally falling into the lake from a high bridge. This has humorous moments and is a characteristic number." *Moving Picture World*, June 17, 1916, p.2063

How Stars Are Made: *Released 06/14/1916 Wednesday.* © 06/06/1916 — 2 reels. DIRECTOR: John G. Blystone. CAST: Alice Howell, Ray Griffith, Dick Smith, Fatty Voss, Gertrude Selby, Reggie Morris
SYNOPSIS: Lillian (Howell) has no luck in landing a job, so she decides to go into the movie industry. She's frustrated in her attempts to get through the L-Ko gates, but finally manages to sneak in behind Fatty Voss. She's finally put to work mopping the floors, but this isn't what she had in mind. Reading of a floral parade to take place and that L-Ko was to have a float in it, she's determined to be part of it. She dresses up in an angel costume intended for Gertie (Selby), while Dick (Smith) and Ray (Griffith) dress up as a devil and a janitor respectively. Mounting the float, the parade begins, and when the real L-Ko comedians learn that their costumes have been appropriated by mere pedestrians, they are furious. Dick is thrown off the float by the real devil, and Gertie rages furiously over Lillian when she spots her in the position that should have been hers. Synopsis adapted from the plot summary in *Moving Picture Weekly*, June 10, 1916, page number illegible
REVIEWS: "Alice Howell and Ray Griffith are sweepers in the L-Ko studio and both have something of a desire to act. When a pageant parades in Hollywood, Alice dresses as an angel, and Ray as the devil, thus usurping the positions of Gertrude Selby and Reggie Morris. A chase of fair character brings the picture to a close. This has some funny stuff in it, but there have been many better L-Ko two reelers." *Motion Picture News*, June 17, 1916, p.3774
"The slavey and janitor decide to become moving picture performers and break into the floral parade, posing as the devil and an angel. There is some roughness in this, but nothing extremely offensive. The humor is hardly up to that of certain predecessors, but there are some moments of a nonsensical sort." *Moving Picture World*, July 1, 1916, pp.108-109

No release 06/18/1916 Sunday

The Jailbirds' Last Flight: *Released 06/21/1916 Wednesday.* © 06/13/1916 — 1 reel. CAST: Gene Rogers, Billy Armstrong, Lucille Hutton, Carmel Myers, Dan Russell
SYNOPSIS: Bill (Armstrong) and Gene (Rogers), two old flirts, both pursue the same young lady (Hutton), who is in actuality an undercover cop. Gene thinks he's outsmarted Bill by telling another cop that Bill is bothering his sister, so Bill is arrested and thrown in jail for five years. Thinking the field now open, Gene once again goes after the young lady, who lures him straight into the police station and has him arrested. He's thrown into the same cell as Bill, and a huge fight follows. Bill is shoved through a wall and into the adjacent room occupied by some card-playing cops, who proceed to give him a thrashing. Bill escapes and takes refuge in an arsenal, but makes the mistake of trying to light a cigarette. The place blows up. Synopsis adapted from the plot summary in *Moving Picture Weekly*, June 17, 1916, p.29

REVIEWS: "This pictures the experiences of two male flirts, lured to the police station by a pretty lady cop. The running scene, explosion in jail and other episodes are laughable. Slightly rough in tone but amusing and acceptable." *Moving Picture World*, June 24, 1916, p.2263

"Showing the manner in which two rounders were taken in by a fair 'cop-ess' and how by their antics in jail they completely destroyed it. Billy Armstrong and Gene Rogers do excellently as the flirts in this while Carmel Myers makes a very pretty foil. The roughhouse in the final scenes is hilariously funny while the comparatively calm action of the opening scenes is equally humorous." *Motion Picture News*, June 24, 1916, p.3935

Dirty Work in a Beanery: *Released 06/25/1916 Sunday.* © 06/15/1916 — 1 reel. CAST: Dave Morris, Gertrude Selby, Reggie Morris, Gene Rogers, Fatty Voss
SYNOPSIS: The restaurant boss (Rogers) makes the mistake of hiring a pretty young cashier (Selby). She immediately attracts the attention of the head waiter (Reggie Morris) and the chef (Dave Morris), which causes conflict between the two. The head waiter buys a gift of flowers and fruit for her, but the chef intercepts it and replaces the card with one of his own. This results in a confrontation, and the boss arrives in time to be dragged into the fight. After receiving a few knocks, the boss gives the chef an earful and sends him back to the kitchen. The boss orders a steak for the cashier, but the chef, still angry with the boss, thinks the steak is for the boss, and poisons it. There's much commotion when it's realized that the cashier was the recipient rather than the boss, but she's saved at the last moment by some quick action on the part of the head waiter. Synopsis adapted from the plot summary in *Moving Picture Weekly*, June 17, 1916, p.20
REVIEWS: "The restaurant scenes contain considerable humor of a characteristic sort. The photography is unusually good and the number fairly strong as a whole." *Moving Picture World*, July 1, 1916, p.108

"Unblushing slapstick is the rule here, and nothing new is introduced. However, it will get a few laughs, if the spectator has not had enough kicks, falls, and the like. Gertrude Selby and Reggie Morris are the leads." *Motion Picture News*, July 8, 1916, p.113

July 22, 1916 *Motion Picture News:* "Lehrman, Director General of L-KO, disposed of interests and severed connection with company previous week. Left for NY, presumably to organize new company. Jack Blystone, director, succeeds Lehrman as Director General."

October 28, 1916 *Moving Picture Weekly:* Stated that the films listed in the article were "made exclusively under the direct supervision of J.G. Blystone, since the advent of Mr. Stern as President of L-KO." The listed film titles that follow are preceded by an asterisk.

It is unclear which of the following were made before Lehrman's departure from L-Ko.

*****Pirates of the Air:** *Released 06/28/1916 Wednesday.* © 06/20/1916 — 2 reels. DIRECTOR: John G. Blystone. CAST: Alice Howell, Fatty Voss, Phil Dunham, Billy Bevan, Joe Moore, Billy Armstrong
(pre-release title: **Pilots of the Air**)
SYNOPSIS: The head waitress (Howell) works in a beanery, along with the proprietor (Voss), waiter (Dunham), and bartender (Bevan). The waitress discovers an airplane model hidden in the attic, stolen from the U.S. Secret Service. The proprietor bribes her to keep her

mouth shut about her discovery, and she agrees, heading out shopping with her newfound windfall. A Secret Service man (Moore) arrives on the scene, searching for the stolen model. He accidentally runs over the waitress, but instead of annoyance she falls head over heels for him. He spurns her when she won't reveal the whereabouts of the stolen model. Overcome with grief, she falls asleep and dreams. She and the Secret Service man are far up in the sky aboard a monoplane, the boss and cook in pursuit. She drops numerous bombs in an attempt to blow them out of the sky, but to no avail. She climbs over the side and drops into the pursuing airplane below, only to be tossed from it. She is saved by the umbrella tossed to her by the Secret Service man, using it to parachute to the ground below. Her landing startles her awake. Synopsis adapted from the plot summary in *Moving Picture Weekly*, June 24, 1916, p.23

REVIEWS: "This two-reel comic production makes an interesting feature of a race between two aeroplanes. The fact that they are suspended in a studio, with a moving background of clouds behind them, does not materially detract from the burlesque. When Alice Howell climbs in her agile way from one aeroplane to another, the scene carries very well for burlesque purposes.

"The aeroplane race is the strong feature of the number. The opening scenes, taken in a country inn, contain considerable laughter, but the humor is not in the best tone. The frequent squirting of water and soup out of the mouths of waiters and customers is overdone and the kitchen scenes lack cleanliness.

"The plot centers about the theft of a newly invented aeroplane. The waitress in the hotel learns it is hidden upstairs and puts her friend, the secret service man, wise. This leads up to the double flight in the air. Simultaneously with this, an automobile on the ground below tears through houses and fences.

"Fatty Voss and Phil Dunham are also in the cast. The number is not as strong as some previous ones, but is better than the average comic in certain respects." Reviewed by Robert C. McElravy, *Moving Picture World*, June 10, 1916, p.1902

"A two-reel comic number.... The scenes in the hotel bar and kitchen contain many flashes of fun, but there is a tendency to the vulgar at times. The airship scenes in the second reel are well staged. Alice Howell climbs from one aeroplane to another, while in midair. Of course this is a studio setting, but it is put on with considerable ingenuity and carries the illusion quite well. An automobile is seen tearing through houses during the rapid-fire portions of the picture. The number is a little rough in places but on the whole an enjoyable one." *Moving Picture World*, July 1, 1916, p.109

"The stellar feature of this rapidly moving L-Ko number is an aeroplane chase. Two machines take part and the passengers think nothing of sprawling all over the wings and dropping from one to another. Now anyone, with half a brain can tell that such action could never transpire on real aeroplanes, and the fact that the machines are palpably products of the L-Ko property department does not detract from the credit that should go to the director for attempting such a difficult bit of comedy. He has succeeded in making these scenes funny although the element of realty is not pronounced.

"As a whole this picture is an average knockabout affair. There have been better L-Kos and there have been others that were not as good. A story, the various episodes of which adhere pretty well to another, has been provided and the incidental humor is of the usual L-Ko sort.

"The cast embraces such names as Alice Howell, Fatty Voss, Billy Armstrong, Phil Dunham and Bill Bevan. Miss Howell has the role of chief importance and cuts a comical figure." Reviewed by Peter Milne, *Motion Picture News*, July 8, 1916, p.111

No release 07/02/1916 Sunday

A Gambler's Gambol: *Released 07/05/1916 Wednesday.* © 06/27/1916 — 1 reel. CAST: Fatty Voss, Harry Coleman
SYNOPSIS: A wife (Voss) objects to her husband's (Coleman) gambling, so he pretends to commit suicide by drowning. She discovers this and returns home to find her husband and his friends gambling, so she appropriates the kitty. None of them have the nerve to take it back, so they all leave. Hubby now decides to end his life for real, but when he spots an alligator waiting for him with jaws spread wide, he thinks better of it. Later, the friends plan to break into the house and steal their money back, but she's on to them and has them all arrested. Her husband returns and life returns to normal. Synopsis adapted from the plot summary in *Moving Picture Weekly*, July 1, 1916, p.29
REVIEWS: "A knockabout comedy number, in which the leading character is a gambler with a pretty wife, impersonated by Fatty Voss. She breaks up a poker game. The closing scenes are very rough and do not get quite the humor a less violent handling would have achieved. Still this will amuse some observers." *Moving Picture World*, July 8, 1916, p.269

"Fatty Voss playing the wife of the gambler creates most of the laughs in this reel. She walks off with the net receipts of a poker game and none of the players are able to collect. Harry Coleman is the gambler. On the whole this is on the average chiefly due to the efforts of Fatty." *Motion Picture News*, July 8, 1916, p.113

Getting the Goods on Gertie: *Released 07/09/1916 Sunday.* © 06/29/1916 — 1 reel. CAST: Reggie Morris, Gertrude Selby, Dave Morris
SYNOPSIS: Hubby (Reggie Morris) is jealous of his wife (Selby), so he hires a detective (Dave Morris) to keep an eye on her. Reggie introduces the detective as his father, but when the wife lavishes a bit too much attention on the fellow Reggie's jealousy grows worse. The detective turns out to be a crook, and enters Reggie's home late one night along with his assistant with the goal of stealing the silverware and other valuables. The assistant spends more time wooing the maid than at thievery, however, with the result that the cops are called and Reggie awakened. Reggie has the crook arrested. Synopsis adapted from the plot summary in *Moving Picture Weekly*, July 1, 1916, p.29
REVIEWS: "A burlesque detective story.... The eccentric situations and trick photography get up some humor, though the production is one of only fair strength." *Moving Picture World*, July 8, 1916, p.269

"Dave Morris and another gentleman who shows fair promise set up as detectives and double cross their clients by burglarizing them. They are employed by a Frenchman to watch his flirtatious wife and Dave poses as the husband's father and consequently receives a full supply of daughterly affection before the riot starts. This is average, although Dave Morris isn't as funny as he has been. Gertrude Selby and Reggie Morris are the other players." *Motion Picture News*, July 8, 1916, p.113

Ignatz's Icy Injury: *Released 07/12/1916 Wednesday.* © 07/03/1916 — 2 reels. CAST: Billy Armstrong, Lucille Hutton, Reggie Morris, Dan Russell, Gertrude Griffith, Carmel Myers
SYNOPSIS: Bogus Baron Ignatz (Armstrong) manages to get invited to a dinner party given by Mr. and Mrs. Rustlebucks (Russell and Griffith) at the Ice Palace. Reno Reggie (Morris) is in attendance as well, and is in love with the Rustlebucks' daughter (Myers). The baron's behavior gets him in all sorts of trouble, causing the manager and some cops to try to throw him out. The baron, on roller skates, attempts to escape by heading to the roof of the fourteen story building, pursued by the cops who are also on skates. A thrilling chase follows with pursued and pursuers skating along the roof's edge, the street seen far below. The baron slips and falls, crashing into the dining room below. He's arrested and taken away, while Reno Reggie remains behind with Miss Rustlebucks. Synopsis adapted from the plot summary in *Moving Picture Weekly*, July 8, 1916, page number illegible
REVIEWS: "Skating with roller skates on ice is the most important bit of business, or it should be said, section of business that this comedy contains. After this the various players, still on roller skates, repair to the roof of a tall building where they indulge in the thrilling pastime of skating along the edge of the roof. This release combines comedy and sensation in proportions that are very suitable. The indoor ice rink makes an unusual scene. Billy Armstrong, Lucile Hudson [sic], Reggie Morris and Dan Russell are the leads. One criticism might be that there is just a little too much of Armstrong." *Motion Picture News*, July 15, 1916, p.282

No release 07/16/1916 Sunday

A Bold Bad Breeze: *Released 07/19/1916 Wednesday.* © 07/11/1916 — 1 reel. DIRECTOR: Noel Smith. CAST: Billie Ritchie, Billy Bevan, Lucille Hutton
(pre-release title: **A Windy Day**)
SYNOPSIS: Lazybones Billy (Ritchie) is in love with the woman Lucile (Hutton) next door, but she strenuously rejects his advances. Her husband (Bevan) is a very jealous man, and when aroused shifts into a murderous state. When Lucile has an accident that threatens to end her life, Billy rescues her. Her husband appears at this moment and misconstrues what is going on. With murder in his eyes, he takes off after Billy and a wild chase ensues. Running to a rooftop, Billy seeks refuge in a tiny rooftop structure. The jealous husband struggles to push the structure off the roof's edge to the street below, and as the structure teeters, Billy pulls the husband in with him. The two topple together as the structure plummets. Synopsis adapted from the plot summary in *Moving Picture World*, July 22, 1916, p.685
REVIEWS: "Billy has a dream in which most of the events take place. There are some vulgarities in this which lower the tone of the production. The action is rapid and the 'cyclone' feature is amusing." *Moving Picture World*, July 22, 1916, p.656

"A heavy wind is the feature in this comedy. It blows Billie Ritchie, bed and all into a married woman's room and this leads to another house top affair with the players falling and hanging all over the edges of the roof. The windy scenes are well done and there is much that is funny in the reel although there is also a little that is too shady for whole hearted enjoyment. Lucille Huton [sic] and Bill Bevan are other players." *Motion Picture News*, July 22, 1916, p.458

Spring Fever: *Released 07/23/1916 Sunday.* © 07/13/1916 — 1 reel. DIRECTOR: Noel Smith. CAST: Billy Armstrong, Gertrude Selby, Phil Dunham, Louise Orth
SYNOPSIS: A poor poet (Armstrong) has a rival (Dunham) for the love of a young lady (Selby) of recent acquaintance. Push comes to shove, the rival ends up in the pond, and the girl runs away. The two rivals encounter each other again later on, and this time the poet is forced to defend himself. Another young lady intercedes and shoves the rival back into the pond. A passerby sees this and decides that the poet has no right to such a sweet girl, so the two of them have a duel. Synopsis adapted from the plot summary in *Moving Picture Weekly*, July 15, 1916, p.28
REVIEWS: "When a company such as the L-Ko, can and do turn out excellent comedies, one is forced to wonder why they should make such a poor picture as 'Spring Fever.' There is no story whatsoever and the business is rather poor, some of the tricks being easily distinguished. Billy Armstrong, Louise Orth and Gertrude Selby are the principals." *Motion Picture News*, July 22, 1916, p.458

"A nonsense number.... Park flirtations, a burlesque duel and acrobatics of various sorts are the main incidents. The humor is only fair." *Moving Picture World*, August 5, 1916, p.947

***Lizzie's Lingering Love:** *Released 07/25/1916 Tuesday.* © 07/15/1916 — 3 reels. DIRECTOR: John G. Blystone. CAST: Alice Howell, Fatty Voss, Phil Dunham, Billy Bevan, Joe Moore
SYNOPSIS: Lizzie (Howell) is released from prison with only the few dollars given her to aid in a new start in life. She's met outside by some members of the gang she worked for when she was arrested, and they want her and her unique skills back working for them. To that end they take her money and haul her back to their underworld den. She's greeted by the group's boss (Voss) who attempts to revitalize her interest in a life of crime. This is no longer the life for her, and she later attempts to take her life by jumping from a bridge. She's saved in the nick of time by a handsome stranger, and convinced not to end it all. Found once again by the thugs, she's forced back into their ranks, and is soon working as the outside lookout while a millionaire's home is robbed. A mouse scares her into the house where she realizes the home belongs to the man who saved her. She turns on the thugs, protects the owner's mother, returns the family jewels, then flees — right into the arms of the arriving police. Synopsis adapted from the plot summary in *Moving Picture Weekly*, July 22, 1916, p.27
REVIEWS: "Another side-splitting comedy has just slipped out of the L-KO studios and promises to eclipse all past efforts. It has been christened 'Lizzie's Lingering Love' and is one of the best comedies Pathe Lehrmann has invented in a long time, with that howl producer Alice Howell as the attraction. The story centers around Lizzie, the jailbird; opium fiends, underworld dens and other cheerful things." *Moving Picture World*, July 8, 1916, p.270

"A rather thin plot, characterized by swift action of the ultra-slapstick variety, and situations not wholly free from coarseness, make this only a fair comedy. The story concerns the experiences which befall Lizzie, after her release from prison, when she is forced by the chief of the crooks to turn burglar, and aid him in a 'job.' It will interest those who like rough-house comedy, unrelieved by anything really ingenious. Alice Howell plays the female lead. Others are Fatty Voss, Phil Dunham and Bill Bevan." *Motion Picture News*, July 29, 1916, p.635

No release 07/30/1916 Sunday

*Where Is My Husband?: *Released 08/02/1916 Wednesday.* © 07/18/1916 — 2 reels. DIRECTOR: Craig Hutchinson. CINEMATOGRAPHY: Park J. Ries. CAST: Dan Russell, Katherine Griffith, Bert Roach, Belle Bennett, Alice Howell
(pre-release title: **Dinty's Daring Dash**)
SYNOPSIS: Poor henpecked Dinty (Russell) can't help himself: He loves to flirt. When his wife (Griffith) finds him with a lovely young lady (Bennett), all hell breaks loose. I.M. Trouble (Roach), the lawyer who is going to get Dinty a divorce, arrives on the scene. He is horrified to find that the other woman is his wife. A dropped cigarette burns a hole in the floor, and Dinty crashes through to the floor below, fleeing via the fire escape wrapped only in a sheet. He boards a passing streetcar, followed by the irate lawyer. The streetcar stalls on a train track, and is soon demolished by a fast-moving express, Dinty sailing into the air on a piece of cowcatcher. Synopsis adapted from the plot summary in *Moving Picture Weekly*, July 15, 1916, p.45
REVIEWS: "A laughable two-reel comedy, featuring Dan Russell as a married man with a penchant for getting into flirtations. One or two scenes verge on the risqué, but taken as a whole the production is filled with a good, healthy sort of humor and much of it is irresistibly funny. The fall from one room to another, the bomb-throwing and chase scenes are all well done. A first rate comic number." *Moving Picture World*, August 5, 1916, p.947
"This is an excellent number. The business is uproarious, and the situations, though delicate, are handled so as to be funny and not offensive. Dan Russell as the man who wants a divorce simply can't keep from getting into precarious situations with his lawyer's wife, and at the end of the last reel a chase is staged. A trolley car is the most prominent feature in it, and this is finally smashed to smithereens when it comes in the path of an engine. The producer has not overworked any of his various comedy appliances at all, and the results will certainly show for themselves. Dan Russell is supported by a cast of capable players." *Motion Picture News*, August 5, 1916, p.793

The Youngest in the Family: *Released 08/06/1916 Sunday.* © 07/28/1916 — 1 reel. CAST: Elsie Cort, Lucille Hutton, Bert Roach, Gene Rogers
SYNOPSIS: Daughter (Hutton) is in love with a well-dressed adventurer (Roach), but little does she suspect that he's a janitor. He is, and coincidentally works for her father (Rogers). When her father fires the janitor for arguing with the head janitor, the janitor spots an open safe on the way out and removes its contents. Daughter and her sweetheart elope, and they live well off of his wealth, in actuality the money stolen from the safe. Daughter reads that her parents are now broke and are homeless, so she convinces her husband to allow father and mother (Cort) to move in with them in their magnificent new home. He agrees, but when father arrives and recognizes his daughter's husband as the former janitor who stole all his money, the fellow flees. Father and the police are in hot pursuit. Synopsis adapted from the plot summary in *Moving Picture Weekly*, July 29, 1916, p.18
REVIEWS: "A very successful comic offering…. The opening scenes are attractive and contain a good burlesque touch. The auto dash in the latter part is a wildly hilarious one and very laughable. There is a big explosion at the close. This is unusually good." *Moving Picture World*, August 12, 1916, p.1104

"The ardent lover robs the girl's father, and then elopes, and there is the L-Ko chase, which in this case is simply uproarious. It is rapid as usual, but the various catastrophes which are caused by the chasers en route leave one breathless and tearless." *Motion Picture News*, August 12, 1916, p.949

*__Unhand Me, Villain:__ *Released 08/09/1916 Wednesday.* © 08/02/1916 — 2 reels. DIRECTOR: John G. Blystone. CAST: Alice Howell, Fatty Voss, Joseph Moore
(advertised in *Moving Picture World* 07/29/1916 and *Universal Weekly* 07/22/1916 as **The Villain Still Pursued Her**)
SYNOPSIS: Poor newsgirl Alice (Howell), threatened by the brutish competitor on the adjacent corner, is "saved" by Ham Actor, the leading man of a local stock company who happens to be passing by. Alice falls head over heels for her protector. Later, when fleeing from some overzealous policemen, Alice takes refuge in the local stock company, hiding in Ham Actor's trunk. There she overhears Ham in conversation with leading lady Lena Genstyou, and it becomes apparent that not only are the two in love, but that they also plan to make off with manager Fuller Bull's (Voss) bank roll. She finally manages to alert Bull of the impending crime, and to show his appreciation he grants her wish: to play lead in a production. Opening night soon follows, and things get off to a rough start, the issues compounded when the paper "snow" catches fire, causing the audience to flee from the theater. Synopsis adapted from the plot summary in *Moving Picture Weekly*, July 29, 1916, p.805
REVIEWS: "It is difficult to classify this series of comics released by the L-Ko company. They are something different from the ordinary slapstick performances, and yet belong to the same general type of fun. The events which take place in this three-reel number makes one think of an animated newspaper cartoon series. Certainly Alice Howell, who has already done good work in previous numbers, gets a firm hold on the risibles in this production and maintains it throughout the entire three reels.

"She first appears as a young lady of the slums, who is overly popular with the police. She dashes up an alley, followed by three or four cops, and breaks into the stage door of the David Tobasco stock company's theater. Here events follow thick and fast. Having eluded the cops she proceeds to make friends with the manager and saves him from a clean-up on the part of the leading man and leading lady, about to depart with all the money in the place.

"Alice gets a bad attack of stage fever and induces the manager to let her play leads. The burlesque scenes are extremely funny. She hangs from the chandelier, milks a fake cow, is tied down before an approaching train and goes through numerous other comic stunts. The snow scene, in which the paper snow gets on fire, is laughable. The whole number winds up with a rapid-fire chase." Reviewed (as **The Villain Still Pursued Her**) by Robert C. McElravy, *Moving Picture World*, July 29, 1916, p.805

"The greater part of this picture is given over to showing diverse appliances of the stage property man in use. His work is burlesqued to a high degree, and the spectator from the vantage point of the audience sees the mechanics of each one of them. These scenes are some of the funniest that have ever made their way into a comedy, and the L-Ko Company deserve all the credit for producing an excellent picture. Alice Howell and Fatty Voss are only two of a large cast that does exceedingly appropriate work." *Motion Picture News*, August 12, 1916, p.949

"A very successful three-reel comic, featuring Alice Howell as a slum girl who breaks into a theater, pursued by cops. She makes herself solid with the manager and gets to be leading lady. Some excellent burlesque scenes are pictured. The fake cow and horse, the railroad scene and the snowstorm, which winds up with fire, are all laughable. The chase at the close is short and well done. A sure laugh-producer." *Moving Picture World*, September 9, 1916, p.1690

No release 08/13/1916 Sunday

* His Temper-Mental Mother-In-Law: *Released 08/16/1916 Wednesday.* © 08/09/1916 — 2 reels. DIRECTOR: David Kirkland. CAST: Billie Ritchie, Lucille Hutton, Margaret Joslin, Harry Todd , Alice Howell
SYNOPSIS: Despite the fact that he's jobless and lacks ambition, Lucille (Hutton) sticks with her husband Billie (Ritchie). Her mother (Joslin) has little patience with Billie, however, and continuously makes his life miserable. Billie decides to find a husband (Todd) for his mother-in-law, thinking this will give her a new person to abuse. He's successful at this, but soon finds that both she and her new husband are ganging up on him. Reaching the breaking point, Billie hires some thugs who sneak into the house and tie the bride and groom to their beds. They then drag the house down to the railroad tracks and leave it there. Meanwhile, Billie has commandeered a locomotive and drives it at full speed towards the abandoned house. The house is demolished, and Billie is beside himself with joy. Climbing to the top of the engine for a better look at his handiwork, Billie accidentally sits on the steam pipe and is blown sky high. Synopsis adapted from the plot summary in *Moving Picture Weekly,* August 5, 1916, page number illegible
REVIEWS: "A three-reel comic number, featuring Billy [sic] Ritchie as a man pestered by his mother-in-law. The action is of the knockabout type, some of it slightly vulgar, though not in an offensive way. The number will probably have a strong appeal in houses that are not too particular. Some of the incidents are certainly funny in their way. The patent bath tub, the traveling soap bubble and the moving of the house to the railroad right-of-way, are features that will bring laughter." *Moving Picture World*, August 10, 1916, p.1265

No release 08/20/1916 Sunday

A Double Double Cross: *Released 08/23/1916 Wednesday.* © 08/10/1916 — 1 reel. CAST: Billy Armstrong, Gertrude Douglas, Charles Inslee, Rich MacAllister, Gertrude Selby
SYNOPSIS: Mac (MacAllister), a sailor, is in love with Gertrude (Douglas). Unfortunately for Mac, his boss Charlie (Inslee) is fond of her as well, and makes life difficult for his underling. Billy (Armstrong), another of Gertrude's suitors, asks her father for permission to marry her, but father tells him in no uncertain terms that he must get a job first. Billy comes up with a plan. He convinces Gertrude to flirt with Mac, hoping it will lead to Mac's firing. And it does, with Billy hired to replace the departed sailor. Billy takes Gertrude for a ride in the boat, but when he loses his temper he throws her into the water. Mac sees this from the shore and rescues her, winning her love. Synopsis adapted from the plot summary in *Moving Picture Weekly*, August 19, 1916, p.37

REVIEWS: "A comic number, featuring Billy Armstrong and others. This is a nonsensical trifle and contains some quick action of a funny sort. The jitney ferryman is an amusing character. It gets several laughs." *Moving Picture World*, August 26, 1916, p.1419

"Staged entirely on the water front and containing some dare devil motor boat chasing this comedy makes a very good impression. The business is quite funny and the players capable. Billy Armstrong is one of the leads while an attractive girl and a capable acrobat-comedian are others." *Motion Picture News*, August 26, 1916, p.1253

Snoring in High C: *Released 08/27/1916 Sunday.* © 08/10/1916 — 1 reel. CAST: Reggie Morris, Gertrude Selby, Kitty Howe, Dave Morris
SYNOPSIS: "Reggie [Morris] was a fortunate man and the ceremony was being duly performed and everything going fine, but just about the finish there happened to appear on the scene an old suitor [Howe] of Gertie's, accompanied by a minister ready to tie the knot for him.

"Gertie [Selby] was called away and the ardent suitor was about to make a bigamist of Gertie before she knew what was happening. But she tartly told the old suitor that he was too late; first come, first served. The old suitor hied himself to the brewery and went home with an overload of the brewer's best. This placed him in no frame of mind to forget the jilting he received.

"Reggie's father in the meantime telegraphed his beloved son that he was on his way with an Eugenic bride for him. So Gertie had to disguise as a boy to be near her hubby and the Eugenic bride-to-be fell desperately in love with Gertie.

"The jilted suitor by this time had gathered enough strength and courage to start on the warpath and Gertie, in trying to elude the fair maiden, ran amuck of the jilted suitor, who took a few shots at her. Things for a while looked rather dubious for Gertie, but love always triumphs and her great love for Reg in the end had to be rewarded." *Moving Picture Weekly*, August 19, 1916, p.36
REVIEWS: "Gertrude Selby, Reggie Morris and others appear in this comic offering. A wedding, a disappointed suitor and a general apartment house scramble are the principal features. This contains a fair amount of humor." *Moving Picture World*, August 26, 1916, p.1419

"A number of fairly humorous situations and a chase roundabout a hotel caused by the ravings of a defeated rival manage to get this comedy over in average style. Reggie Morris, Gertrude Selby and Dave Morris are the principals." *Motion Picture News*, August 26, 1916, p.1253

*Right Car But the Wrong Berth: *Released 08/30/1916 Wednesday.* © 08/16/1916 — 2 reels.
DIRECTOR: Craig Hutchinson. CAST: Dan Russell, Katherine Griffith, Vin Moore, William Irving
(originally advertised 08/05/1916 *Moving Picture World* as **The Right Car But the Wrong Street**)
SYNOPSIS: Mr. Cowbull (Russell) is a floorwalker, and he likes to flirt with the customers. Unfortunately, he flirts with the wife (Griffith) of a mean-tempered man (Moore) who gives Cowbull an ultimatum: Get out of town in five minutes, or else. Cowbull takes heed of this warning and boards the next train out of town, not realizing that the man and

wife have also boarded this same train. Cowbull attempts to escape the man's renewed wrath by jumping on a mail catcher, but the catcher springs him back to the train and the ladies' berth. Cowbull is discovered and flees from the husband, a conductor, a porter, and a confirmed flirt-hater. The chase takes them to the top of the train, where Cowbull and the husband are soon caught on a drawbridge that carries them 250 feet into the air. Synopsis adapted from the plot summary in *Moving Picture Weekly,* August 19, 1916, p.40

REVIEWS: "There can be no question about the laugh-provoking quality of this two-part slapstick comedy, in which Dan Russell is surrounded by an able company. The fun in the first reel develops in a fashionable ladies' tailoring establishment where the philandering proprietor makes love to every woman in sight. Better yet is the comedy in a sleeping car and that on a drawbridge, which carries several struggling men high into the air. As a slapstick number this production may be strongly recommended." *Moving Picture World,* September 2, 1916, p.1559.

No release 09/03/1916 Sunday

*Crooked From the Start: *Released 09/06/1916 Wednesday.* © 08/26/1916 — 2 reels. DIRECTOR: Craig Hutchinson. CAST: Billie Ritchie, Gertrude Selby, Dan Russell (originally announced for Wednesday 08/09/1916 release)

SYNOPSIS: Motorcycle cop Bill (Ritchie) has a nice little side business accepting bribes from all of the speeders he pulls over. When Commissioner Logan learns of this from a friend who was stopped, Logan puts an end to this practice. Annoyed with having to go straight, Bill pulls over the first speeder he sees. It's Gertie (Selby), and he falls for her, and she falls for him. Later, her father, a friend of Chief Schmalz (Russell), Bill's superior, decides that she should marry Schmalz. Gertie and Bill quickly elope in a confiscated auto, foiling Schmalz's plans. The couple accidentally runs afoul of a gang of crooks, and Bill's taken hostage and tied to the railroad tracks. Gertie escapes on foot and calls for help. Schmalz, seeing an opportunity to be a "hero" in Gertie's eyes, rides to the rescue and saves Bill in the nick of time. When Schmalz sees who it is that he's just saved, however, he loses it. Bill flees in one of the cop cars, but its gas tank is leaking. Schmalz sets fire to the trail of gasoline leading from the car, and Bill and the car are blown sky high. Synopsis adapted from the plot summary in *Moving Picture Weekly,* September 2, 1916, p.41

REVIEWS: "A rapid-fire comedy which will produce some hearty laughs. Bill is a motor cycle 'cop' and a successful 'grafter.' His one hobby is to catch 'speeders,' this he is able to do at will. Amongst his many adventures he arrests Gertie. When she is taken before the Chief he immediately falls in love with her, though not before Bill has also fallen victim to her charms. Outwitting the Chief, the two lovers elope; their joy, however, is short-lived, as the Chief overtakes them and in endeavoring to escape, Bill's car is blown up. The cast includes Dan Russell, Billie Ritchie, and Gertrude Selby." *Motion Picture News,* August 12, 1916, p.949

"A two-reel comic number, featuring Dan Russell, Gertrude Selby and Billy [sic] Ritchie. This is very funny throughout and particularly in the opening scenes where the pretty girl speeder is brought to the police court. She escapes and the chief of the force and another member enter into rivalry for her hand. This is full of laughable action and done in the best style for this sort of production." *Moving Picture World,* September 9, 1916, p.1690

No release 09/10/1916 Sunday

*Tillie's Terrible Tumble: *Released 09/12/1916 Tuesday.* © 09/05/1916 — 3 reels. DIRECTOR: John G. Blystone. CAST: Alice Howell, Fatty Voss, Phil Dunham (originally advertised *Moving Picture World* 08/05/1916 as **Tillie's Terrible Trouble**) SYNOPSIS: Washwoman Tillie (Howell) has to work very hard to support her large family and her drunken husband Fat (Voss). When his liquor supply runs low he demands money from her, and when she refuses he takes it all and heads out to tie one on. Later, a stray dog annoys her so she grabs a gun and shoots. Her husband has stumbled on to the scene when this happens, and falls over when he hears the shot; Tillie thinks she's killed him. A few minutes later, though, the "body" is gone. The police arrive and accuse her of the crime, and when they find an old shoe in her stove assume that she's burned the corpse. She's hauled off to jail and sentenced to hang. A neighbor who loves Tillie sneaks in and trades places with her, and she escapes in a cop's uniform. She's found out, though, and a wild chase follows with Tillie finally cornered atop a flag pole. It breaks and Tillie and her pursuer both land in the execution room just as her neighbor is about to be hanged — in her place! And then Fat enters, drunk but still alive, and the execution is halted. Tillie lassoes her husband and drives him out into the street. Synopsis adapted from the plot summary in *Moving Picture Weekly,* September 2, 1916, p.27
REVIEWS: "A three-reel burlesque comedy, featuring Alice Howell, Fatty Voss and others. The opening scenes have an element of humor, but are handled too deliberately. A number of laughs crop out at times, though the development is not strong. The burlesque hanging is quite well done. Two reels would have answered to carry this production." *Moving Picture World*, September 1916, p.1851; reviewed as **Tillie's Terrible Troubles**

No release 09/17/1916 Sunday

*Cold Hearts and Hot Flames: *Released 09/20/1916 Wednesday.* © 09/11/1916 — 2 reels. DIRECTOR: John G. Blystone. CAST: Billie Ritchie, Gladys Tennyson, Vin Moore, Bert Roach, Joe Murphy, James T. Kelly, Mario Bianchi (Monty Banks), Robert McKenzie, Charles Lakin, Eva McKenzie
SYNOPSIS: A dapper-looking Ritchie sits by a mouse hole, Swiss cheese as lure in one hand, upraised hammer in the other. A janitor furiously shovels coal into the basement furnace while a cat looks on. In the lobby so much heat arises from the grate in the floor that a little girl is blown to the ceiling, running in place while held aloft. Ritchie leaps into the blast, is raised to the ceiling, then pulls the girl down; the onlooking guests burst into applause as Ritchie basks in their admiration of his heroics. The girl and her mother are now both blown to the ceiling, and this time when Ritchie rescues the two, he's awarded with a slap from mom. The hotel manager's pretty young daughter (Tennyson) is in the next room, standing over another grate, perspiring profusely in close-up, her skirt billowing seductively about her like a hot air balloon. Ritchie enters, and clearly she's his girl.

The mortgage holder arrives and confronts the manager (Moore) to collect what's due him, threatening eviction if dad can't pay up. Ritchie comes to the "rescue," writing a check in the full amount, and father pays off the mortgage holder and sends him packing. Father and mother are jubilant and now look favorably upon Ritchie until the mortgage holder returns, announcing the check was bad. Fuming, father heads upstairs and gives Ritchie the bum's rush. Ritchie falls through the lobby's heating grate, down the duct work, dancing furious over the furnace's coals until he emerges from the building's chimney and falls through a skylight into the mother's bed. Mother, dressing for bed, doesn't notice, and Ritchie hides under the covers. Father enters and discovers him and drags him out to the hall, kicking him repeatedly with each kick sending Ritchie six feet into the air, then tosses him down to the lobby.

Father pulls a $50,000 fire insurance policy from his drawer, and hatches a plan. Down in the basement, he props a can of gasoline by the furnace, running a ball of string to an upstairs room where he can later pull it to cause a fire. Interrupted by the janitor, father pushes him into the furnace and locks him in! The janitor is blown out the chimney, falling unhurt to the ground below.

Back on the street, Ritchie stops a Western Union boy (Bianchi) and hastily writes a telegram, which the boy delivers to father. It says that Ritchie is to get a huge inheritance, so now dad is immediately fond of Ritchie. He brings Ritchie and his daughter together and forces them to kiss. Iris out and in to a wedding taking place between the two. During this, the cat plays with the string downstairs, tipping the gas can and causing a blaze. The Western Union boy arrives wanting to be paid by Ritchie, and when father catches on he stops the wedding and once again pummels Ritchie in a three-way that includes the boy, then chases Ritchie with pistol blazing. Ritchie jumps out a window and into a rain barrel on the street below.

The mouse makes off with the insurance policy, the fire department is called, and the fire truck races to the scene. The fire has now spread, panicking the wedding guests. Father is in a panic over the missing policy, and his daughter is trapped by the fire spreading in her parents' bedroom. The firemen arrive, but a fireman's ladder isn't long enough to reach a window, so he sits on the blast from a hose and lifts the ladder to the window, hooking it on the sill. Ritchie, wanting to rescue the daughter, rides a hose blast to an adjacent balcony, leaps but misses, dropping to the net below. A second attempt succeeds, and he tries to douse the blaze with a vase. The furnace blows, and the whole building explodes in a clumsy miniature. Ritchie and his girl, standing on a table, are blown into the sky, as is the minister who soon joins them on the airborne table. The minister marries them, and we see faint halos appear over their heads! Synopsis based on the print held by Museum of Modern Art

REVIEWS: "This two-reel number, featuring Billy [sic] Ritchie, contains a number of laughable incidents and is acceptable throughout. It is better staged than common and the settings and costuming are an improvement over the average knockabout comedy. These things all help to give a certain snap to a humorous performance, even of the purely nonsensical type. Billy sends himself a telegram announcing that he has inherited a million dollars, in order to win the girl. The marriage is conducted under difficulties, however, and winds up in midair. The fire scene is unusually good and the small business throughout is funny." *Moving Picture World*, September 23, 1916, p.1994

No release 09/24/1916 Sunday

*A Surgeon's Revenge: *Released 09/27/1916 Wednesday.* © 09/15/1916 — 2 reels. CAST: Dan Russell
SYNOPSIS: When a doctor accidentally runs over Dinty (Russell), a bum, he takes pity on him and takes him home for a meal. Dinty is taken with the doctor's wife, but when he flirts with her the enraged doctor throws him out of the house. Dinty swears revenge. He lures the doctor away from the house with a bogus medical emergency call, then steals the doctor's car and lures the wife into the vehicle. Off he goes, but he isn't much of a driver and crashes near the hospital. Dinty is quickly carried in to surgery. Imagine his horror when the operating doctor turns out to be the very same doctor who ran over him. Dinty escapes before the doctor, now aware of the identity of his patient, can take revenge. The doctor gives chase, and some cops arrive and join in. Dinty ends up back in the doctor's house and hides in a closet. He's discovered, and gets "shoved down the radiator into the cellar." Synopsis adapted from the plot summary in *Moving Picture Weekly,* September 16, 1916, page number illegible

No release 10/01/1916 Sunday

Safe in the Safe: *Released 10/04/1916 Wednesday.* © 09/25/1916 — 2 reels. CAST: Dan Russell
SYNOPSIS: Police corruption is rampant, and there's a close working relationship between the police and the town's crooks. Police Commissioner Jed Doty's daughter brings him a newspaper criticizing him for not firing the chief of police (Russell), so Doty heads to the station to try to improve the situation. When he arrives he finds the chief and the police all singing and dancing and having a good time. Doty tells them to stop, and gives the chief a string of pearls to place in the safe. What he doesn't realize is that the safe has a door in the back, and it's the secret entrance for the crooks to enter the station. The pearls are stolen and Doty is informed as such. Doty tells the chief to retrieve them or be fired. The chief dresses as a woman to gain access to the crooks' lair, and one of them is so smitten with the new "female" arrival that he asks "her" to dance. The dance grows progressively wild, and soon the chief is exposed when his wig falls off. The crooks give chase, the chief in a car with his pursuers close behind. The chief's car crashes off a bridge, and he revives long enough to say his prayers before expiring. Synopsis adapted from the plot summary in *Moving Picture Weekly,* September 30, 1916, p.20
REVIEWS: "A two-reel burlesque number which contains some laughable absurdities. A gang of thieves make themselves at home in the police commissioner's residence and also have a secret chamber at police headquarters. They steal from the police at will. Dan Russell is amusing as the chief, particularly in the scene where he disguises himself as a woman. The automobile chase is well put on, and in spite of its familiarity some new twists occur. This contains a good deal of entertaining nonsense." *Moving Picture World*, October 7, 1916, p.96

No release 10/08/1916 Sunday

Lured But Cured: *Released 10/11/1916 Wednesday.* © 09/28/1916– 2 reels. CAST: Gertrude Selby, Dan Russell, Charles Inslee
SYNOPSIS: Miss Alice Peabody (Selby) arrives in town on a freight car. When she witnesses a murder, she rushes to the police station and reports it. Convincing them she's a wonderful detective, they give her a badge. Alice gets on the trail of the crooks (Russell and Inslee), and they decide to leave town. They know she's the only witness to their crime, so they

decide she has to go. They go after her and she takes refuge in a shack, and she sends her dog for help. The crooks break in and give chase, but help arrives and they are arrested. Alice gets a reward for their capture. Synopsis adapted from the plot summary in *Moving Picture Weekly,* September 30, 1916, page number illegible

REVIEWS: "A two-reel number, in which Gertrude Selby appears as a country girl who enters the city in a box car, accompanied by her dog. She becomes a lady detective and rounds up two villains, whom she sees throw a man over a cliff. The treatment is of a breezy, burlesque style and carries the interest very well, though it is not quite so laughable as some other releases of the type. Dan Russell and another play the villains." *Moving Picture World*, October 14, 1916, p.261

No release 10/15/1916 Sunday

Safety First: *Released 10/18/1916 Wednesday.* © 10/05/1916 — 1 reel.
(the *Moving Picture Weekly* review lists no actors, but refers to the two main characters as Charlie and Moore — perhaps Winninger and Vin Moore?)
SYNOPSIS: Charlie and Moore place the spoils of a robbery in a safe to which only Charlie has a key, planning to divide the take the following morning. When Moore hears Charlie planning to steal the money all for himself at a specific time later on, Moore plants a bomb in the safe timed to go off at that very time. When Charlie goes to steal the money, he hears Moore coming and hides in the safe. Moore and his buddies grab the safe, lower it to the ground, and drag it away behind their auto. Their timing is poor, however, and the bomb explodes at the predetermined time, blowing the crooks into the heavens. Synopsis adapted from the plot summary in *Moving Picture Weekly,* October 14, 1916, p.38
REVIEWS: "An eccentric comedy, featuring two crooks who have made a successful haul. One crawls into the safe, in which the other has placed an infernal machine. He is lowered from the window in the safe. A chase and explosion follow. These latter scenes are best, but, as a whole, the number is only fairly successful." *Moving Picture World*, October 21, 1916, p.418

She Wanted a Ford: *Released 10/22/1916 Sunday.* © 10/09/1916 — 1 reel. CAST: Billie Ritchie, Dan Russell, Gertrude Selby
SYNOPSIS: Gertie (Selby) arrives at a hotel and is spotted by Billie (Ritchie), who falls head over heels for her. He proceeds to flirt with her until she finally gives in, demanding an auto ride. Billie doesn't have a car, but Dan (Russell) lets him know that he can provide one. Which he does, but the vehicle doesn't have an engine. Instead, Dan and his friends hide inside and act as the auto's engine. This works okay at first, but when the auto crests a hill and starts down the other side, they lose control. Gaining speed, the police take notice and go after them. The auto ends up crashing, and Billie and Gertie are left stranded. Synopsis adapted from the plot summary in *Moving Picture Weekly,* October 14, 1916, p.39
REVIEWS: "A knockabout number, featuring Dan Russell, Gertrude Selby and Billy Ritchie. This does not depend very much on plot. The freak automobile proves laughable." *Moving Picture World*, October 28, 1916, p.570

The Sunday and Wednesday release schedule no longer existed from this time on, with most releases now falling on Wednesdays.

*A Rural Romance: *Released 10/25/1916 Wednesday.* © 10/16/1916 — 2 reels. CAST: Dick Smith, Lucille Hutton, Billy Bevan, J. Russell Powell
SYNOPSIS: Dick (Smith) works on a farm, and is in love with the farmer's daughter Lucille (Hutton). The two want to get married, and the farmer is in general agreement with this until his landlord (Powell) suggests his homely rube son (Bevan) as a husband. The farmer thinks well of this, but neither Dick nor Lucille agrees. The farmer forces Lucille and the rube to take a walk in the garden, hoping this will spark a romance. Dick follows and plays all sorts of tricks on the rube, dunking him in a water trough and shoving him into the baler. While the rube attempts to extricate himself from a bale of hay, Dick and Lucille escape in the family auto and head for the parson's home. The landlord, his son, and the farmer get wind of this and set out after the slow-moving auto in a horse-drawn carriage. They lasso the auto but fail to slow it down. Desperate to escape their pursuers, Dick heads for a cliff and drives over it. The pursuers have the horse back up and halt the auto's descent, then gently lower the auto to the ground below. Synopsis adapted from the plot summary in *Moving Picture Weekly*, October 14, 1916, page number illegible
REVIEWS: "A two-reel farm comedy of the burlesque sort. This contains some laughable incidents and keeps the observer well amused throughout. The story concerns a farmhand who elopes with the farmer's daughter when he is about to marry her off to a creditor's son. The elopement and fall of the auto over a cliff are novel in certain respects. An amusing number." *Moving Picture World*, October 28, 1916, p.570

*The Terrors of a Turkish Bath: *Released 11/01/1916 Wednesday.* © 10/17/1916 — 2 reels. CAST: Dan Russell, William Irving, Katherine Griffith
SYNOPSIS: When one of the manicurists quits, Turkish Bath attendant Dan (Russell) hastily calls his wife and tells her to come apply for the position, and to pretend she's single. She's hired, and the manager is immediately taken with her, having her come into his office to perform a manicure. Meanwhile, a female patron has taken a shining to Dan, and her persistent attentions infuriate her husband. He pulls a gun and chases after Dan, who has in turn been chasing the overly-aggressive manager. When Dan finally thinks he's shaken the irate husband, he heads into the nearest house for a well-earned nap. It turns out to be the husband's house, and when he returns and finds Dan he assumes the worst. Dan escapes once again and heads home to the security and comfort of his bed. Synopsis adapted from the plot summary in *Moving Picture Weekly*, October 28, 1916, p.33
REVIEWS: "A two-reel knockabout comedy, featuring Dan Russell as flunkey in a bath house. He manages to extract many laughs from this part. The middle part of the offering slows up a little, but the opening and close are both very funny. Dan smuggles his wife into the bath house and gets her employed as manicurist. The proprietor takes a fancy to her and trouble begins. The action contains nothing offensive, and closes with a general mixup and a chase." *Moving Picture World*, November 4, 1916, p.694

*Alice in Society: *Released 11/07/1916 Tuesday.* © 10/26/1916 — 3 reels. DIRECTOR: John G. Blystone. CAST: Alice Howell, Fatty Voss, Joe Moore, Phil Dunham
(pre-release title: **Astray in a Large City**)
SYNOPSIS: Alice (Howell) and her coworker are treated shabbily by their mean and greedy boss (Voss). Alice is instructed to go out and quietly rip men's pants, then lure them back

to their boss's pressing and mending establishment. She manages to do so with wealthy Mr. Astorbilt, but when the boss finds an invitation to a ball to be held that night, he steals it and then threatens Astorbilt with death unless he signs over a check for a million dollars. Alice rescues the fellow, and as a show of his gratitude he invites both Alice and her coworker to the ball. That night the two arrive and Alice gets into the spirit of things by performing a wild dance. Her boss arrives posing as a count, and while he recognizes them, the two of them do not recognize him in his disguise. The boss sneaks upstairs and steals a bunch of jewels, but as he tries to leave the butler ushers him in to dinner. Alice recognizes him from the familiar slurping of his soup and exposes him, and after a battle the boss is captured. Later, Mr. Astorbilt announces his engagement, but Alice's hope that she is the intended partner are dashed when Astorbilt names her coworker. Synopsis adapted from the plot summary in *Moving Picture Weekly,* October 28, 1916, p.26
REVIEWS: "This burlesque comedy in three reels, extracts numerous laughs from the observer. The action is a little broad in the first reel, but inoffensive and generally acceptable. The last two reels are best and several scenes, particularly those at the reception, are extremely funny.

"Alice Howell, Fatty Voss, Phil Dunham and Joe Moore take the leading parts, the former being seen at her best in certain situations. The plot concerns a tailor and his two assistants. The tailor is a man of fiendish temperament, who eats his soup noisily and swallows wienerwursts whole. He sends the girl out to rip and tear men's clothing in order to increase his patronage.

"The girl finally brings in a wealthy young man named Astorbilt, and the tailor drops him through a trap door into a basement. Here he rigs up an infernal machine and endeavors to get his victim to sign over a check to him for ten thousand dollars. The two assistants lead an amusing rescue.

"The scenes at the Astorbilt reception are very funny. The two assistants have been invited by the grateful host, and the fiendish tailor appears in disguise, without invitation. Numerous complications arise, and Alice Howell does some laughable stunts on the ball room floor and at the dining table. She identifies the tailor by the way in which he eats his soup. The girl imagines the host is in love with her, but learns to her sorrow that his affections are for another." Reviewed by Robert C. McElravy, *Moving Picture World*, October 28, 1916, p.537

"A three-reel comedy of the burlesque, farcical type, featuring Alice Howell, Fatty Voss, Phil Dunham and Joe Moore. This concerns a tailor and his two assistants. The girl's job is to bring customers in the shop and to do this she rips and cuts the clothing of passersby. She brings the rich young Mr. Astorbilt and the tailor devises a fiendish plan for extorting money from him. Some of the humor in the first reel is a little rough, but generally acceptable. The last two reels are full of funny incidents, those at the reception being particularly amusing." *Moving Picture World*, November 11, 1916, p.839

A Million Dollar Smash: *Released 11/15/1916 Wednesday.* © 11/02/1916 — 2 reels. CAST: Lucille Hutton
SYNOPSIS: Jimmie is assistant to the town of Koko's station master, and is in love with his daughter Lucille (Hutton). Large shipments of gold come through Koko on a regular basis, and a huge shipment is scheduled for that day. Nitro Ned and his gang have gotten wind of this, and are aboard the train with intentions of theft, but are caught short when the messenger debarks at Koko with the gold. The crooks debark as well, and Ned goes

to work on Lucille trying to interest her romantically. Her father likes Ned, so he fires Jimmie and gives Ned the job. The crooks learn the combination of the safe holding the gold, but Jimmie, who's been keeping an eye on them, attempts to stop them. They lock him in the safe, and then load the safe into an empty box car. The train leaves town, and soon after the crooks separate the car from the rest of the train. Not a good move, as it turns out, when the car starts rolling away on its own, roaring through town and soaring off a cliff, crashing to earth below. Jimmie has just enough strength to haul himself out of the safe and capture the crooks. He's now the town hero, and Lucille's as well. Synopsis adapted from the plot summary in *Moving Picture Weekly*, November 11, 1916, p.33
REVIEWS: "A two-reel eccentric comedy, with the principal scenes located at a railroad station. The girl's father is agent and her lover the telegraph operator. Two crooks appear at the station and one of them makes love to the daughter. The telegraph operator intervenes and is locked in the safe. The safe is blown out of the station into a passing train. There is not much humor in the opening situations. The runaway freight car furnishes considerable excitement and these scenes are all well handled. The number is one of average interest." *Moving Picture World*, November 18, 1916, p.1034

*Where is My Wife?: *Released 11/22/1916 Wednesday.* © 11/14/1916 — 2 reels. DIRECTOR: John G. Blystone. CAST: Billie Ritchie, Lucille Hutton
SYNOPSIS: Billie (Ritchie) and his wife are proprietors of a hotel, and he's very attentive to the needs of their tenants. A lovely young woman arrives and Billie is immediately taken with her, but his wife observes this and quickly puts an end to it. Or so she thinks, but Billie is persistent. When the young lady rings for soap, Billie etches a love note on it and covers it so that the note won't be seen until the soap is used. The young lady's husband intercepts the "note" when a fan blows the covering off, and the short-tempered fellow goes after Billie. After a wild chase, Billie ends up in a bathtub that sails through the hotel and out into the street, and is dragged away by a passing auto. Synopsis adapted from the plot summary in *Moving Picture Weekly*, November 11, 1916, p.22
REVIEWS: "A comic number, featuring Billy [sic] Ritchie as proprietor of St. Vitus Hotel. This is full of funny antics, some of them of the rougher sort, but none extremely offensive. Billy flirts with a man's wife and endeavors to assist her in obtaining her bath. There is a general mix-up, a chase and considerable shooting." *Moving Picture World*, November 25, 1916, p.1189

Eat and Grow Hungry: *Released 11/29/1916 Wednesday.* © 11/18/1916 — 1 reel. CAST: Phil Dunham
SYNOPSIS: "The tale of a poor janitor in a boarding house whose wife runs the place. She gives the star boarder all the good things to eat, leaving her husband just a little pea soup. Out of desperation the husband rigs up a string so that he can pull things off the dumbwaiter as they go up to the boarder. This affords him some measure of satisfaction. Synopsis adapted from the plot summary in *Moving Picture Weekly*, November 25, 1916, p.33
REVIEWS: "A comic number, picturing the exploits of a janitor and one other man, both of eccentric types. They both lose their trousers in the course of the action, which is rough in character throughout, though quite laughable at times. This is a little too broad for particular houses." *Moving Picture World*, December 9, 1916, p.1512

Tattle-Tale Alice: *Released 12/01/1916 Friday.* © 11/21/1916 — 1 reel. CAST: Alice Howell, Louise Orth

SYNOPSIS: Alice (Howell) is the town tattle-tale, and when an opera singer comes to town Alice's interest and curiosity are aroused. Two of the town's men fall for the singer, and one after the other get into compromising situations with her. Alice, of course, tells on both of them, but ends up getting her comeuppance for doing so. "There is a motor boat race and then a ducking." Synopsis adapted from the plot summary in *Moving Picture Weekly,* November 25, 1916, p.33

REVIEWS: "There is little comedy in this reel which shows the efforts of two old men to win the hand of a young girl and trying to avoid the gossips. The last few scenes featuring the comic police are really funny. Louise Orth and Alice Howell are in the cast." *Motion Picture News,* December 2, 1916, pp.3497-3498

The High Diver's Curse: *Released 12/06/1916 Wednesday.* © 11/28/1916 — 2 reels. DIRECTOR: John G. Blystone. CAST: Dan Russell, Fatty Voss

SYNOPSIS: Dan (Russell), the property man at a vaudeville house, has little patience for the prima donna actors who work there. So little, in fact, that he gets into an argument with one of them, and silently vows to get even. The evening's entertainment goes on, and Dan sabotages each of the performances. The final act, a high diver, sees Dan remove the bucket of water he's to dive into just as he starts his dive; he crashes through the floor. Enraged, he takes off after Dan, both of them ending up in an auto chase. It comes to an end when Dan throws his pursuer into the river and makes a hasty exit. Synopsis adapted from the plot summary in *Moving Picture Weekly,* December 2, 1916, p.38

REVIEWS: "A two-reel comic number, featuring Dan Russell and Fatty Voss. Dan is scene shifter at a theater and Fatty the strong man. Some burlesque vaudeville and a three-part drama bring out many laughs. This is clean and lively and winds up with a hilarious chase." *Moving Picture World,* December 9, 1916, p.1513

*Murdered By Mistake: *Released 12/13/1916 Wednesday.* © 12/04/1916 — 2 reels. DIRECTOR: Craig Hutchinson. CAST: Dan Russell, Lucille Hutton, Bert Roach, Katherine Griffith, William Irving

SYNOPSIS: Mr. Bigbee (Russell) is a flirt, and this causes so much anger with his girl (Hutton) that he decides to end it all. Unfortunately, he's a bad shot and fails miserably at suicide, so he hires assassin Blood Hound Pete (Roach) to finish the task. A tramp (also Russell) who bears an uncanny resemblance to Bigbee gets involved, becomes the confused assassin's target, and almost ends up marrying Bigbee's girl. All is straightened out after a riot. Synopsis adapted from the plot summary in *Moving Picture Weekly,* December 9, 1916, p.40

REVIEWS: "A two-reel comic, featuring Dan Russell in a double role. This is full of laughs and free from vulgarity. The action of the first reel is exceptionally funny and the closing scenes are also good. A society man hires a thug to kill him. A tramp, posing as the victim's double, is followed by the assassin. A good knockabout subject, containing much real humor." *Moving Picture World,* December 30, 1916, p.1978

Shooting His 'Art Out: *Released 12/20/1916 Wednesday.* © 12/13/1916 — 2 reels. DIRECTOR: David Kirkland. CAST: Phil Dunham, Vin Moore, Dick Smith, Margaret Russell
SYNOPSIS: The love has gone out of the marriage between a jealous husband (Moore) and his wife (Russell). She jumps at the chance to model for the artist (Smith) upstairs, donning the costume in which he wants her to pose. The building's janitor (Dunham) has an eye for the collection of good-looking models that make their way into the artist's studio, and falls for this newest girl. Meanwhile, the jealous husband gets wind of this turn of events, and breaks into the studio, revolver in hand. The wife and janitor barely escape via the dumbwaiter, but the husband is persistent and chases them to the rooftop where, confronting the janitor, the two grab opposite ends of a ladder. The two teeter back and forth, each attempting to push the other over the edge. Everything comes to an end with the usual smash-up. Synopsis adapted from the plot summary in *Moving Picture Weekly,* December 16, 1916, p.41
REVIEWS: "A two-reel comic, featuring Phil Dunham and others. A business man, suspicious of his wife, ties a thread to the back of her dress. He traces her by this means to the dumb waiter and finds she is acting as model for an artist upstairs. Trouble at once ensues. The number finishes on the roof tops. This is a characteristic number, with numerous laughs in it." *Moving Picture World*, December 30, 1916, p.1979

The Perils of a Plumber: *Released 12/27/1916 Wednesday.* © 12/16/1916 — 1 reel. DIRECTOR: Craig Hutchinson. CAST: Dan Russell
SYNOPSIS: "The Mr. and the Mrs. live in the closest domestic harmony, until one day when the pipe in the bathroom washstand springs a leak. Mrs. calls hubby and they send for the plumber. The plumber, who is our friend Dan Russell, arrives in top hat and frock coat, followed by his minion with the tools. He is escorted with ceremony to the bathroom and takes off his gloves, coat, shirt and trousers, revealing himself in regulation plumbers' garb. Then he sets to work.

"A young Beau Brummel, a most persistent flirt, annoys the Mrs. in the hall of the hotel. She runs back to her room and begs the majestic plumber, who has now reassumed the garb of fashion, to pretend to be her husband and punish the flirt. The Mr. decided to take the chastisement of the flirt into his own hands, and goes to his room for a gun. Here he finds the plumber. Complications ensue in which Dan vainly tries to pose as the wife in her night cap and kimono. A general scrap brings the situation to an end." *Moving Picture World*, December 30, 1916, p.2004
REVIEWS: "This knockabout number features Dan Russell as a plumber with flirtatious proclivities. He and his assistant create considerable humor in repairing a hotel bath room. A gay wife and an angry husband keep the plot moving. The slapstick work brings numerous laughs and is generally inoffensive. An amusing comic." *Moving Picture World*, January 6, 1917, p.102

Phil's Busy Day: *Released 12/29/1916 Friday.* © 12/20/1916 — 1 reel. CAST: Phil Dunham
SYNOPSIS: "Phil [Dunham] and his jealous wife live in one house, and a father and his pretty daughter live across the way. Phil is a lazy good-for-nothing. He is attracted by the pretty girl and goes through all sorts of adventures in order to meet her. Father does not take to him at all, and his wife is furiously jealous. They both lay plans to restrain him and

the girl from meeting each other. Many complications ensue, with the inevitable chase and firing of revolvers. Phil has to return to the wife of his bosom." *Moving Picture Weekly*, December 23, 1916, p.36

REVIEWS: "A very funny knockabout number, featuring Phil Dunham as a henpecked husband. He gets up late in the morning, flirts with a pretty neighbor and his wife gets after him with the broom. Some of the situations are rough, but not offensive, and some unusually funny stunts are pulled. The chase at the close is a good one." *Moving Picture World*, December 30, 1916, p.1978

1917 Releases:

On the Trail of the Lonesome Pill: *Released 01/03/1917 Wednesday.* © 12/26/1916 — 2 reels. CAST: Phil Dunham, Lucille Hutton, Vin Moore
SYNOPSIS: Janitor Phil (Dunham), having lost his job, searches for another when he wanders into an opium den, is given a pipe and bunk, and lapses into a drug-induced dream. Here he finds himself in the home of a powerful Chinese Mandarin (Moore). His life threatened, a beautiful maiden (Hutton) comes to his aide and convinces the Mandarin to spare his life and place him in charge of the fish pond. Later, the maiden reveals to Phil that she's being held captive against her will, and begs for help to escape. Phil comes up with a plan, such as it is, and the two swap clothes. While the maiden now looks over the fish pond, maiden Phil is taken to the Mandarin, his true identity hidden behind a veil. But not for long, and a struggle soon follows with all involved, and all tangled up in the Mandarin's bedclothes. Phil awakens from his dream as he falls out of the bunk. Synopsis adapted from the plot summary in *Moving Picture Weekly*, December 30, 1916, p.29
REVIEWS: "A two-reel comic featuring Phil Dunham as a hobo who visits a hop joint and smokes opium. Some of the interior scenes are rather dark. The hobo's dream is pictured in full and contains some funny knockabout work. This is not exceptional, but makes a good average feature." *Moving Picture World*, January 6, 1917, p.103

A Limburger Cyclone: *Released 01/10/1917 Wednesday.* © 12/30/1916 — 2 reels. DIRECTOR: Jay A. Howe. CAST: Phil Dunham, Lucille Hutton, Merta Sterling, Charles Inslee
SYNOPSIS: Waiter Phil (Dunham) is in love with the establishment's cabaret dancer, and the two plan to wed. The bartender, himself in love with the dancer, comes up with a plot to get Phil out of the way. Stealing $500 from the cash register, he presents it to Phil stating that it is the bequest of some late lost uncle. Then he informs the landlady that Phil has robbed the register. Meanwhile, Phil and the dancer have married, but now find themselves in jail as a result of their assumed thievery. A cyclone appears on the scene, blowing the prison and its occupants (along with several other cast members) off the side of a cliff, landing in a heap at its base. "The picture fades as explanations, denials and accusations are made by the whole crew lying in the ruins." Synopsis adapted from the plot summary in *Moving Picture Weekly*, January 6, 1917, p.36
REVIEWS: "An unusually good comic offering, sure to bring much laughter. It features Phil Dunham and Lucille Hutton. The restaurant scenes at the opening, picturing the jumping limburger cheese, the game of checkers played with wine glasses, and other

features are good examples of this style of humor at its best. The wind storm at the close is one of the best things of the kind ever staged; in fact it may be a pioneer achievement of the sort. An excellent comic, free from offense." *Moving Picture World*, January 13, 1917, p.246

Heartsick At Sea: *Released 01/17/1917 Wednesday.* © 01/05/1917 — 1 reel. CAST: Dan Russell, Katherine Griffith, William Irving, E. Liserani, Vin Moore
SYNOPSIS: "Mr. Dinty Doozleberry [Russell] gets a letter from his uncle that informs him that he has left him $2.60, and so he starts to Hong Kong, China to collect. A man and his wife are on the boat which Mr. Dinty Doozleberry adroitly takes passage on and trouble starts when he tries to serve them soup. Of course, he's put in the kitchen when he can't pay his fare. The chase after Mr. Dinty Doozleberry finally is staged on an aeroplane and some mighty good pictures and very funny situations are the result." *Moving Picture Weekly*, January 13, 1917, p.33
REVIEWS: "A one-reel comic with some very funny business in it, particularly in the closing scenes. Dan Russell appears as a gentleman hobo, shanghaied by a party of sailors. His adventures on the rocking boat, in the part of a waiter, are full of incident and bring numerous laughs." *Moving Picture World*, January 20, 1917, p.361

Up the Flue: *Released 01/21/1917 Sunday.* © 01/17/1917 — 1 reel. CAST: Billy Armstrong, Louise Orth, Dave Morris
(pre-release title: **Mr. Shoestring in a Hole**)
SYNOPSIS: "Mr. Shoestring [Armstrong] was a burglar, and he made a sad mistake when he robbed a lady [Orth] of her jewelry and presented it to her daughter.

"When the lady recognized the donor and linked him with other 'affairs,' a series of incidents furnish lots of fun until the police arrive." *Moving Picture Weekly*, January 13, 1917, p.33
REVIEWS: "A characteristic knockabout number featuring Billy Armstrong, Louise Orth and Dave Morris. The police force round up a notorious pickpocket after exciting adventures. The reel closes with daring stunts on the roofs of high buildings." *Moving Picture World*, January 20, 1917, p.361

The Battle of "Let's Go": *Released 01/24/1917 Wednesday.* © 01/13/1917 — 2 reels. DIRECTOR: Craig Hutchinson. CAST: Dan Russell, Vin Moore, Marjorie Ray, William Irving, E. Leserani
(pre-release title: **Shot in the Excitement**)
SYNOPSIS: "Dan [Russell, as General Debility] is the general on one side, and Vin [Moore, as General Concarne] of the other. Somebody warns Dan to look out for female spies, and he passes on the warning to his low-comedy sentries. They walk up and down the dividing line of their respective camps, trying to tickle each other with their bayonets. Then appears the Poison Ivy Blossom [Ray]. Dan is so fond of flowers, he just can't resist her. Nobody could, for she's all dressed up and no place to go.

"'Catch me and you may kiss me!' cries the coy little damsel to the susceptible Dan, and he forgets all about home and country on the spot and follows her over the border. The Blossom was a faithful jade and all she wanted was to decoy the head guy of the other side and lead him into the power of General Concarne, a ferocious personage, with an army whose mustaches were even more formidable than the facial decorations of Dan's own men.

"Poor Dan had reason enough to curse the wiles of women, as he saw the elaborate preparations for an exhibition execution, with himself as the piece de resistance. But his fertile brain gave him an idea. Disguise! That's what all heroes do in such predicaments.

"Unfortunately the only disguise available was a female one. Dan looked just too sweet for words, as he lifted his skirt just a trifle, and draped his veil coquettishly over his blushes. Then he minced across the line, secure in the thought that his own mother would not know him.

"But alas! His men had been too well trained. 'It's the spy!' they yelled, and with one accord they were upon him. No use to protest. The dove of peace had flew [sic] the coop, and a battle royal ensued. The last we see of Dan, he is being fired from the muzzle of a huge gun, in the interior of which he has sought a false security." *Moving Picture Weekly*, January 20, 1917, p.17

REVIEWS: "There have been any number of military burlesques since the inauguration of the comic film, but Dan Russell and his assistants, including Vin Moore and Marjorie Ray, prove that good things bear repetition. To follow in the wake of so many previous attempts along this line and still make a favorable impression is no small feat, but it is accomplished in good style in this offering.

"The number is laughable throughout. Dan Russell plays General Debility, the scene being laid on the Mexican border. Here a military camp of considerable size is pitched and the time is spent in drilling awkward squads of very unmilitary looking soldiers.

"The place is infested with Mexican spies, disguised as women. General Debility, after numerous misadventures, puts on female apparel, after which he is made the target for beatings from both sides of the conflict.

"The war scenes in the second reel are uproarious in places and enough gunpowder is burned to satisfy almost any observer. An aeroplane and 'tank' play important parts in the battle episodes; also a war correspondent who writes his story amid bursting shells. The fun is all free from offense." Reviewed by Robert C. McElravy, *Moving Picture World*, January 20, 1917, p.358

Faking Fakirs: *Released 01/31/1917 Wednesday.* © 01/17/1917 — 2 reels. DIRECTOR: Jay A. Howe. CAST: Phil Dunham, Lucille Hutton, Merta Sterling, Charles Inslee, Vin Moore SYNOPSIS: "Springboard Sally [Hutton] and Mabel Carryflesh [Sterling] pull all the sightseers to their sideshow. Phil [Dunham] and Charlie [Inslee], in love with Sally, are in despair when they hit upon a plan to try to get her into their booth. They make love to her until Phil opens and reads a telegram addressed to Sally. In it Takeing Ways, attorney-at-law, informs the diver that she is the heiress to $50,000, left by her aunt.

"To steer Charlie from her, Phil hits on the plan to rewrite the telegram, making Miss Carryflesh the heiress, and when Charlie sees this, sure enough, straightaway to Rev. Dr. Jones does he and the weighty one march. When he discovers that Sally is the heiress, he hates Phil.

"Sally, informed of her legacy, takes a satchel all filled with greenbacks over to her husband's tent, Phil following and receiving a surprise on learning that she is already wed. Consternation follows when he grabs the money and runs away. The entire outfit of side-shows give chase. Phil succumbs when the valise with the coin is taken from him by Sally, and she pins a rose upon his chest as he reclines in peace in the amusement park." *Moving Picture World*, February 3, 1917, p.740

REVIEWS: "A two-reel subject, featuring Phil Dunham as Bonehead Bill, in charge of a ball-throwing concession. The scenes are laid at a beach resort. Phil lets the boys throw at his cranium, three balls for a nickel. This starts off well, but does not develop complications of sufficient interest to prove highly successful. It makes an average release of the nonsensical sort." *Moving Picture World*, January 27, 1917, p.548

That Dawgone Dog: *Released 02/07/1917 Wednesday.* © 01/24/1917 — 2 reels. DIRECTOR: Richard Smith. CAST: Sammy Burns, Katherine Griffith, Vera Reynolds, Grace Jones
SYNOPSIS: "A valuable necklace is stolen from a rich woman [Griffith]. Sammie [Burns], the butler, offers a necklace to the maid [Reynolds] so suspicion points to him. The rich woman notifies the police. Sammie and the maid have an afternoon off and they go to the park. Sammie offers the necklace again; the maid is about to accept it, when she sees it bears the tag of a 5 and 10 cent store and she scornfully returns it to him.

"The real crook looks for a place in his room to hide the necklace, but cannot find one. He catches sight of the dog and puts the jewels in its collar.

"Sammie comes across a girl weeping at the grave of Fido. A little girl appears with a dog. The dog-catchers' wagon also appears and attempt to take a bulldog, but don't succeed.

"The crook goes to the station with his dog and ties it outside. Some one unties the dog, which runs away with the necklace still in its collar. Every one seems to have lost a dog, and a chase ensues. Sammie decides to buy one for the girl who is mourning Fido's loss, and goes to a dog store. He gets a big one and manages to upset several policemen and pedestrians with it. The dog catchers are so determined to arrest all dogs, that they even attempt to arrest a statue of one, which is broken in the scuffle.

"Soon every one is hunting for a dog. After a terrific chase in which the police join, the whole party falls over a cliff, tangled in the remains of the dog catchers' wagon and the police automobile." *Moving Picture World*, February 10, 1917, p.903
REVIEWS: "A two-reel number, featuring Mrs. Griffith, Sammy Burns and Grace Jones. This is a characteristic knockabout comedy. A detective endeavors in the opening scenes to recover Mrs. Lottadough's stolen necklace. Later a Miss Dogberry, whose canine has died, wishes another like it and offers to marry the man who can bring her such a dog. This is not as funny as some by this company, but has a wild and amusing series of chase scenes at the close." *Moving Picture World*, February 10, 1917, p.874

End of a Perfect Day: *Released 02/14/1917 Wednesday.* © 01/29/1917 — 1 reel. CAST: Hank Mann, Gertrude Selby, Reggie Morris
SYNOPSIS: "Gertie [Selby] is an incorrigible flirt. She is sitting on the bank of a lake, and two of her admirers are contending for her favor. She throws a rose into the water and declares, 'Who gets the rose, gets me.' There is a very wet half hour after that.

"Her sweetheart [Morris] comes along and asks her to go for a ride in his car. She is delighted and goes into the house to change her gown. While he is waiting for her, Hank [Mann] slugs his chauffeur over the head, takes his cap and goggles and gets into his seat. Reggie and Gertie climb into the tonneau, and have a lovely spoon, while Hank, as the

chauffeur, drives them all over the town. Finally he drives right off the end of a pier and the joy ride ends in the ocean." *Moving Picture Weekly*, February 10, 1917, p.33
REVIEWS: "It is an 'uproarious 'day,' all right, for the spectators of this well-done slapstick comedy, but it must have been a strenuous one for the actors." *Motion Picture Magazine*, May 1917, p.9

Brave Little Waldo: *Released 02/16/1917 Friday.* © 02/05/1917 — 1 reel. CAST: Fatty Voss
SYNOPSIS: "Colonel Bingo had arranged with Major Godfrey that his son Waldo [Voss] should marry the Major's daughter. But first Waldo had to be sent to college to cure him of his wild and fighting temper. The cure was entirely successful and Waldo returns a perfect example of the genus 'Sissy.' The Colonel is perfectly disgusted and decrees that his son must go west and become a man or die. He goes to the ranch of his uncle. If clothes could make a man, Waldo at the ranch would certainly be a ruffian. He is togged out in Wild West garmens [sic] of the early eighties, including hardware. To the women he is perfectly irresistible. But he does not make such a hit with the cowpunchers.

"They select a 'gentle' horse for him to ride. Waldo just manages to survive the ordeal. Waldo writes home what a daredevil he has become and father and mother come out to see for themselves. Their disappointment is so acute that the result lands Waldo at the bottom of a cliff. Then father repents and goes after his offspring." *Moving Picture Weekly*, February 10, 1917, p.32
REVIEWS: "Fatty Voss acting effeminate and causing an entire ranch of cowboys to assume like ways is a pretty funny though not exactly tasteful sight. There are some good comedy surprises in the reel which should amuse. All the characters go over a cliff for the usual L-Ko ending." *Motion Picture News*, February 4, 1917, p.1260

After the Balled-Up Ball: *Released 02/21/1917 Wednesday.* © 02/08/1917 — 2 reels. DIRECTOR: J.A. Howe. CAST: Phil Dunham, Lucille Hutton, Merta Sterling, Charles Inslee
SYNOPSIS: "Lucille [Hutton] persuades her husband [Inslee] that she must go to Mrs. Highlife's ball, even though he does not want to go. She says that she can easily go with the people who live across the hall, and at last he consents. Phil [Dunham] decides to go, too. He gets into his antiquated dress-suit, and takes a flask in his tail pocket to refresh himself from time to time.

"The fat lady [Sterling] dresses up in her very best gown and goes to the ball, too. Phil gets thirsty from dancing, and finding the punch-bowl, he adds something from his flask to give it a little more flavor. Then he drinks it to the last dregs.

"The fat lady is crossing the hall. Phil bumps into her, falls and lands on her train. He rides around on it, and it is finally torn off. All the guests are very much shocked, and the hostess brings the fat lady her cloak. She is much offended, and goes home. Lucille's husband relents after she has gone, and turns up at the ball. He is jealous of the attentions which his wife receives. As Mrs. Fat Lady is on her way home, a policeman tries to arrest her for not being properly dressed, and so she discovers that half her gown is missing.

"Phil, Lucille and her husband, and the fat lady, all return to the apartment house where they live. Phil has a hard time finding his door. He enters Lucille's room by mistake. Then ensues a general mix-up with everybody in the wrong room.

"The police are called, and chase Phil to the roof. Lucille's husband follows them, shooting madly. They all run around the edge of the roof and down the fire escape. Phil takes a bicycle from an old man, and Lucille's husband chases him in a Ford. The chase takes them all to a pier and they end up in the water." *Moving Picture Weekly*, February 17, 1917, pp.29, 34

REVIEWS: "A two-reel comic subject, featuring Phil Dunham and Lucille Hutton. The former goes to a fashionable ball and consumes all of the punch. There is considerable amusement in these ball scenes. Later a mix-up in an apartment house occurs, the participants finally emerging to the roof tops. This is followed by a lively chase. The number is not particularly novel, but will amuse." *Moving Picture World*, February 24, 1917, p.1213

Spike's Bizzy Bike: *Released 02/28/1917 Wednesday.* © 02/14/1917 — 2 reels. DIRECTOR: Craig Hutchinson. CAST: Dan Russell, Marjorie Ray, Vin Moore

SYNOPSIS: "Dan [Russell, as M.T. Head] is a bicycle rider of renown, and he has entered his name for the six-day race. His rival is Jess Cuckoo [Moore], and both are determined to win, for both love the same girl [Ray] and wish to find favor in her sight. Dan goes into training vigorously for the great occasion. His trainer says that he must reduce, so he goes to work at it. Dan's trainer is a bearded pedagogue, in whose luxuriant whisker Dan finds a little singing bird. He puts on the gloves with Dan and gets decidedly the better of it, until Dan discovers a horseshoe and a hammer head in his gloves. Then everything comes Dan's way for a change. Diet is a great part of the training. Whiskers eats a huge meal, while Dan has to be satisfied with a biscuit and a glass of water. His rival, in the meantime, does most of his training in bed.

"Dan and his rival both go to call on their sweetheart. Jess has brought a piece of mistletoe, which he hangs on the chandelier. Then he stands under it and is rewarded by a kiss from the girl. Dan sneaks in while they are out. He hides a brick in the mistletoe, and attaches a string to it. Then he leads the string over the door and waits outside. Jess again stands under the chandelier, and Dan lowers the brick with a bump onto his head. But when Jess does the same to him he does not find it so funny.

"The day of the race arrives, and both the contestants are ready. There is a large audience, including the girl. Dan has a patent arrangement, concealed by his dressing gown. There is a small gasoline motor attached to his bike, which supplies the power. Jess discovers this in one of the rests, and plans revenge. He removes the gasoline can, and substitutes nitroglycerine for the gas. Dan returns for a surreptitious renewal of the gas, and fills the tank with nitro-glycerine instead. He rides madly around the track, driven by superhuman force, and the crowd flies in terror from the inevitable explosion. The police are called, of course, and the chase proceeds through buildings and houses, until Dan ends in one last explosion, which lands him under a pile of debris." *Moving Picture Weekly*, February 24, 1917, p.28

REVIEWS: "A rapid-fire comic, with a strong 'sporting' flavor, though not in any way offensive. Dan Russell, Marjorie Ray and Vin Moore appear. The former plays the part of a bicycle rider. The scenes at the training quarters contain some laughable incidents of the knockabout sort. The bicycle chase in the second reel is extremely funny. A good offering of the type." *Moving Picture World*, March 3, 1917, p.1375

"Dan Russell as M.T. Head, a bicycle racer, has the leading part in this picture, which is right up to L-Ko standard. The burlesque bike race which M.T. Head wins by attaching a motor to himself is fraught with a number of highly amusing tricks. The direction is good and the supporting players contribute to the best interests of the comedy in a satisfying fashion." *Motion Picture News*, March 3, 1917, p.1426

Fatty's Feature Fillum: *Released 03/07/1917 Wednesday.* © 02/27/1917 — 2 reels. DIRECTOR: Fatty Voss. CAST: Fatty Voss, Gladys Roach, Dick Smith
SYNOPSIS: "Fatty [Voss, as Egbert] is the featured actor of a motion picture company. He is dining in a restaurant when he sees a party of girls watching him, and decides to give them a treat. He sends them a card, on which is written, 'I am featured at the Bazoo.' Then he goes grandly out, trusting them to follow, which they do. He takes up a prominent position at the box office of the theatre, and watches the nickels as they go in.

"First on the screen is the 'Cuckoo Weekly,' with battle scenes 'Nowhere in France,' and the launching of the Dreadnothing, guaranteed to do 470 knots per — haps, in which the bottle of champagne crashes through the hull when it is broken against it. Then come the latest styles from 'Vug,' which close the weekly. Then comes the great feature film, 'Sunshine and Shadows.' Egbert calls on his sweetheart, Blanche [Roach], little dreaming that a vulture is following in his wake. Desmond [Smith] the villain has seen the maiden and is scheming to possess her. He goes to work to get hold of the mortgage on her home, in true villainous fashion, and then force her father to give him the girl, or he will take away their home. Egbert is out maneuvered at every turn, and the villain seizes the girl. So he goes to the side of the stream to commit his shriveled carcass to the waters.

"The villain's cigarette sets fire to the house at the critical moment, and the smoke is blown to Fatty. He suspects the trouble, and rushes to her assistance. He rescues her just in time. As the picture runs its exciting course, Fatty is seated in the audience between the two charmers of the restaurant, and explains the fine points to them, leading the applause at all the thrilling places." *Moving Picture Weekly*, March 3, 1917, p.29
REVIEWS: "A good comic subject, featuring Fatty Voss, Gladys Roach and Dick Smith. The former plays a movie star who goes to the theater to watch himself in the films. Some good burlesque work is done, including excerpts from the 'Cuckoo Weekly' and a melodrama. The snare drummer also makes a funny feature. This contains some amusing novelties." *Moving Picture World*, March 10, 1917, p.1594

"With Fatty Voss playing the part of Little Egbert in a picture and with such amusing features as a burlesque on the animated weekly, this picture ranks high among comedies of its class. Fatty, the actor, is seen in a picture theatre watching himself perform. He leads the applause always and manages to make a hit with several young lady 'movie fans.'" *Motion Picture News*, March 10, 1917, p.1576

Summer Boarders: *Released 03/14/1917 Wednesday.* © 03/03/1917 — 1 reel. CAST: Phil Dunham, Merta Sterling, Lucille Hutton, William Irving, Charles Inslee
SYNOPSIS: "In the summer hotel, there is a call for a decorator. One of the boarders wants her room re-papered. The boss paperer arrives with Phil [Dunham], his assistant. The proprietor's wife is of a flirtatious disposition and her husband is very jealous. He suspects her of casting sheep's eyes at the boss paperer. Phil is hard at work cutting out scraps of paper and pasting them on the desk, the sofa pillows and everywhere else where wallpaper does

not belong. The proprietor starts a chase in which several people become covered with paste, but Phil, as usual, is the chief sufferer." *Moving Picture Weekly*, March 10, 1917, p.38

REVIEWS: "A one-reel comic, featuring Phil Dunham, Merta Sterling, Lucille Hutton and others. The former appears as a paperhanger, engaged to work in a boarding house. He flirts with the girl across the hall and the usual knockabout scenes occur. There is not a great deal to the plot and the subject is only fairly successful as a whole." *Moving Picture World*, March 17, 1917, p.1788

"Phil Dunham as a paper hanger doesn't manage to get his usual number of laughs in this release. The action is not at all spontaneous and the chase at the end is far from funny. Merta Sterling, William Irving, Lucille Hutton and Charles Inslee give support." *Motion Picture News*, March 17, 1917, p.1721

Love On Crutches: *Released 03/16/1917 Friday.* © 03/03/1917 — 1 reel. CAST: Hank Mann (re-titled re-release of **Cupid in a Hospital**)

SYNOPSIS: "Bill gets into a fight with a young interne. They have a scrap over a nurse, and the interne leaves Bill for dead. He and the nurse hurry to the hospital. Bill is found by policemen and carried into the hospital. In the ward an anarchist offers to stand treat. Bill steals his bottle, but the nurse catches him with it. The nurse is sweet to Bill and this arouses the ire of the anarchist, who puts a bomb under Bill's bed. The nurse sits on the bed and the anarchist tries to get her away. Then the bomb is discovered and the entire hospital force tries to get rid of it. In the end both the anarchist and Bill are blown away by the explosion." *Moving Picture World*, March 10, 1917, p.1821

Defective Detectives: *Released 03/21/1917 Wednesday.* © 03/09/1917 — 2 reels. DIRECTOR: J.A. Howe. CAST: Phil Dunham, Charles Inslee, Lucille Hutton, Merta Sterling, Frank Klein

SYNOPSIS: "Phil [Dunham] is about to graduate at the 'School of Detecatufs,' and he and the chief [Inslee] are trying the effect of various disguises on each other. A suspicious party is registered at the hotel, and the detecatufs are called in. They disguise themselves as porters and busy themselves with the baggage, in order to divert the attention of the guests. The bride, Lucille [Hutton], and groom arrive and register at the desk. Soon after another pair, with Merta [Sterling] as the bride, also appear and ask for rooms. Their trunks are delivered and Phil is told to take them upstairs. He takes up Lucille's and leaves it outside her door, going down for Merta's. Charles comes along and takes Lucille's down on the elevator, under the impression that it was left there to be taken away. When Phil staggers up the stairs with Merta's, he is horrified to find Lucille's gone. In the confusion the trunks are delivered to the wrong rooms, and Merta nearly has a fit when she opens the one in her room and finds clothes much too small for her in it.

"Phil and Charles, meantime, have made many changes in make-up and succeeded in deceiving no one but each other. Each thinks the other a suspicious character, until his disguise is removed. The trunks become hopelessly confused, each taking the wrong one into the hall. For some unknown reason, they find themselves on the roof, where they do stunts with the trunks over the edge. One trunk is landed on the telegraph wires, with the detectives and guests after it. There is a battle for the possession of the trunk high up above the city. At last trunk, detective and guests fall together in one heap, and the comedy comes to an end." *Moving Picture Weekly*, March 17, 1917, p.29

REVIEWS: "A two-reel number, featuring Phil Dunham, Lucille Hutton and others. The first reel is given up to some quite amusing scenes in the office of the Star Detective agency, where two rube sleuths operate. Sliding doors and a number of tricks prove interesting. The action is swifter in the second reel, where the detectives are employed in a hotel. Scrambling over the roof tops and across telegraph wires are included in the action, which becomes quite amusing in places." *Moving Picture World*, March 24, 1917, p.1951

"With its roof top chase, its various rough and tumble scrambles and mixups this comedy has more wild action than humor. Phil Dunham hardly appears at his best at any moment throughout the two reels. The closing chase over the house tops introduces the usual number of dare-devil feats of acrobatics, at which the L-Ko aggregation excel. Lucille Hutton, Charles Inslee and Merta Sterling are others in the cast." *Motion Picture News*, March 24, 1917, p.1873

Dippy Dan's Doings: *Released 03/28/1917 Wednesday.* © 03/15/1917 — 2 reels. DIRECTOR: John G. Blystone. CAST: Dan Russell, Vin Moore, Marjorie Ray, Jean Hathaway SYNOPSIS: "The cops put a rope across the street to discourage speeders, but all they could catch was a cow. Later they were more successful, when Dan [Russell, as Speedometer Bill], the chauffeur, came along with the manicure [Ray] in his machine. They were taken to the police station. Both Dan and the judge [Moore] were interested in the manicure, but the judge had the disadvantage of possessing a jealous wife [Hathaway]. She happened to hire Dan's car, and he ran over a terribly rough road, and then was arrested for speeding again, and taken before the judge again. As they have already encountered each other over the manicure, Dan is afraid that he will get a very long sentence. But the little manicure drifts into the court room, carrying the hat which the judge has forgotten and left with her. The officer of the law can see nothing else, and is in terror, because his wife is in the courtroom. Dan thinks he is going to get off after all, but the judge creates a disturbance by pulling a gun, and Dan crawls on a board from the window of the courtroom to that of the opposite hotel. He is not aware that he has entered the judge's rooms.

"The judge comes in, and goes upstairs. Dan hears him coming, and hastily disguises himself in the sheet, putting on a pillow-case for a cap. He takes up a feather duster, and pretends to be the housemaid. The judge enters, and happens to step on the sheet which Dan is wearing. It is pulled off, and the judge recognizes the chauffeur. Dan beats it hastily and hides in the mail-bag in the office of the hotel. The judge and his wife decide to leave town. Dan, in the mail-bag, is loaded onto the same train which they take. The clerk finds him, but allows him to take refuge in a Pullman. The judge and his wife are travelling in the drawing-room. She comes out and seats herself in one of the chairs. A man tries to flirt with her, and the judge angrily sends her back to the compartment. She leaves her coat, and when Dan comes into the car, he disguises in it. The judge takes him for his wife, and sends him into the compartment, too. Dan and Mrs. Judge confront each other, and hearing the judge returning, they hide Dan in the berth. The porter comes in to make it up and Dan is discovered. The chase leads to the top of the car, and they race back and forth over the roofs of the cars. An engine full of police is pursuing them, and Dan finally is forced to dive from a bridge into the river below." *Moving Picture Weekly*, March 24, 1917, p.17
REVIEWS: "Dan Russell seems to have risen to the point where his presence in any comedy is a sufficient guarantee of its success. With his smiling countenance and generally gratifying

presence he fills the bills every time, almost regardless of the story or production. 'Dippy Dan's Doings' has the advantage over many of the L-Kos in that it has a plot, smattered with business enough to give the comedian plenty of opportunities. It stands a chance of sending even the most hypercritical audience into convulsions, while his support, which includes Vin Moore, Marjorie Ray and Jean Hathaway renders good work." *Motion Picture News*, March 31, 1917, p.2037

"Dan Russell is featured in this characteristic number as a taxi driver who is addicted to both speeding and flirting. His affair with the judge's wife leads to all sorts of trouble. The humor in this is but fairly strong. The chase feature at the close is one of the best of the kind shown in a long while, bringing the number to a lively finish." *Moving Picture World*, April 7, 1917, p.117

Nabbing a Noble: *Released 04/04/1917 Wednesday.* © 03/24/1917 — 1 reel. DIRECTOR: J.A. Howe. CAST: Phil Dunham, Lucille Hutton, Charles Inslee, Merta Sterling
SYNOPSIS: "Phil [Dunham] is valet to a noble lord, who is on his way to visit the parents [Inslee and Sterling] of Lucille [Hutton], who are very rich. The lord tells Phil to change places with him till he sees how he likes the looks of the family. Their cook has gone, so Phil makes the valet do duty. They dine after a while, but Phil has great difficulty with the viands. He rushes into the kitchen and catches fire when the valet shoves him against the stove. There is a chase in which all try to act as fire extinguishers for Phil. The valet is left to comfort the daughter. On the day of the wedding, all are waiting for the bride, but she is ready to elope with the valet. They disguise one of the men servants as the bride and send her downstairs to marry Phil. All might have gone well if the ring had fitted, but it wouldn't go on the servant's big fingers. Discovery of the change in positions between Phil and the valet reconciles the parents to their daughter's runaway match." *Moving Picture Weekly*, March 31, 1917, p.32
REVIEWS: "A comic number featuring Phil Dunham as Count Notta Jit, who turns out to be valet to the real count. The fake wedding at the close is a funny feature and is followed by a lively chase." *Moving Picture World*, April 7, 1917, p.117

"In which a noble man changes places with his valet prior to his visit to a family and pays the penalty when the valet runs off with the pretty daughter of the house. Phil Dunham, featured in this, does his usual comical work and is ably supported by Lucille Hutton, Charles Inslee and Merta Sterling." *Motion Picture News*, April 14, 1917, p.2369

Crooks and Crocodiles: *Released 04/08/1917 Sunday.* © 03/23/1917 — 1 reel. CAST: Billy Armstrong, Fatty Voss
SYNOPSIS: "Bill [Armstrong] has had a rough night, and awakes in the morning with an awful head. He goes out to fish in the park lake. While he is gone Fat [Voss] sees his wife hiding a stocking full of money, climbs into the room and steals it. Bill catches an alligator, and is terrified. Fat is on his way to the park, and sees that the cops are after him. He throws the sock into the water. Bill's hook catches it, and he determines to fish for the mate. The big papa alligator comes hunting for his little one. It chases Bill. Fat comes and tries to rescue him. It leads them to the tank where there are many more of the creatures, and there is a furious mix-up of Fat, Bill, the cops and the alligators, during which Bill's wife adds to the confusion by discovering her money in Bill's pail." *Moving Picture Weekly*, March 31, 1917, p.32

REVIEWS: "Mr. Nappy, impersonated by Bill Armstrong, goes fishing. He gets in bad with some alligators, some of the scenes apparently being taken at an alligator farm. This makes an amusing offering of the eccentric, knockabout type." *Moving Picture World*, April 14, 1917, p.288

"Trick work, which causes a number of stuffed crocodiles to have prominent roles in this comedy is sometimes obviously mechanical and sometimes ridiculously funny. Fatty Voss and a good supporting cast disport themselves to advantage in it, although it is an episodic affair with no story as an excuse for its existence." *Motion Picture News*, April 14, 1917, p.2369

Ring Rivals: *Released 04/11/1917 Wednesday.* © 04/03/1917 — 2 reels. DIRECTOR: Noel Mason Smith. CAST: Dan Russell, Dick Smith, Gladys Roach
SYNOPSIS: "Dan [Russell], the Irish Terror, is attracted by the charms of Hot Dog Hattie [Roach], but she does not care for him, as her affections are set upon Battling Bull [Smith]. Both are members of the Stock Yards Athletic Club, and Dan sends Bull a challenge, which is accepted. A curly-haired poodle is the messenger. The fight is fixed for a certain date and both commence to train.

"Dan decides to get a line on Bull's work. He goes to his training quarters, climbs up on a box and peeps through the transom. What he sees there disconcerts him so much that he kicks the box away from under him. The Bull sees him and shuts the transom on his fingers. Dan comes swaggering out, and his appearance is so formidable that all who see him make a dive for the man hole in the middle of the street.

"The day of the fight arrives. Dan has arranged for some dirty work, which fails to operate against Bull, and Dan is knocked out. Dan sneaks away from the ring, passing the guy who is handling the gate receipts. Dan slugs the man and makes off with the dough. He takes it to Hattie, shuts her up in her own hotdog booth, and pushes it off down the steep grade of the street. He clambers on top of it and dresses himself there. The booth falls over a bank, and Dan rescues Hattie from the ruins. They are chased, but he manages to board a Western-bound train with her. Bull finds a lone hot dog which tells him of her fate.

"Out West, Dan's prowess soon makes him master of the town. He shoots up all who oppose his supremacy. Hattie still dreams of Bull, and when he arrives in town in the guise of a tramp she recognizes him. Bull challenges Dan to another fight. Hattie disguises herself as a cow-puncher in order to be present. She pours glue on the seat in Dan's corner, and revives Bull with dope when he threatens to collapse. Dan is knocked out of the ring, and chased down the street, while Hattie and Bull fall into each other's arms." *Moving Picture Weekly*, April 7, 1917, p.28
REVIEWS: "A two-reel comic, featuring Dan Russell, Gladys Roach, Dick Smith and others. This has a strong 'sporting' turn, two ring battles being featured. The action begins in the East and then drifts out to a small Western town. Dan rules the latter place until his old rival shows up and conquers him. This is slightly rough in spots, but does not greatly offend. Some of the small business is very funny." *Moving Picture World*, April 21, 1917, p.453

"Dan Russell, assisted by Dick Smith, proceeds to burlesque ring fighters in this picture with very funny results. The incidental business is clever and the plot coherent enough, with its love element, to hang together. Gladys Roach is the heroine over whom the fighters fight." *Motion Picture News*, April 28, 1917, p.2691

Love and Blazes: *Released 04/18/1917 Wednesday.* © 04/10/1917 — 2 reels. DIRECTOR: Vin Moore and Phil Dunham. CAST: Phil Dunham, Lucille Hutton, Charles Inslee, Merta Sterling
(pre-release title: **Exposition Day in Simpville**)
SYNOPSIS: "The Fire Chief [Dunham] and the Chief of Police [Inslee] are rivals for the fair Lucille [Hutton], daughter of the Mayor. They are preparing to deliver a knockout blow to her, at the annual exhibition of the Fire and Police Departments. Phil is conducting a drill at the fire station, in which his four men exhibit their preparedness.

"At the police station the Chief is preparing his men. His men are troubled with insomnia but the Chief explodes a bomb under their bench, which cures them eventually. The Mayor's fair daughter is the envy of Merta [Sterling], his stenographer, who is a real 'man-eater' by disposition. She sees Phil and at once succumbs to his manly charms.

"The Chief of Police is holding a burglar drill, with the false front of a house, which he is sure will win the commendation of Lucille, while Phil has prepared a demonstration in response to a fire alarm which is sure to take the prize. At last the day comes, and the police and firemen parade. The Mayor makes a speech, and the police are called upon to drill first. They are applauded, and Phil is jealous. The Chief is directing them with blasts on his whistle. Phil blows his own, and upsets the whole drill. Even the cherished burglar drill is put on the blink.

"Then comes Phil's turn. Unfortunately, he sets the fireworks going prematurely, and the fake fire turns into a real one. Phil saves the Mayor's daughter and drives off in a wagon with her. The Police Chief follows in a flivver. The horse balks and the Chief gets the girl. Phil then takes the horse's place and, the flivver balking too, the Chief hitches the horse to the car, while Phil draws Lucille in the wagon. Up and down a steep hill they go, until they reach home. The Chief goes in with the girl, and Phil calls the police and tells them there is a dangerous criminal with Lucille. They throw a bag over his head and arrest him. Then he is recognized, and, returning, sets the house on fire in spite. Phil rushes for his trusty fire laddies. He saves Lucille while the house goes up in smoke." *Moving Picture World*, April 21, 1917, p.487
REVIEWS: "A two-reel subject, featuring Phil Dunham, Lucille Hutton and others. This comic opens in a fire department, where numerous farcical incidents are pictured, done in broad burlesque style. Some of it is a little vulgar, but there is nothing to give great offense. In the second reel the firemen appear in 'Exhibition Day' stunts. This never becomes extremely laughable, but contains a lot of diverting nonsense and makes a fair subject." *Moving Picture World*, April 21, 1917, p.453

"The conventional rivalry of the Police and Fire chiefs for the hand of the Mayor's daughter is brought to the fore in these two reels of slapstick and trickery. The gags are always amusing and the performance of Phil Dunham adds much to the comedy value of the picture. Lucille Hutton, Merta Sterling and Charles Inslee are others." *Motion Picture News*, April 21, 1917, p.2521

Little Bo-Peep: *Released 04/25/1917 Wednesday.* © 04/14/1917 — 2 reels. DIRECTOR: Noel Smith and Richard Smith. CAST: Dan Russell, Lou Bolton, Robert McKenzie, Gladys Roach
SYNOPSIS: "Dan [Russell] was the shepherd at Rushville. Gladys [Roach] was the Rushville beauty, the daughter of the hotel proprietor [McKenzie]. Every day the hotel keeper went to meet the guests who never came, and he grew sad. At last came a day when a guest did

arrive on the 4 o'clock train. She was a vampire, but the proprietor did not know that. He rushed her into the old wagon and drove at top speed to the Rushville house. Gladys was sent upstairs to dust off the furniture in the guest room, and the lady was ushered into her apartment by the full staff. She was given a cow bell with which to make her wants known, and when she sat in the rocker, which promptly went over backwards with her, she rang it furiously.

"Pa disguised himself as the bellboy and answered. She was registered as La Belle Petroleum, a heel dancer, but when Dan saw her practicing in the woods in a Ballet Russe costume he thought it would have been more accurate if she had spelled heel with a double l. Dan had a hard time rescuing his flock from contamination, and the black lamb was determined to attach himself to the dancer.

"Pa invited his guest to drive with him, and Dan was jealous. The horse balked, standing on the railroad tracks, with an engine coming rapidly nearer. Only Dan's presence of mind in lighting a fire under the carriage prevented a tragedy. Then Dan and Pa had a fight, and Dan went off with the dancer, while the wagon burned in front of the hotel.

"Years went by. La Belle Petroleum had become a family drudge, with six husky boys. The hotel had flourished, and Pa had purchased an auto, but he had never forgotten the lovely dancer, and one day he just got into the buzz wagon, drove off to her house, and asked her to elope with him for old times sake. This she was delighted to do, and managed to elude Dan and the children. When they found that she was gone, they set out to follow her, the youngest one carrying his lamb. The elopers got stuck in a mud puddle and abandoned the car, which Dan and his husky boys managed to get going again. They rushed after the train, and just succeeded in catching it. Then they threw Pa off with one mighty heave, and the family were reunited at last." *Moving Picture World*, April 28, 1917, p.675
REVIEWS: "Dan Russell gives one of his inimitable comedy characterizations in this two-reel comedy, one of the good ones put out by the L-Ko organization. Lou Bolton, Robert McKenzie and Gladys Roach are prominent in his support. The comedy is chiefly small country town stuff and the usual burlesque of the city vampire is introduced. Decidedly worth while and well up to the L-Ko standard." *Motion Picture News*, April 28, 1917, p.2691

"Dan Russell is featured as a shepherd boy in this two-reel number. He falls in love with an actress whom he sees dancing over in the meadows. The goat herd makes a good feature; also the large family of boys. This is full of good humor of the nonsensical sort. It is a very successful offering of this type, and is free from offense. A good comic number." *Moving Picture World*, May 12, 1917, p.982

The Cabaret Scratch: *Released 05/02/1917 Wednesday.* © 04/17/1917 — 1 reel. DIRECTOR: Craig Hutchinson. CAST: Dan Russell
SYNOPSIS: "The headwaiter at the 'All Inn' has a lovely wife, who is the star of the cabaret. Dan [Russell] is a frequenter of it, sees the lovely singer and falls in love with her. Mrs. Dan leaves home for a visit and Dan invites the charmer and other guests to his house. They all develop a mysterious illness, which results in spots all over the face. Even the cat is afflicted with it. The Health Department quarantines the house, and when Mrs. Dan returns, she finds it hard to get into her own home. She enters at last, as does the headwaiter, husband of the charmer. Dan has a hard time trying to explain the identity of his various

afflicted guests. The headwaiter is unconvinced, and a chase on horseback, in which the doctor joins, ends the picture." *Moving Picture Weekly*, April 28, 1917, p.32

REVIEWS: "A one-reel comic, featuring Dan Russell. He invades a cabaret, where he flirts with the manager's wife. The 'cabaret scratch,' a disease resembling small pox, breaks out. The reel closes with an auto chase. This is not hilarious, but proves diverting and entertaining." *Moving Picture World*, May 5, 1917, p.813

"The rough and tumble possibilities in a house full of quarantined people are averagely well developed in this L-Ko comedy. Dan Russell contributes his usual highly humorous work and heads a cast of competent comedians." *Motion Picture News*, May 5, 1917, p.2864

Scrambled Hearts: *Released 05/06/1917 Sunday.* © 04/20/1917 — 1 reel. CAST: Billie Ritchie, Anna Darling

SYNOPSIS: "Anne [Darling] had three suitors, Bill [Ritchie], the choice of her dad, Frank, the choice of her mother, and Johnnie, the choice of her own heart. She stood it as long as she could, and then she took matters in her own hands. She sent Frank word to disguise as a woman, and they would elope that night. At the same time she sent word to Bill to do the same thing. Bill and Frank then eloped with each other, and she ran off with Johnnie." *Moving Picture Weekly*, April 28, 1917, p.32

REVIEWS: "A rube comedy number, featuring Billie Ritchie and others. This is a rural burlesque, in which much eccentric action is infused into an elopement story. The knockabout scenes at the close will bring laughter." *Moving Picture World*, May 5, 1917, p.813

Tom's Tramping Troupe: *Released 05/09/1917 Wednesday.* © 04/27/1917 — 2 reels. DIRECTOR: Jay A. Howe. CAST: Merta Sterling, Phil Dunham, Lucille Hutton, Charles Inslee, Harry Lorraine

SYNOPSIS: "The tramping troupers arrive at Punkville Centre, and put up at the boarding house, which is run by the strong-minded landlady [Sterling] and her henpecked husband Phil [Dunham]. He is maid-of-all-work, and she takes the money. He is much attracted to the actress [Hutton] who plays Little Eva, and Merta is jealous.

"That night they are to give a performance of 'Uncle Tom's Cabin.' Phil is head cook and bottle-washer at the theater too, and has to be property man, curtain man, stage manager, ticket taker and everything else but actor. It is he who brings on the soap boxes which do duty as cakes of ice in the river. It is he who barks like hounds on the trail, and who has to shove on the cardboard dogs which pursue Eliza. He has to hurry aloft to drop snow on the sad scene.

"Little Eva appears fascinatingly gowned in a short fluffy frock and a big hair ribbon. Phil can't resist her, and neglects his manifold duties to talk to her. She begins to play tag with him, and chases him into the midst of Uncle Tom's [Lorraine] most touching scene. Merta gets wild. She leaves the audience and is about to jump over the footlights to get after Phil.

"It is time for Eva to die, but she is way up above the stage, eating candy with Phil. Merta jumps on the stage, and hunts for Phil. She interferes considerably with the action, but when Eva cannot be found, the actor who played Eliza grabs Merta, puts a nightgown over her head, and tells her to go on and die. Legree [Inslee] tries to give her the words, but she is struck with stage fright. She is yanked up into heaven, where she promptly discovers

Eva and Phil. In their surprise the men let her fall, and she clutches Phil. They land on the stage together, while Eva laughs at them. This is too much. The audience gives chase and the Tramping Troupe is run out of town." *Moving Picture World*, May 12, 1917, p.1014
REVIEWS: "A two-reel burlesque on 'Uncle Tom's Cabin.' This opens with the arrival of a company of actors in a small town. The performance itself is pictured in the second reel. The humor is not at all strong in this, none of the small business being particularly funny. The dinner scene in the first reel is not a good feature. The company, which includes Phil Dunham, Lucille Hutton and others, has been seen in much better productions than this." *Moving Picture World*, May 12, 1917, p.982

Good Little Bad Boy: *Released 05/16/1917 Wednesday.* © 05/03/1917 — 2 reels. DIRECTOR: Vin Moore. CAST: Phil Dunham, Merta Sterling, Charles Inslee, Lucille Hutton SYNOPSIS: "Phil [Dunham] steals pie from his little sister, and breaks her Teddy Bear. When he makes her cry, her parents try to pacify her by putting money in her bank, and then Phil schemes to steal the bank. For this pa kicks him out, and he wanders into the cruel world.

"Claude Worcestershire [Inslee] and Tabasco Lil [Hutton] read in the paper that the station master is to receive a consignment of $2,000,000. This determines them to stop at Beetville. Phil is in the billiard parlor when the villain and villainess arrive. The sheriff throws Bill out, and falls a victim to the charms of Lil. Phil enters a saloon, where he vainly tries to take some free lunch from the counter. But the proprietor has a sliding cover for it which works by a push button, and Phil is foiled.

"Salvation Liz [Sterling] appears with her concertina, and starts right in to convert Phil. She is successful, and he joins in the singing. She leads him to his home and begs forgiveness for him.

"He meets Tabasco Lil, who decoys him into going for a walk. She gets him to climb a tree for her, and goes off and leaves him there. Then she tries the same tactics on his father, the station master, so that Claude can get to the safe. Phil manages to get down by sawing off the bough and falling with it.

"In the meantime Claude has opened the safe, and is waiting for Lil to make a getaway. Phil has converted Lil, and she leads him to the station to fight Claude. While they fight she gets into the safe with their guns. Claude ties a rope to the safe, after knocking out Phil, and tying him to the track. He jumps on a passing train, and the safe pulls the whole station after the train, while Claude holds the rope. Salvation Liz saves Phil, and on a hand car they pursue the flying station. Phil climbs on the roof and cuts the rope. He drags Lil out of the safe just as a train comes and crashes through station and all." *Moving Picture World*, May 19, 1917, p.1175
REVIEWS: "This touches off one of the funniest comic situations ever devised by this company, in the second reel. It is bound to bring roars of laughter, when the train pulls the station house along the track, pursued by the agent and friends on a hand-car. Phil Dunham Lucille Hutton, Merta Sterling and Charles Inslee have the leading roles. This is full of amusing small business, but has a sure-fire close. An excellent comic subject." *Moving Picture World*, May 19, 1917, p.1145

"Phil Dunham once again in a rapid-fire trick comedy of unusual merit. Much funny business and original gags such as a sliding cover for free lunch make the two reels pass quickly. Dunham is fine and has for support pretty Lucille Hutton, Merta Sterling and Charles Inslee." *Motion Picture News*, May 19, 1917, p.3165

Beach Nuts: *Released 05/23/1917 Wednesday.* © 05/16/1917 — 2 reels. DIRECTOR: Noel Smith. CAST: Dan Russell, Bert Roach, Gladys Varden, Walter Stephens
SYNOPSIS: "Ima Knutt [Russell] was the life saver on the beach and the idol of all the girls. He liked girls to be small and slim, and was much disconcerted when the biggest nut on the beach, an enormous lady in a black bathing suit, insisted upon having his services to teach her how to swim. At the same time Knutt Sunday [Roach], the clerk at the soda fountain, was regaling Hazel Knutt [Varden], his sweetheart, with the sweetmeat named after him. Ima much prefers Hazel to the fat lady.

"Into the bathhouse comes Krazy Knutt [Stephens]. He decides to go in swimming. So does Hazel. Ima brings water wings for her and is delighted with the chance to teach her. He invites her to go for a ride in a beach chair. It runs away with them and Knutt Sunday gives chase. At last they return to the bathhouse. Krazy is pushed into the water and Ima and the girl sit on the edge making eyes at each other. Krazy ties their shoelaces together, and they both fall in when they try to get up. Ima then seizes Krazy and makes him his assistant life saver. He then goes off with the girl to get some ice cream. Knutt ties a weight to his leg as he is eating it and the weight drags him into the pool. Ima pulls Knutt in with him.

"They rush out onto the beach. Ima and the girl hide behind a beach umbrella. Knutt removes the umbrella and puts it over a hideous girl. Ima returns to her and is disgusted. Ima and the girl go for a ride in the flying boats and Knutt follows and spills Ima into the sea. A crab grabs him, and he rushes to the shore. He puts the crab on Sunday. Sunday determines to be revenged. He decoys Ima and the girl into a bathhouse and then chloroforms them with a bicycle pump through the key hole. He hires two confederates to push the machine into the sea and drown Ima and the girl. The police see the suspicious characters and arrive in time to rescue Ima and Hazel. But the men make a mistake in the bathhouse and Knutt Sunday is drowned." *Moving Picture World*, May 26, 1917, p.1335
REVIEWS: "A two-reel comic featuring Daniel Russell, Gladys Varden, Bert Roach and Walter Stephens. Many aquatic stunts are shown in this in a tank and in the ocean by girls and men attired in bathing suits. Certain humorous effects are attained, some of them a little coarse, but not in any way offensive. There is hardly enough plot to hold the action together, but it makes a fairly nonsensical number. A motor chase is the closing feature." *Moving Picture World*, May 26, 1917, p.1304

"Seashore gags with Dan Russell at his best as the heroic life saver. Much action and running about with various summer resort appliances brought in to enhance and speed up the comedy. Bert Roach, Gladys Vardon [sic] and Walter Stephens are in support." *Motion Picture News*, June 2, 1917, p.3474

Roped Into Scandal: *Released 05/30/1917 Wednesday.* © 05/19/1917 — 2 reels. DIRECTOR: Craig Hutchinson. CAST: Harry Lorraine, Eva Novak, Bert Roach
SYNOPSIS: "Mr. Wildcherry [Lorraine] was a menace to society and a trouble to his daughter Eva [Novak]. Right across the hall lived Mr. Samson Hercules [Roach] and his bride. When Hercules goes out Wildcherry goes across the hall and makes a low bow to Mrs. Hercules, taking off his hat. She sees 'I love you' painted on his bald head. But she is adamant. Then Wildcherry ties a string to a purse and pulls it across the hall to get her into his flat. She crawls after it and gets wedged in under the sewing machine. Eva comes to her aid, and she goes home raging.

"Eva has two suitors, Mr. Beer and Mr. Buller. Both come to call at once, and while they are there Papa goes over to Mrs. Hercules. Eva has been sewing on the machine and a thread from his trousers is caught in the needle. As he sits talking, his trouser-leg begins to unravel, and runs right up to his knee. He hears Mr. Hercules coming and hides. Hercules finds his hat, and he is thrown out.

"Eva's suitors are getting into a fight, when Wildcherry arrives and separates them. Mr. Hercules goes out to take his annual bath to sooth his feelings. Beer sends Eva a message asking her to elope, and Buller reads it. He makes a plan with Wildcherry to circumvent them. They take their places with a gun at the rope which is hanging out of the window, but unfortunately in a second fight between Beer and Buller, the latter is caught in the rope and seesaws up and down the side of the house, finally landing in the water tank on the roof. The end of the rope coils around the auto in which the lovers sit and they can't start the car.

"The watertank is upset and Mr. Wildcherry, pulling on the other end of the rope is dragged into the Hercules' bathroom. He makes fast to the bath tub. Mrs. Hercules comes in to take a bath and is dragged out and drawn along the street by the auto of the lovers. En route Mr. Wildcherry falls into the same tub, and the whole outfit crashes through the wall of the bath establishment where Mr. Hercules is bathing. The couples are reunited in the midst of the debris." *Moving Picture World*, June 2, 1917, pp.1494-1495

REVIEWS: "A two-reel comic dealing with the flirtations of a certain Mr. Wildcherry and a neighbor named Mr. Beereyed. Some of the business is pretty rough in this, though most of the antics are funny enough to get over without great offense. The trick effects up and down the high building are very laughable." *Moving Picture World*, June 2, 1917, p.1464

"A jealous husband and a gentleman with designs on his wife and two more jealous suitors for the hand of the gentleman's daughter cavort about in this average L-Ko, which ends with a lot of fine and side-splitting trick stuff. No well-known players in the cast, but all who appear are fairly well versed in comedy tricks of the L-Ko sort." *Motion Picture News*, June 9, 1917, p.3627

Dry Goods and Damp Deeds: *Released 06/06/1917 Wednesday.* © 05/23/1917 — 2 reels. DIRECTOR: Vin Moore. CAST: Phil Dunham, Lucille Hutton, Charles Inslee, Merta Sterling SYNOPSIS: "Phil [Dunham, as A. Wayfarer] arrives in town on top of a freight car, dressed in an autoist's outfit. He sees I.M. Shoddy [Inslee], the proprietor of the dry goods store, persecuting a defenceless [sic] sewing girl [Hutton], and trying to persuade her to enter his car. Phil rescues her and follows her to Shoddy's store, where she works. She gives him an orange as a souvenir, and he saves a piece of the peel. He waits outside, and through the window sees the shadow of Shoddy undressing a wax model. He rushes into the store, and after explanations, is given the position of porter.

"He meets the sewing girl, but Merta [Sterling], the forelady, falls in love with him, and makes it hard for him to meet the girl. Phil has all sorts of adventures in the store. He gives away the goods, and a policeman is called who chases him. He pretends to be a model, and escapes. He waters the flowers on a lady's hat, and finally, when a customer gives him her baby to hold, he puts the child in the cash basket, and swings it to the bundle girl.

"He sees a girl putting stockings for display upon a dummy, and is shocked, and later when a real customer is trying on stockings, Phil gets in wrong by thinking her a dummy. A veiled woman comes in. Phil pursues her, and when he finds she is colored, he faints. At last he finds

Lucille in the sewing room, and plays a song for her on the sleeve-board. Shoddy has been watching him, and now he enters, knocks Phil out, and carries the girl to the cellar. He ties her to a pillar, and turns on the water. Phil follows and there is a fight. Lucille is drowning, and though Phil tries all sorts of ruses, he cannot manage to get into the cellar to rescue her. At last he is thrown out of the window, and falls through a manhole into the flooded cellar, and finds himself with Lucille at last." *Moving Picture World*, June 9, 1917, p.1662

REVIEWS: "A two-reel comic, which features Phil Dunham, Lucille Hutton, Merta Sterling and Chas. Inslee. Most of the scenes occur in a department store, which Phil invades as a hobo. Some of the incidents reveal too much effort at humor; others are more successful. A stronger general idea would have helped this, though it makes a fairly diverting nonsense number as it stands." *Moving Picture World*, June 9, 1917, p.1628

"Or a second title might be 'Fun in a Department Store.' Phil Dunham as the porter in love with the beautiful sewing machine girl gets in some good gags and a fast and furious ending, in which the heroine is tied to a post in the cellar and the place flooded, caps the picture with a good climax. Lucille Hutton, Merta Sterling and Charles Inslee have the supporting parts." *Motion Picture News*, June 9, 1917, p.3626

Chicken Chased and Henpecked: *Released 06/13/1917 Wednesday.* © 05/31/1917 — 2 reels. DIRECTOR: Vin Moore. CAST: Phil Dunham, Merta Sterling, Lucille Hutton, Kathryn Young, Charles Inslee, Al Duffy

SYNOPSIS: "The old man goes away on his vacation, and leaves his son in charge of the house, without any money. The son gets the idea of renting the rooms. He steals a sign and hangs it out. Mr. and Mrs. Henpeck [Dunham and Sterling] with their daughter [Hutton] arrive. They are all loaded into an auto, but it breaks down. Henpeck has to transfer all the bundles to a wagon. The horse makes a meal off Mrs. Henpeck's new hat.

"Filet Mignon of the Follies has rented a room. Hen falls a victim to her charms. Mrs. Hen ties hubby to the bedstead. He, however, transfers the rope to the heaviest bag and goes out. An old man who rooms across the hall is much interested in Filet. She puts on the ballet costume, decorates himself with a lamp shade, and they do a pas de deux.

"Her maid gives a note to the colored porter asking him to meet her in the park at three o'clock. Mrs. Hen finds it and thinks it is from Filet to her husband. She ties a bean bag to his back, with the corner torn out of it. However, the chicken gets out and eats the beans.

"Hen gets through the transom and back to Filet. He orders supper. He connects a tube with the open gas jet and asphyxiates the old man. Mrs. Hen has gone to the park, thinking to trap her husband. She meets the nigger maid instead and they have a fight. Both end in the lake. Meantime, the snake in the grass has seen the supper party. He creeps in. Filet flies, and Hen puts on a suit of armor. The nigger comes to serve the next course and is scared white. Mrs. Hen returns. Hen takes the bellboy's cap and goes in to answer Filet's ring. Mrs. Hen follows, and Hen hides in the folding bed. Mrs. Hen suspects where he is, and there is a mix up in which the bed goes through the wall. Hen climbs a tree. It is in a picnic ground, and the village band is playing. Hen drops into the drum and goes rolling down the hill. He falls over a bank and into the auto which is carrying Filet away from the house." *Moving Picture World*, June 16, 1917, p.1833

REVIEWS: "A boarding house scramble in which hubby, closely watched by wifie, succeeds nevertheless in flirting with a pretty chorus girl. General mixup for all concerned in the end with much rapid-fire action. Phil Dunham, Lucille Hutton and Merta Sterling are the principals." *Motion Picture News*, June 16, 1917, p.3800

Where Is My Che-ild?: *Released 06/20/1917 Wednesday.* © 06/09/1917 — 2 reels. DIRECTOR: Noel Smith. STORY: John G. Blystone. CAST: Dan Russell, Mrs. (Eunice) Moore, Gladys Varden
(pre-release titles: **Where Are My Children?** and **A Baby Mix-Up**)
SYNOPSIS: Henpecked Mr. Weazelbiffer (Russell) rules his office with an iron hand, with a gimmicked chair set up to eject unwanted visitors through the wall and into a pool of water. Flirtatious Mrs. Gilsprev (Varden) arrives at the office looking for a job, and after accidentally being ejected from the trick chair is given the former bookkeeper's job; the bookkeeper swears revenge. Mrs. Weazelbiffer (Moore) shows up and insists on Mrs. Gilsprev's discharge, so hubby writes a final paycheck but includes a note on the back telling Gilsprev to meet him at his home that night. As part of this plan Weazelbiffer tricks his wife into seeing a lawyer about the settlement of her sister's estate. She gets wind of his ruse, however, and returns home. Weazelbiffer just manages to hide Gilsprev before his wife's return. When Mr. Gilsprev learns of his wife's dalliance, he heads to Weazelbiffer's with his baby in tow: "You took my wife, now take my child." Weazelbiffer hides the baby in the stove, but the dog finds the infant and hauls it out to his kennel. Mr. Gilsprev has a change of heart and returns for the baby, but now Weazelbiffer can't find it. A man who has arrived to clean the apartment spots the baby in the kennel, and after some back-and-forth a cop is called in and the baby is now found inside, hanging on the hallway hatrack. The baby is placed on a bed, but the cleaner hides it again. The dog finally locates the child. All in attendance confront the cleaner and demand to know who he is, and he identifies himself as the discharged bookkeeper, now satisfied with his revenge. Synopsis adapted from the plot summary in *Moving Picture World*, June 23, 1917, p.1989
REVIEWS: "A two-reel comic, featuring Dan Russell and Gladys Varden. This has a characteristic nonsense plot, not quite so amusing as in some offerings, but with some laughable moments. Mr. Weazelbiffer's machine for ejecting book agents and other boresome visitors from his office furnishes considerable fun. The baby scenes in the latter part of the picture incline a little too much toward rough handling, though most observers will see that a substitute was used in various instances." *Moving Picture World*, June 23, 1917, p.1955

"More domestic complications done after a typical L-Ko fashion and smattered with the usual number of hilarious gags. Dan Russell was never better than he is in the role of Mr. Weazelbiffer. His style of comedy is catchy and he makes the most of his many chances. The stunts originated by the producers, including the contraption employed by Weazelbiffer to project undesirable clients into a tank of water, are ingenious to the extreme." *Motion Picture News*, June 23, 1917, p.3955

Her Daring, Caring Ways: *Released 06/27/1917 Wednesday.* © 06/21/1917 — 2 reels. DIRECTOR: Vin Moore. CAST: Merta Sterling, Al Forbes, Lucille Hutton, the Donkey, Fritzie Ridgeway
SYNOPSIS: "Lucille [Hutton] is the owner of the ranch, but Little Mert [Sterling] is its pride. She is loved by Al [Forbes]. Chili Ted and Con Carne are scheming to get Lucille into their power. When the two ruffians attack her, she is saved by Mert and Al.

"Chili Ted returns and demands either Lucille or the mortgage. Al is teasing Mert when a bear appears, and he runs away. Mert rushes to the ranch. Al arrives before her and Lucille sends him to the bank to get the money to pay off the mortgage. Chili and Con see him go and chase him. He reaches the bank in safety and rides the donkey to the pay window. On the way back the ruffians waylay him and hang him to a tree. Mert sees him and shoots the rope in two. They both mount the donkey to ride to the ranch to warn Lucille. When they tell her she faints. Al runs to the well for water and falls in. Mert goes to save him and falls in, too. They cling to the ropes and as one comes up the other goes down." *Moving Picture World*, June 30, 1917, p.2148

REVIEWS: "Director Vin Moore has created an L-Ko along different lines than are usually followed in the speedy comedies that firm has been turning out. While there is plenty of dash and 'ginger' in the two reels the laughs are arrived at through unexpected methods. There are several sensations that would fit well into melodrama, indeed one of the incidents, where the men span a chasm by forming a 'human bridge,' recalls one of the big effects of an old time 'thriller' of the stage. 'Her Daring, Caring Ways' is the title, and Myrtle Sterling is the featured one, together with Lucille Hutton. It's a 'wild west' subject, full of dash and chase, and requires, in one of its principal scenes, a numerous company of girls costumed in approved fashion, as shown herewith. Miss Sterling is the leader of the band. This picture was produced under the Supervision of J.G. Blystone, director general of the L-Ko studios." *Moving Picture World*, June 16, 1917, p.1805

Bombs and Bandits: *Released 07/04/1917 Wednesday.* © 06/26/1917 — 2 reels. DIRECTOR: A. Jaeschke. CAST: Vin Moore, Billy Bevan, Charles Inslee, Sammy Burns, Dolly Dimples (pre-release title: **A Mexican Mix-Up**)

SYNOPSIS: "The Mayor [Moore] and the Chief of Police [Bevan] have offices in the same building and are both enamored of the chief's stenographer [Dimples]. She has entangled their middle-aged hearts in her curls and both are determined to win her. Dolly, in the meantime, gives most of her attention to young Sammy [Burns], secretary to the Mayor, a dashing young blade who wears the loudest socks in town.

"The two old chaps each wager ten thousand dollars on the winner of fair Dolly's hand. Each is sure that he is betting on a cinch. They place their money with Sammy, telling him to take it to the bank for them. The temptation is too great. Sammy calls Dolly and tells her that he has just made $20,000 easy money, and invites her to beat it to Mexico with him. She agrees, and they start in his car.

"It is a dull day for Ignatz Tamale and his bandits, for no one has been either killed or tortured thus far, since sunrise. When Sammy and Dolly appear in their car, they fall an easy prey to the bandit chief, who decides to hold them for ransom. He sends a wire to the Mayor, telling him that he is holding the secretary and the stenographer. The Mayor and the Chief remember their ten thousand dollars simultaneously. They call out the police, the railroad cops and the aerial patrol and all set out for Mexico.

"Dolly and Sammy are in a room made of steel, the walls of which are gradually closing in on them. The only open wall leads to a pit of flame. They are pushed nearer and nearer the terrible death. As the hours go on and the ransom money does not arrive. At last, just as they are about to skid over the edge, the advance guard of police arrives. The bride is saved from a fiery death, but Sammy is heartlessly left to be pushed over the edge." *Moving Picture Weekly*, June 30, 1917, p.36

REVIEWS: "A two-reel comic which deals with the love affairs of a city mayor and chief of police, each in love with the same girl. Sammy, the office boy, also loves her, and much of the early part of the offering pictures his various antics. The number has an exceptional whirlwind finish, in which a runaway engine, pursued by a handcar, crashes into freight cars, buildings and other things. The movable floor makes a good humorous feature. This runs ahead of the average for this type of production in several respects." *Moving Picture World*, August 18, 1917, p.1087

Hearts and Flour: *Released 07/11/1917 Wednesday.* © 06/30/1917 — 2 reels. DIRECTOR: Dick Smith. CAST: Eva Novak, Charles Ryckman, Thomas Delmar, Robert McKenzie
SYNOPSIS: Ryck, the grocer boy (Ryckman) and Tom, the butcher boy (Delmar) are both in love with Eva, the boss' daughter (Novak). Eva, however, prefers Ryck, which causes no amount of jealousy on Tom's part. A fight ensues nearly destroying the contents of the store, but the boss (McKenzie) intervenes and restores order. Tom goes on to create all sorts of mischief, each time blaming it on Ryck. The boss falls for this, and he and Tom beat up Ryck. Ryck tries to get even by tampering with a wagon that almost leads to Tom's demise, but he is found out and once again Tom and the boss beat up Ryck. Ryck and Eva plan to elope, but her pa finds out and attempts to stop them. Fleeing in a buggy, the couple is pursued by her pa and Tom, but manages to find a minister and get hitched before they can be stopped. Tom, disappointed, beans his boss with a flower pot. Synopsis adapted from the plot summary in *Moving Picture Weekly*, July 7, 1917, p.37
REVIEWS: "This is a rural slapstick comedy in two reels. The grocer boy and the butcher boy both love the boss's daughter. Nearly all the contents of the shop are thrown at someone in the two reels. This picture is full of action." *Moving Picture World*, July 14, 1917, p.258

Surf Scandal: *Released 07/18/1917 Wednesday.* © 07/09/1917 — 2 reels. DIRECTOR: Noel Smith. CAST: Dan Russell, Walter Stephens, Eunice Murdock [Moore], Gladys Varden, Al Edmunston
(pre-release title: **Physical Torture and Mental Culture**)
SYNOPSIS: "The Sand Dow family are at breakfast. The janitor [Stephens], called by his alarm clock, to which he had attached a feather which tickled his feet, slept underneath the tank in the gym and had a trap door through which he emerged. Gladys [Varden] was the belle of the ladies' department, and Al [Edmunston] of the men's. Sand Dow [Russell] flirted with the girls, and Mrs. [Murdock] with the men. At last each had an idea. They called the janitor and told him to bring disguises in which they would look like each other. When they emerged even the janitor was completely fooled.

"It was too hot so they closed the gym and went to the beach. Sand Dow had a wonderful time with the girls, and Mrs. had a lovely time with the men. But the sweethearts were each planning a chance to get together. Each party got into swimming suits as quickly as possible. The men had brought a lunch, but the girls had none, so Sand Dow decided to go fishing. He used his own carcass for bait, and came up with fishes hanging on his person. The janitor was instructed to cook the fish, and the girls sat down to wait. The other party was lunching, and the janitor got mixed and threw the fish to the men instead of the girls.

Sand Dow went to remonstrate and recognized his wife. He snatched Gladys [Varden] and ran. Mrs. decoys Al. He opens a sandwich and puts sand in it, giving it to her. As she sputters he makes a getaway and rejoins Gladys. Sand Dow comes up and fights Al, while Mrs. fights him for Al. The husband and wife recognize each other. [Sand Dow] beats it with Gladys and Mrs. follows. After a chase, the picture ends in a pie fight." *Moving Picture World*, July 21, 1917, p.534

REVIEWS: "A two-reel broad comedy depicting the troubles of a very strong couple. The janitor lives at the bottom of the swimming pool. His exits and entrances are very funny. When wife quarrels with husband because she wants to drive the comedy auto, she tears it apart bit by bit. The second part shows them at an outing at the seashore. This ends with a pie-throwing episode which is somewhat overdone." *Moving Picture World*, July 21, 1917, p.478

"Dan Russell in the role of Sand Dow, a strong man, puts a lot of laughter in this two-reeler, and is ably assisted in his work by a collection of clever gags, instituted by Director Noel Smith and his staff. The action is staged about a swimming tank and the beach, and has a number of pretty girls among those present. The support includes Gladys Varden and Walter Stephens." *Motion Picture News*, July 21, 1917, p.440

Sign of the Cucumber: *Released 07/25/1917 Wednesday.* © 07/19/1917 — 2 reels. DIRECTOR: Richard Smith. CAST: Thomas Delmar, Bob McKenzie, Eva Novak, Chester Ryckman

SYNOPSIS: "Red Nose Pete [Delmar] arrives in town with his pal [McKenzie], planning to rob the bank. Eva [Novak], the daughter of the Justice of the Peace, is in love with Bob Hardboil, the sheriff [also McKenzie]. He has a cucumber birthmark on his arm. He receives a letter saying that Red Nose and his pal are on the way and sees in the enclosed photograph that the pal is his double. But he thinks that his birth mark will protect him.

"Red Nose gets into the safe and finds four dollars. The sheriff calls a posse. Red Nose and his pal fasten a slice of cucumber on the pal's arm. They hold up the sheriff, tie him to a tree, take his clothes, return to the town and are received with joy. The pal locks Red Nose in jail, intending to return and let him out later, when he has safely captured the ten thousand dollar reward. Eva receives the man who she thinks is her hero.

"When the sheriff appears in town he is taken for Red Nose, and is put in jail. Red Nose begins to fear that his pal is not straight with him so he writes a note and sends it to the sheriff. It says that he can prove that the sheriff is what he claims to be if he will help him to escape. They escape by butting down the wall with a negro's head.

"In the meantime the false sheriff is being married to Eva. The real one comes in. The false one discovers that he has lost his cucumber. There is general shooting. The house blows up and the false sheriff with it. The real lovers are reunited." *Moving Picture World*, July 28, 1917, p.689

REVIEWS: "A two-reel character comedy of the burlesque type. This deals with the efforts of Red Nose Pete and his pal, who is a double of the sheriff, to bunco a rural community. The characters are of the 'rube' type and the humor at no time becomes very pronounced. Perhaps the best scenes are toward the close, where there is a chase on horseback and a burro ride in midair. This is just a fair subject." *Moving Picture World*, July 21, 1917, p.478

Blackboard and Blackmail: *Released 08/01/1917 Wednesday.* © 07/23/1917 — 2 reels. DIRECTOR: Vin Moore. CAST: Phil Dunham, Lucille Hutton, Merta Sterling, Charles Inslee, Al Forbes, Queenie Emery
(pre-release title: **Love Behind Bars**)
SYNOPSIS: Mishap (Dunham) is the cook at a boarding house kept by the president (Inslee) of the board of a district school. Mishap's daughter, Baby Mert (Sterling), attends the school and causes all sorts of mischief. When she and her friends torment a teacher, classmate Angelface (Forbes), son of the president, tells his father. The teacher is let go, soon to be replaced by Lucille (Hutton), a vamp from the city whose sole interest in the position is the $1,000 reward for anyone who can tame the school. Mishap falls for Lucille, and the two take a walk. Baby Mert and Angelface are close behind, and play a prank on the two which deposits them in a stream; Mert steals their wet clothes. Mishap fashions a "skirt" out of weeds, and the president gives Lucille his coat which she wears as trousers. Later, Lucille's pal arrives and attempts to break into the president's safe, but is discovered. After Mishap is tossed into the river by the pal and is rescued by Mert and Angelface, Mishap and the president set out after the pal. Mishap and the pal have a rooftop fight, after which Mishap and Lucille elope along with the retrieved stolen money. A crowd follows and corners the couple in the schoolhouse, which they blow up. The crowd is showered with the stolen money. Synopsis adapted from the plot summary in *Moving Picture Weekly,* July 21, 1917, p.17
REVIEWS: "A comic number, most of the scenes in which take place in a country school. The boys and girls are up to all sorts of juvenile tricks. Just a string of entertaining incidents of the knockabout sort, some of which are quite funny. The explosion at the close will get a laugh. Phil Dunham, Merta Sterling and Charles Inslee are in the cast." *Moving Picture World*, August 4, 1917, p.814

"School day burlesque with Phil Dunham and Lucille Hutton leading the cast. The plot concerns the arrival of a new teacher, who in reality is a crook, and Mishap, the cook, who falls in love with her. Wild chase at the end and many gags, the majority of which register throughout the body of the two reels." *Motion Picture News*, August 4, 1917, p.877

The Little Fat Rascal: *Released 08/08/1917 Wednesday.* © 07/26/1917 — 2 reels. DIRECTOR: Vin Moore. CAST: Merta Sterling, Phil Dunham, Al Gerald, Lucille Hutton, Charles Inslee, Al Forbes
(pre-release title: **Country Lanes and City Lairs**)
SYNOPSIS: Country boy Phil Simpleton (Dunham) and neighbor Saucy Mert (Sterling) are in love, but Mert's dad Pop Snodgrass (Inslee) does not like Phil. Tinhorn Ted (Gerald) escapes from jail and hides in a mailbag, which is delivered to Pop Snodgrass's farm. Pop mistakes the crook for an artist, and decides that he should be married to Mert. Phil watches this from afar, and takes steps to thwart any budding romance. When Phil and Mert attempt to elope, Pop catches them and sends Mert off to a girl's school. Ted hooks up with his accomplice, Melba Sundae (Hutton), and having learned that Mert is to be an heiress scheme to kidnap her. Meanwhile, Phil arrives at the school but is promptly thrown out by the mistress. He regains entrance by dressing as a girl, but his ruse is discovered when the mistress attempts to brush his hair, yanking the wig from his head. Ted and Melba kidnap Mert and take her to the city. Phil follows and follows the kidnappers,

appropriating a bike from a cop and rescuing Mert. The two are scooped up on the safety fender of a streetcar. Synopsis adapted from the plot summary in *Moving Picture Weekly*, July 28, 1917, pp.32, 37

REVIEWS: "A two-reel knockabout comedy, featuring Mert Sterling, Phil Dunham and Lucille Hutton. The story concerns a fat girl whose father sends her to a girls' school. Her country lover follows, and enters the school attired in girl's clothing. There is no particular novelty in this number, and the humor is of the rough type. It is all acceptable in its way, but not at all strong. A fair subject." *Moving Picture World*, August 11, 1917, p.959

Rough Stuff: *Released 08/15/1917 Wednesday.* © 08/03/1917 — 2 reels. DIRECTOR: Noel Smith. CAST: Dan Russell, Eunice Murdock, Al Edmundston [sic], Gladys Varden, Walter Stephens
(pre-release title: **A Hotel Mix-Up**)
SYNOPSIS: Mrs. Doehound (Murdock) runs a hotel with an assist from her henpecked husband (Russell). Mr. Potash (Edmundson), a purveyor of fine gowns, arrives at the hotel for a stay with his wife and model (Varden). She flirts with the receptive Mr. Doehound, and her husband announces that he wants to stage a fashion show at the hotel, and to that end he wants Mr. Doehound to hire the best looking women in town to act as models. Which he does, and on the day of the show a buyer and his wife arrive. Doehound grows jealous of the buyer's access to the models, so he decides to impersonate him. Doehound's wife sees through the disguise, however, and isn't happy about it. Meanwhile, a scientist up on the 65th floor is battling a fire caused by an accidental explosion, assisted by the hotel's bell-hop (Stephens). Compounding problems at the hotel is the arrival of the murderous brother of a former employee discharged due to her flirting with Doehound. A general melee breaks out, and ambulances from several hospitals are called in to cart off the various participants. Synopsis adapted from the plot summary in *Moving Picture Weekly*, August 4, 1917, p.32
REVIEWS: "A knockabout number, as the title aptly suggests, featuring Dan Russell, Walter Stephens and Gladys Varden. The former plays a flirtatious hotel proprietor, with a justly suspicious wife. There is some slight vulgarity in this, but nothing really offensive. It has some very funny moments of the rough house order." *Moving Picture World*, August 18, 1917, p.1087

Street Cars and Carbuncles: *Released 08/22/1917 Wednesday.* © 08/10/1917 — 2 reels. DIRECTOR: Dick Smith. CAST: Eddie Barry, Bob McKenzie, Eva Novak, Chester Ryckman, Bert Roach
(pre-release title: **Battered Hearts and Shattered Faces**)
SYNOPSIS: The president (Roach) of a small town, horse-drawn street car is worried about competition from the owner (Ryckman) of a motorized jitney, and urges his conductor (Barry) and motorman (McKenzie) to solicit passengers in any way possible. Their late arrival doesn't bode well, however, as disgruntled customers have already boarded the jitney. They soon debark, however, when it is found that the jitney's gas tank is empty. The competition escalates from there, with passengers "pulled, by threats, breakdowns and promise" from one vehicle to the other. Meanwhile, the motorman's daughter Eva (Novak), who dutifully brings lunch each day for the street car's two employees, finds

herself falling for the jitney driver. An eventual chase ensues between the jitney and street car, ending with the two vehicles heading off a bluff and landing as a pile of debris at its base. Synopsis adapted from the plot summary in *Moving Picture Weekly*, August 11, 1917, p.33

REVIEWS: "A two-reel comic, featuring Bob McKenzie and others. The fun centers around an old horse car, and winds up with a chase, in which various styles of vehicles participate. The comedy is just fair and at no time becomes very funny. Some of the interior sets and costumes are dirty and unattractive. This always mars the humorous effect." *Moving Picture World*, August 25, 1917, p.1235

Props, Drops, and Flops: *Released 08/29/1917 Wednesday.* © 08/17/1917 — 2 reels. DIRECTOR: Noel Smith. CAST: Bert Roach, Gladys Varden, Walter Stephens, Harry Griffith
(pre-release title: **The Prop's Revenge**)
SYNOPSIS: The head prop man (Roach) and his assistant (Stephens) at the U-Funny Theater are both smitten by the arrival of a soubrette (Varden), accompanied by her fiancé, the traveling troupe's manager (Griffith). Mrs. Morris, the company's star, takes a shining to both the prop man and his assistant, with growing annoyance over their lack of interest in her. Come opening night Mrs. Morris moves to steal the spotlight from the soubrette, jealous over the young lady's dalliance with the assistant. The head prop man gets involved and gains the attention of Mrs. Morris, who proceeds to hurl all sorts of dangerous items at him. Fortunately, all of these missiles just miss him. A thrown torch, however, starts a fire and causes a melee, the fire department arriving in time to extinguish the blaze. The soubrette and the chorus "find that they have left little of their original abbreviated wardrobes." Synopsis adapted from the plot summary in *Moving Picture Weekly*, August 18, 1917, p.22

REVIEWS: "A two-reel comic, featuring Gladys Varden, Bert Roach, Walter Stephens and Harry Griffith. The first reel introduces a number of stage hands and some chorus girls behind the scenes of a theater. Some of the incidental business is funny, but none of it is very strong. The action in the second reel is better and holds the attention closely. There is a lot of good knockabout business and a number of interesting features, including the knife throwing and fire scenes. This will succeed with audiences who like plenty of comic action without much plot." *Moving Picture World*, September 1, 1917, p.1390

Backward Sons and Forward Daughters: *Released 09/05/1917 Wednesday.* © 08/24/1917 — 2 reels. DIRECTOR: Phil Dunham. CAST: Billy Bevan, Lucille Hutton
(pre-release title: **A Rural Caesar**)
SYNOPSIS: Billy (Bevan) occupies his days with fishing, but spinster Lucille (Hutton) holds the mortgage to the property his parents dwell on. Lucille visits the parents and offers an ultimatum: either they vacate the property, or offer their son's hand in marriage. They agree to the marriage, but Billy isn't too thrilled with the idea. He takes Lucille for a boat ride, and drops her in the middle of the lake with a stone tied about her throat. He flees for the city, unaware that Lucille has survived the intended drowning. Taking a job in a hash house, Billy falls in love with the proprietor's daughter. One day, Lucille arrives in the joint for a meal. In a panic, Billy fashions a fake moustache to avoid recognition.

Lucille isn't fooled, however, and professes her love for him. He resists, and a battle follows with many dishes and pasta thrown about, the hash house destroyed in the process. Lucille returns to the farm, as does Billy with his bride, the proprietor's daughter. Synopsis adapted from the plot summary in *Moving Picture Weekly*, August 25, 1917, p.20
REVIEWS: "A knockabout comic, in two reels, featuring Billy Bevan and Lucille Hutton. The former plays a country youth in the city, who falls in love with a restaurant cashier. Some of the action in this is funny, but there is not enough plot to hold the attention well. Some of the restaurant scenes are also disgustingly dirty and unattractive. The number is below this company's average." *Moving Picture World*, September 8, 1917, p.1526

From Cactus to Kale: *Released 09/12/1917 Wednesday.* © 08/31/1917 — 2 reels. DIRECTOR: Noel Smith. CAST: Gladys Varden, Walter Stephens, Harry Griffith, Bert Roach, Katherine Young
(pre-release title: **A Western Romance**)
SYNOPSIS: Restaurant waitress Gladys (Varden) is a bit too friendly with customer Walter (Stephens) for the cook's taste, and a fight follows that nearly demolishes the place. Meanwhile, crooks Miss Young and Harry (Griffith) connive to steal some precious papers, chloroforming their carrier and tossing him from the train he's on. They take their ill-gotten gains and head for town where they meet Walter, and learn that he is heir to a fortune. Using him as a dupe, they take him to the city and set him up as master of a house filled with strange inmates. One of them gives Walter the combination to a safe, then falls over dead. The two crooks gain access to the combination and rob the safe, during which time the fellow from whom they stole the precious papers arrives in town. He joins up with Walter and Gladys to pursue the crooks in a wild race through the streets that leads to the destruction of several buildings before ending up in the middle of the ocean. Synopsis adapted from the plot summary in *Moving Picture Weekly*, September 1, 1917, p.32
REVIEWS: "A two-reel comedy number that has a quite fast and furious finish. There is not much to the earlier parts of the picture, the scenes of which are devoted mostly to a restaurant where the Weasel starts things. When the Weasel inherits money and comes to the city he starts some more things. The chase that finishes the picture is a good one. During the course of it an auto plunges into the sea. A fair comedy of its type." *Moving Picture World*, September 15, 1917, p.1709

A Prairie Chicken: *Released 09/19/1917 Wednesday.* © 09/08/1917 — 2 reels. DIRECTOR: Vin Moore. CAST: Merta Sterling, Kathleen Emerson, Al Forbes, Fay Holderness, Al Edmundson
(pre-release titles: **Railroad Ties That Bind** [unconfirmed] and **From Ranch to Riches**)
SYNOPSIS: Mert (Sterling), the Prairie Chicken, is sent by her father Hank out East to stay with her aunt, Mrs. De Coin (Holderness). Mert's a cowgirl at heart, and arrives riding upon the radiator of a car, decked out in wide-brimmed cowboy hat, chaps and flannel shirt, a six-gun in each hand. Mrs. De Coin and her daughter Kathleen (Emerson) are horrified, but son Algernon (Forbes) is intrigued. They attempt to "civilize" her by dressing her in more "proper" clothes, but Mert insist on wearing her guns over them. Count Notta Cent (Edmundson) schemes to kidnap Kathleen, but Mert intercedes, beats up

the count, and rescues her cousin. Mrs. De Coin is elated, and gives her blessing to the marriage of son Algernon to Mert. The day of the big wedding Mert finds her hoop skirt uncomfortable, so she changes into her chaps. Mrs. De Coin catches her servants robbing her safe, and a chase leads to the rooftop where the thief drops the jewels down a drain pipe, the baubles landing in Mert's lap. Mert joins in the chase, catching him atop a rising drawbridge. She ropes him, returns the jewels to her aunt, then plunges the thief into the river and a watery grave. Synopsis adapted from the plot summary in *Moving Picture Weekly*, September 8, 1917, p.11

REVIEWS: "Myrta [sic] Sterling is featured in this two-reel comic, playing the part of a fat, roly-poly Western girl who goes East to visit relatives. She shocks the effete Easterners with her uncouth ways, and some amusing situations result. This is free from offense and is well up to the average of this company's productions." *Moving Picture World*, September 22, 1917, p.1861

Soapsuds and Sirens: *Released 09/26/1917 Wednesday.* © 09/14/1917 — 2 reels. DIRECTOR: Noel Smith. CAST: Harry Lorraine, Walter Stephens, Bert Roach, Gladys Varden, Jimmy Finlayson

SYNOPSIS: Dance teacher Prof. Thinem (Lorraine) doesn't have a very successful business. When an overweight customer named Babee — "Longs to be a dancing fairy" — comes for some lessons, she is sent packing after the floor gives way and she's deposited into the pool below. The building's janitor Nibbs (Stephens) rescues her and decides to help out, cutting a slit in Babee's purse and then collecting her falling change by the gum stuck to the bottom of his shoe. He presents the change to Prof. Thinem who can now afford to have some hand-bills printed. He sends Nibbs to Mr. Printum (Roach) to have the hand-bills printed. Mrs. Printum (Varden), a devotee of dancing, dances in the room above the print shop, but the weakened floor gives way, depositing her onto the press below, and depositing Printum into a barrel of printer's ink. The hand-bill ad gets printed upon the back of his wife's dress. It reads: "Prof Thinem — Nature and Muscle Dancing — First Two Lessons FREE," the word "FREE" printed square across her bottom. The barrel with her husband falls over and rolls through the wall and down the street, his wife and Nibbs close behind in pursuit. The barrel smashes into a hydrant and the force of the gushing water propels it onto the electrical wires above. Nibbs climbs the pole and frees the barrel, which is scooped up by a passing streetcar. Nibbs and the wife finally release Printum. The imprinted ad on her backside works, though, and soon Thinem's studio is filled with new pupils. Printum, having again fallen into a barrel of printer's ink, resumes his chase. His wife trades clothes with Nibbs in an attempt to elude her hubby. The scantily clad pupils now mistake Nibbs for a woman, and Mrs. Printum for Nibbs, forcing the latter out into the cold. Mrs. Printum and Nibbs end up exchanging clothes again, as Mr. Printum grows increasingly confused as to who is who. They all end up in the park lake. Synopsis based on print held by the Library of Congress along with the plot summary in *Moving Picture Weekly*, September 15, 1917, pp.19, 23

REVIEWS: "A two-reel comic, featuring Bert Roach, Gladys Varden, Walter Stephens and Harry Lorraine. The settings are good, particularly the print shop and dancing school, but several attempts at humor are unfortunately suggestive. Cutting out certain scenes would leave this a fairly good subject." *Moving Picture World*, October 6, 1917, p.74

Counting Out the Count: *Released 10/03/1917 Wednesday.* © 09/20/1917 — 2 reels. DIRECTOR: Phil Dunham. CAST: Billy Bevan, Lucille Hutton (pre-release titles: **High Class Nonsense**, **Entangled Tanglements** and **Complicated Complications**)
SYNOPSIS: Lucille (Hutton) finds that her parents want her to marry the Count de Fromage, who will be arriving shortly. She runs away to the farm of her aunt, uncle, and cousin Bill (Bevan). Her parents follow with the count, and Lucille enlists Bill's aid in thwarting the count, but to no avail. The wedding plans are set in motion. On the big day, the guests are assembled and await the bride's arrival. Lucille changes clothes with one of the footmen, and sends him down for the ceremony. Meanwhile, Bill overpowers the count, tears off his moustache, and disguises himself as the count. He takes the groom's place at the ceremony, not realizing that his bride-to-be is actually the footman. A detective arrives intending to arrest the count. Lucille is gloating over the deception about to be played on the count when she recognizes his feet as those of Bill. She tears the veil from the footman/bride, the real count is arrested, and Bill and Lucille are married. Synopsis adapted from the plot summary in *Moving Picture Weekly*, September 22, 1917, p.32
REVIEWS: "This number, which features Lucille Hutton and Billy Bevan, combines some of the elements of straight comedy and slap-stick humor. The scenes on the country estate are attractively pictured, and the house settings are also good. The story tells the way in which the girl's country cousin outwits a count in winning her hand. The subject is quite pleasing in certain respects; the humor is moderately strong." *Moving Picture World*, October 6, 1017, p.74; reviewed as **High-Class Nonsense**

The Nurse of an Aching Heart: *Released 10/10/1917 Wednesday.* © 09/27/1917 — 2 reels. DIRECTOR: Archie Mayo. CAST: Eddie Barry, Bob McKenzie, Eva Novak, Chester Ryckman, Kathryne Young
SYNOPSIS: Nurse Eva (Novak) has the patients of Dr. Bones' hospital out in the park for an airing. Mr. Winkledinkle (Barry), a typical park Johnnie, takes a shining to her and begins a flirtation. Dr. Bones (McKenzie) arrives and intercedes, leading to an altercation that ends with Bones, Winkledinkle, and an elderly wheel chair-bound patient ending up in the lake. Later, when the group returns to the hospital, Winkledinkle determines to get into the building to once again see Eva. After numerous failed attempts, he's accidentally hit by a Ford and his wish comes true. Admitted to the hospital, Dr. Bones spots his nemesis from the park and vows revenge. Eva attempts to hide Winkledinkle, who eventually seeks refuge in a hospital bed. Unfortunately, the bed's former occupant was to be operated on, and Winkledinkle is hauled into surgery. Winkledinkle seizes Eva and sets up a sail on the operating table, sailing out of the hospital and down a hill with the hospital force in close pursuit. Eva and Winkledinkle arrive at the docks in time to board a steamer about to set sail. They wave farewell to Dr. Bones. Synopsis adapted from the plot summary in *Moving Picture Weekly*, September 29, 1917, p.20
REVIEWS: "An extremely laughable number of the burlesque knockabout type, featuring Eddie Barry as a gay Lothario who falls in love with a hospital nurse. His efforts to gain admission to the hospital and final success are very funny. The scenes and settings are

bright and attractive, the characters are amusing and the action, while slightly rough in places, brings much laughter. A very successful offering of the type." *Moving Picture World*, October 13, 1917, p.253

Vamping Reuben's Millions: *Released 10/17/1917 Wednesday.* © 10/05/1917 — 2 reels. DIRECTOR: Richard Smith. CAST: Bob McKenzie, Chester Ryckman, Eddie Barry, Eva Novak, Harry Lorraine, Katherine Young
(pre-release title: **A Comedy Vampire**)
SYNOPSIS: Jockey Dub L. Cross (Ryckman) is hated by Jim Nastic (Barry), a farmhand who works for farmer Reuben (McKenzie); Cross rides Reuben's horse in the races. Nastic is ill-treated by everyone at the farm, including Reuben's daughter Eva (Novak). Nastic schemes to get Cross fired so that Nastic can take his place, and to that end hangs weights beneath Cross' saddle. Nastic gets his wish, but Cross swears revenge, rigging the scales so that Nastic is disqualified for being overweight. Eva now offers to ride Reuben's horse. Foiled, Cross decides to expose Reuben's illegal bookie site, and engages the services of Miss Gettem (Young), to vamp Reuben and then expose him to the police. The joint is raided, but Reuben escapes in a Ford with bicycle-mounted police in hot pursuit. "Numerous houses were torn down and many citizens maimed before the prey was caught." Synopsis adapted from the plot summary in *Moving Picture Weekly,* October 6, 1917, p.18
REVIEWS: "A two-reel comic of the burlesque type, featuring Bob McKenzie, Eva Novak, Catherine Young and others. The scenes at the Jazztown race track, the farmer-hero who plows with a sail and the later events in which the vampire lady gets the rich old man's roll are all amusing and quite successful for this style of humor. One or two short scenes border on vulgarity, but there is nothing really offensive. The offering as a whole, is a commendable one." *Moving Picture World*, November 3, 1917, p.713

Fat and Furious: *Released 10/24/1917 Wednesday.* © 10/12/1917 — 2 reels. DIRECTOR: Vin Moore. CAST: Merta Sterling, Ted Howland, Al Forbes, Babe Emerson, Russ Powell, Blanche Rose
(pre-release title: **Sunday in Last Chance Valley** [unconfirmed])
SYNOPSIS: Mert (Sterling), the station agent, is in love with foreman Al (Forbes). Her father (Powell) is an engineer. Terrible Ted (Howland) arrives in town with intentions of robbing the station's safe, planning to get into it while Mert is outside flagging the train. Mert catches Ted and his gang in the act, so they lock her in a trunk and load it on a passing train. Al and Babe (Emerson), the local soda jerk, set out on a handcar to rescue Mert. When the train arrives in the big city, the trunk and its contents are taken to a room where Mert is imprisoned. Al and Babe show up, and Mert spots them from her window. She sends them a note in a water pitcher, and Al responds by a bow and arrow borrowed from a passing kid. She makes the escape by rope, the stolen money in hand, and the three of them head back to the station on the handcar. Ted and gang follow in a car, and attempt to overpower the trio with chloroform. Mert throws Ted from the train, and returns triumphant with the stolen money. Synopsis adapted from the plot summary in *Moving Picture Weekly,* October 13, 1917, p.16
REVIEWS: "A two-reel comic number, featuring Merta Sterling and others. She plays the girl at a country railroad station, which is robbed by a gang of thieves. The loot is recovered

by the girl and her lover, who is section foreman. The action is fast and furious in this, particularly in the second reel. The humor is fairly strong in spots and the number as a whole is an enjoyable one of the type." *Moving Picture World*, October 27, 1917, p.526

Even As Him and Her: *Released 10/31/1917 Wednesday.* © 10/19/1917 — 2 reels. DIRECTOR: Phil Dunham. CAST: Billy Bevan, Lucille Hutton, Fred Starr, Fay Holderness, Phil Dunham, Peggy Prevost, Porter Strong
SYNOPSIS: "They eloped and the new Mrs. Snookums [Hutton] telephones her parents, Mr. and Mrs. Lampem [Starr and Holderness], and Ma says: 'Lucille has just married a man we have never seen. Isn't it scandalous?'

"To which Pa answers: 'Well, you did the same thing and you didn't pick such a lemon.' That is the start of a quarrel, and Mrs. Lampem goes out in a huff. The bride soon finds evidence that her hubby [Bevan] had a lovely time before his marriage. She resolves to flirt, too, since that is his taste, and she tries it on the butler, and then goes to the park.

"Out in the park, Mr. and Mrs. Spifflegoofer [Dunham and Prevost] are also having a spat, during which Mr. S. absorbs the family roll. Mrs. Lampem strolls by, and Phil Spifflegoofer follows her, she appeals to the bridegroom, Bill, who also happens to be in the park, and Bill punches Phil. Pa Lampem also seeks the fresh air, and meets Mrs. Phil, with whom he starts a flirtation. Lucille joins the party, and starts flirting with a strange man, who turns out to be a detective [Strong, as Gluck McGlook]. He threatens and she flees, scared of cops from that moment on.

"In the meantime Pa Lampem has taken Mrs. Spifflegoofer to a cafe for some refreshment, and Bill has done the same with Mrs. Lampem. Phil and Lucille find themselves on the same bench in the park, and make eyes at each other. He invites her to the same cafe. When the three couples, all matched up wrong, meet in the same place, there is a general rush for cover. Ma gets under one table, Bill under another, Pa under a third, and Mrs. Spifflegoofer under a fourth. The detective comes crawling in seeking evidence and Phil dives under a fifth table. They shift, and meet each other, and there are general introductions all round. The proper husbands sort out their proper wives, and poor Phil ends his adventure in the cafe fountain." *Moving Picture World*, November 3, 1917, pp.751-752

Double Dukes: *Released 11/07/1917 Wednesday.* © 10/29/1917 — 2 reels. DIRECTOR: Richard Smith and Archie Mayo. CAST: Eddie Barry, Robert McKenzie, Eva Novak, Chester Ryckman, Pat Randy
(pre-release titles: **The Golfers** and **Tickled to De-Feet** [unconfirmed])
SYNOPSIS: Golf enthusiast Sir Muchdoe (McKenzie) receives a telegram informing him that Duke Mixture and Lord Salisbury are expected as guests. He is delighted, but his daughter Eva (Novak) is not, she being in love with Chester (Ryckman), who sells soft drinks at the course. Nibbs De Hobo (Barry) and Nobbs De Bum (Randy) see the telegram and are inspired to pose as the two noblemen. Stealing some golfing togs, they present themselves as Mixture and Salisbury. Muchdoe is delighted, and takes his two guests golfing. New to the sport, their attempts are feeble, and Chester's substitution of eggs for the golf balls doesn't help. Chester is suspicious of the two noblemen, and on the night of the party Chester hires two roughnecks to impersonate two statues that are to be presented

to Muchdoe. When Chester hears Muchdoe announce the engagement of Eva to Duke Mixture, he takes steps to discredit the two noblemen. He has the two roughnecks dress up and pretend to be the real noblemen, and challenge the pretenders to a duel. This doesn't get too far, as the two genuine noblemen arrive with credentials that prove their identities. The four bogus noblemen are kicked out, and Chester embraces Eva. Synopsis adapted from the plot summary in *Moving Picture Weekly*, October 27, 1917, p.20

REVIEWS: "A two-reel comic, featuring Eva Novak, Eddie Barry, Bob McKenzie and others. The action concerns two alleged dukes, who are fond of playing golf. Two hobos, after posing as statues at a lawn party, impersonate the real dukes in order to show up the imposters. There is not much that is new in this plot and the humor is not particularly strong. It is free from offense and makes a subject of fair strength." *Moving Picture World*, November 10, 1917, p.881

Hula Hula Hughie: *Released 11/14/1917 Wednesday.* © 11/02/1917 — 2 reels. DIRECTOR: James D. Davis and Noel Smith. CAST: Hughie Mack, Rae Godfrey, Eva Novak
SYNOPSIS: Hughie [Mack] and his wife take their daughter to the beach. The child goes in for a dip while no one is looking, and the sleepy lifeguard takes her place in her now empty wagon. Meanwhile, Hughie and Purity League head Judge Knott are elsewhere, flirting with some young ladies. The wagon rolls into the sea and Hughie panics, thinking his daughter is in it. His wife spots their actual daughter who is in swimming and, thinking her drowning, enlists the aid of the lifeguard to haul her in. Later, the beach lovelies convince Hughie to dress in a seaweed skirt and perform a rigorous hula dance that eventually leaves him exhausted. The Purity League arrives and has the whole bunch arrested, but when they are hauled into court they recognize Judge Knott; a threat of exposure results in their immediate release. The prettiest girl writes Hughie a note asking him to meet her at the beach that night, and takes advantage of his absence to attempt to rob his house. He returns and finds her there, but when his wife returns he hides her in the bedroom. The wife has brought the lifeguard home with her, so Hughie picks a fight with the fellow. Hughie's daughter comes in and asks for the pretty lady who was there, so his wife expects the worst; she calls in the cops. Synopsis adapted from the plot summary in *Moving Picture Weekly*, November 3, 1917, p.14

REVIEWS: "A two-reel comic of the knockabout sort. There is a note of vulgarity running through many scenes which keep this from becoming really humorous; it is too much like a return to the crude efforts of the early comics. The boat load of 'Water Police' is a good feature, but the fat man's flirtations and the beach scenes generally are too suggestive. This is only a fair subject and will hardly please critical audiences." *Moving Picture World*, November 17, 1917, p.1038

The Joy Riders: *Released 11/21/1917 Wednesday.* © 11/15/1917 — 2 reels. DIRECTOR: Phil Dunham and Frank Howard Clark. CAST: Phil Dunham, Billy Bevan, Lucille Hutton, Robert McKenzie
(pre-release title: **The Judge's Revenge**)
SYNOPSIS: Phil (Dunham) is a speed demon, racing about town in his tiny little car. Lucille (Hutton), daughter of a judge (McKenzie), has a love of speed as well, and presses her poor father to buy her a car. In need of money, the judge pursues the rich widow next door.

She entrusts him with her expensive watch, asking him to take it to the jeweler's to have it repaired. He gets sidetracked, however, and forgets about the watch, leaving it on the table. Meanwhile, daughter Lucille goes for a ride with Phil. Her boyfriend Bill (Bevan) shows up at her house and takes the watch and gets mixed up in a chase with Phil. The watch is stolen several times, and when the widow demands its return, the judge cannot produce it. Bill has been involved in a lengthy chase after the watch, and finally returns with it, handing it over to the widow. Peace is restored. Synopsis adapted from the plot summary in *Moving Picture Weekly*, November 10, 1917, p.21

REVIEWS: "Like all of the popular comedy subjects turned out by L-Ko girls and lots of 'em, in more or less daring costumes and stunts, constitute an attractive adjunct to the onrushing incidents. Mr. Dunham has combined his experience as a comedian with his inventiveness as a director in preparing numerous situations of an unusual sort, depending upon surprises and ridiculous situations, according to L-Ko's publicity man, to advance the frail plot to a more or less plausible solution." *Moving Picture World*, November 17, 1917, p.1051

"A funny knockabout number, featuring Phil Dunham, Lucille Hutton and Bob MacKenzie [sic]. Phil's little runabout brings numerous laughs, being so tractable that it will perform almost any feat. The action in this is free from offense, and the interest is carried along without a break. The plot is of a nonsensical sort and not very much in evidence. The number is a good one of its type." *Moving Picture World*, November 24, 1917, p.1192

The Kid Snatchers: *Released 11/28/1917 Wednesday.* © 11/17/1917 — 2 reels. DIRECTOR: Archie Mayo. CAST: Eddie Barry, Gladys Varden, Bert Roach, Eva Southern, Charles Larkin, Ed Lowry, Robert McKenzie
(pre-release titles: **Cute Kids and Kidsnatchers** and **Gee! What a Mix-up**)
SYNOPSIS: Gladys Zell (Varden) is the pretty young nurse at a day nursery run but older Dr. Soakem (McKenzie). When Soakem spots Simple Jinx (Barry) the janitor flirting with Gladys, and Gladys returning his affections, jealous Soakem promptly fires Jinx. Undeterred, Jinx climbs into a baby carriage, impersonates an infant, and with the assistance of Fatty Lard gains access to the nursery. Meanwhile, Mrs. Washington Mint deposits her little heiress daughter at the nursery. The underworld has its eyes on the little girl, and a gang headed by Terrible Ike arrives in a milk wagon and kidnaps her. Jinx overhears their plan but both he and Gladys are captured and imprisoned near a barrel of dynamite. It's rigged to explode when a burning candle reaches a thread tied to it. Mrs. Mint discovers that her daughter is missing, and accompanied by Soakem rescues Jinx and Gladys in the nick of time. Undaunted, the gang pursues in a Ford, recapturing Gladys. Jinx makes a mad bicycle dash to a bridge where he manages to lasso and rescue both Gladys and the little girl. Synopsis adapted from the plot summary in *Moving Picture World*, December 8, 1917, p.1546

REVIEWS: "A two-reel comedy of the knockabout, nonsensical type, in which a number of children take part. The scenes begin in a day nursery, run by Dr. Perr. The milk man, in love with the nurse, decides to kidnap both the girl and a little child heiress. There is a chase which develops some humorous moments. This should have quite an appeal to children. The situations are not rough, but merely ridiculous." *Moving Picture World*, December 1, 1917, p.1342

A Hero for a Minute: *Released 12/05/1917 Wednesday.* © 11/26/1917 — 2 reels. DIRECTOR: Robert Kerr. CAST: Bobby Dunn, Katheryn Young, Edgar Kennedy, Peggy Prevost, Hank Mann
SYNOPSIS: "Kid Cameraflage [Dunn], the Chief's chauffeur, was secretly married to the maid [Prevost]. She had promised to take good care of him before he married her, but everything was different now, for he was made to do the menial work and became a full-fledged kitchen mechanic to meet the high cost of living. The Chief and his wife were happy. They had a battle every other minute. The Chief [Kennedy] gets an order from the Mayor, advising him that all blackhanders must be clean-shaven. This aggravates one of the blackhanders, who picks himself out a well-fed bomb, and wends his weary way to the office of the Mayor.

"Kid Cameraflage, whose duties varied, was lining up the cuspidors, when he spied the bomb nestling in one of them. Every one looked on to see the Kid's finish, but picking the bomb up he flung it out the window, hitting the blackhanders, and saved the day. 'You're fired!' said the Mayor to the Chief. 'You're hired!' said the Mayor to the Kid, 'You're chauffeur!' said the Kid to the Chief, and so the Chief became the chauffeur, while the chauffeur became the chief. Returning home, the ex-chauffeur and the maid took possession of the Chief's house. Kid Cameraflage fell asleep in Mrs. Chief's [Young] room. The maid tried to detain the Chief by fainting in his arms. Friend wife, seeing her husband's arms full of maid, entered her room, and she found the Kid trembling in her clothes closet. Thereupon she, too, fainted. The ex-Chief's bullets send the Kid to the roof, but they all drop through the skylight and land back where they came from. Explanations are in order, and the Kid relinquishes his right to Chiefdom." *Moving Picture World*, December 15, 1917, p.1675
REVIEWS: "A two-reel comic, featuring Bobby Dunn, Catherine Young and others. The chauffeur is secretly married to the maid, both being employed by the flirtatious chief of police and his wife. The 'Blackhanders' threaten to blow up the police station, and this is attempted. The chauffeur and the chief exchange identities temporarily. The incidents in the chief's bedroom are broadly humorous, though not offensive. There are some funny knockabout incidents in this and the close is quite amusing. It is well up to average." *Moving Picture World*, December 8, 1917, p.1486

Deep Seas and Desperate Deeds: *Released 12/12/1917 Wednesday.* © 12/03/1917 — 2 reels. DIRECTOR: Vin Moore. CAST: Merta Sterling, Al Forbes, Russell Powell, Babe Emerson
SYNOPSIS: Merta (Sterling), of Chicken Center, receives word from her sweetheart (Forbes): He's been taken prisoner by the bank robbers who have escaped on board a ship. The captain has received word that the thieves are on board, so he orders a search of the vessel. The thieves get word of this, so they hide the money in the suite of the bank president who also happens to be on board; having escaped during a gambling raid, he decided on an impromptu vacation. The president finds the money and hides it in the smokestack, but his wife witnesses this and decides to take the money for herself. Meanwhile, Merta has arrived on the boat and gives chase when she spots the woman with the money. The woman jumps overboard and Merta follows, and at the bottom of the sea Merta gains possession of the money. Merta returns the money to its rightful owner, rescues her sweetheart, and promises to marry him at

the earliest opportunity. Synopsis adapted from the plot summary in *Moving Picture Weekly*, December 1, 1917, p.20

REVIEWS: "A two-reel comic, featuring Merta Sterling and Al Forbes. The girl plays a milkmaid who drives a wagon into the city, and the latter is a janitor in love with her. The janitor is shanghaied and the girl climbs hand-over-hand to where the vessel passes under a rope. The makes a good stunt and certain of the situations get up considerable humor as they occur. The number provides a fair amount of entertainment." *Moving Picture World*, December 15, 1917, p.1649

Bullets and Boneheads: *Released 12/19/1917 Wednesday.* © 12/06/1917 — 2 reels. DIRECTOR: Craig Hutchinson. CAST: Dave Morris, Gladys Tennyson, Rube Miller (pre-release title: **Shot in the Excitement**)
SYNOPSIS: Liberty Bell (Tennyson), the beauty of Mushroom Manor, is in love with G. Wattaface (Morris), the town pharmacy's soda jerk. Her father, Blew Bell (Miller) will have none of this. Wattaface and Liberty elope to Allaboola, where General Beetlebuzzer takes a shining to Liberty. When Wattaface objects to this, Beetlebuzzer instructs his army of seven to eliminate Wattaface and kidnap Liberty. Liberty sends a telegram to her father, imploring him to get the army and navy to come to the rescue. The troops arrive along with her father, who accidentally saves Beetlebuzzer. A stray bomb resolves the issue, blowing up both father and Beetlebuzzer. Synopsis adapted from the plot summary in *Moving Picture World*, December 29, 1917, p.1999

Ambrose's Icy Love: *Released 12/26/1917 Wednesday.* © 12/14/1917 — 2 reels. DIRECTOR: William S. Fredericks. CAST: Mack Swain, Rae Godfrey, Jack Perrin
SYNOPSIS: "The two hundred pounds of Ambrose [Swain] was his mother's pride and joy. But his employer, Jack Frost [Perrin], froze him with every look because he loved Rosabelle [Godfrey]. Jack Frost most appropriately was in the ice business. He discovered Ambrose's secret vice — chocolates — the curse of his otherwise perfect manhood, and substituting brandied ones, he started Ambrose on a joy ride on a cake of ice. When Ambrose came to, he not only was disgraced, but the workmen were on strike. 'Give us a steam-heated ice-house,' they demanded. But Ambrose, who was foreman of the cold storage plant, believed in cold comfort. He fired them, and of course they had to have revenge. Another of Ambrose's cute little tricks was a hickory correspondence tree. Jack Frost knew this, and put a decoy letter in the old hickory, apparently from Rosabelle, asking Ambrose to meet her at three o'clock. In the meantime Frost had abducted Rosabelle and chained her to a cake of ice in his ice-house. When Ambrose discovered the perfidy he got so much speed up on the old Ford that he couldn't stop, and bored right through the ice-house." *Moving Picture World*, January 5, 1918, p.138

REVIEWS: "A two-reel comic, featuring Mack Swain in his familiar character of Ambrose. The knockabout action is very funny at times and the leading characterization is laughable as usual. Ambrose is foreman of an ice house. An abduction, a bomb and a bear are features of the number. A good subject of the type." *Moving Picture World*, December 29, 1017, p.1962

1918 Releases:

Cannibals and Carnivals: *Released 01/02/1918 Wednesday.* © 12/21/1917 — 2 reels. DIRECTOR: Vin Moore. CAST: Merta Sterling, Al Forbes, Russell Powell, Babe Emerson, Queenie Emery
SYNOPSIS: "Spareribs Alvicious [Forbes] and Little Spring Fever [Sterling] were sweethearts, and their papas were friendly old hayseeds. This busy quartette hiked themselves over to the Zig Zag Circus. After gallivanting around, the sweethearts finally forsook their papas and went canoeing. They suddenly found themselves in Hula-land, surrounded by Hickydoolas. The Hicky King took a sudden flight into Little Spring Fever's heart.

"The King commanded Little Spring Fever to become his bride, but she was obdurate and would not consent, so the King grew revengeful and ordered Spareribs cooked, baked and served on a platter.

"The object of her love was tied to a tree, but Little Spring Fever uprooted the tree and carried her lover away from the mob, but they were followed, and down the side of a steep mountain went the Hula jitney. This almost broke the lover's heart, so he parachuted down the mountain after her. They were a tough bunch, and as hard to get rid of as the smallpox, but the determined pair gave them the slip, and awoke on the knees of their papas." *Moving Picture World*, January 12, 1918, pp.280-281
REVIEWS: "A two-reel comic, featuring Merta Sterling, Al Forbes and Russ Powell. The number contains much amusing nonsense, picturing the adventures of a young country couple at a county fair. They visit the various amusement concessions and then fall asleep in a canoe and dream they have been captured by a band of cannibals. The humor consists of little tricks and mishaps. Children will undoubtedly like this number." *Moving Picture World*, January 5, 1918, p.99

Torpedo Pirates: *Released 01/09/1918 Wednesday.* © 12/29/1917 — 2 reels. DIRECTOR: Noel Smith. CAST: Hughie Mack, Gladys Varden, Harry Lorraine, Walter Stephens, Catherine Young
SYNOPSIS: Prof. P. Nutt (Lorraine) has invented a flying torpedo worth millions. His happiness is compromised by his daughter's (Varden) crush on his assistant (Mack). The president of the Midnight Thieves' Association wants to get his hands on the torpedo, so he hires a vamp (Young) to go to work on the professor. The vamp conspires to make the professor jealous by flirting with the assistant, which has the desired effect. A terrible storm rolls in, and the thieves use this as cover for their planned theft, but are thwarted by the detective (Stevens) hired by the professor when he got wind of the group's plans. The detective commandeers the torpedo and takes flight, but is eventually rescued by the professor, his daughter, and the assistant. Synopsis adapted from the plot summary in *Moving Picture World*, January 19, 1918, p.418
REVIEWS: "A two-reel comic, directed by Noel Smith. This features Hughie Mack as the rotund hero. He is employed as assistant to Mr. Nutt, who has invented a flying torpedo, and is in love with the daughter. The action is an amusing knockabout character, and has to do with the theft of the torpedo. This contains some funny moments and has a lively chase, on land and in the water, at the close." *Moving Picture World*, January 12, 1918, p.246

Home Run Ambrose: *Released 01/16/1918 Wednesday.* © 01/08/1918 — 2 reels. DIRECTOR: William S. Fredericks. CAST: Mack Swain, Rae Godfrey
(pre-release title: **Baseball Ambrose**)
SYNOPSIS: "Home Run Ambrose [Swain], besides weighing 300 pounds, was over the draft age, but mother still fashioned the child-prodigy to suit her whims. Now, this child was in love with Nell [Godfrey], the village bell, who made up her mind to marry a college man, so mamma mortgaged her bakery shop to send Ambrose to Cornyell College. When Ambrose was conducted to his room by the boys he felt like a million dollars, but during the night, when he was awakened by the shrill cry of a woman in distress he felt more like two cents. It was the president's wife — she saw Ambrose reposing on her bed, and proceeded to 'ventilate' her emotions.

"At a reception given by the Eta Bita Pie Society, Ambrose 'borrowed' Cherry Blossom's dress-suit. 'That's my suit — take it off,' growled Cherry Blossom, one of We boys, to Ambrose, just as Ambrose was about to kiss Nell. This enraged Ambrose beyond repair, and he swore vengeance against the sassy gink, so that the next day at the baseball tournament Ambrose hit the bean-ball right square into a paste-board sign, enabling him to walk home several times, and winning for himself the enmity of Cherry Blossom, the love of his sweetheart and the $500 reward which he used to yank the mortgage off the old homestead. The wedding bells will ring yet." *Moving Picture World*, January 26, 1918, p.578
REVIEWS: "An unusually funny L-Ko, featuring Mack Swain. He helps his mother at home with the cooking, and later goes to 'Cornyell' College. The kitchen scenes are full of amusing small business, and the later events at college are also laughable. Ambrose gets into an entanglement with the president's wife, but redeems himself at the ball game, where he knocks a home run. A very good subject." *Moving Picture World*, January 19, 1918, p.386

Ash-Can Alley: *Released 01/23/1918 Wednesday.* © 01/11/1918 — 2 reels. DIRECTOR: Richard Smith. CAST: Eva Novak, Eddie Barry, Robert McKenzie, Eva Heazlett McKenzie, Pop Jones, Chester Ryckman, Harry Lorraine
SYNOPSIS: "O'Malley [McKenzie] was a bricklayer, and when he fell heir to thirty million dollars, he had a violent attack of social aspiration for himself and his daughter [Novak, as Sally], and nothing would do but he must marry the Widow Sofia Soapsud [Heazlett], and that his daughter must marry a duke.

"But the villains conspired with Wun Lung Woo to marry the daughter and secure the fortune. Wun Lung Woo practiced the gentle art of laundry in the front part of his shop, and the exact science of torture in the torture chamber in the rear. He had various devices such as mechanical beating apparatus, feather ticklers for the soles of the feet, and a wash-wringer adapted to taking the starch out of victims. But the victims survived the ordeals of this torture chamber, and came through triumphantly to the usual movie finale — a wedding, with all of the fuss that Ash-Can Alley could kick up." *Moving Picture World*, February 2, 1918, p.725
REVIEWS: "A two-reel comic which makes an amusing study of alley types, including Grandpop Soapsuds and family, a Chinese laundryman, Sally O'Malley and her lover, and two villains. The banquet, attended in borrowed finery, makes a good feature, and the kidnapping and torture of the hero is funny. There are some laughable knockabout situations and a wild chase at the close." *Moving Picture World*, January 26, 1918, p.531

Barberous Plots: *Released 01/30/1918 Wednesday.* © 01/17/1918 — 2 reels. DIRECTOR: James D. Davis and Robert Kerr. CAST: Hughie Mack, Bobby Dunn, Eva Novak, Katheryn Young, Dick Smith, Gladys Varden

SYNOPSIS: "The establishment of Dr. Beautifier contained everything essential to personal adornment and comfort. It was a hotel, beauty parlor, manicure shop, barber shop, bootblack establishment, swimming pool and gymnasium, and Herr Cutt, the barber, ran a side line for the boss, which gave more revenue than all of the other sources combined. Through the magic force of a wink, the atomizer suddenly produced the satisfaction of a Scotch highball. So many customers came in for atomizer treatment only, that the detectives got wise and tried to get evidence on the boss. Dr. Beautifier thereupon made a present of the shop to Herr Cutt.

"It would have gone hard with this innocent grafter had not Mrs. Poodle, the janitor's wife, decided to adopt the beauty treatment. Dr. Beautifier's wife thought that she ought to have an exhibit of the before-and-after type, so she started to take Mrs. Poodle's picture before. The detective, not knowing what he was walking into, and detecting Mrs. Poodle in next to nothing, made an excellent blackmail photograph. After a 60-horsepower series of incidents, in which the photograph changed hands a dozen times, the detectives, the boss, Poodle's wife and Herr Cutt decided to call it a day and forget about it. *Moving Picture Weekly*, January 19, 1918, p.38

REVIEWS: "A comic number in two reels featuring Hughie Mack and Bobbie [sic] Dunn. This contains no particular plot, but consists largely of nonsensical, knockabout situations, some of which are quite amusing. The chief scenes are in a barber shop operated as a 'blind pig,' a ladies' bath house and beauty parlor, and in a police station. Mixed flirtations of an inoffensive character are the chief centers of action." *Moving Picture World*, February 2, 1918, p.690

The Donkey Did It: *Released 02/06/1918 Wednesday.* © 01/25/1918 — 2 reels. DIRECTOR: Vin Moore. CAST: Merta Sterling, Al Forbes, Babe Emerson, Russell Powell

SYNOPSIS: "Last Chance Valley fairly wallowed in wickedness; its dancehall was so sinful that it made a bank robbery look like a prayer-meeting. To it came Professor Polonius Pinhead [Forbes] upon the back of his donkey and boon companion, King Solomon, and there he found two shrinking flowers of the valley. One's name was Violet [Emerson], warranted fully shrunk, and the other was Molly [Sterling], whose expansion was in direct contrast to Violet's shrinking. She weighed 350 on the hoof and could juggle a bean-shooter as well as any gun-toter. And of course, there was a bad man. His name was Howling Hank [Powell], and he was a union villain licensed by the Moving Picture Theatre Villains' Association, to wear the official black mustache and carry forty-seven shots in his six-shooter. Now, Howling Hank was determined that Violet should work in his dance-hall, and Molly was just as determined that Violet should not. Into this life and death struggle King Solomon, the donkey, kicked Professor Pinhead, and this elongated individual eventually obtained Dutch courage enough to route the villain, to save the shrinking Violet, and to marry the multitudinous Molly." *Moving Picture Weekly*, January 26, 1918, p.34

Pearls and Girls: *Released 02/13/1918 Wednesday.* © 02/02/1918 — 2 reels. DIRECTOR: James D. Davis. CAST: Hughie Mack, Eva Novak

SYNOPSIS: "Hughie [Mack] was in love with the daughter [Novak] of his boss and she was in love with him. But father was so little impressed with Hughie that he fired him. Now, father was a fancier of pearls as well as girls, and he had a necklace which had adorned the stiff neck of a Hindoo idol at a previous time. He was to give it to Eva on the night of her coming out party. The guardians of the Burma Temple had tried in vain to locate the precious necklace, but when they saw a notice in the papers about the gift to be given to Eva they sent a note to father, telling him to give them the necklace of suffer the consequence.

"Father promptly constructed a Hindoo catcher in his home and went ahead with the party. The Hindoos made their plans, but Hughie disguised himself as a Hindoo and copped both Eva and the necklace." *Moving Picture Weekly*, February 2, 1918, pp.38-39
REVIEWS: "A two-reel comic, featuring Hughie Mack, Eva Novak and others. This is a knockabout number, with no special plot interest, but containing a number of funny moments. Hughie plays the part of an office boy, in love with his employer's daughter. A stolen necklace, a masquerade ball and chase scenes at the close are part of the ingredients. A fairly strong comic." *Moving Picture World*, February 23, 1918, p.1140

Beaches and Peaches: *Released 02/20/1918 Wednesday.* © 02/13/1918 — 2 reels. DIRECTOR: Archie Mayo. CAST: Dave Morris, Gladys Varden, Fay Holderness
SYNOPSIS: "That old guy, Father Neptune, certainly knew a thing or two when he picked out the ocean to live in. Ferdy Fishcake [Morris] had it on Neptune, though, for though he had a fright of a wife [Holderness] he was easing himself into forgetfulness by taking a few days' vacation with her at the beach. And the sights he saw! They almost made him forget his wife. He burrowed under the sand to get near Lotta Pepp [Varden] and when his wife woke up she thought he was gone for good. So she hired a detective and they started a search which complicated itself so many times in hotels and cast suspicion on so many marriage vows that we can't bear to tell about." *Moving Picture Weekly*, February 19, 1918, p.35
REVIEWS: "A two-reel knockabout comic, featuring Dave Morris and Gladys Varden. Dave plays a henpecked husband, who becomes entangled with a lady at the beach. Complications with the latter's husband and his own wife follow. Some of the business in this is quite amusing, but as a whole it is an offering of only average strength." *Moving Picture World*, February 23, 1918, p.1140

Ambrose the Lion-Hearted: *Released 02/27/1918 Wednesday.* © 02/18/1918 — 2 reels. DIRECTOR: William S. Fredericks. CAST: Mack Swain, Rae Godfrey, Jack Perrin, Fay Holderness, Mack Ridgway
SYNOPSIS: "Luther Lottercoin [Ridgeway] was the cattle king of Cobweb County, the county seat of which was Slumber Valley, and to this solemnly lent village came one Haroil Hal [Perrin], with his bandit band, intent upon letting a little of Lottercoin's blood. Haroil has a perfectly legal wife, but the only way he saw to annex the cattle man's fortune was to marry the daughter. And this he set out to do attired in an ancient title. His calling card read, Count Lucas De Jazbo, but Lily Lottercoin [Godfrey], the heiress, set her heart upon Ambrose [Swain], and Ambrose had just passed the kindergarten stage in courtship. He was entering upon the post-office-in-the-old-apple-tree grade.

"Love-making wasn't Ambrose's bread-winner, for in private life he kept a shoe store for horses, and when he really wanted to get a horse shoe in quickly he pulled it off with his teeth. That is how good Ambrose was. For this and other manifestations of unusual strength Ambrose was created sheriff of the county, and well it was for Lottercoin that

Ambrose was the sheriff, for in this capacity he was able to foil Haroil's marriage to Lily, and this fact made Lottercoin more willing to give his daughter to him." *Moving Picture Weekly*, February 16, 1918, p.39

REVIEWS: "[T]he determined blacksmith, Ambrose, saves his sweetheart from the clutches of the cruel villain. In spite of his strong arm and lion heart Ambrose is his mother's pet. His blacksmith shop, however, is unable to hold him, for iron is too weak for Ambrose's sturdy arm, so the county appoints him sheriff to take charge of the ruffians and cattle thieves.

"All of the comedy in this picture is of the legitimate kind, being comedy of situation rather than of make-up and slapstick. Rae Godfrey is the leading woman." *Moving Picture World*, February 9, 1918, p.844

"A two-reel comic featuring Mack Swain in the name part. He plays the part of a young blacksmith in love with the daughter of a rich man. His rival is Hairoil Hal, a desperado. The burlesque characterizations and action are very funny in this and the incidents are also laughable. It is one of the best L-KO's recently shown." *Moving Picture World*, March 2, 1918, p.1270

A Flyer in Folly: *Released 03/06/1918 Wednesday.* © 02/23/1918 — 2 reels. DIRECTOR: Bob Kerr. CAST: Hughie Mack, Gale Henry, Bobby Dunn, Russell Powell, Katherine O'Connor, Bartine Burkett
(pre-release title: **The Price She Paid**)

SYNOPSIS: "Jasper Junk [Dunn], the famous author of 'The Psychological Dynamics of Telepathic Concordance,' had a regular job, too. He read gas meters at $8 per, and this vocation led to the highly exciting 'Fyer [sic] in Folly' which dragged down in its train the highly respectable Henrietta Hamaneggs [Henry], and Hector [Mack], her noble husband.

"Henrietta had never seen a cabaret, and probably if Hector had been in the enjoyment of a salary which permitted her even an hour's relaxation from the job of feeding him, she would have seen one under such circumstances as to have satisfied her; but it was not so. For that reason she succumbed to the wiles of Jasper Junk, who had accidentally found out that she had $13.49 put away for a trip to Europe after the war. The cabaret people mistook the gas meter student and the janitor's wife for entertainers, and put up with them until Jasper tried to beat it out with Henrietta's purse. But Hector, who was hot on the trail, and Maximillian Mudguard [Powell], his boss, overtook them just as the cabaret was getting so hot that all of the ice in the ice-chest was melted and a Johnstown flood threatened. After accounts were all squared up, Mudguard, as a parting salutation to Hector, said, 'The next time you let your wife loose, put a gas mask on her.'" *Moving Picture Weekly*, January 23, 1918, p.34

REVIEWS: "A very funny two-reel comic, featuring Gale Henry and Hughie Mack. They appear as a married couple, whose dream of true love is upset by an intrusive gas man and other flirtatious individuals. Trick photography is employed in a laughable way several times and a number of the situations are unusually good." *Moving Picture World*, March 9, 1918, p.1410

Ambrose and His Widow: *Released 03/13/1918 Wednesday.* © 03/02/1918 — 2 reels. DIRECTOR: William S. Fredericks. CAST: Mack Swain, Jack Perrin, Rae Godfrey, Dick Smith

SYNOPSIS: "Ambrose [Swain] had nothing in view. So when a peculiar proposition was put to him, he was ready to embrace it as anything else. The proposition was to marry a beautiful woman and unostentatiously die within twenty-four hours, leaving her to enjoy a fortune which could only be hers in case she was a widow.

"This proposition was put to him by Dr. Despatchem [Perrin], who thereby hoped to get a sufficient slice of the inheritance to enable him to marry his lovely combination assistant, nurse and maid [Godfrey].

"All went well at first. Ambrose, with cheeks chalked to a sepulchral whiteness, dressed in the habiliments of a chronic consumptive, was safely married to the fair one, and with her hustled away to a mountain resort to die. But of course, Ambrose had no idea of dying, and Dr. Despatchem's attempt to blow him up with a bomb was a most brilliant fizzle. The dynamiter was dynamited by his own explosion.

"Finally Ambrose, driven from pillar to post in the hotel in the doctor's frantic endeavor to keep him out of his wife's sight, was cornered by his bride while in the arms of another woman.

"'Haven't you the decency to refrain from flirting on the first day of our married life, and you with only eight hours yet to live?' she hurled at him. And then to her astonishment she saw that the man she had thought to be a consumptive was a very handsome and robust specimen of humanity.

"'Why, hubby,' she cried, 'you're handsome.' Snatching off the funereal gear, she led him downstairs and to the doctor. 'My husband has decided to live, and we're off on our honeymoon,' she said. 'The inheritance can go hang instead.'" *Moving Picture Weekly*, February 2, 1918, p.38

REVIEWS: "A two-reel comic, featuring Mack Swain as Ambrose. He has a series of rather amusing adventures at the beginning and finally weds a woman who desires to get rid of him. She asks a friend to put a bomb under Ambrose, but he escapes death. There is no great amount of plot in this; it is rather a series of amusing small incidents of a knockabout sort." *Moving Picture World*, March 16, 1918, p.1560

Cooks and Crooks: *Released 03/20/1918 Wednesday.* © 03/07/1918 — 2 reels. DIRECTOR: James D. Davis. CAST: Hughie Mack, Gale Henry, Dave Morris, Eva Novak, Jack Connors SYNOPSIS: "Pygmalion Prune [Henry] and Chubby Chumpp [Mack] had combined their interests in matrimony, not so much on account of their similarity in shape — for Chubby was a 350-pound urchin, and Pygmalion a six-foot bean pole — as their similarity in occupation. They were bakers. The two decided to spend their honeymoon in the pleasant land of Mexico. Their pastry cart and lunch wagon had no sooner skidded over the boundary line than they were impressed into service to feed the epicurean bandit, Melachrino Mike [Morris]. All might have gone well with the pair had not Chubby evinced a lively interest in Bambino Soupereeno [Novak], Mike's other interest in life. Between the jealousy of his spouse and the deep-dyed revenge of Mike, Chubby gave every promise of losing all of his tremendous pulchritude, but he made the United States border by the skin of his teeth." *Moving Picture Weekly*, March 9, 1918, p.31

REVIEWS: "A very funny two-reel number of the comic, knockabout type, featuring Gale Henry, Hughie Mack and Dave Morris. The names of the characters in this are well selected, the subtitles are amusing and the burlesque plot is decidedly good. Gale and Hughie appear as proprietors of a traveling lunch wagon. They are captured by a band of brigands, headed by Dave Morris as Melachrino Mike. The action is unusually pleasing." *Moving Picture World*, March 23, 1918, p.1707

Sherlock Ambrose: *Released 03/27/1918 Wednesday.* © 03/16/1918 — 2 reels. DIRECTOR: William S. Fredericks. CAST: Mack Swain, Bill Smithers, Jack Perrin, Rae Godfrey, Lily Butler
SYNOPSIS: "Ambrose [Swain], a greasy immigrant with a wife and six children…" *Moving Picture Weekly*, March 16, 1918, p.39
REVIEWS: "A two-reel comic, featuring Mack Swain as an immigrant who is mistaken for a detective by the president of a school for girls. He finds a diamond ring lost by one of the girls and is duly rewarded. Some very funny spots crop up in this number, which is quite enjoyable." *Moving Picture World*, March 30, 1918, p.1868

Gowns and Girls: *Released 04/03/1918 Wednesday.* © 03/22/1918 — 2 reels. CAST: Hughie Mack, Gale Henry, Eva Novak, Dave Morris, Walter Smith
SYNOPSIS: "Billy Bounce [Mack], proprietor of the Gorgeous Gown Shop, had a cast of stately models which put all of the girl shows in town in the shade, and attracted buyers from miles around. Bessie [Novak] was the leading lady, and the elongated left-angled Theodosia Thimble [Henry] was general utility, in and outfielder, bat-boy and general clean-up woman. In addition to this, Theodosia regarded Billy Bounce as Apollo, Romeo, Don Juan and Sir Gallahad all rolled into one.

"Jazzband Jack [Morris] decided that Bounce's show would make a fine business for him in his own town, and decided to annex it. He chose the moment when Billy was putting on a fashion show of all nations. His bait was an automobile ride, and an attempt to make the girls so independent as to peeve the boss.

"But Theodosia was equal to the occasion. By means of a hand operated elevator and hot-off-the-boat costumes she pulled the show out of the fire, and put it across in fine shape, thereby earning the praise, hand and fortune of the proprietor." *Moving Picture Weekly*, March 23, 1918, p.38

Saved From a Vamp: *Released 04/10/1918 Wednesday.* © 03/29/1918 — 2 reels. CAST: Hughie Mack, Gale Henry
SYNOPSIS: "X.M. Ted [Mack] lived in the Masuma Club on the expectation of inheriting his uncle's fortune. But the foxy old uncle left it in such a way that he could not inherit it unless he was married, and he had to be married within three days. The boys did not want to see Ted lose his fortune, so they scurried around for a bride.

"Luke Loot had a vamp in mind for the bride, who would split fifty-fifty on Ted's fortune, and hurried away to draft her. But the other boys found Lena Thin [Henry], who was even less than that, while Ted was considerably the worse for eighteen highballs, married her to him in the club.

"When Ted woke up he was married but he didn't know it. Lena did, however, and insisted on sticking around the house, much to Ted's embarrassment. But she saved her husband from the cruel vamp, and all came out happily in the end." *Moving Picture Weekly*, March 30, 1918, p.39

Adventurous Ambrose: *Released 04/17/1918 Wednesday.* © 04/05/1918 — 2 reels. CAST: Mack Swain, Jack Perrin, Lilly Loney, Mabel Healy, Bob Higgins, Molly Malone, Bartine Burkett, Coy Watson Jr.
(based on a viewing of the print held at the Library of Congress, this is the "Lehrman" film that Coy Watson Jr. misidentified as **The Mailman** in his autobiography)
SYNOPSIS: "Farmer Ambrose [Swain] was startled out of the self-complacency with which he accepted his wife's admiration by the announcement that he had inherited the Wave Crest Inn at Seaside. His first guest at the Wave Crest Inn was Mrs. R.U. Dun [Loney], wife of a broker [Perrin] who was too busy to come with his wife until the following day.

"In order to make this story complete, there was another U.R. Dunn [Higgins] who manufactured garbage cans, and who caught the train to the Wave Crest ahead of his wife [Healy], who was late as usual.

"Ambrose made the reservation for the broker's wife, and then showed the garbage can manufacturer, supposing him to be the husband of the woman who had registered, into the room reserved. Of course, the other spouses came the next day, and a general mix-up occurred in which Ambrose became utterly bewildered, entangled and enamored of both of the Dunn wives, and a bunch of [illegible] who infested the beach in front of the Wave Crest Hotel. Eventually, Ambrose was very glad indeed to get back to his farm." *Moving Picture Weekly*, April 6, 1918, p.38

A Rural Riot: *Released 04/24/1918 Wednesday.* © 04/12/1918 — 2 reels. DIRECTOR: James D. Davis. CAST: Gale Henry, Hughie Mack, Eva Novak, Dave Morris, Catherine Young
SYNOPSIS: "Gale [Henry] and Hughie [Mack] are sweethearts, and in order to get in right with Gale's dada, they plough the fields for him in their own style auto. Dave [Morris], and his accomplice, are out on a joy ride, when suddenly Catherine [Young] falls out of the machine and rolls down a hill, losing her dress on the way. Dave loses control of the machine, and he, too, tumbles down a hill with the machine. Gale and Hughie see Dave staggering to his feet and bring him to Gale's home. Gale caresses Dave and arouses Hughie's jealousy. The vamp comes there, and together with Dave they try to take all the money away from the farmer and his family. Father's safe was the stove, and Dave was very cold, so he had to take the stove with him, but not before the vamp had lured Hughie into taking the money through a pipe which he had connected from his room to the stove, putting the money in a bag, he dropped in out of the window. Gale is sitting below the window, playing with a pig; she sees the bag, opens it, finds the money, takes the money out, puts the pig in its place. Great complications follow when the vamps [sic] learns he forgot to take the money. She forces Hughie to marry her, but Gale had followed them, and impersonates the minister. Dave comes on, the vamp faints, comes to, and talks to Dave. They plot to rob them in another way, hit Hughie over the head, throw Gale and Hughie down into the cellar. Gale and Hughie escape, Gale telephones father they are being robbed. Father and brother come to the city, fight with Dave and the vamp, and all ends happily." *Moving Picture Weekly*, April 13, 1918, p.34

Fathers' Sons and Chorus Girls: *Released 05/01/1918 Wednesday.* © 04/22/1918 — 2 reels. DIRECTOR: James Davis. CAST: Eva Novak, Rube Miller, Dave Morris, Robert McKenzie, "Frenchy" Bianchi (Monty Banks), Carolyn Wright
SYNOPSIS: "Dave [Morris] and 'Frenchy' [Banks] are dispossessed college chaps, their Fathers [McKenzie is one of them] having disowned them because of their affection for every chorus girl in town. The best thing the boys can do is to dine and wine the girls. They are thrown into prison over night and the Judge phones their fathers in the morning, telling them to keep their sons out of court, as they annoy the other prisoners. The fathers bail the sons and the girls out and gives the boys a chance to sell their merchandise, which is in the dry-goods line. The chorus girls are all fired, and the two leading women [Novak and Wright] apply to the boys' fathers for work. They are made traveling saleswomen and in direct competition to the boys. They pose as their own models and take all the business away from the boys. The other girls are stranded at the same hotel and the proprietor has locked them in because they owe a large bill. The boys get the girls out and dress them up in their merchandise. The buyers all flock back to the boys and they make a big sale. Fathers come over to see how boys are making out, and the proprietor [Miller] calls the police because he can't get his money, and it all ends happily in court." *Moving Picture Weekly*, April 20, 1918, p.38

Her Movie Madness: *Released 05/08/1918 Wednesday.* © 04/27/1918 — 2 reels. DIRECTOR: Robert Kerr. CAST: Hughie Mack, Gale Henry, L-KO Beauties
SYNOPSIS: "The Flabbergasted Film Company was looking for a location on the Pip farm for their latest production, 'Why He Broke Her Heart,' in five parts. Prunella Pip [Henry] was more or less in love with Beafy Ben [Mack], the hired man. But she put him out of her mind resolutely for thoughts of the movies. But Ben got an opportunity to double for the handsome hero, who refused to cross a tree over a six hundred foot drop. Ben didn't cross it either, but he got a job.

"With him in the movies, Prunella, with an inheritance from her Aunt Teek, left home, and when the studio manager discovered she had money, he fired the heroine just before the fifth act commenced, and started on another picture. The manager and the leading man consumed four reels in trying to get Prunella's money, and while they were about it, the deposed leading lady blew the Flabbergasted Film to kingdom come with dynamite." *Moving Picture Weekly*, April 27, 1918, p.34
REVIEWS: "A two-reel comic, with Gale Henry and Hugie [sic] Mack in the cast. Gale plays a farm maiden, who joins a moving picture company; Hughie is her fat country lover. There are some quite amusing knockabout moments in the studio scenes. The subject is one of average strength; it would have been helped by more of a plot idea." *Moving Picture World*, May 11, 1918, p.897

Pretty Babies: *Released 05/15/1918 Wednesday.* © 05/09/1918 — 2 reels. DIRECTOR: James D. Davis. CAST: Dave Morris, Robert McKenzie, Mario Bromo, Rube Miller, Carolyn Wright, Eva Novak, L-KO Beauties
SYNOPSIS: "'Only two more miles.' With these words of encouragement Seekgeld [Bromo] told his Follies they would have to pull him to the next one-night stand. But just then good luck, in the person of the village's Who's Who, accompanied by his not-so-private

secretary [Miller], came up in a regular automobile. After tramping on Seekgeld's toes, they take the Follies into the machine and drive them village-ward. As the chief is due to leave town that day, the secretary decides to improve his hours with a gay little party at the boss' house. Meanwhile the son [Morris] of the village Pooh-Bah chances to meet the soubrette [Novak] of the Follies, but has to leave her to take papa to the station [McKenzie]. Returning to his home he interrupts a tete-a-tete between the secretary and the soubrette of the Follies and the latter mistakes him for a chauffeur. Keeping up the mistaken identity they go for the rest of the girls and return for a big party. Seekgeld plans to spoil the party, and gets a couple of escaped convicts to do the work. Just at this time father returns unexpectedly, and he is told by his secretary that the convicts are men he has sentenced years ago, and have come back to get him. Then sonny gets a brilliant idea to dress up the ingénue [Wright] and soubrette as convicts, feign a capture and ejection, and plays the hero with dad. Of course, complications develop fast and furious, but the scheme works out as planned, and surrounded by all the other members of the Follies, dad forgives every one and all is well." *Moving Picture Weekly*, May 4, 1918, p.30

REVIEWS: "A two-reel subject, featuring Dave Morris, Rube Miller and a group of pretty girls. The latter appear in bathing suits and pajamas, being entertained at a house party by Billy Bingo while his father is away. The story, which is very indefinite in plot, is told in poetical subtitles. The subject is inoffensive, but contains little humor and is not at all strong." *Moving Picture World*, June 1, 1918, p.1334

Who's Zoo?: *Released 05/22/1918 Wednesday.* © 05/14/1918 — 2 reels. DIRECTOR, SCREENPLAY: Craig Hutchinson. CAST: Kathleen O'Connor, Rube Miller, Stan Laurel, Eddie the Ellfa-Nut, Paddy McGuire

SYNOPSIS: "Stanley [Laurel] is the head waiter in a swell hotel and is very much stuck on the job. Rube [Miller], on a sight-seeing expedition to the city, comes to the hotel as a guest and is sighted by Stanley, who proceeds to have sport with him. Katherine [O'Connor] and her husband come to the hotel as guests. Rube and Stanley both lamp her and try to flirt with the pretty wife. The husband gets jealous. Rube gets a job in a zoo. He incurs the displeasure of one of the keepers and is locked in a cage with the animals, the keeper thinking to frighten Rube. Rube, aroused, cleans up the cage. The elephant gets loose and runs amuck. He enters the lobby of the hotel, followed by the bear.

"Rube has returned to the hotel and Katherine is sleeping in a bedroom after a bath. The elephant ascends to the second story, and is prowling around. He reaches through the door and playfully places the bear in the bed with Katherine. She sees the bear and flees, shouting at the top of her voice. The husband hears her and she partially explains. He thinks Rube has gotten into Katherine's bed and rushes in armed with a bed-slat and begins to pummel the bear, who comes out of bed and chases the husband. The husband runs into Rube and Stanley, who are also chased by the bear. Rube and Stanley leap out of windows, run over roofs, and have hairbreadth escapes in fleeing from the animals and once safe, vow never again to tempt fate by flirting with another man's wife." *Moving Picture Weekly*, May 11, 1918, p.38

REVIEWS: "A one-reel comedy, featuring Kathleen O'Connor, Rube Miller and a trained elephant. The latter furnishes much of the comedy, doing some rather surprising stunts. This number is entertaining and will go strong with children." *Moving Picture World*, June 1, 1918, p.1334

An Alice Howell Century Comedy now replaces L-Ko release every fourth week

Merry Mermaids: *Released 06/05/1918 Wednesday.* © 05/29/1918 — 2 reels. DIRECTOR: James D. Davis. CAST: Dave Morris, Rube Miller, L-KO Beauties
SYNOPSIS: "A. Bluffer was everything that his name implied. The son took after the father. Both had a keen eye for beauty, as had also A. Bluffer's partner. When the new stenographer came there was keen competition to see which one should take her out to lunch. The firm was in the law business, and at this moment came a telegram advising that A. Bluffer had been appointed legal advisor to a ladies' gymnasium.

"Bluffer was in such a sweat to accept this new job that he aroused his partner's suspicions, and the latter took his letter of credentials out of his pocket. When Pop reached the gymnasium he felt like a fool. His partner had been there ahead of him, presented the letter, and was in the midst of legal advising.

"The stenographer was a member of the gymnasium class too, and showed up just at this time with Bluffer's son. The son and the partner enter into a compact to beat father out, but when they rolled themselves in an awning which was being painted for the gymnasium they came out with convict stripes on, and the chase which ensued ended up in the gymnasium tank, where their stripes were finally washed out, and they again presented the appearance of clean citizens." *Moving Picture Weekly*, May 25, 1918, p.34
REVIEWS: "Dave Morris, Rube Miller and others appear in this two-reel subject of the knockabout type. A number of good-looking girls appear in gymnasium and swimming-tank scenes. But the plot is of no consequence and most of the action is meaningless and without particular humor." *Moving Picture World*, June 8, 1918, p.1475

A Blind Pig: *Released 06/12/1918 Wednesday.* © 06/04/1918 — 2 reels. DIRECTOR: James D. Davis. CAST: Eva Novak, Eddie Barry, Russ Powell, Rube Miller, L-KO Beauties
SYNOPSIS: "Russ Powell, ticket agent and sheriff, always had trouble with his baggageman and assistant, who both aspire to be his sons-in-law. He receives a telegram that there is a Blind Pig in his town. Russ makes a proposition to the boys that the one who captures the Blind Pig can marry his daughter. So the two boys, not understanding the meaning of Blind Pig, go in search of one in all the pig-pens. Eva [Novak], who overhears, attempts to protect her favorite pig.

"When Eddie [Barry] is looking for Blind Pigs in pig-pens, Rube [Miller], who remembers Eva's favorite pig, goes after him, but has a hard time delivering him to the sheriff. Eddie, not having succeeded in finding a blind pig, goes to visit Eva at the station. Father catches him, and forbids him to visit his daughter until he has caught the blind pig. Eddie gets a telegraph instrument, climbs a pole and telegraphs to Eva. Father gets the message, instead of Eva, and tells Eddie to meet her at the baggage-room. Father exits with Eva, leaving Eddie alone in the baggage-room.

"Rube is still trying to deliver the blind pig, runs into Eddie. He picks up the bag, thinking it is his clothes, but the pig falls out, and Eddie gets scared. Rube tells Eddie it is the blind pig, and they both give chase through the kitchen onto the roof, until they catch it and deliver it to father.

"Father tells them that they are mistaken, a blind pig is a man who sells booze. The perfume salesman arrives at the station and shows his wares to the two girls. At the same time comes the real blind pig man, who hides a box of booze in the outside platform door. The chink hears, and thinks it is the groceryman. While smelling booze the Chink hears perfume talk, sees father coming and, decides to exchange booze for perfume. Father enters the restaurant. The girls want father to smell the perfume (not knowing bottles have been changed). Father mistakes the perfume salesman for the blind pig man and the chase starts all over again." *Moving Picture Weekly*, June 1, 1918, p.34

REVIEWS: "This two-reel comic gets its best effects in the second reel, where some excellent mechanical feats are pictured. The humor of the first reel is of the knockabout order, and only fairly strong. But the second reel is much better, and makes the offering one above the average." *Moving Picture World*, June 22, 1918, p.1758

Romance and Dynamite: *Released 06/19/1918 Wednesday.* © 06/11/1918 — 2 reels.
DIRECTOR: James D. Davis. CAST: Russell Powell, Caroline Wright, Eva Novak, Eddie Barry, Rube Miller, "Charlie from the Orient" Chai Hong, L-KO Beauties
SYNOPSIS: "Father Brownem [Powell] catches his helpers [Barry and Miller] making love to his daughters [Wright and Novak] during working hours. This is strictly against the rules, and he starts a useless chase. Meantime the Chinese cook [Hong] mistakes a bunch of dynamite for kindling wood and the explosion blows the two couples through the roof into the depot. From there they tumble into an automobile, and start for the preacher's. Father extracts himself from the wreckage and follows. When he learns what has taken place, he disowns them all.

"Meanwhile, however, robbers enter the depot. Planning to get back into the good graces of the father, the two couples plan a fake hold-up to show how brave they are. The girls dress in men's overalls and surprise the real crooks, who jump out of the window as the girls enter the door. The girls start to blow up the safe, but seeing the real crooks returning, they run out to get the boys to volunteer to capture the crooks. Of course they think the crooks are the girls, but before it is all over everybody has had a thorough taste of all that is coming to them." *Moving Picture Weekly*, June 8, 1918, p.39

REVIEWS: "A two-reel comic, which features Eddie Barry, Rube Miller, Eva Novak and others. The small Chinaman and young alligator contribute a few laughs in the first reel, and there are some funny mechanical effects in the second. The number, on the whole, strikes a good average for this type of film, though there is little if any plot." *Moving Picture World*, June 29, 1918, p.1892

Phoney Photos: *Released 07/03/1918 Wednesday.* © 06/24/1918 -2 reels. DIRECTOR: Edwin Frazee. CAST: Neal Burns, Rena Rogers, Stan Laurel, Walter Belasco, Lydia Yeamans Titus, Bartine Burkett
(pre-release titles: **The Photographer's Story** and **Skidding Hearts**)
SYNOPSIS: "Grace is at the wagon of a fruit vendor and writes a note telling the buyer to communicate with her. The note is seen by Jules, who sends a letter to Grace. The note eventually falls into the hands of Swift. Swift also communicates with Grace. Jules calls on Grace and takes her out driving. The car is overturned, and Swift rescues her.

"Swift learns she is the girl who wrote the note. Grouch and his wife are determined that Grace shall marry Jules. They lock Grace in her room and forbid Swift from the house. Swift is on the alert and communicates with Grace by talking through a water pipe to Grace. Swift arranges an elopement with Grace. Mrs. Grouch learns of the proposed elopement and plans to checkmate Swift. She induces the colored servant to masquerade as Grace. The colored servant, heavily veiled, goes forth to meet Swift under instructions from Mrs. Grouch. Jules meets the colored girl and, under the impression she is Grace, takes her to the minister. Swift finds Grace and hurries with her to the office of a Justice of the Peace, where they are married.

"Mrs. Grouch, thinking Swift has married the colored servant, is elated. It is all explained, however, when the colored woman removes her veil and Jules and Mrs. Grouch discover that their plans have gone astray." *Moving Picture Weekly*, June 22, 1918, p.38

REVIEWS: "A two-reel comedy number, by Edwin Frazee, featuring Rena Rogers, Stanley Laurel, Neal Burns and others. The action takes place at a girl's school and concerns the efforts of two young men to marry the same girl. One of them succeeds by palming off a colored girl on his rival in a double elopement. The action is of the nonsensical, farcical sort, and while not extremely laughable, has numerous funny spots. The number is one of about average strength." *Moving Picture World*, July 13, 1918, p.251

The Belles of Liberty: *Released 07/10/1918 Wednesday.* © 07/03/1918 — 2 reels. DIRECTOR: James Davis. CAST: L-KO Beauties, Dave Morris, Rube Miller, Eva Novak, Caroline Wright, Frenchie Bianchi (Monty Banks), "Captain" Leslie T. Peacock, Mal St. Clair (pre-release title: **Liberty Belles**)

SYNOPSIS: "In the beautiful garden of girls there grew two poppies who ceased to bloom ever since the Civil War was over, only they didn't know it. They still considered themselves lady killers. Two of the most beautiful flowers in the garden were Trixie [Novak] and Pixie [Wright]. Old Hatband [Bianchi] and Spatts [Peacock] saw them, and no effort seemed too great on their part to win them. Even a liberal contribution to the Liberty Loan was cheerfully forthcoming. But the finances [sic] of the two Liberty Belles happened to be the respective sons [Morris and Miller] of the gay old boys, and much as they disliked it, the fathers became a party to the marriages of their respective sons, just when they fondly thought that they were teaching them the lessons of their young lives." *Moving Picture Weekly*, June 29, 1918, p.28

REVIEWS: "[T]he two-reeler, 'Liberty Belles,' a patriotic laughmaker in which it is sought to drive home the assistance women may be in winning the war for the Allied cause." *Moving Picture World*, June 1, 1918, p.1312

A Clean Sweep: *Released 07/24/1918 Wednesday.* © 07/23/1918 –2 reels. CAST: Merta Sterling, Chai Hong, Bartine Burkett, Russell Powell, Billy Armstrong, Eddie Barry

SYNOPSIS: "It's a sure case between the butcher's [Powell] son and the lady barber's [Sterling] daughter [Burkett], but owing to a falling out between the old people their love is not permitted to run smoothly.

"One day Charlie [Hong], the laundry magnate, receives a mysterious package from the Orient containing a magic ball, and at the suggestion of the frisky son of the butcher he works the ball on the old couple.

"In payment of a laundry bill Charlie gets a Ford, takes the young couple for a joyride where they pick up a lost child. On their arrival home the child is discovered and they're in a tight fix, but finally get out of it by explaining that the child belongs to one of Charlie's customers.

"A reward has been offered for the child and after some lively chases the money finally falls into the hands of the lucky Chinaman." *Moving Picture Weekly*, July 13, 1918, p.34

REVIEWS: "A laughable two-reel comic, one of the best of this company's recent releases. A young Chinaman, 'Charlie of the Orient,' has a leading part, assisted by Merta Sterling, Eddie Barry and others. The number is full of funny tricks and amusing slapstick situations and winds up with a hilarious chase, in which the family washing is carried through the streets between two autos." *Moving Picture World*, July 27, 1918, p.590

Fools and Fires: *Released 08/07/1918 Wednesday.* © 07/30/1918 — 2 reels. DIRECTOR: Craig Hutchinson. CAST: Eddie Barry, Eva Novak, James Donnelly, Billy Armstrong, Rube Miller
SYNOPSIS: "Rube Miller, the fire chief, has a pretty daughter whom the handsome fireman and the notorious crook are both trying to win. By some strange means of mental telepathy both suitors conclude to set the chief's house on fire when the chief will be out of town. But the house is accidentally set on fire by someone other than the suitors and the fire chief, his daughter and the crook are caught in the burning house.

"At twelve o'clock the butler blows the whistle on the engine for lunch and all the firemen leave the burning building to have their lunch. While the firemen are at lunch an opposition fire department composed of women takes up the fight — and the chase is on. All are rescued — but — who gets the beautiful daughter?" *Moving Picture Weekly*, July 27, 1918, p.38

Business Before Honesty: *Released 08/21/1918 Wednesday.* © 08/14/1918 — 2 reels. DIRECTOR: Charles Parrott. CAST: Harry Gribbon, Oliver Hardy, Eddie Barry, May Emory, Helen Lynch
SYNOPSIS: "Babe Hardy is a professional blindman with a tin cup. His boy disguises himself as a lady and gathers in a few stray coins to aid his dark bespectacled papa.

"Willie Steal [Gribbon] a high-class society crook, seeing a beautiful automobile, hangs a 'For Sale' sign on it, and nonchalantly awaits results. Mae [Emory] and her daughter Helen [Lynch], passing by, admire the car, and decide to purchase it, but only pay half of the money, telling Willie to call at their home for the balance.

"On their homeward journey Mae and Helen encounter the poor blind man and his beautiful daughter 'Nellie' [Barry]. Mae is struck by the resemblance of Nellie to her long lost sister and filled with compassion, asks 'Nellie' and her father to live with her.

"That night at Mae's dinner table are Willie, Helen, the beautiful Nellie and the blindman, who in some strange fashion always manages to take the largest portion of everything. Mae brings out a coal scuttle full of gold from the safe with which to pay Willie. The guests gaze in amazement and each one carries his own little plot in his bosom. One by one they leave the table to play with the safe. Willie goes after the money from one side, Eddie from the other, and the blind man is in the safe. A lively general mixup follows." *Moving Picture Weekly*, August 17, 1918, p.29

Her Whirlwind Wedding: *Released 09/04/1918 Wednesday.* © 08/28/1918 — 2 reels. CAST: Eva Novak, Robert MacKenzie, Harry Lorraine, Porter Strong, Chester Ryckman
SYNOPSIS: "Old Man Jellyfish [MacKenzie] thought four years at college would transform his son Algernon [Ryckman] into a veritable 'white hope' and he is chagrined to find when Algy returns to the old home burg, that the pride of his life hasn't much more 'physique' than a table onion. Even pretty Sally Succotash [Novak], who returns from college at the same time,

can't see much to rave about in the 'eddicated' Jellyfish boy until Algernon pulls some gewhilliker hero stuff and rescues her from Hector Hoot [Strong], a little 'wilyun' with lots of coin.

"Of course, a wedding is the only thing that would mean anything in the young lives of Algernon and Sally after that, so the proper arrangements are made.

"Just as the ceremony is about to begin, Hector Hoot walks in and reminds Father Succotash [Lorraine] that the latter's bankroll isn't any more valuable than Swedish matches in war time, and offers to help out the old man on condition that he get Sally. Bridegrooms are switched.

"Then comes a telegram informing Old Man Jellyfish that a relative has left him ten million dollars. Hector is told to evacuate the premises and Algernon again takes Sally into his arms. Just as the ceremony is about to start all over again a bomb, which the fiendish Hector had placed in the house, explodes. Amid the falling walls and flying timbers and clocks and such, the happy pair speak their marriage vows and agree to live happy ever after." *Moving Picture Weekly*, August 31, 1918, p.38

REVIEWS: "This comedy while it may get some laughs has just missed its mark as a burlesque. It follows its story of a courtship and wedding after the fashion of a burlesque on the filming of a moving picture story, and as such is not particularly amusing." *Moving Picture World*, August 31, 1918, p.1310

A Pullman Blunder: *Released 09/18/1918 Wednesday.* © 09/09/1918 — 2 reels. DIRECTOR: Craig Hutchinson. CAST: Harry Gribbon, Harry Mann, May Emory, Eddie Barry, the Cutey Girls

SYNOPSIS: "Leaping Leopold [Gribbon] had been warned against Bevo but persists in indulging until Doctor Gloom [Barry] warns him he will soon be seeing things. However, this isn't any reason why a bill board and an ill wind should blow the same onto Leopold's wall. It does, however, and Leopold then knows he is a Bevo hound.

"Even granting this, was that any reason why Leopold should shake a wicked eye at a nice young bride whose husband was a wild, wild man? Certainly not, but Leo just can't help it and his wife [Emory] hires a detective [Mann] with a bright past to sleuth. This is unsuccessful, however, as another detective with a shady future has to watch the first, and between them, all they catch is a bad cold.

"Leo doesn't even catch a cold, but his wife catches him and he in turn catches the train. The wild, wild husband also catches the train and so does the detective and so does the bride and so do some disagreeable gentlemen with nasty tempers who drink Bevo. This might have been all right but they all meet just when and where they should not and the results are not exactly polite." *Moving Picture Weekly*, September 14, 1918, p.37

REVIEWS: "Occasionally a comic production of the knockabout type gets to skidding along on a series of funny situations that make for real laughter. This two-reel L-KO production, 'A Pullman Blunder,' is one of that kind. It does not differ essentially from the usual comic in plot or situations, but has a certain irresistible swing that gets the giggles going.

"Harry Gribbon, who has had a long and valuable schooling in the comics, appears as an erring husband who has been trifling with too much booze. He is undergoing a certain cure, and while this is in progress his wife gets his pills mixed up with some moth balls and feeds him the latter. The husband so far recovers as to get into further difficulties with a certain bride and groom on a honeymoon trip. Mae Emory appears as his faithful but suspicious wife.

"The number also gets considerable humor out of the 'work or fight' ruling, with Harry Mann playing the role of detective. Eddie Barry appears as the doctor." *Moving Picture World*, September 28, 1918, p.1918; reviewed by Robert C. McElravy

"A lively two-reel comic featuring Harry Gribbon, Mae Emory, Eddie Barry and Harry Mann. This is unusually laughable and contains many situations of a very funny nature. The action throughout is of the best knockabout sort and carries the interest at high speed." *Moving Picture World*, September 28, 1918, p.1921

Hello Trouble: *Released 09/25/1918 Wednesday.* © 09/13/1918 — 2 reels. DIRECTOR: Charles Parrott. CAST: Oliver Hardy, Peggy Prevost, Billy Armstrong, Bartine Burkett, Charles Inslee, Fay Holderness
SYNOPSIS: "Charles Inslee is an undertaker whose business is rotten, due to war conditions, so he has been forced to add as a side line an insurance agency.

"Billy Armstrong and his wife, Bartine Burkett, are a happily married couple as are also Babe Hardy and Peggy Prevost. But Inslee's business is so bad that it is necessary for him to find new fields for his endeavors. Speaking with Peggy and Bartine separately he tells each one their husbands are untrue to them and suggests to Billy and Babe individually that they test their wives' devotion by feigning suicide.

"Babe and Billy, unknown to each other, are told to stand at the end of a pier and signal to their wives their intention of committing suicide by jumping into the water. If the wives are true they will wave to them to stop but Peggy and Bartine have been told by Inslee not to notice their husbands who are only fooling. Babe and Billy jump off the pier and swim out to a little boat which has all been planned by Inslee. Babe and Billy are greatly surprised when they meet on the boat for the first time. Inslee from the shore sees them climb into the boat and pulls a wire which pulls out the bottom of the boat and Babe and Billy disappear. He then takes out Peggy and Bartine to celebrate their husbands' demise.

"A week passed and Babe and Billy are both shown emerging from the water; they return to their homes and discover the treachery of Inslee and then a big chase ensues." *Moving Picture Weekly*, September 21, 1918, p.36
REVIEWS: "The troubles of an undertaker in war times is a theme that brings the comedy talent of L-Ko stars into the high speed of fun. Their film on this subject is 'Hello Trouble.' Charles Inslee, in the role of an dishonest undertaker, stirs up droll, laughable tragedy between two devoted husbands and their loyal wives in his attempt to build up an insurance sideline when the undertaker business fails.

"Charles Parrott directed the picture. Babe Hardy and Billy Armstrong are the devoted husbands. Peggy Prevost and Bartine Burkett are the loving wives." *Moving Picture World*, September 21, 1918, p.1748

Nuts and Noodles: *Released 10/02/1918 Wednesday.* © 09/20/1918 — 2 reels. DIRECTOR: James D. Davis. CAST: Eva Novak, Rube Miller, "Oriental Charlie" Chai Hong, Eddie Boland, Fat Lobeck, James Donnelly
(pre-release title: **A Bum Bomb**)
SYNOPSIS: "Charlie [Hong] is waiter and cook in the Lowlife Café run by Mr. Succotash [Lobeck] with the assistance of his friends and conspirators, Eucalyptus

Sniffle [Miller] and Walter Linseed. Mr. Street [Donnely], together with his daughter [Novak] and son-in-law [Boland] visit the Lowlife Café on a slumming tour where Father Street loses his valuable dog and offers a reward for the return. Old man Succotash gets the dog and, putting him in a satchel, plans to obtain the reward. But satchels all look more or less alike, and so Succotash takes a grip with the bomb and his conspirators get the dog. The natural thing follows — explosion of bomb and conspirators are sent sky high.

"Charlie is given employment by Mr. Street and falls violently in love with Chin-Chin, Miss Street's maid. Charlie returns to Lowlife Café to get the dog, is captured by Succotash and his gang and tied down in the bottom of a well. The water is turned in on him and Charlie is on the verge of drowning when he manages to open the water gate and float out with the water. The crooks, in an effort to capture Eva, seized Chin-Chin by mistake, but eventually capture Eva, tie and bind her, placing a bomb at her feet. She kicks the bomb and it bounces back and burns the rope. A chase ensues which ends up happily for our heroes and heroines." *Moving Picture Weekly*, September 28, 1918, p.34

REVIEWS: "A two-reel comic, with 'Oriental Charlie,' Eva Novak, Rube Miller and others in the cast. The fun consists almost entirely of small stunts which are quite amusing in their way, though a stronger connecting plot would have helped. A burro, goat, a pig and a cow and calf 'assist.' This is of about average strength." *Moving Picture World*, October 12, 1918, p.277

Scars and Bars: *Released 11/20/1918 Wednesday.* © 09/08/1918 — 2 reels. DIRECTOR: Noel Smith. CINEMATOGRAPHY: Irving Reis. CAST: Helen Lynch, Dick Smith, Bobby Richards, Jack Henderson, Henry Gugenheim, Eddie Barry, Charles Lakin
(originally scheduled for 10/16/1918 release; rescheduled due to Spanish influenza theater closings)
SYNOPSIS: "Heinie and Dick attempt to park all night in a farmer's cornfield, but much to their regret they are chased. Dick is caught and put in jail. Heinie, who escapes, runs until he loses almost all his clothes except his underwear. When he stops to rest he leans against a freshly-painted sign with a number on it, and the impression comes off on his back. In such a state he speeds to the city on a bicycle he had secured. In the town there is a bicycle race taking place and as he is coming in he is surrounded by an enthusiastic throng who acclaim him winner of the bicycle race.

"Heinie is royally treated and receives a medal from Henderson, the rich man, who gave the race, and his pretty daughter pins a medal on Heinie.

"One day while Heinie and the girl are slumming they meet Dick Smith in jail, with whom the girl immediately falls for. A rivalry springs up between Heinie and Dick and a chase ensues between them." *Moving Picture Weekly*, October 12, 1918, p.37

REVIEWS: "A two-reel comic with Jack Henderson, Helen Lynch, Dick Smith, Henry Gugenheim and Eddie Barry. The most amusing thing in this is a peculiar vehicle which travels on railroad tracks and which we suspect is a camouflaged Ford car. There are a number of stunts, including a prison vaudeville show. The offering makes a comic of moderate strength." *Moving Picture World*, October 19, 1918, p.447

Painless Love: *Released 11/27/1918 Wednesday.* © 11/09/1918 — 2 reels. DIRECTOR: Charles Parrott. CAST: Oliver Hardy, Billy Armstrong, Peggy Prevost, Charles Inslee, Grace Orma
(originally scheduled for 10/23/1918 release; rescheduled due to Spanish influenza theater closings)
SYNOPSIS: "Billy Armstrong and Peggy Provost [sic] are married secretly. Billy Armstrong is an assistant in the dentist parlor owned by Babe Hardy. Peggy Provost owns a ladies swimming parlor in the building owned by Charles Inslee, which is directly opposite the home where Babe Hardy, the dentist, and his wife live.

"All the trouble starts when Peggy's time is up for paying rent, and she is financially embarrassed, but Babe comes to her rescue and offers a check and an invitation to dinner. Charles, the owner, sees this and becomes desperately mad, because she refused his offer of marriage, and then Charles, swearing revenge, goes to the jealous wife of Babe and tells her all.

"Charles, Babe's wife and all the others are all in a cabaret place and when an explanation is demanded they start a big chase, and the end shows them all struggling in the water." *Moving Picture Weekly*, October 19, 1918, p.34
REVIEWS: "A two-reel comic featuring Babe Hardy, Billy Armstrong and Peggy Prevost. This opens with some funny stunts in a dentist's shop. Later scenes occur in a wine room and in a big plunge, with a contingent of pretty girls. There is no very definite connecting idea in this, but it will bring at least two good laughs and possibly more." *Moving Picture World*, October 19, 1918, p.447

King of the Kitchen: *Released 12/04/1918 Wednesday.* © 11/25/1918 — 2 reels. DIRECTOR: Frank Griffin. CAST: Harry Gribbon, May Emory, Billy Armstrong, Merta Sterling, Eva Novak, Rose Gore, Babe Hardy, Jack Henderson
(pre-release title: **The Chef**)
(originally scheduled for 10/30/1918 release; rescheduled due to Spanish influenza theater closings)
SYNOPSIS: "Billy Armstrong and May Emory, two city crooks, make arrangements to stay at the country boarding-house owned by Rose Gore. The crooks learn that the owner's niece, Eva [Novak], is to get a fortune when she is married to Harry [Gribbon], the chef. Billy poses as an artist and impresses the aunt by a lavish display of fake jewelry for Eva, while May always arranges to make Harry see his fiance with Billy, thereby forcing a break of the engagement, which finally happens.

"Billy, well acquainted now, steals Eva's cash box, locks up the aunt, and places May and Harry in a run-away cab. But Eva arrives in time, saves the cab, and with the aid of Harry captures Billy. They get back their money, arrest the two city explorers, and then Eva and Harry are married, to live happily ever after." *Moving Picture Weekly*, November 30, 1918, p.36
REVIEWS: "A two-reel comic with Harry Gribbon, Mae [Emory], Billy Armstrong and Eva Novak in the cast. This begins in a restaurant, where Harry Gribbon acts as chef. A city couple drop in and make an effort to steal the cash box. This has a number of laughs in it, the action being of the nonsensical, knockabout sort." *Moving Picture World*, November 2, 1918, p.623

Rough On Husbands: *Released 12/11/1918 Wednesday.* © 12/03/1918 — 2 reels. DIRECTOR: Vin Moore. Cinematographer: Park Reis. CAST: Merta Sterling, Eddie Barry, Harry Mann, Helen Lynch, Grace Orma, Charles Dorety
SYNOPSIS: "'It's cheaper to move than to pay rent' was the motto of Albicore Fish [Mann], a shiftless sort of personage, who also lived in the belief that while he loved his wife [Sterling] he should feel sympathetic towards his female neighbors.

"Again and again they move until finally hubby decides that this is the flat they want and here the reason why:

"In the next flat live Ben [Barry] and Lizzie where everything is peaches and cream and cupid reigns supreme, until — wifey's mother comes. Then hubby decides to spend more time at the office, of course leaving wifey alone for several hours.

"Albicore sees this and uses his sympathy in gaining friendship with Lizzie. Friend husband suspects something and goes out on a search for this man-vampire, who is so pleasant to his wife. The trouble then begins when Albicore hears of this search, and hides in the clothes basket in Lizzie's room. When jealous Ben finds him there, in his wife's room, the two men almost strangle each other. Meanwhile Albicore's wife, almost sure that her husband will be killed, is starting her mourning process. While Ben's wife is asking for forgiveness.

"But as ever Albicore is a lucky fish and once more safely lodged in the arms of his Tuna, while Lizzie and Ben become happy once more again." *Moving Picture Weekly*, December 7, 1918, p.38
REVIEWS: "A pleasing two-reel comic, with Harry Mann, Merta Sterling and Eddie Barry in the cast. This has a lot of fun with the moving-day troubles of the Fish family. Later come a series of mixups between the new neighbors, which will get a number of laughs. This is a good subject." *Moving Picture World*, December 21, 1918, p.1384

Work or Fight: *Released 12/25/1918 Wednesday.* © 12/17/1918 — 2 reels. DIRECTOR: Craig Hutchinson. CAST: Harry Gribbon, Eva Novak, May Emory, Harry Mann, James Donnelly
SYNOPSIS: "Harry Gribbon has been exempted from military service due to pretended deafness on his part. His wife, May Emory, takes in washing, does the chores, takes care of the children and does other little sundries around the house. Finally the 'Work or Fight' ordinance is put into effect and Gribbon has to find a job. He lands plenty of them but is unable to hold any. Finally he and Harry Mann, who has also been exempted, after trying numerous times to enlist but being rejected on account of physical disability, secure employment in an overcrowded hotel. Here many things happen as there are not enough accommodations for the crowd and people are sleeping in the elevators, on the roof, etc. Finally, after many vain attempts, Harry Gribbon succeeds in getting into the U.S. Army." *Moving Picture Weekly*, December 21, 1918, p.33

1919 Releases:

Klever Kiddies: *Released 01/01/1919 Wednesday.* © 12/21/1918 — 2 reels. CAST: Eddie Barry, Chai Hong
SYNOPSIS: "To the quiet little village of Muchnoise, came the Flip Flop Film Company to acquire scenery and atmosphere for their billion dollar production. The village school

immediately woke up from its customary lethargy and took notice. Charlie from the Orient [Hong] was usually the originator of all mischief and he suggested that the rest of the pupils assist him in impersonating the stars in the forthcoming drama. To the amusement of a long-suffering public we see depicted before us in rapid succession, Violet Mersereau, the girl who invented curls; Priscilla Dean, who ruins a man's life every time she shrugs her shoulders; Edith Roberts, whose smile would make you forfeit your chance of heaven; Helen Gibson, who stops a couple of runaway engines every morning before breakfast; Eddie Polo, who never uses stairs when the side of the house is steep enough; Hughey [sic] Mack, who shakes up China every time he does a vault in the film, and Harry Carey, who uses his shooting irons for eating utensils.

"While the rehearsal is on, the 'wicious wampire' of the Flip Flop Company takes a dislike to the brand of cigarettes smoked by the villain and tears up her contract, whereupon the manager engages the school children to put on his performance." *Moving Picture Weekly*, December 28, 1918, p.28

Fools and Duels: *Released 01/08/1919 Wednesday.* © *01/02/19 — 2 reels.* DIRECTOR: Henry Lehrman. CINEMATOGRAPHY: Frank D. Williams. CAST: Ford Sterling, Peggy Pearce (copyrighted as © Universal Film Mfg. Co. with Lehrman as director; I assume this to be a re-titled re-release of The Sterling Motion Picture Corp's **Hearts and Swords** [05/28/1914], which was not copyrighted, filling a hole in the schedule caused by the Spanish Influenza studio slowdown. See the synopsis for the Sterling Motion Picture Corp.'s **Hearts and Swords** [05/28/1914] for purposes of comparison)
SYNOPSIS: "Of course Patricia Fishgold was utterly unconscious of the violent and jealous admiration of two chivalrous Frenchmen whom she had endeavored to attract ever since the war started. But now she had them where they could observe her without intruding upon her privacy, for Patricia Fishgold was engaged in the pleasant occupation of rowing upon the miniature lake in the park.

"Count de Fromage thought he was alone in paying his tribute but Baron de Bris was close behind him, and both were so occupied that neither observed the other. When their efforts to attract the fair Patricia became so noticeable that a crowd gathered, their efforts became so athletic that both fell in the pond and had to be dragged out by the uniformed police. The Count emerged first and joined Patricia, whereupon the Baron, in high dudgeon, secured a ballet dancer to divert the Count's attention from Patricia. His efforts were successful and Carmen de Phillipi so worked upon the Count's susceptibilities that they were both soon engaged in dancing a hornpipe on the village green, to the vast edification of the Baron and the jealous contempt of Patricia.

"Of course a duel was planned but, as neither of the gallants cared to approach within swords length of his opponent, the duel was mostly a verbal one." *Moving Picture Weekly*, January 4, 1919, p.29

Charlie the Little Daredevil: *Released 01/15/1919 Wednesday.* © 12/31/1918 — 2 reels. CAST: "Charlie from the Orient" Chai Hong, Helen Lynch
SYNOPSIS: "Chai Chow [Hong] and his chum, Napoleon, were a pair of happy hoboes. In the same baggage car with them were traveling three miners who had gone broke in the cheese mines of Colorado. Chow and Napoleon thought these fellows looked like 'easy

money' because they were smaller. The cheese miners were going East to visit their old pal, Whisk E. Straight, now a wealthy milk bottle manufacturer, where little Claret, his daughter, reigned supreme. Her lover was Nick R. Bocker, a tall one, who didn't have as much of a kick as his would-be father-in-law, Whisk E. Straight. A splendid battle takes place between the cheese miners, Chai Chow and Napoleon. If you can stop laughing long enough to worry about who will come out on top, you will be the only one in the audience who can. And the Chinaman 'bleats it while bleating is good.'" *Moving Picture Weekly*, January 11, 1919, p.35

The Freckled Fish: *Released 01/22/1919 Wednesday.* © 01/13/1919 — 2 reels. DIRECTOR: Joseph LeBrandt. CAST: Oliver Hardy, Merta Sterling, Eva Novak, Chai Hong, Eddie Barry
SYNOPSIS: "If you are thinking of a trout, don't bank on it, for it's just as likely to be clam chowder with no clams in it, for the 'Freckled Fish' is just the name of the restaurant where our old friend, Chai Chow [Hong] masquerades as the head waiter. Solomon Soupmeat [Hardy] commands the kitchen regiment and old Aunt Chloe adds color to his sector. And, of course, there is the cashier, who makes the customers forget how much of the meal was missing, and also their change." *Moving Picture Weekly*, January 18, 1919, p.33
REVIEWS: "A two-reel comic, in which a young Chinaman, a fish, a colored mammy and a barber play important roles. The action is too indefinite to hold the attention closely and the number as a whole is only fair." *Moving Picture World*, February 22, 1919, p.1112

It's a Bird: *Released 01/29/1919 Wednesday.* © 01/17/1919 — 2 reels. DIRECTOR: Joe L Brandt and Anthony Coldewey. CAST: Harry Mann, Eddie Barry, Harry Griffith, Bartine Burkett, Loretta Wilson, Grace Orma
SYNOPSIS: "Eddie Barry and Harry Mann are the owners of a bird and animal store, of which Harry is the crooked partner. Arriving at the store one morning, Harry is unable to unlock the door because a monkey has inserted a hose nozzle in the keyhole, and plays the spray on Harry. Harry goes to Eddie's house for the key and gets into some awkward complications with Eddie's wife, and he also becomes the idol of Eddie's mother-in-law.

"Edie [sic] and his wife have an argument over the mother-in-law, and they say they are going to break up their home. Harry Mann, by mistake, receives the two notes telling of their intentions to leave their home, so he rents Eddie's house to Harry Griffin [sic] and Bartine Burkett, a vaudeville team. Eddie has met Bartine in his store and has a picture of her in tights, without her face showing. Meeting her husband in the park, he shows him this picture, with the address, and then a chase ensues between the husband and Eddie.

"Everything is settled until Eddie and his wife decide to return to their home, which at the same time is occupied by Griffin and Bartine, and a great many complications result." *Moving Picture Weekly*, January 25, 1919, p.40
REVIEWS: "This two-reel subject opens with some pleasing pictures of puppies, kittens, a chimpanzee and a parrot. The plot action is very weak in the first reel, but rather better in the second. It makes a fair subject with some good spots in it." *Moving Picture World*, February 22, 1919, p.1112

Hop, the Bell Hop: *Released 02/05/1919 Wednesday.* © 01/29/1919 — 2 reels. DIRECTOR: Charles Parrott. CAST: Billy Armstrong, Oliver Hardy
SYNOPSIS: "Here we go 'back to the dear old farm' on the Hickory Hills Limited, to where Tiny Toodles, the daughter of the hotel proprietor, is the 'main squeeze,' though a rather tight one, because she is 'built for comfort and not for speed.' Jumping Jupiter is the bell hop of this best Hickory Hills hotel and he is full of monkey shines and shoe shines. Polly Tix, the cashier, has a pair of eyes that travel faster than the fastest traveling salesman. And into this little oasis of contentment comes none other than our fleshless friend — Solomon Soop. He comes because Tiny Toodles has been wigwagging with a matrimonial agency and has succumbed to the winsome charm of Soop's passport picture.

"Now the last thing in the world that you would suspect happens. A slippery fellow called Jerry Jippem, won over by Toodles' offer to give Soop a half interest in her father's hotel and a bonus of $500 for becoming her life partner, impersonates Soop. And then — you just can't get away from the picture till it is over." *Moving Picture Weekly*, February 1, 1919, p.33

Call the Cops: *Released 02/19/1919 Wednesday.* © 02/06/1919 — 2 reels. DIRECTOR: Joseph LeBrandt. CAST: Billy Armstrong
SYNOPSIS: "It was a lucky thing for Bobby Biff [Armstrong] that he was a good lightweight scraper [sic], because he had a pretty wife. Sugar doesn't draw flies any more surely than one good scrapper draws another. So, hist — the Walloping Walrus. Now, Bobby would probably have cavorted royally through a little bout with the Walrus, all by himself, if politics hadn't interfered. But Jasper Jiggs offered him a neat little sum to 'lay down' naturally in the first round.

"In act II the scene shifts abruptly to the fashionable watering place (especially for horses) known as Cobweb Corners. Mrs. Boby [sic] wanted to see the fight, so there she was. And whether memory — anyway Bobby forgot to 'lay down.' And right scored another victory over might." *Moving Picture Weekly*, February 8, 1919, p.38
REVIEWS: "Billy Armstrong is featured in this two-reel comic subject, which abounds in knockabout scenes. Some of the stunts are laughable, but there are one or two traces of vulgarity, which brings down the general average of the production. It is hardly up to the L-KO average." *Moving Picture World*, May 24, 1919, p.1239

Lions and Ladies: *Released 02/26/1919 Wednesday.* © 02/18/1919 — 2 reels. DIRECTOR: Frank Griffin. CAST: Harry Mann, Oliver Hardy, Rose Gore, Bobby Dunn
SYNOPSIS: "Where could you find a more toothsome trio to start a movie with than Henry Hash, Stephen Stew and Peter Pye? And where could you find an easier place to start something than at the crackshaft [sic] of a Ford? And now all you have to do is to add three 'his wives' and 'Moon-struck' Mike, for spice, and things are moving nicely. If you've never had a lion in your front yard or in your library, try a Ford Lizzie.

"Enter, a private picnic, led by the romantic Mike — he, of the moon-struck soul. Having asked a damsel to ride with him on the speedway, he is turned down cold, whereupon an officer and a 'big hippopotamus' give a lively turn to the action." *Moving Picture Weekly*, February 22, 1919, p.37
REVIEWS: "A fractious automobile plays an amusing part in the opening scenes of this knockabout number. There is scarcely a trace of plot, but some of the incidents are laughable.

Animals and birds appear frequently, and the principal human characters all dive into the ocean at the close. The offering strikes a good average." *Moving Picture World*, March 1, 1919, p.1246

A Rag-Time Romance: *Released 03/05/1919 Wednesday.* © 02/20/1919 — 2 reels. DIRECTOR: Noel Smith. CAST: Bobby Dunn, Helen Lynch, Dick Smith
SYNOPSIS: "Countess Creampuff of Denmark decides to come to America to study ragtime. As luck would have it, she put up at the Plunge Inn, where was a wondrous swimming pool, Ragtime Ralph, a musician Jitney Joe, an automobile valet, and Dainty Dolly Dipper, who was an artiste on the piano, and off.

"Previous to her trip to America the Prime Minister of the Prune Industry had favored the Countess with many priceless gems, and as it was just like a Prime Minister to do such a thing, the Countess felt that she must wear the gems to America.

"Swimming pool, ragtime music, with the splash of waves: Ralph and Joe, with eyes for jewels first, let mermaids fall where they may; a charming Countess charmed with synocating [sic] tunes, the sudden descent of Count Rott N. Creampuff, a sudden frigidity of the swimming pool — do you get it?" *Moving Picture Weekly*, March 1, 1919, p.32
REVIEWS: "A two-reel comic, the heroine of which is a beautiful countess who comes to this country to study rag-time music. She creates havoc among the masculine hearts at a certain hotel, and her jealous husband finds his hands full fighting off her various admirers. A crippled Ford car and a bathing pool are features, and the number winds up with an amusing auto chase. The subject is of about average strength, and should please quite well." *Moving Picture World*, March 8, 1919, p.1393

Hearts in Hock: *Released 03/19/1919 Wednesday.* © 03/05/1919 — 2 reels. DIRECTOR, SCREENPLAY: Charles Parrott. CAST: Bartine Burkett, Billy Armstrong, Peggy Prevost, Oliver Hardy, Jack Henderson, William Hutchinson (died during production, and may have been cut from the release print)
SYNOPSIS: "It all happened because a jewelry store was right next door to the court where Judge Barl E. Korn decided the momentous problems of Where, When and Who. Flippant Flossie was the sparkling jewel in the jewelry shop and was used to gentle treatment.

"Somebody lost a purse, and somebody, including Flossie, the judge's wife and Gumshoe Gus all had the purse. A trial took place and the purse was returned to the rightful owner after it was brought out in the evidence that judge Barl E. Korn had given the purse to the thief." *Moving Picture Weekly*, March 15, 1919, p.34
REVIEWS: "A two-reel comic of the strictly knockabout, semi-burlesque type. The chief figure is a judge whose court is connected with a pawnbroker's establishment. A bomb is thrown into the court room from the latter establishment during a trial. This is a number of average quality, with some humorous moments of fair strength." *Moving Picture World*, April 5, 1919, p.128

Gymbelles and Boneheads: *Released 03/26/1919 Wednesday.* © 03/14/1919 — 2 reels. DIRECTOR: Noel Smith. CAST: Dick Smith, Billy Bevan, Peggy Aarup
SYNOPSIS: "Where there is a Purple Peacock Hairdressing Parlor right next to a gym, what chance is there for a happy ending? Of course, there was romance right off the reel,

because the proprietors of the hairdressing parlor were in love with the little hairdresser. And right after romance there is mystery, for the Nutty Nihilists are out with dangerous weapons after business.

"Fish, King Solomon, shimmying, prohibition and ukelelles [sic] all take part in the scramble of this little playlet. How it turns out we will leave to you to see if you can find out." *Moving Picture Weekly*, March 22, 1919, p.37

REVIEWS: "The climax of the comedy is reached when Hy Ball and Glasser Beer, owners of a hairdressing parlor fall in love with one of their customers and exceed the speed limit in proposing to her." *Moving Picture World*, March 22, 1919, p.1689

A Skate at Sea: *Released 04/02/1919 Wednesday.* © 03/24/1919 — 2 reels. DIRECTOR: Vin Moore. CAST: Charles Dorety, Eva Novak, Vera Reynolds
(pre-release title: **Rough on Roller Skates**)
SYNOPSIS: "Anyone who has ever experienced the fatal malady of seasickness knows that it would be just as easy to roller skate on a rolling deck as to stand still and let the railing creep up on you — and far more amusing. This gives the setting, which always happens sooner or later when you try to roller skate.

"You see, Mrs. Lotta Kash, accompanied by her dog and her husband, took a little voyage and Maybelle went along as a maid in America. Whiskey Willy went through the throes of serving a meal and Bouncing Bill saw the pretty maid and wrote her a poem. Unfortunately the poem fell into the hands of Mrs. Kash, who thought it was for her, and then the dog and her husband were angry. Bouncing Billy did not know whether to step off the boat and walk back to land or what. So, just here, unfortunately, the film came to an end." *Moving Picture Weekly*, March 29, 1919, p.34

REVIEWS: "A two-reel comic featuring Charles Dorety. He plays the part of a stowaway on a vessel loaded with monkeys, snakes and other animals and birds. He is discovered and forced to act as cook. This contains some amusing stunts all through, but the strongest feature is the close, which has several new and original chase scenes. The number is well up to the average." *Moving Picture World*, May 17, 1919, p.1077

A Movie Riot: *Released 04/09/1919 Wednesday.* © 03/28/1919 — 2 reels. DIRECTOR: Craig Hutchinson and James Davis. CAST: Chai Hong, Bartine Burkett, Rube Miller
(pre-release titles: **Charlie and the Children** and **Playing Movies**)
SYNOPSIS: "School is out because the village schoolmaster has had his digestion spoiled by the children continually making him sick with their antics. So the two worst culprits, Hoptoad Hal and Tadpole Ted, went to work on the farm. What should arrive but the Filibuster Film Company to stage a few scenes of their great drama, 'The Romance of a Young Butcher.'

"Right here Charlie from the Orient makes his presence felt and Lady Vere de Voop simply cannot escape the tender advances of the young but worldly-wise butcher. Of course, the kids get continually in the way, as they always do when love scenes threaten. Then movies begin to riot all over the place and even 'the child' and the storm — just like 'Way Down East.' But just before you begin to cry the happy ending comes." *Moving Picture Weekly*, April 5, 1919, p.27

REVIEWS: "A two-reel comic featuring Charlie of the Orient and others. A bevy of bathing girls appear in the opening reel. There is not much plot, but several good features. The burlesque melodrama is funny, and the rescue of the baby from the miniature train by a dog makes an exciting close." *Moving Picture World*, May 17, 1919, p.1078

Let Fido Do It: *Released 04/16/1919 Wednesday.* © 04/02/1919 — 2 reels. DIRECTOR: Noel Smith. CAST: Dick Smith, Eva Novak, Peggy Aarup, Billy Bevan
SYNOPSIS: "Right out on the rural front things were happening thick and fast. Father was interested in the livestock, and so was Peggy, though not the same stock, while mother just looked on and got healthy. Handsome Harry and Archibald Acorn both cast fond glances at the youthful Peg. Things were progressing jealously when along came a telegram which got everybody excited, because it said: 'You will receive 50,000 kegs if your daughter is married immediately.' So it was decided that Peg must be married before July 1st.

"Wounded Willie Wimples had just returned from war and was also desirous of marrying Peg, so he changed the wire to fit his purposes. But Peggy took things into her own hands and eloped with Handsome Harry after all." *Moving Picture Weekly*, April 12, 1919, p.34
REVIEWS: "Eva Novak and Dick Smith appear in this two-reel comic. This is full of entertaining stunts, though it does not boast of any particular plot. The work of the trained dog at the beginning is excellent and will surely please. The scenes occur on a farm and wind up with a good chase. This is a first rate comic subject of its type." *Moving Picture World*, May 24, 1919, p.1239

Sambo's Wedding Day: *Released 04/30/1919 Wednesday.* © 04/17/1919 — 2 reels. DIRECTOR: Craig Hutchinson. CAST: Eva Novak, Phil Dunham
(pre-release title: **A Marriage in Black and White**)
SYNOPSIS: "Miss Vera Sweet, sweet bride-to-be, was waiting for her groom, and so were all the guests. Her maid, Mirandy, was to be married the same day in the kitchen. But fate turned against Miss Sweet's sweety, and while he was dressing, a chimneysweep fixing the chimney swept soot all over him. Being late, the doomed groom couldn't stop to fix it, and, arriving at the house, is mistaken for Mirandy's man.

"They are just being married when Sambo appears upon the scene and there is a black and white mix-up which goes to the head of Mr. Hoarse Blankett, and he begins to cry, washing off the soot with his tears. A fade-out shows both couples married two hours — and still happy!" *Moving Picture Weekly*, April 26, 1919, p.41
REVIEWS: "A bridegroom on the eve of his wedding falls down a chimney and becomes so covered with soot that he is mistaken for a colored man. Some real colored folks participate, also some bewhiskered individuals of anarchistic tendencies. This is just a compilation of knockabout stunts, some of which are quite funny, but the production as a whole is not particularly strong." *Moving Picture World*, May 17, 1919, p.1077

Good-Night, Turk!: *Released 05/07/1919 Wednesday.* © 04/22/1919 — 2 reels. DIRECTOR: James D. Davis. CAST: Chai Hong (Charlie of the Orient), Pop Hadley, Harry Keaton, Slim Peppercorn, Dot Farley
SYNOPSIS: "M.T. Head [Hadley], Station Master at Pastop, Tex., sure did work hard — chasing the loafers, Simpleton [Keaton] and Pinhead [Peppercorn], out of his office. The only thing about M.T. that Simpleton liked was his daughter Belindy [Farley]. One day a telegram came from General Nuisance telling of a terrible Turk that was headed in their

direction, and of a box of gold that the General was sending for safe keeping. All the rubes in town began to sit up and take notice when M.T. announced that whoever got the Turk got the only asset in Pastop — Belindy. The Turk scented the gold and made a bee-line for Pastop, but Simpleton the Sheriff had not forgotten M.T. Head's daughter, and when he finished, the Turk was considerably cut up and howling for an armistice." *Moving Picture Weekly*, May 3, 1919, p.35

REVIEWS: "An unusually good two-reel comic of its kind. The burlesque fire scene at the beginning is very funny; also the burro run by the electric trolley. The knockabout scenes are good and the burrowing under ground, while not an unusual stunt, is at the same time very laughable. A successful number." *Moving Picture World*, May 17, 1919, p.1078

In Bad All Around: *Released 05/14/1919 Wednesday.* © 05/01/1919 — 2 reels. DIRECTOR: William H. Watson. CAST: Phil Dunham, Charles Dorety, Eva Novak, Hughie Mack
SYNOPSIS: "Although Luke Warm [Dunham] and Isadore Able [Novak] were married, they were not happy, and the cause of their unhappiness was one Fuller Fat [Mack], who had been a suitor for the hand of the fair bride, and found it difficult to cast himself adrift. He even kidded himself that his was a platonic friendship. Butt Insky [Dorety], however, suspected that it was otherwise, and determined that it should be, anyway. He butted in on a touching scene, when the young wife was attempting to repair a rent in Fuller's trousers. Butt Insky informed hubby, and things in the peaceful village hummed so alarmingly for the next hour or two that the quiet inhabitants thought the Bolsheviki had established a young Soviet there. When the husband's honor had been sufficiently satisfied, Fuller Fat and Butt Insky founded a Home Wrecker's Union, and started out after the next newly-weds." *Moving Picture Weekly*, May 10, 1919, p.34

REVIEWS: "One of the best of recent L-KO subjects, except for a few slight touches of vulgarity, which we think are funny enough to get by without great offense. Phil Dunham, Charles Dorety and Eva Novak are in the cast. This is full of comic action of a pleasing sort, and will bring many laughs." *Moving Picture World*, May 24, 1919, p.1239

His Wicked Eyes: *Released 05/21/1919 Wednesday.* © 05/09/1919 — 2 reels. DIRECTOR: Craig Hutchinson. CAST: Dan Russell, L-KO Beauty Broilers
SYNOPSIS: "Mr. and Mrs. Won Knight Stande traveled de luxe on the Limited Express. Wifey had a mania for curios, and Dan Yell sure was some curio, being the only one of his kind in existence, so naturally wifey was interested. But hubby was curious, too, and proceeded to make Dan Yell, but on account of the evening's performance the battle was postponed.

"That evening all Rummyville attended the big show. Hom and Dearie were all made up 'n' everything, and were rehearsing their act, dearie doing a Nautch dance while Hom walked the tight rope. Everything was going splendidly, when Hom discovered while on the rope that it was not so tight. But too late! He slipped aid [sic] broke his promise, while Dearie and Dannie made their get-away." *Moving Picture Weekly*, May 17, 1919, p.14

All Jazzed Up: *Released 06/04/1919 Wednesday.* © 05/21/1919 — 2 reels. DIRECTOR: William H. Watson. CAST: Dan Russell, Eva Novak, Hughie Mack, Phil Dunham
SYNOPSIS: "The 'Drop Inn,' was the most unpopular place in Four Corners, in spite of the fact that Dainty Dotty's Dad [Russell] owned the place. Dainty Dotty [Novak] was the

whole cabaret show, but she had no audience. The customers passed by just as if the 'Inn' was camouflaged. Then, one day, Wilbur [Dunham], a retired waiter, happened to come in. He immediately saw that there wasn't anything in the 'Inn' except Dottie [sic], and he desired that she get out of the 'Inn' and go with him. Dottie promised that she would, if he would bring some customers to the 'Inn.' So Wilbur bethought himself of the old White Way days and the Jazz bands, and he installed a self-made Jazz band in that 'Inn' that put Sophie Tucker's in the shade. He taught Dottie the 'Shimmie' dance, and after that they had to call out the police force to keep the crowds from coming in the windows." *Moving Picture Weekly,* May 31, 1919, p.37

Four Corners roadside café "Drop Inn" proprietor Russell hits upon a scheme to attract customers: intentionally (and surreptitiously) flatten their tires as they drive by, resulting in a wave of patrons as their tires are replaced (he looks out at the road midway through the film, and there are cars lined up on either side, frustrated drivers pumping up tires, with a title card that suggests heavy cursing).

The café not only provides food prepared by chef "Toddles" (Mack), but entertainment as well in the form of dancing girls featuring "Dainty Dotty" (Novak), the proprietor's daughter, and gambling. The food, served by waiter Wilbur (Dunham), is suspect: one patron's string of sausages arrive after having been dragged all about the place by a hungry dog, and when they finally land on his plate seem to have a life of their own, squirming about in a roughly-pixilated fashion. His first bite reveals a metal dog license inside, and we then cut to a shot of Toddles outside chasing down a bunch of stray dogs!

The gambling is crooked, with it rigged so the house can't lose. In the event that the gambling is going the customer's way, he's quickly dispatched down a chute that leads to the basement where a muscle-strapped black man awaits with a sledgehammer. The customer is conked, the won money sent back upstairs, and the unconscious fellow dumped outside.

The café's waiter heads for the gambling table, and when he wins big, a wild, extended fight and chase ensues with Wilbur pursued by the proprietor and his henchmen. Wilbur escapes with Dotty. Synopsis based on print held by the Library of Congress

Nellie's Naughty Boarder: *Released 06/11/1919 Wednesday.* © 05/28/1919 — 2 reels.
DIRECTOR: Frank Griffin. CAST: Dot Farley, Phil Dunham
SYNOPSIS: "Oleander Olympus and his wife Nellie lived a peaceful existence until one day Nellie decided to take a boarder, by the name of Hemale Vamp. Hemale liked Nellie alright, but couldn't see where Oleander came in, and decided that, if he could help it, Oleander wouldn't come in. So he left a note saying, 'If anything happens to me, Oleander Olympus did it,' and then he dressed a dummy up like himself and drowned it. Later, thoroughly disguised and hiding behind a clump of false whiskers, he presented himself at the Olympus home as a lawyer and accused Oleander of committing the murder. He dragged him to court by the ear and the jury was just bringing in a verdict of 'Guilty,' when the trick-lawyer's sheltering whiskers fell off." *Moving Picture Weekly*, June 7, 1919, p.35
REVIEWS: "A two-part comedy featuring Dot Farley and Phil Dunham. The picture contains some good farce comedy situations and treats of the trials of a husband because of a male boarder who persisted in appropriating his belongings, and sought also to alienate his wife's affections. One of the funniest things in the picture is the method used by the boarder in trying to get rid of the husband. He puts his own clothes on a wax figure and

throws it in the water, leaving a note stating that the woman's husband is his murderer. At the trial he appears in disguise as the defendant's lawyer, and is discovered and duly punished in farce comedy fashion." *Moving Picture World*, July 19, 1919, p.423

Beauty and the Boob: *Released 06/18/1919 Wednesday.* © 06/04/1919 — 2 reels. CAST: Alice Howell

SYNOPSIS: "Calamity Clara was one of those unnecessary beauties whose face was not her fortune. Her husband Percy was in love with her fortune, and that is how she came to have a husband at all. Percy was flirtatious. He always passed roast beef up for chicken.

"Mr. and Mrs. T. Kettle were spending their honeymoon at the Bitless Hotel and when Percy dear invited Mrs. T. Kettle to dinner, Mr. T. Kettle began to boil over.

"Poor Clara's heart was broken when she saw how Percy fell for the beautiful women. She visited the beauty parlor in the hotel and through their machinations was transformed into a beautiful creature. Percy is about to run away with Mrs. T. Kettle when Clara comes along and is espied by Percy. Once again Percy's heart takes flight, and just as he is about to kiss the beautiful unknown he discovers her to be his wife. She scorns him and goes for a dip with Mr. Coff. E. Pott. Ma Coff. E. Pott is greatly stirred up when she discovers friend husband making love to Clara. A general mixup of husbands and wives ensues, which ends in the usual happy everafter." *Moving Picture Weekly*, June 14, 1919, p.33

REVIEWS: "A two-part comedy featuring Alice Howell. Most of the comedy takes place in the apartment of a beauty doctor at a big hotel, and concerns the transformation of a woman who is afflicted with a growth of hair on her face. In her transformed state she dons fine clothes and lures her own husband into a trap. Scenes in which bathing suits, swimming pools and other comedy accessories are used afford considerable action of the broad comedy order." *Moving Picture World*, August 9, 1919, p.884

The Spotted Nag: *Released 07/02/1919 Wednesday.* © 06/22/1919 — 2 reels. DIRECTOR: James D. Davis. CAST: Lois Nelson, Harry Keston

SYNOPSIS: "Hasbeen and Itwas were walking delegates of the Hoboes' Union. They had a valet, Mutt, who carried their baggage and protected them from work. They come upon a Mexican in distress. The Mexicano's horse wouldn't let any one ride him, so Hasbeen and Itwas lead him away and returned with a horse of a different color. They camouflaged the first horse with big white spots and sold it to the Mexican. The same thing happened again, and the Mexican got wise and called the whole Mexican army out to kill the delegates.

"They find refuge in the Shimmy Shack, where you can get a meal and everything for twenty-five cents. The three get into a large pair of trousers, which they had found, and get all they can eat for twenty-five cents.

"Dollyrimples, a former Broadwayite, has been kidnapped by the proprietor of the Shimmy Shack, and is held prisoner by him. Hasbeen and Itwas scheme to save Dolly. Yeabo, the proprietor, demands that Dolly don an Oriental costume and do a 'salome' act. Itwas impersonates Dolly, and while he is dancing, Dolly and Hasbeen make their escape. Itwas entrances Yeabo, runs into another room, locks the door, and escapes through a window. A general chase ensues, wherein to Fords do the shimmy, climb a few trees, and the occupants land safe and sound on the ground, with all forgiven and happy." *Moving Picture Weekly*, June 28, 1919, p.31

A Pair of Deuces: *Released 07/09/1919 Wednesday.* © *06/29/1919* — 2 reels. DIRECTOR: Alf Goulding. CAST: Chai Hong, Claire Alexander
(pre-release title: **The Chinese Blues** [unconfirmed])
SYNOPSIS: "Felecious Foolcap had fallen in love with Patricia Millionbuck, but, being far beneath her, financially, he was lost in despair. But Wun Lung, his valet and spiritual adviser, finds a way out by stealing a suit from a fellow in the pocket of which is an invitation to the Millionbuck's banquet. They force their way into the reception room and find seats at the dinner table. They are enjoying the soup song which is being sung by the guests, when the surprise of the evening comes with Madam Butterflew, a talented 'Salome' dancer. When Wun Lung saw her, he forgot the dinner and started to imitate her. He noticed a bee on her back and heroically attempted to kill it. But it happened to be an ornament which Madam purposely put there, and a general fight followed. 'Pop' Millionbuck was quite furious by that time and challenged Felecious to a duel. The latter thought that he had been killed. 'Pop' offered [one] thousand dollars if he were alive. Felecious comes to life, grabs Patricia and runs away with her. Before Pop catches them they have already been married and are waiting for his parental blessing." *Moving Picture Weekly*, July 5, 1919, p.31
REVIEWS: "A two-reel comic featuring Charlie of the Orient, Claire Alexander and others. Some of the incidents are funny, and the number on the whole is amusing. Charlie's antics in the cabaret contain some vulgar touches which might well be eliminated. The offering is otherwise a fairly good one of the knockabout type." *Moving Picture World*, August 30, 1919, p.1376

Two-Gun Trixie: *Released 07/16/1919 Wednesday.* © *07/03/1919* — 2 reels. CAST: Dan Russell, Marjorie Ray
SYNOPSIS: "Mr. and Mrs. Bonedome are on their honeymoon. They had a special conveyance of a two-wheeled flivver. To balance this flivver Mrs. Bonedome wore a hat with balloons, and as they traveled on their merry way she slackened speed by shooting these balloons one after the other. They arrived at the Hotel DeSwelle and are ushered to the bridal suite. This hotel happens to be at Neptune's beach, where nifty maids are seen galore. Slim Jim, a light-fingered gent with a long reputation, spotted Mr. Bonedome as a good find. He induces friend husband to go down to the beach and watch the maids at their daily play. The girls perform for hubby in their one-piece regalia, 'n' everything.

"In the meantime wifie buys a flivver so she can chase hubby around. After a hair-raising trip she goes for help to get the car out of the sand. Slim Jim sees his chance to sell this flivver to hubby. He puts the girls wise to make him buy the car, and, of course, friend hubby falls. He takes the girls for a joy-ride and lands in a cafe. At the cafe riotous scenes take place. The girls do pretty dances. Friend wifie gets on the trail and discovers hubby having a wild time amongst a bunch of beauties. She beats him up and he escapes getting into a taxi wherein the pretty girls are all ready. Wifie chases with another car.

"Slim Jim is not satisfied with half of hubby's fortune, he must have the while. He is masqueraded as the chauffeur of the taxi and holds up friend husband on a blackmail scheme. He gives hubby ten minutes to get all his money into the hollow of the tree or else he will call his wife and tell her where to find hubby. Hubby, now scared to death, phones the wife, who has returned to the hotel, and tells her of his predicament, and she gets the police force on the job, and a rush to the hollow tree follows. She places the money into the tree and hides herself in the bushes. Slim Jim, in disguise, steals the money and runs. He runs into the road house, where hubby and the girls are hiding. Friend wifie and the cops follow. A rough-and-tumble fight ensues and wifie takes hubby home for a spanking." *Moving Picture Weekly*, July 12, 1919, p.26

REVIEWS: "A two-reel comic of about average interest. Many of the scenes occur on the beach, and there are some close-ups of bathing girls in short suits. Some of the humor has a tinge of vulgarity and seems to lack any particular point, though there are some good special stunts, such as knocking over the bath houses with an automobile. The kitten and white cat at play makes a good feature." *Moving Picture World*, August 9, 1919, p.884

Brown Eyes and Bank Notes: *Released 07/23/1919 Wednesday.* © 07/09/1919 — 2 reels.
DIRECTOR: James D. Davis. CAST: Lois Neilson, Bob Brownie the Dog, Juan Paco
SYNOPSIS: "Paco and Waco ran a shoe-shining shop. They were in hot water all the time, however, because both were in love with Tessie Trim, the manicurist, and Tessie's husband was considerable bar to the effective display of their affection. Waco, who was the general manager of the shoe-shining department, had an assistant in Bobby Brownie, a dog whose intelligence far outweighed that of the proprietor. Bobby had been trained to roll over upon a man's shoes until he had them sufficiently soiled to warrant a shine, and Waco, who was very fond of work, had installed a physical culture machine so that his customers could either work to put on flesh or to take it off, as the case might be. They were blissfully unconscious of the fact that the apparatus was attached to a machine whereby they polished their own shoes. Tessie was extremely fond of bathing and while enjoying this pastime a girlfriend took a picture of her in a bathing suit. This picture fell into the hands of both Waco and Paco and each enjoyed it in secret until Tessie's husband discovered the photo. Then things began to happen which were never supposed to happen in any beauty shop, in fact no beauty shop would stand it, and the fade-out finds it going up in smoke." *Moving Picture Weekly*, July 9, 1919, p.29

A Puppy Love Panic: *Released 08/06/1919 Wednesday.* © 07/23/1919 — 2 reels. DIRECTOR: James D. Davis. CAST: Lois Neilson, Caroline Wright
SYNOPSIS: "Lord and Lady Algeria were engaged in the business of lifting things easily. The town of Slumberville looked good to them and they halted by the side of the road and put on their working clothes. These consisted of a blindman's outfit with a typical hand-organ for Lord Algeria, and his lady went along to collect the dough. Their coming had been announced to the sheriff, but he never expected to find the crooks in this guise. The music was so appealing that the entire population left their homes to listen. When they were all collected, Lady Algeria took a box, entered a rear window and collected the valuables. At least she thought she did. A pair of piggies, who were enchanted by the music, snouted out the valuables and got into the box themselves. When the crooks made their getaway they heard a suspicious sound in the supposed treasure box and when its real contents were revealed the dispute grew fast and furious. The sheriff put in his appearance and Lady Algeria made a break for the river bank, where she disrobed and left her garments under a slip of paper which stated, 'Leave my clothes on the spot from whence I departed this life.' The unsuspicious sheriff did as requested. But a farmer's dog took a liking to them and the poor crookess beat it back to civilization." *Moving Picture Weekly*, August 2, 1919, p.19

Sirens of Suds: *Released 08/13/1919 Wednesday.* © 07/30/1919 — 2 reels. DIRECTOR: William H. Watson. CAST: Dan Russell, Marjorie Ray, Phil Dunham, Vera Steadman SYNOPSIS: "Outside of being chief cook, general housemaid, landlady of the boarding-house and a wife, Lizzie [Ray] had nothing to do. A fire breaks out on the stove and becomes uncontrollable. Lizzie stretches the hydrant over to the stove and puts out the fire. She can't get the faucet back again, so she rests it on the window leading into the dining-room.

"Mme. Swann [Steadman] was the instructress at a swimming pool and her sweetie [Russell] was her assistant. They both boarded at Lizzie's house. Lizzie's husband [Dunham] was infatuated with Mme. Swann and when she smiles sweetly at him, he forgets to collect the money for her board, which amounted to $360. They indulge in a game of tag, and hubby tears his trousers. Mme. Swann tries to sew the trousers together, while hubby leisurely sits behind a screen; he does not see the push button that summons the landlady, which he leans against with his chair. Friend wife answers the summons and discovers Mme. Swann with her hubby's trousers. Sweetie hears the disturbance, lets his bacon fry over the gas jet, and hastens to his sweetheart's rescue. The fight subsides after a lot of shooting and wild excitement.

"Mme. Swann is demonstrating the various strokes and diving stunts to her pupils, when Lizzie's husband is discovered hiding behind a bunch of false whiskers. Lizzie happens along with two great big six-shooters and musses things up.

"Mme. Swann and her sweetie are finally married, and are starting to enjoy a wonderful honeymoon, when along comes hubby, the villain, steals the bride and runs away with her. Sweetie and Lizzie pursue them to a novel finish." *Moving Picture Weekly*, August 9, 1919, p.18

Charlie the Hero: *Released 08/20/1919 Wednesday.* © 08/10/1919 — 2 reels. DIRECTOR: Alf Goulding. CAST: Chai Hong, Hughie Mack, Claire Alexander, Harry Sweet SYNOPSIS: "Charlie [Hong] was fresh from the Orient, and for lack of better work to do, was carrying wash for a couple of his countrymen.

"In the town where Charlie existed there were a bunch of roughnecks so wild that you couldn't walk two blocks without being held up. Charlie overhears a plot to kidnap a banker's daughter and hold her for a ransom.

"He rescues a policeman from the gangsters and is appointed on the staff as an expert policeman.

"Claire [Alexander], the banker's daughter, is having a friendly game of 'craps' with some of her chums, when she is rudely snatched away into the clutches of a big brute gangster. Little Charlie the cop, attempts to take Claire away from the bandits, but is badly beaten up.

"A reward is offered for the capture of the villains. Charlie pursues the kidnapper, and while he is looking for some of his associates, Charlie hides in a baby carriage. He finds out where the hid Claire. The gangster returns to the nurse who has the baby carriage, and insists upon seeing the baby. To the nurse's astonishment and the gangster's joy, they discover Charlie in the baby carriage. A rough and tumble battle ensues, and Charlie manages to beat up the gangster and save the girl. He gets the reward, but one of the other cops gets the girl." *Moving Picture Weekly*, August 16, 1919, p.18
REVIEWS: "A two-reel comic featuring Chai Hong, or Oriental Charlie. A burro, a chimpanzee, and a portly policeman are in the assisting cast. Charlie joins the force and helps run in a gang of villains. This has no highly laughable moments, but is amusing and acceptable all the way through." *Moving Picture World*, September 20, 1919, p.1870

Rainbow Comedies:

A Roof Garden Rough House: *Released 09/10/1919 Wednesday.* © 09/02/1919 — 2 reels.
DIRECTOR: James D. Davis. CAST: Zip Monberg, Lois Neilson
(originally announced as an upcoming L-Ko release *Motion Picture News* 08/30/1919; released as a Universal-Rainbow comedy)

An Oriental Romeo: *Released 09/24/1919 Wednesday.* © 09/12/1919 — 2 reels.
DIRECTOR, AUTHOR: Jess Robbins. CAST: Chai Hong
(originally announced as an upcoming L-Ko release *Moving Picture World* 09/20/1919; released as a Universal-Rainbow comedy)

Foxfilm Comedies & Fox Sunshine Comedies: Lehrman's Films
(released through Fox Film Corporation)

1917 Releases:

The House of Terrible Scandals: *Released 03/19/1917 Monday (originally announced for 02/26/1917, 03/03/1917, and 03/05/1917 release; re-released as a Fox Sunshine on Sunday, 04/20/1919).* © 02/18/1917 — 3 reels. PRODUCER, SCREENPLAY: Henry Lehrman. DIRECTOR: David Kirkland. CAST: Henry Lehrman, Billie Ritchie, Dot Farley, Gertrude Selby, Montana Kid, Victor Potel, Russ Powell, Sid Smith, Bert Roach
(pre-release title: **The Society Buzzard**; released as a Foxfilm Comedy)
SYNOPSIS: "Henry Lehrman and Billie Ritchie, as the result of a gay night, are visited by a joint nightmare which shows them the horrors of their present life. First, a cat knocked a birdcage down upon them then chased a mouse into the yawning face of Henry. Then both Henry and Billie sought to take a bath at the same time in the one bath their hotel boasted. Then Billie found himself on the end of a ladder, balanced over a railing eighteen stories above the street. All of a sudden, the bath overflowed and washed everything in the hotel out into the street.

"Then the two woke up just in time to attend a reception given in honor of the young woman Billie was to wed. Just to queer the affair, Henry held a lighted match in front of Billie's mouth and the breath therefrom, being inflammable because of the previous night's indulgence in firewater, burst into flame.

"At the luncheon table Henry sat next to a lady who ate her soup aloud. He put a carnation in her ear as a sort of silencer, but the lady removed it. Then he placed before her a copy of the song 'I Hear You Calling Me,' and she ate in time to the music, while he marked time with a fork. Finally, he captured the end of a piece of spaghetti which was being inhaled by one of the diners and inserted it in the noisy soup. In a flash the soup disappeared up the spaghetti tube and the noise was stopped.

"Then the house caught fire and Henry rushed out to summon aid. He found a hose lying loose in the street and carried it into the burning building, proceeding to play its contents on the flames. The hose was connected with the traveling equipment of a gasoline vender and what Henry thought was water was gasoline, so that didn't help put out the fire very much.

"The fire and police departments were called and they ran over each other trying to get to the fire. The fire department finally got there, but the police department fell through the street into a sewer. Everybody was rescued. The building was burned to the ground, a runaway locomotive crashed through a string of box cars and that's about it." *Moving Picture World*, March 17, 1917, pp.1824-1825

REVIEWS: "…one of the best slapstick comedies that has been released in a long while, and it had the blasé Broadwayites practically falling out of their seats." *Variety*, May 2, 1919, p. 59

EXHIBITOR REVIEWS: "This comedy was so good that I consider it the week's best picture. It is a combination of Keystone and Chaplin comedy that keeps the audience in one continual roar. Much time and money was spent on this comedy." Charles H. Ryan, Garfield theater. *Motography*, April 28, 1917, p.865

"One of the most wonderful comedies ever produced. My patrons never laughed so much at any other offering. It was liked by everyone." E. Dlouhy, Vitagraph theater. *Motography*, April 28, 1917, p.866

"One of the best comedies Fox has yet produced." A.C. King, Busby theater, McAlester, Okla., *Motography*, August 4, 1917, p. 231

"We played this on a return date and it was another hit. Will likely get it again." Gus Myers, Metropolitan theater, Grand Forks, N.D., *Motography*, August 18, 1917, p. 331

"A very good slap-stick comedy but it would have been even better in two reels instead of three." R.V. Griner, Ideal theater, Centralia, Wash. *Motography*, January 26, 1918, p.149

"Kept them laughing all the time. It's great." George H. Done, Gayety theater, Payson, Utah, *Motion Picture Magazine*, June 1918, p. 6

All of the following films are Sunshine Comedy releases:

Roaring Lions and Wedding Bells: *Released 11/11/1917 Sunday.* © 10/09/1917 — 2 reels. PRODUCER: Henry Lehrman. DIRECTOR, SCREENPLAY: William Campbell and Jack White. CAST: Lloyd Hamilton, Mildred Lee, Jimmie Adams, Tom Wilson, Mario Bianchi, Charles Dorety, Jack Richardson, Jess Welden
REVIEWS: "The first of the new Sunshine comedies released by William Fox for the general service is entitled 'Roaring Lions and Wedding Bells.' Released Nov. 11 with the second, 'A Milk-Fed Vamp,' scheduled to follow Nov. 25. The Sunshine lives up to its trademark. It not only casts a laughing ray from start to finish, but it also has some uproariously funny scenes in which wild animals have as much prominence as the men and women in the film. If the succeeding subjects furnish as much honest laughter as the first film, then their success is assured. Henry Lehrman directed it. Lehrman has staged thousands of funny scenes and directed innumerable camera 'bits,' but he seems to have outdone himself with his first Sunshine. After looking at 'Roaring Lions and Wedding Bells' the task of making film comedies seems to be getting tougher, harder and more difficult and calls for almost superhuman and impossible feats of man and beast to keep up their piston-rod comedy effect. This first Sunshine is funny and capable of handing the most tired business man the surcease from his physical and mental toil he has been looking for. The principals are working all the time. So are some trained lions and ostriches. A trained elephant also shows amazing camera training. All sorts of mixups, confusions, chases, monkeyshines,

clashes, jams, roughhouse, slapstick, photographic tricks, illusions, legitimate screen artifice, natural didoes and the Lord knows what-not are utilized in making the Sunshine subject rank among the best in modern day film comedy. It can't miss, either ahead or following a dramatic." Reviewed by Mark., *Variety*, November 16, 1917, p.50

"'Roaring Lions and Wedding Bells' is just plain farce comedy of the slapstick order, but it is funny enough to bear looking at a second time. William Campbell directed the comedy, and Lloyd Hamilton and Mildred Lee are noticeable in the cast.

"The opening of the picture is more or less of a rehash of former comedy tricks, which are made unusually interesting from the fact that they have been enacted in the vicinity of an ostrich farm. The second reel of the production contains the real comedy situation, where, in revenge, a lover of the bride who is to be joined in the holy bonds of matrimony to a person of her father's choosing sends as a wedding gift a huge box containing a lion. A second lover of the girl, ignorant of this fact, proceeds to impersonate the king of beasts, and the result of the meeting of the twain is all that one could imagine. Then there is the moving platform below the chute to the bath, the breaking up of the wedding party, and the wild rush for safety on the part of all concerned.

"This comedy is clean and quite worth while in its capacity of farce comedy." Reviewed by Margaret I. MacDonald, *Moving Picture World*, November 24, 1917, p.1188

"Two reels taken in and around a menagerie. The chief things [sic] is the rumpus when a couple of lions are turned loose in a big hotel where a wedding party is going on. After the first half reel, it discovers many most amusing situations and laugh follows laugh through all the rest of it. It will pay to book it." *Moving Picture World*, November 24, 1917, p.1191

"'Roaring Lions and Wedding Bells' has convulsed with laughter audiences from coast to coast. Laundry machinery is the medium used by the lions and the comedians in putting over the fun. Chased by the lions through the laundry, Lloyd Hamilton — known as 'Ham' in Fox Sunshine comedies — and his associates find themselves on a treadmill. The lions follow. Of course neither men nor lions can make any progress on the treadmill. At one point water from a powerful fountain raises and lowers one of the comedians — who is always just out of reach of the forest monarchs." "Lions Are Featured in Four Fox Sunshine Comedies," *Moving Picture World*, June 7, 1919, p. 1538

EXHIBITOR REVIEWS: "For a good slapstick comedy, this will keep an audience laughing throughout. Great care in handling the animals has made this comedy much above the ordinary run. It has many special sets." Charles H. Ryan, Garfield theater, Chicago, *Motography*, February 16, 1918, p. 297

A Milk-Fed Vamp: *Released 11/25/1917 Sunday.* © 07/30/1917 — 2 reels. SUPERVISOR, SCREENPLAY: Henry Lehrman. DIRECTOR: David Kirkland. CAST: Dot Farley, Sam Beverly, Ernest Shield, Jack Richardson, Jess Weldon

REVIEWS: "The new Fox-Lehrman Sunshine comedy, 'A Milk-Fed Vamp,' is rich in comic situations, and is what is commonly called a scream. The situations are often both new and delightfully amusing. Nearly all the old situations are well chosen and commendable. It is hardly a picture for a Sunday school entertainment. Theaters are not looking for such all the time, and those things in this which are slightly vulgar are for the people.

"The milk-fed vamp is the daughter of a farmer. She is stuck on her abilities as a charmer of the opposite sex, and elopes with Cobble Stonio, a city youth, who has a wife or two already. She is as good as he at the game of looking out for herself. In the city they come in contact with wife number two, mother of three children. She has an organ and monkey, and this monkey is one of the most amusing things in the picture. Its antics and the things the director has thought up for it to do are both fresh and compellingly laughable.

"The action is decidedly speedy, and oftentimes is exciting. There is a good deal of chasing to and fro among trolley cars, there are near-accidents that give the spectator an instant's apprehension as when an automobile rushes directly at a trolley car, and the next instant we find it running calmly along beside it. The real quality of this kind of farce is indescribable, except that one can safely say that this one is a winner as a laugh maker, and has proved itself out with a good sized audience. I saw it at the Academy of Music in New York, and it made a hit there without a doubt." Reviewed by Hanford C. Judson, *Moving Picture World*, December 15, 1917, pp.1643-1644

"This two-reeler made by the Fox-Lehrman Company is a laughmaker and can be safely depended on to make good in the average theater. It has touches of vulgarity that will make it the more acceptable with most of the people; but are just enough to keep it from being a sure choice for a children's party or a Sunday school entertainment." *Moving Picture World*, December 15, 1917, p1648

"A Sunshine comedy with a full quota of laughs is 'A Milk-Fed Vamp.' The chief fun-maker in this two-reel offering is a monkey that pulls lots of monkey business. Plenty of incident is introduced, and this offering is up to Sunshine's standard. Lots of pep and jazz is introduced in usual fast slapstick manner, and the film maintains a fair rate of speed throughout. All in all it's a thoroughly acceptable comedy number." *Wid's Daily*, June 29, 1919, p.24

His Smashing Career: *Released 12/09/1917 Sunday.* © 10/02/1917 — 2 reels. DIRECTOR, SCREENPLAY: Henry Lehrman. CAST: Billie Ritchie, Gertrude Selby, Billy Bevan, Victor Potel
(reviewed in *Moving Picture World* as **Smashed in the Career**)
REVIEWS: "'His Smashing Career,' the Fox-Lehrman Sunshine Comedy to be released December 9, is a story depicting the exciting and thrilling adventures of Hundred Horsepower Harry, a valiant automobile racing driver, in his efforts to win the Girl, whose father does not fancy Harry in the light of a prospective son-in-law. Various and sundry villains and others do everything they can to prevent Harry from winning. There are declared to be some remarkable automobile stunts in this Sunshiner, which shows the lowly flivver doing things that would tax the versatility of an aeroplane.

"The cast includes Billie Ritchie, who is Little Peter; Gertrude Selby, whose role is that of the Girl; Billy Bevan, who makes a lively Father; and Victor Slim Potel, whose part is that of the judge of the races." *Moving Picture World*, December 15, 1917, p.1662

"The new Fox Lehrman comedy, 'Smashed in the Career,' [sic] has among other properties a swimming pool and a race course for autos and a tall tower for the judges to view the race. It has the expected Lehrman quality in its wealth of dashes, splashes, jumps and almost unthinkable combinations. It is so filled with the unexpected and the astonishing that it baffles any description at all. One noticeable thing will be the costumes of the maids attending the mistress of the house when she is taking her morning dip in the swimming pool — strong armed maids they are to keep the men servants in their place. Then we see the heroine come 'fresh' from her dip to greet father. Her affectionate upper-cut of a love tap breaks the rocking chair. This is only a beginning. There is much of it that made the reviewer laugh. The house was laughing most of the time." Reviewed by Hanford C. Judson, *Moving Picture World*, January 5, 1918, pp.95-96

"Plenty of dash and full of unexpected comic situations mixed with wit, burlesque, comic characterization, and irresponsibility. It made a large audience bellow." *Moving Picture World*, January 5, 1918, p.98

"'His Smashing Career,' a Sunshine slapstick comedy, has enough trick stuff and rough-and-tumble action to put it across as an amusing film of its type. The director pulled something unusual in the handling of a disrobing act when a gracefully formed young woman prepares to dive into a swimming pool. A few of these go close to the border line of what is permissible, but the director always stopped just in time to prevent an argument with the censors. Men, in particular, will find the picture entertaining." *Wid's Daily*, June 29, 1919, p.24

EXHIBITOR REVIEW: "Good settings. There was money spent on this two reel comedy. It is very good and well up to the standard set by these Lehrmann Sunshine comedies." Charles H. Ryan, Garfield theater, Chicago. *Motography*, March 2, 1918, p.397

Damaged — No Goods: *Released 12/23/1917 Sunday.* © 09/09/1917 — 2 reels. SUPERVISOR, SCREENPLAY: Henry Lehrman. DIRECTOR: Jack White and Jay Howe. CAST: Lloyd Hamilton, Gertrude Selby, Mildred Lee, W.E. Lawrence, Max Davidson, Anita Burrell, Dave Morris

REVIEWS: "The greatest fault to be found with the Fox Sunshine comedy, 'Damaged, No Goods,' is the lack of clearness in plot in the opening reel. The rapid action of the play continues from the very start, but fails to make itself thoroughly understood; and the comedy saves its reputation principally by the funny business toward the end of the second reel, where it works up to a hilarious climax.

"Our understanding of the plot from viewing the picture is that father and daughter each have their respective love affairs, and that father, while opposing daughter's choice of a lover, is found out to be considerable of a sport among the feminine kind. To gain entrée to the home of his sweetheart the daughter's lover disguises as a woman, wins the admiration of the father, and is about to elope with the girl, when the plot is discovered. Finally after considerable amusing horse play all parties are caught in a 'young cyclone' in the midst of which the most surprising near accidents occur following each other in rapid action. There are various other touches throughout the picture that are bound to bring laughs, such as the using of a Ford car in pushing a sightseeing bus up-hill, and the spilling off of the back of the bus of all the passengers. A strange and wonderful manipulation of a bed is another amusing feature of the picture." Reviewed by Margaret I. MacDonald, *Moving Picture World*, December 8, 1917, p. 1483

"An excellent slapstick number, in which a father and his daughter have conflicting love affairs. Some of the most amusing things in the picture are a result of a 'young cyclone,' which causes much stir. The number will be thoroughly enjoyed by the majority of audiences." *Moving Picture World*, December 22, 1917, p. 1807

EXHIBITOR REVIEW: "A good knockabout, chase comedy in two reels. The kind much effort and care was taken in the making." Charles H. Ryan, Garfield theatre, Chicago, *Motography*, March 16, 1918, p. 497

1918 Releases:

Shadows of Her Pest: *Released 01/06/1918 Sunday.* © 01/06/1918 — 2 reels. SUPERVISOR: Henry Lehrman. CAST: Dot Farley, Ernie Shield, Vic Potel, Al Ray EXHIBITOR REVIEWS: "One of those spectacular, biff-bim productions. The audience laughed from start to finish. For a rough and tumble comedy, it can't be beaten." Harry C. Miller, Boston and Alcazar theaters, Chicago, *Motography*, February 16, 1918, p. 297 "A good two-reel comedy with many laughs. Up to the standard of the Fox comedies." Charles H. Ryan, Garfield theatre, Chicago, *Motography*, March 30, 1918, p. 597

Son of a Gun: *Released 02/03/1918 Sunday.* © 01/20/18 — 2 reels. SUPERVISOR, PRODUCER, STORY AND SCENARIO: Henry Lehrman. DIRECTOR: Richard Jones. CAST: Billie Ritchie, Winifred Westover, Minnie Ha-Ha, Sid Smith, Hugh Fay, Guy Woodward, Edgar Kennedy
SYNOPSIS/REVIEW: "If some companies must produce comedies, WHY don't they at least produce DECENT ones? I have had to sit and endure many perfectly abominable slapstick comedies to see the feature picture of the evening, but one I saw the other evening, called 'The Son of a Gun,' produced by the Sunshine Comedy co., was the worst ever and my patience is exhausted. From start to finish the picture was tholy [sic] disgusting; in fact, I should call it a satire on the U.S.

"Will you please tell me why the censors allow things like this to pass?

"'The Son of a Gun' was a two-reel slapstick Sunshine comedy. Most of the scenes were supposed to be laid in Mexico and the star of the picture was supposed to be 'General Chronico Appendecito,' who, by the way, was a typical little slapstick 'runt' with the usual mustache about a yard long, cross-eyed, and with his clothes half falling off of him. I wont tell you all the horrors that were in this picture, but only the ones that made me the most provoked.

"'General Appendecito' wanted some excitement and ordered his soldiers to execute two men for him. One of the men was a drunkard and the other was dressed to represent Uncle Sam. While I didn't mind the drunkard getting executed (as I think they all should be) it surely made me peeved to see them shoot Uncle Sam, even if it was only in the movies. Then again the leading-lady, who was supposed to be a second Lillian Gish, goes to the American Consul to save her fiancé, and the Consul is a *very, very* poor representation of Colonel Roosevelt, and my opinion is that it shouldn't be allowed, altho I suppose a great many people would find no fault with this as they don't all admire him as I do. In another scene, the leading-man is all covered up with dynamite, nitro-glycerine, bombs, etc., with the exception of the soles of his feet, and is about to be blown to atoms, when in rushes a typical Keystone policeman, who looks at the leading-man's feet and exclaims: 'He is an American; I must save him.' Now I wish some one would be kind enough to tell me how long since it is possible to distinguish Americans by their feet? An automobile chase then follows of more imitation Keystone 'cops' and another auto full of Red Cross nurses, speeding to the Mexican border. The auto containing the policemen breaks down and they all jump out and hold up the auto containing the Red Cross nurses and have a regular fist-to-fist fight with them to gain possession of their auto, leave them strewn along the road, take the auto and start along again. In all probability the Red Cross nurses were men dressed up as women, but that scene added nothing to the value of the picture nor was it in the least funny.

"Here is the last and, in my opinion, the worst offense. There is a locomotive rushing to the supposed battle laden with still more policemen and it is completely covered with the American Flag. Now if that is the best use the Sunshine Company can think of to put 'Old Glory' to, that of being trampled all over by a lot of crazy-acting, crazy-looking men, I think they had better go out of business until they find something better." Letter by Phyliss Carr, Waterbury, Conn., to the editor of *Motion Picture Magazine*, May 1918, p.130

REVIEWS: "A two-reel farce of comic characters, full of dream-like impossible doings that compel laughter through being so impossible. One of the characters is in a room where a bomb is exploded. He is blown up through the chimney, takes a jump from the roof and lands on a horse quietly waiting below and gallops off. The whole story is of this same material." *Moving Picture World*, January 26, 1918, p.530

EXHIBITOR REVIEWS: "Mexican characters and atmosphere make up this comedy, which is not quite up to the standard set by earlier Fox-Sunshine comedies." Charles H. Ryan, Garfield theatre, Chicago. *Motography*, April 13, 1918, p.697

Hungry Lions in a Hospital: *Released 02/03/1918 Sunday.* © 01/20/1918 — 2 reels.
SUPERVISOR, PRODUCER, SCREENPLAY: Henry Lehrman. DIRECTOR: Jack White and Al Ray. CINEMATOGRAPHY: R.D. Armstrong and A. Vallet. CAST: Lloyd Hamilton, Mildred Lee, Tom Wilson, Ethel the Lion, Gene the Lion, Charles Dorety, Frank Hayes, Gene Rogers, Bert Gillespie, Heinie Conklin, Jimmie Adams, Jess Weldon

SYNOPSIS: Lloyd Hamilton stars as "Ham Bohn," and Mildred Lee co-stars as "Vera Kosher." Ham is in the hospital for some reason. The doctors, all wielding huge, nasty-looking knives, are buddies with the local morticians M. Balmer and Cough Finn, who are constantly on the scene hauling off the doctors' most recent patients. There are a couple of lunatics in the hospital as well, or maybe they are anarchists — it is difficult to tell. Two lions, nicely played by Ethel and Gene, get loose in the place, and some truly scary scenes follow. There is the obligatory scene with a black man sleeping and dreaming of his girl, caressing the lion sleeping next to him, the discovery of which causes his hair and eyebrows to go white with fright.

Ham triumphantly traps one of the lions in a large barrel, but when he enlists the aid of his friends to haul it away, it turns out to have no bottom. The patients in the hospital erect a huge barrier wall of bed-springs turned on their sides and stacked in a futile attempt to keep the lions at bay. The cops are called, and one of the lions ends up in the open-top police car, causing all of the passengers to leap out while driving over a high bridge, all plummeting down to the river far below. The vehicle ends up crashing through the first floors of several buildings.

Synopsis based on a surviving print shown at Slapsticon 2008. This print is incomplete and consists primarily of reel two, although it does retain the opening credits. Plotline clarity suffers due to the absence of the introductory scenes. If Mildred Lee is anywhere in the surviving footage it would only have been in a long shot, perhaps as one of the bathing beauties prancing about in the hospital's indoor pool; her footage is likely missing. Tom Wilson appears to be missing from this version as well.

REVIEWS: "These two reels of fun is sure to bring laughs. Some of it is extremely amusing, and all of it is likely to win favor. The quality is much the same as in the other recent Fox

Lehrman releases, and perhaps its one drawback with the public will be that it reminds of the others and lacks a really rich comedy story." *Moving Picture World*, February 2, 1918, p.689

"In 'Hungry Lions in a Hospital' two lions invade a hospital and come upon a couple of colored attendants sleeping in the same bed. The lion awakens the attendants and the run follows with lightning speed as the hospital is set into an uproar, and patients, doctors and nurses hustle for safety." "Lions Are Featured in Four Fox Sunshine Comedies," *Moving Picture World*, June 7, 1919, p. 1538

EXHIBITOR REVIEWS: "One of the funniest two-reel comedies we have shown. One continuous roar from start to finish." Charles H. Ryan, Garfield theatre, Chicago, *Motography*, May 4, 1918, p. 835

Are Married Policemen Safe?: *Released 02/17/1918 Sunday.* © 01/20/1918 — 2 reels.
SUPERVISOR, STORY, SCREENPLAY: Henry Lehrman. DIRECTOR: Richard Jones. CAST: Billie Ritchie, Charles Conklin, Hugh Fay, Winifred Westover, Guy Woodward, Billy Bevan, Charlotte Mineau, Marvel Rea, Sid Smith
(originally scheduled for 01/13/1918 release)
REVIEWS: "'Are Married Policemen Safe?' [is] a satire on human nature as evidenced in the administration of justice. A crusade against women wearing clothes which are more abbreviated than the law allows results in policemen and juries being captivated by their captives.

"The action ranges all the way from the United States to Mexico with trouble of several sorts developing in both countries. A Mexican who has fallen into the lap of the law here struggles out and finds the way opened to revenge when his American tormentors go to Mexico. It develops then that he is chief of police of a Mexican city and that he knows how to make the most of his authority. A railroad train running straight through a station is a feature of the action." *Motography*, February 23, 1918, p.358

"A rough and tumble comedy which the audience at the Strand theater, New York, seemed to enjoy. The story of the comedy seemed to hinge around the love affairs of a couple of married policemen who tried to marry other wives and were foiled in the attempt with the appliance of much horse play. Some original business has been inserted in this comedy along with much that is old, and, considerable that is unrefined." *Moving Picture World*, March 9, 1918, p.1411

"A Fox Sunshine Comedy with a fast, funny and thrilly climax is 'Are Married Policemen Safe.' The early footage of the film is devoted to ordinary knockabout stuff with only a few laughs. But soon the jazz was injected and automobiles started running every which way, waltzing zippingly around wet streets, and causing no end of fast action of the usual sort. There are as many stunts pulled in this one as in the ordinary serial installment. For instance, two automobiles were shot off into the surf, their occupants spilling all over the screen. The actors sure did take a lot of chances, and there were thrills despite the laughs that accompanied." *Wid's Daily*, July 27, 1919, p.24

EXHIBITOR REVIEWS: "These comedies possess very much more than the average comedies, as many props are destroyed and many specially built sets are used in them and the action is very fast with many thrills." Charles H. Ryan, Garfield theatre, Chicago, *Motography*, May 18, 1918, p. 931

My Husband's Wife: *Released 03/03/1918 Sunday.* © 02/24/1918 — 2 reels. DIRECTOR, SCREENPLAY: Henry Lehrman. CAST: Hugh Fay, Jimmie Adams

A Self-Made Lady: *Released 03/17/1918 Sunday.* © 03/24/1918 — 2 reels. SUPERVISOR, STORY, SCREENPLAY: Henry Lehrman. DIRECTOR: David Kirkland. CAST: Dot Farley, Edgar Kennedy, Bobby Vernon, Victor Potel, John Rand
REVIEWS: "The latest Sunshine comedy release by William Fox is 'A Self-Made Lady.' It is about a 'she crook' who was sentenced to seven days in prison, but through a slight error was behind the bars for seven years. When the 'she crook' gets out she wants to go straight but circumstances won't let her.
"The Lehrman police romp through the picture in characteristic style, automobiles dash recklessly over cliffs and a swimming tank is utilized to speed up the fun. Dot Farley, Bobby Vernon and Ed Kennedy keep the mirth at high pitch from start to finish." *Motography*, March 30, 1918, p.621
"This is a strenuous burlesque of crook characters of the underworld and features Dot Farley, an eccentric comedienne. The two reels contain many ridiculously funny gags. The head crook keeps a package of money lying on a table toward which he leads all disagreeable personages such as policemen. When greedy fingers seize on the package they innocently spring a trap door beneath and the intruder is projected into a tank of water. The first time this is pulled it is uproarious, for the unfortunate cop discovers a dozen of his companions waiting below to welcome him. The action throughout is of a similar type and is surrounded by subtitles that reach the height of good-natured foolishness. When Hedda Holiday (Miss Farley) is released from jail the warden addresses her something like this: 'I'm sorry we kept you here seven years instead of seven weeks. The clerk made a slight error. However, you may consider yourself lucky as two prisoners have died because of his little slips.' David Kirkland directed under Henry Lehrman's supervision." Reviewed by Peter Milne, *Motion Picture News*, April 20, 1918, p. 2417
"These Lehrman Sunshine comedies turn everything to good account to make a laugh. They burlesque everything under the sun from picture melodramas to fresh actualities from the latest newspapers. Nothing is too outrageous for the comical-minded man who makes them up to think up for them. The newest one, 'The Self Made Lady,' opens with a scene in a prison in which is released the heroine who had been in jail for seven years — she had been committed for seven weeks, but through a 'slight mistake of the clerk, who meant well,' her time had been recorded wrong.
"What with the antics of the cameraman and the unexpected twists and turns of the nightmarelike narrative, the picture is pretty sure to fill many a theater with roars of laughter." Reviewed by Hanford C. Judson, *Moving Picture World*, April 20, 1918, p.431

A Waiter's Wasted Life: *Released 04/07/1918 Sunday.* © 04/08/1918 — 2 reels. SUPERVISOR, SCREENPLAY: Henry Lehrman. DIRECTOR: Jack White and William H. Watson. CAST: Lloyd Hamilton, Eileen Percy, Jimmie Adams, Anita Burrell, Tom Kennedy
REVIEWS: "One of the best of the Fox-Lehrmann series so far and a winner surely is 'A Waiter's Wasted Life.' The subtitles are full of wit, and the business of the players, done with the perfect abandon needed for this kind of work, is full of new ideas that exact bursts of hearty laughter again and still again. The unbelievable outrageousness of happenings in

the prison and the nearby cafe that serve as background for the crazy adventures of the inmates of both are indecipherable, because a great deal of the amusement comes from the compelling nonchalance of the players. Then the wit of the description furnished by the leaders gives to much of it the punch given to circus acts by the running comment of the ringmaster. It is one of the best comic pictures that I have seen in a long time." Reviewed by Hanford C. Judson, *Moving Picture World*, April 27, 1918, p.587

"Mr. Lehrman has taken a jail and a quick lunch room and placed them side by side in 'A Waiter's Wasted Life.' The humorous complications that result are numerous and well up to, if not beyond, the Lehrman standard of comedy. The opening reel starts off excellently, there are plenty of gags and a large supply of foolishness that makes one laugh if he will or no. The last reel has to do with a hanging. The prisoner escapes and Ham (Lloyd V. Hamilton) is rushed in to take his place. He escapes in time to start a general mix-up. The director has a good sense of burlesque in everything he undertakes. He introduces the warden of the jail playing with a miniature man dangling on the end of a rope. Such touches, though not of the highest type of comedy, are plentiful in the two reels." Reviewed by Peter Milne, *Motion Picture News*, April 27, 1918, p.2556

"A roaring comic picture with witty subtitles and fresh ideas that positively compel hearty laughter. It is surely a winner, of that there can be no doubt." *Moving Picture World*, April 27, 1918, p.589

A Neighbor's Keyhole: *Released 05/05/1918 Sunday.* © 05/05/1918 — 2 reels. DIRECTOR: Henry Lehrman. PHOTOGRAPHY: A.H. Vallet. CAST: Billie Ritchie, Winifred Westover, Charles Dorety, Hugh Fay, Fritz Schade, George Binns

REVIEWS: "The Sunshine comedy, 'A Neighbor's Keyhole,' by the Fox Film Corporation, is all kinds of a comic and is surely uproarious. The wealth of incident makes it impossible to describe it in detail. One of its characters, Mr. Adam Sapple, has a throat that goes up and down, up and down, whenever he drinks. He and another character are saving a bottle together, and the other wise guy gets a pretty bell to hang around the throat so that when he hears a tinkle, tinkle, he knows what's up and what's going down. There are rivals for the hand of the heroine, school girls in bathing a la Coronado Beach, cops, crazy automobiles, and other wheels of many kinds, an indomitable swan and a most pugnacious ram. It is to laugh all right and that's all one needs to say about one of these fertilly invented Sunshine comedies. It doesn't skimp in anything." Reviewed by Hanford C. Judson, *Moving Picture World*, June 1, 1918, p.1331

"This appears to be one of the most elaborate and extravagant comedies that Henry Lehrman has ever produced for the Fox program. Its special effects include a hurricane and a violent rainstorm which continues throughout the two reels. The wild chasing which goes on through wind and rain contains a number of extremely clever gags which bring hearty response. There is no let-up in stunts and comical business. They present a veritable parade of wild comedy, the like of which has seldom been seen. The two reels must have cost a sum equal to that expended on the average five-reel feature, perhaps more.

"The cast which includes Winifred Westover and Billie Ritchie enters into the spirit of the thing with a vengeance, but it is to the man who directed it that the greatest credit must go. To introduce a succession of funny, ridiculous and marvelous incidents as if they were commonplace occurrences is the secret of the success of this type of comedy. The man who put this one on ranks high in his act." Reviewed by Peter Milne, *Motion Picture News*, June 1, 1918, p.3308

"Has a wealth of incident and situation that is astonishing. It is uproariously funny and a sure winner." *Moving Picture World*, June 1, 1918, p.1333

Wild Women and Tame Lions: *Released 06/02/1918 Sunday.* © 06/02/1918 — 2 reels.
SUPERVISOR: Henry Lehrman. DIRECTOR: William Campbell. CAST: Tom Kennedy, Ethel Teare; Ford Sterling, Hugh Fay, Virginia Rappe
SYNOPSIS: Mack Abdul and his wife visit a park, and while Abdul steps away the wife, her eyes covered, is hoodwinked into accepting kisses from one tramp after another assuming them to be her husband. Mack returns and gives chase, the tramps heading for the zoo where they have bad encounters with a baboon and an alligator. Mack grabs what he thinks is a club, only to find that it is an elephant's trunk; he is deposited in a nearby creek. Back at the zoo, plumbers accidentally knock a hole in the wall of a lions' cage, releasing a trio of lions (Abie, Julius, and Jacob). The plumbers manage to lure them into a trunk, snap the lid close, and dump it from a window. Two tramps find it and thinking that it may contain valuables, haul it back to their rooming house. The lions get loose.

The first makes its way into a lady's room while she braids her hair, unknowingly braiding the lion's tail along with her hair. The lion takes off, dragging the woman behind. She loses her hair.

The second lion makes its way into a bathroom. A guard standing outside to ensure a single occupant at a time eventually loses both his coat and trousers to the lion's claws, and flees when a woman appears intending to take a bath.

The third makes its way into the room of Caesar Sweetbread, a negro gentleman. Not realizing that he has a visitor, Caesar uses the lion's tail as a shaving brush. Noticing this in his mirror, he turns extremely pale with fright.

The lion shenanigans pile up from there. One gets bundled up in some laundry and is hauled off by the laundress, finally clawing his way loose. Another lies down beside a napping man who is woken by the tail draped across his mouth. In a panic he leaps from his window and into another window where he encounters a lovely young lady whose husband is to return any moment. The fellow takes refuge in a Murphy bed, unaware that the third lion is in the room as well. Hubby returns and spots the fellow's shirttail, but when he tries to expose the fellow instead comes face to face with the lion. Hubby chasses the fellow from the room as his wife collapses on the bed, weeping. Feeling a comforting touch on her shoulder, she assumes her husband has returned, only to find a gentle paw instead. She heads out for her husband's gun. The chase finds the two men back in the room and under the bed, reunited with the lion. The wife returns and opens fire but hits her husband instead of the lion. The chase resumes, and all fall into a laundry shoot and end up in the kitchen, terrifying the Chinese cook. The others rush into the cellar where the husband finds some gun powder. He quickly assembles a bomb, intending to feed it to the lion with the thought of blowing it up. Instead of swallowing the bomb, however, the lion merely holds it in his mouth. When the bomb explodes, everything is lost to sight in the smoke. Adapted from the copyright synopsis held by the Library of Congress.

REVIEWS: "The Fox-Sunshine comedy, 'Wild Women and Tame Lions,' is another mark of Lehrman ingenuity. The picture is a series of funny incidents which do not require serious explanation. The tameness of the lions which appear in the picture in conjunction with women of different types, including a sprinkling of men, is something that might be questioned judging from the frequent snarls with which they greet their fellow performers.

"The manner in which these beasts have been made to really act in this production is worthy of mention. The idea of a full-sized lion allowing himself to be tied up in a laundry bundle before entering a single complaint is something that has to be seen to be appreciated. He also allows his tail to be braided in the plait of a maiden lady's hair. By way of further explanation we will say that he found his way unnoticed into said lady's room when she was retiring for the night. The attempt at speedy separation of tail and braid is very funny.

"The picture is full of just such entertaining nonsense, and one wonders at the daring of the players who work with perfect ease apparently unmindful of the danger which must necessarily attend association with the most treacherous of beasts." Reviewed by Margaret I. MacDonald, *Moving Picture World*, June 15, 1918, p.1615

"A comedy which will please the majority of people because of the part taken in it by a couple of apparently tame lions. The picture contains some good slapstick comedy, and the daring of the players in acting in close conjunction with the king of beasts will elicit considerable admiration." *Moving Picture World*, June 15, 1918, p.1616

"Henry Lehrman's late number on the Sunshine bill hits on all four for the course of two reels, and the director had his foot on the accelerator every foot of the way. The 'wild women' are not as much in evidence as the 'tame lions,' but don't be disappointed — the lions will keep you busy. And speaking of lions — these 'pets' can look the camera in the eye without winking an eyelash. When it comes to the rough-house stuff, they use all fours and tear around the sets like a runaway engine.

"Ethel Tearle [sic] and Tom Kennedy are the lions' chief competitors for first place in the running. Miss Tearle might have been reared with a circus, so nonchalantly does she pal with the Sunshine 'pets.' Tom Kennedy strikes up an acquaintance with a sorrowful-looking elephant, and winds up taking a dip in the river with said elephant.

"The element of action is raised to the nith power in this offering. If you can keep account of the 'wild women' and the 'tame lions' you should go in for sleight-of-hand work — you're qualified. The Sunshine brand of comedies loses no prestige by offering this one. If you cannot get excitement out of these two reels of action and lions, you will have to take a turn in the trenches or lead the suicide squad over a mile or two of no-man's-land. Fox has a peppery release in 'Wild Women and Tame Lions' — plenty of action and good comedy." Reviewed by Joseph L. Kelley, *Motion Picture News*, June 29, 1918, p.3951

"Ford Sterling plays the hero in 'Wild Women and Tame Lions,' and is given ample opportunity to show his talents as a tailor and a lover — making a much greater success as the latter despite irate husbands. The lions are used in bedroom and parlor scenes. A fighting kangaroo is one of the features of the comedy.""Lions Are Featured in Four Sunshine Comedies," *Moving Picture World*, June 7, 1919, p. 1538; review of the re-edited and re-released version in 1919 as part of "The Lucky Thirteen"

Who's Your Father?: *Released 06/30/1918 Sunday.* © 07/07/1918 — 2 reels. SUPERVISOR, PRODUCER: Henry Lehrman. DIRECTOR: Tom Mix. CAST: Tom Mix, Gertrude Selby, Charles "Heinie" Conklin, Frank Hayes, Victor Potel, Jimmie Adams, Tom Wilson, Madame Sul-Te-Wan, Guy Woodward
SYNOPSIS: Tom Mix is in love with Colette (Selby), the shopkeeper's daughter. Fernan (Conklin), the town's sheriff, has eyes for Colette, but she wants nothing to do with him. After Mix rescues a baby that has been set afloat in a creek and abandoned, he takes it home and, while trying to figure out what to do with it, offers his six-shooter as a pacifier. The town spinster (Hayes!) thinks that this would be a good time to convince Mix to marry her, but to no avail. Meanwhile, there's a mixup of the baby and a black infant, much to the horror of the latter's parents (Wilson and Sul-Te-Wan).

Sheriff Fernan, frustrated in his attempts to woo Colette, decides to take matters in hand. He enlists the aid of his dimwitted deputy (Potel) and together they knock out Mix and kidnap Colette. Fleeing in their open-top auto, Mix and a hastily rounded up posse give chase on horseback, and Mix manages to rescue Colette. Fernan and his deputy continue on, now pursued by a mob on foot wielding rakes and shovels. Heading into the river, Fernan's vehicle all but disappears from view while the tops of the pursuing mob's rakes and shovels remain visible. Fernan's auto emerges from the river, but when the engine falters the deputy takes a look and is awash in a deluge of dead fish. The auto moves on but Mix catches up and lassos Fernan, pulling him from the moving vehicle. Synopsis based on the print held by the Library of Congress.
REVIEW: "The comedy started with the rescue by the cowboy's dog of a baby that was floating down a gorge toward a cataract in a tiny crib. The cowboy takes the foundling to his cabin. Then the cowboy finds himself not only beset with the troubles of feeding an infant, but also is the object of a spinster who, by claiming the baby, hopes to compromise the cowboy and thus force him to marry her." *Moving Picture World*, June 22, 1918, p. 1734

A Tight Squeeze: *Released 07/28/1918 Sunday.* © 07/28/1918 — 2 reels. SUPERVISOR: Henry Lehrman. DIRECTOR: Jack White and William H. Watson. CINEMATOGRAPHY: George Meehan. CAST: Lloyd Hamilton, Ethel Teare, Jimmie Adams, Tom Kennedy, Charles Dorety, Dave Morris, Frank Coleman, Mae Eccleston, Frank Hayes, Fritz Schade
EXHIBITOR REVIEWS: "This is the best two-reel comedy I have looked at in a long time. Who ever directs the animals around the Fox shop deserves a medal for this." Steve Farrar, Orpheum theatre, Harrisburg, Ill, *Exhibitors Herald and Motography*, September 28, 1918, p.29

"A good comedy; one that you hear loud and continued laughing from. Animals worked very cleverly. Outside of the Mack Sennett comedies these are the best two-reel comedies we run and we show them all." Charles H. Ryan, Garfield theatre, Chicago. — Middle class neighborhood. *Exhibitors Herald and Motography*, October 5, 1918, p.39

A High Diver's Last Kiss: *Released 08/25/1918 Sunday.* © 08/25/1918 — 2 reels. SUPERVISOR: Henry Lehrman. DIRECTOR: Noel Smith and William Beaudine. CAST: Slim Summerville, Bobby Dunn, Mae Eccleston, Betty Carpenter, Frank J. Coleman
REVIEWS: "The ridiculous note sounded in the title is maintained throughout the two reels of ludicrous happenings which constitute 'A High Diver's Last Kiss.' At no time even approximating the plausible, it is well fitted for the purpose it serves — program contrast.

"With the action laid at a seaside resort, bathing girls are brought into play with the customary result. They are good to look at, these Sunshine girls, and they appear in this case with reason.

"The plot has something to do with a high diver who insists upon marrying his employer's daughter before he makes his thrilling leap into the tank of water. When her sweetheart kidnaps him, the girl volunteers to make the dive in his place. A bomb which has been placed at the top of the ladder is discovered by the girl and thrown into the assembled throng, her one-piece bathing suit is snatched from her back by her sweetheart, who seeks to rescue her in an airplane, and she rushes from the tank to his arms, an aerial elopement providing the ending.

"It is well produced, swift of action, and contains new material in quantity. It should thoroughly justify it exhibition." *Exhibitors World*, May 29, 1920, p.74

Roaring Lions on the Midnight Express: *Released 09/22/1918 Sunday.* © 09/22/1918 — 2 reels. SUPERVISOR, PRODUCER, DIRECTOR: Henry Lehrman. CAST: Billie Ritchie, Jimmie Adams, Monty Banks, Hugh Fay, Frank J. Coleman, Jack Cooper, Sylvia Day, Mae Eccleston, Dave Morris, Charles Dudley, Slim Summerville
REVIEWS: "In 'Roaring Lions on the Midnight Express' one of the lions is made to stand on top of a railroad engine glaring at a negro lad in the funnel of the engine. This animal pursues a party of passengers, who flee in ludicrous terror. In one of the funniest scenes the lions invade a sleeping car in which a number of colored porters are slumbering." "Lions Are Featured in Four Fox Sunshine Comedies," *Moving Picture World*, June 7, 1919, p. 1538

Mongrels: *Released 11/17/1918 Sunday.* © 11/17/1918 — 2 reels. SUPERVISOR: Henry Lehrman. DIRECTOR: Jack White. CAST: Lloyd Hamilton, Gertrude Selby, Jimmie Adams, Charles Dorety, Dave Morris, Teddy the Dog
(originally announced for 11/10/1918 release)
REVIEWS: "One of the amusing features of the latest Fox-Lehrman Sunshine Comedy, 'Mongrels,' is an allegory of the war performed by dogs. All the big features of the war are revealed by four dogs, which, with an almost uncanny ability, portray the parts of the four leading nations at war.

"In making the picture, Mr. Lehrman had printed a big sign reading, 'Enemy aliens must not cross this line.' On one side of the line is shown a French poodle gnawing a bone.

"A dachshund, wearing a Hun helmet, comes along, crosses the line and attacks the poodle. The poodle puts up a valiant defense of his rights, but as he is fighting, a vapor bursts, from the dachshund's mouth, representing the Germans' poison gas.

"The English bulldog comes to the aid of the poodle, and the two pursue the dachshund into a kennel, which rocks and rolls violently during the conflict.

"Then, seeing that the dachshund is still full of fight, the poodle runs away and brings back an American terrier. The American terrier, the French poodle and the English bulldog pitch into the German dachshund and clean him up with neatness and dispatch.

"In filming the picture, the fight closed with the band playing 'The Star Spangled Banner' and everybody on the side-lines cheering for victory." *Moving Picture World*, October 26, 1918, p.529

"A strong propaganda picture is 'Mongrels,' the newest sensational two-reel Henry Lehrman Sunshine Comedy. Although the story opens with a number of the cutest and cleverest dogs that ever trotted before a camera, the title, 'Mongrels,' has reference to a gang of Hun spies.

"In their efforts to wreck a munition factory and steal the powder some of the funniest situations imaginable are injected. The comedy, directed by Jack White under the personal supervision of Henry Lehrman, is far above the average two-reel sensational farce.

"In the leading roles are Lloyd Hamilton, who makes the funniest of funny men, and Gertrude Selby. Miss Selby plays the role of the young girl who wins the affections of 'Ham.' The villain, played by Jimmie Adams, meets his just deserts by hanging to a flag pole. As the rope tightens around his neck he sinks out of sight behind the hills and as the picture fades out Old Glory comes peeping over the embankment and rises to the top of the pole." *Oakland Tribune*, November 3, 1918, p.3

EXHIBITOR REVIEWS: "A regular riot. Sunshine comedies are in a class by themselves." F.R. Smith, Bijou theatre, Fond du Lac, Wis. — Mixed patronage. *Exhibitors Herald and Motography*, December 14, 1918, p.33

"Dandy comedy. Everyone liked it. Sunshines all good comedies. Find them the best comedies on the market, not being specials or so-called specials." William Thacher, Royal theatre, Salina, Kan, *Exhibitors Herald*, February 5, 1921, p.93

The Fatal Marriage: *Released 12/15/1918 Sunday.* © 12/15/1918 — 2 reels. SUPERVISOR, PRODUCER: Henry Lehrman. DIRECTOR: William Campbell. CAST: Billie Ritchie, Hugh Fay, Sylvia Day, Charles Dorety, Joe the Orang-utang

REVIEWS: "Henry Lehrman's wild circus tricks were never more amply displayed than in his latest comedy 'The Fatal Marriage.' He starts out with a separate comedy in which dogs, a kitten and an orang' are the principals and then switches into a story of rivalry for a young lady's hand that entails wild chases, smashups, various skiddings and the final plunges of two automobiles off the end of a pier.

"The cast is headed by Billy [sic] Ritchie, Hugh Fay and Sylvia Day. All of them enter into the comedy with a spirit that is remarkable. Miss Day is an ingénue who gives great promise." *Motion Picture News*, December 28, 1918, p.3863

The Son of a Hun: *Released 12/29/1918 Sunday.* © 12/29/1918 — 2 reels. SUPERVISOR, PRODUCER: Henry Lehrman. DIRECTOR: Jack White. CAST: Lloyd Hamilton, Gertrude Selby, Dave Morris, Jimmie Adams, Charles Dorety

REVIEWS: "A riotous two-reel comic, with Gertrude Selby, Dave Morris and Lloyd Hamilton in the cast. This begins with a wedding and winds up with a burlesque battle. There is a Ford car in this that is funnier than any Ford joke ever succeeded in being. The knockabout humor is rough but acceptable, and many laughable stunts are performed. The work of the tank, which completely demolishes a house, is a good feature." *Moving Picture World*, December 28, 1918, p.1555

1919 Releases:

Oh, What a Knight!: *Released 01/26/1919 Sunday.* © 01/26/1919 — 2 reels. SUPERVISOR: Henry Lehrman. DIRECTOR: Fred Fishback. CAST: Mack Swain, Ethel Teare, Jack Cooper, George White
(pre-release title: **Her First Knight**; re-release titles: **Cowboy Ambrose** and **The Sheriff's Mustache**. Originally announced for 01/19/1919 release; aka **Oh! What a Knight!**) SYNOPSIS: Mamma's boy Sunny Jim Arsenic (Swain), the sheriff of Dead Horse, is in love with Black-Eyed Susan (Teare), and she is in love with Jim. Susan lives with her little brother, who is fishing by a creek when a fish leaps out of the water and attaches itself to his rear. Hearing his cries for help, Susan rushes to the creek, as does Handsome Jack Rancid (Cooper), a stranger who rescues the boy. She falls head over heels for the stranger, and returning to her cabin spots the framed photo of Jim on her mantle. She turns it to the wall with a look of disgust, her thoughts now clouded with visions of Jack Rancid.

Meanwhile, Rancid enters the Pink Garter saloon, six-guns blazing, and robs the place. Enter Jim who attempts to stop Rancid, but instead flees in a hail of bullets from the robber's guns. Rancid pursues Jim on horseback, and both dismount at an adobe building where Jim eventually regains possession of the stolen cash. Jim returns to the saloon with the cash in hand, but Rancid follows and, after another confrontation, once again makes off with the loot. Jim pursues on horseback, a quickly assembled posse bringing up the rear.

Rancid arrives at Susan's cabin and enters: "If you love me, gal — hide me!" Rancid hides in the chimney. Jim arrives and sees his photo turned to the wall. Despondent, he sets it afire and tosses it into the fireplace. The smoke drives Rancid from his hiding place and he attempts to escape, but Jim catches him and holds him at gunpoint. Susan intercedes and begs Jim to give Rancid another chance. Moved by her entreaty, he lets Rancid go but retains the stolen money. Jim heads back to the saloon but is intercepted by the posse who find him with the stolen cash. He refuses to betray Susan's trust, so he removes his badge and pins it on another: "Boys, I may be western but I'm squar' — and when a woman's honor is at stake Sunny Jim's lips is sealed!" The posse returns to town.

Returning to his home, Jim opens up to his ma, but when she finds that he has given up his badge, she is furious: "Jim, I may be your mother but I'm human. We ain't never had a coward in the house of Arsenic!" Brought to his senses and with fire now in his belly, Jim exits their apartment, leaps over the railing and rushes down the staircase.

Rancid returns to Susan's cabin and finds that she has now come to her senses and wants nothing to do with him. After an altercation with her little brother, Rancid forces her to leave with him and takes her to a cabin where she is imprisoned. The brother goes for help and enlists Jim's aid. The two head to the cabin where Jim takes on six of Rancid's gang, throwing them one-by-one through the roof and walls. Rancid knocks Jim out with a mallet.

Accompanied by his gang, Rancid once again tries to ride off with the struggling girl, a revitalized Jim in hot pursuit. Jim manages to shoot down Rancid's accomplices and rescue Susan, then resumes his pursuit. Rancid makes it to the saloon with Jim now close on his heels. The patrons scatter as the two horses gallop up one flight of steps to the balcony overlooking the saloon, and down the opposite set, repeatedly until the steps collapse under Jim and his horse. Jim grabs the other set of steps' railing and pulls those down as well. Rancid and horse leap from the balcony onto the bar below. Jim lassoes Rancid, pulling him to the floor. Rancid is hauled off as Jim basks in the cheers from the assembled patrons, his badge returned along with a bouquet of flowers. Jim kisses Susan, at which moment Jim's ma arrives and smacks him on the rear with a rolling pin. "Mother, you've broken my heart!" She drags Jim off by the hair, leaving Susan with the bouquet. Synopsis based on a print held by the author along with a print online at *Youtube.com.*

REVIEWS: "A fine two-reel knockout number, produced by Henry Lehrman. Mack Swain is featured as an overgrown mother's boy who eats enormous meals and loves a girl named Susan. There is a lot of laughable burlesque in this, much better than ordinary. The action is also very good. Ethel Teare plays the heroine." *Moving Picture World*, February 8, 1919, p.805

"Through Sunshine Comedies, rotund Mack Swain remade many of his earlier Sennett hits — and 'Cowboy Ambrose' is a meticulous, but MUCH funnier, reworking of 'His Bitter Pill'. The satire of both western tradition and western action is truly classic; nobody here merely mounts a horse when a spectacular leap will do instead, and although done for comedy purposes, the riding stunts are frenzied and exciting. Not the least of the film's delights are the brilliant subtitles, some of the funniest ever written for a silent comedy." Reviewed by William K. Everson in his film notes for *The Theodore Huff Memorial Film Society*, June 19, 1953, p.1

His Musical Sneeze: *Released 02/23/1919 Sunday.* © 02/23/1919 — 2 reels. SUPERVISOR: Henry Lehrman. DIRECTOR: Jack White. CAST: Lloyd Hamilton, Virginia Rappe, Charles Dorety, Glen Cavender, Jimmie Adams, Madame Sul-Te-Wan, Vera Steadman, Frank J. Coleman
(previously announced for release on 02/16/1919 and 03/23/1919)
SYNOPSIS: A father (Adams) and his son Casper (Hamilton) drive towards the Rocky Bed Lodge in their open-air auto, Caspar with shotgun in hand. When a tire pops Casper thinks it's someone shooting and leaps from the auto, his shotgun at the ready. A disorganized group of hunters are running about nearby, firing wildly at a fast-moving rabbit, each shot causing the ground to erupt in a large explosion. Hunters are thrown in the air as poorly-aimed shots explode nearby. Casper joins the hunt. With feather tucked in bowler and small twig held in front of him as meager camouflage, Casper crawls on his belly unaware of the rabbit standing nearby. The other hunters spot the rabbit and fire in unison, causing a huge screen-filling explosion. As the dust settles, they all scramble towards the huge pit in the ground. Casper emerges, dead rabbit in hand, claiming victory. While the hunters take off looking for more rabbits, another hunter arrives and shoots the dead rabbit out of Casper's hand. The hunt resumes in an ongoing chaotic fashion, another crafty rabbit getting the best of Casper.

Later, back at the lodge, Casper and his father arrive and Woodrow Butts introduces Casper to his daughter Lucy (Rappe). Casper has a sneezing fit, his first launching an Oriental rug into the air, the second clearing a dining room table of its table cloth and settings. The assemblage of guests looks on in shock. Casper returns to the group, but when another sneeze threatens his father hurries him out of the lodge. Outside, Casper's next sneeze is illustrated against a black background — Tra — Ta — Taa — with broken musical notes accompanying. The hunters assembled inside, all decked out in their finest fox-hunting togs, hear Casper's "musical" sneezes. Mistaking them for the horn that's to alert them of a hunt, all scramble outside. There they find Casper, shredded handkerchief in hand; a follow-up sneeze shows them the mistake they've all made. Lucy appears, now dressed for the hunt.

Baron Charles Peabody (Dorety) arrives on the scene. He spots Lucy with her horse, and trots over to profess his undying love for her — in actuality, love for her money. Casper sees the two of them and intervenes, an extended fight the result. Lucy breaks up the conflict by announcing that the one who gets the fox — gets her! The race is now on, but Casper is sidetracked somewhat when he spots a skunk, thinks it to be a fox, chases it down, catches it, and deposits it in a cloth sack. Returning to his mount, his horse takes a couple of whiffs and falls over unconscious. The other hunters see Casper with the sack and assume he's captured the fox. They wander over for a peek in the sack's contents, and they too are rendered unconscious. Utterly confused, Casper tosses the sack into a large hole in the side of a nearby tree.

Peabody arrives, announces that they can't both have Lucy, and proposes a duel.. He hands Casper a pistol, but as the two pace off Casper flees in fright. Peabody follows, firing wildly, and Casper finds that his pistol is unloaded. He tosses it aside and continues his flight, but Peabody catches up and holds him at gunpoint. Peabody pulls a knife and is about to stab Casper when a huge lion appears from behind a boulder. Terrified, Peabody drops the knife and is rendered impotent as his whole body is convulsed with knee-knocking shakes. When Casper finally sees the lion, he too is reduced to violent shakes, and the two of them make off for a barn with the lion hot on their heels. Butts and Casper's father arrive on the scene and the lion now sets his attention on the two newcomers. Casper retrieves the skunk-filled sack from the tree, and with this in hand renders the lion unconscious. Butts and Casper's father have fled and now stand in front of a large statue of a lion. Turning, they take it to be the real thing and flee once more. Lucy arrives and the two men now hail Casper as their savior. Butts awards his daughter to Casper, the new couple now pleased with the result. Synopsis based on the print held by The Danish Film Institute, and the English translations on the print posted at *Vimeo.com*
REVIEWS: "A breezy and laughable knockabout comic in two reels directed by Jack White. The cast includes Lloyd (Ham) Hamilton , Virginia Popple [sic] and others. This pictures many hilarious events occurring at and near a mountain inn. The first reel contains a unique rabbit hunt and the second a fox hunt. Both are joyous affairs, and the number is very successful." *Moving Picture World*, March 8, 1919, p.1393

"A Sunshine comedy, 'His Musical Sneeze,' with Lloyd ('Ham') Hamilton as the featured funmaker, was the second Fox number on the program. It is a comic that lives up to its name at the start, passes that rating before the end of the first reel and keeps going stronger every foot of the second reel. The fun is as broad as it is persistent, and if your doctor has told you a good hearty laugh is what your system needs the theatre which is running this picture is the place to go for it. By the time that rabbit hunt is over you may start for the nearest drug store on a hunt for a plaster for your aching sides, but you have taken an invigorating dose of just what the doctor ordered.

"'His Musical Sneeze' gets its title from the affliction of the hero, who has a bad cold in the head and sneezes so violently but which such musical effect that it sounds like the old call to horse and hounds, 'A Hunting We Will Go.' The guests at a house party at once hurry into their hunting togs and mount their horses. Then comes that rabbit hunt and for fast and uproarious fun it has never been beaten. The director deserves two medals: One for thinking up the scene and the other for the clever way the scene is handled.

"There is also a fox hunt in which 'Ham' mistakes an animal which shall be nameless but under no circumstances can be rendered scentless for the fox. Deprived by his cold of all sense of smell, 'Ham' pops his prize into a bag and is about to take it home in triumph when the strange actions of his horse puzzle him. His mount shows plainly that he is not troubled with a cold and objects to the company of the animal in the bag. While 'Ham' is wondering at the horse's behavior the poor brute falls down, completely overcome. This is another cleverly managed scene.

"'His Musical Sneeze' is one long loud laugh, with a refreshing amount of new material in its two reels." Reviewed by Edward Weitzel, "Fox-Farnum Week at the Rivoli," *Moving Picture World*, March 15, 1919, pp.1467-1468

Money Talks: *Released 03/23/1919 Sunday.* © *03/23/1919* — 2 reels. SUPERVISOR: Henry Lehrman. DIRECTOR: Fred Fishback. CAST: Jack Cooper, Mack Swain, Gertrude Selby, Bobby Dunn
REVIEWS: "'Money Talks,' a Sunshine Comedy in two reels which will go faster than the imagination of any among the spectators who isn't an escape from an asylum, and give him more surprises to the minute than one would think it possible. The subtitles are witty, the action is astonishing and the whole, though indescribable, is certainly amusing." *Moving Picture World*, April 5, 1919, p.128

"Mack Swain and Jack Cooper who play the principal roles in another Sunshine Comedy are a contrasting pair who work well together. There are several very funny bits in which the two figure, all of the slapstick variety of course. Although the offering drags in several places, it has been screened well and includes one very unusual portion, — that in which an automobile travelling at a high rate of speed throws over a line of telegraph poles. Some of the chase stuff included and several other bits are not of any particular value and some of the material lacks cleverness, but the laughs have been distributed so as to keep this going smoothly." *Wid's Daily*, March 21, 1920, p.28

"A Fox Sunshine comedy, 'Money Talks,' closed the film entertainment without getting a laugh." "Rivoli," *Variety*, March 21, 1919, p.55

A Lady Bell-Hop's Secret: *Released 05/04/1919 Sunday.* © 05/04/1919 — 2 reels. SUPERVISOR: Henry Lehrman. DIRECTOR: William Campbell. CAST: Hugh Fay, Betty Carpenter
(pre-release title: **A Lady Bellhop's Millions**; previously announced release dates 02/02/1919 and 02/23/1919)
SYNOPSIS: "[T]he story is that of a girl who works as a bell-hop in a hotel. Her sweetheart has knowledge of the location of six million dollars in gold hidden in a sand pit. The gold is recovered by the villain, who escapes in an aeroplane and drops from the parachute into an open cage of lions, etc., etc." "Negative Stolen," *Moving Picture World*, February 22, 1919, p. 1005
REVIEWS: "Two reels that will surely make a houseful of laughter. A farce of comical characters as well as comical doings, it is replete with good old doings worked up anew. A flood in an upper room of a hotel, caged lions and buried gold are some of its fun-making things." *Moving Picture World*, May 17, 1919, p.1077

The House of Terrible Scandals: *Re-released as a Fox Sunshine: 04/20/1919 Sunday*

Henry Lehrman Comedies
(released through Associated First National Exhibitors Circuit)

A Twilight Baby: *Released 12/20/1919.* 4 reels according to pre-release First National materials and some post-release ads; 3 reels in other post-release ads. DIRECTOR: Jack White. CINEMATOGRAPHY: George Meehan. EDITOR: Charles Hochberg. CAST: Virginia Rappe, Lloyd Hamilton, Billie Ritchie, Harry Todd, Charles Dorety, Harry McCoy, Rube Miller, Ernie Shield, Charles Dudley

SYNOPSIS: Ham's (Hamilton) on a rock pile in striped prison garb, amused that his "father" — Ham is adopted — thinks he's overseas fighting the Germans; in reality he's in the county jail for bootlegging. Elsewhere in his father's general store, his dad (Todd) reads a letter from Ham detailing all sorts of fictitious heroic exploits. A photo of Ham in striped prison garb is included with a note saying that he was in camouflage as a zebra to elude the Germans. Rival bootlegger Nasty Harold (Ritchie) and his son Jake (Dorety) are among the assembled group listening to these exploits. Nasty Harold makes a sarcastic comment, after which a wild pistol-shooting and fist-punching melee breaks out, semi-demolishing the general store's interior.

Ham is made a jail trustee for good behavior, but uses this newfound "freedom" to gather some tools from the tool house and affect an escape down a downspout. He hides in a large barrel on the back of a truck, but as the truck leaves the prison and heads up a hill, the barrel rolls off, down the hill, through the still open gate, bowling over a number of guards. Ham is back in stir.

Virginia (Rappe) is introduced back at the farm, swinging on a swing, her posterior coming in contact with a cactus. Jake, smitten by Virginia, pursues her each day, and is rejected each day — she's waiting for her sweetheart Ham to return.

Ham is released from prison and told to remember the 11th commandment: Thou shalt not get caught. Coming home, he's first greeted by a flock of his chickens that descend upon him, then his faithful dog Happy, and finally by Virginia; she knows full well that he was in jail for bootlegging rather than overseas. Happy trots over to the small idyllic (and still mortgaged) cottage that Ham had bought earlier for when he Virginia get married; Ham tells her it will be their house someday.

Ham and his dad are reunited, but not until Ham has had a painful encounter with both a ram and a mule. Ham crawls to his dad and Virginia; Virginia is very shy and love-struck when with Ham. Meanwhile, Harold has told his rebuffed son Jake that he'll show him how to get rid of Ham. Jake arrives and announces himself as the rival, and punches Ham. A knock-down, drag-out fight ensues with a telephone pole and watermelons used as weapons. Ham grabs Jake by the seat of the pants and rolls him somersaulting into a bunch of bystanders arranged like bowling pins. They all fall down for a strike. Virginia, annoyed, storms off, but the two are eventually reunited and Ham vows to go straight and leave bootlegging behind.

Later on, Ham is in the barn while outside Jake pours a line of gunpowder up to the door. The hens all start pecking at and eating the gunpowder, after which they go to lay their eggs. The first egg drops on a rooster, blowing his tail feathers off. A second egg drops and explodes on Ham's rear. Ham collects the remaining eggs. Ham innocently drops a cigarette onto the trail of gunpowder and it explodes, burning Jake's rear. Harold and Jake go after Ham, but he holds them off with the exploding eggs. When the eggs run out, Ham unsuccessfully suggests calling a truce, but Harold will have nothing of it. Harold chases him off with a gun.

Jake asks Virginia to take a bike ride with him on his tandem, and to test Ham's love she agrees. Ham tells her that if she goes, he'll be a bootlegger when she returns. Jake, trying to impress Virginia with his bike riding abilities, crashes with a passing car.

Later on, Harold pummels Ham, and Virginia urges him to fight back, but Ham announces that he's a coward; Virginia gives up on him, her "dream world coming to an end." She heads off to their old trysting place, a bench by a creek, to sulk.

Happy overhears Harold tell Jake he's going to shoot Ham with his shotgun. Happy rushes to Ham's side just as Harold shoots. Ham's wrist is winged, but Happy sustains a far more serious wound. Ham, unaware of his dog's predicament, heads off to bandage his wound, while Happy struggles to move on, slowly crawling towards the creek. Ham goes to Virginia at the bench and shows her his wound: "A coward deserves no better fate," says she. Happy crawls over, and at first Ham is overjoyed, but when it appears Happy has died, Ham sobs with grief, joined in by a saddened Virginia. Flashback to a dog silhouetted in a window, howling, and a shot of a puppy licking an abandoned infant's face — assumedly Happy and Ham years before. Back to the present: Ham vows revenge, hopping onto a horse, followed by Virginia on same; the two gallop wildly to Harold's house.

Ham confronts Harold, and a wild fight breaks out, Ham's cowardice now a thing of the past. Others attempt to intervene, but one by one Ham tosses them from the building, and into the nearby creek. Ham throws Harold through a wall twice, on either side of a door, leaving two large gaping holes. In spite of this, Harold locks the door from the other side and a stymied Ham tries to figure out how to get to him, peeking in the cracks around the door sill. He finally catches on and runs through the hole in the wall, but Harold quickly opens the door, runs through, and relocks it! Ham finally puts Harold's head through the door and sends both out into the creek. The door floats away like a raft, Harold's squirming body in view and his head beneath the door and under water. Emerging from the building, Ham is greeted by Virginia and Happy, who is indeed alive and now limping with a bandaged leg. Announcing "Beware! I'm a caveman," Ham grabs Virginia under one arm and a minister under the other, hauling them both off, assumedly to be married.

Ham and Virginia, now newlyweds, arrive at their cottage, which is surrounded by many flowers gently blowing in the breeze. They look out at the idyllic scene beyond of a lake, the woods and clouds. The film fades to an abrupt ending. Synopsis based on the print held by the Museum of Modern Art, which appears to consist of the film's final two reels REVIEWS: "Numerable farm scenes in which domestic animals are seen, and bits that carry a considerable appeal will put this slapstick comedy, a three-reeler, over. Ordinarily, it would arouse little enthusiasm but the shots showing the pups drinking milk directly from the cow, and then the baby doing the same, will draw 'Ahs' from the women and bring forth smiles from men. The production has been screened nicely and will fit in well with your program." *Wid's Daily*, December 16, 1919, p.4

"The comedy is 'A Twilight Baby,' a Lehrman two-reeler, containing some exceedingly clever trick photography and an entire zoological garden full of trained domestic animals. These are cleverly interwoven with farce perpetrated by human beings with humorously conceived titles." Reviewed by Jolo., *Variety*, January 16, 1920, p.61

"There is a slender thread of story running through 'A Twilight Baby,' but so much else awakens merriment that it is quickly forgotten. What makes us shake with laughter is a wonderful series of incidents, crowding upon each other, in which all sorts of living things besides the reckless baby take part. Most remarkable is the act of a mothering dog, who leaves her litter of pups to care for the abandoned baby. She drags the tiny helpless human creature to where it can suckle directly from a cow and there stands guard until the infant is fed. There is a really talented rooster, who not only officiates as an alarm clock, but pecks at heavy sleepers to rouse them and raises the shade of their window. There are puppies who follow the baby's example in getting sustenance from the cow. There is a tragic dog who plays his role with startling intelligence, until the human element has to get busy in order to compete for the spectator's interest.

"When the baby, supposedly of noble birth, is grown, the result is a clownish and cowardly fat boy. He is clumsy, awkward and constantly in trouble. Nearly all of his mishaps are worked out by methods both ingenious and novel, and again animals play a part. The fat boy is projected against the side of a barn with such violence that his head drives through it, and there he sticks. The best padded part of his anatomy tempts a goat to butt in. We are treated to a view of the goat delivering the smashing blows of a battering ram on one side, and the agonized expression of the fat boy's face on the other. We laugh at the ludicrous; we laugh at the ridiculous; we laugh anyhow until we are tired. 'A Twilight Baby' made a great hit at the Rialto, and it is one of the best farces ever shown on the screen." Reviewed by Louis Reeves Harrison, *Moving Picture World*, January 24, 1920, p.635

"This purports to be a 'Hank' Mann [sic] starring vehicle, but as a matter of fact much of the merriment, and that is quite some, is furnished by a fox terrier 'purp,' a baby not over a couple of months old and some of the most ingenious business ever devised for a comedy.

"There are really two pictures in a 'Twilight Baby.' The first has to do with what happened to a 'foundling' after it is abandoned by its parents and adopted by the 'purp' we have mentioned, and made one of a rather large family of the canine species. The manner in which this dog performs before the camera is good for both wonderment and much hilarity.

"The next episode begins with the 'twilight baby' all grown up, 'Hank' Mann having the role. The picture then takes on the usual low comedy tempo and keeps going with plenty of pep and punch, with a lot of new stuff, until well toward the last, when it degenerates into the just 'get by' class. However, so much has been crowded into the film, especially in the first episode, which is absolutely new and novel and mirth provoking, that the production may be rated as one of the best of slap-stick comedies to come through in a long time.

"'Hank' Mann contributes to the fun making, although some of his scenes sort of miss fire with us. The supporting cast is good and the camera work is especially fine. All in all, it is a comedy which rates with the topnotchers and worth a million of the majority of releases of its type placed upon the market in the past couple of years." Reviewed by J.S. Dickerson, *Motion Picture News*, January 24, 1920, p.1127

"'A Twilight Baby' promises much for the forthcoming Henry Lehrman comedies for the First National schedule. Care has been lavished upon its preparation, and it shows the results in genuinely laughable incident. Lloyd Hamilton and Virginia Rappe are the leading players." *Exhibitors Herald*, February 21, 1920, p.72

EXHIBITOR REVIEWS: "Something different in this one. First two reels continual laughter, when it begins to drag. Four reels too long. Exceptional comedy. Lots of advertising should get the crowds." W.G. Mitchell, Majestic Gardens, Kalamazoo, Mich., *Exhibitors Herald*, April 3, 1920, p.69

"This picture pulled big." Altman & Trifon, Cozy theatre, Goose Creek, Tex., *Exhibitors Herald*, May 8, 1920, p.89

"Too long. The first half is great, then it begins to drag. Two reels is long enough for a comedy." Jack Cairns, Brooklyn theatre, Detroit, Mich., *Exhibitors Herald*, May 15, 1920, p.77

"Good comedy. Probably too long. Two reels long enough for laughs." Alvin S. Frank, Jewel theatre, Lafayette, Colo., *Exhibitors Herald*, June 19, 1920, p.75

"This comedy became a tragedy. We wonder from what asylum Lehrman escaped. Lost in a night what it has taken all winter to build up, namely, the high quality of First National. No producers are so blind as those who won't see." Philip Rand, Rex theatre, Salmon, Idaho., *Exhibitors Herald*, April 2, 1921, p.81

"Good four reel comedy. Very well liked. Good business." G. Strasser Sons, Emblem theatre, Buffalo, N.Y., *Exhibitors Herald*, June 2, 1923, p.74

The Kick in High Life: *Released 09/13/1920.* © 03/11/21 — 2 reels. DIRECTOR: Al Ray and Al Herman. SCREENPLAY: Henry Lehrman. CINEMATOGRAPHY: George Meehan. CAST: Al Ray, Charles Conklin, Charlotte Dawn, Hugh Fay, Phil Dunham
REVIEWS: "'The Kick in High Life' deals with the troubles of Bud Weiser and Lotta Sherry in attending the birthday party of a precocious youngster who performs remarkable feats in breaking a fall from a ten story window." *Exhibitors Herald*, August 14, 1920, p.79

"This Henry Lehrman comedy for First National presents an assortment of tried and true tricks, with no original effort being visible anywhere. The slapstick brush is applied quite strenuously. There is considerable whacking of head and the hinter portion of one's anatomy. A bathing pool is used to supply the ducking, and another scene is the extension plank outside the window of a skyscraper. A tiny youngster toddles out to the end and manages to stay there, while the burlesquers inside fight to effect his rescue.

"The weakness of this comedy is the absence of spontaneity. The scenes are not inspired. They are conceived and executed for the mere sake of slapstick. It's a knockabout piece with a good deal of tumbling and falling and spanking on the part of the tumblers and spankers. Albert Ray, formerly a star in feature pictures, has the fat part. But it strikes us that he is not exceptionally talented in a comedy direction. He should be used as a straight foil to Charles Conklin or some other player who is gifted with a sense of burlesque. The audience at the Strand, New York, didn't enthuse over the offering with loud guffaws. A trickle of laughter was heard now and then. The fault here is the recourse to old stuff." Reviewed by Laurence Reid, *Motion Picture News*, September 18, 1920, p.2311

EXHIBITOR REVIEWS: "Played this with *Don't Ever Marry* and made a hit. Had large business and kept the house in an uproar continually." I.S. Campbell, Zimm theatre, Winfield, Kan., *Exhibitors Herald*, December 4, 1920, p.101

"One of the best slapstick comedies I have ever run. They laughed so hard that one patron broke a seat back." F.D. Hall, Wonderland theatre, Madelia, Minn., *Exhibitors Herald*, March 12, 1921, p.81

"One of the best slapstick comedies we have ever shown." R.R. Gribble, Grand theatre, New Hamburg, Ont., Can., *Exhibitors Herald*, June 4, 1921, p.98

Wet and Warmer: *Released 11/01/1920.* © 02/14/21 — 2 reels/2,061 feet. DIRECTOR, SCREENPLAY: Henry Lehrman. CINEMATOGRAPHY: George Meehan, Charles Selby. CAST: Charles Conklin, Al Ray, Charlotte Dawn, Billie Ritchie
REVIEWS: "This comedy follows the more or less familiar lines of several others, with hairbreadth escapes along a high ledge outside a large hotel. It concerns a nutty bell hop and a rube guest in a hotel, with some high powered 'hooch' stored in the hotel fire hose. In attempting to extinguish a small blaze the whole place catches fire and the rescues and near rescues furnish the fun." "Reviews," *Exhibitors Herald*, December 10, 1921, p.61

"Henry Lehrman has done a first rate job of it in his latest comedy, 'Wet and Warmer.' It is a sure laugh provoker and carries some incidents which are uproariously funny. The director has taken a hotel, filled it with grotesque comedians and started them running about avoiding water and fire. Albert Ray has installed a Roman bath for his bride but the comic pair use it for a swimming pool while it is empty. The picture moves at its best when Ray puts a hose stream on a fire. The stream is inflammable 'hootch' and the fire spreads. Meanwhile a grotesque guest, provoked at the management, telephones that he is leaving. He makes his exit in his night shirt and finds comfort from the flames far up on a ledge overlooking the street.

"The fun is real snappy at this point and sends forth a deal of suspense. He leans over to catch the telephone receiver and nearly loses his balance and a stream of water sends him scurrying along the ledge. This is knockabout stuff which certainly gets over because it is developed spontaneously. One may be safe in calling it slapstick of the full grown garden variety. Certain comedians are propelled through space; others land through apertures in the floors of the hotel; the cops and firemen are called out and the finish brings a roof chase. The janitor and the porter and the obnoxious guest are hurried away by the collar. Lehrman has taken a page from Mack Sennett's note-book by introducing titles which are snappy and to the point. There is no forced humor in any department of the offering. 'Wet and Warmer' is a sure gloom-chaser." Reviewed by Laurence Reid, *Motion Picture News*, December 4, 1920, p.4339

"A lively little farce produced by Henry Lehrman and shown at the Strand Theatre to an amused audience. The scenes are laid in a bathing establishment and the central figure is a patient guest who is subjected to almost every possible inconvenience devised by the ingenuity of slap-stick producer. The guest decides to give a month's notice when the torments have almost exceeded human endurance. He is almost drowned and nearly knocked to pieces when he declares he will give only a week's notice. Not until jets of fire burn holes through his bed, which no amount of shifting enables him to avoid, does he decide not to stand on the order of his going. There is tireless action throughout and many good laughs at the expense of those who find the bathing establishment decidedly 'Wet and Warmer.'" *Moving Picture World*, December 11, 1920
EXHIBITOR REVIEWS: "An absolute knockout. Run four of these two-reel comedies, and they are great. It is too bad that Lehrman does not make at least one a month. If you want to make your audience laugh, get this one." W.E. Elkin, Temple theatre, Aberdeen, Miss., *Exhibitors Herald*, July 30, 1921, p.63

"Some one should take out Lehrman's brains and cleanse them. People called me down for showing this." Philip Rand, Rex theatre, Salmon Idaho, *Exhibitors Herald*, August 27, 1921, p.72

The Punch of the Irish: *Released 12/20/1920.* © 03/21/21 — 2 reels. DIRECTOR: Noel Smith, Henry Lehrman, and Roy Del Ruth. SCREENPLAY: Henry Lehrman. CINEMATOGRAPHY: George Meehan. CAST: Virginia Rappe, Phil Dunham, Albert Ray, Billy Engle, George Rowe, Frank J. Coleman, Suzanne Avery, Charles Dorety, Bert Gillespie
SYNOPSIS: Two dapper suiters (Ray and Dunham) arrive at a mansion, rivals for the hand of Virginia Rappe. Only Ray has an invitation, requiring Dunham to sneak in over the wall, encountering a puddle of tar on the other side. Ray presents Rappe with a bouquet of flowers, but Dunham has snuck in a note that leaves her furious. Ray catches up to Dunham inside the grounds, where a bunch of partygoers and bathing beauties cavort around the pool. Ray and Dunham get into a brawl, and all of the partygoers — Rappe included — end up in the pool. When Dunham climbs out, his water-logged shoes squirt when a cane pokes them, and his top hat squirts when he sits down.

Soon after, a smaller group sits down for an outside meal at a table overseen by Rappe's father (Engle) and mother (Coleman, in drag). Mother tries the punch and, finding it to be spiked, likes it very much. It goes to her head, though, and when one of the pontificating diners (Rowe) annoys her, she grabs him and tosses him all over the place. That done, she goes after her husband with a vengeance. Momentarily dazed by a falling plant, she revives and tears a small tree from the ground and swings it wildly at her husband. The two square off but it is an uneven match, each one of her punches sending pa eight feet into the air. Bystanders attempt to restrain her to no avail, so Rowe sneaks a horse shoe into pa's glove and now it is ma who flies eight feet into the air with each of pa's punches, crashing into and destroying a sizable pergola. The fight is called and ma is ready to give up, but when she discovers the horse shoe she goes ballistic, pummeling her poor husband senseless and punching the others into the pool. Pa flees into the mansion with his enraged wife in full pursuit. She lunges at him but misses, propelling her out a second story window and crashing to the garden below — twice. Dragging herself back into the house, she tearfully takes time out to grab a large screen and place it over the open window. This time when she charges and misses, she bounces off the screen and back into the room. Pa attempts to escape by climbing up the drapes, ma in hot pursuit. Both ma and pa and several others end up falling into the pool, its contents ejected in a massive gush that pours through the house and out the open window. The closing shot is of the now-waterless pool's drenched occupants. Synopsis based on the prints held by the Museum of Modern Art and the Library of Congress

A Game Lady: *Released 06/27/1921.* © 09/21/21 — 2 reels. DIRECTOR: Noel Smith, David Kirkland, and/or Roy Del Ruth. CINEMATOGRAPHY: George Meehan. CAST: Virginia Rappe, Lloyd Hamilton, Al Ray, Frank J. Coleman, Phil Dunham, Billy Engle
REVIEWS: "Henry Lehrman, the producer of this comedy, has a good time in smashing the conventions to pieces. There is no logic and he did not intend there should be any. He has assembled a cast of fairly clever comedians, a lot of trick incident, some hokum atmosphere, plenty of comedy properties and pieced them together in a crazy quilt pattern — without

any attention being placed to law or order. The wild people are engaged in the pastime of shooting ducks. They are game with their rifles and are after game — all kinds of it.

"It is a crazy chase — with flivvers, ducks, wild geese, and a tromp of merry burlesquers all involved and running around in circles. The offering carries a number of laughs — the antics of the troupers arousing guffaws on several occasions. The titles are snappy and carry double meanings. Phil Dunham and Lloyd Hamilton are in there making the action ridiculous. 'A Game Lady' may be topsy-turvy but it succeeds in sending the 'peepul' forth laughing as they say goodby." Reviewed by Laurence Reid, *Motion Picture News*, July 23, 1921, p.606

Feature Films And Shorts

As Director:

Reported Missing: Owen Moore Picture Corp., for Selznick Pictures; Distributor: Select Pictures. *Released 04/05/1922.* © 04/15/1922 — 7 reels/6,750 feet. DIRECTOR: Henry Lehrman. STORY: Henry Lehrman and Owen Moore. SCREENPLAY, ADAPTATION: Lewis Allen Browne. EDITOR: George M. Arthur. CINEMATOGRAPHY: Jules Cronjager. TITLES: H.I. Phillips, John Medbury, Will B. Johnson, E.V. Durling, and Tom Bret. SUPERVISOR: Myron Selznick. CAST: Owen Moore, Pauline Garon, Tom Wilson, Togo Yamamoto, Frank Wunderlee, Robert Cain, Nita Naldi, Mickey Bennett
(production title: **Love is an Awful Thing**)
SYNOPSIS: "Story: Deals with a rich young man who has inherited a steamship line. His girl wants him to send out all the ships while his crafty advisors desire to sell out to a Chinaman. They manage to kidnap both the girl and the young president. The negro servant follows and all three are landed on a ruffian's brig. 'Robert,' says the girl to the rich young man, 'I wish you would beat up every one of those ruffians.' He replies, 'I hope you get your wish.' Then the boat is stranded upon a reef and the captain commences to dispose of those who eat too much. Fun follows. The hero signals a passing warship while the Chinaman captures the girl and rushes to land in a fast motor boat. The battleship provides an aeroplane and drops a few bombs in the path of the boat. The final climax comes in the home of the Chinaman and a most thrilling fight is carried on by the hirelings of the rich Chinaman and the U.S. sailors who come to the aid of the hero." *Film Daily*, April 16, 1922, p.2

"Romantic melodramatic comedy releasing considerable high jinks aboard a schooner on the high seas. Treats of a wealthy young wastrel who is inspired to go to work by girl with whom he is in love. He inherits the Boyd Company who hold an option on a fleet of ships. Jap merchant desirous of owning fleet arranges to have option elapse during hero's absence and has him 'shanghaied.' Girl is forced to accompany him and his negro valet is faithful enough to follow. The vessel is wrecked. The couple are rescued and picture closes with hero triumphant after a series of hazardous exploits in saving sweetheart from the intricate chambers of Jap's villa." *Motion Picture News Booking Guide*, October 1922, p.60

"Richard Boyd has been left the Boyd Shipping Co. as an inheritance, but he is a young man entirely on a pleasure bent and he takes no interest at all in the business. An Oriental shipping magnate is anxious to get the fleet and he persuades Boyd to give him an option on it. At this point Richard's sweetheart intervenes and makes him promise not to let the option go through. The Oriental captures them both hoping to hold them until after the option expires but the ship is wrecked and they escape. In a battle at home Boyd kills the Oriental leaving his own path clear to marry the girl." *Exhibitors Trade Review*, April 26, 1924, p.51

REVIEWS: "If the title 'Reported Missing' doesn't excite you, you may be sure the picture will. To miss seeing it will be to forfeit an evening of genuine amusement. The film, which was given its initial presentation at a private showing at the Ritz-Carlton on Friday evening is not only one of the best pictures ever made by the Selznick company but one of the most thoroughly satisfactory ever made by any company.

"Owen Moore is delightful in the stellar role, exhibiting real skill as Richard Boyd, a rich young man whose motto, "Early to bed, early to rise and you never meet any regular guys," has caused him to be regarded by his friends as 'senseless, hopeless and useless.'

"The titles, which add considerably to the entertainment of the picture, were written by a group of newspapermen: H.I. Phillips, John Medbury, Will B. Johnstone, E.V. Durling and Tom Brett. The scenario is the work of Lewis Allen Browne, who adapted it from a story by Henry Lehrman. Mr. Lehrman also directed the production, of which he may well feel proud. The photography for which Jules Cronjager is responsible is attractive throughout the production, notably in the scenes of the storm at sea. There are some unusually effective views of a battleship and other vessels on the high sea.

"The picture is full of good moments. One of the most touching of these occurs when a little boy accompanies his father to an employment station in search of work, and then boasts to one of the bystanders about his dad. The boy is not given credit on the program and while he appears only in a scene or two he makes his appearance memorable.

"The happenings during the shipwreck when Boyd, his sweetheart, Pauline, and his man, Sam, are left without food are screamingly funny.

"In addition to Owen Moore, who is at his very best as Richard Boyd, the company includes Pauline Garon, whose simplicity and naturalness as the heroine Pauline is quite refreshing. Togo Yamamoto is good as the Oriental ship merchant, and Robert Cain and Frank Wunderlee do well as Andrew Dunn and the captain of the ship. Running a close second to Mr. Moore is Tom Wilson, whose performance of Boyd's negro servant, kept the audience in paroxysm of laughter on Friday night.

"There isn't space here for all the pleasant things that might be said about this film. It has been many a long day since this reviewer has enjoyed a picture as thoroughly as 'Reported Missing.' Don't miss it." Reviewed by Helen Pollock, *The Morning Telegraph*, April 9, 1922, page number unknown

"Lewis J. Selznick gave a special presentation of 'Reported Missing,' a five-reel comedy directed by Henry Lehrman, starring Owen Moore, at the Hotel Ritz Carlton, New York, last week. It is a whale of a laugh picture and undoubtedly will gross toward the half-million dollar mark as it stands, but if it were taken and re-edited and re-titled the chances are that the picture would prove a second 'Mickey' in the matter of gross receipts.

"The story was written by the director, and it is a real thriller as a melodrama, but the meller is handled in such a slapstick manner as to make it a howling farce.

"Moore plays the role of a wealthy youngster who has more money than brains and who has led a life that has been entirely along the primrose path. To please the girl he wants to marry he consents to purchase a gigantic shipping fleet that the United States Government has and is about to dispose of. Moore, as Richard Boyd, is the head of the directorate board that holds an option on the ships, but the Japanese shipping trust is also planning to lay their hands on the fleet. So their agent plots with a relative of the young man's to get him out of the way until his option expires.

"From this point on the thrills start. Moore and the girl are on the way to the minister after he has delivered his ultimatum to the directors regarding the purchase of the ships, but instead they are driven to a wharf where they are set upon and taken aboard a yacht which is to keep them at sea until the option expires. The yacht is wrecked, the comedy that follows brings howl after howl from the audience. For the rescue a battleship is brought into play, and atop of that Moore starts off in a hydroplane for a chase after a sea-sledge in which the Jap conspirator is running off with the girl. Naturally, there is a happy ending, with Moore getting the girl and arriving on the scene in time to buy the ships.

"Lehrman has taken that plot and dressed it with all the slap-stick hoke that one could ask for, and the general indications are that the picture is going to prove a clean-up for the exhibitor as well as Selznick.

"Moore has a role that is difficult to say the least. He seemingly undertook to take all of the leaps and dives the picture necessitated without resorting to a double.

"Pauline Garon played the lead opposite him and managed to score nicely. But Tom Wilson, working in blackface, managed to clean up on the comedy outside of Moore. He was in all of the battle and took the flops and falls with a wow.

"Five title writers are credited with having provided the reading matter. A number of them are daily paper columnists and humorists, but their titles failed to show any of the alleged humor that they are credited with being possessed of. It was the action of the picture that brought the laughs rather than the subtitles." Reviewed by Fred., *Variety*, April 14, 1922, p.39

"'Reported Missing' is an excellent all around production that combines real humor with some serious melodrama and results in an entertainment that will delight picture-goers. The story unfolds simply and runs along in a consistent manner providing untold opportunities for the star to display his powers of high comedy and ending in a thrilling and smashing climax.

"Owen Moore takes advantage of each situation, dramatic or comic, and gets the utmost result from it. This time he presents a character simple and romantic. He plays the part of a rich young man who is about to do his first day's work as president of a steamship company. Besides having been born a 'nut' he has developed into a fool and a 'boob.' A variety of very comical happenings force him into a situation where he must fight — and it is then that he delivers the goods in a thrilling and whirlwind fashion.

"Director Lehrman has placed the star in a variety of situations all showing him to the best of advantage. The continuity is good and runs along smoothly, speeding up considerably at the finish. The photography helps considerably in heightening the comedy moments and intensifying the drama. Clever camerawork and some unusual perspectives add to the pleasures of this offering.

"In the cast Pauline Garon makes a very satisfactory leading lady, while Tom Wilson, as the darkey valet, is just one long scream. He will get a lot of applause at the climax when he whips out his oversized razor and says that he is going to make yellow confetti out of every oriental. Togo Yamamoto is the crafty oriental and does splendid work in the bad man role. Robert Cain and Frank Wunderlee are also in the support.

"Direction…Splendid. Good selection of types and keeps action running." *Film Daily*, April 16, 1922, p.2

"Lewis J. Selznick has a picture in 'Reported Missing' which he can feel proud of having produced. The foreword which states that no moral is attached to the story and no special aim was in view other than that of entertainment starts the picture off right. And it surely accomplishes what it goes after, for it is one of the cleanest bits of entertainment the screen has had in some time.

"Owen Moore does satisfactory work as Richard Boyd, one of the idle rich who has just succeeded to the presidency of the huge Boyd shipping plant, and who decides to buy up all the idle ships to please his sweetheart, Pauline Dale, played by Pauline Garon. This worthy resolution is not pleasing to one scheming Chinaman, J. Young, played by Togo Yamamoto, who resorts to shanghaiing young Boyd to keep him from taking up his option. Pauline clings to her lover, so is taken aboard, while Sam, Boyd's faithful black man, who nearly runs away with the honors of the picture, as portrayed by Tom Wilson, follows in the row boat. Sam is a wonder — particularly toward the end when he starts out with a razor of alarming size to carve up any yellow man he meets.

"Briefly, the plot is based on the attempt of the Chinaman to get the ships on which Boyd holds an option. To this end he kidnaps Boyd and the girl, the ship in which they are being held runs into a terrific storm, which is as well done as any cinema storm witnessed so far. It is driven on the reefs and the Chinaman starts in a powerful speed boat as soon as he hears of the disaster. Meanwhile, a man-of-war caught the signals and sends a detail to the rescue. The Chinaman gets the girl but leaves Boyd, who is taken upon one of the Navy airplanes in pursuit. The boat ducks into a tiny harbor and Boyd has to follow in a car. He leaves his faithful black on guard outside the Chinaman's house, but Sam is so intent on carving up every yellow man he meets that he is off duty when the whistle blows. However, the commander of the man-of-war arrives with a detachment of Jack Tars, and as exciting a fight as was ever staged takes place all over the mansion of the villainous Chinaman. The blue jackets, of course, win out and Boyd and the girl are saved.

"This is a brief outline of the plot but it is rich in laughs, one to nearly every foot of the film, the black man doing strenuous work throughout.

"Running about seven reels, it will be a pity if it is cut to the usual five-reel length, for every foot of the seven is worth while. Others of the very capable cast are Robert Cain, as 'Andrew Dunn,' and Frank Wunderlee, as 'Captain Ferguson.' There is a small boy in the cast who is quite remarkable, although he has but a bit.

"This is the type of picture that the public is looking for — laughs, thrills, legitimate excitement. A sure box-office attraction. The titles are worthy of special mention. They are responsible for many of the laughs." *Exhibitors Herald*, April 22, 1922, p.61

"The introductory title says this picture is designed as entertainment and nothing else. And that's just what it is — entertainment to the nth degree, a mixture of comedy, slapstick, burlesque, melodrama, so cleverly put together that it is absolutely sure-fire. A certain cure for box-office blues — that's *Reported Missing*. According to our way of thinking all the exhibitor has to do with this picture is to add the proper amount of exploitation and serve — his patrons will do the rest.

"A combination of thrills and eccentric comedy — we use the word eccentric because it has a very apt meaning here — and some of the cleverest titles ever put on the screen — that's the essence of *Reported Missing*. It gives the audience a chance to laugh and laugh hard, which as we understand it, is what most people like to do nowadays in preference to weeping.

"There is just enough plot in *Reported Missing* upon which to hang a series of incidents, ranging from a realistic storm at sea to a remarkably well-staged fight in the stronghold of an Oriental. This latter incident will no doubt come a classic on the screen. It is screamingly funny and yet it thrills. And it is built around the adroit use of the razor by the hero's massive colored servant, who, incidentally, is one of the finest eccentric comedy-characters ever given to pictures.

"The cast is excellent. Owen Moore, in the role of the hero, plays one of those helpless young men, at the mercy of everything and everybody that comes along — for a while. Then, inspired by the girl, he proves himself a man. It is a neat and sympathetic bit of work. Tom Wilson, as the huge servant, scores heavily, and is ideal for the part. He is the life of the picture. The heroine, as presented by Pauline Garon, is pretty and effective, and the rest of the players contribute their share in excellent fashion. A little boy who appears in one sequence must be described as a 'find.' Who is he, we wonder? Though he was on the screen for only a few minutes he registered emphatically as a wonderful type and a remarkably natural actor.

"The direction, staging and technical details are admirably handled. The continuity runs smoothly and the total effect is well managed." *Reported Missing* is a 'pep' picture. And that means 'pep' at the box-office." Reviewed by Oscar Cooper, *Exhibitors Trade Review*, April 22, 1922, p.1515

"If there is one picture which deserves the tribute of 'something out of the ordinary,' that picture is 'Reported Missing,' accurately described by Selznick as its greatest achievement. Henry Lehrman, who wrote and directed this melodramatic comedy, has been given free rein to add to the gayety of a nation. And he has contributed a feature which will be talked about for its adventurous action, its novel gags, its subtle and broad humor, its quaint characterization, its development toward a climax which carries explosive qualities and its overwhelming suspense. This compelling element causes the spectator to grip the arms of his seat despite the fact that the incidents and gags are charged with humor. Even though you wonder if Owen Moore, 'shanghaied' by his enemy, will ever see land again, you laugh over his embarrassing moments.

"The star plays the part of a quiet, unobtrusive chap addicted to idleness and a fondness for liquor. He is always the gentleman. His top hat adorns his head throughout. The idea is a satirical fling at serious melodrama with the author and director punctuating the humor with just enough balancing drama to give it substance. The hero holds an option upon a fleet of merchant vessels — a fleet much desired by a cunning Oriental. Owen takes life and his possession lightly until the girl provokes him to carve his niche in the world. When he threatens to become serious he is 'shanghaied' along with the girl. Here it is that Lehrman says 'Let's Go!' Fun and excitement are running neck and neck. There is Owen in the hands of a crew of vicious cutthroats. And here comes his faithful valet in a rowboat paddling the waves for dear life.

"There is action a-plenty aboard this schooner. For one thing the commissary department is soon emptied. And the skipper shoves the hearty eaters into the briny deep if they take more than their allowance. Money has been spent to make these sequences genuine. The scenes, atmosphere and properties are the real thing. A storm arises which brings more suspense. And the humor is immense as you follow the hero's adventures and the valet's trouble in singing his dying swan song. 'Nearer My God to The,' at the organ, while a veritable Niagara engulfs him. The climax introduces an exciting auto pursuit and the rescue of the heroine who has been brought ashore and hidden in the intricate chambers of the Jap's villa. A hydroplane is employed to give chase to the Oriental's fast motor boat. And the sailors are called upon to help the hero in his distress. It is a healthy melee — a battle royal. Daggers, knives, fists, revolvers are used in combating the enemy. You are laughing one minute and catching your breath the next.

"The titles are genuinely funny and are contributions by humorists associated with New York dailies. Indeed Selznick has not overlooked one department to give the feature a thoroughness of production. The cast is highly efficient. Owen Moore will have to share honors with Tom Wilson whose blackface portrayal and whose antics indicate a born clown." Reviewed by Laurence Reid, *Motion Picture News*, April 22, 1922, p.?

"'Reported Missing,' the hectic vehicle selected by Selznick as a starring vehicle for Owen Moore, and now at the Criterion, is like a chestnut burr. It has many points. Some are good, while others are terrible. Starting out with a real idea, and promising at last to show us what our vast fleet of idle ships is really good for, it soon deteriorates into the slappiest of slapstick. The star, looking more like Harold Lloyd than Lloyd looks like himself, is decidedly unfunny, although he works manfully to rescue the story.

"Never in the wildest days of Mack Sennett did he ever descend to the hokum that Henry Lehrman, the Moore director, does in 'Reported Missing.' The good points referred to are several really excellent photographic shots, many of which are ruined by inaccuracies and absurd carelessness of direction. Moore, as we said, works like a Trojan to get across and keeps everlastingly at it, but the hardest worked man in the whole production is the one who throws spoonfuls of water through the portholes in an effort to simulate a terrific storm at sea. The storm is, indeed, terrible, but not in the sense Lehrman wishes it to be. In fact, the adjective could be used to advantage in describing almost every inch-fraction of the whole too-long footage." Reviewed by Don Allen, (New York) *Evening World*, April 24, 1922, p.18

"'Reported Missing,' the film which has replaced 'The Loves of Pharaoh' at the Criterion, is undiluted slap-stick. It gives the impression, every once in a while, that it is about to become an earnest melodrama, and occasionally there is an unpleasant suggestion of jingoistic propaganda about it, but these are only momentary checks to the irresistible onrush of its horse-play. And this is good, because most of the rough stuff is funny. There's too much of it, of course — these broad burlesques should never be more than three reels long — one grows a little tired after thirty minutes of loud laughter at clowning — but this does not alter the fact that there is riotous merriment in 'Reported Missing,' that the antics of Owen Moore, in various ridiculous costumes, are amusing, that the smashing about of black-faced Tom Wilson is comical, and that there are several ingenious situations in the picture. The story, which doesn't matter at all, is mainly about a youth who is kidnapped and held for three days on a schooner stranded on a reef.

"It may, or may not, be interesting to report that a telegram has been received, ostensibly from David Kirkland, which states that he is 'co-author and co-director' of the film, but that 'through some error' his name 'has been omitted from the screen.' The screen and program give credit for authorship and direction to Henry Lehrman. 'You pays your money and you takes your choice.'" *New York Times*, April 24, 1922, p.18

"'Reported Missing,' the new Selznick film which is at the Criterion, is a photoplay 'Wat-is-it?' but as the rejection slips which magazines send budding authors, usually read: 'This does not imply lack of merit.' Far from it, in fact. The picture is a gorgeous conglomeration of comedy, burlesque, melodrama and hoakum slap-stick, but it is more than that — it is rare entertainment.

"Owen Moore, who is featured in the piece, has never had a vehicle which gave him such glorious opportunity for clowning and funmaking of high order. Henry Lehrman, the director as well as the author of 'Reported Missing,' has produced precisely the sort of film that one would expect from a story such as this placed in the hands of a man who used to make the Sunshine Comedies for Fox Film Corporation.

"Lehrman organized Sunshine Comedies for Fox and supervised all of them for some time, and his training there — and elsewhere — has stood him in good stead in holding a kidnapping drama up to ridicule. The plot of the picture is of least importance. It is the action and the ingenuity in 'Reported Missing' that commend it. Moore, in a bewildering succession of costumes, presents a hilarious conception of his part and he is ably seconded by the big-famed Tom Wilson.

"You'll not regret a trip to the Criterion if you're looking for 'something different.'" Reviewed by Alvin J. Kayton, Brooklyn *Daily Star*, April 25, 1922.

"Owen Moore is a new one on me. I've seen most comedians when they have started to commode and have worked my way through their agonies. But Mr. Moore burst upon me in 'Reported Missing,' at the Criterion Theatre, as a full-fledged funny man who can take it all away from the stereotyped star, and who certainly did it.

"He is of melancholy type, and a bedraggled demeanor, and he wears occasionally the horn-rim glasses that have made a fortune of one Lloyd. Apart from these facts, Moore is agile, sinuous, persuasive, and expressively pantomimic. More cannot be asked for from any picture star. Rah for Owen Moore!

"In 'Reported Missing' he has one of those melodramatic farces that are never wholly melodrama nor farce, but a happy mélange of both. The Picture whirls with incident, with escapes — absurd and otherwise — with rush and push and vigor and vim. There are moments when everybody is racing after everybody else, revolving, circumnavigating and generally rough-housing. Why? There's a reason.

"The agile hero, anxious for his 'option' on certain ships, and persooed [sic] by the Japanese villain, finds himself on board ship with his lady love, and all sorts of sinister characters. The villain always persoos him, but — he is every inch the hero. He is also a humorist, which saves him, as a sense of humor has saved so many! And he is confronted with another humorist, the grimacic [sic] Tom Wilson. Wilson is a scream from start to finish, and he is pitted against Owen Moore with the most felicitous results.

"But 'Reported Missing' needs no more criticism than does the most nimble of comedies. It talks for itself, and it talks loudly. It skulks in no silence, and it is irresistible. There are no custard pies and no lemon meringues. There are moreover, admirable sub-titles, filled with mirth. The heroine was not too frightfully pretty, but just comely enough.

"In a word, don't be 'reported missing' from the Criterion.

"'Tis I as sez it.'" Reviewed by Alan Dale, *New York American*, April 27, 1922, page number unknown

EXHIBITOR REVIEWS: "First showing in Northwest. Raised prices from thirty cents to forty and stood 'em out for three days. Wonderful audience picture. Not even one dissatisfied patron." Guy D. Hasleton, Rialto theatre, Missoula, MO. *Exhibitors Herald*, June 24, 1922, p.106

"A crackerjack, bang-up show. I thought so and so did my patrons. No attempts to register animal desire with a simpletino look a la sheik. No illegitimate children. Drew better than expected. Shows like this and censorship will take care of itself." Joseph Gray, Tru-Art theatre, Spangler, PA. *Exhibitors Herald*, December 30, 1922, p.159

"You can boost this as it's some comedy drama. It sure made them all laugh. Get behind it if you have it booked." H.O. Larson, Majestic theatre, Oakland, NB. *Exhibitors Herald*, December 30, 1922, p.159

"Good comedy, probably because Owen Moore is not the star. All credit should go to the actor who played the darkey." G.W. Yeaton, Ioka theatre, Exeter, NH. *Exhibitors Herald*, December 30, 1922, p.159

"If they don't like it they're dead and don't know it. Comedy and excitement rarely blended. Tom Wilson is a new Bert Williams. Play it up big." E.E. Large, Strand theatre, Ithaca, NY. *Exhibitors Herald*, October 21, 1922, p.67

A Ringer for Dad: Robertson-Cole Pictures Corporation; released through Film Booking Offices of America. Released 1923. © 01/20/1923 — 2 reels. DIRECTOR: Henry Lehrman. STORY: Monty Brice and Ethel Foreman. CINEMATOGRAPHY: Kenneth MacLean. CAST: Mr. and Mrs. Carter DeHaven

SYNOPSIS/REVIEW: "The little Carter De Havens are at the Majestic this week (via the screen) in a little domestic comedy that is not as good as the ones the Sidney Drews put out, but which passes the time away pleasantly enough.

"The De Havens must learn what the Drews KNEW. A comedy as well as a ten reel feature must be convincing to really get across. In 'A Ringer for Dad' there are many scenes that in real life just couldn't be. In the Drew comedies the stories made you live and feel with the players.

"Suburban life is the text of the De Haven sermon. The young husband has a terrible time getting his trains. His young wife leads an awful existence helping him along. The water is shut off at the wrong time. A demon plumber does his part toward making things interesting, but NOT edifying. And then comes the plot, which is perfectly silly and unreasonable, but at times laughable.

"The De Havens have worked together so much on stage and screen that they get along admirably. They share the limelight pleasantly and neither tries to 'hog' the laughs of the other. Both are personable and quick on their feet.

"Left to themselves with a little expert advice…there is no reason why this young couple shouldn't be offering us something pretty good. They have a great field, for EVERYBODY likes good domestic comedies." Reviewed by Mae Tinée, *Chicago Daily Tribune*, January 19, 1923, p.1

Double Dealing: Universal Pictures Corp. *Released 05/21/1923.* © 05/11/1923 — 5 reels/5,105 feet. DIRECTOR, STORY: Henry Lehrman. SCREENPLAY: George C. Hull. CINEMATOGRAPHY: Dwight Warren. PRESENTED BY Carl Laemmle. CAST: Hoot Gibson, Helen Ferguson, Betty Francisco, Eddie Gribbon, Gertrude Claire, Otto Hoffman, Frank Hayes, Jack Dillon
(pre-release titles: **The Poor Worm** and **The Knocker**)

SYNOPSIS/REVIEWS: "Looking at this picture in the most sympathetic light possible we cannot offer many praises for it. Henry Lehrman, who wrote and directed the number, has made nothing else but a two-reel rural comedy, and had he kept to that length it would have passed muster as a good filler for any program. In making it a five-reeler, however, he has shown up its shortcomings, for it carries all the earmarks of exaggerated hokum as it is exposed in rural comedies.

"'Double Dealing' takes Hoot Gibson out of the saddle and off the ranch and places him as a village boob in celluloid collar, ready-made tie, store clothes, et al. — a boob unable to make his drug store pay and who is hounded by the familiar skinflint with his equally familiar mortgage. Gibson is supported by Eddie Gribbon who is best in this type of story. It gives him a chance to exaggerate to the limit in his role of a city slicker who tries to double-cross the boob druggist and the skinflint as well. The star doesn't have any opportunity to show his stuff. He merely plays the grinning boob, but at least he plays IT WELL.

"The idea has been employed since the first slapstick comedy and, being so familiar in its scenes and gags, it contains very few laughs. In fact Lehrman goes the limit in piling on the hokum, so much so, that it appears as if he didn't take it very seriously. The piece is a reminder of his work when he made two-reel comedies. Of course the players could not express themselves except in terms of exaggeration. And Otto Hoffman as the skinflint overplayed to the point of burlesque. He accepts defeat in the end when he sells some valuable property to the hero — property he could have sold at a high figure.

"The only laugh discernible is the scene which shows Hoot's horse being attached by the sheriff and the buggy sliding back into the stream. Otherwise it presents the overdone hokum of outwitting the loan shark." Reviewed by Laurence Reid, *Motion Picture News*, May 26, 1923, p.2539

"Henry Lehrman, erstwhile short reel comedy director, is doubly responsible for this very week Hoot Gibson feature inasmuch as he is both author and director and has done a fairly poor job in each instance. In the first place Lehrman's story is far from suitable for feature purposes. It contains no genuine comedy situations and is too far-fetched for serious treatment. In an apparent effort to cover up the shortcomings, Lehrman has combined drama with slap-stick and burlesque — quite a combination to say the least, and with results that fail to make for entertainment.

"In two reels it might have done nicely, but to take material with such meagre possibilities and try to make a five reel picture of it doesn't show good judgment in the first place. Secondly, the country boob idea has already been worked to death and with each repetition becomes more exaggerated. Gibson is far more at home on a ranch or in the regulation western atmosphere than he is in an ill-fitting suit and celluloid collar and if he is to retain a following, Universal will have to do better in the way of giving him appropriate vehicles.

"The star's admirers have come to expect certain things of him and after several of his recent releases which have supplied entertainments of a good order, they'll surely be disappointed with 'Double Dealing.' The picture is almost entirely without action except for one fight, the only time when the piece threatens to get interesting, but the interest is short-lived.

"Lehrman has only succeeded in dragging his story out to feature length through a lot of unnecessary footage and slap stick that gets laughs not because it is funny but because it is so ridiculous. Eddie Gribbon and Otto Hoffman help consume a lot of time through foolish antics that only impress from the viewpoint of the individual's overacting. Helen Ferguson and Gertrude Claire represent the serious, or dramatic vein, and Betty Francisco is used alternately for comedy and drama. The cast is fair on the whole.

"Story: Hero Ben Slowbell loses his store and is further inveigled by Jobson when he pays him a thousand dollars for property supposed to be worthless. Jobson tries to get back the deed when an out-of-town company offers him $10,000 for it. How Ben discovers the fraud and later sells the deed himself for $30,000 is arrived at after considerable detail that is never funny."

"Direction…Couldn't seem to decide whether to make it a slap-stick or burlesque and not a good job on either." *Film Daily*, May 27, 1923, p.13

"Ben Slowbell [Gibson] loses his little drug store and his horse and buggy, his only possessions in the world. He returns home and finally has to tell his grandmother of his failure. To the town comes Keene [Gribbon], a self styled business advisor and manager. The town's richest and stingiest man seeks Keene's assistance in unloading a tract of worthless land on Ben, who upon being advised of its great value by Keene borrows the necessary amount of cash from his grandmother and completes the purchase. Keene then disappears with Ben's girl and the lad again realizes that he has been cheated. While he is out stirring up trouble some strangers come to town and insist on giving Ben a large profit for his land. Ben also finds that another girl has been waiting for him too.

"Hoot Gibson once again plays the small town fool in a stereotyped sort of picture. However, it is the kind of material that makes a good appeal to the audience and it should not fail to satisfy his admirers. There are a few melodramatic touches, put on with rather a heavy hand in spots, but according to the formula used it is pretty certain that the young hero will finally win out with plenty of money and the true blue girl who sits by and sees him wasting his affections on a frivolous blonde.

"Hoot Gibson gives his usual cleancut, appealing performance and is ably assisted by Helen Ferguson and Betty Francisco playing the two female leads. Gertrude Claire is a lovable character as Grandma Slowbell. Eddie Gribbon gives a good portrayal of the big town sport and manager of the lad's affairs.

"The picture has a great deal of human interest and although the familiarity of the plot detracts from the suspense that might be registered, it is nevertheless a pleasing bit of entertainment and should make a good box office attraction." Reviewed by J.M.D., *Exhibitors Trade Review*, June 2, 1923, p.35

"In 'Double Dealing,' Hoot Gibson probably does less fighting than in his usual stories, but what he does is good and well worth watching. He has a rather peculiar role in this production — that of a small town 'dumbbell' who is 'taken' by a crook, but Hoot rights everything with his fists when he 'gets wise.'

"Excellent support is rendered the star by Helen Ferguson, Eddie Gribbon, Betty Francisco, Otto Hoffman, Frank Hayes and Gertrude Claire.

"If your fans like Hoot Gibson this one should please them. There is a slashing fight in one of the scenes that will delight the hearts of any audience that likes its pathos flavored with thrills.

"Ben Slowbell is swiftly going broke when a tough individual arrives in town, undertakes to be his 'manager' and show him the road to success. First the advisor appropriates the affection of Ben's sweetheart and then he proceeds to fleece him out of a thousand dollars, which he has talked Ben into obtaining from his grandmother. He induces him to invest the money in waterfall land and then splits with the seller. But a couple of capitalists come to town and offer the original seller $10,000 for the land. Meanwhile Hoot has been 'put wise' and is out after his 'manager' hammer and tongs. Hoot cleans up in more ways than one in the grand finish." *Exhibitors Herald*, June 2, 1923, p.48

"It is impossible to extend any praises for this rural opus which treats of a village storekeeper whose mortgage is foreclosed. Such ideas have long since been appropriated by the Sennetts of the comedy lots. Nevertheless, it makes a faint bid for recognition in a story of country yokels — with Hoot Gibson unable to appear in character. They have dressed him up in store-clothes, ready-made tie (*a la* Keaton) and celluloid collar. And this familiar 'hick' is hounded by an equally familiar skinflint — and the — well, equally familiar city slicker. The idea is slapstick, put over by Henry Lehrman of slapstick fame. Thus five reels are too much to swallow. Every detail is exaggerated. Oh yes, the romance. Hoot goes buggy-riding." *Motion Picture Magazine*, November 1923, p.119

EXHIBITOR REVIEWS: "Good picture and Hoot is a real star. You can't go wrong on Hoot pictures. Book it and do not worry." S.H. Elias, Palm theatre, Mund City, Ill. *Exhibitors Herald*, December 29, 1923, p.169

"The first two reels seemed to lag along, but after Hoot woke up to his surroundings he sure did register a wallop that made the house roar. Everybody pleased." Clyde Allen, Casino theatre, Antwerp, N.Y. *Exhibitors Herald*, February 2, 1924, p.63

"This one is awful." Gustine & Roush, Princess theatre, Lewiston, Ill. *Exhibitors Herald*, February 2, 1924, p.63

"Personally liked this one, but our patrons like Hoot Gibson where he belongs, in Western drama. We often wonder why these stars are not put in real Western drama instead of so many comedy-dramas. That makes them just ordinary Western stunt pictures. Let's have some real heavy Western drama." C.A. Whitney, Star theatre, Ottawa, Kans. *Exhibitors Herald*, March 8, 1924, p.76

"Personally I liked it. It demonstrates that Hoot can act other parts than woolly Westerns. Had much good clean comedy. A top-notch fight scene and was clean with a good story." Meece & Hale, New Opera house, Dexter, Kans. *Exhibitors Herald*, March 8, 1924, p.76

Fighting Blood (second series): Robertson-Cole Pictures Corporation; released through Film Booking Offices of America. © various dates 08/04/1923 through 12/23/1923 — 2 reels each. 12 chapter serial. DIRECTORS: Henry Lehrman and Al Santell. ASSISTANT DIRECTOR: Thomas D. Moreno. SCREENPLAY, ADAPTATION: Beatrice Van, from the stories by H.C. Witwer. EDITOR: Harold Young. CINEMATOGRAPHY: Lee Garmes and St. Elmo Boyce. CAST: George O'Hara, Clare Horton, Arthur Rankin, M.C. Ryan, Kit Guard, William Courtwright, Albert Cooke, Ena Gregory, Mabel Van Buren, June Marlowe, Louise Lorraine, Larry McGrath, Joe Rivers, Petey the dog, Mary Beth Milford, Bob Perry

CHAPTERS:

So This is Hollywood (© 08/20/1923; Released 08/05/1923; DIRECTOR: Henry Lehrman)
She Supes to Conquer (© 08/05/1923; Released 08/19/23; DIRECTOR: Henry Lehrman)
Long Live the Ring (© 08/04/1923; Released 09/02/23; DIRECTOR: Henry Lehrman)
The Three Orphans (© 09/24/1923; Released 09/06/1923; DIRECTOR: Henry Lehrman)
The Taming of the Shrewd (© 09/30/1923; Released 09/30/1923)
Wages of Cinema (© 10/14/1923; Released 10/14/1923)
A Comedy of Terrors (© 10/28/1923; Released 10/28/1923; DIRECTOR: Henry Lehrman)
The Merchant of Menace (© 11/10/1923; Released 11/11/1923)
A Midsummer Night's Scream (© 11/24/1923; Released 11/25/1923)
Babes in the Hollywood (© 12/09/1923; Released 12/09/1923; DIRECTOR: Al Santell)
Beauty and the Feast (© 12/17/1923; Released 12/23/1923)
The Switching Hour (© 12/22/1923; Released 01/06/1924; DIRECTOR: Al Santell)

REVIEW OF THE FIRST SERIES:

"A brand new series that looks like ready money and lots of it in the box office. H.C. Witwer, the noted slang writer whose contributions to Collier's Weekly and other publications have made his name a household word is the author, and the first of the series of two reelers based upon the Witwer stories were given a preview last week. In many instances the productions savor somewhat of the famous and very popular series called 'The Leather Pushers' released by Universal. There is a considerable difference between these productions, however. This series shows a large variety of young folks and the types especially are very well selected. Production values are unusual for two reelers and while the fighting and boxing episodes appear in each of the two reelers there is not as much of the actual fighting or the exhibition of the naked body as in the earlier sequences of 'The Leather Pushers.' There is a lot of comedy introduced and if the remainder of the series live up to what developed in the first three stories they are going to prove a mighty good bet.

"Clara Horton plays opposite the star and Mal St. Clair directed. Some exceptionally good camera work appears for which Lee Garmes is given the credit. Nearly all of the stories dwell upon instances in the development of the career of 'Six Cylinder Smith' a nom-de-plume taken by a former dispenser of soda water. The love interest is very well carried out and as a whole the series should prove one of the best bets of the season for short stuff." *Film Daily*, January 21, 1923, p.16

SYNOPSES/REVIEWS OF SECOND SERIES:

Episode 1, **So This Is Hollywood**: "Probably a fight series for R-C by the author who wrote the 'Leatherpushers' in script, later transplanted to the screen.

"The send off for this serial is decidedly weak considering the importance of 'planting' such an undertaking. It shortly develops into nothing more than an ordinary chase comedy and nothing of the fight game in the episode other than to reveal a picture of 'Six Second Smith' (George O'Hara) adorning the cover of a sport magazine. Albert Cooke is cast as the fight manager and Mary Milford plays the girl of the story.

"O'Hara presents a nice appearance although it remains to be seen how he has handled the actual ring stuff. Beyond revealing his arrival in California by means of a freight train this particular episode gives little opportunity for O'Hara to step out other than a couple of prop battles inserted in the chase things.

"The series will need a fluent spice to pick up interest on the next edition for it's away to a poor start and even the usual punch of the Witwer subtitles is missing." Reviewed by Skig., *Variety*, October 11, 1923, p.27

"Gale and his two friends finally reach Hollywood via 'Side-door Pullman.' Stiff and cramped they alight from the train and are amazed at the reception accorded them by a group of friendly people who meet the train, until they learn that this friendly greeting was being filmed in connection with a 'boom California' film. They board a bus which is about to leave the station, but instead of being a public bus as they suppose, it proves to be one belonging to the movie company and takes them with the actors right to a studio. Here they are herded in to the paymaster with the other actors and in spite of their protests are paid for a day's work. But a few minutes later the error is discovered and they are pursued to recover the money. Meanwhile Gale has started to fight an actor whom he suspects of stealing his money, and when other actors join in, a regular battle occurs. The result is that our heroes soon find themselves at work with a road gang under guard. But Gale's fighting ability has been observed and he is offered a movie contract which promises to get them all out of their difficulty and points to a rosy future in California." *Descriptive Catalog of Kodascope Library*, New York, 1926, pp.154-155

Episode 2, **She Supes to Conquer**: "The short subject is billed over the five-reeler which makes up the double bill, a William Steiner production called 'Below the Rio Grande,' and it should be. It has snap and action and, above all, a wealth of low comedy. That would recommend any picture, and this one looks like a clean-up. Any picture that can make a film audience laugh right out loud so you can hear 'em on the sidewalk is in a way to returns.

"At the start they work up a serious situation built around the Roman Christian martyrs, and as quick as it catches hold of attention the camera switches to show the film director working the situation. From that on it is screamingly funny Roman travesty, pure hoke, but tremendously funny. The hero is instructed in the next scene to step into the arena as a lion crouches to spring upon the pale, blonde heroine, and choke the lion to death. It is urged by a nancified lion tamer that it is perfectly safe. They release the lions and for 400 feet or so it becomes a lion chase equal to the classics in some of the earlier Sunshine subjects put out by Fox.

"That passage finished, the story goes on to tell that the leading woman of the picture, and an heiress who aspires to screen stardom, are both seeking the hero's favor. O'Hara is cast as an ex-champion of the prize ring. He invites both girls to a fight, and when one of the contenders in the star bout fails to put in an appearance, an open challenge is made on behalf of the fighter in the ring, one 'Lightning' Kelly. O'Hara wants to get some 'fighting blood' out of his system, so he accepts the challenge. Then they stage a lively two-round fight that has plenty of goodlooking action. The rest is dull, merely the formal courtship of the scrapping actor and the heiress.

"Another funny passage had O'Hara on the street in a hurricane storm on his way to call on the heiress and not a taxi in sight. An old woman leading two poodles by strings against wind that made them stand straight up behind her like a child's balloon was also a strong laugh." *Variety*, October 18, 1923, p.23

"At Hollywood, Gale and his two companions, Nate and Kayo have secured work as actors in the movies. The scenario calls for scenes in a Roman amphitheatre, where Gale has to save Rosemary Du Barry after a fight with lions. But the lion trainer loses control and the lions menace the crowd. Many amusing results before they are recaptured. Gale rescues Patricia Paddington, a wealthy girl who (without her family's knowledge) is a super at the studio. Later, he calls at her home and she accompanies him to the prize fights. One fighter fails to appear and his opponent offers to fight any one present. Gale accepts the challenge and after a few rapid and strenuous rounds knocks him out and wins the fight." *Descriptive Catalog of Kodascope Library*, New York, 1926, p.155

Episode 3, **Long Live the Ring**: "In round three of the second series of 'Fighting Blood,' Gale Galen and his manager and trainer enter the movies at Hollywood. At the request of the leading lady, Gale stages a fight for the newsboys.

"This picture is good entertainment. Besides the usual thrilling fight, there is humor and the added interest that the scenes of the sets always afford." *Exhibitors Trade Review*, October 6, 1923, p.872

Episode 4, **The Three Orphans**: "Round four of the 'Fighting Blood' series is a comedy dramatic offering of good entertainment value. It has a human touch that will warrant exhibitor doing a little extra exploitation, for it is deserving of more than usual attention and treatment as an attraction. Ex-Champion Gale Galem [sic], his trainer and manager advertise for a mother. This brings a deluge of applicants, but only one seems to strike the fancy of the pugilistic trio. However, the pug wins another battle, and once again the movie folks are forced to mark time." Reviewed by Roger Ferri, *Motion Picture News*, October 20, 1923, p.1904

Episode 5, **The Taming of the Shrewd**: "Patricia phones Gale and asks him to go with her to see Rosemary who is acting in a scene on the beach. Just as they arrive a man dressed like Rosemary doubles for her and jumps into the water. Unaware that it is part of the picture and believing that Rosemary has fallen in, Gale dives to the rescue while the others have a laugh at his mistake. That evening Patricia goes to see Gale fight Battling Shrewd. Shrewd is heavier than Gale and expects to have an easy time, but after several strenuous rounds in which both fighters are badly battered, Gale lands the decisive blow and is proclaimed the victor. Patricia waits for him outside and as they start for home Gale is jostled by a young 'fellow' who then takes to his heels with Gale in pursuit. The fugitive proves to be Rosemary who in order to escape attention had attended the fight dressed like a boy. From where she has been left, Patricia sees Gale lock arms with his prisoner and walk off with 'him' in the friendliest manner possible." *Descriptive Catalog of Kodascope Library*, New York, 1926, p.155

"This is round five of the second 'Fighting Blood' series and it is one of the most interesting of the merry group. The ex-champion in this one gets mixed up with the movies while preparing for a fight, which is going to make him a step nearer regaining the fistic crown. Pretty girls run in and out of the picture, a very clever dog actor helps considerably with the action, and the fight scenes are very convincing and realistic. This is the sort of short that has a general appeal and will fill in well on most any kind of a program. It's a good bet to book this one." *Exhibitors Trade Review*, November 3, 1923, p.1054

Episode 6, **Wages of Cinema**: "Gale continues to meet and defeat various opponents in order to demonstrate his right to fight Red Mack, the champion. Red, who is a very conceited chap, refuses to fight Glae whom he does not consider a worthy opponent. But Gale accepts another movie contract, and by a clever ruse the director assisted by Patricia and Rosemary, persuades Red Mack to accept a similar contract and be the 'hero who fights and conquers the villain.' Gale of course is the villain. When the fight occurs, Red finds he has a real battle on his programme and in spite of his best efforts he loses the fight. He angrily promises to get even with Gale and all the others, but his chagrin and rage are unavailing since the camera has faithfully recorded the entire encounter." *Descriptive Catalog of Kodascope Library*, New York, 1926, p.156

"Gale Galem [sic], pugilistically known as 'Six-Second' Smith, almost turns motion picture actor as a means of forcing 'Red' Mack, the champ, into a fight. Fact of the matter was that 'Red' ignored Smith's challenge and an enterprising director conceives the scheme that puts an end to the champ's egotism and incidentally loses the championship for him. This sixth round of F.B.O.'s second 'Fighting Blood' series can be placed in the comedy class, for the business 'on location' and the pranks of the champion border on the burlesque that reaches its climax when the fight is staged. It is a hefty fight with both boys mixing it in one-two fashion. This is a good entertaining release that will please. George O'Hara, as the ambitious challenger, is clever. Mary Beth Milford as Rosemary, the 'girl in the case,' does well as does Kit Guard, Al Cooke and Louise Lorraine." Reviewed by Roger Ferri, *Motion Picture News*, November 3, 1923, p.2139

Episode 8, **The Merchant of Menace**: "Not so gruesome as the title might indicate. However, it's a good title to catch the eye and it's a smooth running, thrilling story.

"Patricia Paddington (Louise Lorraine) comes to the aid of her young friend Galen when Red Mack refuses to fight (because no purse is offered), by staging a pirate tea aboard her father's yacht.

"There's fast and furious fun, one feature of which is 'walking the plank.' The surprise is sprung that an exhibition bout is planned. This time Red Mack can't back out for he has a reputation to uphold and wishes to impress a beautiful blond aboard. The blond is really a movie director, a friend of Galen's in disguise. A good bout is shown on a float but Mack's manager sees his white hope is bound to lose so the police is sent for, and that finishes that.

"These 'Fighting Blood' series are taken from H.C. Witwer's short stories, which has been running in Cosmopolitan. You'll like them, as will each member of your audience." *Exhibitors Trade Review*, December 15, 1923, p.27

Episode 10, **Babes in the Hollywood**: "Gale is approached by a movie director who offers him an attractive contract which Gale accepts. The picture is a melodramatic burlesque and the cast includes Rosemary Du Barry and Patricia Paddington, both of whom are in love with Gale, a fact which at times threatens complications for the movie director.

"As the picture nears completion, Gale starts training for his fight with 'Battling Hawkins.' His hard training stands him in good stead and after several strenuous rounds he lands the winning blow and is proclaimed the victor." *Descriptive Catalog of Kodascope Library*, New York, 1926, p.156

Episode 12, **The Switching Hour**: "Patricia's father meets with financial reverses and tells her that he is ruined and can get no further credit. When Gale hears of it, he promptly sends him a check which saves him. Gale has a hard fight ahead, as he is booked to meet Battling Silva the champion. Just before the battle, he receives a note from Patricia saying that she expects him to win and is planning to marry the world's champion. Thus encouraged, Gale nearly wins in the opening round — then nearly loses. The end of the round finds both fighters almost exhausted. Then Patricia whispers to Gale that her father has bet everything on him. In the next round Gale wins the championship." *Descriptive Catalog of Kodascope Library*, New York, 1926, p.156

EXHIBITOR REVIEWS: "The second series is even better than the first series. These are good short subjects and worthy of a place on anyone's bill." C. Malphurs, Dreamland theatre, High Springs, Fla. *Exhibitors Herald*, March 8, 1924, p.84

"Just finished 'Fighting Blood,' second series, and broke all house records. The most wonderful finish we ever saw for a series or a serial, and the splendid announcement of the director thanking the public for following the series." G. Strasser Sons, Emblem theatre, Buffalo, N.Y. *Exhibitors Herald*, March 8, 1924, p.84

"We have played twelve and not a bad one in the lot. Everyone likes them, all classes alike." D. Filizola, Empress theatre, Fort Scott, Kans. *Exhibitors Herald*, March 15, 1924, p.87

"We have completed the first series and have started on the second. To say that these are good would be putting it mildly. The ending of the first series was a little disappointing but it only served to create more interest in the second series. They are the best two reelers yet." C.L. Reed, Illinois theatre, Newman, Ill. *Exhibitors Herald*, March 15, 1924, p.87

On Time: Carlos Productions; Truart Film Corp. *Released 03/01/1924.* © 03/24/1924 — 6 reels/6,030 feet. DIRECTOR: Henry Lehrman. PRODUCER: Richard Talmadge. SCREENPLAY: Garrett Fort. STORY: Al Cohn. CINEMATOGRAPHY: William Marshall. EDITOR, TITLES: Ralph Spence. CAST: Richard Talmadge, Billie Dove, Stuart Holmes, George Siegmann, Tom Wilson, Charles Clary, Douglas Gerrard, Fred Kirby, Frankie Mann

SYNOPSIS/REVIEWS: "Harry Willis, a spendthrift, has lost a fortune, promises his sweetheart, Helen Hendon, that he will amass another fortune within six months. At the end of the time limit he has failed. At a Hallowe'en party he saves some valuable antiques from being stolen from Helen Hendon. The next day he is approached by a stranger who offers him $10,000 if he will obey instructions for a day. He agrees and action follows. He attempts to rescue a woman in distress, and falls into the hands of an insane doctor who tries to operate on him. Later he is mixed up in a series of exciting incidents in a Chinese temple. He has many fights, but escapes. He later discovers that motion pictures had been taken of all his escapades and is offered a contract. He accepts and wins Helen.

"For those who like thrills and stunts at the sacrifice of plot, 'On Time' will offer great appeal. From start to finish it is a series of stunts and knock-down-drag-out fights in which Richard Talmadge occupies the center of the limelight.

"He does many stunts of daring that are almost lost owing to the weakness of the plot. He has no less than a dozen fights with odds at least ten to one against him and always manages to come out victorious with little or no wear and tear on his personal appearance.

"The picture is much too overdrawn to carry conviction, but it will please that large class of theatre patrons who crave excitement of the serial variety. The same action devoted to a story with more plot would have resulted in an interesting picture.

"It is not the fault of the cast that the picture is not all that it should be. Richard Talmadge works hard and does everything that is required of him. He is strongly supported by Billie Dove and Tom Wilson.

"Tom Wilson, as a colored valet, furnishes the comedy for the picture. He appears in most of the scenes with Talmadge and his antics are really funny.

"The most exciting scenes of the play take place in the doctor's operating room where the insane doctor is about to transplant a human brain to an ape; and the Chinese temple, where Talmadge shows his gymnastic ability.

"In exploiting the picture it should be easy to make large clock dials, with the hands pointing to the hour of showing the picture. Small cards may also bear a clock dial with the words 'Be "On Time" to see Richard Talmadge in his new thriller,' or other similar phrases." Reviewed by Len Morgan, "Action Smothers Picture," *Exhibitors Trade Review*, March 15, 1924, p. 24

"Director Henry Lehrman is responsible for some of the most thrilling and the most humorous action ever combined in a single photoplay. The startling adventures of Harry Willis on his road to success, and the parallel comedy adventures of his valet, Casanova Clay, is 'ON TIME!' which comes to the Orpheum Theatre for a one day stay, are respectively responsible for the thrills and laughs. Richard Talmadge is starred in this photoplay. It was made by Carlos Productions and released by Truart Films." Press notice reprint in (Chatham, New York) *Currier*, August 1924

Children Wanted: Sunshine Comedies; Fox Film Corporation. *Released 06/22/1924.* © 06/22/1924 — 2 reels. DIRECTOR: Henry Lehrman

Sweet Papa: Imperial Comedies; Fox Film Corporation. *Released 08/17/1924.* © 08/18/1924 — 2 reels. DIRECTOR: Henry Lehrman. CAST: Paul Parrott, Sid Smith

The Diving Fool: Sunshine Comedies; Fox Film Corporation. *Released 09/21/1924.* © 09/05/1924 — 2 reels. DIRECTOR: Henry Lehrman *(copyright records credit Charles Lamont)*

Heavy Swells: Imperial Comedies; Fox Film Corporation. *Released 12/13/1925.* © 12/06/1925 — 2 reels. DIRECTOR: Henry Lehrman. STORY: Andrew Bennison

The Fighting Edge: Warner Brothers. *Released 01/08/1926.* © 01/07/1926 — 7 reels/ 6,369 feet. DIRECTOR: Henry Lehrman; ASSISTANT DIRECTOR: Sandy Roth. SCREENPLAY: Edward T. Lowe, Jr. and Jack Wagner; based on the 1922 novel by William MacLeod Raine. CINEMATOGRAPHY: Allan Thompson; additional CINEMATOGRAPHY: Robert Laprell. EDITOR: Clarence Kolster. CAST: Kenneth Harlan, Patsy Ruth Miller, David Kirby, Charles "Heinie" Conklin, Pat Hartigan, Lew Harvey, Eugene Pallette, Pat Harmon, W.A. Carroll

SYNOPSIS/REVIEWS: "Henry Lehrman has been eminently successful in packing action into this story of romance and smuggling along the Mexican border. The picture opens with a very exciting chase after some smugglers and the wreck of their car as it plunges down a mountainside. Then we are introduced to the heroine, who in order to get into the smugglers' mysterious ranch house, purposely dashes her car down a cliff and then feigns unconsciousness. Once we are in the ranch house, there is tense suspense as both hero and heroine seek to locate a missing federal agent. Things happen in swift succession, ending in a battle royal and the escape of the two 'with their man.' However the smugglers still have fight in them and they pursue the trio to a deserted house where the climax comes with more 'free for all,' mixups. Kenneth Harlan has a colorful role as Juan O'Rourke, Spanish-Irish secret service man. Patsy Ruth Miller, who is co-starred, is also good.

"Joyce [Carroll], a government agent, is imprisoned by a gang of smugglers in their ranch house. O'Rourke [Harlan], another U.S. agent posing as half Spanish and living in the enemy's country, is commissioned to rescue Joyce. He meets Phoebe [Miller], Joyce's daughter, who feigns unconsciousness following an accident and is carried into house by smugglers. Eventually two, with aid of cook, get Joyce away to deserted house. Smugglers follow. U.S. troops arrive and save all. Phoebe marries Juan." Reviewed by Frank Elliott, *Motion Picture News*, February 20, 1926, p.912.

"Smuggling aliens across the Mexican border is an exciting subject to begin with and when the story starts off with races, auto spills and disguises and continues such thrills to the end, with plenty of good comedy added, interest never lags. And too there is a happy romance between a brave and charming maiden and a bold young government agent.

"For the family audience, including young people." *National Board of Review Magazine*, March-April 1926, p.19

Private Izzy Murphy: Warner Brothers. *Released 10/30/1926.* © 10/02/1926 — 8 reels/7,889 feet. DIRECTOR: Lloyd Bacon (and Henry Lehrman, uncredited). SCREENPLAY: Edward Clark, Raymond L. Schrock; ADAPTATION: Philip Lonergan. ASSOCIATE PRODUCER: Raymond Schrock. CINEMATOGRAPHY: Virgil Miller. CAST: George Jessel, Patsy Ruth Miller, Vera Gordon, Nat Carr, William H. Strauss, Spec O'Donnell, Gustav von Seyffertitz, Douglas Gerrard, Tom Murray
SYNOPSIS: "Isadore Goldberg [Jessel] changes his name to I. Patrick Murphy because his store is in the heart of an Irish neighborhood. He meets Eileen Cohannigan [Miller], the daughter of a meat packer, and romance begins. He tells her he is Irish. Then comes the war, and Izzy enlists, goes to France and is wounded while engaged in a heroic rescue. He is given up for dead and while in a hospital he writes Eileen and tells her he is not Irish but Jewish. While parading with his regiment in New York he sees Eileen with O'Malley [Gerrard], an old rival. Izzy believes that she has thrown him over because he is Jewish. An Irish lodge comes to bestow honor on Izzy, their supposed Irish hero, but O'Malley tells everyone that Izzy is not Irish and that he is really Izzy Goldberg. But Eileen isn't mad. Despite family objections, the two seek the marriage license bureau." *Reel Journal*, November 6, 1926, p.13

For Ladies Only: Columbia Pictures. *Released 07/20/1927.* © 08/22/1927 — 6 reels/ 5,507 feet. DIRECTORS: Henry Lehrman and Percy Pembroke. PRODUCER: Harry Cohn. SCREENPLAY: Robert Lord; based on George F. Worts' story *Down with Women*. ADAPTATION: Ernest S. Pagano and/or Albert Payson Terhune *(sources vary)*. CINEMATOGRAPHY: J.O. Taylor. CAST: John Bowers, Jacqueline Logan, Edna Marion, Ben Hall, William H. Strauss, Templar Saxe, Kathleen Chambers, Henry Roquemore
SYNOPSIS: "The story hinges on a clash of wills between the hero, Clifford Coleman [Bowers], and his secretary, Ruth Barton [Logan]. Fun is introduced in the persons of Gerty Long [Marion], the switchboard operator, and the office boy, Joe Doakes.

"Coleman, the office manager of the Amalgamated Hallock Company, is a woman-hater. When he is installed in the new office he almost promptly fires the girls; then his secretary plans her revenge, and — she gets it. He falls in love with her." Press notice reprint in *Oelwein Daily Register*, September 28, 1927, p.5

REVIEWS: "Wholly enjoyable comedy romance. Good story nicely handled and replete with entertainment qualities.

"Cast…Jacqueline Logan gets a happy 'break' in this one. Does very well in a good role. Edna Marion a cute little blonde. Ed Hall first rate as the office boy with a trick 'Adam's apple'. John Bowers the handsome 'boss'.

"Story and Production…Comedy romance; from the story 'Down With Women.' They came out to jeer but they remained to cheer…referring to the men in the audience when they read in the introductory title the name of the story from which the picture was adapted. It took the women to make it a picture and the method seemed to thoroughly delight the audience. Henry Lehrman and Scott Pembroke are jointly credited with the direction but if it did take two of them they certainly did a good job. How a certain firm failed to get along after the new boss fired all the women employees and how it took the girls to put the business back on its feet, makes an amusing and entertaining little picture.

"Direction…Henry Lehrman-Scott Pembroke: very good." *Film Daily*, October 16, 1927, p.6

Sailor Izzy Murphy: Warner Brothers. *Released 10/08/1927.* © 09/28/1927 — 7 reels/6,020 feet. DIRECTOR: Henry Lehrman. ASSISTANT DIRECTOR: Frank Shaw. SCREENPLAY, STORY: E.T. Lowe, Jr. CINEMATOGRAPHY: Frank Kesson. CAST: George Jessel, Audrey Ferris, Warner Oland, John Miljan, Otto Lederer, Theodore Lorch, Clara Horton

SYNOPSIS: "Izzy [Jessel], dapper and determined, goes to sell his 'Dream of Love' perfume to Marie's [Ferris] father, M. Jules [Oland], who is a perfumery maker of note. M. Jules, seeing that his daughter's fair face decorates the 'Dream of Love' bottles, wastes no time in ejecting Izzy, by the proverbial swift kick properly placed.

"Jake [Lederer] advices immediate suit for damages. Izzy rushes to the pier, from which he hears that M. Jules and daughter are to sail, to serve the papers. He hurtles from the gang plank just as the yacht puts out to sea and is horrified to find himself surrounded by a crew of crazy men. Not unpleasant crazy men, mind you, but ludicrous, ingratiating loons, who, for a time, make life one heck of a hodge-podge for Izzy and the Juleses. Izzy is appointed Lord High Admiral; Izzy is delegated to do the Lord High Executioner act to his future father-in-law; Izzy is put to stoking in the hold. But through a whirlwind of uproaring situations, Izzy emerges with the girl, the good will of her papa, and a contract for the manufacture of the 'Dream of Love' perfume." Press notice reprint in (Uniontown, Pennsylvania) *Morning Herald*, June 13, 1928, p.14

REVIEWS: "Deep melodrama is served in the guise of comedy in this latest vehicle for George Jessel. Perhaps originally it was intended to be a comedy, as the press sheets so advise, but it goes completely melodramatic as the story progresses. Jessel tries hard to inject some comedy, but surrounded as he is by a crew of lunatics armed with guns and threatening each moment to blow up the pleasure yacht on which the cruise is made, his task is a difficult one.

"Had the tale been handled with a farcical touch it would undoubtedly have hit nearer the mark, but there is hardly the semblance even, of any comedy relief. Jessel assumes a humorous attitude here and there, but in the seriousness of the surrounding circumstances one finds it rather difficult to laugh it off.

"Here is a yacht load of escaped maniacs who have escaped solely for the purpose of doing away with a wealthy perfume manufacturer, who has presumably done their leader wrong. Izzy is unwittingly made a member of the crew after having fallen in love with the wealthy one's daughter. Daughter spends most of her time weeping because of her father's plight. Father is in the deepest despair and even Izzy is uncomfortable in his predicament. It comes to its hilarious climax when Izzy and the girl are locked in the boiler room with the leader of the maniacs and made to shovel coal and more coal as the steam gauge mounts and indicates that soon the yacht and everyone on it are to be blown to atoms." Reviewed by Chester J. Smith, *Motion Picture News*, October 28, 1927, p.1345

"Jessel fails to build comedy atmosphere in story that runs wild with melodramatic trimmings and foolish plot.

"Cast:...Jessel looks like the goat in an impossible story that handicaps him and kills off all his comedy. Warner Oland a sterling player swamped in an unconvincing role. Audrey Ferris does some mechanical posing. John Miljan does his lunatic specialty convincingly. Others Otto Lederer, Clara Horton and Theodore Lorch.

"Story and Production...The press book describes it as 'a battle of wits and half-wits.' And the half-wits win all the way. It is one of the most witless productions of the season's offerings. Jessel finds himself a sailor aboard the yacht of a millionaire whose daughter he loves. John Miljan is the captain, who has shipped a crew of lunatics like himself, to revenge himself of the millionaire and his daughter. From then on the doings are wild and woolly, with Jessel trying to outwit the crazy captain in his plan of destroying the yacht and all aboard. Miljan steals the picture, for the dizzy melo gives Jessel no chance to top it with his comedy antics.

"Direction...Henry Lehrman: handicapped." *Film Daily*, October 30, 1927, p.13

"It is to laugh. There is no other purpose behind this picture and you will laugh. There are moments when Georgie Jessel suggests that in time he will be another Chaplin in the mixing of comedy and pathos. The picture is a sequel to 'Private Izzy Murphy.' There is a suspense sequence that will thrill you, when the hero and heroine are in the power of the escaped lunatic in the yacht boiler room. Audrey Ferris is the girl and very likable. A great performance is contributed by John Miljan as the crazed man. Henry Lehrman directed fairly well." *Photoplay*, November 1927, p.137

EXHIBITOR REVIEW: "What a piece of cheese this turned out to be — no sense to it. Patrons wanted their money back. Leave it alone." H. Goldstein, *Strand*, Sioux City, Iowa.

Husbands for Rent: Warner Brothers. *Released 12/31/1927.* © 12/24/1927 — 6 reels/ 5,200 feet. DIRECTOR: Henry Lehrman. ASSISTANT DIRECTOR: Frank Shaw. SCREENPLAY: Edwin Justus Mayer. ADAPTATION: C. Graham Baker; based on the play *In Name Only*. TITLES: Joseph Jackson and James A. Starr. CINEMATOGRAPHY: Barney McGill and Ed Dupar. EDITOR: Clarence Kolster. CAST: Owen Moore, Helene Costello, Kathryn Perry, John Miljan, Claude Gillingwater, Arthur Hoyt, Helen Lynch, Hugh Herbert

SYNOPSIS: "'Husbands for Rent' is a maze of misunderstanding which results from a rich old uncle's determination that his nephew shall marry his ward. Each finds another attraction and each becomes arbitrarily engaged. On the eve of the disarranged wedding the new-found lovers elope with each other leaving nephew and ward in the lurch. Uncle advises that they marry to avoid society's funmaking. This they do, believing that each wants to marry 'in name only.'

"Then from the blue the errant lovers return, each wanting to reestablish the old ties. Here the chuckles change to roars of delight as the plot rises to its uproarious climax." Studio press release as reprinted in *Huntingdon Daily News*, December 22, 1928, p.9

REVIEWS: "'Husbands for Rent' is the typical Al Woods bedroom farce, embarrassing situations, risky business and what not. No Sunday school picture, this." Reviewed by Lilian W. Brennan, "A Review of Reviews," *Film Daily*," January 3, 1928, p.5

"There is little that can be recommended in this Warner Bros. feature which has Owen Moore and Helene Costello in the leading roles. Its alleged comedy is of the crudest, its plot is slim and moves along at a snail's pace and there is none of the necessary element of suspense. It has one daring touch that goes a little bit beyond the border of the risqué, but otherwise it is without incident.

"While there is little chance for any of the players to do any noteworthy work, they all seem poorly cast. Owen Moore is a somewhat slow moving and slow thinking lover and husband, whose sheer timidity makes him a married man in name only, despite instructions given him by the butler, a sequence that might well have been left out, and thus made of the picture an entire blank.

"Helene Costello, it would seem, would fit better into the role of Moore's wife, instead of the flighty, indiscreet cigarette-smoking vamp type which she depicts. As a matter of fact both Kathryn Perry and John Miljan, the other married couple, give much more capable performances than Miss Costello and Moore.

"The story is slim enough to be told in a single reel and seems interminable when stretched out to five or six. It involves a quartet, none of which seems to know with whom he or she is really in love. Their affections are switched before marriage and they apparently would all be better satisfied if they were switched again after marriage. It does develop, however, that Moore, as Herbert Willis, and Miss Perry as Doris Knight, really did love each other all the time and eventually were glad that Hugh Frazer eloped with Molly Devoe on the night set for the wedding of Molly and Herbert." Reviewed by Chester J. Smith, *Motion Picture News*, January 7, 1928, p.75

"Bedroom farce with a flare for suggestiveness. Impossible to recommend this to admirers of good wholesome comedy.

"Cast…Owen Moore and Kathryn Perry the principals in this marital tangle with John Miljan and Helene Costello the runners up. Claude Gillingwater a 'Mr. Fix-It.' Others Arthur Hoyt, Helen Lynch, Hugh Herbert.

"Story and Production…Farce comedy. The story offers a negligible pick-up of situations that fail to arrive at anything very close to entertainment, at least for those who prefer good clean comedy. The business of the honeymoon and the attempts of the valet to suggest the marital duties to his embarrassed employer immediately taboo the picture for juvenile trade or church going communities. Owen Moore, as the Englishman,, never quite overcomes his timidity until he submits to a 'collusion' frame-up as part of the divorce scheme and then discovers that the 'other woman' is his wife. They wind up by the telephone operator putting up a 'don't disturb' sign on the switchboard plug.

"Direction…Henry Lehrman: poor." *Film Daily*, January 8, 1928, p.6

"Spicy title deceptive, inasmuch as the story does not live up to expectations. Film okey as a filler in the split weeks and down. Helene Costello and Owen Moore, featured, do not figure as box-office attractions of any strength.

"Miss Costello as a blonde vamp fails to impress in one of the major roles. Kathryn Perry photographs becomingly and registers well except in instances when camera shots of her face are too close, creating an angular outline, which spoils appearance.

"John Miljan, Arthur Hoyt and Claude Gillingwater, the latter especially, score nicely in supporting roles. Miljan plays the menace, while the two other boys essay interesting comedy roles.

"Stories of this type, which are being put into production consistently, never carry. Use of material of this kind often raises conjecture regarding the mental balance of the supervisor, director or producer responsible for the choice. Without merit of any kind, timeworn, and lacking a single incident or combination of sequences productive of a laugh or even getting attention, this story could have been taken from any one of 50,000 magazine stories which have appeared in print in the past 20 years. There is no particular idea to the story and very little comedy.

"Concerns a somewhat aristocratic couple whose emotional affairs become complicated. The girl thinks she loves another man who claims to love her. The boy thinks he wants another woman who thinks she loves him. For no particular reason the other pair elope, and the engagement is on, again followed by a marriage. After the marriage the same condition arises, and a divorce is framed when the boy backs out, insisting he loves his wife." Reviewed by Mori., *Variety*, July 25, 1928, p.28

"Dull and draggy comedy of two married couples develops few smiles and grows monotonous through repetition.

"Owen Moore plays a bally monocoled society Englishman who acts and thinks slowly, and picture is slow in consequence, for he has the principal role. Helene Costello as his wife is decorative in a part that has little color. John Miljan and Kathryn Perry are the other couple in the marital mixup. Others Claude Gillingwater, Arthur Hoyt, Helene Lynch, Hugh Herbert.

"Comedy of a mixup between two newly married couples in english society. From the story by Edwin Justus Mayer. This probably was an entertaining story in printed form with clever dialog, but as screen fare it develops little action and the plot travels along one string and grows tedious and tiresome. Moore is engaged to a girl and in his absence she becomes infatuated with Miljan. The latter's fiancée meanwhile forms an attachment for Moore. The mixed couples finally get straightened out and marry, again start flirting, agree on a divorce but a surprise reconciliation is effected." *Film Daily*, September 30, 1928, P.8

Why Sailors Go Wrong: Fox Film Corp. *Released 03/25/1928.* © 03/16/1928 — 6 reels/ 5,112 feet. DIRECTOR: Henry Lehrman. PRESENTED BY William Fox. SCREENPLAY: Randall H. Faye; based on a story by William Conselman and Frank O'Connor. TITLES: Delos Sutherland. CINEMATOGRAPHY: Sidney Wagner. EDITOR: Ralph Dietrich. CAST: Sammy Cohen, Ted McNamara, Sally Phipps, Nick Stuart, Carl Miller, Jules Cowles, Noble Johnson, E.H. Calvert, Jack Pennick
SYNOPSIS: Betty Green (Phipps) is engaged to Jimmy Collier (Stuart), and the two of them, along with her father Cyrus (Calvert), are to take a pre-wedding voyage to the South

Seas on John Dunning's palatial yacht Sultana. Dunning (Miller), Betty and Cyrus take a taxi to the yacht, where we learn that Dunning is in love with Betty, and had hoped to marry her. Meanwhile, Jimmy's riding to the yacht in a horse-drawn hansom cab driven by Angus McAxle (McNamara). When Dunning spots the hansom with Jimmy inside he orders the taxi's driver, Sammy Beezeroff (Cohen), to speed up, leaving the hansom far behind. A race between the two vehicles results, cash changing hands as incentive to the two drivers. Dunning's group arrives first, and boards a small boat to take them out to the huge Sultana. Dunning tells the Greens that his skipper (Pennick) will bring Jimmy out later when he arrives, but palms a note to the skipper instructing him to keep Jimmy from boarding the yacht at all costs. The hansom arrives and Jimmy rushes over to the skipper who tells Jimmy that Betty said if he couldn't arrive on time, he needn't come at all. Jimmy doesn't buy it. A slugfest follows, but when Jimmy realizes he has met his match, he offers Sammy $200 to help him whip the skipper. Sammy enlists Angus' aide, and the two of them push the taxi and pin the skipper to some crates, intending to force him off the pier. The skipper steps out of the way, and only the taxi crashes off the pier.

The skipper hops in his boat and sails out to the yacht, where he tells Betty that Jimmy was insulted that she didn't wait for him, and refused to come. Jimmy, determined to be reunited with his fiancé, swims out to the yacht. He offers Sammy and Angus, who have followed in a row boat, another $50 if they wait for him; he may need to leave quickly. Jimmy boards the yacht and is confronted by the skipper and a burly sailor who thrash him and lock him in a cabin for the trip's duration. Water draining from the yacht swamps Sammy and Angus' row boat, and they are forced to board the yacht. On board, they are spotted by the skipper who finally catches them and forces them into servitude.

A raging late night storm compromises the yacht. Jimmy, now escaped from his cabin, is reunited with Betty and Cyrus, but when Dunning appears the two break into a fistfight. The skipper has Angus, Sammy, Betty, and Cyrus pile into a lifeboat, but without any supplies; they are set adrift. The next morning a passing battleship spots the stranded yacht, and Jimmy explains all to the naval captain who has the skipper and Dunning imprisoned. A search plane is sent out with Jimmy on board to help.

The lifeboat with its four passengers lands at Pogo Pogo Island, and the exhausted group sleeps. Betty is awakened when she mistakes the two cabbies' snoring for a roaring lion. The cabbies are awakened when a playful chimp dumps an opened cocoanut on Sammy's face, and soon after the chimp bombards them with cocoanuts from high above in a cocoanut tree. Fleeing this, the two have various and repeated encounters with a pair of lions, alligators, and the infestation of their clothes by tiny lizards. Stripped of their garments, the two are forced to attire themselves in leaves and such when natives steal their clothing. Jimmy, flying above in the search plane, has spotted the two cabbies below. The naval captain is alerted and rescue boats set sail for the island.

The natives take the two cabbies prisoner. The chief tells them (in English, I suppose) that they are to be beheaded — that is if they don't accept the offer to marry the chief's two husband-hungry daughters. The daughters, overweight and unattractive, quickly make up the minds of the cabbies: they'll both go with being decapitated! Just as they are about to lose their heads the naval captain and a bunch of seamen arrive, guns blazing, scaring the natives away. Angus and Sammy are rescued. Elsewhere, Jimmy and a trio of seamen locate and rescue Betty and her father. The two groups reconnect, and Jimmy tosses the cabbies a roll of $5,000 for their efforts. In their struggle over the wad of bills, it ends up in a nearby alligator's mouth. The closing gag: Having captured the alligator, they make one last try at feeding it castor oil! Synopsis based on a print of the film held by the author REVIEWS: "After witnessing the hectic array of scenes in 'Why Sailors Go Wrong,' the current film offering at the Roxy Theatre, one is no nearer a solution of this all-important question than one was before seeing the picture. During the rowdy moments of the comic contraption the characters travel approximately half way around the world, ending their exciting activities on an island somewhere in the South Seas. A good deal of the fractious fun occurs aboard a sailing yacht, thus giving the producers an opportunity to use the sea as a medium for laughter.

"The presence of landlubbers on shipboard in picture invariably inspires a sea-sick sequence. In this current offering, Mac, whose vocation is driving a ramshackle hansom cab, is attacked with mal de mer after he has succeeded in climbing to the top of the yacht's foremast. He and Sammy, a taxicab driver, are not on the yacht for pleasure or their health, but to obtain $1,000 promised to them by James Collier for putting him aboard. Unfortunately, James's rival, John Hastings, no sooner sets eyes on James than he causes the latter to be locked in a cabin.

"It's bad enough for a hansom cab driver to be out on an angry sea, but it is evidently much more terrifying for him to be awakened from a sound sleep (on the shores of 'Pogo Pogo') by a chimpanzee amusing itself by smacking the poor man's face. The experiences of Mac and Sam go from excitement to spine-chilling ordeals. Little things like being dropped dangerously near the gaping mouths of crocodiles are mild compared to the flight of these two men from a few angry lions. In one scene Mac and Sam fancy themselves at least temporarily safe, if not comfortable, for they have climbed a tree from which they are able to study the snarls and chop-licking of a lion. Imagine then their feelings when they discover that the convenient strip off stuff to which they are clinging is another lion's tail! This beast happens to be just above the two friends. Through agility and what might be interpreted as a quaint sense of humor, Mac and Sam are able to escape from the hungry animals. But they find that they have leaped out of the frying pan into the fire, for they are suddenly surrounded by a group of none too amiable savages, whose chief insists that Mac and Sam be beheaded immediately. The two white men make one last plea — that their heads by chopped off simultaneously on the same block. It's uncomfortable, for there happens to be only one groove on the block, but the savage chief consents. Just when the heads of Mac and Sam are about to fall, there is a fade-out and then a fade-in and our heroes are surrounded by officers and men from an American warship.

"While the pushing of a taxicab off a dock and other such ideas hardly seem worth the expense, there is always fun when wild animals are introduced into a comedy. The lions earn whatever meat they are paid.

"The late Ted McNamara figures as Mac and Sammy Cohen plays the part of his own name-sake. The incidental girl in the case is Sally Phipps, who is an attractive heroine." Reviewed by Mordaunt Hall, *New York Times*, April 9, 1928, p.18

"'Why Sailors Go Wrong' is its diverting title and, true to its label, it has to do with a pair of sea-going comedians who, once they have been shanghaied aboard a yacht bound for the South Seas, go about the mirth provoking business of developing mal de mer. Of course there are other inducements to laughter here once Sammy Cohen and Ted McNamara arrive at their tropical destination, but it is easy to see that the producers considered the seasickness episode the high point of this hilarious structure. The result can hardly be set down as inspired; more likely, it will cause you to shudder at its very vulgarity and to squirm uneasily in the face of as annoying a succession of low comedy effects as you will come across in your attendance of movie classes these next three years.

"It was in the course of filming the yachting scenes, it will be regretfully recalled, that young Mr. McNamara contracted the illness which resulted in his recent death. It is something approaching the irony of such things that this talented comedian should have died for a cause so utterly undeserving." Reviewed by Martin Dickstein, *Brooklyn Daily Eagle*, April 10, 1928, p.12A

"While a too critical reviewer may be justified in condemning the story and veriest slapstick nature of its comedy, the fact remains that it will probably click with the majority of motion picture patrons who are not inclined to delve too deeply in the search for flaws in their entertainment, but are willing to take things as they come.

"Sammy Cohen and Ted McNamara provide most of the fun and aside from their antics there is really nothing much to it. Nick Stuart and Sally Phipps, who are also among the featured players add little to the value of the picture principally because their roles are more or less inconsequential and they have only poor material with which to display their talents.

"Sammy and Ted are a combination bound to provoke mirth and their all too ridiculous exploits here will doubtless be appreciated despite poor direction which prolongs many of the sequences to an impossible point in an effort to promote laughs. There are, however, many humorous situations and quite a number of gags that will meet with the entire approval of the cash customers. Sammy as a taxi driver and Mac as a hansom cab driver are not as funny as they have been on other occasions, but it would seem they are quite funny enough to put even this picture over." Reviewed by Chester J. Smith, *Motion Picture News*, April 11, 1928, p.1213

"Story and Production…Slapstick comedy, made for laughing purposes only. All the newspaper lads and lassies on the metropolitan daily ritzed this one, but the fact still remains that an intelligent and select Roxy clientele laughed in their well-bred way throughout. And if you can get that kind of an audience to chortle, it's a cinch that it will knock 'em off their seats in the popular houses. Just goofy nonsense, but the Hebe and Scotty taxi drivers shanghaied on a private yacht and forced to act as gobs keep the fun going at a fast clip. There's a wild storm and they land on a cannibal island. Here they pull a series of gags with the wild animals and natives that make you laugh in spite of yourself. The story's a flop, but the laughs are undeniably there.

"Direction…Henry Lehrman, fair." *Film Daily*, April 15, 1928, p.4

Chicken a la King: Fox Film Corp. *Released 06/17/1928.* © 05/31/1928 — 6 reels/6,417 feet. DIRECTOR: Henry Lehrman. ASSISTANT DIRECTOR: Virgil Hart. PRESENTED BY William Fox. SCREENPLAY: Izola Forrester and Mann Page; based on the play *Mister Romeo* by Harry Wagstaff Gribble, Isaac Paul, and Wallace M. Mannheimer. TITLES: James A. Starr. CINEMATOGRAPHY: Conrad Wells. EDITORS: Frank Hull and Ralph Dietrich. CAST: Nancy Carroll, George Meeker, Arthur Stone, Ford Sterling, Frances Lee, Carol Holloway, Amber Norman
(pre-release titles: **Mister Romeo** and **Husbands Are Liars**)
SYNOPSIS: "Horace Trundle [Sterling] is a modern, prosperous business man of New York City. He is middle aged, settled in his ways, a chronic grouch, and so careful of his money

that his wife, Effie [Holloway], does not even dare suggest she needs a new dress or hat.

"He comes storming to breakfast one morning waving the month's bills in his wife's face and complaining about expenses. She manages to soothe him and to remind him that it is their twenty-fifth wedding anniversary. He is further mollified and a little ashamed when he finds a bill-fold as her gift to him to celebrate the occasion.

"A telegram arrives for Effie from her brother Oscar [Stone], advising her that he is coming for a visit. Horace goes into another fit of temper and while he is still at it telling his wife what he thinks of her sap brother, Oscar arrives. But he is not a bit put out by the storming of his irate brother-in-law but proceeds to make a hearty meal. In fact, he overdoes it and, as usual, when he is sick or under emotional strain, Oscar goes into a faint and blurts out the truth.

"This time he blurts out that the invention he was telling them about which was to make his fortune is a fake and that Horace is a tightwad.

"When he recovers Horace orders him out of the house but Oscar pleads with him, saying he is about to be married. Horace starts to relent when Oscar further informs him that he is marrying a chorus girl who has 'it,' 'them' and 'those.'

"The family reputation is at stake and Horace makes his decision and quickly. He will find the girl, tell her a few things after which brother Oscar will be glad to crawl into his hole and pull the hole in after him.

"Being a man of action Horace does not delay but hies himself to a burlesque theatre, worms himself back stage, and is immediately taken in tow by two of the merry merry [Carroll and Lee] who intrigue him and cajole him to the extent that he soon forgets his real mission and kicks off the shackles that have bound him for so many years.

"He listens to the song of the sirens, loosens the rubber band from his wallet and shoots the works.

"Eventually he becomes in the butter and egg class and a Broadway rounder, a denizen of the whisper joints, a buyer of fine lingerie and other accessories.

"Oscar has not been idle all this time. He had trailed Horace, made a deal with the two girls, and eventually declares Effie in on it all.

"Which means that after Horace has done a moth and flame act and has succeeded in getting his wings pretty badly burned he is glad to have Effie take him home by the ear with a full realization coming to him that Effie, with the proper raiment looks mighty good to him and so does the home that irked him so much but a short time before." *Chicken a la King* Press Sheet, June 16, 1926

REVIEWS: "Two lithe and pretty girls, competent performances by a couple of mere males and an amusing story make for an excellent diversion at the Roxy Theatre this week. This pictorial effort is known as 'Chicken à la King,' an adaptation of 'Mr. Romeo,' a play by Henry Wagstaff Gribble and Wallace A. Mannheimer, which was presented on Broadway last Autumn. For most of the time this film keeps to more or less gentle fun, but occasionally it has been found necessary to overstep the mark, and at one juncture Ford Sterling is perceived hanging from a window sill, above the sidewalk, more stories than he cares or is inclined to count.

"One might say that Horace Trundle (Mr. Sterling) is extraordinarily solicitous concerning the career of his wife's none too intelligent brother. But, on the other hand, there may be those who will argue that a skinflint like Mr. Trundle would be just the sort who would go out and spend a thousand dollars to save a dime. At any rate Mr. Trundle's parsimonious nature is eased up toward the end of this subject and one gathers that his opinion of his own power of perception is possibly not anything like as exalted as it was.

"It takes the combined efforts of Maisie de Voe and Babe Lorraine, two chorus girls with gold on the brain, to give Horace Trundle a [illegible] picture of the absurdity of being tight-fisted. Babe and Maisie enlist the aid of Oscar Barrows, who is supposed to share with these fascinating creatures all they can wheedle out of Horace. And, in course of time, Mrs. Trundle finds herself also roped into the attack on her husband's purse.

"Quite a number of thousand-dollar bills are displayed as this merry adventure frolics along. And farce comedy or not, the spectators in the big theatre yesterday frequently became audibly nervous regarding the disposition of the currency.

"Maisie is a past mistress in telling sympathetic stories of her mundane needs. To Mr. Trundle it was like listening to an angel saying she is starving and needs having her wings repaired. For a time Mr. Trundle seems to enjoy the fuss made over him as 'Deddy,' but when he begins to suspect that the young bobbed heads do not like him for himself alone, he arranges to close the pleasant platonic friendship. Maisie and Babe, however, have other ideas in mind, and Mr. Trundle falls into their trap. He realizes as he goes back to his wife that his intellect is not sharp enough to cope with brazen gold diggers but that his wife is able to outwit the stage beauties and her own brother.

"Nancy Carroll is so pretty that one almost sympathizes with Mr. Barrow in his helplessness. Mr. Sterling gives an able characterization here, except for an occasional desire to make extravagant gestures. Arthur Stone's acting of the part of the wife's brother is another clever performance. Carroll Holloway and Frances Lee also contribute intelligent portrayals." Reviewed by Mordaunt Hall, "The Screen," *New York Times*, June 11, 1928, p.27

"Nancy Carroll does rather well in the role of a blond gold-digger in 'Chicken a la King,' a mild offshoot of 'Gentlemen Prefer Blondes,' at the Roxy this week. Miss Carroll is the lady who takes Ford Sterling, a granulated sugar daddy, for a series of expensive sleigh rides.

"Mr. Sterling, himself, it may be added, gives an excellent performance and otherwise does much to relieve the plot of its more banal moments.

"'Chicken a la King' is no worse nor is it much better than the average screen comedy of its type. It may be dismissed simply as one of those summer-time program pictures of no definite distinction." *Brooklyn Daily Eagle*, June 11, 1928, p.14a

"Perfect summer diet. Light and frothy. Ford Sterling and Arthur Stone a real comedy team. 3 nifty phrails for the male vote.

"Cast…Nancy Carroll a knockout for looks, and she can troupe. Then there's Carol Holloway and Frances Lee making it a beauty threesome. Ford Sterling and Arthur Stone do the light comedy.

"Story and Production…Light comedy from the stage play 'Mr. Romeo.' It's all nonsensical fun and a lot of whoopee, but ideal hot weather entertainment for any house. Ford Sterling is a tightwad whose wife has a tough time getting money for a new dress every second season. But when Ford meets the dazzling chorus gal he just goes blooey and blows the works. He starts off with the honest intention of saving his sappy brother-in-law, Arthur Stone, who he believes is in the clutches of the fizz dame. But Ford falls hard for the chorus gal's pal. It's a scream as he kids himself into thinking he's only interested in 'uplifting' the poor little gal. Then wifey frames a plot with the two wise babies to cure pa of his philandering. Corking light comedy stuff, done with class. They'll like it.

"Direction, Henry Lehrman, clever." *Film Daily*, June 17, 1928, p.3

"This dish, when properly served, is always tasty. And looming large on the Fox menu it provides light nourishment easily digested because it has been cooked to a turn. The very title suggests a 'kick' and it has been garnished with paprika and plenty of flavor. It doesn't tax the imagination, but speeds through its hour with first rate highlights.

"The cast is excellent. The *chicken*, played by Nancy Carroll, is a treat to the eye in her role of a chorus girl. Nancy is experienced in chorus work, and the part fits her like a glove. It is her job to frame a wayward husband and make him return to his anxious spouse. Ford Sterling has the hubby role, and he gags it to a fare-you-well. He kicked over the traces in the first place to rescue his *sweet* brother-in-law from a chorine. And so the fireworks are released. Arthur Stone, playing the *daffodil*, is good for much laughter.

"Altogether it is a tidy little picture, one which is sophisticated without going too sappy. It is excellently mounted, superbly directed and acted with genuine color." Reviewed by Laurence Reid, *Motion Picture News*, June 23, 1928, p.2117

Homesick: Fox Film Corp. *Released 12/16/1928.* © 12/10/1928 — 6 reels/5,153 feet. Silent, with synchronization. DIRECTOR: Henry Lehrman. ASSISTANT DIRECTOR: Max Gold. PRESENTED BY William Fox. SCREENPLAY, STORY: John Stone. TITLES: William Kernell. CINEMATOGRAPHY: Charles Van Enger. EDITOR: Ralph Dixon. CAST: Sammy Cohen, Harry Sweet, Marjorie Beebe, Henry Armetta, Pat Harmon, Frank Alexander SYNOPSIS: "It all starts in a poolroom in New York, where Cohen, flat as a pancake, financially, reads an ad inserted by a girl in California who wants a husband, but said husband-to-be must have enough wherewithal to buy a chicken ranch.

"Likewise Sammy sees a poster advertising a transcontinental bicycle race from New York to Los Angeles, with a prize of $25,000 for the winner.

"He borrows a dollar and edges into a poker game in the rear room of a pool hall.

"This poker session lasts two days and two nights, sans interruptions. Sammy emerges with enough to pay his entrance fee into the race and purchase a bicycle.

"The man he 'took' in the poker game, Harry Sweet, also enters the race and the feud is on all the way across the continent.

"The riders encounter a cattle stampede, desert hardships, and a forest fire, but nothing serious ever happens." Press notice reprint in *Helena Daily Independent*, February 9, 1929, p.2

REVIEWS: "Packs a lot of laughs, with Sammy Cohen and Harry Sweet the comedy team that keep the mirth bubbling. A pop number.

"Cast…Sammy Cohen, the Hebrew private in 'What Price Glory,' makes this a real laugh fest with a lost [sic] of slapstick fun. Harry Sweet ably seconds him. Marjorie Beebe the girl. Others Henry Armetta, Pat Harmon.

"Story and Production…Comedy. This is a rollicking comedy with the fun coming steadily throughout the reels. It is mostly broad slapstick, but the kind that makes you laugh in spite of yourself. It starts with a poker game that lasts for two days, with Sammy coming out the winner of a big bank roll. He has taken his friend Harry plenty, and the latter is determined to get his roll back, figuring that things weren't just exactly on the level. They both enter a cross-country bicycle race for a big cash prize. Incidentally they are both after a gal in California who has advertised for a hubby with enough dough to buy a chicken ranch. From the time the race starts it is a series of good hearty laughs. Safe pop bookings.

"Direction, Henry Lehrman, box-office." *Film Daily*, January 27, 1929, p.4

"Sammy Cohen, the Hebrew comedian, who has succeeded in knocking them out of their seats in the last few pictures that he made for Fox, succeeds again. It's a cinch job the producers have with Sammy. He doesn't need much story or support. All he needs is to be let in front of the camera, and things take care of themselves.

"This time he starts out as the winner in a two day poker session, with one of the losers trying to get his role back as a side bet on a cross country bicycle race. From then on it looks like a laugh in every state. Broad, slap-stick comedy of the kind that sends the folks away laughing. And that's a good tonic for them as well as for your theater." *Movie Age*, February 2, 1929, p.18

"A reversion to the comedy of the old-time type is the impression gained from 'Homesick,' the Sammy Cohen comedy showing at Everybody's Theatre this week. It incorporates, however, all the modern art of the humorous picture production, and in addition, carries a spontaneity that is seldom found in the present-day film. The inimitable Cohen, whose nasal organ must surely be a libel on the Semitic peoples, is associated with Marjorie Beebe in this story, and unrepressed hilarity is the order throughout. The story opens with Sammy, true to the popular racial characteristics, fleecing a half-dozen of his friends at poker. The venue of the opening scene is New York, but far across the Continent is a very desirable young lady, who is awaiting the time when Sammy or Sammy's bete noir, a particularly fat and greedy young man, amasses sufficient money to launch safely on the sea of matrimony. In order to conserve the funds, the results of much judicious and scientific cheating at cards, Sammy decides to save train fare by entering in the New York to California bicycle race. Sammy's fat poker victim here assumes the conventional villain's role, and does his best to spoil Sammy's chances. The result is ludicrous in the extreme, and in a succession of priceless incidents his many attempts to waylay the indefatigable Sammy come to naught, mainly because Sammy takes full advantage of his rival's one weakness — a particularly sensitive corn on one foot. After the villain has several times been foiled, after having victory — and the money accruing from the poker games — in his grasp, the delightful spectacle is beheld of the villain practicing the gentle art of avoiding missiles aimed at his tender foot. Braving the terrors of a forest fire, a cattle stampede, and other exciting happenings, engineered by his rival, Sammy reaches Los Angeles and crosses the finishing line, the victor, by a few yards. However, in the end wedding bells ring for neither Sammy nor his rival, for the desirable 'Babe' marries the butler in the house in which she is employed." *Press*, Volume LXV, Issue 19672, July 16, 1925, p.15

EXHIBITOR REVIEW: "A sure money-maker if bought when new. Equal to 'Gay Retreat' and better than 'Plastered in Paris.' Will make the audience roar with laughter." "Box Office Reports," *Movie Age*, April 6, 1929, p.17

New Year's Eve: Fox Film Corp. *Released 02/24/1929.* © 02/26/1929 — 7 reels/5,959 feet synchronized sound version/5,909 feet silent version. Silent and synchronization. DIRECTOR: Henry Lehrman. ASSISTANT DIRECTOR: Max Gold. PRESENTED BY William Fox. SUPERVISOR: Kenneth Hawks. SCREENPLAY: Dwight Cummins; based on Richard Connell's story *One Hundred Dollars.* TITLES: William Kernell. CINEMATOGRAPHY: Conrad Wells. MUSIC: S.L. Rothafel. CAST: Mary Astor, Charles Morton, Earle Foxe, Florence Lake, Arthur Stone, Helen Ware, Freddie Frederick, Jane La Verne, Sumner Getchell, Stuart Erwin, Virginia Vance

SYNOPSIS: "Mary, unable to find a job, is in despair while her brother lies home. By chance Mary encounters the town's leading gambler and is told to come to him. She refuses, and later finds a wallet containing ten $100 bills. The girl returns the money to the owner, Edward Warren, played by Charles Morton, who gives her one of the bills as a souvenir.

"She rushes to the toy store where, unknown to her, crooks pick her pocket. The toys are sent home and the landlady pays for them. When it is discovered the money is gone, the landlady orders Mary out. In desperation Mary calls the gambling king. In the meantime Morton has gone to the house of chance. The pickpocket who acquired the $100 bill has also gone there. An altercation results and the pickpocket shoots the gambler and takes his wallet.

"Morton discovers Mary in the apartment with the dead man but before they can escape the butler appears. He calls the police. In a whirlwind finish the pickpocket slips from a rope from the roof in an effort to escape, the gamblers attempt to take Morton 'for a ride' and Mary, discovering the pickpocket's body, prevents this latter catastrophe." Reviewed by Don Ashbaugh, *Motion Picture News*, May 4, 1929, p.1531

REVIEWS: "Fox rushes holiday season with Santa Claus film, but it is excellent program picture with nice action and love story.

"Cast…Mary Astor sweet in a very sympathetic part. Charles Morton who did admirably in 'Christina' is also good here. Other Arthur Stone, Helen Ware, Freddie Frederick, Florence Lake, Sumner Getchell, Virginia Vance, Stuart Erwin.

"Story and Production…Drama. Adapted from story, 'One Hundred Dollars.' Understand this was made originally for the Christmas trade, but held up. Tells the old story of the poor girl's romance with the rich boy with an original angle. Mary is mothering her little brother as Christmas approaches, and penniless she starts out to raise the jack to keep the kid's faith alive in Santa Claus. Works up into a good plot.

Direction, Henry Lehrman, adequate." *Film Daily*, April 14, 1929, p.13

"(Silent Version) Have no illusions about this being one of the current 'whoopee' pictures because of the title. It is a dank, cold drama, with tears aplenty, lots of worry over the poor heroine, with everything hotsy-totsy at the final fadeout.

"The plot is dragged forth for the thousandth time and turned into a picture for Fox under Kenneth Hawk's supervision. It is just one of those so-so pictures, not so good, not so bad. Your audiences won't condemn, neither will they display any ecstatic enthusiasm. It will fill out in a program with plenty of other support…. Mary Astor may mean something to your public. Otherwise you'll have to depend on the title to draw them in on the supposition that it is a wild picture." Reviewed by Don Ashbaugh, *Motion Picture News*, May 4, 1929, p.1531

Sound Your "A": Fox Film Corporation. © 02/25/1929 — 3 reels/1,854 feet– 21 minutes. Sound: all-talking Fox Movietone. DIRECTOR: Henry Lehrman. SCREENPLAY: Paul Girard Smith; based on Sidney Lanfield and William F. Halligan's *The Cornet Rehearsal*. CAST: George Bickel, Arthur Stone, Marjorie Beebe, Jerry Madden, Arnold Lucy, Stuart Erwin, Virginia Sale, Donald MacKenzie, Henry Armetta, Collette Francey
(pre-release title: **The Blew Danube**)
SYNOPSIS: Charlie, the landlord of a series of flats, complains to his friend Steve about the noise all of his tenants make, so much so that one of the quieter ones hung himself the week before. The tenants include a song plugger, a night watchman, "a dame that gives piano lessons," and a chorus girl at perpetual odds with her husband. Henry J. Skinner, another tenant with a wandering eye, also annoys the other tenants with his persistent requests to borrow items.

Elsewhere, German-born Conrad P. Schultz is thrown out of his apartment for making too much noise with his ongoing cornet practices. As Schultz wanders aimlessly down the street tooting on his cornet, Steve hears him and has an idea: Charlie should give Schultz free rent and urge him to practice as much as he wants with the hope that the racket will drive the rest of the tenants out of the building. Charlie agrees and Schultz is soon set up in the flat vacated by the suicide victim.

After various interactions with the other tenants, Schultz's music finally has the desired effect. Unfortunately, it annoys the area dogs as well, and one of them makes off with Schultz's valuable Stradivarius fiddle. Chasing after the dog and cursing in German all the way, Schultz finally catches the dog and retrieves his now-demolished fiddle. He returns to his flat and resumes his cornet practice, only to be confronted by the mob of irate tenants. Charlie and Steve enter to see what all the fuss is about, and are informed by MacGregor, the leader of the mob, that they all are moving out. They do so, after which Steve informs Schultz that he now must never play the cornet again. He agrees and turns the instrument over, and the two leave to dispose of it. When they return, however, they are greeted by more music emerging from Schultz's flat. They enter and inquire: "Here, here, here — what do you mean — didn't you promise not to play that anymore?" Schultz responds: "I ain't playing dot — I'm playing dis!" Synopsis adapted from the dialog summary on file at the New York State Archives.
REVIEWS: "Paul Gerard Smith wrote this one. A little pruning would have helped. Drags somewhat at three-quarter mark, but ends logically and funny. Recording is clear. So is photography. Funny enough to go in anywhere. About a landlord harassed with undesirable tenants. Friend selects a street musician, providing the latter with free rent, so that he will play long and frequent until neighbors get so annoyed they will move out. Situation closes with landlord stuck with street player." *Variety*, November 27, 1929, p.21

The Big Butter and Yegg Man: Universal Pictures. *Released 05/06/1931.* © 04/24/1931 — 2 reels — 21 minutes. DIRECTOR: Henry Lehrman. SCREENPLAY: George H. Plympton, from a story by Henry Lehrman. CAST: George Sidney, Charlie Murray
(other sources erroneously give the title as **A Butter-in-Yeggman, A Butter and Yegg Man**, and **A Butter-In Yegg Man**)
SYNOPSIS/REVIEW: "George Sidney plays the banker, who is threatened with death by a bandit who holds him up, if he should tell the police. The thief is caught, Sidney identifies

him in the belief that he is unconscious, and then the bandit returns to carry out his threat. A few good laughs, and fairly wide appeal. Running time, 20 minutes." *Motion Picture Herald*, April 11, 1931, p.36

"A George Sidney comedy, that fails to click. Sidney is a banker, and gets a tough bank robber pinched for holding up the bank. Later the robber breaks jail, and arrives at Sidney's home as the new butler. Then a lot of horse play with the comedian disguising himself as his wife and trying to fool the robber. Pretty mechanical stuff that lacks any real gags to score the laughs." *Film Daily*, April 12, 1931, p.25

Sink or Swim: Fox Film Corporation. DIRECTOR: Henry Lehrman. CAST: El Brendel, Marjorie White, Cecelia Parker, Rosalie Roy, Peggy Ross, Dixie Lee, Joyce Compton (Unrealized project announced for upcoming 1931-1932 season)

As Screenwriter, Adaptation:

The Poor Millionaire: Richard Talmadge Productions; Distributor: Biltmore Pictures. *Released 04/07/1930.* 5 reels/5,200 feet — 58 minutes. DIRECTOR: George Melford. SCREENPLAY, STORY: Henry Lehrman and Rex Taylor. CAST: Richard Talmadge, Constance Howard, George Irving, Frederick Vroom, John Hennings, Fannie Midgley, Jay Hunt SYNOPSIS/REVIEWS: "Richard Talmadge is a good stunt man. He surely does plenty of them in this wild story. The picture boasts of little besides Dick's antics, and even some of them seem preposterous. Little regard is given for the big loopholes in the too-thin and obvious plot, the main idea apparently having been to load it up with stunt stuff.

"Dick plays a dual role, that of an upright youth who inherits a fortune, and of a twin brother, who is a jailbird and all-around heel. When Dick acquires the estate, he finds it conveniently next door to the home of the girl whose purse he had rescued from a thief. Follows a love affair and the pair are slated to be married when Dick's brother appears on the scene. The brother had escaped from a prison camp, and has made his way to Dick's home. He knocks out Dick, and exchanges clothes with him. Of course, Dick goes back to the prison camp, but escapes in time to prevent the wedding. And that's that.

"The cast supporting Talmadge isn't much, having been selected principally for types. Direction takes plenty for granted, hurdling one inconsistency after another.

"Action fans and kids, who will accept old time film formulas may like this.

"You'll need at least one more feature and some strong shorts." Reviewed by Charles F. Hynes, *Motion Picture News*, May 17, 1930, p.51

"Crude production rates among the lowest seen this season, with amateurish directing and acting.

"Here is one which looks as if it had been made over the week-end. It is pretty terrible any way you figure it. Richard Talmadge plays the double role of hero and villain, he being twins, as it were. His brother is the villain who is an escaped convict, while the hero has inherited a dead man's fortune. The villain steps in, impersonates the hero, and raises the devil before the hero finally straightens everything out. Talmadge was evidently featured in this for his acrobatic stunts, which in some places are so far-fetched that the audience laughed in ridicule. The so-called society scenes are also very laughable. Even for an independent this picture has little excuse, and looks as if it had been shot on a very limited bankroll. The production is handled in the style of the old serial thrillers of 15 years ago and is amateurish throughout. Only good as filler for small stands with uncritical patronage." *Film Daily*, June 22, 1930, p.14

Moulin Rouge: Twentieth Century. *Released 01/19/1934.* © 01/25/1934 — 8 reels. DIRECTOR: Sidney Lanfield. PRODUCER: Darryl F. Zanuck. PRESENTED BY Joseph M. Schenck. SCREENPLAY, STORY: Nunnally Johnson and Henry Lehrman. EDITOR: Lloyd Nosler. CINEMATOGRAPHY: Charles Rosher. MUSIC AND LYRICS: Al Dubin and Harry Warren. MUSICAL DIRECTOR: Alfred Newman. CHOREOGRAPHY: Russell Markert. CAST: Constance Bennett, Franchot Tone, Tullio Carminati, Helen Westley, Andrew Tombes, Hobart Cavanaugh, Ivan Lebedeff, George Revenant, Russ Columbo, Fuzzy Knight, Russ Brown, The Boswell Sisters
SYNOPSIS/REVIEW: "Smart and lively musical with better than usual story, some catchy numbers and gorgeous girls.

"Though it belongs to the backstage school, there are enough individual merits in this production to put it over for the count with any audience that wants musical romance. Story is somewhat in the sophisticated class and stronger than the average musical plot. Constance Bennett plays a dual role, representing two members of a sister act, one of whom went to Paris and became famous under a foreign name, while the other married Franchot Tone, whose refusal to let her go on the stage again results in their separation. Franchot and Tullio Carminati, a producer, engage the foreign star for their show. On her arrival, she lets Connie take her place, after having her transformed so her friends won't recognize her, and thus she proves her talent to her husband — in addition to keeping him and others in hot water for a while as she tests his fidelity by vamping him in her guise as the foreign star. Miss Bennett, Tone and Carminati give swell performances. Music is very good and the girl ensembles are a treat." *Film Daily*, January 10, 1934, p.22
REVIEWS: "Constance Bennett in 'Moulin Rouge'! — What an attraction to conjure with for exhibitors! It is so smart and sophisticated that the wiseacres will have to be alert or they will miss the best points so easily brought to them on a silver platter by the adapters, Nunnally Johnson and Henry Lehrman. When we make this last statement we make it advisedly for the 20th Century Productions surely have in this picture everything that is class in writers, sets, artists, technicians, and above all a star that is worthy of the name. She is supported by an all-star cast, for Franchot Tone, by his work opposite Miss Bennett, proves that he is worthy of a starring role in a picture. He has a close rival in Tullio Carminati, who is going better in the talkies than he ever did in the silent — and they counted him a star back in those days. Helen Westley is so human and real that you just want to put your arms around her neck and give her a real hug and kiss. George Renevant did a fine piece of acting as the real French husband of Constance Bennett, the French actress. In fact, we almost forgot to tell you that Miss Bennett plays three parts — herself, a girl of a sister team ala Dolly Sisters, and the other half of the team who becomes famous in France and is brought here to play in a big musical. Others who give a good account of themselves are Russ Columbo, Hobart Cavanaugh, a sure-fire comedian who is heading for big things; Andrew Tombes, Ivan Lebedeff, Fuzzy Knight, Russ Brown and the Boswell Sisters come in for their share of attention. Constance Bennett sings three

catchy songs from the pen of Al Dubin and Harry Warren. The dance numbers credited to Russell Markert were on a par with the best staged by the Warner's and Goldwyn revue directors. Give a great big hand to Charles Rosher for his beautiful photography and at the same time do not overlook Lloyd Nosler's editing so well handled by William Goetz and Raymond Griffith." *Hollywood Filmograph*, December 16, 1933, p.3

"A snappy romance idea rather than music is the outstanding showmanship feature of this picture. Because of the theatre atmosphere of the theme, music and girl dance features are necessary, but in view of the number of attractions on the screen affording those values, best results with 'Moulin Rouge' should come from emphasizing the comedy romance premise which motivates the story. Naturally the fact that Constance Bennett sings and dances should be called to public attention as it has a definite novelty value.

"Here's the plot. Helen wants a musical career. Douglas, her husband wants her to be a home wife. A French girl (dual role played by Miss Bennett) is imported for the role as Helen and Doug split up. Years before, the two girls, very much resembling each other, played small time vaudeville as a sister act. It is easy for Helen to persuade the other girl to go on a love nest rendezvous with gigolo Ramon, as she fits into her show role. Both Doug and LeMaire, the producer, are entranced by the counterfeit French vision; a note of comedy injected as LeMaire begs Doug to plead his case. The expected developments ensue, both the lovers acclaiming her a great artist both for her musical abilities and her love-making proclivities. Hot as Doug gets for the exotic creature, memories of the missing Helen cool him off, and as the show opens with the Frenchman dragging his wife out of the theatre, Helen goes on to a triumph, finally revealing to LeMaire and Doug who she really is, with the on-the-spot Doug coming up with the tag gag. 'I knew it all the time.'

"While zippy, the situations avoid becoming too daring as an air of suspense which audiences will understand complicates matters for Bennett's principal supports. The modern idea of the theme quickly suggests that the picture be sold with a modern appeal. Exploitation that suggests the comedy value of a man in love with his own wife, but thinking that she is some one else, can be gagged and tricked in all sorts of intriguing ways. Two song numbers, 'Your Kisses in the Morning' and 'Boulevard of Dreams,' basis for the girl-dance sequences, which Miss Bennett sings, supported by Russ Colombo and the radioing Boswell Sisters. Can be tied advantageously on to the comedy romance idea.

"For the show's character, cast names are of more than ordinary importance as advertising assets. Miss Bennett's singing should prove a new attraction for her regular fans, and should make it possible for exhibitors to stir up a new interest in this personality. Tullio Carminati, recently in 'Gallant Lady,' and Franchot Tone in comedy roles, should be given a hefty plug, and Colombo and the Boswells, while appearing only in atmospheric bits, should be capitalized to the fullest extent.

"Merchandising of the girl-spectacle eye appeal should be guided by patron reaction to the chain of musicals. If your audience go for it, sell it enthusiastically. But if you are interested in getting a novel appeal into advance curiosity creating publicity, don't permit folk to be fooled by the title, but don't get that 'wife or no wife, I'll be there tonight' twinkle in your ads in the most intriguing and colorful ways possible." Reviewed by McCarity, *Motion Picture Herald*, December 23, 1933, p.43

Bulldog Drummond Strikes Back: Twentieth Century. *Released 07/20/1934* — 83 minutes. DIRECTOR: Roy Del Ruth. PRODUCER: Darryl F. Zanuck. SCREENPLAY: Nunnally Johnson and Henry Lehrman, based on the novel by H.C. McNeile. CINEMATOGRAPHY: J. Peverell Marley. MUSIC: Alfred Newman. EDITOR: Allen McNeil. CAST: Ronald Colman, Loretta Young, C. Aubrey Smith, Charles Butterworth, Una Merkel, Warner Oland, E.E. Clive, Mischa Auer, Douglas Gerrard, Ethel Griffies, Halliwell Hobbes, Arthur Hohl, George Regas, Creighton Hale, Billy Bevan, Olaf Hytten, Robert Kortman
REVIEWS: "This is a fitting vehicle for Ronald Colman's return to the screen. It is an ideal mixture of comedy and melodrama, with Colman enjoying the adventure of solving a murder and winning decorative Loretta Young, niece of the murdered man. The picture should please every type of audience. Charles Butterworth has his most important role to date and is surefire for comedy. Una Merkel, C. Aubrey Smith, E.E. Clive and Halliwell Hobbes also are among the funmakers. Warner Oland, expert in screen villainy, was never more sinister. All of the action occurs in one night, and there is plenty action. Direction by Roy Del Ruth is excellent. Bows are due to Nunnally Johnson for his sprightly dialogue, and to Peverell Marley for the photography." *Film Daily*, May 4, 1934, p.9

"Not to be confused with 'Bulldog Drummond,' which Ronald Colman made about five years ago, this story is a further narration of the character's adventures. It's a mystery thriller — murders, disappearing corpses, abductions, cryptic code radiograms, gripping detective work, the always popular conflict between the inscrutable Oriental mind and the shrewdness, daring and courage of the Western World. Through this colorful, nerve-tingling atmosphere runs a line of comedy that promises a laugh for every screech and a romantic interest contrasting the melodrama.

"The picture is based on a novel by H.C. McNeile for which the screenplay was prepared by Nunnally Johnson, noted short story writer, recently credited with 'Moulin Rouge' and 'Rothschild.' Direction is by Roy Del Ruth, maker of many popular Warner pictures. Colman is Drummond. It's his first since 'The Masquerader.' All the supports are familiar screen personalities. Loretta Young ('Rothschild') has the leading feminine role. Warner Oland ('Charlie Chan') is the Oriental villain, and important parts are in the hands of such accomplished performers as Charles Butterworth, Una Merkel, C. Aubrey Smith, Arthur Hohl, George Regas, Ethel Griffies, Mischa Auer, Halliwell Hobbes and E.E. Clive.

"Local is London; time is present. It has Drummond swearing off his adventurous career only to meet a girl and to be whirled into a series of thrilling dangerous adventures that promise more exciting entertainment than ordinarily is packed into this type of picture. A thriller all the way through, it appears not only to be a super-baffler for the mystery fans, but a romantic love story with special appeal for the women and a situation — action comedy that opens the door wide to intriguing, spectacular showmanship." Reviewed by Gus McCarthy, *Motion Picture Herald*, May 5, 1934, p.64

"Anytime an actor can hold his own all the way through a photoplay these days, as Ronald Colman does in 'Bulldog Drummond Strikes Back,' screen play by Nunnally Johnson, based on a novel by H.C. McNeile, he is certainly accomplishing all that any producer can hope a star will do. To be truthful, we hated to see the whole mystery cleared up, for Ronald Colman was so delightful in his portrayal that one sort of forgot everything and everybody and wondered what would happen next.

"Next to the great performance of Ronald Colman, we would place Charles Butterworth, who created more real laughs in this picture than in anything he has ever done. Una Merkel came in for her share of laughs. Loretta Young not only looked beautiful, but really did some highly dramatic acting. Warner Oland's villainous performance was superb. He was so ably assisted by George Regas and Mischa Auer. C. Aubrey Smith, as the man from Scotland Yard, was splendid, with Ethel Griffies, Halliwell Hobbes, E.E. Clive, Douglas Gerard and Arthur Hohl rounding out the fine cast.

"Roy Del Ruth is deserving of a world of credit for his direction of 'Bulldog Drummond Strikes Back.' William Goetz and Raymond Griffith were the associate producers on the picture, which was very artistically photographed by Peverell Marley. Edited by Allen McNeil, and musical score by Alfred Newman." Reviewed by Harry Burns, *Hollywood Filmograph*, May 5, 1934, p.3

"Comedy mystery melodrama is the entertainment and showmanship center of this picture. It's a series of surprises. Each prepares the audience to expect a blood-freezing thrill; but instead of provoking screams, shudders, gasps and stopped hearts, it delivers, every time, a healthy thump on the funny bone. With value in performance and presentation continually moving with punch and speed with an unusual brand of suspense utilized, it's both class and mass entertainment.

"The show is based on a tried and proved mystery entertainment idea and every fun-creating possibility of that premise is cleverly worked to the limit. At the same time a novel comedy twist is applied and the fun starts all over again. It deals with the adventures of an amateur detective. There's a girl in the case for romance; the menacing wily Oriental and his henchmen for thrill and mystery; the harassed Scotland Yard Inspector who would rather put the amateur detective in jail than his suspects; cryptic coded radiograms, disappearing corpses, sliding doors, dungeons, all kinds of ruses, traps and deliverances to color the basic plot with a realistic hokum. And to keep the whole thing going, and give it its deft comedy verve, there's a bridegroom who must accompany the amateur detective on his hectic adventures than be with his bride on their wedding night.

"While being catchy entertainment in its own right, 'Bulldog Drummond Strikes Back' points a satirical finger of fun at all the thrill and horror pictures. That information accentuating the fact that the show is a laugh-provoker, should be emphatically brought home to potential audiences." Reviewed by Gus McCarthy, *Motion Picture Herald*, May 19, 1934, pp.67-68

"Ronald Colman, the stellar player in 'Bulldog Drummond Strikes Back,' gives another of his intriguing and flawless performances as the redoubtable Captain Hugh Drummond. Owing to his keen sense of humor, Mr. Colman succeeds in making the extravagant adventures of the master sleuth seem to be almost possible. Drummond faces his antagonists with a coolness that is remarkable and escapes when his life appears to be hanging in the balance.

"In this picture, now on exhibition at the Rialto, Mr. Colman has, if anything, even a better vehicle than he had in his first Bulldog Drummond venture. It is equipped with sparkling comedy and clever dialogue. Charles Butterworth is cast in a role which gives him plenty of opportunities to show his rare skill as a comedian. Then you have the dry villainy of Warner Oland as Prince Achmed, who is willing to go to any extremes to bring ashore from a ship, which has had a case of cholera aboard, furs worth $500,000. He has already killed one man when the story starts, and often several other persons besides Drummond come close to being slain.

"The long arm of coincidence is constantly in evidence in this comedy drama, in which several persons disappear mysteriously from time to time. Drummond frequently disturbs the sleep of his friend, Commissioner Nielson (C. Aubrey Smith), but by the time that official reaches Drummond's apartment or a hotel the witnesses have been kidnapped, and on one occasion Prince Achmed takes the trouble to transform the furnishings of a hotel room." Reviewed by Mordaunt Hall, *New York Times*, August 26, 1934, p.X3

Folies Bergère de Paris: Twentieth Century. *Released 02/22/1935* — 80 minutes. DIRECTOR: Roy Del Ruth. ASSISTANT DIRECTOR: Fred Fox. PRODUCER: Darryl F. Zanuck. ASSOCIATE PRODUCERS: William Goetz and Raymond Griffith. SCREENPLAY: Bess Meredyth and Hal Long, adapted by Jesse Ernst from the play by Rudolph Lothar and Hans Adler. CINEMATOGRAPHY: Barney McGill; DANCE NUMBERS: Peverell Marley. EDITORS: Allen McNeil and Sherman Todd. ART DIRECTOR: Richard Day. SOUND: Vinton Vernon and Roger Heman; Western Electric Noiseless Recording. MUSIC DIRECTOR: Alfred Newman. COSTUMES: Omar Kiam. MUSICAL NUMBERS CREATED BY: Dave Gould. DIRECTOR OF MONTAGE RETAKES *(uncredited):* Henry Lehrman. CAST: Maurice Chevalier, Merle Oberon, Ann Sothern, Eric Blore, Ferdinand Munier, Walter Byron, Lumsden Hare, Robert Greig, Ferdinand Gottschalk, Halliwell Hobbes, Georges Renavent, Phillip Dare, Frank McGlynn, Sr., Barbara Leonard, Olin Howland

REVIEWS: "Besides being one of the most entertaining pictures of the month, this is one of the smartest musicals in a long time. It is a Parisian comedy, with music in the background, and there is one spectacular number, legitimately occurring at the finish. Wonder of wonders, it inspires Maurice Chevalier to act a part instead of being just himself. Most wonderful of all, it lets us see the exquisite Merle Oberon and glimpse for the first time her gleaming sense of humor. Further, it proclaims Ann Sothern a first-rate comedienne and enables her to make her first hit. Superbly staged, it engagingly tells the story of *Baron Cassini*, a financier, whose resemblance to *Eugène Charlier* of the 'Folies Bergère' induces the baron's friends to employ the actor to substitute for him in a drawing-room crisis which extends to the boudoir of the baroness and spicily asks the question if she knows the difference when both visit her separately. Not the newest idea in the world, but it is set forth persuasively and with intelligent restraint." Reviewed by Norbert Lusk, *Picture Play Magazine*, May 1935, p.48

Calm Yourself: Metro-Goldwyn-Mayer Corp. *Released 06/28/1935.* © 06/24/1935. DIRECTOR: George B. Seitz. PRODUCER: Lucien Hubbard. SCREENPLAY: Arthur Kober *(and uncredited Henry Lehrman).* CINEMATOGRAPHY: Lester White. EDITOR: Conrad A. Nervig. MUSIC: Charles Maxwell. CAST: Robert Young, Madge Evans, Betty Furness, Ralph Morgan, Nat Pendleton, Hardie Albright, Claude Gillingwater, Shirley Ross, Raymond Hatton, Herman Bing.

Show Them No Mercy: 20th Century-Fox Film Corp. *Released 12/06/1935.* © 12/06/1935 — 6,838 feet. DIRECTOR: George Marshall. PRODUCER: Darryl F. Zanuck. SCREENPLAY, STORY: Kubec Glasmon. ADAPTATION: Henry Lehrman. CINEMATOGRAPHY: Bert Glennon. EDITOR: Jack Murray. MUSICAL DIRECTOR: David Buttolph. CAST: Rochelle Hudson, Cesar Romero, Bruce Cabot, Edward Norris, Warren Hymer, Edward Brophy, Herbert Rawlinson, Robert Cleckler, Charles C. Wilson, Frank Conroy, Edythe Elliot, William Benedict, Orrin Burke, Boothe Howard, Paul McVey, William Davidson
REVIEWS: "Fans who like tense drama will get a good stretch of it in this kidnapping yarn. It carries suspense from start to finish. The kidnapping part of the story is not elaborated upon in the least, but merely sets the opening groundwork for the campaign of the government men in tracking down the bad men. The main suspense centers on Rochelle Hudson and Edward Norris, a young couple with a baby, who unwittingly seek rainstorm shelter in an abandoned country house picked by the kidnappers for their hideaway. The toughest of the kidnappers, Bruce Cabot, is for bumping off the innocent trio right way, but Cesar Romero holds him off. The danger, however, continually hangs over the heads of the innocent intruders, who finally are saved with the arrival of the G-men. The cast does good work, with Cabot making a particularly hateful killer, and a terrier dog plays an interesting part in the story. Some comedy also is sprinkled along the route." *Film Daily*, December 7, 1935, p.7

"Melodramatic as it capitalizes the entertainment and commercial worth of gangster versus G-man conflict, this picture embellishes that quality with stark but believable human drama. Fast moving and convincing in premise, dialogue and action, assets which fine performances by the entire cast greatly enhance, the show has an appeal that, with merely the aid of a sketchy publicity campaign, should make a deep impression. The ingredients of the novel powerful drama are those with which the public has become familiar through other pictures and news events. But the drama, diverging radically from formula and thus setting the picture entirely apart from any predecessor, is the peg upon which bids for popular interest can be most effectively based.

"The story indicates the character of applicable showmanship. Melodrama colors the opening as a kidnap ransom, paid against advice of Justice Department men, convinces the criminals that theirs is a perfect undetectable crime. Switching, the picture takes on a sympathy stimulating quality as a young couple, Rochelle Hudson and Edward Norris, and their baby seek refuge from a storm in a deserted farmhouse and are surprised to find the kitchen well stocked with needed foodstuffs. It plunges into its dramatic melodrama when the kidnappers arrive to divide their loot and make the little family prisoners. Most vicious of the group, Bruce Cabot wants to kill them immediately. As Edward Brophy and Warren Hymer contribute characteristic tension-easing comedy, ringleader Cesar sees in Norris a medium of spending the supposedly untraceable money. Attempting this, the gang discover they have fallen into a trap as, paralleling a recent sensational case, G-men have so arranged the currency that its serial numbers are positive clues to the criminals.

"Panic stricken, the gang start to quarrel among themselves and with menacing Cabot threatening to make good his determination to kill the family, suspense builds in seething style. Attempting a getaway, Brophy is killed, but Cabot makes his way back to the hideout. Later Hymer is killed by officers as he attempts to pass one of the bills. In the house, murderous Cabot plays Romero, but, in attempting to kill the family, he is sensationally machine-gunned by Miss Hudson.

"While it would be inadvisable not to take full advantage of the entertainment sock of the gangster-G-man basis of the picture, it seems that the element that would surely add to its commercial success would be an intelligent concentration on the drama of the little family held prisoner. It is not a secondary quality, as in any analysis it is the hub about which all else turns. As such it provides something different to talk about. This can be done not only through straight-from-the-shoulder publicity copy, but also by way of ballyhoo exploitation, suggestions for which are almost unlimited." Reviewed by McCarthy, *Motion Picture Herald*, November 2, 1935, pp.60, 62

"At the Rivoli Theatre…is a photoplay that you might easily make the mistake of neglecting unless it were forcibly called to your attention. 'Snatched' was the original and appropriate title for this shockingly realistic casebook of a kidnapping, but the master minds in the Hays office detected a foul odor in that title and it was therefore changed to 'Show Them No Mercy.'

"This is the subjective account of four kidnappers from the time they made a successful 'snatch' and escape to a hideout with $200,000 in unmarked bills until their varied demises. It is, I think, the boldest, most honest and most acutely written melodrama that Hollywood has turned out this year. It is a better film than 'G-Men' because it has a psychological sense and a narrative compactness that the James Cagney film lacked. Kubec Glasmon, a screen playwright who has been in obscurity since he collaborated on 'The Public Enemy' five years ago, writes with a toughness and integrity that rarely finds its way to the screen. The varying moods of the men, their calloused humor and deadly ferocity, are admirably delineated, and the melodrama is original and exciting in its choice of incident.

"There is a nice variety in the way death visits these hunted killers. One of them falls under the bullets of the police as he flees across a field in the dark. His companion, Bruce Cabot, returns to the hideout, lures the leader into a sense of security and then coldly murders him when he turns his back. Mr. Cabot himself, the most fearsome of the quartet, goes to his deserved reward a few moments later when a machine gun slices a stream of bullets across his chest. There is a clever illusion here which persuades you that you see blood bubbling from the perforations.

"Warren Hymer, the crippled and amiable moron of the outfit, is the only one of the gang who earns our sympathy. After exchanging his ransom bills for clean money by the ingenious stunt of making change out of the collection plate in various churches, he arrives hopefully at the railroad station with the $12 that he fondly believes to be the price of a ticket to Phoenix. Unfortunately, $12 was only the weekend excursion rate, and fate has played him a nasty trick. When he offers one of the ransom bills to make up the difference in his fare, he is discovered and shot down. There is something genuinely touching about this episode.

"The film proves some sort of lesson in the notable performances of Bruce Cabot as a mean and ruthless assassin and Cesar Romero as the sleek and slightly human leader. In the past Hollywood has squandered these gentlemen somewhat futilely on romantic roles, when it was obvious that they were not made to be pretty boys. Now they are shrewdly cast and give memorable performances. Perhaps after a little study the producers will be able to put some of our other objectionable charm-boys to equally fascinating use." Reviewed by Andre Sennwald, "On Second Thought," *New York Times*, December 15, 1935, p.X7

Hollywood Cavalcade: 20th Century-Fox Film Corp. *Released 10/13/1939* — 97 minutes. DIRECTOR: Irving Cummings; second unit by Malcolm St. Clair for silent comedy sequences. PRODUCER: Darryl F. Zanuck. ASSOCIATE PRODUCER: Harry Joe Brown. SCREENPLAY: Ernest Pascal, from a story by Hilary Lynn and Brown Holmes, based on an original idea by Lou Breslow. MUSIC: Louis Silvers. CINEMATOGRAPHY: Allen M. Davey and Ernest Palmer. EDITOR: Walter Thompson. ART DIRECTION: Richard Day and Wiard B. Ihnen. GAGS *(uncredited):* Henry Lehrman. CAST: Alice Faye, Don Ameche, J. Edward Bromberg, Alan Curtis, Stuart Erwin, Jed Prouty, Buster Keaton, Donald Meek, George Givot, Al Jolson, Eddie Collins, Ben Turpin, Chester Conklin, Hank Mann, Snub Pollard, Mack Sennett, James Finlayson, Heinie Conklin
(pre-release title: **Falling Star**)

Jitterbugs: 20th Century-Fox Film Corp. *Released 06/11/1943* — 74 minutes. PRODUCER: Sol M. Wurtzel. DIRECTOR: Malcolm St. Clair. SCREENPLAY: Scott Darling; Henry Lehrman uncredited collaborator. CINEMATOGRAPHY: Lucien Androit. EDITOR: Norman Colbert. ART DIRECTORS: James Basevi and Chester Gore. CAST: Stan Laurel, Oliver Hardy, Vivian Blaine, Bob Bailey, Douglas Fowley, Lee Patrick, Noel Madison, Robert Emmett Keane, Charles Halton

The Dancing Masters: 20th Century-Fox Film Corp. *Released 11/19/1943* — 63 minutes. PRODUCER: Lee Marcus. DIRECTOR: Malcolm St. Clair. SCREENPLAY: W. Scott Darling; Henry Lehrman uncredited collaborator; based on a story by George Bricker. CINEMATOGRAPHY: Norbert Brodine. EDITOR: Norman Colbert. ART DIRECTORS: James Basevi and Chester Gore. Musical DIRECTOR: Emil Newman. CAST: Stan Laurel, Oliver Hardy, Trudy Marshall, Robert Bailey, Margaret Dumont, Allan Lane, Nestor Paiva, George Lloyd, Bob Mitchum, Edward Earle, Charles Rogers, Sherry Hall, Sam Ash, William Haade, Arthur Space, Daphne Pollard

The Big Noise: 20th Century-Fox Film Corp. *Released 09/22/1944* — 74 minutes. PRODUCER: Sol M. Wurtzel. DIRECTOR: Malcolm St. Clair. SCREENPLAY: W. Scott Darling; Henry Lehrman uncredited contributor to special sequences. CINEMATOGRAPHY: Joe MacDonald. EDITOR: Norman Colbert. ART DIRECTORS: Lyle Wheeler and John Ewing. MUSICAL DIRECTOR: Lionel Newman. CAST: Stan Laurel, Oliver Hardy, Doris Merrick, Arthur Space, Veda Ann Borg, Bobby Blake, Frank Fenton, James Bush, Philip Van Zandt, Esther Howard, Robert Dudley, Edgar Dearing, Selmer Jackson, Harry Hayden, Francis Ford, Jack Norton, Charles Wilson, Ken Christy

The Bullfighters: 20th Century-Fox Film Corp. *Released 05/11/1945* — 61 minutes. ASSOCIATE PRODUCER: William Girard. DIRECTOR: Malcolm St. Clair. SCREENPLAY: W. Scott Darling; Henry Lehrman uncredited contributor to special sequences. CINEMATOGRAPHY: Norbert Brodine, EDITOR: Stanley Rabjohn. ART DIRECTORS: Lyle Wheeler and Chester Gore. MUSICAL DIRECTOR: Emil Newman. CAST: Stan Laurel, Oliver Hardy, Margo Woode, Richard Lane, Carol Andrews, Diosa Costello, Frank McCown, Ralph Sanford, Irving Gump, Edward Gargan, Lorraine De Wood, Emmett Vogan

Endnotes

Chapter 1: Sambor, The Birth of a Notion

1. Alexander Manor, editor, *The Book of Sambor and Stari Sambor; A Memorial to the Jewish Communities*, published in Tel Aviv, 1980 and translated and posted on the pages of the *Jewishgen.com* web site, *http://www.jewishgen.org/yizkor/sambor/SamI.html*
2. *Sambor PSA AGAD Births 1862-1905*, Lwow Wojewodztwa, Ukraine
3. *Stary Sambor PSA AGAD Births 1856-1903*, Lwow Wojewodztwa, Ukraine
4. According to her birth registry. She gave her birth date as March 1881 years later in an October 27, 1947 deposition.
5. *Sambor PSA AGAD Births 1862-1905*
6. *Kaufmannisches Adressbuch fur Industrie, Handel und Gewerbe, XIV, Galitzien* (The 1891 Galician Business Directory), published by L. Bergmann and Comp., Wien IX Universitutmetr. 6
7. "Henry M. Lehrman," *Los Angeles Times*, January 1, 1915, p.V156
8. Alexandor Manor, editor, *The Book of Sambor and Stari Sambor; A Memorial to the Jewish Communities*
9. The JewishGen, Inc.'s web site gives some different population counts: 14,324 in 1890 and 17,039 in 1900. The population of Jews in 1880 is placed at 4,427.
10. Salka Viertel, *The Kindness of Strangers* (New York: Holt, Rinehart and Winston, 1969), pp.10-11
11. "Henry M. Lehrman," *Los Angeles Times*, p.V156
12. Alexandor Manor, editor, *The Book of Sambor and Stari Sambor; A Memorial to the Jewish Communities*
13. *Sambor PSA AGAD Marriages 1877-1905*, Lwow Wojewodztwa, Ukraine
14. Mlle. Chic, "The Story of the L-Ko Head, H. Pathé Lehrmann," *Moving Picture Weekly*, January 8, 1916, p.15
15. "'Wet and Warmer' at Marlow Theater Soon," *Helena Daily Independent*, July 10, 1921, p.6
16. Salka Viertel, *The Kindness of Strangers*, pp.20-21. Lwow is now known as Lviv.
17. "Henry M. Lehrman," *Los Angeles Times*, p.V156
18. Ibid.
19. Mlle. Chic, "The Story of the L-Ko Head, H. Pathé Lehrmann"

Chapter 2: Biograph, Imp, and Kinemacolor: Baptism By Fire

1. S.S. *Pennsylvania: List or Manifest of Immigrant Passengers for the U.S. Immigration Officer at Port of Arrival*, December 6, 1906-December 23, 1906.
2. S.S. *Karlsruhe: Customs List of Passengers*, December 14, 1896.
3. *Thirteenth Census of the United States: 1910.*

4   Mlle. Chic, "The Story of the L-Ko Head, H. Pathé Lehrmann"
5   Linda Arvidson Griffith, *When the Movies Were Young* (New York: E.P.Dutton and Company, 1925), p.91
6   Terry Ramsey, *A Million and One Nights* (New York: Simon and Schuster, 1926), pp.542-543
7   Mlle. Chic, "The Story of the L-Ko Head, H. Pathé Lehrmann"
8   Henry Lehrman interviewed by Barnet Braverman, *Barnet Braverman Research Collection*, held within the *D.W. Griffith Papers, 1897-1954*, Museum of Modern Art Film Study Center
9   Gene Fowler, *Father Goose: The Story of Mack Sennett* (New York: Covici Friede Publishers, 1934), pp.87-99
10 G.W. Bitzer, *Billy Bitzer: His Story* (Farrar, Straus and Giroux, 1973), p.67
11 Edmund J. McCormick, "Studio Town 1," *Bergen Evening Record*, July 8-12, 1935, page unknown
12 Theodore Dreiser, "The Best Motion Picture Interview Ever Written," *Photoplay*, August 1928, p.24
13 Mack Sennett and Cameron Shipp, *King of Comedy* (Garden City, New York: Doubleday and Company, Inc., 1954), pp.51-52
14 Al Ray interviewed by Barnet Braverman, *Barnet Braverman Research Coll*ection. Ray started working at Biograph at the young age of seven, and in later years would be reunited with Lehrman in both acting and directing capacities.
15 Terry Ramsey, *A Million and One Nights*, p.543
16 Mlle. Chic, "The Story of the L-Ko Head, H. Pathé Lehrmann"
17 Linda Arvidson Griffith, *When the Movies Were Young*, p.182
18 Excerpts from Victor Heerman interviews at his Hollywood home by Kalton C. Lahue on February 21, 1969, and Sam Gill on July 22, 1967 and December 3, 1971
19 Mack Sennett and Cameron Shipp, *King of Comedy*, p.76
20 Gene Fowler, *Father Goose: The Story of Mack Sennett*, p.94
21 *Ibid.*, p.95
22 Mary Pickford, *Sunshine and Shadow* (Garden City, New York: Doubleday and Company, Inc., 1955), pp.128-129
23 Mack Sennett and Cameron Shipp, *King of Comedy*, pp.28-29.
24 Julius Stern, "Reminiscences of a Studio Manager, Part II," *Moving Picture World*, June 12, 1915, p.1763
25 "Henry M. Lehrman," *Los Angeles Times,* p.VI56
26 Gene Fowler, *Father Goose: The Story of Mack Sennett*, p.125
27 *Moving Picture World,* March 16, 1912, p.963
28 Jack Cohn, "Fourteenth Street," *The Film Daily,* February 28, 1926, p.57
29 "Henry M. Lehrman," *Los Angeles Times*
30 Anthony Slide, *Aspects of American Film History Prior to 1920* (Metuchen, New Jersey: The Scarecrow Press, Inc., 1978), p.53
31 "Fox to Produce Comedies," *Motography*, November 4, 1916, p.1021

Chapter 3: Mack Sennett and the Keystone Film Company: Creditless Where Credit is Due

1   Theodore Dreiser, "The Best Motion Picture Interview Ever Written"
2   Victor Heerman interviews by Kalton C. Lahue on February 21, 1969, and Sam Gill on July 22, 1967 and December 3, 1971
3   *Ibid.*
4   "Doings at Los Angeles," *Moving Picture World,* September 21, 1912, p.1160
5   George Blaisdell, "Pacific Coast Number: Mecca of the Motion Picture," *Moving Picture World,* July 10, 1915, p.217

6   "Doings at Los Angeles," *Moving Picture World,* October 19, 1912, p.234

7   Ernest A. Dench, "For the Photo-Play Writer," *Cinema News and Property Gazette*, January 15, 1913, p.33

8   "K-B Active," *Moving Picture World,* February 15, 1913, p.668

9   Ad G. Waddell, "With the Photoplayers," *Los Angeles Times,* March 7, 1913, p.III4

10 Excerpts from interviews with Beatrice Van by Sam Gill, at her home in Manhattan Beach, California, conducted in 1978 on July 8 and 22, August 5, 12, and 26, September 9 and 23, October 14 and 28, and November 11.

11 *Ibid.*

12 *Moving Picture World,* April 26, 1913, p.381

13 *Moving Picture World,* May 3, 1913, p.489

14 *Photoplay*, May 1923, p.34.

15 *Moving Picture World,* April 26, 1913, p.381

16 Other uses of animals in Lehrman-directed films include the trained Boston bulldogs of *Help! Help! Hydrophobia!*, the two bears giving chase in *Mother's Boy*, and the "fractious" goose of *A Rural Demon.*

17 Ray W. Frohman, "Roscoe Arbuckle, Mountain of Flesh, Achieves Fame," *Morning Oregonian*, April 4, 1920, page unknown

18 Excerpts from interviews with Beatrice Van by Sam Gill, conducted on ten Saturdays during the period July 8 through November 11, 1978

19 *Ibid.*

20 *Ibid.*

21 *Ibid.*

22 Sam Gill, "Little Billy Jacobs Grows Up," *Shadowland*, Vol. 1 No. 1., p.12

23 Clarke Irvine, "Little Billy," *Motion Picture Magazine*, September 1915, pp.91-92

24 "Love and Rubbish," *Moving Picture World,* July 19, 1913, p.321

25 "Isch Ga Bibble," *Motion Picture News,* January 31, 1914, p.28.

26 "Another Keystone Kid Production," *Motography*, March 21, 1914, p.200.

27 "Thornby With Keystone," *New York Dramatic Mirror*, January 14, 1914, p.62

28 "This Listens Good," *New York Clipper*, September 6, 1913, p.13

29 "The Firebugs," *Moving Picture World,* August 23, 1913

30 Mack Sennett and Cameron Shipp, *King of Comedy*, pp.108-109.

31 "Auto Registrations," *San Francisco Call*, September 16, 1913, p.8

32 Mack Sennett and Cameron Shipp, *King of Comedy*, pp.107-108, 147

33 Excerpts from interviews with Beatrice Van by Sam Gill, conducted on ten Saturdays during the period July 8 through November 11, 1978

34 *Ibid.*

35 Mack Sennett and Cameron Shipp, *King of Comedy*, p.148

36 Terry Ramsaye, *A Million and One Nights*, p 645

37 David Robinson, *Chaplin: His Life and Art* (New York: McGraw-Hill Book Company, 1985), pp.101-102

38 Harry C. Carr, "Charlie Chaplin's Story, Part II," *Photoplay*, August 1915, p.44

39 Mlle. Chic, "The Story of the L-Ko Head, H. Pathé Lehrmann," p.22

40 Charles Chaplin, *My Autobiography* (New York: Simon and Schuster, 1964), p.138

41 David Robinson, *Chaplin: His Life and Art*, pp.97-98. Chaplin's August 1913 letter to brother Sid regarding the contract is reproduced here.

42. Telegram from the NYMPC to Sennett dated January 13, 1914, as posted by historian Chris Snowden at *www.silentcomedymafia.com* on June 4, 2009.
43. Charles Chaplin, *Charlie Chaplin's Own Story* (Indianapolis: The Bobbs-Merrill Company, 1916), p.200
44. Bo Berglund, "The Day the Tramp Was Born," *Sight and Sound*, Spring 1989, Vol. 58, No. 2, p.110. Berglund quotes from Robert Florey's interview with Henry Lehrman
45. "Studio and Exchange Notes," *Reel Life*, January 24, 1914, p.2
46. Charles Chaplin, *My Autobiography*, pp.143-144
47. "Making a Living," *Moving Picture World*, February 7, 1914, p.678
48. Bo Berglund, "The Day the Tramp Was Born"
49. *Ibid.*
50. Gene Fowler, *Father Goose: The Story of Mack Sennett*, pp.241-242
51. Harry C. Carr, "Charlie Chaplin's Story, Part III," *Photoplay*, September 1915, p.108. Carr said his piece was based on interviews with Chaplin.
52. Mary Pickford interviewed by Tony Thomas, CBC Radio, May 25, 1959.
53. Ann Leslie, "Memories of Old Hollywood," *The Australian Women's Weekly*, March 4, 1970, p.17
54. "In and Out of Los Angeles Studios," *Motion Picture News*, November 14, 1914, p.35.
55. Fred J. Balshofer and Arthur C. Miller, *One Reel a Week* (University of California Press, 1967), p.81
56. Rob Mack, "Clips from the Silent Days," *The Press-Courier*, September 25, 1965, p.5
57. Mlle. Chic, "The Story of the L-Ko Head, H. Pathé Lehrmann," p.22.
58. "Christmas Dinner Dance," *Motography*, January 10, 1914, p.29
59. Gene Fowler, *Father Goose: The Story of Mack Sennett*, pp.223-224.
60. Mack Sennett and Cameron Shipp, *King of Comedy*, p.164
61. Terry Ramsaye, *A Million and One Nights*, p 543

Chapter 4: The Sterling Motion Picture Corporation: The Grass is Always Greener

1. Kalton C. Lahue and Terry Brewer, *Kops and Custards: the Legend of Keystone Films* (University of Oklahoma Press, 1968), p.20
2. Fred J. Balshofer and Arthur C. Miller, *One Reel a Week*, p.92
3. *Ibid.*, pp.108-109. Balshofer said that he included Chaplin among the proposed leads, but that Laemmle nixed the suggestion on the grounds that Chaplin was not sufficiently important or popular. Negotiations with Laemmle took place during the first two weeks of February 1914, and Chaplin's first film for Keystone (*Making a Living*) was released on February 2, so unless Balshofer was sold on Chaplin's comedic abilities prior to its release or on the basis of his performance in this one film, it seems unlikely that Chaplin would have been considered by either.
4. Mack Sennett and Cameron Shipp, *King of Comedy*, p.97
5. Roberta Courtlandt, "Chats With the Players: Ford Sterling, of the Universal Company," *Motion Picture Magazine*, December 1914, pp.115-116
6. Sara Redway, "Passing of the Brown Derby," *Motion Picture Classic*, pp.30-31
7. Mack Sennett and Cameron Shipp, *King of Comedy*, pp.148-149
8. *Ibid.*, pp.150-151
9. "Ford Sterling's Affidavit," *Universal Weekly*, March 21, 1914, inside front cover.
10. "Another Smashing Universal Scoop!," *New York Dramatic Mirror*, February 25, 1914, p.42
11. "Sterling to Universal," *New York Dramatic Mirror*, February 25, 1914, p.30.
12. "Sennett to Act," *New York Dramatic Mirror*, March 4, 1914, p.30

13 "Former Newsboy of Constitution Now Moving Picture Director," *The Constitution*, February 13, 1915, p.7; *Motion Picture Studio Directory and Trade Annual*," October 21, 1916, p.251

14 David N. Bruskin, *The White Brothers: Jack, Jules, & Sam White* (The Directors Guild of America & The Scarecrow Press, Metuchen, NJ, 1990), p.53

15 *Ibid.*, pp.54-55, 97. Given White's sketchy description of the plot, it is impossible to connect this to any of the films Lehrman and Sterling worked on together at the new studio, so it is very possible that his aging memory was playing tricks on him.

16 "Another Smashing Universal Scoop!," *Universal Weekly*, February 28, 1914, p.3.

17 "All of These 'Keystone' Comedy Company Stars Now Join the Universal Staff!," *Moving Picture World*, February 28, 1914, pp.1050-1051.

18 "Another Smashing Universal Scoop!", pp.3-4

19 Mack Sennett and Cameron Shipp, *King of Comedy*, p.255

20 *Ibid.*, p.67.

21 "President Laemmle at the Coast," *Moving Picture World*, February 28, 1914, p.1097.

22 "Ford Sterling Contract Filmed," *Universal Weekly*, March 14, 1914, p.4

23 "New Idea in Censorship," *New York Dramatic Mirror*, March 18, 1914, p.32

24 "Incorporations," *Los Angeles Times*, March 5, 1914, p.II16.

25 In the article "News from Coast Colony," *New York Dramatic Mirror*, February 4, 1914, p.33, the writer claimed that Thornby too was "a stockholder and officer of the corporation," but this assertion has not been found elsewhere. It went on to say that Thornby would teach film acting at a newly organized school at the studio…for tykes, no doubt.

26 Robert Grau, *The Theatre of Science: A Volume of Progress and Achievement in the Motion Picture Industry* (Broadway Publishing Company, New York, 1914), pp.50-51.

27 "Universal Wants Another Name," *Moving Picture World*, March 7, 1914, p.1241. This was an old public relations approach of Laemmle's, who first used it in mid-1909 while seeking a classier name for his Yankee Film Company. The Independent Moving Pictures Co. of America, or "IMP," was the winner, accompanied by a trademark design with the "IMP" legend that was used in the years that followed.

28 "Balshofer Deluged With Suggested Names for New Company," *Universal Weekly*, March 21, 1914, p.9

29 "'Sterling' Name Chosen for New Universal Comedies," *Universal Weekly*, April 4, 1914, p.9.

30 Gene Fowler, *Father Goose: The Story of Mack Sennett*, pp.243-244

31 *Moving Picture World*, July 10, 1915, p.217

32 Fred J. Balshofer and Arthur C. Miller, *One Reel a Week*, p.110.

33 Bert C. Smith, "Ralph Enters Vanderbilt," *Los Angeles Times*, February 6, 1914, p.III1

34 "Goode Skids Near Death," *Los Angeles Times*, February 15, 1914, p.VII7

35 For the record, driver Ralph DePalma won his second Vanderbilt Cup, defeating chief opponent Barney Oldfield by less than a minute. Edwin Pullen won the International Grand Prix race two days later, and Guy Ball — 40 miles behind — came in second. Sennett, it should be added, had his Fiat in the two races as well, driven by Dave Lewis and providing footage for Mabel Normand's *Mabel at the Wheel*.

36 Fichtenberg, of Fichtenberg Amusement Enterprises of New Orleans, controlled the Southwest's largest theater chain.

37 *Albany Evening Journal*, April 3, 1914, p.8. Carter's name is given as "Lon" in this article as reported earlier in Universal Weekly, but more widely and subsequently as "Lou" and "Lew" elsewhere.

38 A. Danson Michell, "Love and Vengeance," *Motion Picture News*, April 18, 1914, p.46

39 Lehrman, dressed in civilian garb in another role, sits on the bleacher to her right, while Paul Jacobs and a little girl both sit on the lap of a fellow sitting behind her.

40 *Moving Picture World* promotional ad, April 18, 1914, pp.300-301.

41 "Love and Vengeance," *New York Dramatic Mirror*, April 29, 1914, p.39

42 George Blaisdell, "Love and Vengeance," *Moving Picture World,* April 18, 1914, p.341.

43 "The Pick of the Programmes: What We Think of Them," *Bioscope*, May 14, 1914, p.767

44 "Emma Clifton," *Moving Picture World,* December 12, 1914, p.1532

45 George Blaisdell, "Love and Vengeance"

46 "Klaw & Erlanger Secure Temporary Injunction Against Universal Film Mfg. Co. — Suit Over 'Fatal Wedding'," *New York Clipper*, May 2, 1914, p.14

47 "Philadelphia Now Has a Fifty-Cent House," *Motion Picture News,* May 9, 1914, p.20

48 "Lasky Sues Eastman," *The Billboard*, May 2, 1914, p.58

49 "Comments on the Films," *Moving Picture World,* May 2, 1914, p.674

50 "Billy Jacobs," *Moving Picture World,* January 30, 1915, p.678

51 "Lehrman Unique in Producing Methods," *Universal Weekly*, April 18, 1914, p.2

52 *Ibid.*, p.2

53 "Doings at Los Angeles," *Moving Picture World,* April 25, 1914, p.529

54 "Papa's Boy," *Motion Picture News,* May 16, 1914, p.56

55 Uncredited review from a Los Angeles paper, quoted in *Motion Picture Magazine*, October 1915, p.170

56 "Woods Heads Authors' League," *New York Dramatic Mirror*, March 25, 1914, p.31

57 "Neighbors," *Motion Picture News,* May 16, 1914, p.56

58 "Doings at Los Angeles," *Moving Picture World,* April 25, 1914, p.529; "Sterling Does Double Role On Baseball Diamond," *Universal Weekly*, June 6, 1914, p.8

59 *Motion Picture News,* March 21, 1914, p.57; "Photoplay Authors' League Pacific Coast Colony," *New York Dramatic Mirror*, June 10, 1914, p.39

60 *Motion Picture Studio Directory and Trade Annual*, October 21, 1916, p.144. Other cameramen that worked for Sterling during its brief existence included W.F. Adler and H.B. Harris ("Motion Picture Cameramen's Organizations in America," *The International Photographer*, October 1933, p.3).

61 "Duelists Plunge From Bridge Sixty Feet High," *Universal Weekly*, May 23, 1914, p.12

62 "Hearts and Swords," *New York Dramatic Mirror*, May 20, 1914, p.3.

63 "The Pick of the Programmes," *Bioscope*, June 25, 1914, p.1361

64 "Hearts and Swords," *Moving Picture World,* May 30, 1914, p.1262

65 "Lehrman Out of Sterling Company," *New York Dramatic Mirror*, May 20, 1914, page unknown.

66 Fred J. Balshofer and Arthur C. Miller, *One Reel a Week*, pp.111-112

67 Gene Fowler, *Father Goose: The Story of Mack Sennett*, p.244

68 "Doings at Los Angeles," *Moving Picture World,* May 23, 1914, p.1103

Chapter 5: L-KO Komedy Kompany: Lehrman's Baby

1 "Newsy Week on the Coast," *New York Dramatic Mirror*, May 27, 1914, p.27

2 "In and Out of Los Angeles Studios," *Motion Picture News,* August 8, 1914, p.59

3 "H. Pathé Lehrman," *Universal Weekly*, June 27, 1914, p.10

4 *Printers' Ink*, September 24, 1902, p.34

5 "Film Show Raided at Park Theatre," *New York Times,* December 20, 1913, p.1

6 "Film Flashes," *Variety,* August 7, 1914, p.16

7 *Ibid.*

8 "Chicago Letter," *Moving Picture News*, October 28, 1911, p.26 and February 10, 1912, p.22

9   "Lehrman Starts Production Work," *Moving Picture World,* August 15, 1914, p.946

10 "Brevities of the Business," *Motography,* July 12, 1913, p.35

11 *Universal Weekly,* August 29, 1914, p.8

12 "Sam Behrendt Funeral Set," *Los Angeles Times,* October 11, 1940, p.A3

13 Gene Fowler, *Father Goose: The Story of Mack Sennett,* p.244

14 Excerpts from interviews with Beatrice Van by Sam Gill, conducted on ten Saturdays during the period July 8 through November 11, 1978

15 "Pacific Coast News," *New York Morning Telegraph,* August 2, 1914, page unknown

16 *Thirteenth Census of the United States: 1910*

17 *Motion Picture News,* January 29, 1916, p.75

18 Clarke Irvine, "Doings at Los Angeles," *Moving Picture World,* August 29, 1914, p.1230

19 "Many Jail Terms for Motorists," *Los Angeles Times,* December 18, 1915, p.II1

20 David Robinson, *Chaplin: His Life and Art,* p.175

21 Much of Ritchie's early life has been reconstructed by Lisa Robins, a surviving great grandniece. By his own account, he joined his mother's act in 1887 rather than 1888.

22 "Billie Ritchie's Make-up Is All His Own," *Universal Weekly,* March 20, 1915, p.12

23 J.P.Gallagher, *Fred Karno: Master of Mirth and Tears* (London: Robert Hale & Company, 1971). pp.23-28, 35, 41-45

24 Their daughter Wyn was born on December 23, 1900.

25 "American Comedies and 'David Garrick'," *Brooklyn Daily Eagle,* November 21, 1905, p.13

26 Frank Cullen, *Vaudeville, Old and New: An Encyclopedia of Variety Performers in America, Volume 1* (New York: Routledge, 2004), p.510. Hill, a founding member of what came to be known as the Columbia Wheel, claimed that he was the first to organize a circuit of bookings that included all of the big cities and towns in rotation. One troupe would follow another throughout the circuit, keeping the theaters full and the troupes continuously employed.

27 *The Park* family theatre program for *Around the Clock,* performances commencing September 17, 1906.

28 According to Lisa Robins, Ritchie's great grandniece, her name at birth was Francis Winifred Kirby. Winifred eventually dropped her surname and shuffled the remaining names for her life on stage.

29 *Universal Weekly,* August 29, 1914, p.8

30 A doubtful influence, since Syd Chaplin's first film would not premiere for another month, and Chaplin did not join Fred Karno's troupe until a year after Ritchie had departed for the U.S. back in 1905.

31 Peter Milne, "For the Love of Mike and Rosie," *Motion Picture News,* April 8, 1916, p.2070

32 *Universal Weekly,* October 3, 1914, p.4

33 Peter Milne, "Love and Surgery," *Motion Picture News,* October 31, 1914, p.48

34 Half-page ad in *New York Dramatic Mirror,* May 20, 1914, p.35

35 J. Stuart Blackton had appeared as "Happy" in a series of shorts for Edison as far back as 1900, eventually moving over to Biograph for the remainder of the series' eleven film, four year run.

36 "Working on 'Happy Hooligan'," *New York Dramatic Mirror,* June 17, 1914, p.29

37 "The Lox Club Outing," *New York Clipper,* June 27, 1914, p.9

38 "The Lox Club Outing," *Billboard,* June 27, 1914, p.13

39 "To Open Nonpareil Exchanges," *New York Dramatic Mirror,* July 1, 1914, p.22

40 Based on the Rays' popular stage play, planned filming of *A Hot Old Time* kept appearing in *Variety*'s pages through the better part of 1915, alternately announced as an upcoming two-, six-, and one-reel comedy to be written by Gus Hill and directed by Paul Arlington. By October, however, the Rays denied any association with Nonpareil. ("Denial," *Variety,* October 8, 1915, p.28)

41 "Happy Hooligan in Court," *Moving Picture World,* November 27, 1915, p.1681

42 Lehrman's name was spelled "Lehrmann" in the opening credits, and this alternate variation of spelling would continue to crop up in articles and reviews for years to come.

43 *Universal Weekly*, December 5, 1914, p.24 and January 2, 1915, p.36

44 "Plot Changed to Fit Accidents," *Universal Weekly*, October 17, 1914, p.9; "No Fatal Results in Auto Accident," *Motion Picture News,* October 17, 1914, p.40

45 "More Universal Comedies," *Motography*, August 3, 1914, p.236

46 "Film Flashes," *Variety,* August 7, 1914, p.16

47 Victor Heerman interviews by Kalton C. Lahue on February 21, 1969, and Sam Gill on July 22, 1967 and December 3, 1971

48 *Ibid.*

49 *Ibid.*

50 Mlle. Chic, "Dancing into Pictures From Texas to the L-Ko," *Universal Weekly*, December 18, 1915, page unknown

51 *Variety,* May 16, 1913, p.25

52 "Film Flashes," *Variety,* August 7, 1914, p.16

53 *New York Clipper*, May 30, 1914, p.9

54 Mary Fuller, "What Thanksgiving is For," *Universal Weekly*, November 21, 1914, p.8

55 "The Players from Ocean to Ocean," *Photoplay*, August 1915, p.110

56 Victor Heerman interviews by Kalton C. Lahue on February 21, 1969, and Sam Gill on July 22, 1967 and December 3, 1971

57 Clarke Irvine, "Doings at Los Angeles," *Moving Picture World,* November 28, 1914, p.1217

58 "Notes of the Trade," *Moving Picture World,* April 3, 1915, p.89

59 Clarke Irvine, "Doings at Los Angeles," *Moving Picture World,* November 14, 1914, p.911

60 Lehrman's comments to Darryl Zanuck, script analysis for *Hollywood Cavalcade*, December 13, 1938

61 David Bruskin, *The White Brothers: Jack, Jules, & Sam White*, pp.55-57, 97

62 Capt. "Jack" Poland, " The Static Club," *Moving Picture World,* July 10, 1915, pp.272-273

63 *Moving Picture World,* August 28, 1915, p.1644. Other cameramen who worked for L-Ko during 1915 included Allen M. Davey and K.D. Gray ("Motion Picture Cameramen's Organizations in America," *The International Photographer*, October 1933, p.3)

64 "Home of L-KO," *Moving Picture World,* July 10, 1915, p.232

65 *Motion Picture Studio Directory & Trade Annual*, 1921

66 Victor Heerman interviews by Kalton C. Lahue on February 21, 1969, and Sam Gill on July 22, 1967 and December 3, 1971

67 *Motion Picture News,* December 12, 1914, p.49

68 *Moving Picture World,* December 12, 1914, p.1524

69 *Motography*, December 5, 1914, p.793

70 *Motion Picture News,* December 19, 1914, p.84. Perhaps the documentary-like scenes were included as part of Lehrman's goal to include a "combination of educational features that will blend and harmonize with comedy"?

71 *Moving Picture World,* December 19, 1914, p.1681

72 "Millionaire is Sentenced to Jail Term," *Los Angeles Herald*, October 3, 1914, p.2

73 "Fortune Can't Buy Him Freedom," *Los Angeles Times,* October 3, 1914, p.II1

74 "Wealthy Auto Speeder is Sentenced to Jail," *Middlebury Register*, October 16, 1914, p.4

75 "Thirty Days His Medicine," *Los Angeles Times,* October 4, 1914, p.II9

76 "Gets Another Chance," *Los Angeles Times*, November 17, 1914, p.II5

77 Clarke Irvine, "Doings at Los Angeles," *Moving Picture World,* October 31, 1914, p.622

78 "Hard Cash Opens Jail for Canine," *Los Angeles Times,* October 6, 1914, p.19

79 *Motion Picture News,* January 2, 1915, p.50

80 "Universal's Challenge on L-KO Comedies!," *Universal Weekly*, December 5, 1914, p.5

81 "From Landscape Artist to Comedian," *Universal Weekly,* February 20, 1915, p.12

82 Mlle. Chic, "A Serious Comedienne," *Moving Picture Weekly*, December 11, 1915, page unknown

83 "The Biggest Man on Broadway!," *Universal Weekly*, January 30, 1915, inside cover

84 "Henry M. Lehrman," *Los Angeles Times,* January 1, 1915, p.VI56

85 J.C. Jessen, "In and Out of West Coast Studios," *Motion Picture News,* April 8, 1916, p.2044

86 "Show Reviews," *Variety,* January 23, 1915, p.21

87 "Billie Ritchie in 'After Her Millions'," *Universal Weekly*, January 23, 1915, p.19

88 *Moving Picture World,* February 6, 1915, p.829

89 "Director Leonard Ill," *New York Dramatic Mirror*, December 30, 1914, p.22

90 *Motography*, March 13, 1915, p.412

91 "Pacific Coast News," *New York Telegraph*, February 7, 1915, page unknown

92 Grace Kingsley, "At the Stage Door," *Los Angeles Times,* December 21, 1914, p.III4

93 "Pacific Coast News," *New York Telegraph*, May 16, 1915, page unknown

94 Victor Heerman interviews by Kalton C. Lahue on February 21, 1969, and Sam Gill on July 22, 1967 and December 3, 1971

95 "Mutual Benefit Ass'n," *Variety,* February 2, 1915, p.32

96 G.P.von Harleman and Clarke Irvine, "News of Los Angeles and Vicinity: The Censorship Question," *Moving Picture World,* February 26, 1916, p.1284

97 *Motography*, September 25, 1925, p.646

98 "Billie Ritchie Now at Lumberg," *Utica Observer*, April 23, 1914, p.8

99 "Billie Ritchie, the Original 'Drunk'," *Moving Picture World,* February 13, 1915, p.991

100 "Billie Ritchie's Make-up Is All His Own," pp.12, 28

101 "Billie Ritchie, Charles Chaplin or Billie Reeves?," *Syracuse Journal*, April 26, 1915, p.12

102 Abel Green and Joe Laurie, Jr., *Show Biz from Vaude to Video* (New York: Henry Holt and Company, 1951), p.47

103 "Answer Department," *Motion Picture Magazine*, November 1915, p.150

104 "Scars and Stripes Forever," *New York Clipper*, April 1, 1916, p.35

105 "Universal City Opened," *Moving Picture World,* March 27, 1915, p.1908

106 "Pacific Coast News," *New York Telegraph*, March 14, 1915, page unknown

107 Letter from Abe Gresenschlag, Mgr., Leland Theatre, Chicago, Illinois to *Universal Weekly*, April 3, 1915, p.31

108 *Motion Picture News,* June 5, 1915, p.13

109 *Motography*, June 5, 1915, p.952

110 "Ritchie Cures Deaf and Dumb Soldier," *Moving Picture Weekly*, September 25, 1915, pp.25, 44. Reprint of the article "The Dumb Soldier Who Spoke" that originally appeared in the August 31, 1915 edition of the London *Evening News and Evening Mail*

111 "Ritchie Excels Chaplin," *Universal Weekly*, May 29, 1915, p.33

112 "George Universal Stevenson Back," *Moving Picture World,* August 21, 1915, p.1303

113 "American Film in London," *Variety,* November 25, 1915, p.21

114 "The Young Picturegoer," *Pictures and the Picturegoer*, July 10, 1915, p.282

115 *Motion Picture News,* May 22, 1915, p.75

116 Peter Pepper, "A Confirmed Optimist — Gene Rogers," *Moving Picture Weekly,* March 25, 1916, p.20

117 *Motion Picture News,* September 11, 1915, p.90

118 "Wants Taxi; Gets a Patrol Wagon," *Los Angeles Times,* June 29, 1915, p.I9

119 "Many Jail Terms for Motorists," *Los Angeles Times,* December 18, 1915, p.II1

120 *Moving Picture World,* December 25, 1915, p.2374

121 *Motography,* March 27, 1915, p.508

122 *Moving Picture World,* April 17, 1915, p.394

123 *Motion Picture News,* July 10, 1915, p.79

124 *Motion Picture News,* August 21, 1915, p.91

125 J.C. Jessen, "In and Out of Los Angeles Studios," *Motion Picture News,* July 3, 1915, p.47

126 *Moving Picture World,* September 18, 1915, p.2012

127 "American Film in London," p.21

128 "Home of L-KO," p.232

129 *Motion Picture News,* June 6, 1914, p.57

130 "Suing Universal," *Variety,* January 16, 1915, p.26

131 "Bernstein is Out," *New York Dramatic Mirror,* April 7, 1915, p.2

132 Victor Heerman interviews by Kalton C. Lahue on February 21, 1969, and Sam Gill on July 22, 1967 and December 3, 1971

133 *Ibid.*

134 "Universal Program Changed," *Moving Picture World,* July 3, 1915, p.72

135 Victor Heerman interviews by Kalton C. Lahue on February 21, 1969, and Sam Gill on July 22, 1967 and December 3, 1971

136 "Doings at Los Angeles," *Moving Picture World,* April 10, 1915, p.221

137 "Live News of the Week," *Motion Picture News,* June 20, 1914, p.45

138 Kirkland's first directorial assignment was the one-reel *In the Claws of the Dragon* with Wallace Reid.

139 "Charles J. Winninger," *Moving Picture World,* June 26, 1915, p.2103

140 Linda Arvidson Griffith, pp.237-238

141 J.C. Jessen, "In and Out of Los Angeles Studios," *Motion Picture News,* May 22, 1915, p.52

142 "Doings at Los Angeles," *Moving Picture World,* July 17, 1915, p.73

143 Co-stars Lehrman and Henry Bergman were joined by a fellow named Ted Mulford. Mulford was in actuality actor Joseph Henabery, appearing here under his vaudeville stage name. Henabery, perhaps best known for his role as Abraham Lincoln in D.W. Griffith's *The Birth of a Nation*, would soon abandon acting for a long career as a director ("At the Temple," *Daily East Oregonian*, November 27, 1915, p.8). In his autobiography, *Before, In and After Hollywood* (Lanham, MD: Scarecrow Press, Inc., 1997) Henabery makes no mention of appearing in vaudeville or of the Mulford pseudonym, although he does cite Universal as his first employer in the film industry. He only mentions working for director Otis Turner, however.

144 "Home of L-KO," p.232

145 J.C. Jessen, "In and Out of Los Angeles Studios," *Motion Picture News,* September 18, 1915, p.67

146 Sam Gill, "Little Billy Jacobs Grows Up," p.12.

147 *New York Telegraph,* January 9, 1916, page unknown

148 "Home of L-KO," p.232

149 *Motion Picture News,* April 1, 1916, p.1894

ENDNOTES

150 "L-Ko Appoints a Special Representative," *Moving Picture Weekly*, October 30, 1915, p.38

151 Victor Heerman interviews by Kalton C. Lahue on February 21, 1969, and Sam Gill on July 22, 1967 and December 3, 1971

152 "A Censored Play," *Film Fun*, January 1916, page unknown

153 *Moving Picture World*, February 12, 1916, p.979

154 Linda Arvidson Griffith, p.238

155 "All About Pacific Coast Players," *New York Clipper*, April 8, 1916, p.36

156 "Space for Exposition Snapped Up by Companies," *Motion Picture News*, April 22, 1916, p.2319

157 *Motion Picture News*, February 19, 1916, p.1033

158 *Moving Picture World*, February 26, 1916, p.1319

159 A print of this film is held by the EYE Filmmuseum.

160 "Billie Ritchie Scorns the Use of a Double," *Moving Picture Weekly*, July 1, 1916, p.20

161 J.C. Jessen, "In and Out of West Coast Studios," *Motion Picture News*, November 13, 1915, p.70

162 *Moving Picture Weekly*, March 11, 1916, p.20

163 *Moving Picture World*, March 25, 1916, p.2032

164 *Motion Picture News*, March 18, 1916, p.1626

165 G.P. von Harleman and Clarke Irvine, "News of Los Angles and Vicinity," *Moving Picture World*, January 15, 1916, pp.408-409

166 "What Coast Companies Spend," *New York Telegraph*, August 6, 1916, page unknown

167 "Producers Forgive Los Angeles," *Motography*, January 29, 1916, pp.231-233

168 *Federal Motion Picture Commission Hearings Before the Committee on Education, House of Representatives Sixty-Fourth Congress, First Session on H.R. 456*, January 13-15, 18-19, 1916, p.232, on file at the University of Michigan Library

169 Vern L. Bullough and Bonnie Bullough, *Human Sexuality* (New York: Taylor & Francis, 1994), p.100

170 "Edwards Will Direct Hamilton and Duncan for Kalem," *Motion Picture News*, March 25, 1916, p.1757

171 "Two Directors for Universal Studios," *Motion Picture News*, March 4, 1916, p.1291

172 "Picture Play Reports," *New York Clipper*, April 22, 1916, p.37

173 "Former Keystone Director With Local Company," *Moving Picture World*, April 8, 1916, p.306

174 Anthony Slide, *Aspects of American Film History Prior to 1920*, p.54

175 *Ibid*.

176 Victor Heerman interviews by Kalton C. Lahue on February 21, 1969, and Sam Gill on July 22, 1967 and December 3, 1971

177 *Motion Picture News*, July 1, 1916, p.4061

178 "Kipling Verse Aids Sennett," *Motion Picture News*, March 25, 1916, p.1744

179 Peter Milne, *Motion Picture News*, July 8, 1916, p.111

180 Peter Milne, *Motion Picture News*, May 20, 1916, p.3103

181 Peter Milne, *Motion Picture News*, April 8, 1916, p.2070

182 "For The Love of Mike and Rosie" synopsis, *Moving Picture Weekly*, April 1, 1916, p.23

183 Peter Milne, *Motion Picture News*, April 8, 1916, p.2070

184 "Notice," *Moving Picture Weekly*, March 18, 1916, p.43

185 "To Have a Male Fashion Show" and "Hear Ye All, Here's Call to Clothes," *Los Angeles Times*, September 25, 1916, p.I3

186 The film was copyrighted, promoted, and reviewed pre-release as *Gertie's Gasoline Glide*, undergoing a last-minute title change a mere two weeks before its release.

187 According to Denise Lowe's *An Encyclopedic Dictionary of Women in Early American Films: 1895-1930* (New York: Routledge, 2014), p.1938, Myers had one previous uncredited bit as part of a crowd scene in a 1915 film titled *Georgia Pearce*. There is little to be found about this film.

188 Anthony Slide, "Silent Stars Speak," *Films in Review*, March 1980, Vol. XXXI, No. 3, p.135

189 "Pegging Away at Ninth 'Ring'," *Motion Picture News*, July 1, 1916, p.4060

190 "Grace Cunard Married to Joe Moore," *Moving Picture World*, February 10, 1917, p.854

191 "Dance to Decide Ownership of Cup," *Los Angeles Herald*, August 25, 1915, p.8

192 "Carl Laemmle Returns East," *Moving Picture World*, February 12, 1916, p.957

193 "Laemmle Guest of Davis," *Motography*, February 5, 1915, p.310

194 "Actors' Fund Feast Shows Coast No Tightwad Locale," *Motion Picture News*, March 25, 1916, p.1734

195 "Movie Stars to Stage Auto Race," *Los Angeles Times*, May 7, 1916, p.VI13

196 "Movie Race Benefit," *Motor Age*, June 8, 1916, p.20

197 G.P.von Harleman and Clarke Irvine, "Film Stars in Unique Stunts at Ascot Races," *Moving Picture World*, June 17, 1916, pp.2037-2038

198 Elizabeth Sears, "Who Wore Them First?," *Film Fun*, April 1916, No. 325, p.7

199 "Author Van Loan Gets One Hundred Dollars a Word," *Motion Picture News*, June 17, 1916, p.3762. No mention was made at this time of the fact that Universal had commissioned Van Loan to write a "six or seven reeled travesty" under this title back in September 1915 to be filmed by either Victor or Nestor ("To Travesty 'Nation'," *Variety*, September 17, 1915, p.22). Thanhauser's Falstaff Comedies used "The Mirth of a Nation" as their motto around that same time, prompting Van Loan to seek damages for copyright infringement ("Van Loan After Users of 'Mirth of a Nation' Title," *Motion Picture News*, January 1, 1916, p.53). None of this got in the way of some fast buck operators cobbling together footage from a number of Chaplin's Keystone comedies and releasing the disjointed, patchwork six-reel *Mirth of a Nation* in April 1916. All this before Lehrman legally acquired the title for a film that was never made by him. To further confuse matters, Van Loan himself in his autobiography (*How I Did It*, Los Angeles: The Whittingham Press, 1922, p.112) claimed that he sold the title to Julius Stern for $250.

200 "Henry Lehrman Sells Interest in L-Ko," *Motion Picture News*, July 22, 1916, p.410

201 Kalton C. Lahue and Sam Gill, p.318. In an email to co-author Gill, he responded "I sure didn't remember such a quote about Henry Lehrman and Carl Laemmle. That definitely did **NOT** come from me, and if I had spotted it, I would have suggested to Kal we drop it." The comment, it would appear, was Lahue's.

202 "Report a New Producing Company," *Moving Picture World*, May 20, 1916, p.1372

203 "Begin Production on Mabel Normand Story," *Motion Picture News*, May 20, 1916, p.3051; "Greater Number of Eastern 'U' Players Now in the West," *Motion Picture News*, June 24, 1916, p.3921

204 "Universal Concentrates in West," *Moving Picture World*, June 10, 1916, p.1862

205 "Removal of 'U' Studios to West Definitely Decided," *Motion Picture News*, June 10, 1916, p.3585

206 "Greater Number of Eastern 'U' Players Now in the West," p.3921

207 "Mr. Stern's Honeymoon," *New York Telegraph*, May 14, 1916, page unknown

208 *Moving Picture World*, May 27, 1916, p.1517

209 "L-Ko Comedy Companies Greet Stern," *Motion Picture News*, July 15, 1916, p.241

210 "Lehrmann Returns to Coast," *Moving Picture World*, December 4, 1915, p.1811

Chapter 6: Foxfilm and Sunshine Comedies: From Rags to Riches

1 "Lehrman Starts Company," *New York Telegraph*, August 27, 1917, page unknown

2 *New York Telegraph*, July 16, 1916, page unknown

3 According to Norman Taurog, there was talk of Lehrman returning to Sennett before the Fox announcement was made. Interview with Norman Taurog by Sam Gill, at Taurog's Beverly Hills home, August 17, 1966

4   "Fox to Produce Comedies," *Motography*, November 4, 1916, p.1021

5   "Lehrman's Comedies," *New York Telegraph*, October 29, 1916, page unknown; Mel Ody, "Screenshine," *Motography*, November 11, 1916, p.1062; Mosgrove Colwell, "Patter from the Pacific," *Motion Picture Magazine*, February 1917, p.13

6   "Fox Film Comedies," *Moving Picture World*, December 9, 1916, p.1481

7   "Tom Mix Will Make Foxfilm Comedies," *Motography*, January 6, 1917, p.27

8   J.C. Jessen, "In and Out of the West Coast Studios," *Motion Picture News*, December 16, 1916, p.3817

9   The final release data is mired in confusion, since earlier release dates of February 26, March 3, and March 5 were all previously announced in the trades, then delayed. The film's title, it would seem, was Lehrman's playful sendup of 1915's Harold Lockwood drama *The House of a Thousand Scandals*.

10 During his brief period of inactivity, Ritchie had been contacted by a British group to open a studio in Canada to make comedies; he turned them down. ("Mystery," *Motography*, September 30, 1916, p.766) Four days after the release of *The House of Terrible Scandals*, Vim Comedies released the one-reel *Nellie's Nifty Necklace* with Billie Ritchie starring. This film had been advertised as an upcoming L-Ko release six months earlier in the September 30, 1916 issue of *Moving Picture World* ("Dan Russell, L-Ko LaughGetter" ad, p.2057). How the L-Ko production ended up in Vim's hands is open for conjecture, the details of which will probably never be known.

11 "Sidelights of the Stage and Screen," *Amarillo Globe*, July 25, 1928, p.9

12 J.H. Walraven, "The Perils of Comedy," *Photo-Play Journal*, January 1919, p.8

13 J.C. Jessen, "In and Out of the West Coast Studios," *Motion Picture News*, December 16, 1916, p.3817

14 "Coming! Foxfilm Comedies," full-page ad, *Moving Picture World*, December 16, 1916, p.1584

15 "Tom Mix Will Make Foxfilm Comedies," p.27

16 "Lehrman Making Fox Comedies," *Moving Picture World*, February 3, 1917, p.698

17 *Moving Picture World*, March 17, 1917, pp.1824-1825

18 Charles H. Ryan, Garfield Theater, quoted in *Motography*, April 28, 1917, p.865

19 E. Dlouhy, Vitagraph Theater, quoted in *Motography*, April 28, 1917, p.866

20 "A.S.C. on Parade," *American Cinematographer*, December 1942, p.518

21 "Fox Forms Comedy Company," *New York Clipper*, March 21, 1917, p.32

22 "Announcement," *Los Angeles Times*, May 20, 1917, p.16

23 *Motion Picture Magazine*, June 1917, p.11

24 *New York Telegraph*, March 4, 1917, page unknown

25 "Fox Wins in Suit," *New York Telegraph*, June 24, 1917, page unknown

26 "Fox Continues Fight," *New York Telegraph*, July 1, 1917, page unknown

27 "Fox Studios Not Wanted," *New York Telegraph*, October 14, 1917, page unknown

28 *Motion Picture Magazine*, January 1918, p.10

29 Lillian Wurtzel Semenov and Carla Winter, *William Fox, Sol M. Wurtzel and the Early Fox Film Corporation* (Jefferson, North Carolina: McFarland and Company, Inc., 2001), p.8

30 Gloria Swanson, *Swanson on Swanson*. (New York: Random House, 1980) p.78.

31 "West Coast Producers Active," *New York Dramatic Mirror*, October 20, 1917, p.23; "New Fox Comedies Soon," *Motography*, October 27, 1917, p.866

32 Sylvia Godwin, "Do You Know Gloria?," *The New Movie Magazine*, February 1930, pp.92, 130

33 M.E.M. Gibsone, "Powers is Star of First Washington Photoplay Film," *New York Dramatic Mirror*, March 16, 1918, p.15

34 "Picture Success Made By Love for Animals," *Ironwood Daily Globe*, March 16, 1921, p.5

35 David Bruskin, *The White Brothers: Jack, Jules, & Sam White*, p.58

36 "Conversations: Norman Taurog, Part I," *Leonard Maltin's Movie Crazy*, Winter, 2006, No. 15, pp.3-4

37 "Lloyd V. Hamilton, The Original 'Ham,' Signed By Lehrman," *Exhibitors Herald and Motography*, July 12, 1919, p.40

38 David Bruskin, *The White Brothers: Jack, Jules, & Sam White*, p.62

39 Mark., "Moving Pictures," *Variety*, November 16, 1917, p.50

40 David Bruskin, *The White Brothers: Jack, Jules, & Sam White*

41 "Studio: Jungle Note," *Los Angeles Times*, September 23, 1917, pp.III14, 19

42 Randolph Bartlett, "The Shadow Stage," *Photoplay*, February 1918, Vol. XIII, pp.66-67

43 Lillian Wurtzel Semenov and Carla Winter, *William Fox, Sol M. Wurtzel and the Early Fox Film Corporation*, pp.7, 12. Letter from William Fox to Henry Lehrman dated October 23, 1917

44 Hanford C. Judson, "A Milk-Fed Vamp," *Moving Picture World*, December 15, 1917, pp.1643-1644

45 "Lehrman's Rise in Comedy Meteoric," *Los Angeles Herald*, June 5, 1917, p.19

46 G.P.Harleman, "News of Los Angeles and Vicinity," *Moving Picture World*, September 29, 1917, p.1986

47 Kalton C. Lahue and Terry Brewer, *Kops and Custards: the Legend of Keystone Films*, p.63

48 "Fox Films Have Daring Stunts," *Moving Picture World*, December 30, 1916, p.1981

49 Sam Gill correspondence with author, March 2, 2016

50 Mark Larkin, "Movie 'Doubles' Face Death to Keep Stars from Harm," *Lowell Sun Sunday Supplement*, July 22, 1917, p.2

51 "Reel Became Real," *Los Angeles Times*, May 24, 1917, p.I9

52 "Burned in Explosion," *Moving Picture World*, February 8, 1919, p.754

53 Interview with Norman Taurog by Sam Gill, at Taurog's home in Beverly Hills, August 17, 1966

54 Interview with William McGann by Sam Gill, at the Motion Picture Country Home and Hospital, Woodland Hills, California, August 10, 1966

55 "Locomotive Upsets Film Players," *Moving Picture World*, June 8, 1918, p.1446

56 "Which Rock Was Worse?" *New York Telegraph*, November 11, 1917, page unknown

57 Kevin Brownlow and John Kobal, *Hollywood: The Pioneers* (New York: Alfred A. Knopf, 1979), p.134

58 "The Double Has Never a Dull Moment," *Lima Daily News*, July 20, 1917, p.17

59 Randolph Bartlett, "Why Aren't We Killed?," *Photoplay Magazine*, April 1916, p.84

60 Hal Jacques, "The Hidden Dangers Stunt Men Faced in Early Days of Hollywood," *National Enquirer*, date and page unknown

61 Ronald Yates, "Lights! Camera! Spectacular, Dangerous Action!," *Chicago Tribune*, July 12, 1981, p.9

62 Henry Lehrman interviewed by Barnet Braverman, *Barnet Braverman Research Collection*

63 "'Damaged Goods' in Films," *Motion Picture News*, August 22, 1914, p.60

64 "Leo White Meets with Accident," *Moving Picture World*, March 1, 1919, p.1239

65 "Comedian Suffers Injuries," *Moving Picture World*, May 31, 1919, p.1333

66 "Players' Checkerboard," *Exhibitors Herald*, October 9, 1915, p.25

67 "Wanda Wiley Injured," *Moving Picture World*, September 20, 1924, page unknown

68 "Perhaps a Little Careless," *New York Telegraph*, August 5, 1917, page unknown

69 *Moving Picture World*, August 5, 1916, p.932

70 *Moving Picture World*, November 25, 1916, p.1169

71 Diana Serra Cary, *Whatever Happened to Baby Peggy*, p.53. Fortunately it was later determined that his blindness was caused by a pituitary tumor. An operation restored his sight, but Earle chose not to return to film, instead spending the next fourteen years working for the Ringling Brothers and Barnum & Bailey Circus.

72 "Film Actress Dead," *Moving Picture World*, September 14, 1918, p.1549

73 "Fall From Airplane Kills Movie Actor," *New York Times*, February 6, 1920, p.17

74 Randolph Bartlett, "Why Aren't We Killed?," p.84

75 "The Week's Hard Luck Film Story," *Exhibitors Herald*, September 2, 1916, p.39

76 "Obliging Mabel Normand," *New York Telegraph*, December 5, 1915, page unknown

77 "Pacific Coast News," *New York Telegraph*, August 29, 1915, page unknown

78 Gene Fowler, *Father Goose: The Story of Mack Sennett*, p.218

79 "Pacific Coast Notes," *Motography*, December 16, 1916, p.1350

80 Michael Campino, "Bernard Harris: The Leap from Keystone to Success," *Slapstick!*, Fall-Winter 2007-08, #13

81 Hanford C. Judson, *Moving Picture World*, January 5, 1918, pp.95-96

82 *Wid's Daily*, June 29, 1919, p.24

83 Margaret I. MacDonald, "Damaged, No Goods," *Moving Picture World*, December 8, 1917, p.1483

84 "The New Fox Pictures," *Moving Picture World*, August 4, 1917, p.804

85 "Fox Sunshine Comedies," *Moving Picture World*, August 25, 1917, p.1239

86 "Lehrman Assaulted," *The Billboard*, September 1, 1917, p.62; "Fight Over Wrecked Car," *New York Telegraph*, August 26, 1917, page unknown

87 G.P.Harleman, "News of Los Angeles and Vicinity," *Moving Picture World*, December 1, 1917, p.1310

88 "Theatre Owners Make Merry," *New York Telegraph*, November 25, 1917, page unknown

89 G.P.Harleman, "News of Los Angeles and Vicinity," *Moving Picture World*, February 3, 1918, p.1106

90 "Film Folk Will Stage Pageant," *Los Angeles Times*, July 26, 1918, p.II2

91 Harry Harding, "Patter from the Pacific," *Motion Picture Magazine*, March 1918, p.130

92 "Costly for Pathé," *New York Telegraph*, December 23, 1917, page unknown

93 "Film Magnate Designs Motor Carriage De Luxe," *Los Angeles Times*, May 5, 1918, p.VI4

94 "Studio Flashes," *Moving Picture World*, April 21, 1917, p.432

95 *Los Angeles Herald*, April 29, 1918, p.17

96 *Los Angeles Herald*, May 4, 1918, p.14

97 Hanford C. Judson, "Two Moon Comedies," *Moving Picture World*, January 26, 1918, p.525

98 "Start Work on New Moon Comedy," *Moving Picture World*, June 14, 1919, p.1675

99 Letter from Phyliss Carr, of Waterbury, Connecticut, to the editor of *Motion Picture Magazine*, May 1918, p.130

100 M.E. Gibsone, "Williams with Western Big V," *The Dramatic Mirror*, December 8, 1917, p.20

101 *Wid's Daily*, July 27, 1919, p.24

102 *Motography*, February 23, 1918, p.358

103 *Moving Picture World*, March 9, 1918, p.1411

104 "Moving Pictures," *Variety*, July 25, 1919, p.45

105 "Are Married Policemen" review held in the Board of Review Collection, Kansas State Historical Society, box number 35-06-06-06

106 "Jones Brings Suit," *New York Telegraph*, August 4, 1918, page unknown

107 *Motography*, March 30, 1918, p.621

108 Peter Milne, *Motion Picture News*, April 20, 1918, p.2417

109 "Los Angeles Gossip," *The Winner*, October 17, 1917, p.10

110 Daisy Dean, "News Notes from Movieland," *Janesville Daily Gazette*, February 26, 1918, p.6

111 *Moving Picture World*, April 27, 1918, p.589

112 "Ham's Friend," *Picture-Play Magazine*, August 1918, p.311

113 Peter Milne, "A Neighbor's Keyhole," *Motion Picture News,* June 1, 1918, p.3308

114 M.E.M. Gibsone, "Coast Colony Looks for Boom in Production," *The Dramatic Mirror*, February 9, 1918, p.12

115 Richard Willis, "Latest News from West Coast Studios," *Motography*, December 8, 1917, p.1187; *Los Angeles Herald*, November 23, 1917, p.19

116 *Moving Picture World,* December 29, 1917, p.1949

117 *Motion Picture Magazine*, February 1918, p.10

118 Harry Harding, "Patter from the Pacific," *Motion Picture Magazine*, March 1918, p.130

119 "Lions Are Featured in Four Fox Sunshine Comedies," *Moving Picture World,* June 7, 1919, p.1538

120 Robert Birchard correspondence with author, May 13, 2013.

121 "Tom Mix Will Make Foxfilm Comedies," *Motography*, January 6, 1917, p.27

122 "Tom Mix Lends a Hand to Henry Lehrman," *Motion Picture News,* June 22, 1918, p.3711

123 "Official Cut-Outs Made By the Chicago Board of Censors," *Exhibitors Herald and Motography*, July 27, 1918, p.43

124 "Ohio Censors Very Active," *Moving Picture World,* August 3, 1918, p.715

125 "Mix Dabbles in Comedy; Says Stuff is Too Fast," *Moving Picture World,* June 22, 1918, p.1734

126 "Ethel Teare to Support 'Ham'," *Moving Picture World,* May 4, 1918, p.682

127 Charles H. Ryan, Garfield Theatre, Chicago, *Exhibitors Herald and Motography*, October 5, 1918, p.39

128 Steve Farrar, Orpheum Theatre, Harrisburg, Ill., *Exhibitors Herald and Motography*, September 28, 1918, p.29

129 Thomas Reeder, "One Shot Fits All: The Rapid-Fire Career of William Beaudine," *Filmfax Magazine*, #44, April/May 1994, pp.78-79

130 Wendy L. Marshall, *William Beaudine: From Silents to Television* (Lanham, Maryland: Scarecrow Press, 2005), p.24-25. Quotes reprinted from Kevin Brownlow, *The Silent Films of William Beaudine: Research Dossier for American Film Institute Oral History Department*, October 1972, pp.11-12; Philip K. Scheuer, "60 Years in Films," *Action*, July-August 1969, p.13

131 "A High Diver's Last Kiss," *Exhibitors World*, May 29, 1920, p.74

132 "Aeroplane Race in New Comedy By Lehrman," *Los Angeles Herald*, August 13, 1918, p.19

133 "Mae Eccleston's High Dive," *New York Dramatic Mirror*, September 14, 1918, p.417

134 "Studio Shorts," *Moving Picture World,* August 24, 1918, p.1103

135 "L-Ko Takes On New Players," *Moving Picture World,* November 9, 1918, p.682

136 Interview with Norman Taurog by Sam Gill, August 17, 1966

137 *Ibid.*

138 J.H. Walraven, "The Perils of Comedy," p.8

139 "A Train Not Under Control of Director McAdoo," *Film Fun*, December 1918, p.20

140 "A Tale of a Bee and a Tail," *Moving Picture World,* September 7, 1918, p.1442

141 Grace Kingsley, "Studio," *Los Angeles Times,* July 29, 1917, p.III2

142 Edward Churchill, "Don't Bring Rover," *Hollywood*, July 1938, p.25. Buster was said to be fifteen years old at the time of the interview, which would place Lehrman's sale of the pup circa 1923.

143 "Lost Dog Star, Not Sirius, but Lehrman's Jess," *Los Angeles Herald*, August 10, 1918, p.13

144 "Daschund Gets Licked by Three Allied Pups," *Moving Picture World,* October 26, 1918, p.529

145 William Thacher, Royal Theatre, Salina, Kan., *Exhibitors Herald*, February 5, 1921, p.93

146 F.R. Smith, Bijou Theatre, Fond du Lac, Wis., *Exhibitors Herald and Motography*, December 14, 1918, p.33

147 "What of Fairbanks and Hart?," *New York Telegraph*, August 11, 1918, page unknown

148 "Solve 'Extra' Problem," *New York Telegraph*, August 18, 1918, page unknown

149 Guy Price, "Coast Picture News," *Variety,* October 18, 1918, p.40

150 "Ten of Lehrman Actors Attend Training School," *Los Angeles Herald*, October 8, 1918, p.20

151 "More Crusaders for Pershing," *Moving Picture World*, August 24, 1918, p.1101

152 Guy Price, "Coast Picture News," *Variety*, October 18, 1918, p.40

153 *New York Telegraph*, July 29, 1917, page unknown; "Raise for Spence," *New York Telegraph*, September 2, 1917, page unknown

154 G.P. Harleman, "Studios Subscribe $1,274,900 to Liberty Loan," *Moving Picture World*, June 8, 1918, p.1421

155 "Studio Shorts," *Moving Picture World*, October 19, 1918, p.363

156 "Sunshine At Tank," *Los Angeles Herald*, October 8, 1918, p.22

157 "Tank Campaign," *The Billboard*, November 16, 1918, p.57

158 Lillian Wurtzel Semenov and Carla Winter, *William Fox, Sol M. Wurtzel and the Early Fox Film Corporation*, p.34. Letter from William Fox to Sol Wurtzel dated January 21, 1918

159 *New York Telegraph*, September 8, 1918, page unknown

160 "Bankruptcy in Pictures Laid to War Conditions," *Variety*, October 25, 1918, p.32

161 John M. Barry, *The Great Influenza* (London, England: Penguin Books, 2004)

162 *New York Telegraph*, November 3, 1918, page unknown

163 A.H. Giebler, "News of Los Angeles and Vicinity," *Moving Picture World*, November 16, 1918, p.728

164 A.H. Giebler, "Coast Studios Curtail Production," *Moving Picture World*, November 9, 1918, p.668

165 "Hollywood Hookum," *Motion Picture News*, January 25, 1919, p.585

166 *Los Angeles Herald*, October 21, 1918, p.11

167 "In New Building," *Wid's Daily*, November 26, 1918, p.1

168 "Del Ruth With Lehrman," *New York Telegraph*, October 20, 1918, page unknown

169 Kevin Brownlow, *The Parade's Gone By...* (New York: Alfred A. Knopf, 1968), p.26

170 "Fishback Joins Fox," *The Billboard*, October 5, 1918, p.51

171 "Interesting Facts About the Clan That Acts," *Photo-Play Journal*, February 1919, p.22

172 "Lehrman Engages Jack Blystone," *Moving Picture World*, December 21, 1918, p.1324

173 "Conversations: Norman Taurog, Part 1," p.4

174 "Fox Films," *Moving Picture World*, January 11, 1919, p.168

175 "Henry Lehrman Enlarges His Producing Activities," *Moving Picture World*, December 21, 1918, p.1374

176 "William Fox to Reissue Two-Part Mix Comedies," *Moving Picture World*, December 28, 1918, p.1540

177 "The Film and Screen." *Oakland Tribune*, December 1, 1918, p.3

178 "Fox Studio Doings," *Motion Picture News*, November 16, 1918, p.2968

179 William K. Everson, *The Theodore Huff Memorial Film Society* notes, June 19, 1953.

180 A.H. Giebler, "Rubbernecking in Filmland," *Moving Picture World*, December 7, 1918, p.1063

181 Edward Weitzel, "His Musical Sneeze," *Moving Picture World*, March 15, 1919, p.1467

182 Cal York, "Plays and Players," *Photoplay Magazine*, April 1919, pp.89-90

183 "Close Ups By Comly," *Wid's Daily*, January 23, 1919, p.3; "Tragedy Victim is Sent Home," *Los Angeles Times*, September 17, 1921, p.I2

184 "Sunshine Comedies Closed," *Variety*, January 24, 1919, p.49

185 "Studio Shots," *Moving Picture World*, February 1, 1919, p.616

186 "Whole Staff Fired," *Los Angeles Times*, January 19, 1919, p.VI12

187 "Fox and Lehrman Part," *Moving Picture World*, February 1, 1919, p.599

188 Lillian Wurtzel Semenov and Carla Winter, *William Fox, Sol M. Wurtzel and the Early Fox Film Corporation*, p.102. Letter from Sol Wurtzel to William Fox dated November 3, 1919

189 "Lehrman at Work on Big Comedy," *Los Angeles Herald*, January 7, 1919, p.22

190 Guy Price, "Facts and Fables of the Foyer," *Los Angeles Herald*, January 29, 1919, p.16

191 "Fox to Continue Making Comedies," *Moving Picture World*, February 8, 1919, p.753

192 "Money Talks," *Moving Picture World*, April 5, 1919, p.128

193 "Short Reels," *Wid's Daily*, March 21, 1921, p.28

194 "Rivoli," *Variety*, March 21, 1919, p.55

195 *Motion Picture News*, January 25, 1919, p.8

196 Buster Keaton and Charles Samuels, *My Wonderful World of Slapstick* (New York: De Capo Press, 1960), pp.151-152. Stunt man "Suicide" Buddy Mason remembered the Dunn incident slightly differently in 1927, stating that it took place while Dunn was making a film for Keystone, not Sunshine; they had to feed him drinks to get him to do it. Mason interviewed by Dick Hylan, "Risking Life and Limb for $25," *Photoplay Magazine*, November 1927, p.125.

197 "Film Flickers," *The Sunday Oregonian*, December 1, 1918, p.4

198 "Negative Stolen," *Moving Picture World*, February 22, 1919, p.1005

199 "Put Sand in Box Instead of Film?" *Los Angeles Times*, February 5, 1919, p.I12

200 "Grand Jury Begins Quiz in Film Case," *Los Angeles Times*, February 20, 1919, p.II1

201 "Indict Two in Film Mystery," *Los Angeles Times*, February 26, 1919, p.II2

202 "Plead Not Guilty," *Los Angeles Times*, April 2, 1919, p.II1

203 "Lehrman Says Stolen Film is of No Value," *Los Angeles Herald*, February 27, 1919, p.11

204 "Film Man is Freed," *Los Angeles Times*, April 11, 1919, p.III4

205 "Film Trial Starts," *Los Angeles Times*, May 7, 1919, p.III4

206 "Hochberg Freed," *Variety*, May 16, 1919, p.57

207 Barry, "Little Trips to Los Angeles Studios," *New York Dramatic Mirror*, date unknown, p.772

208 "Lost Negative Found!" *Wid's Daily*, April 27, 1919, p.23

209 *Moving Picture World*, September 14, 1918, p.1550

210 "A Lady Bellhop's Secret," *Moving Picture World*, May 17, 1919, p.1077

211 A.H. Giebler, "Rubbernecking in Filmland," *Moving Picture World*, December 7, 1918, p.1063

212 "Rivoli," *Variety*, May 2, 1919, p.59

213 "Thirteen Best Comedies for Summer," *Moving Picture World*, May 31, 1919, p.1352

214 "Three Sunshine Comedies Have Been Completed," *Moving Picture World*, June 28, 1919, p.2004

215 Lillian Wurtzel Semenov and Carla Winter, *William Fox, Sol M. Wurtzel and the Early Fox Film Corporation*, pp.102-103. Letter from Wurtzel to Fox dated November 3, 1919

216 *Ibid*, p.139. Letter from William Fox to Sol Wurtzel dated April 15, 1920

217 *Ibid*, p.130. Telegram from William Fox to Sol Wurtzel dated March 23, 1920

218 *Ibid*, pp.152-153. Inter-office memo from W.R. Sheehan to William Fox dated February 21, 1921

Chapter 7: Henry Lehrman Comedies: Overstepping His Bounds

1 "Henry Lehrman" full-page ad, *Moving Picture World*, February 15, 1919, p.832

2 "Lehrman Plans," *Wid's Daily*, February 7, 1919, p.1

3 "Lehrman to Produce Independently," *Moving Picture World*, February 15, 1919, p.882

4 "Chaplin Backing Lehrmann," *Wid's Daily*, March 4, 1919, p.2

5   *Articles of Incorporation of the Henry Lehrman Productions, Inc.*, March 21, 1919

6   "George Meehan," *American Cinematographer*, February 1, 1922, p.31

7   "1st Nat'l's Lehrman Comedies," *Variety*, May 2, 1919, p.63; Telegram from Sid Grauman to Adolph Zukor, dated April 25, 1919

8   "First National Circuit Secures Lehrman Comedies," *Moving Picture World*, May 10, 1919, p.795

9   "Lehrman Forms Company," *Los Angeles Times*, May 14, 1919, p.III4

10 Terry Ramsaye, *A Million and One Nights*, pp.789-791

11 "A Pledge," *Moving Picture World*, May 10, 1919, pp.768-769

12 *Grant Deed*, transfer of property from William M. and Anna E. Waterman to Henry Lehrman, April 7, 1919

13 "New Film Plant," *Los Angeles Times*, April 27, 1919, p.V1

14 "Ground Broken for Studio," *Variety*, May 30, 1919, p.80

15 "New Comedy Plant at Culver City Nears Finish," *Los Angeles Times*, July 6, 1919, p.III13

16 "Lehrman to Build New Plant," *New York Clipper*, May 7, 1919, p.33

17 Brian Taves, *Thomas Ince: Hollywood's Independent Pioneer* (Lexington: University of Kentucky Press, 2012), p.114

18 "Fatty Arbuckle to Share Lehrman Studio," *Moving Picture World*, July 12, 1919, p.207

19 "Arbuckle Is Not a Part Owner of Lehrman Studio," *Moving Picture World*, August 9, 1919, p.840

20 "Lehrman's Diffuser System," *Moving Picture World*, August 2, 1919, p.658

21 J.C. Jessen, "In and Out of the West Coast Studios," *Motion Picture News*, July 19, 1919, p.760. Ritchie took some of the money earned during this down-time to buy a Hudson Speedster for daughter Wyn, who had just graduated from Hollywood High School. ("Winifred Ritchie Graduates," *Camera!*, June 22, 1919, p.5)

22 "Lloyd V. Hamilton, The Original 'Ham,' Signed By Lehrman," *Exhibitors Herald and Motography*, August 16, 1919, p.42; J.C. Jessen, "In and Out of West Coast Studios," *Motion Picture News*, July 19, 1919, p.760; "Thomas Now Lehrman Publicity Chief," *Moving Picture World*, July 12, 1919, p.208; "Coast Brevities," *Wid's Daily*, July 30, 1919, p.4; *Wid's Daily*, October 22, 1919, p.4

23 Guy Price, "In Califilmland: P.A. Faces Breakdown," *Los Angeles Herald*, October 27, 1919, p.24

24 Barrymore, "Little Trips to the Los Angeles Studios," *Variety*, August 28, 1919, p.1381

25 "Olin Patent," *Camera!*, August 2, 1919, p.14; "Patent on Market," *Camera!*, August 16, 1919, p.7

26 "Theater Notes," *Los Angeles Herald*, July 30, 1919, p.23

27 "Merry Mixup," *Camera!*, September 13, 1919, p.9

28 "Film Club of 100," *Variety*, May 2, 1919, p.65

29 "Lehrman Up in the Air," *New York Dramatic Mirror*, June ??, 1919, p.1186

30 "Orvar Meyeroffer, Aviation Pioneer, Dies," *Aerial Age Weekly*, August 9, 1920, p.737

31 *Camera!*, May 4, 1919, p.7; *Camera!*, May 18, 1919, p.6; *Camera!*, August 30, 1919, p.5

32 "Wealthy Young Woman to Be Screen Actress," *Fort Wayne Journal-Gazette*, September 28, 1919, p.IV-4

33 "Comedians Are Added to Lehrman's Staff," *Exhibitors Herald and Motography*, November 15, 1919, p.72

34 "Henry Lehrman Talks Pointedly About Business of Comedy Making," *Moving Picture World*, August 30, 1919, p.1279

35 "Building Massive Set For New Lehrman Comedies," *Exhibitors Herald and Motography*, September 6, 1919, p.64

36 "Deaf Stenographer Caused the Trouble," *Fort Wayne Journal-Gazette*, September 29, 1919, p.4

37 Grace Kingsley, "Flashes," *Los Angeles Times*, October 10, 1919, p.III4

38 "Studio Stories," *Oakland Tribune*, October 12, 1919, page unknown

39 "Bath Tub Sprung Leak and Flooded the Town," *Fort Wayne Journal-Gazette*, September 28, 1919, p.4

40 "'A Twilight Baby,' New Lehrman Comedy, Ready by Nov. 1," *Motion Picture News*, November 8, 1919, p.3450

41 "A Twilight Baby," *Moving Picture World*, January 24, 1920, p.635

42 Assumedly 32-inch tall Julius Daranyi, one of the members of the troupe.
43 "Moving Picture News," *The Morning Oregonian*, October 25, 1919, p.6
44 "Hamilton Dons Old Make-Up; New Player with Lehrman," *Motion Picture News,* November 8, 1919, p.3445
45 Ray W. Frohman, "Virginia Rappe Described As Dashing Beauty of Comedies," *Morning Oregonian*, September 15, 1921, p.6
46 "Billie Ritchie's New Home," *Moving Picture World,* September 28, 1918, p.1880
47 "How the Rooster Lost His Tail and How It Affected His Value," *New York Tribune*, February 29, 1920, p.3
48 "A Twilight Baby," *Motion Picture News,* January 24, 1920, p.1127
49 "A Twilight Baby," *Moving Picture World,* January 24, 1920, p.635
50 "'A Twilight Baby,' Lehrman — First National," *Wid's Daily*, December 16, 1919, p.4
51 "A Twilight Baby," *Exhibitors Herald*, February 21, 1920, p.72
52 G. Strasser Sons, Emblem theatre, Buffalo, NY. *Exhibitors Herald*, June 2, 1923, p.74
53 Altman & Trifon, Cozy theatre, Goose Creek, TX. *Exhibitors Herald*, May 8, 1920, p.89
54 Alvin S. Frank, Jewel theatre, Lafayette, CO. *Exhibitors Herald*, June 19, 1920, p.75
55 Jack Cairns, Brooklyn theatre, Detroit, MI. *Exhibitors Herald*, May 15, 1920, p.77
56 W.G. Mitchell, Majestic Gardens, Kalamazoo, MI. *Exhibitors Herald*, April 3, 1920, p.69
57 Philip Rand, Rex theatre, Salmon, ID. *Exhibitors Herald*, April 2, 1921, p.81
58 "Film Actor On Stand," *Los Angeles Times,* November 29, 1921, p.I2
59 "Cohn's to Feature Edwards," *Wid's Daily*, February 19, 1920, p.2
60 "Promised Kaiser's Shoes," *Sunday Oregonian*, September 22, 1918, p.4
61 "Harry Sherman Sues Lehrman for Alleged Breach of Contract," *Exhibitors Herald*, January 24, 1920, p.53
62 "Lehrman Film Studio Held in Attachment," *Los Angeles Herald*, December 30, 1919, p.B4
63 Telegrams from Joseph R. Darling to Frank Burke, Chief, Bureau of Investigation, dated January 8 and 9, 1920; Burke's telegram responses to Darling dated January 9 and 10, 1920; Burke's letter to Daniel C. Roper, Commissioner, Internal Revenue dated January 10, 1920
64 "Ready to Fight 'Film Trust'," *New York Times,* January 15, 1920, p.8
65 *Articles of Incorporation of the Henry Lehrman Comedies, Inc.*, April 17, 1920, pp.1-4
66 "Heraldgrams," *Exhibitors Herald*, March 20, 1920, p.24
67 *Election to Declare Default in the Payment of Interest of Note Secured by Deed of Trust*, C.L. Logan County Recorder, State of California, County of Los Angeles, dated December 15, 1920, pp.282-283
68 *Trustee's Deed Upon Sale*, State of California, County of Los Angeles, dated November 3, 1920, p.302
69 "Chester Comedies Under Way," *New York Telegraph*, May 2, 1920, page unknown; "Chester Has Lehrman," *Wid's Daily*, May 26, 1920, p.3; "Brentwood Elects Officers," *Moving Picture World,* May 24, 1919, p.1161
70 *Grant Deed, State of California County of Los Angeles*, dated June 4, 1920
71 "Lehrman Plans Special Service," *Los Angeles Examiner*, August 29, 1920, p.IX5
72 "William Fox Engages Two Bright Youngsters," *Moving Picture World,* February 15, 1919, p.887
73 Unless you count the "lunch concession and coffee" that Ray co-operated on the second floor of the Biograph studio when he was a mere seven years old. Ray recounted an amusing story about Sennett's first visit to the Biograph studios, here summarized by Braverman: "While Ray was setting the table, there was a commotion downstairs — a row.... Sennett, chewing a stogie, the juice slopping over his loud check suit. Suit was tight and made him look bigger than he is. Bobby didn't believe he was an actor. 'I want to see Griffith', Sennett said to Bobby.... 'He can't see any bums like you' said Bobby.... Sennett said, 'I'm a strong man. I was told to come here', said Sennett.... 'We don't need any strong men', said Bobby. 'Go on the hell out of here, I have an appointment by Fred Mace to se [sic] Griffith'.... Griffith: 'A strong man? Send him up?'...Bobby: All right bum, go on up.'"

74 "A Star of a New Ray," *Motion Picture Magazine*, October 1919, p.104

75 "Pre-Reviewers Approve of 'The Kick in High Life'," *Exhibitors Herald*, August 14, 1920, p.79

76 J.C. Jessen, "News from the West Coast," *Motion Picture News,* July 31, 1920, p.977

77 "At the Theatres," *Perry Daily Chief*, November 6, 1920, p.4

78 "'The Kick in High Life' at Hex Theater Today," *Semidji Daily Pioneer*, May 7, 1921, p.4

79 Laurence Reid, "The Complete Plan Book," *Motion Picture News,* September 18, 1920, p.2311

80 I.S. Campbell, Zimm theatre, Winfield, KS. *Exhibitors Herald*, December 4, 1920, p.101

81 R.R. Gribble, Grand theatre, Hamburg, Ontario. *Exhibitors Herald*, June 4, 1921, p.98

82 F.D. Hall, Wonderland theatre, Madelia, MN. *Exhibitors Herald*, March 12, 1921, p.81

83 "Chester and Lehrman Part," *New York Telegraph*, July 25, 1920, page unknown

84 "Coast Brevities," *Wid's Daily*, September 20, 1920, p.3

85 Laurence Reid, "The Complete Plan Book," *Motion Picture News,* December 4, 1920, p.4339

86 Richard M. Roberts online post, "Movies," *GroupSrv.com,* August 3, 2006

87 Richard M. Roberts correspondence with author, February 17, 2016

88 Joan Myers, "A Vamp Goes to Cinecon 49," September 3, 2013, *http://nitrateville.com/viewtopic.php?f=4&t=15710&p=115798&hilit=wet+and+warmer#p115798*

89 "Brooksie," "A Vamp Goes to Cinecon 49," September 3, 2013; "missdupont," September 5, 2013

90 "Wet and Warmer," *Moving Picture World,* December 11, 1920, page unknown

91 Laurence Reid, "The Complete Plan Book"

92 W.E. Elkin, Temple theatre, Aberdeen, MS. *Exhibitors Herald*, July 30, 1921, p.63

93 Philip Rand, Rex theatre, Salmon, ID. *Exhibitors Herald*, August 27, 1921, p.72

94 "Wet and Warmer," *Board of Review Collection Review, Kansas State Historical Society*, reviewed December 1, 1920

95 "Lehrman's Fourth Finished," *New York Dramatic Mirror*, October 30, 1920, p.817

96 John Bengston, *Silent Visions* (Solana Beach, CA: Santa Monica Press, 1911), p.162

97 "Says Comedy Needs Elaborate Sets," *Los Angeles Times,* September 28, 1920, p.III4

98 "Lehrman Due," *Wid's Daily*, October 14, 1920, p.1; "Lehrman Not Coming East," *Wid's Daily*, October 20, 1920, p.2; "Schulberg Represents Lehrman in New York," *Exhibitors Herald*, October 30, 1920, p.40

99 "Coast Brevities," *Wid's Daily*, September 11, 1920, p.3

100 "Lehrman's Fourth Finished"

101 "Coast Brevities," *Wid's Daily*, November 27, 1920, p.2

102 Harry Hammond Beale, "With the Procession in Los Angeles," *Exhibitors World*, November 6, 1920, p.109

103 Laurence Reid, "Feature Subjects of Short Length," *Motion Picture News,* July 23, 1921, p.606

104 *Election to Declare Default in the Payment of Interest of Note Secured by Deed of Trust*, C.L. Logan County Recorder, State of California, County of Los Angeles, dated December 15, 1920, pp.282-283

105 *Grant Deed*, State of California, County of Los Angeles, dated January 21, 1921, p.105

106 "Mirth Producer is a Real Public Necessity," *Ironwood Daily Globe*, February 4, 1921, p.5

107 *Behrend-Levy Co. vs. Lehrman Prod*, Superior Court, Los Angeles County, California, January ??, 1921, pp.1-3

108 *Answer to Behrend-Levy Co. vs. Lehrman Prod*, Superior Court, Los Angeles County, California, May 19, 1921, pp.1-2

109 *M.H. Harris vs. H. Lehrman*, Superior Court, Los Angeles County, California, February 3, 1921, pp.1-2

110 *Answer to M.H. Harris vs. H. Lehrman*, Superior Court, Los Angeles County, California, February 9, 1921, pp.1-2

111 *Amended Answer to M.H. Harris vs. H. Lehrman*, Superior Court, Los Angeles County, California, February 21, 1921, pp.1-2

112 "In the Courts," *Wid's Daily*, April 16, 1921, p.4; *Complaint on Judgment M.H. Harris vs. H. Lehrman*, Superior Court, Los Angeles County, California, May 31, 1921, pp.1-2

113 "Switched?" *Wid's Daily*, January 28, 1921, p.1

114 "Lehrman and Educational," *Variety*, March 18, 1921, p.38

115 "Henry Lehrman Signs to Make 13 Comedies for Educational Film," *Exhibitors Herald*, April 9, 1921, p.32

116 "Forthcoming Films," *New York Times*, June 26, 1921, p.VI4

117 *The Film Daily*, June 22, 1924, p.73

118 "The Pulse of the Studio," *Camera!*, January 15 and 22, 1921, p.11. Savo was a popular vaudeville funnyman. His 1910 ad in *Variety* read "SAVO — JUGGLER. Juggling everything from a feather to an automobile." He would go on to star in musical comedies on Broadway that lasted into the mid-1940s.

119 Mlle. Chic, "The Story of the L-Ko Head, H. Pathé Lehrmann," p.22

Chapter 8: Reported Missing *and the Arbuckle Scandal*

1 "Report Lehrman to Return to Fox Lot," *Exhibitors Herald*, April 2, 1921, p.41

2 "Billy Ritchie Says Good Bye to Movies," *Cedar Rapids Evening Gazette*, July 7, 1921, p.15

3 "Plan Funeral for Local Film Star," *Los Angeles Herald*, July 8, 1921, p.A3

4 Lisa Robins correspondence with author, May 8, 2013.

5 Frederick James Smith, "The Youngest Movie Magnate," *Motion Picture Classic*, September 1920, pp.26, 80

6 "Henry A. Lehrman Will Write and Direct Owen Moore Comedy," *Moving Picture World*, July 30. 1921, p.532

7 "Fight Film to Exhibit in New York," *Los Angeles Times*, July 23, 1921; "Owen Moore Features," *New York Dramatic Mirror*, August 13, 1921, p.243

8 Grace Kingsley, "Owen Moore's New One," *Los Angeles Times*, September 9, 1921, p.III4

9 "Avaunt, Slit Skirt! Feminine Sox Now Hold Fashion's Stage," *The Indianapolis Star*, September 22, 1913, pp.1,3

10 Marion Howard, "Spokes from the Hub," *Moving Picture World*, November 3, 1917, p.689

11 Miriam Cooper and Bonnie Herndon, *Dark Lady of the Silents* (New York: The Bobbs-Merrill Company, Inc., 1973), p.178

12 Marjorie Wilson, "Virginia Rappe's Life," *Syracuse Journal*, October 22, 1921, p.11

13 "Life Appealed to Beautiful Virginia, Dead Film Actress," *Seattle Star*, September 17, 1921, p.14

14 "Arbuckle Appears in Court Like Common Criminal," *Janesville Daily Gazette*, September 12, 1921, p.4

15 "Pointers on Sentiment in Case of 'Fatty' Arbuckle," *Logansport Pharos-Tribune*, September 14, 1921, p.9

16 "Miss Rappe's Fiance Threatens Vengeance," *New York Times*, September 13, 1921, p.2

17 "Arbuckle is Jailed on Murder Charge in Woman's Death," *New York Times*, September 12, p.1

18 "Film World is Rended," *Los Angeles Times*, September 12, 1921, p.1

19 "Lehrman Denounces Comedian as 'Beast'," *Los Angeles Examiner*, September 12, 1921, page unknown

20 "Lehrman Sends $150 to Help Mrs. Delmont," *New York Times*, September 15, 1921, p.VII2

21 Louis W. Fehr, "Dead Girl's Fiancé Calls Prisoner Beast — Can't Face Arbuckle: I'd Kill Him," *San Francisco Examiner*, September 12, 1921, page unknown; copyright 1921, *New York American*

22 "Arbuckle Innocent, Declares His Wife," *New York Times*, September 14, 1921, p.3

23 "Lehrman Sends $150 to Help Mrs. Delmont," p.VII2

24 "Fiance of Dead Girl Condemns Arbuckle," *San Francisco Bulletin*, September 12, 1921, p.1

25 Western Union Telegram, from Henry Lehrman to Norman Taurog, dated September 12, 1921, 11:07 PM, c/o Larry Semon Company, Fresno Hotel; courtesy of Robert S. Birchard

26 "Tragedy Victim is Sent Home," *Los Angeles Times,* September 17, 1921, p.I2

27 "Thousands See Body of Dead Girl," *Los Angeles Times,* September 19, 1921, pp.I1-2; "Arbuckle Victim Buried; 7,000 View Body," *Olean Evening Times,* September 19, 1921, p.1

28 "Virginia Rappe is Buried," *Kingston Daily Freeman,* September 19, 1921, p.1

29 "Throng at Girl's Bier," *Indianapolis Star,* September 19, 1921, p.9

30 "Women Weep As Last Rites Are Said," *Los Angeles Herald,* September 19, 1921, p.A8

31 "Virginia Rappe in Final Rest," *Los Angeles Times,* September 20, 1921, p.I2

32 "News of the Films," *Variety,* October 28, 1921, p.34

33 "Many Stars in Moore-Lehrman Comedy Series," *Exhibitors Trade Review,* November 5, 1921, p.1580b

34 "Brown Derby for Sailor Before Mast," *Logansport Morning Press,* May 14, 1922, p.8

35 "New Owen Moore Film Announced," *Exhibitors Trade Review,* January 14, 1922, p.463

36 "'Sink or Swim' Title Selected for Owen Moore Film," *Exhibitors Trade Review,* February 18, 1922, p.815

37 "'Reported Missing' is Title of Moore Special," *Exhibitors Trade Review,* March 25, 1922, p.1165

38 "New Owen Moore Comedy Groomed for Broadway Showing," *Exhibitors Trade Review,* March 11, 1922, p.1035

39 "Lehrman to Face 'Fatty'," *Variety,* March 15, 1922, p.46; "Lover of Miss Rappe Goes to Frisco," *Modesto Evening News,* April 10, 1922, p.1

40 "$1,000 for Lilies, But Not One Cent for a Lovely Fur Wrap," *Ogden-Standard Examiner,* January 8, 1922, p.6

41 "Henry Lehrman Present to Model Told Rappe Girl's Fiance in Costly Gift," *San Francisco Call & Post,* March 24, 1922, page unknown

42 "Lehrman Sued for Rappe Burial Flower Piece," *San Francisco Call & Post,* April 11, 1922, page unknown

43 Western Union Telegram, from Norman Taurog to Henry Lehrman, dated January 26, 1922; courtesy of Robert S. Birchard

44 "De Luxe Showing for Selznick Film," *Exhibitors Trade Review,* April 22, 1922, p.1469

45 Helen Pollock, *The Morning Telegraph,* April 9, 1922, page unknown

46 Laurence Reid, "Reported Missing," *Motion Picture News,* April 22, 1922, page unknown

47 "'Reported Missing' Stops Opposition," *Exhibitors Trade Review,* May 27, 1922, p.1872

48 Guy D. Hasleton, Rialto theatre, Missoula, MO. *Exhibitors Herald,* June 24, 1922, p.106

49 E.E. Large, Strand theatre, Ithaca, NY. *Exhibitors Herald,* October 21, 1922, p.67

50 Don Allen, "Passing in Review," *New York Evening World,* April 24, 1922, p.18

51 "Film Flashes," *The National Advocate,* August 3, 1922, p.1

52 "California Gets Another Rude Blow," *Moving Picture World,* April 26, 1919, p.521

53 "The Screen," *New York Times,* April 24, 1922, p.18

54 The *Film Daily,* April 18, 1922, p.2; "David Kirkland and Clyde Bruckman Are Now on Montana Staff," *Exhibitors Trade Review,* October 21, 1922, p.1352

55 "A Star at Last," *Variety,* September 23, 1921, p.11

56 "Lehrman Ordered to Give Up in Court," *Variety,* January 25, 1923, p.47

57 "Inside Stuff on Pictures," *Variety,* March 24, 1922, p.43

Chapter 9: Treading Water at a Potpourri of Studios

1 "Stern Engages Lehrman as Century Comedy Producer," *Exhibitors Trade Review,* February 25, 1922, p.897

2 "Note from Century Studios," *Exhibitors Trade Review,* April 8, 1922, p.1319

3 "The Pulse of the Studio," *Camera!,* April 15, 1922, p.10

4 Jimmy Starr, *Barefoot on Barbed Wire: An Autobiography of a Forty-Year Hollywood Balancing Act* (Lanham, Maryland: Scarecrow Press, Inc., 2001), pp.35-37

5 "Henry Lehrman Engaged," *Los Angeles Times,* April 17, 1922, p.II7; "Follies Girl Bride of Henry Lehrman," *Wisconsin State Journal*, April 29, 1922, p.4

6 "Judgments," *Variety,* October 24, 1921, p.34

7 "Judgments," *Variety,* April 28, 1922, p.8

8 "Lehrman Sued in Notes," *Los Angeles Times,* November 30, 1922, p.II3

9 "Henry Lehrman is Jailed on Default Charge," *Los Angeles Times,* September 16, 1922, p.II1

10 "Lehrman Pinched," *Variety,* September 22, 1922, p.47

11 "Order Brokers to Quit State," *Los Angeles Times,* March 11, 1919, p.II6; "Thomas Litch Sues Brokers," *Los Angeles Times,* August 18, 1920, p.II1

12 *Answer of C. Fred Grundy*, re *Collection Corp.vs. Lehrman, etc.*, Superior Court of the State of California and the County of Los Angeles, date illegible

13 *Answer to Garnishment*, re *Collection Corp.vs. Lehrman, etc.*, Superior Court of the State of California and the County of Los Angeles, dated June 8, 1922

14 *Affidavit for Citation of Garnishee, Bailee, Debtor, etc.*, Superior Court of the State of California and the County of Los Angeles, dated June 15, 1922

15 *Bittleston etc. vs. Henry Lehrman Comedies et al.*, Superior Court Los Angeles County California, dated June 20, 1922

16 *Answer to Garnishment*, re *Bittleston etc. vs. Henry Lehrman Comedies et al.*, Superior Court of the State of California and the County of Los Angeles, dated July 7, 1922

17 Grace Kingsley, "Flashes," *Los Angeles Times,* October 20, 1922, p.III1; "Lehrman to Direct De Havens," *Exhibitors Trade Review*, November 4, 1922, p.1460

18 Renee Beeman, "Live News of the West Coast," *Exhibitors Trade Review*, November 11, 1922, p.1524

19 Mae Tinée, "The DeHavens Tax Credulity a Bit in This," *Chicago Daily Tribune*, January 19, 1923, p.1

20 "News of the Movie Theaters," *Sunday Oregonian*, December 24, 1922, p.2

21 "Carter De Haven Quits," *Film Daily,* November 4, 1923, p.11

22 Letter to William Traeger, Sherrif, from Film Booking Offices of America, dated October 25, 1922

23 "Coast Brevities," *Film Daily,* January 15, 1923, p.5

24 Laurence Reid, "Double Dealing," *Motion Picture News,* May 26, 1923, p.2539

25 "Probably a Disappointment for Star's Admirers in 'Double Dealing'," *Film Daily,* May 27, 1923, p.13

26 "Double Dealing," *Motion Picture Magazine*, November 1923, p.119

27 "Double Dealing," *Exhibitors Trade Review*, June 2, 1923, p.35

28 "Hoot Gibson in 'Double Dealing'," *Exhibitors Herald*, June 2, 1923, p.48

29 Jenks & Terrill, Dalton Opera House, Dalton, WI. *Exhibitors Herald*, December 29, 1923, p.169

30 Russell Armentrout, K.P.Theatre, Pittsfield, IL. *Exhibitors Herald*, March 22, 1924, p.79

31 Meece & Hale, New Opera House, Dexter, KS. *Exhibitors Herald*, March 8, 1924, p.76

32 "This Must Be a Record," *Universal Weekly*, December 20, 1924, pp.18, 34

33 Universal Film Manufacturing Company, *Answer to Garnishment*, re *H.G.Bittleston Law & Collec Agcy vs. Henry Lehrman,* dated January 23 and 26, 1923; *Sheriff's Return on Execution* dated January 29 and February 2, 1923

34 *Answer to Garnishment*, re *B.P.Schulberg vs. Henry Lehrman*, Superior Court of the State of California and the County of Los Angeles, dated December 6, 1922

35 "What Could Be Sweeter?" *Fighting Blood* full-page ad, *The Reel Journal*, January 5, 1924, p.3

36 Ruth Anne Dwyer , *Malcolm St. Clair: His Films, 1915-1948* (Lanham, MD: The Scarecrow Press, Inc., 1996), p.70

37 "H.C. Witwer Dies; A Noted Humorist," *New York Times,* August 10, 1929, p.13

38 "Louise Lorraine Opposite O'Hara in Fight Series," *Motion Picture News,* August 11, 1923, p.652

39 "Former Professional Boxer Signed for F.B.O. Series," *Motion Picture News,* September 15, 1923, p.1331

40 George Bartlett, "Of All Things," *St. Petersburg Times,* June 24, 1963, p.12

41 Ruth Anne Dwyer, *Malcolm St. Clair: His Films,* p.83. Dwyer states that Lehrman directed the series' first four episodes, and Santell the remainder, but that is not entirely accurate.

42 *Film Year Book 1924,* p.79

43 "Fighting Blood," *Variety,* October 18, 1923, p.23

44 "Fighting Blood," *Film Daily,* January 21, 1923, p.16

45 C. Malphurs, Dreamland theatre, High Springs, FL, and G. Strasser Sons, Emblem theatre, Buffalo, NY, *Exhibitors Herald,* March 8, 1924, p.84

46 D. Filizola, Empress theatre, Fort Scott, KS, and C.L. Reed, Illinois theatre, Newman, IL, *Exhibitors Herald,* March 15, 1924, p.87

47 "Who's Who and What's What in Filmland This Week," *Camera,* June 30, 1923, p.14

48 "Fighting Blood," *Variety,* p.23

49 "H.M. Lehrman Bankrupt," *Variety,* September 27, 1923, p.21; "Henry Lehrman, Ex-Fiance of Virginia Rapp [sic], Bankrupt," New York *Sun and Globe,* September 17, 1923, page unknown

50 "Production," *Exhibitors Trade Review,* November 17, 1923, p.1155

51 "Lehrman Completes Cast," *Film Daily,* December 24, 1923, p.2

52 "'On Time' Finished," *Film Daily,* January 6, 1924, p.9; "Truart Product to Go Through F.B.O. in Majority of Districts," *Exhibitors Herald,* March 15, 1924, p.30

53 Len Morgan, "Action Smothers Film," *Exhibitors Trade Review,* March 15, 1924, p.24

54 "Brief Review of Current Pictures," *Photoplay Magazine,* July 1924, p.14

55 *Harrison's Reports,* March 8, 1924, page unknown

56 *Moving Picture World,* March 8, 1924, page unknown

57 Len Morgan, "Action Smothers Picture," *Exhibitors Trade Review,* March 15, 1924, p.24

58 *Film Daily,* June 22, 1924, p.73

59 "Creating a Laugh a Week," *Exhibitors Trade Review,* August 16, 1924, p.29

60 "A.S.C.," *Film Daily,* June 7, 1925, p.127

61 The film was copyrighted with Charles Lamont named as the director; Lehrman was given credit in articles that ran in *Exhibitors Trade Review, Moving Picture World,* and *Motion Picture News* (all August 16, 1924), albeit from the same Fox press release

62 "Lehrman to Direct Fox Comedy Picture," *Billings Gazette,* May 11, 1924, p.5

63 Interview with George Gray by Sam Gill at the home of Andy Clyde, Hollywood, July 11, 1966

64 "Comedy Head Bids Pie, Bathing Girls, 'Good Bye, Forever'," *Reel Journal,* February 28, 1925, p.12

65 "Buys New Six Sedan," *Los Angeles Times,* July 20, 1924, p.F6

66 "Film Man Jailed in Speeding," *Los Angeles Times,* April 26, 1925, p.13; "Director to Appeal," *Los Angeles Times,* May 3, 1925, p.15

67 "Arrest two in Supposed Plot Case," *Los Angeles Times,* February 11, 1925, p.21

Chapter 10: The Volatile Jocelyn Leigh

1 "Bought Tiger Lily Blanket for Miss Rapp; Loses Heart Again," *The Eau Claire Leader,* May 26, 1922, p.1; "Virginia Rappe's Fiance is Married," *Daily Argus,* May 19, 1922, page unknown

2 "Jocelyn Leigh Weds," *San Francisco Chronicle,* May 21, 1922, p.2

3   "Lehrman Wins Divorce From Jocelyn L. Lehrman," *Variety*, December 24, 1924, p.27

4   "Lehrman Disputes Wife," *Variety*, December 29, 1922, p.7

5   *Complaint on Divorce, Superior Court of the State of California In and For the County of Los Angeles*, October 25, 1924, pp.2-4

6   "Wife Called at 1 A.M. And Became Hysterical," *Variety*, July 16, 1924, p.19

7   *Complaint on Divorce*, pp.4-5

8   "Peace for Director," *Los Angeles Times*, November 18, 1924, p.A8

9   *Interlocutory Judgment of Divorce, Superior Court of the State of California In and For the County of Los Angeles*, December 16, 1924; *Final Judgment of Divorce, Superior Court of the State of California In and For the County of Los Angeles*, December 26, 1924.

10 "What They Say Happens When Red-Headed Jocelyn Loses Her Temper," *San Antonio Light*, November 16, 1930, page unknown

11 Dan Thomas, "Hollywood's Record Year for Wrecked Romances," *Hamilton Daily News*, December 20, 1930, page unknown

12 "Lehrman in Police Toils," *Los Angeles Times*, January 21, 1926, p.A10

Chapter 11: The Brothers Warner Come Calling

1   "Warner Bros. Sign Stars For Stock Co.," *The Reel Journal*, March 7, 1925, p.15

2   Grace Kingsley, "Flashes," *Los Angeles Times*, August 27, 1925, p.A9

3   "Los Angeles," *Variety*, October 7, 1925, p.58

4   Grace Kingsley, "Flashes," *Los Angeles Times*, November 25, 1925, p.A9; "Warners Editing Six Pictures," *Film Daily*, December 6, 1925, p.6

5   *Answering Affidavit of Kenneth D. Harlan, Supreme Court, New York County*, 1921

6   "Music Men," *Variety*, June 30, 1922, pp.28, 30

7   Frank Elliott, "The Fighting Edge," *Motion Picture News*, February 20, 1926, p.912

8   "The Fighting Edge," *National Board of Review Magazine*, March-April 1926, p.19

9   "Pop! Pung! Pow! Ah! Little Girl! You's a Wil' Cat!" (Logansport, Indiana) *Pharos-Tribune*, March 25, 1926, p.12

10 "Lehrman May Go to F.P.," *Variety*, December 16, 1925, p.28

11 "Henry Lehrman Hurt," *Film Daily*, March 14, 1926, p.2; "Henry Lehrman Better," *Film Daily*, March 21, 1926, p.9

12 *Henry Lehrman Director*, contract drawn up by Flint & MacKay, Counselors at Law, dated May 12, 1926, signed by Jack Warner and Henry Lehrman; summary letter from Jack Warner to Henry Lehrman, dated May 12, 1926

13 Grace Kingsley, "Flashes," *Los Angeles Times*, May 21, 1926, p.A8

14 "The 26 Warners," *Film Daily*, April 20, 1926, p.6

15 "Reisner to Direct Jessel," *Film Daily*, May 17, 1926, p.2

16 "Warner Plans Ready," *Film Daily*, July 2, 1926, p.2

17 George Jessel, *So Help Me: The Autobiography of George Jessel* (New York: Random House, 1943), pp.84-85

18 "'Jazz Singer' for Jessel," *Film Daily*, August 1, 1926, p.11

19 Unsigned letter from Jack Warner to P.A. Chase, Warner Brothers comptroller, dated August 20, 1926

20 "Los Angeles," *Variety*, July 21, 1926, p.54

21 George Jessel, *So Help Me: The Autobiography of George Jessel*, pp.86-87

22 Letter from Warner Brothers comptroller P.A. Chase to Warners' attorney William A. Bowen, Flint and MacKay, dated August 21, 1926

23 "Lehrman's Salary Suit," *Variety,* October 20, 1926, p.59

24 Letter from Galen H. Welch, collector, Treasury Department Internal Revenue Service, to Warner Brothers Picture Corporation, dated October 10, 1926.

25 Letter from Warner Brothers comptroller P.A. Chase to William A. Bowen, Flint and MacKay, dated November 29, 1926

26 "Lehrman to Face Trial in October," *Los Angeles Times,* September 3, 1926, p.A2; "Lehrman Trial Again Set," *Los Angeles Times,* December 17, 1926, p.A14

27 "Six Richard Talmadge Productions Under Way for Universal Release," *Universal Weekly,* February 5, 1927, p.11

28 "Differences of Film Producers Taken to Court," *Los Angeles Times,* March 12, 1927, p.A8

29 "The Poor Millionaire," *Film Daily,* June 22, 1930, p.14

30 "Lehrman on Speed," *Variety,* April 6, 1927, p.18

31 "Columbia Starts 'For Ladies Only'," *Film Daily,* June 27, 1927, p.6

32 "Lehrman on Speed," p.18; "Roach Signs Up Henry Lehrman and L.J. Gasnier," *Moving Picture World,* May 7, 1927, p.41; "Studio Briefs," *Motion Picture News,* May 13, 1927, p.1845. Gasnier's affiliation with Roach, according to historian Randy Skretvedt, didn't work out. He directed a single film tentatively titled *Cowboys Cry for It* with Eugene Pallette in the lead. The results were so poor that Pallette's footage was scrapped and scenes with Stan Laurel were reshot by director Clyde Bruckman. The finished film was released as *Should Tall Men Marry?* (Correspondence with the author dated September 5, 2015)

33 George Jessel, *So Help Me: The Autobiography of George Jessel,* p.88

34 "Screen Gossip," *Brooklyn Daily Eagle,* July 8, 1927, p.12A

35 Chester J. Smith, *Motion Picture News,* October 28, 1927, p.1345

36 *Photoplay,* November 1927, p.137

37 *Film Daily,* October 30, 1927, p.13

38 H. Goldstone, *Strand* theatre, Sioux City, IA., publication unknown

39 *Film Daily,* October 30, 1927, p.13

40 *Photoplay,* November 1927, p.137

41 George Jessel, *So Help Me: The Autobiography of George Jessel,* p.89

42 "Studio Briefs," *Motion Picture News,* October 7, 1927, p.1132

43 "New Title for Warners' 'In Name Only'," *Motion Picture News,* November 11, 1927, p.1488; "Warner Bros. Schedules Three December Releases," *Motion Picture News,* December 16, 1927, p.1894

44 Chester J. Smith, "Husbands for Rent," *Motion Picture News,* January 7, 1928, p.75

45 "Husbands for Rent," *Film Daily,* January 8, 1928, p.6

46 Mori., "Husbands for Rent," *Variety,* July 25, 1928, p.28

Chapter 12: Back Home at Fox

1 "Fox Signs Lehrmann," *Film Daily,* December 15, 1927, p.1

2 "Up and Down the Rialtos," *Syracuse Herald,* March 4, 1928, p.4

3 Abel., "The Gay Retreat," *Variety,* October 12, 1927, pp.17, 20

4 "Co-star Cohen-McNamara in Series of 5 Reelers," *Film Daily,* January 26, 1928, p.1

5 "Up and Down the Rialtos," p.4

6 "Why Sailors Go Wrong," *Film Daily,* April 15, 1928, p.4

7 Chester J. Smith, "Why Sailors Go Wrong," *Motion Picture News,* April 11, 1928, p.1213

8 William K. Everson, *The Theodore Huff Memorial Society film notes,* June 4, 1968, p.1

9   Aubrey Solomon, *The Fox Film Corporation, 1915-1935: A History and Filmography* (Jefferson, NC: McFarland & Company, 2011), p.122

10 Martin Dickstein, "Why Sailors Go Wrong," *Brooklyn Daily Eagle,* April 10, 1928, p.12A

11 Jimmy Starr, *Barefoot on Barbed Wire: An Autobiography of a Forty-Year Hollywood Balancing Act,* pp.103-104

12 "News from the Dailies," *Variety,* January 18, 1928, p.58. The divorce was never finalized.

13 Grace Kingsley, "Stage Star Gets Big Film Role," *Los Angeles Times,* February 21, 1928, p.A10; Grace Kingsley, "Flashes," *Los Angeles Times,* March 2, 1928, p.B8

14 "Miss Banky Deeply Moved By Budapest," *New York Times,* April 1, 1928, p.X5; "Secret History of the Month," *Motion Picture Classic,* July 1928, p.35

15 "Utah's Bevy of Filmdom Stars Report Progress at Hollywood," *Salt Lake Tribune,* April 1, 1928, p.10

16 "Fox Sales Convention Starts in N.Y. Today," *Film Daily,* May 23, 1928, p.1

17 Laurence Reid, "Opinions on Pictures," *Motion Picture News,* June 23, 1928, p.2117

18 "Chicken A La King," *Film Daily,* June 17, 1928, p.3

19 Mordaunt Hall, "The Screen: Girls of a Feather," *New York Times,* June 11, 1928, p.27

20 "Chicken A La King," *Film Daily,* June 17, 1928, p.3

21 Mordaunt Hall, "The Screen: Girls of a Feather"

22 "At the Roxy," *Brooklyn Daily Eagle,* June 11, 1928, p.14A

23 Alexander Walker, *The Shattered Silents* (New York: William Morrow and Company, Inc., 1979), pp.23-24

24 "Citrus Turns Into Celluloid," *Los Angeles Times,* June 24, 1928, p.B7; "Film Corner-Stone Laid," *Los Angeles Times,* June 30, 1928, p.A3

25 "Fox Plans for Films Outlined," *Los Angeles Times,* June 3, 1928, p.C7

26 "Fox Plans in Short Feature Field Complete," *Exhibitors Herald and Moving Picture World,* June 2, 1928, p.100

27 "17 Directors Assigned to New Productions," *Exhibitors Herald and Moving Picture World,* June 2, 1928, p.130

28 Ralph Wilk, "A Little from 'Lots'," *Film Daily,* June 12, 1928, p.10

29 "Lehrman Preparing Original," *Film Daily,* June 11, 1928, p.7; "Lehrman Preparing; Stone Scenarizing," *Exhibitors Herald and Moving Picture World,* June 30, 1928, p.57

30 "Lists 52 Features, Comedies for '28-'29," *Film Daily,* May 24, 1928, p.11; "Homesick," *Exhibitors Herald and Moving Picture World,* June 2, 1928, p.97

31 "Cohen Starts New Film," *Film Daily,* July 31, 1928, p.1

32 "Sammy Is A Desert Bicycler," *The Standard-Union,* August 18, 1928, p.14; *The Daily Star,* September 4, 1928, p.8

33 "8 in Work, 5 in Cutting Room, 2 Being Started," *Film Daily,* September 24, 1928, p.3

34 "Homesick," *Film Daily,* January 27, 1929, p.4

35 "Homesick," *Movie Age,* February 2, 1929, p.18

36 "'Blue Danube' in Work," *Motion Picture News,* November 3, 1928, p.1398; "Bickel Here to Act in Films," *Los Angeles Times,* December 14, 1928, p.A11; "Three Stars in Single-Reel Comedy," *Moving Picture World,* May 26, 1917, p.1310

37 "Sound Your 'A': Dialogue As Taken From Screen," January 11, 1929, on file at New York State Archives

38 "Sound Your 'A'," *Variety,* November 27, 1929, page unknown

39 "Mary Astor Stars," *Exhibitors Daily Review,* December 19, 1928, p.4

40 "New Year's Eve," *Film Daily,* April 14, 1929, p.13

41 Don Ashbaugh, "New Year's Eve," *Motion Picture News,* May 4, 1929, p.1531

42 "Marksman Fires at Actor's Head," *Daily Illini,* March 3, 1929, p.11

43 Al Steen, "Exhibitors Respond to Questionnaire," *Movie Age,* March 30, 1929, p.7

44 "Movietone City of Fox Will Provide Talking Pictures," *Stevens Point Daily Journal,* April 1, 1929, page unknown

45   "Silent Product Not to Be Overlooked By Producers," *Movie Age,* April 6, 1929, p.7

46   Jerry Hoffman, "Dotty Jottings," *Motion Picture News,* March 9, 1929, p.782

Chapter 13: Fox, Twentieth Century, and 20th Century-Fox: This Time for Good

1   Myra Nye, "Society of Cinemaland," *Los Angeles Times,* October 13, 1929, p.23

2   "Star Gazing," *Mason City Globe-Gazette,* July 13, 1929, p.11

3   "A 'Triple Tempo' Gives Zip to 'New Year's Eve'," *Morning Herald,* June 15, 1929, p.14

4   "Camera Work for Screen," *New York Times,* June 2, 1929, p.5X

5   Philip K. Scheuer, "Crisis Leaves Directors, Cameramen Unscathed," *Los Angeles Times,* November 9, 1930, pp.B9, 19

6   "Sound Revolutionizing Whole Shorts Industry — Hammons," *Movie Age,* February 16, 1929, p.7

7   "M-G-M Laboratory Head Aboard Chief," *Albuquerque Journal,* December 13, 1929, p.16

8   "U's Short 'Departure'," *Variety,* November 19, 1930, p.12

9   Reviewed and assumedly released under this title, the film has been referenced under a number of variations. It was copyrighted as *A Butter-In Yegg Man,* is listed in the BFI holdings as *A Butter-in-Yeggman,* and advertised in numerous newspaper ads as *A Butter and Yegg Man.*

10   "The Big Butter and Yegg Man," *Motion Picture Herald,* April 11, 1931, p.36

11   "The Big Butter and Yegg Man," *Film Daily,* April 12, 1935, p.25

12   "Lehrman to Direct for Fox," *Film Daily,* February 3, 1931, p.4; "Co-Starring Teams to Be Highlight of Fox Program," *Film Daily,* May 14, 1931, p.6

13   "Personalities Are Featured In Fox's 48 for Next Season," *Film Daily,* April 27, 1931, p.6

14   "Long Rest Over," *Variety,* October 6, 1931, p.6

15   According to historian Sam Gill, who interviewed *Fighting Blood*'s scripter Beatrice Van later in her life, "it was Van who recommended George O'Hara for the lead role. She also had some scathing remarks to make about Darryl F. Zanuck who according to her contributed nothing to the *Fighting Blood* series despite his later claims."

16   "Twentieth Century Lists 12 Features," *Film Daily,* July 17, 1933, p.8

17   "News From the Dailies," *Variety,* August 8, 1933, p.50

18   *Recollections of Nunnally Johnson oral history transcript, http://archive.org/stream/recollectionsofn00john/ recollectionsofn00john_djvu.txt,* p.75

19   "Constance Bennett in 'Moulin Rouge'," *Film Daily,* January 10, 1934, p.22

20   Mordaunt Hall, "The Screen," *New York Times,* February 8, 1934, p.14

21   McCarthy, "Moulin Rouge," *Motion Picture Herald,* December 23, 1933, p.43

22   Harry Burns, "Constance Bennett Gives Her Greatest Performance in 'Moulin Rouge' — Directed By Sidney Lanfield," *Hollywood Filmograph,* December 16, 1933, p.3

23   Ralph Wilk, "A Little from 'Lots'," *Film Daily,* September 8, 1933, p.6

24   "Signed," *Motion Picture Herald,* November 11, 1933, p.53; Arthur Forde, "Seen and Heard," *Hollywood Filmograph,* November 25, 1933, p.2

25   While Del Ruth continued on in a career that would last forty years, not all of his co-workers were enthralled with his personality and technical capabilities. In the opinion of screenwriter John Bright, who worked with Del Ruth back at Warners on such films as *Blonde Crazy* and *Taxi,* "Del Ruth was personally a terrible person, a male chauvinist pig who would leave his mail all over his desk for his secretary to pick up. She hated him." When he asked the Warners editors their opinion of Del Ruth, they reportedly responded something to the effect of "That shit. He plays it safe. He has no imagination. Just watch on the set, and you'll see what we mean. He sets up an establishing shot; he moves in and has a medium shot, an over-the-shoulder shot, a tight two-shot, etc., and then he throws the whole thing into cutting and we make the picture. He's always just protecting himself." Bright quoted in Patrick McGilligan and Paul Buhle, *Tender Comrades* (New York; St. Martin's Griffin, 1997), pp.132-133

26 Gus McCarthy, *Motion Picture Herald*, May 5, 1934, p.64

27 *Film Daily,* May 4, 1934, p.9

28 Norbert Lusk, *Picture Play Magazine*, August 1934, p.37

29 *Recollections of Nunnally Johnson oral history transcript*

30 Joseph Schenck, quoted in Leonard Mosley, *Zanuck: The Rise and Fall of Hollywood's Last Tycoon* (Boston: Little, Brown and Company, 1984), p.152

31 Arthur W. Eddy, "Incorporation of Fox-20th Cent. Completed in Week, Says Schenck," *Film Daily*, June 21, 1935, pp.1, 25

32 Leonard Mosley, *Zanuck: The Rise and Fall of Hollywood's Last Tycoon*, p.155

33 "Studio Placements," *Variety*, May 8, 1935, p.39; M.W. Etty-Leal, "Chatter," *Variety*, June 5, 1935, p.52

34 "New Screen Merger Announces Its Plans," *New York Times*, July 9, 1935, p.24; "Studio Placements," *Variety*, August 21, 1935, p.35

35 Douglas W. Churchill, "Hollywood Sees 'A Midsummer Night's Dream'," *New York Times*, September 29, 1935, p.170.

36 "Screen Notes," *New York Times*, August 21, 1935, p.22

37 "Next Week on the Broadway Screen," *New York Times*, December 1, 1935, p.196

38 Andre Sennwald, "On Second Thought," *New York Times*, December 15, 1935, p.X7

39 Andre Sennwald, "Show Them No Mercy," *New York Times*, December 9, 1935, p.25

Chapter 14: Lehrman Knocks Out Memos

1 "Lehrman Makes Meg Bow On 20th 'Everybody Sing'," *Hollywood Reporter*, March 15, 1937, p.1; Ralph Wilk, "A 'Little' from Hollywood Lots," *Film Daily*, March 29, 1937, p.6

2 Harrison Carroll, "Behind the Scenes in Hollywood," (Tonawanda) *Evening News*, May 15, 1937, p.6

3 "Veteran Director Gets Comedy Job," *San Antonio Light*, March 19, 1937, p.3

4 Mel Gussow, *Don't Say Yes Until I Finish Talking* (New York: Pocket Books, 1972), p.80

5 Ronald L. Davis, *Words Into Images: Screenwriters On the Studio System* (University Press of Mississippi, 2007), pp.51-52

6 Leonard Mosley, Zanuck: *The Rise and Fall of Hollywood's Last Tycoon,* p.119. Sperling misremembered Lehrman's name as Pathé Nathan. It is evident from his comments that he had no real idea of Lehrman's past contributions to film, but given that Sperling was born in 1912 and would have been a mere youngster when Lehrman's career was at its peak, this isn't too surprising.

7 "Sperling Joins Fox," *Film Daily,* May 16, 1935, p.2

8 Inter-Office Correspondence, Twentieth Century-Fox Produced Scripts Collection at the UCLA Theater Arts Library, Lehrman to Zanuck, November 30, 1937.

9 Ibid., Lehrman to Zanuck, March 6, 1939; April 28, 1939; August 14, 1939.

10 Ibid., Lehrman to Zanuck, April 2, 1940

11 Ibid., Lehrman to Zanuck, May 21, 1940

12 Ibid., Lehrman to Harry Joe Brown, July 15, 1938

13 Ibid., Lehrman to Zanuck, July 14, 1937

14 Ibid., Lehrman to Zanuck, August 2, 1937

15 Ibid., Lehrman to Zanuck, January 12, 1939

16 "Driving Case Hearing Set," *Reno Evening Gazette,* December 27, 1937, p.2; "Crash Maims Film Beauty," *Los Angeles Times,* December 28, 1937, p.A8

17 "Lehrman, Film Producer, Faces Drunk-Driving Trial," *Los Angeles Times,* February 12, 1938, p.A3; "Lehrman, Cinema Producer, Fights Drunk-Driving Charge," *Los Angeles Times,* March 1, 1938; p.A3

18 "Girl Tells Crash at Traffic Trial," *Los Angeles Times,* April 13, 1938, p.A10; "Jury Acquits Film Producer," *Los Angeles Times,* April 15, 1938, p.A2

19 "Coast," *Variety,* September 28, 1938, p.62

20 "Film Stars Are Sued Over Income Taxes," *Modesto Bee,* January 18, 1939, p.2

21 Philip K. Scheuer, "Town Called Hollywood," *Los Angeles Times,* July 16, 1939, p.C3

22 "With the *Hollywood Reporter*," *Middlesboro Daily News,* May 15, 1939, page unknown; Paul Harrison, "Hollywood," *Chester Times,* August 29, 1939, page unknown

23 Frank S. Nugent, "The Screen," *New York Times,* October 14, 1939, p.13

24 "Keystone Cops Hit the Come-back Trail," *Film Daily,* October 11, 1939, p.7

25 Inter-Office Correspondence, Twentieth Century-Fox Produced Scripts Collection, Lehrman to Zanuck, December 13, 1938

26 Harrison Carroll, "Behind the Scenes in Hollywood," *Morning Herald,* March 15, 1940, p.28; *Times and Daily News Leader,* April 3, 1940, p.6

27 "Loosening of Economy Grip Brings Relief," *Boxoffice,* June 8, 1940, p.28. It is possible that Zanuck rehired Lehrman in some capacity or other, if only for a short term, as the two of them attended the preview of *The Man I Married* together in July. (Ralph Wilk, "Hollywood Speaking — ," *Film Daily,* July 23, 1940, p.7)

Chapter 15: The End

1 "Film Director Files Bankruptcy Petition," *San Antonio Press*, November 19, 1941, p.5A

2 "Studio Personalities," *Boxoffice*, February 27, 1943, p.43. Lehrman may have had some interim employment with 20th Centruy-Fox during this two-year period: his World War II draft registration card, dated April 26, 1942, lists the studio as his employer.

3 Ivan Spear, "Hollywood Report," *Boxoffice*, March 6, 1943, p.28

4 *AFI Catalog of Feature Films*, American Film Institute, *http://www.afi.com/members/catalog/*

5 Stan Laurel, quoted by daughter Lois in Scott MacGillivray's *Laurel & Hardy, from the Forties Forward* (New York: Vestal Press, 1998), p.8

6 *Creditor's Claim* of Maurice W. Rosenberg, dated February 19, 1947

7 "Henry Lehrman, Producer, Dies," *Los Angeles Times,* November 9, 1946, p.A3

8 Henry Lehrman *Certificate of Death*, State of California Department of Public Health, County of Los Angeles, dated November 8, 1946

9 *First and Final Account and Report, Petition for Distribution, In the Matter of the Estate of Henry Lehrman*, dated April 21, 1949

10 Naturalized Citizen Record # 6916573, issued February 5, 1951 by the U.S. District Court at New York City (at *www.ancestry.com*)

Chapter 16: Lehrman's Legacy

1 Interview with Norman Taurog by Sam Gill, August 17, 1966

2 Anthony Balducci, *Lloyd Hamilton, Poor Boy Comedian of Silent Cinema*, (Jefferson, NC: McFarland & Company, Inc.), pp.147, 157.

3 Charleson Gray, "Salvaging Stars," *Motion Picture*, February 1930, p.130

4 Joan Myers, interviewed by Frank Thompson, *The Commentary Track*, episode 19, November 4, 2012. It is unclear as to whether or not Watson actually worked in any films for Lehrman. The one film he starred in and credited in his autobiography as having been directed by Lehrman is cited as *The Mailman* (Coy Watson, Jr., *The Keystone Kid*, Santa Monica Press, 2001, pp.74-75). The photo accompanying that film is actually from Mack Swain's *Adventurous Ambrose*, made for the Sterns long after Lehrman had moved on to Fox Sunshine.

5 "Henry M. Lehrman," *Los Angeles Times*, p.V156

6 Mlle. Chic, "The Story of the L-Ko Head, H. Pathé Lehrmann," p.15

7 "Joke Not Liked By Joker," *New York Telegraph*, June 3, 1917, page unknown

8 "Men of the Town," *Los Angeles Times*, January 13, 1919, p.II2

9 Lenore Coffee, *Storyline; Recollections of a Hollywood Screenwriter* (London: Cassell and Company, Ltd., 1973), p.74

10 Ray W. Frohman, "Virginia Rappe Described As Dashing Beauty of Comedies," p.6

11 Interview with Dixie Chene Maire by Sam Gill, at the home of her sister Hazel Chene Asher in Hollywood, December 3, 1971

Appendix A: The Sterling Motion Picture Corporation, Post-Lehrman: A Rudderless Ship

1 *Universal Weekly*, May 9, 1914, p.4

2 Walter Lord Wright, "The Sterling Method," *New York Dramatic Mirror*, 1914, date and page unknown

3 *Universal Weekly*, May 9, 1914, p.4

4 "Motion Picture Department," *New York Clipper*, April 11, 1914, p.14

5 *Moving Picture World*, May 23, 1914, p.1056

6 "The Pick of the Programmes," *Bioscope*, October 15, 1914, p.XXI

7 "Nicholls[sic], Sterling Director, Has Made Tradition," *Universal Weekly*, August 29, 1914, p.12

8 "Sensationalism Marks First Nichols Comedy," *Universal Weekly*, June 27, 1914, p.21

9 "…a seven-passenger automobile and two motorcycles plunge over a precipice and fall two hundred feet. Six cameras are to be used to show the entire fall," explained the *New York Morning Telegraph*, August 9, 1914. Direction was attributed to Dave Kirkland rather than George Nichols in this article.

10 "Comments on the Films," *Moving Picture World*, July 18, 1914, p.433

11 "The Pick of the Programmes," *Bioscope*, August 6, 1914, p.598. *Bioscope*'s charity was, I suppose, understandable in that home-grown comedians included Bamforth's "Winky" series and Weston Feature Film Company's "Pimple" series, neither of which could compete with so much of the popular imported product; Sennett's films were the rage, catching on like wildfire in "All-Keystone Nights" as a summer attraction at various locations throughout the British Isles.

12 *Variety*, July 24, 1914, page unknown

13 "The Pick of the Programmes," *Bioscope*, August 27, 1914, p.847

14 According to the *Moving Picture World* only; Sterling's participation in this film has not been verified elsewhere.

15 "Comments on the Films," *Moving Picture World*, September 5, 1914, p.1373.

16 "The Pick of the Programmes," *Bioscope*, October 29, 1914, p.XXI

17 "Balshofer Visits New York," *Universal Weekly*, August 8, 1914, p.33

18 *New York Dramatic Mirror*, August 26, 1914, p.28.

19 Defections from the ranks of Universal's comedy directors was a common occurrence, according to *Variety* ("U's Directors' Upheaval," January 23, 1915), which placed their salary limits at $65 to $75 a week and had them "subjected to the whims, likes and dislikes of those 'higher up'"

20 "Griffin to Sterling," *Moving Picture World*, August 29, 1914, p.1219

21 "Max Asher," *Moving Picture World,* October 24, 1914, p.505.

22 Kalton C. Lahue and Sam Gill, in their *Clown Princes and Court Jesters* (South Brunswick and New York, 1970, p.30), claim that Curtis was the rebuffer, although this seems unlikely in that Curtis served as Asher's director on at least his second film at Sterling, and more than likely followed him over from Joker. Either that, or this was a rebranded Joker release used to plug a hole in the Sterling release schedule.

23 *Motion Picture News* (September 19, 1914, p.61) incorrectly credits actor William Franey as portraying Asher's opponent in this film. It was instead Bobby Dunn.

24 *New York Dramatic Mirror,* September 30, 1914, p.27

25 *New York Dramatic Mirror,* September 2, 1914, p.28

26 "Doings at Los Angeles," *Moving Picture World,* October 31, 1914, p.22

27 *Universal Weekly,* August 8, 1914, p.???

28 Sam Gill, "Little Billy Jacobs Grows Up," p.12

29 "Comments on the Films," *Moving Picture World,* October 3, 1914, p.65

30 Or acknowledged. "The only complaint we have at the present time," wrote Wisconsin exhibitor F.R. Smith, "is the poor titles used on the Sterling comedies. It is almost impossible to keep them in frame." Universal's response was that the problem plagued only the first comedies of the brand, and had already been fixed. "Sterling Titles Fixed," *Universal Weekly,* September 26, 1914, p.33.

31 "In and Out of Los Angeles Studios," *Motion Picture News,* September 26, 1914, p.58

32 H.B. Harris shot 250 feet of extreme closeups of a "hypnotized" cat's eyes for this release, only to find that the resulting (unusable) footage revealed the cat's eyes to be acting as a perfect mirror, with Harris to be seen cranking away at the camera with the studio visible behind him.

33 "Emma Clifton," *Moving Picture World,* December 12, 1914, p.1532

34 *Motion Picture News,* October 31, 1914, p.52

35 "The Pick of the Programmes," *Bioscope,* December 10, 1914, p.X

36 *Motion Picture News,* October 17, 1914, p.54

37 *Motion Picture News,* October 31, 1914, p.63

38 "Daily Release Reviews," *Variety,* October 31, 1914, p.26

39 "Sterling Co. Dissolving?," *Variety,* October 10, 1914, p.22

40 "In and Out of Los Angeles Studios," *Motion Picture News,* November 14, 1914, p.35

41 According to *Universal Weekly* (May 2, 1914, p.25), Fazenda wished to move out of comedy and into serious roles. Numerous applications to show her dramatic capabilities had finally taken their toll on Universal's West Coast studios' General Manager Isadore Bernstein, who was considering giving her the chance. Obviously, this never came to fruition, and the assumedly frustrated thespian was forced to continue making comedies until the twenties when other opportunities became available.

42 Dunn according to *Universal Weekly*; *Bioscope*'s reviewer insists that the actor is Bill Franey.

43 *Motion Picture News,* January 2, 1915, p.50

44 "In and Out of Los Angeles Studios," *Motion Picture News,* December 5, 1914, p.29

45 "Doings in Los Angeles," *Moving Picture World,* December 19, 1914, p.1661

46 "Doings in Los Angeles," *Moving Picture World,* December 26, 1914, p.1825

47 *New York Dramatic Mirror,* December 23, 1914, p.27

48 Fred J. Balshofer and Arthur C. Miller, *One Reel a Week,* p.112

49 "In and Out of Los Angeles Studios," *Motion Picture News,* December 26, 1914, p.32

50 "Moving Pictures," *Variety,* February 6, 1915, p.20

51 *New York Dramatic Mirror,* December 30, 1914, p.22

52 "Doings in Los Angeles," *Moving Picture World,* December 5, 1914, p.1363

53 "In and Out of Los Angeles Studios," *Motion Picture News,* December 12, 1914, p.38

54 *Universal Weekly*, December 26, 1914, p.9

55 *New York Dramatic Mirror*, December 23, 1914, p.27

56 "John E. Brennan, the Famous Funny Man," *Universal Weekly*, December 26, 1914, p.25

57 Actress Ethel Teare's sister. Both Betty and Ethel had worked at Kalem before Betty hooked up with Brennan.

58 "Break in Mutual Co. Healed; N.Y.M.P.CO. Gets Here," *Variety,* December 25, 1914, p.1

59 "Film Flashes," *Variety,* January 14, 1915, p.26

60 "Sennett Feature Film Company?" *New York Dramatic Mirror*, January 20, 1915, p.26

61 "Balshofer Goes East," *New York Telegraph*, January 17, 1915, page unknown

62 *Universal Weekly*, November 21, 1914, p.32

63 The studio ended up being used — if only briefly — by Balshofer's next venture, Quality Pictures, featuring his newest acquisition Francis X. Bushman. "Pacific Coast News," *New York Telegraph*, May 30, 1915, page unknown

64 *Motion Picture News,* January 2, 1915, p.36

65 *Ibid.* Not about to let inclement weather hinder production, Balshofer improvised and hurried Fazenda and Erdman out into a rainstorm for additional scenes. It would appear that this footage influenced the eventual title of the film.

66 *Motion Picture News,* November 28, 1914, p.49

67 Fred J. Balshofer and Arthur C. Miller, *One Reel a Week*, p.113

68 *Motion Picture News,* May 15, 1915, p.73

69 "In and Out of Los Angeles Studios," *Motion Picture News,* September 12, 1914, p.64

70 "Comedy Film Artist is Also Famed as a Light Opera Star," *Exhibitors Herald*, February 16, 1916, p.20

71 "Pacific Coast News," *New York Telegraph*, March 21, 1915, page unknown.

72 "In and Out of Los Angeles Studios," *Motion Picture News,* November 14, 1914, p.36

73 Wells' first name Mae would alternately be spelled "May" and "Mai" over the course of her career

74 "Sennett Feature Film Company?," *New York Dramatic Mirror*, January 20, 1915, p.26

75 "In and Out of Los Angeles Studios," *Motion Picture News,* July 10, 1915, p.57

Appendix B: The L-Ko Komedy Kompany, Post-Lehrman: Soldiering On

1 *Moving Picture World,* October 7, 1916, p.60

2 "Lured But Cured," *Moving Picture Weekly*, September 30, 1916, page unknown

3 *Moving Picture World,* October 7, 1916, p.60

4 "Lehrman Starts Company," *New York Telegraph*, August 27, 1916, page unknown; "Pathé Lehrman to Open Studio," *Moving Picture World,* September 9, 1916, p.1679

5 "J.G. Blystone," *Moving Picture Weekly*, November 25, 1916, p.4

6 "List of Winning L-KO Releases Growing Bigger All the Time," *Moving Picture Weekly*, October 28, 1916, p.1

7 "How Do They Do It?" *Moving Picture Weekly*, June 3, 1916, pp.14-15

8 *A Mid-Air Mixup* may have been an early working title for Alice Howell's *Balloonatics*, which ended up as a Century Comedy

9 Letter from Michael Edelstein, Mount Morris Theatre, 116th St. & 5th Ave., New York City, reprinted in *Moving Picture Weekly*, October 28, 1916, p.39

10 "Julius Stern," *Moving Picture World,* November 4, 1916, p.633

11 "Twenty Five Million Attend Film Shows Every Day in U.S.," *Exhibitors Herald*, August 5, 1916, p.20

12 Julius Stern, "Reminiscences of a Studio Manager, Part II," p.1764
13 "A Rural Romance," *Moving Picture Weekly*, October 14, 1916, page unknown
14 "Merta Sterling Laughs at Fate," *Moving Picture Weekly*, March 10, 1917, p.15
15 Sterling and Dunham had appeared together in at least one film for Joker, *Luttie's Lovers*, April 22, 1914
16 *Moving Picture World*, January 13, 1917, p.246
17 "L-KO's for August and September Release," *Moving Picture World*, August 4, 1917, p.821
18 "The Donkey Did It," *Moving Picture World*, February 2, 1918, p.692
19 "L-KO's Ingenue," *Moving Picture Weekly*, May 12, 1917, p.19
20 Robert C. McElravy, *Moving Picture World*, January 20, 1917, p.358
21 "Dippy Dan's Doings" review, *Motion Picture News*, March 31, 1917, p.2037
22 *Moving Picture World*, November 25, 1916, p.1169
23 "Alice Howell Howls," *New York Telegraph*, May 13, 1917, page unknown
24 "Long Acre Will Market Comedies," *Moving Picture Weekly*, July 28, 1917, p.33
25 "New Chief for Universal City," *Moving Picture World*, December 11, 1915, p.1994
26 "Combine Rumors Fill the Air; Millions Flying Everywhere," *Variety*, March 24, 1916, p.21
27 "Laemmle to Start New Film Company, is Report," *New York Clipper*, October 14, 1916, p.32
28 "Universal's Efficient Editorial Force," *Motography*, December 2, 1916, p.1242
29 "Tribute to Fatty Voss," *New York Telegraph*, May 6, 1917, page unknown
30 One of the actors in this film was Billie Ritchie's former vaudeville partner, Rich McAllister. This is his only known appearance in an L-Ko comedy.
31 *Motion Picture News*, June 24, 1916, p.3935
32 *Motion Picture News*, July 15, 1916, p.282
33 *Motion Picture News*, June 24, 1916, p.3902
34 "Some L-KO Announcements," *Moving Picture World*, May 19, 1917, p.1152
35 Interview with Norman Taurog by Sam Gill, August 17, 1966
36 "An Innocent Crook" review, *Motion Picture News*, January 29, 1916, p.571
37 *Moving Picture World*, January 6, 1917, p.89
38 "Frank Klein, Circus Strong Man, Joins L-KO," *Moving Picture World*, February 24, 1917, p.1190
39 "L-KO Notes," *Moving Picture Weekly*, August 4, 1917, p.22
40 "L-KO Notes," *Moving Picture Weekly*, September 29, 1917, p.20
41 "Comedian Dies in Camp," *Moving Picture World*, November 30, 1918, p.938
42 "L-KO Notes," *Moving Picture Weekly*, September 29, 1917, p.20
43 Jas. S. McQuade, "Chicago News Letter," *Moving Picture World*, August 18, 1917, p.1076
44 "Five Directors Making L-Ko'S," *Moving Picture World*, September 8, 1917, p.1555
45 "Schedule of Forthcoming L-Ko's," *Moving Picture World*, October 13, 1917, p.265
46 "L-Ko Increasing All Its Forces to Supply Comedy Demand," *Motion Picture News*, October 20, 1917, p.2733
47 "L-Ko Adopts Star System for Comedy Companies," *Motion Picture News*, December 12, 1918, p.418
48 "Gale Henry Transfers to L-Ko Comedies," *Moving Picture World*, December 1, 1917, p.1354
49 "Gale Henry Forms Company," *Moving Picture World*, August 10, 1918, p.828
50 *Moving Picture World*, January 19, 1918, p.386
51 *Moving Picture World*, March 2, 1918, p.1270

52 J.C. Jessen, "In and Out of West Coast Studios," *Motion Picture News,* August 18, 1917, p.1145

53 "New Arrangement of L-Ko Directors," *Moving Picture World,* December 29, 1917, p.1960

54 "L-Ko Increasing All Its Forces to Supply Comedy Demand," p.2733

55 "Bullets and Boneheads," *Moving Picture World,* December 15, 1917, p.1660

56 "Activities at L-O [sic] Studios," *Moving Picture World,* September 22, 1917, p.1868

57 "A Few L-KOmiums," *Moving Picture Weekly*, October 27, 1917, p.21

58 "Los Angeles Camoufleurs," *New York Telegraph*, November 18, 1917, page unknown

59 "Laemmle Explains Curtailment," *Motography*, November 10, 1917, p.960

60 "Universal Stops Short Subjects," *Motography*, November 3, 1917, p.906

61 "Universal Tries an Experiment," *Motion Picture News,* May 11, 1918, p.2838

62 "Fate of Industry Lies in Hands of Exhibitors," *Exhibitors Herald,* January 5, 1918, p.13

63 "Alice Howell Release to Be Issued Monthly," *Moving Picture World,* May 25, 1918, p.1165

64 "Cut By Broken Glass," *Moving Picture World,* September 28, 1918, p.1862; *Moving Picture World,* October 5, 1918, p.64

65 John McCabe, *The Comedy World of Stan Laurel* (Garden City, NY: Doubleday & Company, Inc., 1974), pp.26-27

66 Or at least he was promoted as being Chinese; *IMDb.com* gives Korea as his place of birth.

67 "L-Ko to Feature Chinaman," *Moving Picture World,* July 27, 1918, p.574

68 *New York Telegraph*, November 19, 1916, page unknown

69 *Los Angeles Evening Herald*, October 7, 1919, p.19

70 It is possible that Hong had a small, uncredited role in *Ash-Can Alley* (January 13, 1918) as well; both the supplied synopsis and reviews mention a Chinese laundryman as part of the plot.

71 *Moving Picture World,* June 29, 1918, p.1892

72 "Century and L-Ko Companies Expand," *Moving Picture World,* August 10, 1918, p.815

73 *Photoplay*, July 1925, p.45

74 *Moving Picture World,* November 17, 1917, p.1038

75 *Motion Picture News,* July 22, 1916, p.458

76 Adding to the confusion, Sennett biographer Gene Fowler attributed the quote to Keystone title writer Johnny Grey, *Father Goose*, p.355

77 But not by King Vidor, who later attributed the quote to Abe in his book *A Tree is a Tree* (New York: Harcourt, Brace and Company, 1952). Given the fog of time, it very well may have been brother Julius who uttered these famous words.

78 "Close-Ups," *Photoplay*, September 1918, p.67. Abe Stern was also credited by King Vidor as having made the memorable and oft-used quote "A rock is a rock, and a tree is a tree. Shoot it in Griffith Park." Silent era cameraman and director Harry Arthur Gant recalled a variation of this quote in his memoirs of 1959 as "A rock is a rock, a tree is a tree, shoot it on the back ranch," and attributed it to Carl Laemmle (Harry Arthur Gant, *I Saw Them Ride Away*, Castle Knob Publishing, 2009, p.244)

79 *Motion Picture News,* May 15, 1915, p.73

80 "Merit Won His Start in Films," *Los Angeles Times,* September 27, 1925, p.31

81 "L-Ko Has New Scenario Editor," *Moving Picture World,* October 12, 1918, p.206

82 "Moving Pictures," *Variety,* September 27, 1918, p.43

83 "What L-Ko Has to Offer," *Moving Picture Weekly*, December 21, 1918, p.8

84 "Death Alters Plot of Comedy," *Moving Picture World,* October 12, 1918, p.244

85 "Edith Roberts and the L-Ko Beauties Take Bathing Suit Prizes," *Moving Picture Weekly*, August 4, 1917, pp.18-19. Babe Henderson, as reported in the article, was likely a misreported Babe Emerson.

86 "L-Ko President Back from Coast," *Motion Picture News,* March 23, 1918, p.1709

87 Eddie Cline, as quoted in Frederick C. Othman, "With the *Hollywood Reporter,*" *Middlesboro Daily News*, June 20, 1942, page unknown

88 The cast list for September's *A Pullman Blunder* includes "the Cutey Girls," which may have been a later, last gasp incarnation of the group

89 "L-Ko Beauty Sextette Breaks Into Broadway," *Moving Picture World,* June 22, 1918, p.1739

90 "Official Cut-Outs Made By the Chicago Board of Censors," *Exhibitors Herald*, May 18, 1918, p.31

91 Alfred A. Cohn, "The Spanish Invasion," *Photoplay*, January 1919, p.76

92 "Universal Opened on November 18," *Moving Picture World,* December 14, 1918, p.1195

93 "Moving Pictures: Deaths," *Variety,* November 15, 1918, p.45

94 A.H. Giebler, "Where the L-Ko Laughs Come From," *Moving Picture World,* November 16, 1918, pp.729-730; "What L-Ko Has to Offer," *Moving Picture Weekly*, December 21, 1918, p.8

95 "L-Ko Producing Again," *Wid's Daily*, January 13, 1919, p.1

96 Diana Serra Cary, *Hollywood's Children* (Boston: Houghton Mifflin Company, 1979), p.78

97 Diana Serra Cary, *What Ever Happened to Baby Peggy?* (New York: St. Martin's Press, 1996), p.26

98 "Close-Ups by Comly," *Wid's Daily*, January 27, 1919, page unknown

99 "L-Ko and Century Move," *Moving Picture World,* September 7, 1918, p.1417

100 "L-Ko Moves into Bigger Quarters," *Moving Picture World,* February 15, 1919, p.878

101 "Fred Fishback Joins Universal," *Moving Picture World,* May 3, 1919, p.669

102 "L-Ko Notes," *Moving Picture Weekly*, April 12, 1919, p.10

103 "News of the Film World," *Variety,* February 21, 1919, p.66

104 "'Rainbow' Comedies are to Supersede L-Ko," *Motion Picture News,* June 14, 1919, p.3982

105 "New Century Policy in the Fall Announced," *Motion Picture News,* July 5, 1919, p.353

106 "L-Ko Changed to Century," *Moving Picture World,* July 19, 1919, p.363

107 "Stern, Universal Treasurer," *Wid's Daily*, April 22, 1920, p.1

108 The number of shares would be further increased to five thousand three years later. *Certificate of Increase of Capital Stock of L-Ko Motion Picture Kompany*, August 25, 1920; *Certificate of Increase of Capital Stock of Century Film Corporation*, April 23, 1923

109 *Decree of Dissolution of Corporation*, June 5, 1928

110 *In the Matter of the Petition of L-Ko Motion Picture Kompany, a Corporation, for a Change of Name*, October 26, 1920

Bibliography

Books:

Balshofer, Fred and Miller, Arthur C. *One Reel a Week*. University of California Press, 1967

Barry, John M. *The Great Influenza*. London: Penguin Books Ltd., 2004

Bengston, John. *Silent Visions*. Solana Beach, CA: Santa Monica Press, 1911

Bitzer, G.W. *Billy Bitzer: His Story*. New York: Farrar, Straus and Giroux, 1973

Bowser, Eileen. *Biograph Bulletins 1908-1912*. New York: Octagon Books, 1973

Brownlow, Kevin and Kobal, John. *Hollywood: The Pioneers*. New York: Alfred A. Knopf, 1979

Brownlow, Kevin. *The Parade's Gone By...*. New York: Alfred A. Knopf, 1968

Bruskin, David N. *The White Brothers: Jack, Jules, and Sam White*. Metuchen, NJ: The Scarecrow Press, Inc., 1990

Cary, Diana Serra. *Hollywood's Children*. Boston: Houghton Mifflin Company, 1979

_____. *What Ever Happened to Baby Peggy?* New York: St. Martin's Press, 1996

Chaplin, Charles and Lane, Rose Wilder. *Charlie Chaplin's Own Story*. Indianapolis: The Bobbs-Merrill Company, 1916

Chaplin, Charles. *My Autobiography*. New York: Simon and Schuster, 1964

Coffee, Lenore. *Storyline; Recollections of a Hollywood Screenwriter*. London: Cassell and Company, Ltd., 1973

Cooper, Miriam and Herndon, Bonnie. *Dark Lady of the Silents*. New York: The Bobbs-Merrill Company, Inc., 1973

Cullen, Frank. *Vaudeville, Old and New: An Encyclopedia of Variety Performers in America, Volume 1*. New York: Routledge, 2004

Davis, Ronald L. *Words Into Images: Screenwriters On the Studio System*. University Press of Mississippi, 2007

Drinkwater, John. *The Life and Adventures of Carl Laemmle*. London: William Heinemann Ltd, 1931

Dwyer, Ruth Anne. *Malcolm St. Clair: His Films, 1915-1948*. Lanham, MD: The Scarecrow Press, Inc., 1996

Fowler, Gene. *Father Goose: The Story of Mack Sennett*. New York: Covici Friede Publishers, 1934

Fox, Susan and Rosellini, Donald G. *William Fox: A Story of Early Hollywood, 1915-1930*. Baltimore, MD: Midnight Marquee Press, Inc., 2006

Gallagher, J.P. *Fred Karno: Master of Mirth and Tears*. London: Robert Hale & Company, 1971

Graham, Cooper C., Higgins, Steve, Mancini, Elaine, and Viera, João Kuiz. *D.W. Griffith and the Biograph Company*. Metuchen, N.J.: The Scarecrow Press, Inc., 1985

Grau, Robert. *The Theatre of Science: A Volume of Progress and Achievement in the Motion Picture Industry*. Broadway Publishing Company, New York, 1914

Green, Abel and Laurie, Joe. *Show Biz from Vaude to Video*. New York: Henry Holt and Company, 1951

Griffith, Linda Arvidson. *When the Movies Were Young*. New York: E.P. Dutton and Company, 1925

Gussow, Mel. *Don't Say Yes Until I Finish Talking*. New York: Pocket Books, 1972

Hayde, Michael J. *Chaplin's Vintage Year*. Albany, GA: BearManor Media, 2013

Henabery, Joseph. *Before, In and After Hollywood*. Lanham, MD: Scarecrow Press, Inc., 1997

Henderson, Robert M. *D.W. Griffith: The Years at Biograph*. New York: Farrar, Straus and Giroux, 1970

Jessel, George. *So Help Me: The Autobiography of George Jessel*. New York: Random House, 1943

Keaton, Buster and Samuels, Charles. *My Wonderful World of Slapstick*. New York: Da Capo Press, Inc., 1960

Lahue, Kalton C. and Brewer, Terry. *Kops and Custards: the Legend of Keystone Films* Norman: University of Oklahoma Press, 1968

MacGillivray, Scott. *Laurel & Hardy from the Forties Forward*. New York: Vestal Press, 1998

Manor, Alexander, editor. *The Book of Sambor and Stari Sambor; A Memorial to the Jewish Communities*, published in Tel Aviv, 1980 and translated and posted on the pages of the Jewishgen.com web site, *http://www.jewishgen.org/yizkor/sambor/SamI.html*

Marshall, Wendy. *William Beaudine: From Silents to Television*. Lanham, MD: The Scarecrow Press, Inc., 2005

Massa, Steve. *Lame Brains & Lunatics*. Albany, GA: BearManor Media, 2013

McCabe, John. *The Comedy World of Stan Laurel*. Garden City, NY: Doubleday & Company, Inc., 1974

Mosley, Leonard. *Zanuck: The Rise and Fall of Hollywood's Last Tycoon*. Boston: Little, Brown and Company, 1984

Pickford, Mary. *Sunshine and Shadows*. Garden City, New York: Doubleday and Company, Inc., 1955

Ramsey, Terry. *A Million and One Nights*. New York: Simon and Schuster, 1926

Robinson, David. *Chaplin: His Life and His Art*. New York: McGraw-Hill Book Company, 1985

Sennett, Mack and Shipp, Cameron. *King of Comedy*. Garden City, New York: Doubleday and Company, Inc., 1954

Semenov, Lillian Wurtzel and Winter, Carla. *William Fox, Sol Wurtzel and the Early Fox Film Corporation: Letters, 1917-1923*. Jefferson, NC: McFarland & Company, Inc., 2001

Slide, Anthony. *Aspects of American Film History Prior to 1920*. Metuchen, New Jersey: The Scarecrow Press, Inc., 1978

Solomon, Aubrey. *The Fox Film Corporation, 1915-1935: A History and Filmography*. Jefferson, NC: McFarland & Company, 2011

Starr, Jimmy. *Barefoot on Barbed Wire: An Autobiography of a Forty-Year Hollywood Balancing Act*. Lanham, Maryland: Scarecrow Press, Inc., 2001

Stone, Rob. *Laurel or Hardy: The Solo Films of Stan Laurel and Oliver "Babe" Hardy*. Temecula, CA: Split Reel Books, 1996

Swanson, Gloria. *Swanson on Swanson*. New York: Random House, 1980

Taves, Brian. *Thomas Ince: Hollywood's Independent Pioneer*. University Press of Kentucky, 2012

Viertel, Salka. *The Kindness of Strangers*. New York: Holt, Rinehart and Winston, 1969

Walker, Alexander. *The Shattered Silents: How the Talkies Came to Stay*. New York: William Morrow and Company, Inc., 1979

Walker, Brent E. *Mack Sennett's Fun Factory*. Jefferson, NC: McFarland & Company, Inc., 2010

Articles:

Berglund, Bo. "The Day the Tramp Was Born," *Sight and Sound*, Spring 1989, Vol. 58, No. 2

Carr, Harry C. "Charlie Chaplin's Story, Part II," *Photoplay*, August 1915; "Charlie Chaplin's Story, Part III," *Photoplay*, September 1915

Caslavsky, Karel, "American Comedy Series: Filmographies 1914-1930," *Griffithiana*, No. 51/52, La Cineteca del Friuli, October 1994

Dreiser, Theodore. "The Best Motion Picture Interview Ever Written," *Photoplay*, August 1928

Gill, Sam. "Little Billy Jacobs Grows Up," *Shadowland*, Vol. 1 No. 1.

Maltin, Leonard. "Conversations: Norman Taurog, Part 1," *Leonard Maltin's Movie Crazy*, Winter, 2006, No. 15; "Conversations: Norman Taurog, Part 2," *Leonard Maltin's Movie Crazy*, Spring, 2006, No. 16

Redway, Sara. "Passing of the Brown Derby," *Motion Picture Classic*, date unknown

Slide, Anthony. "Silent Stars Speak," *Films in Review*, March 1980, Vol. XXXI, No. 3

Newspapers, Trade Publications, Periodicals:

Aerial Age Weekly, 1919
Albany Evening Journal, 1914-1918
Albuquerque Journal, 1929
Amarillo Globe, 1928
American Cinematographer, 1922-1942
Australian Women's Weekly, 1970
Bergen Evening Record, 1935
Billboard, 1914-1918
Billings Gazette, 1924
Bioscope, 1914-1915
Boxoffice, 1940, 1943
Brooklyn Daily Eagle, 1905
Camera, 1923
Cedar Rapids Evening Gazette, 1921
Chester Times, 1939
Chicago Daily Tribune, Chicago Tribune 1923, 1981
Cinema News and Property Gazette, 1913
Daily Argus, 1922
Daily East Oregonian, 1915
Daily Illini, 1929
Daily Star, 1928
Eau Claire Leader, 1922
Exhibitors Herald, 1915-1928
Exhibitors Trade Review, 1921-1924
Exhibitors World, 1920
Film Daily, 1918-1940
Film Fun, 1916-1918
Filmfax Magazine, 1994
Fort Wayne Journal Gazette, 1919
Hamilton Daily News, 1930
Harrison's Reports, 1924
Helena Daily Independent, 1921
Hollywood, 1938
Hollywood Filmograph, 1933
Hollywood Reporter, 1937
Indianapolis Star, 1913, 1921
International Photographer, 1933

Ironwood Daily Globe, 1921
Janesville Daily Gazette, 1918, 1921
Kingston Daily Freeman, 1921
Lima Daily News, 1917
Logansport Daily Press, 1922
Logansport Pharos-Tribune, 1921, 1926
Los Angeles Examiner, 1920-1921
Los Angeles Herald, 1914-1921
Los Angeles Times, 1913-1946
Lowell Sun, 1917
Mason City Globe-Gazette, 1929
Middlebury Register, 1914
Middlesboro Daily News, 1939, 1942
Modesto Bee, 1939
Morning Herald, 1929, 1940
Morning Oregonian, 1919-1921
Morning Telegraph, 1922
Motion Picture Classic, 1920
Motion Picture Herald, 1931-1934
Motion Picture Magazine, 1914-1923
Motion Picture News, 1914-1929
Motion Picture Studio Directory and Trade Annual, 1916, 1921
Motography, 1913-1925
Motor Age, 1916, 1929
Moving Picture News, 1911-1912
Moving Picture World, 1912-1927
National Advocate, 1922
National Board of Review Magazine, 1926
National Enquirer, 197?
New York Clipper, 1913-1919
New York Dramatic Mirror, 1914-1921
New York Evening World, 1922
New York Sun and Globe, 1923
New York Telegraph, 1914-1920
New York Times, 1913-1939
New York Tribune, 1920
Oakland Tribune, 1918-1919

Ogden-Standard Examiner, 1922
Perry Daily Chief, 1920
Photoplay, 1915-1927
Photo-Play Journal, 1919
Picture-Play Magazine, 1918
Press Courier, 1965
Printers' Ink, 1902
Reno Evening Gazette, 1937
St. Petersburg Times, 1963
San Antonio Light, 1930, 1937
San Antonio Press, 1941
San Francisco Bulletin, 1921
San Francisco Call, 1913
San Francisco Call and Post, 1922
San Francisco Chronicle, 1922
San Francisco Examiner, 1921
Seattle Star, 1921
Semidji Daily Pioneer, 1921
Slapstick!, 2007-2008
Stevens Point Daily Journal, 1929
Sunday Oregonian, 1918, 1922
Syracuse Herald, 1928
Syracuse Journal, 1906, 1915, 1921
Syracuse Post-Standard, 1906
The Constitution, 1915
The Dramatic Mirror, 1994
The New Movie Magazine, 1930
The Reel Journal, 1924-1925
The Winner, 1917
Tonawanda Evening News, 1937
Trenton Evening Times, 1908
Universal Weekly/Moving Picture Weekly, 1914-1927
Utica Observer, 1914
Variety, 1913-1938
Wisconsin State Journal, 1922

Miscellaneous Sources:

AFI Catalog of Feature Films (afi.com)

Barnet Braverman Research Collection, held within the D.W. Griffith Papers, 1897-1954, Museum of Modern Art Film Study Center

Internet Archive (archive.org)

Lantern: Search, Visualize and Explore the Media History Digital Library (lantern.mediahist.org)

Library of Congress (chroniclingamerica.loc.gov)

Mary Pickford interview by Tony Thomas, CBC Radio, May 25, 1959

Media History Digital Library and the University of Wisconsin-Madison Department of Communication Arts (mediahistoryproject.org.)

Newspaper Archive (newspaperarchive.com)

NitrateVille (nitrateville.com)

Old Fulton NY Post Cards (fultonhistory.com)

Silent Comedians Forum (silentcomedians.com)

Silent Comedy Mafia Forum (silentcomedymafia.com)

William K. Everson, *The Theodore Huff Memorial Film Society* notes

Index

101 Bison Film Company 37-38, 50, 73-75, 94, 371
20th Century-Fox 10, 346, 350, 356, 358-361, 690, 695, 697
Aarup, Peggy 422, 424, 624, 626
Abalone Industry, The 438
Abbott and Costello 359
Actors' Fund 173
Adams, Eugene 195
Adams, Frankie 297
Adams, Jimmie 13, 18, 201, 209, 211, 214-215, 217, 220, 223, 225-226, 236, 634, 639, 641, 645-647, 649
Adams, Maude 149
Adler, Hans 694
Adler, William F. 380
Adventures of Dollie, The 26
Adventures of Hi Holler, The 384
Adventuress, An 278
Adventurous Ambrose 406, 609
Aero Marine Works 284
AFI Academic Network 10, 208
AFI Catalog of Feature Films 10, 208
After Big Game of the Sea 477
After Her Millions 129-130, 489
After the Balled-Up Ball 390-391, 572
A-Haunting We Will Go 359
Air Raid Wardens 359
Aitken, Harry 37, 54
Albert, Dan 440
Alexander Graham Bell 350
Alexander, Claire 424, 630, 632
Alexander, Frank 180, 328, 685
Alexander, Gus "Shorty" 201
Alexandria Hotel (see Hotel Alexandria)
Algy On the Force 42, 435
Alice in Society 166, 388, 563
Alice in Wonderland 113
Alkali Ike series 85, 384
All Jazzed Up 398, 400, 423-425, 627
All the Dog's Fault 368
Allen, Don 289, 663

Allen, Phyllis 82, 224
Allister, Claud 343
Almost a Scandal 123, 125-126, 491
Almost Married 371, 450
Ambrose and His Widow 406-407, 606
Ambrose the Lion-Hearted 406, 409, 605
Ambrose's Icy Love 406-407, 601
Ameche, Don 356, 697
American Éclair Company 75, 85, 368, 371
American Film Institute 10, 208
American Film Manufacturing Company 380
American Miracle 351
American Mutoscope and Biograph Company 24
American Theatre 54
American Vitagraph Company 25, 50, 76, 83, 87, 94-95, 152, 213, 221, 368, 404, 412, 414-415
Anderson, Dave "Andy" 375, 436, 455-456, 458, 460, 480
Anderson's Gaiety Company 171
Andrews, Carol 697
Androit, Lucien 697
Angelus Publicity Bureau 102
Anger, Lou 245
Animated Weekly 80, 149, 410, 574
Anthony, Earle C. 200
Arbuckle, Minta Durfee (see Durfee, Minta)
Arbuckle, Roscoe 13, 45-48, 59, 68-69, 71, 139, 195-196, 242, 244-245, 255, 257-258, 279-282, 284, 290-291, 311, 340, 351, 356, 379, 384, 435-442
Arcadian Maid, An 429
Are Married Policemen Safe? 199, 203, 205-206, 233, 468, 640
Arling, Charles 180-181
Arlington, Paul 112
Arliss, George 339
Armetta, Henry 328, 330, 685, 688
Armistead, Charles 365
Armstrong, Billy 171-172, 233, 387, 396-398, 414-416, 420, 539, 544, 548-549, 51-553, 556-557, 569, 577-578, 614-615, 617, 619, 623-624
Armstrong, R.D. 639

Arnold, Edward 352
Around the Clock 105-107, 132
Arrowhead Springs 151, 156
Arsenal of Lloyd at Triest, The 368
Arthur, George M. 658
Arvidson, Linda 15, 23, 31, 151, 427-428, 430, 432
As the Bells Rang Out! 429
Asch, Jerry 397
Ascot Speedway 173, 277
Ascott, "Funny Face" 201
Ash, Jerome 182, 537
Ash, Sam 697
Ash-Can Alley 401, 603
Asher, Max 84, 92, 94, 374, 377-378, 383, 446, 458, 460-462, 464, 466-468
Ashton, Sylvia 147, 502, 511-512
Associated First Pictures, Inc. 258
Associated Publications 333
Astor, Mary 331-332, 687
Astra Studios 246
Astray in a Large City (see *Alice in Society*)
At Coney Island 38
At It Again 39
At the Shoot (see *Shooting Match, A*)
At Three O'Clock 371, 373, 454
Auer, Mischa 692-693
August, Edwin 94, 430-432
Austro-Hungarian Empire 19
Authors' League of America 95
Automaniacs 394
Automobile Fashion Show 173, 277
Avenged By a Fish 149-150, 154, 513
Avenging Dentist, The 134, 493
Avery, Charles 41, 49, 59, 94, 433-439, 441-442
Avery, Suzanne 267, 657
B.H. Dyas Sporting Goods Company 95
Babes in the Hollywood 296, 298, 669, 672
Baby Ben 293
Baby Mix-Up, A (see *Where is My Che-ild?*)
Backward Sons and Forward Daughters 391, 592
Bacon, Lloyd 311, 675
Baffles, the Gentleman Burglar 65, 440
Baggot, King 31, 85
Bailey, Robert "Bob" 697
Baker, C. Graham 677
Balboa Feature Film Company 69, 378, 384
Balboa Park 320
Balducci, Anthony 364
Balloon Bandits, The (see *Balloonatics*)
Balloonatics 196, 394
Balmain, Rollo 104
Balshofer, Fred 38, 47, 66, 73-76, 81-84, 87, 93, 97-99, 107, 277-278, 367, 369, 371-372, 378-383, 385-386, 443, 472, 475
Bandit, A 70
Bangville Police 42, 44-45, 66, 70, 435

Bankoff, Ivan 156
Bankruptcy of Boggs and Schultz, The 168, 542
Barberous Plots 398-399, 404-405, 604
Barker, Florence 428-431
Barnes, A.L. 244, 259
Barnett, Chester 84
Barnold, Charles 134
Barnold's Drunken Dog 134
Barnyard Flirtation 47
Baron Long's Vernon Country Club 69, 173
Baron Long's Watts Tavern 200
Baron Near Broke 132
Baron's Bear Escape, The 119, 484-485
Barry, Eddie 401-402, 410-411, 417, 420-421, 591, 595-599, 603, 612-618, 620, 622
Bartholdi Inn 31, 115
Bartholdi, Polly 31
Bartlett, Randolph 188
Baseball Ambrose (see *Home Run Ambrose*)
Baseball Teams (All Stars, Comics, Photo-Players League, Sunshines, Tragics) 76, 95, 99, 200
Basevi, James 697
Bath Between, The 327
Bath House Tragedy, A 147, 154, 515
Battered Hearts and Shattered Faces (see *Street Cars and Carbuncles*)
Battle of "Let's Go", The 394, 569
Battle of Gettysburg, The 51
Battle of Running Bull, The 383, 479
Battle of Who Run, The 68, 441
Battle, The 376, 459
Baum, L. Frank 375
Baumann, Charles O. 37-38, 40, 54, 58, 73, 75, 78
Baxter, Warner 346
Beach Birds 153-154, 512
Beach Nuts 392, 394, 583
Beach Romance, A 371, 450
Beaches and Peaches 605
Bear Escape, A 378, 465
Beast at Bay, A 432
Beat At His Own Game 34, 432-433
Beaudine, William 211, 213, 645
Beauties and Bombs 154
Beauty and the Boob 629
Beauty and the Feast 669
Beauty Brigade 234
Beban, George 245
Bébé series 368
Beck, Robert 136
Beebe, Marjorie 327, 329-330, 685-686, 688
Beery, Wallace 92
Behrendt, Sam 101-102, 148
Behrendt-Levy Company 272
Behrman, Miss 32
Belasco, Walter 613
Bell, Spencer 363

INDEX

Belle Starr 351
Belles of Liberty, The 420, 423, 614
Bells, The 131
Ben Hur: A Tale of the Christ 172
Benedict, William 695
Bennett, Belle 173, 554
Bennett, Constance 339-342, 690-691
Bennett, Mickey 658
Bennison, Andrew 674
Bergman, Henry 103-104, 107-108, 113, 116-119, 125, 127, 129, 134-138, 140, 143-144, 154, 159, 390, 480-485, 487, 490-491, 493, 495, 497-499, 501, 503-505, 510, 512-514, 516, 518-520, 526
Berkley, Busby 342, 346
Bernard, Dorothy 431-432
Bernstein Film Productions 148
Bernstein, Isadore 69, 101-102, 107, 148, 412
Between Showers 62, 64-65, 71, 440
Bevan, Billy 158, 171-172, 192, 391, 422, 523, 534, 540, 543-544, 547, 549, 552-553, 563, 587, 592-593, 595, 597-598, 624, 626, 636, 640, 692
Beverly, Sam 635
Beware of Married Men 317
Bianchi, Mario "Frenchie" (see Banks, Monty)
Bickel and Watson 330
Bickel, George 330-331, 688
Big Butter and Yegg Man, The 337, 688
Big Noise, The 360, 697
Bill's Blighted Career 135, 501
Bill's Narrow Escape 159-160, 542
Bill's New Pal 134, 493
Billie's Reformation 159, 416, 526
Billie's Strategy (see *Billy Was a Right Smart Boy*)
Billie's Waterloo 157-158, 547
Billy Was a Right Smart Boy 382, 473
Billy's Charge 378, 467
Billy's Riot 368, 448
Billy's Vacation 370, 449
Billy's Waterloo (see *Billie's Waterloo*)
Biltmore Pictures 312, 689
Binns, George H. 420, 642
Biograph Company, The 10, 13, 15, 24-29, 31-35, 50, 64, 70, 76, 78, 81, 90, 95-96, 109, 115-116, 135, 153, 165, 201, 211, 276, 427-432, 382
Biograph Girl, The 33
Birchard, Robert S. 10, 16, 208
Birdwell, Russell 337
Birth of a Nation, The 174
Bison 101 Film Company (see 101 Bison Film Company)
Bitzer, G.W. "Billy" 26-27, 35, 430, 432
Blache, Alice Guy 276
Black Hands 378, 382, 466
Blackboard and Blackmail 391, 393, 590
Blackmail in a Hospital 152, 522, 524
Blaine, Vivian 697
Blaisdell, George 89-90, 444

Blake, Bobby 697
Blew Danube, The (see *Sound Your "A"*)
Blighted Spaniard, A 118, 483
Blind Pig, A 420, 612
Blind Princess and the Poet, The 33, 432
Blondeau Tavern 83
Bloomer Girls 116
Blore, Eric 694
Blue Bird, The 351
Blue Blood and Black Skin 168, 535
Blue Blood and Yellow Backs 149, 502
Blue, Monte 307
Bluebird Photoplays, Incorporated 180
Blystone, John "Jack" G. 13, 130, 145, 149, 158, 164, 166, 223, 229, 234, 387-389, 392, 394, 398, 408, 415, 480, 492, 494-495, 497-500, 504, 508, 510, 515, 517, 544-545, 548-549, 553, 555, 559, 563, 565-566, 576, 586-587
Bob Brownie the Dog 393, 424, 631
Bobbed Hair 307
Boehm's Picnic Grounds 113
Bogus Baron, A 376, 456
Bogus Uncle, The 201
Boland, Eddie 130, 384, 420, 617
Bold Bad Breeze, A 157-159, 552
Bolivar the Baby Bear 129, 487
Bolton, Lou 397, 579-580
Bombs and Bandits 400-401, 587
Booker, Harry 197
Borg, Veda Ann 697
Borzage, Frank (as "Berzage") 245
Boston Lyric Opera Company 141
Boswell Sisters, The 690
Bout-de-Zan series 368
Bowen, William A. 311
Bowers, John 313-314, 675-676
Boyce, St. Elmo 668
Bracey, Clara T. 429-431
Brand, Harry 291
Brave Little Waldo 396, 399, 572
Braverman, Barnet 24
Breaking Into Society 76
Breen, Joseph I. 346
Brendel, El 338, 689
Brennan, John E. 380-381, 383-384, 466, 470, 472-474, 479
Brenon, Herbert 35
Brentwood Film Corporation 260
Breslau, Al 201
Breslow, Lou 359, 697
Brett, Tom 658-659
Brettinger, A.M. 291
Brice, Monty 293, 665
Bricker, George 697
Bringing Up Father comic strip 112
Brodine, Norbert 697
Brodsky, Benjamin 414
Broken Blossoms 43

Broken Cross, The 431
Broken Doll, The 376, 457
Broken Hearts and Pledges 145, 500
Bromberg, J. Edward 697
Broncho Film Company 37, 69, 75, 95, 222
Brophy, Edward 347-348, 695
Brown Eyes and Bank Notes 631
Brown, Harry Joe 354, 356, 697
Brown, Phoebe 156
Brown, Rowland 352
Brown, Russ 690
Browne, Lewis Allen 283, 658-659
Brownie, the dog (see Bob Brownie the dog)
Browning, Tod 171
Bruce, Kate 427-429, 431-432
Bruskin, David N. 79-80, 186
Buck Privates 359
Buckham, Hazel 432
Bulldog Drummond 342-344
Bulldog Drummond Strikes Back 10, 343-344, 692-693
Bullets and Boneheads 408, 411, 601
Bullfighters, The 360, 697
Bulls Eye Film Corporation 196
Bum Bomb, A (see *Nuts and Noodles*)
Bunny, John 76
Burgess, Earl 196
Burkan, Nathan 272
Burke, Orrin 695
Burkett, Bartine 417-418, 420-421, 606, 609, 613-614, 617, 622, 624-625
Burnham, Bertha 384
Burns, Al 201
Burns, Bobbie 383, 478
Burns, Neal 413-414, 500, 613-614
Burns, Sammy 400-401, 546, 571, 587
Burr, C.C. 319
Burrell, Anita 235, 637, 641
Bush, James 697
Bushman, Francis X. 298
Business Before Honesty 410, 615
Busted Honeymoon, A 168, 545
Buster Brown series 368
Butcher's Bride, The 490
Butler, Lily 608
Butler, William J. 427, 429, 431-432
Butler's Busted Romance, The 382, 476
Butter and Yegg Man, A; *Butter-In-Yeggman, A* (see *Big Butter and Yegg Man, The*)
Butterworth, Charles 343-344, 692
Buttolph, David 695
Byron, Walter 694
C.L. Chester Productions, Inc. 259
Cabanne, William Christy 337
Cabaret Scratch, The 394, 580-581
Cabot, Bruce 347-348, 695-696
Café Nat Goodwin 69

Cahill, Lily 430
Cahuenga House, The 83
Cain, Robert 658-659, 661
Call the Cops 453, 623
Calm Yourself 346, 694
Calvert, E.H. 320, 679
Cameo Comedies 301
Camp Kearney 223
Campbell, Eric 200
Campbell, William 66, 186-188, 201, 220, 223, 232, 260, 634-635, 643, 647, 651
Cannibals and Carnivals 392, 602
Cannon, Raymond 337
Career in "C" Major 350
Carlisle, Lucile 245
Carlos Productions 298, 312, 673-674
Carlos, Abraham "Abe" 188, 190, 298, 312
Carmen, Jewel 48
Carmen's Romance 378, 469
Carmen's Wash Day 378, 382, 462
Carminati, Tullio 342, 690-691
Carney, Augustus 85, 116, 384
Carpenter, Betty 194, 211, 220, 232-233, 235, 645, 651
Carr, Harry C. 64
Carr, Nat 675
Carr, Phyliss 201, 639
Carroll, Nancy 323-325, 682, 684-685
Carroll, William A. 309, 432, 674
Carter, Lew 87, 114, 443, 482
Cary, Diana Serra 196, 421-422
Case, Theodore 324
Caudebec Inn 10, 32-33
Caught On a Skyscraper 538
Caught with the Goods 39, 129, 487-488
Cavanaugh, Hobart 690, 342
Cavender, Glen 220, 223, 649
Century Comedies/Century Film Corporation 196, 218, 230, 291, 293, 327, 366, 389, 393-394, 398-399, 410, 415-416, 420-422, 424-426, 612
Century Lions 215, 424
Chabas, Paul Émile 155
Chadwick Pictures Corporation 319
Chambers, Kathleen 675
Champion, The 439
Champion Film Company 75
Chaney, Lon 131
Change in Lovers, A 145, 495
Chaplin, Charles 13, 54-62, 64-66, 69-71, 88, 96, 128, 132-137, 143, 154, 159, 169-171, 182, 184, 194, 200, 220-221, 234, 237, 239, 241, 245-246, 258, 281, 316, 338, 340, 379-380, 383, 385, 390, 414, 439-440, 634, 677
Chaplin, Syd 109, 310
Chaplin: His Life and At 103
Charles Levy and Son 295
Charlie and the Children (see *Movie Riot, A*)
Charlie Chan series 359, 692

Charlie from the Orient (see Hong, Chai)
Charlie the Hero 414, 632
Charlie the Little Daredevil 414, 621-622
Chase, P.A. 311
Cheese Special, The 84, 374, 379
Chef, The (see *King of the Kitchen*)
Chef's Revenge, The 379, 382, 470, 477
Chene, Dixie 82, 365
Chester, C.L. 259-260, 262, 271-272
Chesterfield Motion Pictures Corporation 319
Chester-Outing Scenics 259, 362
Chevalier, Maurice 344-345, 694
Chic., Mlle. 24
Chicago Board of Censors 209
Chicago Daily Tribune 293
Chicken a la King 323-326, 384, 682-685
Chicken Chased and Henpecked 391, 585-586
Chicken in the Case, The 289
Child Needs a Mother, The 146, 504-505
Child of the Ghetto, A 429
Child Players Co. of America 368
Child's Faith, A 429
Child's Impulse, A 429
Child's Stratagem, A 430
Children Wanted 301, 674
Chinese Blues, The (see *Pair of Deuces, A*)
Chip Off the Old Block, A 437
Christian Herald 102
Christie Film Company 129, 179, 184, 220-221, 402
Christie, Al 48, 84-85, 129, 132, 153, 180, 360, 386
Christie, Charles 386
Christy, Ken 697
Christy, Nell 418
Cinderella 132
Circus Princess, The 330
Circus, The 371, 450-451
Cisco Kid, The series 359
City Girl 327
Claire, Gertrude 666-667
Clansman, The 326
Clarges, Verner 429-431
Clark, Bobby 327
Clark, Edward 310, 675
Clark, Frank Howard 598
Clark, June 453
Clary, Charles 298, 673
Clean Sweep, A 414, 614-615
Cleckler, Robert 695
Clifford, Jack 491
Clifford, William 131
Clifton, Emma 46, 62, 65, 78, 86-91, 93, 95-96, 370, 375-376, 379, 382, 439-440, 443-446, 449, 453, 456-458, 460, 462-463, 470, 473, 477
Clifton, Wallace C. 90
Cline, Eddie 233, 418
Clive, E.E. 692-693

Cloister's Touch, The 428
Close Call, A (see *Close Call, The*)
Close Call, The 378, 443, 460-461
Clown Princes and Court Jesters 9, 174
Cochran, R(obert).H. 133, 410
Cody, Lew 245, 415
Coffee, Lenore J. 364
Cogley, Nick 41, 43-44, 46, 53, 433-438, 441-442
Cohen Saves the Flag 51-52, 438
Cohen, Milton M. 231, 272
Cohen, Sammy 13, 318-323, 327-329, 679-682, 685-686
Cohn, Al 300, 673
Cohn, Harry 258, 675
Cohn, Jack 34
Colbert, Norman 697
Cold Hearts and Hot Flames 94, 143, 159, 162-164, 388, 559-560
Coldewey, Anthony W. 418, 622
Coleman, Frank J. 220, 224, 267-268, 271, 283, 499, 645-646, 649, 657
Coleman, Harry 531, 540-541, 551
Collection Service Corporation 292, 294
Collier's Weekly 296, 669
Collins, Eddie 356, 697
Colman, Ronald 342-344, 692-693
Columbia Pictures Corporation 34, 313, 334, 363, 675
Columbo, Russ 690
Comedy of Terrors, A 296, 298, 669
Comedy Vampire, A (see *Vamping Reuben's Millions*)
Comique Film Corporation 47
Comly, Sam H. 398
Complicated Complications (see *Counting Out the Count* [L-Ko])
Compton, Joyce 338, 689
Comrades 33, 109, 431
Comstock, Anthony 155
Conklin, Charles "Heinie" 84, 203, 209, 212, 260-266, 307, 309, 439-440, 697
Conklin, Chester 59, 62-63, 65, 196-197, 200, 222, 233, 356, 639-640, 645, 655-656, 674, 697
Conley, Lige 363
Connell, Richard 332, 687
Connelly, Bobby 368
Connors, Jack 607
Conroy, Frank 695
Conscience 431
Conselman, William 679
Continental Players 165
Cook, Clyde 234
Cooke, Albert 296, 668-669, 672
Cooks and Crooks 406, 607
Cooley, Frank 63, 439
Cooper, Earl 439
Cooper, Jack 222-223, 225, 230, 356, 646, 648, 651
Cooper, Miriam 278
Copelin, Agnes 468, 476

Corner in Wheat, A 30, 427
Cornet Rehearsal, The (see *Sound Your "A"*)
Cort, Elsie 546, 554
Costello, Helene 315-317, 677-679
Coudray, Peggy 510
Counihan, William 112
Count Your Change 415
Counting Out the Count [L-Ko] 391, 595
Counting Out the Count [Sterling] 382, 478
Country Lanes and City Lairs (see *Little Fat Rascal, The*)
Course of True Love, The 428
Courtwright, William 668
Cowboy Ambrose (see *Oh, What a Knight!*)
Cowles, Jules 679
Craig, Charles 427-430
Crash, The 369-370, 449
Crescent Film Company, The 73
Crest Film Company 195
Crimmons, Dan 420
Crisp, Donald 427, 430
Crompton, Frank 118
Cronjager, Jules 658-659
Crooked From the Start 159-160, 388, 558
Crooks and Crocodiles 396-397, 577-578
Cross, Leach 168, 220, 296
Crusaders Exhibiting Company 102
Crystal Film Corporation 84, 103, 368, 380
Cub Comedies 172, 424
Cuddebackville, New York 32-33
Culver City Film Company 242
Cummings, Constance 339
Cummings, Irving 346, 356, 697
Cummins, Dwight 332, 687
Cumpson, John R. 34, 432
Cumpson, W.R. (see Cumpson, John R.)
Cunard, Grace 173, 175
Cupid and the Scrub Lady 153, 518
Cupid At the Polo Game 168, 530
Cupid in a Dental Parlor 42, 48, 434
Cupid in a Hospital 122-123, 177, 400, 486-487, 575
Cure That Failed, The 39, 433
Current Events and Screen Magazine 410
Curse of a Name, The 149, 505-506
Curse of Work, The 135, 503-504
Curtain Pole, The 28
Curtis, Alan 356, 697
Cute Kids and Kidsnatchers (see *Kid Snatchers, The*)
Cutey Girls 616
Dad's Dollars and Dirty Doings 166, 534
Daly, Bob 31
Damaged – No Goods 199, 233, 637
Dana, Viola 245
Dancing Masters, The 360, 697
Daniels, Bebe 278
Dare, Phillip 694
Darling Twins, The 399

Darling, Anna 399, 542, 545-546, 581
Darling, Joseph R. 258
Darling, W. Scott 360-361, 697
Dary, René 368
Daub Has a Dream 380
Davenport, Alice 46, 63, 435-437, 439, 441-442
Davey, Allen M. 697
Davidson, Max 637
Davidson, William 695
Davis, H.O. 394, 396
Davis, James D. 404-405, 418, 420, 423, 598, 604, 607, 609-610, 612-614, 617, 625-626, 629, 631, 633
Davis, Joan 349
Davis, Richard Harding 301
Dawn, Charlotte 261-262, 264-265, 655-656
Dawn, Jack 291
Day After, The 428
Day, Richard 694, 697
Day, Sylvia 194, 218, 223-224, 646-647
De Bri, Lajon 340
De Comas, Eddie 420
De Foe, Annette 180
De Garde, Adele 427
De Jardins, Sylvion 84
De Lea, Charles 420
De Wood, Lorraine 697
Deaf Burglar, A 41, 433
Dean, Priscilla 173, 621
Deane, Hazel 220, 235
Dearing, Edgar 697
Death of Simon La Gree, The 129, 488-489
Decker, Frieda 83
Deep Seas and Desperate Deeds 392, 600-601
Defective Detective 391, 402, 575-576
DeForest, Lee 324
DeForrest, Charles 84
DeHaven, Carter 293-294, 665
Del Ruth, Hampton 84, 220-222, 233-234, 440
Del Ruth, Roy 201, 220, 234, 266, 270, 301, 317, 343-344, 354, 657, 692-694
Delmar, Thomas 588-589
Delmont, Maude 280
Dempster, Carol 156
Denishawn School 156
Denny, Reginald 296
DeRue, Carmen 368, 378, 384, 448, 451-452, 455, 457, 462, 464-465, 467, 469, 473
Dickerson, J.S. 256, 654
Dickenson, Clarence 201
Dickstein, Martin 322
Dietrich, Ralph 679, 682
Dillon, Edward 32, 173, 429-432
Dillon, John T. "Jack" 453, 666
Dimples, Dolly 401, 587
Dintenfass, Mark 75
Dinty's Daring Ways (see *Where Is My Husband?*)

Dippy Dan's Doings 392, 395, 576-577
Dirty Work in a Beanery 549
Disguised, But Discovered 147, 520
Dismantled Beauty, A 149, 503
Diving Fool, The 301, 674
Divorce of Convenience, A 283
Dixon, Ralph 328, 685
Dixon, Thomas 326
Dodd, Reverend Neal 275
Does Flirting Pay? 150-151, 516
Dog Raffles, The 379, 382, 465, 472
Dollar Did It, A 434
Domino Films 37, 75
Donkey Did It, The 392, 604
Donnelly, James 420, 615, 617, 620
Doomed Groom, The 151, 524
Doomed Hero, A 135-136, 505
Dorety, Charles 207-208, 215, 220, 226-227, 246, 251-252, 255-256, 620, 625, 627, 634, 639, 642, 645-647, 649-650, 652, 657
Dot's Chaperone 379, 464
Dot's Elopement 379, 466-467
Double Dealing 294-295, 305, 666-668
Double Double Cross, A 396, 556-557
Double Dukes 402, 597-598
Double's Trouble, A (see *Double's Trouble, The*)
Double's Trouble, The 166, 540-541
Dougherty, George S. 112
Dougherty, Lee 26, 32
Douglas, Gertrude 556
Douglaston Manor 276
Dove, Billie 298-300, 673
Down With Women 313, 675-676
Doyle, Jack 170, 396
Doyle, Johnny 382, 478
Dramatic Mistake, A 371-372, 453
Dressler, Marie 90
Drew, Sidney 293, 665
Drury Lane Company 107
Dry Goods and Damp Deeds 391, 584-585
Dubin, Al 690-691
Dude Raffles 382, 472
Dudley, Allen 259-260, 271-272
Dudley, Charles 121, 246, 485-486, 646, 652
Dudley, Robert 697
Duffy, Al 585
Dumont, Margaret 697
Dunbar, Dixie 349
Duncan, Bud 165, 186, 196, 211, 390
Dunham, Phil 167, 170-172, 218, 263, 268, 270-271, 387, 390-393, 396-398, 414, 417, 420, 423-424, 527, 534, 542, 544, 549-551, 553, 559, 563-565, 567-568, 570-577, 579, 581-582, 584-586, 590-592, 595, 597-599, 626-628, 632, 655, 657-658
Dunn, Bobby 49, 92, 200-201, 211, 213, 230, 373-374, 379, 404-406, 455, 458, 469, 600, 604, 606, 623-624, 645, 651

Dunn, Herbert Charles (see Russell, Dan)
Dunne, Philip 350, 352, 354
Dupar, Ed 677
Durand of the Badlands 209
Durfee, Minta 282, 440
Durling, E.V. 658-659
Dwan, Allan 371
Dwyer, Ruth Anne 296
Earl Auto Works 200
Earle, Edward 697
Earle, Jack 196
Early Birds 104, 132
East Coast Ramo Film Company 261
Eastman Kodak Company 90
Easy Money 153, 494
Eat and Grow Hungry 565
Eccleston, Mae 194, 213, 220, 235, 645-646
Eddie the Ellfa-Nut 611
Edendale, California 37, 74
Edeson, Robert 149
Edison, Thomas H./Edison Manufacturing Company 24-25, 28, 105, 368, 370
Edmunston, Al 588
Educated Roosters 503-504
Educational Exchange 80, 258, 272-273, 301-302, 337, 363
Edwardes-Hall, George 118
Edwards, Gus 103
Edwards, Harry 116, 119-120, 134-136, 144, 165, 180, 387, 483, 493, 495-499, 501, 503, 505, 508, 513, 521-522
Edwards, Neely 258, 301
Egan, Gladys 427-432
Egyptian Theater 200
Elevating Father 168, 533
Elliot, Edythe 695
Elliott, Frank 308
Elmore, S.A. 199
Eltinge, Julian 116, 278
Emerson, Babe 391-392, 596, 600, 602, 604
Emerson, Kathleen 397, 593
Emery, Queenie 392-393, 420-421, 590, 602
Emmons, Buster 465, 469
Emory, May 146, 150, 154, 407, 412, 420, 506-509, 512-513, 516, 518, 538-539, 615-617, 619-620
Empire Film Exchange 73
Empress Theatre 54
End of a Perfect Day 400, 571-572
Engel, Joe 75, 385
Engle, Billy 267-268, 657
Enoch Arden: Part II 432
Entangled Entanglements (see *Counting Out the Count* [L-Ko])
Erdman, Gus 375, 378-380, 382, 463, 465-466, 468, 470, 472, 474-476
Erlanger, A.L. 90, 153, 390

Ernst, Jesse 694
Erwin, Stuart 330, 687-688, 697
Essanay Film Manufacturing Company 25, 40, 85, 92, 137, 149, 153, 171, 185, 194, 242, 368, 379-380, 385, 390, 402
Ethel the Lion 13, 203, 639
Ettinger, Dot 355
Evans, Frank 427-430, 432
Evans, Madge 346, 694
Evans, Owen 420
Even As Him and Her 391, 597
Everson, William K. 9, 225, 322
Every Inch a Hero 117, 129, 488
Everybody Sing 349
Everything Happens at Night 351
Ewing, John 697
Exposition Day in Simpville (see *Love and Blazes*)
EYE Film Institute; EYE Filmmuseum 11, 119, 182
F.B.O. (see Film Booking Offices of America)
Face At the Window, The 429
Fairbanks, Douglas 219, 246, 298
Faking Fakirs 390, 570-571
Falling Star (see *Hollywood Cavalcade*)
False Alarm 293
False Friends and Fire Alarms 159, 416, 536
Fame and Fortune 209
Famous Players-Lasky Corporation 64, 155, 241, 270, 309, 385
Farley, Dot 13, 40-42, 180, 190, 205-206, 424, 433-435, 438, 626, 628, 633, 635, 638, 641
Farmer's Daughter, The 327
Fascinating Widow, The 116
Fat and Furious 392, 596-597
Fatal Flirtation, A 116
Fatal Hansom, The 379, 469
Fatal Marriage, The [Fox] 199, 223-224, 228, 647
Fatal Marriage, The [L-Ko] 114, 482
Fatal Note, The 136, 143, 496
Fatal Wedding, A (see *His Wedding Day* [Sterling])
Fatal Wedding, The [Fox] 327
Fatal Wedding, The [Klaw and Erlanger] 90
Father Goose: The Story of Mack Sennett 24
Father Was a Loafer 123-124, 490-491
Father Was Neutral 135, 498-499
Father's Choice 434
Father's First Murder 147, 153, 517
Fathers' Sons and Chorus Girls 610
Fatty at San Diego 116
Fatty's Feature Fillum 396, 574
Fatty's Infatuation 153, 492-493
Fatty's Magic Pants 398
Faversham, William 276
Fay, Hugh 201, 203, 205-208, 210, 215, 218, 220, 223-224, 229, 232-233, 258, 261, 638, 640-643, 646-647, 651, 655
Faye, Alice 354, 356, 697

Faye, Randall H. 679
Fazenda, Louise 84, 197, 307, 374, 379, 382, 384-385, 468, 472, 475-476
Feathered Nest, The 197
Federal Motion Picture Commission 164
Feeding Time 436
Fehr, Louis 280
Fejos, Paul 337
Fenton, Frank 697
Ferguson, Helen 666-667
Ferris, Audrey 314, 316, 676-677
Fetchit, Stepin 356
Fichtenberg, Herman 87, 443
Fiction Pictures 384
Fido's Dramatic Career 119, 483-484
Fields, Lew 151
Fighting Blood 293, 295-298, 305, 339-340, 668-673
Fighting Edge, The 307, 309, 674-675
Film Booking Offices of America 293-296, 298, 313, 338, 360, 665, 668, 672
Film Johnnie, A 51, 71, 440
Film Service Association 24
Fine Arts Studio 36, 131, 172-173, 184
Finlayson, James "Jimmy" 356, 402, 405, 594, 697
Fire Bug, The (see *Firebugs, The*)
Firebugs, The 51, 68, 441
Firing the Butler or The Butler Fired (see *Firing the Butler; or, The Butler's Fire*)
Firing the Butler; or, The Butler's Fire 532
First National Exhibitors Exchange/ First National Pictures 13, 240-241, 248, 257-258, 260-262, 266, 272-274, 323-324, 652, 654
First National Motion Picture Exposition 157
Fishback, Fred 220, 222-223, 225, 229-230, 245, 279, 424, 648, 651
Fitzpatrick, Charlotte 51, 438, 440
Flash of Light, A 429
Flint and MacKay Law Firm 311
Flirt, The 368, 448
Flirtation A La Carte 166, 527
Florey, Robert 56
Flyer in Folly, A 404, 406, 606
Flying A (see American Film Manufacturing Company)
Foiling Fickle Father 41, 434
Folies Bergère de Paris 344-345, 694
Fonda, Henry 352
Fools and Duels 420, 446, 621
Fools and Fires 615
For Art's Sake 196
For Ladies Only 313, 675-676
For the Love of Mabel 45
For the Love of Mike and Rosie 168-170, 394, 396, 399, 539-540
Forbes, Al 391-392, 586, 590, 593, 596, 600-602, 604
Ford Sterling: His Life and Films 16
Ford, Charlotte 448

Ford, Francis 175, 182, 697
Ford, John 354
Forde, Victoria 85, 99, 180, 209, 245, 442
Foreman, Ethel 293, 665
Forest Lawn Cemetery 275
Forgetters, The 276
Formes, Carl 464, 466
Forrester, Izola 682
Fort Lee, New Jersey 28, 276, 283
Fort, Garrett 300, 673
Four Sons 351
Four Times Foiled 259
Fourth Liberty Loan Tank 220
Fowler, Gene 15, 24, 30-31, 33-34, 62, 64, 70, 83, 98, 103, 198
Fowley, Douglas 697
Fox Animal Comedies 327
Fox Film Corporation 179, 229, 231, 233-234, 258
Fox Movietone Entertainments 330
Fox Movietone Sound System 324, 326-327, 330
Fox Trot Craze, The 382, 473-474
Fox, Fred 694
Fox, William 179-182, 185, 188, 191, 199, 228, 298, 300, 324, 679, 682, 685, 687
Foxe, Earle 331-333, 687
Foxfilm Comedies 180-182, 184, 186, 191-192, 209, 220, 633
Frances, Winifred 105-107, 283
Francey, Collette 688
Francisco, Betty 666-667
Franey, William 84, 92, 379, 384, 458
Franklin, Chester 41, 433, 438
Freckled Fish, The 412, 414, 622
Frederick, Freddie 687
Fredericks, William S. 406, 601, 603, 605-606, 608
French, Charles 73
Freuler, John R. 37
Friend, But a Star Boarder, A 157-158, 538
Frisky Lions and Wicked Husbands 215
Frohman, Ray W. 252, 364
From Beanery to Billions 153, 524-525
From Cactus to Kale 402, 593
From Ranch to Riches (see *Prairie Chicken, A*)
Frontier 85, 89, 111, 186, 368, 371, 375, 380
Fuehrer, Bobby 85
Gaby's Gasoline Glide 171-172, 396, 544-545
Galicia 19-20, 22
Gallagher, J.P. 104
Gambler's Gambol, A 170, 551
Gamboling On the Green 546
Game Lady, A 270-273, 278, 657-658
Game of Love, A 153, 510
Gangsters, The 45, 153, 435
Garage, The 258
Garcia, Al 370-371, 452-453
Gardner, Willard 153, 492-493

Gargan, Edward 697
Garmes, Lee 668-669
Garon, Pauline 283, 287-288, 658-662
Gasnier, Louis J. (as "Gasinier") 245
Gates, Crane and Earl Mortuary 275
Gay Retreat, The 319, 686
Gay, Charles 218
Gay's Lion Farm 218
Gebhardt, George 521
Gee! What a Mix-Up (see *Kid Snatchers, The*)
Gem Motion Picture Company 33, 50, 116
Gems and Germs 121, 486
Gene, the Lion 13, 203, 639
General Film 383
George Bickel Fun Subjects 330
George Eastman House 141, 514
George White's Scandals 330
Gerald, Al 590
Gerrard, Douglas 299, 673, 675, 692
Gertie's Awful Fix 535-536
Gertie's Busy Day 527
Gertie's Gasoline Glide (see *Gaby's Gasoline Glide*)
Gertie's Joy Ride 147, 152, 172, 510
Getchell, Sumner 687
Getting the Goods on Gertie 551
Gibbons, Willie 368
Gibney, Sheridan 351
Gibson, Art 196
Gibson, Hoot 294-295, 666-668
Giebler, A.H. 227, 233
Gilbert, Billy 437, 439-440
Gill, Sam 7-9, 15-16, 31, 47, 153, 174, 192, 194, 213, 363, 365, 375
Gillespie, Bert 639, 657
Gillingwater, Claude 677-679, 694
Girard, William 697
Girl from Moulin Rouge 340
Givot, George 697
Glasmon, Kubec 346, 695-696
Glaum, Louise 116
Glennon, Bert 695
Globe Theatre 101
Godfrey, Rae 404, 406-407, 409, 572, 598, 601, 603, 605-608
Godwin, Sylvia 186
Goetz, William 339-340, 343, 346, 691, 693-694
Gold, Max 685, 687
Goldberg, Nathan 298
Goldwyn, Samuel 339, 416
Golfers, The (see *Double Dukes*)
Good Little Bad Boy 391, 582
Goode, Frank B. 86-89, 375, 443
Good-Night, Turk! 414, 626-627
Gordon, Huntley 307
Gordon, Vera 675
Gore, Chester 697

Gore, Rose 619, 623
Gotham Productions 319
Gottschalk, Ferdinand 694
Gould, Bobbie "Dot" 375, 379-380, 382-384, 463-464, 466-467, 470-474, 479
Gould, Dave 346, 694
Goulding, Alf 630, 632
Gowns and Girls 406, 608
Graham, Fred H. 132
Grandin, Ethel 85
Grandon, Francis J. 428-432
Grau, Robert 82
Grauman, Sid 200, 246
Gray, George 301
Graybill, Joseph 429-432
Great Guns 359
Great Smash, The 168-169, 543-544
Great Universal Mystery, The 371
Great War Parade 200
Greed and Gasoline 153, 525
Gregory, Ena 668
Gréhan, Réne 85
Greig, Robert 694
Grey Nun of Belgium, The 384
Gribble, Harry Wagstaff 323, 682-683
Gribbon, Eddie 294, 666-667
Gribbon, Harry 145-146, 149-151, 153-154, 173, 410, 412, 420, 500-503, 505-507, 509, 513, 516, 518, 538-539, 615-617, 619-620
Griffies, Ethel 692-693
Griffin, Frank C. 197, 234, 372, 374, 378, 385, 418, 420, 460, 466, 470, 619, 623, 628
Griffith, Beverly 79, 376, 433, 435, 438-439, 456
Griffith, David Wark 13, 24-27, 29, 31-36, 43, 116, 131, 148, 171-172, 174, 221, 371, 379, 414, 427-432
Griffith, Gertrude 217, 552
Griffith, Gordon 50-51, 173, 370-371, 384, 437-438, 440, 442, 452, 455, 457
Griffith, Harry 420, 453, 592-593, 622
Griffith, Katherine 173, 397, 455, 554, 557, 563, 566, 569, 571
Griffith, Lawrence (see David Wark Griffith)
Griffith, Linda Arvidson (see Arvidson, Linda)
Griffith, Raymond 131, 152-153, 155-156, 166, 168, 340, 343, 346, 510, 512,515, 517, 521-522, 524-526, 528-530, 533, 535, 542-545, 548, 691, 693-694
Groom's Doom, The 118, 483
Grundy Comedies Company 292-293
Grundy, C. Fred 292-293
Guard, Kit 296, 668, 672
Gugenheim, Henry 618
Gump, Irving 697
Gusher, The 70
Gussow, Mel 349
Gymbelles and Boneheads 417, 624-625
H. & H. Film Service 37

H.G. Bittleston Law and Collection Agency 293, 295
Haade, William 697
Hadley, Pop 626
Hagenios, Charles 375, 456
Ha-Ha, Minnie 638
Haldeman, Edith 427-428, 430
Hale, Creighton 692
Hall Room Boys 258
Hall, Ben 675
Hall, Charley 332
Hall, Mordaunt 324
Hall, Sherry 697
Halligan, William F. 330, 688
Halsted and Company Funeral Home 282
Halton, Charles 697
Ham and Bud series 165, 186, 196, 203, 211, 390
Ham, Harry 184
Hamberg, Alfred P. 101-102, 115, 148
Hamilton, Lloyd 13, 165, 186-187, 189, 201, 203, 205, 207, 211, 214-215, 217, 220, 223, 225-227, 229, 244, 246, 248, 250-252, 254, 256, 258, 260, 271, 283, 301, 363-364, 390, 634-635, 637, 639, 641-642, 645-647, 649-650, 652, 654, 657-658
Hammerstein Theatre 54
Hammerstein, Elaine 276
Hammerstein, Oscar 105
Hammond Lumber Company 292
Hammons, E.W. 301, 337
Hamp, Charles 355
Hamp, Virginia 355
Hanneford, Poodles 266
Hansen, Helen 278
Happ, Fred 41, 435
Happy Hooligan 112-113
Happy Hooligan comic strip 112
Happy Jack, a Hero 430
Harbaugh, Carl 310
Hardebeck, Joe 278
Hardebeck, Kate 278
Hardy, Oliver "Babe" 283, 359-360, 406, 412, 420, 615, 617, 619, 622-624, 697
Hare, Lumsden 694
Harlan, Kenneth 200, 245, 307-309, 674-675
Harmon, Pat 328, 674, 685
Harris, Bernard 198
Harris, Buddy/Buddie 51, 465
Harris, H(arry). B. 91
Harris, Mildred 258
Harron, Robert 427, 431-432
Harry Manley's Circus 104
Hart, Florence "Flo" 307-308
Hart, Ruth 427-429
Hart, Virgil 682
Hart, William S. 219-220
Hartigan, Pat 309, 674
Hartman, Ferris 420

Harvey, Lew 309, 674
Hastings, Seymour 466
Hatch, Olive 358
Hathaway, Jean 576-577
Hatton, Raymond 41, 435, 694
Hauber, William "Bill" 41, 49, 180, 196, 435-440, 442
Hawks, Kenneth 687
Hayden, Harry 697
Hayes, Frank 209-210, 212, 224, 639, 645, 666-667
Hays Office 346, 364, 696
Hayseed, The 258
Healy, Mabel 406, 609
Hearn, Tom 106
Hearst, William Randolph 284
Heart of Nora Flynn, The 153
Hearts and Flames 135, 495-496
Hearts and Flour 397, 588
Hearts and Saddles 209
Hearts and Swords 95-96, 98, 420, 446-447, 621
Hearts in Hock 412, 418, 624
Heartsick At Sea 168, 392, 569
Heavy Swells 301, 674
Hedlund, Guy 165, 428-432
Heerman, Victor 31, 36, 38, 115-116, 118, 131, 148-149, 153, 156, 165, 289, 387, 522, 541
Heinie's Outing 377-378, 461-462
Heinze's Resurrection 68, 442
Hellinger, Mark 351
Hellman, Sam 351
Hello Bill 135, 508
Hello Trouble 412, 617
Help! Help! Hydrophobia! 45, 48, 436
Heman, Roger 694
Henabery, Joseph 337
Henderson, Babe 418
Henderson, Dell 31, 211, 361, 428-432
Henderson, Grace 427, 429-432
Henderson, Jack 420, 618-619, 624
Henie, Sonja 351
Hennings, John 689
Henry Lehrman Comedies, Inc. 187, 239-274, 366, 652-658
Henry Lehrman Productions, Inc. 239-240, 259-260, 272, 274, 292
Henry, Gale 84, 155, 379, 405, 408, 420, 606-610
Her Birthday Present 39, 41, 114, 433
Her Daring, Caring Ways 392, 586-587
Her Filmland Hero 384
Her First Knight (see *Oh, What a Knight!*)
Her Majesty's Guests 104
Her Movie Madness 406, 418, 420, 610
Her Naughty Eyes 166, 531-532
Her New Beau 434
Her Sacrifice 432
Her Ups and Downs (see *Cupid and the Scrub Lady*)
Her Whirlwind Wedding 615-616

Herbert, Hugh 677-679
Herman, Al 201, 211, 220, 229, 244, 261, 283, 655
Hero for a Minute, A 404, 600
Hickory Hiram 412-413
Hide and Seek 48-49
Higgins, Bob 406, 609
High Class Nonsense (see *Counting Out the Count* [L-Ko])
High Diver's Curse, The 566
High Diver's Last Kiss, A 199, 211, 645-646
Hilarity 104-105
Hill Street Tunnel 266
Hill, Gus 105, 112, 132
Hill, Mary 104
Hill, Thomas 104
Hillyer, Lambert 337
Hinshaw Conservatory of Music 116
His Bitter Pill 225, 649
His Finish 201
His Home Sweet Home 415
His Musical Sneeze 223, 226-227, 278, 649-651
His New Job 379, 467-468
His Own Fault 35, 432
His Second Childhood 82
His Sister-in-Law 430
His Smashing Career [Fox] 192-194, 196, 198, 233, 382, 636-637
His Smashing Career [Sterling] 477
His Temper-Mental Mother-In-Law 159-161, 556
His Ticklish Job 181
His Wedding Day 90-91, 445
His Wicked Eyes 627
His Wife's Flirtation 371, 454-455
Hite, Charles 37
Hobbes, Halliwell 692-694
Hochberg, Charles 79, 118, 158, 201, 231-232, 244, 652
Hodges, A.B.W. 259-260, 271-272
Hoffman, Gertrude 103
Hoffman, Otto 666-667
Hogan, James 337
Hogan's Romance Upset 384
Hohl, Arthur 692-693
Holden, Irving 349
Holderness, Fay 593, 597, 605, 617
Hollenbeck Park 195, 266
Holloway, Carol 324-326, 682-684
Hollywood Cavalcade 351, 356-357, 697
Hollywood Cemetery 282, 286, 361
Hollywood Officers' Training School 220
Holmes, Brown 697
Holmes, Stuart 298, 673
Home Run Ambrose 406, 409, 603
Homesick 327-329, 685-686
Hong, Chai "Charlie of the Orient" 412, 414-415, 420, 613-614, 617, 620-622, 625-626, 630, 632-633
Honor System, The 326
Hooligan at the Lox Outing 113

Hop O' My Thumb 107
Hop the Bell Hop 412, 623
Hope, Edward 346
Hopper, E. Mason 337
Hornbeck, William 222
Horne, James W. 245, 337
Horse Thief, The 438
Horsley, David 75, 83, 107, 131
Horsley, William 102
Horton, Clara 296, 368, 668-669, 676-677
Hot Old Time, A 113
Hotaling, Arthur D. 382
Hotel Alexandria 33, 121, 132, 145, 148, 246, 414
Hotel for Women 351
Hotel Mix-Up, A (see *Rough Stuff*)
Hotel Virginia 69
Houck, Leo 194
House of Rothschild, The 343, 692
House of Terrible Scandals, The 180, 182-184, 233, 326, 366, 633-634, 651
House That Karno Built, The 105
House, Chandler 368, 384, 448, 452, 462, 464-465, 467, 469
How Green Was My Valley 351, 353
How Stars Are Made 168, 548
How Villains Are Made 50-51, 440
Howard, Boothe 695
Howard, Constance 689
Howard, Esther 697
Howard, Marion 278
Howe, Jay A. "Kitty" 146-147, 199, 387, 390, 392, 504, 508, 514-515, 557, 637
Howell, Alice 13, 123-124, 126, 130-131, 136, 143-145, 151-153, 165-167, 170, 173, 177, 196, 387-389, 394, 397-399, 410, 490, 492, 494, 499, 502, 505-508, 515-518, 522-525, 527, 531-532, 534, 540-545, 548-551, 553-556, 559, 563-564, 566, 612, 629
Howl Comedies 394
Howland, Olin 694
Howland, Ted 596
Howling Lions and Circus Queens 215
Hoyt, Arthur 677-679
Huachuca Crawl 328
Hudson, Rochelle 348, 695-696
Hudson's Bay 351, 355
Hudson's Bay Company 351
Huff, Louise 276
Hughes, Ray 154
Hula Hula Hughie 404-405, 416, 598
Hull, Frank 682
Hull, George C. 666
Hungry Lions in a Hospital 199, 203-205, 233, 639-640
Hunn, Bert 41, 433, 435, 437-440, 476
Hunn, William 474
Hunt, Jay 689
Husbands Are Liars (see *Chicken a la King*)

Husbands for Rent 315-317, 677-679
Hutchinson, Craig 66, 152-153, 387-388, 392, 398, 412, 418, 420, 440, 517, 521-522, 524-525, 528, 546, 554, 557-558, 566-567, 569, 573, 580, 583, 601, 611, 615-616, 620, 625-627
Hutchinson, Samuel 37
Hutchinson, William 624
Hutton, Lucille 158, 161, 171, 390-391, 393, 397, 541, 547-548, 552, 554, 556, 563-566, 568, 570, 572-577, 579, 581-582, 584-587, 590-593, 595, 597-599
Hyde, Harry 430-432
Hymer, Warren 347-348, 695-696
Hypnotic Power 376, 460
Hytten, Olaf 692
Iconoclast, The 430
Idle Rich, The 150, 518
Ignatz's Icy Injury 396, 552
Ihnen, Wiard B. 697
Ill Wind, An 379, 464-465
Illinois Exhibiting Company 102
IMP (Independent Motion Picture Company) 31, 33-35, 75, 85, 118, 180, 186, 387, 418, 432
Imp Abroad, The 85
Imperial Comedies 237-238, 300-301, 327, 674
In and Out [Essanay] 92
In and Out [Pyramid] 154
In and Out [Sterling] 92, 374, 458
In and Out of Society 134, 493-494
In Bad All Around 627
In Life's Cycle 32, 430
In Little Italy 30, 428
In Name Only 317, 677
In the Border States 429
In the Claw of the Law 149, 507
Ince, Thomas H. 51, 78, 131, 222, 242
Independent Motion Picture Company (see IMP)
Independent Woman, An 384
Ingraham, Lloyd 379, 470-471, 477
Innocent Dad 380, 470
Inside of the White Slave Trade, The 101
Inslee, Charles 73, 369-371, 375, 390-391, 397, 415, 439, 441-442, 449, 451-453, 456, 536, 556, 561, 568, 570, 572, 574-577, 579, 581-582, 584-585, 587, 590, 617, 619
International Association of Theatrical Stage Employees and Motion Picture Operators 220
International Feature Service, Inc. 284
Intolerance 172
Iola's Promise 432
Irene the Onion Eater's Daughter 85
Irving, George 689
Irving, William 224, 397, 557, 563, 566, 569, 574-575
Isle of Bang Bong, The 116-117
Isle of Love, The 278
It's a Bird 417, 421, 622
It's a Boy 369, 371, 449

Italian Barber, The 431
Itching for Revenge 153, 507-508
Ivey, Luciebelle 518, 526, 532
Jack Doyle's Vernon Athletic Club 396
Jackson, Grant 426
Jackson, Joseph 677
Jackson, Selmer 697
Jacobs, Jessie 175
Jacobs, Louis 175, 209, 387, 398, 420, 424-425
Jacobs, Oscar 245, 425
Jacobs, Paul 48-51, 66, 78, 91-95, 153, 165, 170, 368-369, 371-372, 375-376, 378, 381-382, 384, 436-440, 442, 445, 448-452, 454-455, 457, 459, 467, 469, 471, 473, 475-476, 522, 541
Jaeschke, A. 587
Jaeschke, George (see Jeske, George)
Jail Birds 104
Jailbird's Last Flight, The 396, 548-549
Jameson, Jean 280
Jamison, Bud 424
Janios, Nick 349
Jazz Singer, The 310, 314, 326
Jealous Husband, A 369, 448-449
Jenkins, L.B. 198
Jerome, Amy 180
Jeske, George 382, 384, 437, 440, 466, 474
Jesse L. Lasky Feature Play Company 90
Jessel, George 310-311, 314-317, 675-677
Jessen, J.C. 181
Jewish Relief Fund 200
Jitterbugs 359-360, 697
Joe the Orang-outang (see Martin, Joe)
John, Al St. 245, 437, 439, 442
Johnny Apollo 351
Johnson, Arthur V. 427-428
Johnson, Emory 337
Johnson, Noble 679
Johnson, Nunnally 10, 340-344, 346, 690, 692
Johnson, Olive 153, 375, 378, 382, 384, 450, 455, 457, 459-460, 471, 473, 475-476, 522, 541
Johnson, Will B. 658
Joker Comedies 75, 84, 130, 149, 170, 196, 211, 260, 374, 378-380, 383-384, 386, 402, 405, 410
Jolson, Al 314, 697
Jones, Grace 571
Jones, Pop 603
Jones, F. Richard 201, 205, 343, 638, 640
Joslin, Margaret 161, 556
Jourjon, Charles 75
Joy Riders, The 391, 598-599
Joy, Leatrice 330
Judge's Revenge, The (see *Joy Riders, The*)
Judson, Hanford C. 201
Just Kids 48, 371, 437
K.B. Clarendon Comedies 400
Kaiser There Was, A 415

Kalem Company 25, 112, 152-153, 165, 170, 184, 186, 196, 211, 371, 375, 380, 383, 390
Kansas Board of Review 205
Karno, Fred 54, 56, 104-105, 132, 134, 143, 171, 382, 396
Karnophone 105
Kay-Bee Studios 37, 75
Keane, Robert Emmett 697
Keaton, Buster 230, 237, 245, 291, 356-357, 360, 697
Keaton, Harry 626
Keith-Proctor Circuit 94
Kelly, James T. 559
Kennedy, Edgar 41, 200, 202, 205, 225, 306, 404, 435-437, 439-442, 600, 638, 641
Kennedy, Tom 201, 208-209, 211, 363, 641, 643-645
Keno, the Boy Clown 76
Kenton, Earl C. 398
Kenyon, Curtis 352, 355
Kernell, William 685, 687
Kerr, Robert 405, 600, 604, 606, 610
Kerrigan, J. Warren 64, 69
Kershaw, Elinor 428
Kessel, Adam 37-38, 40, 54, 58, 73, 75-76, 78-79
Kessel, Charles 54
Kesson, Frank 676
Keston, Harry 424, 629
Keystone Cops 39, 44, 356
Keystone Film Company 16, 37-71, 75
Keystone Kids 66, 368
Kiam, Omar 694
Kick in High Life, The 261-263, 655-656
Kid Auto Races at Venice, Cal. 58-62, 71, 439
Kid Snatchers, The 599
Kids 368, 448
Kids Komedy Kompany 384
Kids of the Movies 368
Kindness of Strangers, The 20
Kinemacolor Company of America, The 35-36, 115, 277
Kinetoscope 25
King Bee Comedies 220, 412
King Cole Comedies 400
King of Comedy 7, 24
King of the Kitchen 410, 619
King, Nana 475
Kingsbury, Stanley C. 155, 176
Kingsley, Grace 130, 217
Kingston, Jerome 342
Kipling, Rudyard 166
Kirby, David 674
Kirby, Fred 299, 673
Kirkland, David 149, 151, 180, 184, 190, 205, 220, 270, 283, 289, 337, 365, 369-371, 376, 378-379, 382, 385, 387-388, 453-454, 458, 460, 465-466, 470-472, 476, 502, 505, 516, 518, 556, 567, 633, 635, 641, 657, 663
Kirkwood, James 427-429
Kirtley, Virginia 436, 439, 441-442
Klaw and Erlanger 153, 390

Klaw Theatre 283
Klaw, Marcus 90
Klein, Charles 337
Klein, Frank 402, 575
Kleine, George 330
Klever Kiddies 414, 620-621
Knickerbocker Star Features 385
Knight of the Road, A 431
Knight, Fuzzy 690
Knocker, The (see *Double Dealing*)
Knockout Wallop, The 382, 474-475
Knocks and Opportunities 159, 529-530
Kober, Arthur 346, 694
Kohler, Roy 121
Kohlmar, Lee 151
Kolb and Dill 374-375
Kolle, Herman 73
Kolster, Clarence 674, 677
Komic Comedies 383
Kortman, Robert 692
Kremer, Theodore 90
Kriterion Films Exchange 117
La Badie, Florence 431-432
La Cava, Gregory 337, 339
La Verne, Jane 687
LaBarba, Fidel 350
Lady Bellhop's Millions, A (see *A Lady Bell-Hop's Secret*)
Lady Bell-Hop's Secret, A 231-233, 651
Lady Lion, The 238
Laemmle, Carl 13, 33, 37, 74-76, 78, 80-81, 84, 87, 98-99, 101-102, 107, 134, 149, 173-175, 177, 239, 381, 394, 408, 410, 443, 666
Laguna Beach 329
Lahue, Kalton C. 9, 15, 31, 174, 176, 191
Lake, Florence 332, 687
Lakin, Charles 559, 618
Lamont, Charles 674
Land Salesman, The 434
Landlord's Troubles, A 442
Lane, Allan 697
Lane, Richard 697
Lane, Rose Wilder 56
Lanfield, Sidney 330, 339, 341-342, 688, 690
Lang, Walter 339
Langdon, Harry 266
Langley, Ramona 85
Lanning, Frank 486
Lanoe, J. Jiquel 430
Laprell, Robert 307, 674
LaRose, Joseph 259
Lasky, Jesse 90, 131, 153, 173, 184, 220-221
Last Deal, The 428
Latham Film Loop 28
Lauer, Benisch Benjamin 21, 362
Lauer, Heinrich 362
Laurel and Hardy Feature Productions 359

Laurel, Stan 148, 159, 360-361, 384, 412-414, 611, 613, 697
Lawrence, Florence 33, 76
Lawrence, W.E. 637
Leather Pushers 296, 339
Lebedeff, Ivan 690
LeBrandt, Joseph 418, 420, 622-623
Lederer, Otto 676-677
Lederman, Ross 201
Lee, Dixie 338, 689
Lee, Dorothy 234
Lee, Frances 324-326, 682, 684
Lee, Jocelyn (see Leigh, Jocelyn)
Lee, Mildred 187, 189, 235, 634-635, 637, 639
Left At the Alter, or Love in a Pullman Car 356-357
Leggewie, Edward 349
Lehrman Comedies (see Henry Lehrman Comedies)
Lehrman Knock-Out 101, 479
Lehrman, Henry (aka "Pathé" Lehrman, Henry "Pathé" Lehrman, H. Pathé Lehrman, Henry Mauritz Lehrman, Henry Max Lehrman, Moritz Lehrman, Moses Lehrman, Moshe Lehrman)
   Early days in Sambor 18-22
   Arrival in the U.S. 23-24
   With Biograph 24-33, 35
   With IMP 33-35
   With Kinemacolor 35-36
   With Keystone 37-71
   With Sterling 73-99
   With L-Ko 101-177
   With Fox: Foxfilm and Sunshine Comedies 179-238
   With First National: Henry Lehrman Comedies 239-274
   With Selznick and the Arbuckle Scandal 275-290
   For Hire with Robertson-Cole, Universal, Richard Talmadge Productions, Fox Comedies 291-302
   Marriage to Jocelyn Leigh 303-306
   Warner Brothers, Richard Talmadge Productions, Columbia 307-317
   With Fox 318-334
   With Fox, Twentieth Century, and 20th Century-Fox 335-348
   Script Reader at 20th Century-Fox 349-358
   Final Days 359-362
   Legacy 363-366
Lehrmann, Ester Bina (Sabina) 20-21, 354, 362
Lehrmann, Kreincze 20, 362
Lehrmann, Osias 20
Lehrmann, Rachel 20
Lehrmann, Sara 19-21
Lehrmann, Sime Liebermann 19
Lehrmann, Simon Josef 19-21
Leigh, E.L. 432
Leigh, Jocelyn 285-286, 292-293, 303-304, 306
Leonard, Barbara 694
Leonard, Gus 532

Leonard, Jack 41, 435
Leonard, Marion 427-428
Leonard, Robert 85, 95
Lestina, Adolph 428, 431
Let Fido Do It 422, 626
Levy, S.G. 292
Lewis, Grace 34, 432-433
Lewis, Mitchell 245
Liberty Belles (see *Belles of Liberty, The*)
Library of Congress 10-11, 111, 117, 122, 130, 137, 144, 146-147, 168, 208, 211, 268, 402, 406, 425, 455
Liebermann, Karoline 362
Life and Moving Pictures 136, 506-507
Ligon, Grover 82, 439
Lilies of the Field 283
Lillian Russell 351
Limburger Cyclone, A 391, 568-569
Linder, Max 76
Lindsay, Laura 259
Line-Up at Police Headquarters, The 112
Lions and Ladies 412, 623-624
Lions and Tin Horn Sports 215
Liserani, E. 569
Little Angels of Luck 430
Little Billy (see Jacobs, Paul)
Little Billy's City Cousin 51
Little Billy's School Days 153, 170, 384, 541
Little Billy's Strategy 51
Little Billy's Triumph 51
Little Bo-Peep 394, 579-580
Little Fat Rascal, The 391, 590-591
Little Old New York 351
Little Orphant Annie 153
Live Wires and Love Sparks 160-163, 536-537
Lizzie's Escape 114, 482-483
Lizzie's Fortune 379, 468
Lizzie's Lingering Love 166-167, 388, 553
Lizzie's Shattered Dreams 151, 171, 523
Lizzie's Watery Grave 153, 384, 522
L-Ko Beauties 415, 418-419, 610, 612-614
L-Ko Beauty Broilers 627
L-Ko Komedy Girls 418
L-Ko Motion Picture Company 16, 101-177, 387-426, 479-633
  During Lehrman's Ownership 101-177
  After Lehrman's Departure 387-426
Llewellyn, Richard 353
Lloyd, George 697
Lloyd, Harold 200, 237, 266, 338, 415
Loback, Marvin 420, 617
Lockwood, Harold 278, 420
Logan, Jacqueline 313-314, 675-676
London Comedy Company 105-106
London Fire Brigade, The 106
London Pantomime Company 105-106
Lonergan, Philip 310, 675

Lonesome Hearts and Loose Lions 218
Loney, Lilly 609
Long Live the Ring 296, 669, 671
Long, Hal 694
Longacre Distributing Company 394
Longfellow, Stephanie 428-431
Looney Lions and Monkey Business 215
Lorch, Theodore 676-677
Lord, Robert 675
Lorraine, Harry 220, 397, 402-403, 405, 581, 583, 594, 596, 602-603, 615
Lorraine, Louise 296, 668, 672
Los Angeles Athletic Club 173
Los Angeles Benevolent Order of Elks 135, 508
Los Angeles Herald 190, 229, 245
Los Angeles Times 20, 22, 34-35, 47, 57-58, 86, 127, 130, 200, 222, 242, 290, 292, 337, 361, 364
Lost in the Studio 372, 454
Lothar, Rudolph 694
Love and Lunch 154, 371, 450-451
Love and Blazes 391, 579
Love and Courage 45, 437
Love and Dough 382, 472-473
Love and Gasoline 69, 442
Love and Lunch 154, 371, 450-451
Love and Pain 42, 434
Love and Rubbish 48-49, 70, 436
Love and Sour Notes 139-140, 499-500
Love and Surgery 107-112, 114, 116, 203, 366, 480-481
Love and Vengeance 87-90, 96, 192, 366, 443-444
Love and Water 379, 471
Love Behind Bars (see *Blackboard and Blackmail*)
Love in a Tub 104-105
Love is an Awful Thing (see *Reported Missing*)
Love of Lady Irma, The 428
Love On an Empty Stomach 146, 508
Love On Crutches 400, 575
Love School, The 342
Love, Luck, and Candy 379, 467
Lowe, Jr., Edward T. 307, 674
Lowry, Ed 599
Lox Club 113
Lubin Manufacturing Co. 25, 50, 90, 116, 372, 383, 402
Lubin, Sigmund 73, 382
Lucas, Wilfred 50-51, 65, 431-432, 439-440
Lucille Love, the Girl of Mystery 380
Lucky Thirteen, The 233
Lucy, Arnold 330, 688
Lung Yep Building Company 102
Lured But Cured 561-562
Lusk, Norbert 344
Luther, Anna 180
Lynch, Helen 418, 420, 615, 618, 620-621, 624, 677
Lynn, Charles (see Conklin, Charles "Heinie")
Lynn, Hilary 357, 697
Lynn, Julian 362

Lynne, Ethel 245
Lyons, Eddie 85, 95, 99, 137, 410
Ma Gosse 148
Mabel's New Hero 68, 70, 441
Mabel's Strange Predicament 61-63, 439
MacAllister, Rich 105-107, 556
MacDonald, Donald 85
MacDonald, Joe 697
MacDonald, Margaret I. 199
MacDonald, Wallace 118-119, 130, 483-484, 492
Mace, Fred 33, 38-45, 54, 66, 76-77, 132, 173, 432-436, 441-442
Mack Sennett's Fun Factory 16, 37
Mack, Bobby 491
Mack, Hughie 200, 398, 404-406, 416, 424, 598, 602, 604-610, 627, 632
Mack, Wayne 242
Mack, Willard 337
MacKenzie, Donald 330, 688
MacLean, Kenneth 665
MacPherson, Jeannie 427-432
Madame Butterfly 131
Madame Q 306
Madame Rex 431
Madden, Jerry 330, 688
Madison, Noel 697
Maghull Military Hospital 136
Mahony, Jack 112
Mailes, Charles Hill 432
Majestic Film Service 37
Majestic Motion Picture Company 54, 130, 384
Making a Living 55-58, 71, 79, 109, 439
Malone, Molly 406, 609
Mandaville, Molly 349
Manicure Girl, The 116, 121, 485
Mann, Frankie 673
Mann, Hank 13, 49, 121-125, 130-131, 145-147, 152-154, 177, 179-182, 186, 200, 220, 256, 356, 400, 435, 437, 439-442, 455, 481, 485-486, 490-492, 494-495, 497-500, 504-505, 508, 510-512, 514-515, 517, 520, 571, 575, 600, 616, 654, 697
Mann, Harry 417, 420-421, 616, 620, 622-623
Mannheimer, Wallace M. 323, 682-683
Marcus, Lee 360, 697
Marie, Renee 327
Marion, Edna 675-676
Markert, Russell 342, 690-691
Marley, J. Peverell 344, 346, 692-694
Marlowe, June 668
Marquis, John B. 86
Marriage in Black and White, A (see *Sambo's Wedding Day*)
Married in Hollywood 335-336
Married On Credit 140-141, 513-514
Marsh, Mae 432
Marsh, Marguerite 432
Marshall, George 99, 301, 346, 696

Marshall, Trudy 697
Marshall, William 673
Martin, Joe 223, 424, 647
Martin, Tony 349
Mary Glouster 166
Mary Hill's Concert Company 104
Maryland 351
Massa, Steve 10, 13-14, 415
Master Comedies 415
Matheson, Detective Captain Duncan 279
Matinee Girl, The 147
Matrimonial Tangle, A 147
Matthews, Harry 153
Mayer, Edwin Justus 317, 677, 679
Mayer, Louis B. 339
Mayo, Archie 404, 595, 597, 599, 605
McCabe, John 414
McCarey, Leo 306
McCown, Frank 697
McCoy, Alberta 453
McCoy, Harry 84, 246, 374, 379, 439-440, 442-443, 652
McCoy, Kid 296
McCullough, Paul 327
McCutcheon Jr., Wallace 25
McCutcheon, Wallace "Old Man" 25-26
McDaniel, J.H. 121
McDermott, Bill 201
McDonald, Catherine 258
McDowell, Claire 430
McElravy, Robert C. 394
McEvoy, Tom 76
McGann, William 194
McGill, Barney 677, 694
McGlynn, Sr., Frank 694
McGrath, Larry 201, 296, 668
McGrath, Tim 245
McGuire, Paddy 611
McKenzie, Eva Heazlett 398, 401, 559, 603
McKenzie, Robert "Bob" 397-399, 401-402, 404, 559, 579-599, 603, 610-611, 615
McKinley Mansion 266, 268
McLean, Barbara 349
McMackin, Archer 384
McNamara, Ted 13, 319-323, 679-682
McNeil, Allen 694
McNeile, H.C. 343, 692-693
McRae, Henry 394
McVey, Paul 695
Mecca Building 127-128, 394, 424
Medbury, John 284, 658-659
Meehan, George B. 196, 220, 239-240, 244, 283, 301, 645, 652, 655-657
Meek, Donald 697
Meeker, George 323-325, 682
Meeting for a Cheating, A 157-158, 541
Melford, George 312, 689

INDEX

Méliès Company 149
Melies, George 25
Memories of a Trunk 370-371
Merchant of Menace, The 669, 672
Merchants and Manufacturers of Los Angeles 185
Meredyth, Bess 346, 694
Merkel, Una 344, 692-693
Mermaid Comedies 258, 301
Merrick, Doris 697
Merritt, Greg 279
Merry Jailbirds, The 230
Merry Mary's Marriage 129, 489
Merry Mermaids 420, 612
Message of the Violin, The 430
Metro Pictures 221, 385
Metro-Goldwyn-Mayer 172, 317, 334, 342, 346, 358-359, 384, 694
Mexican Mixup, A (see *Bombs and Bandits*)
Meyer and Holler 242
Meyerhoffer, Orvar "Swede" 246
MGM (see Metro-Goldwyn-Mayer)
Mid-Air Mixup, A 388
Midgley, Fannie 689
Midnight Marauder, The 431
Midnight Soaring 84
Midsummer Night's Scream, A 669
Mike and Jake series 84, 374
Mile-A-Minute 273-274
Milford, Mary Beth 296, 668, 672
Miljan, John 314-317, 676-679
Milk-Fed Vamp, A 190, 233, 634-636
Miller, Carl 319, 321, 679-680
Miller, Joe 194
Miller, Patsy Ruth 307-310, 674-675
Miller, Rube 41, 68, 94, 116-117, 129, 177, 200, 246, 384, 410-412, 415, 418, 420, 423, 433, 435-436, 487-488, 490-491, 601, 610-615, 617-618, 625, 652
Miller, Virgil 675
Miller, W. Chrystie 427-432
Millington, Norris 368
Million and One Nights, A 24
Million Dollar Smash, A 171, 564-565
Millionaire's Son, A (see *Great Smash, The*)
Millsfield, Charles A. 420
Milne, Peter 111, 168-169, 205, 207
Milwaukee Building Company 242
Mineau, Charlotte 640
Mintz, Sam 342
Mirth of a Nation, The 174
Mister Romeo 323, 682
Mitchum, Robert 697
Mix, Tom 180, 186, 199, 209, 211, 223, 245, 398, 645
Mohawk's Way, A 430
Monberg, Zip 633
Monday Morning in a Coney Island Police Court 24, 27
Money Talks 230-231, 651

Mongrels 199, 217, 219, 646-647
Monopole Film Company 102
Montana Kid, the Dog 121, 180, 217, 486, 633
Montgomery, "Baby Peggy" 196
Moon Comedies 201
Moore, Colleen 153
Moore, Eunice (see Murdock, Eunice)
Moore, Ewell D. 361
Moore, Joe 11, 173, 527, 549, 553, 563-564
Moore, Matt 173
Moore, Owen 276, 278, 282-284, 287-289, 317, 427-428, 658-665, 677-679
Moore, Tom 173
Moore, Vin 145-146, 149, 162, 215, 233, 387, 390-392, 394, 397, 399, 418, 420, 501, 504, 508-509, 538, 557, 559, 562, 567-570, 573, 576-577, 579, 582, 584-587, 590, 593, 596, 600, 602, 604, 620, 625
Moorhouse, S.A. 196
Moran, Lee 85, 95, 99, 131, 137, 291, 293, 410
Moran, Polly 222
Moreno, Antonio 245, 432
Moreno, Thomas D. 668
Morgan, Ira H. "Joe" 118
Morley, James 245
Morosco Stock Company 171, 221
Morris, Dave 153, 170, 223, 404, 408, 410-411, 423, 525, 527, 530, 532, 535-536, 543-544, 546, 549, 551, 557, 569, 601, 605, 607-612, 614, 637, 645-647
Morris, Lee 180, 373, 379, 392
Morris, Reggie 135, 144-145, 147, 153, 159, 170, 495, 497, 502, 508, 510, 512-513, 521-522, 525-527, 529-530, 532, 535, 538-539, 543, 546-549, 551-552, 557, 571
Morrison, Helen 101, 229, 282, 361
Mortgage On His Daughter, A 147, 514-515
Morton, Charles 332-333, 687
Mosher and Harrington Film Exchange 73
Most Dangerous Game, The 332
Mother's Boy 437
Motion Picture Conservation Association 164
Motion Picture Day 132
Motion Picture Producers and Distributors Association 165
Motion Picture Producers' Association 131, 164
Motion Picture War Service Association 200
Motion Pictures Patents Company 25, 28, 33, 74-75
Moulin Rouge 10, 340-342, 690-692
Movie Riot, A 414-415, 625-626
Movietone City 334
Movietone Sound System 324, 326-327, 330, 688
MPPDA (see Motion Picture Producers and Distributors Association)
Mr. Buddy Briggs, Burglar 543
Mr. Flirt in Wrong 150-151, 509
Mr. McIdiot's Assassination 168, 528-529
Mr. Moto series 359

Mr. Romeo (see Chicken a la King)
Mr. Shoestring in a Hole (see Up the Flue)
Mr. Suicide 114, 191
Mud Turtle, The 327
Mulford, Ted 490
Mulhall, Jack 53
Mumming Birds 143
Munier, Ferdinand 694
Munro, Willie 104
Murdered By Mistake 388, 566
Murdock, Eunice 392, 588, 591
Murnau, F.W. 329
Murphy, Joe 162, 536-537, 559
Murphy's I.O.U. 40, 42, 434
Murray, Charlie 81-82, 197, 200, 337, 384, 688
Murray, Jack 695
Murray, Tom 675
Museum of Modern Art 10, 140, 146, 162, 250, 370
Musselman, Morris 355
Musty Suffer series 330, 420
Mutoscope 24-26, 29
Mutt and Jeff comic strip 112
Mutual Film Corporation 37, 54-55, 75, 82, 98, 112, 151, 159, 396
My Husband's Wife 199, 205, 641
My Lucky Star 350-351
Myer's Mistake 377-378, 460
Myers, Carmel 172
Myers, Isadore 172
Myers, Joan 9, 266, 364
Nabbing a Noble 391, 577
Naldi, Nita 283, 658
Nation, Carrie 258
National Association of the Motion Picture Industry 165
National Board of Censorship 87, 164
National Board of Review Magazine 308
National Drama Corporation Studio 179
National War Labor Board 412
Neighbor's Keyhole, A 199, 207-208, 233, 642-643
Neighbors 94, 374, 446
Neilan, Marshall 258, 380
Neill, Roy William 337
Neilson, Lois 424, 629, 631, 633
Nellie's Naughty Boarder 628-629
Nelson, Eva 107-109, 116-117, 124-126, 136, 145, 150, 157-160, 162, 177, 390, 440, 480, 486, 490-491, 495, 498, 506, 518, 521, 535-536, 541-543, 547
Nelson, J. Arthur 85
Neptune's Naughty Daughter 394, 398
Nestor Motion Picture Company 45, 48, 75, 83, 85, 107, 111, 118, 137, 149, 170, 371, 378, 400, 402, 410, 412-414
Neversink River 32
New Baby, The 50, 437
New Dress, The 432
New Neighbor, The 68, 441-442

New Woman's Club, The 104
New Year's Eve 331-335, 687
New York Motion Picture Company 37-38, 50 54-55, 73-75, 79, 82, 381
New York Society for the Suppression of Vice 155
Newman, Alfred 344, 690, 692-694
Newman, Emil 697
Newman, Lionel 697
Nichols, George 46, 50-51, 64, 116, 372, 427-431, 435, 440, 449-450
Night in a Music Hall, A 105, 107
Night in a Pullman, A 327
Night in an English Music Hall, A 54, 105, 132, 520
Night in the Show, A 143
No Flirting Allowed 147, 511-512
No Money—No Fun 201
Nolan, Eddie 439-440
Nolan, Edwin P. 165
Nolan, Lloyd 352
Nonpareil Feature Film Co. 112-113
Noodle's Return 466
Norman, Amber 682
Normand, Mabel 13, 34, 37-39, 42-43, 45, 47, 51, 53-54, 61-64, 66-67, 69, 76, 90, 103, 173, 184, 197, 356, 384, 433-439, 441-442
Norris, Edward 348, 695
Norton, Jack 697
Nosler, Lloyd 690-691
Novak, Eva 397-398, 400-402, 404-405, 410-411, 415, 418, 423-425, 583, 588-589, 591, 595-598, 603-605, 607-615, 617-620, 622, 625-628
Nurse of an Aching Heart, The 402, 595-596
Nursing a Viper 25, 30, 427
Nuts and Noodles 414, 617-618
Nuts in May 148, 412
Nutty series 85
NYMPC (see New York Motion Picture Company)
O'Brien, Eugene 276
O'Conner, Frank 319, 337, 679
O'Connor, Kathleen/Katherine/Catherine 418, 606, 611
O'Donnell, Spec 675
O'Hara, George 296-297, 668-670, 672
O'Neil, Blanche 147
O'Sullivan, Anthony 427-429
Oakley, Laura 41, 85, 433-434, 438, 442
Oberon, Merle 694
Oh Professor 276
Oh What a Nurse 310
Oh! Buoy! 400
Oh, Papa! 151
Oh, What a Knight! 223, 225-226, 648-649
Okeh Comedies 425
Oland, Warner 314-316, 343-344, 346, 676-677, 692-693
Old California 94
Oldfield, Barney 439
Olin, Earle 244-245, 283

INDEX

Olive's Hero 382, 475-476
Olive's Love Affair 382, 471
Olive's Pet 382, 475
On Again, Off Again Finnegan 130
On the Trail of the Lonesome Pill 391, 568
On Time 298-301, 673-674
One for All 351
One Hundred Dollars 332, 687
One Reel a Week 66
Opper, Frederick Burr 112
Opperman, Frank 46, 82, 432, 440-442
Oriental Romeo, An 633
Orma, Grace 420, 619-620, 622
Orr, Harry 456
Orth, Louise 81, 116-117, 121-122, 124-127, 134-135, 140, 142-145, 149, 151-152, 154, 159, 168, 170, 177, 390, 485-488, 490-491, 493, 495, 501, 503-504, 507-508, 510, 512-514, 516, 518, 520-522, 524-526, 528-530, 533-535, 539-540, 542, 553, 566, 569
Other Man's Wife, The 310
Our Children 50-51, 438
Our Daily Bread 327
Out and In 48, 436
Over the Rhine 278
Owen Moore Picture Corp. 658
Oz Film Company 375
Pacific Coast Electrical Company 292
Package Party, The 147
Paco, Juan 631
Pagano, Ernest S. 675
Page, Mann 682
Paget, Alfred 428-429, 431-432
Painless Love 412, 619
Pair of Deuces, A 414, 630
Paiva, Nestor 697
Palace Theatre 136
Pallette, Eugene 674
Palmer, Ernest 697
Pancakes and Lunatics 129
Pantages Theatre 54, 252
Pants and Petticoats 525-526
Panzer, Paul 103
Papa's Boy 93-95, 445-446
Paradise Garden 277
Paramount Pictures Corporation 282
Paramount-Artcraft Pictures 242
Park Johnnies 149, 501
Parker, Albert 337
Parker, Cecelia 338, 689
Parks, E.O. 302
Parrott, Charles 179-180, 186, 207, 412, 418, 420, 615, 617, 619, 623
Parrott, James "Paul" 300-301, 674
Parry, Harvey 191, 194-196, 203
Partners in Crime 109, 113-114, 481-482
Pascal, Ernest 697

Passions—He Had Three 45, 436
Pathé Frères 25, 29, 33
Pathé, Henry 34, 432
Patrick, Lee 697
Patterson, Helen 277
Paul, Isaac 323, 682
Peacock, Captain Leslie T. 614
Peacock, Lillian 84, 173, 196
Pearce, Peggy 78, 95-96, 117-118, 129, 134-137, 139-140, 146-147, 149, 152-154, 157-160, 370-371, 373, 376, 380, 383-384, 420, 439-440, 446, 449, 451, 454-456, 462b, 483-484, 487-488, 491, 493-501, 504-507, 511-512, 514-515, 517, 520-522, 524, 533-534, 536-538, 621
Pearls and Girls 405, 604-605
Peck's Bad Boy 368
Peddler, The 436
Peerless Pictures 276
Peg O' the Ring 175
Peggie, the Dog 379, 465, 472
Peggy's Sweethearts 117, 491
Pembroke, Percy "Perc" Scott 153, 313, 675-676
Pennick, Jack 319-320, 323, 327, 679-680
Peppercorn, Slim 626
Percy, Eileen 641
Perils of a Plumber, The 567
Perils of Pauline, The 103
Perley, Charles 428
Perrin, Jack 406-407, 601, 605-609
Perry, Bob 668
Perry, Kathryn 276, 283, 317, 677-679
Petey, the Dog 296, 668
Phil's Busy Day 567-568
Phillips, Carmen 131, 180, 433
Phillips, H.I. 284, 658-659
Phipps, Sally 11, 318-321, 327, 679, 681-682
Phoney Photos 413-414, 613-614
Phonofilm Sound System 324
Phony Teeth and False Friends 547-548
Photographer's Story, The (see *Phoney Photos*)
Photoplay Authors' League 95
Physical Torture and Mental Culture (see *Surf Scandal*)
Pickford, Jack 431
Pickford, Lottie 200, 245, 430-431
Pickford, Mary 32-33, 64, 69, 76, 278, 428-432
Pierce Brothers Mortuary 361
Pierce, Eleanor 530
Pilots of the Air (see *Pirates of the Air*)
Piltz, William J. 118
Pirates of the Air 166, 388, 396, 549-551
Pixley, Gus 81, 201
Plastered in Paris 327, 686
Playing Movies (see *Movie Riot, A*)
Playmates 382, 476-477
Plump and Runt series 406
Plympton, George H. 688

Pokes and Jabbs 383, 478
Pollard Opera Company 171
Pollard, Daphne 697
Pollard, Snub 356, 384, 697
Pomeroy, Roy 337
Poor But Dishonest 147, 517
Poor Millionaire, The 312-313, 337, 689-690
Poor Policy 137-139, 497-498
Poor Prune, A 400
Poor Simp, The 289
Poor Worm, The (see *Double Dealing*)
Popper, E.M. 244
Post, Charles 397
Potel, Victor 192, 194, 206, 209, 212, 356, 633, 636, 638, 641, 645
Powder My Back 317
Powell, Frank 32-33, 427-428, 431
Powell, J. Russell " Russ" 397, 420, 563, 596, 600, 602, 604, 606, 612-614, 633
Power, Tyrone 352
Powers, Pat 75, 425
Powers' Picture Plays 75, 85, 118, 153, 170, 296, 368, 371, 374, 378
Poyen, René 368
Prairie Chicken, A 392, 593-594
Praskins, Leonard 355
Preferred Pictures 319
Prescott, Vivian 84, 429, 431-432
Pretty Babies 420, 610-611
Pretty Lady 236
Prevost, Marie 307
Prevost, Peggy 420, 597, 600, 617, 619, 624
Price She Paid, The (see *Flyer in Folly, A*)
Primrose and West's Minstrels 380
Prince of Pilsen, The 390
Priscilla and the Umbrella 431
Private Izzy Murphy 10, 310-311, 313, 675, 677
Professor Bean's Removal 437
Prop's Revenge, The (see *Props, Drops, and Flops*)
Props, Drops, and Flops 402, 592
Protecting San Francisco from Fire 439
Prouty, Jed 356, 697
Przemysl 22
Public Enemy, The 346, 696
Public Welfare Committee 131
Pullman Blunder, A 410, 616-617
Punch of the Irish 266-270, 273, 278, 364-366, 657
Puppy Love Panic, A 631
Putnam, B.M. 302
Pyramid Comedies 154
Quality Pictures Corporation 385
Quick, Evelyn 41, 45, 47-48, 433-435, 438
Quirk, William 427-429
Rabjohn, Stanley 697
Race for a Bride, A 378, 463-464
Race for Life, A 371, 452-453

Race, The 87
Radcliffe, Violet 381-382, 384, 449, 462, 471, 490
Rag-Time Romance, A 624
Railroad Ties That Bind (see *Prairie Chicken, A*)
Rainbow Comedies 327, 415, 424-425, 633
Raindrops and Girls 380, 382, 475
Raine, William MacLeod 674
Ramage, George 49
Ramsey, Terry 24, 29, 71
Rancho Rincon de Los Bueyes 242
Rand, John 145, 194, 490, 641
Randy, Pat 597
Rankin, Arthur 668
Rappe, Virginia 9, 13, 174, 208, 210, 222, 226-228, 246, 250-252, 254-255, 261, 266, 268, 270-271, 277-283, 285, 290-292, 303, 361, 364-365, 643, 649, 652, 654, 657
Rawlinson, Herbert 95, 99, 695
Ray, Albert "Al" 29, 203, 205, 245, 260-265, 267-268, 270-271, 274, 301, 638-639, 655-657
Ray, Charles 258
Ray, Emma 113
Ray, John 113
Ray, Leah 349
Ray, Maggie (see Ray, Marjorie)
Ray, Marguerite (see Ray, Marjorie)
Ray, Marjorie 147-148, 218, 387, 392, 394, 397, 569-570, 573, 576-577, 630, 632
Raymaker, Herman 310
R-C Studios 293
Rea, Marvel 206, 234, 640
Ready for Reno 152, 521
Realart Pictures Corporation 319
Red Feather Photoplays 180
Redman's View, The 30, 427
Reed, Luther 305-306
Reed, Walter C. 180-181
Reedscale, Clarence 196
Reelcraft Pictures Corporation 384, 398, 400
Reeves, Billie 134, 382-383, 478
Regas, George 692-693
Reichenbach, Harry 155
Reid, Laurence 261-262, 271, 288, 294, 324
Reid, Wallace 173
Reis, Irving 618
Reisner, Charles "Chuck" 310
Reliance Motion Picture Company 95, 112, 384
Renavent, Georges 690, 694
Renfro, Rennie 217
Reported Missing 275-277, 282-284, 287-289, 291, 295, 298, 658-665
Rescued from an Eagle's Nest 25
Rest for the Weary 276
Return of Frank James, The 351-353
Rex Motion Picture Company 50, 75, 85, 95, 149, 180, 379
Reynolds, Vera 571, 625
Rich, Irene 307, 317

Richard Talmadge Productions 300, 312-313, 689
Richards, "Shorty" 397
Richards, Bobby 618
Richardson, Jack 634-635
Richardson, Larry 302
Ridgeway, Fritzie 586
Ridgway, Mack 605
Ries, Park J. 554
Riesenfeld, Hugo 254
Right Car But the Wrong Berth 388, 557-558
Right Clue, The 34, 432
Ring Rivals 394, 578
Ring, Blanche 116, 151
Ring, Eddie 245
Ringer for Dad, A 293-294, 665
Ringling Brothers Circus 330
Rin-Tin-Tin 339
Riot, The 68, 442
Ritchie Comedy Company 107
Ritchie, Billie
  Arrival in U.S. 103
  Death 275, 277-278
  Foxfilm Comedies 180-183, 366, 633
  Henry Lehrman Comedies 239-240, 244, 246, 248, 251-253, 262, 264, 652, 656
  L-Ko Comedies 107-114, 116-118, 120-130, 132-145, 153-154, 157-163, 165, 174, 177, 192, 387, 390, 399, 416, 480-491, 493, 495-508, 510, 513-514, 516, 518, 520-523, 526, 529-530, 533-534, 536-538, 541-542, 547, 552, 556, 558-560, 562, 565, 581
  Nonpareil Feature Films and Happy Hooligan 112-113
  Early Days in Scotland, British Music Hall 104-105
  Sunshine Comedies 192, 196, 199-201, 203, 207, 215-216, 218, 220, 223-224, 228-229, 636, 638, 640, 642, 646-647
  U.S. Vaudeville 105-107
Ritchie, Winifred 105-107, 283
Ritchie, Wyn 275
Ritchie's London Comedy Company 106
Ritchie's London Pantomime Company 105
Ritchie-Hearn London Pantomime Company 106
Ritz Brothers, The 359
Ritz Carlton Hotel 288, 659
Rivers, Joe 296, 668
Roach, Bert 131, 158, 392, 397-398, 400, 402, 490, 536, 539, 554, 559, 566, 583, 591-594, 599, 633
Roach, Gladys 392, 400, 525, 536-537, 546, 574, 578-580
Roach, Hal 205, 273, 306, 313, 359, 366, 402, 424
Roaring Lions and Wedding Bells 186-189, 233, 634-635
Roaring Lions on the Midnight Express 199, 215-218, 233, 646
Robbins, Herman 233
Robbins, Jess 237, 633
Roberts, Arthur 244
Roberts, Bob 118
Roberts, Edith 418, 424, 621
Roberts, Joann 198
Roberts, Richard M. 10, 262, 264, 266

Robertson-Cole Pictures Corporation 293-294, 340, 665, 668
Robins, Lisa 11, 275
Robinson, David 103
Robinson, Gertrude 427-429
Robinson, Kite 201
Robinson, W.C. 430-432
Robust Romeo, A 46
Rocky Road, The 428
Rogers, Charles 697
Rogers, Gene "Pop" 13, 135, 138, 140-141, 143-146, 152, 158-159, 162, 390, 396, 497, 503-504, 508, 510-511, 513, 515, 517-519, 522, 526, 530-531, 533-534, 536-538, 542, 546-549, 554, 639
Rogers, Rena 245, 413, 613-614
Rogers, Will 245-246
Roland, Richard 385
Roland, Ruth 380
Rolin Film Company 412, 415
Roman Cowboy, A 209
Romance and Dynamite 414, 420, 613
Romero, Cesar 347-348, 695-696
Roof Garden Rough House, A 424, 633
Room 1219 279
Room and Board a Dollar and a Half / Room and Board – $1.50 516
Roped Into Scandal 398, 402, 583-584
Roquemore, Henry 675
Rose Maid, The 101
Rose O'Salem Town 430
Rose, Blanche 596
Rosenberg, Dr. Maurice W. 361-362
Rosher, Charles 342, 690-691
Ross, Bud 81, 507-508
Ross, Peggy 338, 689
Roth, Sandy 674
Rothacker Labs 261
Rothafel, S.L. 687
Roubert, Matty 50, 368, 438, 440
Rough But Romantic 145, 494
Rough On Husbands 620
Rough on Roller Skates (see *Skate at Sea, A*)
Rough Stuff 394-395, 591
Rowe, George 268-269, 657
Roy, Rosalie 338, 689
Royal Comedies 383, 400
Ruge, Billy 406
Rumwell, Dr. Melville 281
Runaway Closet, The 382, 474
Runaway Wardrobe, The (see *Runaway Closet, The*)
Rural Affair, A 375, 455
Rural Caesar, A (see *Backward Sons and Forward Daughters*)
Rural Demon, A 47, 71, 440
Rural Demons, The 120, 484
Rural Love Affair (see *Rural Affair, A*)
Rural Riot, A 404, 406, 609

Rural Romance, A 388, 455, 563
Rush, June 418
Russell, Dan 13, 147-148, 152, 158, 160, 166, 168, 170, 218, 387, 392, 394-398, 400, 424-425, 517, 521-522, 524-525, 528-530, 533-535, 539-541, 546, 548, 552, 554, 557-558, 561-563, 566-570, 573, 576-581, 583, 586, 588-589, 591, 627-628, 630, 632
Russell, Harry 486
Russell, Margaret 567
Russell, Raymond 476
Ryan, M.C. 668
Ryckman, Charles 397, 402, 588-589, 591, 595-597, 603, 615
Rydzewski, Steve 11, 196
S.S. *Pennsylvania* 23
Sabichi, Katherine "Kay" 358
Safe in the Safe 561
Safety First 562
Sailor Izzy Murphy 313-317, 676-677
Sale, Virginia 330, 688
Sally, Irene and Mary 350, 355
Salter, Thelma 51, 437-438, 440
Sambo's Wedding Day 626
Sambor 9, 18-22, 354
Sammy Burns Comedies 400
Sampson, Teddy 98, 245, 323, 385
San Diego Exposition 132, 394
San Francisco and Her Environs 441
Sanford, Ralph 697
Santa Ynez Canyon 74-75
Santell, Al 296, 668-669
Saphead's Revenge, A 152, 522
Saved From a Vamp 406, 608
Saving Mabel's Dad 442
Saving Susie from the Sea 166, 527-528
Savo, Jimmy 274
Sawmill, The 283
Saxe, Templar 675
Say It With Diamonds 294
Scandal At Sea, A 152, 525
Scandal in the Family 147, 152, 512-513
Scardon, Paul 428
Scars and Bars 618
Scars and Bars Forever (see *Scars and Stripes Forever*)
Scars and Stripes Forever 159, 537-538
Schade, Betty 40
Schade, Fritz 642, 645
Schenck, Joseph M. 291, 339-340, 346, 690
Scheuer, Philip K. 337, 356
Schraeder, Anna (see Darling, Anna)
Schreiber, Lew 349
Schrock, Raymond L. 310-311, 675
Schulberg, B.P. 270, 295, 309, 319, 356
Schulsinger, Ester Ryfka 21
Scrambled Hearts 399, 581
Sea Dogs and Land Rats 530

Seal Beach Bathing Suit Contest 418-419
Sears, Elizabeth 174
Sebastian, Alla 312
Sebastian, Charles E. 312
Secret Service Snitz 376, 382, 462-463
Sedgwick, Edward 295
Seeley, Blossom 342
Seiler, Lewis 301
Seitz, George 346
Selburn Comedies 180
Selby, Charles 656
Selby, Gertrude 103-104, 107-109, 112-114, 116, 120, 123-124, 129, 131, 134, 136, 145, 147, 151-153, 155-156, 158, 160, 165, 170, 172, 177, 180, 182, 192-193, 209, 214, 217, 220, 223, 229-230, 387, 390, 400, 480-484, 489-491, 493-495, 497, 500, 502, 506-507, 509-510, 512-513, 515, 517, 522, 525-527, 530-532, 535-536, 538-539, 543-544, 548-549, 551, 553, 556-558, 561-562, 571, 633, 636-637, 645-647, 651
Selby, Olga 103
Selby, William 103
Select Pictures 658
Selective Service Act 408
Self-Made Lady, A 199, 205-206, 233, 641
Selig Polyscope Company 25, 40, 45, 90, 153, 180, 186, 194, 209, 371, 418
Selig, William 102
Selznick Pictures Corporation 276, 658-660, 662, 664
Selznick, Lewis J. 276, 659, 661
Selznick, Myron 275-276, 282-284, 288-289, 658, 663
Semnacher, Al 280
Semon, Larry 245, 282-283, 363, 404, 414-415
Sennett, Mack 7, 13, 15-16, 24-28, 30-35, 37- 43, 47-56, 58, 61-64, 66, 68-71, 75-80, 82, 94, 103, 115, 131-132, 166, 171-174, 185-186, 192, 200-201, 205, 207, 211, 215, 220-222, 225, 230, 239, 260, 262, 266, 289, 338-339, 356-360, 366, 368-369, 371, 381, 384, 386, 397, 399, 404-406, 418, 420, 424, 427-434, 438-442, 645, 649, 656, 663, 668, 697
Sennwald, Andre 348, 696
September Morn 155-157, 530-531
September Mourning, A 155-157, 530-531
Sergeant Hofmeyer 77, 91-93, 109, 445
Seyffertitz, Gustav von 675
Seymour, James 306
Shadows of Her Pest 199, 233, 638
Shaved in Mexico 145, 498
Shaw, Frank 676-677
Shawn, Ted 156
She Supes to Conquer 296, 669, 670-671
She Wanted a Ford 157-158, 562
Sheehan, Winfield "Winnie" R. 179, 228-229, 235, 238, 326, 346
Shepard, David 10, 160
Sheriff's Mustache, The (see *Oh, What a Knight!*)
Sherlock Ambrose 406, 608

Sherman Productions, Inc. 240
Sherman, Harry A. 240, 258
Sherman, Lowell 279, 339
Shield, Ernest "Ernie" 130, 190, 246, 380, 383-384, 473-474, 476, 479, 635-638, 652
Shields Lantern Slide Company 73
Ship Café 245
Shooting His 'Art Out 567
Shooting Match, A 375-376, 458-459
Short, George 492
Short, Gertrude 153, 492
Shot in a Bar Room (see *Itching for Revenge*)
Shot in the Excitement (see *Battle of "Let's Go", The* and *Bullets and Boneheads*)
Show Them No Mercy 346-348, 695-696
Sidney, George 337, 688-689
Siegmann, George 298, 429, 673
Sign of the Cucumber 402, 589
Silk Hose and High Pressure 94, 140-144, 342, 510, 518-520
Silver, Sam 349
Silvers, Louis 697
Silverstein, Leo V. 312
Simpson, Mary Alice (see Leigh, Jocelyn)
Simpson, Russell 245
Sin On the Sabbath 144-145, 522-523
Sing and Be Happy 349
Singer Midgets 252
Singer, Leo 252
Sink or Swim (Fox Film) 338-339, 689
Sink or Swim (Selznick; see *Reported Missing*)
Sinnott, Michael 26-27
Sirens of Suds 632
Six-Cylinder Love 209
Skate at Sea, A 625
Skidding Hearts (see *Phoney Photos*)
Slapstick Encyclopedia 160, 537
Slapsticon 10, 262, 639
Sleuths at the Floral Parade, The 40, 43, 433
Slide, Anthony 36
Slim of Bungville series 85
Smaltz Loves (aka *When Smaltz Loves*) 369, 447-448
Smashed in the Career 636
Smith, C. Aubrey 344, 692-694
Smith, Chester J. 316
Smith, George 474
Smith, Noel Mason 158-159, 220, 266, 270, 387, 391-392, 402, 404-405, 416, 418, 420, 527, 552-553, 578-579, 583, 586, 588-589, 591-594, 598, 602, 618, 624, 626, 645, 657
Smith, Paul Girard 330, 688
Smith, Richard "Dick" 123, 135, 145, 147, 153-154, 387, 391, 397, 400, 407, 420, 422, 493-495, 497, 499, 505-506, 511-512, 515, 517, 520, 524, 527, 531, 534, 542-544, 548, 563, 567, 571, 574, 578-579, 588-589, 591, 596-597, 603-604, 606, 618, 624, 626

Smith, Sid 184, 202, 206, 301, 363, 633, 638, 640, 674
Smith, Stanley W. 302
Smith, Walter 608
Smithers, Bill 608
Snakeville series 149
Snatched! (see *Show Them No Mercy*)
Snitz Joins the Force 369-370, 447
Snookee's Day Off 375, 378, 463
Snookee's Disguise 371, 373, 455-456
Snookee's Flirtation 370, 448-450
Snooky the "Humanzee" 259-260
Snoopee's Day Off (see *Snookee's Day Off*)
Snoring in High C 557
So This is Hollywood 296, 669-670
Soapsuds and Sirens 402-403, 594
Social Pirates 181
Society Buzzard, The (see *House of Terrible Scandals, The*)
Soft Tenderfoot, A 209
Son of a Gun 199, 20`1-202, 233, 638-639
Son of a Hun , The 190, 223, 225, 647
Song of the Islands 351
Sonja Henie No. 4 351
Sonny Jim series 368
Sothern, Ann 694
Sound Your "A" 330-332
Southern California Edison Company 292
Southern Feature Film Association 148
Southern, Eva 599
Space, Arthur 697
Spanish Influenza Epidemic 136, 221, 229, 402, 420, 618-619
Speed Boy, The 312
Speed Kings, The 51-52, 66-67, 439
Spence, Ralph 220, 300-301, 673
Sperling, Milton 350
Spike's Bizzy Bike 397, 573-574
Sponable, Earl 324
Spotted Nag, The 629
Spreckels, John D. Jr. 280
Spreckels, Sydia "Sidi" 278, 280-281
Spring Fever (see *Mr. Buddy Briggs, Burglar*)
Springtime (see *The Kick in High Life*)
Squaw Man, The 91
St. Clair, Malcolm 293, 295-297, 339, 356, 359-360, 614, 669, 697
St. Louis Motion Picture Company 40
Stanley Comedies 412
Star Company 113
Star Films 25
Starr, Fred 597
Starr, James A. "Jimmy" 291-292, 323-325, 677, 682
Static Club 118
Steadman, Vera 220, 227, 234, 632, 649
Steck, Velma 375, 377, 461
Stein, Albert O. 286
Steiner, William 75, 670

Step Lively, Jeeves! 349
Stephens, Walter 397, 402, 583, 588-589, 591-594, 602
Steppling, John 85
Sterling Kids 368, 384, 462
Sterling Kids comic strip 76
Sterling Motion Picture Corporation 16, 73-99, 367-386, 404, 420, 442-479, 621
Sterling, Ford 7, 9, 13, 16, 31, 37-39, 41, 44-46, 49-54, 59, 62, 65-66, 68-70, 76-99, 107, 109, 115, 127, 173, 207-210, 222, 233, 323-326, 356, 367, 369-373, 375-376, 378-382, 384-386, 420, 433-451, 453-460, 462-463, 477, 621, 643-644, 682-685
Sterling, Merta 390-393, 397-398, 405, 420-421, 568, 570, 572, 574, 579, 581-582, 584-587, 590-591, 593-594, 596, 600-602, 604, 614-615, 619-620, 622
Stern, Abe 101-102, 148, 173, 175-177, 182, 389, 398, 416, 425
Stern, Julius 33, 175-176, 200, 209, 215, 221, 231, 389, 394, 405, 408, 414, 418, 422, 424-425
Stern, Recha 102
Stevenson, George 136
Stewart, Anita 258
Stich, George Ford (see Sterling, Ford)
Stolen Glory 442
Stolen Hearts and Nickels 136, 521
Stolen Purse, The 39-40, 433
Stoloff, Benjamin 301, 319, 327
Stone, Arthur 323-326, 330, 332, 682, 684-685, 687-688
Stone, John 327, 685
Stonehouse, Ruth 175
Stool Pigeon's Revenge, A 145, 418, 499
Story of Alexander Graham Bell, The 350
Stradling, Walter 121
Strauss, William H. 676
Street Cars and Carbuncles 402, 591-592
Strobach, Rudolph and Eugenie 23
Stromeyer and Wyman 73
Strong Affair, A 375, 453
Strong, Porter 397, 597, 615
Strother and Dayton Funeral Home 282, 286
Stuart, Nick 319-321, 327, 679, 682
Studebaker, Hale 433
Studio Liberty Loan Campaign 220
Stull, Walter 383, 478
"Suicide" Lehrman 114, 191
Sullivan and Considine Circuit 54
Sul-Te-Wan, Madame 227, 645, 649
Summer Boarders 391, 574-575
Summerville, George "Slim" 200-201, 211, 213, 218, 236, 301, 645-646
Sunday in Last Chance Valley (see *Fat and Furious*)
Sunshine Comedy Company 10, 44, 66, 179-238, 278, 301, 319, 327, 384-385, 399, 633-652, 664, 674
Sunshine Film, Inc. 201
Sunshine Sue 430
Sunshine, Marion 430-431

Surf Scandal 588-589
Surgeon's Revenge, A 168, 388, 561
Surmagne, Jacques 350
Sutherland, Delos 679
Swain, Mack 59, 220, 222-223, 225-226, 230, 405-410, 439-440, 601, 603, 605-609, 648-649, 651
Swan Life 474-475
Swanson, Gloria 185-186
Swanson, William 75
Sweet Papa 300-301, 674
Sweet, Blanche 428, 431-432
Sweet, Harry 327-329, 632, 685
Swickard, Joseph 41, 434
Switching Hour, The 296, 669, 672-673
Symonds, Henry Roberts 118, 244
Tail Spin 351, 354
Tale of a Black Eye, The 436
Tale of a Hat, The 375, 456
Tale of Twenty Stories, A 146, 508-509
Talley, Thomas L. 241
Tally's Kinema 248
Talmadge, Constance 205, 258, 270, 289
Talmadge, Norma 258
Talmadge, Richard 298-301, 312-313, 337, 673-674, 689
Taming of the Shrewd, The 669, 671
Tangled Affair, A 442
Tattle-Tale Alice 166, 566
Taurog, Norman 13, 186-187, 194, 213, 223, 244, 282-283, 286, 301, 363-364, 399
Tavares, Arthur 41, 370-371, 377, 383-384, 433-434, 441-449, 451, 453-454, 456, 460-461, 463, 465, 467-468, 470-475, 477, 479
Taylor, J.O. 675
Taylor, Rex 310, 312, 689
Taylor, Robert 342
Teare, Betty 380
Teare, Ethel 208, 211, 214, 220, 222-223, 225, 229, 643, 645, 648-649
Tears and Sunshine 152, 517
Teddy the Dog 217, 646
Telephone Girl, The 339-340
Temperamental Husband, A 39, 433
Temple, Shirley 346
Tenbrook, Harry 99
Tennyson, Gladys 162-163, 559, 601
Terhune, Albert Payson 675
Terrors of a Turkish Bath, The 563
Tetzlaff, Teddy 439
Thanhouser Company 33, 50, 115-116, 298
Thank You, Jeeves! 349
That Dark Town Belle 42, 435
That Dawgone Dog 400, 571
That Little Band of Gold 384
Theatre of Science: A Volume of Progress and Achievement in the Motion Picture Industry, The 82
Theatre Unique 24

Their Downfall 201
Their Last Haul 130, 492
Their Unexpected Job 201
Thief Catcher, A 66-67, 440
Thief in the Dark, A 323
Thomas Ince Studios 242
Thomas, Chester 201
Thomas, Edward C. 244
Thomas, Olive 276
Thompson, Allan 307, 674
Thompson, Walter 697
Thornby, Robert 50-51, 66, 78, 80-81, 83, 87, 94, 98, 368-369, 371, 375, 378, 385, 448, 450, 452, 454, 457, 459, 465-466, 469, 471
Those German Bowlers 380, 472
Thou Shalt Not Flirt 129, 487
Three Carnoes, The 104-105
Three Karnos, The 104
Three Musketeers, The 351
Three Orphans, The 296, 669, 671
Through a Knot Hole 117, 487
Through the Breakers 30, 427
Tickled to De-Feet (see *Double Dukes*)
Tides of Barnegat, The 153
Tierney, Gene 352
Tight Squeeze, A 199, 211, 214, 233, 645
Tillie's Nightmare 90
Tillie's Punctured Romance 136, 174
Tillie's Terrible Tumble 166, 388, 559
Timely Interception, A 171
Tinling, James 337, 349
Titus, Lydia Yeamans 613
To Live or Die 298
To Save Her Soul 428
Todd, Harry 246, 251-252, 256, 556, 652
Todd, Sherman 694
Tom and Jerry Mix 209
Tom's Tramping Troupe 166, 391, 581-582
Tombes, Andrew 690
Toncray, Kate 431-432
Tone, Franchot 341, 690-691
Too Many Bachelors 153, 495
Too Many Brides 439
Toonerville Trolley Comedies 273
Toplitsky and Company 44-46, 435
Torpedo Pirates 404-405, 602
Tough Luck On a Rough Sea 400, 546
Tourneur, Maurice 337
Trans-Atlantic Film Company, Ltd. 122, 136
Trapped in a Closet 375, 457-458
Trapped in a Wardrobe (see *Trapped in a Closet*)
Trask, Wayland 197
Treasure Seekers, The 382, 472
Triangle Film Corporation 75, 225, 384, 406
Triangle-Fine Arts Company 172, 185-186, 211, 221, 242, 406

Trouble Inn 201
Troublesome Pets 452
Truart Film Corp. 298, 673-674
Trust, The (see Motion Picture Patents Co.)
Tunberg, Karl 355
Turpin, Ben 196, 200, 222, 356, 697
Tuxedo Comedies 301
Twentieth Century Films 339, 341-342, 346, 690, 692, 694
Twentieth Century-Fox (see 20th Century-Fox)
Twenty Legs Under the Sea 238
Twenty Minutes At the Fair 157-158, 416, 533-534
Twilight Baby, A 246, 248-257, 259, 266, 271, 278, 348, 366, 652-655
Twixt Love and Fire 435
Two Old Tars 438
Two Paths, The 431
Two Widows, The 41, 48, 433
Two-Gun Trixie 630-631
UCLA Film and Television Archive 145, 262, 317
Unconquered 153
Under New Management 152, 515-516
Under the Table 145, 497
Underwood and Underwood 73
Unhand Me, Villain 166-167, 388, 555-556
Unique Theater (see Theatre Unique)
United Artists Corporation 270, 334, 339, 342-343, 346
United States v. Motion Picture Patents Co. 75
Universal Animated Weekly (see *Animated Weekly*)
Universal City 107, 134, 175, 387, 395
Universal Film Manufacturing Company 74, 127, 129, 176, 442, 479, 621
Universal Ike Jr. series 85, 116
Universal Ike series 85, 111, 116
Universal Pictures Corp. 666
Unknown Purple, The 298
Up the Flue 397, 569
Valentino, Rudolph 53, 278
Valiants of Virginia, The 153
Vallet, A.H. 118, 639, 642
Vamping Reuben's Millions 402, 404, 596
Vampire a la Mode 327
Van Bibber series 238, 301
Van Buren, Mabel 668
Van Enger, Charles 685
Van Loan, H.H. 174
Van Zandt, Philip 697
Van, Beatrice 41, 47-48, 53, 103, 296-297, 436, 668
Vance, Virginia 687
Vanderbilt Cup Race 86, 88, 444
Vanity Fair 107, 132
Vannuy's Hotel 78
Vendetta in a Hospital 137-138, 510-511
Venice Miniature Railway 50
Venice-By-The-Sea 371
Venus, Lola 201
Vernon Country Club 69, 173

Vernon, Bobby 84, 205, 379, 641
Vernon, Vinton 694
Victim of Jealousy, A 429
Victor Film Company 33, 85, 149, 378
Victoria Theater 105
Vidor, King 258
Viertel, Salka 20-22
Vignola, Robert 337
Villain Still Pursued Her, The (see *Unhand Me, Villain*)
Vim Comedy Company 261, 383, 406
Vitagraph (see American Vitagraph Company)
Vitaphone 310, 326
Vogan, Emmett 697
Vogt, George E. 355
Vogue Motion Picture Company 184, 384, 400, 405
Voss, Franklin "Frank" H. "Fatty" 139-140, 146, 151-154, 158, 167, 170, 387, 396, 398-399, 498-499, 501, 504, 507-510, 512-513, 515, 518, 521, 523-527, 530, 532, 534, 541, 545-546, 548-551, 553, 555, 559, 563-564, 566, 572, 574, 577-578
Vroom, Frederick 689
Wages of Cinema 669, 671-672
Wagner, Jack 307, 674
Wagner, Sidney 320, 679
Waiter's Wasted Life, A 199, 205, 211, 641-642
Waiting At the Church 380
Wakefield Sanitarium 281
Walker, Brent 11, 16, 35, 37, 39, 53, 61, 66, 68-69, 121, 198, 439, 441-442
Wall Between, The 378, 464
Wall Street Girl, The 151
Walraven, J.H. 180-181
Walsh, Felix 378, 460, 466
Walsh, Raoul 319, 326
Walters, Wake 173
Walthall, Henry B. 298, 427-430
Waltham, J. 427, 429
War Squad 219
Ward, Lucille 88, 90, 384, 443, 446, 449, 458
Wardell, Harry 349
Ware, Helen 687
Warner Brothers Pictures, Inc. 10, 155, 307-317
Warner, Jack 310-312
Warner, Sam 310
Warren, Dwight 666
Warren, Harry 690-691
Water Nymph, The 66
Watson, Coy Jr. 364, 408, 418, 609
Watson, Harry 330
Watson, William H. 211, 220, 424, 627, 632, 641, 645
Watts Tavern (see Baron Long's Watts Tavern)
Way Down East 380, 625
Weber and Fields Music Hall 115
Weed, Frank 354
Welden, Jess 634
Wells, Conrad 682, 687

Wells, Mae/May 370, 384, 440, 450, 453
Werker, Alfred L. 359
West, Billy 196, 412
West, Charles H. 427, 429-432
West, Dorothy 427-432
Westcott, Frederick John 104
Western Exchange Service 37
Western Romance, A (see *From Cactus to Kale*)
Western Union Telegraph Company 292
Westley, Helen 342, 349, 690
Westover, Winifred 207-208, 638, 640, 642
Wet and Warmer 7, 10, 262, 264-266, 366, 656-657
What Happened to Father? 311
What Price Glory? 319, 685
Wheeler, Lyle 697
When Claudia Smiles 151
When Snitz Was "Married" 382, 474
Where Are My Children? (see *Where Is My Che-ild?*)
Where Is My Che-ild? 392, 586
Where Is My Husband? 168, 388, 554
Where is My Wife? 159-160, 388, 565
Where Our Morning Paper Comes From 476
Whisler, Margarete 370, 452
White Roses 431
White, George 648
White, Jack 8, 13, 79-80, 118, 158, 186-187, 199, 201, 203, 211, 217, 220, 223, 226, 229, 244, 246, 258, 271, 301, 363, 634, 637, 639, 641, 645-647, 649-650, 652
White, Jules 363
White, Leo 196
White, Marjorie 338, 689
White, Pearl 84, 103
White, Wendy Warwick 9, 16
Whittier, George 76
Who's Your Father? 199, 209-212, 214, 645
Who's Zoo? 412, 414, 611
Why Sailors Go Wrong 318-323, 679-682
Wife, Husband and Friend 350
Wilbur Opera Company 141
Wild Ride, A 371, 451-452
Wild Women and Tame Lions 199, 207-210, 233, 278, 643-644
Wiley, Joseph E. 361
Wiley, Wanda 196
Wilful Peggy 32, 430
Willat, Irvin 337
Williams, Bert 289, 665
Williams, Billy 195
Williams, Earle 245
Williams, Frank D. 60, 95, 384, 446, 621
Williams, Harry 207
Williams, J.D. 241
Willie Walrus and the Awful Confession 378
Willie Walrus and the Baby 378
Willie Walrus, Detective 378
Wilson, Charles C. 695, 697

Wilson, Loretta 42, 622
Wilson, Tom 283, 288-289, 298-299, 634, 639, 645, 658-665, 673-674
Windy Day, A (see *Bold, Bad Breeze, A*)
Wine, Women and Sauerkraut 237-238
Winninger Family Variety Company 151
Winninger, Charles 150-151, 155-157, 509, 523-524, 530-531, 562
Winter Garden Theatre 314
Winter, Eva 355-356, 358
Withers, Jane 359
Wittgenstein, Victor 351
Witwer, H.C. 295-296, 668-670, 672
Wizard Comedies 383
Wodehouse, P.G. 349
Wolbert, William 378-380, 382-383, 466, 468-469, 472
Wolgast, Al 296
Woman from Mellon's, The 428
Woman from Warrens, The 171
Woman Haters, The 438
Wonder Models of Fashion 277
Woode, Margo 697
Woodward, Guy 202, 396, 638, 640, 645
Work or Fight 410, 412, 620
World Film 383
World Pictures 385
Worshippers of the Cuckoo Clock, The 394
Worthington, William 131

Worts, George F. 313, 675
Wounded Feelings (see *Avenging Dentist, The*)
Wright, Carolyn/Caroline 411, 418, 423, 610-611, 613-614, 631
Wright, Walter 440
Wright, William Lord 367
Wulze, Harry W. 380
Wunderlee, Frank 658-659, 661
Wurtzel, Sol M. 190, 231, 234, 298, 335, 359-360, 697
Yamamoto, Togo 288, 658-659, 661
Yankee Film Company 75
Yankee Girl, The 116, 151
Yorke Film Corporation 386
York-Metro Company 184, 277
Young, Catherine/Katherine/Kathryn 402, 585, 593, 596, 600, 602, 609
Young, Harold 668
Young, Loretta 339, 343-344, 692-693
Young, Robert 346, 694
Youngest in the Family, The 554-555
Zanuck, Darryl F. 10, 13, 338-340, 343-344, 346, 349-351, 353-354, 358-359, 690, 692, 694-695, 697
Ziegfeld Follies 292, 307, 382
Zimmerman, Josef 19
Zimmerman, Malka 19
Zip and His Gang 153, 490
Zukor, Adolph 241

Bear Manor Media

Classic Cinema.
Timeless TV.
Retro Radio.

WWW.BEARMANORMEDIA.COM